LEVITICUS
17–22

VOLUME 3A

THE ANCHOR BIBLE is a fresh approach to the world's greatest classic. Its object is to make the Bible accessible to the modern reader; its method is to arrive at the meaning of biblical literature through exact translation and extended exposition, and to reconstruct the ancient setting of the biblical story, as well as the circumstances of its transcription and the characteristics of its transcribers.

THE ANCHOR BIBLE is a project of international and interfaith scope: Protestant, Catholic, and Jewish scholars from many countries contribute individual volumes. The project is not sponsored by any ecclesiastical organization and is not intended to reflect any particular theological doctrine. Prepared under our joint supervision, THE ANCHOR BIBLE is an effort to make available all the significant historical and linguistic knowledge which bears on the interpretation of the biblical record.

THE ANCHOR BIBLE is aimed at the general reader with no special formal training in biblical studies; yet it is written with the most exacting standards of scholarship, reflecting the highest technical accomplishment.

This project marks the beginning of a new era of cooperation among scholars in biblical research, thus forming a common body of knowledge to be shared by all.

William Foxwell Albright
David Noel Freedman
GENERAL EDITORS

THE ANCHOR BIBLE

LEVITICUS
17–22

◆

A New Translation
with Introduction and Commentary

JACOB MILGROM

THE ANCHOR BIBLE
Doubleday
New York   London   Toronto   Sydney   Auckland

THE ANCHOR BIBLE
PUBLISHED BY DOUBLEDAY
a division of Random House, Inc.
1540 Broadway, New York, New York 10036

THE ANCHOR BIBLE, DOUBLEDAY, and the portrayal
of an anchor with the letters A and B are trademarks
of Doubleday, a division of Random House, Inc.

LIBRARY OF CONGRESS CATALOGING-IN-PUBLICATION DATA
Bible. O.T. Leviticus XVII–XXII. English. Milgrom. 2000.
Leviticus 17–22: a new translation with introduction and commentary /
by Jacob Milgrom.—1st ed.
    p.   cm.   (The Anchor Bible; v. 3A)
Includes bibliographical references and index.
1. Bible. O.T. Leviticus—Commentaries. I. Title: Leviticus seventeen
through twenty-two. II. Milgrom, Jacob, 1923– III. Title.
IV. Bible. English. Anchor Bible. 1964; v. 3A.
BS192.2A1   1964.G3 vo. 3A
[BS1255.3]   220.7′7 s—dc21
[222/.130]   99-089367

ISBN 0-385-41255-X
Copyright © 2000 by Doubleday, a division of Random House, Inc.

First Edition

10 9 8 7 6 5 4 3 2 1

FOR JO

ʿēzer kĕnegdî
My Enabler

CONTENTS

◆

TRANSLATION, NOTES, AND COMMENTS

IV. THE HOLINESS SOURCE (Chapters 17–27)

BIBLIOGRAPHY
*See Volume 3B for complete bibliography
for Volumes 3A and 3B.*

INDEX
*See Volume 3B for cumulative indexes
for Volumes 3, 3A, and 3B.*

PREFACE

◆

A word of explanation regarding the Introduction. From the start, I decided not to repeat anything I had written in the Commentary. The Introduction is thus not a compendium, but a supplement. Frequent references to the Commentary are made throughout. Such is the case with H's distinct terminology (I B); style (I D); law and narrative (I G); polemic against P, JE, and D (I I); holiness (II G); ethics (II H); jubilee (II K); and reflections on the biblical *gēr* (II N). Hence, just as necessity dictated that the Commentary be *written* before the Introduction, so also the Commentary should be *read* before the Introduction.

Frequent reference is also made to three seminal books on H, which appeared during the past five years: Knohl (1995), Joosten (1996), and Schwartz (1999 Hebrew). Moreover, wherever chapters 17–27 (H) allude to or assume chapters 1–16 (P), I refer the reader to the discussion in my earlier work, *Leviticus 1–16* (AB3). The Introduction also omits the state of research, since it is thoroughly covered by Hartley (1992: 251–60) and Joosten (1996: 5–16).

The other commentators and studies I have consulted—Reventlow (1961), Kilian (1963), Feucht (1964), Elliger (1966), Cholowinski (1970), Zimmerli (1980), Hurvitz (1982), Levine (1989), Paran (1989), and Sun (1990)—have contributed to this Commentary and are gratefully acknowledged. As in volume 1, the insights of the medieval Jewish commentators and their rabbinic predecessors illuminate these pages. Once again, I have benefited from the perceptive questions and comments of my graduate students in both Berkeley and Jerusalem. They are noted by first initial and surname. Several of them have also contributed excurses: The Missing Family Members in the List of Sexual Prohibitions (Dr. S. Rattray); Parallelism and Inversion in 21:1b–15 (C. E. Hayes); Hittite and Israelite Festive Calendars (Dr. S. Stewart); and Ancient Seed Mensuration (J. Sheldon).

The Introduction is in two parts. The first is called Structure, justifying reference to chapters 17–27 as H, a discrete priestly source, which differs from chapters 1–16 (P) in form (I A), terminology (I B), style (I D), and precision (I C). H exhibits inner growth (I F), supplements and revises P (I H), polemicizes against P (I I), and extends into Exodus and Numbers (I E). Hence the book of Leviticus remains a distinctive organic creation (I L), composed, with the exception of several verses, in preexilic times (I K). The second part, Theology, deals with topics found in H, such as revelation (II A), rationales (II B), ancestor worship (II C), idolatry (II D), covenant (II F), holiness (II G), ethics (II H), land (II I), Sabbath (II J), jubilee (II K), crime (II O), and YHWH (II Q).

My deepest appreciation is extended to the librarians of the Hebrew Union College, Jerusalem, for their cooperative and efficient bibliographical help. I cannot close without expressing my thanks to my indefatigable and faithful editor, David Noel Freedman. My indebtednerss is implicit on every page by its improved style and clarity and is explicit on occasion by his perceptive comments.

The introduction is preceded by my translation of the entire book of Leviticus, thereby obviating the need to flip to volume 1 each time my rendering is sought. The volume concludes with appendices A–F, giving my comments to some of the scholarly reactions to volume 1.

> *tam weniŝlam*
> April 23, 1999
> This is the day YHWY made;
> let us rejoice and exult in it.
> Ps 118:24

ABBREVIATIONS

◆

'Ab.	'Abot
AB	Anchor Bible
ABD	Anchor Bible Dictonary
'Abod. Zar.	'Aboda Zara
'Abot R. Nat.	'Abot Rabbi Nathan
AHw	W. von Soden, Akkadisches Handwörterbuch (Wiesbaden, 1965–81)
AJSR	Association of Jewish Studies Review
Akk.	Akkadian
ANET	J. B. Pritchard, ed., Ancient Near Eastern Texts Relating to the Old Testament (Princeton)
AoF	Altorientalische Forschugen
'Arak.	'Arakin
Aram.	Aramaic
ARM	Archives royales de Mari
ARN¹	Abot Rabbi Nahman, ms.1
AH³	Biblia hebraica stuttgartensia (3d edition)
b.	Babylonian Talmud
B. Bat.	Baba Batra
B. Meṣ.	Baba Meṣiʿa
B. Sot.	Talmud Babli, Soṭah
BAM	F. Köcher, Die babylonisch-assyriache Medizin in Texen und Untersuchungen (Berlin, 1963–)
bar.	baraita
BBR	H. Zimmern, Beiträge zur Kenntnis der babylonischen Religion (Leipzig, 1901)
B.C.E.	Before the Common Era; corresponds to B.C.
BDB	F. Brown, S. R. Driver, and C.A. Briggs, Hebrew and English Lexicon of the Old Testament (Oxford, orig. 1907; I cite the 1953 ed.)
Bek.	Bekorot
Ber.	Berakot
Beṣ	Beṣah
BH	biblical Hebrew
BHS	Biblia Hebraica Stuttgartensia
BH³	Biblia hebraica stuttgartensia (3rd edition)
BI	Biblical Interpretation

BM	*Beth Mikra*
BO	unpublished Boğazköy Tablets
BR	*Bible Review*
CAD	*The Assyrian Dictionary of the Oriental Institute of the University of Chicago*
CD	Damascus Document
C.E.	Common Era
CH	Code of Hammurabi
col(s).	column(s)
CT	*Cuneiform Texts from Babylonian Tablets*
CTA	A. Herdner, *Corpus des tablettes en cunéiformes alphabétiques découvertes à Ras Shamra-Ugarit de 1929 à 1939* (Paris, 1963)
CTH	designation of compositions after Laroche 1971
D	Deuteronomist
Deut. Rab	*(Midrash) Deuteronomy Rabbah*
Deut. Re'eh	Deuteronomy Rabbah, parashat *re'eh*
DISO	C.-F. Jean and H. Hoftijzer, *Dictionnaire des inscriptions sémitiques de l'ouest* (Leiden, 1965)
DJD V	J. Allegro, ed. *Discoveries in the Judean Desert*, V (Oxford, 1968)
E	Elohist Source
EBWL	*Encyclopedia of the Biblical World, Leviticus* (Jerusalem: Revivim) (Hebrew)
'Ed.	*'Eduyyot*
EJ	*Encyclopaedia Judaica*
EM	*Encyclopaedia Miqra'it*
EQ	*Evangelical Quarterly*
Eth.	Ethiopic
fem.	feminine
frg.	fragment
GAG	W. von Soden, *Grundriss der akkadischen Grammatik samt Erganzungsheft, AnOr* 33/47 (Rome, 1969)
Giṭ.	*Giṭṭin*
GKC	W. Gesenius, ed. E. Kautsch, trans. A. Cowley, *Gesenius' Hebrew Grammar* (Oxford, 1983)
H	Holiness Code
Ḥag.	*Ḥagiga*
Ḥal.	*Ḥallah*
HALAT	*Hebräisches und Aramäische Lexikon zum Alten Testament*
HAL³	W. Baumgentmer et al, eds., *Hebräisches und aramäisches Lexicon zum Alten Testament*, 3 ed.
Heb.	Hebrew
Heliod.	Heliodorus, *Aethiopica*

Herod.	Herodotus
Hitt.	Hittite
HL	Hittite Laws
Hor.	*Horayot*
HSS	Harvard Semitic Studies
HUCA	*Hebrew Union College Annual*
Ḥul.	*Ḥullin*
IBHS	B. Watke and M. O'Connor, *An Introduction to Biblical Hebrew Syntax* (Winona Lake, Ind: 1990)
IDBS	*Interpreters Dictionary of the Bible, Supplement*
J	Yahwist Source
JE	Jewish Encyclopedia
JLAS	*Jewish Law Association Studies*
Jos.	Josephus (Loeb Classical Library editions)
Ant.	Antiquities of the Jews
Con. Ap.	Contra Apion
Wars	The Jewish Wars
JPS	Jewish Publication Society
Jub.	*Jubilees*
KAI	H. Donner and W. Röllig, *Kanaanäische und aramäische Inschriften* (Wiesbaden, 1968–71)
KAR	*Keilschrifttexte aus Assur religiösen Inhalts*
KAT	*Kommentar zum Alten Testament*
KB	L. Koehler and W. Baumgartner, *Lexicon in Veteris Testamenti libros* (Leiden, 1958)
KBo	*Keilschrifttexte aus Boghazkoy*
Ker.	*Keritot*
Ket.	*Ketubot*
Kil.	*Kil'ayim*
KJV	*King James Version*
KTU	*Die keilalphabetischen Texte aus Ugarit*
KUB	*Keilschrifturkunden aus Boghazkoy*
LB	Late Bronze
LBH	late biblical Hebrew
LE	Laws of Eshnunna
lit.	literally
LKA	E. Ebeling, *Literarische Keilschrifttexte aus Assur* (Berlin, 1953)
ll.	lines
LXX	Septuagint
MAL A	Middle Assyrian Laws, Tablet A
m.	Mishna
Ma'aś.	*Ma'aśerot*
Mak.	*Makkot*
MAL	Middle Assyrian Laws

MAOG	Mitteilungen der Altorientalischen Gesellschaft
masc.	masculine
Meg.	Megilla/construct Megillat (e.g., Megillat Ta'anit)
Mek.	Mekilta
Mekh.	Mekhilta
Men.	Menahot
Menah.	Menahot
Mid.	Middot
Midr. Gen. Rab.	Mirdash Genesis Rabbah
Midr. Lev. Rab.	Midrash Leviticus Rabbah
Midr. Num. Rab.	Midrash Numbers Rabbah
MMT	Ma'ăśê Miqṣat Hattôrâ, Qumran Cave 4, 394–99
MMT B	Miqṣat ma 'ăśê Tôrâ, B
Mo'ed Qaṭ.	Mo'ed Qaṭan
MSL	Materialen zum sumerischen Lexikon, (Rome, 1937–)
MS(S)	manuscript(s)
MT	Masoretic Text
NAB	New American Bible
Naz.	Nazir
NEB	New English Bible
Ned.	Nedarim
Nid.	Niddah
NJPS	New Jewish Publication Society Bible
NRSV	New Revised Standard Version
OB Gilg.	Old Babylonian text of Gilgamesh
P	Priestly Source
par(s).	paragraph(s)
Pesah.	Pesahim
Pesh.	Peshitta
Pesiq. R.	Pesiqta Rabbati
Pesiq. Rab Kah.	Pesiqta de Rab Kahana
Philo	Philo
Plant.	De plantatione
Virt.	De virtutibus
pl.	plural
PRU	C. F.-A. Schaeffer and J. Nougayrol, eds., Le Palais royal d'Ugarit (Paris, 1955–65)
Q	Qumran
Qidd	Quiddishun
QL	Qumran Literature
Qoh.	Qohelet (Eccl, Ecclesiastes)
1QM	Qumran, War Scroll, Cave 1
1QS	Qumran, Manual of Discipline, Cave 1
1QS	Serek hayyahad (Rule Of The Community, Manual Of Discipline) Cave 1

1QSa	Qumran, *Rule of the Congregation*, Cave 1
4Q	Qumran, Cave 4
4Q365	Qumran fragment 365, Cave 4
4QD^b	Qumran fragment D^b, Cave 4
4QD^e	Qumran fragment D^e, Cave 4
4QLev^e	Qumran, Leviticus, fragment e
11QPaleoLev	Qumran, Paleo Leviticus, Cave 11
11QT	Qumran, Temple Scroll, Cave 11
11QT^a	Qumran, Temple Scroll fragment a, Cave 11
R.	Rabbi
REVQ	*Revue de Qumran*
RIH	J. de Rouge, *Inscriptions hiéroglyphiques en Égypte*, 3 Vols. Études égyptoloiques 9–11 (Paris, 1877–78)
RLA	E. Ebeling and B. Meissner, eds., *Reallexikon der Assyriologie* (Berlin, 1928)
RS	Ras Shamra, field numbers of tablets
RŠbY	*Rabbi Simeon ban Yoḥhai*
RSV	*Revised Standard Version*
Šab.	*Šabbat*
Šabb.	*Šabbat*
Sam.	Samaritan Pentateuch
Sanh.	*Sanhedrin*
SbTU	H. Hunger, ed., *Spätbabylonische Texte aus Uruk* (Berlin: Mann, 1976–)
SDB	*Supplément, Dictionnaire de la Bible*
Šebu.	*Šebu ʿot*
Seder Elijah Rab.	*Seder Elijah Rabbah*
Šek.	*Šekalim*
sing.	singular
Sot.	*Sotah*
Sukk.	*Sukkot*
Sum.	Sumerian
t.	Tosefta
T. Levi	*Testament of Levi*
TA	*Tel Aviv*
Ta ʿan.	*Ta ʿanit*
Targ. Jon.	*Targum Jonathan*
Tam.	*Tamid*
TCS	Texts from Cuneiform Sources
Tem.	*Temura*
Ter.	*Terumot*
tg(s).	targum(s)
Tg. Neof.	*Targum Neofiti*
ThR	*Theologische Rudschau*
Tg. Onq.	*Targum Onqelos*

Tg. Ps.-J.	*Targum Pseudo-Jonathan*
Tg. Sam.	*Targum Samuel*
Tg. Yer.	*Targum Yerušalmi*
ThWAT	G. J. Botterweck and H. Ringgren, eds., *Theologisches Wörterbuch zum Alten Testament*
Tos.	*Tosafot*
Ug.	Ugaritic
UT	C. H. Gordon, *Ugaritic Textbook* (Rome, 1965)
VAB	*Vorasiartische Bibliotek* (Lipzig, 1907–16)
Vg	Vulgate
VTE	D. J. Wiseman, ed., *Vassal-Treaties of Esarhaddon* (London, 1958)
WHJP	*World History of The Jewish People*
Y.	Talmud Yerušalmi = Jerusalem Talmud
YBC	tablets in the Babylonian Collection, Yale University Library
y.	*yerushalmi*
y. Pe'a	*(Talmud) yerushalmi, Pē'â*
Yeb.	*Yebamit*
Zeb.	*Zebaḥim*
Zebaḥ.	*Zebaḥim*
Zuṭ	*Zûṭâ*

TRANSLATION OF THE BOOK OF LEVITICUS

◆

THE BOOK OF LEVITICUS IN OUTLINE

◆

PART I. THE SACRIFICIAL SYSTEM (CHAPTERS 1–7)

1. *The Burnt Offering (1:1–17)*

Introduction

[1]YHWH summoned Moses and spoke to him from the Tent of Meeting, and said: [2]Speak to the Israelites, and say to them: When any person among you presents an offering of livestock to YHWH, he shall choose his offering from the herd or from the flock.

The Burnt Offering: From the Herd

[3]If his offering is a burnt offering from the herd, he shall offer a male without blemish. He shall bring it to the entrance of the Tent of Meeting, for acceptance on his behalf before YHWH. [4]He shall lean his hand on the head of the burnt offering, that it may be acceptable on his behalf, to expiate for him. [5]The bull shall be slaughtered before YHWH, and Aaron's sons, the priests, shall present the blood and dash the blood against all sides of the altar that is at the entrance to the Tent of Meeting. [6]The burnt offering shall be flayed and quartered. [7]The sons of Aaron the priest shall stoke the fire on the altar and lay out wood upon the fire. [8]Then Aaron's sons, the priests, shall lay out the quarters, with the head and suet, on the wood that is on the fire upon the altar. [9]Its entrails and shins shall be washed with water, and the priest shall turn all of it into smoke on the altar as a burnt offering, a food gift of pleasing aroma to YHWH.

From the Flock

[10]If his offering for a burnt offering is from the flock, of sheep or of goats, he shall offer a male without blemish. [11]It shall be slaughtered on the north side of the altar before YHWH, and Aaron's sons, the priests, shall dash its blood against all sides of the altar. [12]When it has been quartered, the priest shall lay out the quarters, with the head and suet, on the wood that is on the fire upon the altar. [13]The entrails and the shins shall be washed with water, and the priest shall present all of it and turn it into smoke on the altar. It is a burnt offering, a food gift of pleasing aroma to YHWH.

From Birds

[14]If his offering to YHWH is a burnt offering of birds, he shall present a turtledove or a young pigeon as his offering. [15]The priest shall present it to the altar, pinch off its head and turn it into smoke on the altar; and the blood shall be drained out against the side of the altar. [16]He shall remove its crissum by its feathers, and cast it into the place of the ashes, at the east side of the altar. [17]The

priest shall tear it open by its wings, without severing [them], and turn it into smoke on the altar, upon the wood that is on the fire. It is a burnt offering, a food gift of pleasing aroma to YHWH.

2. *The Cereal Offering (2:1–16)*

Raw Flour

[1]When a person presents an offering of cereal to YHWH, his offering shall be of semolina; he shall pour oil upon it, lay frankincense on it, [2]and present it to Aaron's sons, the priests. [The priest] shall scoop out therefrom a handful of its semolina and oil, as well as all of its frankincense; and this token portion the priest shall turn into smoke on the altar, as a food gift of pleasing aroma to YHWH. [3]And the remainder of the cereal offering shall be for Aaron and his sons, a most sacred portion from YHWH's food gifts.

Cooked: Baked, Toasted, Fried

[4]When you present an offering of cereal baked in an oven, [it shall be of] semolina: unleavened cakes mixed with oil, or unleavened wafers smeared with oil.

[5]If your offering is a cereal offering [toasted] on a griddle, it shall be a semolina mixed with oil, unleavened. [6]Crumble it into bits and pour oil upon it; it is a cereal offering.

[7]If your offering is a cereal offering [fried] in a pan, it shall be made of semolina in oil.

[8]If you bring to YHWH a cereal offering prepared in any of these ways, it shall be presented to the priest, who shall deliver it to the altar. [9]The priest shall set aside the token portion from the cereal offering and turn it into smoke on the altar as a food gift of pleasing aroma to YHWH. [10]And the remainder of the cereal offering shall be for Aaron and his sons, a most sacred portion from YHWH's food gifts.

Injunctions Concerning Leaven, Honey, and Salt

[11]No cereal offering that you offer to YHWH shall be made leavened, for you must not turn into smoke any leaven or any honey as a food gift to YHWH. [12]You may offer them to YHWH as a first-processed offering; but they shall not be offered up on the altar as a pleasing aroma. [13]You shall season all your cereal offerings with salt; you shall not omit from your cereal offering the salt of your covenant with your God: on all your offerings you must offer salt.

Natural Grain

[14]If you bring a cereal offering of first-ripe fruits to YHWH, you shall bring milky grain parched with fire, groats of the fresh ear, as a cereal offering of

your first-ripe fruits. [15]You shall add oil to it and lay frankincense on it: it is a cereal offering. [16]And the priest shall turn into smoke its token portion: some of its groats and oil, with all of its frankincense, as a food gift to YHWH.

3. The Well-Being Offering (3:1–17)

[1]If his offering is a sacrifice of well-being—

From the Herd

If he offers from the herd, whether male or female, he shall present it without blemish before YHWH [2]and lean his hand upon the head of his offering. It shall be slaughtered at the entrance of the Tent of Meeting, and Aaron's sons, the priests, shall dash the blood against all sides of the altar. [3]He shall then present from the sacrifice of well-being a food gift to YHWH: the suet that covers the entrails and all the suet that is around the entrails; [4]the two kidneys and the suet that is around them, that is on the sinews; and the caudate lobe on the liver, which he shall remove with the kidneys. [5]Aaron's sons shall turn it (this food gift) into smoke on the altar, with the burnt offering that is upon the wood that is on the fire, as a food gift of pleasing aroma to YHWH.

From the Flock

[6]And if his offering for a sacrifice of well-being to YHWH is from the flock, whether male or female, he shall offer it without blemish. [7]If he offers a sheep as his offering, he shall present it before YHWH [8]and lean his hand upon the head of his offering. It shall be slaughtered before the Tent of Meeting, and Aaron's sons shall dash its blood against all sides of the altar. [9]He shall then present, as a food gift to YHWH from the sacrifice of well-being, its suet: the broad tail completely removed close to the sacrum; the suet that covers the entrails and all the suet that is around the entrails; [10]the two kidneys and the suet that is around them on the sinews; and the caudate lobe on the liver, which he shall remove with the kidneys. [11]The priest shall turn it into smoke on the altar as food, a food gift to YHWH.

[12]And if his offering is a goat, he shall present it before YHWH [13]and lean his hand upon its head. It shall be slaughtered before the Tent of Meeting, and Aaron's sons shall dash its blood against all sides of the altar. [14]He shall then present as his offering from it, as a food gift to YHWH, the suet that covers the entrails and all the suet that is around the entrails; [15]the two kidneys and the suet that is around them on the sinew; and the caudate lobe on the liver, which he shall remove with the kidneys. [16]The priest shall turn these into smoke on the altar as food, a food gift of pleasing aroma.

The Law of Suet and Blood

All suet is YHWH's. ¹⁷*It is a law for all time throughout your generations, in all your settlements: you must not eat any suet or any blood.**

4. *The Purification Offering (4:1–35)*

Introduction

¹YHWH spoke to Moses, saying: ²Speak to the Israelites thus:

When a person inadvertently does wrong in regard to any of YHWH's prohibitive commandments by violating any one of them—

Of the High Priest

³If it is the anointed priest who so does wrong to the detriment of the people, he shall offer for the wrong he has done a bull of the herd without blemish as a purification offering to YHWH. ⁴He shall bring the bull to the entrance of the Tent of Meeting before YHWH, lean his hand upon the head of the bull, and slaughter the bull before YHWH. ⁵The anointed priest shall take some of the bull's blood and bring it into the Tent of Meeting. ⁶The priest shall dip his finger in the blood, and sprinkle some of the blood seven times before YHWH against the veil of the shrine. ⁷The priest shall put some of the blood on the horns of the altar of perfumed incense, which is in the Tent of Meeting, before YHWH; and all the rest of the bull's blood he shall pour out at the base of the altar of burnt offering, which is at the entrance of the Tent of Meeting. ⁸He shall set aside all of the suet from the bull of the purification offering: the suet that covers the entrails and all of the suet that is around the entrails; ⁹the two kidneys and the suet that is around them, that is on the sinews; and the caudate lobe on the liver, which he shall remove with the kidneys—¹⁰just as it is set aside from the ox of the well-being offering. The priest shall turn them into smoke on the altar of burnt offering. ¹¹But the hide of the bull, and all its flesh, together with its head and shins, its entrails and dung—¹²all the rest of the bull—shall be taken away to a pure place outside the camp, to the ash dump, and burned with wood; it shall be burned on the ash dump.

Of the Community

¹³If it is the whole community of Israel that has erred inadvertently and the matter escapes the notice of the congregation, so that they violate one of YHWH's prohibitive commandments, and they feel guilt ¹⁴when the wrong that they committed in regard to it becomes known, the congregation shall offer a bull of the herd as a purification offering and bring it before the Tent of Meeting. ¹⁵The elders of the community shall lean their hands upon the head of the bull be-

---

* Italic block type here through page 1294 (Chs. 3–16) stands for H.

fore YHWH, and the bull shall be slaughtered before YHWH. [16]The anointed priest shall bring some of the bull's blood into the Tent of Meeting, [17]and the priest shall dip his finger in the blood and sprinkle some of it seven times before YHWH, against the veil. [18]Some of the blood he shall put on the horns of the altar that is before YHWH in the Tent of Meeting, and all the rest of the blood he shall pour out at the base of the altar of burnt offering, which is at the entrance of the Tent of Meeting. [19]He shall set aside all of its suet from it and turn it into smoke on the altar. [20]He shall treat the bull as he treated the [first] bull of the purification offering; he shall treat it the same way. Thus the priest shall effect purgation for them that they may be forgiven. [21]The bull shall be taken away outside the camp, and it shall be burned as the first bull was burned; it is the purification offering of the congregation.

Of the Chieftain

[22]When the chieftain does wrong by violating any of YHWH's prohibitive commandments inadvertently, and he feels guilt [23]or he is informed of the wrong he committed, he shall bring as his offering a male goat without blemish. [24]He shall lean his hand upon the goat's head, and it shall be slaughtered at the spot where the burnt offering is slaughtered, before YHWH: it is a purification offering. [25]The priest shall take some of the blood of the purification offering with his finger and put it on the horns of the altar of burnt offering; and (the rest of) its blood he shall pour out at the base of the altar of burnt offering. [26]All of its suet he shall turn into smoke on the altar, like the suet of the well-being offering. Thus shall the priest effect purgation on his behalf for his wrong, that he may be forgiven.

Of the Commoner

[27]If any person from among the populace does wrong inadvertently by violating any of YHWH's prohibitive commandments and he feels guilt [28]or he is informed of the wrong he committed, he shall bring as his offering a female goat without blemish for the wrong he committed. [29]He shall lean his hand upon the head of the purification offering, and the purification offering shall be slaughtered at the spot (of the slaughter) of the burnt offering. [30]The priest shall take some of its blood with his finger and put it on the horns of the altar of burnt offering; and all the rest of its blood he shall pour out at the base of the altar. [31]All of its suet he shall remove, just as the suet was removed from the well-being offering; and the priest shall turn (it) into smoke on the altar as a pleasing aroma to YHWH. Thus the priest shall effect purgation on his behalf, that he may be forgiven.

[32]If the offering he brings is a sheep, he shall bring a female without blemish. [33]He shall lean his hand upon the head of the purification offering, and it shall be slaughtered for purification purposes at the spot where the burnt offering is slaughtered. [34]The priest shall take some of the blood of the purification offering with his finger and put it on the horns of the altar of burnt offering, and all the rest of its blood he shall pour out at the base of the altar. [35]And all of its

suet he shall remove, just as the suet of the sheep of the well-being offering is removed; and the priest shall turn it (lit., them) into smoke on the altar, with the food gifts of YHWH. Thus the priest shall effect purgation on his behalf for the wrong he committed, that he may be forgiven.

5. *The Graduated Purification Offering (5:1–13)*

The Four Cases

¹If a person does wrong:
   When he has heard a public imprecation (against withholding testimony)— and although he was a witness, either having seen or known (the facts)—yet does not testify, then he must bear his punishment;
   ²Or when a person touches any impure thing—be it the carcass of an impure wild quadruped or the carcass of an impure domesticated quadruped or the carcass of an impure swarming creature—and, though he has become impure, the fact escapes him but (thereafter) he feels guilt;
   ³Or when he touches human impurity—any such impurity whereby one becomes impure—and, though he has known it, the fact escapes him but (thereafter) he feels guilt;
   ⁴Or when a person blurts out an oath to bad or good purpose—whatever anyone may utter in an oath—and, though he has known it, the fact escapes him but (thereafter) he feels guilt in any of these matters—

Resolution: Confession and Sacrifice

⁵When he feels guilt in any of these matters, he shall confess that wherein he did wrong. ⁶And he shall bring as his reparation to YHWH, for the wrong that he committed, a female from the flock, sheep or goat, as a purification offering; and the priest shall effect purgation on his behalf for his wrong.
   ⁷But if his means do not suffice for a sheep, he shall bring to YHWH as his reparation for what he has done wrong, two turtledoves or two pigeons, one for a purification offering and the other for a burnt offering. ⁸He shall bring them to the priest, who shall offer first the one for the purification offering, pinching the head at its nape without severing it. ⁹He shall sprinkle some of the blood of the purification offering on the side of the altar, and what remains of the blood shall be drained at the base of the altar; it is a purification offering. ¹⁰And the second he shall sacrifice as a burnt offering, according to regulation. Thus the priest shall effect purgation on his behalf for the wrong that he committed so that he may be forgiven.
   ¹¹And if his means do not suffice for two turtledoves or two pigeons, he shall bring as his offering for what he had done wrong one-tenth of an ephah of semolina for a purification offering; he shall not put oil upon it or place frankincense on it, for it is a purification offering. ¹²He shall bring it to the priest, and the priest shall scoop out a handful as a token portion of it and turn it into smoke on the altar, with YHWH's food gifts; it is a purification offering. ¹³Thus

the priest shall effect purgation on his behalf for the wrong he committed in any of these matters so that he may be forgiven. It shall belong to the priest, like the cereal offering.

The Reparation Offering (5:14–26)

For Sacrilege Against Sancta

5 [14]YHWH spoke to Moses, saying: [15]When a person commits a sacrilege by being inadvertently remiss with any of YHWH's sancta, he shall bring as his penalty to YHWH a ram without blemish from the flock, convertible into payment in silver by sanctuary weight, as a reparation offering, [16]and he shall make restitution for that item of the sancta wherein he was remiss and shall add one-fifth to it. When he gives it to the priest, the priest shall effect expiation on his behalf with the ram of the reparation offering so that he may be forgiven.

For Suspected Sacrilege Against Sancta

[17]If, however, a person errs by violating any of YHWH's prohibitive commandments without knowing it and he feels guilt, he shall bear his responsibility [18]by bringing to the priest an unblemished ram from the flock, or its assessment, as a reparation offering. The priest shall effect expiation on his behalf for the error he committed without knowing it so that he may be forgiven. [19]It is a reparation offering; he has incurred liability to YHWH.

For Sacrilege Against Oaths

[20]YHWH spoke to Moses, saying: [21]When a person sins by committing a sacrilege against YHWH in that he has dissembled to his fellow in the matter of a deposit or investment or robbery; or having withheld from his fellow [22]or having found a lost object he has dissembled about it; and he swears falsely about any one of the things that a person may do and sin thereby—[23]when one has thus sinned, and feeling guilt, he shall return that which he robbed or that which he withheld, or the deposit that was entrusted to him, or the lost object he found, [24]or anything else about which he swore falsely; he shall restore it in its entirety and add one-fifth to it. He shall pay it to its owner as soon as he feels guilt. [25]Then he shall bring to the priest, as his reparation to YHWH, an unblemished ram from the flock, or its assessment, as a reparation offering. [26]The priest shall effect expiation on his behalf before YHWH so that he may be forgiven for whatever he has done to feel guilty thereby.

6. Sacrifices: The Administrative Order (6:1–23)

Introduction

[1]YHWH spoke to Moses, saying: [2]Command Aaron and his sons thus:

The Burnt Offering

This is the ritual for the burnt offering—that is, the burnt offering that stays on the altar hearth all night until morning, while the altar fire is kept burning on it. ³The priest, having put on linen raiment, with linen breeches next to his body, shall remove the ashes to which the fire has reduced the burnt offering on the altar and put them beside the altar. ⁴He shall then remove his vestments and put on other vestments, and take the ashes outside the camp to a pure place. ⁵The fire on the altar shall be kept burning on it [the hearth]; it shall not go out. Every morning the priest shall feed wood to it, lay out the burnt offering upon it, and on top turn into smoke the fat parts of the well-being offerings. ⁶A perpetual fire shall be kept burning on the altar; it shall not go out.

The Cereal Offering

⁷This is the ritual for the cereal offering. Aaron's sons shall present it before YHWH, in front of the altar. ⁸A handful of the semolina and oil of the cereal offering shall be set aside from it, with all of the frankincense that is on the cereal offering, and this token of it shall be turned into smoke on the altar as a pleasing aroma to YHWH. ⁹The remainder Aaron and his sons shall eat; it shall be eaten unleavened in a holy place; they shall eat it in the court of the Tent of Meeting. ¹⁰It shall not be baked with leaven; I have assigned it as their portion from my food gifts; it is most sacred like the purification offering and the reparation offering. ¹¹Any male of Aaron's descendants may eat of it, as a due for all time throughout your generations from YHWH's food gifts. Whatever touches them shall become holy.

The High Priest's Daily Cereal Offering

¹²*YHWH spoke to Moses, saying:* ¹³*This is the offering that Aaron and his sons shall present to YHWH from the time of his anointment: one-tenth of an ephah of semolina as a regular cereal offering, half of it in the morning and half of it in the evening.* ¹⁴*It shall be prepared with oil on a griddle. You shall bring it well soaked, and present it as tūpînê, a cereal offering of crumbled bits, of pleasing aroma to YHWH.* ¹⁵*And so shall the priest, anointed from among his sons to succeed him, sacrifice it; it is YHWH's due for all time; it shall entirely go up in smoke.* ¹⁶*So every cereal offering of a priest shall be a total offering; it shall not be eaten.*

The Purification Offering

¹⁷*YHWH spoke to Moses, saying:* ¹⁸*Speak to Aaron and his sons thus:* this is the ritual for the purification offering. The purification offering shall be slaughtered before YHWH, at the spot where the burnt offering is slaughtered; it is most sacred. ¹⁹The priest who offers it as a purification offering shall enjoy it; it

shall be eaten in a holy place, in the court of the Tent of Meeting. [20]Whatever touches its flesh shall become holy; and if any of its blood is spattered upon a garment, the bespattered part shall be laundered in a holy place. [21]An earthen vessel in which it is boiled shall be broken; if it has been boiled in a copper vessel, that shall be scoured and flushed with water. [22]Any male among the priests may eat of it: it is most sacred. [23]No purification offering, however, may be eaten from which any blood is brought into the Tent of Meeting to effect purgation in the shrine; it shall be consumed in fire.

7. Sacrifices: The Administrative Order (Continued) (7:1–38)

The Reparation Offering

[1]This the ritual for the reparation offering: it is most sacred. [2]The reparation offering shall be slaughtered at the spot where the burnt offering is slaughtered, and he [the priest] shall dash its blood against all sides of the altar. [3]All of its suet shall be presented: the broad tail, the suet that covers the entrails; [4]the two kidneys and the suet that is around them on the sinews; and the caudate lobe on the liver, which shall be removed with the kidneys. [5]The priest shall turn them into smoke on the altar as a food gift to YHWH; it is a reparation offering. [6]Any male among the priests may eat of it; it shall be eaten in a holy place, it is most sacred.

The Priestly Prebends from the Most Holy Offerings

[7]The reparation offering is like the purification offering. There is a single rule for both: it shall belong to the priest who performs expiation therewith. [8]The priest who sacrifices a person's burnt offering shall keep the hide of the burnt offering that he sacrificed. [9]Any cereal offering that is baked in an oven, and any that is prepared in a pan or on a griddle shall belong to the priest who offers it. [10]Any cereal offering, whether mixed with oil or dry, shall belong to all the sons of Aaron alike.

The Well-Being Offering

[11]This is the ritual for the sacrifice of well-being that one may offer to YHWH. [12]If he offers it for thanksgiving, he shall offer together with the sacrifice of thanksgiving unleavened cakes mixed with oil, unleavened wafers smeared with oil, and well-soaked cakes of semolina mixed with oil. [13]This offering, with cakes of leavened bread added, he shall offer together with his thanksgiving sacrifice of well-being. [14]Out of this he shall present one of each [kind of] offering as a contribution to YHWH; it shall belong to the priest who dashes the blood of the well-being offering. [15]And the flesh of his thanksgiving sacrifice of well-being shall be eaten on the day that it is offered; none of it shall be put aside until morning.

¹⁶If the sacrifice he offers is a votive or freewill offering, it shall be eaten on the day he offers his sacrifice, and what is left of it shall be eaten on the morrow. ¹⁷What is then left of the sacrificial flesh shall be consumed in fire on the third day. ¹⁸If any of the flesh of his sacrifice of well-being is eaten on the third day, it shall not be acceptable; it shall not be accredited to him who offered it. It is desecrated meat, and the person who eats of it shall bear his punishment.

¹⁹Flesh that touches anything impure shall not be eaten; it shall be consumed in fire. As for other flesh, anyone who is pure may eat such flesh. ²⁰But the person who, while impure, eats flesh from YHWH's sacrifice of well-being, that person shall be cut off from his kin. ²¹When a person touches anything impure, be it human impurity or an impure quadruped or any impure detestable creature, and eats flesh from YHWH's sacrifice of well-being, that person shall be cut off from his kin.

No Suet or Blood May Be Eaten

²²And YHWH spoke to Moses, saying: ²³Speak to the Israelites thus: you shall not eat the suet of any ox, sheep, or goat. ²⁴The suet of an animal that died or was mauled by beasts may be put to any use, but you must not eat it. ²⁵If anyone eats the suet of an animal from which a food gift is presented to YHWH, that person shall be cut off from his kin. ²⁶And you must not ingest any blood, whether of bird or animal, in any of your settlements. ²⁷Any person who ingests any blood shall be cut off from his kin.

The Priestly Prebends from the Well-Being Offering

²⁸And YHWH spoke to Moses, saying: ²⁹Speak to the Israelites thus: the one who presents his sacrifice of well-being to YHWH shall bring his offering to YHWH from his sacrifice of well-being. ³⁰His own hands shall bring YHWH's food gifts: he shall bring the suet together with the breast, the breast to be elevated as an elevation offering before YHWH. ³¹The priest shall turn the suet into smoke at the altar, but the breast shall belong to Aaron and his sons. ³²And the right thigh from your sacrifices of well-being you shall give to the priest as a gift; ³³the one among Aaron's sons who offers the blood of the well-being offering and the suet shall receive the right thigh as his prebend. ³⁴For I have taken the breast of the elevation offering and the thigh of the contribution from the Israelites, from their sacrifices of well-being, and have assigned them to Aaron the priest and to his sons as a due from the Israelites for all time. ³⁵This shall be the perquisite of Aaron and the perquisite of his sons from YHWH's food gifts once they have been inducted to serve YHWH as priests, ³⁶which YHWH commanded to be assigned to them, once they had been anointed, as a due from the Israelites for all time throughout their generations.

Summary

[37]This is the ritual for the burnt offering, the cereal offering, the purification offering, the reparation offering, the ordination offering, and the sacrifice of well-being, [38]which YHWH commanded Moses on Mount Sinai, when he commanded the Israelites to present their offerings to YHWH, in the Wilderness of Sinai.

PART II. THE INAUGURATION OF THE CULT (CHAPTERS 8–10)

8. *The Consecration of the Priests (8:1–36)*

[1]YHWH spoke to Moses, saying: [2]Take Aaron and his sons with him, the vestments, the anointing oil, the bull of purification offering, the two rams, and the basket of unleavened bread, [3]and assemble the whole community at the entrance to the Tent of Meeting. [4]Moses did as YHWH commanded him. And when the community was assembled at the entrance of the Tent of Meeting, [5]Moses said to the community, "This is what YHWH has commanded to be done."

[6]Moses brought Aaron and his sons forward and had them washed with water. [7]He put the tunic on him, girded him with the sash, clothed him with the robe, put the ephod on him, and girded him with the decorated band, which he tied to him. [8]He put the breastpiece on him, and put into the breastpiece the Urim and Thummim. [9]And he set the turban on his head; and on the turban, in front, he put the gold plate, the holy diadem—as YHWH had commanded Moses.

[10]Moses took the anointing oil and anointed the tabernacle and all that was in it, thus consecrating them. [11]He sprinkled some of it on the altar seven times, and he anointed the altar, all of its utensils, and the laver with its stand, to consecrate them. [12]He poured some of the anointing oil upon Aaron's head, thereby anointing him to consecrate him. [13]Then Moses brought Aaron's sons forward, clothed them in tunics, girded them with sashes, and tied caps on them—as YHWH had commanded Moses.

[14]He had the bull of purification offering brought forward. Aaron and his sons leaned their hands on the bull of purification offering, [15]and it was slaughtered. Moses took the blood and with his finger put [some] on the horns around the altar, decontaminating the altar; then he poured out the blood at the base of the altar. Thus he consecrated it to effect atonement upon it. [16]All of the suet that was about the entrails, and the caudate lobe of the liver, and the two kidneys and their suet, were then taken up and Moses turned [them] into smoke upon the altar; [17]but the [rest of the] bull—its hide, its flesh, and its dung—was put to fire outside the camp—as YHWH had commanded Moses.

[18]Then the ram of burnt offering was brought forward. Aaron and his sons leaned their hands upon the ram's head, [19]and it was slaughtered. Moses dashed

the blood against all sides of the altar. ²⁰The ram was cut up into its quarters, and Moses turned the head, the quarters, and the suet into smoke. ²¹The entrails and shins were washed in water, and Moses turned all of the ram into smoke on the altar. This was a burnt offering for a pleasing aroma, a food gift to YHWH—as YHWH had commanded Moses.

²²Then the second ram, the ram of ordination, was brought forward. Aaron and his sons leaned their hands upon the ram's head, ²³and it was slaughtered. Moses took some of its blood and put [it] on the lobe of Aaron's right ear, and on the thumb of his right hand, and on the big toe of his right foot. ²⁴Then the sons of Aaron were brought forward, and Moses put some of the blood on the lobes of their right ears, and on the thumbs of their right hands, and on the big toes of their right feet; and Moses dashed the [rest of the] blood against all sides of the altar. ²⁵He took the suet—the broad tail, all of the suet about the entrails, the caudate lobe of the liver, and the two kidneys and their suet—and the right thigh. ²⁶From the basket of unleavened bread that was before YHWH, he took one cake of unleavened bread, one cake of oil bread, and one wafer, and placed [them] on the suet pieces and on the right thigh. ²⁷He placed all of these on the palms of Aaron and on the palms of his sons, and presented them as an elevation offering before YHWH. ²⁸Then Moses took them from their palms and turned [them] into smoke on the altar with the burnt offering. This was an ordination offering for a pleasing aroma, a food gift to YHWH. ²⁹Moses took the breast and presented it as an elevation offering before YHWH; it was Moses' portion of the ram of ordination—as YHWH had commanded Moses.

³⁰Then Moses took some of the anointing oil and some of the blood that was on the altar and sprinkled [it] upon Aaron's vestments, upon his sons, and upon his sons' vestments with him. Thus he consecrated Aaron's vestments, his sons, and his sons' vestments with him.

³¹And Moses said to Aaron and his sons: Boil the flesh at the entrance of the Tent of Meeting and eat it there with the bread that is in the basket of ordination—as I commanded: "Aaron and his sons shall eat it." ³²The remainder of the flesh and the bread you shall destroy by fire. ³³You shall not go outside the entrance of the Tent of Meeting for seven days, until the day that your period of ordination is completed; for your ordination will require seven days. ³⁴Everything done today, YHWH has commanded to be done, to make atonement for you. *³⁵You shall stay at the entrance of the Tent of Meeting day and night for seven days, observing YHWH's prohibitions, so that you do not die—for so I have been commanded.*

³⁶And Aaron and his sons did all of the things that YHWH had commanded through Moses.

9. *The Inaugural Service (9:1–24)*

The Sacrificial Procedure

¹On the eighth day, Moses summoned Aaron and his sons and the elders of Israel. ²He said to Aaron, "Take a calf of the herd for a purification offering and

a ram for a burnt offering, both without blemish, and bring [them] before YHWH. ³And speak to the Israelites, saying, 'Take a he-goat for a purification offering; a calf and a lamb, both yearlings without blemish, for a burnt offering; ⁴and an ox and a ram for a well-being offering to sacrifice before YHWH; and a cereal offering mixed with oil. For today YHWH will appear to you.'"

⁵They brought what Moses had commanded to the front of the Tent of Meeting, and the whole community came forward and stood before YHWH. ⁶Moses said, "This is what YHWH commanded that you do, that the Glory of YHWH may appear to you." ⁷Then Moses said to Aaron, "Come forward to the altar and sacrifice your purification offering and your burnt offering and make atonement for yourself and for the people; and sacrifice the people's offering and make atonement for them—as YHWH has commanded."

⁸Aaron came forward to the altar and slaughtered his calf of purification offering. ⁹Aaron's sons presented the blood to him; he dipped his finger in the blood and put [it] on the horns of the altar; and he poured out [the rest of] the blood at the base of the altar. ¹⁰The suet, the kidneys, and the caudate lobe of the liver from the purification offering he turned into smoke on the altar—as YHWH had commanded Moses; ¹¹and the flesh and the skin were consumed in fire outside the camp. ¹²Then he slaughtered the burnt offering. Aaron's sons passed the blood to him, and he dashed it against all sides of the altar. ¹³They passed the burnt offering to him in sections, and the head, and he turned [them] into smoke on the altar. ¹⁴He washed the entrails and the legs, and turned [them] into smoke on the altar with the burnt offering.

¹⁵Then he brought forward the people's offering. He took the he-goat for the people's purification offering, and slaughtered it, and performed the purification rite with it, as with the previous [purification offering]. ¹⁶He brought forward the burnt offering and sacrificed it in the prescribed manner. ¹⁷He then brought forward the cereal offering and, taking a handful of it, he turned [it] into smoke on the altar—*in addition to the burnt offering of the morning.* ¹⁸He slaughtered the ox and the ram, the people's sacrifice of well-being. Aaron's sons passed the blood to him—which he dashed against all sides of the altar—¹⁹and the suet pieces of the ox and the ram: the broad tail, the covering [suet], the kidneys, and the caudate lobes. ²⁰They laid these suet pieces upon the breasts; and he turned the suet pieces into smoke upon the altar. ²¹Aaron presented the breasts and the right thigh as an elevation offering before YHWH—as Moses had commanded.

Blessing and Theophazny

²²Then Aaron lifted his hands toward the people and blessed them; and he came down after sacrificing the purification offering, the burnt offering, and the well-being offering. ²³Moses and Aaron then entered the Tent of Meeting. When they came out, they blessed the people; and the Glory of YHWH appeared to all of the people. ²⁴Fire came forth from before YHWH and consumed the burnt offering and the suet pieces on the altar. And the people saw, and shouted for joy, and fell on their faces.

10. *The Tragic Aftermath of the Inaugural Service (10:1–20)*

Nadab and Abihu

[1]Now Aaron's sons, Nadab and Abihu, each took his pan, put coals in it, and laid incense on it; and they offered before YHWH unauthorized coals, which he had not commanded them. [2]And fire came forth from YHWH and consumed them; thus they died before YHWH. [3]Then Moses said to Aaron, "This is what YHWH meant when he said: 'Through those near to me I shall sanctify myself, and before all of the people I shall glorify myself.' " And Aaron was silent.

[4]Moses called Mishael and Elzaphan, sons of Uzziel the uncle of Aaron, and said to them, "Come forward and carry your kinsmen away from the front of the sacred precinct [to a place] outside the camp." [5]They came forward and carried them out of the camp by their tunics, as Moses had ordered. [6]And Moses said to Aaron and to his sons, Eleazar and Ithamar, "Do not dishevel your hair and do not rend your clothes, lest you die and anger strike the whole community. But your kinsmen, all the house of Israel, shall bewail the burning that YHWH has wrought. [7]You must not go outside the entrance of the Tent of Meeting, lest you die, for YHWH's anointing oil is upon you." And they did as Moses had ordered.

The Conduct and Function of the Priests

[8]And YHWH spoke to Aaron, saying: [9]Drink no wine or ale, you or your sons after you, when you enter the Tent of Meeting, that you may not die; it is a law for all time throughout your generations. *[10]You must distinguish between the sacred and the common, and between the impure and the pure. [11]And you must teach the Israelites all of the laws that YHWH has imparted to them through Moses.*

On Eating the Priestly Portions

[12]Moses spoke to Aaron and to his remaining sons, Eleazar and Ithamar: "Take the cereal offering that remains from YHWH's food gifts and eat it unleavened beside the altar, for it is most holy. [13]You shall eat it in the sacred precinct, inasmuch as it is your due and your sons' due from YHWH's food gifts; for so I have been commanded. [14]But the breast of the elevation offering and the thigh of contribution you, and your sons and daughters after you, may eat in any pure place, for they have been assigned as a due to you and your children from the Israelites' sacrifices of well-being. [15]Together with the food gifts of suet, they must present the thigh of contribution and the breast of the elevation offering, which shall be elevated as an elevation offering before YHWH, and which shall be a due to you and to your children after you for all time—as YHWH has commanded."

[16]Then Moses insistently inquired about the goat of the purification offering, and it had already been burned! He was angry with Eleazar and Ithamar, Aaron's remaining sons, and said, [17]"Why did you not eat the purification offering in the sacred precinct? For it is most holy, and he has assigned it to you to remove the iniquity of the community to effect purgation on their behalf before YHWH.

[18]Because its blood was not brought into the interior of the sacred precinct, you certainly ought to have eaten it in the sacred precinct, as I commanded." [19]And Aaron spoke to Moses, "See, this day they brought their purification offering and burnt offering before YHWH, and such things have befallen me! Had I eaten the purification offering today, would YHWH have approved?" [20]And when Moses heard this, he approved.

PART III. THE IMPURITY SYSTEM
(CHAPTERS 11–16)

11. *Diet Laws (11:1–47)*

Introduction

[1]YHWH spoke to Moses and Aaron, saying to them: [2]Speak to the Israelites thus:

Quadrupeds

These are the creatures that you may eat from among all of the quadrupeds on the land: [3]any quadruped that has hoofs, with clefts through the hoofs, and that chews the cud—such you may eat. [4]The following, however, of those that chew the cud or have hoofs, you shall not eat: the camel—although it chews the cud, it has no hoofs: it is impure for you; [5]the rock badger—although it chews the cud, it has no hoofs: it is impure for you; [6]the hare—although it chews the cud, it has no hoofs: it is impure for you; [7]and the pig—although it has hoofs, with the hoofs cleft through, it does not chew the cud: it is impure for you. [8]You shall not eat of their flesh or touch their carcasses; they are impure for you.

Fish

[9]These you may eat of all that live in water: anything in water, whether in the seas or in the streams, that has fins or scales—these you may eat. [10]But anything in the seas or in the streams that has no fins and scales, among all of the swarming creatures of the water and among all of the [other] living creatures that are in the water—they are an abomination for you [11]and an abomination for you they shall remain: you shall not eat of their flesh and you shall abominate their carcasses. [12]Everything in water that has no fins and scales shall be an abomination for you.

Birds

[13]The following you shall abominate among the birds; they shall not be eaten, they are an abomination: the eagle, the black vulture, the bearded vulture, [14]the kite, and falcons of every variety; [15]all varieties of raven; [16]the eagle owl, the

short-eared owl, and the long-eared owl; hawks of every variety; [17]the tawny owl, the fisher owl, the screech owl, [18]the white owl, and the scops owl; the osprey, [19]the stork, and herons of every variety; the hoopoe, and the bat.

Flying Insects

[20]All winged swarming creatures, that walk on all fours, shall be an abomination for you. [21]But these you may eat among all the winged swarming creatures that walk on all fours: all that have, above their feet, jointed legs to leap with on the ground. [22]Of these you may eat the following: locusts of every variety; all varieties of bald locust; crickets of every variety; and all varieties of grasshopper. [23]But all other winged swarming creatures that have four legs shall be an abomination for you.

Purification Procedures

[24]And you shall make yourselves impure with the following—whoever touches their carcasses shall be impure until evening, [25]and whoever carries any part of their carcasses shall wash his clothes and be impure until evening—[26]every quadruped that has hoofs but without clefts through the hoofs, or does not chew the cud. They are impure for you; whoever touches them shall be impure. [27]Also all animals that walk on flat paws, among those that walk on all fours, are impure for you; whoever touches their carcasses shall be impure until evening. [28]And anyone who carries their carcasses shall wash his clothes and remain impure until evening. They are impure for you.

[29]The following shall be impure for you from among the creatures that swarm on the earth: the rat, the mouse, and large lizards of every variety; [30]the gecko, the spotted lizard, the lizard, the skink, and the chameleon. [31]Those are for you the impure among all the swarming creatures; whoever touches them when they are dead shall be impure until evening. [32]And anything on which one of them falls when they are dead shall be impure: be it any article of wood, or fabric, or skin, or sackcloth—any such article that can be put to use shall be immersed in water, and it shall remain impure until evening; then it shall be pure. [33]And if any of those falls into any earthen vessel, everything inside it shall be impure and [the vessel] itself you shall break. [34]Any food that might be eaten shall become impure when it comes into contact with water; and any liquid that might be drunk shall become impure if it was inside any vessel. [35]Everything else on which the carcass of any of them falls shall be impure. An oven or a stove shall be smashed; they are impure, and impure they shall remain for you. [36]A spring or cistern in which water is collected shall remain pure, however, but whoever touches such a carcass [in it] shall be impure. [37]If such a carcass falls upon seed grain that is to be sown, it remains pure; [38]but if water is put on the seed and such a carcass falls upon it, it shall be impure for you.

[39]If a quadruped that you may eat has died, anyone who touches it shall be

impure until evening; ⁴⁰and anyone who eats of its carcass shall launder his
clothes and remain impure until evening; and anyone who carries its carcass
shall launder his clothes and remain impure until evening.

Land Swarmers

⁴¹All creatures that swarm upon the earth are an abomination; they shall not be
eaten. ⁴²You shall not eat anything that crawls on its belly, or anything that walks
on all fours, or anything that has many legs, comprising all creatures that swarm
on the earth, for they are an abomination. *⁴³You shall not defile your throats
with any creature that swarms. You shall not make yourselves impure therewith and thus become impure, ⁴⁴for I YHWH am your God. You shall sanctify
yourselves and be holy, for I am holy. You shall not contaminate your throats
with any swarming creature that moves upon the earth. ⁴⁵For I YHWH am he
who brought you up from the land of Egypt to be your God; you shall be holy,
for I am holy.*

Summary

⁴⁶These are the instructions concerning quadrupeds, birds, all living creatures
that move in the water, and all creatures that swarm on the earth, ⁴⁷for dis-
criminating between the impure and the pure, between creatures that may be
eaten and creatures that may not be eaten.

12. *Childbirth (12:1–8)*

¹YHWH spoke to Moses, saying: ²Speak to the Israelites thus: When a woman
at childbirth bears a male, she shall be impure for seven days; she shall be impure as during the period of her menstrual infirmity. — ³On the eighth day the
foreskin of his member shall be circumcised. — ⁴She shall remain in [a state of]
blood purity for thirty-three days; she shall not touch any consecrated thing, nor
enter the sacred precinct until the period of her purification is complete. ⁵If she
bears a female, she shall be impure for two weeks, as at her menstruation, and
she shall remain in [a state of] blood purity for sixty-six days.
　⁶On the completion of her period of purification, for either son or daughter,
she shall bring a yearling lamb for a burnt offering, and a pigeon or turtledove
for a purification offering to the priest, at the entrance of the Tent of Meeting.
⁷He shall offer it before YHWH and effect expiation on her behalf, and then
she shall be pure from her source of blood. This is the ritual for the woman who
bears a child, male or female. *⁸If, however, her means do not suffice for a sheep,
she shall take two turtledoves or two pigeons, one for a burnt offering and the
other for a purification offering. The priest shall effect expiation on her behalf,
and she shall be pure.*

13. *Scale Disease (13:1–59)*

Introduction

¹YHWH spoke to Moses and Aaron, saying:

Shiny Marks

²When a person has on the skin of his body a discoloration, a scab, or a shiny mark, and it develops into a scaly affection on the skin of his body, it shall be reported to Aaron the priest or to one of his sons, the priests. ³The priest shall examine the affection on the skin of his body: if hair in the affection has turned white and the affection appears to be deeper than the skin of his body, it is scale disease; when the priest sees it, he shall pronounce him impure. ⁴But if it is a white shiny mark on the skin of his body that does not appear deeper than the skin and its hair has not turned white, the priest shall quarantine [the person with] the affection for seven days. ⁵On the seventh day, the priest shall examine him, and if the affection has retained its color and the affection has not spread on the skin, the priest shall quarantine him for another seven days. ⁶On the seventh day, the priest shall examine him again: if the affection has faded and has not spread on the skin, the priest shall pronounce him pure. It is a scab; he shall wash his clothes, and he shall be pure. ⁷But if the scab should spread on the skin after he has presented himself to the priest and been pronounced pure, he shall present himself again to the priest. ⁸And if the priest sees that the scab has spread on the skin, the priest shall pronounce him impure; it is scale disease.

Discolorations

⁹When a person has a scaly affection, it shall be reported to the priest. ¹⁰If the priest, on examining [him], finds on the skin a white discoloration and it has turned some hair white, with a patch of raw flesh in the discoloration, ¹¹it is chronic scale disease on the skin of his body, and the priest shall pronounce him impure; he shall not quarantine him, for he is impure. ¹²But if the scales break out over the skin so that they cover all of the skin of the affected person from head to foot, wherever the priest can see—¹³if the priest sees that the scales have covered the whole body—he shall pronounce the affected person pure; because he has turned all white, he is pure. ¹⁴But as soon as raw flesh appears in it, he shall be impure; ¹⁵when the priest sees the raw flesh, he shall pronounce him impure. The raw flesh is impure; it is scale disease. ¹⁶If the raw flesh again turns white, however, he shall come to the priest, ¹⁷and the priest shall examine him: if the affection has turned white, the priest shall pronounce the affected person pure; he is pure.

Boils

¹⁸When a boil appears on the skin of one's body and it heals, ¹⁹and a white discoloration or a reddish-white shiny mark develops where the boil was, he shall

present himself to the priest. [20]The priest shall examine [it]; if it appears lower than his skin and the hair in it has turned white, the priest shall pronounce him impure; it is scale disease that has broken out in the [site of the] boil. [21]But if the priest on examining it finds that there is no white hair in it, and it is not lower than his skin, and it is faded, the priest shall quarantine him for seven days. [22]If it has spread on the skin, the priest shall pronounce him impure; it is an affection. [23]But if the shiny mark remains stationary, not having spread, it is the scar of the boil; the priest shall pronounce him pure.

Burns

[24]When the skin of one's body sustains a burn by fire, and the patch of the burn becomes a reddish-white or white shiny mark, [25]the priest shall examine it. If some hairs in the shiny mark have turned white and it appears deeper than the skin, it is scale disease that has broken out in the burn. The priest shall pronounce him impure; it is scale disease. [26]But if the priest on examining it finds that there is no white hair in the shiny mark, and it is not lower than the skin, and it is faded, the priest shall quarantine him for seven days. [27]On the seventh day, the priest shall examine him: if it has spread on the skin, the priest shall pronounce him impure; it is scale disease. [28]But if the shiny mark has remained stationary, not having spread on the skin, and it is faded, it is the discoloration from the burn. The priest shall pronounce him pure, for it is the scar of the burn.

Scalls

[29]If a man or a woman has an affection on the head or in the beard, [30]the priest shall examine the affection. If it appears deeper than the skin and the hair in it is yellow and sparse, the priest shall pronounce him impure; it is a scall, scale disease of the head or jaw. [31]But when the priest examines the scall affection and finds that it does not appear to go deeper than the skin, yet there is no black hair in it, the priest shall quarantine [the person with] the scall affection for seven days. [32]On the seventh day, the priest shall examine the affection. If the scall has not spread, and there is no yellow hair in it, and the scall does not appear deeper than the skin, [33]the person [with the scall] shall shave himself, without shaving the scall; the priest shall quarantine him for another seven days. [34]On the seventh day, the priest shall examine the scall. If the scall has not spread on the skin, and does not appear deeper than the skin, the priest shall pronounce him pure; he shall wash his clothes, and he shall be pure. [35]If, however, the scall should spread on the skin after he has been pronounced pure, [36]the priest shall examine him. If the scall has spread on the skin, the priest need not look for yellow hair; he is impure. [37]But if [subsequently] the scall has retained its color, and black hair has grown in it, the scall has healed; he is pure. The priest shall pronounce him pure.

Tetters

[38]When a man or woman has numerous shiny marks on the skin of the body and they are white, [39]the priest shall examine [them]. If the shiny marks on the skin of the body are dull white, it is a tetter that has broken out on the skin; he is pure.

Baldness

[40]When a man's hair falls out from his head, he is bald [on the crown] but pure. [41]If the hair falls out from the front of his head, he is bald on the forehead but pure. [42]But if a reddish-white affection appears on the bald crown or forehead, it is scale disease that is breaking out on his bald crown or forehead. [43]The priest shall examine him: if the discolored affection on his bald crown or forehead is reddish white, like scale disease of fleshy skin in appearance, [44]the man has scale disease; he is impure. The priest shall not fail to pronounce him impure; he has an affected head.

The Comportment of a Certified Carrier

[45]As for the person stricken with scale disease, his clothes shall be rent, his hair shall be disheveled, he shall cover his mustache, and he shall call out, "Impure! Impure!" [46]He shall be impure as long as the affection is on him. He is impure: he shall dwell apart; his dwelling shall be outside the camp.

Fabrics

[47]When mold disease occurs in a fabric, either a wool or a linen fabric, [48]or in the warp or woof of the linen or the wool, or in a skin or in anything made of skin: [49]if the affection in the fabric or the skin, in the warp or the woof, or in any article of skin, is bright green or bright red, it is mold disease. It shall be shown to the priest. [50]The priest shall examine the affection and shall quarantine the [article with the] affection for seven days. [51]On the seventh day, he shall examine the affection: if the affection has spread in the fabric, or in the warp, or in the woof, or in the skin, for whatever function the skin serves, the affection is malignant mold disease; it is impure. [52]The fabric, or the warp, or the woof, whether in wool or linen, or any article of skin that contains the affection, shall be burned, for it is a malignant mold; it shall be destroyed by fire. [53]But if the priest sees that the affection in the fabric, or in the warp, or in the woof, or in any article of skin, has not spread, [54]the priest shall order the affected material to be washed, and he shall quarantine it for another seven days. [55]And if, after the affected material has been washed, the priest sees that the affection has not changed its color and that it has not spread, it is impure. You shall destroy it by fire; it is a fret, whether on its inner side or on its outer side. [56]But if the priest examines [it] and finds the affection faded after it has been washed, he shall cut it out from the

fabric, or from the skin, or from the warp, or from the woof; [57]and if it reappears in the fabric, or in the warp, or in the woof, or in any article of skin, it is breaking out afresh; you shall destroy the affected material by fire. [58]If, however, the affection disappears from the fabric, or warp, or woof, or any article of skin that has been washed, it shall be washed once more, and it shall be pure. [59]This is the procedure for mold disease of fabric, woolen or linen, or of warp, or of woof, or of any article of skin, for pronouncing it pure or impure.

14. *Purification after Scale Disease (14:1–57)*

Rite of Passage

[1]YHWH spoke to Moses, saying: [2]This shall be the ritual for a scale-diseased person at the time of his purification. When it is reported to the priest, [3]the priest shall go outside the camp. If the priest sees that the scale-diseased person has been healed of scale disease, [4]the priest shall order two wild pure birds, cedar wood, crimson yarn, and hyssop to be brought for the one to be purified. [5]The priest shall order one bird slaughtered into an earthen vessel over spring water; [6]and he shall take the live bird, along with the cedar wood, the crimson yarn, and the hyssop, and dip them together with the live bird in the blood of the bird that was slaughtered over the spring water. [7]He shall then sprinkle [the blood] seven times on the one to be purified of the scale disease. When he has thus purified him, he shall release the live bird over the open country. [8]The one to be purified shall launder his clothes, shave off all of his hair, and bathe in water; then he shall be pure. After that he may enter the camp, but must remain outside his tent for seven days. [9]On the seventh day, he shall shave off all of his hair — of his head, chin, and eyebrows — indeed, he shall shave off all of his hair. He shall launder his clothes and bathe in water; then he shall be pure.

Purification Sacrifices

[10]On the eighth day, he shall take two male lambs without blemish, one yearling ewe without blemish, three-tenths [of an ephah] of semolina mixed with oil for a cereal offering, and one log of oil. [11]The priest who performs the purification shall place the one to be purified, together with these [offerings], before YHWH at the entrance to the Tent of Meeting. [12]The priest shall take one of the male lambs and present it as a reparation offering, together with the log of oil, and offer it as an elevation offering before YHWH. [13]The lamb shall be slaughtered at the spot in the sacred precinct where the purification offering and the burnt offering are slaughtered. For the reparation offering is like the purification offering; it [goes] to the priest; it is most holy. [14]The priest shall take some of the blood of the reparation offering, and the priest shall put [it] on the lobe of the right ear of the one who is being purified, and on the thumb of his right hand, and on the big toe of his right foot. [15]The priest shall then take some of the log of oil and pour [it] into the palm of his own left hand. [16]And the priest

shall dip his right finger in the oil that is on his left palm and sprinkle some of the oil with his finger seven times before YHWH. [17]And some of the oil left on his palm the priest shall put on the lobe of the right ear of the one being purified, on the thumb of his right hand, and on the big toe of his right foot—on top of the blood of the reparation offering. [18]The remainder of the oil on the priest's palm shall be put on the head of the one being purified. Thus the priest shall make expiation for him before YHWH. [19]The priest shall then offer the purification offering and effect purgation for the one being purified for his impurity. After this, the burnt offering shall be slaughtered, [20]and the priest shall offer up the burnt offering and the cereal offering on the altar. And the priest shall make expiation for him. Then he shall be pure.

Purification Sacrifices for the Poor

[21]If, however, he is poor and his means are insufficient, he shall take a reparation offering of one male lamb for an elevation offering to make expiation for him, one-tenth [of an ephah] of semolina mixed with oil for a cereal offering, a log of oil; [22]and two turtledoves or two pigeons, whichever are within his means, the one to be the purification offering and the other the burnt offering. [23]On the eighth day of his purification, he shall bring them to the priest at the entrance of the Tent of Meeting, before YHWH. [24]The priest shall take the lamb of reparation offering and the log of oil, and elevate them as an elevation offering before YHWH. [25]When the lamb of reparation offering has been slaughtered, the priest shall take some of the blood of the reparation offering and put it on the right ear of the one being purified, on the thumb of his right hand, and on the big toe of his right foot. [26]The priest shall then pour some of the oil on the palm of his own left hand, [27]and with the finger of his right hand the priest shall sprinkle some of the oil that is on the palm of his left hand seven times before YHWH. [28]The priest shall put some of the oil on his palm on the lobe of the right ear of the one being purified, on the thumb of his right hand, and on the big toe of his right foot, on top of the blood spots of the reparation offering; [29]and the remainder of the oil on the priest's palm shall be put on the head of the one being purified, to make expiation for him before YHWH. [30]He shall then offer one of the turtledoves or pigeons that are within his means—[31]whichever he can afford—the one as a purification offering and the other as a burnt offering together with the cereal offering. Thus shall the priest make expiation before YHWH for the one being purified. [32]This is the ritual for the one who has scale disease [and] whose means are insufficient at [the time of] his purification.

Fungous Houses: Diagnosis and Purification

[33]*YHWH spoke to Moses and Aaron, saying:* [34]*When you enter the land of Canaan, which I give you as a possession, and I inflict a fungous infection upon a house in the land you possess,* [35]*the owner of the house shall come and tell the priest, saying, "It appears to me that there is something like an infection in*

my house." ³⁶The priest shall order the house cleared before the priest enters to examine the infection, so that nothing in the house may become impure; after that the priest shall enter to examine the house. ³⁷If, when he examines the infection, the infection in the walls of the house is found to consist of bright green or bright red eruptions, which appear deeper than the wall, ³⁸the priest shall come out of the house to the entrance of the house, and quarantine the house for seven days. ³⁹On the seventh day, the priest shall return. If he sees that the infection has spread on the walls of the house, ⁴⁰the priest shall order the stones with the infection in them to be pulled out and cast outside the city into an impure place. ⁴¹The house shall be scraped inside all around, and the mortar that is scraped off shall be dumped outside the city in an impure place. ⁴²They shall take other stones and replace those stones [with them], and take other coating and plaster the house.

⁴³If the infection breaks out again in the house, after the stones have been pulled out and after the house has been scraped and replastered, ⁴⁴the priest shall come and examine: if the infection has spread in the house, it is a malignant fungus in the house: it [the house] is impure. ⁴⁵The house shall be demolished—its stones and timber and all of the mortar of the house—and taken to an impure place outside the city.

⁴⁶Whoever enters the house during the whole time it is quarantined shall be impure until evening. ⁴⁷Whoever lies down in the house must launder his clothes, and whoever eats in the house must launder his clothes.

⁴⁸If, however, the priest comes and sees that the infection has not spread in the house after the house was replastered, the priest shall pronounce the house pure, for the infection has healed. ⁴⁹To decontaminate the house, he shall take two birds, cedar wood, crimson thread, and hyssop. ⁵⁰One bird shall be slaughtered over spring water in an earthen vessel. ⁵¹He shall take the cedar wood, the hyssop, the crimson yarn, and the live bird, and dip them in the blood of the slaughtered bird and the spring water, and sprinkle on the house seven times. ⁵²Having decontaminated the house with the blood of the bird, the spring water, the live bird, the cedar wood, the hyssop, and the crimson thread, ⁵³he shall release the live bird over the open country outside the city. Thus he shall perform purgation upon the house, and it shall be pure.

Summary of Chapters 13–14

⁵⁴This is the procedure for all [fleshy] scale diseases, for scalls, ⁵⁵for mold in fabrics and houses, ⁵⁶for discolorations, for scabs, or for shiny marks—⁵⁷to determine when they are impure and when they are pure. This is the procedure for scale disease.

15. *Genital Discharges (15:1–33)*

Introduction

¹YHWH spoke to Moses and Aaron, saying: ²Speak to the Israelites and say to them:

Abnormal Male Discharges

When any man has a discharge, his discharge being from his member, he is impure. ³This shall be his impurity in his discharge—whether his member runs with his discharge or his member is blocked by his discharge, this is his impurity. ⁴Any bedding on which the man with a discharge lies shall be impure; and every object on which he sits shall be impure. ⁵Anyone who touches his bedding shall launder his clothes, bathe in water, and remain impure until evening. ⁶Whoever sits on an object on which the man with a discharge has sat shall launder his clothes, bathe in water, and remain impure until evening. ⁷Whoever touches the body of the man with a discharge shall launder his clothes, bathe in water, and remain impure until evening. ⁸If the man with a discharge spits on one who is pure, the latter shall launder his clothes, bathe in water, and remain impure until evening. ⁹Any means for riding that the man with a discharge has mounted shall be impure. ¹⁰Whoever touches anything that was under him shall be impure until evening; and whoever carries such things shall launder his clothes, bathe in water, and remain impure until evening. ¹¹Anyone whom a man with a discharge touches without having rinsed his hands in water shall launder his clothes, bathe in water, and remain impure until evening. ¹²An earthen vessel that a man with a discharge touches shall be broken; and any wooden implement shall be rinsed with water.

¹³When a man with a discharge is healed of his discharge, he shall count off seven days for his purification, launder his clothes, and bathe his body in spring water; then he shall be pure. ¹⁴On the eighth day, he shall obtain two turtledoves or two pigeons and come before YHWH at the entrance of the Tent of Meeting and give them to the priest. ¹⁵The priest shall offer them up, the one as a purification offering and the other as a burnt offering. Thus the priest shall effect purgation on his behalf, for his discharge, before YHWH.

Normal Male Discharges

¹⁶When a man has an emission of semen, he shall bathe his whole body in water and remain impure until evening. ¹⁷All fabric or leather on which semen falls shall be laundered in water and remain impure until evening.

Marital Intercourse

¹⁸[This applies to] a woman, with whom a man has sexual relations; they shall bathe in water and remain impure until evening.

Normal Female Discharges

¹⁹When a woman has a discharge, her discharge being blood from her body, she remains in her menstrual impurity seven days; whoever touches her shall be impure until evening. ²⁰Anything she lies on during her menstrual impurity

shall be impure; and anything she sits on shall be impure. ²¹Anyone who touches her bedding shall launder his clothes, bathe in water, and remain impure until evening; ²²and anyone who touches any object on which she has sat shall launder his clothes, bathe in water, and remain impure until evening. ²³If it [the object] is on the bedding or on the seat on which she is sitting when he touches it [the object], he shall be impure until evening. ²⁴And if a man proceeds to lie with her, her menstrual impurity is transmitted to him, and he shall be impure seven days; any bedding on which he lies shall become impure.

Abnormal Female Discharges

²⁵When a woman has a discharge of blood for many days, not at the time of her menstrual impurity, or when she has a discharge beyond the time of her menstrual impurity, as long as her impure discharge lasts, she shall be impure, just as during her menstrual period. ²⁶Any bedding on which she lies while her discharge lasts shall be for her like bedding during her menstrual impurity; and any object on which she sits shall be impure, as during her menstrual impurity: ²⁷whoever touches them shall be impure; he shall launder his clothes, bathe in water, and remain impure until the evening.

²⁸When she is healed of her discharge, she shall count off seven days, and after that she shall be pure. ²⁹On the eighth day, she shall obtain two turtledoves or two pigeons, and bring them to the priest at the entrance of the Tent of Meeting. ³⁰The priest shall offer up the one as a purification offering and the other as a burnt offering; and the priest shall effect purgation on her behalf, for her impure discharge, before YHWH.

Consequences for the Sanctuary and for Israel

³¹You shall set apart the Israelites from their impurity, lest they die through their impurity by polluting my Tabernacle which is among them.

Summary

³²This is the procedure for the one who has a discharge: for the one who has an emission of semen and becomes impure thereby, ³³and for the one who is in her menstrual infirmity, and for anyone, male or female, who has a discharge, and for a man who lies with an impure woman.

16. *The Day of Purgation* (Yôm Kippûr) *(16:1–34)*

Introduction

¹YHWH spoke to Moses after the death of the two sons of Aaron who died when they encroached upon the presence of YHWH.

Precautions and Provisions

²YHWH spoke to Moses: Tell your brother Aaron that he is not to come whenever he chooses into the adytum, inside the veil, in front of the *kappōret* that is upon the Ark, lest he die; f*or by means of the cloud I shall appear on the* kappōret. ³This is how Aaron shall enter the adytum: with a bull of the herd as a purification offering and a ram for a burnt offering; ⁴he shall put on a sacral linen tunic, linen breeches shall be on his body, and he shall gird himself with a linen sash, and he shall don a linen turban. These are the sacral vestments he shall put on after bathing his body in water. ⁵And from the Israelite community he shall take two he-goats for a purification offering and a ram for a burnt offering.

The Purgation Ritual

⁶Aaron shall bring forward his own bull of purification offering to effect purgation for himself and for his household; ⁷and he shall take the two he-goats and set them before YHWH at the entrance of the Tent of Meeting. ⁸Aaron shall place lots upon the two goats, one marked "for YHWH" and the other "for Azazel." ⁹Aaron shall bring forward the goat designated by lot "for YHWH" to sacrifice it as a purification offering; ¹⁰while the goat designated by lot "for Azazel" shall be stationed alive before YHWH to perform expiation upon it by sending it off into the wilderness to Azazel. ¹¹When Aaron shall bring forward his bull of purification offering to effect purgation for himself and his household, he shall slaughter his bull of purification offering. ¹²He shall take a panful of fiery coals from atop the altar before YHWH, and two handfuls of finely ground perfumed incense, and bring [these] inside the veil. ¹³He shall put the incense on the fire before YHWH so that the cloud from the incense covers the *kappōret* that is over [the Ark of] the Pact, lest he die. ¹⁴He shall take some of the blood of the bull and sprinkle it with his finger on the *kappōret* on its east side; and in front of the *kappōret* he shall sprinkle some of the blood with his finger seven times.

¹⁵He shall then slaughter the people's goat of purification offering, bring its blood inside the veil, and manipulate its blood as he did with the blood of the bull; he shall sprinkle it upon the *kappōret* and before the *kappōret*. ¹⁶Thus he shall purge the adytum of the pollution and transgressions of the Israelites, including all of their sins; and he shall do likewise for the Tent of Meeting, which abides with them in the midst of their pollution. ¹⁷No one shall be in the Tent of Meeting when he goes in to effect purgation in the adytum until he comes out. Thus he shall effect purgation for himself and his household and for the entire congregation of Israel. ¹⁸He shall then come out to the altar that is before YHWH and effect purgation upon it. He shall take some of the blood of the bull and of the goat and put it upon the horns around the altar; ¹⁹and he shall sprinkle some of the blood upon it with his finger seven times. Thus he shall purify it of the pollution of the Israelites and consecrate it.

The Scapegoat Ritual

²⁰When he has finished purging the adytum, the Tent of Meeting, and the altar, he shall bring forward the live goat. ²¹Aaron shall lean both of his hands upon the head of the live goat and confess over it all of the iniquities and transgressions of the Israelites, including all of their sins, and put them on the head of the goat; and it shall be sent off to the wilderness by a man in waiting. ²²Thus the goat shall carry upon it all of their iniquities to an inaccessible region.

The Altar Sacrifices

When the goat is set free in the wilderness, ²³Aaron shall go into the Tent of Meeting, take off the linen vestments that he put on when he entered the adytum, and leave them there. ²⁴He shall bathe his body in water in a holy place and put on his vestments; then he shall go out and sacrifice his burnt offering and the burnt offering of the people, effecting atonement for himself and for the people. ²⁵The suet of the purification offering he shall turn into smoke on the altar.

The Purification of the High Priest's Assistants

²⁶He who sets free the goat for Azazel shall launder his clothes and bathe his body in water; after that he may reenter the camp. ²⁷The purification-offering bull and the purification-offering goat whose blood was brought in to effect purgation in the adytum shall be taken outside the camp, and their hides, their flesh, and their dung shall be burned in fire. ²⁸He who burned them shall launder his clothes and bathe his body in water, and after that he may reenter the camp.

The Date: An Appendix

²⁹And this shall be for you a law for all time: In the seventh month, on the tenth day of the month, you shall practice self-denial; and you shall do no manner of work, neither the native-born nor the alien who resides among you. ³⁰For on this day shall purgation be effected on your behalf to purify you of all your sins; you shall become pure before YHWH. ³¹It shall be a sabbath of complete rest for you, and you shall practice self-denial; it is a law for all time. ³²The priest who has been anointed and ordained to serve as priest in place of his father shall effect purgation. He shall put on the linen vestments, the sacral vestments. ³³He shall purge the holiest part of the sanctuary, and he shall purge the Tent of Meeting and the altar; he shall effect purgation for the priests and for all the people of the congregation. ³⁴This shall be for you a law for all time: to effect purgation on behalf of the Israelites for all their sins once a year.

Summary

And he [Aaron] did as YHWH had commanded Moses.

PART IV. THE HOLINESS SOURCE
(CHAPTERS 17–27)

17. *The Slaughter and Consumption of Meat (17:1–16)*

Introduction

[1]YHWH spoke to Moses, saying: [2]Speak to Aaron and to his sons and to all the Israelites and say to them: This is what YHWH has commanded:

No Nonsacrificial Slaughter

[3]If anyone of the house of Israel slaughters an ox or a sheep or a goat in the camp, or does so outside the camp, [4]and has not brought it to the entrance of the Tent of Meeting to present (it as) an offering to YHWH, before YHWH's Tabernacle, bloodguilt shall be imputed to that person: he has shed blood; that person shall be cut off from among his kinspeople. [5](This is) in order that the Israelites may bring their sacrifices which they have been sacrificing in the open field—that they may bring them to YHWH, at the entrance of the Tent of Meeting, to the priest, and offer them as sacrifices of well-being to YHWH; [6]that the priest may dash the blood against the altar of YHWH at the entrance of the Tent of Meeting, and turn the suet into smoke as a pleasing aroma to YHWH; [7]and that they may offer their sacrifices no longer to the goat-demons after whom they stray. They shall have this (statute) as an eternal law, throughout their generations.

No Sacrifices to Other (Infernal) Gods

[8]And say to them further: If anyone of the house of Israel or of the aliens who may reside among them offers up a burnt offering or a (well-being) offering, [9]and does not bring it to the entrance of the Tent of Meeting to offer it to YHWH, that person shall be cut off from his kinspeople.

[10]And if anyone of the house of Israel or of the aliens who reside among them ingests any blood, I will set my face against the person who ingests blood, and I will cut him off from among his kinspeople. [11]For the life of the flesh is in the blood, and I have assigned it to you on the altar to ransom your lives; for it is the blood that ransoms by means of life. [12]Therefore I say to the Israelites: No person among you shall ingest blood, nor shall the alien who resides among you ingest blood.

[13]And if any Israelite or any alien who resides among them hunts down a beast or bird that may be eaten, he shall pour out its blood and cover it with earth. [14]For the life of all flesh—its blood is with its life. Therefore I said to the Israelites: You shall not ingest the blood of any flesh, for the life of all flesh is its blood; anyone who ingests it shall be cut off.

Eating of a Carcass Requires Purification

[15]And any person, whether citizen or alien, who eats what has died or has been torn by beasts shall launder his clothes, bathe in water, and remain impure until the evening; then he shall be pure. [16]But if he does not launder (his clothes) and bathe his body, he shall bear his punishment.

18. *Illicit Sexual Practices (18:1–30)*

Opening Exhortation

[1]YHWH spoke to Moses, saying: [2]Speak to the Israelites and say to them: I am YHWH your God. [3]As is done in the land of Egypt where you dwelt, you shall not do, and as they do in the land of Canaan to which I am bringing you, you shall not do; you shall not follow their statutes. [4]My rules alone shall you observe and my statutes alone shall you heed, following them: I YHWH your God (have spoken). [5]You shall heed my statutes and my rules, which if one does them, he shall live by them: I YHWH (have spoken).

The Prohibitions

[6]No one shall approach anyone of his own flesh to uncover nakedness: I YHWH (have spoken). [7]The nakedness of your father, that is, the nakedness of your mother, you shall not uncover; she is your mother—you shall not uncover her nakedness. [8]The nakedness of your father's wife you shall not uncover; it is the nakedness of your father. [9]The nakedness of your sister, the daughter of your father or the daughter of your mother—whether of the household clan or of an outside clan—do not uncover her nakedness. [10]The nakedness of your son's daughter or of your daughter's daughter—do not uncover their nakedness; for their nakedness is your own nakedness. [11]The nakedness of your father's wife's daughter who is of your father's clan—she is your sister; do not uncover her nakedness. [12]The nakedness of your father's sister you shall not uncover; she is of your father's flesh. [13]The nakedness of your mother's sister you shall not uncover; for she is your mother's flesh. [14]The nakedness of your father's brother you shall not uncover, (that is,) you shall not approach his wife; she is your aunt. [15]The nakedness of your daughter-in-law you shall not uncover: she is your son's wife; do not uncover her nakedness. [16]The nakedness of your brother's wife you shall not uncover; it is your brother's nakedness.

[17]The nakedness of a woman and her daughter you shall not uncover; neither shall you marry her son's daughter or her daughter's daughter to uncover her nakedness: they are kindred; it is depravity. [18]And you shall not marry a woman producing rivalry to her sister, uncovering her nakedness during her (sister's) lifetime. [19]You shall not approach a woman during her menstrual impurity to uncover her nakedness. [20]You shall not have sexual relations with your neighbor's wife and defile yourself through her. [21]You shall not dedicate any of

your offspring to be sacrificed to Molek, and thereby not desecrate the name of your god: I YHWH (have spoken). [22]You shall not lie with a male as one lies with a woman: it is an abomination. [23]You shall not have sexual relations with any animal to defile yourself thereby; nor shall any woman give herself to an animal to mate with it; it is a perversion.

Closing Exhortation

[24]Do not defile yourselves in any of these (practices), for by all these (practices) the nations I am casting out before you defiled themselves. [25]Thus the land became defiled; and I called it to account for its iniquity, and the land vomited out its inhabitants. [26]You, however, must keep my statutes and my rules and commit none of these abominations, neither the citizen nor the alien who resides among you; [27]for all these abominations the people in the land who (were) before you did, and the land became defiled. [28]So let not the land vomit you out for defiling it, as it is vomiting out the nation that was before you. [29]For all who commit any of these abominations—such persons shall be cut off from their kin. [30]So you will heed my prohibitions not to commit any of these statutory abominations that were done before you, and not defile yourself by them: I (who speak) am YHWH your God.

19. *Ritual and Moral Holiness (19:1–37)*

Opening: Call to Holiness

[1]YHWH spoke to Moses, saying: [2]Speak to the entire Israelite community and say to them: You shall be holy, for I, YHWH your God, am holy.

Religious Duties

[3]You shall each revere his mother and his father, and keep my sabbaths: I YHWH your God (have spoken).
   [4]Do not turn to idols, and molten gods do not make for yourselves: I YHWH your God (have spoken).
   [5]When you sacrifice a well-being offering to YHWH, sacrifice it so it may be accepted on your behalf. [6]It shall be eaten on the day you sacrifice (it), or on the next day; but what is left by the third day must be consumed in fire. [7]But if it is eaten at all on the third day, it is rotten meat; it will not be acceptable. [8]Anyone who eats of it shall bear his punishment, because he has desecrated what is sacred to YHWH; that person shall be cut off from his kin.
   [9]When you reap the harvest of your land, you shall not destroy the edge of your field in reaping, and the gleanings of your harvest you shall not gather. [10]Your vineyard you shall not pick bare, and the fallen fruit of your vineyard you shall not gather. For the poor and the alien shall you leave them: I YHWH your God (have spoken).

Ethical Duties

[11]You shall not steal; you shall not dissemble, and you shall not lie to one another. [12]And you shall not swear falsely by my name, lest you desecrate the name of your God: I YHWH (have spoken).

[13]You shall not exploit your fellow, and you shall not commit robbery. The wages of your hireling shall not remain with you until morning. [14]You shall not insult the deaf, and before the blind you shall not place a stumbling block, but you shall fear your God: I YHWH (have spoken).

[15]You shall not do injustice in judgment. You shall not be partial to the poor or favor the rich; in righteousness shall you judge your fellow. [16]You shall not go about as a slanderer among your kin; you shall not stand aloof beside the blood of your fellow: I YHWH (have spoken).

[17]You shall not hate your brother (Israelite) in your heart. Reprove your fellow openly so that you will not bear punishment because of him. [18]Rather, you shall not take revenge or nurse a grudge against members of your people. You shall love your fellow as yourself: I YHWH (have spoken).

Miscellaneous Duties

[19]You shall heed my statutes.

You shall not let your cattle mate with a different kind; you shall not sow your field with two kinds of seed; and clothing made of two kinds of yarn you shall not put on yourself.

[20]*If a man has sexual intercourse with a woman who is a slave betrothed to another man, but has not been ransomed or given her freedom, there shall be an inquest; they shall not be put to death because she has not been freed.* [21]*But he shall bring to the entrance of the Tent of Meeting, as his penalty to YHWH, a ram of reparation offering.* [22]*And the priest shall make expiation for him before YHWH with the ram of reparation offering for his wrong that he committed, so that he may be forgiven of his wrong that he committed.* *

[23]When you enter the land and plant any kind of fruit tree, you shall treat its foreskin with its fruit as foreskin. Three years it shall be forbidden to you; it shall not be eaten. [24]In the fourth year, all of its fruit shall be sacred, an offering of rejoicing to YHWH. [25]In the fifth year, you may use its fruit that its yield may be increased for you: I YHWH your God (have spoken).

[26]You shall not eat over the blood. You shall not practice augury or divination. [27]You shall not round off the side-growth on your head, and you shall not destroy the edge of your beard. [28]Gashes in your flesh you shall not make for the dead, and tattoos you shall not put on yourselves: I YHWH (have spoken).

[29]You shall not degrade your daughter by making her a prostitute so that the land may not be prostituted and the land be filled with lewdness.

---

*Vv. 20–22 are an insertion from the P source.

Closing

[30]You shall keep my sabbaths and my sanctuary you shall revere: I YHWH (have spoken).

[31]Do not turn to ghosts and do not search for wizard-spirits to become impure by them: I YHWH your God (have spoken).

[32]In the presence of the elderly you shall rise, and thereby you will show respect to the aged; you shall fear your God: I YHWH (have spoken).

Appendix

[33]When an alien resides with you in your land, you shall not oppress him. [34]The alien residing with you shall be to you as a citizen among you. You shall love him as yourself, for you were aliens in the land of Egypt: I YHWH your God (have spoken).

[35]You shall not do injustice in judgment, (namely,) in measures of weight or capacity. [36]You shall have an honest scale, honest weights, an honest ephah, and an honest hin.

Closing Exhortation

I YHWH am your God who freed you from the land of Egypt. [37]You shall heed all my statutes and all my rules, and you shall do them: I YHWH (have spoken).

20. *Penalties for Molek Worship, Necromancy, and Sexual Offenses (20:1–27)*

[1]And YHWH spoke to Moses: [2]Say further to the Israelites:

Penalties for Molek Worship

Any man from among the Israelites, or among the aliens residing in Israel, who dedicates any of his offspring to Molek, must be put to death; the people of the land shall pelt him with stones. [3]And I myself will set my face against that man and cut him off from among his people, because he dedicated his offspring, thus defiling my sanctuary and desecrating my holy name. [4]And if the people of the land indeed shut their eyes to that man when he gives of his offspring to Molek by not putting him to death, [5]I myself will set my face against that man and his family, and I will cut off from among their kin both him and all who whore after him in whoring after Molek.

Penalty for Necromancy

[6]And if any person turns to ghosts and wizard-spirits to whore after them, I will set my face against that person and I will cut him off from among his kin.

Opening Exhortation

[7]You shall sanctify yourselves and be holy, for I YHWH am your God. [8]You shall heed my statutes and do them: (Thereby) I YHWH make you holy.

Penalties for Sexual Violations

[9]If any man dishonors his father or his mother, he must be put to death; he has dishonored his father or his mother—his bloodguilt is upon him.
   [10]If a man commits adultery with a married woman—committing adultery with his (Israelite) neighbor's wife—the adulterer and the adulteress must be put to death. [11]If a man lies with his father's wife, it is the nakedness of his father that he has uncovered; the two of them must be put to death—their bloodguilt is upon them. [12]If a man lies with his daughter-in-law, the two of them must be put to death; they have committed a perversion—their bloodguilt is upon them. [13]If a man lies with a male as one lies with a woman, the two of them have done an abhorrent thing; they must be put to death—their bloodguilt is upon them. [14]If a man marries a woman and her mother, it is a depravity; by fire they shall burn him and them, that there be no depravity among you. [15]If a man has sexual relations with a beast, he must be put to death, and you shall kill the beast. [16]If a woman approaches any beast to mate with it, you shall kill the woman and the beast; they must be put to death—their bloodguilt is upon them.
   [17]If a man marries his sister, the daughter of either his father or his mother, so that he sees her nakedness and she sees his nakedness, it is a disgrace; they shall be cut off in the sight of their people. He has uncovered the nakedness of his sister; he shall bear his iniquity. [18]If a man lies with a woman in her infirmity and uncovers her nakedness, he has laid bare her source and she has exposed the source of her blood; the two of them shall be cut off from among their kin. [19]You shall not uncover the nakedness of your mother's sister or your father's sister, for that is laying bare his own flesh; they shall bear their punishment. [20]If a man lies with his uncle's wife, it is his uncle's nakedness that he has uncovered. They shall bear their sin: they shall die childless. [21]If a man marries the wife of his brother, it is repulsive. It is the nakedness of his brother that he has uncovered; they shall remain childless.

Closing Exhortation

[22]You shall heed all my statutes and all my regulations and do them, so that the land to which I bring you to settle in will not vomit you out. [23]You shall not follow the statutes of the nations that I am driving out before you. It is because they did all these things that I loathed them [24]and said to you: You shall possess their land, and I myself will give it to you to possess, a land flowing with milk and honey. I YHWH am your God who has set you apart from other peoples. [25]So you shall distinguish between the pure and the impure quadrupeds

and between the impure and the pure birds. You shall not defile your throats with a quadruped or bird or anything with which the ground teems, which I have set apart for you to treat as impure. [26]You shall be holy to me, for I YHWH am holy; therefore I have set you apart from other peoples to be mine.

Appendix: Penalty for Mediums

[27]A man or a woman who is a medium for a ghost or wizard-spirit shall be put to death; they shall be pelted with stones—their bloodguilt is upon them.

21. *Instructions for the Priests (21:1–24)*

[1]YHWH said to Moses: Say to the priests, the sons of Aaron, and say to them:

Mourning

None shall defile himself (mourning) for any dead person among his kin, [2]except for his closest relatives: his mother, his father, his son, his daughter, and his brother; [3]also for his marriageable sister, closest to him, who has no husband, for her he may defile himself. [4]But he shall not defile himself among his kinspeople, thereby desecrating himself.

[5]They shall not make any bald patches on their heads, or shave off the edge of their beards, or make gashes in their flesh. [6]They shall be holy to their God and not desecrate the name of their God; for they offer the gifts of YHWH, the food of their God, and so must be holy.

Marriage

[7]They shall not marry a promiscuous woman or one who was raped, nor shall they marry a woman divorced from her husband. For each (priest) is holy to his God, [8]and you must treat him as holy, since he offers the food of your God; he shall be holy to you, for I YHWH who sanctifies you am holy.

Addendum on a Priest's Daughter

[9]When the daughter of a priest desecrates herself by harlotry, it is her father whom she desecrates; she shall be burned by fire.

The High Priest

[10]The priest who is preeminent among his fellows, on whose head the anointing oil has been poured and who has been ordained to wear the (priestly) vestments, shall not dishevel his hair or rend his vestments. [11]He shall not go in

where there is a dead body; even for his father or mother he shall not defile himself. [12]He shall not leave the sacred area so that he not desecrate the sacred area of his God, for the distinction of the anointing oil of his God is upon him. I (who speak) am YHWH.

[13]He is to marry a young virgin. [14]A widow, a divorcee, a raped woman, or a harlot: these he shall not marry. Only a young virgin of his kin may he take to wife [15]that he not desecrate his offspring among his kin, for I am YHWH who sanctifies him.

Blemished Priests

[16]YHWH spoke to Moses: [17]Speak to Aaron and say: A man of your offspring in any generation who has a blemish shall not be qualified to offer the food of his God. [18]No one at all who has a blemish shall be qualified: a man who is blind, lame, disfigured, or deformed; [19]a man who has a broken leg or broken arm, [20]or who is a hunchback, or a dwarf, or has a discoloration of the eye, a scar, a lichen, or a crushed testicle. [21]Every man among the offspring of Aaron the priest who has a blemish shall not be qualified to offer YHWH's gifts; having a blemish, he shall not be qualified to offer the food of his God. [22]He may eat the food of his God, of the most holy and of the holy. [23]But he shall not enter before the veil or officiate at the altar, for he has a blemish. And he may not desecrate my sanctums. (Thereby) I am YHWH who sanctifies them.

Subscript

[24]Thus Moses spoke to Aaron and his sons and to all the Israelites.

22. *Instructions for the Priests and Lay Persons (22:1–33)*

[1]YHWH spoke to Moses, saying: [2]Instruct Aaron and his sons to be scrupulous concerning the sacred donations that the Israelites consecrate to me so they do not desecrate my holy name, I am YHWH. [3]Say (further) to them: Throughout your generations, if any man of your offspring, while he is impure, encroaches upon the sacred donations that the Israelites may consecrate to YHWH, that person shall be cut off from my presence: I YHWH (have spoken).

Concerning Sacred Food

[4]Any man of Aaron's offspring who has scale disease or a chronic discharge [or is contaminated by a corpse], may not eat of the sacred donations until he is pure. [One who touches anything contaminated by a corpse, or] If a man has an emission of semen, [5]or if a man touches any swarming thing by which he is

made impure or any human being by whom he is made impure whatever (be) his impurity, [6]the person who touches any of these shall be impure until evening, and he shall not eat of the sacred donations unless he has washed his body in water [7]and the sun has set. Then, he shall be pure; and afterward he may eat of the sacred donations, for they are his food. [8]He shall not eat of any animal that died or was torn by beasts to become impure by it. I YHWH (have spoken). [9]They shall heed my prohibition lest they bear sin by it and die thereby when they desecrate it; I am YHWH who sanctifies them.

[10]No lay person shall eat sacred food; neither may a priest's resident hireling eat sacred food. [11]But if a priest purchases a person with money, he may eat of it; and those born into his household may eat of his food. [12]If a priest's daughter marries a layman, she may not eat of the sacred gifts; [13]but if a priest's daughter is widowed or divorced and without children, and returns to her father's house as in her youth, she may eat of her father's food. But no lay person may eat of it.

[14]If any (lay) person inadvertently eats of a sacred donation, he shall add one-fifth of its value to it and pay to the priests the (combined) sacred donation. [15]They (the priests) shall not desecrate the sacred donations of the Israelites that they set aside for YHWH [16]by causing them (the Israelites) to bear the penalty of reparation when they (the Israelites) eat their (own) sacred donations; for it is I YHWH who sanctifies them (the priests).

Concerning Blemished Sacrificial Animals

[17]YHWH spoke to Moses, saying: [18]Speak to Aaron, to his sons, and to all the Israelites, and say to them:

Whenever any person from the house of Israel or from the aliens in Israel presents an offering for any of his vows or any of his freewill gifts, which may be presented to YHWH as a burnt offering, [19]to be acceptable on your behalf (it must be) a male without blemish, from cattle, sheep, or goats. [20]You shall not present any that has a blemish, because it will not be acceptable on your behalf.

[21]And whenever any person presents, from the herd or the flock, a well-being offering to YHWH for an expressed vow or as a freewill offering, (it must be) perfect in order to be acceptable; it shall not have any blemish. [22]Anything blind, (has a) broken (limb), is maimed, (has) a seeping sore, a scar, or a lichen—such you shall not present to YHWH; you shall not put any of them on the altar as a food gift to YHWH. [23]You may, however, sacrifice as a freewill offering a herd or flock animal with an extended or contracted (limb), but it will not be accepted for a votive offering. [24]You shall not offer to YHWH (an animal) with bruised, crushed, torn, or cut-off (testicles). You shall not do (this) in your land. [25]And from the hand of a foreigner, you shall not offer the food of your God from any of these. Because of deformities and blemishes in them, they will not be accepted on your behalf.

Additional Criteria for Sacrificial Animals

²⁶YHWH spoke to Moses, saying: ²⁷Whenever an ox or a sheep or a goat is born, it shall remain seven days with its mother, and from the eighth day on it will be acceptable as a food-gift offering to YHWH. ²⁸However, no animal from the herd or from the flock shall be slaughtered on the same day as its young.

²⁹When you sacrifice a thanksgiving offering to YHWH, sacrifice [it] so that it will be acceptable on your behalf. ³⁰It shall be eaten on the same day; you shall not leave any of it until morning. I YHWH (have spoken).

Exhortation

³¹You shall heed my commandments and do them. I YHWH (have spoken). ³²You shall not desecrate my holy name that I may be sanctified in the midst of the Israelites. I am YHWH who sanctifies you, ³³your deliverer from the land of Egypt to be your God; I am YHWH.

23. *The Holiday Calendar (23:1–44)**

¹YHWH spoke to Moses, saying: ²Speak to the Israelites and say to them: **(As for) the fixed times of YHWH, which you shall proclaim as sacred occasions, these are my fixed times.**

The Sabbath

³Six days' work may be done, but the seventh day is a sabbath of complete rest, a sacred occasion. You shall do no work; it is a sabbath of YHWH throughout your settlements.

The Festivals

⁴These are the fixed times of YHWH, the sacred occasions, which you shall proclaim at their fixed times:

The Paschal Offering and the Unleavened Bread

⁵In the first month, on the fourteenth (day) of the month, at twilight, a paschal offering to YHWH, ⁶and on the fifteenth day of that month the Pilgrimage-Festival of Unleavened Bread to YHWH. Seven days you are to eat unleavened bread. ⁷The first day shall be for you a sacred occasion: You shall do no la-

---

*In chap. 23, italic block type (as in v. 1) stands for H, boldface block type (as in v. 2b) for H_R, standard type (as in v. 10b) for Pre-H₁, and boldface standard type (as in v. 11b) for Pre-H₂. For details see the commentary on chap. 23, COMMENT A.

borious work. *8Seven days you shall offer food gifts to YHWH. The seventh day is a sacred occasion: You shall do no laborious work.*

The First Barley Offering

9YHWH spoke to Moses, saying: 10Speak to the Israelites and say to them:

When you enter the land I am giving to you and you reap its harvest, you shall bring the first sheaf of your harvest to the priest. 11He shall elevate the sheaf before YHWH. For acceptance on your behalf **from the day after the sabbath-week** the priest shall elevate it. 12On the day that you elevate the sheaf, you shall sacrifice an unblemished male lamb in its first year as a burnt offering to YHWH. 13Its accompanying cereal offering shall be two-tenths of an ephah of semolina mixed with oil, a food gift of pleasing aroma to YHWH; and its accompanying libation shall be one-fourth of a hin of wine. 14Do not partake (from the new crop) of any bread or parched or fresh grain until the very day you have brought your God's offering—*a law for all time, throughout your generations, in all your settlements.*

The First Wheat Offering

15And **from the day after the sabbath-week,** from the day on which you bring the elevation offering of the sheaf, you shall count for yourselves **seven sabbath-weeks. They must be complete:** 16**You shall count until the day after the seventh sabbath-week** fifty days. Then you shall present a new cereal offering to YHWH. 17You shall bring from your settlements as an elevation offering of two bread (loaves), comprising two-tenths (of an ephah) of semolina and baked after leavening, as firstfruits for YHWH. *18With the bread you shall offer seven unblemished yearling lambs, one bull of the herd, and two rams; (they) shall be a burnt offering to YHWH, and with their cereal offerings and libations, a food gift of pleasant aroma to YHWH. 19You shall sacrifice one he-goat as a purification offering* and two yearling lambs as a sacrifice of well-being. 20And the priest shall elevate them *with the bread of firstfruits* as an elevation offering to YHWH *with the two lambs;* they shall be holy to YHWH for the priest. *21On that very day, you shall proclaim: It shall be for you a sacred occasion; you must do no laborious work—a law for all time, in all your settlements, throughout your generations. 22And when you reap the harvest of your land, you shall not complete (it) to the edge of your field, or gather the gleanings of your harvest; you shall leave them for the poor and for the alien; I am YHWH your God.*

The Festival of Alarm Blasts

23YHWH spoke to Moses, saying: 24Speak to the Israelites thus: In the seventh month, on the first day of the month, you shall observe a rest, a sacred occasion, commemorated with short blasts. 25You shall do no laborious work; and you shall present a food gift to YHWH.

The Day of Purgation

²⁶*YHWH spoke to Moses, saying:* ²⁷*However, the tenth day of this seventh month is the Day of Purgation. It shall be a sacred occasion for you; you shall afflict yourselves, and you shall offer a food gift to YHWH;* ²⁸*you shall do no work on that very day. For it is a purgation day, to effect purgation on your behalf before YHWH your God.* ²⁹*Indeed, any person who does not afflict himself on that very day will be cut off from his kin;* ³⁰*and any person who does any work on that very day I will cause that person to perish among his people.* ³¹*You shall do no work; it is a law for all time, throughout your generations, in all your settlements.* ³²*It shall be a sabbath of complete rest for you, and you shall afflict yourselves; on the ninth day of the month at evening, from evening to evening, you shall observe your sabbath.*

The Festival of Booths

³³*YHWH spoke to Moses, saying:* ³⁴*Say to the Israelites thus: On the fifteenth day of this seventh month [there shall be] the pilgrimage-festival of Booths, [lasting] seven days to YHWH.* ³⁵*The first day shall be a sacred occasion; you shall do no laborious work.* ³⁶*Seven days you shall present food gifts to YHWH. On the eighth day, you shall observe a sacred occasion and present a food gift to YHWH. It is a solemn assembly; you shall do no laborious work.*

Summary

³⁷*These are the fixed times of YHWH, which you shall proclaim as sacred occasions, to present food gifts to YHWH—burnt offerings, cereal offerings, sacrifices, and libations, the daily protocol on each day—*³⁸*apart from the sabbath offerings of YHWH, and apart from your gifts, and apart from your votive offerings, and apart from your freewill offerings that you give to YHWH.*

Addendum on the Festival of Booths

³⁹However, on the fifteenth day of the seventh month, when you have ingathered the yield of the land, you shall celebrate the pilgrimage-festival of YHWH seven days: on the first day, rest and on the eighth day, rest. ⁴⁰On the first day you shall take for yourselves the boughs of majestic trees: fronds of palms, branches of leafy trees, and willows of the brook, and you shall rejoice before YHWH your God seven days. ⁴¹*You shall celebrate it as a Pilgrimage-Festival to YHWH for seven days in the year as a law for all time, throughout your generations. You shall celebrate it in the seventh month.* **⁴²In booths you shall live seven days; all citizens in Israel shall live in booths, ⁴³in order that your generations may know that I made the Israelites live in booths when I brought them out of the land of Egypt; I am YHWH your God.**

⁴⁴*Thus Moses declared the fixed times of YHWH to the Israelites.*

24. *Tabernacle Oil and Bread; the Case of Blasphemy (24:1–23)*

Oil for the Tabernacle Lamps

¹YHWH spoke to Moses, saying:

²Command the Israelites to bring you clear oil of beaten olives for lighting, for kindling a flame regularly. ³Aaron shall set it up in the Tent of Meeting outside the veil of the Pact [to burn] from evening to morning before YHWH regularly; it is a law for all times, throughout your generations. ⁴On the pure (golden) lampstand shall be set up the lamps before YHWH [to burn] regularly.

Bread for the Tabernacle Table

⁵You shall take semolina and bake it (into) twelve loaves; two-tenths of an ephah shall be in each loaf. ⁶You shall place them (in) two piles, six to a pile, on the table of pure (gold) before YHWH. ⁷With each pile you shall place pure frankincense, which shall be a token offering for the bread, a food gift for YHWH. ⁸Every sabbath day it shall be set it up before YHWH regularly, (a commitment) of the Israelites as a covenant for all time. ⁹It shall belong to Aaron and his descendants; and they shall eat it in a holy place; it is a most sacred portion for him from the food gifts of YHWH, a due for all time.

The Case of the Blasphemer

¹⁰There came out among the Israelites a man whose mother was Israelite and whose father was Egyptian. And a fight broke out in the camp between the son of an Israelite woman and a certain Israelite. ¹¹The son of the Israelite woman pronounced the Name, cursing it, and he was brought to Moses—now his mother's name was Shelomith, daughter of Dibri, of the tribe of Dan—¹²and he was put in custody, (until) the decision of YHWH should be made clear to them.

¹³And YHWH spoke to Moses, saying: ¹⁴Take the blasphemer outside the camp; and have all who were within hearing lean their hands on his head; then have the whole community stone him. ¹⁵And to the Israelites speak thus: Anyone who curses his God shall bear his punishment; ¹⁶but if he (also) pronounces the name of YHWH he must be put to death. The whole community shall stone him; alien as well as citizen, if he has (thus) pronounced the Name, he must be put to death.

The Talion Laws

¹⁷If anyone kills any human being, he must be put to death. ¹⁸But anyone who kills an animal shall make restitution for it, life for life. ¹⁹If anyone maims another, as he has done so shall it be done to him: ²⁰fracture for fracture, eye for eye, tooth for tooth. The injury he has inflicted on the person shall be inflicted

on him. [21]One who kills an animal shall make restitution for it; but one who kills a human being shall be put to death. [22]You shall have one law for the alien and citizen alike: for I YHWH your God (have spoken).

The Compliance Report

[23]Moses spoke (thus) to the Israelites. And they took the blasphemer outside the camp and pelted him with stones. The Israelites did as YHWH had commanded Moses.

25. Jubilee, the Priestly Solution for Economic Injustice (25:1–55)

Introduction

[1]YHWH spoke to Moses on Mount Sinai: [2]Speak to the Israelites and say to them:

The Sabbatical Year

When you enter the land that I give you, the land shall observe a sabbath to YHWH. [3]Six years you may sow your field, and six years you may prune your vineyard and gather in its produce. [4]But in the seventh year there shall be a sabbath of complete rest for the land, a sabbath to YHWH; you may neither sow your field nor prune your vineyard. [5]The aftergrowth of your harvest you shall not reap, nor the grapes of your untrimmed vines shall you pick; it shall be (a year of) complete rest for the land. [6]But the sabbath (-yield) of the land will be for you to eat: for you, for your male and female slaves, your resident hirelings, who live under your authority, [7]your livestock and the wild animals in your land—all of its yield will be (available for you) to eat.

The Jubilee Year

[8]You shall count for yourself seven weeks of years—seven times seven years— so that the period of seven weeks of years gives you (a total of) forty-nine years. [9]Then you shall sound the horn loud; in the seventh month, on the tenth day of the month—the Day of Purgation—you shall have the horn sounded throughout your land, [10]and you shall sanctify the fiftieth year, proclaiming release throughout the land for all its inhabitants. It shall be a jubilee for you, when each of you shall return to his holding and each of you shall return to his kin group. [11]That fiftieth year shall be a jubilee for you; you shall not sow, nor shall you reap its aftergrowth or pick its untrimmed vines. [12]Since it is a jubilee, sacred it shall be to you; you may only eat its produce (direct) from the field. [13]In this year of jubilee, each of you shall return to his holding.

[14]When you sell property to your fellow, or buy (any) from your fellow, you shall not cheat one another. [15]On the basis of the number of years since the jubilee shall you buy from your fellow; on the basis of the number of (remaining) crop years shall he sell to you; [16]the more such years, the more its purchase price; the fewer such years, the less its purchase price; for it is the number of crops that he is selling you. [17]Do not cheat one another, but fear your God; for I YHWH am your God.

[18]You shall perform my laws, and my rules you shall heed and you shall perform them, that you may dwell on the land in security. [19]The land shall yield its fruit and you shall eat your fill, and you shall dwell upon it in security. [20]And should you say, "What are we to eat in the seventh year, if we may not sow or gather in our crops?" [21]I will ordain my blessing for you in the sixth year, so that it will yield a crop (sufficient) for three years. [22]When you sow (in) the eighth year, you will (continue to) eat from the old crop; until the ninth year, until its crop comes in, you shall eat the old.

Redemption of Property: The Basic Principle

[23]Furthermore, the land must not be sold beyond reclaim, for the land is mine; you are but resident aliens under my authority. [24]Therefore, throughout the land you hold, you must provide redemption for the land.

The Three Stages of Destitution

Stage One: Sold Land and Houses and Their Redemption

[25]When your brother (Israelite) becomes impoverished and has to sell part of his holding, his closest redeemer shall come and redeem the sold property of his brother. [26]If a man has no redeemer but prospers and acquires enough for his redemption, [27]he shall compute the years since its sale, refund the difference to the man to whom he sold it, and return to his holding. [28]If he does not acquire sufficient means to recover it, his sold property shall remain with its buyer until the jubilee year; it shall be released in the jubilee, and he shall return to his holding.

[29]If a man sells a dwelling house (in) a walled city, it may be redeemed until the end of a year of its sale; its redemption period shall be a year. [30]If it is not redeemed before the completion of one full year, the house in the walled city shall belong to its purchaser beyond reclaim throughout the ages; it shall not be released in the jubilee. [31]However, houses in hamlets that have no encircling walls shall be classed as open country; they may be redeemed, and in the jubilee they shall be released. [32]As for the Levitic cities—the houses in the cities they hold—the Levites shall forever have the right of redemption. [33]Whoever of the Levites redeems (should know that) the house sold (in) the city of his possession shall be released in the jubilee; for the houses in the cities of the Levites are their holding among the Israelites. [34]But the field of

the livestock enclosures (about) their cities may not be sold, for that is their holding forever.

Stage Two: Lost Land

[35]If your brother, being (further) impoverished, falls under your authority, and you (would) hold him (as though he were) a resident alien, let him subsist under your authority. [36]Do not exact from him advance or accrued interest. Fear your God, and let your brother subsist under your authority. [37]Do not lend him money at advance interest, or lend him food at accrued interest. [38]I, YHWH, am your God, who freed you from the land of Egypt, to give you the land of Canaan, to be your God.

Stage Three: "Slavery"

[39]If your brother, being (further) impoverished under your authority, is sold to you, do not make him work as a slave. [40]He shall remain under you as a resident hireling; he shall work under you until the jubilee year. [41]Then he and his children with him shall be released from your authority; he shall return to his kin group and return to his ancestral holding.—[42]For they are my slaves, whom I freed from the land of Egypt; they shall not be sold as slaves are sold.—[43]You shall not rule over him with harshness; you shall fear your God.

[44]Male and female slaves as you may have—(it is) from the nations around about you, from them that you may buy male and female slaves. [45]Also from among the children of residents (aliens) who live under your sway, from them you may buy (slaves), or from their kin groups that are under your sway, whom they begot in your land. These shall become your property; [46]you may keep them as a possession for your children after you, for them to inherit as property for all time. These you may treat as slaves, but as for your Israelite brothers, no one shall rule over the other with harshness.

[47]If a resident alien under you has prospered, and your brother, being (further) impoverished, comes under his authority and is sold to the resident alien under you, or to a branch of the alien's kin group, [48]after he is sold he shall have the right of redemption. One of his brothers shall redeem him, [49]or his uncle or his uncle's son shall redeem him, or anyone of his kin group who is of his own flesh shall redeem him; or if he prospers, he may redeem himself. [50]He shall compute with his buyer the total from the year he was sold to him until the jubilee year: the price of his sale shall be applied to the number of years, as the term of a hired laborer he shall be under the other's authority. [51]If many years remain, he shall pay back (for) his redemption in proportion to his purchase price; [52]and if few years remain until the jubilee year, he shall so compute; according to the years involved, he shall pay back (for) his redemption. [53]As a worker hired by the year shall he be under his (the alien's) authority, who (however) shall not rule over him with harshness in your sight. [54]If he has not been redeemed in any of these ways, he and his children with him shall go free in the jubilee year. [55]For it is to me the Israelites are slaves.

They are my slaves whom I freed from the land of Egypt. I am YHWH your God.

26. *Blessings, Curses, and the Recall of the Covenant (26:1–46)*

The Essence of God's Commandments

¹You shall not make idols for yourselves, and a carved image or pillar you shall not set up for yourselves, and a figured pavement you shall not place in your land to worship upon it, for I YHWH am your God. ²You shall keep my sabbaths and venerate my sanctuary: I YHWH (have spoken).*

The Blessings

³If you follow my laws and keep my commandments and observe them, ⁴I will grant you rains in their season, so that the earth will yield its produce, and the trees of the field will yield their fruit. ⁵Your threshing shall overtake the vintage, and the vintage will overtake the sowing; you shall eat your fill of food and dwell securely in your land.

⁶I will grant peace in the land, so that you shall lie down, and no one shall make you afraid; I will eliminate vicious beasts from the land, and no sword shall traverse your land. ⁷You shall give chase to your enemies, and they shall fall before you by the sword. ⁸Five of you shall give chase to a hundred, and a hundred of you shall give chase to ten thousand; your enemies shall fall before you by the sword.

⁹I will look with favor upon you, and make you fruitful and multiply you; and I will uphold my covenant with you. ¹⁰You shall eat old grain long stored, and you shall have to clear out the old to make room for the new. ¹¹I will establish my presence in your midst, and I will not expel you. ¹²I will walk about in your midst: I will (*continue to*) be your God, and you shall be my people. ¹³I YHWH am your God who freed you from the land of Egypt from being their slaves; I broke the bars of your yoke and made you walk erect.

The Curses

¹⁴But if you do not obey me and do not observe all these commandments, ¹⁵if you despise my laws and loathe my rules, so that you do not observe all my commandments, thereby breaking my covenant, ¹⁶I in turn will do this to you: I will bring panic upon you—consumption and fever wearing out the eyes and

---

*Boldface block type (vv. 1–2, 33b–35, and 43–45) stands for H$_R$. For details see Chap. 26 NOTES.

drying out the throat; you shall sow your seed to no purpose, for your enemies shall eat it. ¹⁷I will set my face against you: you shall be routed by your enemies, and your foes shall dominate you. You shall flee though nobody pursues you.

¹⁸And if, for all of that, you do not obey me, I will go on to discipline you sevenfold for your sins, ¹⁹and I will break your proud strength. I will make your skies like iron and your earth like copper, ²⁰so that your strength shall be spent to no purpose. Your land shall not yield its produce, nor shall the trees of your land yield their fruit.

²¹And if you continue in opposition to me and refuse to obey me, I will go on smiting you sevenfold in measure for your sins. ²²I will let loose wild beasts against you, and they shall bereave you of your children and wipe out your cattle. They shall make you few (in number), and your roads shall be deserted.

²³And if, in spite of these (things), you are not disciplined for me, and you continue in opposition to me, ²⁴I too will continue in opposition to you: Yes, I myself will smite you sevenfold for your sins. ²⁵I will bring a sword against you, executing vengeance for the covenant; and if you withdraw into your cities, I will send pestilence among you, and you shall be delivered into enemy hands. ²⁶When I break your staff of bread, ten women shall bake your bread in a single oven; they shall dole out your bread by weight, and though you eat, you shall not be satisfied.

²⁷But if, despite this, you disobey me and continue in opposition to me, ²⁸I will continue in wrathful opposition to you; Yes, I myself will discipline you sevenfold for your sins. ²⁹You shall eat the flesh of your sons, and the flesh of your daughters you shall eat. ³⁰I will destroy your cult places and cut down your incense stands, and I will heap your carcasses upon your lifeless fetishes.

I will expel you. ³¹I will lay your cities in ruin and make your sanctuaries desolate, and I will not smell your pleasant odors. ³²I myself will make your land desolate, so that your enemies who settle in it shall be appalled by it. ³³You, however, I will scatter among the nations, and I will unsheath the sword after you.

When your land will be a desolation and your cities a ruin, ³⁴then the land shall be paid its sabbath years throughout the time that it is desolate. When you are in the land of your enemies, then the land shall rest and pay off its sabbath years. ³⁵Throughout the time it is desolate, it shall have the rest it did not have on your sabbaths when you were living on it.

³⁶As for those of you who survive, I will bring faintness in their hearts in the land of their enemies. The sound of a driven leaf will put them to flight. They shall flee as though from the sword, and they shall fall though nobody is pursuing. ³⁷They shall stumble over one another, as if (to escape) a sword, though pursuing is nobody. You shall not be able to stand (your ground) before your enemies. ³⁸You shall be lost among the nations, and the land of your enemies shall devour you. ³⁹And those of you who survive shall rot because of their iniquities in the land of your enemies; also they shall rot because of the iniquities of their ancestors (adhering) to them.

Remorse and the Recall of the Covenant

⁴⁰But if they confess their iniquity and the iniquity of their ancestors, in that they committed sacrilege against me and, moreover, that they continued in opposition to me—⁴¹so that I, in turn, had to continue in opposition to them and disperse them in the land of their enemies—if, then, their uncircumcised heart is humbled and they accept their punishment in full, ⁴²then I will remember my covenant with Jacob; also my covenant with Isaac and also my covenant with Abraham I will remember, namely, I will remember the land. **⁴³For the land shall be deserted by them that it may be paid its sabbath years by being desolate without them, as they accept their punishment in full for the very reason that my rules they spurned and my laws they loathed. ⁴⁴Yet, for all that, while they are in the land of their enemies I have not spurned them or loathed them so as to destroy them, annulling my covenant with them: for I YHWH am their God. ⁴⁵But I will remember in their favor the covenant with the ancients whom I freed from the land of Egypt in the sight of the nations to be their God: I YHWH (have spoken).**

Summation

⁴⁶These are the laws, rules, and the rituals that YHWH established between himself and the Israelites on Mount Sinai through Moses.

27. *Consecrations and Their Redemption (27:1–34)*

Vows of Persons and Animals

¹YHWH spoke to Moses, saying: ²Speak to the Israelites and say to them: When a person makes an extraordinary vow to YHWH concerning the (fixed) valuation of a human being, ³these shall be the valuations: If it is a male from twenty to sixty years of age, the valuation is fifty shekels of silver by the sanctuary weight. ⁴If it is a female, the valuation is thirty shekels. ⁵If the age is from five years to twenty years, the valuation is twenty shekels for a male and ten shekels for a female. ⁶If the age is from one month to five years, the valuation for a male is five shekels of silver, and the valuation for a female is three shekels of silver. ⁷If the age is from sixty years and over, the valuation is fifteen shekels in the case of a male and ten shekels for a female. ⁸But if he is too poor (to pay) a valuation, he shall be presented before the priest, and the priest shall assess him; the priest shall assess him according to what the vower can afford.
⁹If [the vow concerns] any quadruped that may be brought as an offering to YHWH, any such that may be dedicated to YHWH shall be holy. ¹⁰One may not exchange it or substitute it—a healthy with an emaciated one or emaciated with a healthy one; if one does substitute one animal for another, it (the vowed one) and its substitute shall be holy. ¹¹If [the vow concerns] any impure quadruped that may not be brought as an offering to YHWH, the quadruped

shall be presented before the priest, [12]and the priest shall assess it. Whether high or low, whatever is the valuation of the priest, so it shall stand; [13]and if he wishes to redeem it, he must add one-fifth to its valuation.

Consecrations of Houses and Fields

[14]If a man consecrates his house to YHWH, the priest shall assess it. Whether high or low, as the priest assesses it, so it shall stand; [15]and if he who consecrated his house wishes to redeem it, he must add one-fifth to the sum at which it was assessed, and it shall be his.

[16]If a man consecrates to YHWH any part of his tenured field, its valuation shall be according to its seed requirement: fifty shekels of silver to a homer of barley seed. [17]If he consecrates his field as of the jubilee year, its valuation stands. [18]But if he consecrates his field after the jubilee, the priest shall compute the price according to the years that are left until the jubilee year, and its valuation shall be so reduced; [19]and if he who consecrated the field wishes to redeem it, he must add one-fifth to the sum at which it was assessed, and it shall pass to him. [20]But if he does not redeem the field but has sold the field to another, it shall no longer be redeemable; [21]when the field is released in the jubilee, it shall be holy to YHWH, as a proscribed field; it belongs to the priest.

[22]If he consecrates to YHWH a field that he purchased, which is not of his tenured field, [23]the priest shall compute for him the proportionate valuation up to the jubilee year, and he shall pay the valuation as of that day, a sacred donation to YHWH. [24]In the jubilee year the field shall revert to him from whom it was bought, to whom the tenured land belongs. [25]All valuations shall be by sanctuary weight, the shekel being twenty gerahs.

Firstlings

[26]However, a firstling of quadrupeds—designated as a firstling to YHWH—cannot be consecrated by anyone; whether bovine or ovine, it is YHWH's. [27]But if it is of impure quadrupeds, it may be ransomed at its valuation, with one-fifth added; if it is not redeemed, it may be sold at its valuation.

Proscriptions

[28]However, anything a man proscribes to YHWH of what he owns, be it persons, quadrupeds, or his tenured land, may not be sold or redeemed; every proscribed thing is totally consecrated to YHWH. [29]No human being who has been proscribed can be ransomed: he must be put to death.

Tithes

[30]All tithes from the land, whether seed from the ground or fruit from the tree, are YHWH's; they are holy to YHWH. [31]If a man wishes to redeem any of his

tithes, he must add one-fifth to them. [32]All tithes of the herd or flock—of all that passes under the shepherd's staff, every tenth one—shall be holy to YHWH. [33]He must not seek out the healthy as against the emaciated and substitute (the latter) for it (the former). If he does provide a substitute for it, then it and its substitute shall be holy: they cannot be redeemed.

Summary

[34]These are the commandments that YHWH commanded Moses for the Is-raelites on Mount Sinai.

INTRODUCTION

◆

I. STRUCTURE, VOCABULARY, EXTENT, AND DATE

◆

Lev 17–27 is conventionally called the Holiness Code. More accurately, these chapters are part of the Holiness Source. I will, however, refer to them by the accepted siglum H. They are distinguished from the previous chapters, 1–16 (P), by structure, vocabulary, style, and theology.

A. THE LITERARY STRUCTURE OF H

a. INTROVERSIONS AND PARALLEL PANELS

In vol. 1.39–42, I illustrated by two indisputable H interpolations within the P complex, chaps. 1–16, namely, 11:43–44 and 16:29–31, that H stands out from P by its structural artifices. The following is a sample of H's introversions (large chiasms) and parallel panels. To fully appreciate the artfulness of their composition and theological kerygma, they should be viewed in situ—the diagrammatic form followed by commentary. Supplementary evidence can be found in Paran (1989).

1. **17:10–12.** This is an example of a law stated twice in order to envelop and accentuate its rationale by means of an AXA′ structure. Thereby, the rationale for the absolute prohibition against slaughtering sacrificial animals profanely (17:3–4) is made prominent: meat for the table is permitted only if the animal's blood is brought to the altar to ransom the slaughterer from the charge of murder.

2. **17:13–14.** These two verses form an ABCC′B′A′ introversion that extends to game the prohibition against ingesting the blood of sacrificial animals.

3. **Chap. 18, introduction.** All of chap. 18 is an AXA′ introversion in which the rationales envelop the laws. The rationales take the form of exhortations whose hammering effect is amplified by their distribution before and after the prohibitions. The prohibitions are duplicated, in the main, in chap. 20.

4. **18:24–30.** This exhortatory conclusion may be divided—among other options—into parallel panels ABCDEFA′B′C′D′E′F′, in effect separating the fate of the Canaanites in the past from a similar fate awaiting Israel if it adopts the former's ways.

5. **19:1–18, 30–37.** Possibly, these form two parallel panels with two elements in chiastic relation, serving to lock the panels. The chapter would thus fall into an AXA′ pattern, the center X being the intermediate vv. 19–29.

6. **Chap. 20, introduction.** All of chap. 20 is a grand introversion ABCXC'B'A'. It explains that the necromancy prohibition (A') may have been pulled out of its original context (A) in order to create this structure.

7. **20:5–6.** The punishments for Molek and necromancy are identically structured, forming the parallel panels ABCA'B'C'. That they share the same form and punishment possibly may allude to their similar nature, namely, both are aspects of ancestor worship (see chap. 20, COMMENT B).

8. **20:10–21.** This example of a meaningless introversion (ABCXC'B'A'; see INTRODUCTION to vv. 9–21) provides a warning that structure, regardless of its perfect form, may be a matter of chance or, more likely, a purely aesthetic exercise.

9. **Chap. 20, COMMENT A.** Chap. 20 is the introversion of chap. 18, forming an ABXB'A' structure. With chaps. 18–20, the center (X) stands for chap. 19, which may well be the intended climactic center for the book of Leviticus and even for the Torah as a whole (see I L).

10. **Chaps. 21 and 22.** These are the only two chapters that deal exclusively with priests and sacrificial animals. They are bound together in an ABXB'A' chiasm (see INTRODUCTION to chap. 21). In moving from priests (AB) to animals (B'A'), the commands also include Israel as the addressee. This transition emphasizes that both priests and Israelites are responsible to detect sacrificial blemishes. The center (22:1–16, X) merges priests as consumers and animals as their food.

11. **Chaps. 21 and 22.** These chapters also contain two parallel panels. Chap. 21 (A, above) breaks down twice into instructions for the priest (vv. 1–9, 16–22) and high priest (vv. 10–15, 23), yielding an ABB'A' pattern, and thereby resolving the otherwise enigmatic v. 23 (see its NOTE).

12. **21:17b–21.** This is an AXA' introversion containing two parallel panels and two chiasms, which manages to keep the word *mûm* 'blemish' always at the center—a summit of H's consummate artistry (explicated in vol. 1.40–42).

13. **21:1b–5, 10–11.** The order of prohibitions of corpse-contamination followed by prohibitions of certain mourning rites for priests is reversed for the high priest (even for the terms "mother" and "father"), yielding an ABB'A' chiastic pattern (see COMMENT A).

14. **22:10–13.** These verses comprise an introversion ABCC'B'A', where the keyword *'akal* appears seven times (see COMMENT).

15. **22:17–25.** This marks a minor literary summit: two matching panels, each in chiastic order, AXB CYD || B'X'A' D'Y'C'. The centers X and Y are the same in both panels (*tāmîm laYHWH*), emphasizing the message of this pericope. The panels end with the same warning in matching minor panels: a blemished animal is not acceptable (see COMMENT).

16. **23:1–4.** The sabbath is linked to the festival calendar in an ABCDEXE'D'C'B'A' introversion, emphasizing at its center (X) that each sabbath is a sacred occasion, like all other festivals, but one requiring complete rest because it is YHWH's day.

17. **23:27–32.** It is only fitting that the one festival requiring complete rest, the Day of Purgation, should be distinguished by its structure. It forms an ABCDXD'C'B'A' introversion. Its key injunctions, self-denial and abstention from all work, are found three times, in the center (DD') and in the flanks (BB'

and CC′). This structure also vitiates the common critical view that v. 32 is an interpolation. Admittedly, the possibility also exists that a later H tradent added v. 32 in order to create the inverted structure, but this is hardly likely.

18. **24:13–23.** This introversion ABCDEFGXG′F′E′D′C′B′A′ is surely another major summit of H's structural artistry. First and foremost, law (talion) and narrative (blasphemy) are inextricably integrated. Talion is the heart (GXG′). It trumpets its central message: disfiguring the divine image in the human is blasphemy. D is expanded by the inner chiasm axa′, extending the blasphemy prohibition to the alien, but center stage is held by talion (GXG′). Verse 21a is not a superfluous repetition of v. 18, but is essential to the structure, forming FF′. Other stylistic points are discussed in COMMENT A.

19. **25:10aγ–13.** This has an ABB′A′ construction, thrice commanding the observance of the jubilee year, emphasizing its sanctity and its association with the prohibitions of the sabbatical year (vv. 4b–5a). The clause missing in A′ regarding the return to the kin group is explicated in the following verses (14–19).

20. **25:14–17.** This is an ABCDEE′D′C′B′A′ introversion, surrounding the mundane business of computing crop years by the injunction not to cheat one another (ABB′A′). Missing C′ is covered in E′.

21. **25:18b–22.** These verses are arranged in a complex axa′ABXB′A′bxb′ construction, an introversion flanked by two chiasms, where the center of the entire pericope (X) emphasizes that it is YHWH's blessing that provides for two successive fallow years. Admittedly, the flanks are weak. A more precise example of this structure is Num 11–12 (Milgrom 1990a: 376–80).

22. **25:39–40.** The parallel panels ABCDA′B′C′D′ contrast the Israelite with the non-Israelite slave. The laws dealing with the Israelite slave (vv. 36–43) subdivide into an ABXA′B′ introversion, whose center (X) stresses that an indebted Israelite may never be treated as a slave.

23. **25:47–53.** These verses stand parallel to vv. 16–28, forming the panels ABCDEFGHIJKA′B′C′D′E′F′G′H′I′J′K′. The pericope itself (vv. 47–53) comprises two inner introversions, ABXB′A′ (vv. 47–49) and ABB′A′ (vv. 50–53), where X states emphatically that an Israelite enslaved by a non-Israelite creditor must be redeemed. It constitutes an example of *imitatio dei*: just as YHWH redeems sold land or indentured Israelites (at the jubilee), so must the nearest relative (the redeemer). S. Chavel points out to me that in this regard, H takes a giant step forward in making practical use of the rationale that God has redeemed Israel from Egypt (v. 55), for it now becomes the paradigm for active, redemptive brotherly love among the Israelites. Thus H goes beyond the concern for the poor in JE and D, which require essentially self-restrictive steps, such as not taking clothing as collateral (Exod 22:24–26; cf. Deut 24:12–13, 17), not charging interest on loans (Deut 23:20), and not delaying payment to the impoverished laborer (Deut 24:14–15). These measures do not involve the active investment toward long-term relief demanded by H.

24. **25:53b–55, 42–43.** The alien master is matched with the Israelite master in an introversion ABCC′B′A′, each half being supplemented by the rationale that Israel is pledged to the God of the covenant; hence the Israelite debtor must not be treated as a slave and must be released in the jubilee. The resulting construction is ABCDC′B′A′D′.

25. **26:3–12.** These verses form an ABCDEE′D′C′B′A′ introversion, where the center EE′ itself is a minor introversion of continuous chiasms, E_1 (ab) E_2 (cd) $E_2′$ (dc) $E_1′$ (ba).

These twenty-five examples suffice to reveal the profusion of large structural units in H. They not only demonstrate the aesthetic impulse of H, but, more often than not, ensconce a message. H's aesthetic arrangement of the text may primarily have a kerygmatic goal. Hence structure is theology.

b. SMALLER CONSTRUCTIONS: CHIASMS AND PANELS

As expected, many single verses or contiguous verses are chiastically structured. The following samples are chosen not only for their form, but also for their disclosure of the meaning of the text.

1. **18:7, 8, 10, etc.** Many of the verses in the list of forbidden sexual unions (18:6–16) have an abxb′a′ or axa′ form in order to add a rationale to the prohibition.

2. **19:4, 5, 9, 14, etc.** Many of the injunctions in chap. 19 are chiasms (19:5 uses the same verb) in order to add a new provision.

3. **21:6, 12.** These two verses, though removed from each other, form parallel panels, abcda′b′c′d′, indicating that the priest and the high priest—despite the more severe regimen of the high priest—require the same fastidious care to sustain their holiness (see COMMENT A).

4. **23:11.** Removing *mimmāḥŏrat haššabbāt* from this verse restores the original chiastic structure (using the same verb) and simultaneously provides the key to understanding the inner evolution of the grain festivals.

5. **23:41.** This third repetition to observe the Festival of Booths in the seventh month is chiastically added to the verse and leads to the suspicion that Israelites either were not observing it or, more likely, were observing it during another (the eighth) month.

6. **23:42.** The repetition to live in *sukkôt* for seven days points to the *Sitz im Leben* of this innovation.

7. **25:25.** This intricate chiasm (abcxc′b′a′) exegetically clarifies the enigmatic term *mimkār* (bb′) and emphasizes in its center (x) the responsibility of the nearest kinsman to redeem the sold land.

8. **25:38.** This verse forms the chiasm abb′a′. The purpose of YHWH's salvific act freeing Israel from Egypt was to give it the land of Canaan (bb′) and to be its God (aa′), implying that Israel's occupation of the land is contingent on its observance of YHWH's commandments.

9. **25:44.** The unbalancing and otherwise superfluous a′ in this chiasm (abxb′a′) lays stress on "from them" (non-Israelites); slaves may be acquired, but not from Israelites.

10. **26:39.** This chiasm (abxb′a′) lays stress on the iniquity of the ancestors (b′) as an equal component with Israel's iniquities (b) for rotting (aa′) in exile (x).

c. INCLUSIONS

Below are ten examples of inclusions, illustrating how they resolve exegetical, structural, compositional, and even theological issues.

1. **18:2, 30** These verses enclose chap. 18, which opens with YHWH's self-declaration of the Decalogue, implying that the forbidden sexual unions are Sinaitic.

2. **19:36b–37 and 18:2b–5.** The former provides the rationale for the latter: YHWH's redemption of Israel from Egypt was for the purpose that Israel should serve him by obeying his commandments. Furthermore, the structure of 19:36b–37 is explicable on the basis of 18:2b–5.

3. **20:8, 22.** Verse 22a encloses vv. 9–21 as the similarly worded v. 8 encloses vv. 1–7; v. 22b also encloses vv. 9–21 as the similarly worded v. 18:28aα encloses (with its peroration) vv. 6–23, indicating respectively the unity of chap. 20 and the unity of chaps. 18 and 20.

4. **21:1, 4.** The fact that these two verses form an inclusion provides strong grounds for regarding *ba'al* in v. 4 as a dittography (partial) of *bĕ'ammāyw* (see its NOTE).

5. **22:2aβ, 2b, 32.** This inclusion not only binds chap. 22, but equates Israelites with priests in a double chiastic form (abcd ∥ b'a'd'c') concerning their common obligation to prevent the desecration of the sacred.

6. **22:29–30 and 19:5–6.** This inclusion envelops chaps. 19–22, containing all the references to human and divine holiness. It explains why the *tôdâ* offering was severed from the discussion of the *šĕlāmîm* (19:5–6), where it belongs: it was brought down to 22:29–30 so it could create this inclusion.

7. **23:4, 37a.** This inclusion demarcates the *original* festival calendar from its subsequent appendices, the sabbath (vv. 1–3) and the supplement to the Festival of Booths (vv. 39–43a).

8. **24:13–15a, 23.** This inclusion proves structurally that the narrative (blasphemy) and law (talion) make up a unitary composition.

9. **25:1–2 and 26:46.** The specific reference to Mount Sinai as the place where these two chapters were revealed may be due to their content: release of persons and property (chap. 25) and the covenant imprecations (chap. 26). The inclusion forms an abcdd'c'b'a' introversion, whose center (dd') stresses that Israel's retention of the land hinges on its observance of the laws of Leviticus.

10. **25:23, 55.** This inclusion forms a parallel panel (aba'b'), implying that both the land and Israel belong to YHWH; therefore, Israelites who live on the land are his tenants.

d. THE NUMBER SEVEN

A favorite structural device in H is its frequent use of the number seven—that is, seven attestations of a word in a pericope to indicate its importance. The number seven stands for perfection, completion, not only in the Bible, but in the literature of the ancient Near East (see the convenient summary and bibliography in Freiberg 1992). The following list will indicate its prevalence in H.

1. In **chap. 18**, YHWH occurs seven times (vv. 1, 2, 4, 5, 6, 21, 30), uniting the entire chapter. Its redactor, who added the opening and closing exhortations to an existing list of prohibitions (see INTRODUCTION to chap. 18), used this number of completeness to demonstrate that the chapter is a unity. The first verse states that the chapter is YHWH's command. The six remaining attestations, in the formula *'ănî YHWH* 'I YHWH (have spoken)', reiterate his authorship of the prohibitions (see NOTE on v. 5) and warn any potential offender that he will not escape punishment.

2. In **chap. 19**, the formula *'ănî YHWH 'ĕlōhêkem* occurs 1 + 7 times (vv. 2, 3, 4, 10, 25, 31, 34, 36). Verse 2, however, is the heading and is unattached to a specific law. By the same token, the shorter formula *'ănî YHWH* is found 7 + 1 times (vv. 12, 14, 16, 18, 28, 30, 32, 37), but its final attestation is in the conclusion and not attached to a law. This can hardly be an accident. The author made a concerted effort to achieve the perfect number, seven, for each formula, balancing the two by a 1 + 7, 7 + 1 construction (note P's similar technique in the purging of the sanctuary, chap. 16; cf. vol. 1.1038–39).

3. In **chap. 21**, the key root *qdš* occurs seven times in the prohibitions incumbent on the priest (vv. 6–8), stressing that the priest's innate holiness can be diminished by violating these prohibitions.

4. In **chap. 22**, the word *yiśrā'ēl* occurs seven times (vv. 2, 3, 15, 18 [thrice], 32), tying the three sections of the chapter together and emphasizing that Israel has a shared responsibility with the priests to offer unblemished sacrifices. Perhaps that is why another keyword, *rāṣôn*, also occurs seven times (vv. 19, 20, 21, 23, 25, 27, 29), again laying stress on Israel's responsibility that its sacrifices will be acceptable to YHWH.

5. In **chap. 23**, *yiśrā'ēl* again occurs seven times (vv. 2, 10, 24, 34, 42, 43, 46). Perhaps this is why the redactor was forced to omit the clause *dabbēr 'el bĕnê yiśrā'ēl* in the heading of v. 26. Note as well that there are seven festivals in the calendar. The key terms *miqrā' qōdeš* 'sacred occasion' and the sacrificial requirement *lĕhaqrîb 'iššeh laYHWH* (vv. 2, 7, 8, 18, 21, 24–25, 27, 35, 36 [twice], 37) also occur seven times. (Neither is attested for *pesaḥ*, but they are compensated for in the summary, v. 37.) Also the root *qṣr* 'harvest' is found seven times (vv. 10 [thrice] and 22 [four times]), thereby enveloping both grain festivals (Barley and Wheat) into a single unit—that is, a continuous festival.

6. In **chap. 24**, YHWH occurs seven times in the two ritual requirements (vv. 1–9), the menorah oil and the bread of presence. Seven laws compose blasphemy and talion (vv. 15–21), affirming that they are a unified pericope (see COMMENT A). The roots for blasphemy *qll* and *nqb* (indicating the desecration of God's name) appear, all together, seven times, perhaps midrashically explaining the juxtaposition of this pericope with the menorah oil and shewbread, where God's name appears seven times (S. Chavel).

7. In **chap. 26**, the verb *'ākal* 'eat' occurs seven times (vv. 5, 10, 16, 29 [bis], 38), acknowledging that the basic laws for the septennate and the jubilee are

economic concerns. The *ʾăḥuzzâ* 'holding' occurs seven times in regard to the real property of lay persons and Levites (vv. 25–34), which unifies the two pericopes (the section on houses, vv. 29–34 being a supplement).

8. In **chap. 26**, vv. 34–35, the *šbt* occurs seven times, thereby setting off these two verses from the surrounding curses and supporting the supposition that they are an interpolation.

e. MISCELLANEOUS DEVICES

Chapter 19 contains two structural devices that link it to its neighbors. Verse 19 serves as a break in the middle of this chapter and separates its two units (vv. 1–18, 20–37). Simultaneously, it forms a symmetrical inclusio with the final verse (37aα) and with the preceding chap. 18 (vv. 5aα, 26aα). "I YHWH am your God who freed you from the land of Egypt" (v. 36b) provides a rationale for caring for the alien (vv. 33–34) and is both the beginning of the closing exhortation of chap. 19 (vv. 36b–37) and a grand inclusio for chaps. 18–19 (18:2b–3a; details in INTRODUCTION to 19:36b–37).

The exhortation to Israel that it strive for holiness (20:7–8) functions as a bridge between two seductive practices that threaten to assimilate Israel to its neighbors: Molek worship (20:1–5) and sexual license (vv. 6–21). Simultaneously, it corresponds with the opening exhortation of 18:1–5, which also warns Israel not to follow the (sexual) mores of its neighbors.

Thus the interlocking capabilities of such breaks and inclusios provide a tool of multiple applicability that can connect larger and smaller units simultaneously.

A word should also be added about the artfulness of H's structural skills as exemplified by the comminations of chap. 26. They comprise five units of increasing severity (vv. 16–17, 18–20, 21–22, 23–26, 27–39). Each unit is provided with an introduction expressing YHWH's intention, which also is of increasing length and severity. This is accomplished by repeating the preceding intention and adding to it words or phrases expressing greater emphasis.

B. VOCABULARY: H's DISTINCTIVE TERMINOLOGY

Knohl (1995: 108–10) provides a comprehensive list of H words and idioms, which differ from equivalent expressions in P. I suggest certain refinements to this list as well as a number of terms that receive a unique nuance in H. The following are some examples:

1. *wĕhikrattî . . . miqqereb ʿammāh* (Lev 17:10; 23:3, 5), in contrast with P's *wĕnikrĕtâ . . . mēʿammêhā* (7:20, 25, 27), is used when the divine punishment

is *imminent*. H's exact parallel with P *wĕnikrĕtâ . . . mē ʿammêhā* is also attested (19:8; 23:29; Num 9:13 H). The singular *ʿam* illustrates H's tendency to fudge P's precision (details in NOTE on 17:10).

2. As correctly noted by Knohl (1995: 1, n. 3), a basic characteristic of H's style is that YHWH speaks in the first person to second-person Israel. A parade example is the closing formula *ʾānî YHWH*. This expression requires nuancing. I submit that it is equivalent to the prophetic *nĕum YHWH*, literally 'the declaration of YHWH'; indeed, as S. Chavel reminds me, Ezekiel fuses the two expressions (Ezek 26:14; 37:14). The formula should be rendered "I YHWH have spoken," implying that he is certain to punish if his commands are not fulfilled (see NOTE on 18:2).

3. I have long noted (1976a: 86–89) that P's term for 'desecration', *ma ʿal*, is expressed by H as *hillēl šēm YHWH* 'desecrate the name of YHWH'. I further remarked that *ma ʿal* appears once in H (26:40), but in a metaphoric sense. Knohl (1995: 109, n. 165) claims that *ma ʿal* also appears in passages outside Leviticus: Num 5:6; 31:16; Deut 32:51. It should be noted, however, that *ma ʿal* in these verses is also metaphoric, and it is even doubtful that Num 5:6 can be attributed to H (see I E). In any event, the consistent pattern holds: wherever H uses *ma ʿal*, it is metaphoric, but in P and P alone it refers to a specific desecration of sanctums (see NOTE on "and thereby not desecrate the name of your God," 18:21).

4. H's metaphoric use of P's cultic terms is highlighted by *ṭāmēʾ*. In P, it is ritual impurity; in H, moral impurity. Ritual impurity (P) is remediable by ritual purification, but moral impurity is irremediable. It is a capital crime, punishable for the individual by *kārēt* and for the community by exile (details in INTRODUCTION to 18:24–30).

5. Israel's land is always called *ʾăhuzzâ* in H, whereas it is always called *nahălâ* in D and both *ʾăhuzzâ* and *nahălâ* in P. H's *ʾăhuzzâ* dovetails with its theology: the land is YHWH's, and the Israelites are but resident aliens. Thus the land is not Israel's *nahălâ* '(permanent) inheritance', but its *ʾăhuzzâ* '(conditional) holding' (see the discussion in NOTE on "his holding," 25:10, and in I C).

6. H's use of *rāṣâ* in 26:34–35, 41, 43 is unique. Regardless of how it is rendered (I suggest "be paid," *Qal*; "pay off," *Hip ʿil*), I tentatively propose that H used it as a synonym of *kipper* 'atone, expiate', a P term that implied a cultic rite, which Israel in exile could not perform (see NOTE on 26:34–35).

7. H's *mōrek* 'faintness' (26:36) is a hapax, probably from *rkk*. The idiom *mōrek bilbābām* 'faintness in their heart' would correspond with *rak hallēbāb* 'fainthearted' (Deut 20:8; see NOTE on 26:36).

8. *usĕmartem mišmeret/mišmartî* 'heed the guarding of/my guarding' (cf. Milgrom 1970: 10–12). The verb is found in Exod 12:17 (bis), 24; 31:14; Lev 18:5, 26, 30; 19:3; 20:22; 22:31; 28:8; Num 18:5 — all H; the idiomatic form of the noun is also found in H (18:30; 22:9; Num 9:19, 23), except for Lev 8:35, which ostensibly belongs to P, but because of the use of the rationale *wĕlōʾ tāmûtû* 'lest you die' is suspect of being an H addition.

C. VOCABULARY: H'S DISSOLUTION OF P'S PRECISION AND EXTENSION OF P'S USAGE

As detailed in vol. 1.36–38, H blurs many P terms. For convenience, I repeat their essence:

1. In P, *ma'al* is limited exclusively to the sacrilege of sanctums, and it can bear only one rendering, "sanctum desecration." In H, however, it metaphorically connotes "rebellion, treachery" (e.g., 26:40 and Num 31:16; Deut 32:51 [also H]) and thus assumes a figurative meaning (see no. 3, above).

2. P also distinguishes punctiliously between *šeqeṣ* and *ṭāmē'* (see NOTE on 10:11; Milgrom 1992a), whereas H fuses and confuses the two.

3. P's *miškān* invariably designates the inner curtains of the Tabernacle or, by extension, the structure on which the inner curtains rest (e.g., Exod 26:7, 30). H, however, interprets it metaphorically as the "(divine) presence" (26:11; cf. Ezek 37:27) that "walks about" (*hithallēk*) in Israel's midst (26:12), implying first that YHWH is to be found throughout the land and not just in the sanctuary (the latter is P's doctrine) and, second, that if Israel observes the divinely revealed commandments, it can regain the conditions of paradise in which God also "walked about" (Gen 3:8; see NOTES on 26:11–12).

4. P meticulously distinguishes between feminine *ḥuqqâ/ḥuqqôt* 'statute(s), law(s)' and masculine *ḥōq/ḥuqqîm* 'due(s), assigned portion(s)' (see NOTE on 10:13), whereas H blurs the two (e.g., 10:11 [H]; 26:46).

5. The term *ṭāmē'* in P strictly denotes "(ritually) impure," whereas H employs this term metaphorically in nonritualistic contexts, such as adultery (18:20), all sexual violations (18:24), Israel's land (18:25–28), and necromancy (19:31; see the discussion in INTRODUCTION to 18:24–30).

6. H fuses and confuses the terms *ḥillēl* 'desecrate' and *ṭimmē'* 'defile'. The high priest who is defiled by a corpse pollutes the sanctuary, a far more grievous sin than *yĕḥallēl* 'desecrate' (21:12). Similarly, the ordinary priest who eats sacred food in a state of impurity becomes defiled, not desecrated (22:9). Yet in both cases, H uses the verb *ḥillēl* 'desecrate'.

7. P scrupulously distinguishes between the divine punishments *mût* 'death' and *kārēt* 'excision' (vol. 1.457–61). H, however, interchanges them indiscriminately. For example, H prescribes *mût* for the impure priest who partakes of sacred food (22:9; cf. vv. 4–8), whereas P prescribes *kārēt* for the same offense (7:20). In light of the fact that *kārēt* is the severer penalty, is it conceivable that H would designate *mût*, a lesser penalty, for the priest? Furthermore, H explicitly prescribes *kārēt* for sancta desecration by a lay person (19:8; contrast 7:18[P]). Again, would H prescribe only *mût*, the lesser penalty, not for desecration (*ḥillēl*), but for the severer offense of defilement (*ṭāmē'*) if it is committed by a priest (22:9)? This example alone, I contend, suffices to indicate H's cavalier disregard of P's terminological precision.

8. As shown by Knohl (1995: 87), P distinguishes meticulously between *nepeš*

and *ʾîš ʾô ʾiššâ/ʾîš ʾîš*, the former being reserved for the sacrificial laws (2:1; 4:2, 27; 5:1, 2, 4, 15, 17, 21; 7:18, 20, 21) and the latter for the impurity laws (13:29, 38; cf. 15:5 with 7:21). H, however, mixes the two indiscriminately in the same law (17:3, 8; 22:4–6). In this instance, Knohl's point must be amended. P, it seems, also uses *ʾîš ʾîš* and *ʾîš ʾô ʾiššâ* in the heading of sacrificial laws (15:2; Num 6:2). If, however, this formula is followed by *mibbêt/mibbĕnê yiśrāʾēl ʾăšer*, it becomes a distinctive H expression (17:3, 8, 10, 13; 22:18).

9. In P, the word *niddâ* is a technical term for menstrual discharge (12:2, 5; 15:19, 24, 25, 26, 33). In H (20:21), however, and in derivative literature (e.g., Ezek 7:19, 20; Lam 1:8, 17; Ezra 9:11), it becomes a metaphor for impurity, indecency, or disgrace, which stems from moral rather than physical causes.

The list can be supplemented by three more examples:

10. P's precision has completely broken down in the formula *wĕnikrĕtâ hannepeš hahiʾ* . . . . It consistently ends in P with the plural *ʿammîm* 'kin' (Gen 25:8, 17; 35:29; 49:33; Exod 30:33, 38; Lev 7:20, 21, 25, 27; Num 20:24; 27:13; 31:2), whereas H interchanges it frequently with the singular *ʿam* 'people', a different term (17:4, 10; 20:3, 6, 17, 18; see NOTE on 17:10, and no. 1, p. 1325).

11. In 23:17, H refers to loaves of bread offered on the Festival of First Wheat as *bikkûrîm*, and in 23:10, it calls the firstfruits of raw barley *rēʾšît*. This, however, contravenes P's terminological distinction, by which, in contrast, *bikkûrîm* stands for the raw produce and *rēʾšît* for the processed product—another example of how H blurs and, in this case, reverses P's precise definitions.

12. H consistently calls Israel's home *ʾăḥuzzâ* 'holding', whereas D just as consistently uses the term *naḥălâ* 'inheritance', and P employs both terms *ʾăḥuzzâ* and *naḥălâ*. In each source, theology is the determining factor. From the expression that recurs in D, *ʾăšer YHWH ʾĕlōhêkā nōtēn lĕkā naḥălâ* '(the land) that YHWH your God gives you (as) inheritance' (Deut 4:21; 15:4; 19:10; 20:16; 21:23; 24:4; 25:19; 26:1; cf. 4:38; 19:14), one can readily see that YHWH gifted Israel (*nātan* 'give, gift') with permanent inheritance (*naḥălâ*). H, on the contrary, posits (despite the use of *nātan* in 23:10; 25:2) that Israel resides in YHWH's land as resident aliens (25:23). Hence H is constrained to refer to the land as *ʾăḥuzzâ* 'holding', namely, subject to recall by its divine owner. P (what we have of it), concerned exclusively with the sanctuary and its sanctums, has no doctrine of the land; hence it fluctuates indiscriminately between *ʾăḥuzzâ* and *naḥălâ*. Strikingly, here is manifested a reversal in terminological precision between H and P. Whereas H generally fudges and expands P's precise definitions, here we find the reverse, namely, that H added precision to P's broader usage (see NOTE on "his holding," 25:10, and no. 5, p. 1326).

Throughout his book, Knohl has amassed a mountain of evidence distinguishing P's terminology from that of H (1995: 46–121, esp. 106–10). He is not always correct. In vol. 1.16–17, I have taken issue with his declaration (1995: 46–55) that *ḥuqqat ʿôlām lĕdōrōtêkem/ām* is always a telltale sign of H. Here I wish to demonstrate that on the basis of style, terminology, and theology, Knohl wrongly assigns a whole pericope to H. I refer to Num 5:6–8 (Knohl, 1995: 86–87).

In regard to style, Knohl offers seven bits of evidence:

1. *hēšîb ʾāšām* (vv. 7, 8) is found in H (Num 18:9), but not in P.
2. *těrûmâ* (v. 9), referring "to all Priestly gifts," is found only in H (22:12; Num 18:8).
3. *gōʾēl* (v. 8), "a name for family relation," is found only in Lev 25:25–26.
4. The *gōʾēl* implies "a law that refers primarily to resident aliens," a concern of H.
5. The use of *milbad* (v. 8) typifies H's editorial additions (1995: 178, n. 38).
6. *ʾāšām* (vv. 7, 8) means "monetary compensation," not "sacrifice," as in P (1995: 86, n. 80).
7. P always resorts to *nepeš* as the subject of its sacrificial laws and *ʾîš*, *ʾiššâ* or a combination of the two as the subject of its laws of purity, whereas H uses both indiscriminately (17:10; 20:5–6; 22:3, 4–6), precisely as it does in this pericope (v. 6). Knohl discusses this last point at length in the main body of his text and says that it "can tip the scales" (1995: 87).

Initially, I accepted Knohl's conclusions (vol. 1.369). I have changed my mind. I shall deal with his evidence seriatim.

Points 1 and 2 can be dismissed out of hand. They are arguments from silence. The absence of *hēšîb ʾāšām* and the special status of *těrûmâ* from P would be significant only if P were substituting for them with equivalent items. Moreover, point 2 is wrong. First, *těrûmâ* occurs in v. 9, which falls outside the *ʾāšām* pericope (cf. Milgrom 1990a: 36). Then, *těrûmâ* does mean "a priestly gift" in Exod 29:28; 30:13–15; and Lev 7:14—all admitted by Knohl as P. That *těrûmâ* applies to several specific gifts—for example, the priestly prebends from the well-being offering and the half-shekel contributed by adult Israelite males—implies that *těrûmâ* stands for any or all "priestly gifts" in P. Point 3 is again an argument from silence; P has no use for a term that refers to a redeemer of sold land (Lev 25:25–26) or of a slain person (Num 35, claimed for H by Knohl 1995: 99–100). And it is not true that the *gōʾēl* refers "primarily" to the resident alien (point 4), since the latter is incidental to and only a by-product of the laws bearing on destitution (25:25–55); these laws are derived from the postulate of 25:23–24 dealing with only the redemption of land, a subject of no concern to the resident alien since, according to H, he is barred from possessing inherited land.

The use of *milbad* (point 5), indeed a mark of the H redactor (Knohl 1995: 56–58), appears in the final clause of the pericope (v. 8b); it may, however, have been appended by an H tradent, who thought that Num 5:6–8, being a condensed text of 5:20–26 (see below), should state explicitly that an *ʾāšām* sacrifice is due to the deity, and since *ʾāšām* has been usurped for the monetary payment, he coins the unique term *ʾêl hakkippurîm* 'ram of expiation' (recognized by Dillmann and Jackson, cited by Knohl 1995: 178, n. 33). Knohl's sixth point cannot be sustained: *ʾāšām* in P also bears the meaning of "reparation, penalty" (5:6, 7, 25a, its primary meaning, vol. 1.339–45), just as in Num 5:7. Thus *ʾāšām* in

P, as both sacrifice and monetary compensation, constitutes reparation. H, no differently, also uses *'āšām* in both senses (cf. 19:21, 22; Num 18:9).

Finally, Knohl's main point (no. 7), his terminological analysis of the subject in P and H, has to be challenged.

1. Knohl (1995: 87, n. 82) is able to muster only two P verses, found in two contiguous pericopes, in which *'îš 'ô 'iššâ* occurs: 13:29, 38. Let us look at both verses from the point of view of text and context. Verse 29 specifies *zāqān* 'beard'. How, then, could the subject be designated by the gender-neutral *nepeš*? Verse 38 begins a new law with *wě'îš 'ô-'iššâ kî-yihyeh b*. The previous law (v. 29) begins identically, *wě'îš 'ô-'iššâ kî-yihyeh b*. Thus for the sake of stylistic uniformity, P adopts the same initial wording of v. 29 in v. 38. Besides, v. 38, as the only instance of *nepeš* with its attendant feminine verbs and suffixes within an entire chapter couched in the masculine, would have been glaringly inconsistent and stylistically gauche.

2. In Num 5:6 (1995: 87), stylistic reasons are again responsible for *hannepeš* following *'îš 'ô 'iššâ*: the repetition of the latter—in the same verse—would have been awkward.

3. In Num 9:1–14, which Knohl (1995: 90) assigns to H, he notes a shift from *'îš 'îš* to *hannepeš* (v. 13). However, the latter occurs in P's formula *wěnikrětā hannepeš*, which H regularly uses (Gen 17:14; Exod 12:15, 19; Lev 19:8; 22:3; 23:29; Num 9:13; 15:30; 19:13, 20—all H, according to Knohl). Only in 17:4, 9 does H write *wěnikrat hā'îš*, perhaps for stylistic reasons, because both H's laws begin with *'îš 'îš* (vv. 3, 8), though the legist clearly had both sexes in mind (the switch to *nepeš* in 17:10 is motivated differently; see its NOTE).

4. Turning finally to P's usage, its alleged distinction between sacrificial and purity contexts breaks down in the Nazirite pericope, Num 6:1–21. Though it is concerned mainly with sacrifices, it uses the heading *'îš 'ô 'iššâ*. Knohl (1995: 89), realizing this anomaly, divides the pericope into two sections (vv. 1–12, 13–21), the latter dealing exclusively with the sacrifices brought by the Nazirite upon the completion of his term. This division is of no help because both sections stem from P, and the first section (vv. 1–12) deals mainly with the sacrifices the Nazirite must bring in the event that his term is interrupted by corpse-contamination. Nothing, however, is said about his purificatory procedures! Thus we have a sacrificial text, indisputably the handiwork of P, which according to Knohl's analysis should be headed by *nepeš*, but instead it begins with *'îš 'ô 'iššâ*. The distinction between the usage of these two terms in P and H is, therefore, proved untenable (but see no. 8, above; concerning the theological significance of this pericope, see I E).

D. H's Style

Examples of H's style can be found in Paran (1989), Knohl (1995), and Schwartz (forthcoming). In the section on structure (I A), I have discussed H's favorite stylistic devices: chiasms, introversions, parallel panels, and inclusions. The following are additional examples listed sequentially, by verse.

1. **17:3.** *'îš 'îš* 'anyone'. This idiom must be followed by *mibbêt yiśrā'ēl* (and not otherwise; *pace* Knohl 1995: 87, n. 83) in order to become an *exclusive* H expression (17:8, 10; 22:18; cf. 17:13).

2. **17:5–7.** The first of three asides to Moses (17:5–7, 11–12, 14; Schwartz forthcoming). The rationales are given to Moses privately (cf. esp. NOTE on "Say to them further," vv. 8–9, and no. 16, below). The necessity of providing rationales in this chapter is to underscore the innovative nature of the law banning nonsacrificial slaughter.

3. **18:2 and passim.** H's *'ănî YHWH* is equivalent to prophetic *nĕ'ûm YHWH* (see NOTE on 18:5).

4. **18:30.** *'ănî YHWH 'ĕlōhêkem* 'I (who speak) am YHWH your God' encloses chap. 18 with v. 2.

5. **19:2.** This formula also encloses chap. 19 (vv. 2, 36) and chaps. 18–19 (18:4–5; 19:36b–37).

6. **19:3.** Seidel's (1955–56) law is intensively utilized. H inverts the Decalogue's order of father and mother (Exod 20:12) and commandments 4 and 5 (v. 3). H also inverts the order of commandments 1, 2 (v. 4) and 4, 5 (v. 3). Thus there can be no doubt that H is referring to the Decalogue. Two other examples are H's reversal of P's order of the *zebaḥ šĕlāmîm* (7:11–15, 16–18) by placing the one-day *tôdâ* (22:29–30) after, and removed from, the two-day *šĕlāmîm* (19:5–8). H also employs this law of reversal when it wishes to cite itself (25:53b–55a inverts vv. 42a–43b; see NOTE on v. 55).

7. **19:5–8, introduction.** In quoting P, H trims and simplifies P's style—the sign of a redactor at work (Paran 1983: 144–49).

8. **19:9.** The imperative of the initial prohibition comes before the object, whereas in the following three prohibitions the imperative follows the object— H's device to emphasize a novel law (Paran 1989: 144–49; cf. NOTES on 23:18; 26:1).

9. **19:13.** The entire unit (vv. 13–14) is set up as a series of prohibitions of increasing length (Schwartz 1987: 141–42).

10. **19:18.** There is an increase in the variety of terms designating the Israelite in vv. 11–18, reaching a crescendo in vv. 17–18 (Magonet 1983; Wenham 1979a; cf. NOTE on "you shall love," v. 18).

11. **22:3.** *'ĕmōr 'ălêhem* 'Say (further) to them.' This is H's stylistic device to indicate that the general command of scrupulousness toward sacred donations, mentioned in the previous verse (v. 2), can be worded as Moses and Aaron desire. The list of prohibitions that now follows, however, must be the *ipsissima verba* of YHWH, received as dictated.

12. **22:4.** When P begins a casuistic law with *'îš 'îš* or *'îš* (*'îššâ*), the relative conjunction *kî* always follows (e.g., 12:2; 15:2, 19, 25). H, however, will generally use the relative conjunction *'ăšer* (e.g., 17:3, 8, 10, 13; 20:2, 9, 10–21; 21:17, 18, 19, 21; 22:5, 18).

13. **23:8.** H's redactional technique is displayed in 23:7–8, which condenses Num 28:18–25.

14. **23:11.** H's stylistic use of *lirṣōnĕkem* betrays that the term *mimmāḥŏrat haššabbāt* (also in 23:16) is a gloss.

15. **23:22.** In repeating 19:9a, H improves the style, clearly indicating that 19:9a is the original.

16. **24:15.** *wĕ'el-bĕnê yiśrā'ēl tĕdabbēr lē'mōr* 'And to the Israelites speak thus'. The reversal of object and verb in the usual address formula to Israel indicates that the previous word to Moses, the oracle's response (vv. 13–14), was addressed to Moses alone (Muraoka 1985: 38–39; see no. 2, above).

17. **25:3–4.** H's reworking of Exod 23:10–11 is distinguished stylistically by the omission of *'et*, word pairs, and the use of a refrain with variations (Paran 1983: 15–19, 259–61).

18. **25:22.** *wa'ăkaltem . . . tō'kĕlû.* This presents a circular inclusio with change of verb pattern, typical of H's style (Paran 1983: 35; cf. NOTE on 26:4).

19. **26:34.** Since there is no ritual atonement for the land, H substitutes for *kippēr* the verb *rāṣâ* in a new usage. The *Hip'il wĕhirṣāt* that follows is H's circular inclusio with a change of verbal aspect and pattern.

E. THE TERMINI AND EXTENT OF H

a. LEVITICUS

Thus far it has been tacitly assumed that H produced Lev 17–27. Before examining whether H is found outside this bloc, it must first be demonstrated that chaps. 17 and 27 are its actual termini in Leviticus.

There is overwhelming evidence for placing chap. 17 at the head of H. Its distinctive style (YHWH addressing Israel in the first person, vv. 10–12, 14), structure (large and small introversions throughout the chapter, vv. 10–12, 13–14), emphasis on motivations (asides to Moses, vv. 5–7, 11–12, 14), proliferation of penalties (vv. 4, 9, 10, 14, 16), and polemic (against P!, v. 11) identify it with the succeeding chapters and set it apart from those preceding it (details in INTRODUCTION to chap. 17).

However, it has also been noted that chap. 17 lacks either of the two key terms that characterize H: the root *qdš* and the formulaic ending *'ănî YHWH*. Moreover, chap. 17 is tied to the preceding chap. 16 by the verb *kippēr* (16:6, 10, 16, etc.; 17:11 [bis]) and the chthonic *śā'îr* (see NOTES on *Azazel*, 16:8, 21–22; 17:7). Furthermore, as argued by Douglas (1995), the similar sacrificial vocabulary of chaps. 1 and 17 indicates that the latter serves as a latch to bind chaps. 1 and 17 into a (minor) ring structure (see INTRODUCTION to chap. 17). Thus the position of chap. 17, a distinctive H composition, while exhibiting links with chaps. 1–16, may best be explained as the work of the H redactor (H_R), who intentionally set chap. 17 at its present place as a bridge between the two major blocs that compose the book of Leviticus. His choice of this rather than some other chapter would have been motivated by his desire to begin with a prescription on sacrifice, in keeping with the practice of other law corpora (Exod 20:22–26 [JE]; Deut 12 [D]).

What can be said of the other terminus, chap. 27? On the one hand, chap. 27 is linked to chap. 25 by the law of jubilee (27:17–24; 25:10–54) and by its supplementation (consecrated and sold usufruct). On the other hand, it is clearly an appendix, not only for the reason usually given: that it follows blessings and comminations (chap. 26), which normally conclude a law corpus (Exod 23:20–33; Deut 28). A firmer textual argument is that both chapters have fairly similar subscripts (27:34; 26:46). The subscript of chap. 26, moreover, contains the term *tôrōt*, found only in P (6:2, 7, 18; 7:1, 11; 13:59; 14:2; 15:32; Num 6:13, 21), indicating that chap. 26 is the closure to the entire book of Leviticus.

What, then, is the function of the appendix, chap. 27? Four answers are ventured in the scholarly literature: chaps. 26 and 27 share the same votive context; chap. 27 provides the funding for the sanctuary; it obviates ending Leviticus with a series of curses; and it concludes Leviticus with the same content as its opening, chap. 1 (see the discussion in chap. 27, COMMENT B).

I shall substantiate only the last explanation, the one that I favor (Hertz 1941; Douglas 1995). The same redactional structure that accounts for the placement of chap. 17 as a latch for chap. 1 (above) is now exhibited for the entire book. Chapter 26 concludes with blessings and comminations. Nonetheless, the redactor (H$_R$) found it more important to ignore the covenantal form (chap. 26) in favor of his larger goal: to use chap. 27 as the supplement to and redaction of the *relevant* P material that lay before him.

Knohl (1995: 47–55, 61–103, 201, n. 5) discusses the pentateuchal passages he attributes to H. He lists them (1995: 104–6) as follows: Gen 17:7–8, 14*; 23*; 36*; Exod 4:21b; 6:2–7:6; 9:35; 10:1–2, 20–23, 27; 11:9–10; 12:1–20, 43–49; 16**; 20:11; 24:12–18**; 25:1–9; 27:20–21; 28:3–5; 29:38–46; 30:10; 31:1–17, 18**; 32:15**; 34:29–35**; 35:40; Lev 1:1; 3:17; 6:10–11; 7:19b, 22–36; 9:16b; 10:6–11; 11:43–45; 14:31; 15:31; 16:29–34; 17–22; 23:2–3, 9–22, 28–32, 38–43 (but cf. my objections in chap. 23, COMMENT A); 24–26; Num 1:48–5:10; 5:21, 27b; 6:21b (?), 22–10:28; 13:1–17a; 14:26–35; 15; 16:1–11, 16–24, 26–27a, 35; 17–18; 19:2a, 10b–13, 20–21a; 20:1–13**, 22–29; 25:6–18; 27:1–23; 28:2b, 6, 22–23, 30, 31a; 29:5–6, 11, 16, 19, 22, 25, 28, 31, 34, 38; 31; 32:6–15; 33:52–53, 56; 35–36; Deut 32:48–52 (the single asterisk means "partially"; the double asterisks are JE passages edited by H$_R$).

Recently, two dissertations have appeared, which throw doubt on the *narrative* passages in this list. Frankel (1994) has demonstrated convincingly that the murmuring narratives (Exod 16; Num 13–14; 16–18; 20:1–3) contain early priestly narratives embedded in P units (attributed by Knohl to H), which may be even earlier than the nonpriestly (JE) units. King (1996) presents the challenging thesis that the priestly texts in Gen 1:1–Exod 6:1 are from a pre-Hezekian source (PN) that stems from North Israel. Finally, just before this manuscript went into publication, I read a challenging article by Wehnham (1999: esp. 241–45) arguing compellingly—as does Frankel—that in Genesis, several whole P sections are framed by supplements of J, implying that P antedates J. One flaw in Frankel's and Wenham's arguments surfaces immediately: there is no distinction between P and H. Though P could be claimed as prior to J, H—the source subsequent to P—might also turn out to be subsequent to J. Nonetheless, their conclusions are in part ensured. Some priestly texts in the Torah's epic are early, even earlier than J. Perhaps, I might add, Frankel's and Wenham's early P may be identical with King's PN.

I have heretofore hesitated to be drawn into the quagmire of the priestly narrative because I will not have any terminological controls. Bereft of the distinctive cultic and legal vocabulary whose currency throughout the biblical period can be traced, I have no reasonable assurance that my identification of any priestly narrative is correct, not to mention its date. At least within the cultic texts some terms fall out of use (e.g., *ḥuqqâ* 'due'), some lose their precision (e.g., *šeqeṣ*), others change in meaning (e.g., *ʿăbōdâ*), while still others are replaced by different terms (e.g. *maṭṭeh* by *šēbeṭ*). In other words, the *history* of the terms can be approximated and, with that, the date of their context. For me, a distinctive vocabulary does not suffice as a bona fide criterion. Moreover, so many purported priestly passages are mere snippets without any distinctive traits and their attribution is purely guesswork. Now along come Frankel's (1994) and King's (1996) dissertations and Wenham's (1999) article, and the identification and dating of the priestly narrative is thrown into turmoil. And if these questions linger regarding the priestly narrative per se, the doubts are compounded manyfold if one tries to identify the text as either P or H, as Knohl (1995) and many others have done. I shall therefore concentrate exclusively on the *legal* passages attributable to H. Even here I shall be more conservative than Knohl and confine myself to passages whose H identity can be substantiated. I, too, hold that the H redactor (H$_R$) has left his fingerprints in Exodus and Numbers—but not to Knohl's extent.

b. NUMBERS: THREE EXAMPLES

Let me illustrate first with Num 3:11–13. This pericope explains YHWH's choice of the Levites: they replace the firstborns. It clearly bears the hallmarks of H. YHWH speaks in the first person and concludes his words with his signature *ʾănî YHWH*, and, in typical H fashion, a rationale is provided (see further no. 6, p. 1340). Remove this pericope, and the text reads smoothly. Now there is nothing in the rest of the chapter regarding style, language, or content that can be ascribed to H. Yet Knohl assigns not only all of chap. 3, but the entire "Levite treatise" (Num 1:48–5:10; 6:22–10:28; 17–18) to H. These passages serve his goal to identify the creation of the priests' assistants, the Levites, with the employment of Levite refugees, who flooded Judah after the destruction of the Northern Kingdom at the end of the eighth century—the age of H (Knohl 1995: 209–12).

Note that no reason is given in Num 3:11–13 (nor in Num 8:16–19) to explain why the original priests, the firstborns, were replaced by the Levites. This is one of the many instances where H demonstrates familiarity with the golden calf episode and with the entire JE corpus (after J and E have been combined, namely, R$_{JE}$). Perhaps that is why the verb *hiqdîš* 'consecrate' is deliberately used by H in connection with the firstborns (Num 3:13; 8:17; cf. Exod 13:2), in order to allude to their priestly role in worshiping the golden calf.

To cite another example, Knohl (1995: 31, n. 68) has excised the requirement of a male goat as a *ḥaṭṭā't* from every public offering in Num 28–29 (P) as an H addition, except that of the new moon, on stylistic grounds only, without accounting for its alleged absence. Yet in P's account of the first in public offering (Lev 9), which sets the pattern for all subsequent public offerings, the *ḥaṭṭāt* plays an integral role. (One cannot argue that it is sacrificed first, Lev 9:8–12, but in Num 28–29 it is listed last. The reason is obvious: the descriptive and prescriptive orders do not correspond; see the case of the Nazirite, Num 6:14–16, and NOTE on the parturient's offerings, vol. 1.756.) Moreover, as shown by Marx (1989), in a sacrificial series the *ḥaṭṭāt* is integrally connected with the *ʿōlâ*, and together they form an inseparable tandem (cf. vol. 1.289–92). Finally, I would point to the recent article of Zatelli (1998) on the function of a goat in the purgation of a royal (hence, sacred) mausoleum in third-millennium Ebla and its obvious parallels with the goat's function in the annual Day of Purgation of Israel's sanctuary (Lev 16). Is it not conceivable, indeed essential, particularly in view of the probability that originally the purgation of the sanctuary was more frequent (see NOTE on 16:2, vol. 1.1012–13), that in P's system the sanctuary had to be purged with a single goat on every festal occasion?

As the final example, I cite Knohl's (1995: 86–87, 176–78) claim that H achieved a major theological breakthrough by revising Lev 5:20–26 (P) in Num 5:5–8. (Knohl also includes vv. 9–10, but these constitute a separate unit; see Milgrom 1990a: 36.) He writes, H "presents moral injustice as ritual guilt" (179, n. 36) whereby "a transgression against moral and social justice is also a breaking of faith with God (*maʿal baYHWH*), even if no false oath accompanies it" (172). Thus, according to Knohl, whereas P will consider a crime against man (*jus*, 'fraud') only when it involves a crime against God (*fas*, 'false oath'), H declares categorically that the former is always *maʿal*, a crime against God. H has thereby released the term *maʿal* from the limited confines of sanctum desecration to a "breaking of faith." Immediately, an objection springs to mind:

Knohl overlooks the penalty prescribed in Num 5:6–8, a reparation ram—the most expensive ovine! I can understand that if the sinner had denied his crime under oath (Lev 5:22, 24) and thus had desecrated the name of YHWH, then severe expiatory reparation to YHWH is required. But if the sinner experiences remorse without being apprehended and confesses his crime to God (not to a court; vol. 1.301–3), it makes sense that he must pay his *victim* a 20 percent fine in addition to the capital (for the juridical reason for this small penalty, see Milgrom 1976a: 114–16). But if he has not taken a false oath—that is, desecrated the name of YHWH—why is his crime also *maʿal* against God, and why is it expiated by a costly ram?

If, indeed, H wished to express the thought that any sin against a person is a *maʿal* against God expiable by a reparation ram, why didn't H say so unambiguously? All that H had to do was to transpose P's *ûmāʿălâ maʿal baYHWH*

(5:21) from the protasis to the apodosis, as follows: *'îš 'ô 'iššâ kî ya'ăśû mikkol-ḥaṭṭō't hā'ādām ûmā'ălû ma'al baYHWH* 'If a man or woman commits any wrong against a person, he has committed a sacrilege against the Lord (when that person feels guilt . . . '; on the remainder of the text, see vol. 1.368). Instead, it resorts to an infinitival construction *lim'ōl ma'al*, which can be only part of the protasis. The sacrilege is not the result, but a condition of his act, namely, the wrongdoer commits a sin against a person *whereby* he commits sacrilege. That condition is explained explicitly in Lev 5 and presumed in Num 5: he has taken a lying oath.

Thus I find that Knohl's claim that any breach of moral or social justice is *ma'al baYHWH*, even if no oath accompanied it, cannot be sustained. Rather, the *'āšām* law of Num 5:6–8 is a reference to and a contraction of Lev 5:20–26 (with Ramban 1960, changing my earlier opinion, 1976a: 105, n. 388), and its opening should be rendered, "If a man or woman commits any wrong against a person *in the course of which* he commits sacrilege against the Lord," namely, by a lying oath.

That the repetition of a law can be abbreviated (such as the omission of an oath in Num 5:6–8) is exemplified frequently in the priestly writings. For example, within P, compare Lev 1:1–9 with 1:10–13; 14:10–20 with vv. 21–31; 9:8–10, citing the *ḥaṭṭā't* procedure of chap. 4, but omitting the required hand-leaning (*sāmak yād*). So, too, Num 15:27–28 (H) takes for granted the entire *ḥaṭṭāt* procedure of Lev 4 (P). H uses the term *'iššeh* in Lev 23 to allude to the schedule of public offerings in Num 28–29 (P). Similarly, Num 5:6–8 relies on the telltale *ma'al* to refer to P's explicatory statement (5:22, 24) that it is a lying oath.

If Num 5:6–8 is a restatement of Lev 5:20–28, what does it add to its Leviticus *Vorlage*? The answer is obvious: *it adds the criterion of confession.* Implied is that this defrauder of man and God cannot hope for expiation by "feeling guilt"; he must express his guilt verbally. Confession is a prerequisite only for expiating deliberate sin (5:1–4; 16:21; 26:40; Num 5:6–7; cf. Milgrom 1976a: 108–9; vol. 1.374). Confession is made to the injured party: God, man, or both (as in the case of Lev 5:20–26). The verbalization of confession to man is neatly captured by the rabbis' *'ad šeyyĕraṣṣeh 'et ḥăbērô* '(he is not expiated) until he appeases his fellow' (*m. Yoma* 8:9). The rabbis also foresee the possibility that the injured party may not be appeased, in which case they prescribe that the confession take place before ten men, and God will then forgive him (*Pesiq. R.* 38; *Tanḥ B* Vayera 30).

In sum, Num 5:6–8 is not H's giant breakthrough, calling every immoral or unjust act a sacrilege against God that requires the sacrifice of a reparation ram. It is either P or, preferably, a composition of later P tradents (P₂) who added the confessional requirement to the case of defrauding one's fellow and then denying the act under oath.

Knohl (1995: 86–87, nn. 80–82) also claims that Num 5:6–8 employs a terminology different from that of Lev 5:20–26. I shall refute his arguments seriatim as I state them.

1. In Num 5, *'āšām* is a monetary reparation, not P's sacrifice (following Well-

hausen 1963: 174). However, P also uses *'āšām*, meaning "monetary reparation," not "sacrifice" (Lev 5:6, 7).

2. The expression *hēšîb 'āšām* appears again in the Torah only in Num 18:9 (H). However, it remains to be proved that all of Num 18 is H. Note also that *'āšām* in Num 18 stands for sacrifice, not the monetary penalty. Moreover, in Num 18:20–22, the tithe is the perquisite of the Levites; in Lev 27:20–22 (H), of the priests. It is hardly conceivable that H, the alleged author of Num 18, would record such a major change from Levites to priest without an explanation. Admittedly, my proposal that Num 18:20–22 is P is also questionable, since Lev 27 is older than Num 18 (Kaufmann 1938: 1.147–60), and one would expect the tithe recipients to change from priests (Lev 27) to Levites (Num 18). However, H has also been found to contain older laws—for example, sending the corpse-contaminated and the genitally diseased outside the camp (Num 5:1–3H)—and popular folk observances in its cultic calendar (Lev 23:11, 16 [pre-H₁ and pre-H₂]). Similarly, Lev 27 (H) is the repository for older, never again repeated laws, such as the death penalty for persons under *ḥērem* (vv. 28–29) and the animal tithe (vv. 32–33). So, too, it may be presumed, its vegetable tithe (vv. 30–31) reflects a law older than Num 18:20–22 (P) because, like the unique animal tithe, it originally was the prebend of the priest. Finally, the expression *hēšîb 'āšām* cannot be an H invention. It is found in an indisputably ancient narrative (1 Sam 6:3, 8, 17). The fact that P does not use it in one pericope (5:20–26) is inconsequential. Note that the verb *hēšîb* indeed is used (v. 23), but it is followed by *specific* embezzled items, and the *general* term *'āšām* would be out of place.

3. The term *tĕrûmâ* must be ruled "out of court"; it occurs in Num 5:9–10, an independent pericope.

4. H's *gō'ēl* cannot be the *gēr*. The *gō'ēl* is limited to *blood* relations of Israelites (Lev 5:48–49). Thus other Israelites may also be without redeemers.

5. According to Knohl (1995), P's purity laws use *'îš 'ô 'iššâ*, never *nepeš*, a term reserved for the sacrificial laws. In Num 5:6–8, both terms are used. This law, therefore, cannot be P, but H. However, P's alleged distinction requires examination: (a) in Lev 13:29, 38, *'îš 'ô 'iššâ* is used because of *'îš* in v. 40. An insertion of *nepeš* would be stylistically awkward. (b) *'îš*/*'iššâ* is used in Lev 12, 15 because each gender is given discrete prescriptions; and (c) Lev 7:21 and 15:5 are not analogous; 7:21 applies to both sexes. Thus the terminology of Num 5:6–8 can accord with P's language and thought (see also I C).

In sum, Num 5:5–8 is not an H pericope. It may be P₂, to which H has appended vv. 9–10. The vocabulary of vv. 5–8 is not distinctly H, and the innovation is just confession and not an extension covering all sins.

c. EXODUS AND NUMBERS: H INSERTIONS

Of all the passages listed above, the ones that are, for me, indisputably H are those that have established H criteria and also are textual interpolations serving as transitions between P and non-P passages. These can be attributed to only the H redactor. The following are a sample:

1. **Exod 27:20–21 and Num 8:1–4.** These two passages on the menorah were inserted by H between the P prescriptions on the Tabernacle (Exod 25:1–27:19) and the priestly consecration (Exod 28) and between the gifts of the chieftains (Num 7) and the ordination of the Levites (Num 8). They do not fit their context, and without them the text reads logically without a ruffle (cf. Knohl 1995: 48, and Milgrom 1990a: 60, n. 4).

As will be demonstrated, Lev 24:2–3 and Exod 27:20–21 are duplicates. They exhibit two ideological differences: (1) in Exod 27:21, Aaron and his sons, rather than Aaron alone, are responsible for setting up the lamps; and (b) *mē'ēt běnê yiśrā'ēl* 'from the Israelites' has been added at the end of Exod 27:21 (using the language of Lev 24:8bα), imposing on all Israel the obligation to supply the oil for the menorah.

Note that these two verses are located in the interstices between units of P. It can only be the work of a redactor. This fact characterizes all units written outside the main corpus (Lev 17–27). Moreover, the addition of "for the Israelites" and "and his sons" (Exod 27:21) must be attributed to a later H tradent. Thus whereas H leaves the P text intact and inserts its additions at the beginning or end of P, but never "revises and rewrites PT legal passages" (Knohl 1995: 1027), it does not hesitate to alter its own scrolls (Knohl 1995: 47–49).

2. **Exod 29:38–46.** At the end of the passage on the purgation and consecration of the altar (Exod 29:36–37), H appends a prescription on the Tamid (vv. 38–42) and a rationale for the Tabernacle (vv. 43–46). The Tamid is copied and condensed mainly from Num 28:3–8 (P). A significant deletion in Exod 29 is *baqqōdeš hassēk nesek šēkār laYHWH* 'to be poured as a libation of beer inside the sanctuary' (Num 28:7b), implying that the beer (cf. Milgrom 1990a: 240) was poured on the incense altar, which H emphatically prohibits (Exod 30:9H). The *golden* libation vessels, stored on the table containing the bread of presence, were intended for use, *'ăšer yussak bāhēn* 'with which (libations) would be poured' (Exod 25:29; 37:16), and being of gold could be used only inside the Tent—that is, on the incense altar. H, however, eliminated the golden libation vessels from his recapitulation of the Tamid and explicitly prohibited their use, because it was a gross anthropomorphism; it implied that the deity imbibed drink in his chambers (details in Milgrom 1990a: 240, and NOTES). Since the passage on the Tamid (Exod 29:38–42) is borrowed from Num 28:3–8 (P), it contains no H expressions. The reverse holds true for the remaining verses, 43–46. H's imprint is implicit throughout. YHWH speaks in the first person and concludes with his formulaic signature *'ănî YHWH.*

3. **Exod 31:12–17; 35:1–3.** The attachment of the sabbath injunctions at the close of the prescriptions for the Tabernacle construction and priestly consecration (Exod 25:1–31:11) and at the beginning of the prescriptions for the manufacture of the Tabernacle furniture and priestly clothing (Exod 35:4–39:43), with their quintessential H characteristics— *'ănî YHWH,* YHWH the sanctifier of Israel (Lev 20:8; 21:8, 15, 23; 22:16, 32), plural construct *šabbětôt* (Lev 19:3,

30; 23:38), superlative *šabbat šabbatôn* (Lev 16:31; 23:3, 32; 25:4), and direct address to Israel (Exod 31:13, 15; 35:2, 3 LXX)—all testify to the work of the H redactor (cf. Kuenen 1886: 278; Driver 1913: 38; Paran 1989: 167; Knohl 1995: 16). I demur, however, regarding Knohl's (1995: 64) assignment of the appointment of Bezalel (Exod 31:1–11) to the pen of the H redactor. It is fully an independent unit (contra 1995: 64, n. 13) and need not be attached to vv. 12–17.

These sabbath passages share with the one inserted at the head of the festival calendar (Lev 23:1–3) the aim of highlighting the central importance of the sabbath. Since, as I propose, Lev 23:1–3 was composed by the exilic H redactor (see NOTE on "the fixed times of YHWH," 23:2, and chap. 23, COMMENT A), it is likely that these two sabbath passages in Exodus were composed by the same exilic H tradent.

The rabbis held that these passages warn Israel not to construct the Tabernacle on the sabbath (*y. Ber.* 9:5). A historical explanation is more likely: Israel in exile is informed (by H_R) that the observance of the sabbath is just as acceptable to God as worship in the Temple. That these passages precede the Tabernacle instructions, just as the sabbath precedes the suspended festivals (Lev 23:4–38), may be a sign that according to H_R the sabbath is more important than the Tabernacle.

As suggested by S. Chavel, H_R has inserted 32:15 and appended 34:29–35 into JE (32*–34*) and has thereby created a grand introversion, as follows:

A: Theophany/Moses' ascent (Exod 24:15–18)

   B: Instructions (25:1–31:11)

      C: Sabbath (31:12–17)

         X: Apostasy (Golden Calf [JE]), Theophany (to Moses [JE]), Theophany (Moses' radiating face) (31:18–34:35)

      C': Sabbath (35:1–3)

   B': Instructions + fulfillment (35:4–40:33)

A': Theophany/Moses cannot enter the Tabernacle (40:34–35; cf. Lev 1:1).

One can see how the sabbath passages (CC') frame the climactic center (X), which serves to highlight the importance of the sabbath.

4. There can be no doubt that H_R interpolates his laws according to some preconceived logical plan. This certainly is the case in Leviticus, where he inserts **3:16b–17; 6:12–18aα; 7:22–29a; 9:17b;** and **10:10–11** at the point where he expands P's sacrificial laws (vol. 1.61–63). For example, the prohibition against the ingestion of all suet and blood is appended to the law of *šĕlāmîm* (3:16b–17), because it is the only sacrifice whose meat is permitted to lay persons. This prohibition is inserted at the head of another *šĕlāmîm* passage (7:22–29a), for the purpose of allowing nonsacrificial suet to be used, but not eaten (v. 24). The absolute blood prohibition occurs a third time (17:10–14),

where H states that the purpose of the blood is to ransom (*lĕkappēr*) the offerer of the sacrifice from the charge of murder (17:3–4, 11; see above). The integral association between blood ingestion and the *šĕlāmîm* offering in the first two passages (3:16b–17; 7:22–29a) provides further evidence that the ransoming (*kippēr*) function of the blood in 17:11 must also refer to the *šĕlāmîm*—and to no other offering. Furthermore, P apparently presumes that since the *šĕlāmîm* is a sacrifice of joy (thanksgiving, vow fulfillment, or spontaneity, 7:11–12, 16), it has no expiatory function. H negates that presumption and states expressly that the blood of the *šĕlāmîm* ransoms (*kippēr*, 17:11).

The placement of 10:10–11 (an H passage; see vol. 1. 616–17) is, at first glance, puzzling. Both syntactically and contextually, it has nothing to do with the inebriation prohibition (vv. 8–9) to which it is attached. The chapters that follow provide the answer. This proleptic insert stands at the beginning of the impurity laws (chaps. 11–15[P]). H is clearly fearful that Israel will not be aware of what precisely is *ṭāmē'* 'impure' and *qādōš* 'holy'. The difference means life and death; contact with *ṭāmē'* can be fatal for the entire community (15:31 [H]). Hence the priests are charged with the pedagogic responsibility to teach Israel the difference between *ṭāmē'* 'impure' and *ṭāhôr* 'pure' and between *qādōš* 'holy' and *ḥōl* 'common'.

5. In P's impurity laws, H inserts **11:43–45** (vol. 1.684–88, 694–96). As demonstrated in vol. 1.683–84, 11:43–45 subdivides into an introverted structure $AB_1B_2B_1'B_2'A'$, which comprises an inner parallel panel $B_1B_2B_1'B_2'$ within the chiasm AA'. Thus *ṭāmē'* 'impure' is pitted against *qādōš* 'holy', vv. 43b–44aα (B_1B_2) versus v. 44aβ $(B_1'B_2')$, and all *šereṣ* 'swarming creatures' are designated *ṭāmē'* 'impure' (AA'). The antithetical relationship between *ṭāmē'* and *qādōš* is substantiated by YHWH himself (B_1B_2), and the identification of *šereṣ* as *ṭāmē'* (AA') explains why H placed vv. 43–45 at this spot in chap. 11. P had distinguished between *šeqeṣ* and *ṭāmē'* (Milgrom 1992a) and designated the *šereṣ* as *šeqeṣ* (v. 42bβ). H, therefore, appends its difference with P: *šereṣ* (and all *šeqeṣ*) is also *ṭāmē'* (AA'; see I I A). To make sure that, henceforth, it should be understood that *šeqeṣ* and *ṭāmē'* are synonymous terms and, hence, the other species P called *šeqeṣ* are *ṭāmē'*, namely, forbidden fish and birds (11:10–12, 13, 20, 23), H repeats this injunction in 20:25, where forbidden birds are explicitly called *ṭāmē'* (concerning the missing fish, see NOTE on "pure and impure birds," 20:25; for H's metaphoric meaning of *ṭāmē'*, see INTRODUCTION to 18:24–30).

6. That **Num 3:11–13** and **8:14, 15b–19** are H interpolations is shown by YHWH's first-person address with the subject *'ănî* (3:12, 13) and the object *lî* (3:12, 13; 8:16 [bis], 17 [bis]), the characteristic formula *'ănî YHWH* (3:13), the use of rationales (3:13; 18:16, 17), and *kippēr* meaning 'ransom' (8:19; cf. Milgrom 1990a: 369–71). The passage 3:11–13 is an insert to explain 3:5–10, namely, by what right Levites assumed a cultic office (Loewenstamm 1971c). Thus H informs us that the Levites replaced the firstborns, who hitherto had officiated at the family hearth in worship of the departed ancestors (cf. Milgrom 1990a: 17–18). That the Levites replaced the firstborns is repeated in 8:16–17. Furthermore, 8:19 provides a rationale explaining the purpose of the Levites'

service—to ransom Israel (cf. Milgrom 1990a: 369–71). This unit, 8:14, 15b–19, also resolves the perplexing problem caused by v. 15b, which inexplicably and illogically repeats the purificatory prescriptions (vv. 13, 15a). Verses 14 and 15b have been inserted by H at the beginning of the unit to explain why the Levites qualified to undergo the purificatory and dedicatory process (8:5–13, 15a). Remove vv. 14, 15b–19, and the text reads smoothly: vv. 20–22 reports Israel's compliance with the prescriptions of vv. 5–15a. H's opening statement, the transfer of the Levites from Israel to God (v. 14), takes place when they are dedicated to God (*těnûpâ,* v. 13). For that reason, it could not be placed after v. 15a.

7. That the entire chapter Num 15 stems from H had already been observed by Kuenen (1886: 96, n. 37). This can be substantiated by examining each of its pericopes. The prescription for adjacent cereal, oil, and wine offerings (vv. 1–16) begins with *kî tābô'û 'el-'ereṣ môšěbōtêkem 'ăšer 'ănî nōtēn lākem* 'When you enter the land of your settlements that I am giving you'. This clause contains a number of H characteristics: the clause itself, cf. 23:10, 25:2, and 14:34 (H); YHWH referring to himself in the first-person *'ănî; môšěbōtêkem* 'your settlements' (Exod 12:20; 35:3; Lev 3:17; 7:26 [vol. 1.866–68]; 23:3, 14, 21, 31; Num 31:10; 35:29 [cf. Knohl 1995: 96–100]); the opposition of *gēr* and *'ezrāḥ* (vv. 13–14) and their equality in civil (*jus*) and religious (*fas*) law (vv. 15–16); and the similar vocabulary and construction of v. 3 and Lev 22:21, noted by Wellhausen (1963: 175).

8. Cereal, oil (olive), and wine are products of an agricultural society. Hence they were projected for settled conditions in Canaan. The land, in addition to the sanctuary, is H's field of concern, and all its inhabitants, including the *gēr* 'the resident alien,' are subject to its laws. It is taken for granted that the non-Israelite may worship YHWH at his sanctuary. He is therefore cautioned that he must follow all the sacrificial regulations. Moreover, H categorically rules that the same laws, both *mišpāṭ* 'civil regulation' and *tôrâ* 'ritual,' apply to the *gēr* 'resident alien' and *'ezraḥ* 'citizen' alike (cf. vv. 15–16, 29). Elsewhere, H's rule is restricted to *tôrâ* 'ritual' (Exod 12:49; Num 15:29) and *mišpāṭ* 'civil regulation' (Lev 24:22) or is expressed by the nonspecific term *ḥuqqâ* 'law' (Num 9:14; 15:15). Only here does H explicitly and unambiguously state that the alien is entitled to equal protection and privilege under the law (for the qualifications, see II N; chap. 17, COMMENT B; and II O).

9. The prescription of the first of the kneading trough (*'ărîsâ*), namely, dough (vv. 17–21), begins with *běbô'ăkem* (*'el-hā'āreṣ*) literally 'in your coming' (v. 18) rather than the usual *kî tābô'û* 'when you come' (v. 2) to indicate that this law was given simultaneously with the preceding one. This makes sense, since both pericopes deal with agricultural products. Note again the first-person pronoun *'ănî* (v. 18) for the deity. Also, the expression *kitěrûmat gōren* 'like a gift from the threshing floor' (v. 20) presumes the knowledge of Num 18:12, 30, which are demonstrably H (Knohl 1995: 71–73, with reservations).

10. In vol. 1.264–69, it was demonstrated that Num 15:22–31 is a reworking of chap. 4 for the chief purpose of making the performative and not only the prohibitive commandments subject to the laws of *ḥaṭṭā't* and *kārēṭ.*

This is at once suggested by the lack of a heading to this pericope, implying that it is continuous with the preceding laws. Since the latter are performative commandments, the *ḥaṭṭā't* requirement and *kārēt* penalty therefore apply to them. Telltale H signs are the inclusion of the *gēr* (vv. 26, 29, 30), the change of the *kārēt* formula from *mēʿammekâ* (P) to *miqqereb ʿammāh* (v. 30; cf. Knohl 1995: 53), and the employment of a rationale (v. 31).

11. The pericope of the wood-gatherer (vv. 32–36) resembles the narrative of the blasphemer (24:10–14, 23) by its similar use of *pārāš* (Pi ʿel) 'make clear' and *mišmār* 'custody' (Kuenen 1886: 96, n. 38). Kuenen terms Num 15:32–36 a *"novella* regarding the observance of the sabbath"; he renders the same opinion concerning H's authorship in regard to the sabbath pericopes Exod 31:12–17 and 35:1–3 (H). H's emphasis on the sabbath is also evident in 19:3, 30; 26:2; and especially 23:1–3. H is obsessed with the sabbath, because its violation pollutes the land. This is explicitly the case with the septennate, the seventh-year rest for the land (25:1–6; 26:34–35, 43), to which H_R, the exilic redactor, adds the weekly sabbath (26:2), whose violation contributes to Israel's exile. The case of the wood-gatherer in the wilderness demonstrates that Israel was warned *in advance* that nonobservance of the sabbath is fatal (cf. also Exod 31:15[H]).

12. In the concluding passage on the *ṣîṣīt* 'tassels' and its *pĕtîl tĕkēlet* 'blue cord' (vv. 37–41), we find the characteristic H term *zānâ 'aḥărê* 'whore after' (Lev 17:7; 20:5 [bis], 6; cf. 19:29 [bis]; 21:9), which elsewhere in the Torah is found in only two places: Exod 34:15–16 and Deut 31:16. All the earmarks of H, however, are concentrated in the concluding verses (vv. 40–41). Note: *wihyîtem qĕdōšîm lē'lōhêkem* 'so you shall be holy to your God' (v. 40b; cf. 19:2; 20:26; 11: 45 [H]) and H's concluding formula *'ănî YHWH 'ĕlōhêkem* 'I am YHWH your God (v. 41aα), a reminder of YHWH's self-declaration at the opening of the Decalogue as Israel's redeemer from Egypt (Exod 20:2; Lev 19:36; 22:33; 25:55; 26:13, 45). This formula repeated at the end of the pericope (v. 41b) should be rendered 'I YHWH your God (have spoken)' (see NOTE on 18:2b).

As pointed out in I I, H breaks with the exclusive preserve of *šaʿaṭnēz* (a mixture of wool and linen) by commanding the lay person to wear it on the outer garment in the form of linen tassels, each containing one blue, woolen thread. Their being in constant sight will remind every Israelite to strive for holiness by observing the commandments. The blue further symbolizes that Israel belongs to royalty. Thus Israel can become "a kingdom of priests and a holy nation" (Exod 19:6; see NOTE on "clothing made of two kinds of yarn," 19:9, and the complete discussion in Milgrom 1990a: 410–14).

The pericope ends not only chap. 15, but also the larger unit Num 13–14, with the failure of the scouts chosen by YHWH to reconnoiter Canaan. It forms an envelope with the unit's opening verse by the similar term *tātûrû* 'scout' (13:2; 15:39; cf. v. 25; 14:34) and further on with *zānâ* 'whore, lust' (14:33; 15:39). Also, that you (Israel) should not lust (*zānâ*) after what is scouted (*tār*) by your eyes (*'ênêkem*, v. 39) negates the report of the scouts *wannĕhî bĕʿênênû kahăgābîm* 'we became like grasshoppers in our own eyes' (Num 13:33). Thus keeping the blue-corded tassels in sight may prevent Israel from disobeying YHWH, as did the scouts (cf. Milgrom 1983e: 21–22; 1990a: 127, 410–14).

The tassels pericope also points forward to the Korahite rebellions (chap. 16). Korah's argument against the Aaronides was his ostensibly irrefutable claim *kol-hāʿēdâ kullām qĕdōšîm* literally 'the entire congregation, all of them, are holy' (Num 16:3). This actually is a basic plank in the theology of D (not H), which maintains that Israel is genetically holy, by dint of YHWH's choice of the patriarchs. Korah's theological challenge is not answered in what follows in chap. 16, but in what precedes, the tassels unit (15:37–41). The H redactor anticipates Korah's challenge by quintessential kerygma: Israel can become holy only if it fulfills the divine commandments. Holiness is not hereditary; it is not genetically transmitted except in YHWH's chosen, the Aaronide priests.

It should be clear, then, that Num 15:37–41 serves as a transition between the two larger blocs (Num 13–14 and 16–18; see also Knohl 1995: 90). The larger question, however, remains: Why did the H redactor place chap. 15 in its present position? In my commentary on Numbers (1990a: XV–XVI), I noted that the book consists of an alternation of law and narrative, totaling twelve units: 1:1–10:10 (L); 10:11–14:43 (N); 15 (L); 16–17 (N); 18–19 (L); 20–25 (N); 26:1–27:11 (L); 27:12–13 (N); 28–30 (L); 31:1–33:49 (N); 33:50–36:13 (L). Douglas (1993: 102–22) refines my observation in an extensive treatment and demonstrates that twelve alternating units (differently defined) form a ring (see her diagram, p. 1365) such that chap. 15 matches chaps. 18–19 in that both deal with cultic provisioning and defilement. An equally satisfying reason is suggested by the medieval commentators (e.g., Ibn Ezra 1961, Ramban 1960, Ḥazzequni 1981 at the beginning of chap. 15) that after the generation of the Exodus is told that it must die in the wilderness (Num 14:32), it is given some laws that will take effect in the promised land, "when you enter the land . . . " (15:2, 18). Thus the members of that generation are assured that though they will die in the wilderness their children will inherit the land. Another reason may be the equality granted to the *gēr* with the citizen (15:14–16, 26, 29), which may have been motivated by the good deeds of the loyal *gēr* Caleb (13:30; 14:6, 24; cf. Josh 14:7–9; see also Milgrom 1990a: 391–92), who was awarded choice territory in the promised land (Josh 14:7–9). These three reasons adequately explain the placement of 15:1–31. Thus the concluding pericope (vv. 37–41), as demonstrated, serves as a bridge between the major blocs (13–14 and 16–18)—the work of the H redactor.

The examples discussed above outside of Leviticus—Exod 27:21; 29:38–46; 31:12–17; 35:1–3; Num 3:11–13; 8:15b–19; 15—illustrate what, I believe, are certain H passages. I have attributed the following to H: Lev 3:16b–17; 6:12–18aα; 7:22–29a, 38b (?); 9:17b; 10:10–11; 11:43–45; 12:8; 14:34–53 (?), 54–57 (?); 15:31; 16:2bβ, 29–34a (vol. 1.61–63). I would add 8:35 (see I B, no. 8), but I am no longer sure about 6:17–18aα; 7:28–29a; 9:17b; and 12:8. If they are, indeed, additions to the basic text (P_1), they may be the handiwork of P_2. Other passages that probably should be assigned to H are Exod 6:2–8; 12:17–20,

43–50; Num 3:40–51; 5:1–3; 9:9–14; 10:10; 15; 19:10b–13; 28:2b; 29:39; 33:50–56; and 35:1–36:13. The remaining passages in Knohl's (1995) list are possibly H, but they lack, in my opinion, adequate evidence.

The above passages are characterized by H formulas, style, vocabulary, and ideology. Moreover, they do not disrupt P units with the intent of altering them, but are attached to or inserted between units. It should also be noted that P's narratives are at times integrated with those of JE (e.g., Num 13:1–17a; 14:26–35, which Knohl [1995: 90–92] assigns to H), an indication that the attached H (e.g., Num 15) is subsequent to and familiar with both JE and P (see I R). The only logical conclusion is that if H_R edited the fused JE and P passages in these narratives, there is a strong possibility that it is the redactor of Exodus and Numbers as well as Leviticus.

I have deliberately omitted the few passages in Genesis attributed to H (see Knohl 1995) because of their speculative nature. But one Genesis passage, overlooked by Knohl, clearly accords with H criteria. As noted by Amit (1997: 25*), Gen 2:2–3 (she wrongly includes v. 1) contains basic H terms, such as the verbs *qiddēš* (this root is totally absent in P) and *šābat* (a metaphoric usage breaking with P's cultic term, Num 28:9–10). As noted by Cassuto (1965: 30–40), the noun *šabbāt* has deliberately been avoided lest it be deduced that non-Israelites are also bound to observe it. Moreover, these two verses are replete with anthropomorphic vocabulary typical of H and antithetical to P, such as *wayyĕkal*, *'āsâ*, *wayyĕbārēk*, *wayyĕkaddēš*, *šabat*. I should also note the rationale (*kî* beginning v. 3b), a sure sign of H (see II B). Furthermore, the attribution of Gen 2:2–3 to H solves the enigma concerning the twice mentioned fact that God completed (*klh*) his work. H has added *vayyĕkal* (v. 2) to P's *vayyĕkullû* to continue his work beyond the sixth day to create the sabbath. Thus there is no need, with all the versions, to emend the first *haššĕbî'î* to read *haššiššî*.

Finally, the addition of Gen 2:2–3 breaks P's sophisticated structure marked by two chiastic panels:

Introduction: *haššāmayim, hā'āreṣ* (1:1)

Day	Element	User	Day
1	Light (3–5)	Luminaries (14–19)	4
2	a. sky	b. marine life	5
	b. terrestial waters (6–8)	a. sky life (20–23)	
3	c. dry land	c. land animals	6
	d. vegetation (9–13)	d. humans (24–31)	

Conclusion: *haššāmayim, hā'āreṣ* (2:1)
7. The sabbath (2:2–3)

The balanced panels, locked by the central chiasm (abba) and enveloped by a similarly worded introduction and conclusion, make it graphically clear that the addition of the sabbath is a glaring intrusion.

F. THE INNER GROWTH OF H AND P

a. THE INNER GROWTH OF H

I begin this section with chap. 23. It is the only chapter that exhibits all four strata that, in my opinion, make up the continuum of H's thought in the Torah. I do not use the term "school," as invented by Knohl (1995: passim), because in my opinion over 95 percent of the H material can be attributed to the product of the eighth century. It may be the product of a single generation of "young Turks," who radically changed the priestly thought, but I find no signs of continual literary activity that would justify using the term "school."

1. Pre-H$_1$ is a pre-Hezekian stratum (vv. 10aβ–11a*, 12–14a, 15*, 16*, 17, 19*, 20*, 39*, 40; the single asterisk means "partially"). It prescribes the *individual's* rites with the grain crop whenever it ripened. It also ordains the (processional) use of branches during the seven-day celebration at the local sanctuary to rejoice over the past year's yield and to pray for adequate and timely rain for the following year's yield (see NOTES).

Pre-H$_2$ (vv. 11b*, 15*, 16a*) prescribes that the barley firstfruits be brought to each local sanctuary on the first Sunday of the harvest, which automatically sets the wheat offering, fifty days later, also on Sunday. Pre-H$_2$ introduces the notion of *šabbāt* as a sabbath-week, giving rise to schismatic differences in later Judaism (see NOTE on v. 15). Thus it can be seen that Pre-H$_2$ is a series of glosses in the early stratum Pre-H$_1$.

H comprises the main text of chap. 23 (vv. 4–38*). Its composition can be attributed to the Jerusalem Temple. It preempts the individual's grain offering and standardizes the date of the Festival of Booths. It adopts the catalogue of the regional (Jerusalem) sanctuary reflected in P (Num 28–29) and indulges in detail whenever it is innovative (barley) or different (wheat; see NOTE on v. 8, and INTRODUCTION to vv. 15–22). The name of the fall festival, the Festival of Booths, probably derives from the Jerusalem scene when its surrounding hills were blanketed with pilgrims' booths (see NOTE on v. 36).

H$_R$ represents the end product of the H continuum, probably composed in the Babylonian Exile. In this chapter, H$_R$ focuses particularly on the sabbath (vv. 2aβ–3) and makes the living in booths during the seven-day festival mandatory, while supplying a historic rationale (vv. 42–43). For details on H's calendar, see chap. 23, COMMENT A, and for the discussion on H$_R$'s role in the redaction of Exodus and Numbers, see I E.

2. An older list of sexual prohibitions (18:6–23) has been incorporated into two exhortations that have been reworded and made into the frame of the prohibitions (vv. 1–5, 24–30). An indication that there are two layers embedded in chap. 18 is that only one prohibition is called *tôʿēbâ* (v. 22), whereas all the prohibitions are labeled *tôʿēbâ* in the closing exhortation (vv. 26, 27, 29).

3. Three H pericopes differ on the theme of Israel's expulsion from the land: Lev 18:24–30 (20:22) states that the land will evict Israel (like the Canaanites

previously) for violating the enumerated sexual prohibitions; in Num 33:50–56, God declares that if Israel does not drive out the Canaanites, God will drive them (Israel) out; and Lev 26 avers that if Israel breaks the covenant by violating all the commandments, God will blight the land, making the land ripe for invasion and the people ripe for expulsion.

In contrast with Lev 26 and Num 33, which posit a human enemy, Lev 18 (20) metaphorically describes automatic ejection by the land. In this respect, it is closest to P: just as P's sanctuary (seemingly) expels its resident YHWH, so H's land expels its resident Israel—both ostensibly automatic processes. Though the agents of expulsion are human or terrestrial, YHWH is behind the scene pulling the strings (details in INTRODUCTION to 18:24–30).

4. One of the reasons that 19:5–8 was placed near the top of the chapter is to have its rationale *kî-'et-qōdeš YHWH ḥillēl* (v. 8aβ) correspond with the equivalent expression *lō' tĕḥallĕlû 'et-šēm qodšî* (22:32), thereby encompassing all the attestations of the root *qdš* commanding Israel to be holy (chaps. 19–22). Effecting this inclusio for these four chapters of the Holiness Source is clearly the handiwork of a redactor.

5. In chap. 19, the units on the *gēr* (vv. 33–34) and honest trading (vv. 35–36) may be supplements (see NOTES). Once removed, the chapter's close (vv. 30–32) forms an inclusion with its opening (vv. 3–4) (see INTRODUCTION to chap. 19).

6. Chapters 18 and 20 flank chap. 19, thereby projecting it as the pinnacle of Leviticus and, possibly, of the entire Torah (see I L). These two chapters, 18 and 20, contain identical prohibitions (20:9–21; 18:6–23) and parallel final exhortations (20:22–26; 18:24–30), and the prohibitions are headed by kerygmatic exhortations (20:7–8; 18:2b–5).

7. The singular verb in *môt-yûmat hannō'ēp wĕhanō'epet* 'the adulterer and the adulteress must be put to death' (20:10) indicates that, originally, only the paramour was slain; the wife was added later. In narrative, though the verb agrees with the first subject, it may agree with both. In law, however, this fluidity would create chaos.

8. The compliance report (21:24) is clearly an addition, since nowhere in chap. 21 is Moses commanded to speak to the Israelites. It corresponds with Lev 16:29–34a (H), which also shifts the addressee from the high priest (16:2) to all Israel (*lākem*, 16:29, 31). This shift in chap. 21 signifies that the responsibility for the priests' impeccable body (chap. 21) and the high priest's performance on the Day of Purgation (chap. 16) ultimately rests with Israel.

9. The *tôdâ*, the 'thanksgiving offering' (22:29–30), should have been placed by 19:5–8 (the *šĕlāmîm*, the 'peace offering'), where it rightfully belongs (cf. 7:11–18), but it was located instead where it would further chaps. 19–22 (see no. 3, above).

10. Lev 24:4 is a redactional supplement to vv. 2–3, clarifying that the lampstand did not consist of just a single lamp (as implied by *nēr*, v. 1).

11. The final, exilic tradent (H$_R$) has inserted 26:1–2 as a prologue to the blessings and comminations (26:3–46). He has selected three commandments of the Decalogue (nos. 1, 2, and 4): the worship of one God, but not with im-

ages, and the observance of the sabbath as determinative for suspending Israel's continuous presence on its land.

12. The verses 26:33b–35, 43–44 are also an insert by H_R, explaining to Israel in exile that the delay in its restoration to the land is due to the fact that the land has not yet made up its neglected sabbaticals.

13. Whereas 26:1–39 (with the addition of vv. 40–45) forms the epilogue to the Holiness Source, v. 46 is the closure to the entire book of Leviticus (prior to the addition of chap. 27).

14. Chapter 27, an appendix, belongs to Leviticus. It supplements 5:14–26. Both speak of a 20 percent fine. Whereas in chap. 27, it is a *charge* imposed for the *right* to convert the sacred into the profane, in 5:14–16 it is a *penalty* for the *crime* of doing the same. Thus all the cases of sanctification, legitimate and illegitimate, are covered. The placement of chap. 27 is clearly the work of the redactor H_R.

15. The subscript 27:34 supplements the previous subscript (26:46) so that both effect a proper closure for the book of Leviticus.

b. THE INNER GROWTH OF P

It should not be forgotten that P also is a composite of two or more strata and that its rightful designation is the School of P. I have already argued that 11:24–38, 47 is the contribution of P_2 (vol. 1.61–63). I have also intimated that chaps. 8 and 9 (and possibly 10), as well as the prescriptive text Exod 29:10–14, contain a description of the *ḥaṭṭā't* offering that preserves an older form of the *ḥaṭṭā't* ritual, which presumes the absence of the incense altar (vol. 1.636–37). It should not go unnoticed that the description of the inaugural service of the Tabernacle (chap. 9) is not based on any prescriptive text, abetting the possibility that this chapter stems from an older narrative source. Similarly, the unique vocabulary of 16:1–28 indicates the probability that it also stems from an older P source, which portrayed the total purgation of the sanctuary as an emergency rite (vol. 1.1038).

G. LAW AND NARRATIVE IN H

In the INTRODUCTION to 24:10–23, I cite at length the jurist Robert Cover (1983: 4–68) and the biblicist James W. Watts (1995: 540–57), who argue that narrative and law are mutually interdependent (see also Milgrom 1996a). In chap. 24, COMMENT A, I argue that the talion laws are integrated into the structure of the blasphemy narrative and that the narrative provides an indispensable *Sitz im Leben* for the laws. Thus it may be surmised that behind every law lies a (narrative) case and that the narrative is not an artificial, fictive case and not a midrashic

construction or an ancient tradition (Carmichael 1985b) to justify the inclusion
of an existing law; rather, both law and narrative arise simultaneously, the narrative (case) providing the motivation for the emergence of the law. Thus the
wilderness narratives to which laws are attached must be taken seriously as providing the actual grounds for the formulation of a law—for example, the blasphemer (Lev 24:10–23), the second *pesaḥ* (Num 9:1–14), the wood-gatherer
(Num 15:32–36), and the inheritance rights of women (Num 27:1–11). This is
not to preclude that these narratives have been reworked (e.g., Num 9:1–8 and
vv. 9–14; within chap. 36; cf. Milgrom 1990a: 511–12). But at their core, they
apparently are authentic. These cases and the laws they generated occurred in
the distant past; hence, they could be attributed to the Mosaic period. For an in-
cisive analysis of the interpenetration of law and narrative in Exodus, see Daube
(1963) and Smith (1997: 264–84, esp. 277–84; see also Nasuti 1986: esp. 15–19).

Greenstein (1984: 84) argues differently: the Torah's laws were, indeed, generated by the accompanying narratives, but they seem to have served less as a
tool for the judiciary than as a vehicle for religious instruction. This heuristic
nature of the law is expressed by such pedagogic terms as *tôrâ* 'teaching' and
the priestly function *lĕhôrōt* 'to teach' (Lev 10:11; Deut 33:10; cf. Lev 14:57;
Exod 24:12; Deut 17:9–11; 24:8, 12; Ezek 44:23; Mic 3:11). He further analo-
gizes from the Code of Hammurabi (CH): just as it is not reflected in the vast
jurisprudence of ancient Mesopotamia, so it can be inferred that the Torah does
not constitute the actual jurisprudence of ancient Israel.

In either view, the antiquity of both law and narrative is presumed (on Mosaic origins, see II A). However, Greenstein's thesis is subject to challenge. The
Torah's laws state not only what should be (imperfect) heuristically, but also
what occurred (perfect) historically. Limiting myself to priestly texts, note the
following: the blasphemer and wood-gatherer *were* (reportedly) put to death
(24:23; Num 15:36); the impure Israelites *were* (presumably) granted a postponed *pesaḥ* (Num 9:8); and the daughters of Zelophehad *were* awarded inheritance rights (Num 27:7; Josh 17:4–6), but *were* (reportedly) restricted in marriage to their own tribe (Num 36:10–13; actually to their own clan; cf. Milgrom
1990a: 511–12).

Thus even if the other laws of the Torah are not such test cases, there is every
likelihood that they were actually carried out. For example, some sexual violations were initially adjudicated and punished by the paterfamilias (Lev 20:9–16),
but in subsequent, urbanized Israel they were administered by the city elders
(Deut 22:13–29, esp. 15–18), and the execution of the deliberate homicide was
turned over to the blood redeemer by the *ʿdâ* (Num 35:19–27) and subsequently
by the city elders (Deut 19:12; cf. Milgrom 1985c). The possibility is thus strong
that the change of juristic authority bespeaks a living law. Finally, Scripture
records a law, which ostensibly appears advisory but was reportedly carried out
in practice: the death penalty for cursing God or king (Exod 22:27) is cited in
the trial of Naboth (1 Kgs 21:13). Therefore, CH notwithstanding, it may be
concluded that the Torah's laws, far from being a guide for behavior, were, at
least in part, the living code of Israel.

H. H PRESUMES, SUPPLEMENTS, AND REVISES P

As expounded in chap. 21, COMMENT B, H's law on priestly and sacrificial blemishes cannot be complete, but must rely on earlier (P) traditions (Gerstenberger 1996: 318). So, indeed, all of H presumes and even revises earlier P traditions. In addition to those examples in Lev 17–27 cited by Knohl (1995: 111–23), I adduce the following:

1. Game animals *'ăšer yē'ākēl* 'that may be eaten' (17:13) are permitted for the table. What are they? A knowledge of forbidden game (P)—birds (11:13–19) and quadrupeds (11:24–28)—as well as the criteria for permitted quadrupeds (11:2–8) must be presumed.

2. The carcass of *every* animal transmits impurity. This law of 11:39–40 (which is not P₃, as I conjectured in vol. 1.681–82, 93–95) agrees with H (17:15), not P (e.g., 5:2–3; 7:21), which asseverates that only carcasses of *impure* animals convey impurity. The same verdict, namely, that, in contrast to P, H holds that the carcasses of pure animals convey impurity, must apply to 22:8: eating from a carcass subjects a priest to death by divine agency (22:9), whereas a lay person need but undergo purification (17:15). Nonetheless, in regard to *touching* a carcass, the law for both priest (22:4b–7) and lay person (H's silence presumes the law of 5:2; 7:21[P]) is the same: there are no penalties in H once the required purification is observed. Here, where the law is the same, a true comparison can be made. H (11:39–40; 17:15; 22:5a, 8) maintains that all animal carcasses, of pure as well as impure animals, convey impurity. This differs from P (noted above), which holds that carcasses of pure animals convey no impurity at all.

Thus the fact that 11:30–40 (H) is an interpolation into P's diet laws is confirmed by two indisputably H passages, 17:15 and 22:8, thereby supporting the thesis that H is both subsequent to and the redactor of P.

3. In the INTRODUCTION to 19:5–8, this unit is shown to be a near verbatim repetition of 7:16–18 (P), whose superfluous and confusing wording is clarified and to which a rationale is added, "because he has desecrated what is sacred to YHWH" (v. 8a*β*). This rationale qualifies this unit to be subsumed under the rubric of holiness.

4. Many of the categories of 19:11–13 are found in 5:20–26 (P). H must have had the P text before him, because he supplements it with a series of furtive transgressions and, thereby, converts the P text from a unit on illegal expropriation of property into a broad category of basic ethical violations (details in Milgrom 1976a: 84–101).

5. The description of the high priest *kî nēzer šemen mišḥat 'ělōhāyw 'ālāyw* (21:12) must be adjudged as awkward because of its three words in construct. Its construction can be explained as an amalgamation of *kî šemen mišḥat YHWH 'ălêkem* (10:7a*β*[P]) + *nēzer* (8:9). The change from YHWH to *'ělōhāyw* is explicable by the need for a suffix on the latter designating the deity. It underscores that each successive high priest must undergo the distinctive consecra-

tion rites (Exod 29; Lev 8) during which his head would be anointed with sacred oil. These changes are a clear indication that H presumes and revises P.

6. The prescription that the priest afflicted with scale disease (ṣārûaʿ) or a genital flow (zāb) may not eat sacred food ʿad ʾ̌ašer yiṭhār 'until he becomes pure'
(22:4a) omits purificatory rites. That such details should be expected can be deduced from the adjoining unit on minor impurities, which specifies that ablutions and sunset are required (vv. 6b–7). These rites do not apply to the ṣārûaʿ
and zāb who are sources of impurity, requiring a more complex and prolonged
purification. Thus 22:4a depends on a prior knowledge of all the purificatory
details in chaps. 13–15 (P).

The same verdict, namely, that the oblique statement depends on prior elaboration, must be assigned to bĕ'ādām ʾ̌ašer yiṭmā'-lô lĕkōl ṭumā'tô 'any human
being by whom he is made impure whatever (be) his impurity' (v. 5b), which
is modeled on 5:3 (P)! But who are the humans who defile? Again, they must
include those identified and discussed in chaps. 12–15 and Num 19, namely,
the parturient (chap. 12), mĕṣōrāʿ (chaps. 13–14), zāb (chap. 15:1–5), the menstruant (15:24), the zābâ (15:25–30), and the corpse-contaminated (Num 19).

7. What did the priest do with the ʿōmer of barley (23:10–11)? Was it kept by
the priest as his perquisite, or was it an ʾiššeh to God (on the altar)? H is silent,
because it presumes 2:14–16 (P), which states that it was an ʾiššeh (cf. 7:9). That
2:14–16 deals with the ʿōmer, see vol. 1.192–94.

8. In the discussion of H's festival calendar (Lev 23), it is demonstrated that
the referent of the repeated formula wĕhiqrabtem ʾiššeh laYHWH 'you shall offer food gifts to YHWH' (23:8, 25, 27, 36 [bis], 37) is Num 28–29 (P). When H
agrees with Num 28–29 on sacrificial requirements, it uses this formula. When
H prescribes the firstfruits of the grain, however, it advisedly avoids this formula
and, instead, enumerates the required sacrifices (23:12–13, 18–19). The reason
is obvious: P has no barley (ʿōmer) offering; H must therefore prescribe it. P does
have a wheat offering (Num 28:26–31). In this case, however, H differs with P's
sacrificial regimen; H therefore must prescribe its version. Can there remain any
doubt that Lev 23 (H) has adapted the text of Num 28–29 (P)?

It always can be (and has been) argued that H's awareness of P's laws does
not mean that H is also aware of P's text. This argument, however, collapses in
points 2, 4, and 6 (above), which, I submit, confirm that H was fully aware of
the MT of P.

9. H's pericope on the Festival of Alarm Blasts (23:23–25) is brief due to its
derivation from Num 29:1–6 (P), as follows:

Num 29:1–6	Lev 23:23–25
[1](û)baḥōdeš haššĕbîʿî bĕ'eḥad laḥōdeš miqrā'-qōdeš yihyeh lākem kol-mĕleket ʿăbōdâ lōʾ taʿăśû (yôm) tĕrûʿâ (yihyeh lākem [2]wa'ăśîtem ʿōlâ . . .[6b] lĕrêaḥ niḥōaḥ) ʾiššeh laYHWH	[23][wayyĕdabber YHWH ʾel-mōšeh lēʾmōr] [24]dabbēr ʾel-bĕnê yiśrāʾēl lēʾmōr] baḥōdeš haššĕbîʿî bĕ'eḥad laḥōdeš yihyeh lākem [šabbātôn zikrôn] tĕrûʿâ miqrāʾ qōdeš [25]kol-mĕleʾket ʿăbōdâ lōʾ taʿăśû [wĕhiqrabtem] ʾiššeh laYHWH

The parentheses in the Numbers passage enclose the words deleted in Leviticus, while the brackets in the Leviticus passage enclose its additions to the Numbers passage. Lev 23 (H) takes for granted the rites as detailed in the text of Num 29 (P), and it innovates two new H concepts: *šabbātôn* and *zikkārôn* (details in NOTES on 23:24).

10. H's pericope on the Day of Atonement (23:26–32) is also constructed on the basis of its prototype in Num 29:7–11 (P), but this time H appends a large section of its own:

<table>
<tr><td>Num 29:7–11</td><td>Lev 23:26–32</td></tr>
</table>

^{7}(*û*)*bĕʿăśôr laḥōdeš haššĕbîʿî hazzeh miqrāʾ-qōdeš yihyeh lākem wĕʿinnîtem ʾet-napšōtêkem kol-mĕlāʾkâ lōʾ taʿăśû wĕhiqrabtem* (*ʿōlâ*) *laYHWH* (…) ^{12} …

[*wāyyĕdabbēr YHWH ʾel-mōšeh lēʾmōr* ^{27}*ʾak*] *bĕʿăśôr laḥōdeš haššĕbîʿî hazzeh* [*yôm hakkippūrîm huʾ*] *miqrāʾ-qōdeš yihyeh lākem wĕʿinnîtem ʾet-napšōtêkem wĕhiqrabtem* [*ʾiššeh*] *laYHWH* ^{28}[*wĕ*]*kol-m̆lāʾkâ lōʾ taʿăśû* […] ^{33} …

The long passage prescribing the sacrifices (Num 29:8–11) is characteristically encapsulated in H by the term *ʾiššeh* (see no. 8, above). H's own long (and unique) addition (23:28aβ–32) summarizes the day-long purgation rites for the sanctuary detailed in Lev 16, in particular, in its own appendix to Lev 16: vv. 29–34a. Thus 23:26–32 is a blend of H's summary of Num 29:26–28aα (P) and its own supplement to Lev 16 (vv. 29–34a). The result is an artfully constructed introversion diagrammed and diagnosed in the INTRODUCTION to 23:26–32.

11. This H text on the Festival of Booths, as others in Lev 23 (exemplified above), presumes the equivalent prescriptions in the P text of Num 28–29, namely, 29:12–38. Note the similarity of the opening lines (the parallel words are boldfaced):

<table>
<tr><td>Num 29:12–13</td><td>Lev 23:34b–36</td></tr>
</table>

^{12}**ûbaḥămiššâ ʿāśār yôm laḥōdeš haššĕbîʿî miqrāʾ-qōdeš yihyeh lākem kōl-mĕleʾket ʿăbōdâ lōʾ taʿăśû** *wĕhaggōtem* **ḥag laYHWH šibʿat yāmîm** ^{13}*wĕhiqrabtem ʿōlâ ʾiššeh rēaḥ niḥōaḥ* **laYHWH**

^{34b}**baḥămiššâ ʿāśār yôm laḥōdeš haššĕbîʿî** *hazzeh* **ḥag** *hassukkôt šibʿat yāmîm laYHWH* ^{35}*bayyôm hāriʾšôn* **miqrāʾ-qōdeš kol-mĕleʾket ʿăbōdâ lōʾ taʿăśû** ^{36}*šibʿat yāmîm taqrîbû ʾiššeh* **laYHWH**

H's major addition is the name of the festival, *sukkôt*. For its significance, see NOTES on 23:34, 42.

12. The narratives Lev 24:10–23 (H) and 10:1–7 (P) supplement and expand the basic postulate of P's pericope on the reparation offering: whereas *inadvertent* or *unwitting* desecration of YHWH's sanctums (5:14–16, 17–19) or YHWH's name (5:20–26, also a sanctum) may be expiated by sacrifice (see vol. 1.319–78), *advertent, brazen* desecrations of YHWH's sanctums (10:1–4) or name (24:10–16) are punishable by death (through divine agency). Thus H$_R$ added

his story of the deliberate desecration of the divine name (24:10–16, 23) to balance the corresponding story in P (10:1–4) of the deliberate desecration of the sanctuary.

13. H's ethics do not comprise a code. They consist of a series of moral injunctions, occasionally reaching sublime heights (see II H). These disconnected ethical statements (e.g., 19:3a, 9–18, 32–36; 5:6, 17, 25–43) clearly presume a code, namely, legislation covering a logically continuous range of human interaction. The entire priestly tradition (both P and H) rests on this base, part of which is adumbrated in P (in Genesis, see above), and the rest mentioned explicitly or allusively by P and supplemented by H. For example, the prohibition against murder is given to humanity (Gen 9:5–6[P]), but Num 35, probably an H composition (Knohl 1995: 99–100), separates out unintentional from intentional homicide and provides remedies for both.

I. H'S POLEMICS AGAINST P, JE, AND D

a. AGAINST P

H's controversies with earlier traditions are readily discernible. H does not delete them in favor of its own differing views, but respectfully preserves them. It is apparent, however, that H does omit other laws, such as P's presumed ethical code (see II H). H's choice of one or the other option is not haphazard, but based on its basic redactional principle: H cites P when it wishes to polemicize or supplement. Thus H (rather, the H redactor) incorporates P's laws on sacrifices and impurities (Lev 1–16) because it needs them as the basis for its own remarks on these subjects. However, when H takes no issue with P's rulings, it takes them for granted and does not cite them. So, for example, H's laws on physical blemishes of priests and sacrifices (21:16–20; 22:22–25) are noticeably incomplete, but rely on unmentioned criteria preserved by P's sacrificial term *tāmîm* (1:3, 10; 3:1, 6; 4:3, 23, 28; 5:15, etc.). I find that D operates with the same principle in regard to its forerunner E (Milgrom 1976h). Examples of the polemics follow. They are listed sequentially as they occur in H.

1. P painstakingly distinguishes between Moses' address to priests and to laity (itemized and categorized in the NOTE on 17:2). H obliterates this distinction. On issues of common concern, priests and laity are addressed simultaneously—for example, sacrificial slaughter (17:1–7) and sacrificial defects (22:17–25). Even where the context is purely priestly (priestly disqualifications, 21:1–23), a colophon adds that Israel is also addressed (v. 24; see its NOTE).

H's egalitarian thrust is clear: no differently from priests, all Israel is enjoined to follow a distinctive regimen by which it, too, can attain a holy status (19:2; 20:8; 22:32; see COMMENT to chap. 19). Moreover, the laity herewith become divinely authorized to supervise the sanctuary and the priests (see II L, and NOTE on 21:24).

2. H breaks with past tradition by mandating that all meat must initially be offered as a *šĕlāmîm* because slaughtering a sacrificial animal constitutes murder (see NOTE on 17:4). H has not invented this reason. This is also P's tacit basis for its prescription that blood may not be ingested, but must be drained— that is, returned to God (Gen 9:4; Lev 3:17; 7:26). H, however, adds a rationale: the blood of sacrificial animals must be returned on the altar to ransom the life of the offerer (see NOTE on 17:11).

3. H demands that the blood of game be covered with earth (17:13). It constitutes a polemic against Gen 9:4 (P) and against P in general, whose silence implies that it harbors no such requirement. Various suggestions are offered as to H's rationale (see NOTE on *wĕkissāhû bĕ'āpār* 'and cover it with earth', 17:13).

4. Originally, I assumed that P does not mention any penalty for cohabiting with a menstruant (15:24) because it focuses on only the generated impurity. Perhaps P's silence betrays its lack of concern with or even denial of any penalty (reversing vol. 1.940), except when the impure couple comes in contact with sanctums (vol. 1.258–92) or when they neglect to purify themselves (vol. 1.307–19). H overturns P by subsuming this act under the rubric of moral impurity, which cannot be expunged by purificatory rituals. It is punishable by *kārēt* (20:18) and, if rampant among the people, by exile (see NOTE on 18:9, and INTRODUCTION to 18:24–39).

5. In P's theology, the advertent and the inadvertent sinner can share the same ultimate punishment: their continual and unexpiated pollution of the sanctuary leads to their abandonment by God (vol. 1.258–64). H differs on the nature of the joint penalty and in distinguishing between the two sinners. The advertent sinner suffers an additional penalty. He will be exiled with the inadvertent sinner, but he will also suffer *kārēt*, implying the termination of his earthly line and excision from his clan in the afterlife (vol. 1.457–61).

6. Many categories in 19:11–13 are found in 5:20–26 (P), but whereas P deals exclusively with illegal expropriation of property, H breaks out of P's limited mold and converts P's cases into basic ethical prohibitions (see NOTES on 19:11–13).

7. In H, the concept of holiness undergoes a radical change. Whereas P limits holiness to the sacred precincts (*temenos*), H extends holiness to the land (by virtue of YHWH's proprietorship, 25:23) and its occupants, Israel (as its goal, 19:2). Moreover, endowed holiness is not static, but dynamic: Israel attains it and priests sustain it by their observance of the commandments (see II G, and the (lengthy) discussion in COMMENT on chap. 19).

8. Whereas physical impurity in P pollutes the sanctuary from afar (vol. 1.254–61), H's *metaphoric* impurity apparently pollutes only by direct contact. This can be deduced from the fact that the land can be polluted only by those living in it. To be sure, the worship of Molek pollutes the sanctuary (20:3), ostensibly from afar, but Ezek 23:29 relates that Molek devotees (in the Valley of Hinnom below the Temple) would also worship in the Temple on the same day and thereby pollute by direct contact.

9. H reflects the conversion of the firstfruits offering from P's private, individual rite (2:14; 23:10–17 [minus 14b, 15b, *mimmāhŏrat haššabbāt*]; Num

28:26) into a public, collective rite (see the discussion in INTRODUCTION to 23:15–22, and NOTES on 23:18–19, 21).

10. H changes the order and number of sacrifices (Num 28:27[P]) for the wheat (two loaves) offering (23:18) and the components of the public purification offering (Num 15:22–31; see no. 21, below).

11. Exod 29:42b–46 is not P (Levenson 1986: 37), but H (Knohl 1995: 18, n. 24; 65, n. 17, and passim). It states that God will meet (i.e., reveal himself to) Israel directly (v. 43a), countering P's insistence that God's word will be transmitted solely through the mediation of Moses (but cf. LXX, Sam on *lākem*, v. 42b).

12. Num 15:22–31 (H, Knohl 1995: 18, 170–72) includes all the commandments, performative as well as prohibitive, in the prescription of the *ḥaṭṭāʾt* for inadvertent sinners and *kārēt* for advertent sinners (vol. 1.264–69), in contrast to P, which limits the *ḥaṭṭāʾt* and, presumably, *kārēt* to prohibitive violations (vol. 1.457–61).

Equally significant is H's declaration that the *gēr*, the resident alien, is also subject to *ḥaṭṭāʾt* and *kārēt* for violating the prohibitive commandments. H's ruling derives from its theological premise that the land can be polluted by *any* of its inhabitants (see II I). To be sure, P does not expressly exclude the *gēr*. But from its postulation that violators of prohibitions pollute not the land, but the sanctuary, and that the *ḥaṭṭāʾt* requirement falls solely on Israelites (4:2, 13), it may be inferred that P has no cultic interest in the behavior of the *gēr*.

13. The "sacred" constituent of the priestly clothing is whatever contains a mixture of wool and linen. This *šaʿaṭnēz* is forbidden to a lay person (19:19 [H]) and permitted to only a priest. In biblical times, wool could be dyed, but not linen. Thus according to P, the high priest's clothing in its entirety is *šaʿaṭnēz*, since a totally blue (woolen) tunic covers his underlying linen garments (Exod 28:31) and a blue woolen band encircles his linen turban (v. 37). The garments of the ordinary priest, however, are linen, except for the woolen belt encircling his body (Exod 39:29; see NOTES on 8:7–9, 13).

H breaks with the *šaʿaṭnēz* taboo and ordains that linen tassels should be attached to the outer garment of every lay person, each containing a blue woolen thread (Num 15:37–41 [H]). In this manner, every Israelite will be declaring publicly that he or she can also be holy, not as a birthright, but as a result of following YHWH's commandments (Milgrom 1981, 1990; see COMMENT on chap. 19).

Three ostensible differences between H and P rate particular attention:

1. Num 5:1–4 (H Knohl 1995: 53) banishes the scale-diseased (*ṣārûaʿ*), genital-diseased (*zāb*), and corpse-contaminated (*ṭĕmēʾ nepeš*) from the camp. Lev 15 and Num 19 (P) allow the latter two to remain at home, within the settlement (vol. 1.909–10, 995). The difference is chimerical. Numbers prescribes for the wilderness war-camp in which the divine presence rests (v. 3) and where more stringent purity exists (1 Sam 21:5–7; 2 Sam 11:11). Thus H and P are legislating for two different locales in which variant rules prevail. Note that Num 5:1–4 (H) banishes bearers of sporadic impurity, not normal ones (such as the men-

struant, parturient), but D even excludes one who has a seminal emission from the (war-)camp (Deut 23:10–15).

2. Num 4:15 and 20 (presuming they are H) prohibit the Levites (whose cultic status is equivalent to that of laymen) from touching the sanctums when they are stationary or to view them when they are being dismantled (Milgrom 1990a: 29). However, P ordains that these same sanctums are contagion to objects, but not to persons (vol. 1.443–56). Again, the difference is chimerical. H's penalty for contact with sanctums is death. P and H may be in agreement, however. P might have ruled that sanctums do not sanctify persons for the purpose of abolishing sanctuary asylum to criminals, but it would have affirmed, with H, that persons who contact sanctums are punished with death through divine agency. Contrariwise, though H punished with death by divine agency those who touched sanctums, it might have declared, with P, that sanctums do not sanctify persons.

3. There can be no question that Num 5:6–8 and Lev 5:20–26, the ʾāšām prescription for a false oath, differ from each other. Knohl (1995: 86–87) attributes the Numbers passage to H. I question this ascription (see I E).

The thirteen examples of H's polemics against P cited above should suffice in demonstrating that H responds to P (see I H) and that H cannot be only a continuation and supplement of P (Schwartz, forthcoming: Introduction); at significant points, it breaks with P and forges a new theology and jurisprudence (see part II).

b. AGAINST JE

H shows awareness of the epic narrative (JE). According to the primeval tradition, the sexual immorality of the Egyptians and Canaanites is attributed to their ancestor Ham (Gen 9:22, the father of Egypt, Gen 10:6) and his son Canaan (Gen 9:25; 10:26). Since only the Canaanites polluted the land and were expelled from it (Lev 18:28), the purported sexual debauchery of the Egyptians (18:3; see its NOTE) serves no function in chap. 18, except to allude to Ham's sin with Noah (Gen 9:18–27).

Even the laws preserved in the epic tradition were apparently known to H. As shown by Jackson (1996: 12–21), the thematic parallels and the talion formulation in Lev 24 stem from the Covenant Code (Exod 21–22; details in NOTE on 24:9). Thus H is cognizant of JE, but similar to the relation of H to P shown above, H alludes to JE only when it differs with it.

1. One such example is H's homicide law (24:21). As noted by Joosten (1996: 78), H's choice of the term ʾādām 'person' may be its way of polemicizing against JE's ʾîš in its similar legislation (Exod 21:12, 20–21). That ʾîš is restricted to the meaning of "free citizen" is shown by JE's exclusion of slaves from this law (Exod 21:21, 32). For H, the life and body of all human beings is sacred.

2. As shown by Paran (1983: 15–19, 259–61), the text of Lev 25:2aβ–7 is based on Exod 23:10–11. A total of sixteen stylistic, grammatical, and ideational dif-

ferences can be detected. Among them is a fixed sabbatical year, hitherto rotational (Exod 23; see chap. 25, COMMENT C) on the entire, not just inherited, land (Falk 1964: 90). The landowner and all those dependent on him benefit from the sabbatical aftergrowth (Lev 25:6–7), not the community's indigent (Exod 23:11). For the other differences, see the NOTE on "a sabbath to YHWH" (25:2).

3. In contradiction to JE's slave law, H's Israelite can never be a slave, his wife cannot be indentured, and his children are released with their father (cf. Exod 21:2–11; see NOTES on Lev 25:40–41).

4. To be sure, JE's slave is manumitted after six years, whereas H's "slave" has to wait for the jubilee. However, after the seventh year, JE's slave, having no resources, will soon be reindentured, which is precisely why D lays so much rhetoric on the owner that he shower his manumitted slave with gifts (Deut 15:13–15). H, however, does not appeal to the owner's impulse toward charity, but lays down a law that if the slave can pay off his debt (a possibility because he pays no interest) or on the advent of the jubilee—whichever is earlier—he "returns to his ancestral land" (25:41). The status quo is reestablished; he is on a par with his fellow Israelites.

The examples above lend support to the theory espoused in II R that H was fully cognizant of the laws of JE and P—not just their content, but their text as preserved almost perfectly in the MT.

c. AGAINST D

Eleven such instances are discussed in I J. One further consideration is herewith appended. I cite from Joosten (1996: 87–88):

> From H we learn nothing about the existence—even the future existence—of a king (contrast Deut 17), nor of an institution of elders (as elsewhere in Deuteronomy), nor of a tribal ruler, *nāśî'* (as in Ex 22 and in D) [or of priests in juridical roles (Deut 17:9, 12; 19:17; 21:5; Joosten, n. 273); or of the replacement of the kin group's patriarch with the state-appointed judge (Deut 1:13–15; 21:29); cf. Milgrom (1983d: 134–39)—J.M.]. It is sometimes supposed that in H as in P, the priests, and especially the high priest, hold the power which in other sources is ascribed to the king; these texts are then said to point to the hierocratic Jewish society of the Persian period. This view . . . can in no way be supported by the data from H. . . . The responsibility of the priests is great, and the demands imposed on them are stricter than those on the other Israelites. . . . Yet all these provisions result from the great holiness of the priest, not from his greater political power.

As pointed out in my article (1983d: 134), D fashions a national constitution under state-controlled officials. The earlier powers of the village elders are restricted to a few cases of domestic law—that is, the rebellious son (21:19–20) and the suspected adulteress (22:15–18). Moreover, even in these cases, jurisdiction has been withdrawn from the patriarchal head of the kin group and transferred to the *elders of the city* (21:19–20; 22:15). Contrast this urban-based society with the socioeconomic setting presumed in H. The authority to punish violators of forbidden unions (chaps. 18 and 20) is vested with the patriarch. (The elusive ʿam hāʾāreṣ is of certainty not an urban body [see NOTE on 20:2], and the pericope on urban homes is a later interpolation [see INTRODUCTION to 25:29–34].) Thus the city as a juridical unit is nonexistent in H. H's nearly exclusive focus on the Israelite countryside and its agriculturally based economy precludes that the city, with the possible exception of Jerusalem (and Lachish), was a major socioeconomic factor at the time of the composer of chaps. 18 and 20:9–27 (H).

J. H AND D

A consensus exists that the D Code is preexilic. Moreover, it is indisputable that there are no traces of D's language or concepts in H. However, the reverse proves otherwise: there is ample evidence that D is dependent on and reacting to H. I shall select eleven such instances:

1. There is good reason to believe that the status of the resident alien (gēr) in H served as a model for D's concession of profane slaughter to the Israelite. When D abolished the local altars, it became impossible to require the Israelite to journey to the one legitimate sanctuary each time he desired meat for his table. Hence the Israelite was permitted to slaughter his animals at home, with the proviso that he would abstain from ingesting the blood (Deut 12:15–16, 20–25; 15:23). By declaring that all animals eligible as food were to be treated as the gazelle and the deer, D bestowed on them the status of game (cf. Lev 17:13–14). Is this de novo legislation? Not at all. D's concession to the Israelite corresponds precisely to H's concession to the gēr, who also may slaughter his animals profanely (Lev 17:3–4).

D, however, creates one distinction between the gēr and the Israelite. A něbēlâ, a carcass of an animal that died a natural death, is forbidden to the Israelite, but is turned over to the gēr (Deut 14:21a). H, though, offers no objection to the consumption of a něbēlâ by either Israelite or gēr as long as ritual purification follows (Lev 17:15–16). That H relaxes D's prohibition of něbēlâ to the Israelite would make no sense. Rather, H is simply consistent with the entire matrix of priestly rules concerning the eating of any ineligible meat: it engenders impurity (requiring purification), but does not constitute a violation; that is, it is not a sin (cf. Lev 11, esp. vv. 39–40). However, since D promulgates the ubiquitous holiness of Israel, it is crucial for D to make an explicit distinction between the Israelite and the gēr, which it does by prohibiting the něbēlâ to the former and transferring it to the latter.

2. H's prohibition against mixed seed (Lev 19:19b) needs to be compared with the equivalent prohibition in D (Deut 22:9). As already observed by Ramban, D explains and expands H. Fishbane (1985: 58–63) substantiates Ramban's insight by pointing to D's use of *mĕlē'â* 'the full crop'. This term describes the firstfruits in two different verses, but in different senses: in Exod 22:28 (E), it refers to the firstfruits of grains (LXX; *Mek.*; *b. Tem.* 4a), and in Num 18:27 (P), it refers to the firstfruits of the vat. Therefore D, according to Fishbane, is forced to say that the *mĕlē'â* refers to both: the yield of the sown and of the vineyards. Fishbane's conclusion is correct, but his argument is in need of improvement. The term *mĕlē'â* refers to the firstfruits of the vat not only in Num 18:27, where the identification is explicit (*min hayyeqeb* 'from the vat'), but also in Exod 22:28 (with Haran 1962b), where the parallel term *dema'* refers to grain (Milgrom 1976a: 61, n. 216), leaving *mĕlē'â* to be identified with the vat. In Deut 22:9, however, *mĕlē'â* is used in its literal sense "fullness" to include the produce of both the seed and the vine (Kutscher 1956–57), indicating that the entire crop of this overcultivated field is forfeit to the sanctuary.

3. D's injunction against false measures (Deut 25:13–16) is an expansion and exposition of Lev 19:35–36a:

[13]*lō'-yihyeh bĕkîsĕkâ 'eben wā'eben gĕdôlâ ûqĕtannâ* [14]*lō'-yihyeh lĕkā bĕbêtêkâ' epâ wĕ'epâ gĕdôlâ ûqĕtannâ* [15]**'eben šĕlēmâ wāṣedeq yihyeh-lāk** 'epâ sĕlemâ **wāṣedeq** yihyeh-lāk lĕma'an ya'ărîkû yāmêkā 'al ha'ădāmâ 'ăšer-YHWH 'ĕlōhêka nōten lāk* [16]*kî tô'ăbat YHWH kol-'ōšeh 'ēlleh kōl 'ōšeh 'āwel.*

The core of the H passage is contained in Deut 25:15a (boldface). The rest is an expansion, indicated by the addition of *šĕlēmâ* 'completely' and the transferral of *'ōšeh 'āwel* 'who does injustice' to the end of the passage.

4. Whereas H, in agreement with JE (Exod 19:6; 22:30), regards holiness as only an ideal toward which Israel should aspire (e.g., Lev 19:2; 20:7), D establishes Israel's holiness as inherent in its biological nature (e.g., Deut 7:6; 14:2). Thus, from the diachronic viewpoint, D has extended H's (and P's) axiom that only priests are genetically holy (e.g., Exod 29:1, 21, 33; Lev 8:30; 21:6–8) to embrace all of Israel.

5. I have attempted to demonstrate that the diet laws of D (Deut 14:1–21) are modeled on those of Lev 11 (vol. 1.698–704), which were edited by H, mainly by the addition of vv. 39–40 and 43–45.

6. H's idiom *dāmâyw bô* 'his bloodguilt is upon him (the miscreant)' (Lev 20:9, etc.) is an assurance to the executioner, appointed by the court of elders, that he will not be held responsible (by God or man) for slaying the convicted person. It is significant that this idiom is not found in D. Even though family and sexual crimes continue to be adjudicated by elders of the city (cf. Deut 19:12; 21:20; 22:17–18)—but not by the elders of his clan, H's basic socioeconomic unit—they are not given a free hand but are closely supervised by state-appointed officers (Deut 21:2) and judges (Deut 25:1–3) in every community ("in all your gates," Deut 16:18). No longer is there fear of divine or human

(i.e., blood revenge) retribution for taking the life of a person. The responsibility for the execution of a criminal by the clan elders henceforth devolves upon the state and its officials. This, I submit, is telling evidence that family crimes in D reflect a later period than those preserved in H.

7. There is no consensus concerning the different kinds of interest represented by the terms *nešek* and *m/tarbît* (Lev 25:36–37). Ramban holds that *nešek* is yearly interest and *tarbît*, interest paid at the end—that is, accrued interest. Eliezer of Beaugency (on Ezek 18:18) derives *nešek* from *nāšak* 'bite off', hence, advance interest. The tannaitic sages register the view that *nešek* is interest paid at the end, and *tarbît* is food that has increased in price (based on Lev 25:37b). Deut 23:20 relates *nešek* to both money and foodstuffs. To deepen the confusion, the amoraitic sages disagree with the tannaim and (in apparent agreement with Deut 23:20) conclude that both terms mean "interest," without any distinction between them (*b. B. Meṣ.* 60b).

Loewenstamm (1969: 11–12) brings order to this semantic chaos by postulating a chronological development: Originally, the terms were distinguished (as in Lev 25:37), *nešek* for money, *m/tarbît* for victuals. Subsequently, as a money economy became predominant, *nešek* became the exclusive term for "interest," and was extended to cover victuals as well (as in Deut 23:20). If Loewenstamm is correct, then D reflects a later period than H. This also is the implication of Seeligmann's (1978: 183–206, 209–20) study of biblical interest and of Fishbane's (1985: 175–76) stylistic analysis of the two laws: namely, that Deut 23:20–21 expands Lev 25:36–37 to include as interest any commodity and to exclude the foreigner as a beneficiary.

8. Scripture records two different sabbaticals, aptly titled by the rabbis (*b. Giṭ.* 36a, *b. Moʿed Qa.* 2b) as *šĕmiṭṭat qarqāʿôt* 'release of lands' (Exod 23:10–11; Lev 25:2–7) and *šĕmiṭṭat kĕsāpîm* 'release of monetary claims' (Deut 15:1–13). Are they complementary (the rabbinic view) or contradictory? I opt for the former for two reasons. First, "no debtor could be expected to repay his loans while prohibited from tilling and reaping his land" (Neufeld 1958: 68). Second, D prescribes a debt release *kî qārā šĕmiṭṭâ laYHWH* 'because YHWH's release has been proclaimed' (Deut 15:2). This is not deuteronomic language; not a single one of its laws, institutions, or festivals is described by such terminology. Whence its origin? A hint by Ibn Ezra supplies the answer. The phrase is modeled on *šabbāt laYHWH* (Lev 25:2b, 4a, H's designation for the land-sabbatical; see also Lev 23:3; Exod 16:25; 20:10 [= Deut 5:14]; 31:15). Moreover, the use of *qārā* 'proclaim' is unique in D. Again, it is H's terminology, employed in regard to the sabbath (Lev 23:3) and the festivals (Lev 23:4–37; cf. Exod 12:16; Num 28–29).

9. The slave laws occur in three sources: Exod 21:1–11 (E); Lev 25:39–43 (H); and Deut 15:12–18 (D). The term *ʿimmāk/mēʿimmāk* occurs five times in D, four times in H, but is totally absent in E. Whence did D draw this term? One can argue that since it appears nineteen times in the rest of Deuteronomy, it is normal D usage. However, in its five occurrences in D's slave law, it means "under your authority," the same as in H, whereas in the rest of Deuteronomy

it never bears this specialized meaning, only its usual connotation: "with." What alternative remains except to agree that D must have drawn it from the slave law of H?

10. A major difference between the slave laws of E and D is that the word 'ebed 'slave' does not appear in D, except in the two verses on the lifelong slave (Deut 15:16–17). In H it does not appear at all. Its absence makes sense, since for H the indentured Israelite is no longer a slave, but a śākir tôšāb 'a resident hireling' (Lev 25:40; cf. v. 53). D, however, implores the master to shower his manumitted slave with gifts, and reminds him that he has benefited from the slave twice as much as from a śākir. Thus, for D, he is not a śākir, as in H, but an 'ebed. I submit that the best explanation of this difference is that D has been influenced by H to ameliorate its attitude toward the slave; but without H's theological postulate that all Israelites are only YHWH's slaves (Lev 25:42, 45), D has no basis for abolishing Israelite slavery.

11. The comminations of Lev 26 and Deut 28 invite comparison:

a. The short, tight phrases of Lev 26 are repeated and lengthened in Deut 28 — for example, disease (Lev 26:16; Deut 28:23, 27–28, 59–61), enemy (Lev 26:17; Deut 28:25–26, 30–33, 48–52), drought (Lev 26:19–20; Deut 28:23–24, 38–40, 42).

b. The schema of increasing torment in Lev 26 has no analogue in Deut 28. The former is grouped in five sets with the same refrain (vv. 16–17, 18–20, 21–22, 23–26, 27, 29), a typology that is found in eighth-century Amos 4:6–11 and Isa 9:7–10:4.

c. The comminations of Lev 26 are provincial in character, whereas those of Deut 28, except for a few verses (38–42), derive from the punitive imagery of contemporary Assyrian vassal treaties. In this respect, Lev 26 resembles the antecedent Sefire treaty (cf. Weinfeld 1972d: 123–26). A particularly striking contrast is offered by Lev 26:25, which implies that Israelites normally reside in rural areas and gather in cities only for protection against invading armies, whereas the focus of Deut 28:3, 16 is equally divided between the city and the countryside (cf. Joosten 1996: 159–60).

d. I wish to apply an additional argument, which for me is decisive. Deut 28 has no consolatory epilogue comparable to Lev 26:40–45. For that, one must turn to Deut 30:1–10, a passage that may originally have served as the epilogue to Deut 28:1–68. Indeed, Deut 30:1–10 and its verbal and contextual counterpart (Deut 4:25–31) may be seen as an inclusio for the original book of D (cf. Weinfeld 1991: 216). This fact suffices for most scholars to decide that Lev 26 (at least its epilogue) is a later text because it purportedly reflects the despair of the Babylonian exiles.

Unfortunately, inadequate attention has been paid to the difference between the two consolatory additions. Deut 30:1–10 stresses that God will restore Israel only on condition that Israel repents (wěšabtā, v. 2; tāšûb, v. 10). The root šwb is an unambiguous reference to prophetic repentance, which calls for a radical change in behavior (e.g., Isa 1:16–17). This root is missing in Lev 26, which calls on Israel only to confess (wěhitwaddâ, v. 40), feel remorse (yikkāna' lěbābām,

v. 41), accept the divine punishment (*yirṣû ʾet-ʿăwōnām*, vv. 41, 43), but nothing else. This is only embryonic repentance; it is a far cry from the subsequent demands of Israel's prophets. I cannot conceive that any exilic text exhorting "Israel to repent would have ignored the prophetic insistence that repentance involves action, not just emotion, and, instead, would substitute an older, inchoate—and for the prophets inadequate—form of repentance. Thus there exists a qualitative and, hence, chronological gap between Lev 26 and Deut 28.

My net deduction from this comparison is that Lev 26 is an older text. I cannot prove, nor do I claim, that Lev 26 was the *Vorlage* of Deut 28. But the signs in points a–c—namely, the lengthy and repetitive phrases of Deut 28; the typology of the form and locale of Lev 26, resembling the earlier models in Amos, Isaiah, and Sefire; and, especially, the earlier, incipient repentance of Lev 26—argue strongly for the conclusion that Lev 26 reflects an older form than Deut 28 (published in expanded form in Milgrom 1999).

K. H IS PREEXILIC (EXCEPT H_R)

With the exception of a few verses (23:2aβ–3, 39b, 42–43; 26:33b–35, 43–44, the product of H$_R$ [see below]), all of H is preexilic. My arguments (annotated in Milgrom 1999) follow.

1. There is no ban on intermarriage in H (and P)—neither opposition nor prohibition. This absence would be inconceivable in postexilic times, when a national purge of intermarriages was initiated (cf. Ezra 9–10). This purge is perfectly understandable demographically. The returning exiles were a small enclave surrounded and interpenetrated by non-Israelites. However, when Judah had full control of its land, and the Canaanites were reduced to a small subservient minority, intermarriages—the relatively few that would occur—would have been one-directional: the resident alien would have become a worshiper of YHWH and a (possibly zealous) follower of his laws (e.g., Uriah, 2 Sam 11:11). Intermarriage could not have been a threat and, hence, would not have been banned. H, therefore, must be set in the preexilic period (see chap. 18, COMMENT A).

2. The fact that D and all the writing prophets use only one verb *šwb* to denote "repent," whereas H resorts to only *niknaʿ* 'be humbled' and *hitwaddâ* 'confess' (and P to *ʾāšām* 'feel guilt', a meaning that disappears from use from the exile onward), indicates that H (as well as P) stems from a time before *šwb* became the exclusive term for repentance (Milgrom 1976a: 119–27). In any event, it is hardly conceivable that after the refugees from North Israel brought with them the writings of Amos and Hosea, and the Judahite prophets Isaiah and Micah promulgated their kerygma of repentance, their term *šwb* would not have dominated, perhaps exclusively, the priestly doctrine of repentance.

3. H utilizes the term *ʿam hāʾāreṣ* 'people of the land' (Lev 20:2), also found in P (Lev 4:27). It is possible that in H (but not in P) the term bears a specific,

technical meaning that refers to a political group in the kingdom of Judah composed of loyal supporters of the Davidic dynasty (e.g., 2 Kgs 11:4, 18, 19, 20; 21:24; 23:30). If so, it would betray the time of the writer (H), who abandoned (accidentally?) his fiction of the wilderness ʿēdâ and substituted the corresponding body operative in his own day. In any case, the entirely different and contradictory connotation of ʿam hāʾāreṣ 'foreign people' in the postexilic books (e.g., Neh 9:30; 10:31) lends certainty to the preexilic provenience of H (see NOTE on 20:2).

4. All commentators have noted the extraordinary correspondence between the language of Ezekiel and that of H in general and Lev 26 in particular. Who borrowed from whom? Or did Ezekiel and H borrow from a third source? The issue, I submit, can be settled only by examining those passages where there is irrefutable evidence that one source has indisputably *altered* the other. My investigation demonstrates nine such instances, all of which point in one direction, from Lev 26 to Ezekiel: Ezek 4:16; 5:10, 17; 11:12; 14:15, 17; 24:23; 34:24–28; and 36:9–11 have borrowed from Lev 26:3–39. It is Ezekiel, then, who expands, omits, and reformulates (see chap. 26, COMMENT C).

Moreover, there are thirteen additional cases in the rest of H that, again, point to Ezekiel as the borrower: Lev 10:10–11a (H) > Ezek 44:23; Lev 17:10; 20:3 > Ezek 14:8; Lev 17:13b > Ezek 14:7b; Lev 18:5 > Ezek 20:11 (cf. vv. 13, 21); Lev 18:7a > Ezek 22:10a; Lev 18:19–20 > Ezek 18:6b; Lev 19:16a > Ezek 22:9a; Lev 19:30a (26:2a) > Ezek 23:38b; Lev 19:34aα > Ezek 47:22; Lev 20:9 > Ezek 22:7aa; Lev 21:1bβ > Ezek 44:25a; Lev 22:8a > Ezek 44:31; Lev 25:43a (46bβ, 53b) > Ezek 34:4b (in addition, cf. Hurvitz 1982). There are many other such cases, but I have set these aside because the direction of influence is not as compelling. In any event, there is not a single case which shows that H borrowed from Ezekiel.

Recently, Rooker's (1990) work on Ezekiel has come to my attention. Following Hurvitz (1982 and others), he provides additional evidence that Ezekiel's lexemes and phrases form a transitional stage between BH, exemplified in the priestly texts (and other early books), and LBH, the language of the postexilic books.

In sum, Ezekiel had all of H (except for its few exilic additions) before him, the language and ideas of which he refashioned in novel ways. Thus nearly all of H is preexilic, and all the more so P, which was supplemented and redacted by H.

5. As accurately observed by Blenkinsopp (1995: 15–16), the Josianic reform and the other reforms in the history of Judah, as narrated by the Deuteronomist, "deal exclusively with the removal of cultic abuses, never with the kind of social abuses excoriated by the eighth-century prophets." However, H endorses the prophetic program (see below). There are, to my count, fifty-five individual ethical commandments in H, most of which are directed against social abuses: thirteen in Lev 18:6–17; twenty in 19:9–18, 32–35; one in 20:9; one in 23:22; three in 24:17–22; sixteen in 25:6, 10, 17, 25–54; and one in 26:15, 25, 45. In contrast, H virtually ignores Judah's cultic abuses, a hardly likely occurrence were H a product of the seventh century or later.

6. H posits multiple sanctuaries (see chap. 17, COMMENT D). No one will deny that in the postexilic age, the deuteronomic doctrine of the absolute central-ization of worship ruled supreme. Thus any source that posits multiple sanctu-aries must ipso facto be preexilic.

7. The superscript and subscript to Lev 23 stem partially from the Babylon-ian Exile. There is no other way to account for the glaring editorial seams, the proclamation that the sabbath is a festival (*môʿēd*) and the absence of a sacrifi-cial ritual for the sabbath (see NOTES on 23:2aβ–3). Similarly, the mandatory seven-day residence in a *sukkâ* (for the Israelite, but not the *gēr*) and the Exo-dus rationale for the Festival of Booths are explicable only in the context of the Babylonian Exile (see NOTES on vv. 42–43). The only other H passage (in Leviti-cus) with an exilic provenience is 26:33b–35, 43–44 (see their NOTES), where the failure to observe the land-sabbatical provides a rationale for the prolonga-tion of the exile. All other H passages are preexilic.

8. As argued in Lev 26, COMMENT E, the exilic allusions in 26:40–42, 45 are a probable reference to the exile of North Israel at the end of the eighth cen-tury, a conclusion that follows from the fact that Ezekiel is thoroughly suffused with the language of chap. 26 (see chap. 26, COMMENTS C–D). Furthermore, chap. 26 reflects the Hezekian atmosphere (see NOTES on "[pagan] cult prac-tices," v. 30, and "your [multiple] sanctuaries" and "[enemy] who resides in it," v. 31). Above all, the absence of prophetic repentance, represented by the verb *šub*, betrays its preexilic provenience (see chap. 26, COMMENT B).

9. Since the high priest was not anointed during the Second Temple period, his description as the "one on whose head the anointing oil has been poured" (21:10; see its NOTE) is an unambiguous reference to the preexilic period.

10. As shown by Joosten (1996: 151), the expression "the land of Canaan" as a territorial designation is confined to the preexilic parts of the Pentateuch, Joshua, and Judges; hence it is a preexilic term.

11. Finally, I again revert to the term *ʿăbōdâ*. I have concluded that in all its occurrences in the priestly texts in the Pentateuch, it denotes "physical labor," but in postexilic texts dealing with the functioning of the Temple, it denotes "cultic service" (Milgrom 1970a: 82–87; cf. vol. 1.7–8). These two meanings, however, contradict each other and, hence, could not coexist. Levites, on pain of death, are forbidden to officiate in the cult (Num 18:3b), and thus *ʿăbōdâ* is confined to the physical labor of dismantling, transporting, and reassembling the Tabernacle. But in postexilic texts, only the priests perform Temple *ʿăbōdâ*, because this term now means "cultic service," for which the priests alone are eligible; its usurpation by Levites is punishable with death. The singular ad-vantage of this term is that it undermines the counterclaim that P and H are in-dulging in anachronisms (advanced by Wellhausen 1963: 9; Cross 1973: 322–23; Joosten 1996: 15).

Smith's (1997: 167) assertion that "J. Milgrom admits: 'the possibility must be granted that the priestly redaction may have succeeded in concealing its true (later) period'" (1992: 5.549) has been pulled out of context. My argument there was that *even if we would concede* that P could have concealed its period, "another control (P's use of *mišmeret* and *'ăbōdâ*—J.M.) can vitiate the charge of anachronisms" (Milgrom 1992: 5. 549).

L. THE STRUCTURE OF LEVITICUS

The integrity and unity of the book of Leviticus can be demonstrated. It is visibly distinct from Numbers. Whereas Leviticus is static, Numbers is dynamic. Throughout Leviticus, Israel is encamped at Mount Sinai; in Numbers, Israel is preparing for, undertaking, and completing its journey through the wilderness. Leviticus's boundary with Exodus, however, is not sharp. To be sure, there is a break in content: Exodus closes with the construction and erection of the Tabernacle (Exod 35–40), and Leviticus begins with the laws of sacrifices (Lev 1–7). But the transition point is blurred: Lev 1:1 is an incomplete verse; it is semantically and grammatically bound with Exod 40:34–35 (cf. vol. 1.139). Nonetheless, disjoining Leviticus from Exodus can be substantiated. Exodus 40:36–38, briefly describing the role of the divine fire-cloud in leading Israel through the wilderness, has been inserted as a prolepsis of the detailed account in Num 9:15–23. Recently, Frankel (1998) has demonstrated that these closing, but intrusive verses are a late priestly stratum, which I identify as H_R, the exilic redactor. That is, Exod 40:36–38 is an advance notice of the book of Numbers, and it represents the view of the redactor who has inserted it in the interstice between Exodus and Leviticus.

However, is Leviticus itself a unity? Is there a comprehensive design for the entire book? The most commendable attempt to account for the organization of Leviticus has, in my opinion, been proposed by Mary Douglas. Using as a model the ring structure attested in contemporary Greek poetry (e.g., eighth-century B.C.E. Hesiod), she arranges the chapters of Leviticus in the form of a ring (1995: 247–55). I prefer her diagram (Figure 1) in an earlier work (1993a: 11; 1995: 253) for its greater precision, which I slightly amended.

The virtues of the ring construction (overlooking its terminological imprecision) are, moving upward, as follows:

1. The central turning point (chap. 19) is flanked by two chapters of equivalent content (18 and 20) in chiastic relation.
2. The beginning of the central turning point (19:1–4) is matched in content (the Decalogue) by the beginning of the closing turning point (26:1–2) and offers a reason why the latter was inserted as the prefix to a chapter on blessings and curses (26:3–46). The two chapters share a theme: the holy righteousness of Israel (19) and God (26).
3. Chapter 17 is not a summary, but a bridge between the two parts of Leviticus: chaps 1–16 and 18–27 (see INTRODUCTION to chap. 17).
4. Chapters 11–16 and 21–23 form a giant introversion in the center of the ring (ABB'A'). Carcasses are innately "blemished" (chap. 11, *šeqeṣ* or *ṭāmē'*;

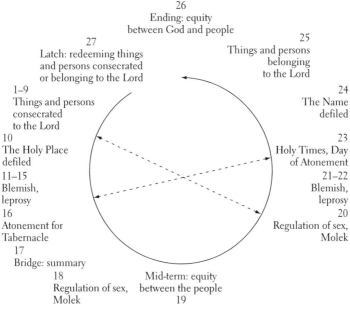

26
Ending: equity
between God and people

27
Latch: redeeming things
and persons consecrated
or belonging to the Lord

25
Things and persons
belonging
to the Lord

1–9
Things and persons
consecrated
to the Lord

24
The Name
defiled

10
The Holy Place
defiled

23
Holy Times, Day
of Atonement

11–15
Blemish,
leprosy

21–22
Blemish,
leprosy

16
Atonement for
Tabernacle

20
Regulation of sex,
Molek

17
Bridge: summary

18
Regulation of sex,
Molek

Mid-term: equity
between the people
19

FIGURE 1. Leviticus in a Ring

Milgrom 1992a), as are certain sacrificial animals (22:17–25) and certain priests (21:16–23) (AA′). Carcasses of common animals also create "blemishes" (lit. *ṭum'â* 'impurity') to persons (11:24–38), especially to priests (22:3a–9). Impure issues and scale disease in laity (12–15) and priests (22:3–9) are identical in diagnosis and treatment; these form the center of the chiasm. The holiest day (16) corresponds chiastically with the holy (festival) days (BB′).

5. The two narratives in Leviticus (10:1–4; 24:10–23) face each other in the ring; they share a theme: defilement of the Tabernacle (10) and of God's name (24). Chap. 24 was placed in its present spot for the sake of this ring structure, even though its subject matter is alien to its context. A more detailed analysis is presented below (and in I E).

6. Holy things, sacrifices (1–9), are complemented by holy land and its sabbatical and jubilee regulations (25).

7. The latch (27) was appended after the logical ending (blessings and curses, 26) in order to lock with the opening topic (1–9). Both deal with sanctifications of sacrifices (1–9) and of persons, animals, houses, and land (27).

In my opinion, there exists a striking parallel in the structure of the book of Isaiah. Isaiah, too, can be divided into two major parts: Isa 1–39 and 40–66. They are distinguished chronologically (and by theme and vocabulary as well), the second indisputably later than the first. Moreover, Liebreich (1955–56; 1956–57), in a seminal study written forty-five years ago, demonstrated that chaps.

65–66 reflect chap. 1, and chap. 40 is connected with chap. 39. Liebreich's verbal parallels have been expanded verbally, thematically, and theologically by Lack (1973), Sweeny (1988: 21–24), Tomasino (1993), and others (but note Carr's [1993: 61–81] reservations).

In effect, Liebreich and his followers have argued that the book of Isaiah bears a ring structure. Its two parts resemble the book of Leviticus in being linked by their outer and inner ends: Isa 1 and 65–66 are akin to Lev 1 and 27 (no. 7, above), and Isa 39 and 40 are like Lev 16 and 17 (no. 3, above). Thus a redactor has composed (or worded) chaps. 40 and 65–66 as verbal clasps that link the two parts of Isaiah in the shape of a ring. One can, therefore, no longer say that the ring structure is a hypothetical (even imaginary) peculiarity of Leviticus, but concede that it must be recognized as a substantive macrostructural, redactional technique in the Bible.

Returning to the Leviticus ring, I shall not dwell on the themes of each of its chapters. They are fully expounded in the Notes. Instead, I shall focus briefly on the purpose behind H_R's choice of chaps. 1–16 from the P material at his disposal, and on the overall theme that unites the chapters that compose H.

It is clear that P (chaps. 1–16) comprises two major themes: sacrifices (1–10) and impurities (11–16). These were selected by H_R, as I surmise (in APPENDIX C), out of a larger body of P regulations, because they constitute an indispensable base for H's own laws concerning sacrifices (e.g., 17; 19:5–8, 20–22; 23) and impurities (e.g., 17:15–16; 18:19; 22:3–8). This body of P is lastly annotated by H_R (3:16b–17; 6:12–18aα; 7:22–29a; 8:35; 9:17b; 10:10–11; 11:43–45; etc.; see I E). H_R adds his own material (17–27 [H]), which comprises three strata. Nearly all of it is (end of) eighth-century H, but earlier strata (pre-H_1 and pre-H_2) are detectable (e.g., 18:6–23; 20:9–21; 23:10–17*; 24:17–21). The common denominator of this material (chaps. 17–27 [H]) is the theme of holiness. Its source and rationale is chap. 19. Logically, this chapter would have introduced this holiness material, were it not for the redactor's desire to underscore its centrality for the entire book of Leviticus by flanking it with two similar collections of sexual prohibitions (chaps. 18 and 20) in chiastic relation. This is followed by holiness precautions for priests and Israelites (chaps. 21–22), the holiness of time (chap. 23), YHWH's name (chap. 24; for its placement, see below), land (chap. 25), the covenant (chap. 26), and consecrations (chap. 27; for greater detail, see II G). The root qdš 'holy' appears throughout, except, notably, in the beginning (chaps. 17–18). qdš appears in sixteen of the twenty DS (Divine Speeches), and, as explained (I E), the anomalous chap. 17 was needed by H_R because of its associations with and allusions to P's closing chap. 16 and, thus, could form a needed bridge between P and H. The theme of holiness thus accounts for the choice of these H chapters. For their integration with P (chaps. 1–16), I rely on Douglas's ring structure (1995: 247–55).

In truth, the root qdš does not appear in the narrative on blasphemy (24:10–23), but in the preceding material (vv. 1–9). What, then, accounts for the choice of the blasphemy narrative? Douglas (1995) is on the right track in suggesting a structural reason, namely, a parallel to the Tabernacle defilement narrative (10:1–4) in the ring structure. But other subjects actually specify the desecration (*ḥll*) of YHWH's *Name* (18:21; 19:12; 20:3; 21:6; 22:2, 32). Why did the redactor H$_R$ select the story of blasphemy where neither the root *qdš* nor its antonym *ḥll* appears? I propose that he needed it not only as a structural counterpart to the only other narrative in Leviticus (10:1–4), but also for legal reasons: to complete the subject of the desecration of YHWH and his sanctums. The desecration of YHWH's sanctums (5:14–16, 17–19) and YHWH's name (5:20–26) are inadvertent sins expiable by sacrifice; the desecration of YHWH's sanctuary (10:1–4) is an advertent sin, punishable by death. A lacuna prevails: the advertent sin of desecrating YHWH's name. This is supplied by the narrative on the blasphemer (24:10–23; see the discussion in NOTE on 24:24). Its placement in an unrelated context, between chaps. 23 and 25, however, may be owing to the structural needs of the ring. A similar structural reason may prevail for the absence of *qdš* in the fourth and last DS: the list of twelve sacrifical imperfections (22:17–25). H needed it to balance the twelve priestly imperfections (21:16–23).

Finally, just as the logical opening of H, chap. 19, was preempted by two other chapters, 17 and 18, for structural reasons, so the logical terminus of Leviticus, the blessings and curses (26), was preempted by an appendix (27), also for H's structural needs (for the discussion, see I E).

In sum, the unity and integrity of Leviticus become evident on realizing its structural and thematic design.

Just as my manuscript was about to be sent to press, Warning's (1999) book came to my attention. I have found several pleasing observations, which I have dutifully noted. His basic conclusion is that "Leviticus reveals a text where a distinction between P and H is seemingly irrelevant and even non-existent." This makes no sense in view of H's distinctive terminology (I B), terminological imprecision (I C), different style (I D), redactorial work on P (I H), and, especially, outright polemics with P (I I). Warning states that he plans a follow-up volume on his literary observations. Until it appears, I shall suspend final judgment.

II. THEOLOGY

◆

A. THE NATURE OF REVELATION AND MOSAIC ORIGINS

When the scroll of the Torah is raised during the synagogue service, the congregation intones *wĕzō't hattôrâ 'ăšer-śām mōšeh lipnê bĕnê yiśrā'el 'al-pî YHWH bĕyad-mōšeh* 'This is the Torah that Moses set before the Israelites by the command of YHWH through Moses' (Deut 4:44 + Num 4:37). Do they really believe what they say? Indeed, is it possible to affirm the Mosaic origin of the entire Torah not as blind faith but with conviction—rationally, critically? I resort to a rabbinic story:

> Moses requested of God to visit R. Akiba's academy. Permission was granted. He sat down in the back and listened to R. Akiba exposit a law purportedly based on the Torah. Moses didn't understand a word; *tāšaš kôḥô* 'his energy was drained'. At the end of R. Akiba's discourse, the students challenged him: *minnayin lāk* 'What is your source?' R. Akiba replied, *hălākâ lĕmōšeh missînay* '(It is) an oral law from Moses at Sinai'. The story concludes that Moses was reinvigorated, *nityaššēbâ da'atô*, lit. 'his mind was put to rest' (*b. Menaḥ.* 29b).

The obvious deduction from this story is that between the time of Moses and Akiba, the laws of the Torah had undergone vast changes, to the extent that Moses was incapable of even following the exposition. But the story conveys a deeper meaning. After all, why was Moses pacified when Akiba announced that his law is traceable to Moses? It could not be true. Moses never said it! The answer, however, lies on a different plane. After Akiba announced that it was an oral law from Moses at Sinai, Moses recognized that it was based on Mosaic foundations. Akiba was not creating a new Torah, but was applying the Torah's law to problems generated by the law. Moses had been given general principles and rules; successive generations derived their implications. Thus Moses did not author Akiba's legal decision, but he would have intended it. That is, had Moses lived in R. Akiba's time he would have concurred with Akiba's conclusion.

This interpretation is explicitly confirmed in Scripture. I cite two examples. The first is 'They (the priests and Levites) took their accustomed stations *kĕtôrat mōšeh 'îš-'ĕlōhîm* according to the law of Moses, the man of God' (2 Chr 30:16). Obviously, no such stations are attributed to priests and Levites in the Torah. However, the priests and Levites did have stations in the Tabernacle, albeit different ones (Num 3:5–10; 18:6–7; on *mišmeret* 'guard duty', see Milgrom 1970: 8–10). This suffices for the Chronicler to declare that the clerical stations in his own time are of Mosaic authorship.

A more impressive example is Nehemiah's *'ămānâ* 'covenant/agreement' sub-scribed by Israel's leaders and accepted on oath by the people (Neh 10:1–40ff). The *'ămānâ* comprises eighteen laws (Kaufmann 1977: 381–89) *bĕyad mōšeh 'ebed 'ĕlōhîm* 'given through Moses the servant of God' (Neh 10:30; cf. vv. 35–37), yet none of them can be found in the Torah precisely as prescribed in Nehemiah's *'ămānâ*. Nonetheless, each law can be derived from a pentateuchal precedent (details in Kaufmann 1977 and Willamson 1985: 333–39). Again, since Nehemiah's eighteen laws are built on Moaic foundation, Nehemiah feels authorized to attribute them to Moses (cf. Japhet 1993: 950).

Nevertheless, it must be conceded that Nehemiah and the Chronicler prob-ably had the complete written Torah before them. The question, however, still remains. What were the Mosaic principles that lay behind the traditions *within* the Torah? It could well be that each of them derives from the Decalogue. This specifically is the case for the priestly tradition (see Lev 19:3–4, 30–32; 26:1–2; and, with reservations, Kaufmann 1979). The kernel of the Decalogue is terse. Without penalties, it is more like directions or *principles* rather than laws. In-deed, Patrick (1985) has mounted an impressive argument that all pentateuchal codes are compilations of instructions in the form of principles, concepts and values (but see some reservations in the NOTE on "for you," 25:6). No wonder, then, that these traditions stemming from different authors and times might dif-fer from each other in form and content.

In effect, the Torah's *wayyĕdabbēr YHWH 'el-mōšeh lē'mōr* 'YHWH spoke to Moses, saying' is equivalent to rabbinic *hălākâ lĕmōšeh missînay* '(their law is) an oral law from Moses at Sinai'. The anonymous authors of the Torah's legis-lation were certain that the laws they proposed were not of their invention, but were derivable from Mosaic principles (i.e., traceable to Moses himself). They might have agreed, for example, that the dire economic conditions of eighth-century Judah would have been remedied by the laws of jubilee and redemp-tion (chap. 25; see II K) *stemming from Moses* (25:1).

I owe this insight to Halivni (1989; 1993), who clarified my inchoate insight by his systematized perspective on divine revelation in rabbinic literature. He refers to the story of Moses and Akiba as the minimalist position, averring that only general principles were revealed at Sinai, in contrast to the maximalist po-sition, which dogmatically asserts that the entire oral, as well as written, Torah, including "whatever novelum an earnest scholar (*talmîd wattîq*) will someday teach[,] has already been declared to Moses at Sinai" (*p. Pe'ah* 17a). Halivni also cites an ancillary minimalist position, illustrated by the following rabbinic midrash: "R. Yannai said: The words of the Torah were not given as clear-cut decisions. . . . When Moses asked, 'Master of the Universe, in what way shall we know the true sense of the law?' God replied, 'The majority is to be followed' (play on Exod 23:2bβ)—when a majority declares it is impure, it is impure; when a majority says it is pure, it is pure" (*Midrash Tehillim* 12:4; cf. fuller ver-sion *b. Ḥag.* 3b; Greenberg 1996b). As Halivni (1989: 30) perceptively concludes: "Contradictions are thus built into revelation. Revelation was formulated within the framework of contradiction in the form of argumentation pro and con. No legitimate argument or solution can be in conflict with the divine opinion, for all such arguments and solutions constitute part of God's opinion."

These two minimalist stories about Moses portray the human role throughout the generations in the revelatory process. Revelation was not a onetime Sinaitic event. It behooves man—indeed, compels him—to be an active partner of God in determining, as well as implementing, the divine will.

I submit that what Halivni has discovered in rabbinic tradition applies *mutatis mutandis* to the written Torah. If it can be maintained that insights of, or disagreements among, the rabbis are traceable to Sinai, all the more so is it true for innovations or discrepancies ensconced within the biblical text. Legal formulations may be presuming earlier, reputedly Sinaitic precedents (Moses in R. Akiba's academy), and conflicting laws may be justifiable claimants to Sinaitic origin (Moses in R. Yannai's midrash).

Both positions are frequently attested in H. For example,

1. The formulation of H's sabbatical law, Lev 25:2–7, is clearly constructed on its prototype, Exod 23:10–11 (JE), but differs with it regarding the nature of the sabbatical and its beneficiaries (see its NOTE).
2. H repeats almost verbatim JE's homicide law (Lev 24:21; Exod 21:12), but introduces one change: *'ādām* instead of *'îš*. That the latter means "free citizen" is shown by JE's exclusion of slaves from this law (Exod 21:20–21). For H, however, all human life is sacred (see II G, L). (It should not go unnoticed that in JE's code [Exod 20:22–23:33], the *mišpāṭîm* 'rules' [Exod 21:1–23:19] are revealed to Moses together with the *děbārîm* 'commands'— that is, the Decalogue [Exod 20:2–17], atop Mount Sinai [Exod 24:3].)
3. H fully accepts the teaching of its own tradition (P) that holiness inheres in the sanctuary *temenos*, but it differs radically from P by extending holiness to the entire land and, potentially, to its occupants, every Israelite (see NOTES to 19:2 and 25:23; see also II G).
4. H is in full accord with P that a community that has inadvertently violated a prohibitive commandment must bring a *ḥaṭṭā't* 'purification offering' (Lev 4:13–21), but it differs from it by adding all the commandments— performative and prohibitive—to its sway as well as changing the nature of the public offering (Num 15:24–26; for further examples, see I I).

As is well known, JE's claim concerning the divine sanction of multiple altars (Exod 20:24) is flatly contradicted by D, which repeatedly avers that YHWH authorized only a single altar (e.g., Deut 12:4–7, 11–14, 18, 26–27). Most critics would therefore concur with Levinson (1997: 48) that D is a pseudepigraph whose authors "attempted to camouflage the innovations by feigning a cunning piety with respect to the very authoritative texts that they had subverted." Note, however, that in this case D explicitly concedes that Exod 20:24 was also divinely revealed to Moses. D also argues that JE's law was time-bound, possessing validity only until Israel attained "rest and inheritance" (Deut 12:9; cf. Fishbane 1985: 252). In other words, had Moses lived in the time of D he probably would have pronounced D's interpretation of the altar law as correct.

We should therefore acknowledge that each school that contributed to the composition of the Torah had a valid claim that its laws were traceable to Mosaic origins. The schools were theologically pluralistic. None proclaimed exclusive access to the divine word. None labeled the other *šeqer* 'false,' as the classic prophets labeled their rivals (e.g., Jer 5:31; 28:15). As for their divergences, they would have answered in words similar to those coined by a later generation of rabbis concerning the different schools of Rabbis Hillel and Shammai: *ʾēlû wāʾēlû dibrê ʾĕlōhîm ḥayyîm* 'Both are the words of the living God' (*p. Ber.* 1:7).

B. RATIONALES ARE THEOLOGY

H's rationales (one of its distinctive features; see I B), also termed "motive clauses," will be discussed as they sequentially appear in Leviticus.

1. I have, however, decided to open this discussion with an out-of-sequence rationale (20:24–25) because it fuses two major theological planks in H's program—separation and holiness—and anchors their foundation in the basic themes of creation and life. Separation (*hibdîl*, 20:24, 25 [bis], 26) is the leitmotif of P's creation story (Gen 1:4, 7, 14, 18). Separation of the elements and species produces order out of chaos (cf. Douglas 1966: 55–57) and allows for life to multiply and fill the earth (Gen 1:22, 28). Similarly, Israel's dietary code (Lev 11), which declares most of the animal kingdom off limits (*šeqeṣ* 'abomination' or *ṭāmēʾ* 'impure'), is based on a reverence-for-life principle, an aspect of P's life-versus-death theme (vol. 1. 732–35; corrected by chap. 17, COMMENT D) throughout all its impurity laws (chaps. 11–15).

As shown recently by Boersema (1997: 156), P does not limit this principle to forbidden flesh. It states that a carcass (of the eight impure *šereṣ*, vv. 29–30) falling on wet seed—but not on dry seed—renders the seed impure (11:37–38) probably because the wet seed has germinated; it has produced life, and life must not come into contact with death (the carcass). Thus the life–death antipodes are the basis of all the dietary laws. H propels it one giant step forward. It declares *ṭāmēʾ* 'impure' to be the incompatible antithesis of a quality of YHWH expressed by the term *qādôš* 'holy', a quality that should be emulated by all of Israel (11:44; 19:2; 20:26). Thus adherence to the dietary laws, namely, eschewing contact with the world of *ṭāmēʾ* 'impure', forms an indispensable step in Israel's ascent on the ladder of holiness (see below).

Israel's separation from the nations is the continuation (and climax) of the cosmic creation *process*. Just as YHWH has separated the mineral, vegetable, and animal species to create order in the *natural* world, so Israel must separate from the nations to create order in the *human* world. Israel is thus charged with a universal goal.

It should not be forgotten that H was well aware (at least by oral transmission) of the antediluvian legends. The creation of the first human pair ends in fail-

ure: the violence of Cain and his descendant Lamech, miscegenation with celestial beings (Gen 6:1–4), and *ḥāmās*, universal "violence" (Gen 6:13). The polluted earth is cleansed by a flood; God tries again with the righteous survivor
Noah, hoping to avert failure by imposing a law (Gen 9:1–6; Frymer-Kensky
1977). This experiment also fails with Noah himself (Gen 9:21) and with his
descendants, who defy God by building up instead of spreading out (Gen 11:1–9;
contra 1:28). Furthermore, H (at least H_R) is fully cognizant of JE's patriarchal
narrative. Thus God decides on an individual who willingly "spreads out" from
his sinful society and builds a model family (Gen 18:19). P's Abraham is commanded, "Walk in my ways and be blameless (*tāmîm*)" (Gen 17:1). Just as the
life of Abraham will be a standard for blessing throughout the nations (Gen
12:3), so will the exemplary life of his progeny (cf. Gen 26:4).

Israel that follows YHWH's commandments will evoke admiration and emulation throughout the world, indicated by the *Nip'al* and *Hitpa'el* of *brk* followed by the preposition *be* (Gen 12:3; 18:18; 22:18; 26:4; 28: 14; cf. 48:20; Isa
65:16; Jer 4:2; Ps 72:17). The *Nip'al* here bears a reflexive connotation, equivalent to the *Hitpa'el*, both meaning "bless themselves by" (Rashi 1946 and Luz-
zatto 1965 on Gen 12:3; see also Ehrlich 1899–1900: 1.32; Driver 1906: 145;
Jacob 1934: 337–39; Orlinsky 1969: 85; Weinfeld 1975b: 61). Abraham, Jacob,
and their progeny will be a standard for blessing chiefly because they exemplify
ṣĕdāqâ ûmišpāṭ 'justice and righteousness' (Gen 18:18–19; 22:18).

I presume that H was fully aware of the Genesis narratives for no other reason than that it was the heir to P's narrative strand, which by the time of H had
been intertwined and integrated with JE (see II R). But even if the cosmologi-
cal and patriarchal legends were known to H tradents only by means of oral
transmission, they would have recognized that the patriarchs, in spite of (or
through) their faults, were credible models of behavior. Thus when H demands
that Israel separate from the nations, it has in mind that Israel's *imitatio dei* will
generate a universal *imitatio Israel*.

It does not happen. In the time of H (Hezekiah) and the author of Lev 17–27
(with few exceptions), social injustice and individual criminality are rampant.
H thereupon devises a plan whereby Israel's purpose on earth can be achieved.
To P's life–death principle, which governs its impurity laws, H attaches prescriptions for attaining holiness (see II G, and COMMENT on chap. 19). The separation from all things *ṭāmē'* 'impure' is the first rung on the ladder of holiness;
H's rungs are specified in chap. 19 (see below).

When H prescribes separation from Egypt and Canaan (18:3) because of their
immoral sexual mores (18:6–23), it should be borne in mind that these serve as
only an illustration of all their practices (*ma'ăśê*) and laws (*ḥuqqôt*) that Israel
should avoid. Instead, it should follow the life-giving laws of YHWH (18:5). In
truth, nowhere does H state explicitly that the purpose of Israel's separation is
to create a model people for nations to emulate. But H did inherit the tradition
that the moral behavior of the patriarchs, the model for the descendants, was
intended to influence the behavior of their neighbors (Gen 12:3; 22:18; 26:4).

Separation does not mean isolation. Israel is completely integrated into its sur-
roundings commercially and culturally. If, in H's view, non-Israelites will wit-

ness how Israel treats the *gēr* (24:22; see II N) and the poor (19:9–10), abolishes slavery (25:39–43; see NOTES, and II H), cancels debts, and restores confiscated land (25:8–17; see II K)—for which Israel's God will reward it with prosperity and security (26:3–13)—how could the non-Israelites not be induced to behave similarly (see also Deut 4:8). How far, indeed, is this incipient transnational role from the servant poems of the exilic Isaiah, which predict that Israel will be *lĕʾôr gôyim* 'for a light of the nations' (Isa 42:6–7; 49:6; 51:4; cf. 61:1)? After all, the divine promise to the patriarchs (mentioned above) and H's concrete plan of achieving holiness by separation from the ways of others and obeying YHWH's commandments lie before exilic Isaiah. Is he not standing on the shoulders of the patriarchal traditions and H's legislation?

2. Chap. 17 is small (16 vv.), yet rife with rationales—all dealing with the same theme. Since blood is life (v. 14, repeating v. 11aα, the aside to Moses) and, hence, forbidden to be ingested by both the Israelite and the alien (v. 10, repeated in vv. 12, 14, the aside to Moses), then nonsacrificial slaughter is declared a capital crime punishable by YHWH with *kārēt* (v. 4; see II O). Moreover, nonsacrificial slaughter is banned permanently to prevent the worship of chthonic deities (v. 7; see II C). The blood of sacrificial animals must be drained on the altar (v. 4a). YHWH has empowered the blood of an animal killed for its flesh to ransom its killer if the blood has been returned to YHWH via the altar (v. 11)—which adds a new dimension to P's function for altar-sacrificial blood: purging the sanctuary of pollution (chaps. 4, 16) and expiating inadvertent wrongdoing (1:4; 5:16, 18, 26).

3. Whereas P speaks of only the pollution of the sanctuary and its sancta, H holds that the entire land of Israel is vulnerable to pollution (18:24b–25). Israel had the right to possess the inhabited land of Canaan because Canaan had polluted the land by its gross sexual misconduct (18:24a, 26–28; 20:22; see II I). The resident alien (*gēr*) is also subject to this rule because he lives on the land (see II N), and violations of prohibitive commands committed by any of the inhabitants pollute the land (18:26).

In essence, H does not differ from P regarding the end result of disobeying YHWH's commandments. P also posits that the pollution of the sanctuary leads to YHWH's abandonment of Israel and its ejection from its land. H differs in this regard: whereas P presumes Israel's banishment by hostile *human* forces, H presumes a natural ecological cause and effect: Israel pollutes the land; the land becomes infertile; Israel is forced to leave. (H combines the two rationales in the maledictions of chap. 26.)

The forbidden sexual unions are mainly incest, defined by either blood or affinity (18:8b, 10b, 11aα, 12b, 13b, 14bβ, 15bβ, 16b, 17bγ). Blood is the more important factor. The reason for prohibiting *ʿerwat ʾābîkā wĕʿerwat ʾimmekā* 'the nakedness of your father, that is, the nakedness of your mother' is *ʾimmĕkā hi(w)ʾ* 'she is your mother' (v. 7b). In this case, the sin against the father is by affinity and not by blood and, hence, is secondary. A rationale is missing only in the case of sex with the half sister (v. 9). The reason may be stylistic: the awkward length of the needed rationale, "she is the nakedness of your father or your mother," which would further burden the already overlaid sentence.

In the forbidden nonincestual unions (18:17–21), the rationale switches to condemnatory terms: *zimmâ* 'depravity', *tô'ēbâ* 'abomination', *tebel* 'perversion', *ḥesed* 'disgrace'. Deprived of the natural revulsion evoked by sex with blood relations, the writer resorts to the artifice of condemnatory words—indicating that Israel had developed a shame culture. Thus all the sexual prohibitions in chap. 18 consists of rationales intended to arouse shame in the would-be violator. He is reminded that the forbidden union either is a blood relation or is shameful.

4. Molek worship is included among the sexual prohibitions (18:21; 20:1–5) because it destroys human seed, thereby aborting procreation; it constitutes murder. It also desecrates YHWH's name (18:21b) and pollutes his sanctuary (20:3). The reason for the latter rationale is that YHWH's name is invoked during the worship of Molek on the presumption that YHWH commanded the sacrifice of children to this chthonic god; on the same day, its devotees would ascend from the Valley of Hinnom, where they worshiped Molek, to the Temple Mount to worship YHWH (see Ezek 23:39; II C; and NOTES on 18:21b). No other idolatry is condemned by H or its eighth-century prophetic contemporaries, presumably because it was not considered a threat to YHWH (see II D).

5. Chap. 19 contains fifty-two laws grouped into fifteen subjects (see INTRODUCTION to chap. 19). Yet only four laws are given a rationale. None but the first is needed, however. The first rationale covers all the others: *qĕdōšîm tihyû* 'you shall be holy', *kî qādôš 'ānî YHWH 'ĕlōhêkem* 'for I YHWH your God am holy' (19:2). YHWH demands obedience to his commandments. Obedience produces godliness, a quality encapsulated by the term *qādôš* 'holy' (see II G). Just as the priests, who are innately holy, are qualified to enter into YHWH's presence (*qĕrōbay* 'those near to me', 10:3), so if Israel obeys YHWH's commands (19:37), it will attain holiness (19:2) and qualify for admission into the presence—that is, the providence and protection—of God. For JE, as D. N. Freedman reminds me, the ultimate blessing is to be in YHWH's presence—literally, that is, to see him (Exod 33:18–23; Num 12:8)—but the priestly sources would not permit such license. H sharply differs from Isaiah on the eligible recipients of holiness. Isaiah holds that only the repentant survivors of YHWH's purge of the wicked will be called holy (Isa 4:3–4; 10:21–22). H rejects this dismal prediction. All of Israel, including its worst sinners, can attain holiness.

6. Two prohibitions are singled out with the rationale that their violators desecrate sanctums: the consumption of sacred food beyond its allowable time (19:7) and the desecration of God's name with a lying oath (19:12). Those who resist harvesting the fruit of a tree during the first three years of its growth and offer YHWH the harvest of the fourth year will be rewarded with an abundant yield in the fifth year (19:23–25). This rationale is also practical; it is confirmed by agronomics (see NOTE on 19:23). Lastly, H adapts the rationale for supporting the *gēr* (19:33–34) found in earlier legal tradition—for example, *kî yĕda'tem et-nepeš haggēr* 'you should know the feelings of the alien' (Exod 23:9 NJPS; cf. 22:20). Israel should recall that it was once an alien in Egypt, where it was exploited and persecuted. The concern for the *gēr* is attested in all the pentateuchal codes (Exod 23:9; 22:20; Lev 19:10, 33–34; 24:22; Num 15:14, 15, 29; 35:15; Deut 10:19; 14: 21, 29; 16:11, 14; 23:8; 24:19–21). This suffices to indicate the

vulnerability of the *gēr* and the necessity for this rationale (see further II N).

7. The injunctions to the priests (21:1–22:16) contain four rationales. H uniquely stresses that priests must *sustain* their holiness (21:8, 15, 23), while Israel must *attain* it (19:2; 20:26). Priests must watchfully avoid impurity because they offer YHWH's food (21:6). Israel, for its part, must show priests respect due to their sacred work (21:8). The high priest may not follow the bier even for his father or mother because he is anointed with the sacred oil and will "desecrate" (rather "pollute"—H's imprecision) himself and the sanctuary (21:12). Priests may eat sacred food after their ablutions from minor impurity (22:7b), as do the Israelites, because this is their major source of food. This is language of concession; it may indicate that originally priests had to wait until the following morning (see NOTE to 22:7b). Indeed, purificatory procedures are the same for priests and lay persons (cf. chaps. 11, 14, and 15), though Ezekiel enjoins severer procedures for priests (44:25–27).

8. Since God provided Israel with booths for housing in the wilderness "exile," Israel should recall this event by living in booths (23:43) in the new exile of Babylonia. For the argument that this passage stems from an exilic H tradent, see NOTE on 23:42 and COMMENT A.

9. Because YHWH owns the land, Israel is his tenant; it may continue to lease the land as long as it fulfills the owner's condition to redeem confiscated land and restore it to its original tenant at the jubilee (25:24, 38). Thus selling the land is in reality leasing it until the jubilee, and what is sold is not the land but its usufruct (see NOTES on 25:24; see also II I). YHWH is also Israel's owner because he is their redeemer. Hence Israel cannot be owned by any other person or power (25:42, 45), and the enslavement of an Israelite is totally forbidden.

10. In chap. 19, the motive clause *’ănî YHWH* (*’ĕlōhêkem*) 'I am YHWH (your God)' appears sixteen times (in the long and short formulas of YHWH's self-presentation)—always where the prohibition can be violated in secret. Thus if by ignorance or intent the infringer is not prosecuted in a human court, he will not escape the attention of the divine judge. This motive clause appears in a similar context in chap. 25: cheating (25:17), taking interest on loans (25:38), and redeeming kin from non-Israelite masters (25:55). In chap. 26, this motive changes complexion: it alludes to the faithfulness of YHWH to fulfill his promises (26:13) and to keep his covenant (26:44–45; cf. Rashi on 26:13; Exod 6:2; and Saadiah on 26:45). A further rationale appears in explaining Israel's exile: it has loathed YHWH's laws, in particular, by neglecting the septennates (v. 43; cf. vv. 34–35).

C. Provincial Perspectives and Ancestor Worship

I have already argued (vol. 1.1066–67) that *originally* the tenth of the seventh month was a day of rejoicing because it was the climax of a ten-day New Year festival. This would explain why the jubilee year was proclaimed on this day and not on the first of the year. The proclamation of the jubilee by shofar blasts throughout the land as a "year of liberty" (Ezek 46:17; cf. Lev 25:10) is another indication of the joyousness of this day. That it was a day of unbridled joy, which in no way reflected the sober character of the subsequent yôm hakkipûrîm, is attested in a much later tannaitic source: "Rabbi Simeon b. Gamliel said: There were no happier days for Israel than the fifteenth of Ab and the Day of Purgation, for on them the daughters of Jerusalem used to go forth in white raiments . . . to dance in the vineyards. And what did they say? 'Young man, lift up your eyes and see what you would choose for yourself; set your eyes not on beauty, but set your eyes on family' " (m. Ta'an. 4:8).

I believe I am correct in suggesting that the image of nubile maidens dancing in the vineyards recalls the Shilonite maidens dancing in the vineyards on the annual "Festival of YHWH," snatched as brides by surviving Benjaminites (Judg 21:19–24). This day, then, marked by feasting, merriment, and the dancing of maidens in the vineyards, is a far cry from the 'innûy nepeš 'self-denial' that characterizes this day's successor. (On the transformation, see vol. 1.1067–70; for another view, see Knohl 1995: 32–34, 195–96.)

H's pericopes on the Day of Purgation (16:29–34a; 23:26–32) indicate that folk observances, which burgeoned sporadically and spontaneously in the countryside, have been suppressed or supplanted. Another excellent example is the firstfruits festivals of grain. I have argued that standard H (termed H) is built on two earlier layers (Pre-H$_1$ and Pre-H$_2$), which presumed that the individual farmer brought to his regional sanctuary the firstfruits of barley whenever they ripened, followed fifty days later by the firstfruits of wheat. It is H, I submit, which standardized the day and converted the previous, individual rite into a public, collective rite (see INTRODUCTION to 23:15–22). H thereby abolishes the individual farmer's offerings by ordaining that henceforth the responsibility to supply the firstfruits of the barley and wheat falls on the sanctuary.

Thus the common assumption that, in contrast to P, H reflects the provincial character of the festivals is misleading. H, to the contrary, only hints at the provincial nature of the observances that it suppresses or supplants. But H, no differently than P (cf. Num 28:29), institutionalizes the festival observances by imposing a fixed date and sanctuary ritual for each of them.

Folk observances surface in the final, exilic stratum (H$_R$) dealing with the appendix to the Festival of Booths (23:39–43). Were it not for the need to salvage some holiday observance in the absence of the Temple pilgrimages and sacrifices, the chances are that we would not have been informed of the custom of building booths during the great, seven-day postharvest festival or of the custom of circumambulating the altar with branches (a rain rite; see NOTES on 23:40) — though they are documented in rabbinic sources. But with the Temple destroyed, the calendric observances became totally inoperative except for the sabbath, which rose to prominence (see INTRODUCTION to 23:1–3), and the Festival of Booths, for which new rituals were mandated: Israel must construct booths, and live in them (23:42) as well as rejoice with branches (23:40) during this entire seven-day festival.

That H did not incorporate all the firstfruit festivals as celebrated by the populace may be reflected in the calendar of Qumran, which ordains celebrations of the firstfruits of the grapes and olive harvests (in the form of wine [i.e., must] and oil) at the Temple, fifty days apart, followed by a six-day wood festival. These additional festivals are found in the sect's supplement to the Pentateuch, 11QT 19:11–25:1 (a sixth book of the Torah?), and in its version of the pentateuchal text, as attested by the recently published 4Q365 fragment 23, in which the festivals appear at the end of Lev 23 and the beginning of Lev 24 (details in chap. 23, COMMENT D). These festivals are also attested in the teachings of (the Karaite?) Judah the Alexandrian (cf. Yadin 1983: 1.119–23).

Regional evidence of these extracanonical festivals may be reflected in the *ḥag laYHWH*, a grape harvest celebration at the Shiloh sanctuary (Judg 21:19–21; see above). In other words, the sectaries of Qumran were not theoretically extrapolating these festivals from the fifty-day interval between the Festivals of Barley and Wheat, but were rendering actual folk observances that, they averred, were commanded by YHWH and were recorded in the Torah itself. If so, why did H suppress them? I can only speculate:

The Festival of New Wine was celebrated by sacrifices and wine drinking at the Temple. The priests drank first, followed by the Levites, chieftains, and all the people. That everyone drank of the new wine (must) probably indicates that each was given a sip or the equivalent of a small glass so that the drinking would be strictly controlled by the Temple authorities (11QT 21:4–7)—a far cry from the bacchanals that probably prevailed in Israel and outside it (cf. the great seven-day Anthestria and the older Mycenaean Festival of the Thirsty; details in chap. 23, COMMENT D). Thus it may have been the unrestrained indulgence that attended the wine festival, adumbrated directly by the Qumran Temple Scroll, that led to its deletion from the priestly firstfruit festivals. And with the fifty-day nexus between the festivals broken, the following Festival of New Oil (Oil) was also deleted.

The provincial element in H is adumbrated in H's "National Perspective" (see II E), where it is pointed out that central authority figures, such as the king and his bureaucracy (*śārîm, śōpĕtîm*, etc.), are missing in favor of the family within its kin group (*mišpāḥâ*; see II M). The urban atmosphere is also totally missing and is made even more conspicuous by the interpolation of cities (25:29–34) into the exclusively agronomic background of the septennial and jubilee laws (chap. 25; cf. Loewenstamm 1958a: *EM* 3:579–80). The adventitiousness of the city interpolation is further projected into view by H's ruling that houses in unwalled villages are reckoned as fields (v. 31). Presumably, the reference is to farmers' dwellings huddled together for economic and protective advantages, entailing a short commute to their fields. In other words, the interpolation on the city is worded to the advantage of the farmer.

Joosten (1996: 157) makes the astute observation that the Israel that H is addressing must be living in the countryside because *wĕneʾĕsaptem ʾel-ʿārêkem* . . . *wĕnittatem bĕyad-ʾōyēb* 'if you withdraw into your cities (when your land is occupied by foreign troops) . . . you shall be delivered into enemy hands' (26:25). Joosten (1996: 158–59) also contrasts H with D to good advantage:

> In H, one finds no information on a central court of justice (contrast Deut 17:8–13), on the king (Deut 17:14–20), on military service (Deut 20:1–9), warfare (Deut 20:10–20; 23:9–14), or captives of war (Deut 21:10–14), nor on the attitudes to be adopted towards the neighboring peoples (Deut 23:1–8; 25:17–19). . . . In Deuteronomy, nothing is said about the land or agriculture; . . . in Deuteronomy, the seventh year signifies an interruption of the money economy, in H the suspension of agricultural activities . . . whereas Deuteronomy accentuates the independent value of personal freedom, the conception of H is without land no man is entirely free, since he will not be able to support himself.

Here, however, I must enter a slight demurrer. D is very much concerned about the farmer. As I remark in the NOTE on 23:8, D compromises the celebration of the Passover at the central sanctuary precisely because it falls at the beginning of the grain harvest. Not only does D omit any mention of aliens, widows, orphans, Levites, or even sons and daughters (Deut 16:1–8), as found in the texts dealing with the Festivals of Weeks and Booths (Deut 16:11, 14), but it even *urges* the family head, who is required to offer the paschal sacrifice (though theoretically all males should be present as well, Deut 16:16; cf. Exod 23:17; 34:23), *ûpānîtā babbōqer wĕhālaktā lĕ'ōhālêkā* 'in the morning you may start back on your journey home' (Deut 16:7b, JPS). The reason is rooted in agricultural reality. The spring is a time of anxiety and trepidation lest an unseasonable rain or some other blight, such as the dreaded Sirocco/*ḥamsîn*, wipe out the ripening crops (see NOTE on 23:15).

I must enter stronger objection to Joosten's (1996) conclusion that "the provincial outlook of H . . . could not have arisen in the capital" (164), but, instead, "H is the product of a priestly school in the countryside" (163), which he explains by his admittedly speculative hypothesis that "a priest might have his home in the countryside while executing his priestly duties in the capital" (163–64). The evidence adduced by Joosten (1996: 164, n. 103), namely, the twenty-four priestly classes officiating in the Second Temple two weeks a year (Hoffmann 1904: 151), cannot be used for the much smaller priestly cadres of the First Temple (not to speak of the multiple sanctuaries until the time of Josiah). Nor are the Aaronite cities in the land of Judah (Josh 21:4, 9–19) cited by Haran (1961: 51–52), which may be purely a utopian construction, valid evidence. As for Abiathar's land in Anatoth (1 Kgs 2:26), it should not be forgotten that his village is walking distance from the Temple—hardly representative of the Judahite countryside. Rather, to cite the example of First Isaiah (e.g., 5:1–10; 17:4–6; 18:4–6), it is certainly possible for a sophisticated urbanite (even with close ties to the royal court!) to have rural knowledge and concerns. Note the following:

[23]Listen, and hear my voice;
   Pay attention and hear my speech.
[24]Does he who plows to sow
   Plow all the time,
   Breaking up and furrowing his land?
[25]When he has leveled its surface,
   Does he not scatter dill, sow cumin,
   And plant wheat in rows,
   Barley in a strip
   And spelt as the border?
[26]For he is well instructed;
   His God instructs him.
[27]Dill is not threshed with a threshing sledge,
   Nor is a cartwheel rolled over cumin;
   But dill is beaten with a stick,
   And cumin with a rod.
[28]Grain is crushed for bread,
   But one does not crush it forever;
   One drives the cartwheel and horses over it,
   But one does not pulverize it.
[29]This also comes from YHWH of hosts;
   He is wonderful in counsel,
   And excellent in wisdom. (Isa 28:23–29)

Rather, I would concur with Knohl (1995: 222–24) that the Temple priesthood itself was stung by the prophetic indictments of the Judean leadership, including the priesthood (e.g., Hos 4:6–9; Zeph 3:4), which heretofore had ignored the growing social and economic injustices that caused widespread landlessness (due to latifundia) and destitution. It is not hard to conceive the rise of a new generation of "Young Turks" within the Jerusalem priesthood who, like the prophet Isaiah, probably circulated among the people and became sensitized to their plight.

The provincial concern of H finds its clearest, most outspoken voice in the popular religion it opposes. In the repeated indictments against Molek worship (18:21; 20:1–5) and necromancy (19:31; 20:6, 27) its condemnation becomes strident and clamorous. Why was H exercised to that extent and why wasn't its venom directed against other idolatrous worship? The latter question will be discussed in the next excursus (II D); the former in the discussion that follows.

I have argued that Molek worship must be distinguished from other idolatries because the people-at-large believed that it was not only tolerated by YHWH, but approved and even demanded by him. The evidence is manifold: Jeremiah's thrice-repeated emphatic denials by YHWH that he had commanded it (Jer 7:31; 19:5; 32:35a); its inclusion among the magical means of divining YHWH's will (Deut 18:10–11; cf. 12:29–31); and its worship followed on the same day (*bayyôm hahû*') by worship of YHWH in his Temple (Ezek 23:29). These are only part of the arsenal I have mounted to demonstrate that Molek and YHWH coexisted in the mind-set and practice of the people (see NOTES on 18:21; 20:1–5; chap. 20, COMMENTS B–C; and II D). They probably pronounced *hammolek* 'the Molek' as *hammelek* 'the King', namely, of the underworld, whom some circles may have conceived as a member of the divine assembly assigned by YHWH to supervise the infernal realm.

Why this obsessive drive to worship this chthonic deity? I have argued that Molek, as master of the underworld, controled access to the ancestral spirits, and to attain his intervention child sacrifice was essential. Both factors combined to create the enormity of the sin: ascribing to Molek the attributes of a deity who can demand the murder of one's child and, at the same time, claiming that Molek is an agent of YHWH carrying out his will. (See the detailed discussion in NOTE on "and thereby not desecrate the name of your God," 18:21b, and in II D.)

Molek worship is coupled with necromancy (20:1–5, 6; cf. Deut 18:10–11), indicating that Molek, a subterranean deity, is associated with the cult of the ancestors. That ancestor worship was rife in Israel is demonstrated by a multitude of biblical passages. The most obvious are Lev 19:31; 20:5, 27; Deut 18:9–12; 26:14; 1 Sam 28; 2 Sam 18:18; and Isa 8:19–20; 19:2; 29:4; 57:6–9; and 65:4. To be sure, these verses speak of the dead, not of the ancestors. However, it stands to reason that in this cult one turned not to the dead in general, but to one's ancestors. Besides the desire to venerate them, a utilitarian motivation was also present: ancestors bestow favors on descendants who regularly tend their cult. Such a background is clearly manifest in Isa 8:19–20a, which associates ancestor worship with necromancy:

> When they say to you: Consult the ghosts (*hā'ōbôt*) and the wizard-spirits (*hayyidě'ōnîm*) who chirp and mutter; shall not a people consult its ancestral spirits ('*ĕlōhāyw*) on behalf of the living, (consult) the dead (*hammētîm*) for an oracle and a message?

The vehement opposition of prophets (and priests) to ancestor worship stemmed, at heart, from their suspicion that it harbored an incipient dualism, particularly since the belief was rife among the masses that the dead existed outside YHWH's realm (e.g., Isa 38:18; Pss 6:6; 88:11–13; 115:17; see Toorn 1991). Even if, in theory, Molek would have been reckoned a member of the divine assembly, and even if the ancestral spirits, despite their capriciousness, could be thought of as always subject to YHWH's overall control, it is difficult to see that these very sophisticated views were more than the belief system of an elite. As will be shown in II D, throughout the First Temple period, the people-at-large worshiped female figurines that may have represented (YHWH's consort?) Asherah. A more authentic monotheism was championed by priests and prophets, who constituted only a small minority of the people.

Toorn (1990: 211–17) has mounted a convincing case that teraphim were ancestor figurines used in divination. Moreover, the teraphim in 1 Sam 19:13, 16 and Hos 3:4 are not condemned, nor are they listed among the divinatory practices prohibited in Deut 18:10–14. The indications are that the practice of consulting the ancestors on behalf of the living, though lampooned by the prophets (cf. Isa 8:19–20a), was deeply rooted in popular worship and could not be extirpated.

It has been suggested that H's attempts to control (if not eradicate) ancestor worship are adumbrated in the very first law of its corpus, Lev 17. The fact that it repeats P's prescriptions that the blood and suet of the animal must be offered on the altar (17:6; cf. 3:2b–5, 8b–11; 13b–16) may well be a polemic against a chthonic (i.e., ancestor) cult, which required that these animal ingredients be poured on the ground (see chap. 17, COMMENT A). Moreover, as was pointed out (vol. 1.1072), the terms "open field" (17:5) and *midbār* 'wilderness' (16:21) are also synonyms of the underworld (cf. Akk. *ṣēru*), and the goat/satyr that was worshiped (17:7) is identified with the Ugaritic god of the underworld, Mot (= *māwet* 'death' [Heb.]; vol. 1.1021).

S. Chavel remarked (oral communication) that H would have been horrified at D's concession of secular slaughter, whereby the blood of the animal would be poured on the ground (Deut 12:16, 24)—opening the door to chthonic worship! However, no such reaction is recorded in H. Rather, H seems oblivious not only to D's disposal of the blood, but to its very innovation of secular slaughter. Does this mean that H and D were working in separate, independent tracks, in total ignorance of each other? This is hardly likely in view of the evidence that H was familiar with parts of D (see II I–J). It more likely implies that D's doctrine of secular slaughter was composed after H. This option is more probable, since H (but not H$_R$) is the product of the Hezekian period whereas D's doctrine of secular slaughter reflects the Josianic period (see chap. 17, COMMENT D, and I K).

In the NOTES on 19:27–28 and 21:5, with the assistance of Deut 14:1 and Ezek 44:20aα, I have argued that ostensible mourning rites such as shaving the head, polling the hair, and lacerating the body are aspects of the cult of the dead, equally incumbent (with a slight variation) upon lay person and priest. The deuteronomic passage is particularly significant, since it is preceded by the injunction "You are children of YHWH your God" (Deut 14:1a), which sets a contrast between the worship of the dead and the worship of Israel's God (von Rad 1966: 101). H's rationale for equating priests and laity is straightforward: those who are (priests) and those who aspire to holiness (Israel) are desecrated by these practices.

In view of the inseverable hold that the ancestor cult has exhibited down to the present time even in the most sophisticated religions (documented in chap. 20, COMMENT C), it is understandable that H did not ban the worship of ancestors outright, but instead reserved its fire both for Molek worship, which became fused and confused with the worship of YHWH, and for necromancy because its practitioners usurped YHWH's exclusive authority to direct Israel's destiny via his appointed agents, the prophets, and perhaps because of the fear of the potential power of the ancestors to undermine the established government and cult (see further chap. 20, COMMENT C).

In sum, H discloses a subculture of popular religion. It is particularly evident in the description of the festivals of the seventh month (23:23–43), which are exceptionally not rooted in nature. The national element is supplied by the missing rain rites of the people. As discussed in chap. 20, COMMENT C, the priests exercised firm control over rituals that they performed in the sanctuary. Thus they transformed the firstfruits festivals of grain from spontaneous offerings of the individual farmer to fixed, public offerings at which they officiated (see NOTES on 23:10–21). But rites performed by the people even in the sanctuary, such as processions and water libations for rain, and rites performed outside the sanctuary, such as ancestor worship, were beyond priestly control. The priests neither approved nor disapproved, but by their suppression of these rites in the holy text, they hoped that ultimately these and other quasi-magical practices of the masses would disappear.

Their hopes were in vain.

D. PROPHETS AND ARCHAEOLOGY REGARDING IDOLATRY IN THE EIGHTH–SEVENTH CENTURY

a. THE BIBLICAL TEXT

I define idolatry broadly: the worship of all images, not just of other gods but also of YHWH. My definition, therefore, covers the first and second commandments of the Decalogue (Exod 20:3–6; Deut 5:7–10, following Philo, *Decal.* 52–174; Josephus, *Ant.* 3.91–92; *Sipre* Num. 112; *b. Sanh.* 99a; *b. Hor.* 8b; see the Addendum, p. 1390).

The study is grounded in these statistics: the datable biblical literature of the eighth century accuses Israel of idolatry 15 times; in the following seventh century, there are 166 accusations. These totals break down as follows: eighth century: H (Lev 19:4; 26:1), Amos (5:26), Hosea (5:3b–4; 6:10), Isaiah (2:8, 18, 20; 10:11; 17:8; 27:9; 30:22; 31:7), and Micah (1:7; 5:12–13a). In the seventh century, the citations are too many to itemize; here are the totals for each book: Deuteronomy (36), Jeremiah (46), Ezekiel (82), Zephaniah (1), and Habakkuk (1).

At once I must enter two qualifications. First, these statistics are approximate. Admittedly, I have not distinguished between the *ipsissima verba* of the prophets and those of tradents (to cite one obvious example, the prose sections of Jeremiah). However, even if we could identify the latter and remove them from our count, the total would still increase by adding the seventh-century statements in the book of Kings, which most likely underwent an initial preexilic redaction (tentatively cf. the summary in McKenzie 1992; Cross 1973: 278–85; Nelson 1981: 119–28; Friedman 1981). Indeed, even without a "Josianic" edition, commonly accepted by scholars (see, most recently, Halpern and Vanderhooft 1991; Knoppers 1995: 1.17–56, esp. 46–54; 2. 5–14 *inter alia*; Eynikel 1996: passim), there may even be a "Hezekian" edition (Halpern 1981b: esp. 48–53; Barrick 1996: esp. 636–40) and a North Israel prophetic document (McCarter 1980: 18–23; Campbell 1986: 139–202). Nevertheless, since there is no consensus on the extent of this redaction, the book of Kings will be excluded from consideration.

The second qualification concerns the book of Hosea. I accept the theory proposed by Kaufmann (1948: 93–107; cf. Kaufmann 1960: 368–72) and amplified by Ginsberg (1971: esp. 1011–17) that Hos 1–3 (henceforth, Hos I) constitutes the work of a ninth-century northern prophet. Among the compelling reasons for this distinction, one is especially relevant for this study. Hos I is replete with accusations of Baal worship, but they are absent from Hos II (chaps. 4–14). Hos II refers to either idolatry of the past, the sin of Baal-peor (9:10; 13:1) or "idolatry" of the present, the worship of the golden calves (8:4–6; 13:2), which, as recognized, symbolizes the presence of YHWH, not the Baal. Lastly, the country altar is the scene of *zenût*, not idolatry, but literally "fornication," enhanced by drunkenness (4:10–18; 7:3–7; 9:1–2; cf. 5:1–4; 6:8–10; Kaufmann 1945: 130–34; 1960: 374–75). It is significant that Amos, the only other eighth-century writing prophet of North Israel, never mentions the Baal (Kaufmann 1945: 83).

What could have caused the disappearance of the contemporaneous Baal from Amos and Hosea II? The answer in the book of Kings should be taken literally: Jehu wiped out the official, royally sponsored Baal cult from the land (2 Kgs 10:1–28). Private idolatry was ridiculed by the prophets as fetishistic *ʿăṣabbîm* (Hos 4:17, but cf. Ginsberg 1967: esp. 74–75; Mic 1:7 = *pĕsîlêha*, but see below), *bĕʿālîm* = *pĕsîlîm* (Hos 11:2, but cf. Kaufmann 1945: 117, n. 36), *ĕlîlîm* (Isa 2:8, 18, 20; 31:7, but see below), *maʿăśēh yād / ʿāśâ-lô* (Isa 2:8; 31:7; 37:19; Hos 14:4; Mic 5:12), but since it was not state-sponsored, it was not a threat to the worship of YHWH. True, Amos 5:26 mentions the Mesopotamian astral deities Sikkuth (possibly, the Hebrew transliteration of ᵈSAG.KUD; see Loretz 1989: 286–89; Paul 1991: 194–95; Stol 1995b) and Kiyyun (Akk. *kajamānu*; see Loretz 1989: 286–89; Paul 1991: 194–95; Stol 1995), which may have penetrated into North Israel through Aramean mediation (see Paul 1991: 194–96, esp. n. 87). But it is the only reference to these gods in all of Scripture. Note their total absence from Hosea and from the list of Mesopotamian gods worshiped in the land after the exile of its inhabitants (2 Kgs 17:29–34). This indicates that their cult was neither widespread (perhaps limited to the aristocracy of Samaria) nor long-lasting.

In Judah, the major writing prophet of the eighth century is Isaiah. Only one of the seven references to idolatry (cited above) refers to Isaiah's own time (2:8). It is part of Isaiah's larger denunciation against the proliferation of magic, chariots, fortified walls, towers, large ships—and even the high places in nature: cedars, oaks, mountains. All are extensions of or contribute to human pride. It is man's hubris that is responsible for idolatry: he "makes" his own gods (Kaufmann 1948: 202–3, 1960: 387). This notion is neatly captured by the rabbis: "Rabbi Joḥanan said in the name of R. Simeon b. Yoḥai: Every man in whom there is haughtiness of spirit (*gassût rûaḥ*) is as though he worships idols" (*b. Sot.* 4b). Psychological insight is provided by Fromm (1955: 121–22): "Man spends his energy, his artistic capacities, on building an idol, and then he worships this idol, which is nothing but the result of his own human effort. His life forces have flowed into a 'thing,' . . . (is experienced) as something apart from himself, over and against him, which he worships and to which he submits."

Isaiah does not call for an immediate end to idolatry. Nor does he warn his people that their paganism will lead to imminent disaster. On the contrary, the abolition of idolatry, so graphically portrayed in 2:6–8, will be carried out only in the unpredictable future (vv. 18–21). The remaining references to idols say the same (17:8; 27:9; 30:22; 31:7). Thus Isaiah, as his northern counterparts, does not see paganism as a threat to YHWH. The reason is the same as that of the North: state-sponsored idolatry had been abolished. As described in the book of Kings, the high priest Jehoiada destroys Athaliah's Baal temple in Jerusalem as a consequence of the covenant struck between YHWH and the king (2 Kgs 11:17–18).

Micah's prophecy on Judean apostasy is clearly influenced by his older contemporary, Isaiah. In an eschatological passage (*bayyôm hahûʾ*, 5:9), he predicts the destruction of idols together with horses, chariots, fortresses, cult pillars, and cities (5:12–13). Micah's one other mention of idolatry refers to the imminent destruction of North Israel (1:7). There is no future for the North: its doom is sealed. But, as in Isaiah, there is no mention of a foreign god. The idolatry of the masses is home grown. This would include the sacred poles (*ʾăšērîm*) and incense stands (*ḥammānîm*) set up alongside or atop local altars (Isa 17:8) or in homes.

Finally, Lev 17–27 (H), which I attribute to eighth-century authors, contains three references to idols: 19:4 and 26:1, which encapsulate the first two commandments of the Decalogue, the latter most likely a product of the sixth-century Babylonian Exile; and 26:30, a result but not a cause of Israel's threatened destruction.

In H, the telltale word *ṭāmēʾ* is used to indicate the contaminating effects of Molek worship (20:3, on which see below) and necromancy (19:31). *Ṭāmēʾ* is not used with idolatry. This indicates that idolatry does not render the sanctuary, the land, or its practitioners impure. Neither do the eighth-century prophets characterize idolatry as *ṭāmēʾ*. It is not that they are unfamiliar with this term; they use it in connection with foreign lands (Amos 7:17; Hos 9:3–4), drunkenness (Hos 5:3; 6:10), harlotry (Hos 6:10), social injustice (Mic 2:10; cf. LXX; Ehrlich 1908–14; and vv. 1–9) and general immorality (Isa 6:5), but not with idolatry. To be sure, H does stigmatize Molek worship as *ṭāmēʾ*: it pollutes the sanctuary and desecrates YHWH's name (Lev 20:3; cf. 18:21, 24). But the people-at-large felt no inconsistency in worshiping both Molek and YHWH in tandem. The importance of this verse (Lev 20:3) should, however, not be overlooked. It is the first time, in my opinion, that any non-YHWHistic worship is condemned using either the verb *ṭimmēʾ* or the adjective *ṭāmēʾ*. I would suggest that it constitutes a precedent adopted by the seventh-century prophets to extend H's limited usage of *ṭimmēʾ* from Molek worship to idolatry in all its forms and effects, and idolatry henceforth will become a factor in determining Israel's destiny. Elsewhere I have argued that there was a widespread belief in Judah that the worship of Molek was compatible with the worship of YHWH—hence H twice calls it a desecration of his name (18:21; 20:3). Supportive textual evidence comes from Jeremiah, who repeats YHWH's disclaimer three times: "which I did not command, and which did not come to mind" (7:31; 19:5; 32:35). Moreover, Deut 18:10–11 attests to the common belief that the worship of Molek was licit, as further indicated in Ezek 20:39, namely, that YHWH and Molek could and would be worshiped successively *on the same day*. Extrabiblical evidence can be mustered that Molek (= Malik) was an infernal god, identified by its worship in the depths of a valley (rather than on a hill), and by its juxtaposition with *ʾôb* and *yiddĕʿōnî* (20:1–6), thus indicating that it was a form of necromancy tied to ancestor worship.

Turning to the seventh century, the prophets repeatedly stated that idolatry pollutes (*mĕṭammēʾ*) its adherents, the Temple, and the land (Jer 2:7–8, 23; 7:30; 19:13; 32:34; Ezek 20:7, 18, 26, 31; 22:3–4; 23:7, 13–14, 17, 30; 37:23). The quantitative difference in the number of statements on idolatry between the eighth and seventh centuries (15 versus 166) is accentuated by the difference in the effects of idolatry, as illustrated by the distribution of the term *ṭāmēʾ*: 0 times in the eighth century versus 17 in the seventh.

How can we account for this stupendous change? First, as mentioned above, we must take the book of Kings at its word: Jehu in North Israel and Jehoiada in Judah wiped out the Baal cult during the second half of the ninth century (2 Kgs 10:1–29; 11:17–18). In effect, *state*-sponsored paganism ceased. It is absent throughout the eighth century. Moreover, there was *private* fetishism (see below), but the eighth-century prophets were virtually unconcerned: it was no threat to the worship of YHWH in his sanctuaries or to Israel's existence on its land. To be sure, Molek worship and necromancy are indicted by H (19:31; 20:1–6), but the general populace did not view these acts as incompatible with their allegiance to YHWH, a misconception that the priestly tradents of H and the prophets tried to correct. They may have been aided independently by refugees from the North who brought with them the deuteronomic tradition, which vehemently attacked the ancestor cult, as can be seen by its prohibition against offering sacrifices to the dead (Deut 26:14) or participating in funerary rites of mourning (Deut 14:1; 26:14), and banned outright all aspects of magic, including necromancy and Molek worship (Deut 18:10–11; Toorn 1996b: 357–58).

The dominant prophets of the seventh century, Jeremiah and Ezekiel, were influenced by the thought, if not the language, of Deuteronomy (cf. Kaufmann 1945: 613–25, 1960: 415–17). In the book of Jeremiah, however, the issue is far from clear. Many of its prose passages are attributed to deuteronomic tradents, but there is no consensus concerning their extent and date. Despite the near absence of deuteronomic language in Ezekiel (confirmed by the paucity of Ezekielian citations in Weinfeld's [1972d: 320–61] exhaustive list of deuteronomic phraseology), the same does not hold for deuteronomic thought (contra Zimmerli 1979: 46). Uppermost is Ezekiel's advocacy of cultic centralization (e.g., 20:40), an innovative deuteronomic doctrine. Ezekiel excoriates his people for their worship on *bāmôt* (note his sneering pun, 20:29), and he repeatedly condemns them for "eating on the mountains" (18:6, 11, 15; 22:9; 34:6), figurative language for their sacrificial (*šĕlāmîm*) meals at the *bāmôt*. True, Deuteronomy's language is hardly recognizable in Ezekiel, but understandably so. Ezekiel is a priest and would be expected to clothe his ideas in priestly language. Nevertheless, he is imbued with deuteronomic teachings. In sum, Jeremiah, probably a disciple of D (e.g., Jer 11:1–51; cf. McKane 1986: 235–46), is permeated by D's language, and Ezekiel, who speaks in priestly language, is permeated by D's thought. It therefore is D's demand to remove every trace of idolatry, private as well as public, that accounts for the proliferation of statements against idolatry in the seventh and sixth centuries.

But to trace the prophetic denunciations of idolatry to D only begs the question. What accounts for D's obsession with idolatry (thirty-six references)? First of all, it is a reflex of Manasseh's official sponsorship of foreign gods not just in Judah and Jerusalem, but in the Temple itself (2 Kgs 21:3–7). Deuteronomy, however, also alludes to *private, superstitious* idolatry, *bassēter* (13:7; 27:15). D thus anticipates (or reflects) a situation that even after the obliteration of the state-sponsored cults, private ones will continue furtively, as evidenced by the worship of the Queen of Heaven (Jer 7:18; 44:17–18, 25; Smith's [1975a] objections notwithstanding), the astral gods on rooftops (Jer 19:13; 32:29), the "image rooms" (Ezek 8:12), and child sacrifice in the open country (Isa 57:5; cf. Ezek 20:31). That these cults were private and unofficial is substantiated by the absence of a clergy, the quintessential component of an officially sponsored cult (cf. Kaufmann 1948: 274–75; Greenberg 1983a: xxiii, n. 47); contrast the royally established cult places extirpated by Josiah (2 Kgs 23:4–7, 11–15, 19; Kaufmann 1948: 452). Thus alongside official, state-sponsored idolatry there sprouted a widespread, individual or family-centered cult, which existed uninterruptedly after the destruction of the official Baal cult in North Israel and Judah and even after the Josianic reform successfully annihilated all the royally sponsored cult places in Judah.

The biblical evidence of idolatry has yielded thus far the following picture: the difference in the state-endorsed religion of Judah between the eighth and the seventh century is largely summarized by a single word—rather, by a single person: Manasseh. By force majeure (2 Kgs 21:16), he reintroduced idolatry into Jerusalem and Judah, completely undoing the reform of his father, Hezekiah (2 Kgs 21:3), and, even succeeding the previous status quo, he installed idols in the Temple courtyards and in the sanctuary itself (2 Kgs 21:5, 7; 23:4–7). Also, alongside the official cult, there flourished an ongoing popular cult that continued unabated throughout the eighth and seventh centuries until Judah's destruction in the sixth century.

b. ARCHAEOLOGY

These deductive conclusions receive substantive support from the ancillary discipline of archaeology. First, however, I must credit Yehezkel Kaufmann (1938: 672–76, 1960: 142–47) for possibly being the first to draw a sharp distinction between the official and the popular cult. The problem is that he did not investigate the biblical references and allusions sufficiently in order to ferret out the unofficial religion of the masses. Had he done so, he would not have ascribed monotheism to them. For this failing, however, he should not be faulted completely because in his day (the 1930s and 1940s) he did not possess the massive archaeological data now available to us, and the staggering number of figurines explained initially as magical (like lucky rabbits' feet) not as idols or images of deities, which they were.

Archaeological evidence for the popular cult exists, and in profusion. Among the artifacts, the most likely candidate is the figurine. Its widespread distribution in time (throughout Iron Age II) and space (in sites throughout Judah) warrants certain conclusions concerning the extent and nature of idolatry in eighth- and seventh-century Judah. The entire figurine collection reveals a consistent pattern: the figurines cluster in "tolerated, *nonconformist* worship" (Holladay 1987: esp. 269–75) and are virtually absent from "establishment sanctuaries, whereas a total of 862 figurines were found throughout the countryside of Judah" (Kletter 1995: 384–85, fig. 3). These, in Kletter's terms, "were cheap, everyday objects representing the goddess Asherah in private homes, (mainly) in front of ordinary people" (81). The "homespun" Asherah is not to be confused with the cult statue of the biblical Asherah, which "was sacred because it was made of expensive materials, situated in a public temple, and represented the goddess in front of all the population" (81; contra Meyers 1988: 162).

Parade examples of the former are found in Jerusalem Cave I and the City of David. The cave was excavated by Kenyon (1967; 1974); its figurine hoard was first discussed by Holland (1977), who claims that 597 figurines were found in Jerusalem up to 1975. Shilo's excavations at the City of David (1978–85) uncovered over 1300 additional ceramic figurines; they were recently analyzed by Gilbert-Peretz (1996). Again, the locus of these figurines is outside the Temple *temenos.* This category contrasts with Judahite "establishment" sanctuaries, such as Lachish (stratum V) and Arad (strata VIII–XI), which are devoid of figurines. Figurines, also standing idols, were found in strata V and VI (ninth to sixth century) of 'En Hatzevah in the southern Negev, but these most likely belong to an Edomite shrine (Cohen and Israel 1996; cf. Beit-Arieh 1996).

To be sure, as shown by Mettinger (1995), imageless worship pervaded the entire ancient Near East from earliest time, but as correctly critiqued by Hurowitz (1997), it is a far cry from passive acceptance (Israel's ambiance) to fastidious opposition (Israel's state religion). Moreover, of the two forms of aniconism that Mettinger distinguishes in his exhaustive study—"material" (e.g., *maṣṣēbôt, ʾăšērâ,* see below) and "empty seat" (e.g., Ark throne flanked by cherubim)—Israel legitimated the latter because it allowed the deity not to inhere in it but to be totally transcendent.

The lack of figurines in the official cult centers in Judah motivated Holladay (1987: 281) to deduce:

The most economic hypothesis covering the above data seems to be to assign the aniconic shrine-sanctuary–centered to an officially established hierarchically organized state religion (or religions, in the case of the divided monarchy) operative in close coordination with the state's political apparatus. The "distributed" cultic remains and iconically "clustered" phenomena, both of which seem totally isolated from the life of the official shrines and sanctuaries, are best explained as popular phenomena, probably dependent upon traditions of folk religion stretching back into the Bronze ages.

Of the City of David figurines, 19 percent are anthropomorphic (and pillared), and 73 percent are animal. Of the 211 animal heads, 174 are horses. Are they related to the Assyrian "horses of the sun" (2 Kgs 23:11)? In any case, these and some of the other represented animals are levitically forbidden either as offerings or as food. The large number of female figurines show the woman clutching her breast(s), and they seem to be naked. Thus they bear a likeness to the *dea nutrix* pose of many Late Bronze figurines (undermining Steiner 1997: esp. 22), and perhaps they can be associated with the fertility goddess Asherah (see the addendum, below). Alternatively, they may be only votive offerings, expressing a desire for fertility (Meyers 1988: 161–63; Smith 1990: 93–94; Bloch-Smith 1992a: 94–101). I would, however, concur with Lewis (1998: esp. 11) that even if they did not represent Asherah, "they nonetheless may have been thought by the ancients to have derived their efficacy through a goddess." The explanation of this hoard can only be speculated. The possibility might be entertained that they are a favissa of the Temple under Manasseh or are objects cleansed from the Temple by Josiah. But this scenario is highly unlikely for the figurines stemming from the eighth century, since no such objects appear in Hezekiah's reform. Thus they probably represent the popular religious practice in Jerusalem—indeed, in the very shadow of the Temple—or if Kletter's (1995: 63) conclusions concerning Cave I also hold here, they represent "disposal patterns rather than use patterns" and possibly were a "protecting figure in domestic houses, more likely a figure which bestowed 'plenty,' especially in the domain of female lives" (81).

What makes the City of David finds so striking is that *the distribution of the figurines over the eighth to the sixth century is homogeneous.* This means that after the Josianic reform (621 B.C.E.), the profusion and practice of figurine worship continue unabated—all in the proximity of the Jerusalem Temple. The deduction is nigh inescapable: "The evidence from the City of David lends no support to a postulation of an iconoclastic reform between 8th and 6th centuries B.C.E." (Sharon 1996: esp. 105).

c. CONCLUSIONS

Thus the cult practices attested by the Judahite figurines conform with and confirm the biblical evidence. A distinction has to be made between the official "establishment" cult centers in sanctuaries and the private, occasionally clandestine, worship practiced by the people. The Josianic (and Hezekian) reform occupied itself solely with the former—public cult sites served by YHWHistic or idolatrous priests—but it did not penetrate into the private, domestic worship of the masses. This does not imply that Josiah was in principle a monotheist; probably he was henotheist, believing in the existence and potency of other gods. His reform (and Hezekiah's) only affirmed that YHWH was Israel's national God, who alone should be worshiped in *his* land. Manasseh, to be sure, broke with this pattern, but he continued to maintain YHWH (and his assumed consort, Asherah) as Israel's national God (see the addendum, below).

The biblical evidence reveals that in the eighth century (state idolatry having been abolished), there was no opposition to the idolatry of the population by either the prophets or the priests. First, it was no threat to official YHWHism; the sanctuaries were now devoted exclusively to the worship of YHWH. Then, one need but ask: What could the prophets have done? They constituted only an infinitesimal minority of YHWH purists. Isaiah parades their impotence. He cries out three times in succession *mālĕ'û . . . wattimālē' . . . wattimālē'* (2: 6–8), namely, that the land is overflowing with idolatrous practices, "They bow down to the work of their hands, to what their fingers have wrought" (v. 8). This outburst only reflects his helplessness and frustration. Instead of excoriating his people, he figuratively shrugs his shoulders and throws up his hands. Since Isaiah has no alternative, he can only prophesy that on some future day (*bayyôm hahû'*) "the idols will vanish completely . . . on that day (*bayyôm hahû'*) men shall fling away, to the moles (?) and the bats, the idols of silver and the idols of gold, which they made for worshiping" (vv. 18, 20).

In the seventh century, the picture begins to change. The doctrine of One God strikes roots and spreads among the masses. One reason, in the main, is responsible: the book of Deuteronomy (or its kernel), which testifies that YHWH has placed all idols in all their forms—either for YHWH or for other gods, public or private—under total ban. Furthermore, the Deuteronomist wages an ongoing polemic against Asherah (Olyan 1988: 73), especially to dissociate her from the worship of YHWH (Binger 1997: 125). And Deuteronomy's adoption and promulgation by Josiah, the king, and Hilkiah, the high priest, become a permanent, irreversible turning point in the history of Israelite religion. This time, the prophets and the Deuteronomist's disciples declare war on idolatry. Apparently they persuaded many to discard their idolatrous practices so that when struck by the catastrophe of 586, they could justifiably protest that "the parents have eaten sour grapes and the children's teeth are set on edge" (Jer 31:28 [29]; Ezek 18:2; see Lam 5:7). And perhaps precisely because the deuteronomic campaign succeeds so well, the editors of Kings have no choice but to make Manasseh the scapegoat for the destruction (2 Kgs 21:10–11; 23:26–27; 24:3–4, 20; cf. Jer 15:4). In the meantime, the Hezekian and Josianic reforms come and go, but domestic idolatry persists, despite its explicit and vehement denunciation by Deuteronomy and its protagonists. In turn, this arouses the ire of Jeremiah and Ezekiel, which accounts for the lopsided numbers of biblical condemnations of idolatry between the eighth and the seventh to sixth century.

Addendum: *Asherah*

I would like to add a speculative suggestion on the nature of Manasseh's idolatry. After the finding of the Kuntillet Ajrud and Khirbet El Qom inscriptions, the possibility has been raised that the people-at-large worshiped Asherah as YHWH's consort (Margalit 1990; Hadley 1994; Binger 1997: passim). This supposition would explain the proliferation of Asherah in the vicinity of Israelite *bamôt* (2 Kgs 21:3). In particular, it would throw light on "the idolatry" of Manasseh, who installed a sculpted image (*pesel*, 2 Kgs 21:7; *pesel hassemel*, 2 Chr 33:7; *hassemel*, 2 Chr 33:15) of Asherah within the Jerusalem Temple. One should pay close attention to the Deuteronomist's wording of 2 Kgs 21. Whereas Manasseh is smeared with the sweeping but vague accusation that he constructed altars for Baal in the land (2 Kgs 21:3; cf. 23:5) and for astral deities in the Temple courtyards (2 Kgs 21:5), the text reaches its strident climax when it indicts Manasseh for having placed an image of Asherah in the sanctuary proper (2 Kgs 21:7; cf. 23:6; see also Binger 1997: 125–26). Did Manasseh set the Asherah image within the Holy of Holies alongside the Ark and its cherubic throne? If so, Manasseh was thereby not abandoning his loyalty to YHWH, but worshiping him together with his consort Asherah. That references to Asherah are not necessarily negative is exemplified by King Asa, who is looked upon with favor by the deuteronomistic historian (1 Kgs 15:11), though he cuts down Asherah's *mipleṣet* 'abominable thing(?)' but not Asherah herself (1 Kgs 15:13)!

Moreover, one is surprised by only four references to Asherah among the prophetic indictments (Isa 17:8; 27:9; Jer 17:2; Mic 5:13), all voiced in the masculine plural and, hence, even if not additions to the text, denoting cult objects rather than the goddess. Thus the objections in the Bible to Asherah are scant and betray a greater acceptance of Asherah worship than the Deuteronomist would allow (with Hadley 1994: 240). This deduction from the text could also be abetted by logic: since YHWH may have been associated with Palestinian forms of El (Miller 1980), it stands to reason that the El–Asherah (Ilu–Athirat) relationship obtaining in Ugarit was transferred by the people to YHWH–Asherah.

Why, then, did Manasseh and the general populace, who bought or carved statues or figurines representing Asherah, arouse the ire of the deuteronomistic YHWH priests? If the Decalogue is used as a grid, the conflict raged over the second commandment, not the first. Popular opinion could well have declared that Asherah was not just another god, but an indispensable adjunct of YHWH, and an image of Asherah need not diminish fealty to him. Monotheistic priests, however, would reply that YHWH forbade all images, and for support they would cite the hallowed Sinaitic prohibition *lō' ta'áśûn 'ittî 'ĕlōhê kesep wē'lōhê zāhāb lō' ta'áśû lākem* 'With me you shall not make any gods of silver, nor shall you make for yourselves any gods of gold' (Exod 20:20 [23]), an exegetical application of the second commandment (cf. Ibn Ezra; Cassuto 1951a; etc.). That is, YHWH forbids any image to be associated with himself, possibly a veiled reference to Asherah.

Moreover, it is even possible that the YHWH exclusivists would not have taken offense if Asherah were aniconic, because it was not the concept of Asherah as consort that incensed them, but that she was imaged in a physical form (just as later rabbinic literature expressed the concept of the earthly presence of God by the feminine but incorporeal Shekina; details in Urbach 1979: 37–65).

Recently, Lutzky (1996) has made a strong case for rendering Ezekiel's *sēmel haqqin'â hammaqneh* as "the image of the Creatress which provokes to jealousy" (Ezek 8:3). (Freedman, however, informs me [correctly] that *haqqin'â*, indeed, is YHWH's consort, but she is not "the Creatress" [from the root *qnh*] but the female equivalent of *'ēl qannā'* 'The Zealous One'.) It already had been suggested by scholars that Ezekiel was referring to Manasseh's time, and this statue was the one set up by Manasseh (e.g., Greenberg 1983a: 168). On the basis of Ugarit's description of Asherah as *qnyt 'lm* 'Creatress of the gods' (CTA 4, I, 23; IV, 32) and the nearly obsolete BH verb *qānâ* 'create' (Gen 14:19, 22; Deut 32:6; Ps 139:13; Prov 8:22), as well as the theophoric name *'elqānâ* (1 Sam 1:4–8; Exod 6:24; etc.) and the inscriptional evidence for *'l qn 'rs* (at eighth-century Karatepe and Jerusalem; see Miller 1980), it is possible to hypothesize that what outraged the deuteronomistic reformers even more than finding Asherah's image in the Temple was attributing to her creative powers that were independent of those of YHWH. This study will be published separately in *HUCA* (forthcoming).

E. NATIONAL PERSPECTIVES

Joosten (1996: 86–88) points to the following national characteristics in the H corpus:

1. The sabbatical and jubilee are national institutions. Whereas heretofore the sabbatical—that is, the determination to leave the land all or partially fallow—was left to the discretion of each landowner (see chap. 25, COMMENT C), H imposes the sabbatical on all the land and in the identical year (25:2b, 4). The jubilee is proclaimed on a fixed date by sounding a shofar "throughout your land" (25:9; see also II J).
2. The festivals are fixed calendrically (chap. 23).
3. The commandments are addressed to the people as a whole.
4. If the commandments are not followed, the catastrophe will befall the entire nation (18:24–28; 26:13–39).
5. "Transgression of the commandments by any individual brings guilt on the people, it defiles the land, it profanes the sanctuary." Correct. But this represents not H but P, a theology that H adopts and extends to the land.

6. "This conception (above) creates a certain tension between the freedom of the individual and his responsibility towards the collective." I deduce no tension. The doctrine of collective responsibility endorsed by P (and H) states that the sins of each individual affect the collective. However, herein lies a disagreement (polemic?) between H and P. P presumes that the sinner will receive his comeuppance together with the collective (vol. 1.258–61). But H will not allow the sinner to go scot-free in the meantime. The sinner who violates the sexual prohibitions (18:7–23; 20:10–21) is assuredly *contributing* to the *ultimate* exile of his people (18:28), but *in the meantime* he is subject to the punishment of *kārēt* (18:29).

I would add two small indications of H's national dimension:

7. The bread of presence functions as a reminder to God of his *bĕrît 'ôlām* 'eternal covenant' with the *entire* people of Israel (24:8b).
8. Both the bread of presence and the oil for the menorah (24:1–9) are to be provided by *all* of Israel.

Joosten (1996: 86–88) also notes the absence in H of the *nāśî* 'chieftain' and *zĕqēnîm* 'elders', found in P (4:22, 15, 22; 9:1), and the *melek* 'king', found in D (Deut 17:13–20). Priests in H are central figures, but they lack political power; nor do they hold judicial functions as in D (Deut 17:9, 12; 19:17; 21:5). Here several demurrers must be entered: The institutions of the elders and chieftains are taken for granted in P. That they rise to the fore is almost by accident: the elders because of their appearance as representatives of the people in the inaugural service (9:1, Bekhor Shor), and the elders together with the chieftains in their respective roles in the *ḥaṭṭāʾt* offering (4:12, 14, 22). There is no reason per se for denying that they existed in the time of H. But H throughout is directed to the individual *within his kin group* (*mišpāḥâ*) under the control of the paterfamilias. The chieftains and elders as representatives of the larger sociopolitical units—the kin group (*mišpāḥâ*), the tribe (*maṭṭeh*), the national assembly (*ʿēdâ, qāhāl*; cf. Milgrom 1979a; 1990a: 335–36), or subsequently the city (*ʿîr*)— are beyond H's juridical horizon. True, in H's theology, the action of the individual affects the collective, but judgment and punishment are carried out within the kin group by the paterfamilias.

It should be emphasized that the *zāqēn* is not synonymous with the paterfamilias. Though every *zāqēn* was a paterfamilias, not every paterfamilias was a *zāqēn*. Irrespective of the sociopolitical body, be it the kin group, the tribe, or the city, leadership was vested in the most powerful families, and it was their heads, acting in concert, who were responsible for the administrative and judicial decisions of their respective groups. The elders are "the grown-up men of powerful families who *de facto* have the power to rule" (Pederson 1926: 1.36). Thus the office of *zāqēn* undoubtedly existed in the time of H, but H had no need to refer to it. Its laws calling for the *kārēt* penalty were executed by the divine court. Those calling for the death penalty (*môt yûmāt*) would *theoretically* fall into the province of the paterfamilias. Here, however, the possibility exists that a weak paterfamilias may have, of necessity, had to turn to the *zāqēn* of his kin group (*mišpāḥâ*) to confirm and execute the death sentence. But these exceptions were not noted by H. It sufficed for H to state the law and its punishment. It was assumed that the paterfamilias was authorized to adjudicate and execute the law. The paterfamilias would also have had the authority to refer the case to the head of his kin group, the *zāqēn*. (For the equivalent office, the *šībum* in Mari and Babylon, see Klengel 1960; LU′ᴹᴱˢ ŠU.GI in Hatti, see Klengel 1965; see the summations of the evidence by Conrad 1980: 126–31 and van der Toorn 1996b: 192–94.)

There are only two crimes in Lev 17–27 that require the intervention of bodies larger than the kin group. The first is blasphemy (24:10–23). Like murder (Num 35), it is considered a national crime that can be adjudicated, sentenced, and punished only by the national assembly (*ʿēdâ*). Here, too, the tribal chieftains and elders play no judicial role. The only actors are the *šōmĕʿîm* 'those who hear (the blasphemy)' and the *ʿēdâ* 'assembly' (24:14). The other crime is Molek worship, which evokes the *immediate* intervention of the *ʿam haʾareṣ*. But as I contend (see NOTE on 20:2), this term does not designate a sociopolitical body. No differently from its attestation in P (4:27), it refers to the masses, the unorganized amorphous masses, literally "the people of the land," who for the egregious crime of Molek worship are empowered to act on their own (authorized lynching!) in order to quickly stamp out the source of pollution to the sanctuary and the name of YHWH (18:21; 20:3).

Thus the *ʿam haʾareṣ* cannot be the equivalent in the settled land to the wilderness *ʿēdâ*, as claimed by Joosten (1996: 44–47). As Joosten (almost) admits (46, n. 79), the mention of the *ʿēdâ* and *ʿam haʾareṣ* as two distinct bodies in the *ḥaṭṭāt* pericope (4:13, 27) creates difficulty for his theory. Nor can the *ʿam haʾareṣ* be related to the *ʿam* 'kin group' of the Shunammite (2 Kgs 4:13)—another suggestion of Joosten (1996: 92). First, it must not go unnoticed that the *ʿam haʾareṣ* is distinguished from the Molek worshiper's *mišpāḥâ* 'kin group' (20:4–5). There, the *mišpāḥâ* is punished for "covering up" the crime (see NOTE on 20:5), but not the *ʿam haʾareṣ*, even though the latter is guilty for having failed to put the miscreant to death! The only explanation for this ostensible lapse in divine justice is that the *ʿam haʾareṣ* is not an organized, responsible body. It refers, I submit, to the masses. Since this amorphous, unidentifiable mass did not spontaneously act, YHWH intervenes, imposing *kārēt* on the culprit and on all who may have assisted him.

Is there any sociopolitical term that can be associated with the *ʿam haʾareṣ*? I propose the *ʾezrāḥ* 'citizen, native'. This term always appears in tandem with the *gēr* 'alien' (16:29; 17:15; 18:26; 19:34; 24:16, 22; Exod 12:48, 49; Num 9:14; 15:13–14, 29, 30 [all H]; cf. Jos 8:33; Ezek 47:22). The only exception is 23:42 (stemming from exilic H_R), where it is uncoupled from the *gēr* because the latter applies to only aliens resident in the Promised Land, but not in Babylonia (see NOTE on 23:42). P's unspecific expression *nepeš ʾaḥat mēʿam hāʾareṣ* 'a person of the people of the land' becomes in H the concrete term *ʾezrāḥ* in order to contrast it with the term *gēr*.

F. COVENANTS: SINAITIC AND PATRIARCHAL

The Sinaitic covenant is first encountered in H in 18:2b. This is the only place where the long formula *'ănî YHWH 'ĕlōhêkem* 'I am YHWH your god' stands at the head of a legal pericope. Elsewhere, it closes a legal pericope, where its rendering is 'I YHWH your god (have spoken)' (e.g., 18:4b), and its short formula *'ănî YHWH* is rendered 'I YHWH (have spoken)' (e.g. 18:5b; see the discussion in NOTE on 18:2). The exceptional placement of the long formula in chap. 18 is redolent of the self-declaration formula at the head of the Decalogue (Exod 20:2), and it may imply that the laws of Lev 18 are equivalent in importance to the Decalogue.

The placement of the more complete Sinaitic self-declaration at the end of the blessings pericope (26:3–13) "I YHWH am your god who freed you from the land of Egypt" (26:13a) is a deliberate attempt to embody the thrust of the Sinaitic covenant: the blessings will occur if Israel deserves them by obeying YHWH's commandments (26:3).

There are many indications that the term *bĕrît* in the blessings and curses of chap. 26 nearly always refers to or includes the Sinaitic covenant: *lĕhaprĕkem 'et-bĕrîtî* '(your) breaking my covenant' (26:15) refers at least to all the commandments of priestly authorship, whereas the single occurrence of the same idiom *'et-bĕrîtî hāpēr* in regard to the patriarchal covenant (Gen 17:14b) refers to the nonobservance of one commandment, circumcision, the sign of P's covenant.

Again, the broken covenant avenged by the sword (26:25) must refer to the Sinaitic covenant. In contrast, elements of rewards and punishments are missing in the patriarchal covenant (cf. Knohl 1995: 141–45). The triad of punishments—sword, plague, famine (26:25–26)—explicitly follows in the wake of breaking a covenant (Jer 34:17; cf. Isa 33:8; Ezek 17:11–21), indicating that we are encountering the Sinaitic covenant.

Finally, the Sinaitic covenant is the exclusive reference of the binding formula between Israel and YHWH *wĕhāyîtî lākem lē'lōhîm wĕ'attem tihyû-lî lĕ'ām* 'I will (continue to) be your God, and you shall be my people' (26:12). Only half of this formula is found in the patriarchal covenant (Gen 17:8; the patriarchs are not an *'ām*!). The full formula occurs in Exod 6:7 (H), which adumbrates the Mosaic covenant (cf. Ibn Ezra [long] 1961; Ramban 1960; Sforno 1980; evidence of an H text).

The patriarchal covenant is explicitly mentioned in 26:42 (see also v. 9); it alone specifies the promise of land and seed. It is a conditional covenant (contrary to the consensus). Older covenantal references imply conditionality (e.g., Lev 18:19 [JE]). Moreover, since Gen 17:14 (cited above) is a priestly text, it posits P's basic doctrine that if the sanctuary is defiled by Israel's sins, God will abandon Israel to conquest, subjugation, and expulsion (see vol. 1.254–61, and NOTE on 26:42). This reciprocality is absent in patriarchal covenantal accounts.

All these observations on the nature of the covenant so frequently mentioned or implied in chap. 26 demonstrate that the word *bĕrît* refers mainly to the Sinaitic covenant (vv. 3, 12, 13, 15, 25), whereas the patriarchal covenant is the explicit subject of only a single verse (v. 42, possibly in v. 9). And even the latter two verses are not governed by unconditionality, as shown above. Thus it can no longer be proposed that chap. 26 refers to postexilic times when the alleged unconditional covenant was invoked to justify and spur Israel's return to its land.

The identification of the final covenantal reference in chap. 26, *bĕrît rī'šōnîm* (v. 45), has been debated for ages. The decision, I submit, is weighted in favor of the Sinaitic covenant. The syntax tips the scales. The adjoining clause *'ăšer hôṣē'tî-'ōtām* can only be rendered "whom I freed" or "for whose sake I freed" (Rashbam 1969). In either case, the reference is to the generation of the Exodus (see the discussion in NOTE on 26:45).

Why, then, was this covenant not called by its known designation *bĕrît sînay*, as in the envelope of chaps. 25–26 (25:1; 26:46)? I would suggest that H deliberately chose the rare term *rī'šōnîm* 'ancients' in order to refer to both covenants simultaneously. When *rī'šōnîm* occurs without the article (Deut 19:14; Isa 61:4; Ps 79:8), it denotes "prior *multiple* generations or ancients" (Joüon § 137 i). Thus this term is ideal in embracing the two covenants.

Therefore, the reciprocal obligations implied by H's covenant (26:15, 25a, 44a), the association of H's covenant with the Exodus generation (v. 45a), and the explicit references to the Decalogue (19:3–4) can only lead to the conclusion that H presumes a knowledge of the Sinaitic covenant. How, then, can one explain the absence of an account of the Sinaitic covenantal ceremony in H? I concur with Cross (1973: 320) that the H redactor relied on E's account (Exod 24:1–8). Moreover, H's redactional hand is clearly visible in the placement of priestly texts (Exod 19:1–2; 24:15b–18) as the encasement of the Sinaitic pericope, further indicating that H adopted the entire epic tradition of the Sinaitic events (see further NOTE on 26:45).

It can be demonstrated that the priestly term *hēqîm bĕrît* does not mean "establish a covenant," but "uphold/maintain a covenant" (see chap. 26, COMMENT A). Thus *wĕhăqîmōtî 'et-bĕrîtî* (26:9) should be rendered "I will uphold my covenant." In the reverse of this blessing, Israel annuls the covenant *lĕhaprĕkem 'et bĕrîtî* (26:15), which YHWH refuses to do (*lĕhāpēr bĕrîtî*, v. 44). The theological import of this antithesis between *hēqîm* and *hēpēr* is YHWH's commitment that he will never desert Israel however much it violates the covenantal terms. YHWH will punish Israel with increasingly severe natural and human scourges and finally banish it into exile. But since YHWH has never broken his commitment to the covenant, he is ready to restore Israel to its land once it contritely confesses its sins (see the discussion in NOTE on 26:44 and in COMMENT A).

Ezekiel reaffirms (*hēqîm*) the eternity of YHWH's covenant with Israel (16:60, 62). In addition, he avers that YHWH will make a new covenant (*kārat*): the blessings peace from enemies and voracious beasts, rain in its season, fertile crops, cessation of famine, breakage of "the bars of their yoke," and the (marriage) bond specifying that Israel will be YHWH's people, and YHWH will be Israel's God, which in H is a *conditional* promise (Lev 26:3–13)—in keeping with the Sinaitic covenant—in Ezekiel becomes an everlasting (i.e., *unconditional*) covenant (Ezek 34:26–30; see 37:26, and the discussion in Greenberg 1985: 291, 303–4).

Another indication that H is fully aware of the Sinaitic covenant is its artful interpretation of the Decalogue in structuring its message. For example, the original core of chap. 19 (Schwartz 1987: 120–23) consists of an inclusio (vv. 3–4, 30–32) based on commandments 1, 2, 4, 5, but nearly in reverse order 5, 4, 1, 2 in vv. 3–4 (parents, sabbath, idolatry, images) and chiastically 4, 2, 5, 1 in vv. 30–32 (sabbath, images [mediums], parents [elders], YHWH only). In the present MT, the appendix vv. 33–36 (Schwartz 1987: 120–23 see INTRODUCTION to chap. 19) ends with a restatement of the Decalogue's prologue (Exod 20:2), thereby forming an inclusio with v. 2b. Thus the H tradent responsible for the appendix was aware that chap. 19, which he had before him, contained an inclusio based on the Decalogue (vv. 3–4, 30–32). He therefore decided to give his expanded chap. 19 (including vv. 33–36) the form of the Decalogue by basing the inclusio on the prologue to the Decalogue. The Decalogue, however, is secondary to the content of chap. 19. That is, the God who freed Israel from Egypt (v. 36b) is also the holy God who can and should be emulated by his people through their fulfillment of the Decalogue as well as the additional duties enjoined upon Israel in this chapter (see further NOTE on 19:2aβ, b).

That the fifth and fourth commandments were chosen to head chap. 19's list (in that order) may reflect an attempt to show that ethics (respect for parents) and ritual (sabbath observance) are of equal importance, with a nod in favor of ethics. As to why the third commandment (*šāw'* vain oath) was omitted from the inclusio, the reason is perhaps due to the author's decision to place a lying (*šeqer*) oath into the pericope where he needed it, namely, in his supplement to 5:20–26 (19:11–12; see their NOTES). Alternatively, and preferably, H may have chosen commandments that deal with group (national) rather than individual wrongs (see below).

The comparison of 25:55b–26:2 with Exod 20 and Lev 19 (see also INTRODUCTION to 26:1–2, TABLES) shows that the former is a rephrasing of commandments 1, 2, and 4 of the Decalogue. The author, whom I identify as the exilic H tradent and redactor (H$_R$), bypassed the commandments that relate to individual behavior (3, 5, 6–10) in favor of the three commandments that, I maintain, are the determinants of Israel's existence and, hence, appropriate as a prolepsis of the curses (vv. 26:14–25) that follow.

This tradent (H$_R$) did not want the term *šabbāt* limited to the septennate (26:34–35, 43). He therefore added the weekly sabbath (26:2)—simply by quoting 19:30—so that Israel's exile would be extended by an additional ninety years (see the calculation and discussion in INTRODUCTION to 26:1–2). The content of 26:1–2—its stress on idolatry, rather than H's specification of sexual violations (18:24–30; 20:22), as the cause of Israel's exile; the use of *maśkît*, a late term (Num 35:42; Ezek 8:12); and the reference to the septennate (26:34–35, 43, exilic passages)—lead inexorably to the conclusion that 26:1–2 is also of exilic provenance. This conclusion is buttressed by the absence of any mention of idolatry in all of H (except for the Molek), a sign that 26:1–2 stems from a period later than the eighth century—the main provenance of H.

Thus 25:55b–26:2 (H$_R$) sums up in a condensed form the divine laws determinative of Israel's (return to and) continuous presence on its land by selecting and rephrasing three commandments of the Decalogue: exclusive adherence to YHWH, his aniconic worship, and the sabbath observance. Since H$_R$ is interested in only national factors of Israel's destiny, he cites 19:30 as his support text for the sabbath (rather than 19:3), because it includes another national factor: reverence for the sanctuary (i.e., the cult).

In sum, H$_R$, the redactor, is heir to four covenantal traditions: two patriarchal (Gen 15 [JE]; 17[P]) and two Sinaitic (Exod 19–24 [JE]; Lev 9[P]). Whereas the early priestly tradition (P) contains no verbal revelation (like the Decalogue) and ratification ceremony, but only YHWH's acceptance of the priestly service by incinerating the inaugural sacrifices (Lev 9:24), the later priestly redaction (H$_R$) incorporates the texts of both covenants of the epic source (Gen 15; Exod 19–24) alongside its own priestly tradition (Gen 17; Lev 9). In effect, we are witnessing the formation of the pentateuchal canon (see II R).

G. HOLINESS

The topic of holiness is discussed at length in the COMMENT to chap. 19, but it is limited to examples taken from that chapter. What follows here are introductory remarks omitted in the COMMENT and some illustrations from other chapters in H.

From a broader perspective, the theme of the entire book of Leviticus is holiness. Chapters 1–10 deal with the sanctuary service; 11–16, with the purification for access to the sanctuary; 17, with blood on the altar; 18–22, with how Israel can attain and priests retain holiness and how sexual violations and ancestor worship defile the sanctuary and the land; 23, with the sanctification of time; 24, with Israel's upkeep of the sanctuary and the desecration of YHWH's holy name; 25, with the laws of the "holy" land; 26, with how breaking the covenant causes God's abandonment of his sanctuaries leading to Israel's exile; and 27, with the laws of consecrations.

H's main distinction from P is that P restricts holiness to sanctified persons (priests) and places (sanctuaries), whereas H extends holiness in both its aspects to persons, the entire people of Israel, and to places, the entire promised (YHWH's) land (see II A). Moreover, his holiness is dynamic: Israel must attain it (19:2; 21:8 LXX; 22:32; see their NOTES), and priests must sustain it (21:15; 22:16; see their NOTES).

Israel is enjoined to be holy because YHWH is holy (19:2). This does not mean that Israel can achieve or even imitate YHWH's holiness. There is an unbridgeable gap between them. Holiness implies separation, distinction (see COMMENT on chap. 19). In the priestly texts, the Masoretes consistently and meticulously distinguish between divine and human (Israelite, priestly, Naziritic) holiness. When holy refers to God, it is written *plene*, *qādôš* (six times); referring to Israel, it is defective, *qādōš* (ten times). Note the following parade examples:

wihyîtem qĕdōšîm kî qādôš 'ănî (11:44, 45)

qĕdōšîm tihyû kî qādôš 'ănî YHWH (19:2)

wihyîtem lî qĕdōšîm kî qādôš 'ănî YHWH (20:7)

qādōš yihyeh-lak kî qādôš 'ănî YHWH (21:8)

But, when the prescriptions (for holiness) in chap. 19 are examined, though most of them are negative (approximately thirty), many are positive (approximately fourteen). In this latter sense, holiness implies *imitatio dei*, namely, Israel should emulate God by living a godly life. Observance of the divine commandments leads to God's attribute of holiness, but not to the same degree—not to God, but to godliness. Just as the priests, who are innately holy, are qualified to enter into God's presence in the sanctuary, so Israel, by following all YHWH's commandments (19:37), can attain holiness (19:2) and qualify for admission metaphorically into the providence (i.e., the presence and protection) of God.

Nonetheless, when one examines the holiness contexts outside chap. 19, they are nearly all negative. That is, Israel's separation from God has to be emulated by Israel's separation from other peoples. This is explicitly stated in 20:24–25. As YHWH has separated (*hibdîl*) Israel from the nations, so Israel must separate itself *from them* by its dietary system (see also the context of 11:43–45). Conversely, observing the dietary laws will ipso facto keep Israel from intermingling with others. The necessity to keep apart from the neighboring peoples is spelled out in chaps. 18 and 20. Incest and other sexual abominations attributed to Egypt and Canaan are defiling to Israel and to the land and lead to *kārēt* for their indulgers and exile for the people (18:24–30; see the reservations in NOTES on 18:3).

Mary Douglas (1999: 35) defines purity as "adequately segregated." This can also serve as a definition of holiness. Indeed, both purity and holiness have to be carved out of areas of the impure and the profane, respectively, and they must be safeguarded (segregated) against incursions of the ever virulent impurity. The two priestly traditions, P and H, differ in that H ascribes a dynamic quality to holiness, which counters the aggressive, malevolent force of impurity and empowers it to advance on and reduce the area and control of impurity (see the diagram and its detailed explanation in COMMENT, chap. 19). Thus the notion of segregation (or separation) bridges the two major systems in Leviticus, P's purity (chaps. 11–16) and H's holiness (constellated in chaps. 19–22 and passim). To be sure, since all these qualities in H's monotheistic thought are inert, they possess no intrinsic power. They can be activated only by human deeds. Israel's sins generate impurity, but it can be transmuted into the pure by purificatory rituals. YHWH has bestowed upon Israel an additional power. It can transmute the pure (and the profane) by observing the divine commandments.

Selected examples of holiness not discussed in the COMMENT to chap. 19 are the following:

1. The only sanctums available to Israel are the meat of the well-being offering (*šĕlāmîm*; 7:11–21; 19:5–8; 22:29–30) and the use of YHWH's name (e.g., in oaths). Desecration is caused by eating sacrificial portions in a state of impurity (7:20–21; cf. 22:3–7), swearing a false oath (19:12), worshiping ancestors (20:1–6; see their NOTES), and faulty sacrificial procedures (see NOTE on 22:32). These rules hold for priests as well as Israelites. The result is the loss of whatever holiness the Israelite has attained or the priest has inherited. Worst of all, in H there is neither remedy nor expiation for this indiscretion.

I have argued that 22:24–25 comprises a single taboo on animals with defective genitals intended for the altar: animals brought to the altar (v. 24a), animals in the land (v. 24b), and imported animals (v. 25). Thus gelded animals and castrated priests are barred from the altar, but not from the land. Moreover, a sanctuary could own gelded beasts of burden, castrated priests could benefit from the sacrifices (21:22), and castrated Israelites could enter the sanctuary to present their sacrifices. Perhaps this implied stance of H influenced the reversal of D's edict barring castrated Israelites from "entering the congregation of YHWH" (Deut 23:12) in the prophecy of Isaiah of the exile (Isa 56:3–5). Thus H compromises its rigid stance on the "holy land" and allows for the gelding of the flocks and herds so essential for better-quality meat, manageable beasts of burden, and the production of wool (Wapnish and Hesse 1991: 34–35).

2. As Israel sanctifies the sabbath by abstaining from work (Exod 20:8–9; Deut 5:12–14; Jer 17:22, 24), so Israel is commanded to sanctify every fiftieth year (Lev 25:1–12). In both cases, *qiddēš* (*Pi'el*) is used, but for the sabbath it means "treat as holy." The jubilee, in contrast, is sanctified by the positive act of proclamation by the blowing of a shofar—a rite of sanctification.

3. The doctrine of the "holy land," though not explicitly stated in Scripture, is implied (cf. Exod 15:17; Isa 11:9; 57:13; Jer 31:23; Ps 78:54). But H, which in legislation extends P's sacred sphere from the sanctuary to the land, never calls the land "holy." There are two basic theological reasons. The first is the implication that holiness inheres in nature, a notion that monotheistic H implicitly rejects (see NOTE on "do not desecrate the name of your God," 18:21). As pointed out by Joosten (1996: 176, 169, n. 1), H refrains from using expressions like *'ereṣ/'admat/naḥălat YHWH*, though they are found elsewhere, "lest it be inferred that there was a natural relationship between YHWH and the land." Secondly, since YHWH is the owner of the land (25:23), the "holiness" of the land is but a reflection of YHWH's holiness, and it is palpable in the land only when Israel fulfills his commandments (see NOTES on 26:11–12).

4. Inherited land must revert to the owner at the jubilee. If he consecrates (or sells) its usufruct, he, in effect, leases the land until the jubilee. Only if he consecrates the land *after* selling it (27:20) is he indicating that he does not want the land back, and the land then becomes sanctuary property after the jubilee. The basic postulate is that the *sanctuary takes no priority over the landowner.* Inherited land always reverts to the owner except if by word (27:28)

or act (27:20–21) he consecrates his land (and not just its usufruct) to the sanctuary.

Perhaps this is the priestly response to the condemnation by the eighth-century prophets of the growing latifundia of the time, both by avaricious creditors (e.g., Isa 5:8–10; Mic 2:1–2) and by covetous priests, who might have looked enviously at the vast land tracts owned by their counterparts in Egypt and Mesopotamia. Thus H devised the jubilee system whereby the status quo ante concerning the land would be restored and indentured Israelites would be released (25:8–43). Also, H made consecrated land subject to the jubilee so that priests could not participate in the land-grabbing practices of their priestly neighbors.

H. ETHICS

P's ethics—rather, its alleged absence—have been discussed in vol. 1. 21–26 (see also APPENDIX C). H's ethics are touched on in the pericopes on the resident alien (II N), women's rights (II L), democratization (II L), the jubilee (II K), holiness (II G), and the rationales (II B). Here, two topics will be treated: H's postulate (implied) that ethics rank equally with ritual, and H's concern for the underprivileged and helpless. The examples are culled from chaps. 19 and 25.

The bonding of ethics and ritual is not unique to Israel. It abounds in Mesopotamia—for example, Surpu, tablet II (Reiner 1958; for the text, see vol. 1.21–23), the Bilingual Hymn to Nanurta, ll. 3–7 (Lambert 1960: 119), the Nanshe Hymn, ll. 136–71 (Heinpel 1981: 90–93)—and is exemplified in Egypt's sacral sphere by an inscription on a door of the temple of Edfu (Weinfeld 1982a: 233–35; for the text, see APPENDIX C). What, however, is unique to Israel—rather, to H—is the subsumation of ethics in addition to rituals under the rubric of holiness. All the pentateuchal codes raise the issue of holiness. Here, H takes a giant step forward. Other codes restrict holiness to ritual commandments (abstention from sabbath labor, Exod 20:8–11 [JE]; Deut 5:12–15 [D]; eating carcasses, Exod 22:30 [JE]; Deut 14:21 [D]; idolatry and mourning rites, Deut 7:5–6 and 14:1–2 [D]), whereas H lists ethical prescriptions alongside rituals as determinants of holiness. H also differs from the prophets, but in the other direction. The prophets rank ethics as supreme. YHWH's holiness is characterized mainly by ethics: *wayyigbah YHWH ṣĕbā'ôt bammišpāṭ wĕhā'ēl haqqādôš niqdaš biṣdāqâ* 'YHWH OF HOSTS is exalted by justice and the holy God is shown holy by his righteousness' (Isa 5:16); indeed, for some of the prophets, Israel's national destiny is determined *exclusively* by its ethical behavior (Kaufmann 1947: 3.76–79; 1960: 365–67). H, however, insists on the equal and inseparable role of ritual in the prescription for the holy life. Possibly, the fourth and fifth commandments of the Decalogue (sabbath and parents) were chosen to head the list of the prescriptions of holiness (19:3), even ahead of the first and second commandments (19:4), in order to illustrate from the start that ethics (respect for parents) and ritual (sabbath observance) are of equal importance.

Note that 19:9–18 deal exclusively with ethical prescriptions (see also vv. 29, 32, 33–34, 35–36).

H's concern for the underprivileged and helpless is exemplified not only by its numerous citations of them, but also by its formulaic and lexical characteristics. A number of examples should suffice. The closure of nearly every prescription in chap. 19 is *'ănî YHWH 'ĕlōhêkem* 'I YHWH your God (have spoken)'. This formula is explicitly defined at the opening of the chapter by the addition of the word *qādôš* 'holy': *qādôš 'ănî YHWH 'ĕlōhêkem* 'I YHWH your God *am holy*' (v. 2). Hence anyone who disobeys YHWH's injunctions concerning the care of the underprivileged and the alien is desecrating YHWH's holiness. Similarly, chap. 25 resorts to this formula to close its major units (vv. 17, 38, 55) and uses exhortative admonitions as an inclusio: *lō' tônû* 'do not cheat/oppress' (vv. 14, 17); *lō'-tirdeh bô bĕpārek* 'do not rule over him with harshness' (vv. 43a, 46bβ). Both chapters also utilize the closing formula *wĕyārē'tā mē'ĕlōhêka* 'you shall fear your God' (19:14, 32; 25:17, 36, 43). Is it no accident that this formula is attached to those prescriptions where the handicapped are the most vulnerable (the deaf and blind, elders, the indentured servant)? Their case cannot be adjudicated in a human court, but YHWH has witnessed the exploitation *and will prosecute*.

H also has a penchant for generalizations (in contrast to P, see I D). Thus the injunction "do not curse (*tĕqallēl*) a deaf person, and before a blind person do not place a stumbling block (*mikšōl*)" (v. 14) cannot be taken literally; rather, "deaf" and "blind" are metonyms for all the helpless, and "curse" and "stumbling block" stand for abuse and harm, respectively. The full importance of this injunction is that though the deaf does not know who insulted him or the blind who hurt him, God knows and he will punish accordingly. In contrast to the codes of the ancient Near East, in which only verifiable injury or loss is adjudicable, Israel's law has moved beyond them to ethical laws under the surveillance of a caring God (D. Stewart).

To be sure, concern for the underprivileged—the poor, the widow, the orphan, and the alien—is consistently reiterated throughout Scripture (Exod 22:20–23; Lev 19:9–10, 13, 33–34; Deut 15:18–19; 24:14, 17; 27:15; Jer 7:6; 22:3; Zech 7:10). The prophets repeatedly rail against their neglect and exploitation (Isa 1:17, 23; 3:14–15; 10:2; Jer 5:8; Ezek 16:49; 18:17; 22:7, 29; Amos 8:4; Mal 3:5; cf. Pss 82:3; 94:6). H differs from them in going beyond outcries and implorations. It legislates concrete measures in order *to prevent their impoverishment* (see the jubilee laws, II K).

Ostensibly, H has no concern for the needy persons listed above since they are not mentioned in H, except for a single law affirming the indigent's rights to the "leftovers" of the harvest (19:9–10; repeated in 23:22). But it must be borne in mind that H discards empty implorations and focuses on concrete efficacious measures. H, moreover, is mainly the product of the eighth century, when family ties were strong and the patriarchal structure was still in place. The widow and orphan would be the charge of the nearest relative of the deceased (*gō'ēl*; see Ruth 3:13; 4:4). The alien (*gēr*) would be the responsibility of the owner of the land on which he resided (25:6), and the Levites were in most part employed in the flourishing regional sanctuaries throughout the land (but see II Q).

The eighth century was characterized by national prosperity, which brought in its wake urbanization, latifundia, and other social injustices decried by the prophets (cited above) and solved (in theory) by the priestly H (see the jubilee laws, II K). In the main, however, every poor Judahite belonged to some household (*bêt 'āb*) or, if that was wanting, to a kin group (*bêt 'ābōt, mišpāḥâ*). The situation changed rapidly for the worse when Judah was inundated by hordes of landless, destitute Northern refugees, among whom the widow, orphan, alien, and Levite abounded.

The paucity of references to the poor in H (a single verse and its copy, 19:10; 23:22) should not be misjudged. On the one hand, despite D's plethora of references to the gifts from the produce for the orphan and the widow, namely, of tithes (Deut 14:29; 26:12, 13), of the harvest (Deut 24:19–21), and of the Festivals of Weeks and Booths (Deut 16:11, 14), the poor are excluded from these gifts and, instead, Israel is exhorted to grant them interest-free loans (Deut 15:7–11; 23:20–21; 24:10–13; cf. Exod 22:24–26 [JE]), the assumption being that the poor can work off their debts but the orphan and widow cannot. H, on the other hand, does not discriminate between these groups. As long as they are poor, they are entitled to glean from the crops; they need not depend on the unpredictable beneficence of the rich (but see my reservations, II Q).

The refinement and sensitivity of H's concerns toward the helpless can be illustrated by the following examples:

1. *lō' ta'amōd 'al-dam rē'ekā* 'You shall not stand aloof by the blood of your fellow' (19:16b). If this rendering is correct, then it is not permitted to remain on the sidelines of one's endangered fellow. The rabbis correctly infer, "If one sees someone drowning, mauled by beasts, or attacked by robbers, one is obligated to save him, but not at the risk of one's life" (*b. Sanh.* 73a). In H's court, the "silent majority" would be guilty.

Not surprisingly—though I was surprised when I realized it—a similar ethical law derives from P's concept of sin: the *inadvertent* sinner also pollutes the sanctuary and must "repair" the damage by an appropriate purification (*ḥaṭṭā't*) offering (vol. 1.254–61). Nonetheless, it should be clear that H has raised the culpability to unparalleled heights. It includes not only unintentionality but also passivity, a nonexistent category, as far as I can tell, in world jurisprudence, both late and modern.

2. The structured sequence in Lev 19:17–18 clearly addresses the needs of the helpless.

19:17

Prohibition:	You shall not hate your kinsperson in your heart;
Remedy:	Reprove your fellow openly,
Rationale:	so that you will not bear punishment because of him.

19:18

Prohibition:	Rather you shall not take revenge or nurse a grudge against members of your people.
Remedy:	You shall love your fellow as yourself.
Rationale:	I YHWH (have spoken).

These two verses form parallel panels (Schwartz 1987: 145), which may aid in discerning the intent of the author. For example, the remedy for taking revenge and nursing a grudge is extending love (for the meaning of love, see below). The ethical emphasis here is on thought, the perils of which were sensitively apprehended by the rabbis who declare that *śin'at ḥinnām* 'causeless hatred' was responsible for the destruction of the Second Temple (*b. Yoma* 9b).

3. The verb *'āhab* 'love' (19:18) signifies not only an emotion or attitude, but also deeds. Such is its meaning in suzerainty treaties (Moran 1963) and elsewhere (see NOTE). The medieval exegetes come to the same conclusion by noting that *'āhab* takes the preposition *le*, which they render as "for," that is, do good as you would do for yourself. Indeed, all four attestations of *'āhab le* (19:18, 34; 1 Kgs 5:15; 2 Chr 19:2) imply doing, not feeling (Malamat 1963).

4. That the injunction to love the alien "as yourself" (19:34) is the exact counterpart of "you shall love your fellow as yourself" (19:18) is shown by the switch to the singular *wĕ'āhabtā* within a plural context and by the use of the dative *lô*, which matches *lĕrē'ăkā*. This, arguably, is the ethical summit not only in this chapter, but in all of Scripture.

5. The theological innovation of H's law of redemption is that YHWH is the ultimate redeemer (25:24; see the jubilee laws, II K). If indebtedness causes the sale of any of YHWH's land, the nearest kinsperson is obligated to redeem it and return it to the owner. He may retain it only to cover his costs, but by the unilateral decree of the divine owner, he must return it to the human owner at the jubilee. Here, H has broken with the hoary institution of clan ownership of property (cf. Jer 32). Henceforth, the concern of the law is to guarantee property rights for the individual.

Ethical concerns are also visible in the sale of city houses, which (in distinction to farmhouses) are not subject to the law of the jubilee (for the rationale, see the jubilee laws, II K). Why, then, allow their redemption even for one year (25:29)? Here we touch on the merciful foundations of the jubilee legislation. No differently from the destitute farmer (25:25), the urbanite may have been driven by economic constraints to sell his home. Hence for a short time, no more than a year, an opportunity is granted to him (and his kin group) to regain his holding.

6. Do not charge the Israelite debtor interest as if he were a resident alien (25:35; see NOTES). This constitutes a reversal of antichresis prevalent elsewhere. In this way, whatever the debtor earns amortizes the principal in addition to supporting his family. If his destitution forces him to become an indentured servant, his status is that of a hireling, not a slave. He may not be treated "harshly"

(25:43, 46b). Implied is that if he finds the creditor's conditions too severe or the wages too low, he can seek another employer. Again, his work amortizes the principal, pays off the loan, retrieves his land, so he can make a fresh start. If he does not succeed on his own, the safety net of the jubilee awaits him (or his heirs). The institution of slavery is totally abolished for the Israelite. This constitutes a practical advantage over the slave laws of Exod 21 (JE) and Deut 15 (D). The latter legislation does not provide him with resources, there is no indication that his land is returned to him, and the probability is strong that it will not be long before he is indentured once again.

I. LAND

Joosten's (1996: 137–92) discussion of "land" is the centerpiece of his book. Among his many well-argued points is his convincing demonstration that H predicates an Israel in control of its land. For example, it can impose its laws on the gēr (II N), issue prohibitions on food and sex (10–21, 25), prescribe the release of Israelite debt-slaves at the jubilee (25:39–43), and impose the death penalty (20:9–16; 24:23). The conclusion is inescapable that H is preexilic (see I J).

Rather than repeating what he says so excellently, I would offer a few corrections and add a few comments of my own.

1. I differ with Joosten on one of his cardinal positions. He (1996: 189, 92) claims that the "land is YHWH's because his sanctuary is located there, and after the expulsion of the Israelites (26:33–34), YHWH will no longer dwell in the land, for his sanctuaries will have been destroyed" (26:31). If so, by what right did YHWH have the land expel the Canaanites for polluting the land (18:24–30)—unless the land was already his! Besides, the epic (JE) Song of the Sea expressly states that "you brought them and planted them in the mountain of your inheritance" (Exod 15:17a; cf. Ps 78:54). Again, the land must have been YHWH's even before Israel's arrival. Thus, YHWH chose this land as the future residence of Israel, a grant not abrogated even if Israel would be expelled from it (see 26:40).

2. That sexual violations (among others) pollute the land is expressly stated by D (Deut 24:1–4; cf. Jer 3:1–10). But only H states that the punishment is inexorably exile (18:24–28; 20:22–23). H's concept of pollution is noncultic, but it is real. Indeed, it is more devastating than P's cultic impurity: it is nonexpiable (see II O). Nonetheless, the polluted land must be cleansed. When the entire earth was polluted in Noah's time, it was cleansed by a flood. Presumably, Israel's polluted land is purified by time. This can be deduced from the explicit statements that the land must be allowed to make up for the sabbaths that Israel has failed to observe (26:34–35; for the nuanced difference, see NOTE on 26:43–44).

3. Israel's possession of the land is called naḥălâ 'inheritance' in D, 'ăḥuzzâ 'holding' in H, and both in P. H insists on calling the land YHWH's and Israel

its *gērîm* 'alien residents, tenants' (25:23); hence, H eschews the term *naḥălâ* which implies permanent possession.

4. All of H's laws, though given to Israel in the wilderness, are intended to be operative in the land. According to Joosten (1996: 139), four laws are laid down for life in the wilderness camp: blood disposal (chap. 17), the menorah oil (24:1–4), the bread of presence (24:5–9), and blasphemy/talion (24:10–23). That all four laws are expected to be in force in the land is indicated by the term *ḥōq/ḥuqqat 'ōlām* in the first three, and since the blasphemy incident gives rise to a series of talion laws (24:15–22), permanence is obviously intended. Joosten, however, overlooks the law of Num 5:1–3 (H), which states that the corpse-contaminated (*ṭāmē' lānepeš*), the scale-diseased (*ṣārûa'*), and the genitally diseased (*zāb*) must be sent out of the camp. This omission is important because it undermines his claim that the camp is a paradigm for the land. Those persons might have been expelled from the city (as in the explicit case of the *ṣārûa'*, e.g., 2 Kgs 7:3), but certainly not from the land. In fact, Num 5:1–3 indicates that the camp is a paradigm of *the city* (see also 14:45).

5. Israel and its land belong to YHWH. Of Israel, YHWH declares *'ăbāday hēm* 'they are my slaves' (25:42) and of the land YHWH declares *kî-lî hā'āreṣ* 'for the land is mine' (25:23). Neither can be sold, but only leased. The buyer purchases only the usufruct of the field or the labor of the "slave" calculated as a yearly wage. Even then, the buyer's hold on the purchased land or slave is limited. The land and slave are subject to the laws of redemption and jubilee. The purchase price is calculated according to the years remaining until the jubilee (see the jubilee and redemption laws, chap. 25). The relationship of consecrated land to the jubilee is discussed in II G, and a résumé on the jubilee laws is given in II K, with details in chap. 25, COMMENTS A–B.

J. SABBATH AND SABBATICAL

The sabbath, the sabbatical, and the Day of Purgation are the only times designated by the superlative *šabbat šabbātôn*, literally 'a most restful rest' (Exod 31:15; 35:2; Lev 23:3; 25:4; 16:31; 23:32 [all H]), when the total cessation from *kol-mělā'kâ* 'all labor' is enjoined.

The sabbath is the only ritual observance commanded in the Decalogue (Exod 20:8–11) and the only commandment grounded in creation (Exod 20:11; cf. 31:17). It is a *miqrā'-qōdeš* 'sacred occasion' (Lev 23:3), literally 'a proclamation of holiness'. Normally, the phrase would be followed by *yihyeh lākem* 'it shall be for you' (cf. 23:21, 24 [split], 27, 36). Its inclusion in 23:3, however, would contradict the following attribution, *šabbāt hi(w)' laYHWH* 'it is YHWH's Sabbath' (23:3; Exod 31:15; 35:2). In H, YHWH always refers to the sabbath as *šabbětōtay* 'my sabbaths' (Exod 31:13; Lev 19:3, 30; 26:2). That is, it is not for Israel to proclaim the day. Its septiminal regularity was set at creation (Gen 2:3).

It is independent of the lunar calendar, whose months, hence its festivals, must be set and proclaimed by Israel.

The sabbath is holy because God sanctified it (Gen 2:3; Exod 20:11; 31:15; 35:2; Neh 9:14). But for H and H-influenced passages, it is incumbent upon Israel to sanctify the sabbath (Exod 20:8; Deut 5:12; Jer 17:24, 27; Ezek 20:20; 44:24; Neh 13:22) and not to desecrate it (Ezek 20:13, 16, 24, 38; 22:8; Neh 13:8). This accounts for the sabbath as the very first injunction in chap. 19 under the rubric "You shall be holy" (Lev 19:2, 3). Moreover, in the "holiness" list of Lev 19, it is the only repeated injunction (vv. 3, 30). In the latter verse, it is coupled with the sanctuary, indicating that its sacred time shares equal importance with the sacred space of the sanctuary (see II G).

In the NOTE on *mô ʿădê YHWH* 'the fixed times of YHWH' (23:2), I have argued that the sabbath pericope (23:2aβ–3) is the product of H$_R$, an exilic tradent who calls the sabbath a *mô ʿēd*, a term found in no other references to the sabbath. Moreover, in contrast to the rest of the festivals listed in the calendar, the sabbath contains no mention of sacrifices. Thus I have concluded that its tradent (probably the H redactor of Leviticus; see II R) lived among the exiles in Babylonia, where the Temple and the sacrificially bound *mô ʿădîm* of Lev 23:4–38 and Num 28–29 were inoperative. He therefore composed the passage Lev 23:2aβ–3 and framework Num 28:2aβ, b; 29:39 to indicate that the sabbath is one of the *mô ʿădê* YHWH 'fixed times of YHWH', and it is incumbent on Israel to observe it scrupulously.

The structure of the sabbath injunction (Lev 23:3) is clearly the basis of H's prescription for the sabbatical year (25:1–7; cf. 23:2aβ, b with 25:4). The differences in the wording are slight but significant.

1. The sabbatical is not for YHWH, but for the land (*šabbat hāʾareṣ*).
2. Total rest (*šabbat šabbātôn*) falls on the land, not on the Israelites. Hence Israelites may work during the sabbatical year at all occupations other than farming.
3. Whereas God instituted the sabbath during the world's creation, Israel — not God — will henceforth institute the sabbatical. Hence the land's sabbath is not of, but "to YHWH."

A structural comparison between the two land-sabbatical passages, Lev 25:2–7 and Exod 23:10–11, demonstrates that the former is an expansion of the latter (Paran 1989: 29–34). The four stylistic and eight factual differences between the two are detailed in the INTRODUCTION to 25:2–7. Of special significance is that in contrast to Exodus's vague (and impractical) prescription *wĕʾākĕlû ʾebyōnê ʿammekā* 'may the needy of your people eat (of the aftergrowth)' (Exod 23:11a), H shows once again its pragmatic side (see II K) by ordaining that in the sabbatical year, the landowner is personally responsible to distribute the aftergrowth to all those under his authority (*haggārîm ʿimmāk*; for this interpretation, see NOTE on 25:35). Thus the *gēr*, who is included in Exodus (23:9–11) is omitted in Leviticus, because he does not live on the landowner's property. H, therefore, groups him with the poor (Lev 19:10; 23:22) to be a recipient of charity.

K. JUBILEE, REDEMPTION, AND DESTITUTION

The basic postulate of the jubilee is 25:23–24:

> Furthermore, the land must not be sold beyond reclaim, for the land is mine; you are but resident aliens under my authority. Therefore, throughout the land you hold, you must provide redemption for the land.

"Land" here is Canaan, the promised land, and "you" refers to the people of Israel. They are to keep in mind that the owner of the land is YHWH and they are only resident aliens; that is, YHWH is the landlord, and the Israelites are his tenants.

The notion of YHWH's ownership of the land is found throughout Scripture (e.g., Exod 15:17; Isa 14:2, 25; Jer 2:7; Ezek 36:5; 38:16; Hos 9:3; Pss 10:16; 85:2). Divine ownership of the land of Canaan does not, however, delimit the boundaries of YHWH's control. The God who created the world by fiat (Gen 1[P]) and "whose glory is the fullness of the earth" (Isa 6:3; Levenson 1985: 141, 170–71) is also, of certainty, the ruler of the earth (cf. Halpern 1987: 96). An unbridgeable distinction between the two spaces is manifest: the land Canaan/Israel occupies a special place in the divine schema. It is set apart from all other earthbound territory; it is holy (implicit in H; see II G) and, hence, it imposes special requirements on its inhabitants.

Each Israelite clan has been assigned a plot of land (Num 26:52–56) that must always remain in its possession (Milgrom 1990a: 219, 480–82). Even when it is sold, it can always be reclaimed through a process called redemption (gě'ullâ), and every fiftieth year, called jubilee (yōbēl), it must be restored to its original owner. Nationwide institutions of debt cancellation and return of forfeited land were known in the ancient Near East (Weinfeld 1990a; 1995). It usually occurred when a king acceded to the throne. Its purpose was to "prevent the collapse of the economy under too great a weight of private indebtedness" (Edzard 1965: 225). However, it was generally limited to the king's retainers (Bar Maoz 1980) and subject to his whim. The biblical jubilee, in contrast, was immutable and periodic, and its laws were binding on every Israelite (for details, see NOTES on 25:9–10).

The text assumes that in the jubilee, the original owner is automatically restored to the land and kin group and that he no longer remains indebted to his creditor (see further NOTES on 25:25–49). The jubilee was intended to preserve the economic viability of the peasant farmer, but it did not protect urban property from alienation (cf. Bess 1963: 121). The jubilee provisions are directed solely to the land, since God owns the land, not to the cities, which are a human achievement (Muffs 1965b: 4. 11). The jubilee is also of pragmatic benefit to the creditor: a fifty-year period would give him ample time to recoup his loan (except if it was contracted close to the jubilee).

The institution of the jubilee (and redemption) is unavailable to the resident alien (gēr tôšāb). It is ironic that H has unambiguously proclaimed the absolute equality (in civil matters) between native and alien (24:22). This blatant contradiction can be resolved only by presuming that the axiom of YHWH's bestowal of inheritable land exclusively to the Israelite takes priority over the principle of the alien's equality before the law. Thus the discrimination against the alien rests not on his inaccessibility to the jubilee, but his inaccessibility to the land (remedied in Ezekiel's Law of the Temple, 47:22–23).

The principle of redemption is based on *imitatio dei*. YHWH redeems Israel whenever it is subjected (i.e., enslaved) by a foreign nation (e.g., the Egyptian bondage, Exod 6:6; 15:13, and the Babylonian Exile, Isa 35:5, 9; 43:1; 44:22, 23, etc.). Therefore, the nearest relative (gō'ēl 'redeemer') redeems his kinsman's sold land or the kinsman himself when he is enslaved by a non-Israelite. If, however, the human redeemer fails to intervene, then the divine redeemer acts—by his law of the jubilee.

The fundamental principle of redemption (with Pedersen 1926: 1.81–85) is that ancestral lands should never be alienated from the family (kin). At the moment the land is sold, the obligation falls on the redeemer to reclaim it. Contrary to general practice, as attested in Jer 32, H ordains that the property does not belong to the redeemer. He retains it until the jubilee; its usufruct will repay him his redemption costs. At the jubilee, the land reverts to the original owner, not to his clan. Thus H breaks the time-honored institution of clan ownership of property.

If an Israelite is forced by his utter destitution to sell his land and himself to his creditor, he never becomes a slave. His status is that of a śākîr 'hireling'. He receives a regular wage with which he can support his family and amortize his interest-free loan. If he still cannot pay off his loan, the safety net of the jubilee will rescue him (25:39–41). In this case, however, there is no redemption. Redemption applies, as stated above, only to sold land and to Israelites sold to non-Israelites. The redeemer might lend him the money, but he cannot hold him until the jubilee.

The jubilee and redemption laws are measures founded on theological principles to assist the Israelite farmer in times of economic stress. My reconstruction of his successive stages of impoverishment reads as follows:

1. In the event of crop failure, the Israelite farmer takes out a loan to purchase seed for the next year's crop. If the new crop fails, he is forced to sell part of his land to cover his debt. If he cannot redeem his land, his redeemer does, and the latter retains it until the jubilee (25:25–28).

2. The farmer takes out a new loan. He defaults again and loses the land (but not its title) to his creditor. If he still owes on his loan, he works his land as a tenant farmer. Though he has lost the land, its usufruct is still his. It amortizes

his loan (on which he pays no interest) or the land reverts to him at the jubilee (25:35–38).

3. If he still cannot pay off his loan, he forfeits not only his land but also its usufruct. He and his family enter the household of the creditor (25:41a, 54b). The debtor's status is that of a resident hireling, not a debt-slave. He receives wages that amortize his debt (vv. 39–43). He is a free person. If he finds his creditor's treatment too harsh, he is at liberty to find another employer. In stages two and three, the redeemer need not intervene. But if the indentured kinsman sells himself to a non-Israelite, his redeemer must intervene, and until the jubilee, the kinsman works for the redeemer (vv. 47–55).

The above is only a sampling of the significant laws and their implications, which are discussed in detail in NOTES on chap. 25, esp. vv. 25–54.

L. ISRAELITES: LAYMEN, PRIESTS, AND WOMEN

Both H and P presume that the people are responsible for supplying the sacrificial animals in the public cult. This is evidenced by the second-person plural *taqrîbû, wĕhiqrabtem* 'you (Israel) shall offer, present' (Num 28:3, 11, 19, 27[P]; Lev 23:8, 25, 27, 36 [bis] [H]). This grammatical usage is preceded by the explicit statement that opens P's public sacrificial calendar: *wayyĕdabbēr YHWH ʾel-mōšeh lēʾmōr ṣaw ʾet bĕnê yiśrāʾēl wĕʾāmartā ʾălēhem* 'YHWH spoke to Moses saying: Command the Israelite people and say to them' (Num 28:1–2aᵃ, substituting *lāhem* in v. 3 for H's *ʾălēhem*). Providing for *the altar* is, therefore, Israel's task. What about the shrine? P is noncommittal. It prescribes bread for the table (Exod 25:30; 39:36), oil for the menorah (Exod 39:37), and incense for the inner altar (Exod 30:34–38), with no indication of their supplier. H removes all doubt. It is emphatic in its demand that bread for the table and oil for the menorah stem *mēʾēt bĕnê yiśrāʾēl* 'from the Israelites' (Lev 24:8; Exod 27:21 [H]). H has no corresponding prescription regarding the incense. This omission, I submit, is explicable on economic grounds: flour and olive oil were relatively cheap; spices for the incense were out of reach for the masses. Judging by the fact that the initial supply of incense was donated by the chieftains (Num 7:14, 20, etc.), it is safe to assume that spices for the incense were supplied by the wealthy (details in INTRODUCTIONs to 24:1–9 and 24:1–4).

Moreover, the use of the verb *ʿāśâ* 'sacrifice' in the second-person plural (e.g., Num 28:4, 8, 21–24 [P]; Lev 23:12, 19 [H]) suggests the possibility that Israel's role in the public cult goes beyond supplying the ingredients for the service, but also includes a supervisory function. In H, this misty impression precipitates into words. The compliance report of Moses' instructions to and for the priests regarding their mourning taboos and their physical disqualifications reads *vayyĕdabbēr mōšeh ʾel-ʾahărōn wĕʾel-bānāyw wĕʾel-kol-bĕnê yiśrāʾēl* 'Moses spoke to Aaron and to his sons and to all the Israelites' (21:24). Even without a direct object such as *haddĕbārîm hā'ēlleh* 'these words' (e.g., Gen 20:8; Exod 19:7; Num 14:39; cf. Lev 8:36; 23:46), it is clear that the reference has to be to the previous words of the chapter. But why was the direct object omitted? I submit that the H tradent responsible for interpolating 21:24 was intent on only rephrasing the heading to the chapter *'ĕmōr 'el-hakkōhănîm bĕnê 'ahărōn* 'speak to the priests, the sons of Aaron' (21:1aβ) so that Moses was commanded to speak not only to the priests, but to *all* of Israel. The implication is clear: Israel is charged with the responsibility of overseeing the priests so they do not officiate if in mourning or if physically disqualified.

The same conclusion must be rendered concerning the heading and compliance notice of the festival calendar *dabbēr/vayyĕdabbēr 'el-bĕnê yiśrā'ēl* 'Speak/spoke to the Israelites' (23:2aα, 44). The priests' role in the observances is barely mentioned (and only in the third person, vv. 11, 20). The manifold obligations fall on the Israelites: complete sabbath rest (v. 3), *pesaḥ* offering and unleavened bread (vv. 5–8), *'ōmer* of new barley (vv. 10–11, 14), two loaves of new wheat (v. 17), grain for the needy (v. 22), sounding alarm blasts (v. 24), fasting and complete rest (vv. 27–28), and altar processions and domestic booths (vv. 40–42). This nearly exclusive address to the lay Israelites sows the suspicion that, as mentioned above, when the priestly role is commanded in the same second-person plural *wa'ăśîtem* 'you shall sacrifice' (v. 12, 19), the community of Israel bears the ultimate responsibility for the correct cultic observance of each festival *bĕmô'ădô* 'at its fixed time' (Num 28:2bβ [H]).

H defines the pedagogic responsibility of the priest as *ûlĕhabdîl bên haqqōdeš ûbên haḥōl ûbên haṭṭāmē' ûbên haṭṭāhōr* 'to distinguish between the sacred and the common, and between the impure and the pure' (10:10; cf. vol. 1.615–17). What the priests teach, Israel must practice. Thus Israel is also enjoined to distinguish between the pure and the impure in regard to its diet (20:25), a responsibility also found in P (11:47). In H, however, observing the dietary laws is a sine qua non for attaining holiness (11:43–45; 20:25–26)—an objective that is unknown and unthinkable to P.

Nowhere is Israel explicitly commanded to distinguish between the holy (*qōdeš*) and the common (*ḥōl*). It is implied in H's doctrine of holiness. Israel's basic task is to transform the common into the holy *within itself*. It should espouse to become a holy people. How? By adding to every possible moment and activity a dimension of holiness. This technique is exemplified in chap. 19 (and discussed in II G and in the COMMENT on chap. 19).

On the basis of the colophon of the New Year's rite (*ANET* 331a, 336a), which demonstrates that the priestly lore of the Babylonians was a carefully guarded secret, Ginsberg, 1963 (followed by C. Cohen 1969; Haran 1981b) infers that Israel's priestly laws were also the private, secret preserve of the priestly guild (see also Egypt: The Book of the Dead 161, ll.11ff.). However, as demonstrated by Paul (1970a: 38–39) and Greenberg (1995b: 11–17), all the priestly texts of the Bible belie this analogy. In contrast to the impersonal address of Mesopotamian law, the priestly laws of the Bible begin with YHWH's charge to Moses *dabbēr 'el-bĕnê yiśrā'ēl* 'speak to the Israelite people', except where priests are exclusively concerned, specifically: the sacrificial service (6:1–7:21), sobriety and prebends (10:8–15), scale-disease diagnosis (13), sanctuary purgation (16:2–28), mourning and physical defects (21), contamination or desecration of sacred food (22:1–16), the priestly blessing (Num 6:22–27), the menorah (Num 8:1–4), and guarding responsibilities and prebends (Num 18:1–24). These, however, constitute only a small fraction, less than 4 percent of the priestly corpus. Moreover, in one case (mourning and physical defects, chap. 21), as noted above, the priestly H turns over the responsibility of supervising the priests to the Israelites (21:24). Also, the entire cultic calendar, including the priestly role but with emphasis on the people's participation, is broadcast to the entire people (Num 28:2a; 30:1 [H]). Finally, that the priestly corpus is the patrimony of all of Israel is made explicit in the summary statements at the closure of the book of Leviticus (26:46) and of the appendix (27:34; see their NOTES).

Thus it can be assumed that Israel's priests took their pedagogic role seriously. They publicized all their laws—not in writing, but orally. If I am correct that P and H each represents the legal lore of the Jerusalem sanctuary (with antecedents at Shiloh), but that other sanctuaries abounded throughout the land, then the people-at-large had ample opportunity to be in contact with their local priest(s) (whenever they wanted to eat meat, according to H), and they would have heard the laws pertaining to their visits recited and interpreted by the resident priest(s). And if the latter was (were) truly conscientious, the instruction would also contain moral teaching. Levenson (1985: 178) remarks on Pss 23:6; 27:4; 84:6–8 that the Psalmists

> wish to spend their lives within the Temple—came to be taken as lyrical hyperbole, for the religious traditions recorded in the Hebrew Bible include no parallel to the monasticism that was to develop in the church, or, *mutatis mutandis*, in the Buddhist tradition. At any given time, there were a few individuals whose employment, as it were, lay within the Temple, but *these did not develop an ideal of religious life that was demarcated from the daily concerns of the masses.* (italics mine).

Indeed, had Israel's priests been cloistered within and around the Temple (Knohl 1995: 152–56), we might have seen the emergence of a monastic community or something resembling the ascetic sect of Qumran.

To be sure, all of Israel is commanded to separate from the nations (20:24). This is exemplified by the divine directive not to follow the ways of Egypt and Canaan in general (18:3). Their immoral behavior is incurable; it is a genetic trait, traceable to their epynomic ancestor Ham (see NOTE on 18:3). Since it is ingrained in their nature, Israel must try to avoid any contact with them.

Separation from the nations becomes a cardinal plank in H's theology when it is associated with the term *qādōš* 'holy'. Its model is YHWH himself. Israel is enjoined to become holy because YHWH is holy (19:2). Holy (*qādōš*) implies separation (see COMMENT on chap. 19), explicitly expressed by *hibdîl* 'separate'. This verb describes YHWH's act of separation in creating his world (Gen 1:4, 14, 17, 18), and it is used in Israel's requirement to separate from the nations

(20:25). Separation of the elements and species created order, and their distinctions must remain intact lest the world collapse into chaos. So, too, Israel must apply the word *hibdîl* 'separate' to distinguish between acts of life and acts of death.

Thus *hibdîl* is applied to certain foods (20:25; cf. 11:47). Those that must be eschewed are called *ṭāmē'* 'impure' (or *šeqeṣ* 'abomination'), and this term is generalized to apply to all things God has designated as impure (10:10), specifically the sexual prohibitions (18:24–25, 27–28; see also 19:31; 22:5, 8). Impure (*ṭāmē'*) is the antonym of holy (*qādōš*), and these represent the implacable opposition between death and life. Thus the God of life (the quintessence of the holy, *qādōš*) enjoins Israel to obey his commandments because they generate life (18:5).

The same juxtaposition of holiness and separation is found in Deut 7:6; 14:2, but there, instead of H's verb *hibdîl* 'separate', D resorts to the verb *bāḥar* 'choose' (Paschen 1970: 48). For D, Israel's election is traceable to God's demonstrable love of the patriarchs (Deut 4:37; 7:8). For H, as for P (Milgrom 1992a), the choice of Israel is a continuation (and climax) of the process of creation. The implication is clear: just as YHWH created order out of chaos in the *natural* world by his act of separation, so the separation of Israel from the nations—as the continuation of creation—is essential not just for Israel's survival, but for an orderly, *moral* world.

The patriarchal blessing had stated that if they are loyal to YHWH, follow his commandments, and live an exemplary moral life, then their prosperity will become proverbial, and all nations will adopt the formula: "May you be blessed like Israel" (Gen 12:3; 18:18; 22:18; 26:4; cf. Gen 4:2). H implies a deeper message. It is not only Israel's blessing but also its source—Israel's moral life—that will arouse envy and inspire emulation among the nations.

Thus a first, but essential step has been taken for the development of the prophetic doctrine of "a light to the nations" (Isa 42:6; 60:3; cf. Radak and Abravanel. The program to attain holiness, therefore, carries universal implications.

There is no doubt that H's Israel was a patriarchal society. The sexual prohibitions (chaps. 18 and 20) are addressed to the paterfamilias and other male family members, more explicitly: the paramour (19:20–22), the prostitute's father (19:29), the Molek worshiper (18:21; 20:1–5), the farmer (19:9–10, 23–25; 23:9–11, 15–17, 22; 25:2–7, 14–55), the merchant (19:35–36), and the vower (27:1–13; note "if *she* is female," 27:4). Indeed, Joosten (1996: 30–34) has conjectured that *běnê yiśrā'ēl*, the normal addressee of the laws, is limited to adult male Israelites, whereas *bêt yiśrā'ēl* includes everyone. However engaging his theory, it is marred by flaws (see NOTE on 17:10) and the mixed textual evidence in Amos (Andersen and Freedman 1989: 128–41).

Since there is no directive addressed specifically to the woman, we can deduce her status, rights, and safeguards from only indirect evidence. We know from P's rules that a woman could make vows (Num 30; cf. 1 Sam 1:11; details in Milgrom 1990a: 488–90)—even be a Nazirite (Num 6:2–21; Milgrom 1990a:

355–58)—but she could be vetoed by her father or husband. If, however, she becomes or remains single, her vows stand (Num 30:10). Thus one must be careful about the use of "patriarchal" to describe Israel's early society. Only while dependent on the father or husband is the woman in a subservient position. But if widowed or divorced, she is theoretically no longer under patriarchal or any other male control. I say theoretically because under pressure from the social norms, she could be forced to abide by communal decisions. For example, a woman could inherit the patrimony if she had no brothers (Num 27:1–11), but subsequent legislation (Num 36) limited her marital opportunities, initially, to members of her kin group and, then, to her tribe (Milgrom 1990a: 511–12).

If the woman is dependent on her father, she is under his total control. This is implied by the exhortation addressed to the father not to turn his daughter to prostitution (19:29). This is an H passage, but it also reflects similar cases of impoverished (or venal) fathers in the days of P and in all times (e.g., contemporary Southeast Asia; see INTRODUCTION to 25:39–43). The same unqualified and unchallengeable control over the woman passes, upon marriage, from her father to her husband. This can be inferred from the case of the suspected adulteress (Num 5:12–31 [P]). On mere suspicion that she was having an extramarital affair, the husband could probably put her to death with full communal (male) support (e.g., Gen 38:24). P, however, legislates that she should first be subjected to an ordeal. From the construction of the ordeal, it becomes evident that its purpose is to protect the woman against the uncontrollable rage of her husband (and community). It transfers the authority to punish the woman (if the ordeal proves her guilty) from her husband to her God (details in Milgrom 1990a: 346–54) and thus saves her from a communal lynching.

Thus we see that P's laws regarding the woman are concerned as much with her protection as with her rights, so that even while under her husband's control, she would not be abused. Does H continue this trend?

Ziskind (1996: 128–29) has set forth the attractive proposal that H's purpose in repeating the expression *legallōt ʿerwâ* 'to uncover nakedness' in the sexual prohibitions (18:6–19) is to indicate that even if the woman is divorced or widowed, she is not subject to the whim or will of the paterfamilias or other powerful males. Neither can she be bandied from one man to another. To the contrary, she is free to marry whom she will or not marry at all. *Once she regains her single status, she is her own person, the only determiner of her life.*

I submit that Ziskind is correct. I find support in the text itself. It should be noted that *legallōt ʿerwâ* occurs in every heterosexual prohibition but one—the last, adultery (18:20). There is only one possible reason: adultery means cohabiting with a married woman. Adultery does not apply to women in a postmarital state. In the previous cases, however, the problem of the woman's postmarital status exists, hence *legallōt ʿerwâ* is used; and, conversely, wherever *legallōt ʿerwâ* is found, the woman is unmarried. Indeed, this conclusion is deducible on other grounds: sex with any of these women, if they are married, would be adultery and prohibited by 18:20. Hence these women are in a pre- or postmarital state (either widowed or divorced). This deduction is even more manifest in chap. 20, where adultery heads the prohibition list (20:10), implying that the prohibitions that follow deal with cases where the woman is no longer married. This also explains why the adultery prohibition in chap. 18 was placed at the bottom of the list: it does not contain *legallōt ʿerwâ*.

Furthermore, on the basis of the valuation scale of males and females, cited in 27:1–8, one can infer that the relatively high percentage of women, at or near 40 percent, demonstrates that they were an indispensable part of Israel's labor force and, therefore, must have achieved a respectable and respected status in Israelite society (Meyers 1983: 584–87; 1988: 170–73). This economic factor may also account for her autonomy once she is released from her patriarchal and marital bonds, as indicated above. Also, I have conjectured that, in contrast to and in polemic with Exod 21:3, the woman may not be indentured with her husband (see NOTE on 25:41).

M. THE MISSING KING

The absence of a Davidic theology is recurringly advanced by scholars as proof that the composition and redaction of P and H are postexilic, when the political control of the Judean state was in priestly hands. That P would not mention the king is obvious: its concern focuses exclusively on the sanctuary. Moreover, it may be echoing the only viable social structure of its time, namely, the clan — at whose head stood the *nāśî'* 'chieftain' (Lev 4:22–31) — before the kingship became entrenched. And even then, the organs of the central state did not obliterate the control of local organs such as *ziknê hāʿîr* 'city elders', particularly in domestic issues. Take Deuteronomy as a case in point. Written during the time of the kingdom (Deut 17:14–20), it defers often to the authority of the elders (Deut 19:12; 21:1–9, 18–21; 22:16–18; 25:5–9).

H, in contrast to P, centers in the land and brings into play a series of decrees concerning the sale and redemption of land and persons (chap. 25) and the proper sexual and ethical behavior (chaps. 18–20), which will prevent the contamination of the land and simultaneously assist the people of Israel to achieve holiness. Why, then, is there no mention of the king's behavior or of his rights and responsibilities in regard to the land? This question will be addressed briefly, by surveying the role of the king in Ezekiel and D.

Ezekiel (or his tradent) reapportions the land of Israel to the future returnees from exile so that each tribe receives an equal portion of the land stretching from the eastern boundary (the Jordan or the desert) to the sea. Between Judah and Benjamin, the king (*nāśî'*) receives an equivalent portion, in the middle of which a 2500 square area is set aside for the sanctuary, priests, Levites, and city (Ezek 45:7; 48:21). His land grant is affixed with the warning not to encroach on any other tribe by evicting its inhabitants (45:8–9). After enacting a stipulated (honest) weights and measures system, the king has to supervise the people's stipulated contribution to the sanctuary (vv. 10–16). The king himself, however, is responsible for contributing all the public sacrifices for the sabbaths, new moons, and festivals (v. 17). He is provided a private (eastern) gate to which he brings his own offerings, but he proceeds no farther; he never enters the inner (priestly) court (46:1–2, 12). The king is warned once again not to dispossess the people of their land (46:18).

The admonition to the king, given twice, that he must not expropriate land (45:9; 46:18) is a clear reference to the attested practice of the monarch's presumed right of "eminent domain" (e.g., 2 Sam 9:7 [see Radak]; 1 Kgs 21:7–16). To curb this royal prerogative and temptation, Ezekiel endows the king with ample land of his own—nearly equivalent in size to a tribal portion. Ezekiel even ordains that royal land grants to his subjects (but not to his sons) must revert to him at the jubilee (46:16–17).

Of equal significance is the implied prohibition against the king entering the priests' (inner) court, even for his own sacrifice. He is granted a special (eastern) gate (an honorific privilege), but he may only watch from the gate's threshold while the officiating priests offer his sacrifice (46:1–2, 12). Ezekiel has thus, with one stroke, eliminated the right of kings, heretofore unrestricted, to officiate on the altar (e.g., 1 Kgs 8:63–64; 2 Kgs 16:15; 2 Chr 26:16–20). In a word, Ezekiel has severed church and state. In the sanctuary, the king's royal status is acknowledged by his exclusive gate, but the priestly domain is off-limits to him.

Although D purports to be a constitution of the ideal Israelite polity, it begrudgingly concedes a role to the king (Deut 17:14–20). D puts the king under the control of its Torah, as interpreted (and supervised?) by the priests. The king's powers are clipped—at best, a limited monarch.

What Ezekiel legislates, H presumes. In H, too, church and state are separated. The king is missing in H because he is given no special gate, no special land, no special duties. Presumably, he is just one of the people. His only distinction is that prescribed by P: as the successor to the *nāśî'* (vol. 1.246–47), his purification offering is a male goat and not the commoner's female of the flock (4:22–35). Other than this "honor," H's king is indistinguishable from the layman. Thus both Ezekiel and H remove the king from the sacred realm: Ezekiel by legislation, and H (and P) by the king's presumed lay status.

H, moreover, is uninterested in the organization of the state. In distinction from D, H does not legislate a state-appointed judiciary (Deut 16:18) and a central court of appeals (Deut 17:8–13). Nor does it create a people's army (Deut 20:1–9) or regulate the rules of warfare (Deut 20:10–20; 21:10–14; 23:10–16). H is vitally concerned with the land, but only insofar as it is affected by disobedience to the divine commandments (chaps. 18, 20, 26). It is also concerned with righting the socioeconomic injustices stemming from latifundia (see chap. 25, COMMENT A), since they violate H's basic principle: YHWH, the owner of the land, has ordained that the land must periodically revert to its original tenants (chap. 25; see further II K).

The possibility should be entertained that H—in contradiction to D—does not hold that the kingship was ordained by God. Divine approval of the Davidic dynasty was vouchsafed by a prophet, not a priest (2 Sam 7). Interestingly, H cites only the prophet's *opposition* to building the Temple (2 Sam 7:6b and Lev 26:11–12a; see NOTES). Indeed, it would seem that in H's view, Israel could do well without a king. Rather, obedience to YHWH's commandments suffices to bring fertility to the land and peace to its inhabitants (26:3–13). To be sure, an organized civil administration is presumed, but there is no indication that its head is a king. In contrast with D's comminations, there is not a word about the king suffering the consequences of his people's infidelity to YHWH (cf. Deut 28:36). Does this indifference to kingship indicate that H is registering hostility toward the institution itself? Do we hear an echo of the antimonarchical tendency attributed to the time of Samuel and the first king Saul, namely, that Israel would be better off under the kingship of YHWH?

The absolute powers of the king, as Samuel had warned (1 Sam 8:11–17), will lead to land confiscation, burdensome taxation, slavery, and other socioeconomic abuses (see NOTES on 25:25–43). D tries to curb the king's arbitrariness by having him read daily from a copy of the Torah under the supervision of the priests (Deut 17:18–19). H, apparently, would have no truck with such palliatives. The kingship of man is too dangerous per se. Better the kingship of YHWH, who rewards those who obey his commandments with peace, prosperity, and life (26:3–13; cf. 18:5).

N. REFLECTIONS ON THE BIBLICAL *GĒR*

The term *gēr* or its compound form *gēr tôšāb* is generally rendered "resident alien." Hence one might think that it always refers to a non-Israelite. However, this is not its meaning in Genesis and Exodus. Abraham declares to the residents of Hebron, "I am a resident alien among you" (Gen 23:4). Moses in Egypt also admits, "I have been a *gēr* in a strange land" (Exod 2:22; see Gen 15:13). Indeed, from a divine perspective, the people of Israel has the status of a *gēr* on its own land: "For the land is Mine; you are but resident aliens under my authority" (Lev 25:23). Moreover, according to the testimony of the Psalmist, "I am only an alien in the land" (Ps 119:19); all human beings are but tenants on the earth charged with the responsibility "to work it and take care of it" (Gen 2:15).

How does the *gēr* differ from other persons in Israelite society? He is neither the Israelite native (*'ezrāḥ*) nor the foreigner (*nokrî*). True, the *gēr* is also of foreign origin, but there the distinction ends. The foreigner is either a visiting merchant or a mercenary (2 Sam 15:19); he is attached to his homeland and intends to return to it. The *gēr*, however, is a resident alien; he has uprooted himself (or has been uprooted) from his homeland and has taken permanent residence in the land of Israel.

By the same token, the historical *gēr* must be distinguished from the *'ebed*, 'the slave'. He is a free person with the same civil rights as the Israelite. There is, however, one notable exception. The *gēr* may not own landed inheritance, and in an agricultural economy, which describes ancient Israel, this means that the *gēr* had to work for an Israelite farmer as a hired hand. Moreover, having severed his ties with his original home, he has no family to turn to for support. Thus deprived of both land and family, he was generally poor, listed together with the Levite, the fatherless, and the widow among the wards of society (Deut 26:12), and exposed to exploitation and oppression (Ezek 22:7).

To be sure, some resident aliens managed to become rich (Lev 25:47) and achieve high social status. Note the cases of Doeg the Edomite (1 Sam 21:8), Zelek the Ammonite (2 Sam 23:37), and Uriah the Hittite (2 Sam 11:3)—all high officers in the royal court or army. However, though they totally assimilated into Israelite society, even to the point of being zealous worshipers of Israel's God (a matter emphasized in the Doeg and Uriah accounts), they retained their ethnic label and were not reckoned as Israelites. The parade example is Ruth the Moabite. When she entered Israel's land with her mother-in-law, Naomi, she declared herself a foreigner (Ruth 2:10). Eventually she became a resident alien, a *gēr*, but not an Israelite. Even after her marriage to Boaz, an Israelite "of substance" (Ruth 2:1), she probably retained her alien status. In the long run, marriage was the only way the *gēr* could become an Israelite, not the *gēr* himself or herself, but only the progeny—of the fourth generation of limited ethnic stock, but only of the tenth Moabite generation, according to the rigid scruples of Deuteronomy (23:2–9).

Let it be emphasized that in biblical times, religious conversion was not an option. Though the notion that one joins a people by adopting its faith is an Israelite invention, it is now clear that it was not a biblical experience but the creation of the following period. Thus when Ruth declares to Naomi, "Your people shall be my people, your God, my God" (Ruth 1:16), she was only fulfilling the law of cause and consequence: by casting her lot with the people of Israel, she automatically accepted the God of Israel. This "conversion," however, did not make her an Israelite.

According to the Bible, the *gēr* is completely equivalent to the Israelite in civil law: "the same *tôrâ* and the same *mišpāt* shall apply to the *gēr* who resides among you" (Num 15:16). Here *mišpāt* stands for civil law and *tôrâ*, for religious law. However, though the legal status of the *gēr* matches that of the Israelite in civil law, the same is not true in religious law. In fact, the *gēr* is held to a more lenient regime. He or she is obligated to observe only the negative commandments, the prohibitions, but not the positive commandments, the performative ones. The rationale for this legal distinction rests on a theological premise. The violation of a prohibition generates a toxic impurity that radiates into the environment, polluting the sanctuary and the land. Sexual offenses and homicide, for example, pollute the land (Lev 18:27–28; Num 35:34–35), and Molek worship and corpse-contamination pollute the sanctuary (Lev 20:3; Num 19:13). It therefore makes no difference whether the polluter is an Israelite or a *gēr*: anyone in residence in YHWH's land is capable of polluting it or the sanctuary. Performative commandments, however, are violated by refraining from or neglecting to do them (in rabbinic language, "sit and do nothing"). These violations are not sins of commission, but of omission. They, too, can lead to dire consequences, but only for the Israelite, who is obligated by his covenant with God to observe them. The gēr, however, is not so obligated. Since violations of performative commandments are acts of omission, of nonobservance, they generate no pollution. As a result, the gēr need not, for example, observe the paschal sacrifice. But if he wishes to, he must be circumcised (Exod 12:48) and, presumably, must be in a state of ritual purity (Num 9:6–7, 13–14). Under no circumstances, however, may he possess leaven during the festival (Exod 12:19; 13:7). Similarly, the sukkâ-booth is a positive, performative commitment. Since the gēr generates no impurity when he refrains from constructing the sukkâ, the commandment falls solely on the Israelite (Lev 23:42). To give the principle a more modern application, the gēr living in the state of Israel could not be required to light sabbath candles or recite the qiddûš over the wine (performative commands), but would be forbidden to work on the sabbath (a prohibition).

The implications of the biblical gēr in the sociopolitical sphere are far-reaching. Every nation (at least among the Western democracies) has a status equivalent to that of the gēr: the permanent resident. Such a person is granted the same rights and accepts the same responsibilities as the citizen, except the right to vote. The Tôrâ, however, mandates to the gēr more than equality under the law. The Tôrâ, first, calls on us to remember our Egyptian experience: "You shall not oppress a gēr, for you know the feelings of the gēr in having yourselves been gērîm [plural] in the land of Egypt" (Exod 23:9). Since our experience as gērîm in Egypt sensitized us to the "feelings" of the gēr, just how are we to empathize with him or her? The Tôrâ then tells us: "You must befriend [wa'ăhabtem] the gēr, for you were gērîm in the land of Egypt" (Deut 10:19); "You shall love [wĕ'āhabtā] him [the gēr] as yourself for you were gērîm in the land of Egypt" (Lev 19:34).

The same verb 'āhab is rendered both "love" and "befriend" (JPS, The Torah). The latter translation is more felicitous. The Hebrew 'āhab is related to its semantic cognates in the diplomatic vocabulary of ancient Near Eastern treaties, which denote the fidelity and loyalty pledged by a vassal to his suzerain as well as the reciprocal obligations of support owed by the suzerain to the vassal. Thus when Israel is commanded "You shall love the Lord your God," it follows logically that this love is fulfilled if "these words [of the Tôrâ] shall be upon your heart" (Deut 6:5–6); that is, if we obey them. By the same token, when we are commanded "Love your [Israelite] fellow as yourself" (Lev 19:18) and "You shall love him [the gēr] as yourself" (Lev 19:34), the term "love" is not an abstraction. It connotes obligation, commitment, reaching out—providing not only our fellow Israelite but also the local alien with his or her essentials. Strikingly, this formula of love is found in one of the ancient Near Eastern treaties: "You shall love [King] Ashurbanipal as yourself." Of course, this love is not familiar or intimate affection, but it designates the devotion owed to the king. It is characteristic of the Tôrâ that it transfers the allegiance demanded by a human ruler to the allegiance we pledge solely to God (see NOTES on 19:18, 34).

The gēr is discussed at length in chap. 17, COMMENT B, where it is demonstrated that gēr means "the resident alien," and his status can be derived from the laws of chap. 17. Additional aspects of his status will now be adduced from his appearance mainly in chaps. 24 and 25.

First, I shall extract the essence of chap. 17, COMMENT B, regarding the basic law of the *gēr*. He is expected to observe all the prohibitive commandments lest their violation lead to the pollution of YHWH's sanctuary and land, which, in turn, results in YHWH's alienation and Israel's exile. In this regard, the *gēr* is equivalent to the Israelite, with one exception: the *gēr* does not have to slaughter his animal at an authorized altar (17:3–4, 11), but may slaughter it like game (17:13). This concession is a concomitant of the main distinction between the *gēr* and the Israelite: the *gēr* must observe the prohibitive commandments, such as not worshiping other gods (17:8–9), but he is not compelled to observe YHWH's positive, performative commandments, such as sacrificing at YHWH's altar.

The distinction between the *gēr* and the Israelite is also apparent in the corollary prohibition concerning the animal's suet: the *gēr* may eat it, but the Israelite may not (3:17; 7:25). This leniency toward the *gēr* follows logically from his distinction from the Israelites regarding the meat: if the *gēr*'s meat need not be offered as a sacrifice, why then his suet?

The *gēr* is required to follow the same sacrificial procedures as the Israelite (Exod 12:48–49; Lev 17:8, 12, 13; Num 9:14; 15:14, 29), observe the same prohibitions (16:29; 18:26), and receive the same punishments (20:2; 24:16, 22) — all verses of H. The observance of both civil and (prohibitive) religious law is incumbent on the *gēr*, as shown in chap. 24 by the juxtaposition of the law of blasphemy (v. 16) and the talion laws for injuries (v. 22). H's repeated concern for the *gēr* is explicable — rather, derivable — from theology. H has expanded P's horizon of holiness from the sanctuary to Israel's land. Since the *gēr* is a resident of the land, he is capable of polluting the land to no lesser degree than the Israelite; hence the Amorites in Gen 15:16 and the Canaanites and Egyptians in Lev 18:24–30 and 20:23 were driven out. The *gēr* must, therefore, heed all the prohibitive commandments incumbent on the Israelites, such as blasphemy (14:10–23), but he is exempt from all the performative commandments because they are nonpolluting. Thus it is the fear that the *gēr* may pollute the land by infractions of the prohibitive laws, such as blasphemy, that accounts for his inclusion in the talion laws (24:17–22) and for their attachment to the narrative about the blasphemous *gēr* (24:10–16, 23).

In three successive verses, the words *tihyeh lākem* 'shall be for you' occur in connection with the jubilee (25:10, 11, 12), emphasizing that the observance of the jubilee is incumbent on the Israelite, not on the *gēr*. This staccato emphasis is required because farming the land in the jubilee is a prohibition, and hence it should be expected of the *gēr* (see II K). But in this case, he is free to work the land and benefit from its produce. This exception for the *gēr* explains why the term "sabbath" is never applied to the jubilee. The sabbatical law, by contrast, falls on the land, not on the Israelite (25:4); hence the *gēr*, no differently from the Israelite, is forbidden to work it. The labor laws for the jubilee and sabbatical are not equivalent, and, therefore, the jubilee cannot fall on a sabbatical (forty-ninth) year.

The Israelite may never be enslaved. If he is sold for his indebtedness, he must be treated as a hireling. He repays his creditor from the remainder of his wages—after feeding himself and his family. His payments amortize his interest-free loans. If he fails to repay the creditor completely, the jubilee takes over; it cancels his loan and restores him to his family and land (see NOTES on 25:40–41). In this case, there is no resemblance between the gēr and the Israelite. The indentured or purchased gēr is a chattel-slave, not a debt-slave (note the verb qānâ 'bought', vv. 44–45). The institutions of jubilee and redemption are unavailable to him. He is landless, and without land to lose to a creditor, these remedies are of no meaning. Thus this discrimination against the alien— which ostensibly flies in the face of the alien's equality before the law (24:22)— rests not on his lack of access to the jubilee, but on his inaccessibility to land. Even Ezekiel, who legislates that the alien may possess and bequeath landed property (Ezek 47:21–23), remains silent concerning the remedies of redemption and jubilee for the gēr.

O. Crime, Punishment (Talion), and Restitution

a. CRIME

From the outset, the distinction must be made between crimes against persons and crimes against God. The basic principle observed in P (Milgrom 1970: 5–8) also holds in H: crimes against persons are adjudicable and punishable by a human court; crimes against God are judged and punished by God, with the exception of Molek worship and blasphemy, which must be punished by human agency. These exceptions are explicable on the grounds that their consequences *for Israel* are too grave to wait for divine punishment (kārēt) to take effect. Kārēt, it will be recalled, probably refers to the extirpation of the line and denial of an afterlife (vol. 1.457–60), but not the immediate death effected by a human court. Molek worship actually straddles both spheres. Homicide (the murder of children) is a crime against persons, and its violator must be executed by human agency (see NOTE on "must be put to death," 20:2). Failure to put him to death results in kārēt for his family and associates (20:3–5; see below). Blasphemy, to be sure, is purely an offense against the deity. But the inexpiable impurity generated by the curse threatens the very survival of the community (see INTRODUCTION to 24:17–22) unless its source, the blasphemer, is slain.

A clear case of the division between crimes against persons and God is adultery. If the criminal is apprehended, his or her prosecution is a human responsibility; if the criminal is not apprehended, the case is off-limits to humans and is prosecuted by divine agency via the ordeal (Num 5:12–31; see NOTE on Lev 20:10). Adultery throughout the ancient Near East was considered a crime against the gods, "the great sin" (see NOTE on 19:21). In Israel, this is echoed in the provision of capital punishment for various sexual offenses (20:9–16); if they are not punished by man, then God himself will intervene with *kārēt* (see NOTE on 18:29).

Molek worship also straddles both jurisdictional spheres. The Molek worshiper is subject to immediate death by the *'am hā'āreṣ* 'people of the land' *and* by divine *kārēt* (20:2–3). If they fail to execute him, YHWH will punish him, his family, and all who acquiesced in (or covered up) his idolatrous act with *kārēt* (20:4–5). Thus the Molek worshiper is punished by his immediate death and the excision of his line. If his community does not execute him, YHWH will inflict *kārēt* not only on the idolatrous miscreant, but on his family, who may be protecting him by their silence, and all those whom he may have influenced (see NOTES on 20:2–5).

Sabbath violators are also subject to death by human agency, even in the borderline case of the wood-gatherer (Num 15:32–36 [H]). But clear-cut, brazen violators will be punished by both human agency and divine agency, *môt yûmāt* and *kārēt* (Exod 31:14 [H]). The sinner will be deprived of his life in this world and denied access to the departed (kin) in the next world.

It should be noted as well that the priest suffers severer penalties than the lay person for his infractions. If the latter eats carrion, he is impure for one day (11:39–40, an H interpolation; see NOTE on "He shall not eat," 22:8). If he fails to purify himself, he is liable for a purification offering (see NOTE on 17:16). In reality, he suffers no penalty, since his sin is remediable. But the same offense committed by a priest is inexpiable: he suffers death (*ûmētû*) at the hands of God (22:8–9).

The case of the impure priest (22:1–9) clarifies the difference in degree between the sins punished by *kārēt* and those punished by death at the hands of God (*yāmût*). *Kārēt* is imposed for advertent violations of sacred donations (22:3), specifically for eating or touching them in an impure state (vv. 4–7). A pure priest suffers death (*mût*) if he (advertently) eats of carrion (22:8–9). Thus *kārēt*, a severer penalty, is prescribed for a severer crime—contacting sacred food while in an impure state. Death (*mût*) is the lesser punishment for the same act because the priest is pure; the impure priest should have taken greater precautions.

'ărîrî 'childlessness' is a divinely caused punishment (20:20–21). *Kārēt* 'excision, extirpation (of the line)' also results in childlessness, but in addition, it implies being cut off from the ancestral spirits. Thus the *'ărîrî* is not barred from the afterlife, but he leaves no one to lament him (see NOTE on "they shall remain childless," 20:21, and 2 Sam 18:18).

Death by human agency presumably is by stoning (see NOTE on "he must be put to death," 20:9). Death by burning is exceptional and presumably is a severer execution. It is inflicted on a woman and her mother who are married to the same man. Presupposed is that they conspired with the man that he take them both in marriage (see NOTE on "and them," 20:14). That an illegal ménage à trois is contemplated in this law may be indicated by the condemnatory term *zimmâ* from the root *zmm* 'connive, conspire'. It is no accident that the only other occurrence of this term in the sexual domain is the similar case of a mother and her daughter (18:17b; see its NOTE). Death by fire is also prescribed for the promiscuous daughter of a priest (21:9), in contrast to a promiscuous daughter of a lay person, who was probably stigmatized socially, but was unpunished by human agency. If, however, she was betrothed or married, she and her paramour would be put to death by stoning for having committed adultery (20:10; Deut 22:23–24).

Blasphemy (24:10–23) brings us again to the thin borderline between crimes punished by divine and those punished by human agency. The distinction lies in whether the blasphemer has cursed God while pronouncing his name or while omitting it. The former falls under human jurisdiction; the latter, under divine jurisdiction (vv. 15–16; see II Q). Both cases presume acts performed in public, reported by witnesses, and decided by court. If the witnesses report that the blasphemer's curse did not mention the Name (YHWH), the court is powerless to act; the blasphemy is punishable only by God. Thus the basic postulate undergirding this distinction—observable in all priestly legislation (Milgrom 1970: 5–8; 1990a: 346–54)—is once again confirmed: sins against God are punishable only by God, and humans have no right to intervene.

As for the obvious objection that curses including the Name are all the more an offense against God and yet a human court is empowered to pass a death sentence on the offender, the answer has been given above: like Molek worship—also an offense against the deity—the impurity generated by the blasphemer threatens the survival of the community, which must act quickly in self-defense to eliminate the impurity by eliminating its source: the sinner (for the exegesis of this difficult passage, see NOTES on 24:15–16).

This conclusion is congruent with the postulates underlying the sexual crimes (18:24–30) and the curses of Lev 26 (vv. 34–35, 40–45). They posit that the pollution of the land is nonexpiable *culticly*, but is "expiable" by Israel's exile. This is the basic message of 26:40–45: YHWH's covenant with Israel is not broken, and a penitent Israel will be restored to its land. Israel's expulsion, however, predicates that the *entire community* is guilty, for its sexual and/or covenantal violations (18:6–23; 26:14–39). But if these sins can be nipped in the bud, by the death of the initial miscreants, the community can be saved.

Thus the alleged difference between H and P regarding the nature of expiation has to be sharply modified. H, after all, speaks of *advertent*, unrepentant sins (18:24–30; 26:14–39). P, however, deals with *inadvertent* violations, which are expiable by sacrifice. But P also posits—as can be derived from its laws— that advertent sins committed by the community result in Israel's exile (vol. 1. 258–64). They differ, however, on the target of the generated pollution: P's sanctuary and H's land. This difference is consequential. H's land concept holds all its residents responsible, including the *gēr* (see II N).

Joosten's (1996: 45) underlying notion of collective guilt resulting from the crime of one man, exemplified in 20:2–8; 24:10–23, must be rejected. The reason why YHWH punishes the Molek worshiper's *mišpāḥâ* is that they are probably guilty for having covered up the crime or otherwise protected their kinsman (see NOTE on 20:5). Furthermore, YHWH does not punish the community

(ʿēdâ) for the blasphemer's sin (24:10–23). Note that only the šōmĕʿîm, those who heard the curse and have absorbed it, must transfer it back to the blasphemer (by hand-leaning, v. 14) lest it endanger *their* lives. Nonetheless, the community must put him to death lest they be considered as conspirators (20:5). Also, in the case of the wood-gatherer (Num 15:32–36 [H]), there is no indication that the ʿēdâ is imperiled by the violator of the sabbath. As I have posited, the sanctuary/land (i.e., God) can tolerate a limited amount of pollution caused by a few, but if the ʿēdâ is culpable, Israel is driven from its land.

b. PUNISHMENT (TALION)

In H, talion for either death or injury (24:17–22) is literal (see NOTE on "he has inflicted on," 24:20). Moreover, it is imposed on all human beings (ʾādām), not just on Israelites (ʾîš, Exod 21:12, 20–21 [JE]; Joosten 1996: 78). Was it ever carried out? There is one such recorded incident (Judg 1:6–7); its talion, however, was inflicted on a captured enemy and is, hence, irrelevant. But no decree of talion for injury was ever issued by a court. Nor could one ever be executed: "It could sometimes happen while the offender is being blinded, his life might depart from him" (*b. B. Qam.* 84a). Talion for injury in Israel is theory. In practice, monetary compensation must have been the rule. But the *principle* of talion for injury did have a practical, heuristic goal: equivalent compensation to the victim without regard to his social or economic status. The one exception is intentional homicide. Talion and a prohibition on monetary compensation was strictly prescribed (Num 35:32)—but not always obeyed (cf. Prov 6:35).

Talion exists in ancient Near Eastern legislation, but it differs fundamentally from its biblical analogue.

1. In Mesopotamian laws, talion is applied only to a person of the same rank. In H (but not in JE), it applies to all human beings (see NOTE on 20:17).
2. In ancient jurisprudence, there is no provision for the principle of intention. For example, inadvertence is unattested in Mesopotamian law; biblical law prescribes inadvertence for homicide (Num 35; Deut 19:1–10), for wrongs against God (Lev 4; 5:20–26), and, by inference, for injuries (see NOTE on 24:19).
3. Biblical law rejects vicarious talion (Exod 21:31; Deut 24:16), but it is present in Mesopotamian law (see chap. 24, COMMENT B).

God alone punishes by the principle of talion (measure for measure), but not consistently (see below). For example,

1. The Molek worshiper thought that by sacrificing one child he would be granted many more and receive access to his ancestors, but YHWH will terminate his line and will deny him access to his ancestors in this life and in the afterlife (20:3, 5).

2. He who turns to (*pôneh 'el*) mediums will find that YHWH turns against (*pôneh be*) him (20:6).
3. He who cohabited illicitly in secret will be punished by YHWH in public (*lĕ'ênê bĕnê 'ammām*, 20:17): he will die prematurely (correcting vol. 1. 458), his children will die before him, and he will be cut off from his kin in the afterlife.

Divine talion is not always precise. YHWH also punishes collectively (note Moses' complaint, Num 16:22). This is particularly evident in the case of the blasphemer. The punishment, stoning (demanded by God, 24:10), does not correspond to the crime, cursing God, and yet the penalty can be called talion (*nepĕš taḥat nepĕš*, 24:18b). Divine punishment operates both vertically and horizontally. H accepts the doctrine that the fathers' sins are transferred to their children (Exod 34:7b [JE]). God also adds the fathers' sins to those of the children (Lev 26:39–40). H's horizontal retribution is illustrated in the case of the Molek worshiper, where his extended family (*mišpāḥâ*) also suffers his punishment (but see NOTE on 20:5). D rejects vertical retribution (Deut 7:9–10; 24:16; but cf. 5:2–10), and Ezekiel abolishes both vertical and horizontal retribution (Ezek 18, 33).

YHWH actually admits that his talion is inexact. Four times he declares that he will punish sevenfold for Israel's sins (26:18, 21, 24, 28). When YHWH's fury is at its fiercest (*baḥămat-qerî*, v. 28), he exacts punishments that have no counterpart in Israel's behavior: cannibalism, destruction, exile. Yet in this very chapter, YHWH's curse proves to be an exact reversal of his blessings. Levine (1989a: 276) cites the following examples:

The fertile land (vv. 4–5, 10) will become unproductive (vv. 16, 19–20, 26) | God will turn his face (i.e., with favor) toward his people (v. 9) or will set his face against them (v. 17) | Israel will repulse its enemies (v. 9) or be battered by them (vv. 17, 23) | wild beasts will disappear (v. 6) or devour the people (v. 25) | the sword will not traverse the land (v. 6) or it will bring destruction (v. 25) | obedience brings secure settlement (v. 5) whereas disobedience brings exile (v. 33a).

Other, more graphic examples abound:

One crop will follow another (v. 5a) or you will sow your seed in vain (v. 16bα) | you shall eat your fill of your food (v. 5b) or your enemy will eat it (v. 16bβ) | you will rout your enemies (v. 7a) or be routed by them (v. 17b) | God breaks (*šābar*) the burden of your yoke (v. 13a) or he breaks (*šābar*) your proud strength (v. 19a) | the skies will yield rain and the earth will produce (v. 4a) or they will become iron and copper (v. 19b) | instead of multiplying (v. 9aγ) you will become few (v. 22aβ) | no sword will traverse your land (v. 6bβ) or it will be brought against you (v. 25aα) | God will break (*šābar*) the bars (*mōtōt*) of your yoke (v. 13bα) or he will break (*šābar*) your staff (*maṭṭeh*) of bread (v. 26aα) | YHWH (his gullet) will not expel you (v. 11b) or he (his gullet) will expel you (v. 30b).

Gerstenberger (1996: 432) has pointed out that in chap. 26 YHWH's measure-for-measure principle is broken. Israel's remorse and confession will break YHWH's resolve to punish it any further. Israel will continue to be his people, and his covenantal promises will remain in force (26:40–45). In theological terms, YHWH's attribute of mercy will override his attribute of justice.

b. RESTITUTION

In vol. 1.373–78, it was argued that the verb *'āšēm* was P's word for experiencing contrition, and it is rendered "feel guilt." I deliberately chose the noun "guilt" over the common adverb "guilty" in order to convey its substantive nature. It is not a metaphor or mental abstraction, but a physical reality, felt in pain or illness—literal pangs of conscience.

In 5:20–26, the full power of *'āšēm* comes into view. A basic postulate of P's sacrificial system, accepted and amplified by H, is that the brazen, deliberate sinner is barred from the sanctuary. His sin not only has polluted the sacrificial altar in the court, but has penetrated into the inner sanctum, the Holy of Holies. Hence YHWH will not tolerate his presence. "The person, be he citizen or alien, who acts defiantly reviles YHWH; that person shall be cut off from his people. Because he has spurned the word of YHWH and violated his commandment, that person shall be cut off—he bears his sin" (Num 15:30–31 [H]). His sin is *pešaʿ* 'rebellion', a priestly term that appears in only Lev 16:16, 21. The *pešaʿ* that has polluted the very seat of the godhead can (and must) be purged only by the high priest in an emergency rite, which subsequently becomes annual, fixed for the tenth day of the seventh month (16:29; 23:27; Num 29:7).

Lev 5:20–26 violates this postulate. It cites cases where the defrauder has denied his act under oath. Thus he has committed a deliberate crime not only against his fellow, but also against YHWH. And yet if he experiences *'āšēm* 'remorse', pangs of conscience, and confesses his crime (Num 5:6–8 [P₂], disputed by Knohl 1995; see I E), he has first to pay his victim a 20 percent fine in addition to the principal and bring a reparation offering (*'āšām*) to YHWH. The admission of the deliberate sinner into the sanctuary is explicable on the grounds that his voluntary contrition (*'āšēm*) has the power to correct retroactively his advertent sin into an inadvertent offense, which is expiable by sacrifice (for details, see vol. 1.373–78; for a fuller discussion, see Milgrom 1976a: 84–125).

Thus P has innovated the doctrine of repentance. In this initial stage, however, it is linked to sacrifice. The penitent must bring an *'āšām*, a reparation offering, without which he cannot be forgiven. H takes repentance a giant step farther. Even if Israel is in exile, its remorse and confession will be met by YHWH's covenantal fidelity, and he will restore Israel to its land (26:40–45). Thus in one stroke, H has removed the sacrificial requirement for the absolution of sin, and, perhaps for the first time in recorded history, a people is granted restoration and renewal by its repentance (see INTRODUCTION to 16:40–45). This is still a far cry from the fully developed repentance found in the prophets. They, too, dispense with sacrifice. As indicated by the prophetic term for repentance *šûb* 'return', the sinner must "cease to do evil; learn to do good" (Isa 1:10–11). Remorse must be followed by deeds, a change of heart *and* behavior (see the fuller discussion in vol. 1.375–78).

Nonetheless, H's contribution, though falling short of prophetic repentance, should not be underestimated. It is to the everlasting credit of H, of the *priestly* school, for liberating repentance from the constraint of sacrifice. A repentant person anywhere—even in the privacy of his home—can win absolution for his sins. That innovation rendered the final, prophetic step possible and inevitable. The prophets only add that when the repentant leaves his home his actions must testify that he has discarded his evil ways. One cannot read the prophets again without realizing that they stand on the shoulders of the priests—in particular, the priestly author of H.

P. THE SANCTUARY OF SILENCE AND OTHER MISCONCEPTIONS REGARDING P

a. THE SANCTUARY OF SILENCE

Knohl's book (1995) and subsequent article (1996) emphasize a major theme in his comprehensive treatment of the P source. Earlier, Kaufmann (1946: 2. 476–78; 1960: 303–4) had posited the bold thesis that Israel's priests had officiated exclusively in (ritual) acts and never in words. Knohl (1995: 148–52; 1966: esp. 21, 23) augments Kaufmann by adding to the priests of silence a realm of silence: not only did priests officiate in silence, but silence also reigned in the sacrificial court where the priests officiated. His argument itself is from silence (the lack of evidence for prayer or song); its only textual support is an unambiguous statement in the Letter of Aristeas: "The ministering of the priests was absolute, unsurpassable in its vigor and the arrangement of its well-ordered silence. A general silence reigns, so that one might think there was not a single man in the place" (ll. 92, 95; trans. R. J. H. Shutt 1995).

The inherent fallacy of this evidence is that its source, the Letter of Aristeas, stems from the second century B.C.E., when the Jerusalem Temple had two courts of which the inner one was the exclusive domain of the priests (except for its entrance area, where the offerer would present sacrifice). Nonetheless, there is irrefutable evidence that the Levites, who stood at the entrance to the priests' court, sang *during* the sacrificial service (*t. pesaḥ.* 3:11; cf. Also the people, *m. pesaḥ.* 5:10). The preexilic Jerusalem Temple, however, had only one court (Exod 27:9–19; 1 Kgs 7:9, 12; Haran (1968b: 5:349). This was also true of the sanctuaries of Dan and Arad. The biblical texts certify that the people had access to this court (e.g., Lev 1:3–5; 4:15).

In P's system, the Tabernacle court does not have the "most sacred" status of its structure and sanctums, but belongs to the lower category of the "sacred." A simple proof of the inferior holiness of the court is evidenced by the purgation rites on Yom Kippur (Lev 16). Only "most sacred" areas are purged. These are the adytum, shrine, and outer altar, but not one drop of purgation blood is sprinkled on the court's floor or curtains. Note also that when the Tabernacle was consecrated, every area was anointed except the court (Exod 30:26–30; 40:9–16). According to P, the "most sacred" is off-limits to the lay person, but no harm ensues from his or her contact with the "sacred." Thus in P's system, the lay worshiper theoretically is not barred from any part of the entire court. True, the inner portion of the court *bên hā'ûlām wĕlammizbēaḥ* 'between the porch and the altar' (Joel 2:17) was regarded by the priests as their private reserve, but this (possibly Second Temple) distinction is not recognized by P or any other pentateuchal source; on the contrary, the Psalmist declares, "I wash my hands in innocence and go around your altar, O YHWH" (Ps 26:6). The processions around the altar during the Festival of Booths (*m. Suk.* 4:5; *m. Mid.* 2:6) show that even in the late postexilic Temple, the people reclaimed their ancient right of complete access to the Temple court. Indeed, one can infer from Nehemiah's mortal fear of entering the Temple building (Neh 6:10–11) that he had no such fear of being in the Temple court. The blasphemy of the twenty-five men in the Temple court (Ezek 8:16) is not where they stood, but what they did (worshiping the sun). Finally, Aaron and Solomon blessed the people (Lev 9:22a; 1 Kgs 8:55) while they stood about the sacrificial altar in the court.

Gluklich (1999) projects the bold thesis that the sacrificial preparations of the priest, i.e., abstention from sex, purificatory rites, special clothing, find traces in the cultic acts of the paleolithic and Minoan bull races and Greek Olympian races. He errs in claiming that the silence of the priest (sic) while slaughtering the animal originates in the alleged analogy of priests in other ancient cultures. Without disputing the latter (itself requiring evidence) it has been demonstrated that sacrificial slaughter in Israel was done by the lay offerer and that some words passed between the offerer and the officiating priest to determine which sacrifice corresponded to the offerer's needs.

With Kaufmann (2: 476–78; 1960: 303–4), I presume that the officiating priests were silent. But were the assembled people also silent? Amos 5:23 and 8:10 speak of songs and music during the festival celebrations at the sanctuaries. Sennacherib records (700 B.C.E.) that among the tribute he exacted from King Hezekiah were "male and female singers" (*ANET* 288a). Early psalms (e.g., Ps 68:26; cf. Pss 33:2; 92:4; 150:3) attest to music and song in the Temple by lay worshipers and professional clergy (Mowinckel 1967: 2.79–84) *all within a Temple that had a single court.*

The inner sanctuary (*hêkāl*) of Solomon's Temple contained *mĕzammĕrôt* (1 Kgs 7:50; 2 Kgs 12:14; 25:14) 'musical instruments' (*Ps. Targ. Jon.*, Ibn Janaḥ 1968, Rashi 1946), which indicate that they were used in the Temple services (details in Hurowitz 1995: 155–56). Thus the cultic service at Solomon's Temple (and probably at Shiloh and other sanctuaries) was anything but silent.

These data do not negate "the sanctuary of silence" for officiating priests, but they affirm that music accompanied the performance of their rites in the one and same court. One should hardly be surprised. Israel was at one with the ancient Near Eastern sanctuaries that boasted of a rich musical tradition in their temples. Israel's priests, however, were constrained to silence, but the assembled people suffered no such constraints.

b. WELFARE

Knohl (1995: 156) maintains that P exhibits a "total lack of concern with basic human needs or social legislation," which he justifies by the absence of any reference to priestly participation in war (156) and a priestly role in the popular ceremonies for abundant rain and harvest (43–45).

From the outset, it is clear that Knohl is arguing from silence. He presumably does admit that the holidays celebrated at the sanctuary were occasions of thanksgiving and petition, but without any supporting evidence, he cavalierly declares that "in those cases PT had to incorporate popular practices with which it was not in sympathy" (44). Moreover, the possibility exists that P had a wide-ranging manual dealing with ethical and other personal concerns (see I H, and APPENDIX C), but H chose only those P elements—the cultic prescriptions (chaps. 1–16)—that served as a basis for his own agenda. Admittedly, this, too, is a hypothesis *ex silentio*, but at least it follows logically from the demonstrable supposition that H is the redactor of P and that *selection* was one of his options.

Moreover, there are intimations that the priests were ardently involved in promoting the welfare of the people. The obvious example is the priestly blessing (Num 6:22–26). Knohl (1995: 89) assigns it to H, but his evidence, the first-person passage of the God speech in v. 27, is not part of the blessing, and it could well be the editorial remark of the H redactor on a P text. Moreover as shown by Chaim Cohen (1993), the language of the priestly blessing has many analogues in anterior Mesopotamian literature. For example:

ila alšīma ul idimma panīšu
usalli ištarrī ul ušaqqâ rēšīša

I invoked the god, but he did not direct his face;
I beseeched my goddess, she did not raise her head. (Lambert 1960: 38, ll. 4–5)

The antiquity of the Priestly Benediction has been dramatically verified by the discovery of its inscription on two cigarette-size silver plaques dating back to the late seventh (Barkai 1989) or early sixth (Yardeni 1991) century. Accordingly, Levine (1993) dates them to the late preexilic period. However, one should not overlook the fact that if this blessing was in wide currency, it had been composed much earlier. And if it originated in priestly circles, it took a long while before its use spread among the populace in the form of an amulet. Finally, even if we were to disallow Num 6:22–26 as a P composition, there is no gain-saying that Aaron's blessing of the people at the inauguration of the cult (Lev 9:22) assuredly stems from P. The text, however, is not provided. If not Num 6:24–26, what could it have been? Blessing implies providence, favor, and concern—the very content of the Priestly Benediction.

Let us now consider the *šĕlāmîm*, the 'well-being offering'. P breaks it down into three categories: *tōdâ* 'thanksgiving', *neder* 'vow', and *nĕdābâ* 'free-will'. The thanks-giving offering is occasioned by escape from danger (cf. Ps 107, esp. v. 22); the votive offering expresses the hope that God will fulfill one's most urgent desires; and the free-will offering springs from the spontaneous outburst of joy. Thus the widest possible range of positive emotional needs are covered by the *šĕlāmîm*. The negative motivations—sanctuary pollution and sacrilege and other violations of prohibitive and performative commandments—are not overlooked. They are the grounds for the expiatory sacrifices, *ʿōlâ*, *ḥaṭṭāʾt*, and *ʾāšām* (details in vol. 1.133–490). Thus the sacrificial system is geared toward answering all the emotional and psychological needs of the people. Through the medium of sacrifice, the individual is urged to come to the sanctuary, and in the presence of YHWH, he or she can seek personal blessing or forgiveness. How can anyone now say that P exhibits a "total lack of concern with basic human needs" (Knohl 1995: 156)? Furthermore, a direct challenge to Knohl (1993) has been issued by Frankel (1994), who argues that the earliest stratum of the P narrative reveals YHWH as directly and intimately concerned with the fate and welfare of the people (Exod 16:9; Num 13; 14:26–27, 35, 37; 16:5, 23–24; 17:2–5, 16–20; 18:1–5; 20:7–11).

Knohl (1995: 160) also claims that "God's meeting with Moses in the priestly Tent of Meeting is merely a listening to the commandments of God." However, on a number of occasions, the Tent serves an oracular function. The blasphe-mer and the wood-gatherer are held in custody until God specifies (*prš*) their fate (24:12; Num 15:34). Moses explicitly "brings their [Zelophehad's daugh-ters'] case [*mišpāṭ*] before the Lord" (Num 27:5). Is one to assume that Moses entered the Tent just to listen? Or does the text presume that Moses verbalized each problem before God inside the *priestly* Tent and then awaited the heav-enly response? If one argues that these three H texts do not reflect P, then evidence that God and Moses were in dialogic relation is expressed in an unam-biguously explicit P statement, *ûbĕbōʾ mōšeh ʾel-ʾōhel môʿēd lĕdabbēr ʾēlâyw wayyišmaʿ ʾet-haqqôl middabbēr ʾēlāyw* 'When Moses went into the Tent of Meet-ing to speak with him, he would hear the voice speaking to him' (Num 7:89aα). This verse is an elaboration of another P verse: *wĕnôʿadtî lĕkā šām wĕdibbartî ʾittĕkā mēʿal haqqappōret mibbēn šnê haqqĕrubîm ʾăšer ʿal-ʾărôn hāʿēdut ʾēt kol-ʾăšer ʾăṣawweh ʾôtĕkā ʾel-bĕnê yiśrāʾēl* 'There I will meet with you, and I will im-part to you—from above the cover, from between the two cherubim that are on top of the ark of the Pact—all that I will command you concerning the Israelite people' (Exod 25:22). I concur with Levine's (1993: 258) conclusion that "the priestly tradition, while laying great stress on cult and sacrifice, nonetheless en-dorses the oracular role of the Tent" (see also Licht 1985: 1.111–12).

Thus it is clear that in P, no differently than in the epic (JE) tradition, Moses could commune with God and lay his people's needs before him, namely, food and water, military advice, or how to manage this contentious people. The Tent in the camp's center was, therefore, the oracular center of Israel's concerns (see further Milgrom 1990a: 386–87).

According to Kaufmann (1945: 2.476–80; 1960: 303–4), P desires to break away from the magical moorings of the cult. It is the ubiquitous use of magical incantations in idolatrous temples, forcing the deity to obey the will of the magician, that accounts for the priests' silence in the sanctuary. Knohl (1995: 148–49) rejects this explanation on the grounds that the very rituals "which, externally, most closely resemble idolatrous ritual (see Lev 16:21; Num 5:19–22)" are accompanied by speeches.

I opt for Kaufmann. In fact, I go even further. I maintain that Moses, the quintessential prophet, was constrained to silence while *performing* miracles lest he be taken as a magician. For the same reason, he would *initiate* the miracles when no one was in sight (with the occasional exception of picked elders, Exod 17:6). In fact, that Moses broke his silence at the waters of Meribah "in sight of the Israelites" (Num 20:13) is, in my opinion, why his punishment (death) fits his crime (heresy) (for the substantiation of my claim, see Milgrom 1990a: 448–56).

Turning to Knohl, I aver that he has misunderstood his two prooftexts. P's innovation in 16:21 is that the people's advertent sins, not the sanctuary's impurities, are removed by the scapegoat (see vol. 1.1034, 1043–44). Thus the confession recited by the high priest is not an incantation, but the verbalization of Israel's deliberate transgressions—a far remove from magic.

Regarding Num 5:21, which ascribes the effect of the bitter waters to God, whereas I maintain it is P's interpolation into an older magical formula (1981b; 1985d; 1990a: 353–54), Knohl (1995: 88) asserts it is H's interpolation into P's magical text. The difference between us hinges on the relationship between the term *'ālâ* 'imprecation' in the curse and in the pericope's summary (v. 27b as well as in v. 21). I maintain that since the notion of the curse rendering the adulteress an object of derision is found in only these two verses, P, the author of the summation (vv. 27–28), must have had v. 21 before him. Thus P is responsible for the interpolation of v. 21. Knohl (1995: 88–89, n. 90), however, would sweep away my argument by also declaring v. 27b an H interpolation. Here, I submit, he has erred. If the suspected adulteress is acquitted, she will bear seed (v. 28b). What is her punishment if found guilty? The answer is *wĕhāyĕtā hā'iššâ lĕ'ālâ bĕqereb 'ammāh* 'the woman shall become a curse among her people' (v. 27b). This sentence is the exact balance of v. 28 and, therefore, an essential component of P's summation (vv. 27–28) and cannot be an interpolation. It is based on v. 21, which, therefore, must also stem from P. Hence it is P that eliminates the automatic operation of an ordeal—probably in vogue in the Canaanite environment—by attributing its results to YHWH.

Knohl (1995: 149–50) also claims that "the inner cultic enclosure and its vessels are imbued with a 'contagious' substantive holiness and may be neither touched nor seen." This undoubtedly holds true for Israel's folk belief (e.g.,

1 Sam 6:19; 2 Sam 6:6–7). However, P has effectively and permanently eliminated the contagion of sanctums to persons by its formula *kol-hannōgēaʿ yiqdāš* 'whatever (not 'whoever) touches (it) will become sanctified' (Exod 29:37; 30:26–29; Lev 6:11, 20; details in vol. 1.443–56). Ironically, a reflex of the folk tradition is attested in Num 4:15, 20, which declares that the inner sanctums of the Tabernacle are contagious to touch when they *are stationary* and contagious on sight when they *are moved* (Milgrom 1990a: 29, on v. 20). Since Knohl holds that these verses stem from H, then H has been influenced by folk belief and has endowed the sanctums with power contagious to persons. Knohl has reversed the purported roles of H and P. In this case, it is H that displays a magical face! That H actually preserves a more primitive (folk) practice in contrast to a more sophisticated P is exemplified by Num 5:1–4 (H) and Lev 15 (P). Whereas P allows the *zāb* (and the corpse-contaminated person, Num 19) to remain at home, H sends them out of the camp, Num 5:1–4 (details in vol. 1.920).

My comments on Knohl's treatment of other P passages follow the pagination of his book.

1. Knohl (1995: 24–25) avers that P's firstfruits prescription (2:14) is voluntary. In vol. 1.192–93, however, I argue that this verse refers to the firstfruits of barley (*ʿōmer*), the prescription for which originally was mandatory for all farmers (see also NOTE on 23:10). The opening particle *wĕʾim* bears the notion of "when"; this verse is separated from the rest of the *minḥâ* prescriptions (2:1–10) because the latter are composed of wheat (*sōlet*); firstfruits of every crop are compulsory (Num 18:13; Neh 10:36). Knohl also claims that P's prescription of firstfruits of wheat (Num 28:26) is voluntary. To the contrary, this verse prescribes the mandatory public (not private) firstfruits offering by the sanctuary (see INTRODUCTION to 23:15–22).

2. Knohl (1995: 126) claims that by the use of the passive conjugations *Nipʿal* and *Hopʿal*, "God no longer forgives, cuts off or shows; rather the sin is forgiven (*wĕnislaḥ*); the sinner is cut off (*wĕnikrat*); Moses is shown the Tabernacle's vessel (*horʾâ*)." In this matter, one has to tread with caution. These verbs may be part of stock formulas that have no bearing on the "distancing" of the subject. For example, the terms *ʿammîm* and *nepeš* are as much fixed terms in formula of excision as *wĕnikrat*; *wĕnislaḥ* is governed by preceding *wĕkipper* (*Piʿel*), where the subject (active) has to be the officiating priest.

Note as well that P is not averse to anthropomorphisms—for example, *bĕʿênê* YHWH, literally 'in the eyes of YHWH' (10:19). It is perhaps no accident that the verse is part of a narrative. Where P is narrational, such anthropomorphisms might recur noticeably. (On Num 30, see no. 6, below.)

3. With Dillmann (1886), Knohl (1995: 126, n. 7) declares *ḥelqām nātattî ʾōtāh mēʾiššay* 'I have assigned their portion from my gifts' (6:10aβ) an interpolation. In vol. 1.17, I mount a number of arguments objecting to the removal of this sentence from the P corpus. If I am right, P is not averse to the deity speaking and referring to his sacrifices in the first person.

4. Knohl (1995: 127–28) exhibits confusion about the "sanctity" of Moses and Aaron in regard to entering the adytum. He claims that Moses would enter it at

random, but Aaron only at fixed circumstances and with preliminary safeguards (Lev 16). Not true. Moses *never* entered the adytum. He spoke to God *before* the Veil in the Shrine (Num 7:89). According to JE, only on Mount Sinai did he enter the divine cloud (= adytum). For details, see Milgrom 1990a: 365–66.

P, as customary, is consistent and logical. The distinction between Moses and Aaron is clear. Aaron's consecration marks the watershed. Moses is superior to Aaron before the latter becomes a priest. Moses, not Aaron, is invited to enter the divine cloud (Exod 24:18 [JE]), and Moses officiates at Aaron's consecration (Lev 8). But once Aaron is consecrated, he alone officiates. He alone enters the adytum. Moses neither officiates again nor enters the adytum.

5. When Knohl (1995: 132, n. 24) categorically declares that P's Tent of Meeting "serves as the permanent dwelling place of God," he overlooks the plain meaning of Exod 40:36–38 and Num 9:18–23. P also holds (with JE) that the deity is not immanent in the Tent of Meeting (*môʿēd*), but enters it only when he meets with Moses (*wĕnôʿadtî lĕkā šām*, Exod 25:22; cf. Num 7:89). Otherwise, the divine presence (*kābôd*) is suspended within a cloud *over* the Tent, presumably to provide guidance in the wilderness. When YHWH wished to speak with Moses, his *kābôd* (in the form of fire) would leave the cloud and descend into the Tent and reside on his Ark-throne, between the two cherubim.

6. It is no surprise, as claimed by Knohl (1995: 135), that the cereal offering for purification (5:11–12) or for the suspected adulteress (Num 5:15, 26) contains no frankincense because the frankincense symbolizes an occasion for joy, which is certainly not the case for expiatory sacrifices or for a *mazkeret ʿāwōn* 'a reminder of sin' (vol. 1.306), the offering of the suspected adulteress.

7. Knohl (1995: 135) argues that the omission of *rēaḥ nîḥōaḥ* 'appeasing/pleasing aroma' from the expiatory sacrifices par excellence, the *ḥaṭṭāʾt* and *ʾāšām* (except in 4:31) "lies in PT's desire to eliminate anthropomorphic overtones." But he overlooks that in P, the function of the *ʿōlâ* is exclusively expiatory (1:4; cf. 12:6–8; 14:19–20; 15:14–15, 29–30; 16:24; Num 6:10–11) and *rēaḥ nîḥōaḥ* is not eliminated (1:9).

8. In contradiction to Knohl (1995: 135, n. 42), the clause *YHWH yislaḥ lāh* (Num 30:9) implies automatic forgiveness. The woman receives divine assurance that if the father or husband cancels her vow, God will assuredly forgive her. Elsewhere, passive *wĕnislaḥ* (*Nipʿal*) is deliberately chosen (avoiding *Qal* active *sālaḥ*) to indicate that not the sacrifice, but only YHWH's will is the determinant of forgiveness (Lev 4:20bβ, 26bβ, 31bβ, 35bβ, etc.; see also vol. 1.17–18).

9. Knohl's (1995: 148, Appendix C) claim that Lev 16:21 and Num 5:19–22 are magically based rituals containing speech has been answered above. I would only add that in the priestly system, speech is prohibited only during sacrifice (Kaufmann's and Knohl's sanctuary of silence). But in Lev 16:21, the high priest's confession is made while leaning his hands on a goat, and the goat is not sacrificed, but dispatched into the wilderness. In Num 5:19–22, the priest addresses the woman (note the second-person address). Thus the speech of the priests in Lev 16:21 and Num 5:19–22 is not an incantation.

10. Knohl (1995: 151–52) claims that *wĕnirṣâ lō lĕkapper ʿālāyw* 'that it may be acceptable on his behalf to expiate for him' (Lev 1:4b) "expresses the idea that the very approach to the holy requires atonement and appeasement." Really? What of P's thanksgiving, votive, and free-will *šĕlāmîm* (7:11–21), which are occasioned by joy (the expiatory *šĕlāmîm* of ransom is the innovation of H; see NOTE on 17:11). It makes no sense to aver that merely entering the sanctuary "engenders feelings of guilt and the need for atonement" (note the influence of Otto 1958: 34–50). Surely, the authors of Pss 27:4; 65:5; 84:11, and so on did not think that way. Rather, Lev 1:4b (see above) refers to expiation for the violation of any of the performative commandments (vol. 1.858).

11. Knohl (1995: 164, n. 157) claims that the Urim and Thummim were placed *permanently* inside the Breastpiece of Decision to prevent "viewing the cult as a means to obtain God's help and intervention" (cf. Exod 28:29–30). Rather, the reason for "hiding" the Urim and Thummim is that they are for the exclusive use of the high priest, and no one else should be tempted to use them. Otherwise, the people were theoretically free to consult them by the mediation of the high priest.

12. Knohl's argument that Gen 2:1–3 (P) does not command sabbath rest for Israel is effectively parried by Smith (1999: 165, n. 20). There remains, however, Knohl's (1995: 18–19) ostensibly telling textual argument that P omits any mention of a work prohibition (*kol-mĕlākâ lōʾ taʿăśû*) and of the sabbath's sacred day (*miqrāʾ qōdeš*) in its calendar (Num 28:9–10).

First, the term *miqrāʾ qōdeš* literally means "a proclamation of holiness." This term, however, was inappropriate for the sabbath as long as Israel's day began in the morning. The sabbath, falling automatically on each seventh day, did not have to be proclaimed (see details in NOTE on 23:2). Once the nexus between the two was broken, the second term—the work prohibition—was not mentioned, even though the prohibition could have remained in force.

Second, it should be noted that a number of sacrifices consistently required for the following festivals (Num 28:11–38) are missing for the sabbath, namely, the bull and ram (burnt offerings) and the goat (purification offering). In fact, the sacrifices for the sabbath are the precise duplicate of those for the previous pericope, the daily *tāmîd* (vv. 3–8). Moreover, note that v. 9 is an incomplete sentence because it is lacking a verb such as *taqrîbû* (see v. 11). Thus there can be no doubt that the sabbath is only an extension of—indeed, an appendix to—the *tāmîd*. Its purpose (only two verses!) is merely to indicate its similarity with the *tāmîd and nothing else*. There is no reason to deny P's sabbath a priori a work prohibition.

Q. YHWH: A CAMEO

Knohl has observed that in P, YHWH always addresses Israel in the third person, whereas in H, YHWH speaks in the first person (*ʾănî*) when he addresses Israel in the second person. Thus there is "unmediated contact between God and the entire community" (Knohl 1995: 169). This generalization must be sharply amended. In all such recorded instances, God's address mainly opens with the introduction *wayyĕdabbēr YHWH 'el-mōšeh lē'mōr dabbēr 'el-bĕnê yiśrā'el wĕ'āmartā 'ălēhem* 'YHWH spoke to Moses, saying, speak to the Israelites and say to them'. Indeed, nowhere do we find the introduction *wayyĕdabbēr YHWH 'el-bĕnê yiśrā'el lē'mōr* 'YHWH spoke to the Israelites, saying'. Nor should we ever expect to find it. According to the Sinaitic account, Israel only once heard the voice of God, at Sinai, and it was so frightened by his voice that it requested of Moses that henceforth he should be its mediator (Exod 20:19 [E]; Deut 5:24). If, as I have surmised (see II S), the H redactor (H_R) had incorporated the Sinaitic traditions, he was fully aware that Moses was the indispensable conveyor of YHWH's messages to Israel. Moreover, since in the priestly tradition, after the construction of the Tabernacle, YHWH communicated his messages from within the Holy of Holies, only Moses (and Aaron) could have access to his word. Thus according to H, YHWH always spoke to Israel through the mediation of Moses. In effect, H does not differ from P: both require Moses' interposition.

There is one text ascribable to H (see I E) that ostensibly avers that God spoke directly and immediately to Israel. But as shown by an examination of this text and its immediate context, this deduction is chimerical:

Exod 29:42b–43a

'ăšer 'iwwā'ēd lākem šāmmâ lĕdabbēr 'ēlêkā šām wĕnō'adtî šāmmâ libnê yiśrā'el

for I will meet with you [pl.] there to speak with you [sing.] there, and there I will meet the Israelites

As noted by the critics, in YHWH's direct speech to Moses ("you," sing.), the word *lākem* ("you," pl.) is out of place (cf. Exod 30:6, 36 contra Num 17:19). The reading *lĕkā*, as found in the LXX and Sam., is therefore preferable. Thus here, too, Moses intervenes between YHWH and Israel. Also, instead of *wĕnō'adtî*, other readings are found in the versions *wĕnidraštî* 'and I will be sought' (Sam.) and *taksomai* 'I will command' (LXX Heb.?). But even presuming that the MT is correct, sense can be made of the text. YHWH will meet both Moses and Israel in the Tent of Meeting—Moses inside the Tent to receive YHWH's speech and the people at the altar where YHWH receives their sacrifices (Dillmann 1886). In any case, though YHWH speaks in the first person in H, in both P and H, YHWH's speech is always transmitted to Israel via Moses.

What is the nature of YHWH that can be gleaned from his addresses? Scanning H in Leviticus, we find the following:

17:1–7   YHWH does battle against chthonic worship (vv. 5–7; cf. 18:21; 20:1–5) by banning common slaughter (vv. 3–4). In this chapter, but not elsewhere in H, rationales are given to only Moses; the people, however, receive the straight commandment. For H, it seems, Israel is told what to do, not what to think.

17:10–14	Though God had already banned the ingestion of blood (3:17[P]) for all humanity (Gen 9:4[P]), H provides a positive motive to Israel for prohibiting common slaughter: the blood of sacrificial animals must be brought to the altar (17:3–4) to ransom (*kippēr*) them for the murder of these animals (17:11).
18:2, 5	YHWH uniquely introduces his laws with his formula of self-presentation, but all usages following this formula (except 19:2) denote "I YHWH (have spoken)," which is equivalent to the prophets' *něʾûm* YHWH 'the declaration of YHWH', implying that YHWH intends to punish if his command is not fulfilled.
18:5	YHWH asseverates *wāḥay bāhem*; that his, commandments generate life.
18:21	YHWH denies that he sanctions or even tolerates Molek worship (see NOTES).
18:24–30	YHWH declares that the violation of the sexual prohibitions pollutes (noncultic and nonexpiable *ṭāmēʾ*) the land and leads to Israel's exile.
19:2	YHWH declares that holiness is his essence, a quality that Israel gains by fulfilling his commandments.
19:11–18	The quintessence of divine and human holiness is ethics.
19:19	Mixing boundaries is forbidden because God has created an ordered world.
20:8	YHWH continuously judges Israel by its level of holiness; priests must sustain it, and laity must attain it.
20:24b–26	An indispensable way to holiness is by abstaining (*hibdîl* 'separate') from the ways of the nations.
22:1–16	YHWH warns the priests that the *qodāšîm* 'sacred food' are bound with special precautions.
22:26–33	When Israel abstains from desecrations, YHWH's holiness becomes more visible (v. 32).
23:3	YHWH sanctifies time (sabbath, festivals, septennate, and jubilee).
23:22	(= 19:9) YHWH cares for the indigent (of Israel) and the *gēr*, but only at harvest time (see below).
23:27–32	YHWH's *repeated* emphasis (three times) on fasting and no work implies that for YHWH's forgiveness the annual purgation of the sanctuary is insufficient without Israel's self-purgation.
24:14–16	YHWH will punish anyone who curses him, but if YHWH's name is cursed, the effect is so powerful that those within earshot must lean their hands on the blasphemer (i.e., "returning" his curse) and the community must slay him by stoning.
24:17–22	The talion laws affect the citizen and *gēr* alike. Aliens who settle in YHWH's land (*gēr tôšāb*) enjoy his protection.
25:2	The sabbatical is justified not economically, but theologically: YHWH's seventh day of rest (sabbath) is extended to YHWH's land every seventh year (sabbatical).

25:6–7   That H excludes the poor from benefiting from the sabbatical's af-
            tergrowth gives the impression that God is not concerned with their
            care. The reason may be practical: the aftergrowth is so skimpy that
            it is insufficient even for those under the direct responsibility of
            the landowner.

25:20–22   Practical economic considerations are tossed aside. Pure, unadul-
            terated faith in God will be rewarded with ample produce during
            the fallow seventh and unripe eighth years (also in the forty-ninth
            to fifty-first years).

25:23–24   YHWH's basic postulate: as only *tenants* in (not owners of) his land,
            they must obey YHWH's laws of jubilee and redemption.

25:39–43   The abolition of slavery is justified theologically: the Israelites are
            YHWH's own slaves; therefore, they cannot become slaves of any-
            one else.

26:11–12   "My (YHWH's) presence" (*miškānî*, a metaphoric usage) will bless
            Israel by circulating (*wĕhithallaktî*) about the land, possibly
            throughout many of its extant sanctuaries. As S. Chavel reminds
            me, I already observed in the NOTE on 26:11 that this verse is a di-
            rect reference to *wā'ehyê* **mithallēk** *bĕ'ōhel* **ūbĕmiškān** 'I have
            moved about in tent and **tabernacle**' (2 Sam 7:6b). Thus as YHWH
            (i.e., his Ark) circulated among the major sanctuaries before (and
            probably after) the construction of Solomon's Temple (see chap.
            17, COMMENT D), this blessing projects the recurrence not of the
            Ark, but of the divine presence. This image is also a literary allu-
            sion to the Garden, where God also circulated (Gen 3:8), an in-
            dication that the paradisiacal conditions can be restored (see
            NOTES).

26:13–39   The divine wrath is nowhere so vividly illustrated as its mounting
            ferocity in these five sets of curses, reaching a crescendo with
            YHWH's pursuit of Israel in the exile (vv. 38b–39). In the main,
            however, YHWH's punishments operate measure for measure—
            the perfection of justice.

26:39–41   Vertical retribution also operates in divine punishments: YHWH
            will punish Israel for the sins of its fathers and will hold it respon-
            sible for confessing those sins as well as its own (but see NOTE on
            v. 39). Proto-(prophetic) repentance (see NOTES) is attested here.

26:42–45   God's mercy is based not on sentiment, but on his unbreachable
            fidelity to his covenant: he keeps his promises (to the patriarchs).

A synopsis of these verses follows:

If the one God, YHWH, forbids the worship of other gods, it is not attested
in H except in regard to the Molek (20:1–5; see II D). The reason is that Molek
worship is practiced by the people on the assumption that it is sanctioned (even
commanded!) by YHWH. The worship entails the sacrifice (i.e., murder) of children (to earn access to the ancestral spirits)—a further desecration of YHWH's

name (18:21). That he is vexed by the illegitimate use of his name is attested by the existence of two categories of blasphemy: whoever curses him is punished by him, but if his name is cursed, the resulting pollution is so powerful that those within earshot "return" his curse (via hand-leaning) and the community slays him (and his curse) by stoning (24:14–16).

YHWH is a God of fidelity. His signature *'ănî YHWH/'ĕlōhêkem* (except where it reflects his self-presentation, as in 18:2; 19:2) is the equivalent of prophetic *nĕ'ûm YHWH*, indicating that YHWH keeps his word (of blessing and curse) and will punish its violation—again, a sign of his fidelity (see NOTE on 18:2b). His fidelity to his word is so unbreachable that he will keep his covenantal promise to the patriarchs and will restore exiled Israel to God's land, even if it has broken the (Sinaitic) covenant again and again—but only if it shows remorse and repents of its sins. YHWH's reconciliation with Israel is not an act of mercy, but fidelity (26:42–45). Indeed, the words for mercy never appear in H (or in P); (Friedman 1988: 238–39).

D shows deep compassion for the poor (Deut 15:7–8), in the form of inter-est-free loans (Deut 23:20), but provides no legislative relief. H, however, shows no concern at all for the poor other than at harvest time (19:9–10; 23:2). In fact, H actually denies the poor access to the sabbatical aftergrowth (25:6–7, in con-trast with Exod 23:11). However, this may be based on pragmatic grounds: to preserve the meager produce for those under the landowner's exclusive respon-sibility (family, slaves, and *resident* workers and aliens). Also, in theory, the land-less will be nonexistent (the laws of redemption and jubilee will be in effect) and, in general, the poor will be taken care of by their kin group (see further the apologia in II H). But the poor must have existed in large numbers, as tes-tified by the following: the loss of landed property due to its inability to support growing families; the increased latifundia, which the jubilee laws tried to rec-tify; and, above all, the massive influx of homeless and landless Northern refugees. D had it right: *lō yeḥdal 'ebyōn miqereb hā'āreṣ* 'the poor will not cease from the midst of the land' (Deut 15:11a). Thus the question remains unan-swered: Why does H ignore the poor? Rephrasing the question theologically: Why is there no instruction from YHWH—if not a law, at least some concern—for the poor? I have no answer.

YHWH's punishments are mainly exemplified by the principle of measure for measure—the ultimate in precise justice (26:13–38). He also punishes by verti-cal retribution, holding the children accountable for their sins and for the sins of their fathers (26:39). This is not unjust. The fathers, presumably, did not atone for their sins. The responsibility falls on the children. Reflected here is an im-age of disorders in creation that must be rectified. In H's theology, YHWH had created an ordered world. Hence he has prohibited admixtures of species, even between priests and lay persons (19:19?). What is true in nature also holds in morality. Sins cause a breach in the world, and they must be expiated, if not by the sinners, then by their children. The required expiation, remorse and con-fession, is H's contribution to the development of prophetic repentance (see NOTES on 26:40–41).

H's explicit image for the disruptions caused by sins is pollution of the land. Here, H has expanded the literal pollution caused by homicide (illegally spilled blood) to the surrounding earth (Gen 4:10–12; Num 35:33–34; Deut 21:4) to cover all violations, which metaphorically pollute (noncultic *ṭāmē᾿*) the entire land (18:24–30). The land is YHWH's; he has redeemed Israel from Egypt and granted it this land. The people of Israel are his tenants (25:23–24) and slaves (25:39–43). Hence they must obey his laws, specifically, to return the land to its original tenants and release indentured Israelites to their kin groups. They are not slaves; they receive daily wages as resident hirelings. They are slaves of YHWH, not of anyone else.

The postulate of the land also explains the legal equality of the resident alien (*gēr tôšāb*) with the citizen (24:17–22). Because they settled on his land, they are entitled to the owner's (YHWH's) protection.

YHWH's presence (*miškānî*, metaphoric usage) blesses (obedient) Israel by circulating (*wĕhithallaktî*) about the land—a literary image that recalls the divine voice circulating (*mithallēk*) in the primordial Garden and thereby suggests that paradisiacal conditions can be restored (26:11–12).

Israel in the wilderness is a recalcitrant, rebellious horde (JE). Faithless and feckless, it exasperates its leader Moses. How will Israel become a disciplined people, obedient to YHWH's laws as transmitted to Moses? It is this wilderness dilemma, true also for H in his own time, that may be the basis for H's greatest teaching: the doctrine of holiness. It serves as a heuristic technique. It is a ladder on which Israel can climb symbolically toward YHWH, the quintessence of holiness (19:2). The totality of *miṣwôt* need neither overwhelm nor deter. Step by step, rung by rung, Israel can transform itself spiritually and be ever more deserving of YHWH's blessing.

There is nothing that better illustrates Israel's immature dependence and dire need for such an aid than H's beginning: chap. 17. Israel is incapable of absorbing the divine commandments rationally. Israel has to be told what to do, not what to think. Only Moses is provided with rationales (vv. 5–7, 11, 14a). Perhaps it is no accident that the term *qādōš* 'holy' appears only two chapters later (19:2). Thereafter, Israel begins to be capable of receiving and internalizing rationales (see II B).

Simp(listical)ly put, Israel should strive to attain holiness, and (holy) priests should strive to sustain it (20:8). That is, YHWH awards increased holiness with each ascent on the ladder. Conversely, violation of the divine commandments causes slippage. Thus holiness is a dynamic concept, and priests, no differently from laity, must be on the alert concerning their own spiritual standing. Indeed, their very holiness always stands in jeopardy. Moreover, priests, by virtue of their right to officiate on the altar, are not allowed to make mistakes (10:1–3[P]). They are subject to severer regulations than the laity (22:1–16).

The ethics that Israel is bidden to follow (19:11–18, etc.) is the essence of divine holiness (*imitatio dei*). Equally important and even more operative in daily life is negative holiness, namely, to abstain from violating the divine prohibitions. Here, too, a divine model is invoked. As YHWH has separated the species

(Gen 1) and separated Israel from the nations, so should Israel separate itself from their contaminating ways (20:24b–26). The more Israel succeeds in abstaining from violating the commandments, *wĕniqdaštî* 'I will be sanctified' (22:32); that is, the more YHWH's holiness becomes visible in Israel (22:32).

In sum, though the text speaks of YHWH who sanctifies (*mēqaddēš*) Israel, the reality is that Israel sanctifies itself. If it obeys YHWH's commandments, its sanctification is automatic, a built-in result of the commandments. It will be recalled that the antithesis holy versus impure stands symbolically for life versus death (see II G; chap. 11, COMMENT A; COMMENT on chap. 19). Thus the self-sanctification produced by observance of the commandments is life-generating. This is pronounced succinctly and precisely by H: if one follows YHWH's commandments, *wāḥay bāhem* 'he shall live by them' (18:5b).

R. TOWARD THE COMPOSITION OF THE PENTATEUCH

It has been shown that H_R, the last stratum along the continuum of H's thought (Lev 23:2aβ–3, 42–43; 26:1–2, 33b–35, 43), dates to the exile (see their NOTES, and I F). It was also shown that this stratum is located both inside and outside Leviticus (see I E). The sabbath, for example, was inserted by exilic H_R at the head of the festival calendar (Lev 23:2aβ–3), before the concluding blessings and comminations (26:2), and also in Exod 31:12–17 and 35:1–3. These and other extra-Leviticus H_R passages are clearly later than their respective contexts because they have been interposed or appended, resulting in the discontinuance of those contexts (see the texts cited in I E). These considerations have led me to the conclusion that H_R is the redactor of all three books: Exodus, Leviticus, and Numbers.

This conclusion gathers support from the fact that H was aware of P. Note, however, that the source of the public calendar (Num 28–29, in the fourth book of the Torah) appears *subsequent* to its derivative (Lev 23, in the third book of the Torah), and the purificatory rites for the corpse-contaminated (e.g., *'ad 'ăšer yiṭhar*, Lev 22:4; *bĕyôm ṭoharătô*, Num 6:9) are taken for granted in Leviticus *prior* to their appearance in the MT of Numbers (Num 19; noted by the rabbis, *Tanḥ Buber* B, Num 115; *Pirq. R. Kah.* 69). This means that H (and, of course, P) had crystallized, and the redactor was limited to prefixes and supplements or, as in the above cases, to the rearrangement of their pericopes (for the possible motivations, see Milgrom 1990: 237, 443).

Why did H_R become the redactor? That is, why was he impelled to bring together the extant *Torah* traditions (JE, P, H, and D) and organize them at times (as illustrated above) in an ostensibly illogical order? I presume that H_R was motivated by two major factors, one internal and the other external.

The inner force is a conflation of three factors: (1) the threat of assimilation in the exile, (2) the hope (and preparation) for return to the homeland, and (3) the challenge of Babylonian mythology. There are no hard facts to support the first two factors, except for the indirect evidence of the small number of Israelites who actually did return (Ezra 2) and the rousing prophecies of exilic Isaiah. The Babylonian belief system is reflected and refuted in Gen 1–11, an exilic composition, the date for which I shall argue below. First, however, I shall cite five examples of the anti-Babylonian polemic (partially noted by Cassuto 1944: 49):

1. *Deep, tēhôm* (Gen 1:2). It reflects the goddess *tiamat* (note the absence of an article), from whose body Marduk creates the earth. In the Bible, there is no theomachy; Tiamat is inert material in the hands of the monotheistic creator (e.g., Gen 7:11; Isa 51:10; Ezek 26:19; Hab 3:10).

2. *Lights, mĕʾôrōt* (Gen 1:15, 16). A reference to the sun and moon, which are not called their proper names *šemeš wĕyārēaḥ*. In Babylonian, their names are *šamaš* and *śîn*, respectively. The precise equivalence between *šemeš* and *šamaš*, in particular, provided sufficient cause for alarm to the author that he disguised its name lest Israel identify the two and attribute autonomous force to the sun. Moreover, light was created by God on the first day (v. 3), and the function of the celestial bodies was reduced to *memšālâ* 'rule, management' of the light. Note as well that the creation of the sun and moon is demoted to the fourth day, the *last* of the inanimate objects in the cosmos.

3. *Our image after our likeness, bĕṣalmēnû kidmûtēnû* (Gen 1:26). The human being is not formed with the flesh and blood of a slain god, as reported by the Babylonian creation epics (Enūma Elish and Atraḥasis), but according to the divine likeness/image. Indeed, the former Babylonian epic served as political propaganda promoting the supremacy of Marduk and his city, Babylon. Biblical creation is apolitical. It contains no allusion to Israel, Jerusalem, or the Temple.

4. *The Flood.* Ever since the discovery first of Enūma Elish and subsequently of Atraḥasis, it has become clear that the biblical account is modeled after Babylonian prototypes. The differences between them reveal the biblical polemic. The rationale for the flood in Atraḥasis is overpopulation due to extensive fertility. In contrast, the cause for the biblical Flood rests entirely on moral grounds. Man is guilty of *ḥāmās* 'violence' (Gen 6:11; cf. Ezek 9:9; Job 16:17). The earth has been polluted in increasing measure by Adam (3:17), Cain (4:11), Lamech (4:23–24), and miscegenation with heavenly beings (6:5–7).

The Babylonian remedy is birth control: barrenness, infant mortality, and celibate women. The Bible, instead of reducing the birthrate, commands the reverse: "be fruitful and multiply." This command is given three times: once to the first human pair (1:28) and twice to Noah (9:1–7), as an inclusio to Noah's law code (cf. Exod 23:26). Indeed, these laws provide the remedy. The Flood has purged the earth of its pollution. Henceforth, it is hoped, man will heed the prohibition not to take life, because God will be the redeemer of the slain (9:5–6).

5. *The tower and Abraham* (chaps. 11–12). Mankind settles in the Sumer Valley. Instead of spreading out, in keeping with the divine desire (11:4), it builds up (Harland 1998: 527–33). It constructs a tower, an echo of Babylon's giant Etemenaki. The writer lampoons this building (11:3) and its builders. They are forcefully dispersed when YHWH confuses their language (vv. 7–9). In contrast,

Abraham unhesitatingly hearkens to YHWH's command to be "dispersed" from overly crowded Babylonian civilization, and he is accordingly rewarded (12:1–3). Zakovitch (1995: 54–55) points to other contrasts: whereas the people (i.e., the Babylonians) want to build (*bnh*) a tower for themselves (11:4), Abraham builds (*bnh*) an altar for God (12:4). Therefore, those who sought a name (*šēm*) for themselves (11:4) will be rejected and ejected, but Abraham, who sought neither name nor any other gain, will be granted a great name (*šēm*, 12:2).

Ostensibly, an objection can be invoked from source criticism in regard to these examples: Isn't it literarily impossible to claim that Gen 1 (P) lampoons Gen 11:1–4 (J)? This assumes the unlikely case that P had before him the written text of J! This objection is sustainable as worded. But we are dealing not with P the author, but with H_R, the redactor. He has artfully utilized both *written* texts in his composition of the primeval history. His editorial privilege may have allowed him the right to pare down his received texts or to slightly reword them in order to sharpen the contrast. In any event, J and P can coexist in the MT in the final, redactional stage.

Other examples abound regarding Mesopotamian references in Gen 1–11 (Cassuto 1961; Speiser 1964: 3–77), which justify, in my opinion, the conclusion that they were edited (and possibly reworded) in the Babylonian Exile. Thus the need to counter Babylonian mythology as part of the effort to combat assimilation and bolster hope of restoration to the homeland may have contributed, within the exilic community, to the composition of the Pentateuch.

The outer pressure to redact the Mosaic Torah at the close of the Babylonian Exile was supplied by the Persian emperor, Darius I. According to ample testimony culled from Darius's monumental inscription, the Demotic chronicle and the Edjahoresne inscriptions, Darius assembled the religious and secular leaders of Egypt in the third year of his reign (519–518 B.C.E.) and commanded them to codify all the Egyptian laws that had been in force (Spiegelberg 1914; Lichtheim 1980: 3. 36–41; Blenkinsopp 1987: 412–13; Tuell 1992: 90–94). Considering that the Persian imperial rule was (wisely) based on maximum tolerance of the religious beliefs and customary practices of its diverse subject populations, and especially that Darius was reputed in the ancient world for his legislative reforms throughout his kingdom (Plato, *Epis.* 8. 332 B), it is most reasonable to assume that the Jewish community in Jerusalem adjacent to Egypt was ordered to do the same.

Tuell (1992: 93) surmises that the Jewish community in Jerusalem responded to Darius's command with Ezekiel's Law of the Temple (chaps. 40–48), whereas their Babylonian counterparts responded with the Mosaic Torah. Tuell's conjecture lacks support (cf. Greenberg 1995b: 43–44). Furthermore, the Jews of Babylonia probably would have been exempted from Darius's prescript; they were not politically autonomous! Finally, had Ezekiel's laws been enforced in Jerusalem (note the radically different prescriptions for the sacrificial cult, Ezek 43:13–27; 45:12–46:15), they would have been expressly negated by Ezra.

It would be more reasonable to presume that the nascent, minuscule Jerusalem community would have requested their large and better established

Babylonian counterparts to assist them in composing the required laws. The result of this purported joint effort would have been the extant Book of the Torah — for both communities.

The question persists, though: nearly a century later, Ezra brings the Torah to Jerusalem and on the first day of the seventh month (Festival of Alarm Blasts, Lev 23:24) reads it to his assembled people (Neh 8:3), which signifies, ostensibly, that they heard it for the first time. Moreover, the people burst into tears during the reading (v. 9) — again, a likely sign that they heard it *for the first time*. Doesn't this imply that the Mosaic Torah was nonexistent before Ezra?

Williamson (1985: 291) has plausibly suggested that the people heard for the first time not the Torah, but its interpretation, and their tears stemmed from hearing not the words of the Torah, but its exposition (and, no doubt, its application). Further support for this inference can be garnered from the events of the following day. Ezra persuades a small group of civil leaders, priests, and Levites to remain behind (v. 13) to study (*lĕhaśkîl*) a particular law, the building of ceremonial booths, an observance falling due in less than two weeks (Lev 23:42). As explained in chap. 23, COMMENT B, this laconic text was subject to more than one interpretation. That Ezra (and probably the Babylonian Jews) chose an interpretation that was not in accord with the plain meaning of the text (see NOTE on 23:42) is an indication of its ambiguity. It therefore required textual exposition and "study." The Jerusalemites may have known and observed the Festival of Booths, but they were confused about the booths themselves, namely, their materials and their location. Again, clear evidence that the Torah text was probably not new, but only Ezra's interpretation (for Ezra's misinterpretation, see chap. 23, COMMENT B).

There is textual evidence concerning a major problem facing the redactor. Recently, my attention was arrested by Loewenstamm's (1968: 625) observation that the two largest law corpora, P (+ H) and D differ from each other in the following telling way. The priestly corpus is a collection of small, independent laws that probably existed in separate scrolls. Many open with *wayyĕdabbēr YHWH 'el-mōšeh lē'mōr* 'YHWH spoke to Moses saying' (over eighty times) and conclude with *zō't tôrāt (YHWH)* 'This is the ritual (of YHWH)', *wĕhāyâ lāhem . . . lĕhuqqat 'ōlām* 'It shall be for them . . . an eternal statute' (7:37; 11:46; 12:7; 13:59; 14:32, 54, 57; 15:32; 17:7), *ûšĕmartem 'et* 'And you shall guard' (Exod 12:17 [bis], 24; 31:14; Lev 18:5, 26, 30; 19:3; 20:8, 22; 22:31; Num 18:5), or *tôrâ 'aḥat . . . lā'ezraḥ wĕlaggēr* 'The same law . . . for citizen and alien' (Exod 12:19, 49; Lev 17:15; 24:22; Num 9:14; 15:15–16). Deuteronomy's laws, to the contrary, lack introductions and closures, but form a single unified bloc. For me, this sharp distinction is instructive. It signifies that D's laws were composed and *edited* before the exile. The priestly corpus, however, composed in preexilic times (see I K), existed only in disparate documents until it was assembled and edited by the exilic redactor, H$_R$. Since H alludes to E's corpus (e.g., Lev 25:1–7; Exod 23:10–11), E preexisted H. That E's Book of the Covenant existed as a single corpus (Exod 21–23) is also shown by the same D characteristic: it contains no inner introductions or conclusions (i.e., postscripts, summations, compliances). Thus the priestly corpus (P + H) must have been the last to be redacted, though—it should never be kept out of mind—all its disparate laws (except the few added by the redactor H_R) were composed in preexilic times.

It was demonstrated (see I E) that H redacted both the laws and the narratives of P (e.g., Exod 27:20–21; 31:12–17; Lev 11:43–45; Num 15), and it was also suggested that H redacted the JE narratives as well. The illustration I chose here is Num 13–14. There is no doubt that priestly material (Num 13:1–17a; 14:26–35) has been grafted onto JE (13:17b–14:25), which independently is a continuous, smooth-running story, leaving the combination despite its harmonious structure rife with logical contradictions (Milgrom 1990a: 386–90). Knohl (1995: 90–92) assigns the priestly texts to H. I am not so sure. Be that as it may— whether P or H—there can be no doubt that H, the redactor of Num 15 (see I E), has attached Num 15 to Num 13–14. In other words, H or H_R has added its legal material (chap. 15) to a fused JE and P (H?) narrative (chaps. 13–14). His reasons for placing chap. 15 between the narratives of the reconnaissance of Canaan (chaps. 13–14) and the Korahite rebellions (chap. 16) are explained in my analysis of the tassels pericope (see I E, no. 11). I need but add that chap. 15 can be read into the text without disturbing the flow between the two narratives. Thus chap. 15 must be an insert by the redactor H_R.

In conclusion, if H_R had the fused JE and P (H?) narratives (Num 13–14), it stands to reason that H_R is also the redactor of the central books of the Torah: Exodus, Leviticus, and Numbers; mainly in agreement with Knohl (1995: 101–102). In addition, if it will be proved that H_R's hand is also detectable in Genesis (17*, 23 [?], 36 [?]; see Knohl 1995: 104; and possibly Gen 1–11, see above) and Deuteronomy (32:48–52), and that these are the *final* insertions into these two books, the possibility must be considered that H_R is the redactor of the entirety of the Mosaic Torah.

Moreover, in agreement with Freedman (1992: 6–12) that the Former Prophets were also edited in the Babylonian Exile, the likelihood must be considered as well that H_R was their final redactor (note the priestly passages in Josh. 20:6, 9; 22:16–20; 1 Kgs 8:10–11, etc.).

TRANSLATION, NOTES, AND COMMENTS

◆

PART IV. THE HOLINESS SOURCE (CHAPTERS 17–27)

◆

17. THE SLAUGHTER AND CONSUMPTION OF MEAT

TRANSLATION

Introduction

[1]YHWH spoke to Moses, saying: [2]Speak to Aaron and to his sons and to all the Israelites and say to them: This is what YHWH has commanded:

No Nonsacrificial Slaughter

[3]If anyone of the house of Israel slaughters an ox or a sheep or a goat in the camp, or does so outside the camp, [4]and has not brought it to the entrance of the Tent of Meeting to present (it as) an offering to YHWH, before YHWH's Tabernacle, bloodguilt shall be imputed to that person: he has shed blood; that person shall be cut off from among his kinspeople. [5](This is) in order that the Israelites may bring their sacrifices which they have been sacrificing in the open field—that they may bring them to YHWH, at the entrance of the Tent of Meeting, to the priest, and offer them as sacrifices of well-being to YHWH; [6]that the priest may dash the blood against the altar of YHWH at the entrance of the Tent of Meeting, and turn the suet into smoke as a pleasing aroma to YHWH; [7]and that they may offer their sacrifices no longer to the goat-demons after whom they stray. They shall have this (statute) as an eternal law, throughout their generations.

No Sacrifices to Other (Infernal) Gods

[8]And say to them further: If anyone of the house of Israel or of the aliens who may reside among them offers up a burnt offering or a (well-being) offering, [9]and does not bring it to the entrance of the Tent of Meeting to offer it to YHWH, that person shall be cut off from his kinspeople.

No Ingestion of Blood: Sacrificeable Animals

[10]And if anyone of the house of Israel or of the aliens who reside among them ingests any blood, I will set my face against the person who ingests blood, and I will cut him off from among his kinspeople. [11]For the life of the flesh is in the blood, and I have assigned it to you on the altar to ransom your lives; for it is the blood that ransoms by means of life. [12]Therefore I say to the Israelites: No person among you shall ingest blood, nor shall the alien who resides among you ingest blood.

No Ingestion of Blood: Game

[13]And if any Israelite or any alien who resides among them hunts down a beast or bird that may be eaten, he shall pour out its blood and cover it with earth. [14]For the life of all flesh—its blood is with its life. Therefore I said to the Israelites: You shall not ingest the blood of any flesh, for the life of all flesh is its blood; anyone who ingests it shall be cut off.

Eating of a Carcass Requires Purification

[15]And any person, whether citizen or alien, who eats what has died or has been torn by beasts shall launder his clothes, bathe in water, and remain impure until the evening; then he shall be pure. [16]But if he does not launder (his clothes) and bathe his body, he shall bear his punishment.

Comments

Chthonic worship in 1 Sam 14:31–35, COMMENT A; the gēr, COMMENT B; the blood prohibition, COMMENT C; and the alleged centralization of worship in H, COMMENT D.

COMPOSITION AND STRUCTURE OF CHAPTER 17

Chapter 17 comprises five laws revolving about a single pivot: the prohibition against ingesting blood. The prohibition itself is confined to the third (middle) law (vv. 10–12). The rest of the chapter, however, either leads up to it (vv. 1–9) or depends on it (vv. 13–16). Further emphasizing the centrality of this theme is a stylistic criterion. The word dām 'blood' and its verb 'ākal 'ingest' occur, respectively, ten and seven times (all in vv. 10–15; dām also appears in v. 4, where its meaning, however, is "bloodguilt, murder").

Another motif unifying this chapter is the kārēt penalty (vv. 4, 9, 10, 14, 16; on its distinction from nāśā' 'āwōn, see NOTE on v. 16). In the first two laws, it is voiced in the passive, wěnikrat (vv. 4bβ, 9b); the fourth law only alludes to it (v. 14bβ), and the fifth (vv. 15–16) does not mention it by name, but implies that kārēt may ultimately happen (see NOTE on "he shall bear his sin," v. 16). The third and middle law (vv. 10–12) contains the active, emphatic, and highly personalized *wĕhikrattî*, which emphasizes the urgency and centrality of this law within the chapter. Thus "the first three paragraphs contain three prohibitions, arranged in ascending order of severity. The last of these three, which is of course the most absolute and most severe, draws in its wake two positive commands . . . in descending order of severity. The five paragraphs thus make up an inverted 'V' [an introversion—J.M.], at the zenith of which stands the absolute prohibition of partaking of blood and its rationale. This section, vv. 10–12, is therefore the axis upon which the chapter revolves" (Schwartz 1991: 42–43).

The common denominator of all five laws is the ritual procedure in the slaughter and consumption of meat. The first law (vv. 3–7) mandates that permitted domesticated quadrupeds must be sacrificed at a legitimate sanctuary. The second law (vv. 8–9) prohibits both the Israelite and the resident alien from sacrificing to other gods. The third law (vv. 10–12) lays down the absolute prohibition against ingesting blood, incumbent on Israelite and resident alien alike. The fourth law (vv. 13–14) prescribes that the blood of game killed by the Israelite and resident alien must be buried, and the fifth law (vv. 15–16) states that the Israelite or resident alien who eats of an animal that has died must purify himself. The first, third, and fourth laws contain rationales (vv. 5–7, 11–12, 14). They take the form of asides to Moses and are not intended to be repeated to Israel (Schwartz 1991: 45–46). Details follow in the NOTES.

NOTES

The structure of Lev 17 can be represented by the following outline:

Introduction (vv. 1–2)
A. Nonsacrificial slaughter prohibited (vv. 3–7)
    1. Sacrificeable animals must be sacrificed at a legitimate sanctuary (vv. 3–4)
    2. Rationale: wean Israel from idolatry (vv. 5–7)
    B. Israelites and aliens forbidden to sacrifice to other gods (vv. 8–9)
        1. A link with the previous law (v. 8aα)
        2. The law (vv. 8aβ–9)

        X. Ingestion of blood prohibited (vv. 10–12)

            1. Of all animals (v. 10)
            2. Rationale for sacrificeable animals: ransom for murder (vv. 11–12)
    B'. Ingestion of blood prohibited (vv. 13–14)
        1. Of game (v. 13)
        2. Rationale: blood is life (v. 14)
A'. Eating of a carcass requires purification (vv. 15–16)
    1. The law (v. 15)
    2. The consequence (v. 16)

I presume that chap. 17 forms the beginning of the Holiness Source. To be sure, this chapter does not mention the root *qdš*, nor does it contain H's quintessential term *'ănî YHWH* (*'ĕlōhêkem*), which has led some scholars to deny any connection between this chapter and those that follow (e.g., Hoffmann 1953; Kilian 1963: 176–79; Feucht 1964: 63–64). Moreover, the word *śā'îr* 'goat' (17:7) occurs in the previous chapter (16:5–10, 21–22; cf. Ibn Ezra), as does the term *kippēr* 'purge, ransom' (17:11 [bis]; 16:6, 11, 16–18, etc.; cf. Hallo 1991: 68), which might indicate that Lev 17 belongs with the preceding chapters. Indeed, this is the conclusion of Douglas (forthcoming: chap. 9), who finds that chaps. 1–17 form a ring closed by chap. 17 with a latch to the beginning: chap. 1. Both chap. 1 and chap. 17 speak of the correct sacrificial procedure (note the parallel vocabulary: 1:2–4 ‖ 17:3–4; 1:5, 9 ‖ 17:6).

		Latch		
	1	17		
	2		16	
SACRIFICE	3		15	IMPURITY
	4		14	
	5		13	
	6		12	
	7		11	
		8 9 10		
		NARRATIVE		

Nonetheless, as demonstrated by most scholars (most recently, Schwartz 1987: 89–90; Joosten 1994: 3–4), the evidence overwhelmingly favors placing chap. 17 at the head of the Holiness Source. Their main arguments are the following:

1. Like other pentateuchal law corpora, H begins with prescriptions on sacrifices (chap. 17) and concludes with a series of blessings and curses (chap. 26; cf. the Book of the Covenant, Exod 20:22–26; 23:20–23; Deut 12, and 28; concerning the appendix, Lev 27, see Introduction I E).

2. The exhortatory sections giving the motivations for the laws are typical of the chapters that follow (e.g., 17:5–7, 11; 18:2–5, 24–30) and are alien to those that precede (P). The contention that paraenesis is not foreign to P, on the basis of 11:43–45 (Cholewinski 1976: 31, n. 60; Blum 1990: 322), is refuted because that passage is demonstrably an addition by H (see vol. 1.683–88, 95–96).

3. Chap. 17 shares with H its same distinctive style (e.g., God addressing Israel in the first person, vv. 10–12; 19:2; 20:5–7), structure (Schwartz 1991: 42–43), and theology (see Introduction I I; Knohl 1995: 125–37), specifically, the emphasis on motivations (vv. 5, 7, 11–12, 14), the declaration of penalties (vv. 4, 9, 10, 14, 16), and the reform of non-Yahwistic practices (vv. 7, 9; cf. Budd).

4. Budd (1996: 16) argues that since the prohibitions against imbibing blood (vv. 10–14) and eating carcasses (vv. 15–16) "have already been explicitly affirmed (Lev 7:22; 11:39–40)," chap. 17 belongs with the following chapters. He

is right, but his argument requires nuancing. The reason for repeating these laws is that H amends them: the blood of the *šĕlāmîm* ransoms its offerer (v. 11), and eating carcasses mandates purification, or else divine sanctions are certain to follow (v. 16) (see Introduction II P).

Nevertheless, the possibility exists, for the reasons mentioned above, that chap. 17 was intentionally positioned by H to form a link with the preceding chapters, thereby indicating that H was a continuation and elaboration of P (see Introduction II P).

Vv. 1–2. Introduction

Some scholars hold that this introduction applies solely to vv. 5–7 (Elliger 1966) or to the first two laws, vv. 3–9 (Ibn Ezra; Wessely 1846; Dillmann and Ryssel 1897; Hoffmann 1953). However, since ritual instruction is a priestly responsibility (cf. 10:10–11), there is no reason to doubt that vv. 1–2 head up the entire chapter.

2. *Speak to Aaron and to his sons and to all the Israelites.* This salutation occurs again only in 21:24 and 22:18, a possible indication that it stems from the pen of H. The priests are included because they are the promulgators of ritual laws (10:10–11). As a signature of H, it is theologically significant. P carefully distinguishes between Moses' statements to priests and to laity: laity (Exod 25:2; 27:20; Lev 1:2; 4:2; 7:29; 8:5; 9:5–6; 12:2; Num 5:2; 9:10; 15:2, 18; 28:2; 30:2; 34:2; 35:10); priests (Lev 6:2, 18; 8:31; 9:2, 7; 10:3, 6, 8, 12; 13:1; 14:33; 16:2; Num 18:1, 8, 26). Even where priests and laity share a concern, either one party or the other is addressed (e.g., Num 2:2; 5:6, 12; 6:2). Indeed, on two such occasions, Moses directs the priests to speak to the Israelites (Lev 11:1–2; 15:1–2).

H, however, breaks down this distinction. On issues of common concern, priests and laity are addressed simultaneously: sacrificial slaughter (17:1–7) and sacrificial defects (22:17–25). In H, one salutation projects its viewpoint into greater prominence: even where the context is of purely priestly concern (priestly disqualifications, 21:1–23), a colophon is added that the Israelites are also addressed (v. 24; see its NOTE).

H's egalitarian thrust is clear: no differently from the priests, the Israelites are enjoined to follow a distinctive regimen of holiness (19:2; see COMMENT on chap. 19). No matter that concerns the sanctuary and its personnel is, therefore, out of their purview. Indeed, the sociopolitical implications are even more fundamental: the laity is divinely ordained to supervise the priests while they carry out their functions (see Introduction II L). In the same vein, Crüsemann (1996: 308–10) points out that whereas the other pentateuchal law codes are addressed to property owners, in P (rather H) "all social distinctions based on ownership of land or legal freedom are gone. . . . The law applied for landowner and wage owner, slave and free, rich and poor, even Israelite and non-Israelite."

This. zeh haddābār. Judging by other attestations of this phrase in the priestly texts (Exod 16:16, 32; 29:1; 35:1, 4; Lev 8:5; 9:6; Num 30:2; 36:6), it always refers to the speech that follows. According to the rabbis (*Sipra* Aḥare, par. 1:2;

cf. Wessely 1846), it emphasizes that YHWH's words may not be paraphrased by Moses, but must be delivered verbatim (see NOTES on 8:5 and 9:6).

Vv. 3–7. The First Law: No Nonsacrificial Slaughter and Its Two Rationales

Vv. 3–4. Rabbinic writings record a debate between R. Akiba and R. Ishmael (b. Ḥul. 16a–17a; cf. Lev. Rab. 22:6). R. Akiba holds that since the verb šāḥaṭ means "slit the throat (for sacrifice)," this first law (vv. 3–7) deals solely with animals intended for the altar. Hence slaughter by other means (e.g., bludgeoning, strangling, stabbing), not intended for sacrifice (but for nonsacrificial slaughter), is also permitted. This view is echoed in most commentaries (Sipra Aḥare, par. 1:5; b. ʿAbod. Zar. 51b, 52b; b. Zeb. 106a; Tanḥ Naso 21; Saadiah, Rashi, Rashbam, Abravanel; among the moderns: Paton 1897; Driver 1913; Reventlow 1961; Levine 1989; Hartley 1992; also the oldest witness—the Samaritan addition to v. 4, see below). R. Ishmael, however, holds that this law ordains that all animals intended for food must be offered up as a sacrifice, thereby prohibiting nonsacrificial slaughter. This view is also championed in some rabbinic commentaries (Sipre Deut. 75; Deut. Rab. 4:6; cf. Ramban, Bekhor Shor, Sforno, Shadal). R. Akiba apparently read vv. 3–4 as if the words lĕhaqrîb qorbān laYHWH followed lammaḥăneh, yielding "If anyone . . . slaughters . . . an offering to the Lord in the camp" (Schwartz, forthcoming).

R. Akiba's view cannot be maintained. First, the verb šāḥaṭ refers to only the method of slaughter, not its purpose. Note that in H, where all slaughter is sacrificial, šāḥaṭ is used in the same context as zābaḥ (e.g., 22:28–29). But there is a difference between these two terms: whereas zābaḥ is used strictly for the šĕlāmîm, where it connotes not just slaughter but the bringing and presentation (hiqrîb) of the sacrifice (contrast 7:16aβ with 19:6a; cf. Paran 1989: 248), the verb šāḥaṭ, in priestly texts, is not limited to the šĕlāmîm but applies to all quadrupedal sacrifices (details in Milgrom 1976h: 13–15). Indeed, nonsacrificial slaughter employing šāḥaṭ is also attested (e.g., Gen 37:31; Num 11:22; 1 Sam 14:32; Isa 22:13), also in P (e.g., 14:5, 50). Second, if the first law (vv. 3–7) dealt with only sacrificial animals, demanding that all sacrifices be offered up solely to YHWH, then the second law (vv. 8–9), banning sacrifices to other gods, would be superfluous (Bekhor Shor; Cassuto 1954a: 884). Third, R. Akiba would not be able to explain the absence of the gēr from the first law, since the gēr, like the Israelite, is required to bring all his sacrifices to YHWH (vv. 8–9). In R. Ishmael's view, however, the omission of the gēr makes sense: even if he resides within the camp, he is permitted nonsacrificial slaughter (see NOTE on "of the house of Israel").

Nonetheless, R. Akiba's position cannot be entirely rejected. The very fact that the prohibition against nonsacrificial slaughter is the radical innovation of H implies that heretofore—in the time of P—nonsacrificial slaughter was practiced and approved (vol. 1.28–34), provided that the slaughter took place on an improvised stone and that the blood was drained (vol. 1.28–29; cf. COMMENT A).

Thus R. Akiba's view, even if held invalid for the present MT (stemming from H), holds logically for the prior historical situation prevailing under P.

The theory that in Israel and among other Semites all slaughter was originally a sacrifice is based on Wellhausen's (1897: 117–18) investigations into customary rites of pre-Islamic Arabs, a theory that most scholars have followed (e.g., Paton 1897: 32; Baentsch 1903: 388; Elliot-Binns 1955: 40; Cholewinski 1976: 266). But as correctly challenged by Aloni (1984), Wellhausen had no evidence except for the *tahalil*, the shrill calls to the deity during the act of slaughter—a far cry from any known sacrificial procedure. Eventually, a law is decreed that all slaughter in Israel is required to be a sacrifice, but it stems from the innovative mind of H, and to judge by D's subsequent reversion to nonsacrificial slaughter, H's law—if enacted at all—could not have lasted very long.

3. *anyone.* ʾîš ʾîš. This idiom is distributive in meaning. Knohl (1995: 87, n. 83) claims it for H (vv. 8, 10, 13; 18:6; 20:2, 9; 22:4, 18; 24:15), whereas P, for similar (sacrificial) laws, uses only *nepeš* (e.g., 2:1; 4:2; 5:1), restricting ʾîš ʾîš (and ʾîš ʾ ô ʾiššâ) for its laws of purity (e.g., 15:2, 5, 16). However, the latter verses refer to a male! Besides P also uses ʾîš ʾîš and ʾîš ʾ ô ʾiššâ in sacrificial laws (15:2; Num 6:1–21). Nonetheless, once this idiom is followed by *mibbēt yiśrāʾēl ʾăšer* (see below), it becomes a distinctive H expression (vv. 8, 10; 22:18; cf. 17:13).

of the house of Israel. mibbēt yiśrāʾēl, attested in vv. 8, 10; Ezek 14:4, 7. The LXX[BA] adds ʾo[?] *min haggēr haggār bĕtôkĕkem* (cf. v. 8; 16:29), but it is rightly dismissed by Dillmann and Ryssel (1897: 586, 588) and Baentsch (1903: 389). The rabbis would also have rejected this reading on logical grounds: "The non-Israelite is not subject to the law of slaughtering and sacrifice outside (the sanctuary); moreover, non-Israelites may erect altars everywhere (provided) they sacrifice to (the Lord of) heaven" (*Sipra* Aḥare, par. 6:1; cf. *b. Zeb.* 16b). The requirement to offer the blood of sacrificeable animals on the altar falls solely on the Israelite ("I have assigned it to you," v. 11), which forms another bond between the first and third laws of this chapter (see its INTRODUCTION). The *gēr* is bound by the Noahide law to drain the blood (Gen 9:4), but since he is required to worship Israel's God, he need not bring the blood to his altar. Moreover, there exists a deeper, more basic, reason for this exemption, one that is grounded in the priestly theology or, rather, ecology: it is incumbent on the *gēr* to obey only YHWH's prohibitive commandments, since their violation generates impurity that pollutes the land and ultimately results in Israel's exile. The violation of performative commandments, however, is characterized not by action, but by neglect. No pollution is generated by inaction, and the ecology is not upset (details in Milgrom 1982a). Thus in H's view, the *gēr* does not belong in this law.

slaughters. yišḥaṭ. This is P's technical term for "slit the throat" (Milgrom 1976h). It refers to only a method of slaughter, but not its purpose. Hence it can be applied not only to sacrifice but also to nonsacrificial slaughter (e.g., Gen 37:31; Num 11:22; 1 Sam 14:32; Isa 22:13). This fact leads to the conclusion that this law prohibits all common, nonsacrificial slaughter and, instead, demands that meat for the table initially be offered up as a sacrifice. Heretofore, those who could not readily make the journey to the sanctuary would slaughter their animals at home. Not that they would have been permitted to drain the animal's blood on the ground (as later allowed by D, of Deut 12:16, 24), but, more likely, in keeping with Saul's remonstrances (1 Sam 14:31–35), they would have slaughtered their animals on a stone (see COMMENT A). Indeed, since H insists that the blood of game be buried (vv. 13–14), one must assume that special slaughtering conditions, such as those imposed earlier by Saul, would have been required for domesticated animals (see further COMMENT A).

Thus one might explain H's ban on historical grounds: Saul's exhortations were not obeyed. Israel continued to slaughter on the ground, arousing suspicion that it was surreptitiously indulging in chthonic worship. Hence H bans all nonsacrificial slaughter, forcing the people to bring their animals to the sanctuary where the preliminary sacrificial rites performed by the offerer—including slaughtering—would be supervised by the priests. D, however, polemicizes with H and restores the right of nonsacrificial slaughter. This concession can be explained by positing that D may have feared that espousing Saul's method of slaughtering on a stone would have led to the construction of field altars, just as it happened in the case of Saul (1 Sam 14:35).

However, H's ruling may be better understood on the basis of its theological postulates. As will be unfolded in the rest of this chapter, H believes that the charge of murder against an Israelite who takes the life of an animal can be expiated if the animal's blood is returned to its divine creator via the sacrificial altar (vol. 1.704–13). D, on the contrary, permits nonsacrificial slaughter because it has no choice: it is mandated by centralization.

Although the verb *šāḥaṭ* is the technical term for all sacrificial slaughter (e.g., 1:5; 3:8; 4:22, 33; 7:2), its use here probably refers to the well-being offering (Hartley 1992). This certainly is how H understands it (vv. 5–7; see NOTE on *zābaḥ*). Besides, the sacrifice of a *šôr* 'ox' occurs only as a well-being offering (4:10; 9:4, 18; 22:23, 27; Num 15:11).

an ox or a sheep or a goat. šôr 'ô-keśeb 'ô-'ēz. This triad comprises all the sacrificial quadrupeds. It is found elsewhere only in 22:27, with the copulative waw in 7:23, and in construct with *bĕkôr* 'firstling' in Num 18:17—all probably H. Alternatively, one finds the expression *šôr 'ô śeh* 'ox or flock animal' (e.g., 22:28; cf. Exod 34:19; Lev 27:26; Deut 18:3)—*śeh* referring to the young of either a sheep or a goat (e.g., Exod 12:5; Num 15:11). Why are not permitted domesticated birds (e.g., doves or pigeons) included in this list? The rabbis reply (*Sipra* Aḥare, par. 6:4) that birds are not slaughtered sacrificially by slitting the throat (*šāḥaṭ*), but by pinching the neck (*mālaq*; cf. 1:15). The rabbis are partially right. Sacrificial birds, indeed, are not "slaughtered." The conclusion, however, must follow that the context here is nonsacrificial (unless one follows R. Akiba's sentence rearrangement; see INTRODUCTION to vv. 3–4). Moreover, the verb *šāḥaṭ* does not denote sacrificial slaughter unless it is directly followed by sacrificial modifiers; otherwise, it refers to nonsacrificial slaughter (e.g., Exod 12:6; Lev 14:5, 50).

in the camp. The *maḥăneh* 'camp' is the prototype of the city (14:3, 40; cf. 2 Kgs 7:3–4), and Israel's wilderness camp with the Tabernacle at its center is the prototype for a city with a regional sanctuary (for P, initially Shilo; for H, Jerusalem).

outside the camp. In the wilderness camp, no one presumably would have left in order to slaughter an animal. Hence this phrase clearly indicates a provenance in Canaan—not to all of it, but to the area surrounding the central sanctuary and within easy reach of it (Raban 1956: 234; Aloni 1984: 35). The phrase *miḥûṣ lammaḥăneh* always implies the vicinity of the camp (13:46; 14:3; 24:14; Exod 33:7–8; Deut 23:13; see also Gen 19:16; 24:11; Exod 26:35; Lev 14:8). If, however, a greater distance from the camp were intended, then this expression would have been supplemented (e.g., *miḥûṣ lammaḥăneh harḥēq min-hammaḥăneh* 'outside the camp, at some distance from the camp,' Exod 33:7 [E]), and in Canaan a spot not within reach of a sanctuary is described by *derek rěḥōqâ lākem*, literally 'a long way for you' (Deut 12:21 [D]). Since there is no area in the land that is not accessible to some sanctuary, all common slaughter is interdicted.

If, however, it is assumed, as it is by most scholars (most recently Schwartz 1996b: 24), that P (not just H) totally banned nonsacrificial slaughter after the construction of the Tabernacle, what is H stating that is new? If H merely repeats an extant P law code, it is offering no innovation at all! Indeed, once it is granted that H continues P's assumed policy of multiple sanctuaries (see COMMENT D), the only possible remaining innovation of this first law (vv. 3–7) is the total abolition of common slaughter. Moreover, if H is not innovating but "illucidating the underlying intent of the *šělāmîn*-law" (Schwartz 1996b: 32), why wasn't all of chap. 17, which deals with the problems ensuing from consuming meat, appended at the end of chap. 7, where it logically belongs? Contrast each of the four following laws of this chapter, and note that each of them contains a singular innovation, indicating that the first law must have one as well.

Rofé (1988: 15–16) plausibly suggests that Deut 12:20–28, which permits nonsacrificial slaughter only in instances when the person's residence is far from the (centralized) sanctuary, is an attempt to reconcile the *absolute concession* of nonsacrificial slaughter in the previous pericope, vv. 13–19, with the *absolute prohibition* against nonsacrificial slaughter in Lev 17:1–7. Rofé has supplied another bit of evidence that D is fully aware of H, at least in its law of slaughter.

This position, that the ban on nonsacrificial slaughter applies to only the sanctuary's vicinity, is adumbrated in the writings of the rabbis (*Sipre* Deut. Re'eh 75; *fb. Kidd.* 57b), the Dead Sea sectaries (11QT 52:13–21), and the Karaites (e.g., *Seper Hamibḥar, Keter Torah*). Neither P/H (Num 9:10) nor D (Deut 12:21) specifies the radius of the area in which nonsacrificial slaughter is banned. Qumran defines it as four miles (thirty stadia) for blemished animals and a three-day journey for pure animals (11QT 52:13–21; cf. Schiffman 1995). The Karaites specify 2000 cubits (S. al-Maghribi, chap. 16; see the discussion in Yadin 1983: 1.315–20).

4. *has not brought it. lō'hĕbî'ô*. This pluperfect implies that the animal must be brought alive (Wessely 1846). If the verb had read *yĕbî'ennû*, an imperfect (as in v. 9), one could have reasoned that the animal may be slaughtered outside the sanctuary and only its carcass must be brought to the sanctuary.

The LXX and Sam. follow with a long addition: *la ʿăśōt ʾōtô ʿōlâ ʾô šĕlāmîm laYHWH lirṣōnĕkem lĕrēaḥ nîḥōaḥ wayyišḥāṭēhû baḥûṣ wĕʾel-petaḥ ʾōhel mōʿēd lōʾ hĕbîʾô* 'to sacrifice it as a burnt offering or well-being offering to YHWH on your behalf as a pleasing aroma, but has slaughtered it outside and has not brought to the entrance of the Tent of Meeting'. It is ostensibly authentic because it is a classic homoeoteleuton (ending with *lōʾ hĕbîʾô*) and is confirmed by two independent witnesses (LXX and Sam.). Nonetheless, it must be rejected because it would render the second law of this chapter (vv. 8–9)—the banning of all sacrifice outside an authorized sanctuary—completely redundant; it contradicts its context, which deals solely with the *šĕlāmîm* (v. 5); and—what betrays its inauthenticity—it uses the plural-suffixed *lirṣōnĕkem* (perhaps based on 19:5; 22:19, 29) within a singular context. Thus this addition, despite its attractive homoeoteleuton, must be dismissed as a clever attempt to harmonize the first law (vv. 3–7) with the second (vv. 8–9) (cf. also Geiger 1865: 606–7; Elliger 1966).

the entrance of the Tent of Meeting. petaḥ ʾōhel mōʿēd. This expression and its synonym *lipnê ʾōhel mōʿēd* 'before the Tent of Meeting' are used solely for the slaughter of well-being offerings (3:2, 8, 13), whereas the slaughter of other sacrifices takes place *lipnê YHWH* 'before YHWH' (1:5, 11; 4:15, 24; Exod 29:11 and Lev 4:4 conflate the two), another indication that the subject of this law— as, indeed, of the entire chapter—is procuring meat for the household, the chief function of the well-being offering (vol. 1.217–26). The sanctuary area covered by *petaḥ ʾōhel mōʿēd* is discussed in the NOTE on 1:3.

before YHWH's Tabernacle. lipnê miškan YHWH. This expression is found in 1 Chr 16:39 and 2 Chr 1:5; *miškan YHWH*, in Num 16:9; 17:28; 19:13; 31:30, 47; Josh 22:19; 1 Chr 21:29; and 2 Chr 29:6; and the related term *miškānî*, in Lev 15:31. The chances are that all the citations in Numbers (as well as Lev 15:31) are H. Thus its occurrence here must also be assigned to H (cf. Elliott-Binns 1955: 32). H delights in multiple synonymous or near-synonymous phrases (e.g., "to YHWH," "to the priest," "at the entrance of the Tent of Meeting," v. 5).

It should not go unnoticed that the Tetragrammaton occurs seven times in the first two laws (vv. 4 [twice], 5 [twice], 6 [twice], 9, but not in the remaining laws) in order to emphasize both the prohibition incumbent on the Israelite and *gēr* against sacrificing to other gods (vv. 8–9) and the requirement that the Israelite's meat must originate as a sacrifice to YHWH (vv. 3–7).

Thus it must be concluded that H deliberately added the phrase *lipnê miškan YHWH* (as it added the otherwise superfluous *laYHWH* twice in v. 5) in its polemic against the extant blood rites offered to the goat-demons of the underworld (see NOTE on v. 7).

bloodguilt. dām. In this sense, it is equivalent to *dāmîm* (Num 35:27; Ezek 33:5; cf. Exod 22:1; Ps 51:16). The word *dām* is used to create a linguistic balance with *dām* (*šāpak*), thereby enhancing the ideological balance of the measure-for-measure principle, employed chiefly by God (see NOTE on "life for life," 24:18): The offender has shed *dām*; therefore, God shall impute *dām* against him (Schwartz, forthcoming). The accusation is one of murder, "equivalent to the one who by spilling blood of a human being forfeits his life" (Rashi; cf. *Tgs. Neof., Ps.-J.,* Saadiah, Ramban, Rashbam, who declares explicitly "guilty of death").

shall be imputed. yēḥāšēb. This is a legal apronouncement (cf. von Rad 1966) that, however, is punishable by God (cf. 7:15; Num 15:27, 30; Ps 32:2), in contrast with *dāmāyw / dāmô bô* 'his bloodguilt is upon him' (e.g., 20:9, 11, 12, 13, 16, 27; Ezek 18:13; 33:5) or *dām / dāmîm lô* 'there is bloodguilt in his case' (Num 35:27; cf. Exod 22:1), which connotes execution by a human court.

I disagree with Schwartz (1996b: 21), who interprets this pronouncement "*as if* the (antediluvian) prohibition of theriocide were still in force, though no *real* bloodguilt exists." This primordial law is indeed restored, but not for the entire animal kingdom—only for three sacrificeable animals: the ox, the sheep, and the goat. The formulation *dām yēḥāšēb lā'îš hahû'* implies a final sentence that will issue from the (divine) court based on existing law. Incidentally, the expression *kĕšôpēk dām* in Ramban and Sforno (n. 16) means "*equivalent* to murder," not "as if it were murder."

he has shed blood. dām šāpak. Elsewhere this phrase connotes the intentional murder of a human being (Gen 9:6; 37:22; Num 35:33; Zeph 1:17; Prov 1:16). In Ezekiel, it is linked with the sins of idolatry, sexual violations, blood consumption, and ethical wrongs (Ezek 16:38; 18:10; 22:3, 4, 6, 9, 12, 27; 23:45; 33:25; 36:18). Bloodshed disqualifies David from building the Temple (1 Chr 22:8), and iron, the instrument of violence, is similarly invalidated (Exod 20:22). Paran (1989: 270–71) notes, however, that when this expression is followed by the prepositions *'el* or *'al*, the blood shedding is legitimate (e.g., 4:30, 34; Deut 12:16, 27; contrast 19:10 and see NOTE on v. 13).

The murderer—indeed, the perpetrator of any premeditated crime—is banned from the sanctuary (Milgrom 1990a: 122). Hence the priestly legists abolished altar asylum for fear it would be polluted by murderers and assorted criminals. Instead, they invented the asylum city, but limited its use to the involuntary homicide (Milgrom 1990a: 504–9). Greek Orphics who totally eschewed blood regarded all sacrifice as murder (Detienne 1979). Blum (1990: 324, n. 139) objects to my interpretation on the grounds that slaying wild animals is not considered murder (v. 13). True, but this precisely is the point: only animals eligible for the altar, which excludes game, are subject to the charge of murder and the penalty of *kārēt* (see below). Game, however, is treated like all animals in the Noahide laws: its blood must not be ingested, but drained (vv. 13–14; Gen 9:4).

It is hardly accidental that the prohibition against ingesting blood in the Noahide laws is the obverse of the law prohibiting and punishing homicide (Gen 9:5–6; note the same idiom as in our verse, *šōpēk dām, dāmô yiššāpēk*). That is, theriocide becomes equivalent to homicide if the animal's blood is ingested. Here, however, H has applied this universal Noahide law to Israel, but insisting that the altar must be the depository of the animal's blood.

H adds a rationale (in an aside to Moses, vv. 5–7), to prevent Israel from engaging in chthonic worship (see NOTES and COMMENT A), and later in the chapter offers an additional rationale (again, only to Moses, v. 11) for the indispensability of the altar as the blood's recipient—as ransom for the murder of the animal. This rationale is already intimated in early Sumerian myths (vol. 1.713). The difference between P and H, then, is reduced to this: H bans *all* nonsacrificial slaughter (except for sacrificially unqualified animals, vv. 13–14). It is an incremental and logical development from P. What is radical is not the law itself, but its implementation (see COMMENT D).

shall be cut off. wĕnikrat. For an exposition of the *kārēt* penalty, see vol. 1.457–60, but see now NOTE on "they shall remain childless," 20:21, and chap. 20, COMMENT C (cf. Rashi also on *b. Šabb.* 25b, and *Tos. b. Yeb.* 2a, s.v. *'ēšet 'āḥiyw*). Punishment is by divine agency. Banishment is ruled out; as pointed out by Saalschütz (1848: 472–79, n. 595), it is unthinkable that an Israelite would be doomed to worship foreign gods (1 Sam 26:19; see NOTE on "I will cut off," 20:5). The rabbis are fully aware of a wide range of ritual and ethical violations that are not enforceable in a human court—chiefly, because they occur clandestinely (see NOTE on "you shall fear your God," 19:14). They coined the judicial category *pāṭûr middînê 'ādām wĕḥayyāb bĕdînê šāmayim / wĕdînô māsûr laśśāmayim* 'exempt from human laws but guilty in divine (lit., heavenly) laws / his case is passed on for divine judgment (lit., to heaven)' (*m. B. Qam.* 6:4; *t. B. Qam.* 6:16–17). Among the ethical cases are frightening a neighbor or his animal, causing his deafness by shouting in his ear, the court's authorized agent who flayed the convicted party but caused him injury, and the professional physician authorized by the court who healed a person but caused him injury (cf. Berman 1972: 1482–83).

If illegitimate slaughter of animals is equivalent to homicide, why is it not punished with death by human agency? Bekhor Shor answers this question on purely legal grounds—the absence of testimony: there are neither witnesses to the crime nor witnesses who warn the criminal in advance of the crime (a rabbinic requirement). A sounder legal basis has been suggested by Wold (1979: 20): the innocent animal has no blood redeemer other than the deity.

from among his kinspeople. miqqereb 'ammô. An idiom of H (cf. Exod 31:14; Lev 17:4, 10; 18:29; 20:3, 5, 6, 18; 23:30; Num 15:30). On *'ammô* 'his kinspeople', see NOTE on v. 10.

Vv. 5–7. Nonsacrificial Slaughter Banned: An Additional Rationale

This is the first aside to Moses (see NOTES on vv. 11–12, 14). The stylistic and linguistic differences between this passage and the preceding one (vv. 3–4) are so apparent that it seems certain that we are encountering a new source (Elliger 1966). Note the following changes: (1) plural instead of singular (indeed, the fact that the second law [vv. 8–9] is also couched in the singular [except for its introduction *wa 'ălēhem tō'mar*] lends support to the supposition that vv. 5–7 are a late insertion); (2) *zābaḥ* instead of *šāḥaṭ*; (3) *zebaḥ šĕlāmîm* instead of *qorbān*; (4) *'al-pĕnê haśśādeh* instead of *miḥûṣ lammaḥăneh*; (5) new rationale (vv. 5a, 7a); (6) scene shift from the wilderness to Canaan (Reventlow 1961).

However, another source need not be postulated:

1. Since vv. 5–7 are not directed *to* Israel but are an aside to Moses *about* Israel, the use of the plural is to be expected (Schwartz, forthcoming).
2. The verbs for slaughter, *zābaḥ* and *šāḥaṭ*, are not synonymous: as explained

in the introduction to vv. 3–4, *zābaḥ* is reserved exclusively for the well-being sacrifice, while *šāḥaṭ* is employed for all sacrifices.

3. Point no. 2 is further corroborated here.

4. The change from *miḥûṣ lammaḥăneh* to *ʿal-pĕnê haśśādeh* is deliberate, from the vicinity of the wilderness camp to the entire land.

5. We have a new rationale in v. 7a; indeed, the sanctuary vicinity now shifts to the countryside where chthonic worship, in H's time, is widespread (see NOTE on 18:21, and chap. 20, COMMENT B).

6. Reventlow is correct—partially; the explicit reference to chthonic worship (v. 7a) betrays H's *Sitz im Leben* more distinctly than vv. 3–4, where, but for the oblique reference to sacrifices outside the wilderness camp, H's time is successfully disguised.

5. *in order.* *lĕmaʿan.* The initial rationale *dām šāpak* 'he has shed blood' (v. 4) is now supplemented by a second one. Two rationales, the second also beginning with *lĕmaʿan*, characterize another H pericope (Num 15:37–41; cf. vv. 39–40). Thus it should not occasion surprise that H appended a second rationale to the law of vv. 3–4. Its purpose is a radical change in the existing law of vv. 3–4; nonsacrificial slaughter, tacitly permitted beyond the vicinity of the sanctuary, is now totally banned.

their sacrifices. *zibḥēhem*, 'that they are likely to offer' (Saadiah). The nonsacrificial slaughter performed illicitly within the vicinity of the camp and licitly at a distance from the camp is, in effect, a *zebaḥ*, a sacrifice. As this pericope explicitly states further on (v. 7), the blood of the slaughtered animal is suspect of being offered to chthonic deities. The noun *zebaḥ* always denotes a well-being sacrifice, the meat of which is eaten by the offerer (details in vol. 1.217–26)—an indication that the subject of this law is the proper procedure for providing meat.

have been sacrificing. *zōbeḥîm.* This verb denotes "sacrifice" in all the pentateuchal sources (e.g., Gen 31:54; 46:1; Exod 8:23; 23:18; 34:15; Deut 16:4; 17:1), but in P (9:4) and H (17:5, 7; 19:5; 22:29) it has the more restricted meaning of "sacrifice the *zebaḥ*" (cognate accusative)—an indication once again that the subject of this first law (and of the chapter) is providing meat for the table (see NOTE on 9:4). Moreover, the root *zbḥ* occurs seven times in vv. 5–7 (5 [four times], 6, 7 [twice]), in order to emphasize its centrality—sacrificial slaughter alone is permitted.

in the open field. *ʿal-pĕnê haśśādeh.* The word *śādeh* means "open space" (e.g., 1 Sam 14:25; 2 Sam 11:11; 2 Kgs 9:37; Ezek 16:5; 39:5) or, as glossed succinctly—and accurately—by Ibn Ezra (1961) on 14:7: "where people do not dwell." (The claim that "*śādeh* throughout the Holiness Source . . . refers only to cultivated land" [Fager 1993: 89] is mistaken.) Note that the certified scale-disease bearer resides *miḥûṣ lammaḥăneh* (13:46; 14:3)—that is, in the camp environs—but the bird, which symbolically carries away his disease/impurity, is released *ʿal/ ʾel-pĕnê haśśādeh* (14:7, 53)—that is, far beyond the camp.

The change from *miḥûṣ lammaḥăneh* 'outside the camp' (v. 3) to *ʿal-pĕnê haśśādeh* 'in the open field' was not done for the sake of style. These terms are not synonymous. The former, as noted, indicates the area within range of the camp; the latter, anywhere outside the camp, thereby indicating that the interdiction against nonsacrificial slaughter has been translated from the wilderness camp to the land of Canaan.

Furthermore, 'al-pĕnê haśśādeh literally means "on the surface of the field," an apt phrase for chthonic worship, which entails forming a circle of earth and grass and digging a trench in its center into which the blood of the sacrifice is poured (details in COMMENT A). The occurrence of this phrase in Num 19:16, which speaks of corpses and tombs, may also be an allusion to a fear of chthonic worship. Knohl (1995: 219, n. 67) claims that satyrs were worshiped at bāmôt, which he bases on 2 Kgs 23:8 and 2 Chr 11:15. The former, however, requires an emendation, and the latter is unreliable: it is not in the Kings Vorlage (1 Kgs 12:31–32), and it is probably the Chronicler's tendentious effort to heap the violation described in our verse on to Jeroboam's sins.

Douglas (forthcoming: chap. 5) remarks acutely that if H were advocating centralization, it would have contrasted the Tabernacle with other sanctuaries and not exclusively (if at all) with the open field (see further COMMENT D).

that they may bring them. wĕhebî'ūm. This verb is repeated because of the long objective clause following the first occurrence of the verb (Hoffmann 1953; Cholowinski 1976: 30, n. 58).

to YHWH. laYHWH occurs twice in this verse, emphasizing the absolute rejection of the worship of goat-demons or any other deity. Indeed, the fact that the Tetragrammaton occurs seven times in the first two laws of this chapter (vv. 4 [twice], 5 [twice], 6 [twice], 9), but not in the subsequent laws, proves that the priestly legist is decreeing that the proper worship of YHWH requires banning both nonsacrificial slaughter (vv. 3–7) and worship of other gods (vv. 8–9).

to the priest. 'el-hakkōhēn. The term "priest" is missing in vv. 3–4 for good reason. That context speaks solely of šāḥaṭ, slaughtering, a lay responsibility. Here, however, where zābaḥ is employed, denoting not just slaughtering but performing the entire sacrificial rite, the priest's role is paramount. He is to supervise the slaughtering of the animal in the sanctuary and to see to it that its blood is dashed on the altar, thereby preventing any semblance of chthonic worship.

sacrifices of well-being to YHWH. zibḥê šĕlāmîm laYHWH. The illicit sacrifices (zebāḥîm) to goat-demons offered by the people on the open field (see below) are due to be converted to well-being offerings to YHWH (Rendtorff 1967a: 120, 157, 163, with reservations; see vol. 1.217–18).

Kugler (1997: 21, n. 44, 27) asserts that on the basis of this verse, H marginalizes the usefulness of sacrifice for the priest, since he receives only "some meat portions." But these portions are the right thigh and the breast (7:34) of every animal that provides meat for the table! Kugler's second piece of evidence boomerangs as well. He claims that in 15:22–26, H provides the priest with the meat of a ḥaṭṭā't goat, whereas for the same communal sin, P endows the priest with the meat of a bull (4:13–21). Kugler errs with both sacrifices. H's goat and P's bull are burned on the altar, and nothing is given to the priest (4:20–21; cf. vv. 11–12; 9:10–11, 15). Besides, a priest never receives any part of a sacrifice for his own sin, and since the priest is a member of the sinning community he, too, requires expiation (Exod 29:14; Lev 8:17; cf. 6:16). In sum, there is absolutely no difference between P and H regarding a purported prebend for the priest from his *own* purification offering.

them. ʾōtām. Proper syntax would require this vocable, the direct object, to follow the verb *wĕzābĕḥû* and precede the indirect objective phrase (Ibn Janaḥ 1968: 360; Ḥazzequni). Perhaps this irregular transposition is explicable as a result of the customary juxtaposition of the verb *zābaḥ* with its cognate accusative noun (in H, 19:5; 22:29; elsewhere, e.g., Gen 46:1; Exod 24:5; Deut 33:19; Judg 16:23; 1 Sam 2:13; 6:15; 10:8; 1 Kgs 8:62; Isa 57:7; Jon 1:16; Pss 4:6; 116:17; 2 Chr 7:4).

6. This verse should be compared with *ʾak bĕkôr-sôr ʾô bĕkôr keśeb ʾô-bĕkōr ʿēz lōʾ tipdeh qōdeš hēm ʾet-dāmām tizrōq ʿal-hammizbēaḥ wĕʾet-ḥelbām taqṭîr ʾiššeh lĕrēaḥ nîhōaḥ laYHWH* 'But the firstling of an *ox, sheep,* or *goat* may not be redeemed; they are consecrated. *You shall dash their blood against the altar,* and *turn their suet into smoke* as a gift-offering *for a pleasing aroma to* YHWH' (Num 18:17). The same animal sequence is also found in v. 3; 7:23; 22:27 (all H), and the prescription for the disposition of the blood and suet in these verses is worded the same way—a strong argument that Num 18:17 (and perhaps all of Num 18) stems from the hand of H.

that the priest may dash the blood against the altar of YHWH. wĕzāraq hakkōhēn ʾet-haddām ʿal-mizbaḥ YHWH. Why repeat the *šĕlāmîm* procedure already detailed in chap. 3? One answer is that the *šĕlāmîm* offering of chap. 3 is restricted to three specific motivations—thanksgiving, vows, and free-will offerings (7:11–21)—whereas the motivation for the *šĕlāmîm* in this passage is to provide meat; the instructions are therefore repeated to indicate that the procedure remains the same (Wessely 1846). In truth, however, not all the instructions are repeated, just the disposition of the blood and suet; the reader would still have to refer to chap. 3 for the complete procedure. A more likely answer is that the blood and suet prescriptions are emphasized as a pointed polemic against chthonic worship, the object of which is the pouring of the blood and suet into the ground (see COMMENT A). For the authorized ritual procedure, see the NOTES on 1:5 and 3:2b.

Schwartz (1996b: 25) makes the salient point that *zāraq* 'dash', the sacral term for the blood used on the altar, is employed in pointed contrast to *šāpak* 'pour, spill' (v. 4). Henceforth, Israel will not "spill" blood (for the nonsacral attestation of *šāpak* within a sacrificial context, see 4:7, 18, 26), but will slaughter all sacrifices at the sanctuary and "dash" their blood on the altar.

the altar of YHWH. mizbaḥ YHWH. This phrase is found in Deut 12:27; 16:21; 26:4; 27:6; Josh 9:27; 22:19, 28, 29; 1 Kgs 8:22, 54; 18:30; 2 Kgs 23:9; Mal 2:13; Neh 10:35; 2 Chr 6:12; 8:12; 15:8; 29:19, 21; 33:16; 35:16. It is not true that this is an exclusively deuteronomistic expression (Aloni 1984: 40), since the citations from Josh 22 (note esp. in v. 19: *ṭĕmēʾâ hāʾāreṣ,* the root *ʾḥz, miškan YHWH*) stem from the priestly (H) layer of the chapter. In any case, this term was deliberately chosen for a specific polemical purpose: it is prohibited not only to pour the blood into the ground (a chthonic rite), but also to slaughter the animal on an improvised stone platform (Saul's method for nonsacrificial slaughter, 1 Sam 14:31–35; see COMMENT A). Not only must the animal be brought to the entrance of the Tent of Meeting (v. 4a), but its blood (and the suet) must be offered on an authorized sanctuary altar.

turn the suet into smoke as a pleasing aroma to YHWH. For the details of this procedure, see the NOTES on 1:9 and 3:3–5.

7. *no longer.* *'ôd.* This word proves that in the mind of the legist, Israel had worshiped goat-demons in the wilderness (*Sipre* Num. 116; *Lev. Rab.* 22:8).

goat-demons. *śĕ'îrîm* (see Isa 13:21; 34:14). The demonic aspect of goat worship was known to the rabbis (*Lev. Rab.* 22:8; *Sipra* Aḥare 9:8, citing Isa 13:21; see also Maimonides, *Guide* 3:46; Sforno). The possibility must be considered that the demon *'azā'zēl* (*'ēz* = goat) was a satyr (cf. Ibn Ezra on 16:8) and that the *šēdîm* 'demons' (Deut 32:17) also refers to satyrs (note that *Tg. Onq.* renders here *šēdîn*). Satyrs are said to inhabit open fields, ruins, and desolate places (Isa 13:21; 34:14). As has been pointed out (vol. 1.1072), the "open field" (v. 5) and *midbār* 'wilderness' (16:21) are also synonymous with the underworld (cf. Akk. *ṣēru*), and the goat is identified with the Ugaritic god of the underworld, Mot (= *māwet,* Heb. "death"; see vol. 1.1021). At Ebla, a goat rite is attested for the purification of the mausoleum NE-naš in connection with royal ceremonies (Zatelli 1998). Gerstenberger (1996: 237), who claims that all of the priestly literature is postexilic, has to admit that the statement alleging Israelite worship of satyrs is anachronistic. Janowski (1995: 1382) suggests that our verse is a "postexilic polemic against foreign gods," support for which is 2 Chr 11:15, which avers that Jeroboam established *śĕ'îrîm* and calves for his shrines. However, it is more likely that the Chronicler utilized our verse to label North Israel as worshiping satyrs (Japhet 1993: 668). Levine (1989) acutely recognizes that 17:7 forbids the worship of satyr-demons, which were *mandated* by the official religion in chap. 16 (i.e., Azazel). This blatant contradiction can be explained by positing that Lev 17 belongs to a new source. Namely, it is part of a polemic against P (see the Introduction I I), and it may account for the contiguity of these two chapters. For details on chthonic rites, see COMMENT A, and chap. 20, COMMENTS B and C.

after whom they stray. *'ăšer hēm zōnîm 'aḥărêhem.* The verb *zānâ* literally means "whore, commit harlotry," and is used in Scripture as a metaphor for Israel's infidelity to God (e.g., Jer 2:20; 3:1–3). As a metaphor for idolatry, see Exod 34:15–16; Lev 20:5, 6; Num 15:39; Deut 31:16, among other verses, and Adler (1989: 1.1–4). For a capsule summary of the expansion of this metaphor among the prophets, see Greenberg (1983a: 297–99). It is hardly accidental that the verb *zānâ* is used for worshiping Molek and consulting the spirit of the dead (Lev 20:5–6), since both practices indulge in chthonic rites (see chap. 20, COMMENT B).

an eternal law, throughout their generations. *ḥuqqat 'ôlām . . . lĕdōrōtām.* It is claimed that in view of Deuteronomy's subsequent restoration of nonsacrificial slaughter for nonsacrificial purposes (Deut 12:15–16, 21–25), the "eternal law" mentioned in this verse refers either to the prohibition against satyr worship (R.

Ishmael, Abravanel, Ḥazzequni, Sforno, Wessely 1846) or to the priestly control over the *šĕlāmîm* sacrifice (in keeping with R. Akiba's view that the subject of this law is the correct sacrificial procedure; cf. Rendtorff 1967a: 119–68). Neither of these answers can be correct. Satyr worship is worded not as a prohibition, but as a rationale. It is but another reason why nonsacrificial slaughter is permanently banned. Rabbi Akiba's view already has been rejected (see INTRO-DUCTION to vv. 3–4).

   The plain meaning of this declaration is that the ban on nonsacrificial slaughter is to be permanent (a ban that Deut 12 nullifies). Rather than regard it as a sheer idealization and utopian legislation (Schwartz 1987: 37; Werman 1994) or as a reflection of the writer's unconcern with the historical application of the wilderness to his own time (Joosten 1994: 205, n. 45; 1996: 148, n. 45), it is more logically the pragmatic consequence of H's assumption that there always will be multiple sanctuaries, one in easy access of every Israelite (see COMMENT D). Schwartz (1996b: 41), however, recently claimed otherwise: "P [by which he includes H–J.M.], as distinct from D, is not programmatic: its aim is not to convince and to reform but rather to concretize its beliefs in idealized, utopian laws" (cf. Haran 1981b: 328). This categorical statement flies in the face of every H chapter, which, as will be shown, grapples with reality, attempts to reform, and adds rationales at every turn in order *to convince its audience* (see the discussion in Introduction II B). This clause also settles once and for all a question that, admittedly, has gnawed in the back of my mind: if Num 5:1–3 (H) (cf. Introduction I E) attempts to be faithful to the wilderness background, in conflict with the laws of settled conditions of Lev 13–15 (scale disease and chronic genital discharge) and Num 19 (corpse-contamination), why wouldn't H in Lev 17 be doing exactly the same, namely, retrojecting wilderness conditions? The answer: our pericope is a permanent statute, and, in the view of its H author, it has to apply to his own time.

   Admittedly, other reasons may account for the promulgation of this law. For example, Plato (*Laws*: 909–10) also forbids private shrines and insists that worshipers must seek public temples in order to put an end to the fraudulent practices prevailing at the private shrines. Plato's motivation resembles that of H (v. 7), which also is aimed at putting an end to the *theologically* fraudulent practices of worshiping chthonic deities.

Vv. 8–9. The Second Law: No Sacrifices to Other (Infernal) Gods

Since the first law (vv. 3–4) bans nonsacrificial slaughter and, instead, demands that all meat originate as a sacrifice to YHWH at an authorized sanctuary, why is the second law, the banning of sacrifices to other gods, necessary? The following answers have been given: (1) to include the *gēr* (Noth); (2) to include the *ʿōlâ* (Wessely 1846); (3) lest one think that slaughtering to other deities is forbidden, but that sacrificing to them is permitted (Shadal, Hoffmann 1953). All three answers are correct. The *gēr* is included because even if he is allowed nonsacrificial slaughter, he may not sacrifice to infernal gods. The *ʿōlâ* is included, since the subject is no longer meat for the table—the concern of one sacrifice, the *šĕlāmîm*—but sacrifices in general. Finally, since the first law is limited to the proper procedure for slaughter, a second law is required to deal with the proper procedure for sacrifices.

The difference between the two laws is projected by their key verbs, *yišḥaṭ* 'slaughter' (v. 3) and *yaʿăleh* 'offer' (v. 8), indicating that the first law is concerned with an animal as food, and the second with an animal as sacrifice. Both laws, however, share a clause *wĕʾel-petaḥ ʾōhel môʿēd loʾ hēbîʾ* . . . *laYHWH* literally "and to the entrance of the Tent of Meeting does not bring . . . to YHWH" (vv. 4a, 9a), namely, that the animal must be sacrificed at the sanctuary to YHWH. The emphasis on YHWH (seven times in both laws) as the recipient of the sacrifice is explicated by the rationale, lest it be offered to infernal deities (vv. 5–7). This rationale, as shown, is an aside to Moses. It is followed immediately by *waʾălēhem tōʾmar* 'And say to them' (v. 8aα). This can only mean that the rationale, recited to Moses privately, also applies to what is now said to Israel (Wold 1979: 20; Schwartz 1987: 44). Thus whether animals are slaughtered for food or for sacrifice, this text is apprehensive that they will end up as offerings to infernal deities. In effect, worship of all other gods is herewith proscribed. But as will be demonstrated throughout the following chapters, H is obsessed only with infernal deities (see esp. NOTES on 20:1–5, and COMMENTS B and A).

Nonetheless, the integral connection of vv. 8–9 with the preceding and following laws cannot be denied. The subject still is the blood, *sacrificial blood*: it must be offered on only the authorized altar of YHWH.

8. *Say to them further. waʾălēhem tōʾmar.* The fact that the pronoun object is in the plural as, are vv. 5–7, whereas the following law (vv. 8aβ–9) is in the singular, indicates the possibility that this clause was added by the interpolator of vv. 5–7 to form a link with the following law (Kilian 1963).

In the divine speech formula, the inversion of subject and object indicates a change in addressee. There are seven such cases:

1. In Exod 30:31, the warning to the Israelites not to manufacture or misuse the anointment oil follows instructions to Moses on its manufacture and proper use (vv. 22–30).
2. In Lev 9:3, the instruction to the Israelites concerning their sacrificial obligation for the inaugural service of the Tabernacle follows the instruction to Aaron concerning his sacrifices (v. 2).
3. In Lev 24:15, the law of the blasphemer proclaimed to all Israel is preceded by a private address to Moses concerning the fate of an apprehended blasphemer (vv. 13–14).
4. In Num 11:18, the command to the Israelites to purify themselves in preparation for the arrival of the quail is preceded by God's private assurances to Moses that he will be granted assistants (vv. 16–17).
5. In Num 18:26, the instruction to the Levites to tithe their tithes follows God's personal address to Aaron concerning the Levites' responsibility and reward (vv. 21–24).

6. In Num 27:8, the Israelites are given the law of inheritance after Moses receives divine assurance that the daughters of Zelophehad may inherit (vv. 6–7).

7. Lev 20:2 probably has another purpose in mind: to connect chap. 20 with chap. 18, which contains the same topics—Molek worship and illicit sex relations.

All seven cases are priestly texts (P and H), except for Num 11:18 (JE).

However, the law under discussion (vv. 8–9) is ostensibly an exception. It is addressed to Israel—"say to them further"—and so is the previous law 'say to them' (v. 2). Schwartz (1991: 45–46), following the lead of Ehrlich (1908), has come up with a convincing solution. He suggests that vv. 5–7, H's rationale for the ban on nonsacrificial slaughter, is an aside to Moses and is not intended to be delivered to Israel. That is, Israel is informed of the law (vv. 3–4), but only Moses is told of its rationale (vv. 5–7). Thus "say to them further" indicates a change in the recipient of the message, from Moses (vv. 5–7) to Israel (vv. 8–9). The same literary phenomenon surfaces twice more in a subsequent law of this chapter: Moses alone is privy to the rationale (vv. 11–12, 14; see NOTE on vv. 11–12 and 24:15).

Joosten (1994: 39–43, 45–46; 1996: 30–34) marshals a strong case that the four cases of *mibbêt yiśrā'ēl* 'from the house of Israel' attested in H (17:3, 8, 10; 22:18) imply that women are included as addressees, whereas *běnê yiśrā'ēl*, the usual addressee, should be rendered "sons of Israel," meaning that only the adult Israelite males are being addressed. The rationale for the latter expression is that the adult male, as the head of the family, is solely responsible for overseeing the fulfillment of the law by all members of his household. Particularly compelling are his citations of 18:23 and 19:29, addressed in the second person to the male and the third person to the female, under the rubric of *běnê yiśrā'ēl*. The use of *bêt yiśrā'ēl*, Joosten argues, is limited to cases where women would naturally be included: they may slaughter an animal (17:3), bring a sacrifice (17:8; 22:18), or be liable to eat blood (17:10). Strikingly, whereas the first three laws of chap. 17 (cited above) are addressed to *bêt yiśrā'ēl*, the fourth is addressed to *běnê yiśrā'ēl* (17:13–14) because its subject is hunting, an activity in which women are unlikely to engage. Finally, I might add, if the MT of Num 27:21 *wěkol- běnê-yiśrā'ēl 'itto wěkol-hā'ēdâ* 'and all the Israelites with him and all the congregation' (Milgrom 1990a: ad loc; contra Lohfink 1994: 202, n. 68) is H, then *běnê yiśrā'ēl* refers to the able-bodied *males* of Joshua's future *army* (pace Lohfink 1994: 197–99). For new, but less persuasive arguments, see Melcher (1996: 91–93).

However, Joosten (1994: 46, n. 28; 1996: 34, n. 20) is forced to reverse himself when he explains the other attestation of *běnê yiśrā'ēl* in chap. 17, namely in v. 5, which also deals in sacrifice, by averring "that sacrifice by a woman was probably the exception." This is hardly the case, since the only other injunction in H dealing with the people's sacrifice (22:17–33) uses *bêt yiśrā'ēl* (v. 18), which, according to Joosten's contention, includes the woman! Moreover, although the other occurrences of *bêt yiśrā'ēl* in P (Exod 16:31, the sabbath; Exod 40:38, sighting God's cloud-encased fire; Lev 10:6; Num 20:29, mourning the departed) surely apply to women, so does *běnê yiśrā'ēl* in P, since their sins also pollute the sanctuary (16:16, 19, 21, 34 [H!]) and they, too, must be careful not to eat forbidden food (11:2), especially since they work alone in the kitchen (cf. 11:29–38) outside the surveillance of their husbands and fathers. Furthermore, in the opening address to the sacrificial section (chaps. 1–7), and to the book (1:2), the antecedent of *mikkem* is clearly *běnê yiśrā'ēl*. Then, *'ādām* 'person' cannot include the non-Israelite, as elsewhere in P (Gen 1:27; 9:6; Lev 5:3; 13:2; Num 19:14), but applies to the woman (unless *mikkem* is to be deleted, for which, however, there is no textual warrant; see NOTE). Thus *běnê yiśrā'ēl* must also be addressed to the woman.

Finally, if it is argued that in P the distinction between the two addressees does not hold, it would appear strange that H, in this one case (v. 5), is more precise than P (vol. 1.35–39). Thus Joosten's thesis that the terms *běnê yiśrā'ēl* and *bêt yiśrā'ēl* refer to two different addressees, attractive as it is, is not watertight. To be sure, many of H's prescriptions are addressed solely to men: incest (18:2), priestly rules (21:24), ingredients for the shrine (24:2), sabbatical and jubilee (25:2), vows (29:2; note telltale *'im něqēbâ hi(w)'* 'if *she* is female,' 27:4). But in laws of holiness (19:2), Molek and mediums (20:2), private sacrifices (22:18), festivals (23:2, 44), and the total commandments (26:46; 27:34), *běnê yiśrā'ēl* surely includes the woman. Nonetheless, the last word has not been written. For now, my judgment is suspended.

the aliens. haggēr. As I argue (see NOTE on "of the house of Israel," v. 3), the *gēr* is exempt from the performative commandment to drain the animal's blood on the altar, but may, instead, pour it on the ground (see COMMENT B). If so, isn't there a danger that the *gēr*, even less likely bound by YHWH's commandments than the Israelite, will offer the blood to some chthonic deity? This possibility (even probability) is parried by H's second law: the *gēr* may slaughter the animal as he pleases, but only to gain meat for his table, not for the purpose of sacrificing the animal to any other god but YHWH.

offers up. ya'ăleh. Literally, this means "makes ascend," though in sacrificial contexts the *Hip'il* of *'ālâ* bears the special meaning "burn" (vol. 1.172–74). This verb, a denominative of *'ōlâ*, is quite apt since the *'ōlâ*, the burnt offering, is completely "burned" (except for its skin, 7:8) and completely "ascends" (Judg 13:16; Jer 33:18). Yet here this verb also serves the *zebaḥ*, which, except for its suet and the blood, does not entirely burn and ascend but is consumed by the offerer and the officiating priest (vol. 1.217–26). Indeed, this is the only attestation in the Bible for *zebaḥ* as the object of *he'ělâ*. Hence it is not surprising that the LXX and Sam. read *ya'ăśeh*, the usual verb for executing the entire sacrificial rite (e.g., Num 15:3, 8; 2 Kgs 10:24). That such is the intent of this verse is proven by the next verse, which utilizes the expression *la'ăśôt 'ōtô laYHWH*. (For other examples of *'āśâ* with the *'ōlâ* and *šělāmîm*, see Ezek 46:2, 12; cf. 43:27; 45:19.)

The possibility exists that we are faced with an ellipsis *ya'ăleh 'ōlâ 'ô [yizbaḥ] zebaḥ* (Schwartz 1987: 43–44), a formula that is attested elsewhere (Exod 24:5;

Josh 8:31; 1 Sam 6:15; 1 Chr 29:21). However, there is good precedent for this ellipsis in similar cases where the ʿōlâ is listed first. Note the following examples: *heʿĕlâ ʿōlâ ʾō/ûminḥâ* (Josh 22:23; Jer 14:12; Amos 5:22) and *heʿĕlâ ʿōlâ ʾō/ûšĕlāmîm* (Judg 20:26; 21:4; 2 Sam 6:17–18; 24:25). The verb *heʿĕlâ* 'burn' is appropriate for the *minḥâ*, since in public sacrifices the *minḥâ* accompanied by the ʿōlâ is completely burned. However, this does not hold for the *šĕlāmîm*. Hence one can only conclude that *heʿĕlâ* can be the equivalent of *ʿāśâ* and connote the entire sacrificial rite—that is, "offer up."

a burnt offering or a (well-being) offering. ʿōlâ ʾō zebaḥ. This formula is found in, among others, Num 15:3, 5, 8; cf. Deut 12:6, 11; 1 Sam 15:22; 2 Kgs 5:17; Isa 43:23; 56:7; Jer 7:22; Ezek 44:11. These attestations show it is not of priestly origin. Either it is a merism for all the sacrifices (*b. Zeb.* 109b) or it is literally limited to the ʿōlâ and *zebaḥ* (i.e., the *šĕlāmîm* and *tôdâ*; cf. 22:21, 29) and excludes the *minḥâ* 'cereal offering' and *nesek* 'drink offering'. The latter alternative might be considered more likely, since the subject in this chapter is the consumption of meat. But since this law's intent is to ban all sacrifices, the former alternative is more attractive. In either case, the omission of the other blood sacrifices, the *ḥaṭṭāʾt* and *ʾāšām*, is unaccounted for. Perhaps the term *zebaḥ* is inclusive of all blood sacrifices that were not completely immolated, and hence would include the *ḥaṭṭāʾt and ʾāšām* (McConville 1984: 52; see NOTE on 23:37).

Alternatively, the answer might be that H reflects the popular religion, which hardly knew, if knew at all, the *ḥaṭṭāʾt* and *ʾāšām*. I have proposed (vol. 1.172–77) that originally the ʿōlâ was the only expiatory sacrifice, but in the Temple of Jerusalem and possibly in earlier regional sanctuaries, the demand for more nuanced expiatory sacrifices led to a splitting off of the *ḥaṭṭāʾt* and *ʾāšām* from the ʿōlâ. In the folk tradition, however, much of which is represented in H, the original tandem ʿōlâ ʾō *zebaḥ* was preserved. However, as will be shown in the NOTES on chap. 23, H not only was aware of P's sacrificial system, but used it (i.e., Num 28–29) to formulate its festival calendar. Hence the solution of the inclusion of all blood sacrifices but the ʿōlâ under the term *zebaḥ* is preferable.

Childs (1986: 173) followed by Anderson (1992: 882) claim that Jeremiah's condemnation of ʿōlâ *wāzābaḥ* (7:21–22) embraces public as well as private sacrifices—indeed, the entire sacrificial cult. Neither scholar has paid sufficient attention to the fact that Jeremiah's Temple address is directed exclusively to the sacrifices done by the people (see esp. vv. 10, 16), not to those offered in the daily and festival cult by the priests. Moreover, even assuming that the term *zebaḥ* is inclusive of the expiatory sacrifices, it is never part of the public cult (for the ostensible exception of 23:19, see its NOTE) but is exclusively a sacrifice brought by the people. It makes no difference whether the expression ʿōlâ *wāzābaḥ* emanates from circles that are priestly (17:8; 22:18–21; Num 15:3, 8) or nonpriestly (e.g., Deut 12:6, 11; Josh 22:26–29; 1 Sam 6:15; 10:8); these are sacrifices brought by the people on their own initiative and are not part of the routine cult. Thus Jeremiah is not attacking the Temple service, but only the private offerings of individuals who live under the illusion that their immoral life is expiated by their sacrifices (details in Milgrom 1977b; 1983c: 119–21).

Recently, Schwartz (forthcoming) has made the attractive proposal that the *ḥaṭṭāʾt* and *ʾāšām* were excluded on the grounds that their purpose was to repair the pollution and desecration, respectively, of the sanctuary. Hence there was no fear of their being offered anywhere outside. His suggestion makes sense, but not in the way he thinks. Since he holds that this law indicates the principle of centralization, then heretofore there must have been multiple sanctuaries. Whether or not they were contaminated by Canaanite practices (the assumption of Deut 12:30–31), they were dedicated to the worship of YHWH. That being the case, they may have followed the priestly theory of the pollution and desecration of the sanctuary and would have demanded the appropriate *ḥaṭṭāʾt* or *ʾāšām* from their constituency. Thus the legist of 17:8–9 would have been as apprehensive about the *ḥaṭṭāʾt* and *ʾāšām* as about the *ʿōlâ* and *zebaḥ*!

However, assuming the existence and *acceptance* of multiple sanctuaries, then Schwartz's proposal works. Persons have to offer the *ḥaṭṭāʾt* and *ʾāšām* at whatever sanctuary they worship. The only existing fear is that they may offer a sacrifice falling in the range of *ʿōlâ* and *zebaḥ* to an outside deity, more likely an infernal one associated with ancestral worship (see NOTE on 18.21, and chap. 20, COMMENTS B and C).

Thus the first two laws, vv. 3–7, 8–9, are unified by a common theme, or, rather, a common fear: worshiping a foreign deity (specified to Moses as a satyr, v. 7). The first law prohibits the profane slaughter of the *šĕlāmîm* lest it be offered to a satyr (an aside to Moses). The second law broadens this law to include all the sacrifices a person could bring to these deities. A question still remains, at least for now: If antagonism to the ancestral cult is behind this legislation, why isn't it banned outright? This question will be discussed in chap. 20, COMMENT C. Here, let it be said that the legist was plainly afraid that his audience would recoil with hostility from his categorical demand and perhaps turn a deaf ear to everything else he had to say. The holiness school apparently knew that on an issue so personally meaningful as reaching out to the departed beloved, one had to tread carefully.

9. *to offer it to YHWH. laʿăśôt ʾōtô laYHWH.* Both the first and second laws are bound by the same motive: to prevent chthonic worship, since the second rationale for the first law (vv. 5–7) applies equally to the second law (Wold 1979: 20). The *kārēt* penalty is prescribed in both laws for the same reason: nonsacrificial slaughter (vv. 3–7) can lead to the worship of infernal gods as much as can sacrificing to these deities directly (vv. 8–9). Once again, the text assumes, as it does in v. 4, that there exists multiple sanctuaries.

shall be cut off. wĕnikrat. However, a similar law mandates a different penalty: *zōbēaḥ lāʾĕlōhîm yoḥŏrām biltî laYHWH lĕbaddô* 'Whoever sacrifices to a god other than YHWH alone shall be proscribed' (Exod 22:19). The *ḥērem* penalty is executed by man (see chap. 27, COMMENT F), whereas the *kārēt* penalty is executed by God (vol. 1.457–61). How can these two penalties be reconciled? The key to the answer is found in the passage dealing with the Molek worshiper (20:2–5): if the people do not put the culprit to death, God will punish him, his family, and all who have aided him, with *kārēt*. Thus the two laws are not in conflict. The Exodus version posits that the idolater has been apprehended. The Leviticus version presumes that his heresy is practiced furtively; although undiscovered by man, he will be punished by God.

Vv. 10–12. The Third Law: The Blood Prohibition and Its Rationale Regarding Sacrificial Animals

Two main reasons for the blood prohibition are cited by the medieval commentators: (1) to prevent the worship of other gods (Maimonides, *Guide* 3:46), including the rite of imbibing the blood to commune with the spirits of the dead (Sforno; see COMMENT A); and (2) the blood, or, rather, its *nepeš* 'life', belongs to God: "All lives [*nĕpāšôt*] are mine" (Ezek 18:4; Ramban 1960; cf. Dillmann and Ryssel 1897; Driver and White 1894–98). Both reasons are partially correct. The first reason connects the blood prohibition with the first law: the ban of chthonic worship (v. 7; see COMMENT A). The second reason cites the rationale for the blood prohibition (v. 11a), but does so incompletely (see NOTES on v. 11, and vol. 1.704–13).

The structure of this pericope consists of a law, stated twice (vv. 10, 12), enclosing its rationale (v. 11). The rationale is introduced by *kî*, the repetition of the law by *ʿal-kēn*. This form is attested elsewhere in biblical law (e.g., Deut 15:10–11 [double *kî*]; 19:6–7 [triple *kî*]). The closest parallel, however, is Num 18:23b–24 (H):

A   *ûbĕtôk bĕnê yiśrāʾēl lōʾ yinḥălû naḥălâ*
B   *kî ʾet-maʿăśar bĕnê-yiśrāʾēl ʾăšer yārîmû laYHWH tĕrûmâ nātattî lalĕwiyyim lĕnaḥălâ*

A′   *ʿal-kēn ʾāmartî lāhem bĕtôk bĕnê yiśrāʾēl lōʾ yinḥălû naḥălâ*

A   But they shall have no territorial share among the Israelites;
B   for it is the tithes set aside by the Israelites as a gift to YHWH that I assign to the Levites as their share.

A′   Therefore I have said concerning them: They shall have no territorial share among the Israelites.

The tripartite structure should be noted; the first and third parts state the law, and the middle part contains the rationale (the *kî* sentence). The purpose of the repetition of the law, the *ʿal-kēn* sentence, is thereby clarified. It creates an introversion, the chiastic structure ABA′, which frames the rationale (B) as an inclusion (AA′). In this way, the center, the rationale (B), is highlighted (Schenker 1983: 197–98; Schwartz 1991: 45–46). Thus the reason for not granting territorial rights to the Levites is emphasized: they are recipients of the tithe.

Lev 17:10–12 is similarly structured. The law (v. 10) repeats in an *ʿal-kēn* sentence (v. 12); envelops the rationale, the *kî* sentence (v. 11); and thereby stresses its importance. The theological significance of the rationale is discussed in the NOTES on v. 11.

10. *the aliens.* Just as they are forbidden to worship other gods (vv. 8–9), so are they forbidden to ingest blood. The alien is subject to all the prohibitive commandments (for the exposition, see COMMENT B). Another reason for specifying the *gēr* is that the non-Israelite world of which he was a part not only lacked a blood prohibition, but savored blood in its diet. Thus most of the recipes collected by Bottéro (1995) call for blood. That the alien refers primarily to the displaced Israelite, as recently claimed by Greger (1992), is unlikely (see COMMENT B) and, for H, impossible. H assumes that all Israelite families are landed, and hence alienation from the land caused by their forfeiture to creditors is only temporary, but in principle it is always theirs (see NOTES on 25:24, 35–43). In H's retrojection, in the wilderness the "landless" *gēr* would have to have been the aliens who attached themselves to Israel when they left Egypt (Exod 12:38, 48; Num 11:4; cf. Lev 24:10).

ingests. *yō'kal.* That the verb *'ākal* is employed indicates that the blood is ingested in the course of eating meat. The deuteronomic version of this prohibition makes this explicit: *raq ḥăzaq lĕbiltî 'ăkōl haddām . . . wĕlō'-tō'kal hannepeš 'im-habbāśār* 'But make sure you do not ingest the blood . . . and you must not ingest the life *with the flesh*' (Deut 12:23). If the prohibition were directed against imbibing the blood by itself, the text would have resorted to the verb *šātâ* 'drink' (e.g., Num 23:24; Ezek 39:17–19), *'ila''sip'* (= *lā'â*, Job 39:30), or *lāqaq* 'lick' (1 Kgs 21:19). It is significant that all attestations of imbibing the blood alone refer only to animals. That YHWH ingests the sacrificed blood dashed on the altar is vigorously denied by the Psalmists (Ps 50:13); citations containing this notion (Deut 32:42; Isa 34:6; Jer 46:10) are simply metaphors.

The objection has been raised that in Akkadian, the exact cognate *ākil dami* occurs in a context where "eating [blood] with the flesh is not required" (Rodriguez 1979: 241). Not so. The text speaks of demons who are *a-kil šīri* 'flesh eaters' and that, when consuming the blood separately from the flesh, are depicted as *šātū ušlāti* '(they) drink (the blood of) the arteries' (CT 1426–27, cited in CAD A1, 246). Thus Akkadian distinguishes carefully between drinking blood (alone) and eating blood (with its flesh).

The blood prohibition is common to most of the pentateuchal sources (Gen 9:4; Lev 3:17; 7:26–27; Deut 12:16, 23–25), which bespeaks its importance. In the priestly view, it stands even higher than the ten commandments: the Decalogue was given solely to Israel, but the blood prohibition was enjoined on all humankind. It alone, according to the priestly legists, forms the basis of a viable human society. Although God intended that the human race be vegetarian (Gen 1:29), beginning with Noah he concedes it animal flesh (Gen 9:3), but on condition that the blood be eschewed (Gen 9:4); it must be drained and returned to its source: God (details in vol. 1.704–13).

any blood. *kol-dām.* Since the blood of game is the topic of the next law (vv. 13–14), one might argue that "any blood" in this verse refers to only sacrificial animals. The rabbis, however, claim that this blood prohibition is total: it includes nonsacrificial animals as well (*Sipra* Aḥare, par. 3:3; *b. Ker.* 4b). This view is corroborated by the occurrence of the same phrase in another attestation of the blood prohibition (7:27), which contains the added words *lā'ôp wĕlabbĕhēmâ* 'of birds and beasts', a phrase intended to include every nonsacrificial category: game, blemished animals, and carcasses. The absence of fish implies that it was considered a bloodless creature. Contrast the Qumranites (1QS 12:13–14), who claimed that the blood of fish must be spilled. (On the rarity of fish in the Israelite menu, see NOTE on 11:12. On the expression *'ākal 'al-haddām*, which has a totally different meaning, see COMMENT A.)

I am reminded by Boersema (1997: 28, n. 68) that blood always remains present in meat. The reference is to "blood that flows through the body and in biological terms forms an independent organ."

I will set my face. wenātattî pānay be. The phrase *nātan pānîm* is an H idiom (20:3, 6:26–27; cf. Ezek 14:8), one whose bold anthropomorphism would have been avoided by P. Its synonymous counterpart *śām pānîm* is attested more frequently (e.g., 20:5; Jer 21:10; 44:11; Ezek 15:7). Both terms are neutral, connoting that the subject is turning his attention to or setting his mind on the object (e.g., Dan 9:3; 11:17; 2 Chr 20:3). However, when these two expressions are followed by the preposition *be*, they become menacing. This is the *beth* of hostility that causes *Tg. Onk.* to render *pānay* 'my face': "I (YHWH) turn [*pôneh*] from all my affairs to deal with him" (*Sipra* Aḥare, par. 7:4). *Tg. Ps.-J.* follows suit by rendering *pānay* as *pĕna'y* 'leisure'.

the person who ingests. bannepeš hā'ōkelet. The word *nepeš* was chosen for "person," though elsewhere in this chapter, person is expressed by *'îš* or *'îš 'îš*, and *nepeš* has the meaning "life" (see NOTE on v. 11). The root meaning of *nepeš*, however, is "throat, appetite" (see NOTE on "life," v. 11), a most apt word to be paired with *'ākal*. That the choice of *nepeš* for "person" was deliberate is proved by the fact that only twice more in this chapter does *nepeš* denote "person," and both times the verb is once again *'ākal* (vv. 12a, 15a). The centrality of this idiom is emphasized by the sevenfold occurrence of *'ākal* and *nepeš* (twice more with a suffix) in vv. 10–16.

and I will cut him off. wĕhikrattî. The school of H will occasionally abandon the impersonal *kārēt* formula of P, *wĕnikrat* 'shall be cut off' (*Nip'al* passive; e.g., Lev 7:20, 21 [P]; 17:14; 22:3; 23:29 [H]), when it wishes to make the punishment emphatically imminent (e.g., 20:3, 5, 6; 26:30). This verse clearly served Ezekiel as a model in *wĕnātattî pānay . . . wĕhikrattiyw . . . 'ammî* (Ezek 14:8).

from among his kinspeople. miqqereb 'ammâ. That *qereb* indicates the H version of the *kārēt* formula, see the NOTE on v. 4, and for the meaning(s) of *kārēt*, see vol. 1.457–61. In the formula, *'am* 'people' interchanges with *'ammîm* 'kin'. Undoubtedly, the latter is more original, since in the antonymous expression *ne'ĕsap 'el-'ammāyw* 'gather to his kin' (Gen 25:8, 17; 35:29; 49:33; Num 27:13; 31:2; Deut 32:50), *'ammîm* is replaceable by *'ābôt* 'fathers, ancestors' (Judg 2:10) or *qĕbārôt* 'family tomb' (2 Kgs 22:20 [= 2 Chr 34:28]; note the plural). Certainly to render the singular *'am* as "people" in this expression would be meaningless (e.g., Gen 49:29), particularly since the punishment includes the *gēr*, who has no "people" (contra Gerstenberger [1996: 285], who renders "his fellows in faith or his people"; cf. COMMENT B). Rather than reading *'ammāyw* instead of *ʿammô*, regard the two as synonymous. It is probably no accident that all P occurrences of this formula consistently read the plural *ʿammîm* (Gen 25:8, 17; 35:29; 49:33; Exod 30:33, 37; Lev 7:20, 21, 25, 27; Num 20:24; 27:13; 31:2), whereas H reveals the variation with the singular *ʿam* (17:4, 10; 20:3, 6, 17, 18). To be sure, four priestly verses (Exod 12:15, 19; Num 19:13, 20) substitute *yiśrā'ēl* or *qāhāl* for *ʿam* in the *kārēt* formula, as argued by Zimmerli (1954: 17–25). But all these instances are interpolations of exilic H (cf. Ezek 14:8–9), reflecting a shift from kinspeople to people (contra Joosten 1994: 116; 1996: 82). Thus the interchange between *ʿam* and *ʿammîm* would be in keeping with the attested phenomenon of H fudging P's precision (see Introduction I K, and vol. 1.35–39).

Vv. 11–12. The Rationale

Another aside to Moses (see NOTES on vv. 5–7, 14). Only the law is given to Israel, not its rationale. Thus the repetition of the law (v. 12, and again in v. 14) is not superfluous, but is part of an aside meant for Moses' ears alone. From the fact that the wording of the law repeated to Moses (12aβ, b; 14aβb) does not correspond to its wording to Israel (v. 10), Schwartz (1991: 45–46) draws the conclusion that Moses and, subsequently, the prophets were not compelled to deliver God's message verbatim, but were free to couch it in their own language. This deduction is unwarranted. The law given to Israel (v. 10) is formulated in typical casuistic style, and there can be no doubt that it was so transmitted and recorded. Its variations (vv. 12, 14), as Schwartz has correctly noted, are a personal aside to Moses and can therefore be given in a precis form.

What is the meaning of this aside to Moses? Surely, it is not H's intention to hide its rationales from Israel; they occur in nearly every law in subsequent H chapters. Note, for example, the next chapter: 18:5, 7bα, 8b, 10b, 12b, 13b, 16b, 21b, 23b, 24–25, 27–29. Here, I submit, the rationales underscore the innovative nature of the law banning nonsacrificial slaughter. H is forced to explain, repetitively and emphatically (vv. 5–7, 11–12, 14), that Israel may have been ignorant of the law because its rationale was revealed only to Moses.

11. This verse, the center of the larger chiasm, (vv. 10–12), has its own chiasm, with v. 11aβ, the ransoming power of the altar (not the blood), as its center.

life. nepeš. The ancients realized early on that death ensued following the loss of breath or blood. The notion that the source of life is in the breath is attributable to JE (Gen 2:7; 7:22). It can be surmised how these two different concepts arose. The word *nepeš*, which ultimately came to mean "life," originally denoted "throat, appetite," a meaning still attested in Scripture (e.g., Isa 32:6; 58:10; Jer 4:10; 31:14, 25; Jon 2:6; Pss 69:2; 107:9; Prov 10:3; 11:25; 13:4; 27:7; Qoh 6:2, etc.). Since the throat contains both the esophagus and the trachea, one can readily understand that *nepeš* denotes both "appetite" (see NOTE on "the person who ingests," v. 10) and "breath, life." Finally, following Ruesche (1930), it can be assumed that once life (breath) became equated with *nepeš* (throat), it became inevitable that a similar equation would develop between *nepeš* and blood, the other life-containing organ. For the meaning of *nepeš* 'life', see, for example, Josh 2:13; 1 Kgs 19:10; Ezek 13:19; Ps 40:15.

and I. waʾănî. In the priestly writings (P and H), the emphatic *waʾănî* always refers to God (e.g., 20:3, 24; Gen 6:17; 9:9; Exod 9:3; 14:17; 31:6; Num 3:12; 6:27; 18:6, 8).

I have assigned it. nětattiyw. The priest is the subject of *nātan* whenever *dām* 'blood' is the direct object, in which case the meaning is "place the blood" (on a person, Exod 29:20; Lev 14:14, 25; on doorposts, Exod 12:7; Ezek 45:19; on the altar, Lev 4:7, 25; Ezek 43:20). Here, however, the subject is God, and the meaning of the verb *nātan* is "assign" (e.g., Num 3:9; 8:16, 19; 18:6, 8, 19; contra Schwartz 1991: 50). This distinction is important to prevent the association of this verse with the *ḥaṭṭāʾt* offering, the blood of which is indeed "placed" by the priest on the horns of the altar (cf. 4:7, 18, 25, 30, 34).

to you. lākem. A shift in person has occurred for Israel, from the third to the second person. This pattern regularly occurs following the expression *waʾănî nātattî*. God, the subject, is in the first person; the indirect object, a person, is in the second person; and the direct object, a thing, is in the third person (Gen 1:29; 9:3; 27:13; 48:22; Exod 31:6; Num 18:6, 8; cf. 6:27).

As observed by the rabbis (*Sipra* Aḥare, par. 7:5), the *gēr* is excluded. This is as it should be. The *gēr* may not worship other gods (vv. 8–9), but he need not worship Israel's God; neither need he slaughter his animals at the altar, but may slaughter them at home (see NOTE on v. 3, and COMMENT B). My student S. Nikaido has challenged me on the basis of the similarly structured law of blemished sacrifices (Lev 22:17–20), which also begins with an introduction in the third person, referring to both Israelites and aliens, but then switches to second person *lākem*, ostensibly addressed only to Israel. He asks: Are we to conclude that the prohibition against bringing a blemished sacrifice applies only to the Israelite and not to the alien? The import of his question is that, as in Lev 17:11, *lākem* should also include the alien. If, then, the alien is not required to offer his meat as a well-being offering (vv. 3–5), the ransoming power of his blood offerings must refer to other sacrifices! The answer is provided by the nature of v. 11. It is an aside to Moses. Whereas God commands Moses to prohibit the ingestion of blood during the consumption of meat to Israelite and alien alike (v. 10), he confides to Moses the rationale for this prohibition as it concerns his people Israel: the life blood of an *Israelite's* meat must be offered on the altar to ransom his life. Thus v. 11 complements and completes the law of vv. 3–5. It explains why the Israelite, but not the alien, must first offer up all his meat as a sacrifice (i.e., a well-being offering)—to ransom his life for spilling the life blood of the animal in order to enjoy its meat. The structure of 22:17–20 will be explained in the discussion of those verses.

Finally, the relationship of subject and object bears theological significance. YHWH declares here: it is not that you (Israel) give (*nātan*) the blood to me, but I (*waʾănî*) give (*nātan*) the blood to you (*lākem*). This statement would not apply to the *ʿōlâ*, 'the burnt offering', and *minḥâ* 'the cereal offering', which, in the main, are gifts to the deity (vol. 1.172–77, 195–202), but it most definitely fits the rationale of the *šĕlāmîm* 'the well-being offering', as explained below (see also vol. 1.217–26, 704–13, and Schwartz 1991: 51).

on the altar. 'al-hammizbēaḥ. The blood manipulation is the only rite mentioned and, hence, must be the most important rite of whatever sacrifice(s) is (are) intended here. A comparison of the sacrifices regarding the prebends awarded the officiating priest identifies only the *šĕlāmîm* with the dashing of the blood on the altar (7:8, 10, 14; see NOTE on v. 14). Also, merely to mention the blood rite suffices to identify the *šĕlāmîm* (Ezek 43:18; cf. v. 27). Details are given in vol. 1.217–26.

ransom your lives. lĕkappēr 'al-napšōtēkem. The remarks here supplement the detailed COMMENTS in vol. 1.253–54, 704–13, and 1079–84, where it has been demonstrated that (1) the preposition 'al following *kipper* means "on behalf of"; therefore, the *kippûr* rite is performed on behalf of the person offering the sacrifice; (2) *nepeš* 'life' in a legal context connotes capital crime or punishment, and expressions compounded with it often imply that life is at stake (see esp. Num 17:3); therefore, the phrase lĕkappēr 'al-napšōtēkem implies that human life is in jeopardy unless the stipulated ritual is carried out; and (3) *kipper* in this phrase means "ransom," as shown by the occurrence of kippēr 'al-napšōtēkem in the same pericope as kōper napšô 'a ransom for his life' (Exod 30:12; cf. vv. 15, 16), leading to the conclusion that *kipper* is a denominative of kōper (Ibn Ezra on Num 8:19; cf. Milgrom 1970: 28–31; vol. 1.1082–83; see Schwartz 1991: 54, n. 1).

Certainly, whenever God's deadly plague (*negep*) or anger (*qeṣep*) comes into play, a ransom is sought, expressed by the verb *kipper*—for example, the census (Exod 30:16; Num 31:50; cf. 2 Sam 24:10–25), idolatry (Num 25:12; cf. Josh 22:17–18; Ps 106:29–30), homicide (Num 35:33; 2 Sam 21:3)—extended in wisdom literature to assuaging the anger of a king (Prov. 16:14). The notion of "ransom" becomes so significant in rabbinic Hebrew that a new word, the *Pi'el* denominative *kappārâ*, emerges.

Thus the function of the blood on the altar is to ransom the life of the one who offered it. Is it the blood of all sacrifices or that of a particular sacrifice? The answer already has been given: the expression *'ākal dām*, repeated four times in this law (vv. 10 [twice] 12 [twice]) implies that the blood is ingested with the meat and that the only sacrifice eaten by its offerer is the *šĕlāmîm*, the well-being offering. Thus the blood of the *šĕlāmîm* serves as the ransom for the life of its offerer.

Ostensibly, this conclusion faces two contradictions:

1. The *šĕlāmîm* is the one sacrifice that has no *kippûr* function.
2. No sacrifice can expiate a deliberate sin, not to speak of a capital crime!

The resolution of both objections is found in the opening law of this chapter: animal slaughter is murder except at an authorized altar (vv. 3–4). V. 11 offers the remedy: the blood ransoms the offerer's life and clears him of the charge of murder.

Objection to my interpretation that the *šĕlāmîm* has no attested expiatory (*kippûr*) function has been voiced by Schenker (1983: 209), Gorman (1990: 184–87), Schwartz (1991: 58–60), Hartley (1992: 275), and Rendtorff (1992:

169). Instead, these critics champion the customary interpretation that Lev 17:11 is addressing all other sacrifices, which expressly expiate. Their interpretation, however, must be rejected out of hand. Why should the blood of the *ḥaṭṭāʾt* and *ʾāšām*, the exclusive expiatory sacrifices, brought for *inadvertent* wrongs, ransom the offerer's life? What capital crime has he committed to warrant the forfeit of his life? In particular, as I argued thirty years ago (Milgrom 1970), is the new mother, whose *ʿōlâ* and *ḥaṭṭāt* offerings expressly expiate on her behalf (*wĕkip-per ʿālêhā*, 12:7, 8), deserving of death because she had a baby?

Conversely, Blum (1990: 324–25) denies that v. 11 deals at all with expiation, but refers, instead, to the need, via the altar, to bring a gift to God. However, the term *kippēr* 'purge, atone, ransom' implies some form of guilt and, hence, never connotes a guilt-free "gift."

Thus, reasoning indirectly, the only sacrifice left that might answer the criteria of Lev 17:11 is the *šĕlāmîm*, a conclusion confirmed by the context of the entire chapter, which focuses on the mortal danger of imbibing blood in the process of eating meat, which, according to H, must first be sacrificed as a *šĕlāmîm*; otherwise, the animal's slaughter is regarded as murder (v. 4).

Nonetheless, the question remains: Why is the *kipper* function of the *šĕlāmîm* never mentioned? The answer, I submit, is that, paradoxically, the *šĕlāmîm* does not have an expiatory function—*in P!* Nor could it. P, we may recall, allows for nonsacrificial slaughter; it does not require that the blood of meat for the table be drained at an authorized (i.e., priest-controlled) altar (vol. 1.28–29). H, how-ever, having broken with past tradition by mandating that all meat must initially be a *šĕlāmîm*, is forced to supply a rationale: slaughtering an animal constitutes murder. Of course, H did not invent this rationale. This is also P's tacit basis for its demand that the blood may not be ingested but must be drained—that is, returned to God. H, however, adds a new stipulation: it must be returned *ʿal-hammizbēaḥ* 'on an authorized altar'.

Other objections have been voiced that do not require a lengthy rebuttal. One is that no sin is incurred, above all murder, in the legitimate slaughter of a sac-rificial animal (Kiuchi 1987: 102–3). In answer, one has to keep in mind that all sacrifices, save the well-being offering, become the property of God (which he, with certain sacrificial portions, allots to the priests). Thus the life blood of the animal reverts to its creator, and therefore no crime has been committed. The well-being offering, though, is solely for the benefit of its offerer. He kills it for its flesh. For an Israelite, it is a capital crime, unless he returns its life force, the blood, to its creator via an authorized altar. The objection has also been posed that since *ʿōlâ ʾô zebaḥ* (v. 8) is a merism for all sacrifices, it provides the immediate context for the next law (vv. 10–12). This means that the ransoming power of the blood (v. 11) refers to all blood sacrifices (Schenker 1983: 209–10). The absurdity of applying v. 11 to the expiatory sacrifices has been pointed out (above; see also Janowski 1982: 191). Furthermore, the law of vv. 8–9 is not re-lated to the following law, but to the preceding one (vv. 3–7), indicated by its special introduction "say to them further." Their common function is to pro-hibit idolatry.

Another objection is that since the following two laws (vv. 13–16) deal with the issue of eating nonsacrificial animals, the handling of the blood in this law (vv. 10–12) is of general concern and is not limited to well-being offerings (Füglister 1977: 197). This objection overlooks the common denominator of these three laws (and the first, vv. 3–7), namely, the prohibition of "eating" the blood, an eventuality that can occur only in the sacrificial system with the well-being offering.

Finally, it has been argued that "since blood cannot be separated from the life, a sacrificial animal's blood cannot serve as payment for its own life which has been taken" (Hartley 1992, quoting and agreeing with Schenker 1983: 209). This sophistry is alien to the Bible. For biblical man (and his Near Eastern antecedents, as shown by the Sumerian myth of Lugulbanda; see below), taking the *nepeš* 'life' of an animal invokes the vengeful wrath of the deity in the same measure as taking the life of a person (Gen 9:4–5). Unless the blood is drained—returned to God—for the Israelite on an authorized altar, the slaughter of the animal is murder (vv. 3–4). This answer also helps rebut Schenker's (1983: 209) additional argument that no compensatory ransom is required for killing game. Paradoxically, in this argument Schenker is correct, but he draws the wrong conclusion. As spelled out in the NOTE on "Therefore I said to the Israelites" (v. 14a) only the blood on the altar, not the blood per se, serves as *kippēr* 'ransom'.

The ethical sensitivity displayed by P's ancient rule should not be underestimated. It must be recalled that according to P's account of creation, man was meant to be a vegetarian (Gen 1:28). God, however, concedes to man's carnivorous appetite: his craving for meat is indulged, but he must abstain from ingesting the blood (Gen 9:3–4). H imposes a greater restriction on Israel: the blood of sacrificeable animals must be drained on the authorized altar "to ransom your lives" when you take the animal's life for its flesh.

Anthropological evidence reveals that the fear of killing an animal harks back to a very early period in the history of humanity. Indeed, an early Sumerian myth relates that a ritual and a sacred meal are devised by the gods in order to sanction the killing of an animal (Hallo 1987; elaborated in 1996: 217–20; see vol. 1.712–13). However, Israel is the only people that codifies this sensitivity, converting the ethic into law. Life is inviolable. Hence all people must eschew the blood, the symbol of life. Israel is enjoined to obey an additional safeguard: the blood must be drained on the authorized altar. In either case, the blood must be drained and returned to the universe, to God.

By way of contrast, Zoroastrian religion (as practiced in Cappadocia) also prohibits blood, not only its consumption but also its contact, as indicated in sacrificial preparations: "taking care that nothing of the water nearby is soiled with blood, because thus they will defile it" (Strabo, *Geography* 15.3.13–15).

A closer examination of sacrificial ransom is in order. Ransom is a specialized aspect of expiation. The blood of all sacrifices expiates (*kipper*; see vol. 1.1079–84): the *ḥaṭṭāʾt* for the inadvertent contamination of sancta (hence *kipper* means "purge"; see vol. 1.253–58), the *ʾāšām* for the inadvertent desecration of sancta (see NOTE on 5:15), and the *ʿōlâ* and *minḥâ* for sins of omission (vol.

1.172–77, 203–17). H now adds the šĕlāmîm to this list. It also expiates, not for a prior wrong, as do the other sacrifices, but for the slaughter of the sacrificial animal. The reason is clear: other sacrifices belong to God (which, in whole or in part, he turns over to his priests), but the šĕlāmîm is returned to its offerer. If the animal is solely for the benefit of its owner, then killing it requires expiation. The expiation is for a capital crime: murder. Thus the form of expiation— pouring the animal's blood on the altar for an Israelite, burying it for a non-Israelite—is, in effect, a ransom for life.

Hence the substitutionary theory of sacrifice, based largely on this verse and championed by so many in the scholarly world, must once and for all be rejected. It should have been dismissed out of hand long ago if for no other reason than that given by Füglister (1977): If the death of an animal is so important, why is it performed by a layman and not a priest? It should now be clear that the animal on the altar never replaces the person who offered it. Blood as life is indispensable for expiating inadvertent wrongs against the deity. In the case of the šĕlāmîm, however, the sin is aggravated. Killing for food is a capital, nonexpiable crime, but it is conceded by God if the blood, the life of the animal, is drained and returned to its creator—in P anywhere, in H only on the authorized altar.

The midrash makes a statement about the blood of the ḥaṭṭāʾt that applies more accurately to the šĕlāmîm: "Ordinarily blood is a despised thing—it is the food of dogs. Yet the Holy One, Blessed be He says it should be offered on the altar! However, the Holy One Blessed be He—if one dare impute such a request to Him—said: Bring me an offering and take its blood and daub the blood on the horns of the altar that blood may yĕkappēr [ransom] for blood [that you shed]. It is because of your need and kappārātĕkā [your ransom] that I request an offering" (Pesik. R. 194b).

Rendtorff (1995: 26–28) raises the possibility that 17:11 indeed refers to a ḥaṭṭāʾt. For evidence he cites the P narrative of 10:17–18, where a vocabulary similar to that of 17:11 obtains. However,

1. The formulas expressing the *function* of the respective sacrifices are different, which makes all the difference: lĕkappēr ʿălêhem 'to purge (the sanctuary) on your behalf' (10:17) versus lĕkappēr ʿal-napšōtêkem 'to ransom your lives' (17:11). The meaning of the *verb* is different, "purge" versus "ransom," and the *object* is different, "sanctuary" versus "life."

2. The *cause*: polluting the sanctuary (vol. 1.254–58) versus taking life. (Rendtorff correctly points to the emphasis in the priestly texts [Gen 9:10, 12, 15; Lev 17:10–12] that animals as well as humans are endowed with nepeš 'life'.)

3. The *effect*: kārēt for the sinner (Num 19:13, 20) and, ultimately, for the community (vol. 1.258–61) versus kārēt for the sinner (Lev 17:4).

4. The *procedure*: consumption by priests (6:22; 10:17) versus consumption by the offerer (7:15–16). Whereas the lay person is forbidden to eat of the

flesh of the *ḥaṭṭā't*, a most sacred offering (6:23), the context of 17:11 and, indeed, of all of chap. 17 is the consumption of meat by the lay offerer, which can only refer to the *šělāmîm*.

Thus the limitation of 17:11 to the *ḥaṭṭāt* cannot be sustained.

Finally, I submit another piece of evidence that supports and, perhaps, vindicates my case. The truth (conveniently ignored) is that a *kipper* function for the *šělāmîm* is attributed to H in Ezek 45:15, 17 (differing with vol. 1.709). What is Ezekiel's source? It is not in P. The only possible answer is that he derived it from this chapter. And it should occasion no surprise. It has been shown that Ezekiel was manifestly influenced by the vocabulary and thought of H—indeed, of this very chapter (see NOTE on "he shall pour out its blood," v. 13; chap. 26, COMMENT D; and Introduction I L).

In sum, H has innovated a new function for the *šělāmîm*, which differs radically from that of P. Rather than being another kind of P's *šělāmîm* of joy, H's *šělāmîm* is an expiatory sacrifice—ransoming (*kpy*) the offerer for the sin of murder by slaughtering the sacrificed animal. H's innovation is not without some precedent. P ordains that the non-Israelite commits murder if he does not drain the slain animal of its blood (Gen 9:4). H extends this notion to the Israelite and revises it: to ransom the Israelite from the charge of murder, for taking the life of the animal, he must drain the animal's blood on a sanctuary altar—that is, offer the animal as a *šělāmîm*.

for it is the blood. kî-haddām hû'. The pronoun *hû'* is added for emphasis of the subject (contra Schwartz 1991: 48), which probably led the rabbis to generalize: *'ên kappārâ 'ellâ bĕdām* 'Expiation is only with blood' (*Sipra* Nedaba 4:9; *b. Yoma* 5a; *b. Zeb.* 6a; *b. Men.* 93b; cf. *Jub.* 6:2), a statement, however, that is in need of qualification (e.g., Exod 29:33; Lev 5:11–13; 16:10; cf. Brichto 1973: 31–35; the other verses he cites are inapplicable). In particular, see the NOTE on "to the Israelites," v. 12.

by means of life. bannepeš. This is the *beth instrumentii* (correcting Milgrom 1971: 149; Levine 1974: 69; Brichto 1976: 28), since, as pointed out by Schwartz (1991: 47, n. 2; cf. Füglister 1977: 147; Janowski 1982: 245–46; Schenker 1983: 209), this is the only attested meaning of the *beth* in the adverbial prepositional phrase *kipper b* (Gen 32:21; Exod 29:33; Lev 5:16; 7:7; 19:22; Num 5:8; 35:33; 1 Sam 3:14; 2 Sam 21:3; Isa 27:9; Ezek 43:22; Prov 16:6), except where the *beth* indicates place (e.g., 6:23; 16:17, 27). So, too, was it understood by the rabbis (*Sipra* Aḥare, par. 7:5; *b. Ker.* 2b, 22a), the medieval commentators (Ibn Ezra, Abravanel), and other moderns (Kalisch 1867–72; Dillmann and Ryssel 1897; Baentsch 1903; Bertholet 1901; Elliger 1966).

The nouns *dām* and *nepeš* in the third clause (v. 11b) are also present in the first clause (v. 11a) but in reverse order, thereby forming a chiastic inclusion that endows the verse with an ABA' structure, highlighting B—the instruction to Israel to place the blood of its meat-producing animals on the altar as a ransom for taking their lives.

Another point arguing on behalf of the *beth instrumentii* is that *nepeš* in both parts of the inclusion must have the same meaning; since *nepeš* indisputably refers to the life of the animal in the first part (v. 11a), it must denote the same in the second part (v. 11b). Thus the *kipper*—action of the blood must be of the slain animal—and not "for" (*beth pretii*) the human being, who is the offerer.

12. *Therefore.* ʿal-kēn. This prepositional phrase generally introduces a repetition of a previous command (e.g., Num 18:23–24; Deut 15:8, 11) or introduces its summation (e.g., Deut 5:15; 15:11, 15; 24:18, 22). The latter usage is applicable here, since the initial blood prohibition (v. 10) is not repeated verbatim—the *kārēt* penalty is missing. Thus there is no reason to flounder with Gerstenberger (1996: 238), searching in vain for an antecedent text, such as Gen 9:4; Deut 12:16, 23; or 1 Sam 14:32–34. It is located in the same unit: v. 10.

I say. ʾāmartî. Through the medium of Moses—that is, "I told you to say"—this is an indication that this verse continues the aside to Moses.

to the Israelites. But was not the blood prohibition directed also to the *gēr* (v. 10a)? Was not Moses commanded to warn the *gēr* about the fatal consequences of ingesting blood (v. 10b)? The answer is that the previous verse, the prescription to drain the blood on the altar, is delivered solely to Israel. For that reason, the third person of v. 10, inclusive of the *gēr*, becomes the second person of v. 11, directed solely to Israel. This verse continues in the second person: *mikkem*, *bĕtôkĕkem* 'among you'. Hence the instruction concerning the *gēr* must be supplemented (v. 12b).

It is apparent from this verse that the *gēr* requires no expiation for taking the life of animal. This is so because, according to the priestly theology, he may kill any animal for its meat (Gen 9:3–4). There is no restriction on where or how he may perform the slaughter. All he has to remember is to obey the blood prohibition: not to ingest it (since it is the animal's life, v. 10) and to bury it (so he is not tempted to engage in chthonic worship, see NOTE on v. 13). Thus draining the blood, whether performed by the *gēr* or by the *Israelite*, does not effect expiation/ransom. Once again, the rabbinic dictum "Expiation is only with blood" has been modified (see NOTE on "for it is the blood," above). It is not the blood per se that expiates, but only blood on the altar. To be more precise, it is not the blood *at all*; it is the altar. It should not be forgotten that bloodless sacrifices also expiate—for example, the bread loaves accompanying the consecration ram (Exod 29:32–33; note the plural: "expiated by them") and the *ḥaṭṭāʾt* cereal offering (Lev 5:11–13).

This point is of no small importance. Blood is life. Hence it is powerful, but only God can activate it. This happens when the blood is sanctified; that is, when it is in contact with the altar and other sancta. The blood that consecrates the priest and his clothing must come from the altar (8:30). The altar itself is consecrated from blood that has been sanctified inside the adytum and shrine (16:14–19). This principle also holds for blood as apotropaic. In all such instances, the blood stems from sacrifices—that is, from animals that have been consecrated, and hence belong, to God (e.g., 8:22–24; 14:13–14; cf. Exod 12:21–23).

Vv. 13–14. The Fourth Law: No Ingestion of Blood: Game

This law is stylistically, structurally, and ideologically an integral part of the previous law (vv. 10–12). As observed by Paran (1983: 117), together they form an introverted structure:

A   *wĕnātattî pānay bannepeš* **hā'ōkelet** . . . *wĕhikrattî 'ōtāh miqqereb 'ammāh* (v. 10b)

B   *kî nepeš habbāśār baddām hw(î)'* (v. 11a)

C   *'al-kēn 'āmartî libnê yiśrā'ēl kol-nepeš mikkem lō'-tō'kal dām* (v. 12a)

C'   *wā'ōmar libnê yiśrā'ēl dam kol-bāśār lō' tō'kēlû* (v. 14a)

B'   *kî nepeš kol-bāśār dāmô hw(î)'* (v. 14bα)

A'   *kol-'ōklāyw yikkārēt* (v. 14bβ)

This structure is rejected by Schwartz (1991: 37, n. 1), presumably for the reason (none is given) that the parallel lines are imperfect and that they cover only half of the verses (vv. 10a, 11b, 12b, 13 are omitted). Both scholars are correct, but for another reason: the parallels exist, but they share a vocabulary (boldface) because they comprise the rationales for each respective law. The prohibition against ingesting blood is here extended to game. Moreover, as a precaution lest the drained blood be utilized in chthonic rites, the performative commandment is issued that the blood has to be buried (see "and cover it with earth," below).

Hunting is attributed in the Bible to pre-Israelite personalities—Nimrod (Gen 10:9), Ishmael (Gen 21:20), and Esau (Gen 25:27)—an indication that it played an important role in early times. After the settlement in Canaan and, certainly, by the monarchic period, hunting became an insignificant factor in the national economy. To be sure, the royal menu featured specimens of game: *'ayyāl* 'deer', *ṣĕbî* 'gazelles', and *yaḥmûr* 'roebuck' (1 Kgs 5:3). These three animals are supplemented by four others whose identification is uncertain: *'aqqô, dîšōn, tĕ'ô,* and *zemer* in the list of wild animals permitted in the Israelite cuisine (Deut 14:4–5). Once Israel's pastoral economy shifted almost exclusively to agriculture, hunting also changed from a necessity to a sport, one that could be indulged in only by a leisure class, namely, the royal aristocracy. Nevertheless, this law and the one specifying the permitted game, mentioned above, demonstrate that since hunting continued to be practiced—even by relatively few—it had to be controlled by legislation.

The prohibition against game on the altar was not followed in every regional sanctuary, to judge by the evidence of Tel Dan, which reveals fragments of deer and gazelle bones from its altar complex dating from the Israelite (Iron Age II), ninth and eighth centuries B.C.E., as well as small amounts of bones of forbidden quadrupeds (see NOTE on 11: 3–8, 24–28), such as donkey, turtledove, bear, and lion (Wapnish and Hesse 1991: 46). Game was also sacrificed at Ugarit (*CTA* 6 I: 18–29; Levine 1963) and probably by the Canaanites.

13. *hunts down. yāṣûd ṣēd.* This root occurs in Arabic *ṣāda/ṣaid* and Syriac *ṣwd* 'hunt, fish' and, perhaps, in Canaanite (the Phoenician-Punic god of the hunt is *ṣd*; Heltzer 1987). It means "kill in the hunt" (Gen 27:5, 33; Lam 3:52) and, hence, the translation "hunt down." This is one of the reasons why the clause *wĕšāpak dāmô* 'he shall pour out its blood' cannot be considered part of the protasis (see NOTE on "he shall pour out its blood").

The textual and iconographic evidence from other countries in the ancient Near East abounds in descriptions and depictions of hunting—by the king, not commoners. Excelling in the hunt was a means of extolling the king's manliness, skill, and courage. Even the gods were depicted as engaging in hunting. The Assyrian emperors from the ninth to the seventh century regularly boasted of their hunting prowess. They and subsequent royal figures among the Babylonians and, especially, among the Persians established vast game parks to provide sufficient (and easy) prey for royal hunting expeditions. These parks were called *paradesu* in Akkadian, *paradaidā* in Persian, and *paradaisos* in Greek, whence late biblical Hebrew *pardes* (Koh 2:5) and modern English "paradise" are derived (Heltzer 1987).

a beast. ḥayyâ. This refers to an undomesticated animal (11:27, but not in 11:2, where it is the generic for all animals).

that may be eaten. 'ăšer yē'ākēl. Assumed is a knowledge of 11:13–19, 24–28, another indication that H is later than P. But what of the forbidden animals, those whose flesh may not be eaten? Is their blood to be drained and buried? A positive reply must be presumed, especially in view of the absolute prohibition against ingesting the blood (Gen 9:4). The fact, however, that this phrase is used—despite the questions that may arise—indicates that the subject here and throughout the chapter is meat for the table. Indeed, the absence of any reference to predatory (hence, forbidden) animals shows that the notion of hunting as sport is not even envisaged—a far cry from the practices of Israel's neighbors (see NOTE on "hunts down").

he shall pour out its blood. wĕšāpak 'et-dāmô. Is this clause part of the protasis or the apodosis? The former is favored by some scholars (e.g., Wessely 1846; Brichto 1974: n. 10) on stylistic grounds: Were it the apodosis, it should have read *wĕšāpak 'et-dāmô 'al-hā'āreṣ* 'he shall pour out its blood *on the ground*'. As part of the protasis, it assumes that the blood pouring is a condition, not a requirement; that is, only in a case where the *animal* spills its blood must it be buried. Abetting this hypothesis is the fact that a favorite method of hunting, especially of birds, was by trapping (e.g., Amos 3:5; Ps 124:7; Prov 6:5; cf. Job 18:8–10), in which case there would be no bloodletting at all.

The protasis option, however, must be rejected. The stylistic argument is unconvincing: Where else shall the hunter pour the blood, if not on the ground? The trapping argument is irrelevant. Trapping and traps are expressed by a different vocabulary—*yāqaš, môqēš*—whereas the verbal root used here, *ṣād*, connotes kill in the hunt, hence the translation "hunt down." Moreover, trapped animals are generally taken alive. After the hunter slaughters them, this law, the requirement to bury the blood, would be still invoked. However, if they are found dead, the law of the carcass (vv. 15–16) applies.

The notion that the blood must be spilled "on the ground" is taken for granted is further corroborated by the fact that the expression *šāpak dām*, if left unqualified, implies murder (v. 4; Gen 9:6; 37:22; Num 35:33; 1 Kgs 2:31; Ezek 22:27); if it connotes licit killing, it must be followed by the preposition *'al* (Deut 12:16; 1 Kgs 18:28) or *'el* (4:30, 34; Paran 1983: 194).

Thus with MT and LXX, the apodosis option is preferred. The text then states that when the animal is brought down in the hunt, the hunter should see to it that all its blood is spilled on the ground and buried.

This verse clearly lay before the prophet Ezekiel: "For the blood (Jerusalem shed) is (still) in her; she set it on a bare rock [*lō' šĕpākathû 'al-hā'āreṣ lĕkassôt 'āpār*]; she did not pour it on the ground to cover it with earth" (Ezek 24:7). The prophet adroitly turns the theriocidal language and context of Leviticus into homicidal accusations against his people, enabling him to invoke the penalty— inexorable divine retribution. The illicit shedding of human blood pollutes the soil (Num 35:33–34; Ezek 36:17–18) so that it refuses to yield its fruit (Gen 4:10–12; 2 Sam 21:1) and, ultimately, vomits out its inhabitants (Lev 18:28).

and cover it with earth. wĕkissāhû bĕ'āpār. A number of explanations are given for this requirement:

1. So that other people will not ingest it (Rashbam, Ḥazzequni, Abravanel, Ralbag; Schwartz 1991: 61–62). If so, why should human blood—clearly not a comestible—be buried (Gen 37:26)?
2. So that no other animal will ingest it (Rosenmüller, cited by Shadal; Noth 1977). To be sure, it is the worst of curses for the blood of the slain to be licked up by an animal (e.g., Ahab, 1 Kgs 21:19; 22:38). Yet there is no indication that it was considered an affront to God for one animal to ingest the blood of another.
3. So that it would not be suspected of being human blood that could pollute the ground (Shadal). Far-fetched.
4. So that it would be returned to God, who granted *nepeš* not only to human beings but also to animals (Dillmann and Ryssel 1897). This argument is worthy of consideration, especially since it is the rationale provided by the text itself (v. 14a).
5. So that the blood does not cry out for vengeance (cf. Ezek 24:7; Kalisch 1867–72; Ehrlich 1908; Snaith 1967). A bold midrash emphasizes this point: "the Holy One Blessed Be He said, If you slaughter an ox, sheep, or goat, do not cover their blood. Why? Because they stem from your possessions and are under your authority. But those that are under his [i.e., God's] authority [i.e., the wild animals], if you slaughter (them), cover their blood. Why? *Lest he become your prosecutor and slayer* [my emphasis]" (Mid. Yelammedenu, 170). However, the citation of Ezek 24:7 is invalid. It proves only that human blood spilled illicitly cries out for divine retribution, which would not apply to animals that may be killed with impunity.

6. A vestige of an ancient apotropaic rite (Elliger 1966), which explains nothing.
7. So that the blood will not be used in chthonic rites—that is, for divination.

Whereas earlier (1971: 152) I opted for explanation no. 5, I now prefer no. 7. It complements the ban on animal slaughter outside the sanctuary, which, in my view, is also directed against chthonic worship (details in COMMENT A). I also like explanation no. 4, blood as life, the very one offered by the text (v. 14a). These two (nos. 4 and 7) are not mutually exclusive: the ban on using blood in chthonic worship (no. 7) implies that, instead, the blood should be returned to God (no. 4).

The Greek addition to *T. Levi* 18:2 mentions a Book of Noah, which prescribes that Levi (i.e., a priest) must bury the blood in earth before eating (sacrificial) flesh, presumably adding to the Noahide prohibition against ingesting blood (Gen 9:14) the Leviticus requirement to bury the blood.

14. This verse comprises the third aside to Moses (in addition to vv. 5–7, 11–12). It consists of two parallel *stichoi*: aα // bα and aβ // bβ. Both halves begin with *kî* and, hence, are rationales, the first explaining why the blood of game must be buried and the second explaining why the blood may not be ingested. In effect, this verse is a repetition of vv. 10–11a (Schwartz 1991: 62).

all flesh. kol-bāśār. This phrase is used twice, in contrast with *habbāśar* 'the flesh' (v. 10), to emphasize that the blood of all flesh, including nonsacrificial meat, must not be ingested but buried.

its blood is with its life. dāmô bĕnapšô hû'. This is a syntactically difficult phrase that has resulted in a number of solutions: (1) cutting the Gordian knot by deleting *bĕnapšô*, yielding "For the life of all flesh is its blood" (Bertholet 1899–1900; Ehrlich [H], Elliger 1966; Brichto 1976: 24; Hartley 1992; cf. LXX, Pesh., Vg., Philo, *Laws* 4:123, Sforno); (2) reversing the nouns, *bĕdāmô napšô*, yielding "its life is in its blood," equivalent to v. 11a (cf. Ibn Janaḥ 1964: 1.357; Ḥazzequni 1981); (3) understanding the *beth* as the *beth essentiae*, yielding "its blood is its life" (Kalisch 1867–72; Keil and Delitzsch 1874; NJPS; cf. *Seper Ha-Mibḥar*) and requiring no emendation; however, the very validity of the *beth essentiae* has been questioned (Brichto 1976: 26, n. 18); (4) considering the word *bĕnapšô* 'in its life' as a scribal error brought down from v. 11b (Gerstenberger 1996: 239); and (5) rendering the *beth* as "with," yielding "its blood is with its life" (i.e., its blood is attached to, inseparable from, its life) (Ibn Ezra, Abravanel; Mendelssohn, Dillmann and Ryssel 1897; Hoffmann 1953). This usage of *beth* is attested (e.g., Exod 14:13, 20), especially in a similar context: *ak-bāśār bĕnapšô dāmô*, which Shadal, following the Masoretic cantillation, renders literally as: "However, flesh *with* its life, that is, its blood" (Gen 9:4), or, more idiomatically, "However, flesh *with* its life-blood" (cf. NJPS; Sabourin 1966). That this may be the correct interpretation, at least as far as Deuteronomy is concerned, is shown by the statement *wĕlō'-tō'kal hannepeš 'im-habbāśār* 'You may not ingest the life with the flesh' (Deut 12:23b). Note that the same syntax prevails as in our verse: *nepeš* connected to *bāśār* by a preposition, but using *'im* instead of *be*. Thus vv.

10–14 records three different usages of the preposition *beth*: "in" (v. 11a), "by" (v. 11b), and "with" (v. 14a).

Therefore I said to the Israelites. wā'ōmar libnê yiśrā'ēl. The reference is to v. 10, which is now repeated, but not verbatim (see NOTE on vv. 11–12). Two blatant omissions need be accounted for: the rationale (*kippēr* 'ransom') and the *gēr*, the resident alien. One cannot argue that since the rationale was a private communication to Moses, it is therefore omitted in this recap of God's statement to Israel. The fact is that part of the rationale is repeated, indeed repeated twice: blood is life (v. 14aα, bα). Why, then, should the other part of the rationale—the blood as ransom (v. 11b)—be omitted? The answer can only be that in this case, the burial of the blood of game does not serve as a *kippēr* 'ransom'. All blood must be drained, but only blood on the altar is endowed with the power to expiate or ransom. Moreover, certain bloodless offerings also expiate (see NOTE on 5:13, and vol. 1.195–202). This can only mean that *it is the altar, not the blood, that expiates*. For this reason, the *gēr*, who does not have to resort to the altar (vv. 3–4), requires no ransom for slaughtering a sacrificeable animal. That is his divinely endowed right (Gen 9:3); he need but bury its blood. Only the Israelite risks his life in taking the life of an animal: a higher order of morality is incumbent on Israel. The omission of the *gēr* from this verse is thereby also explained: since part of the rationale—intended solely for Israel and inapplicable to the *gēr*—was included, the verse had to exclude the *gēr*.

for the life of all flesh is its blood. kî nepeš kol-bāśār dāmô hû'. The equation of life with blood is made explicit; it is repeated in Deuteronomy's version of the blood prohibition: *kî haddām hû' hannapeš* 'For blood is life' (Deut 12:23).

anyone who ingests it shall be cut off. kol-'ōklāyw yikkārēt. The particle *kol* is distributive and therefore takes a singular predicate (e.g., Gen 27:29; Exod 31:14; Lev 19:8, etc.; cf. GKC 145).

Vv. 15–16. The Fifth Law: Eating of a Carcass Requires Purification

The fifth law follows the fourth (vv. 13–14) logically: once game is killed, it becomes a carcass requiring the purification of the hunter (Ibn Ezra) and, therefore, both laws, vv. 13–14 and 15–16, compose the rules of hunting game (Wenham 1979). This view, however, must be rejected. As will be shown, this law deals mainly with the carcasses of domesticated animals. In fact, these two laws are related reciprocally. Their juxtaposition implies that the hunter must purify himself (with Ibn Ezra) and that whoever eats of carcasses must first drain and bury the blood, symbolically if it has congealed.

15. *And any person. wĕkol-nepeš.* This is a break from the *'îš 'îš* formula. The change is explicable: since the following verb is *'ākal, nepeš* is the preferred subject because of its primary meaning, "throat" (see NOTES on "the person who ingests blood," v. 10; see also at v. 12a). Hence there is no reason to regard this law as an appendix, and a very good reason to attribute it to the author of the entire chapter.

That the same legist should be willing to break the consistency of his introductory formula should occasion no surprise. For example, a change of formula occurs five times in one section of the Laws of Eshnunna: (1) statement of price, LE 8; (2) conditional (casuistic) sentence (*šumma awīlum*), LE 43; (3) split protasis, LE 17; (4) apodictic command, LE 166; and (5) relative formulation (*awīlum ša*), LE 13 (Yaron 1969: 59–71; Paul 1970).

whether citizen or alien. bāʾezraḥ ûbaggēr. Instead of *mibbêt/mibbĕnê yiśrāʾel ûmin-haggēr haggār bĕtôkām* (vv. 8a, 10a, 13a). The change may have been necessitated because this clause had to be transposed after the verb and direct object in order to bring the verb *ʾākal* in close contact with the subject *nepeš*. For the purported etymology of *ʾezrāḥ*, see NOTE on 19:34.

There are three laws regarding carcasses that concern the *gēr*: Exod 22:30 states that carcasses should be discarded as dog meat; Deut 14:21 claims that the *gēr* (and the foreigner) may benefit from carcasses; and Lev 17:15–16 insists that the *gēr* who eats of a carcass must undergo purification. The position of Exodus (JE) is unclear; since it is addressed to the Israelites, it may be implying that anyone else may benefit from carcasses. Deuteronomy (D), in its concern for the underprivileged, including the *gēr* (e.g., Deut 10:18; 24:17, 19, 20, 21; 26:12–13), recommends that the carcass be given to the *gēr*. Leviticus (H), obsessed with the fear that the land may be polluted by its inhabitants, concedes the carcass to the *gēr* on condition that he purify himself.

Regarding the Israelite (called "citizen" here), there are four carcass laws: the three mentioned above and a fourth, Lev 22:8 (H), which bans the consumption of carcasses by priests. Van Houten (1991: 82) mistakenly thinks that this last law conflicts with this verse, which ostensibly forbids the consumption of a carcass to an Israelite and a resident alien. This is not true. Lev 17:15 does not prohibit a carcass to the laity. But the stringency for priests is not surprising. Since priests are inherently holy (21:6; 22:9), deliberate contact with impurity is punishable by *kārēt* (22:3, 9). Lay persons, however, not being holy, are only warned not to perpetuate any impurity that they have incurred (5:2–3; see vol. 1.307–19), but there is no penalty for becoming impure. To be sure, Israel is enjoined to a *life* of holiness (e.g., 19:2). This concept, however, goes beyond ritual holiness to embrace ethics (see COMMENT on chap. 19). Deuteronomy, however, considers every Israelite inherently holy (e.g., Deut 7:6; 14:2) and, for that reason, prohibits the eating of carcasses (Deut 14:21a).

Cohen (1990a; 1993) has argued that the *nĕbēlâ* laws of both H and D (contra Hoffmann 1953: 2.323) presume that it is forbidden for an Israelite to partake of a carcass. However, there is no such prohibition in P, Lev 11:8a notwithstanding. The axiom of biblical (or any) jurisprudence is this: a prohibition that entails no penalty is not a law, but an appeal to conscience. Lev 11:8a is composed of two laws: "You shall not eat of their flesh or touch their carcasses." At the outset, it must be stated that the antecedent of "their" is the four named quadruped anomalies of 11:4–7, not the entire animal kingdom. Furthermore, it can be shown that this apodictic statement is not a prohibition. The Israelite is not forbidden to touch a human corpse (only a priest is prohibited, 21:1–4).

Then all the more so he is not forbidden to touch an animal carcass. Of course, he *should* not touch a carcass or eat of it. If he does, he is impure and must undergo laundering and ablutions (11:40; 17:15). It is only if he contacts sancta or prolongs his impurity that sanctions are imposed (7:20; 11:16; see vol. 1.307–19). By contrast, note that if a priest eats of a carcass he is punished with death by divine agency (21:8–9). Thus, in his case, the prohibition has teeth; it is truly a law. Finally, the general warning that Israelites whose impurity pollutes the sanctuary will suffer death (15:31) applies only to severe impurities requiring a purification offering. However, minor impurities, such as eating of a carcass, have no effect on the sanctuary unless the impurity is prolonged (vol. 1.307–19, 976–1004).

Therefore Hoffmann is correct. There is no priestly law prohibiting an Israelite or a resident alien from eating of a carcass unless he or she does not undergo the prescribed laundering and ablutions.

what has died. nĕbēlâ. As indicated by the Akkadian cognate *napultu*, rendered in Mesopotamian dictionaries as *mitti* or *mittitum* 'dead body' (*CAD* 11.1, s.v. *napištu*), Hebrew *nĕbēlâ* denotes "a dead person or animal." It had been assumed that this law shares with the previous one a concern about the ingestion of blood; that is, since the blood is still inside the carcass, the flesh might be eaten with the blood (Kalisch 1867–72; Dillmann and Ryssel 1897; Driver 1895: 165; Snaith 1967). Indeed, although the blood of a *ṭĕrēpâ* 'torn by beasts' (see NOTE on "has been torn by beasts") may have drained by itself, the blood of a *nĕbēlâ* probably would have coagulated and could easily be partaken with the flesh. Perhaps, from the H legist's perspective, since congealed blood is inseparable and indistinguishable from the flesh, it loses its symbolic association with the life of the animal. In any event, the apprehension lest the blood be eaten is nowhere expressed in this law. Indeed, if there were any anxiety about the ingestion of blood, the *kārēt* penalty would have been invoked (v. 10).

Moreover, this law cannot be an extension of the previous one. If it were, it would have been worded something like *wĕʾōkēl minniblātām bāʾezraḥ ûbaggēr* 'And whoever eats of this carcass, whether citizen or alien', not as a separate law. Furthermore, the subjects of these two laws are not the same; whereas vv. 13–14 focus on game, vv. 15–16 deal with the carcasses of all animals, including the domestic ones (in consonance with 11:40). Finally, it would make no sense that eating the carcass of game is legislated, but eating the carcass of domesticated species—those in one's own corral—is ignored!

The fact that the carcass of every animal transmits impurity puts this law in agreement with 11:39–40 (H), but not with other priestly statements (e.g., 5:2–3; 7:21[P]) which asseverate that only carcasses of impure animals convey impurity—indicating again the lateness of H relative to P (for the development, see vol. 1.13–35).

has been torn by beasts. ṭĕrēpâ. The verb *ṭārap* means "tear apart, rend" and refers to the manner in which wild animals kill their prey (cf. Gen 37:33; 49:27; Exod 22:12; Ezek 22:25; Nah 2:13; Ps 22:14).

The tandem *nĕbēlâ ûṭĕrēpâ* is attested elsewhere in prohibitions (7:24; 22:8;

Ezek 4:14; 44:31), the first citation dealing with the carcasses' suet (banned as food, 3:17; 7:25) and the other three, with the priest to whom all carcasses are forbidden. Only in the verse under discussion is this phrase directed to the laity. The Exodus law speaks only of *ṭĕrēpâ* (Exod 22:30); the deuteronomic law, only of *nĕbēlâ* (Deut 14:21). Why is only one member of the pair mentioned? I submit that the socioeconomic *Sitz im Leben* of these two laws provides the answer. The older Covenant Code (Exod 21–22) has its setting in a largely pastoral economy. The most likely accident befalling one's livestock is *ṭārōp yiṭṭārēp*: it will fall victim to a wild beast (Exod 22:12). To salvage something of the loss, the owner is tempted to eat it. After all, the meat is edible and relatively fresh. In contrast, Deuteronomy bespeaks an agricultural and commercial society. Animals reared for food are part of the homestead or graze close by. The chances of their becoming prey to wild animals is slim.

The juxtaposition of vv.15–16 to the laws that thrice mention the prohibition against ingesting blood (vv. 10,12,14) presumes that an animal that died naturally or violently (v. 15) will be drained of its blood before it is eaten.

Yet whereas Exod 22:30 (JE) and Deut 14:21 (D) prohibit the consumption of animals torn by beasts and those that have died naturally, respectively, H permits them, requiring only subsequent purification. Why has H turned lenient (for the lay person, not the priest; see 22:8 and its NOTE)? First, it should be noticed that P is even more lenient than H, since it, by inference, does not prohibit touching (and presumably, eating) the carcass of a pure animal at all (the prohibition of 11:39–40 I now assign to H; see NOTE on 22:8). Thus the question needs to be directed to the priestly tradition, in general. The answer can only be surmised. The priests who were in close contact with the people were more sensitive to the economic plight of their worshipers. The loss of an animal through either natural death or attack by a wild beast was a substantial economic loss to the ordinary farmer or herdsman. The priests, therefore, allowed them to benefit from their carcasses, H however insisting on subsequent purification.

launder his clothes, bathe in water. For an explanation of this method of purification, see the NOTE on 11:25 and vol. 1.957–68, 986–1000. Bathing the whole body is required (see v. 16). Akkadian texts contain the recurrent expression "water of the large ocean where the impure woman did not wash her hands (and) the woman under taboo did not wash her clothes" (*SbTU* I 44:72–74; var. *BAM* 543 III 70'–VI 1). Thus even in Mesopotamia, which did not develop a contamination system, ablutions and laundering were essential in order to eliminate the miasma of contamination. That the clothes are likely to become contaminated because of their contact with the body, as hypothesized in the NOTE on 11:24, is supported by the explicit statement in a Sabaean (pre-Islamic), South Arabian inscription "(after sexual intercourse he) wore his clothes without purification . . . he moistened his clothes with ejections" (*ANET* 665a).

and remain impure until the evening. For the meaning of this one-day impurity, see vol. 1.957–68, 986–1000.

16. *and bathe his body.* *ûbĕśārô.* This word is added here so that the conjunctive *waw* can be rendered "or" (Saadiah).

he shall bear his punishment. wĕnāśā' 'awōnô. When a person is the subject of *nāśā' 'awōn* or its synonym *nāśā' ḥēṭ'*, he literally bears the sin "and eventually perishes under its weight" (Schwartz 1991: 38, n. 4). However, God, as the subject, "lifts off" the sin from the erstwhile sinner; that is, he forgives him. (Schwartz suggests that God consents to "bear the sin," but that is carrying literalism too far.) For *nāśā'* meaning "lift," see Ps 116:13 (cup), Isa 18:3 (standard), Gen 31:10 (eyes), Ps 134:2 (hands), Gen 29:1 (feet), and 2 Kgs 9:32 (face). Interestingly, when God is the subject, this idiom appears in only nonpriestly texts (Gen 4:13; Exod 34:7; Num 14:18, etc.). Either the priestly legists were repelled by the implied anthropomorphism, or, more likely, they objected on theological grounds: sin does not "lift off" and then disappear; it adds to the pollution of the sanctuary and must be penalized.

Since behavioral terms also have extended consequential meaning (Milgrom 1976a: 1–13; vol. 1.339–45), *'awōn* may also be translated as "punishment"; that is, the person is liable for punishment, or, conversely, God "lifts" his punishment (cf. also Rashi on Num 5:31; Ibn Ezra on Gen 4:13; 1 Sam 28:10). This consequential meaning "bear sin/punishment" is also attested in Akkadian *ḥiṭam našû, arnam našû, šertam našû* (*CAD* N 11/2: 103, 104, 108), which contravenes Schwartz (1994; 1995). A parade example of this usage is *wĕnāśĕʾû 'et-zĕnûtêkem* (Num 14:33), which already Yeshuʿah ben Yehudah's Arabic translation had rendered "and they will *bear the harmful consequences* of your excessive behavior" (cf. Polliack 1993–94: 218; contra Paran 1989: 87; Schwartz 1995: 12, n. 31). Among moderns, note the more idiomatic "suffering for your faithlessness" (*NJPS*).

Schwartz (1991: 38, n. 4; 1994; 1995) persistently argues that the idiom *nāśā' 'awōn / ḥēṭ'* is a metaphor with the single, consistent meaning "carry, bear sin" or "carry off, remove sin." I concur with the latter in three P cases (Exod 28:38; Lev 10:17; 16:22; see vol. 1.1045), but unequivocally reject the former. I claim, instead, that in all other attestations in priestly texts, *nāśā' 'awōn / ḥeṭ'* means "bear, suffer punishment." In other words, the sinner does not carry his sin as if it were a weight, but must pay the consequences for his sin. Schwartz (1995: 11–12) supports his position by examining all the occurrences of this idiom in P and H, and, although he admits that in the preponderant number of cases punishment is implied, he cites four cases where remedial expiation is prescribed (see below), thereby obviating punishment. Because of the theological significance of this idiom, I shall review the twenty cases, adding their consequences and analyzing them: (1) Exod 28:43 (*mwt*); (2) Lev 5:1 ('*āšām*); (3) Lev 5:17 ('*āšām*); (4) Lev 7:18; 19:8 (*kārēt*); (5) Lev 17:16 (*kārēt*, implied); (6) Lev 19:17; (7–9) Lev 20:17, 19, 20 (*kārēt*, *'arîrî*); (10) Lev 22:9 (*mwt*); (11) Lev 22:16 ('*āšām*); (12) Lev 24:15; (13) Num 5:31 (*'arîrî*, implied); (14) Num 9:13 (*kārēt*); (15) Num 14:33 (*mwt*, implied); (16) Num 18:1 (*mwt*, implied); (17) Num 18:22 (*mwt*); (18) Num 18:23 (*mwt*, implied); (19) Num 18:32 (*mwt*); (20) Num 30:16.

Schwartz contends that nos. 2, 3, and 6 imply no punishment. His case for Lev 5:1 (no. 2) is based on the parallelism of *wĕnāśā' 'awōn* (v. 1) and *wĕ'āšēm* (vv. 2, 3, 4). The purported parallelism is vitiated because *wĕ'āšēm* is part of the

protasis (see NOTES), whereas *wĕnāśā' 'āwōn* is, here and always, part of the apodosis. Besides, it can be shown that 5:1 was originally a separate law that was
only subsequently, and artificially, incorporated into this pericope (vol.
1.314–15). Lev 5:17 (no. 3), to be sure, explicitly states that the sin is expiated
by a reparation offering. However, considering that the sin is a suspected *ma'al*
committed unwittingly, incurring an expensive ram as a fine is hardly a remedy,
but a steep penalty. (Indeed, that the word *'āšām* means "reparation, penalty,"
see especially 5:6, 19, 25a; Num 5:7.)

Lev 19:17 (no. 6) mentions no punishment, but neither do 7:18 (no. 4), 20:19
(no. 8), 24:15 (no. 12), Num 5:31 (no. 13), Num 18:1 (no. 16), Num 18:23 (no.
18), and Num 30:16 (no. 20). Indeed, these additional unspecified punishments
will prove my case: 7:18 (no. 4) is explicated by 19:8, which specifies *kārēt*. That
is, H (19:8) explains that *nāśā' 'āwōn*, in 7:18 (P) means *kārēt*. The punishment
in 19:17 (no. 6) may be inexplicable in its context, but it is elucidated in Ezekiel:
if you fail to "warn the wicked man of his wicked course in order to save his
life—he, the wicked man will die for his iniquity, but I will require a reckoning for his blood from you" (Ezek 3:18; cf. v. 19; 33:8). Lev 20:19 (no. 8) contains the only instance in the entire list of illicit unions (20:9–21) without an
explicit punishment. Surely, one is intended; it would be incredulous if in this
case the sinner merely "bears his sin." Perhaps, the placement of this verse between the *kārēt* and *'ărîrî* punishments indicates that the legist was unsure to
which of the two categories 20:19 belongs (see its NOTE).

Lev 24:15 (no. 12) is followed by the *môt yāmût* case of v. 16. The sequence
is clear: whereas one who curses God will be punished by God (*wĕnāśā' ḥeṭ'ô*),
one who curses him and also pronounces his name is not left to God's inevitable
punishment but must immediately be put to death by the community (see
NOTES). If the suspected adulteress (Num 5:31 [no. 13]) is convicted by the ordeal, she will not bear seed (vv. 22, 27); her punishment is equivalent to *'ărîrî*.
In Num 18:1 (no. 16), *mwt* is implied: if infractions of the Levitic guards are
punishable by death (v. 3), all the more so infractions committed by the priestly
(and Kohatite) guards. In Num 18:23 (no. 18), just as encroaching Israelites are
subject to *mwt* (v. 22), so, we can assume, are the Levitic guards who failed to
stop them. That unfulfilled vows (Num 30:6 [no. 20]) are inexorably punished
by God is explicitly stated in Koh 5:2–3. Finally, the construct *'ăwōn 'ašmâ* in
22:16 (no. 11) makes no sense if rendered "sin of (reparation)"; *'ăwōn* here clearly
must mean "penalty of."

Other evidence adduced by Schwartz (1995: 14) is, in my opinion, equally
erroneous:

1. *ba'ăwōn* does not mean "*in* the sin." In all its attestation (26:39; Num 27:3;
   Ezek 4:17; 18:17, 19, 20; 33:6; etc), the *beth* of means is employed, which
   must be rendered "by means of (the sin)."
2. In 20:11, 12, 13, 16, *dĕmêhem bām* is not a statement of condition. It *follows môt yûmātû*; it gives the *reason* for the death penalty. Thus it is not
   in parallel with *nāśā' 'āwōn* (vv. 17, 19, 20).

3. *tôʿēbâ / zimmâ, taznût* (Ezek 16:58; 23:35) make no sense as objects of *nāśāʾ* unless punishment for these sinful conditions is implied.

While denying that *nāśāʾ ʿāwōn* refers to punishment, Schwartz (1994: 170, n. 69) admits to the consequential meaning "incur fine" but restricted to judicial torts (e.g., Prov 19:19). However, he fails to contend with the cognate Mesopotamian terminology, cited above. Indeed, *arnu* 'sin' also means punishment in the theological as well as the judicial realm: note *arnum kabtam šēressu rabītam . . . līmussuma* 'may (Šamaš) inflict upon him as grievous punishment, his greater penalty' (*CAD* 1/2: 298; for other examples, see *CAD* 1/2: 299).

In sum, *nāśāʾ ʿāwōn* is a nonexpiable, irremediable divine sentence. In all cases where the punishment is not stated, it is forthcoming—irrevocably. In theological terms, perhaps one might say that the punishment (usually *mwt* or *kārēt*, see above) expiates for the sin (explicitly, *m. Yoma* 8:8), but the punishment itself is unavoidable.

COMMENTS

A. Chthonic Worship and Saul's Remedy (1 Sam 14:31–35)

[31]*wayyakkû bayyôm hahûʾ bappĕlistîm mimmikmāś ʾayyālōnâ wayyāʿap hāʿām mĕʿōd* [32]*wayyaʿaś[ṭ (Q)] hāʿām ʾel-[ha]śśālāl wayyiqḥû ṣōʾn ûbāqār ûbĕnê bāqār wayyišḥāṭû-ʾarṣâ wayyōʾkal hāʿām ʿal-haddām* [33]*wayyaggîdû lĕśāʾûl lēʾmōr hinnēh hāʿām ḥōṭʾim[ṭĕʾîm (Q)] laYHWH leʾĕkōl ʿal-haddām wayyōʾmer bĕgadtem gōllû-ʾēlay hayyôm ʾeben gĕdōlâ* [34]*wayyōʾmer šāʾûl pūṣû bāʿām waʾămartem lāhem haggîśû ʾēlay ʾîš šôrô wĕʾîš śĕyēhû ûśĕḥaṭem bāzeh waʾăkaltem wĕlōʾ-teḥṭĕʾû laYHWH leʾĕkōl ʾel[ʿal mlt (MSS)] -haddām wayyaggîśû kol-hāʿām ʾîš šôrô [ʾăšer (LXX)] bĕyādô hallaylâ wayyišḥāṭû-šām* [35]*wayyiben šāʾûl mizbēaḥ laYHWH ʾōtô hēḥēl libnôt mizbēaḥ laYHWH.*

[31]They struck down the Philistines that day from Michmas to Aijalon, and the troops were famished. [32]The troops pounced on the spoil; they took the sheep and cattle and calves *and slaughtered them facing the ground,* and the troops *ate over the blood.* [33]When it was reported to Saul that the troops were sinning against YHWH, *eating over the blood,* he said, "You have acted treacherously. Roll a large stone over to me here." [34]And Saul ordered: "Spread out among the troops and tell them that everyone must bring me his ox or his young sheep and slaughter it here, and then eat. You must not sin against YHWH and *eat over the blood.*" Everyone of the troops brought whatever he had in his possession *that night* and slaughtered it there. [35]Then Saul built an altar to YHWH; that one (the rock) he began to build into an altar to YHWH.

The key that unlocks the meaning of this passage is the threefold mention of the expression *ʾākal ʿal-haddām.* It cannot be rendered "eat with the blood" (most recently McCarter 1980), since it would become virtually synonymous with *'ākal 'et-haddām* 'eat blood' (vv. 10–12; 3:17; 7:26–27). It must be translated literally "eat over the blood" and refer to some illicit cultic rite that kindled the zealous wrath of King Saul. The nature of this rite is intimated in another law of the Holiness Source: *lo' to'kĕlû 'al-haddām lo' tĕnaḥăšû wĕlō' tĕ'ônēnû* 'You shall not eat over the blood: you shall not practice divination or soothsaying' (19:26). Thus the act of eating over blood must be related to some form of divination (see NOTE on 19:26, and Ibn Ezra, Rashbam, and Ramban on this verse).

Grintz (1966; 1970–71) must be credited as having correctly identified both the troops' illicit act and Saul's antidote. First he points out that Saul's rock is not an altar; nor is the slaughtering method he proposed a sacrifice:

1. The animal suet is not burned (cf. Lev 3:3–5).
2. The blood is not dashed on the rock (cf. Lev 3:2a), but only drained.
3. The rite takes place at night, contrary to authorized sacrificial procedure: "The whole of the day is a proper time . . . for handleaning, slaughtering" (*m. Meg.* 2:5–6; cf. *b. Zebaḥ.* 56a; *b. Tem.* 28b; Maimonides *'Abodah* 4:1).

Thus the conclusion is inescapable: the rock was not an altar, but only a foundation for a subsequent one (v. 35), and the slaughtering was a secular act and not a sacrifice to YHWH. What, then, was its purpose?

Grintz has assembled ample evidence from the ancient Greek world that clearly indicates that Saul attempted to prevent his troops from engaging in chthonic worship. He contrasts the worship of the celestial (Olympian) and subterranean (chthonic) gods as follows: (1) *sacrifice:* the verb for the Olympians is *thuein* 'raise smoke'; for chthonians, *enagízein* 'consecrate (by destroying)' (i.e., a burnt offering); (2) *slaughtering:* Olympians, the animal's throat is turned upward; chthonians, downward; (3) *place:* Olympians, *bomós* 'altar'; chthonians, *éschara,* a circle of earth and grass containing a *bóthros,* a deep trench; (4) *color:* Olympians, white animal; chthonians, black; (5) *animal:* Olympians, bull; chthonians, ram or pig (see NOTE on 11:7); (6) *site:* Olympians, high spot (temple); chthonians, caves, dark recesses; and (7) *time:* Olympians, daylight; chthonians, night, especially midnight.

Reflexes of chthonic worship are found in the Bible (1 Sam 28:3, 13; Isa 8:19; 20:4; 65:4; see chap. 20, COMMENTS B and C) and the Talmud (*m. Ḥul.* 2:9; *b. Ber.* 18b; *b. Sanh.* 65b; *y. Meg.* 1:12 [*b. Zebaḥ.* 120a]; cf. Maimonides, *Guide* 3:46). The classic description of chthonic worship is found in the *Odyssey* (11.24–26), when Odysseus raises from the dead the seer Teiresias:

There Perimedes and Eurylochus held the victims, but I drew my sharp sword from my thigh, and dug a pit, as it were a cubit in length and breadth, and about it poured a drink-offering to all the dead, first with meal and thereafter with sweet wine, and for the third time with water. And I sprinkled white meal thereon. . . . But when I besought the tribes of the dead with vows and prayers, I took the sheep and cut their throats over the trench, and the dark blood flowed forth, and lo, the spirits of the dead that be departed fathered them from out of Erebus.

Similar descriptions of chthonic worship are attested in the ancient Near East. In Egypt, "deities, whose bloodthirsty character is emphasized, are summoned to drink the blood of sacrificial animals" (Bergman 1978: 238). In Mesopotamia, Etana beseeches Shamash daily: "Thou hast eaten, O Shamash, the fat of my sheep, *The Netherworld has drunk the blood of my lambs* [my emphasis]); the gods I have honored, the ghosts [*eṭimmu*] I have revered" (*ANET* 1955: 117, ll.34–36; see also McCarthy 1969). In Ugarit, *nps ʿgl* [ ]*xxnxk. ašt. n. bḫrt. ilm. arṣ* 'throat of a calf . . . let me place in the hole of the underworld gods' (*KTU* 1.5 V: 4–6; cf. Gibson 1978: 72) and *npš. ʿgl* [*iṯ.lb*]*nk. ašt. n. bḫrt. ilm. arṣ* 'Your s[on will hav]e the soul of a bull-calf, for him I will put into a grave of the earth-gods" (*CARTU* 34 restoring *ARTU* 77). Above all, the technique common to all these passages is reminiscent of the pit (Heb. *ʾôb*; Akk. and Hitt. *apum*) utilized in the ancient Near East to raise the spirits of the dead (see NOTES on 19:31, and chap. 20, COMMENT B).

The relationship of 1 Sam 14 to Lev 17:5–7 is now rendered plausible. Israelites were sacrificing to *śēʿîrîm*, satyrs (i.e., chthonic goat deities) (v. 7); slaughtering *ʿal-pĕnê haśśādeh* 'on the open field' (v. 5), not on Saulide stones but on the ground; and consulting with spirits of the dead (Isa 8:19) for purposes of divination (Lev 19:26). That Saul's army ate "over the blood" (1 Sam 14:32–33), so that the spirits of the dead might imbibe it, is demonstrated in Homeric Greece (Homer *Odyssey* 11.24–34) and in Israel by surreptitious worship clearly identified with the cult of the dead: "As to the deified dead (*qĕdôšîm*; cf. Ps 89:6–8) who are in the underworld . . . I will have no part of their bloody libations" (Ps 16:3a, 4aβ; see chap. 20, COMMENT C). Clearly, the priestly legists of chap. 17 did not accept Saul's remedy. Rocks were convertible to altars (as proved by Saul), which—as shown by Olympian rites—lent themselves to the worship of other gods. Hence the Holiness legislation bans nonsacrificial slaughter, insisting that the slaughter of animals take place at an authorized sanctuary where the blood can be sacrificed on the altar. For the rationale for this prescription, see NOTE on v. 11, and COMMENT D.

The reasons why the troops "pounced" on the animal spoil can be stated simply (perhaps simplistically): they had fasted all day (1 Sam 14:24, 28) and were famished. There may, however, be a deeper, more fundamental reason. Fasting is a prerequisite for divination (e.g., Saul at En-dor, 1 Sam 28:20; cf. Exod 34:28; 2 Chr 20:3–4). Moreover, we are told that when Saul consulted God by the officially sanctioned oracle (presumably the Urim and Thummim), he received no answer (v. 37) (Grintz 1966). To be sure, the present order of 1 Sam 14 MT seems to indicate that Saul consulted the oracle after the slaughtering rite episode (vv. 31–35). However, the narrative also states that Saul requested that the oracular instrument be brought to him before the battle (v. 18 LXX, reading *ʾēpōd* instead of *ʾărôn hāʾĕlōhîm*; cf. Exod 28:30; Lev 8:8), a more logical time for divination since Saul would have wanted to know in advance how the battle would fare. Thus in view of the silence of God, Israel was forced to turn to illegitimate oracular means. The troops (probably their officers) sought to consult the departed spirits (as Odysseus consulted Teiresias). Saul, however, refused (contrast Saul at En-dor, 1 Sam 28), and it was left to Jonathan's successful strike to point the way to victory (1 Sam 14:13–23).

Grintz's (1966) thesis, however, is open to question:

1. If *'ākal 'al-haddām* refers to chthonic worship, why does D omit it from its list of banned magical practices (Deut 18:10–11), and why does it permit the blood of animals slaughtered commonly "to be poured on the ground like water" (Deut 12:16, 24).
2. The Greek analogy is not quite exact: chthonic sacrifices are mainly burnt offerings, rarely well-being offerings, that is, they are not intended as food for the offerer (note: "Meilichios will have all or nothing"; cf. Harrison 1922: 15, 28, 32, 57–58).
3. There is nothing in the text that indicates that the conflict between Saul and the troops rested on the proper procedure for divination.

Nonetheless, these objections do not impinge on Grintz's (1966) main thesis. The probability remains strong that the background of 1 Sam 14:31–35 is chthonic worship. Particularly compelling is Grintz's argument that in Greek sacrificial slaughter, the animal's head was always turned toward the gods—heavenward to the Olympians, earthward (as in 1 Sam 14:32) to the chthonians. A reflection of this rule lies in the following rabbinic prescription: "The sacrificial animal stands in the north and faces west, the one performing the handleaning in the west facing west" (*t. Men.* 10:12; cf. *b. Yoma* 36a [bar.]); thus both animal and offerer must face west, toward the shrine and adytum, the symbolic presence of YHWH. Again: "(The high priest) approaches his bull. The bull stands between the porch and the altar; *its head toward the south but facing west* [my emphasis]. The priest stands in the east facing west" (*m. Yoma* 3:8). Thus the high priest faces God (the west) and so does his sacrifice, *even if its head must be turned.* The handleaning and slaughter follow with both offerer and animal in the same position (*m. Yoma* 4:2–3).

A question, however, remains: Is the satyr worship of 17:7 identical with the chthonic worship of 19:26 and 1 Sam 14:31–35? Here the evidence for an affirmative answer is lacking. We miss the telltale idioms: *'ākal 'al-haddām, wayyašḥîṭû 'arṣâ, laylâ.* The massive evidence for the ancient Near East, partially cited above, renders Grintz's (1966) theory plausible, but until further evidence is marshaled, it will have to remain just that—plausible but unproved.

B. The gēr, "Resident Alien"

In return for being loyal to his protectors (Gen 21:23) and bound by their laws (e.g., Lev 24:22), the gēr, as indicated by its Arabic cognate *jâr*, was a "protected stranger" (Smith 1927: 75–79). Israel regarded itself as a gēr both in its own land (during the time of the forefathers, Gen 15:13; 23:4) and in Egypt (Exod 2:22; Lev 19:34). Moreover, since the land belonged to God, Israel's status on it was theologically and legally that of a gēr (Lev 25:23). Strangers had attached themselves to Israel during its flight from Egypt (Exod 12:38, 48; Num 11:4), as did many Canaanites after the conquest (e.g., Josh 9:3–27). Indeed, the Canaanites whom Solomon enslaved for his work projects (1 Kgs 9:20–21) are referred to in the later literature as gērîm (2 Chr 2:16; Paran 1987: 116). Therefore, gērîm could not own landed property and were largely day laborers and artisans (Deut 24:14–15) or were among the wards of society (Exod 23:12). Indeed, since the Levites—although Israelites—were also landless, they were dependent on the tribes in whose midst they settled, and, hence, they could be termed gērîm (e.g., Judg 17:7; 19:1; Deut 18:6; however, Cohen's [1990a; 1990b; 1993] repeated attempts to establish that the gērîm are North Israelite refugees in Judah are groundless; cf. Bultmann 1992: 11–12, 213). Although some gērîm did manage to amass wealth (Lev 25:37), most were poor and were bracketed with the poor as recipients of welfare (cf. Lev 19:10; 23:22; 25:6; for fuller details, see Seeligmann 1954). These latter verses indicate only too clearly that the gēr was landless. Thus the rabbis are at a loss to explain Ezekiel's prophecy (47: 22–23) that the restoration to the land will see the gēr inheriting land on a par with the Israelite (Sipre Num. 78, on Num 10:29).

Bultmann (1992) argues that the gēr in D does not designate a resident alien, but a landless, impoverished yet legally free member of Israelite rural society (34–119), a concept extending into exilic Dtr (129–74)—that is, not an ethnic label but a socioeconomic class. The analysis of his thesis would take us beyond the pale of this commentary. Here, however, I wish to cite one verse that challenges his thesis.

Deut 14:21a concedes a carcass as food for the gēr, whereas it is forbidden to the Israelite because he belongs to a "holy people" ('am qādôš) (Bultmann 1992: 84–93, 213). One might agree that D partially adopts H's concession that all Israelites may partake of a carcass (Lev 17:15a)—although Bultmann, uncritically maintaining Cholewinski's (1976) thesis that H enlarges and modifies D, would argue that the borrowing occurred in the reverse direction—but would limit the concession to the gēr and jettison H's purificatory requirements (Lev 17:15b-16). However, to exclude an Israelite gēr from the category of an 'am qādôš 'holy people' for socioeconomic reasons is, for me, inconceivable.

Moreover, I suspect that D's oft-repeated expression haggēr 'ăšer biš 'ārêkā, literally "the gēr within your gates" (e.g., Deut 5:14; 14:21, 29; 16:14; 26:12; 31:12; cf. 16:11; 24:14), refers to an alien, not to an Israelite, as implied by this expression's ancient Near Eastern equivalents (cited in Weinfeld 1991: 348): Ugaritic gr ḥmyt ugrt 'alien at the walls of Ugarit' (KTU 1.40:18, 35–36); Ugaritic Akkadian "the people of Ugarit / Carcemish together with the men living within their gates" (amēli ša bābišunu, RS 18: 115, ll. 4, 13; PRU 4.158–59); Nuzi Akkadian, which mentions a category of people ša bābi 'those of the gate', or noncitizens (HSS 19, 79).

Another indication that D's *gēr* is a non-Israelite can be derived from Deut 10:18–19:

ʿōśeh mišpaṭ yātôm wĕʾalmānâ wĕʾōhēb gēr lātēt lô leḥem wĕśimlâ waʾăhabtem ʾet-haggēr kî-gērîm heyîtem bĕʾereṣ miṣrāyim

(God, who shows no favor and takes no bribe, but) upholds the cause of the orphan and the widow, and loves the alien, providing him with food and clothing. Therefore you too must love the alien, for you were aliens in the land of Egypt.

First, the analogy of the *gēr* to Israel's status in Egypt would make sense only if the *gēr* were an alien (similarly in Exod 22:20; 23:9; Lev 19:34; Deut 23:8). Second, the *gēr* is contrasted with the orphan and widow. Although all three are subject to exploitation, the orphans and widows are Israelites and ties of blood entitle them to turn to authorities—be they judicial or social—for help. The *gēr*, however, cannot call on any ethnic bond. Israel is therefore admonished to think empathetically of its similar experience in Egypt. Then it too, like God, will love the alien (for the meaning of "love" as love in action, see NOTE on 19:18).

I do not deny the possibility that a "mindere rang der *gēr*" (the heading of Bultmann 1992: 84–93) may be ensconced in some layer of D. A definitive solution awaits a new investigation that would eschew Bultmann's source critical assumptions and methodology. In the meantime, one conclusion remains certain: one cannot accept Bultmann's categorical assertion that "es lässt sich für keiner Beleg . . . nach der der *gēr* eine Gestalt nicht-israelitischer Herkunft wäre" (213). Rather, one must assume, with most critics, that the *gēr* is an alien. Regarding Bultmann's even more dissatisfying remarks concerning the *gēr* in H, see the discussion on chap. 17 and NOTE on 19:33–34.

Recently, Gerstenberger (1996: 279, 326 inter alia) has claimed that the *pesaḥ* law (Exod 12:48) demonstrates that the circumcised *gēr* was a member of "the faith community." His thesis is undermined in the same pericope (v. 44) by the law that the circumcised slave—surely not a member of the faith community—could also partake of the *pesaḥ*. Furthermore, the *gēr*, as our chapter teaches us, may eat meat (or its suet, see below) without first slaughtering the animal at an authorized sanctuary and pouring its blood on the altar (see NOTES on 17:3 and 11). Indeed, Gerstenberger himself has to admit that the *gēr* "quite possibly was not an adherent of YHWH" (279). Thus he, just like the slave, was not a convert and certainly not a member of "the faith community."

In my critique of Gottwald (1979), I had shown that individual *gērîm* continued to be designated by their ethnic origin even though they worshiped the God of Israel (Milgrom 1982b). My argument has been countered by van Houten (1992: 60), citing de Vaux (1961: 4), that the tribe of Caleb "the Kenizzite" (Num 32:12), patently non-Israelite, was absorbed into the tribe of Judah. Thus, ostensibly, large groups or tribes did convert. However, as Kaufmann (1977:

670–72) has demonstrated, there is no Kenizzite tribe. Rather, Kenaz is one of the shared names between Israel and Edom (Gen 36:11), referring to an ancient pre-Israelite tribe. Thus Kenaz is neither Israelite nor Edomite, but one of the early ethnic groups out of which Judah was formed (Gen 15:19). As for Caleb, he is never referred to as a gēr, and all narratives testify that Caleb was an Is-raelite, a leader in the conquest of the land. Thus intermarriage and fusion with Israel, indeed, took place, but long before there was an Israel.

Although the gēr enjoyed equal protection with the Israelite under the law, he was not of the same legal status; he neither enjoyed the same privileges nor was bound by the same obligations. Whereas the civil law held the citizen and the gēr to be of equal status (e.g., Lev 24:22; Num 35:15), the religious law made distinctions according to the following underlying principle: the gēr is bound by the prohibitive commandments, but not by the performative ones. For example, the gēr is under no requirement to observe the festivals. The paschal sacrifice is explicitly declared a voluntary observance for the gēr: whereas an Israelite ab-stains from the sacrifice on pain of kārēt, the gēr may observe it provided that he is circumcised (Exod 12:47–48; Num 9:13–14). In fact, the injunction to dwell in sukkôt is explicitly directed to the "Israelite citizen" (Lev 23:42), which, by implication, excludes the gēr. Similarly, the gēr may participate in the vol-untary sacrificial cult if he follows its prescriptions (Num 15:14–16; Lev 22:17–25; details in Milgrom 1982b).

The injunction that "there shall be one law for you and for the resident stranger" (Num 15:15; cf. Exod 12:48–49; Lev 7:7; 24:22; Num 9:14; 15:29–30) should not be misconstrued. It applies only to the case given in the context; it is not to be taken as a generalization (contra van Houten 1991: 150, 156; cf. Ibn Ezra). Yet, according to the priestly legislation, the gēr is equally obligated to observe the prohibitive commandments. This conclusion can be derived from the following prohibition incumbent on the gēr: "Any person, whether citizen or gēr, who eats what has died or has been torn by beasts shall launder his clothes, bathe in water, and remain impure until the evening; then he shall be pure. But if he does not launder (his clothes) and bathe his body, he shall bear his punishment" (Lev 17:15–16). Thus the gēr and the Israelite are not forbidden to eat carrion, but are required to clean themselves of the impurity. The ratio-nale is clear: failure to eliminate impurity threatens God's land and sanctuary. The welfare of all Israel residing in God's land and under the protection of his sanctuary is jeopardized by the prolongation of impurity. The principle is un-derscored by the requirement to bring a communal purification offering to atone for the individual wrongs not only of the Israelites but of the gērîm as well (Num 15:26).

No wonder, then, that the gēr and the Israelite are equally obligated to refrain from violations that produce impurity. The penalty is wĕnāsā' 'awōnô 'he will bear his punishment' (Lev 17:16), which, in the priestly system, means a pu-rification offering for inadvertent violations (Lev 4) and kārēt for presumptuous ones (Num 15:30–31). Moreover, the requirement of a purification offering is imposed for the inadvertent violation of any prohibitive commandment (Lev 4:2,

13, 22, 27). Perhaps, originally, this sacrifice was limited to those cases where it was explicitly required: the parturient (Lev 12:6, 8), the *zāb* (Lev 15:14–15, 29–30), the *mĕṣōrāʿ* (Lev 14:13, 22, 27), and so on. These cases, it should be noted, deal explicitly with ritually impure persons. However, the heading of Lev 4 makes it emphatically clear that this sacrifice is called for upon the inadvertent violation of all prohibitive commandments (vol. 1.21–26). Again, the underlying principle is that the violation of all prohibitive commandments creates impurity and consequently pollutes God's sanctuary and land: sexual offenses and homicide, for example, pollute the land (Lev 18:27–28; Num 35:34–35), and Molek worship and corpse contamination pollute the sanctuary (Lev 20:3; Num 19:13, 20). It therefore makes no difference whether the polluter is Israelite or non-Israelite. Anyone in residence on YHWH's land is capable of polluting it or his sanctuary.

Performative commandments, however, are violated by refraining or neglecting to do them (in rabbinic terms *šēb wĕ-'al taʿăśeh* 'sit and do nothing'). These violations are sins not of commission, but of omission. They, too, can lead to dire consequences, but only for the Israelite, who is obligated by his covenant to observe them. The *gēr*, however, is not so obligated. And since they are acts of omission, of nonobservance, they generate no pollution either to the land or to the sanctuary. Thus the *gēr*, the resident non-Israelite, does not jeopardize the welfare of his Israelite neighbor by not complying with the performative commandments. As a result, he need not, for example, observe the paschal sacrifice. But if he wishes to, he must be circumcised (Exod 12:48) and, presumably, must be in a state of ritual purity (Num 9:6–7, 13–14). However, under no circumstances may he possess leaven during the festival (Exod 12:19; 13:7).

Does this mean that the *gēr* is required, as is the Israelite, to observe the minutiae of ritual and ethical prohibitions, such as not wearing garments of mixed seed (Lev 19:19) or not spreading gossip (Lev 19:16)? The answer is not clear. Most likely, the *gēr* is limited in his obligations to refrain from only those violations that engender ritual impurity (Lev 17:15). However, it would seem from Num 15:27–29 that the *gēr* is required to bring a purification offering for the violation of all commandments (vol. 1.264–69).

Ostensibly, there is one exception, but it only proves the rule. The exception is the right of the *gēr* to slaughter his animals profanely—that is, not as a sacrifice. The priestly tradition equates the *gēr* and the Israelite in almost all laws of Lev 17 that deal with legitimate means of providing meat for the table (vv. 8–9, 10, 12, 13–14, 15–16). There are two exceptions: the prohibition of profane slaughter (vv. 3–7) and the requirement to bring the blood of the slain animal to the altar (v. 11). The *gēr* is conspicuously absent in the first of these two laws (v. 3, 5). The second law (v. 11) implies this as well by its pronominal suffixes. In vv. 10–14, the larger context of which v. 11 is part, the Israelite is addressed in the second person; the *gēr* is always in the third person. Thus "to you" and "your lives" (v. 11) can refer to only the Israelites ("to you," but not to others; *Sipra* Aḥarei Mot, par. 8). These two laws complement each other perfectly. The first states that an Israelite who slaughters the animal for its meat without

offering it as a sacrifice—indeed, of dousing the animal's blood on the altar—
is to atone for killing it (see NOTES on v. 11, and vol. 1.704–13). The omission
of the gēr from this law now becomes understandable. The gēr is permitted nonsacrificial slaughter because (like the non-Israelite in Gen 9:3–4) he need only
drain the blood (the animal being treated like game, vv. 13–14). Conversely, he
need not bring his animal as a sacrifice, since its slaughter is not sinful for him
and requires no sacrificial expiation. This conclusion suffices by itself to undermine Bultmann's (1992) thesis that the gēr is a subordinate class of Israelite
(see below).

This distinction between the gēr and the Israelite is also apparent in the corollary prohibition concerning the animal suet: the gēr may eat it, but the Israelite
may not (Lev 3:17; 7:25). The reason is clear: suet of sacrificial animals must
be offered on the altar (Lev 7:25), from which may be inferred that suet of game
may be eaten. (Note also the contrast: whereas the prohibition against eating
suet falls on sacrificial animals alone, the prohibition against eating blood falls
on all animals, including birds; Lev 7:26.) This leniency toward the gēr in regard to suet follows logically from his distinction from the Israelites regarding
the blood: if the gēr's meat need not be offered as a sacrifice, why, then, his suet?

There is good reason to believe that the status of the gēr in the priestly laws
served as a model for Deuteronomy's subsequent concession of profane slaughter to the Israelite. When D abolished the local altar and declared that the central sanctuary was the only legitimate one, it became impossible to require the
Israelite to journey to the central sanctuary each time he desired meat for his
table. Thus the concession was made to the Israelite that he might slaughter his
animals profanely, at home, but with the proviso that the blood would not be
ingested (Deut 12:15–16, 20–25).

By suspending the rules of purity that governed the eating of sacrificial flesh
(Lev 7:16–21) and by declaring that, henceforth, all animals eligible to be used
as food were to be treated as the gazelle and deer (Deut 12:15, 22), Deuteronomy bestowed on them the status of game (cf. Lev 17:13–14). Moreover, although Deuteronomy takes great pains to reiterate the blood prohibition, it is
conspicuously silent on the suet. This silence is explicable in the light of the
limitation of the suet prohibition to sacrificial animals alone (Lev 7:25). Thus
in allowing the Israelites to treat all animals as game—in suspending the laws
of purity regarding the eating of animals and in conceding, implicitly, the suet
of animals as food—Deuteronomy accorded the Israelite the same status as the
gēr. Placed in its historical perspective, the legislation concerning the gēr served
as the model for the deuteronomic concession to the Israelite concerning the
slaughtering and eating of animals.

However, Deuteronomy allowed, or rather created, one distinction between
the gēr and the Israelite. In the older legislation, the Israelite is forbidden to eat
ṭĕrēpâ, flesh torn by beasts in the field (Exod 22:30); Deuteronomy forbids him
to eat nĕbēlâ, carrion of animals that died a natural death (Deut 14:21). The
priestly tradition prohibits neither ṭĕrēpâ nor nĕbēlâ to the Israelite and the gēr,
but requires only a purification ceremony in the event they are eaten (Lev

17:15–16). Deuteronomy, in forbidding the *nĕbēlâ* to the Israelite, has thereby added a prohibition not found in the early sources, presumably so as not to obliterate completely the distinction in this regard between the *gēr* and the Israelite; at the same time, it imposes the knowledge and the fulfillment of its Torah on the *gēr* (Deut 31:12).

In sum, the *gēr* was expected to observe all the prohibitive commandments, lest their violation lead to the pollution of God's sanctuary and land, which, in turn, results in God's alienation and Israel's exile. In this regard, both the *gēr* and the Israelite are subject to the same law, with the exception—explicitly stated—that the *gēr* does not have to slaughter his animal at the authorized altar but may slaughter it, like game, in the field. In essence, this concession is only a concomitant of the main distinction between the *gēr* and the Israelite: the *gēr* must observe the prohibitive commandment not to worship other gods (Lev 17:8–9), but he is not compelled to observe YHWH's performative commandments.

It must be remembered that the *gēr*, the resident alien of biblical times, is far removed from the *gēr*, the convert of rabbinic times. Conversion as such was unknown in the ancient world. Ethnicity was the only criterion for membership in a group. The outsider could join only by marriage (e.g., Ruth). In fact, it was not those who intermarried but the subsequent generations that succeeded in assimilating, and even then not always (e.g., Deut 23:1–9). Some *gērîm*, like the Kenites (Moses' family, Judg 1:16), were ultimately absorbed into Israel, presumably by marriage. Others, like the Gibeonites, maintained their slave status throughout the biblical period (Josh 9:27; cf. Ezra 2:58).

Barrick (1996: 640, n. 88) questions whether my criteria for conversion hold up in the cases of Naaman (2 Kgs 5:17–18) and the transplantees (2 Kgs 17:24–34a). The former, of course, is technically not a *gēr*; he does not reside in Canaan. Moreover, that he adds YHWH to his pantheon hardly warrants the designation "convert." Although the latter do fall under the rubric *gēr*, they too are polytheists; they do not forsake their own gods. And their so-called conversion stems not from faith, but from expediency.

The *gēr* never lost the connotation of "resident alien" in the Older Testament (Smith 1971: 178–79). Van Houten (1991: 151–55), however, claims that the priestly laws of the *gēr* refer to the Israelites who remained in the land during the exile, were considered impure by the returnees, and were compelled to undergo a ritual of purification before being readmitted into the community of Israel. Her theory must be dismissed out of hand. The only "purity" requirement imposed on the *gēr* is circumcision, but only if he wished to partake of the paschal sacrifice (see below). But Israelites who hypothetically were not exiled must have been circumcised. Besides, would the opposition to building the Temple have stemmed from Israelites (Ezra 4:4; cf. 3:3)?

Rather, the first glimmer of a new status for the *gēr* is found in the words of the Second Isaiah at the end of the sixth century B.C.E. In the Babylonian Exile, non-Jews had been attracted by the Jewish way of life, particularly by the sabbath. Isaiah calls on these would-be proselytes to "make *ʿaliyah*" with the Israelites; and although he cannot promise them that they will be part of the *'am*, the peoplehood of Israel—conversion as such was unknown—he assures them that the Temple service will be open to them because "My house will be called a house of prayer for all peoples." (Isa 56:7; for a close reading of Isa 56:1–8, see Greenberg, forthcoming; see also Ezra 6:21; Neh 10:29–30; 2 Chr 30:25; and the discussion in Japhet 1977: 286–99).

One postexilic passage, however, states unequivocally that the *gēr* will become part of the people of Israel: *wĕnilwâ haggēr 'ălêhem wĕnispĕḥû 'al-bêt ya'ăqōb* 'and the resident alien shall join them and attach themselves to the House of Jacob' (Isa 14:1; for the meaning of *sāpaḥ*, see 1 Sam 26:19). The assimilation of the *gēr* may also be intimated in Ezek 47:22–23 "You shall allot it (the land) as an inheritance [*bĕnaḥălâ*] for yourselves and the aliens who reside among you, who have begotten children among you. You shall treat them as Israelite citizens; they shall receive allotments along with you among the tribes of Israel. You shall give the alien an allotment within the tribe where he resides—declares YHWH your God." With this last barrier between the Israelite and the *gēr* removed, total assimilation is apparently envisioned.

Another indication of the outreach to the *gēr* to join the community of Israel is the requirement that he must be circumcised in order to participate in the paschal offering (Exod 12:48), which may belong to H's final, exilic stratum (see Introduction I E, and vol. 1.27–28). Circumcision is a sign of the covenant (Gen 17:11), a reminder to YHWH (e.g., Gen 9:13–16) to fulfill his promise of great progeny (Gen 17:5–6; cf. Fox 1974: 586–96). Initially, Ishmael as well as Isaac are recipients of this promise (Gen 17:5–6). Though the covenant is transferred to Isaac (Gen 17:19, 21). Ishmael still retains the blessing of posterity (v. 20). But if any Israelite remains uncircumcised, he automatically forfeits the blessing: instead of progeny, his line is cut off (*kārēt*, v. 14). Thus the *gēr* who is circumcised and upholds the covenantal obligations (e.g., Exod 12:48; Num 15:27–31) is eligible for its blessing of posterity. This is the first step—a giant one—on the road to conversion. Also, as pointed out by Gammie (1989), followed by van Houten (1991: 133), since Egyptians, Edomites, Ammonites, and Moabites also practiced circumcision (Jer 9:24–25), it did not function to separate Israelites from non-Israelites. But because the Babylonians did not practice it, it became an effective sign of membership in Israel's exilic community (see also Westermann 1985: 265).

There is another marker of this progression toward conversion. Of the eighteen verifiable cases of the *kārēt* formula attributable to H, eight mention the *gēr*, four use the customary object *'am / 'ammim* 'kinspeople', but four have the following objects: *yiśrā'ēl* (Exod 12:15; Num 19:13; cf. Knohl 1995: 93, n. 111), *'ădat yiśrā'ēl* (Exod 12:19), and *qāhāl* (Num 19:20). How is it possible that the *gēr* is reckoned as belonging to Israel's *'ēdâ* and *qāhāl?* The possibility looms that the H author (rather, redactor) of these passages already envisioned the inclusion of the *gēr*, at least in theory, among the people of Israel. That is, since the *gēr* was obligated to observe Israel's prohibitive commandments and was allowed to observe Israel's performative commandments, he was, for all intents and purposes, bound by Israel's covenant. If this conjecture holds, I would further speculate that these four passages were written by Hr, the H tradent of the exile. It is hardly accidental that this tradent was (roughly) the contemporary of exilic Ezekiel, who prophesied that the *gēr* would be eligible to inherit land (see above), and the exilic Isaiah, who granted the *gēr* full participation in Israel's cult (see above), and that the *gēr*'s full acceptance in the *pesaḥ* rites (note that two of these four cases deal with the *pesaḥ*) may also be exilic (see above). Thus it may be postulated that the change in attitude to the *gēr* occurred in the exile, and the movement toward conversion was under way.

The way was now open to the next stage of religious conversion, a stage discernable by the year 200 B.C.E. At that time, Antiochus III issued a decree fining any foreigner who entered the Israelite court of the Temple (equivalent to "the entrance of the Tent of Meeting") the sum of 3000 silver drachmas, payable to the priests (Jos. *Ant.* 12: 145–46)—a far cry from the biblical *gēr*, who could enter the Tabernacle court to offer his sacrifices. Clearly, the Jews of the third century B.C.E. were not in violation of the Torah, for by then they had reinterpreted the Torah's *gēr* to denote the convert. That the institution of religious conversion was heretofore unknown not just in Israel but also in its contemporary world is indicated by the need of the Septuagint translators to invent a new word, *prosēlutos* 'proselyte' (Tov 1982: 793), for the convert, a term they consistently use for *gēr* in all legal contexts. The sole exception is Exod 12:19, where they use the transliterated (Aramaic) form *geiōras*, and Deut 14:21, where, in order to prevent concluding that the convert may eat of a *nĕbēlâ*, they translate *gēr* as *pároikos* 'alien' (B. Elliot).

C. The Blood Prohibition (Continued)

The blood prohibition was discussed in chap. 11, COMMENT C, "The Ethical Foundations of the Dietary System" (vol. 1.704–13). What follows is an excursus on the priestly text Gen 9:1–4, a passage that bans the ingestion of animal blood to the entire human race:

> *wayyĕbārēk ʾĕlōhîm ʾet-nōaḥ wĕʾet-bānāyw wayyōʾmer lāhem pĕrû ûrĕbû ûmilʾû ʾet-hāʾāreṣ. ûmôraʾăkem wĕḥittĕkem yihyeh ʿal kol-ḥayyat hāʾāreṣ wĕʿal kol-ʿôp haššāmayim bĕkōl ʾăšer tirmōś hāʾădāmâ ûbĕkol-dĕgê hayyām bĕyedkem nittānû. kol-remeś ʾăšer hûʾ-ḥay lākem yiheh lĕʾoklâ kĕyereq ʿēśeb nātatti lākem ʾet-kol. ʾak bāśār bĕnapšô dāmô lōʾ tōʾkēlû*

[1]God blessed Noah and his sons, and said to them, "Be fertile and increase, and fill the earth. [2]The fear and dread of you shall be upon all the beasts of the earth and upon all the birds of the sky, on everything that creeps on the ground, and upon all the fish of the sea; into your hand are they given. [3]Every creature that lives shall be yours to eat; as with the green grasses, I give you all (these). [4]Only, you shall not eat flesh with its life, that is, its blood."

The fundamental question is this: Why does the priestly account concede meat to Noah rather than to Adam, who instead is explicitly described as a vegetarian (Gen 1:29)? Was there an earlier tradition that man the carnivore represents a later stage in the history of the human race? In my initial treatment of the blood prohibition, I cited the Sumerian "Myth of Lugulbanda" (vol. 1.713), which clearly indicated that such a transition, indeed, was a widespread belief (details in Hallo 1983; 1987; 1996: 216–20). There is another text, however, one that was more likely known to the Israelites, which strikes pervasive roots into much of the Bible's antediluvian epic. I refer to the *Epic of Gilgamesh.*

The key to this channel of influence is the expression "the fear and dread of you" (Gen 9:2aα), implying that heretofore man was not just a vegetarian but a friend of the animals; however, with the concession of meat, he became a hunter. Note the relevant passages from *Gilgamesh* (I, ii, 24–34; II, iii, 3–7 [*ANET* 75, 77]): "On seeing him, Enkidu, the gazelles ran off. The wild beasts of the steppe drew away from his body. . . . But now he had [wi]sdom, [br]oader understanding. . . . [The harlot] says to him, to Enkidu: 'Thou art [wi]se, Enkidu, art become like a god! Why with the wild creatures dost thou roam over the steppe? . . . " Food (meat) they placed before him. He gagged . . . nothing does Enkidu know of eating food."

Elsewhere I am preparing to set forth the thesis that biblical Adam was modeled on Mesopotamian Enkidu. Before each of them experienced sex, they were vegetarians (Gen 1:29; *Gilgamesh* I, iv, 2–4), naked (Gen 2:25; 3:7; *Gilgamesh* II, ii, 27–28), and friends and protectors of the beasts (Gen 2:20; 3:1–4; *Gilgamesh* I, iii, 9–12). After sex, they eat meat (*conceded* to Noah, Gen 9:3, but presumably illegally eaten by Adam and his progeny; *Gilgamesh* II, iii, 3–7), wear clothes (Gen 2:25; 3:21; *Gilgamesh* II, ii, 27–29, iii, 26–27), and become enemies of the beasts (Gen 3:15; 9:2; *Gilgamesh* I, iv, 24–25; II, iii, 28–32).

However, the most significant parallel between the heroes of the two epics is that sex makes them wise and thereby enables them to become civilized. "Thou art wise, Enkidu, art become like a god" (*Gilgamesh* I, iv, 34) is matched by Adam and Eve's eating the forbidden fruit, the "source of wisdom" (Gen 3:6), which empowers them to "know good and evil" (Gen 2:7, 17; 3:4, 21). That the latter expression is a euphemism for sex is proved by Deut 1:39 and, especiallyl, 2 Sam 19:36 (Milgrom 1994b), by the more obvious euphemism that they were naked (see NOTE on 18:6) before they ate the fruit (another metaphor for sex) and immediately afterward realized their nakedness (Gen 2:25; 3:7), and by the fact that the woman had her name changed to Eve, "the mother of all living," only after she ate the fruit (Gen 3:19), implying that previously she had been a "helpmate (helpmeet)" (Gen 2:20), but not a sexual partner.

To be sure, the line of Cain also knows both good and evil. Cain himself is "a builder of a city" (Gen 4:17), and his progeny creates the first arts and sciences of civilization (Gen 4:20–22). But Cain is also the first homicide, and his descendant Lamech more brazenly follows suit (Gen 4:23–24). The sapiential empowerment from "eating the fruit" of certainty leads to good and/or evil consequences.

It is probable that with their eviction from paradise, man and woman illicitly began to eat meat (Brichto 1976). With Noah, the carnivorous appetite of the human being is legitimized (Gen 9:1–4). This concession forms part of his first law code (Gen 9:1–6). He will kill to have meat. Therefore, let him do so only if he drains the animal's life-blood and returns it to its divine creator.

It is also of interest to note the obsessive fear that permeates the book of *Jubilees* regarding the Noahide prohibition against blood consumption. The biblical text (Gen 9:4–5a) reads:

> 'ak- bāśār běnapšô dāmô lō' tō'kēlû wě'ak 'et-dimkem lěnapšôtêkem 'edroš miyyad kol-ḥayyâ 'edrěšennû. . . .

> You must not, however, eat flesh with its life-blood in it. But for your own life-blood I will require a reckoning. I will require it of every beast. . . .

Jub 6:7–8, 12b interprets this passage: "But flesh which is (filled) with life, (that is) with blood, you shall not eat—because the life of all flesh is in the blood—lest your blood be sought for your lives. . . . And the man who eats the blood of the beasts or cattle or birds throughout all the days of the earth shall be uprooted, he and his seed from the earth."

Jubilees has artfully combined the following biblical verses sequentially: Gen 9:4; Lev 17:14aα, 4b, 10. That is, blood should not be ingested because it contains life; so whoever ingests blood is guilty of murder, and he and his line will be cut off. *Jubilees* has correctly interpreted *kārēt* to mean "excision" (which it explains in detail, 7:28–29; see vol. 1.457–61), but has applied the charge of murder, levied against one who slaughters an animal illicitly—that is, who does not sacrifice the animal on the authorized altar (see NOTES on v. 4b)—to one who ingests blood. Moreover, *Jubilees* even condemns the person who does sacrifice the animal properly but allows any of the blood to splatter on his clothing to "be seen upon you" (*Jub* 7:30; cf. vv. 31–33; details in Werman 1994).

Philo (*Laws* 4.122) provides a rationale: "they prepare sacrifices which ought never be offered, strangling their victims, and stifling the essence of life, which they ought to let depart free and unrestrained, burying the blood, as it were in the body. For it ought to have been sufficient for them to enjoy the flesh by itself, without touching any of those parts which have a connection with the soul or life."

D. Does H Advocate the Centralization of Worship?

According to Kuenen, Wellhausen, and their immediate followers, P (and H) does not explicitly espouse the centralization of worship because it took it for granted an attitude that could be expected by a postexilic source, which would have been influenced by Deuteronomy. This notion, I submit, was exploded by Kaufmann (1937: 1.113–42; 1960: 175–99), and no one to date has offered a point-by-point refutation of his challenge. Even Blenkinsopp (1996), who, to his credit, has read Kaufmann's four massive volumes on the history of Israelite religion in the original Hebrew, unfortunately neglects to confront Kaufmann's most potent arguments, such as the laws of the firstfruits and the tithes (for an itemization of these and other of Blenkinsopp's omissions, see Introduction I K and Milgrom 1999). I have argued (vol. 1.28–34) that P, indeed, maintains a limited doctrine of centralization at a regional sanctuary (possibly Shiloh), thereby admitting to the existence and legitimacy of other regional sanctuaries. Furthermore, P must have allowed the slaughter of animals anywhere (see vol. 1.28, and COMMENT A). Otherwise, one cannot explain H's polemic against sacrifice in the open fields, the prevailing practice *up to his time*. Indeed, the very beginning of the *šĕlāmîm* pericope implies this reading. It is a protasis *wĕ'im zebaḥ šĕlāmîm qorbānô* 'If his offering is a sacrifice of well-being' (3:1). That is, only if he wishes to offer a *sacrifice* of well-being, then the following rules apply. But if he wants meat for the table, he need not bring his animal to a sanctuary. Of course, he was expected to drain the blood in the manner exemplified by Saul (1 Sam 14:34), lest he engage in chthonic worship. That this expectation frequently was not met provides the *Sitz im Leben* for H's drastic measure banning all nonsacrificial slaughter. Thus the evidence points in one direction: P presumes both multiple sanctuaries and nonsacrificial slaughter.

But what of H? Since the Hezekian reform both endorsed and implemented centralization (2 Kgs 18:1–4), did it do so under the influence of H? Haran (1973; 1978: 141) and Knohl (1995: 199–224) think so, not because H takes it for granted, but because it states at the opening of its corpus (17:3–7) that all slaughter is banned except that which occurs at the one legitimate altar at the Tabernacle. Kaufmann (1937: 1.113–42; 1960: 175–99) is the only one, to my knowledge, who maintains that H posits multiple sanctuaries (also Elliott-Binns 1955, but without substantiation). I believe he is right (reversing vol. 1.29). These are my (and his) reasons:

1. The unexpected and otherwise inexplicable burgeoning of the plural *miqdĕšêkem* 'your **sanctuaries**' (Lev 26:31; correcting vol. 1.754) can now be understood as revealing the true intent of the writer. These are *maḥănêhem 'ăšer 'ānî šōkēn bĕtôkām* 'their camps in whose midst [lit. 'middles'] I dwell' (Num 5:3 [H]) and *miqdĕšêkem* 'your **sanctuaries**' (Lev 26:31; correcting vol. 1.754). The former clearly is a reference to the writer's cities (the wilderness camp stands for cities, 14:1–3; 33:53), in which God's presence dwells, namely, those that have sanctuaries. The latter is even more revealing. As pointed out by Kaufmann (1937: 1.133; 1960: 182), Ezek 6:6 omits this item from his citation of Lev 26:30–31a (see chap. 26, COMMENT C) because multiple sanctuaries had been abolished (in the deuteronomic reform). Not only does *miqdĕšêkem* attest to the existence of multiple sanctuaries in the time of the H writer, but it also confirms the divine (and his) approval of them. For he adds *wĕlō' 'ārîaḥ bĕrēaḥ nîḥōḥăkem* 'and I will not smell your pleasant odors' (chap. 26; see its NOTE). Furthermore "your sanctuaries" is placed in parallel with "your cities," which certainly were not condemned by God (Elliott-Binns 1955: 32). H therefore admits that heretofore (before Israel is punished for its disobedience), God did ac-

cept Israel's sacrificial service in these sanctuaries. (Also the singular *miqdāšî*, 19:30; 26:2 may be an erroneous Masorete vocalization of the original plural *miqdāšay*; Kaufmann 1937: 1.134.)

2. That H inherits P indicates that H recognizes the *legitimacy* of multiple sanctuaries until its time. The Bible itself attests to the existence of regional sanctuaries (*bayit* or *miqdaš*) at Bethel (Gen 28:17, 22; 1 Kgs 12:31a), Shechem (Josh 24:26; cf. Judg 9:27), Shilo (1 Sam 1:24; cf. 3:15; Judg 18:31), Gilgal (Amos 4:4; 5:5), and Beer-sheba (Amos 5:5; 8:14) and in JE's prescription that firstfruits must be brought to *bêt YHWH ʾĕlōhêkā* (Exod 23:19; 34:26)—that is, a regional sanctuary (cf. Kraus 1966: 125–73; Olyan 1991). Moreover, this fact corresponds with historical reality, as verified by the findings of archaeology. Iron Age cult places have been discovered at Dan, Arad, Megiddo, Lachish, Gezer, Shechem, Tell Beit-Mirsim, Tell Qadesh (in the Jezreel Valley), and Beer-sheba, to which Scripture adds Gilgal, Mizpah, Bethel, and Shilo (Judg 2:1; 20:1, 26–28; 1 Sam 1–3; details in Shilo 1979). Thus there is no need to scrounge for a reason to explain the "aboutface" taken by H by allegedly demanding centralization. It continues to sanction the regional sanctuaries presumed by its priestly (P) predecessors. H's innovation banning all nonsacrificial slaughter is radical enough (see below).

3. Both pro- and anticentralization positions hold that the wilderness setting of Lev 17 is programmatic for the promised land. Kaufmann (1938) argues that just as Moses, Aaron, and the camp are archetypes for future prophets, priests, and camps (i.e., cities), respectively, so the Tent of Meeting is the archetype for future sanctuaries. In Douglas's (forthcoming) words: "A projectile universe constantly reconstituting itself in objects and places is the essence of its microcosmic thinking. The multiplication of tabernacles is implicit in the idea of replicable holy space. . . . Correctly mapped on to space, the temple once consecrated will be as sacred as the original tabernacle, and they can build as many as they need." Here I differ with Kaufmann (as presumably would Douglas), who holds that the *bāmâ* (by which he means an open-air altar) is the successor to the wilderness Tabernacle. Such a simple installation could be improvised by every householder, mainly for providing meat for the table (1 Sam 14:32–35; cf. COMMENT A) or for worshiping the deity (e.g., Num 23:14; Judg 13:19). However, the names *miškān* and *ʾōhel môʿēd* imply a structure that in landed conditions would have to be a building. Indeed, the requirement that there be (at least) one officiant *kōhēn* implies the storing of ample equipment, which only a building (*bayit*) can provide. The wilderness model, however, does not mean that its structure, sacred objects, and sacrificial functions have to be precisely duplicated (Haran 1973: 121). Rather, the names *ʾōhel môʿēd* and *miškān* chiefly imply that YHWH's presence is there to meet with Moses and Israel (Exod 29:42b-43 [H]), namely, for oracular purposes. If one assumes, however, that the model was intended to be duplicated, the only communal rites purportedly conducted in the wilderness sanctuary are daily sacrifices (Exod 29:39–42a), lighting the candelabrum (Exod 27:20–21), incense offering (Exod 30:1–9), bread of presence (Exod 25:30), and purgation (Lev 16)—all per-

formable at any sanctuary (but not at an open-air altar). Indeed, there is textual evidence that the regional sanctuaries had a candelabrum (Shilo, 1 Sam 3:3) and the bread of presence (Nob, 1 Sam 21:7). Only the wilderness Ark seems to be missing. This lack can be explained. One cannot fail to notice that in the premonarchic period, the Ark was variously located at Gilgal (Josh 4:19; cf. 3:11–15), Bethel (Judg 20:26), Shiloh (Josh 18:1; 1 Sam 4:4), and, most likely, other sanctuaries. The Ark's unceasing movement is recorded in the statement that until it was installed permanently in the Jerusalem Temple, it (God) *mithallēk bě'ōhel ûmběmiškān* 'moved about in a tent and tabernacle' (2 Sam 7:6). This means that the Ark was never in the permanent possession of any one sanctuary, but was shared by all of them. The possibility should also be reckoned with that each of these sanctuaries may have had its own Ark (cf. Toorn and Houtman 1994).

It is presently not clear how the *bāmâ* differs from *bayit* (see the discussion in NOTE on 26:30). My tentative (and tremulous) speculation is that the *bāmâ* is for sacrifice; hence it consists of a *bayit* 'building' and an outside altar. The *bayit*, however, is of necessity devoid of a sacrificial altar. Note that the repeated description of *bêt mikâ* (Judg 17–18) omits any mention of an altar. This would mean that its function was purely divinatory, as indicated by the quest of the Danite scouts (Judg 18:5–6). Thus we see that *bêt mîkâ* (Judg 17:9, 12; 18:13, 15, 18) was provided with an ephod, a molten image (*pesel ûmassēkâ*), and teraphim (Judg 18:17, 18, 20)—but no altar—which subsequently were set up in a more elaborate building(s) at Dan (Judg 18:31; 1 Kgs 12:31; cf. Biran 1992: 14).

The Wellhausanian centralizers hold, instead, that satyr worship (17:7) is specified because satyrs are associated with wildernesses (Isa 13:21; 34:14) and symbolically are emblematic of all illicit worship, namely, any worship taking place outside the one authorized sanctuary and its altar. A Kaufmannian, however, would explain the satyr reference as an allusion to the time of H, when satyr worship may have been an aspect of the rampant ancestor cult (see COMMENT A; chap. 20, COMMENTS B and C). Knohl (1995: 219) adds to the centralizer's portfolio by claiming that centralization enabled the priests to ensure that satyr sacrifices "would not be incorporated into the worship of God." For this, however, centralization was not required. The ban on nonsacrificial slaughter would have put all sacrifices under the total supervision of the priests.

Furthermore, I submit, there exists one priestly text that does indicate H's program for worship in the promised land—Num 33:50–56. It can be attributed to H on the basis of the terms *maśkît* and *bāmôt* (v. 52), both found in H (Lev 26:1, 30) but absent in P (see also Kuenen 1886: 98, n. 39). In this passage, H states explicitly that *bāmôt* should be destroyed, meaning those of the Canaanites. Had H wished to ban the construction of *bāmôt* for YHWH, it would have added some statement, the equivalent of D's: "You shall not worship YHWH your God in such ways" (Deut 12:4). The fact that it refrained from doing so can only mean that it had no scruples about multiple sanctuaries in the land.

Finally, since P does not deny the validity of other sanctuaries (admitted by

Haran 1962a), one would have expected a centralizing H to have rung the alarm against them in the strongest possible terms. It does so neither in Lev 17 nor in Num 33, where it had such a golden opportunity.

Haran (1981b) argues that Israel's priests were unconcerned with their contemporary world and, hence, did not wrestle with its pressing ills. Instead, they constructed an idealistic, utopian picture removed from historical reality. As an example, he cites the encampment of Israel in concentric squares around an ornate Tabernacle during its wilderness sojourn (Num 2; Exod 25–31). I have contended (1990a: 340–41), to the contrary, that their conception of the wilderness camp corresponds to the Egyptian war camp during the second half of the second millennium. Thus the details may be imaginary, but the kernel is grounded in reality.

To be sure, one cannot deny the utopian elements in the priestly reconstruction of Israel's past and in its vision for the future. But the latter, particularly in H, rather than being removed from its world, is reacting vigorously and concretely to the socioeconomic injustices prevailing in its own time, as will be demonstrated throughout this commentary. And even if its solutions for Israel's faults (beginning with this chapter) are, at times, so idealistic as to be beyond realization, there can be no doubt that the tradents of the H school are sensitively aware of the problems besetting their fellow Israelites outside the sanctuary precincts, problems for which they propose far-reaching remedies and a comprehensive blueprint for achieving an ideal society.

4. The realistic setting for H's absolute ban on nonsacrificial slaughter is resolved. There is no longer any need to posit strained (and patently unsatisfactory) conditions that would allow for such a ban to be implemented, such as meat meals were rare (Haran 1963: 551–52; 1973: 120), Judah was reduced to the environs of Jerusalem following Sennacherib's invasion (Weinfeld 1985b: 86, n. 35; cf. Cogan 1974: 66–67), and sheer idealization (Schwartz 1987: 37; Joosten 1994: 205, n. 45; 1996: 148, n. 45). The first rationale is refuted below. The third is refuted by the frequent occurrence of the phrase *ḥuqqat 'ōlām lĕdōrōtêkem / lĕdōrōtām* 'an eternal law throughout your / their generations' (Exod 12:17; 27:21; Lev 3:17; 7:36; 10:9; 16:31; 17:7; 23:14, 21, 31, 41; 24:3; Num 10:8; 15:15; 18:23; 35:29; cf. Knohl 1995: 46–55, but note my reservations in vol. 1.16–17). In each case, the law is realistic and attainable. Thus there is no reason why Lev 17:1–7 is not meant to be implemented as and when decreed. Also, since H's presumed centralization was to take effect permanently (v. 7b), H clearly did not have the limited territory of Hezekiah in mind (the second rationale), but all of the promised land (reversing Milgrom 1992c: 459). In this respect, then, H is no different from D. One would have expected that H would secularize all slaughter or at least state, as did D, "When YHWH your God extends your boundaries" (Deut 12:20). Instead, H absolutely prohibits nonsacrificial slaughter! However, if, as I claim, multiple sanctuaries are allowed to persist, Israelites would simply be required to bring their animals to their closest sanctuary. Thus this ban on nonsacrificial slaughter is severed from any alimentary, historical, or fictional rationale. It becomes doable and, hence, manda-

tory for all time. In H's words, it is a *ḥuqqat ʿôlām . . . lĕdōrōtām* 'an eternal law throughout their generations' (Lev v. 7b).

Moreover, if centralization had occurred in Hezekiah's time, the logistical problems would have been insurmountable. Oded (1966: 6–7) has plausibly suggested that Sennacherib's incredible statement that he exiled 200,150 Judeans (Luckenbill 1924: 33, 144; *ANET* 288a) actually refers to the Assyrian estimate of the total population of Judah (the 150 being added to make the number sound precise). Even assuming that Jerusalem and its immediate environs contained half that number, it is difficult to conceive that the Jerusalem Temple of *Hezekiah's time*—considering its small size and staff—could have supplied the year-long meat requirements of about 25,000 families (of the countryside 100,000), not to speak of the paschal requirement of the total population.

Regarding the first rationale (rarity of meat meals), Mary Douglas (personal communication) has provided me with another argument in this regard. Citing Dahl and Hjort (1976: 29, 88–89), she points to the indispensable necessity to cut down the number of males among the herd and flock to avoid a waste of grazing land—all the more essential in marginal-rain areas, such as that of ancient Israel. The only solution is either castration (for improved quality of meat) or sacrifice. Since the former is forbidden by H (22:24), sacrifice remains the sole alternative. In sheep farming in seminomadic conditions, the general minimum of uncastrated males to ewes is 1:60; as for cattle, one mature bull can serve fifty to sixty females. This means that fifty-nine out of sixty males in the country would have to be brought to the altar. These facts adduced by Dahl and Hjort (courtesy of Douglas) explain, first, why all the public sacrifices were males and, conversely, why it was all the more burdensome to the commoner who had to bring a female for his or her purification offering (4:27–35) and why he or she was allowed in certain cases a cheaper alternative (5:1–13); second, contrary to the scholarly consensus, why the Israelite farmer or herder had an ample diet of meat; and third, why it is evident that multiple sanctuaries must be posited to accommodate the frequent need for sacrificial slaughter. As Douglas states acutely: "If a sacrifice was the regular occasion for thinning the herds, I suspect that it would be impossible and even ridiculous to require livestock farmers to do every killing at a central place." For D, however, H's enigma would present no problem, since it permits common slaughter to provide meat for the table.

5. There is one priestly text that unmistakably points to a single sanctuary: Josh 22:9–34 (esp. vv. 19, 29). This ostensible difficulty, however, can be fully resolved in view of the larger, contextual narrative of which this text is a part. According to the priestly tradition, Shilo is the final resting place of the wilderness Tabernacle, where lots are drawn for the distribution of the land to the remaining seven tribes (Josh 18:1–6; 19:51). Indeed, later tradition acknowledged that Shilo had been the site of the wilderness Tent of Meeting/Tabernacle (1 Sam 2:22; Ps 78:60). And it is from Shilo that a representative delegation of the tribes under the leadership of the high priest Phineas is sent to the Transjordanian tribes to remonstrate with them for having built an altar on "impure" land (Josh 22:13–19). This is their sin. Had any of the Cisjordanian tribes built

an altar, the same outburst would not have ensued. The altar could not have been labeled as *mered baYHWH* 'a rebellion against YHWH' or as *ma'al bĕ'lōhê yiśrā'ēl* 'sacrilege against the God of Israel' (v. 16).

Thus this priestly narrative presumes that immediately upon entry to the land, the existence of a single sanctuary, which had prevailed during the wilderness journeys, continued to be maintained. As Kaufmann (1959: 239) astutely observes, at this point there are no other Israelite cultic sites in the land, neither sanctuary complexes (*miqdāšîm*) nor smaller sanctuaries (*bāmôt*). The Tabernacle is not yet installed in a building (which already existed when Samuel was born, 1 Sam 1–3). It was only subsequent to the time presumed by this chapter that other cultic sites (enumerated in no. 2, above) begin to proliferate in the land. (Even the book of Joshua predicates a *miqdaš YHWH* 'sanctuary to YHWH' in Shechem [Josh 24:26].) To be sure, Josh 22:19 and 23 state explicitly that the only legitimate altar is *lipnê miškānô* 'before his Tabernacle' (v. 29b)—that is, at Shilo. This is indubitably correct in view of the historical setting. For if the tribes of Gad and Reuben would have abandoned their holdings in Transjordan, and had crossed over to Cisjordan, they could not have built their altar until they would have been assigned and had *conquered* their land. In the meantime, they would have had no choice but, together with the other tribes, to worship at the existing altar at the wilderness Tabernacle resting at Shilo.

Knohl (1995: 208, n. 26) claims that a few verses in Josh 22 contain H expressions. Be that as it may, but the author (or compiler) of Josh 22 remained true to his reconstruction of events; he did not betray his own chronologically later situation. An analogy comes to mind. D mentions *mizbāḥôt* 'altars', but neither *miqdāšîm* 'sanctuary complexes' nor *bāmôt* 'smaller sanctuaries'. The purpose, again, is to prevent anachronisms. Moses worshiped on an altar, but he knew nothing of the existence of Canaanite sanctuaries. The tradition of a single sanctuary in the wilderness and for a while at Shilo (cf. Jer 7:12) may have been used as a precedent by the deuteronomic centralizers. But even they would have conceded (as did rabbinic tradition; see *m. Zebaḥ.* 14:6–8) that from that time on, cult sites proliferate. Moreover, they would also have admitted that nowhere in Scripture, before the deuteronomic reform, are altars, built not in "impure" territory but in YHWH's (holy) land, ever condemned. Hence the ostensible evidence of a permanent single sanctuary from Josh 22 must be ruled out of court.

6. If H was promoting centralization, is it not strange that there is no mention of the place where the single sanctuary is to be located? Nor should the choice of Jerusalem be taken for granted. There would be many claimants for the site—for example, those in which Iron Age sanctuaries have been discovered (listed above). Moreover, H would have been challenged by the Shechemite tradition brought by the North Israelite refugees, as manifested in Deut 27:1–8. Thus the term *'ōhel mô'ēd* could not have been understood as a code name for Jerusalem. To mask his true intention, the H tradent, at least, should have resorted to a subterfuge like D's *hammāqôm 'ăšer-yibḥar YHWH* (Deut 12:11 inter alia). Moreover, as astutely remarked by Douglas (1999: 94), if H was advo-

cating centralization, it would have contrasted the Tabernacle with other sanctuaries and not exclusively (if at all) with the open field.

7. Had H motivated Hezekiah's centralization (2 Kgs 18:4, 22), Hezekiah would have based it on the explicit command of God. Its words would have been read in public or, at least, before Israel's elders (cf. 2 Kgs 23:1). Then the high priest Hilkiah (2 Kgs 22:8–10) would have buttressed D's demand for centralization by pointing to the century-old precedent set by H. In any event, even if we postulate that H had remained confined to the esoteric circle of Jerusalem's priesthood, Hilkiah would have known of it!

Furthermore, there are two significant items in Hezekiah's reform that are conspicuously absent in H: the 'ăšērâ and nĕḥaš hannĕḥōšet (2 Kgs 18:4). Indeed, as pointed out by Ginsberg (1982: 37), Hezekiah's extirpation of the 'ăšērâ may have been based on Deut 16:21 (and Exod 34:13 [D]), but not on H. Conversely, Hezekiah did not destroy H's ḥammānîm (Lev 26:30). And whereas the bāmôt destroyed by Hezekiah included those laYHWH (2 Kgs 18:22), the bāmôt of H are idolatrous (Lev 26:31; Num 33:52). These inconcinnities in themselves should suffice to unhinge Hezekiah's reform from its alleged moorings in H.

8. If centralization had been advocated, much less had occurred, one could expect the insertion of some proviso to allow priests of *legitimate* sanctuaries to be absorbed by, or at least benefit from, the central sanctuary, similar to the prescription in the deuteronomic legislation (Deut 18:6–8), which demonstrably was implemented, if unsuccessfully, during Josiah's reign (2 Kgs 23:9). Furthermore, there is no indication that Hezekiah herded the rural priests of Judah in the Jerusalem Temple (for opposing evidence, see 2 Chr 31:15–20), a policy adopted by Josiah (2 Kgs 23:8a).

9. Knohl (1995: 211) proposes that the changeover of tithe ownership from priests (27:30) to Levites (Num 18:21) ordained by H (presuming that Num 18 stems from H; see Knohl 1995: 53–55) was adopted by Hezekiah when he was confronted by many Levites among the refugees from the collapsed North. However, how could H have justified the tithe transfer on the basis of ḥelep 'ăbōdātām 'ăšer-hēm 'ōbĕdîm 'et- 'ăbōdat 'ōhel mô'ed 'in return for the work they do: the work of the Tent of Meeting' (Num 18:21b; cf. Milgrom 1970: 76)? Hezekiah certainly could not have employed them all in his centralized sanctuary (Knohl's assumption), nor would he have endowed them with such a largesse as the tithe if they were unemployed! Rather, he must have distributed the Levites among the existing sanctuaries in his realm.

10. Finally, one is compelled to ask: What would have been the driving force behind H's centralization? The apostasy of the Baal and that of the golden calves of Bethel and Dan, the two cardinal heresies of the deuteronomistic historiography, occurred in North Israel, outside the boundaries of Hezekiah's kingdom. In fact, idolatry is not an issue with the H legislation. The mention of 'ĕlîlîm 'idols' (H's term for 'ĕlōhîm 'ăḥērîm 'other gods', perhaps Isaiah's coinage [2:8, 18, 20; 10:10, 11; 19:1, 3; 31:7]) in Lev 19:4 and its reflex in Lev 26:1 alludes to the Decalogue. But other than these two tangential citations, there is no polemic in H against idolatry (see Introduction I I). As already indicated (see

COMMENT A) and as will be further substantiated (see chap. 20, COMMENTS B and C), H's main battle is waged against chthonic worship, particularly the ancestor cults. The molten gods (19:4), carved images, pillars, and figured pavements (26:1), against which H inveighs, are probably directed to the worship of YHWH (see NOTES). So, too, I claim, is Molek worship (see NOTES on 18:21).

In sum, there are two oblique references to idolatry: reflexes of the Decalogue and, possibly, the curse of 26:30. What is totally missing in H is the frontal attack, like the repeated gunfire of D (4:19, 25; 6:13–14; 7:4; 8:12; 11:16; 13:2–19; etc.). Possibly, some illicit cultic activities were practiced at the *bāmôt*; hence, the prediction of their destruction (26:30). At the same time, however, the sanctuaries (*miqdāšîm*, H's *'ōhel mô'ēd*) are not condemned; they will be "made desolate," but not destroyed (26:31). Thus, with idolatry removed as the possible reason for centralization, why the urgency to centralize? To disrupt the economy of the entire land, flood the countryside with unemployed and homeless priests and their staffs, and, above all, deprive the populace of its familiar and accessible houses of worship—why?

It has even been doubted that Hezekiah actually centralized the cult (Hoffmann 1980; Spieckermann 1982; Handy 1988; Zwickel 1994: 316–18; Na'aman 1995). In his frontal attack, Na'aman marshals the following arguments:

1. Except for the archival notice on the bronze serpent, 2 Kgs 18:4, 22 were composed by the deuteronomic historian, who (following Ben Zvi 1991b) wished to fit Hezekiah into his scheme of alternating four good and bad kings. As Ahaz is the prototype for Manasseh, Hezekiah is the prototype for Josiah. The historian therefore portrayed Hezekiah as fulfilling precisely the injunctions of Deut 7:5; 12:3.

2. Isaiah and Micah, contemporaries of Hezekiah, are strangely silent concerning his alleged cultic reform, and 2 Chron 29–31 is historically unreliable.

3. Tel Arad and Tel Beer-sheba show no signs of Hezekiah's cultic reform.

4. The existence of a cult place at Lachish, destroyed by Sennacherib in 701 B.C.E., proves that Hezekiah's alleged cultic centralization did not affect his largest city after Jerusalem.

If Na'aman (1995) is correct, then H, a Hezekiahan product in the main, could not have advocated centralization simply because Hezekiah did not implement it. However, Na'aman's argumentation can be challenged:

1. Na'aman pays inadequate attention to the differences between 2 Kgs 18:4 and Deut 7:5, 12:3. Whereas the former uses terms such as *hēsîr* and *bāmôt*, the latter employs *nātaṣ* and *mizbāḥôt* (there are no *bāmôt* in Deuteronomy). These terms are not synonymous. That *hēsîr* literally means "remove," not "tear down" (*nātaṣ*), is shown by the deuteronomistic historian's use of the same expression *hēsîr bāmôt* in conjunction with *ma'ăkâ . . . wayĕsîrehā* (1 Kgs 12–13). Surely, the queen mother was not torn down! Hence, Hezekiah is said to have removed the *bāmôt*, not that he tore them down, an act attributed by the same historian subsequently to Josiah (2 Kgs 23:8, 15; note *nātaṣ*).

As for the Rab-shakeh's first speech (2 Kgs 18:19–25), there can be no doubt that it is not a verbatim citation. However, as pointed out by Weinfeld (1992:

160, n. 15), in view of the fact that Hezekiah's deeds were well known a full century later (Jer 26:18), the historian would have undermined the creditability of his account had he attributed to Hezekiah such a major but nonexistent cultic reform. Moreover, as demonstrated by Cohen (1979), there are many expressions reflecting a neo-Assyrian background in the Rab-shakeh's first speech, which contains no deuteronomistic elements (contra Ben Zvi 1990: 91).

2. It is hardly to be expected that Isaiah and Micah, who focus on the grievous moral injustices in the land, would be concerned with cultic matters. On the contrary, even if worship were centralized in the Jerusalem Temple, they roundly condemned it (Isa 1:11–17; Mic 6:6–7). Furthermore, Na'aman errs concerning the prophets' silence. Isa 17:7–8 and 27:9 express the hope that the altars—even those dedicated to the worship of YHWH—will be torn down (cf. Weinfeld 1992: 161). Also, the possibility exists that the prophecy of Mic 5:9–14 was delivered to promote Hezekiah's religious reform (cf. Willis 1969).

The *Tendenz* of the Chronicler is well known (see NOTE on 27:31, and Japhet 1993: 958–73). However, as pointed out by Borowski (1995), Hezekiah's centralization and accumulation and distribution of supplies, as described by the Chronicler (2 Chr 31:11–12, 15, 19), do not make sense, except against the backdrop of preparations for a revolt against Assyria (see also Halpern 1991: 26–27, 41–49).

3. The stratification of Tel Arad and Tel Beer-sheba is presently disputed. Nonetheless, if it is finally established that the cessation of worship at the Tel Arad altar and the reuse of the Tel Beer-sheba altar stones in the repair of a storehouse occurred in an eighth-century layer, then a number of facts begin to make sense in the light of Hezekiah's cultic reform. That the two altars were not destroyed but, respectively, were buried and dismantled reflects Hezekiah's reform, which only "removed" the altars (Aharoni 1974; Herzog 1981; Herzog et al. 1984: 87). Moreover, Halpern (1991: 26–27, 41–49) has mounted a strong case that Hezekiah dismantled the local cult as part of his *political* policy to herd the peasantry into forts in anticipation of Sennacherib's invasion, which would explain the removal of the altar at Beer-sheba, where there was no enclosed shrine, but did not dismantle the cult at fortresses such as Arad and Lachish (see further below). In addition, the survival of the Arad incense altars may be an indication that Hezekiah's reform affected only sacrificial, not incense, altars. Abetting this hypothesis is the fact that in the more drastic centralization demanded by Deuteronomy, probably mirrored in 2 Kgs 23, there is no prohibition against the burning of incense (see also Jer 41:5; Cowley 30:25–26; 32:9–10, for the persistence of sanctioned incense offerings even after the destruction of the Temple; cf. Milgrom 1976g; 1979).

4. The same holds for Na'aman's hypothesis concerning Lachish. The only evidence for the existence of its cult place is the portrayal on Sennacherib's relief of two large incense stands carried off as booty. Again, this suggests that incense burning legitimately continued after Hezekiah's reform (Borowski 1995: 152).

Thus it must be concluded that Hezekiah *did* centralize the cult. His radical action, however, did not stem from H, but was most likely motivated by socioeconomic and, chiefly, political considerations, namely, in preparation for the invasion of Sennacherib (705–701 B.C.E.) (see Oesterley and Robinson 1930: 1.393; Rowley 1962; Miller and Hayes 1986: 353, 357; Ben Zvi 1991b; Halpern 1991: 41–49; Tatum 1991; Borowski 1995). Even David initiated the construction of a centralized sanctuary more out of political and economic considerations than religious ones (Heltzer 1989). A religious factor may also have been operative. Deuteronomy's demand for centralization may possibly be traced to North Israel of the eighth century, when Hosea fulminated against multiple altars (8:11–14; cf. Ginsberg 1982: 21; Levine 1997: 247–49). In any case, Hezekiah invalidated local altars (*bāmôt*), but in view of Halpern's study, he would have retained the regional sanctuaries ensconced within Judahite fortresses. H, to the contrary, following the P tradition, validated all the regional sanctuaries.

Another possibility, proposed by Ginsberg (1982: 115–16), is that Hezekiah's centralization was influenced by the kernel of D brought to Judah by exiles from North Israel. As support, he points to Hezekiah's action in cutting down (*krt*) the cult post (*ʾăšērâ*, 2 Kgs 18:4), which may be "a response to the prohibition of Deut 16:21 against the planting (*nṭʿ*) of such an object next to the altar of YHWH. For within the Pentateuch the word *ʾăšērâ* only occurs again in Deut 12:3 (as object of *śrp* 'to burn'), in Deut 7:5 as object of *gdʿ* 'to cut down', and in Exod 34:13 . . . adapted from Deut 7:5 [cf. ad loc. 62–64—J.M.]—as object of the other Hebrew word for 'to cut down,' the very *krt* of 2 Kgs 18:4! P [and H—J.M.], on the other hand, exhibits not a single instance of *ʾăšērâ* or any other expression that might conceivably mean the same thing." Moreover, there is no reference in H to the *nĕḥaš hannĕḥōšet* 'the copper snake' (2 Kgs 18:4). Conversely, Hezekiah did not destroy H's *ḥammānîm* 'incense stands' (Lev 26:30). Also, Hezekiah's disqualified *bāmôt* were dedicated to the worship of YHWH (2 Kgs 18:4, 22), whereas H's *bāmôt* are idolatrous (Lev 26:30; note the contiguous *ḥammānîm* and *gillûlîm* 'fetishes'). These points, in themselves, undermine Knohl's (1995: 207) claim of the "correspondence of the king's reform to the laws of HS." In any event, whether motivated by political or by religious considerations, Lev 17:3–9 was not a factor (see also Welch 1924; Alt 1953: 2.250–75; Wright 1953: 2.323–26; Nicholson 1967: 58–82, 121–23; Weinfeld 1972d: 366–70; 1991: 44–57; Tigay 1996: xxiii-xxiv).

One by-product of this conclusion is that, once and for all, it sounds the death knell for all those who continue to date the priestly material after the exile (most recently, Otto 1994: 219–56). No one will deny that in the postexilic age, the deuteronomic doctrine of total centralization ruled supreme. Thus any source that posits multiple sanctuaries must ipso facto be preexilic. Moreover, the bulk of H must be attributed to the eighth century B.C.E. If it stemmed from the seventh century, then no differently from Deuteronomy, Jeremiah, and Ezekiel, it would have had to confront the state-endorsed idolatry promulgated by Manasseh (see Introduction II D).

If H does not advocate centralization, what, then, is its innovation? It can only be the absolute ban on nonsacrificial slaughter. H demands that all meat for the table must be brought to a sanctuary as a well-being offering (šĕlāmîm) so that its blood can be poured out on the altar. Here H takes issue with P, which permits nonsacrificial slaughter (vol. 1.28–29). What is H's rationale? It unfolds throughout this chapter, reaching its climax in v. 11: lĕkappēr 'al napšōtêkem 'to ransom your lives' for having "murdered" the animal (see its NOTE, INTRODUCTION to chap. 17; and vol. 1.253–54, 704–13, 1079–84). For H, the real threat to the worship of YHWH is the proliferation and persistence of ancestor worship, whose main rite consists of offering blood to the chthonic gods and ancestral spirits, exemplified by satyr (and Molek) worship (see COMMENT A; chap. 20, COMMENTS B and C). Hence H adopts a theology prescribing that all animal slaughter, heretofore permissible anywhere, must be performed at a sanctuary of YHWH (vv. 5–7).

In sum, H accepts and continues P's tradition of regional sanctuaries. There is, however, an important difference between the two. P reflects the cultic practice of a particular regional sanctuary, possibly Shilo, as supplemented by the pre-Hezekian Jerusalem Temple (vol. 1.29–34). However, there can be no doubt that worship was also conducted at regional sanctuaries throughout the land. H similarly represents the cultic practice of a single sanctuary, probably Jerusalem, and no differently from P it does not advocate centralization, but legitimates worship of YHWH at other sanctuaries. Nonetheless, the royal Temple of Jerusalem, fairly accessible from all parts of Judah, was preferred for the pilgrimage-festivals (maṣṣôt and sukkôt; concerning the absence of šābû 'ôt in H, see NOTE on "all your settlements," 23:21) over the regional sanctuaries of Judah. Thus the booths that sprang up on Jerusalem's hills for the seven-day autumnal festival gave rise to its name, Festival of Booths, in H and D (see NOTE on 23:42). However, this distinctiveness of Jerusalem was a matter of preference, not requirement. It was only with D that all worship was centralized at the Jerusalem Temple. No differently from P, the devotee of H could have worshiped at the regional sanctuary of his choice. The legal, hence mandatory, innovation of H is that whereas P permits nonsacrificial slaughter for meat, H prohibits it in toto, lest its practitioners be charged by the deity for the capital crime of murder (v. 4) and chthonic worship (v. 7). The real innovator of centralization remains D; it must therefore concede nonsacrificial slaughter. Thus it turns out that only H imposes an absolute ban on nonsacrificial slaughter, a far-reaching and unrealistic demand that probably always remained a dead letter.

18. ILLICIT SEXUAL PRACTICES

TRANSLATION

Opening Exhortation

¹YHWH spoke to Moses, saying: ²Speak to the Israelites and say to them: I am YHWH your God. ³As is done in the land of Egypt where you dwelt, you shall

not do, and as they do in the land of Canaan to which I am bringing you, you shall not do; you shall not follow their statutes. ⁴My rules alone shall you observe and my statutes alone shall you heed, following them: I YHWH your God (have spoken). ⁵You shall heed my statutes and my rules, which if one does them, he shall live by them: I YHWH (have spoken).

The Prohibitions

⁶No one shall approach anyone of his own flesh to uncover nakedness: I YHWH (have spoken). ⁷The nakedness of your father, that is, the nakedness of your mother, you shall not uncover; she is your mother—you shall not uncover her nakedness. ⁸The nakedness of your father's wife you shall not uncover; it is the nakedness of your father. ⁹The nakedness of your sister, the daughter of your father or the daughter of your mother—whether of the household clan or of an outside clan—do not uncover her nakedness. ¹⁰The nakedness of your son's daughter or of your daughter's daughter—do not uncover their nakedness; for their nakedness is your own nakedness. ¹¹The nakedness of your father's wife's daughter who is of your father's clan—she is your sister; do not uncover her nakedness. ¹²The nakedness of your father's sister you shall not uncover; she is of your father's flesh. ¹³The nakedness of your mother's sister you shall not uncover; for she is your mother's flesh. ¹⁴The nakedness of your father's brother you shall not uncover, (that is,) you shall not approach his wife; she is your aunt. ¹⁵The nakedness of your daughter-in-law you shall not uncover: she is your son's wife; do not uncover her nakedness. ¹⁶The nakedness of your brother's wife you shall not uncover; it is your brother's nakedness.

¹⁷The nakedness of a woman and her daughter you shall not uncover; neither shall you marry her son's daughter or her daughter's daughter to uncover her nakedness: they are kindred; it is depravity. ¹⁸And you shall not marry a woman producing rivalry to her sister, uncovering her nakedness during her (sister's) lifetime. ¹⁹You shall not approach a woman during her menstrual impurity to uncover her nakedness. ²⁰You shall not have sexual relations with your neighbor's wife and defile yourself through her. ²¹You shall not dedicate any of your offspring to be sacrificed to Molek, and thereby not desecrate the name of your god: I YHWH (have spoken). ²²You shall not lie with a male as one lies with a woman: it is an abomination. ²³You shall not have sexual relations with any animal to defile yourself thereby; nor shall any woman give herself to an animal to mate with it; it is a perversion.

Closing Exhortation

²⁴Do not defile yourselves in any of these (practices), for by all these (practices) the nations I am casting out before you defiled themselves. ²⁵Thus the land became defiled; and I called it to account for its iniquity, and the land vomited out its inhabitants. ²⁶You, however, must keep my statutes and my rules and commit none of these abominations, neither the citizen nor the alien who re-

sides among you; ²⁷for all these abominations the people in the land who (were) before you did, and the land became defiled. ²⁸So let not the land vomit you out for defiling it, as it is vomiting out the nation that was before you. ²⁹For all who commit any of these abominations—such persons shall be cut off from their kin. ³⁰So you will heed my prohibitions not to commit any of these statutory abominations that were done before you, and not defile yourself by them: I (who speak) am YHWH your God.

Comments

Intermarriage, COMMENT A; the sacrifice of the firstborn, COMMENT B; and Carmichael on chaps. 18 and 20, COMMENT C.

NOTES

Chapter 18 comprises three parts: (1) exhortation (vv. 2b–5), in second-person plural; (2) prohibitions (vv. 6–23), in second-person singular (v. 6, a transition); and (3) exhortation (vv. 24–30), in second-person singular. Part 2 is not connected with part 1, linguistically or contextually. However, part 3 is connected linguistically with part 1 (*ûšĕmartem*, vv. 5, 26, 30; *ḥuqqôt hattôʿēbōt* and *ḥuqqōtay* (vv. 3, 4). That only one prohibition in this list is called *tôʿēbâ* (v. 22), whereas all of them are labeled as such in part 3 (vv. 26, 27, 29), indicates editorial activity: an older list has been incorporated by the H redactor into his exhortations. He may deliberately have used *ʾĕlōhîm* only in vv. 2, 4 and 30 to create an envelope for the chapter, whereas he used the Tetragrammaton seven times (M. Hildenbrand).

Wenham (1979) suggests that the order of this chapter loosely resembles that of the covenant treaty (exemplified by Exod 20; Deuteronomy; Josh 24):

v. 2.	Preamble: "I am YHWH your God"
v. 3.	Historical retrospect: "Egypt where you dwelt"
v. 4.	Basic stipulation: "My rules alone shall you observe"
v. 5.	Blessing: "he shall live by them"
vv. 6–23.	Detailed stipulations
vv. 24–30.	Curses

However, the separation of the (single!) blessing (even that is doubtful, see NOTE on "by," v. 5) from the curses and the fact that the historical retrospect lacks any of YHWH's past salvific acts render the covenant treaty analogy unusable.

This chapter forms an AXA′ introversion:

Introduction (vv. 1–2a)
A. Opening exhortation (vv. 2b–5)
   1. YHWH's self-introduction (v. 2b)
   2. Two prohibitions against following foreign practices (v. 3)
   3. Two exhortations to keep God's laws (vv. 4–5)

X. The prohibitions (vv. 6–23) [details in INTRODUCTION to vv. 6–23]

A'. Closing exhortation (vv. 24–30)
1. Admonition with historical substantiation (vv. 24–25)
2. Threat of expulsion and excision (vv. 26–29)
3. Exhortation to heed these prohibitions (v. 30a)
4. YHWH's self-introduction (v. 30b)

Vv. 2b–5. The Opening Exhortation

The exhortation consists of an opening (v. 2b), prohibition (v. 3), command (v. 4a), close (v. 4b, an inclusio with opening, v. 2b), coda (v. 5a, chiastic with v. 4a), and echo of the close (v. 5b) (Schwartz 1987: 63, following Cholewinski 1976: 34–35, except the latter holds that v. 5 is an interpolation). The practices and statutes of Egypt and Canaan are banned (*maʿăśeh* and *ḥuqqōtêhem*, v. 3) in contrast to God's rules and statutes (*mišpāṭay* and *ḥuqqōtay*, vv. 4–5), which must be obeyed.

2. *I am YHWH your God. ʾănî YHWH ʾĕlōhêkem.* This formula occurs in three contexts of H (Wenham 1979): (1) redemption from Egypt (e.g., 11:45; 19:34, 36; 23:43; 25:38, 55; 26:13, 45; Exod 6:7; Num 15:41); (2) *imitatio dei* (11:44; 19:2; 20:7, 24); and (3) motive for observing a partial law (18:4, 30; 19:3–4, 10, 25, 31; 23:22; 24:22; 25:12; 26:1). It is H's signature seal. Its import is neatly caught by Alshekh (cited by Leibowitz 1984: 190): "It is as if the Lord himself spoke to them (to Israel) face to face."

This formula is usually rendered as either "I am YHWH your God" or "I YHWH am your God." The former may be preferred because of its shorter form *ʾănî YHWH* (v. 4b), usually rendered "I am YHWH" (Masoretic cantillation; Zimmerli 1982: 3–4). The latter rendering, "I YHWH am your God," is probably correct in other citations (e.g., Exod 6:7; 16:12; Shadal; Orlinsky 1969: 157). The rendering "I YHWH" for the shorter formula is also correct in many passages (e.g., Exod 12:12; 15:26; 31:13; Num 14:35; 35:34). Schwartz (1987: 68–69, 239–40, nn. 39–41), however, argues that since *ʾănî YHWH* in v. 5b must be translated "I am YHWH," it must be so translated in vv. 2b, 4a. Both renderings presume that this formula is equivalent to God's self-declaration at the beginning of the Sinaitic covenant (Exod 20:2; Deut 5:6). Its import would therefore be that which was aptly expressed by the rabbis: "I am the one who said (at Sinai), 'I am the Lord your God' and you accepted my hegemony; henceforth, then, accept my decrees" (*Mekh.* Baḥodesh, par. 6; *Sipra*, addition).

To be sure, self-identification formulas "I am . . . " do abound (e.g., Gen 27:19; 45:3; Ruth 3:9), but it seems far-fetched that the only purpose of this formula in legal contexts is to identify its divine author with the God of the Sinaitic covenant. Equally remote is Ibn Ezra's suggestion—a variation of the self-declaration formula—that it signifies that YHWH will be Israel's God only if Israel follows his laws.

A third option, I submit, should also be given consideration: the inclusion vv. 2a, 4b, 5b gives literary expression to the divine source of the laws. It states the reason why Israel must follow the specified commandments. In that sense, it is equivalent to prophetic *nĕ'ûm YHWH*, literally "the declaration of YHWH." Therefore, when these two formulas are found at the end of a law pericope, they should be regarded as ellipses for "I YHWH your God (have spoken)" (e.g., v. 4b) and "I YHWH (have spoken)" (e.g., v. 5b). In fact, as pointed out by Cassuto (1951a: 50), the complete formula is found in another H statement *'ănî YHWH dibbarti 'im-lō' zō't 'e'ĕśeh* 'I YHWH have spoken: Thus I will do' (Num 14:35; for its attribution to H, see Knohl 1995: 91–92), a formula beloved by Ezekiel: *'ănî YHWH dibbarti wĕ'āśîtî* 'I YHWH have spoken and will act' (17:24; 22:14; 36:36; cf. 5:13, 15, 17; 17:21; 21:22, 37; 24:14; 26:14; 30:12; 34:24; 37:14—fourteen times!). Thus *'ănî YHWH* (*'ĕlōhêkem*) is an abbreviated form of the statement that YHWH has spoken and is certain to punish if his words are not fulfilled. Weinfeld (1993: 223, n. 3) has brought to my attention that Poebel (1932) suggested that the phrase "I am the lord," which opens many of the royal land-grant documents of the ancient Near East, should be rendered "I am the one who did so and so, etc." This supports my contention that this phrase is not an independent statement of self-introduction where it stands at the end of a pericope. However, v. 2b is the only place, to my knowledge, where the long formula stands at the head of a legal pericope. In this case, the probability rests with the assumption that the legist consciously wished to recall the Sinaitic covenant and, thereby, make the laws of Lev 18 equivalent in importance to the Decalogue.

Vv. 3–4a. Structurally, this passage consists of three sentences in which the objects precede the verbs to emphasize the opposition of YHWH to Egypt and Canaan (Malbim)—"My rules alone" (*NJPS*). In each case, the verb followed by its object is attested elsewhere: *šāmar ḥuqqôt* (Exod 12:17; 13:10; Lev 19:19; 20:8); *hālak bĕḥuqqôt* (20:23; 26:3); *'āśâ mišpāṭîm* (Ezek 5:7; 18:17; 20:24). The third sentence (v. 4a) negates the previous two (v. 3), as follows: *ḥuqqōtay* (v. 4a) and *ûbĕḥuqqōtêhem lō'* (v. 3b); *ta'ăśû* (v. 4a) and *lō' ta'ăśû* (vv. 3a, 3b); *lāleket bāhem* (v. 4a) and *lō' tēlēkû* (v. 3b); *mišpāṭay* (v. 4a) and *ma'ăśēh* (the nations, v. 3a; *ma'ăśay* 'my [YHWH's] practices / doings' would be inappropriate here; cf. Schwartz 1987: 64–65).

3. *As is done. kĕma'ăśēh,* literally "as the doings of" (the people of; see Saadiah). In P, it is found only in the singular but always as a subjunctive genitive—for example, *ma'ăśēh ḥōšēb* (Exod 26:31) / *rōqēm* (Exod 26:36) / *rōqēaḥ* (Exod 30:25) / *'ōrēg* (Exod 28:32) / *'ăbōt* (Exod 28:14) / *hammĕnōrâ* (Num 8:4) / *'izzîm* (Num 31:20). It is also found in parallel with *ḥuqqôt* (Mic 6:16), all of which lead to the conclusion that it is a collective verbal noun, literally "doings"—that is, practices, mores (construct: Deut 11:7; 15:10; Josh 24:31; absolute: Exod 23:12; 18:20; BDB 795b).

in the land of Egypt. Egypt was reputed for its licentiousness (Ezek 16:26; cf. 23:3, 20–21; see also Potiphar's wife, and Sarah in Pharaoh's harem). That brother–sister marriage prevailed among Egyptian royalty was well known. It was even practiced by the patriarch Abraham (Gen 20:12; cf. Lev 18:9). Moreover, as shown by Monkhouse (1989), consanguineous marriages (father–daughter, brother–sister, aunt–nephew, uncle–niece, and others) prevailed in Egypt in every period, in *nonroyal* as well as royal cases (see, e.g., Breasted 1906: 386–88, 390–91; Murray 1927: 45–46; Černy 1954).

Carmichael (1997: 41) suggests that Moses prohibited the very union (aunt–nephew) that his parents contracted—in Egypt (Num 26:59). However, he has no warrant—other than his imagination—to hypothesize that the legist was living in Babylon and feared to criticize the mores of the lost culture except "in a coded way."

The sexual immorality of the Egyptians and the Canaanites is attributed to their ancestors Ham (9:22; the father of Egypt, Gen 10:6) and his son Canaan (Gen 9:25). Indeed, since only the Canaanites are responsible for polluting the land and being expelled from it (vv. 24–25, 27), the purported sexual debauchery of the Egyptians has no function in chap. 18 except to allude to Ham's sin with Noah. Ibn Ezra, followed by Abravanel, suggest that the *maʿăśeh* of Egypt refers to the chthonic worship of 17:5–7, whereas the *maʿăśeh* of Canaan refers to the following incest prohibitions. However, the similar style and language of the exhortative framework of chap. 18 indicate the organic and contextual unity of the entire chapter. The omission of the Babylonians, Assyrians, and Hittites can hardly be accidental. As suggested by Greengus (1992: 246), the cumulative evidence below demonstrates that H must have been fully cognizant that these peoples shared many taboos.

That Canaan was cursed (Gen 9:25) instead of his father, Ham, the real perpetrator of the sexual crime against Noah (Gen 9:22), has been a conundrum that has vexed the ages. Now, however, a likely explanation is at hand. According to the recently discovered Pesher Genesis 4Q252, col. 2 (Wacholder and Abegg 1992: 2.212–15; Eisenman and Wise 1992: 86–89), as analyzed by Fröhlich (1994), Canaan was cursed instead of his father, Ham (Gen 9:20–22), because the sons of Noah were blessed by God (Gen 9:1); thus Ham's curse was passed down to his son Canaan (confirming R. Judah, *Gen. Rab.* 36:7).

Fröhlich (1994) makes the attractive suggestion that Abraham is juxtaposed to the story of Noah's drunkenness because the latter was given the land (col. 2, l.8 [broken]) when the former lost it. In addition, the priestly memory that the land of Canaan was once an Egyptian province (the borders of the promised land, Num 34:1–5 [P], correspond to those under New Kingdom Egypt; see Mazar 1954; de Vaux 1968) may be responsible for the inclusion of Egypt in our verse. Moreover, it may be more than an accident that the sexual violations in chaps. 18, 20 and in Gen 9:2 are couched in identical euphemisms (but with different meaning; see NOTE on "that is, the nakedness of your mother," v. 7), namely, *gillâ ʿerwâ* [18:8, 10, 16] and *rāʾâ ʿerwâ* [20:17; cf. Fröhlich 1994: 84, n. 7].

It could therefore well be that the author of the exhortatory envelope (vv. 1–5, 24–30) had the Noahide episode in mind. Canaan and Egypt (Ham's sons, Gen 10:6) lost their rights to the land of Canaan because their sexual immorality polluted the land, and the land vomited them out (v. 25). Israel is therefore warned that it faces the same fate if it behaves similarly. One caution, however, should be borne in mind. Intertextual allusions such as these to an earlier (and different) source, even as far back as Genesis, may be sought in exhortations, in comminations (e.g., Lev 26), and in narratives—but not in law (Milgrom 1996a).

in the land of Canaan. Canaan was identified with homosexuality (Gen 9:20–26; 19:5–8) and bestiality (van Selms 1954: 81–82). Sex crimes are referred to as a *něbālâ běyiśrā'ēl* 'an outrage in Israel' (Gen 34:7; Deut 22:21; Judg 20:6; 2 Sam 13:12; Jer 29:23). Seven times is Israel warned not to behave as the nations that inhabited Canaan (vv. 3 [twice], 24, 26, 27, 29, 30). But there is no extrabiblical evidence that the Canaanites were steeped in sexual immorality (Nussbaum 1974: 34–89). Where, then, did H get that idea? As cogently argued by Nussbaum (1974: 90–115), sexual depravity was a means of both stigmatizing an ancient enemy, the Canaanites, and sending a dire warning to Israel that it will suffer the same fate, expulsion from the land, if it follows the same practices. Alternatively, H may have exaggerated the sexual sins of the Egyptians and Canaanites so that Israel would break off all ties with them (Schwartz, forthcoming).

Joosten (1994: 209–10; 1996: 151) demonstrates that the term "land of Canaan" appears in the Pentateuch, Joshua, and Judges but, thereafter, in its territorial sense as Israel's land, it does not occur. In the prophetical books, it bears a different meaning: the Phoenician coast (Isa 23:11; cf. Zeph 2:5), the Hebrew language (Isa 19:18), or merchants (Ezek 16:29; 17:4; Hos 12:8; Zeph 1:11). In reply to the possible objection that the priestly author was archaizing, Joosten points out (n. 63) that even though Ezekiel or a tradent borrows the map of Israel's land, he does not call the land *'ereṣ kěna'an,* as in his *Vorlage* (Num 34:2 [bis]), but "the land" (Ezek 47:15) and "the land of Israel" (Ezek 47:18). Thus one may safely conclude that at least from the Babylonian Exile on, the term *'ereṣ kěna'an* fell out of use and that this entire chapter, including its redactorial framework, was composed before the exile.

I am bringing you. 'ănî mēbî' 'etěkem. One would expect the second person *'attem bā'îm* (cf. 14:34; 23:10; 25:2; Num 15:2). The emphasis is clearly on the subject *'ănî* 'I'. That is, God will drive out the Canaanites only if Israel does not follow their practices (Beer Yitzhak, cited by Leibowitz 1964: 194).

you shall not follow their statutes. ûběḥuqqōtêhem lō' tēlēkû. This sentence applies to both Egypt and Canaan, a point verified by the plural "their." Thus the *'atnaḥ* should be moved to the second *ta'ăśû.*

All their statutes (and "doings") are intended (Rashi, Maimonides, *Idolatry* 11:1). However, the rabbis logically inquire: "Does this mean that they should not build or plant like them? Therefore, the verse reads "their statutes," i.e., the laws governing the relationships between them, their parents, and grandparents. What were they wont to do? A man would be married to a man, a woman to a woman, a man to mother and daughter, and a woman to two men" (*Sipra* Aḥare, par. 8:8).

The term *ḥuqqâ* is derived from the verb "inscribe," and it denotes a law inscribed by God, "a boundary line for the sea which it may not cross (e.g., Jer 5:22)" (Wenham 1979). For P's distinction between *ḥōq* and *ḥuqqâ,* see NOTE on 10:13.

4. *My rules alone* (with *NJPS*). This emphatic sense is caused by beginning the sentence with the object *mišpāṭay*. These are the rational laws (Saadiah), "that even if they were not written, they would have been deduced logically" (*Sipra*, addition). According to Wenham (1979), the common denominator of *mišpāṭîm* is a legal decision, the sentence passed by a judge. This is true regardless of whether the judge is human or divine; that is, this term applies to oracular as well as court decisions. Perhaps the best rendering for *mišpāṭîm* is "jurisprudence."

The poetic ring of this verse was recognized by Reventlow (1961: 58) and Bigger (1979: 191), and is characteristic of H, in general (e.g., 19:32; 20:3; 25:3, 18; 26:1; cf. Paran 1989: 109). The word pair *mišpāṭ* / *ḥuqqâ* is prevalent in Ezekiel (e.g., 18:17; 20:11, 13, 19), particularly in reference to this verse.

Note that *mišpāṭ* replaces *maʿăśeh* (v. 3): what *they* do is simply *maʿăśeh* 'behavior'; what *you* should do are *mišpāṭay* 'my rules' (Schwartz, personal communication).

shall you observe. taʿăśû. Compare with *mišpāṭîm* (Ezek 5:7; 11:12; 18:17) and with *ḥuqqôt* (18:30; 25:18; Ezek 20:11). As opposed to *ḥuqqôt* 'statutes', concerning the violation of which one must be on guard (*šāmar*; see below), God's *mišpāṭîm* 'rules', must be executed (*ʿāśâ*) (Leibowitz 1964: 198).

shall you heed. tišměrû. The root meaning of this verb is "guard." Hence it is generally used in the context of prohibitions—that is, to guard against their violation. Note *ûšěmartem . . . lěbiltî ʿăśôt* 'heed . . . not to commit' (v. 30); *ʾet-ḥuqqōtay tišmōrû* 'you shall heed my statutes', followed three times by *lōʾ* (19:19). Thus one heeds (*šāmar*) the sabbath by not desecrating it (Exod 31:14; note that the parallel verb is *yārēʾ* 'fear', 19:3; 26:2).

This basic meaning is not always kept; *šāmar* occasionally applies to performative commandments (see NOTES on v. 5, and 19:37; 20:22). Its Akkadian cognate *naṣāru* (Heb. *nāṣar* = *šāmar*) means "to obey, follow commandments, to observe laws, decrees, heed, respect an institution, a word "(*CAD* 11.2: 42–44), indicating a similar application to both performative and prohibitive laws.

The word pair *ʿāśâ* / *šāmar* abounds in Ezekiel, particularly in reference to this verse (e.g., Ezek 11:12; 18:19, 21; 20:19; cf. Paran 1989: 108, n. 48).

following them. lāleket bāhem. The verb *šāmar* never appears as the auxiliary of *hālak*. Therefore, it belongs solely with *ḥuqqotay*, leaving the phrase *lāleket bāhem* to apply to both "rules" and "statutes"; so, too, according to the cantillations. That *hālak* takes the object *mišpāṭîm*, see Ezek 37:24.

I YHWH your God (have spoken). ʾănî YHWH ʾělōhêkem. For this rendering, see NOTE on v. 2b. Note that this phrase (using *ʾānōkî*) opens and (nearly) closes the first (and second) commandment (Exod 20:2a, 5b). This similarity leads R. Yishmael to declare: "The laws of incest are severe since they open and close with the Tetragrammaton" (*Sipra*, addition). Although R. Yishmael had in mind vv. 6 and 30, his statement applies as well to the entire chapter (vv. 2, 30) and to the opening exhortation (vv. 2, 4, 5).

5. Is this verse an interpolation? The fact that in the closing exhortation (vv. 26–30), v. 30 repeats v. 26 shows that v. 5, which repeats vv. 3–4, is an integral part of the composition. Moreover, this verse adds a significant new element, "if

one does them, he shall live by them" (see below). And this clause declaring the fate of the obedient nation is countered by the fate of the disobedient nation (*kārēt*, v. 29, the opposite of *ḥay*; Schwartz, personal communication). Note as well that v. 5a stands in chiastic relation to v. 4a (Paran 1983: 112), as well as within itself.

You shall heed . . . does them. ûšĕmartem . . . ya 'ăśeh 'ōtām. According to *Sipra* (Aḥare, par. 8:10), this proves that *mišpāṭîm* 'rules' and *ḥuqqôt* 'statutes' require both guarding (*šāmar*) and performing ('āśâ). Indeed, both verbs are attested for these two kinds of laws (18:5, 26; 19:19; Ezek 20:18). Furthermore, the parallelism between v. 5aα and v. 26aα and between v. 5aβ and v. 26aβ underscores the correctness of the *Sipra*'s observation.

Thus since *mišpāṭîm* includes positive, performative commandments (which a person "does") this verse may have more than the prohibitions of chap. 18 in mind. It, therefore, urges the *gēr* (see below) to follow all of God's laws (Joosten 1994: 109; 1996: 77, contra Schwartz 1987: 66); however, to speak of "the universal tenor" of this message is carrying things too far, since it applies solely to residents of God's land, Canaan.

one. hā'ādām, literally "person." Why the switch to third person? Why not simply *wĕḥeyîtem* 'you shall live'? The answer is obvious: "person" includes the *gēr*, who also must observe these incest prohibitions or face the death sentence of *kārēt* (v. 29). Indeed, the parallelism between v. 5 and v. 26, indicated above, reinforces this identification, since *hā'ādām* (v. 5aβ) is matched by *hā'ezrāḥ wĕhahggēr* (v. 26b). The language of this phrase has left its mark in QL (e.g., CD 3:16; 4Q5046 1.17; 4QDᵇ18 V.12). On the basis of this phrase, the rabbis declared: "The non-Jew who observes the Torah is equivalent to a high priest" (*Sipra* Aḥare 13:12).

shall live. wāḥay. The observance of these incest laws is essential for a viable human society (Ramban; cf. Bekhor Shor). Since the violation of these laws leads to *karēt* (v. 29), this latter term must signify the opposite of "live," namely, death (by divine agency).

The influence of this passage on Ezekiel is paramount (Ezek 20:11, 13, 21, and, in negation, *lō' yiḥyû bāhem*, 20:25; cf. Neh 9:29). Ezekiel also regards exile as the penalty for violating these incest laws (Ezek 20:23), as does his Leviticus *Vorlage* (18:25; so too Neh 9:29–30). That Ezekiel is quoting this expression from Lev 18 is shown by his use elsewhere in his book of the neologism *ḥāyāh* (Ezek 18:23; 33:11), which appears in postexilic literature (e.g., Koh 6:6; Est 4:11; Neh 9:29). He resorts to the older, and for him antiquarian, *ḥay* when he is discussing contexts similar to those in Scripture, such as interest (Lev 25:36; cf. Ezek 18:13, 24) and, as mentioned, is citing the formula in this verse (see above). For details, see Hurvitz (1982: 46–48).

by them. bāhem. The *beth instrumenti,* by means of doing them, connotes that the fulfillment of these laws gives life. In other words, life is built into these laws. Without *bāhem*, the implication would be that God, not the laws, gives life to those who fulfill them, as in Num 21:8–9; Deut 19:4 (Schwartz 1987: 66–67). Thus disobeying these laws by engaging in foreign incest practices shortens or deprives life (R. Simeon, *m. Mak.* 3:15). Note the absence of *bāhem* in Deut 4:1; 5:30; 8:1; 11:8; 30:15,19. In D, God grants life as a reward for obeying his laws, but only H states that the laws themselves have the inherent power to grant life. Indeed, this is also its clear meaning in Ezekiel—for example, "I gave them my laws and taught them my rules [*ʾăšer yaʿăśeh ʾōtām hāʾādām wāḥay bāhem*] by means of doing them one should live" (Ezek 20:11; also v. 25; Neh 9:29).

I YHWH (have spoken). *ʾănî YHWH.* The short form (see NOTE on v. 2b) is preferred when (1) no second person either precedes (e.g., Exod 6:2, 29) or is even briefly interrupted (e.g., 18:5aα; 22:3); (2) the formula is asyndetic (18:21; 19:14); (3) it is attached to the preceding (21:8, 15, 23); (4) or it is attached to the following (22:9); (5) it echoes the full formula (11:45; 19:12; 20:26; 22:33); and (6) it is equivalent to prophetic *nĕʾûm YHWH* at the end of a unit (e.g., 19:37; 22:33; 26:2). For details, see Schwartz (1987: 70, 240, nn. 45–48 [beware of typos]). In particular, the full formula containing "*your* God" (*ʾĕlōhêkem*) would be inappropriate here, since the subject is *hāʾādām*, namely all persons, not just Israelites.

Vv. 6–23. Forbidden Sexual Relations

Two chapters list them (18:6–23; 20:9–21). That two chapters are required probably indicates that the violation of these laws was widespread, as recognized by the rabbis. Rendering the verse *bōkeh lĕmišpĕḥōtāyw* as (the people) wept *concerning* (the breakup) of their families' (Num 11:10), R. Nehorai used to say: "This teaches us that Israel was distressed when Moses told them to withdraw from (i.e., sever) forbidden marriages, and it teaches us that man married his sister, his father's sister and his mother's sister. Thus when Moses told them to withdraw from forbidden marriages they were distressed" (*Sipre* Num. 90; cf. *b. Yoma* 75a). It may not be off the mark to suggest that R. Nehorai had in mind Moses himself, who was the product of a forbidden marriage: Amram, his father, had married Jochebed, his father's sister (Exod 6:20).

Furthermore, Carmichael (1997: 1–3) makes the fascinating observation that the incest rules of the Bible and Lev 18 and 20, in particular, have left a greater impact on Western law than any comparable body of biblical rules. For example, the Table of Levitical Degrees set out by the Church of England in 1603 held sway until 1907.

These are two sets of prohibitions:

I. Prohibitions against incest (vv. 6–18), which can be defined as "the infraction of the taboo upon sexual relations between any two members of the nuclear family, except husband and wife" (Mead 1968: 115).
   A. Primary relationships (vv. 6–17a)
      1. General law (v. 6)
      2. With a mother (v. 7)
      3. With a father's wife (v. 8)
      4. With a half sister (v. 9)
      5. With a granddaughter (v. 10)
      6. With a stepsister (v. 11)

    7. With a paternal aunt (v. 12)

    8. With a maternal aunt (v. 13)

    9. With an aunt, wife of father's brother (v. 14)

    10. With a daughter-in-law (v. 15)

    11. With a brother's wife (v. 16)

    12. With a mother and daughter (v. 17a)

  B. Additional prohibitions (vv. 17b–18)

    1. Against sexual relations with a woman and her granddaughter (v. 17b)

    2. Against marriage to a wife's sister (v. 18)

II. Prohibitions against certain sexual practices and sacrifice to Molek (vv. 19–23)

  A. Against sexual relations with a menstruating woman (v. 19)

  B. Against sexual relations with a neighbor's wife (v. 20)

  C. Against offering up children to Molek (v. 21)

  D. Against male homosexuality (v. 22)

  E. Against bestiality, male and female (v. 23)

Paton (1897: 47) groups these prohibitions as follows. Vv. 6–23 contain two pentads (vv. 6–15): first-degree kinship (vv. 6–10) and second-degree kinship (vv. 11–15). Both pentads close with prohibitions in which the relationship is traced through children (vv. 10, 15). Vv. 16–23 describe remote relationships: through marriage (vv. 16–19) and outside the family (vv. 20–23).

Elliger (1955) and Kilian (1963: 21–36) called attention to vv. 7–18 as a "Decalogue" using the prohibitive pattern 'erwat . . . lō' tĕgalleh. However, Halbe's (1980) analysis that these laws follow two basic patterns undermines this assertion.

V. 7aβ–b illustrates Halbe's *Sentence Type A:*

A   'erwat 'immĕka

B   lō' tĕgalleh

C   'immĕka hi(w)'

B'   lō' tĕgalleh

A' 'erwātāh

This pattern, A:B::C::B':A', contains the prohibitive in AB, and its chiastic *Wiederaufnahme* in B'A'. Together, they form a ring figure around the motivation clause in C. V. 15 is a second clear example of this type.

Vv. 8 and 16 form a larger ring figure and illustrate Halbe's *Sentence Type B:*

A   'erwat 'ēšet-'ābîkā

B   lō' tĕgalleh

A' 'erwat 'ābîkā hi(w)'

A   'erwat 'ēšet-'aḥîkā

B   lō' tĕgalleh

A' 'erwat 'aḥîkā hi(w)'

Here the repetition of *Leitwörter* accentuates the structural scheme. Vv. 12–13 also follow this pattern, but introduce a new word in the A′ *stichos*:

A   *ʿerwat ʾăḥôt-ʾābîkā*
B   *lōʾ tĕgalleh*
A′   *šĕʾēr ʾmmĕkā hi(w)ʾ*

A   *ʿerwat ʾăḥôt-ʾimmĕkā*
B   *lōʾ tĕgalleh*
A′   *kî šĕʾēr ʾimmĕka hi(w)ʾ*

The ring figures in vv. 7 and 15, 8 and 16, and 12 and 13 create an "interim balance" (*Zwischenbilanz*). Vv. 9–11, 14, however, must be emended in order to fit either pattern. These laws are directed to the head of the household, and their enforcement was left entirely in his hands (Phillips 1973: 350). This accounts for the lack of stipulated penalties in this chapter (Hartley 1992). Ziskind (1996: 127–28) cogently suggests that the repeated use of the second-person singular possessive adjective with regard to a given relative (in contrast to the use of the third person in the casuistic list of chap. 20) makes the prohibition "more immediate and personal, and not something abstract or somebody else's family. It is not just a sister but your sister; not just a mother but your mother, and so on." Its purpose "was to impress upon the men to whom these laws were addressed a moral priority that went beyond an exhortation to stay away from these female relatives because they are the possessions of his close relatives.

"The result is some curious circumlocutions and cumbersome expressions" (Ziskind 1996: 129). This point, however, must be challenged. A sister is defined as the daughter of a father or mother (vv. 9, 11) because the half sister prohibition affects either parent. (The omission of the full sister prohibition from the list is unexplained by Ziskind's theory; see below). A granddaughter is referred to as the daughter of a son or daughter (v. 10) because despite the attestation of *neked* 'grandson' (Gen 21:23; Isa 14:22; Job 18:19), the term *nekdâ* 'granddaughter' does not make its appearance until post-talmudic times. An aunt is not an aunt (*dôdâ*), but the sister of a father or mother (vv. 12–13), first, because *dôdâ* is only the paternal aunt (Exod 6:20) and, second, because in H, the term *dôdâ* stands for the wife of the paternal uncle (v. 14), but for neither the paternal nor the maternal aunt. The paternal uncle's wife is not prohibited in her own right because it is important to stress that she is banned only due to the principle of affinity, and her husband is called "your brother's father" (rather than *dôd* 'uncle') to distinguish him from the maternal uncle, whose wife is not one of the prohibited unions because she is not an affine (see NOTE on v. 14). A stepmother is called a father's wife (v. 8; cf. Ziskind 1996: 130, n. 12) because BH has no specific term for her; *ʾēm ḥôreget* is a post-talmudic invention whose etymology is still a mystery. And, finally, a daughter-in-law and sister-in-law are called "your son's wife" and "your brother's wife" (vv. 15–16) in order to justify their prohibition as affines. Moreover, although the daughter-in-law is explicitly termed *kallâ*, there is no equivalent BH word for sister-in-law; the term *gîsâ* is post-talmudic.

In sum, each of these terms and all those used in the list of vv. 6–23 are purposeful and essential in their context.

The basic sociological unit was the *bêt 'āb* 'father's house'. It included three to five generations consisting of fifty to a hundred people living in close proximity. Although the average Israelite house could accommodate four persons (father, mother, two children), the kin-related group, numbering about twenty persons, lived in close quarters around a common courtyard. Such compounds are evidenced at Raddana and Ai and at the later Iron Age settlements Tell Beit Mirsim, Tell Far'ah, and Tell en-Naṣbeh (Stager 1985: 18–23; van der Toorn 1996b: 195–97). When this family grew too large, the younger sons would break away to form their own "father's house," but familial bonds would still unite them into a *bêt 'ābôt* / *mišpāḥâ* 'family association' (popularly called a clan). Several of these associated families would form a *maṭṭeh* / *šēbeṭ* 'a tribe' (Milgrom 1978; 1990a: 335–36). The tribe, however, was probably a later, artificial sociopolitical construct: "The clan has its judiciary—not so the tribe. When dissatisfied with the judicial proceedings at the level of the clan, one had to ask the king to intervene (2 Sam 14:4–11; 15:1–6; 2 Kgs 8:1–6) since there was no court of appeal at the level of the tribe. The clan engaged in corporate rituals (1 Sam 20:6–21)—not so the tribe" (van der Toorn 1996b: 204).

Surprisingly, intermarriage—that is, between Israelites and non-Israelites—is not prohibited (see NOTE on 18:21, and COMMENT A).

A rationale for the sexual prohibitions is proposed in the NOTE on v. 22.

Vv. 6–23. The prohibitions are listed in the following order:

1. vv. 6–11. Your closest blood relations: mother (7), stepmother (8), the addressee's: half sister (9), granddaughter (10), stepsister [= sister] (11).
2. vv. 12–14. Your parents' closest blood relations and affines: father's sister (12), mother's sister (13), father's brother's wife (14).
3. vv. 15–16. Your relatives by marriage: daughter-in-law (15), brother's wife (16).
4. vv. 17–18. Your wife's closest relatives: wife–daughter (17a), wife–granddaughter (17b), wife–sister (18).
5. vv. 19–23. Unrelated: copulation with menstruant (19), someone's wife (20), a male (22), an animal (23). Molek worship is placed among these copulation prohibitions (21).

The main distinction between these laws is that nos. 1–3 (vv. 6–16) concern relations between the addressee and a forbidden woman, whereas nos. 4 and 5 (vv. 17–23) focus not on the relations, but on the act (Schwartz 1987: 96; Hartley 1992). Also the first group (vv. 6–16) is characterized by the lack of syndetic connection between prohibitions. The reason is that the women are the addressee's relatives; hence there is no need for a *waw*. This division is recognized by the Masoretes, who insert a space indicated by a *samek* (a "closed" division marker) between each prohibition but not in the second list (vv. 17–23) (Schwartz 1987: 71–72).

Alternative ways of listing these prohibitions might have been: (1) *by generation*: mother, stepmother, father's sister, mother's sister, father's brother's wife; (sister), half sister, stepsister, brother's wife, wife's sister; (daughter), daughter-in-law, granddaughter, wife's granddaughter; (2) *by blood*: mother, sister, (daughter), granddaughter, father's sister, mother's sister; stepmother, father's brother's wife, brother's wife, daughter-in-law (Schwartz 1987: 87); and (3) *by relationship*: addressee's mother, daughter, sister (see below): wife's mother, daughter, sister, granddaughter; father's wife, (mother), daughter, sister; father's wife's daughter of his patrilineage; mother's (mother), daughter, sister; son's wife, (mother), (sister), daughter; daughter's (mother), (sister), daughter; father's brother's wife, (mother), (sister); brother's wife, (mother), (sister); sister's (mother), (sister) (Rattray 1987: 543, including the omissions in parentheses).

The value of Rattray's list is that it clarifies that prohibitions are limited to four generations (accounting for the omission of grandparents) and that the basic postulate is that affinity is equivalent to consanguinity (already recognized by Kalisch 1868: 359); that is, the declaration of Gen 2:24 that husband and wife are of one flesh must be taken literally (accounting for the remaining omissions). Also, by the absence of first cousins and nieces from the consanguineous list, it may be deduced that unions with them are permitted.

The major contribution of Rattray's list is that she has, in my opinion, satisfactorily accounted for the ostensible omission of the full sister and, especially, of the daughter from the list. I quote her solution (1987: 542):

> The key lies in the opening verse to the incest prohibitions (Lev 18:6): one may not marry close kin (*šĕʾēr bĕśārô*). Who are they? In Lev 21:2 we have the expression *šĕʾērô haqqārōb ʾēlāyw*, which is spelled out as follows: mother, father, son, daughter, brother, and maiden sister (sister who never married). Hence mother, sister and daughter, as close kin, are automatically forbidden by Lev 18:6. The purpose of the list of Leviticus 18 is to indicate *who else* is forbidden by extension from these basic relationships.

Her view receives indirect support from Daube (1973: 132) who, noticing the absence of direct damage by the paterfamilias from the Roman XII Tablets and from Exod 21–23, concludes: "The more fundamental an institution . . . the more apt it is to be accepted without ado and to remain unformulated" (brought to my attention by S. Nikaido). Daube's (1973: 130–31) "self-understood in the legal history" is confirmed by the absence of a sister-incest prohibition in Hittite law. Yet Suppiluliuma I refers to such a customary prohibition in his treaty with Huqqana of Hayasa, §§ 25–26, 29 (*CTH* 42; Beckman 1996). Suppiluliuma I forbids his treaty partner to commit incest with his sister, sister-in-law (by wife or brother), and female cousin, claiming this is the custom of Hatti (brought to my attention by D. Stewart). In truth, however, the omissions are not taken for granted but subsumed under the word *šĕʾēr* (see its NOTE below).

What for me clinches Rattray's solution is that the *se'er besaro* in v. 6 refers to the addressee's closest *blood* relatives, as they are spelled out in 25:49. V. 6, therefore, cannot be a general heading for the list, since the forbidden women that follow are mainly affines, and some are even unrelated. Thus, v. 6 concerns only the missing blood relatives, namely, the sister and daughter.

Thus there is no longer a need to argue that a law about the daughter fell out after v. 9 as a result of homoeoarcton (Elliger 1955: 2; 1966: 234; Kilian 1963: 21) or that the daughter is taken for granted as proved by the "she is your sister" rationale in the prohibition concerning the half sister (Daube 1973). Nor need one theorize that the addressee did not hesitate having sex with his daughter since his only loss would be the marriage price of a virgin (Luria 1965; Basset 1971: 236; Cardascia 1980: 10; Bendavid 1986: 23; Ziskind 1988; 1996; cf. Wegner 1992). The absence of such a law in two other incest regulations (Lev 20:11–21; Deut 27:20–23) does not support inserting such a law here (Bendavid 1986: 23; Rattray 1987; Hartley 1992). Rather, the daughter (and the full sister) is subsumed under the term for close relative, *šě'ēr bāśār* (v. 6). As for the assumption of "sex rights" for the father, it has no basis either in the Bible or in the ancient Near East. Indeed, Ziskind (1996: 125) admits (contra Cardascia 1980: 9–10) that "the Laws of Hammurabi and the Hittite Laws, which do not treat incest as fully as does Leviticus, both prohibit a daughter" and, citing Gen 19:30–38 and the priestly demand that daughters were expected to behave virtuously (Lev 19:29; 20:16; 21:7–9; Num 5:12–31), that neither in the Bible nor in its environment was father–daughter sex approved (see further Bigger 1979). Ziskind's (1996: 129–30) assumption of paternal "sex rights" forces him to theorize that had the legist explicitly banned sex with a daughter, in language such as *'erwat bittěkā lō' těgalleh 'erwātěkā hî'* " 'The nakedness of your daughter you shall not uncover; it (her nakedness) is your nakedness,' (it) could be interpreted as using the cover of the law to undermine a father's authority within his family" and, hence, he chose language "neither condemning incest with a daughter nor explicitly permitting it either." This strained argumentation needs no further comment. Finally, Ziskind's theory concerning father–daughter sex leaves unexplained the absence of the full sister from this list.

Most recently, Meacham (1997) has theorized that father–daughter and brother–full sister prohibitions were omitted because neither the patriarchs (or Israel's early leaders) nor the House of David violated them, but were guilty of violating the rest of the listed prohibitions. Thus Abraham married his half sister on his father's side (Gen 20:2, 12; Lev 18:9, 20:17), Jacob married two sisters in their lifetime (Gen 29:28; Lev 18:8, 20; 20:10–11), Judah committed incest with his daughter-in-law (Gen 38:18; Lev 18:15; 20:12), Reuben committed adultery with his father's wife during his lifetime (Gen 35:22, a double violation; Lev 18:20; 20:10, 11), and Amram married his aunt Jocebed and fathered Aaron and Moses (Exod 6:20; Lev 18:12; 20:19). Concerning the House of David, David committed adultery (2 Sam 11; Lev 18:20; 20:10), Absalom slept with his father's concubines (2 Sam 16:22; Lev 18:8; 20:11), and Amnon raped his half sister, Tamar (2 Sam 13:12, 14; Lev 18:19; 20:17). Meacham, therefore, concludes that Lev 18 and 20 constitute an apologia for the patriarchs who preceded the promulgation of these chapters at Sinai, and a polemic against the House of David for transgressing them. She offers the noteworthy aside that Ezek 22:10–11 indicts Israel with the same four violations committed by the House of David: father's wife, adultery, daughter-in-law (Judah and Tamar, David's ancestors), and half sister on the father's side. Thus, Ezekiel selected them from Lev 18 and 20, which he had before him, because he, too, wished to indict the Davidic line for incest. This attractive suggestion perhaps is corroborated by the charge *wĕʾîš ʾet- ʾăḥōtô bat-ʾābîw ʿinnâ-bāk* 'in you (Israel) they have ravished their own sisters' (Ezek 22:11b), precisely the same charge levied against Amnon (note the same use of the verb *ʿinnâ*, 2 Sam 13:12, 14).

On consideration, this fascinating proposal must be rejected. Even were we to regard, as Meacham (1997) proposed, the other prohibitions in Lev 18 and 20 as logical extensions of those committed by the early leaders and the House of David, we could not account for the list's inclusion of Molek, sodomy, bestiality (18:21–23), and heterosexual relations with the sister-in-law (18:18) and the menstruant (18:19)—none of which was committed by the aforementioned persons. As for Ezekiel, his alleged indictment against the Davidic line also includes the menstruant (22:10b)! Furthermore, chaps. 18 and 20 were intended to be inclusive; their violation would subject the individual to the penalties of chap. 20 and the nation to exile predicted by 18:24–30. Are we therefore to presume that incest with a mother or full sister would be unpunishable? If, however, one would derive these penalties a fortiori, we would be left in the dark concerning the full sister: Is the punishment *kārēt*, on the basis of 20:17, or death, as one would naturally expect? Meacham's explanation of Ezek 22 is similarly questionable. Ezekiel's *j'accuse* also includes the abuse of parents (v. 7) and sexual relations with a menstruant, neither of which is levied against the patriarchs or the House of David.

The question for Rattray, however, remains: Since the mother is also included in the term *šĕʾēr bĕśārô*, why need she be explicitly mentioned at the head of the list (v. 7)? Rattray responds: "The reason for beginning the list with the mother (v. 7) is to establish the principle with one case least likely to occur and most universally abhorred. In other words, just as one would 'not expose the nakedness of one's father, that is of one's mother' so one must not expose the nakedness of one's father's wife, half sister, etc."

A more satisfactory answer, however, has been suggested by Horton (1973: 29–31), who notes that *ʿerwat ʾābîkā* 'the nakedness of your father' (v. 7) is superfluous and, besides, overburdens the structure of this verse. He therefore concludes that mother and father have been placed in tandem in order that this law may serve a heuristic function, to classify all the following incestuous unions as a violation of either one's father or one's mother (see also Hartley 1992: 287). That the mother was exceptionally singled out in order to head the list (both Rattray's and Horton's conclusion) and normally would be taken for granted is proved, in my opinion, by the fact that she is absent from the corresponding list of prohibitions in chap. 20, where a different order prevails and there is no need for the mother to head the list (see NOTE on 20:11). As for the similar absence of the daughter and full sister in the penalty list of 20:9–21, see NOTE on 20:17.

Sun (unpublished paper) questions the analogy of Lev 18 to the priest's šĕ'ēr of Lev 21: "the rules of conduct normative for the one are not necessarily the rules for the other." Rattray (personal communication) responds: "The rules regarding incest were normative for all Israel, including priests . . . . There is no indication that priests had a different kinship system than the rest of Israel, or that they had special terms for family members that were not also used by lay Israelites."

The prohibited unions and their relations in the family tree are shown in Fig. 2.

David Stewart (dissertation proposal) postulates that the mother, father, son, daughter, brother, and virgin sister (21:2) used by Rattray (1987) to define šĕ'ēr bĕśārô should also include father–son and brother–brother taboos. The homosexuality prohibition occurring at the end of illicit sexual unions (v. 22) would therefore extend to the male family members of the same degree as the prohibited females in the preceding verses: grandfather–grandson, uncle–nephew, and stepfather–stepson.

Halpern (1991: 52) suggests perceptively that a kin group, which ordinarily would favor exogamous marriages in order to ensure its growth, would also endorse partial endogamy in order to minimize the alienation of property. Hence the incest taboos stop short of prohibiting cousin marriage; rather, Gen 24:15; 28:8–9; 29:10 indicate that cousin marriage was the preferred pattern.

Motives are attached to all the laws. These, however, are words of derogation and disgust. In addition, the laws are rationalized in several ways: they stem from God (v. 4); they lead to life (v. 5); the land will not tolerate their violation (vv. 25, 27, 28); and their violators will be defiled (v. 24) and cut off (v. 29) (van Houten 1991: 141). These reasons, however, do not penetrate to the quintessential rationale that lies behind the laws. Many suggestions have been offered in this regard. The one that seems, in my opinion, to be the common denominator is a social rationale. Ibn Kaspi finds its clue in the word liṣrōr 'producing rivalry' in the prohibition against marrying two sisters (v. 18), and he opines (as transmitted by Abravanel) that the purpose of these laws is the prevention of family quarrels and the maintenance of šālôm bayit, literally "household peace," an insight that Shadal wryly glosses: "It is well known that the hostility between relatives is greater than the hostility between strangers." For similar views, see Elliger (1955: 8–12), Porter (1976), and Taber (1976: 574, 810). For other views, see Bekhor Shor, Maimonides (Guide 3.49), Ramban, Sforno, Wessely (1846), Kalisch et al. in Schwartz (1987: 244, n. 12).

The social rationale, however, falls short in explaining the entire list. It works for interpersonal relations that might erupt in rivalry and quarrels. But the acts described in the final prohibitions in this list—sex with a menstruant, Molek, sodomy, and bestiality (vv. 19, 21–23)—are patently private matters. With Ramban (on vv. 22–23), I hold that the basic rationale is procreation within the ordered, patriarchal structure. Thus vv. 6–18, 20 presuppose the production of seed destructive of the family (the social rationale), whereas vv. 19, 21–23 pre-

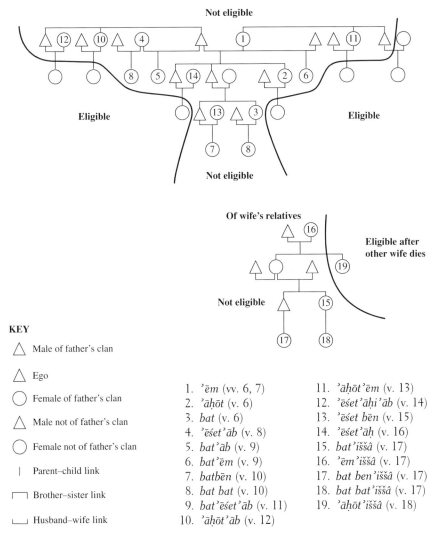

Not eligible

Eligible

Eligible

Not eligible

Of wife's relatives

Eligible after other wife dies

Not eligible

KEY

△ Male of father's clan

△ Ego

○ Female of father's clan

△ Male not of father's clan

○ Female not of father's clan

| Parent–child link

⊓ Brother–sister link

⊔ Husband–wife link

1. 'ēm (vv. 6, 7)
2. 'āḥōt (v. 6)
3. bat (v. 6)
4. 'ēśet 'āb (v. 8)
5. bat 'āb (v. 9)
6. bat 'ēm (v. 9)
7. batbēn (v. 10)
8. bat bat (v. 10)
9. bat 'ēśet 'āb (v. 11)
10. 'āḥōt 'āb (v. 12)

11. 'āḥōt 'ēm (v. 13)
12. 'ēśet 'āḥi' āb (v. 14)
13. 'ēśet bēn (v. 15)
14. 'ēśet 'āḥ (v. 16)
15. bat 'iššâ (v. 17)
16. 'ēm 'iššâ (v. 17)
17. bat ben 'iššâ (v. 17)
18. bat bat 'iššâ (v. 17)
19. 'āḥōt 'iššâ (v. 18)

FIGURE 2. Prohibited relationships according to Lev 18:6–18 (S. Rattray, SBLASP 26 [1987] 544). Used by permission of Susan Rattray.

suppose the reverse: relationships that would produce no seed (see NOTE on 18:22).

It can well be that these rationales need no further rationale. They constitute a "shame" theology that is sufficiently adequate to exact adherence. Daube (1969) argued for the existence of such a vocabulary in the deuteronomic code, as in its threefold warning against "hiding yourself" (Deut 22:1–4) and its warning that "your brother should not be degraded in your eyes" (Deut 25:3). Of direct relevance is its expression *wĕlō'-yireh bĕkā 'erwat dābār* 'see anything un-

seemly' (Deut 23:15; cf. 24:1). This is the identical expression for a sexual offense (Gen 9:23; Lev 20:17), to which D adds the object *dābār*, giving it the extended, figurative meaning "unseemly, shameful," an indication that Lev 18,
rooted in the literal vocabulary of Genesis, is earlier than its metaphoric use in
D.

The difference between H and D, however should not be overlooked. H's
shame vocabulary is both the *justification* and the *punishment*. D's shame vocabulary is found mainly in the case; it does not constitute the punishment. Of
course, H presumes that its shame rationales will fall on disciplined ears, a situation that can prevail only when the extended family (*bêt 'āb*) is a cohesive,
communal unit, an intimation that this list may stem from early or even premonarchic times. The power of a shame culture to control societal behavior is
witnessed in modern Japan, where individual honesty and a low crime rate prevail. As indicated at the opening of this introduction, the series of shame rationales is a further indication that incest was prevalent and that the text had repeatedly to appeal to Israel's shame culture in order to win obedience.

What precisely is prohibited: Is it marriage or copulation? In favor of the former is the argument that prima facie, free sex is forbidden: the couple who indulge in sex must marry (Exod 22:15–16; Deut 22:28–29; cf. Kaufmann 1945:
2.561–64). Thus this chapter must be speaking of forbidden marriages (Kalisch
1867–72; Neufeld 1944: 191–92; Driver and White 1894–98; Baentsch 1903;
Hoffmann 1953; Ehrlich 1908; see also Schwartz 1987: 244, n. 17). Those who
hold to the copulation theory counter with linguistic arguments: *gillâ 'erwâ* and
qārab connote only sex (Noordtzij 1982); otherwise, would forbidden intercourse
with a menstruant (v. 19) be limited to only one's wife? To be sure *lāqaḥ* (vv.
17b, 18; 20:14, 17, 21) does mean "marry" (21:7, 13, 14; Gen 25:20; 26:34, etc.).
It indeed occurs in vv. 17b and 18. The truth, however, is that the interdictions
fall on both copulation and marriage. Incest can never be legitimated by marriage (Gottwald 1979: 302; cf. Dillmann and Ryssel 1897). Moreover, the text
distances itself from the sexual practices of Egypt and Canaan regardless of the
status of their women (Schwartz 1987: 77–78). The question, therefore, is academic. The closing exhortation warns Israel not to commit the purported sexual sins of the Canaanites lest they, too, suffer expulsion from the land.

The prohibitions can be divided into two groups: vv. 6–16 (17) and 18–23; v.
17 is a transitional verse (see its NOTE). The first grouping (vv. 6–17) is characterized by the lack of syndetic connection between prohibitions. The reason is
obvious: the women are relatives; hence there is no need for a *waw*. This division is recognized by the Masoretes, who insert a space indicated by a *samek* (a
"closed" division marker) between each prohibition, but not in vv. 18–23
(Schwartz 1987: 71–72). The order in the first list is logical: mother, stepmother,
sister, granddaughter, aunt (both), stepaunt (father's), daughter-in-law, sister-
in-law.

6. This verse heads the list of prohibitions, as indicated by its special vocabulary *'îš 'îš, kol-šĕ'ēr bĕśārô, lĕgallôt 'erwâ* (all other prohibitions employ the
construct *'erwat*), its ending *'ănî YHWH* (duplicated only in v. 21), and its use

of the plural. The last point also indicates the transitional nature of this verse, which connects the opening exhortation (vv. 1–5), voiced in the plural, with the following prohibitions, expressed in the singular, thereby addressing both nation (pl.) and individual (sing.). Some maintain that this verse serves as a heading for only vv. 7–16, which focus on šĕ'ēr, 'erwâ 'blood relatives'. However, the following section also contains the terms ša'ărâ (v. 17b) and lĕgallôt 'erwâ (vv. 17b, 18, 19). Thus the context of v. 6 may apply to only vv. 7–16, but its formulation alludes to vv. 17–23 (Cholewinski 1976: 32; for the discussion, see Schwartz 1987: 70–71). However, whether heading or transition, the aforesaid reasoning overlooks the possibility that v. 6 also includes its own prohibitions—indeed, those ostensibly missing from the following list (see below).

No one. '*îš* '*îš*. The incest laws are directed to the man, since he initiates the sexual act. Also, the absence of *mibbêt* / *mibbĕnê yiśrā'ēl* indicates that these laws are also incumbent on the *gēr*, the resident alien (Ibn Ezra; cf. 20:2).

anyone of his own flesh. kol-šĕ'ēr bĕśārô, literally "any flesh of his flesh," *bāśār* referring to the outer flesh and *šĕ'ēr* to the flesh with its blood (Wolff 1974: 29; Hartley 1992). That *šĕ'ēr* basically means "flesh," see Akkadian *šīru* / *šēru*, and Ugaritic *š'r* (paralleled by *dm* 'blood', RS 225:3–5; Loewenstamm 1963–64: 295; Exod 21:10; Mic 3:2; Ps 78:20, 27). The expression is a superlative, as in *miqdaš haqqōdeš* (16:33), *śimḥat gîlî* (Ps 43:4), and *'admat 'āpār* (Dan 12:2; cf. Kalisch 1867–72; Ehrlich 1908), implying that the subject is the close relatives (cf. *qĕrêb biśrēh*, Tgs.). Thus Paran's (1989: 84) claim that *šĕ'ēr* by itself in H means "relative" is incorrect. Also his claim that this alleged uniqueness in H is due to its precise and distinctive vocabulary, to separate itself from the language of the common people must equally be rejected: H's language is anything but precise, and it incorporates many of the idioms and customs of the people (see Introduction I C).

The addition of *kol* 'anyone' indicates that all the close relatives, even those missing from the list, are included. Accordingly, my erstwhile student S. Rattray, initially in a graduate seminar and then in a publication (1987: 537–44), has seized on the generic meaning of this term to locate the missing family members in the list of prohibitions (see INTRODUCTION to vv. 6–23). An objection might be filed against her interpretation on the grounds that this idiom in 25:49 (also H) ostensibly refers, on the contrary, to just distant relatives (Schwartz 1987: 246, n. 3). Not so. There, too, the term is generic, and its use is essential to specify that not only may the redeemer be one of the enumerated kin, but the term may include anyone from the kin group, *provided he is a blood relative* (see NOTE on 25:49). Finally, that *tiqrĕbû* is the only verb in the entire list (vv. 6–23) in the plural may be an editorial hint that more than one incestuous relationship is implied.

In sum, the very fact that v. 6 serves as a heading for the list of forbidden unions with kinswomen automatically implies, as Lev 21:2 specifies, that all close blood relatives absent from the list are also included. Thus Schwartz's forthcoming claim that this verse is a general heading for the entire list must be rejected.

shall approach. tiqrĕbû. This is a euphemism for sex (Gen 20:4; Isa 8:3; cf. Lev 18:6, 14, 19; 20:11; Ezek 18:6), as indicated by its parallel terms gillah (v. 14), šākab (20:18 || 18:19), nāgaš (Exod 19:15), bā' (Deut 22:13). The legal term qāreb means "encroach" (Milgrom 1970: 16–37). Here it means "encroach sexually." This meaning also holds for its exact Akkadian cognate qerēbu (*CAD* 13:233b; cf. Milgrom 1970: 34, n. 127; Moran 1973: 66–67, ll. 1, 3; Caplice 1974: 22). More conclusively, the very verb in Akkadian for "approach," ṭeḫû, also means "copulate." For example:

a-na bît tap-pe-šu i-te-ru-ub a-na aššat tap-pe-é-šú iṭṭe₄-ḫi

He entered his neighbor's house, had intercourse with his neighbor's wife. (Šurpu 2:47–48 [Reiner 1958: 14])

Cassuto (1964: 148–63), however, derives from the semantic field of qārab, rā'â 'see', gillah 'uncover', and especially from the use of these verbs in Gen 9:21–22 (he understands Ham's crime as literally seeing Noah's genitals; cf. Heb 2:15; versus *b. Sanh.* 70a), that originally approaching / seeing were prohibited and only later were these taboos treated figuratively. Rabbinic tradition also prohibits "approaching" (*Sipra* Aḥare 13:15; ARN[1] 2). The sectaries of the Dead Sea (if the textual reconstruction is correct) apparently endorse a euphemistic connotation of qūrab, since they append it with an explanatory gloss WLW' [YQRB] '[L] 'ŠH LD'TH LMŠKBY ZKR 'He shall not [approach] a woman to have sexual relations with her' (1QSa 1:10).

It should be noted that these euphemisms are used in reference to only man–woman relationships, but not others (vv. 22–23). The list in chap. 20 is not so squeamish, an indication that it is an independent composition (see INTRODUCTION to chap. 20).

to uncover nakedness. lĕgallôt 'erwâ. This is another euphemism for "copulate," as demonstrated by comparing 18:6–19 with 20:11–13, 18, 20 (šākab, lit. "lie"). Also, note its use in describing harlotry (Ezek 16:36; 23:18; Hos 2:11–12) and the fate of captive women (Isa 47:3; Ezek 16:37; Lam 1:8). The use of this synonymous term of tiqrĕbû functions the same way as the doubling up of flesh in šĕ'ēr bĕśāro, namely, as a superlative.

Indeed, there is no biblical term for genitals, only euphemisms: 'erwâ, bāśār (15:2), raglayim (Judg 3:24), šĕkōbet (Lev 18:20), šōpĕkâ (Deut 23:2). The root of 'erwâ is 'rh 'uncover', implying that "nakedness" (i.e., genitals), is customarily covered (Ibn Ezra), as indicated by its idiomatic antonyms kissâ 'erwâ (Exod 28:42; Ezek 16:8; Hos 2:11) and rā'â 'erwâ (Gen 9:23). The word 'erwâ applies to both sexes (20:17; cf. *Tg. Onk; m. Meg.* 4:9; *b. Meg.* 25a) and is clearly distinguished from 'ārôm 'nudity, nakedness' (Horton 1973: 20).

Ziskind (1996: 128–29) offers an attractive rationale for the use of this idiom:

[Its author] intended these prohibitions to be absolute, to transcend the laws of rape, seduction or adultery and to be lifelong, i.e., from the time that the relationship was established by either birth in marriage, and not to end with death or divorce. . . . Accordingly, a man would now be forbidden to have sex with his stepmother not only in his father's lifetime but after his father died. He was also barred from sex with his daughter-in-law and sister-in-law on the death of his son or brother (hence no levirate). . . . Women could no longer be handed around to other men in the family as wives and concubines. A widow could now marry anyone she wished outside the family or could be free not to remarry at all. . . . The rules forbidding a man to marry a woman and then to marry or make a concubine of her mother, daughter or sister prevented the unseemliness of a man moving about from one member of a woman's family to another, and thus ended an abuse in the practice of polygamy (Lev. xviii 17–18). P [rather, H–J.M.] did not wish any dilution of affection to take place among sisters or between mother and daughter by reason of a circumstance in which these women were forced to compete for the attention of the same man.

Maimonides (*Guide* 3.49) seems to have alluded to the same rationale:

All illicit unions with females have one thing in common: namely, that in the majority of cases these females are constantly in the company of the male in his house and that they are easy of access for him and can easily be controlled by him—there being no difficulty in making them come to his presence; and no judge could blame the male for their being with him. Consequently if the status of the woman with whom union is illicit were that of *any unmarried woman*, I mean to say that if it were possible and that the prohibition with regard to them were only due to their *not being the man's wives*, most people would have constantly succumbed and fornicated with them. (my italics)

I submit that Ziskind (1996) is correct, and I can bring support from the text itself. It should be noted that *lĕgallōt ʿerwâ* occurs in every heterosexual prohibition but one—the last, adultery (18:20). There is only one possible reason: since adultery means cohabiting with a married woman, *lĕgallōt ʿerwâ* does not apply. Therefore, since the previous cases contain *lĕgallōt ʿerwâ*, they are dealing with a woman who is no longer or has never been married. This conclusion is also deducible on purely logical grounds. The fact that the legist found it necessary to include a prohibition of adultery implies that all other prohibitions deal with cases where the woman is unmarried. In fact, the expression *lĕgallōt ʿerwâ* is apparently an organizing factor in this list, which explains why adultery, being without it, is found at the bottom of the list (v. 20).

Ziskind's view is further supported by (royal) Hittite practice (*Jub* 33:15; Philo, *Laws* 3.12–18; the rabbis, *m. Sanh.* 7:4) and the sequence of incest prohibitions in chap. 20, where adultery precedes all the others (see NOTE on v. 8), implying that the following prohibitions focus on cases where the woman is again unmarried, namely, if she is divorced or widowed but still living in the family compound.

Initially, it may seem puzzling that five of the listed prohibitions were blatantly violated, as related by the narratives (JE) about Israel's founding fathers. Abraham's marriage to his half sister, Sarah (Gen 20:12), is forbidden in v. 11 and punished by kārēt in 20:17. That such unions were the accepted practice is indirectly proved by Tamar's statement to her half brother, Amnon, that their father, King David, would not object to their marrying (2 Sam 13:13). Jacob's marriage to Rachel in the lifetime of her older sister, Leah (Gen 29), is prohibited by v. 18. Moses, Aaron, and Miriam were the offspring of a union between an aunt and her nephew (Exod 6:20), forbidden in v. 12 and punishable in 20:19 (by either kārēt or childlessness; see its NOTE). Tamar is vindicated for having seduced her father-in-law, Judah (Gen 38:26), a liaison condemned in v. 15 and punishable with death in 20:12. Judah admits his wrong in withholding his last surviving son from performing his levirate duty with Tamar (Gen 38:26), a union prohibited by v. 16 and punished with kārēt in 20:21.

The answer to these incontrovertible contradictions rests with Ziskind (1988: 104) who concludes that H's laws of forbidden sexual unions constitute nothing less than a reform: "the priestly writer was not only compiling rules relating to the purity of family life but was reforming them with the objective of improving the status of women within the framework of ancient Israel's patriarchal family structure."

I YHWH (have spoken). 'ănî YHWH. Since the blood relatives in this list (vv. 6–16) live in the family compound, they are under the authority and complete control of the addressee, the paterfamilias. The forbidden liaisons may be consensual, and, even if discovered, there is no one to bring the paterfamilias to justice, except YHWH: and he will punish. The only other occurrence of this formula in the list is in v. 21. Possibly, it is an envelope marker for enclosing all the forbidden liaisons between persons in this list. Molek is included, not only because of the enormity of the sin—idolatry and murder—but also, like the preceding prohibitions, because the decision and responsibility rests with the paterfamilias: again, YHWH will surely punish.

7. The nakedness of your father. 'erwat ābîkā. What could this phrase mean in a prohibition against having sex with one's mother? The following answers are worthy of consideration:

1. It emphasizes that his mother is also his father's wife: "The nakedness of his father" (20:11) proves that "just as his wife is specified there so is it intended here" (Rashi). Abravanel cites broader evidence: "Everywhere the word 'erwat (of the man) is mentioned his wife is intended" (cf. 18:8, 14, 16; 20:11, 20, 21).

2. Its purpose is to include his mother even if her husband is his stepfather or she is no longer his wife, as evidenced by 18:8; 20:11, 20, 21; Deut 23:1 (Hoffmann 1953).

3. The son is encroaching on the father's exclusive possession: "One is trespassing upon the spot where the nakedness of one's father has been exposed" (Eilberg-Schwartz 1990: 171).

4. Since the text emphasizes the motive "she is your mother," her relationship to her husband can no longer be the motive, as in v. 8b; it is, therefore, shifted into the prohibition (Schwartz 1987: 91).

5. Since the father is the head of the family, this—the first prohibition—must emphasize that the crime is against him (Ibn Ezra).

6. "Marital intercourse makes a man and wife as closely related as parents and children. In the words of Gen 2:24: 'they become one flesh' " (Wenham 1979; cf. Patai 1959: 156).

7. Daube (1947: 81) and Phillips (1980), followed by Ziskind (1988: 98–99) and Cohen (1990), proposes that this constitutes a discrete injunction against homosexual intercourse with one's father. This view was long ago suggested by R. Judah (*b. Sanh.* 54a), but objected to by Ramban, as follows: (a) why has a similarly worded phrase not been inserted concerning the son, namely, *ʿerwat binkā hîʾ* (v. 15), and, one might add, concerning the neighbor, namely *ʿerwat ʿămîtĕkā hîʾ* (v. 20); and (b) this would be the only verse containing two prohibitions, thereby breaking the structural pattern of the chapter.

8. As pointed out by Melcher (1996: 94), whereas *ʿerwâ* denotes the sexual organs of a woman, in construct with a man it denotes his jurisdiction over the woman's sexual function (see NOTES on vv. 8b, 10,14, 16b, and its exceptional use in 20:17). Thus v. 7a reads as follows: "The sexual jurisdiction of your father, namely, the sexual organs of your mother you shall not uncover." This interpretation also requires the *waw* explicative.

9. Ramban's objections (no. 7) themselves can be parried if *ʿerwat ʾābîkā* is an interpolation by the H redactor (cf. Elliger 1966), who thereby connected the exhortatory prelude (vv. 1–5), alluding to the homosexual crime of Ham (Egypt) and Canaan (Gen 9:22) regarding their father Noah (see NOTE on "in the land of Egypt," v. 3), with the palpably older list of sexual prohibitions. This structural link, however, was not the redactor's objective. This verse and equivalent statements in vv. 8, 12 (cf. vv. 10, 16) simply imply that a liaison with one's mother is tantamount to having sex with one's father—a taboo so deeply embedded in the Israelite (and universal) psyche that it requires no legislation. Nonetheless, Elliger's hypothesis seems the most likely.

The juxtaposition of father and mother also serves a heuristic purpose. Precisely because this is the first specific prohibition in the list, it lays down the principle of consanguinity and affinity as the two bases for prohibited unions (cf. Horton 1973: 29–31). Subsequently, *ʿerwâ* also designates affinity (vv. 8, 14–16; see no. 1).

that is, the nakedness of your mother. wĕʿerwat ʾimmĕkā. The *waw* is explicative (Ramban, who cites asyndetic v. 14). It has been suggested Ham's crime against his father, Noah—*wayyarʾ ḥām ʾăbî kĕnaʿan ʾēt ʿerwat ʾābîw*, literally "And Ham, the father of Canaan, saw the nakedness of his father" (Gen 9:22a)— really intends to say that Ham committed incest with his mother (*ʿerwat ʾābîw = ʿerwat ʾimmô*, as in this verse) and that Canaan was a product of this incest, thereby explaining the subsequent incest of Lot's daughters, the progenitresses of Moab and Ammon (Gen 19:30–38; Basset 1971: 232–36). However, based on the literal interpretation of *gillâ* and *rāʾâ*, Ham's offense has also been identified as seeing his father's genitals (Cassuto 1964: 148–63). That genitals were considered sacrosanct, so that an unauthorized person was forbidden to see them, is ostensibly supported by the prohibition against seizing a man's genitals (Deut

25:11–12) and the ancient custom of taking an oath by holding one's genitals (Gen 24:2–3; 47:29–31; Countryman 1988: 35). Both interpretations of the ambiguous sexual crime against Noah are ingenious but speculative.

That *'erwâ* can have a sexual connotation is illustrated by another narrative context. Saul excoriates his son Jonathan for siding with David *lĕbōšet 'erwat 'immekā* 'to the shame of your mother's nakedness' (1 Sam 20:30). Rather than saying that he is betrayed by the product of his loins, Saul adds that the mother with whom he produced his son has also been shamed.

you shall not uncover; she is your mother—you shall not uncover. lō' tĕgalleh 'immĕkā hi(w)' lo' tĕgalleh. The prohibition is mentioned twice because there is double incest, with the father (v. 7a) and with the mother (v.7b; cf. Ramban). Also, the stress on the motive "she is your mother" necessitates the repetition (so, too, in v. 15). Indeed, the motive indicates the primary reason: "she is your mother"; the incest with the father is secondary (Schwartz 1987: 93).

you shall not uncover her nakedness. lō' tĕgalleh 'erwātāh. This is a chiasm with *'erwat . . . lō' tĕgalleh* (cf. v. 15; Halbe 1980: 69; Paran 1983: 112), a stylistic characteristic of H. It is not surprising that this form of incest—the basis of *Oedipus Rex* and other Greek tragedies—is universal (cf. CH § 157; HL § 189).

8. *The nakedness of your father's wife. 'erwat 'ēšet-'ābîkā.* It is clear from the law codes that this violation was a major concern. It is punishable by death (20:11) and national destruction (Deut 27:20; Ezek 22:10), and it is the only incest law mentioned in the prohibitions of Deut 23 (cf. v. 1, a clear sign of its prevalence; see Driver 1895: 259). The matter is unclear whether the addressee's mother is alive. Clearly, there is no ban on polygamy (it may even be assumed in vv. 9, 11). That is, she need not be his stepmother, whom his father marries after his uterine mother dies. Indeed, it is a polygamous marriage that evokes a grown son's interest in a stepmother, for no blood relationship would be violated. This prohibition, then, would follow from the experience that such unions lead to disaster, as attested by the cases of Reuben (Gen 35:22; 49:4) and Adonijah (1 Kgs 2:13–25). Furthermore, this prohibition may also include concubines (Keil and Delitzsch 1956: 2.414) in order to prevent a son from usurping his father's position (2 Sam 16:21–22; 1 Kgs 2:22; cf. 1 Sam 20:30; 2 Sam 12:8). "All these references indicate that such relations were a real possibility. This is probably due to the young age at which girls married, which often resulted in a situation where a later wife of a man would be about the same age as his son by an earlier wife, if not younger" (Tigay 1996: 209).

One can argue that union with the stepmother is permitted once she is widowed (MAL § 46; HL § 190; CH § 158, if she is childless). Then her position in the kinship network changes. Indeed, if she is not single (either divorced or widowed), the crime would be adultery, covered in a separate prohibition (v. 20). Ancient Near Eastern codes also distinguish between offenses with a woman during the husband's lifetime and after his death (e.g., CH §§ 129, 157–58; HL §§ 189–98). However, that an affine is prohibited even after the death of her spouse is clearly expressed in a letter from the Hittite king Šuppiluliumaš to his Armenian vassal Huqqanaš, who has married the king's sister (contradicting HL § 190, unless the king's prohibition applied only to royalty): "My sister whom I, the Sun, have given you in matrimony has many sisters of different degrees; and you have acquired these (as sisters) too since you have (taken) their sister (as a wife). But in the land of the Hittites there is an important rule: a brother does not take his own sister or cousin (as a wife); it is not permitted . . . when you return to Hajaša (i.e., Armenia), you should no longer take the wives of your brothers (*who are, as it were*) your (*sisters?*)" (cf. Greengus 1975: 9; Wenham 1979: 38–39, n. 12). That affines are forbidden even when divorced or widowed is also held by *Jub* 33:15; 41:23; Philo, *Laws* 3.12–28; *m. Sanh.* 7:4. That this would seem to be the plain meaning of this prohibition is bolstered by the sequence of the prohibitions in chap. 20: adultery precedes the father's wife (vv. 10–11). Indeed, it must be assumed that all the following prohibitions in this list are in force even if the woman in question is widowed or divorced (unless otherwise specified, e.g., v. 18).

it is the nakedness of your father. *'erwat 'ābîkā hī(w)'.* B. *Sanh.* 54a and some moderns, including Elliger (1966) (details in Schwartz 1987: 254, n. 15), claim that this sentence constitutes a separate prohibition against sodomy with the father. Besides the redundancy it creates with v. 22, this suggestion must be rejected as a distortion of the text (see NOTE on "The nakedness of your father," v. 7a).

This verse, as noted by Melcher (1996: 94), actually connotes that the sexual organs (*'erwâ*) of the father's wife is the father's jurisdiction. Thus *'erwâ* '(female) sexual organs' in construct with a man bears an extended meaning of the jurisdiction over the function of the female's sexual organs (see also NOTES on vv. 10, 14, 16b; 20:17).

9. *The nakedness of your sister, the daughter of your father or the daughter of your mother.* *'erwat 'ăhôtĕkā bat-'ābîkā 'ô bat-'immekā.* Alternatively, this can be rendered ". . . your sister, *even* (a half sister)," thereby including a full sister among the prohibitions. The Torah acknowledges that marriages with half sisters were permitted before Sinai (Gen 20:12); they also occurred afterward (Ezek 22:11; CD 5: 8–11; see below). Brother–sister marriages were practiced among royalty in Egypt and Phoenicia (Černy 1954; *KAT* 14:13–15; *ANET* 662b). Half-sister marriages are attested in pre-Islamic Arabia (Smith 1907: 191–98).

No rationale is given, perhaps due to the length of the sentence or its presence in v. 11, "she is your sister" (Schwartz 1987: 98). Perhaps, none was needed: "Sister or paternal half sister could expect protection from sexual advances . . . as a successful marriage depended entirely on her retaining her virginity" (Bigger 1979: 198). The Qumranites derive the rationale by analogy from v. 13: "And they marry each man the daughter of his brother and the daughter of his sister, though Moses said: 'You shall not approach [*lō' tiqrab 'el,* instead of *'erwat . . . lō' tĕgalleh* 'the nakedness of . . . you shall not uncover', a euphemistic rendering forbidden by *m. Meg.* 4:9; cf. Rabin 1954: 19—J.M.] your mother's sister; she is your mother's flesh', and the rules of incest are written with reference to males and apply equally to women [lit. "and women the same as they"]" (CD 5:7–10). The document then continues to apply this principle to ban marriage with nieces (CD 5:10–11), a practice permitted by the rabbis (see NOTE on v. 12). But 11QT 66:14 supplies the motive *tô'ēbâ hî'* (cf. v. 22); 20:17, though, calls it *ḥesed*. I would suggest, however, that the added rationale *'erwat 'ābîkā ō' 'immĕkā hi(w)'* 'she is your father's or mother's nakedness' is awkward stylistically, and it would further burden the existing overlong sentence.

As pointed out by Sarna (1989: 143), marrying a half sister was not considered consanguineous by the people and hence, permitted (Gen 20:5, 12; 2 Sam 13:13), a position condemned by H (Lev 18:9, 20:17) and Ezekiel (22:11).

whether of the household clan or of an outside clan. môledet bayit 'ô môledet ḥûṣ. There is no doubt that the antonyms *bayit* and *ḥûṣ* mean "inside" and "outside," respectively (e.g., Gen 6:14; Exod 25:11; 37:2; 1 Kgs 7:9). But what is the meaning of *môledet?* This word and, hence, the entire phrase have been variously interpreted:

1. Legitimate or illegitimate birth (*b. Yeb.* 23a; Ibn Ezra[1], Ramban, Abravanel, Hoffmann 1953; Noth 1977).
2. Born of your father (at home) or from another woman, coupling *môledet bayit* with the father's daughter and *môledet ḥûṣ* with the mother's daughter (*Tgs.*, Saadiah, Radak, Bekhor Shor).
3. Raised at home or abroad (cf. Gen 50:23; Ibn Ezra[2], Neufeld 1944: 197; *NEB*; Porter 1976; Wenham 1979).
4. "Whether of the household clan or of an outside clan." The entire phrase refers to only "the daughter of your mother" (Porter 1967: 3; Wenham 1979, Rattray 1987). Here *môledet* applies to a wider grouping than the nuclear family; it includes cousins and therefore refers to the extended family or clan (Dillmann and Ryssel 1897; cf. Gen 11:28; 12:1; 24:4–38; 31:3, 13; 32:10; 43:7; 48:6 [P]; Num 10:30; Jer 22:10; 46:16; Ezek 16:3, 4; 23:15; Ruth 2:11; Est 2:10, 20; 8:6). That *ḥûṣ* can refer specifically to those outside the clan, see Deut 25:5.

Bigger (1979: 194) objects that it is: "unlikely that the half sister's own family would have allowed her to leave with her mother, since she was a valuable economic asset, capable of commanding a substantial bride-price." On the contrary, the assumption is that the daughter is a young child and the mother is widowed (or divorced); thus the likelihood is that no one in the father's family is willing to assume responsibility for rearing the daughter.

The emphasis of this prohibition is on *môledet ḥûṣ*: even though your half sister belongs to another clan, she is your mother's daughter and, therefore, forbidden. The additional advantage of this interpretation is that it alone will satisfactorily render the expression *môledet 'ābîkā* in v. 11. Moreover, it will allow v. 11 to follow logically on this verse: a half sister—whether she is part of your household (*bayit*) or not (*ḥûṣ*) or is a sister by marriage (not consanguineous) who, however, becomes part of your father's household—is forbidden.

her nakedness. 'erwātān. Read *'erwātāh* with LXX, Sam., Pesh., and fifteen MSS. The MT possibly was contaminated by the same word in the following verse (Sun 1990: 116), or, preferably, it refers to *both* sisters, and its presence in v. 10 is influenced by its occurrence here (see below).

10. *The nakedness of your son's daughter or of your daughter's daughter.* The

startling absence of the daughter has been rationalized as derivable as an a fortiori argument from the case of the daughter of the father's wife (v. 17; Rashi, Ibn Ezra), the granddaughter (v. 10; *b. Sanh.* 76a; Abravanel), and the mother; that is, as the son–mother union constitutes incest, so does the daughter with the father (Shadal). It has also been proposed that it fell out by homoeoarcton (Dillman and Ryssel 1897; Ginzburg). Even arguments permitting such unions have been put forth. I have preferred Rattray's (1987) solution, slightly amended by Horton (1973), that the missing daughter (and full sister) is subsumed under v. 6 (see INTRODUCTION to vv. 6–23).

Bendavid (1986: 22) wonders why the daughter's daughter is in this list, since her mother may have married outside her kin group. He speculates that her father may have taken residence with her grandfather, as Jacob did with his father-in-law, Laban. However, Bendavid adheres to Elliger's (1955) theory that the main criterion is that the prohibitions fall on those family members who are living together, whereas I maintain that it makes no difference where the relative lives as long as he or she is a blood relation (or an affine). The structure and style of this verse may have been influenced by v. 9; otherwise, one would expect the two granddaughters to each have received a discrete prohibition as in vv. 12–13 (Schwartz 1987: 92).

their nakedness. ʿerwātān. This word seems superfluous, and it breaks the pattern set by vv. 7 and 8. Its occurrence here may be due to its presence in the previous verse, v. 9. Indeed, the threefold use of ʿerwâ in the case of the granddaughter underscores that copulation, not marriage, is intended (J. Thompson).

for their nakedness is your own nakedness. kî ʿerwātĕkā hēnnâ. Bigger (1979) claims that this motive clause is more fitting for a daughter than for a granddaughter, since the latter is not the offspring of his loins. This argument does not hold, since ʿerwâ 'genitals' here implies blood relationship (Wenham 1979: 39). Besides, one would have expected the singular hîʾ, not MT's plural hēnnâ. Porter's (1967: 12) claim that the granddaughter must be living in the addressee's household must also be dismissed, since, again, the determining factor is their blood ties regardless of where she lives.

The semantic awkwardness is resolved once it is realized that ʿerwâ in construct with a male refers to the jurisdiction over the function of the named female's sexual organs. Thus ʿerwātĕkā hēnnâ means that the paterfamilias "has jurisdiction of his granddaughter's sexual function until she is married. At that point, exclusive jurisdiction over the woman's sexual function passes to the male" (Melcher 1996: 94).

11. *The nakedness of your father's wife's daughter.* ʿerwat bat-ʾēšet ʾābîkā. The expression ʾēšet ʾābîkā 'your father's wife' always denotes the stepmother (v. 8; 20:11; Deut 23:1; 27:20). The "sister" is not the daughter of the addressee's father or mother. His father married another woman who had a daughter from a previous marriage; she is a stepsister whom the father raises (R. Eliezer b. Jacob in *B. Sot.* 43b; *y. Yeb.* 2:4; Karaites). As a stepsister, she is not the addressee's šĕʾēr or ʿerwâ. This prohibition follows logically after vv. 9–10, which do speak of blood relations.

of your father's clan. môledet ʾābîkā. Bigger (1979: 197) renders this as "begotten by your father"—that is, a consanguineous offspring. He may have been influenced by the LXX, which inserts lō' tĕgalleh before môledet 'ābîkā, making the latter part of motive: "she is your sister *by the same father* [my emphasis]." This interpretation must be rejected out of hand; it is redundant of v. 9.

Another rendering is "raised by your father" (Karaites, who also add this exception: if the wife has no children from his father [i.e., produces no half siblings], the marriage is permitted). Dillmann and Ryssel (1897) also follow this rendering by reading *mûledet* (Hop'al)—that is, begotten in a separate marriage and adopted by the new father (cf. Neufeld 1944: 199). Loewenstamm (1971a: 388) objects on the grounds that the institution of adoption does not exist in the Torah. However, no formal adoption need be presumed: a minor daughter automatically enters the father's household with her mother.

As elucidated in the NOTE on v. 9, *môledet* means "clan." If this phrase forms part of the motive (cf. LXX, above), then once she enters the father's family—even though her own father is of a different clan—she is your sister. But if it is a motive clause, it should have been followed by *hî'* (Rattray 1987: 537, n. 2). It must, then, be part of the case: if she is related to you—that is, her father is of the same clan as your father, no matter how distant—she is your sister and prohibited to you. However, if she is of a different clan—there being no common blood—the implication is clear: she may marry you (Ehrlich 1908).

she is your sister. 'āḥôtĕkā hî'. The rationale here stands out even more in view of its absence in v. 9. That is, to say: even if she is totally unrelated to you, if she is of your father's clan, she is still your sister. For this reason, she is placed within the list of prohibited blood relatives (vv. 6–14).

12. *your father's sister. 'āḥôt-'ābîkā*. This relation is also called *dōdâ* (Exod 6:20; see NOTE on v. 14). Normally, aunts would not reside with the family, which indicates that these incest laws applied to blood relations regardless of where they lived. Another factor may be the high status held by a paternal uncle (cf. v. 14), which also was extended to a paternal or maternal aunt (v. 13). It is perhaps no accident that although Saul was sent by his father to look for lost donkeys, he reported back to his uncle (1 Sam 10:14–16).

How did Moses feel when he learned through this law that he was a bastard? His mother Jocheved was his father Amram's aunt (Exod 6:20). For that matter, some of the patriarchs were also guilty of illicit unions: Abram married his half sister (Gen 20:12, cf. Lev 18:9), Jacob married two sisters (Gen 29, cf. Lev 18:18), and Judah had sex with his daughter-in-law (Gen 38, cf. Lev 18:15)—thereby bastardizing all their progeny, the people of Israel! Comparing the books of Exodus and Numbers helps us resolve this paradox. Irasel's murmuring against God before receiving the law at Sinai goes unpunished; after Sinai the same offenses are severely punished (cf. Exod 15:24–25 with Num 21:4–6; Exod 16:1–12 with Num 11:1–5, 31–34; Exod 16:22–27 with Num 15:32–36; Exod 17:1–7 with Num 20:1–13). Sinai is the watershed; its laws do not apply ex post facto.

your father's flesh. šĕ'ēr 'ābîkā. The motive stresses the blood relationship (also on v. 13). 11QT 66:15 supplies for vv. 12–13 a different motive, *zimmâ hî'* (cf. v. 17b)—that is, a moral, not a biological, rationale.

The similarity of vv. 12–13 to 20:19 might suggest that the latter imitates the

style and content of the former (Bigger 1979: 187, n. 2), but the basic form of
20:9–21 (*wĕ'îš 'ăšer*; see INTRODUCTION to this pericope) suggests a different origin.

13. *your mother's sister.* However, unions between uncles and nieces were permitted—for example, Nahor and Milcah, daughter of his brother, Haran (Gen
11:29); and Othniel and Achsah, daughter of Caleb, brother of Kenaz (Josh
15:17; Judg 1:13). Indeed, such marriages were considered meritorious by the
rabbis (*b. Yeb.* 62b), perhaps because the affection a man has for his sister will
be extended to her daughter (Rashi). Marriages between uncles and nieces were
repeatedly and emphatically forbidden at Qumran (CD 5:8; 11QT 66:16–17;
4Q274, fr. 7:2–3, 4–5) and by early Christians (Matt 14:4; Mark 6:18).

Elliger (1966) questions the validity of this prohibition on the grounds that
the maternal aunt is probably married to a man from another kin group and
therefore does not live with her family. However, as pointed out in the NOTE on
v. 12, this condition is not a factor. What counts regardless of where the aunt
lives and to whom she is married is that she is a blood relation.

She is not called *dōdātĕkā* 'your aunt', as in v. 14, in order to preserve the
symmetry with v. 12. The more likely reason, however, is that *dōdâ* refers exclusively to the wife of the *dôd*, the father's brother (see v. 14).

14. The structure of this law, ABB'C, breaks the ABB'A' pattern (see INTRO-
DUCTION to vv. 6–23), perhaps due to the inclusion of "you shall not approach
his wife." This sentence—the essence of the prohibition—overloads the verse
due to the necessity of explaining that she is "the nakedness of your father's
brother;" vv. 7, 11 (LXX) proved overloaded for a similar reason.

This verse, however, can be seen as forming a new structure—a chiastic one—
that is followed in vv. 15 and 16 as well (M. Hildenbrand):

A   *'erwat 'ăḥî- 'abîkā*   A   The nakedness of your father's brother
  B   *lō' tĕgalleh*   B   you shall not uncover,
    X   *'el- 'ištô*   X   (that is,) his wife;
  B'   *lō' tiqrab*   B'   you shall not approach
A'   *dōdātĕkā hi(w)'*   A'   she is your aunt

The aunt is identified three times, each using a different expression *'erwat . . . ,*
'ištô, dōdātĕkā 'nakedness of, his wife, your aunt' (AXA'). BB' form synonymous
statements. That *qrb* and *glh* are synonymous, see the NOTE on "you shall not
approach," v. 6. The motive clause, rather than being in the center (vv. 7, 11,
15), is delayed until the end (A').

This verse actually reads "The sexual function of your father's brother you
shall not uncover, (that is,) . . . (see NOTES on vv. 8 and 10).

your aunt. dōdātĕkā. It cannot go unnoticed that the expected rationale *kî 'er-*
wat dōdĕkā hî' 'for she is the nakedness of your paternal uncle' is missing. It is
possible that these words accidently fell out, since they are ostensibly found in
the LXX *suggenēs gar sou ĕstin.* However, the LXX also renders the words *dōdātô*
and *dōdô* as *suggenous* and *suggeneias*, respectively. Thus the LXX does not designate *dōd / dōdâ* as specific family members, but as their attestations elsewhere
in Scripture suggest (e.g., 25:45; 2 Sam 3:39), the LXX interpreted *dōdātĕkā* as

"your relative, kinsperson"—highly inaccurate, considering that she is only the wife of the relative.

Rather, the omission is probably deliberate. It reflects the all-powerful position of the paternal uncle in the family. Consider Laban, the paternal uncle of Jacob's wives (Gen 29–31, assuming that their father was alive); David's adviser, his paternal uncle (1 Chr 27:32); and the paternal uncle's obligation to care for the dead (Lev 10:4; Amos 6:10), to inherit (Num 27:9–10), and to redeem (Lev 25:48). Van der Toorn (1996b: 216–17) may be correct in suggesting that the dôd was the paterfamilias who presided over the family banquet at the local bāmâ and to whom Saul first reported the results of his search for the lost asses (1 Sam 10:14–16) rather than to his father.

Thus, I submit, it sufficed for the text to state her title dōdātěkā, namely, the wife of the dōd, without having to explain that she was an extension of his person. Note, finally, that the only ones in the list whose persona embraces their wives are, in this order: father (v. 8), paternal uncle (v. 14), son (v. 15? see its NOTE), and brother (v. 16). Such, indeed, is the ranking of the paternal uncle in the internal family structure.

All members of the avuncular list (vv. 12–14) are accounted for except the wife of the mother's brother. Is she, perhaps, included in the term dōdātô (20:20; Philo, Laws 3.26; cf. LXX)? This verse allows for such an interpretation, since it does not specify whether her husband is the father's or the mother's brother. This solution, however, must be rejected because the term dwd in Aramaic and Old South Arabic and probably in the Bible denotes the paternal uncle (Sanmartin-Ascaso 1978: 148–50), and, hence, the dōdâ refers, as in this verse, to his wife. It cannot refer to the blood aunt (paternal or maternal), who is listed in a separate prohibition (20:19; Yahel Or). But it clearly means the paternal aunt in the case of Jochebed, who explicitly is called Amram's father's sister (Exod 6:20). Either the term developed a more restricted meaning in legal terminology or it always referred to both the paternal aunt and the wife of the paternal uncle, but was avoided in 20:19 for stylistic reasons—to list the paternal and maternal aunt (who is not a dōdâ) in tandem. A third possibility is that dōdâ means only "paternal aunt" (Exod 6:20) but was, by extension, applied here to the wife of the paternal uncle, implying that she is equivalent to the paternal aunt (b. Sanh. 28b; Ibn Ezra; Hoffmann 1953; Schwartz 1987: 99). In any event, the wife of the maternal uncle is not a dōdâ.

It is more likely that the maternal uncle's wife was excluded from the list because her husband and, hence, she are not part of the family. Thus the principle of affinity does not apply (b. B. Bat. 109b; b. Yeb. 54b; Wessely 1846; Shadal; Hoffmann 1953). Although the maternal aunt is also not part of the father's family, she is the "mother's flesh" (v. 13), which is not true for her sister-in-law (Shadal).

15. your daughter-in-law. kallātěkā. This violation is labeled tebel and is punishable by death (20:12). Ezekiel calls it zimmâ (Ezek 22:11), the designation for unions with mother and daughter (v. 17a), which it resembles. The union with a widowed daughter-in-law is clearly implied in the narratives (cf. Gen 19:30–38 and esp. 38:11–26). It was also permitted elsewhere in the ancient Near East (cf. MAL § 33). However, as argued in the NOTE on v. 6 (see also

NOTE on v. 8), H forbids union with affines, even if they are divorced or widowed.

your son's wife. ʾēšet bǐnĕkā. Why does it not read ʿerwat bǐnĕkā 'the nakedness of your son', the form it takes in v. 16? Bigger (1979: 197) suggests that since "a son was dependent on his father and under his authority," his own "nakedness" is not violated by his father's incest. A simpler and more reasonable explanation is at hand: since the term kallâ can also mean "bride" (e.g., Isa 49:18; 61:10; 62:5; Jer 2:32; 7:34), the text in this case had to specify that "she is your son's wife" (Rattray 1987: 540).

do not uncover her nakedness. lōʾ tĕgalleh ʿerwātāh. The repetition of this verb is due to the insertion of the motive "she is your son's wife." (For similar reasons, it is repeated in v. 7 because of "she is your mother.") The repetition also transforms the verse into a chiasmus: abcbʹaʹ (Paran 1983: 113).

16. *your brother's wife.* ʾēšet-ʾāḥîkā. The presence of a younger brother is not surprising, since he would not always be given the opportunity to head his own household (Bigger 1979: 198). The rabbis extend this prohibition to the wife's sister-in-law (b. Yeb. 55a). However, the wife's brother is not of the father's family, and the rule of v. 14 (absence of the maternal uncle's wife) applies; she is not "your mother's flesh" (v. 13).

Does this verse oppose levirate marriage (Deut 25:5–9), an institution attested in Israel and the ancient Near East (e.g., Gen 38; Ruth 4; Matt 22:23–33; MAL A §§ 30–33; HL § 193)? Both opinions have been registered:

1. This verse is not in contradiction with Deut 25, since it implies that the brother is alive (Snaith 1967; Noth 1977). However, its parallel verse (20:21) uses the verb lāqaḥ 'marry'. Therefore, she must be single, either widowed or divorced. Besides, if she were married, the offense would be adultery, covered by v. 20. A stronger argument is that Lev 18 is the rule and Deut 25, the exception (Sipre Deut. 289: 7; b. Qid. 75b–76a; Driver and White 1894–98; Wenham 1979). Nonetheless, it is hard to believe that Deut 25 would bother to mention this law unless the norm were that it is prohibited (Schwartz, personal communication).

2. The two verses are in contradiction. H would not allow levirate marriage, since once your brother married, his wife is a "blood relative" (hence the repetition "it is your brother's nakedness") and his death is irrelevant. Tellingly, Philo (Laws 3.27 N) omits this law from his discussion of incest rules, perhaps because he could not reconcile it with Deut 25.

This verse, ostensibly, is also in conflict with v. 18: if a deceased wife's sister is permitted, why not the deceased brother's wife (Kalisch 1867–72)? The answer is again in keeping with the rule enunciated in the NOTE on v. 14: relations on the female side are not as close, since they are not members of the father's family (Paton 1897: 48). Therefore, affinity does not apply.

it is your brother's nakedness. ʿerwat ʾāḥîkā hi(w)ʾ. This sentence could be rendered "it is your brother's jurisdiction" (see NOTES on vv. 8 and 10).

17. From the point of view of both content and structure, v. 17 represents a transition. The consanguineous relations end with v. 16, but their formula persists in v. 17a, leading some scholars to claim that the change begins with v. 17b

(Elliger 1966; Reventlow 1961; Kilian 1963; Cholewinski 1976: 32, n. 3). However, v. 17b is still grammatically linked to v. 17a (*bĕnāh* 'her son, *bittāh* 'her daughter', and "they are kindred" refers to 17a). Furthermore, the change in relationship is apparent in v. 17a: mother and daughter are kindred to each other, not to the addressee. Thus v. 17a is part of the transition. It is formulated according to the preceding pattern, but contextually it is related to the following cases (e.g., the wife and her sister, v. 18).

The change is gradual: the expression *lĕgallôt ʿerwâ* 'to uncover nakedness' persists in three more cases (vv. 17b, 18, 19); that is, it is still the same shameful act. After v. 20, all previous characteristics disappear, but the prohibited object still precedes the predicate (except in v. 21). The unique syntax of the final prohibition (v. 23) and its change to third person are due to the fact that the female is addressed; all previous prohibitions are addressed to males (details in Schwartz 1987: 72).

a woman and her daughter. ʾiššâ ûbittāh. The question is: Did he take or marry the second woman while the first was alive or after she was dead? The second option must be ruled out on legal grounds: if the daughter were dead, he would be taking his mother-in-law (*ḥôtenet*, a term missing here), a union that is not prohibited in this list. To be sure, the mother-in-law is forbidden in Deut 27:23, but there the probability is that her daughter—his wife—is alive. But if the mother were dead, he would be taking his stepdaughter, again a union that is not forbidden. But are not both unions forbidden in 20:14? This prohibition reads:

wĕʾîš ʾăšer yiqqaḥ ʾet-ʾiššâ wĕʾet-immāh zimmâ hi(w)ʾ bāʾēš yiśrĕpû ʾōtô wĕʾethen wĕlōʾ-tihyeh zimmâ bĕtôkĕkem

If a man takes a woman and her mother, it is a depravity; both he and they shall be put to the fire, that there be no depravity among you.

The words "he and they" (*wĕʾethen*) imply that both women are alive. Hence it is permissible to marry one after the death of the other (so R. Akiba, *Sipra* Kedoshim 9:18). But R. Ishmael, who avers that each is forbidden even after the death of the other (*Sipra* Kedoshim 9:18), might argue that since the first one, being the only one, is obviously permitted, the word *ʾethen* must refer to either one. Moreover, if the text intended to imply that one is permitted after the demise of the other, it would have specified that the prohibition is incurred *bĕḥayyêhen* 'in their lifetime'. Saadiah (on Koh 4:10 and 1 Kgs 8) supports this view with the following argument: despite the fact that the Temple had ten candelabra (2 Chr 4:7, 20) and ten tables (2 Chr 4:8), only one candelabrum was lit (2 Chr 13:11) and one table held the Bread of Presence (1 Kgs 7:48). Thus the intent was that any one of the ten sancta could have been used. Similarly, only one wife is permitted and the second is guilty of incest.

These arguments, however, cannot be sustained. The plural *ʾethen* (20:14) implies that both women were married *simultaneously*, and, hence, both are guilty. The conclusion is then inescapable: marriage with one is permitted as long as the other is not alive. The violation of this prohibition is punished more severely, by burning (20:14), perhaps because it leads to promiscuity in the father's household (Hoffmann 1953). Coincidentally, from the wording of HL §§ 191, 195, it can be inferred that the Hittites prohibited cohabitation with a mother and daughter during their lifetimes and also declared it a capital crime, unless the liaisons took place in different countries (§ 191, in which case the man is presumed to have been ignorant of their relationship).

marry (to uncover . . . nakedness). tiqqaḥ (lĕgallot 'erwâ). The verb lāqaḥ here and frequently elsewhere refers to marriage (Keter Torah; Noth 1977; Elliger 1966, who cites 18:17, 18; 20:14, 17, 21; 21:7, 13, 14; Gen 25:20; 26:34; 27:46; 28:1, 2, 6, 9; Exod 6:20, 23, 25), a meaning that is assumed in non-H passages by the addition of 'iššâ / lĕ'iššâ. Since lĕgallot 'erwâ refers to only the sex act, the addition of tiqqaḥ must refer to marriage (cf. Wessely 1846).

It is equally plausible, however, to argue that lāqaḥ does not mean "marry" unless it takes the object 'iššâ (e.g., Gen 24:4, 7, 38, 40) or lĕ'iššâ (e.g., Gen 25:20; 28:9). Indeed, there are instances where lāqaḥ by itself cannot mean "marry" (e.g., Gen 20:2; 24:48).

Thus the verb lāqaḥ cannot be used as proof of either meaning. Each attestation must be judged according to its context. In this verse, I have rendered lāqaḥ as "marry" on the basis of this argument: whereas the addressee knows that marriage with his own granddaughter is forbidden (and, hence, the warning concerning copulation suffices, v. 10), he might well assume that the marriage taboo does not apply to the unrelated granddaughter of his wife. Surely, the presence of a vulnerable granddaughter in the same household makes her an accessible victim (cf. Ramban on 20:17). It should be kept in mind that in our own society it is no longer an oddity to find teenage mothers and grandparents in their early thirties, so that a grandparent need not be more than thirty years older than a grandchild.

kindred. ša'ărâ (i.e., to each other; see Rashi, Ramban). That is, the consanguinity principle applies between the wife and her progeny. The LXX reads ša'arĕkā 'your kindred'. However, they are not the addressee's blood relations. Dillmann and Ryssel (1897) revocalize it to read šĕ'ērāh 'her (the wife's) flesh' (accepted by BHS). However, a fifth mappiq in this verse is stylistically awkward: one would expect šĕ'ēr 'ištĕkā. It should be considered an abstract collective noun as 'ōrḥâ 'travelling persons, caravan' (Gen 37:25), dāgâ 'a shoal of fish' (Gen 1:26, 28), and rabbinic ḥammeret 'donkey-drivers', gammelet 'camel-drivers' (m. Sanh. 10:5; Hoffmann 1953; GKC § 122s).

Porter (1967: 20–21) applies this law (v. 17a) to a woman and her widowed mother-in-law, as in the case of Ruth and Naomi, but once Boaz marries Ruth, he is forbidden to Naomi. Hittite law permits cohabitation with free women who are daughters and mothers if they are in different lands but not if they are in the same place; but if they are slaves, cohabitation is permitted everywhere (HL §§ 191, 194; ANET 196).

Greengus (1992: 246) surmises that there was a comparable prohibition against father and son to have sexual relations with the same woman, a situation condemned in Amos 2:7, and can be inferred from HL § 194, which voids the penalty if the woman was a slave.

depravity, zimmâ. The root *zmm* is rendered by *rsn* 'bridle, restrain' in Aramaic. Hence the meaning "suppressed thought, plot," mostly evil (Shadal; cf. *Tg. Onk.*, Ramban). It connotes (neutral) purpose (Job 17:11), evil purpose (Deut 19:19; Isa 32:7; Pss 26:10; 37:12; Prov 24:9), and unchastity (Judg 20:6; Jer 13:27: Hos 6:9–10; Job 31:11; cf. CD 8:6–7; 11QT 66:15 [= Lev 18:13, 14]), but in H (18:17; 19:29; 20:14) and Ezekiel (22:11; 23:35), the meaning is only sexual (Paran 1983: 179).

This condemnatory term is not a legal basis for incest; similarly, *tô'ēbâ* (22bβ); *tebel* (23bβ). They deter because they are shameful. The shame culture that Daube (1969) found in Deuteronomy also prevails in H (see NOTE on 20:12bα).

Two rationales *ša'ărâ* and *zimmâ* are specified perhaps because there are two prohibitions, but the terms apply to both; note that the mother and daughter prohibition (20:14) is also called *zimmâ* (Schwartz 1987: 100). The reason is apparent. The wife's mother, daughter, and granddaughter live in the addressee's household. Hence he can easily find an opportunity—that is, scheme (*zmm*)—to take advantage of them. The most likely scenario, however, is that he has plotted (*zāmam*) with both women to accept a ménage à trois arrangement (see NOTE on 20:14; also 19:29).

18. *And.* The *waw* (here and in the subsequent prohibitions, vv. 18–23) indicates a new section. The previous one dealt with incest (*Keter Torah*); the next one (vv. 18–20) consists of cases that are time-bound—a deceased sister, a menstruant, a widow, or a divorcee (Shadal)—and the final one (vv. 21–23) deals with exceptional situations (see INTRODUCTION to vv. 6–23).

marry. tiqqaḥ. In this verse, *lāqaḥ* can only mean "marry."

a woman . . . to her sister. wĕ'iššâ 'el-'ăhōtāh. The preposition *'el* bears the meaning "with, in addition to." Note the same phrase *'iššâ 'el-'ăhōtāh* 'one to the other' (Exod 26:3), referring to the tabernacle curtains (cf. Josh 13:22; *m. Yeb.* 11:1). The meaning of the prohibition has been subject to vigorous (and vitriolic) debate:

1. The Karaites (in view of analogous wording in Exod 26:3) render *'ăhōtāh* not as "her sister," but as "another (woman)." Then, rendering *liṣrōr* metaphorically as "to inflict pain, misery" on the basis of its primary meaning "to bind" (cf. 2 Sam 20:3), they interpret the verse as prohibiting polygamy only if the husband deprives his wives of their conjugal rights (*Seper Ha-Mibḥar, Keter Torah*). As proof, they cite chap. 20, which contains no punishment for polygamy, an argument that Ibn Ezra dismisses because chap. 20 does not cite any punishment for sex with a granddaughter (v. 17a).

2. The sectaries of Qumran maintain the opposite view. They, too, read *'ăhōtāh* as *'iššâ 'aheret* 'another woman', but fixing their gaze on the word *bĕhayyêhā* 'in her (the wife's) lifetimes', claim that this verse prohibits not only polygamy but also divorce (11QT 57:17–18; CD 4:21; supported by Yadin 1983: 1.347; Tosato 1984; Kampen 1993, but disputed by Sun 1990: 119).

3. The prohibition bans marriage to a sister-in-law during the lifetime of the wife (Philo, *Laws* 3.27; *m. Qid.* 2:7). This, the plain meaning of the words, is

reinforced by the context: the women are related to each other (as in v. 17), the prohibition is time-conditioned (as in v. 19), and 'āḥôt in this chapter means only "sister" (e.g., vv. 12, 13). Sororate marriage (after death) is known among the Assyrians (MAL A § 31) and Hittites (HL § 192), but forbidden during the wife's lifetime (inferred from HL § 194). The rabbis regard such a union as meritorious: no other woman would show the same affection to the orphaned children of a deceased sister (Hertz 1941: 1.180). In other cultures as well, it is considered a preferred marriage (Murdock 1949: 13, cited by Rattray 1987: 539).

producing rivalry. liṣrōr from the root ṣrr 'vex, show hostility' (Exod 23:22; Num 10:9; 25:17–18; 33:55; cf. Ug. ṣr 'vex' and ṣrt 'hostility'; Akk. ṣerru 'enemy' and ṣerretu, the exact cognate of ṣārâ 'second wife, rival' [cf. 1 Sam 1:6]; *Tgs. Onk., Ps.-J., lĕʾa ʿăqā*' and *Tg. Neof., lĕma ʿăqā* 'to cause distress'). The nominal feminine form ṣārā means "rival-wife" (1 Sam 1:6; Sir 37:11; cf. Akk. ṣerretu). The suggestion that this word should take the 'Atnāḥ must be rejected, since it would resemble the implausible Karaite interpretation that marrying a second woman is forbidden only in the case of mistreatment (cf. Ibn Ezra).

her nakedness. ʿerwātāh (i.e., of the second woman). The following word ʿālêhā (untranslated here), literally "in addition to her," i.e. the first wife (cf. Gen 31:50), is rendered by Saadiah and Ḥazzequni as "with her" (cf. 25:31).

during her (sister's) lifetime. bĕḥayyêha. Even if she were divorced (*b. Yeb.* 8b; cf. *m. Yeb.* 4:13). Since this qualification is missing in the prohibition against union with mother and daughter (v. 17a), one must assume that the prohibition continues in force even after the death of either party (Ramban).

Jacob clearly violated this prohibition, leading to domestic strife (Gen 29:28–35; 30:1–2, 14–24). His deed is exonerated by Ibn Ezra on the legal grounds that the prohibition applies solely to Canaan, not to the diaspora. Ramban supports this interpretation by pointing to fact (not a coincidence) that Rachel died upon entering the land. Abravanel objects rightly on two counts: the patriarchs preceded and therefore were exempt from Sinaitic law, and the prohibition is not limited to the holy land but applies everywhere (but see INTRODUCTION to vv. 24–30, and chap. 20, COMMENT D).

19. *approach. tiqrab* (see NOTE on v. 6). That this term refers to sexual relations and not to marriage is shown by its cognate in a similar context in a South Arabic inscription: "Harim, son of awbân, avowed and did penance to Tû-Sanâwî because he drew near [*qrb*] a woman during a period illicit to him [or her]" (*ANET* 665).

The final four sexual prohibitions (menstruation, adultery, sodomy, bestiality, vv. 19–20, 22–23) refer to nonrelatives of either party (Wessely 1846).

during her menstrual impurity. bĕniddat ṭumʾātāh, literally "the menstrual impurity of her impurity." The terms are reversed in *bĕṭumʾat niddātāh*, literally "the impurity of her menstrual impurity" (15:26). This inversion is attested for near synonymous pairs (e.g., in P, *tôlaʿat šānî*, Exod 25:4; *šĕnî tôlaʿat*, Lev 14:4; Yalon 1971: 158, 330), a reference I owe to Greenberg (1995: 75, n. 17). Moreover, the nearly exact quotation of v. 6aβ, *lo'tiqrab lĕgallot ʿerwâ*, v. 19b "signals that the latter verse begins a new paragraph" (D. Stewart, forthcoming dissertation).

Both vv. 18 and 19 deal with time-bound prohibitions; after death (v. 18) and purification (v. 19) cohabitation is permitted (Abravanel; cf. Shadal); v. 20 also falls into this category (see below). No rationale is given. Surely, one was readily at hand: *lĕṭom'â-bāh* 'to defile yourself through her' (v. 20)! The only possible answer is that this verse presumes a knowledge of 15:24 (Kalisch 1867–72), one of the many indications that H is cognizant of P (see Introduction I H). The violation of this prohibition is scored by Ezekiel (18:6). The silence of P concerning the penalty is explained by Abravanel, that P focuses on the effect of impurity on persons and objects but not on divine sanctions for its bearers (cf. vol. 1.940). Nonetheless, the possibility must be considered that P's silence actually betrays its unconcern for or even denial of a penalty (reversing vol. 1.940), except in the instance where impurity bearers come in contact with sancta or neglect to purify themselves. H, however, holds that impurity pollutes not just sancta but the land (see INTRODUCTION to vv. 24–30). YHWH resides not only in the sanctuary but throughout the land. The land, as it were, is also a sanctum, and thus, no differently from P, furtive, unapprehended violations are punishable with *kārēt* (18:29; 20:17–19). Alternatively, and more likely, H overturns P. H subsumes this act under its rubric of moral impurity, which cannot be expunged by purificatory rituals. It is punishable by *kārēt* (20:18) and, if rampant among the Israelites, by exile (see INTRODUCTION to vv. 24–30, and NOTE on v. 24).

The basis for H's penalty is further discussed in the NOTE on 20:18.

20. *You shall not have sexual relations.* *lō-titten šĕkobtĕkā lĕzāra'*, literally "You shall not use your lying for seed" or, more exactly, "You shall not use your penis for sex." According to the former rendering, "for seed" is essential; otherwise, "your lying" would be punishable even for an embrace or a kiss (Ramban). That *šĕkōbet*, however, means "penis," see Orlinsky (1944) and the discussion in vol. 1.927. All other attestations of *nātan šĕkōbet* become clearer in this meaning because they are followed by the preposition *b* 'in' (v. 23; 20:15; Num 5:20).

The term *'erwâ* is not used, since we are not dealing with blood relatives (Hartley 1992). A preferable reason is that *lĕgallōt 'erwâ* is found in every other heterosexual prohibition but this one; hence adultery is found at the bottom of this sublist (vv. 6–18). This expression connotes, according to Ziskind's 1996 attractive theory, that we are dealing with cases where the woman in question is not married; she is widowed, divorced, or as yet unmarried. The same charge is cited by Ezekiel (18:6; 22:11). Ehrlich 1899–1900 (H) takes *lĕzāra'* literally "for seed"; that is, one is forbidden to be contracted by infertile husbands to fertilize their wives. However, there is no evidence for the custom of surrogate fatherhood in antiquity, and this interpretation defies the plain meaning of the text.

One should note that in Israel, adultery is strictly a religious crime. In the ancient Near East, despite the fact that adultery is a "great sin" against the gods, it is a civil crime, commutable and pardonable (details in Milgrom 1990a: 348–50; see now Greengus 1992: 247).

your fellow. *'ămîtĕkā* (5:21; 18:20; 19:11, 15, 17; 24:19; 25:14, 15, 17; Zech 13:7 [abstract]). The root is disputed: *'mm* (Wessely 1846), *'mt* (Ibn Janaḥ), *'mh*

(KB³; its derivation from Akk. *emu* 'father-in-law' > *emūtu* must be rejected since the latter is probably related to *ḥāmôt* 'mother-in-law'). Ezekiel replaces *ʿămît* with *rēaʿ* or *ʾāḥ* (Ezek 18:6, 15, 18; cf. Lev 19:11–13), and thereafter it is lacking in biblical and postbiblical literature, indicating that it is a preexilic term (Hurvitz 1982: 74–78; see NOTE on 19:11).

with your fellow's wife. wĕʾel-ʾēšet ʿămîtĕkā. This wording might imply that sexual relations with a widow or divorcee are forbidden (Ehrlich 1899–1900 [H]). Thus this prohibition must be time-conditioned: it is operative only as long as she is his wife. It should be kept in mind that adultery does not apply to the extramarital relations of a married man with an unmarried woman. Since it was essential to be certain of the paternity of heirs, only the extramarital affairs of the wife is of concern to the legislator (cf. Abravanel on Deut 24:1; Coulanges n.d.: 97).

defile yourself. lĕṭomʾâ. Permanently (Ibn Ezra), since there is no antidotal purification rite. Wessely (1846) cites *nôʾēp ʾiššâ . . . mašḥît napšô* 'He who commits adultery . . . destroys himself [lit. "his soul"]' (Prov 6:32) as proof that we are dealing with nonritual, moral impurity. So, too, 18:23; 19:31; 22:8 (all H; see Introduction I B). Other applications of the root *ṭmʾ* to adultery are found in Num 5:13, 14, 20, 27, 28, 29 and Ezek 18:6, 11, 15; 33:26. However, it is not related to the notion of disgust (Gruber 1990, 1992: 84).

Carmichael (1997: 52, n. 9) disputes my claim (vol. 1.37) that *ṭāmēʾ* in H bears a nonritual sense by arguing that the plague of sterility befalling Abimelech's house—the alleged narrative behind the prohibition of 18:20—falls in the *ṭāmēʾ* categories of Lev 13–15. This is patently wrong. Only scale disease and genital flows generate ritual impurity, not sterility. Note, however, that Carmichael apparently changes his mind: a few pages later, he writes of "the *metaphorical* uncleanness attaching to the adulterer in Lev 18:20."

Adultery and bestiality (v. 23) are the only prohibitions in the entire list containing the root *ṭmʾ*. They are proleptic of the peroration (vv. 24–25), which states that one's own impurity contributes to the impurity of the land. That is, one's own sin affects the welfare of the community, an echo of the basic priestly doctrine of collective responsibility (vol 1.258–61). Considering that of all the listed prohibitions, this one, adultery, was by far the most widespread, the legist may have purposefully attached the impurity label here to allude to its grave implications.

Is not this prohibition superfluous in view of the seventh commandment *lōʾ tinʾāp*? Not at all. The term *nîʾûp* implies the consent of both parties. This prohibition, however, applies even in cases of rape (S. Rattray). Also note that this prohibition, as all the others, is directed to the addressee (except in v. 23b, for obvious reasons). Hence there is no mention of the woman, who also must become defiled (but cf. 20:18).

21. The prohibition against offering child sacrifices to Molek (see the discussion, below) adds a new rationale for eschewing Canaanite practices. The Canaanites were expelled from the land for polluting it not only by their sexual aberrations, but also by their Molek worship. A lopsided imbalance, however, is

thereby created: one idolatrous practice over against seventeen itemized sexual violations, which the redactor tried to rectify in chap. 20 by placing the Molek prohibition first and expanding it over five verses.

dedicate. tittēn. For this meaning, see Exod 30:14 (gift); Num 3:9; 8:16 (Levites); Num 18:12 (first-processed); 1 Sam 1:11 (son). This verb may have been chosen because of its use in vv. 20, 23 (Schwartz 1987: 83). However, it never carries the meaning "sacrifice" (see below, and COMMENT B).

any of your offspring. ûmizzar 'ăkā. This word was chosen because of its use in v. 20 (*Leqah Tob*; Wessely 1846; Noth 1977), or because of its contextual association with the destroyed seed in acts of sodomy (v. 22) and bestiality (v. 23; Abravanel), or, more likely, to include grandchildren who reside with the family and over whom the family head (the addressee) has control (see NOTE on 20:2 (and 20:4), showing that *zera'* is always associated with Molek).

to be sacrificed. lĕha 'ăbîr, literally "to transfer." In matters of property, *nātan* is used for inheriting males, whereas *he 'ĕbîr* is used for bequeathing daughters (*Num. R.* on Num 27:7), or it can connote the transfer of the property from the daughter to her husband or her son (*Sipre* Num. 134; *b. B. Bat* 109b). Thus *he 'ĕbîr* refers to the transfer from one domain to another, but from the qualified to the unqualified. Bequeathing sons, however, does not constitute a transfer; sons are the extension of their fathers and technically part of the same domain (details in Milgrom 1990a: 232).

Here, then, children are transferred to the (unqualified) Molek. What is their fate? There are four main interpretations:

1. Ramban claims that the children are employed in some mantic practice, to judge by the association of this rite with magic (Deut 18:10; 2 Chr 33:6; 2 Kgs 17:17; 21:6). As will be demonstrated in chap. 20, COMMENTS B and C, he is probably correct: Molek worship is associated with necromancy and ancestor worship. But what was of the fate of the child?

2. *Tg. Ps.-J.* reflects the rabbinic view *bĕtasmîštā' lĕšêd bat 'ammĕmîn limĕ 'abbĕrā'* (or *lĕmā 'ĕbĕrā'*) *lĕpûlhānā' nûkrā'â* 'to lie carnally with the daughters of gentiles for impregnation (or transfer) for idolatrous worship', wherein *lĕha 'ăbîr* is related to Rabbinic Hebrew *'ibbēr* 'make pregnant' (already appearing in Job 21:10) and *zar 'ăkā* is rendered literally "your seed" (cf. *Jub* 30:7–16; *m. Meg.* 4:9, but see Albeck 1952: 505; *Sipre* Deut. 171). For details, see Vermes (1981).

Wiesenberg (1986) has provided a new justification for the correctness of the rabbinic view. He cites a number of verses where the verb *nātan* can be rendered as "pour" (Exod 30:18; 40:7; 1 Kgs 8:36; 2 Chr 6:27), with water or rain as the object (he also might have cited Lev 11:38), and, especially, cases where *nātan* is used with the object *šĕkōbet* in a decidedly sexual context (Lev 18:20, 23; 20:15; Num 5:20). The root *škb*, in turn, Wiesenberg points out, has the sense of "pouring out" in *šikbat hattal* (Exod 16:13–14) and, more relevantly, in *šikbat zera'* (Lev 15:16–18, 32, 19:20, 22:4; Num 5:13; see Ibn Ezra, and vol. 1.957).

Of course, Wiesenberg (and the rabbinic view) has the decided advantage of being able to explain why the Molek prohibition was placed among sexual offenses. However, Wiesenberg's "proof" cannot be sustained: (1) *nātan mayim / māṭār* can also—and preferably—be rendered "grant water / rain" (e.g., Deut 11:14; cf. v. 15), and *yuttan mayim ʿal-zeraʿ* (Lev 11:38) can only mean "if the seed is moist"; that is, water has been in contact with and not necessarily poured on the seed; (2) the phrase *nātan šĕkōbet* 'spill a spilling' would be a redundancy; (3) in our verse, what sense would *nātan lĕhaʿăbîr* have? (4) above all, the key term *lammōlek*, clearly a reference to a god (see below), would be left unexplained; (5) Wiesenberg explains the objection in *m. Meg.* 4:9 to the public expression of this interpretation—sexual intercourse with gentiles—as the fear of inciting anti-Jewish acts by the Romans. However, since intermarriage with gentiles is explicitly and disparagingly banned in Exod 34:15–16; Deut 7:3 (not to speak of Ezra 9), why the need to resort to the alleged circumlocutions and euphemism of Lev 18:21?

In my opinion, the rabbis were fully aware that they were not imparting the plain meaning of the text. Their purpose (and that of *Jubilees*), I submit, was to include sexual intercourse with a gentile among the forbidden sexual liaisons (Cohen 1983). They resort to this forced exegesis since, surprisingly, intermarriage is not included in this list (or in chap. 20) of forbidden sexual unions. It is, in fact, startling that there is no prohibition against intermarriage in *all* the priestly texts, in H as well as P. This puzzle is explored in COMMENT A. One deduction needs to be made here: this chapter cannot be a product of the exilic or postexilic age, when intermarriage became a cardinal issue.

3. R. Judah ben Elai (*Sipre* Deut. 171; cf. *m. Sanh.* 7:7), taking *lĕhaʿăbîr* literally as "transfer," holds that it refers to the dedication of a child to pagan service. This view has been revived and amplified by Weinfeld (1969; 1971a; 1972a; 1978; cf. Deller 1965; Platorati 1978; Albertz 1994: 192–93), who cites evidence from ancient Near Eastern and classical sources (see also Gaster 1962: 154a) that such dedications did indeed take place. This interpretation is further supported by the LXX reading *la ʿăbōd* 'to worship' (see also Sam. *leha ʿăbîd* 'to enslave').

Smith (1975a) has challenged Weinfeld's argument on the grounds that the evidence from the rabbis must be discounted, since they wanted to eliminate all references to killing. In particular, Smith cites Num 31:23, where *ta ʿăbîru bāʾēš* must imply that an inflammable object would be burned. However, his scriptural argument has already been parried by Ibn Ezra[2], who points out that our verse omits the decisive word *bāʾēš* 'in fire'. Moreover, it can be argued that Num 31:23 applies only to metals, which can undergo burning, but is inapplicable to human beings (Paran 1983: 207, n. 522). Also Weinfeld (1978: 412), in a rebuttal to Smith (1978), adds the argument that "the conventional verbs for sacrificing such as: *zbḥ, šḥṭ, hqryb* are never used in the context of offering to Molek."

Weinfeld's new argument, however, cannot be sustained. It is precisely the words for sacrificial slaughter *zbḥ* and *šḥṭ* that occur together with *nātan* and *he ʿĕbîr* in another verse, Ezek 16:21. And if the objection is raised that this verse refers to idolatrous worship in general, which does not necessarily include the

Molek, it still should be noted that it offers a clear case where *he ʿĕbîr* by itself, without the addition *bāʾēš*, refers to sacrificial slaughter (see also 23:37–39, and below). Finally, *bāʾēš* may have been added for emphasis (not for qualification) in order to make clear that the "transference" is into fire. Undoubtedly, the issue remains vexed, but no decision can be attempted until the chief rival solution has its say.

4. There is no doubt that child sacrifice was practiced in the ancient world (Ackerman 1992: 117–26). Especially impressive are the archaeological excavations in Phoenician colonies, especially Carthage, that have unearthed special precincts in cemeteries containing hundreds of urns, dating as early as the eighth century B.C.E., that contain bones of children and animals (but no adults), many of which are buried beneath steles inscribed with dedications to gods (Stager and Wolff 1984). Reliefs from about 500 B.C.E. found at Pozo Moro, Spain, a site bearing Phoenician influence, show an open-mouthed, two-headed monster receiving offerings of children in bowls (Almagro-Gorbea 1980; Kennedy 1981).

Neither can there be any question that the practice of "burning babies" in pagan worship is attested in the Bible (Deut 12:31bβ; 18:10; 2 Kgs 16:3b [= 2 Chr 28:3]; 17:17a, 31; 21:6; 23:10; Isa 30:33; Jer 7:31; 19:5; Ezek 16:21; 20:31; 23:37; Ps 106:37–39). Particularly strong is the evidence of 2 Kgs 23:10:

> *wĕṭimmēʾ ʾet-hattōpet ʾăšer bĕgê bĕnê(K)/ben(Q)-hinnōm lĕbiltî lĕha ʿăbîr ʾîš et-bĕnô wĕʾet-bittô bāʾēš lammōlek*

> He also defiled Topheth, which is in the Valley of Ben-hinnom, so that no one might consign his son or daughter to the fire of Molek.

All the identifying words are here: *tōpet* 'cauldron' (see below), Ben-hinnom (the site of the cult), *lĕha ʿăbîr bāʾēš* (burning), and *mōlek* (the god). The argument that "the legal-historical, in contrast to the prophetic-poetic, sources do not mention real burning" (Weinfeld 1971a: 230) can be challenged. The cited verse, 2 Kgs 23:10, is embedded in a chapter that contains bona fide historical information. Moreover, the fact that the cultic practice described in this verse is attributed to Josiah's immediate predecessors, who did, indeed, sacrifice their children (2 Kgs 16:3; 21:6), lends weight to the identification of the other instances of sacrificing children with Molek worship (e.g., Deut 12:31; 18:10 [a legal passage!]). Furthermore, the attestation of the telltale words, especially *tōpet*, in Jer 7:31 (cf. Isa 30:33), and Ezekiel's unambiguous statement that *bayyôm hahûʾ* 'on the same day' *he ʿĕbîrû lāhem lĕʾoklâ* 'they consigned (their children) to them (idols) for consumption' (Ezek 23:39) clearly indicates that both prophets are referring to the sacrifice of children at the Topheth of Molek in the Valley of Ben-hinnom at the foot of the Temple Mount.

Ezekiel's use of the verb *ʿābar* is again attested in Ezek 39:11. Irwin (1995) argues compellingly that this entire verse is a word play on the Molek sacrifice. It describes how the forces of Gog are passing through (*hā ʿōbĕrîm*) on their way to their burial in *gê' hămôn gôg*, an obvious reference to the site of the Molek sacrifice *gê-hinnōm* (Josh 15:8 = *gê' ben-hinnōm*, Jer 7:31).

For other possible references to the god Molek/Malik, see Isa 30:33; Heider (1985) on Isa 57:5, 9; Day (1989: 58–64, 6a) on Amos 5:26 LXX; and Knohl (1995: 219, n. 67) on Ps 106:37 (where *šēdîm* = *šĕ'îrîm*) (see NOTE on Lev 17:7).

Krahmalkov (1996) has demonstrated that the euphemistic language used by the Phoenicians for child sacrifices, "brought or carried to the gods," indicates that they denied and concealed from themselves the enormity of the cruelty they practiced. This suggests that perhaps in Israel the language *nātan* / *he'ĕbîr* functioned similarly as a euphemistic cover for the identical rite. It is surely significant that in both cultures the term *zābaḥ* 'sacrifice' is never employed.

Finally, Schwartz (1987: 82, 250, nn. 38–40) adds an indirect, but telling, argument. First, he cites my observation that the induction of the Levites is described as a sacrifice (Milgrom 1985a: 59; 1990a: 369–71) and, in particular, that the *tĕnûpâ* ritual is required for the Levites (Num 8:11, 13, 15, 21), but for no other human being (Milgrom 1973: 40; 1983c: 141). Then, he remarks that a whole battery of sacrificial terms is employed regarding the transfer of the Levites from the profane to the sacred realm: *hapqēd* 'appoint' (Num 1:50); *haqrēb* 'advance' (Num 3:6); *wĕhibdaltā* 'you shall separate' (Num 8:14); *wĕlāqaḥtā* 'you shall take' (Num 3:41; cf. Num 3:12, 45; 8:16, 18); *wā'ettĕnâ* 'I assigned' (Num 8:19), but not the most obvious term of all—*he'ĕbîr* (the term *hiqdîš* 'sacrificed' is also assiduously avoided, but for another reason entirely: not to endow priestly status on the Levites; Milgrom 1990a: 64). The only reason can be that the sacrificial term *he'ĕbîr* is exclusively reserved to denote burning, immolation.

Thus the evidence tilts toward the view that Lev 18:21 is expressly prohibiting the practice of sacrificing children to Molek. Concerning the question of whether this worship was limited to the sacrifice of the firstborn male, see COMMENT B. And concerning the misbegotten view (Elliger 1955: 17; Zimmerli 1979: 1.344) that only newly born children of cult prostitutes were sacrificed to Molek, see the NOTE on 19:29.

to Molek. The name is found five times in Leviticus (18:21; 20:2, 3, 4, 5) and in 2 Kgs 11:7 (where, however, for *mōlek*, read *milkōm*, BHS); 23:10; Jer 32:35, and probably Isa 30:33; 57:9 and Zeph 1:5 (*melek* > *mōlek*). It probably means "ruler." But who is Molek? A number of proposals follow in their chronological order:

1. The oldest is that of R. Ḥanina b. Antigonus: the name Molek "teaches that the same law applies to whatever they proclaimed as king, even a pebble or a splinter" (*b. Sanh.* 64a). According to his statement, Molek relates to the noun *melek* 'king' or the participle *mōlēk* '(the one who) rules' (supported by LXX *archon*), but also to idolatry of any kind. However, despite the definite article, the word must be a proper name, as will be discussed below.

2. *Mōlek* stands for (or should be read as) the Ammonite god *milkōm* (Ibn Ezra, Ramban). Supporting this identification is that one attestation of *mōlek* (1 Kgs 11:7) should be read *milkōm* (LXX[L]; Pesh.). However, this identification

must be rejected not only because 1 Kgs 11:7 expressly labels this god as "the abomination of the Ammonites" (cf. 1 Kgs 11:5, 7), but also because 2 Kgs 23:10, 13 clearly distinguish between the two deities and specify that the cult center of Milcom was not in the Hinnom Valley but at a site south of Jerusalem.

3. The rabbinic view (no. 1) was revived by Geiger (1857: 301), but explained differently: the original name *melek* was distorted as *mōlek* in order to echo the word *bōšet* 'shame'. As evidence, Geiger pointed to Ishbaal (1 Chr 8:33; 9:39) also attested as Ish-bosheth (2 Sam 2:10), Merib-baal (1 Chr 8:34; 9:40) occurring as Mephibosheth (e.g., 2 Sam 4:4), Jerubbaal (Judg 6:32) as Jerubbesheth (2 Sam 11:21), and the goddess Astarte/Ashtart regularly found as Ashtoreth (e.g., 1 Kgs 11:5, 33). This view is vigorously supported by Day (1989: 56–58). It is contested by Tsevat (1975), who argues for the retention of MT *mōlek*, and by Heider (1985: 223–28), who opts for the participle *mōlēk*, but their own proposals have, in my opinion, been decisively refuted by Day (1989: 56–58).

4. In 1935, Eissfeldt (later amplified by Mosca 1975; Ackerman 1992: 131–37; Müller 1995) proposed the radical view that Molek was not the name of a deity, but a kind of sacrifice (accepted but modified by de Vaux 1964: 73–90; Müller 1984; Stager and Wolff 1984: 47) on the basis of alleged Punic evidence. Eissfeldt's thesis, however, has been challenged by a number of scholars (see Weinfeld 1972a: 133–40; Day 1989: 4–13), and today, to my knowledge, only few seriously adhere to this view (Edelman 1987; Smith 1990: 132–38). Decisive evidence is provided by the Bible itself: the expression *liznôt 'aḥărê hammōlek* 'to go astray after Molek' (20:5) can in no way refer to a sacrifice; on the contrary, the expression *zānâ 'aḥărê* consistently refers to the pursuit of other gods (e.g., Exod 34:15, 16; Deut 31:16; Ezek 6:9; 20:30)—a point overlooked by Edelman in her defense of Eissfeldt and Mosca.

A preliminary reading of the recently discovered (as yet unpublished) eighth-century Incirli (eastern Turkey) stele contains the terms *mlk swsym, mlk 'dm, mlk bn bkr*, namely, *mlk* of horses, men and cattle, which certainly demonstrates that *mlk* denotes "gift, tribute." However, the language is Phoenician, and in the latter's ambience, as Eissfeldt (1935) has shown, this is precisely the meaning of *mlk*—but not in the Bible. A note from Stephen Kaufman (Feb. 20, 1997), who together with Bruce Zuckerman is publishing the inscription, informs me that they have a completely new reading. The term *mlk*, however, remains the same, "sacrifice," but it seems to refer to prisoners of war.

5. Berlin (1994: 76–77) following Ehrlich among others, translates *malkām* (Zeph 1:5) as "their melekh"—that is, their Molek god—and therefore proposes "that Molekh or *melek* is not the personal name of a specific god, but rather an epithet that could be applied to any god connected with the fire ritual." For support, she points to "the Sepharirtes burned their children to Adrammelech (= Adadmelech: Mazar 1950: 116–17) and Anammelech" (2 Kgs 17:31) and the fact that Molek always appears with a definite article (except in 1 Kgs 11:7, where the reference is to Milcom; see no. 2).

However, *melek* in the above-cited theophoric names can just be proper names, an instance where two gods have been fused, as Hadadrimmon (Zech

12:11), meaning "Hadad is Rimmon" (Rimmon / *rammān* 'the thunderer' [cf. Greenfield 1976] is an independent deity; cf. 2 Kgs 5:18); Ba'lu-Haddu in the Amarna letters; Šamši-Adad, an Assyrian monarch; and *'ēl 'elyôn* (Gen 14:18–20, 22). That the last originally referred to two deities is conclusively demonstrated by *'ēl wĕ 'alyān* in Sefire A11; so, too, among the Phoenicians (cf. Philo of Byblos) and the Hurrians-Hittites. To be sure, in the Bible *'elyôn* is an epithet of El 'the most high', but there can be no doubt that originally it was an independent deity (cf. Lack 1962; Rendtorff 1967b; Cross 1973: 50–52). Finally, it is not insignificant that most scholars date the composition of Zephaniah in the reign of Josiah, as stated in the superscription, in the prereform period—when Molek worship still flourished (cf. 2 Kgs 23:10). Thus I regard *malkām* (Zeph 1:5) as an error for *mōlek* (but see the reservations of Berlin 1994: 33–43, based on Ben Zvi 1991a). As for the definite article, the MT must be evaluated by the millennium-older LXX, which consistently omits the article in all its attestations. It may have been deliberately inserted by the Masoretes to eliminate its association with a specific deity in conformance with the rabbinic interpretation (no. 1).

Nonetheless and notwithstanding all the above objections, it cannot be doubted that the consistent presence of the definite article is a weighty contention. The *mōlek* is comparable to the *ba'al*, which similarly is always affixed with a definite article. That *ba'al* can serve as a generic and not as the name of a specific deity is evidenced by the many occurrences of the plural *bĕ 'ālîm*. The evidence is marshaled in the NOTE on "and thereby not desecrate the name of your God," below. Thus the possibility must be granted that *mōlek* is also not a personal name but a title, in which case Geiger's (1857:301) suggestion *mōlek* < *melek* 'king' (no. 3) might be sustained. A doubt, however, still remains concerning Berlin's (1994) proposal as the plural *mĕlākîm* is not attested. Thus if *mōlek* / *melek* is a title, it could be that of a specific deity (see further below).

6. There can be no question that a deity *mlk* was known in the ancient Near East, as attested by the theophoric element in Akkadian *Adad-milki* (Weinfeld 1972a: 144–49; but cf. Day 1989: 41–46; Ackerman 1992: 128–30); Ugaritic *mlk* (*KTU* 1.100, l. 41; 1.107, l. 17); a god *mlk*/Malik, who appears in various personal names from Ebla and Mari; and an angel of hell, Mālik, attested in the Koran 43:77. His original provenance, however, is disputed: Phoenicia (de Vaux 1964: 75–90), Mesopotamia (Weinfeld 1972a), or Syro-Palestine (Heider 1985; 1995). The origin of the cult would by itself not be a productive inquiry, but the evidence produced by Heider that biblical Molek stems from a chthonic Mesopotamian deity Malik is of extreme significance, and it is developed in chap. 20, COMMENT B. Suffice it here to add that Day (1989: 24–31; now supported by Heider 1992: 897b) supports Heider's view but argues, convincingly in my opinion, that Israel derives its Molek cult directly from the Canaanites. It is also possible that the cult of Molek was imported by the Sepharvites whom the Assyrians settled in North Israel at the end of the eighth century (2 Kgs 17:31). They probably stemmed from Syria, to judge by the name of their god Adrammelekh, a misspelling of Adadmelekh 'Adad-is-King' (Levine 1989a: 260;

see also Cogan and Tadmor 1988: 212). MT Adrammelekh, however, is defended by Millard (1995), who derives it from *'addîr-melek* 'The glorious one is king' or *'addîr-molek* 'Molek is king'. Molek sacrifices were offered in the Valley of Hinnom, just below the western side of the Temple Mount at the Topheth (a word cognate with Aramaic *tapyā* and Syriac *tĕpayā/tĕpāyā* meaning "furnace, fire-place"; see Day 1989: 24–28).

7. The most recent view is that of Gerstenberger (1996: 292), who is presumably forced by his postexilic assumptions to postulate that Molek is a "fictitious deity" invented by later theologians in order "to cleanse YHWH from the suspicion of having actually demanded such an abomination" as child sacrifice. No comment required.

In sum, only interpretations nos. 3, 5, and 6 thus far remain viable. As will be argued below (see NOTE on "and thereby not desecrate the name of your God"), all three are partially correct. Most likely, *mōlek* stands for Malik, a Mesopotamian chthonic deity whose cult was transmitted to Israel via the Canaanites (no. 6), and, possibly, it is the title of a (other?) chthonic deity (deities?) (no. 5). Many in the populace (in contrast to priestly and prophetic circles) vocalized the name as *hammelek*, 'the king', and thereby believed that their worship was entirely legitimate. The Masoretes, on their part, vocalized Malik as *mōlek* in order to deride it. It may be of significance that the one case that seems to have escaped the notice of the Masoretes is the word *lammelek* in Isa 30:33. To be sure, the Masoretes retained this pronunciation because they assumed that this title referred to the king of Assyria, who, in their view, would be offered on the Tophet as part of YHWH's forthcoming universal purge (see also v. 31). However, the greater likelihood is that this vocalization preserves the actual name of the deity worshiped by the general populace, an indication of its association with YHWH. In any case, the medium of worship was child sacrifice.

Finally, the question of why Molek worship was inserted among laws banning illicit sexual practices must be addressed: six solutions have been offered, the first four of which are cited by Hartley (1992: 336–37):

1. "The offering of children to Molek (could) threaten a clan's solidarity or cause great discord among family members." But what if the clan accepts child sacrifice as part of its culture, as did the Carthaginians and other Punic settlements?

2. Molek worship is "considered abhorrent and extremely defiling." But so are other idolatrous practices labeled *tô'ēbâ* 'abomination' (cf. Deut 12:31; 13:15; 17:4; 27:15), and yet they are not included in Lev 18. Moreover, Molek worship is singularly condemned as a desecration of God's name (v. 21b), not as an abomination.

3. "The Israelite social consciousness connected them"—that is, incest with idolatry. Again, the exclusive focus on Molek is left unexplained.

4. "Molek worship may be associated with ancestral worship, making it more understandable why these laws against Molek have been placed with other laws regarding intimate family matters." As will be shown (see chap. 20, COMMENT

B), the assumption that Molek was an underworld deity associated with the worship of the dead can be validated. It will also be shown (see chap. 20, COMMENT C) that ancestor worship was rife in ancient Israel, particularly during the eighth century, the time of the composition of most of H, and that, plausibly, Molek was a vaunted instrument by which the departed ancestors could be consulted (hence the juxtaposition of necromancy with Molek, 20:1–6). However, the *'ôb* and *yiddĕ'ōnî*, whose necromantic credentials are beyond question (see chap. 20, COMMENT B), are not listed in Lev 18. Indeed, as I shall argue, what singles out Molek from all other necromantic mediums is his identification with YHWH, the god of Israel, as intimated by the motive clause attached to the Molek prohibition (v. 21b; see below).

5. Child sacrifice, particularly on the scale practiced in Carthage, may have been a means of controlling population, of consolidating patrimony, or of providing a hedge against poverty (Stager and Wolff 1984: 50). The inalienable worth of each individual as having been created in the divine image would, for the biblical authors, have led to the designation of child sacrifice as murder, punishable by death (20:2). This reason, however, might have applied to urbanized, territorially limited Carthage, but not to Israel, in any period. Moreover, Molek worship was sporadic, infrequent. For population control, one would have expected child sacrifices on an extensive scale, like that in Carthage.

6. Schwartz (forthcoming) suggests that Molek worship was included among prohibited sexual unions because both were labeled *tô'ēbōt* 'abominations' for which the expulsion of the Canaanites did, and the Israelites would, take place (vv. 25–28). Strikingly, the same rationale is cited by the deuteronomist: "Let no one be found among you who consigns [*ma'ăbîr*] his son or daughter to the fire. . . . For anyone who does such things is abhorrent to YHWH [*tô'ăbat YHWH*], and it is because of these abhorrent things [*hattô'ēbōt hā'ēlleh*] that YHWH your God is dispossessing them before you" (Deut 18:10–12). Thus both H and D cite Molek worship as a cause for the expulsion of the Canaanites, but whereas D lists Molek among other abominable magical rites, H adds it to its list of abominable sexual practices. Furthermore, elsewhere the H legist uses the verb *zānâ* 'whore' in describing Molek worship (20:5 [bis]), thereby associating it with a sexual offense (M. Hildenbrand).

As for the placement of the Molek prohibition after v. 20, Schwartz (forthcoming) points to the repetition of the words *tittēn* and *zera'* in v. 21, which has caused the redundance of *tittēn* and *lĕha'ăbîr*, both meaning, in essence, "dedicate," instead of the use of either *tittēn* or *ta'ăbîr*.

Finally, what makes Molek worship such an egregious crime is that it was practiced in God's land by the Canaanites, causing its pollution and the expulsion of its inhabitants (a view also held by D; cf. Deut 18:9–12), a fate that awaits Israel if it does the same (Lev 18:24–30).

In sum, H found it necessary to incorporate Molek into this chapter because it held that the violation of two prohibitions incumbent on and practiced by the Canaanites — Molek worship and illicit sexual unions — would also condemn Israel to destruction and exile.

and thereby not desecrate the name of your God. wĕlōʾ tĕḥallēl ʾet-šēm ʾĕlōhêkā.
Of the seventy-five loci of the root *ḥll* in the Bible, fifty are concentrated in
priestly texts and Ezekiel. Yet of those fifty, forty-nine are found in H and Ezekiel,
and only one in P (Num 30:3, but tellingly not with the name of God). The statistics reveal more: the idiom *ḥillēl šēm* 'desecrate the name of (God)' occurs six
times in H (18:21; 19:12; 20:3; 21:6; 22:2, 32), nine times in Ezekiel (20:9, 14,
22, 39; 36:20, 21, 22, 23; 39:7), four times elsewhere (Isa 48:9–11; Jer 34:16;
Amos 2:7; Mal 1:11–12)—but *not once in P.* Furthermore, both P and H have
pericopes dealing with false oaths (5:20–26; 19:11–13), but whereas the former
labels this offense as *maʿal baYHWH,* the latter condemns it as *ḥillēl šēm YHWH.*
This leads ineluctably to the conclusion that *ḥillēl šēm* is H's term for *maʿal*
'desecration', and thereby provides an unassailable linguistic criterion for distinguishing between P and H (details in Milgrom 1976a: 86–89).

In the priestly lexicon, the verb *ḥillēl* is a precise, technical term. To desecrate implies a holy object. Thus the expression *ḥillēl ʾet- haššabbāt* (Exod 31:14;
Ezek 20:13, 21, 24; 22:8; cf. Neh 13:17, 18) presumes that the sabbath is holy,
a presumption confirmed in 23:3. In our case, the holiness of the divine name
is made explicit.

The question is: Why is Molek worship, but not the other prohibitions in
chap. 18 (and in chap. 20; see v. 3), called a desecration of God's name? To
put the question differently: What is it about Molek worship that warranted this
designation? Three of the remaining instances of this phrase in H can be explained; they deal with priests or sacrifices (21:6; 22:2, 32), which, being
YHWH's sancta, are associated with his name. The remaining instance, the false
oath (19:12), is more illuminating. It involves using the name of God in a false
oath—that is, making YHWH an accomplice in a crime—most likely, in offering false testimony in court. The tentative conclusion deriving from the analogy is clear: the sin of Molek worship is egregious because the name of YHWH
is associated with it.

Can this conclusion be substantiated? Berlin (1994: 77) has suggested that
hannišbāʾîm laYHWH wĕhannišbāʾîm bĕmalkām 'swearing loyalty to YHWH and
swearing loyalty to Molek' (Zeph 1:5b, see her interpretation of Molek, no. 5,
above) indicates that YHWH's name was invoked during the Molek rite. Thus
for the people-at-large, the worship of Molek is compatible with the worship of
YHWH.

Also, if *melek* in Isa 30:33 stands for Molek, then the verse is stating that Molek
is acting on behalf of YHWH to bury Assyria (cf. v. 31) in the underworld. And
even if *melek* stands for the king of Assyria (unmentioned in context, but see Isa
14:3–23, 24–27, where the Assyrian king prefigures his kingdom), the fact that
he will be incinerated in the Topheth, where sacrifices to Molek were offered
(see no. 6, above), indicates that Molek worship was a licit practice.

In addition, three (deuteronomistic) passages from Jeremiah can be marshaled
for support:

*ûbānû bāmôt hattōpet ʾăšer bĕgēʾ ben-hinnōm liśrōp ʾet-bĕnêhem wĕʾet-
bĕnōtêhem bāʾēš ʾăšer lōʾ ṣiwwîtî wĕlōʾ ʿālĕtâ ʿal-libbî*

And they built the shrine [sing. with the LXX and *Tg.*] of Topheth, which is in the valley of Hinnom, to burn their sons and daughters in the fire—which I did not command, and which did not come into my mind. (Jer 7:31)

ûbānû ʾet-bāmôt habbaʿal liśrōp ʾet-běnêhem bāʾēš ʿōlôt labbāʿal ʾăšer lōʾ-ṣiwwîtî wělōʾ dibbartî wělōʾ ʿālětâ ʿal-libbî

And they built the shrines of Baal to burn their sons in fire as burnt offerings to Baal—which I did not command, and did not decree, and which did not come into my mind. (Jer 19:5)

wayyibnu ʾet-bāmôt habbaʿal ʾăšer běgēʾ ben-hinnōm lěhaʿăbîr ʾet-běnêhem wěʾet běnôtêhem lammōlek ʾăšer lōʾ-ṣiwwîtîm wělōʾ ʿālětâ ʿal-libbî laʿăśot hattôʿēbâ hazzōʾt

They built the shrines of Baal that are in the valley of Hinnom to offer up their sons and their daughters to Molek—which I did not command, and which did not come into my mind (that they should) do this abomination. (Jer 32:35a)

The explicit mention of Topheth, Hinnom, and Molek and the critical verb *heʿěbîr* in Jer 7:31 and/or Jer 32:35a ensures the identification of these two verses with the Molek cult. The occurrence of the phrase "which I did not command, and which did not come into my mind" in all three passages raises the possibility that Jer 19:5 is also a reference to Molek worship. This possibility turns to probability in view of the following verse: "Assuredly, a time is coming—declares YHWH—when *this place* shall no longer be called Topheth or Valley of Ben-hinnom, but Valley of Slaughter" (Jer 19:6; cf. 7:32). The reason that in the future the Topheth will be called the "Valley of Slaughter" is explicated further on in the chapter: God will place Jerusalem under siege when *wěhaʾăkaltîm ʾet-běśar běnêhem wěʾēt běśar běnôtêhem* 'I will cause them to eat the flesh of their sons and the flesh of their daughters' (Jer 19:9). God punishes by the principle of measure for measure. They who cause Molek to eat the flesh of their sons and daughters will now be compelled to do the same. Note that Jeremiah uses the same verb *heʾěkîl* in a similar fashion. Israel is guilty because "Its tongue is a sharpened arrow; through its mouth it speaks deceit" (Jer 9:7). Hence YHWH says, "I am causing that people to eat [*maʾăkîlām*] wormwood and to drink poisonous water." Once again, measure for measure (see the discussion of this principle in INTRODUCTION to 26:3–39).

The juxtaposition or confusion of Baal with Molek is explained by Heider (1985: 340) as the attribution of "all competition to the strictly monotheistic Yahweh worship . . . as the cult of Yahweh's ancient foe in the North, Baal." It should be recalled that in popular religion, Baal could syncretistically be equated with YHWH, to judge by Hosea's declaration: "And in that day—says YHWH—you will call me 'my husband' and no longer will you call me 'my Baal' (Hos 2:18; cf. also the name Bealiah, lit. "Yahweh is [my] Baal," 1 Chr 12:6), where *baʿal* is used paronomastically to mean "Baal" and "master." The fact that in all fifty-eight occurrences of the singular *baʿal*, it always contains the definite article and, especially, that it also appears as the plural *habbě'ālîm* (Judg 2:11; 3:7; 8:33; 10:6; 1 Sam 7:4; 12:10; 1 Kgs 18:18; Jer 2:23; 9:13; Hos 2:15, 19; 11:2; and throughout Chronicles) clearly indicates that it is not a proper name but a title. Either it is a synonym for idols—that is, images of other gods (Hos 11:2)—or, as argued by Halpern (1987: 93–95), it is a generic for the divine assembly, the *şěbā' haššāmayim* (1 Kgs 22:19 = 2 Chr 18:18)—that is, the stars (Judg 5:20; Jer 8:2; 19:13; 33:22; Dan 8:10), YHWH's celestial troops (Josh 5:14–15; Isa 13:4; 24:21). Indeed, the *ba'al* may be identified with the heavenly bodies in 2 Kgs 23:5, where the series that follows "the sun, the moon, the constellations and all the host of heaven" is not introduced by the conjunctive *waw* (see also Ps 148:1–3).

Furthermore, the fact that *ba'al* is also equated with *mōlek* (Jer 19:5; 32:35a, see above) indicates that *mōlek*, attested only with the definite article, may be a title. Or just as *ba'al* may be a generic for the divine assembly, as argued above, so *mōlek* may be a generic for the divinities associated with the underworld (Berlin 1994; see no. 5, above). Unlike *ba'al*, however, *mōlek* is never found in the plural. Thus it is just as likely that the purported underworld deities have been subsumed under one title and identified with a specific deity, Malik (see no. 6, above).

In any event, that the definite article is always affixed to *mōlek* indicates that Scripture has presumed the pronounciation of this name by the people-at-large: *hammelek* 'the king', even though it actually refers to the deity Malik. Whether *hammelek* is a title that stands for the plurality of the underworld deities or the name of a specific deity, the fact that it may be subsumed under YHWH (as the *ba'al*[?]), shows how easily the popular mind could fuse the two without finding any incongruity in worshiping the one alongside the other.

As Molek became associated with YHWH or Baal, so he may have been linked with other gods. Alternatively, each deity may have been worshiped separately, as in any polytheistic system (cf. 2 Kgs 5:17–18; 17:24–34a). Thus the near total attestation of YHWH elements in the theophoric names in Tigay's (1986: 37–41) onomastic and inscriptional collection does not necessarily indicate a preexilic monotheism in Judah, but, as trenchantly argued by Knauf (1989–90: 238–40; cf. Niehr 1996: 54), it only points to YHWH as the supreme state deity, which might represent the beliefs of townspeople, not the peasantry. The latter may have harbored a different loyalty to the gods in its pantheon.

Thus there can be no doubt that the phrase "which I did not command and which did not come to my mind" can only mean that the Molek devotees harbored the belief that YHWH had acquiesced to this worship, which Jeremiah vigorously and repeatedly repudiates. This folk belief and Jeremiah's repudiation of it are adumbrated in the prophet's (or his tradents') theological source— Deuteronomy. First, *'ăšer lō'-şiwwîtî* 'which I did not command' is D phraseology. In Deut 18:20, it refers to false prophecy uttered in YHWH's name. In Deut 17:3, it describes astral worship associated with the worship of YHWH (but not that the heavenly bodies are his images: Taylor 1994; Schmidt 1996b: 88).

That astral bodies, including the sun, were worshiped by Israelites is expressly indicated by Deut 4:19; 17:3; 2 Kgs 21:3–5; 23:4–9; Jer 8:1–3; 19:13; Ezek

8:16–18; Zeph 1:4–6 (*m. Suk.* 5:4; cf. McKay 1973: 45–49; Cogan 1974: 84–87; Tigay 1996: 50). Moreover, archaeological evidence points, in particular, to the sun as an object of worship (Greenberg 1979: 104):

> That the people should have revered them is no wonder, since even the biblical authors ascribed "dominion" to the sun and moon (Gen 1:15 [cf. Pss 103:20–21; 136:8–9—J.M.]). Psalm 83 [82—J.M.] reflects a protest against the entrenched idea that the government of the world was parcelled out among the divine beings. . . . Divine government thus had two levels: a higher, that of the "Gods of gods" (Deut 10:17), who at the beginning reserved Israel for himself (32:9), and a lower, that of his suite, to whom the rest of the peoples were allocated (Deut 4:19 LXX and Qumran fragment). Now, if the biblical authors themselves assigned dominions to members of the divine suite, simple folk could hardly be blamed for rendering them homage.

Even more significant is Deut 18:9–22, which deals with the prophet, the fourth and final national authority figure projected in D (after the judiciary, king, and clergy, 16:18–18:8). The ten illegitimate communications of the divine will, with which this pericope begins (vv. 10–11), do not include consultants of other gods; the term *ʾĕlōhîm ʾăḥērîm* (eighteen times in D), *ʾĕlōhêhem* (for child sacrifice! 12:31) would have been used. In D's strict monotheism, other gods are "no-gods" (32:17) or pejoratives—for example, *gillûlîm* (29:16), *tôʿēbâ* (7:26; 12:35; 18:12), *šiqqûṣîm* (29:16). Note that *ʾăšērâ* (7:5; 12:3; 17:2) is not a proper name, but refers to wooden pillars. In fact, other gods are nameless (except for *baʿal pĕʿôr*, a sin of the past, 4:3). Perhaps this accounts for the absence of Molek as the designee for child sacrifice (v. 10a; see below). Among the illegitimate channels for consulting YHWH, we find *wĕšōʾēl ʾôb wĕyiddĕʿōnî wĕdōrēš ʾel-hammētîm* (v. 11b). The first two are discussed in chap. 20, COMMENT B; the third is explicated by Ramban as "one who performs necromancy by any other means" (described in *Sipre* and *t. Sanh.* 10:7). Tigay (1996: 173) offers "one who sits in tombs" (Isa 65:4) as an example. But what is *maʿăbîr bĕnôûbittô bāʾēš* (v. 10a) doing in this list? As demonstrated in the texts cited above, the telltale phrase *maʿăbîr bāʾēš* indicates that the reference is to Molek worship. This passage emphatically denies that YHWH reveals his will through any of these pretenders. Rather, "YHWH your God will raise up for you a prophet from your own people, like myself (Moses); him you shall heed" (v. 15).

Deut 12:29–31 leads to a similar conclusion; lest Israel be seduced by the Molek cult, saying *wĕʾeʿĕśśeh-kēn gam-ʾānî* 'and I shall do the same' (v. 30bγ), D exhorts *lōʾ-taʿăśeh kēn laYHWH ʾĕlōhêkā* 'You shall not do the same for YHWH your God' (v. 31a). As pointed out by Heider (1985: 260–61), this dialogic exchange implies that Israel intends to worship YHWH the same way that the Canaanites worship the Molek, a clear indication that in the Israelite popular mind the two deities are associated (but not identified, see below).

The thesis must therefore be seriously considered that many Israelites saw no incongruity in worshiping Yahweh and Molek simultaneously. This practice is clearly what Ezekiel had in mind when he condemns those who "On the very day that they slaughtered their children to their fetishes, they entered my sanctuary to desecrate it. That is what they did in my house" (Ezek 23:39). This interpretation is buttressed by another Ezekielian statement:

we'ēt-šēm qodšî lō' tĕhallĕlû-ʿôd bĕmattĕnôtêkem ûbĕgillûlêkem

And you shall not desecrate my holy name anymore with your gifts and your fetishes. (Ezek 20:39b)

In this verse, the prophet is explicitly declaring that the syncretic practice of serving YHWH with gifts and at the same time worshiping idols constitutes a desecration of God's name! By the same token, then, the labeling of Molek worship in Lev 18:21 as a desecration of God's name is due to the notion current in the popular mind that the worship of Molek is not incompatible with the worship of YHWH. One need not go so far as to suggest that "the clear implication (of Ezek 20:39) is that the rejected forms of worship were directed toward YHWH" (Greenberg 1983a: 374). Here, I follow Day (1989: 67–69), who, in my opinion, argues convincingly that YHWH was not equated with Molek. In the popular mind, YHWH and Molek (*hammelek* 'the king') were distinct deities, governing distinct spheres—the world and the underworld, respectively (cf. Pss 6:6; 88:11–13)— each with his own demands (human sacrifice for Molek) and rewards (consultation with departed ancestors through Molek) and worshiped at discrete sites (the Topheth in the Valley of Hinnom for Molek). Moreover, if the distinction between the worship of celestial and that of chthonic deities (on an altar versus in a trench) that prevailed in the Greek world also held in Israel (see chap. 17, COMMENT A), then even in official religious circles, YHWH was a celestial deity (cf. Gen 11:5, 7; Exod 19:11, 18, 20; 20:22; etc.), whose control did not extend into the underworld (cf. Zevit 1996: 57). This incipient dualism is forcefully repudiated by H (and other monotheistic circles), which labels it a desecration of God's name. This point is developed further in chap. 20, COMMENT B.

The only remaining question is: Why did the populace assume that YHWH would approve—indeed, command—Molek worship? Day (1989: 68) sidesteps this question by claiming that *'ăšer lō' ṣiwwîtî* in Deut 17:3 cannot mean "which I commanded," but "which I forbade." However, in the Jeremiah passages, cited above, which specifically refer to Molek worship (in distinction to Deut 17:3), there can be no doubt that this expression, followed by "which did not come to my mind," unambiguously implies that the people actually believed that their worship of Molek was desired by YHWH. "It was more than that the Molek 'cult' was not felt incompatible with YHWH" (Day 1989: 68); in the popular religion it actually played a role in the worship of YHWH.

The two postulated reactions to Molek worship are polaric: either compatible or incompatible with the worship of YHWH. Can this antology be resolved? The answer I would suggest is that each view reflects a different circle in eighth- and seventh-century Judah. Those adhering to pure monotheism hold that

Molek and YHWH are incompatible (see above), but the people-at-large apparently believe that the two are bridgeable. Their position is not represented in Scripture, but it is ensconced in the popular pronunciation of Molek as *hammelek* 'the king'. Whereas in priestly and prophetic circles, Molek and YHWH were discrete deities, in the popular mind Molek was *hammelek* 'the king' *appointed by* YHWH to rule the underworld. That is, Molek / *hammelek* held a status equivalent to that of other negative, malevolent forces in the divine pantheon, such as *hammašḥît* 'the Destroyer', the executioner of YHWH's death sentence, and *haśśāṭān* 'the Adversary', YHWH's prosecutor and persecutor of humanity. It should not be overlooked that these divine agents possessed some autonomy so that YHWH, in effect, had to defend Israel against the Destroyer's wanton force (Exod 12:23; see NOTE on "a paschal offering," 23:5) and to check the Adversary's desire and power to harm the human race (Zech 3:1–2; 1 Chr 21:1). It is significant that these forces are also affixed with definite articles and capitalized titles and hence are personified forces: divine beings, agents of the heavenly court, capable of exerting independent (though limited) power. It is this autonomy that Molek possesses *in his realm*. It is he whom his devotees beseech by child sacrifice, a crime compounded by being performed in YHWH's name, and it brings down the wrath of Israel's priests and prophets. Herein may lie the difference between Molek and the other capitalized forces. The latter are not worshiped; their demonic intent cannot be blunted by sacrifice. But Molek controls access to the ancestral spirits, and to attain his intervention, sacrifice — child sacrifice — is essential.

Thus both factors combine to create the enormity of the sin of Molek worship: ascribing to Molek the attributes of a deity who can demand child sacrifice and, at the same time, averring that Molek is an agent of YHWH and carries out his will.

I YHWH (have spoken). *'ănî YHWH.* This ending is found with certain prohibitions to indicate that they are ethical rather than legal precepts, unenforceable in courts but punishable by God (see NOTE on 19:3). It is, therefore, no accident that the Molek prohibition is the only one in this list that ends this way (except for v. 6; see its NOTE). In this instance, moreover, the (royal) court itself promoted Molek worship. It lends support to the thesis expounded above that many circles, including official ones, fused or confused the worship of Molek with the worship of YHWH. This syncretism certainly prevailed in the royal court during the end of the eighth century and the beginning of the seventh (2 Kgs 16:3; 21:6; cf. 23:10). Hence this admonitory crescendo: YHWH says no!

22. Sodomy is attested in all periods (e.g., Gen 19:5; Judg 19:22; Rom 1:27; 1 Cor 6:9; Gal 5:19; 1 Tim 1:10; cf. Deut 22:5) and is most often reviled, if not proscribed. The sodomy of the Sodomites (hence, its name) is a cause for their destruction. The homosexual drive of the men of Gibeah, protected by their tribe, Benjamin, leads to the tribe's proscription. (It can hardly be accidental that Gibeah is the city and capital of King Saul. Whether historical or fictional, this story is an attempt to taint the Benjaminites, Saul's tribe, with a revulsive crime.)

Egyptian mythology relates that the god Seth had carnal relations with his younger brother Horus (Westendorf 1977: 2.1272–73). The Book of the Dead (§ 125) includes the confession: "I have not copulated with a boy"; however, an adult consenting man is omitted. The Hittites declare sodomy with one's son— but not with any other male—a capital crime (HL §189). Thus sodomy (like heterosexuality) is subject to regulation, but not to interdiction. Moreover, Hittite legislation for sexual offenses "does not belong to the category of torts and personal offenses, such as do the bulk of the laws in the corpus. Ḫurkel [see NOTE on "an abomination," below] constitutes an offense against the culprit's city. By committing such an act, he has brought impurity upon his fellow townsmen and made them liable to divine wrath. Thus the townsfolk must protect themselves by eradicating the cause of the divine wrath, i.e., either by executing the offender(s) or removing them permanently from the town" (Hoffner 1973: 85). This description of the Hittite rationale for punishing the sodomizer corresponds to biblical law. Here, too, sodomy is a sin against the deity (punishable by divine agency, kārēt; v. 29), but all of Israel faces expulsion from its land (vv. 26–28; 20:22) unless the malefactors are put to death (20:13). Assyrian law ostensibly also issues a blanket prohibition against sodomy (MAL § 20); however, the case seems to be that of rape (see the discussion in Olyan 1994).

Thus the difference between the biblical legislation and other Near Eastern laws must not be overlooked: the Bible allows for no exceptions; all acts of sodomy are prohibited, whether performed by rich or poor, higher or lower status, citizen or alien.

Many theories have been propounded to provide a rationale for this prohibition. One must surely exist, since this absolute ban on anal intercourse is unique not only in the Bible but, as shown in Olyan's (1994; 1997a) recent, comprehensive study, in the entire ancient Near Eastern and classical world. To be sure, a rationale is given with staccato emphasis—the pollution of the land—in the concluding exhortation (vv. 25, 27, 28), but it does not explain the individual prohibitions in the list, which, as shown (see INTRODUCTION) must be older. Olyan (1994: 197–204) faults the regnant explanations, namely, idolatry (Snaith 1967; Boswell 1980), blurring of boundaries (Douglas 1966: 41–57; Thurston 1990), wasting of male seed (Eilberg-Schwartz 1990: 183; Biale 1992: 29), and mixing of semen with other defiling liquids (Bigger 1979), on the grounds that either they do not share the same universe of discourse of the list or, conversely, their rationale for the list does not fit this very prohibition.

Olyan's own explanation is based on his theory that our verse comprises two layers: an earlier one in which only the insertive partner is addressed, and the receptive partner (in 20:13) is not punished or even mentioned. His second layer is that "the laws of Lev 18:22 and 20:13 in their final setting may well be part of a wider effort to prevent the mixture of semen and other defiling agents in the bodies of receptive women, men, and animals, mixing that results in the defilement of the individuals involved" (1994: 205).

Olyan's two-source theory for this verse (and the list) is based mainly on Daube's (1947: 74–101) claim that originally the male adulterer was punished and only subsequently the adulteress was added (20:10). However, Daube's analysis of 20:10 is not analogous. There all the verbs are singular, and the adulteress (*hannōʾāpet*) is attached at the end. But to fit Olyan's theory, the latter half of 20:13 would have to be rewritten by changing its verbs and suffixes to singular and deleting *šĕnêhem*. Rather, 20:13 is constructed like 20:18, which also is voiced in the singular except for the punishment *wĕnikrĕtû šĕnêhem*. In this case, it would be inconceivable that originally only the male was punished, but the consenting menstruant would go scott free, since her guilt is made amply clear by the charge *wĕhûʾ* (*wĕhîʾ* Q) *gilta ʾet- mĕqôr dāmêhā* 'and she has exposed the source of her blood'. Thus 20:13 bears no signs of an earlier text, and the two-source theory of Olyan is put into doubt.

Olyan's (1994: 205) rationale for this verse (the MT) is "the defilement of the individuals involved" (but not of the land, the redactor's rationale). It represents, in effect, the position of P, which is concerned with only the persistence and spread of impurity lest it pollute the sanctuary (vol. 1.254–61). P, therefore, institutes purificatory measures by which this impurity can be contained or eliminated (chaps. 11–16). By contrast, H provides no countervailing measures for the polluted land. The land stores its defilement nonstop until it vomits out its inhabitants (vv. 25, 28). Unlike P's sanctuary, which can be purged of its pollution by the high priest's purification offerings (chaps. 4, 16), there is no purificatory rite in H's system that the high priest can perform for the land (see INTRODUCTION to vv. 24–30). Our verse and the list, in general, enumerate those cases where semen emissions, though normally unimpeachable (15:16–18), are strictly forbidden, but this observation fails to disclose the overarching purpose of either this verse or the list.

The common denominator of all the prohibitions, I submit, is that they involve the emission of semen for the purpose of copulation, resulting in either incest and illicit progeny or, as in this case, lack of progeny (or its destruction in the case of Molek worship, v. 21). In a word, the theme (with Ramban) is procreation. This rationale fully complements (and presupposes) P's laws of 15:16–18. Semen emission per se is not forbidden; it just defiles, but purificatory rites must follow. But in certain cases of sexual congress, it is strictly forbidden, and severe consequences must follow.

Indeed, it is the assumption that H is fully cognizant of P that throws light on an anomaly that, to my knowledge, no previous scholar has dealt with: Why is masturbation—the willful spilling of seed—not proscribed? First, it must be recognized that masturbation was not condemned by the ancients. What Hippocrates considered harmful is not masturbation, but excessive expenditure of semen (Marcus and Francis 1975: 384). In Israel, moreover, the spilling of seed, by itself, is not the issue. As illustrated by the story of Onan, sin occurs if seed is deliberately spilled during coitus (Gen 38:9–10). Indeed, all the cases cited in our chapter refer to illicit intercourse. But the ejaculation of semen results in only a one-day impurity that requires laundering and ablutions (15:16–18), regardless of whether the act takes place during (legitimate) intercourse or by the self, deliberately (masturbation) or accidentally (nocturnal emission). The rab-

bis, to be sure, condemned masturbation (*b. Nid.* 13a, b), but it is their enact-
ment, not that of Scripture. However, as has been demonstrated by Satlow (1994),
this text and all others in rabbinic literature that purportedly condemn nonpro-
creative emission of semen per se cannot be found in Palestinian and earlier rabbinic sources, or even in their contemporary classical world. Rather, they are limited and attributable to the redactors of the Babylonian Talmud, who may have
been influenced by Zoroastrian notions to which they were exposed.

An ancillary question concerns birth control. May a married couple practice
coitus interruptus? The example of Onan (Gen 38:8–10) is irrelevant. His act
is condemned because he refused to act as the levir and thus denied an heir to
his deceased brother. Analogously to the case of masturbation, the silence of our
text would permit the inference that birth control was not prohibited as long as
the couple reproduced itself. This, indeed, is the opinion of the tannaitic rabbis (*m. Yeb.* 6:6; *t. Yeb.* 8:4), two males according to R. Shammai (on the basis
of Moses' two sons, 1 Chr 23:15), and one male and one female, according to
R. Hillel (Gen 1:27b–28a).

If the rationale of procreation proves correct, I would have to presume that
Israel's priests might have frowned on sexual congress during certified pregnancy,
but they would not have forbidden it; their prohibitions focused on illicit intercourse. They would, however, have had only a positive attitude concerning sexual relations after the onset of menopause. They would have held up the example of Abraham and Sarah, as passed down by tradition, who by the grace of
God were blessed with a child despite their advanced age (Gen 18:9–13). Similarly, as I have argued (see NOTE on "she shall remain," 12:4), with the rabbis
(versus the sectarians), the priests would have permitted the parturient to reen-
gage sexual union with her husband, despite her lochia, after the initial seven
or fourteen days of severe impurity had passed.

Female sexual relations are nowhere prohibited in Scripture, nor anywhere
else (to my knowledge) in the ancient Near East. Surely, lesbianism was known!
Gerstenberger's (1996: 297) conjecture that these prohibitions, composed by
men for men, evidence neither knowledge nor interest in female relations is a
stab in the dark; besides, it is refuted by one of the main rationales behind these
prohibitions (see NOTE on "to uncover nakedness," v. 6). Hebrew Scriptures ignored it (contrast Rom 1:26) because in the act no bodily fluids are lost (cf. Pope
1976: 417). The *legal* reason for interdicting anal intercourse (see below) is the
waste, the nonproductive spilling, of seed—the equivalence of Onanism (Gen
38:9–10)—which, in this case, does not occur.

Finally, it is imperative to draw the logical conclusion of this discussion for
our time. If my basic thesis is correct that the common denominator of the entire list of sexual prohibitions, including homosexuality, is procreation within a
stable family, then a consolatory and compensatory remedy is at hand for Jewish gays (non-Jews, unless they live within the boundaries of biblical Israel, are
not subject to these laws; see chap. 20, COMMENT D): if gay partners adopt children, they do not violate the *intent* of the prohibition. The question can be
asked: Why didn't the biblical legist propose this remedy? The answer simply is
that this option was not available, since ancient Israel did not practice adoption

(cf. Tigay 1972; Knobloch 1992; the alleged cases of Est 2:7; Ezra 10:44 [the latter MT is suspect; cf. Williamson 1985] reflect foreign practice). See the more detailed discussion in, chap. 20, COMMENT D.

as one lies with a woman. miškĕbê 'iššâ, literally "as the lyings down of a woman" (cf. *miškab zakar*, Num 31:17, 18, 35 [P], referring to vaginal penetration, i.e, defloration; hence, in this case it must indicate anal penetration; Olyan 1994: 183–85). It is a technical term (cf. 20:13). The plural is always found in the context of illicit carnal relations (Gen 49:4; Lev 18:22; 20:13); contrast *miškāb* (Num 31:18), the singular implying licit relations.

Thus since illicit carnal relations are implied by the term *miškĕbê 'iššâ*, it may be plausibly suggested that homosexuality is herewith forbidden for only the equivalent degree of forbidden heterosexual relations, namely, those enumerated in the preceding verses (D. Stewart). However, sexual liaisons occurring with males outside these relations would not be forbidden. And since the same term *miškĕbê 'iššâ* is used in the list containing sanctions (20:13), it would mean that sexual liaisons with males, falling outside the control of the paterfamilias, would be neither condemnable nor punishable. Thus *miskĕbê 'iššâ*, referring to illicit male–female relations, is applied to illicit male–male relations, and the literal meaning of our verse is: do not have sex with a male with whose widow sex is forbidden. In effect, this means that the homosexual prohibition applies to Ego with father, son, and brother (subsumed in v. 6) and to grandfather–grandson, uncle–nephew, and stepfather–stepson, but not to any other male.

an abomination. tô'ēbâ. This word occurs 116 times, and the verb *ti'ēb* (*Pi'el*), obviously a denominative, occurs 23 times. The term also occurs in the Tabnit inscription from Sidon (*KAI* 13, 1.6), referring to opening a grave. Some claim that its root *y'b* is related to *'yb* 'darken, contaminate, stain' (cf. Lam 2:1). The equivalence of I-*yodh* and II-*yodh/waw* (e.g., *'yp/y'p, gwr/ygr, twb/ytb*) is frequently attested. Also the Egyptians had an equivalent (related?) term *bwt*, used in similar contexts (Humbert 1960).

This term proliferates in wisdom literature (e.g., twenty-one times in Proverbs), including seventeen times in Deuteronomy (Weinfeld 1972d: 267). In Deuteronomy, it appears in the following contexts: idolatry (12:31; 13:15; 17:4; 27:15), defective sacrifice (17:1), invalid offerers (23:19), magic (18:12), false weights (25:13–16), transvestism (22:5), and remarriage with a remarried divorcee (24:4). D places its emphasis on idolatry and magic. Only the last-mentioned instance (Deut 24:4) deals with sexual aberrations (cf. Hoffner 1973: 84; Picket 1986: 131–50). H, however, limits its use solely (as does Hittite *ḫurkel*) to sexual relations (18:22, 26, 27, 29, 30; 20:13). And Paran (1983: 253) may be right that the inclusion of *taḥăṭî' 'et-hā'āreṣ* 'you will bring sin upon the land' in Deut 24:4 betrays the priestly (H) origin of this case (cf. Lev 18:25–28; Num 35:34; Josh 22:19 [all H]; see Introduction I E). What is striking is the total absence of *tô'ēbâ* from P, and its few *specialized* (incest) attestations in H (and its derivatives, e.g., Ezek 33:25–26) indicate that the priestly texts were not influenced by wisdom literature (Milgrom 1982c).

It should not be forgotten that the term *tô'ēbâ* is used to characterize all the illicit cohabitations (vv. 26, 27, 29, 30). It carries "moral (rather than legal) weight and serves primarily to characterize the undesirability and unacceptability of the (referred) offenses" (Picket 1986: 127; on the alleged equivalence of Sum. *níg-gig* and Akk. *ikkibu*, see Geller 1990). The word *tô'ēbâ* is chosen, like *ṭāmē'* for adultery and bestiality (see NOTE on v. 20), as proleptic of all the listed prohibitions summed up in the peroration (vv. 26, 27, 29). Just as the choice of *ṭāmē'* may point to its widespread occurrence, so too homosexuality. That the latter is labeled *tô'ēbâ* may indicate that it was not a rare occurrence. Moreover, this word may have been chosen, as well as condemnatory *tebel* for bestiality (v. 23), because these two violations would probably never come to the attention of the paterfamilias, whereas all the other cases would likely become known, especially if pregnancy resulted.

23. *You shall not have sexual relations with. bĕ . . . l'-titten šĕkobtĕkā*, literally "You shall not inject your penis/flow in" (also 20:15). For the meaning of *šĕkōbet*, see the NOTE on v. 20. Note the decisive use of the preposition *bĕ* (rather than *'el*, v. 20). LXX and Pesh. add *lzr'* which, as pointed out by Miller (2000) would make *zera'* 'semen' the unifying factor in the nonincest laws (v. 19:23).

any animal. ûbĕkol-bĕhēmâ. The emphasis is on "any" (cf. Exod 22:18, Deut 27:21). In the Hittite laws, bestiality is permitted with a horse or mule (HL § 200A), but is interdicted (*ḫurkel*) with an ox (§ 187), a sheep (§ 188), or a dog (§ 199). If the man is the victim, he is not held responsible (§ 199); if the initiator, he is killed, but the king could spare his life (§§ 187, 188, 199). *Ḫurkel* is punishable by death or, if spared by the king, by banishment. Nonetheless, the spared criminal "shall not appear before the king nor shall he become a priest" (§ 200H). Thus the Hittites distinguished between the holy and the profane, demanding more rigorous behavior in the realm of the former (cf. Moyer 1969: 51–61, 84).

References to bestiality in Mesopotamian and Ugaritic texts are limited to the realm of mythology. For example, the Sumerian "Ninegala Hymn" refers to Inanna's copulation with horses; in the *Epic of Gilgamesh*, Ishtar is depicted as the wanton lover of a bird, lion, and stallion (*ANET* 84, ll. 48–56); Baal copulates with a cow and fathers an ox, a heifer, and a buffalo (*ANET* 142). Eichler (1976: 96) claims that "mythology is not a direct reflection of human behavior." However, if it does not mirror society's norms, it surely reflects society's ideals. In any case, the probable practice of bestiality in the Egyptian cult at Mendes (= Dedet) illustrates the ideal being put into practice (Krebs 1963: 20). In the rabbinic period, the belief was prevalent that bestiality was practiced by pagans: the Mishna prohibits the placing of animals in inns kept by pagans, since they are suspected of having intercourse with them (*m. 'Abod. Zar.* 2:1).

Gerstenberger (1996: 299) appropriately concludes: "Hence in view of the ancients, sodomy [bestiality—J.M.] is not a private matter. It directly affects the welfare of the community, either because deities are angered or because monstrous hybrids are generated. Accordingly, the 'legislator' must intervene."

to defile yourself thereby. lĕṭom'â-bāh. The antecedent of the feminine suffix of *bāh* is not *bĕhēmâ* 'animal'. It refers to the entire relationship. The defilement is not cultic, but moral (see NOTE on v. 20).

give herself to. ta'ămōd lipnê. The idiom *'āmad lipnê* bears the sense of "pre-

sent oneself before" (e.g., Gen 43:15; Exod 9:10; Num 27:2, 21) and, more relevantly in this case, "put oneself at the service of" (e.g., 1 Sam 16:22; 1 Kgs 1:2).
On the one hand, the use of the *Qal*, rather than *tiššākab*, *Nip'al*, shows that
her act is voluntary (Wessely 1846). On the other hand, as pointed out by
Schwartz (personal communication), the verb *šākab* is irrelevant here, since as
a transitive verb, *šākab* can be used of only men. In either case, it is the woman
who initiates the intercourse.

to mate with it. lĕrib'āh. This is an Aramaic loan word for the equivalent Hebrew *rbṣ* 'lie down, crouch, recline' (e.g., Ps 139:3). Its occurrence in 19:19 for
the crossbreeding of plants indicates its special use in H. Ibn Ezra claims that
the root is related to *'arbā'â* 'four' (generally derived from a homonymous *rb'*)
due to the fact that an animal copulates standing. The woman, however,
crouches on all fours.

Driver and White (1894: 30) aver that the Masoretic *mappiq* is incorrect, since
rb', *Qal*, is not transitive (note *lĕrib'â 'ōtāh*, 20:16), as it is subsequently in Rabbinic Hebrew, and it should therefore be rendered "for mating."

perversion. tebel. It has been suggested that the root of this word is *bll* 'mix'
(Ibn Janaḥ, Rashi[2], Ibn Ezra[2])—that is, the untoward mixture of man and beast.
So, too, the father's and son's semen in the daughter-in-law is also labeled a *tebel*
(20:12; see Rashi and Ramban on 18:17). Presumably, the husband's and adulterer's semen in the wife could be similarly designated (v. 20), though the root
ṭm' is employed. Another suggestion is that the root *tbl* is related to Arabic *ta-
bala* 'arousement of the male by the female' (*EM* 8:407–8). Its relationship to
tĕballul (21:20) is unclear.

The mixture of species and social roles is anathema to Scripture (cf. Bigger
1979: 203). "Holiness requires that different classes should not be confused"
(Douglas 1976: 53). "The cosmology of the Old Testament places barriers between the divine realm and the human realm and between the human realm
and the animal realm; any mixing of these barriers is considered unnatural, a
confusion (*tebel*)" (Hartley 1992:298).

Vv. 24–30. The Closing Exhortation

Schwartz (1987: 106–7) finds a complex structure for this unit. Cholewinski
(1976: 37) offers this simpler one ABCA'B'C', which is more satisfying:

A   *'al- tiṭṭammĕ'û bĕkol- 'ēlleh*
    kî bĕkol- 'ēlleh niṭmĕ'û haggôyim
    'ăšer- 'ănî mĕšallēaḥ mippĕnêkem (v. 24)
    B   *wattiṭmā' hā'āreṣ*
        wā'epqōd 'ăwōnāh 'ālêhā
        wattāqî' hā'āreṣ 'et-yōšĕbêhā (v. 25)
        C   *ûšĕmartem 'attem 'et-ḥuqqōtay wĕ'et mišpāṭay* (v. 26aα)
A'   *wĕlō' ta'ăśû mikkōl hattô'ēbōt hā'ēlleh*
    hā'ezrāḥ wĕhaggēr haggār bĕtôkĕkem
    kî 'et-kol- hattô'ēbōt hā'ēl 'āśû 'anšê-hā'āreṣ 'ăšer lipnêkem (vv. 26aβ–27a)

B′   *wattiṭmā᾿ hā᾿āreṣ*
      wĕlō᾿- tāqî᾿ hā᾿āreṣ ᾿etkem bĕṭammăkem ᾿ōtah
      ka᾿ăšer qā᾿â ᾿et-haggôy ᾿ăšer lipnêkem
      kî kol-᾿ăšer ya᾿ăśeh mikkōl haṭṭô᾿ēbōt hā᾿ēlleh
      wĕnikrĕtû hannĕpāšôt hāʿōśōt mikkereb ʿammām (vv. 27b–29)
      C′   *ûśĕmartem ᾿et- mišmartî*
            lĕbīltî ʿăśot mēḥuqqôt haṭṭô᾿ēbōt ᾿ăšer na᾿ăśû lipnêkem (cf.
            v. 26aβ)
            wĕlō᾿ tiṭṭammĕ᾿û bāhem (cf. v. 24a)
            ᾿ănî YHWH ᾿ĕlōhêkem (v. 30; cf. v. 2b)

AA′ consist of a prohibition followed by *kî* and *᾿ăšer*. BB′ state that the earth,
which thereby becomes polluted, vomits out its inhabitants. CC′ completes the
structure with a positive general command followed by three inclusions in C′:
the first corresponds with the second half of the peroration (v. 26aβ); the second,
with the entire peroration (v. 24a); and the third, with the entire chapter (v. 2b).

The violation of prohibitions listed in chap. 18 leads to banishment from the
land (see also 20:22–23). The rationale is that the land becomes polluted and
vomits out its inhabitants. This ecological theology is not the innovation of H.
It is already adumbrated in the punishment for the first human sin: "Cursed be
the ground because of you" (Gen 3:17). As pointedly observed by R. Meir, "Three
entered to be judged at the beginning of creation and four emerged condemned.
Adam, Eve, and the serpent entered to be judged and the earth was cursed because of them" ('*Abot R. Nat.* 42).

Not by accident, I submit, is sex the first couple's sin: they engaged in it, defying God's prohibition. This is the meaning *tôb wāraʿ* (Gen 2:17, 3:22) and the
immediate consequence of eating the fruit. Neither, I submit, is it accidental
that the Flood is triggered by an egregious sexual crime (Gen 6:1–4). To be sure,
the earth is polluted by *ḥāmas* (Gen 6:11, 13), probably an accumulation of vi-
olent crimes committed by previous generations. But these, according to the
plain meaning of the text, have been committed by the offspring of boundary-
crossing cohabitation of divine and human beings, which pinpoints this act as
the cause of the Flood. But I must reserve this subject for separate treatment.
In any event, that sexual violations can pollute the land is found in Deuteronomy (Deut 24:1–4) and the prophets (Jer 3:1–10). But only here, in H, are they
itemized, categorized, and penalized (cf. 20:10–21).

That human sin pollutes the land is an axiom that pervades all of Scripture
(e.g., Gen 4:12; 8:21; Lev 26:34–35, 43 [presumed]; Num 35:33–34; Deut 2:23;
24:4; Isa 24:5–6; Jer 3:2; Ezek 36:17; Ezra 9:11; cf. Frymer-Kensky 1979: 223).
But nowhere is it so clearly stated as here that exile is the automatic, built-in
punishment for land pollution. The verb *ṭāmē᾿*, therefore, must be understood
in a real but noncultic sense (cf. Wright 1991: 162–63; see NOTE on "defiled
themselves," v. 24).

Supporting this view of *ṭāmē᾿* is the fact that H never calls the land "holy."
As a priestly source, which held that the contact between *qādōš* 'holy' and *ṭāmē᾿*

'impure' is dangerous and, at times, fatal (see 22:3), it had no choice but to avoid any reference to the land as holy. Indeed, the concept of "holy land" is totally absent from the Hebrew Bible (even though it is implied; see NOTE on 25:23) and does not surface until the Apocrypha (e.g., 2 Macc 1:7) and Philo (e.g., *Laws* 4.215). The term *'admat haqqōdeš* (Zech 2:15), as pointed out by Weinfeld (1993: 203), refers to the land around the Temple. Indeed, as a matter of principle, H rejects the notion of innate holiness in nature. This perhaps explains why H never designates God's land as holy (for other reasons, see NOTE on 25:23). Moreover, as pointed out by Melcher (1996: 102, n. 30; correcting Milgrom 1991: 48–49), the land need only be initially clean (not holy) for it to become impure, and then automatically regurgitate its inhabitants in the process of cleansing itself. Furthermore, in contradistinction to P, which claims that it was Moses who sanctified both the Tabernacle and the priests (with the sacred anointment oil, Lev 8 [P]), H states emphatically that the sanctification was the act of God: "I will sanctify [*wĕqiddaštî*] the Tent of Meeting and the altar, and I will consecrate [*'ăqaddēš*] Aaron and his sons to serve me as priests" (Exod 29:44 [H]). Thus H implies that neither the sacred anointment oil nor its manipulator, Moses, is responsible for the sanctification, but only God's condescending presence (*wĕniqdaš bikbōdî*, Exod 29:43b [H]).

Ritual impurity always allows for purification and atonement. But the sexual abominations of Lev 18 (and 20) are not expiable through ritual. There is but one solution: the land must disgorge its inhabitants: "Land was rendered unfit for habitation *by them*, not permanently polluted (land waste) but polluted remediably in that it was cleansed *of them*" (Goodman 1986: 26). The violation of the sabbaths (both weekly and septennial) also leads to exile, but in this case a healing period is specified: the time the land was worked on the sabbath is prescribed for its rest (26: 34–35; cf. *'Abot R. Nat*[1]. 38). No period, however, is set for the pollution limits of the land. God alone keeps the reckoning: "And they shall return here in the fourth generation, for the iniquity of the Amorites is not yet complete" (Gen 15:16).

Murder, also, allows for atonement—the death of the murderer(s) (Num 35:33). Otherwise, destruction and exile are once again the consequence (cf. Ezek 24:6–14). The punishment decreed upon Cain—wandering, and his ultimate settlement in the land of "the wanderer" (Gen 4:16)—is, in reality, not exceptional. His homicide is declared involuntary, for he knew not the consequence of his act (*Gen. R.* 22:26), and his punishment is codified in the prescribed exile to the asylum city for the involuntary homicide (Num 35:22–28; cf. vol. 1.510).

In sum, ritual impurity (P) is always subject to ritual purification, but no ritual remedy exists for moral impurity (H). Indeed, the sinner(s) cannot expunge moral impurity. It is a capital crime. If committed by the individual, it is punished by God with *kārēt* (e.g., sexual offenses, 18:29) whenever it is overlooked or neglected by man (e.g., Molek worship, 20:1–5; see NOTES). If, however, the entire community is guilty of moral impurity, the irrevocable result is the pollution of the land (18:25; Num 34:33–34) and the exile of its inhabitants (18:28;

26:14–38). These radically differing concepts of *ṭum'â* 'impurity' is one of the terminological hallmarks that distinguish H from P. For other examples, see Introduction I B.

It is noteworthy, even startling, that the Qumran sectarians averred that non-cultic sins are expiable. Their biblical license for such a daring deviation would most likely have been Ezek 36:25:

wĕzāraqtî 'ălêkem mayim ṭĕhôrîm ûṭĕhartem mikkōl ṭum'ôtêkem

I shall pour upon you pure waters, and you will be purified from all your sins

Commentators, both ancient (e.g., Radaq) and modern (e.g., Zimmerli 1979), take this passage as a metaphor. *Tg. Ps.-J.*, which also holds that the projected image is but a simile for eschatalogical purification, nonetheless specifies that the purificatory waters should contain the ashes of the red cow prescribed for purification from corpse contamination (Num 19). The *Tg.* was anticipated by Qumran:

WYT[H]RW MṬM'T HNPŠ B[WMKL ṬM'H] 'ḤRT [BZ]RWQ 'LYHM
[HKW]HN 'T MY HNDH LṬHR[M

and they shall be purified of corpse-contamination [. . . and of all] other [impurity when the pr]iest throws the purificatory waters upon them to purify them. (4Q277, frg. lii, ll. 8–9 [reconstructed and explicated by J.M. Baumgarten, forthcoming]

Most likely, the Qumranites would have interpreted this Ezekielian passage in the light of Num 19; note the use of the same verb *zāraq* (v. 20) and that *mê niddâ* (vv. 9, 20, 21) is synonymous with *mayim ṭĕhôrîm* 'purificatory waters'.

This admittedly speculative interpretation of a reconstructed text (4Q277), I submit, is supported by the *explicit* fusion of Ezek 36:25 and Num 19 in 1QS 3:8–9 (Vermes 1987: 64):

WBRWḤ QDWŠ LYḤD B'MTW YṬHR MKWL 'WWNWTW
WBRWḤ YWŠR W'NWH TKWPR ḤṬTW
WB'NWT NPŠW LKWL ḤWQY 'L YṬHR BŚRW
LHZWT BMY NDH WLHTQDŠ BMY DWKW

He shall be cleansed from all his sins by the spirit of
    holiness uniting him to His truth,
and his iniquity shall be expiated by the spirit of
    uprightness and humility.
And when his flesh is sprinkled with purifying water
    and sanctified by cleansing water,
it shall be made clean by the humble submission of
    his soul to all the precepts of God.

The essence of this passage is that by following the precepts of God (i.e., the sect) in a spirit of righteousness and humility, the purificatory waters of the red cow (*mê niddâ*) can expiate *all one's sins* (*kol 'ăwônôtăyw*). Thus if my reading of 1QS 3:8–9 is correct, Qumran holds that sprinkling the waters containing the ashes of the red cow is both essential and effective to purify a person not just of corpse contamination, but broadly "of all his iniquities" (Baumgarten, forthcoming).

What is significant is that the sectaries of Qumran have effectively eliminated H's notion of irremediable (moral) impurity. Their reading of Ezek 36:25 led them to this radical doctrine: all one's sins can be washed away by the waters containing the ashes of the red cow if one's life is conducted in the right "spirit" (cf. Licht 1965: 75). This doctrine is not in the Bible: the priests (H) deny it. The prophets affirm it, but in their view, one's correct behavior (spirit) by itself suffices. Qumran adds that the proper "spirit" must be accompanied by the rite of sprinkling with the purificatory waters of the red cow.

Ezek 22:1–16 comprises a list of Israel's violations of H prohibitions (drawn mainly from this chapter) whose punishment is exile: dishonoring parents (v. 7; cf. 20:9), violating the sabbath or the sancta (v. 8; cf. 19:30), causing an unjust death by slander (v. 9; see NOTE on 19:16), copulating with the father's wife (v. 10a; cf. 18:8), copulating with a menstruant (v. 10b; cf. 18:19), adultery (v. 11aα; cf. 18:20), copulating with a daughter-in-law (v. 11aβ; cf. 18:15), copulating with a half sister (v. 11b; cf. 18:19), taking interest (v. 12bα; cf. 25:36), and exploiting one's fellow (11bβ; cf. 19:13). To this list, Ezekiel adds murder (*šāpak dām*, vv. 3, 4, 6, 12; seven times elsewhere) and idolatry (*gillûlîm*, vv. 3, 4; thirty-five times elsewhere) as defiling (*lĕṭom'â*, v. 3; cf. v. 4).

That murder pollutes the land is stated (or implied) by every pentateuchal source (e.g., Gen 4:11–12 [JE]; Num 25:33–34 [P]; Deut 21:4 [D]) and hence it need not be emphasized by Ezekiel. However, that idolatry is defiling is nowhere mentioned in the Pentateuch. This is the innovation of the seventh-century prophets Jeremiah (2:7–8, 23; 7:30; 19:13; 32:34) and Ezekiel (using his favorite pejorative *gillûlîm*, 20:7, 18, 31; 22:3, 4; 23:7, 30; 36:18; 37:23), once stating emphatically that idolatry (but not murder! see above) pollutes the land (*ûbĕgillûlêhem ṭimmĕ'ûhā*, 36:18). For Ezekiel's heavy indebtedness to H, see chap. 26, COMMENTS C and D.

Weinfeld (1993: 185) suggests that the older notion predicated that Israel possessed the land forever *unconditionally*; as evidence, he cites Gen 13:15; 17:8; Exod 32:13, and he submits that it was the fall of Samaria and the loss of the northern territories that gave birth to the doctrine of conditionality. But pace Weinfeld, other old texts do imply conditionality (Gen 15:10; 18:19, admitted by Weinfeld), and, above all, Gen 17:14 is a priestly text, which posits that if the sanctuary is defiled by Israel's sins, God abandons Israel to conquest, subjection, and expulsion (vol. 1.254–61). Indeed, as demonstrated, it is axiomatic for all sources, including the oldest, that heinous sins such as murder (Gen 4:5; 2 Sam 1:21–22; 21:1–14) contaminate the land. Is it then conceivable that conditionality was not *always presumed*, if not explicit, in any of the land-grant passages? Nonetheless, it is important to note that the mass deportations practiced by the Assyrians in their imperial conquests would have *lent great force and immediacy* to the doctrine of conditionality.

As noted by Avishur (1987: 128), the closing exhortation is structured as an introversion (ABCC'B'A'):

A   [24]*'al tiṭṭammĕ'û bĕkol-'ēlleh*

B   *kî bĕkol-'ēlleh niṭmĕ'û haggôyîm . . .*
     [25b]*wattāqî' hā'āreṣ 'et-yōšĕbêhā*
     [26]*ûšĕmartem 'attem 'et-ḥuqqōtay . . .*
     C   *wĕlō' ta'ăśû mikkōl haṭṭô'ēbōt hā'ēlleh . . .*
     C'   [27]*kî 'et-kol-haṭṭô'ēbōt hā'ēl 'ăśû*
   B'   *'anšê hā'āreṣ 'ăšer lipnêkem wattiṭmā' hā'āreṣ*
     [28]*wĕlō' tāqî' hā'āreṣ 'etkem bĕṭamma'ăkem 'ōtah . . .*
     [30]*ûšĕmartem . . . lĕbiltî 'ăśôt mēḥuqqôt . . .*
A'   *wĕlō' tiṭṭammĕ'û bāhem*

A   [24]Do not defile yourselves in any of these (practices),

B   for by all these (practices) the nations . . . defiled themselves
     [25b]and the land vomited out its inhabitants
     [26]You, however, must keep my statutes . . .
     C   and commit none of these abominations
     C'   [27]for all these abominations . . . did
   B'   the people in the land who (were) before you . . . and the land became defiled
     [28]So let not the land vomit you out for defiling it . . .
     [30]So you will heed . . . not to commit any of these statutory . . .
A'   and not defile yourself by them

Schwartz (forthcoming), basing himself on Cholewinski (1976: 36–38), but differing with the latter's conclusions, subdivides this pericope into two parallel panels, whose identical or synonymous words are represented below:

A   *'al-tiṭṭammĕ'û . . . 'ēlleh* (v. 24a)   A'   *wĕlō' ta'ăśû . . . haṭṭô'ēbōt hā'ēlleh . . .*
                                                 (v. 26aβ, b)

B   *kî . . . haggôyim* (v. 24bα)   B'   *kî . . . 'anšê hā'āreṣ* (v. 27a$\alpha\beta$)
C   *'ăšer . . . mippĕnêkem* (v. 24bβ)   C'   *'ăšer lipnêkem* (v. 27aγ)
D   *wattiṭmā' ha'āreṣ . . .* (v. 25a)   D'   *wattiṭmā' hā'āreṣ* (v. 27b)
E   *wattāqî' hā'āreṣ 'et-yōšĕbêhā* (v. 25b)   E'   *. . . tāqî' hā'āreṣ 'etkem . . .* (vv. 28–29)
F   *ûšĕmartem 'attem 'et-ḥuqqōtay . . .*   F'   *ûšĕmartem 'et-mišmartî* (v. 30aα)
    (v. 26aα)
        A''   *lĕbiltî 'ăśôt . . . haṭṭô'ēbōt . . . wĕlō' tiṭṭammĕ'û bāhem* (v. 30aβ–b)

The virtue of these parallel panels is that they neatly separate the fate of the Canaanites in the past from a similar fate awaiting Israel if it adopts the former's ways. Moreover, the validity of this structure is reinforced by the fact the beginning of each panel (AA') is reproduced in the conclusion (A''); that is, A'' = A+A'. F, as the opening of v. 26, actually begins the section on Israel. It is placed at the end of the first panel as a contrastive warning to Israel (the con-

trast provided by *'attem* 'you, however'), and it is matched by F', the true beginning of the conclusion to the second panel (v. 30).

Concerning the expulsion of the Canaanites, H expresses itself once again in
Num 33:50–56 (for the attribution, see Introduction I E). As pointed out by
Schwartz (forthcoming), this passage agrees with the earlier epic tradition (JE)
that the Canaanite cultic objects must be destroyed and the Canaanites themselves must be forcibly expelled by Israel and/or by God (cf. Exod 23:24–33;
34:11–13). Our pericope, however, presents a different view: just as the Canaanites were not ejected by the Israelites, but beforehand by the action of the land,
so Israel will not be ejected by some outside invading force, but by the automatic regurgitation of the land of the pollution inflicted on it by sinful Israel.
This implies that Israel would be forced to leave because the consequent sterility of the land would no longer yield any produce. This notion, adumbrated in
the first homicide (Gen 4:11–12) and developed by the Holiness tradents for all
subsequent homicides (Num 35:33–34), is fully exposited in H's blessings and
curses (26:3–5, 10, 19–20). Here, however, the pollution of the land is not caused
by homicide (Num 35), by Israel's neglect to drive out the Canaanites (Num
33), or by the adoption of Canaanite cultic practices (Exod 21, 34), but by its
sexual aberrations (and by Molek worship; see NOTE on v. 21).

Lev 26 modifies H's metaphysical hypostasization of the land as the agent of
Israel's expulsion (chaps. 18 and 20) by adopting a position closer to Num 33.
The process is initially begun by natural causes blighting the land's fertility (vv.
16–22), leaving the coup de grâce to the human enemy (vv. 5–32). Even at this
point, Israel's woes are not at an end. YHWH is portrayed graphically as pursuing Israel in exile, breaking its ethnic cohesion by scattering the people (v. 33a)
and its psychological stability by destroying their morale (vv. 36–37) until they
rot (v. 39).

In effect, Lev 18 (20) adheres to P's conceptual explanation of Israel's expulsion by its image of impurity "forcing" YHWH to abandon his sanctuary, but it
transfers the barometer of Israel's moral and spiritual status from the sanctuary
to the land. But in contrast to P's sanctuary, which pictures the sanctuary as
evicting its resident YHWH, Lev 18 images the land as evicting its resident Israel (and previously the Canaanites). Both Lev 26 and Num 33, however, real-
istically attribute the expulsion to human agency. Num 33 is closer to older JE
in that it, too, lays down one condition for Israel's residence in the land—the
expulsion of the Canaanites. Lev 26 is rooted more in actual historical experience—the destruction and exile of North Israel (see chap. 26, COMMENT E). But
the entire scenario, as in Num 33 (see v. 56), is directed by YHWH.

That three H pericopes betray substantively differing concepts of the same
theme—Israel's tenure in the land—clearly indicates that they are the work of
different H tradents separated in time. Speculatively, one would be inclined to
regard Lev 18 (20) as the oldest by its unabashed anthropomorphic imagery and
closer resemblance to older P. The more realistic conceptualization of Lev 26
and Num 33, I find difficult to separate chronologically.

The main theme of this peroration that sexual immorality pollutes the land may have left its mark on Deut 24:1–4 (cf. Jer 3:1–2, 9), though the specific sin in these cited passages—remarrying a former wife who meanwhile married someone else—is not among the sexual crimes listed in our chapter. The prophets picture Israel as the consort of YHWH who commits harlotry (*zānâ*) by worshiping other gods (e.g., Jer 2:20–25; 3:1–8; Hos 1:2; 2:3–15; 3:1–5; 4:12; Ezek 16:15–41, already adumbrated in the Torah by the use of *zānâ* for idol worship, Exod 34:16; Deut 31:16; especially in H, 17:7; 20:5 [bis], 6), in Ezekiel (e.g., 6:9; 16:15–17; 20:5, 30; 23:5, 19, 30, 43), and in the framework of Judges (2:17; 8:27, 33).

24. *Do not defile yourselves.* '*al-tiṭṭammĕ'û.* This is a *Hitpa'el* (Ibn Ezra) or an orthographically identical *Nip'al* (Schwartz, personal communication). In either case, the meaning is reflexive (see NOTE on "defiled themselves," below). Note the use of the negative particle '*al*, not *lō*'. This is exhortation, not commandment (for the difference, see Bright 1973; for its application, see vol. 1.536, 608, 611, 1012).

The use of the root *ṭm*' in H constitutes a radical departure from its usage in P. No ritual, be it ablution or sacrifice (P's purification technique), can expunge the pollution of the land (v. 25). The violator is punished with *kārēt* (v. 29) and the community, with exile (v. 28). H, however, is not negating P (except in v. 19; see its NOTE; see also 22:4–8, which clearly presumes P's notion of impurity). Each source speaks of a different kind of impurity: in P, it is concrete, cultic—ritual impurity; in H, it is abstract, inexpungeable—moral impurity.

One should not, hence, conclude that H's impurity is metaphoric. It is just as real and potent as P's impurity. It is engendered by wide-ranging violations that, in effect, are congruent with all the divine prohibitions. This is also true for P, as I have already argued in vol. 1.21–26. Its effect, however, is more devastating. It leads not only to the pollution of the Temple (20:3), but explicitly, as emphasized in this pericope, to exile from the land (which may actually be implicit in P; vol. 1.254–61). Moreover, H's impurity is nonexpiable. Perhaps it is analogous to the final stage in the pollution of the sanctuary, according to P. Once the impurity has accumulated to a sufficient degree, the consequence is inevitable and irreversible. God abandons his sanctuary (in H's theology, God's land is his sanctuary; see NOTE on 25:23), and his people, unprotected and vulnerable, are subject to invasion and exile (see Introduction II E).

in any of these (practices). bĕkol-'*ēlleh.* Not just those ways specified in prohibitions, vv. 19, 20, 23, containing the root *ṭm*', but all of them (Wessely 1846).

the nations I am casting out before you. This refers to the Canaanites. "The nations" (*haggôyim*) clearly allude to the composite of peoples that composed the Canaanites. The "sin of the Amorites" (Gen 15:16) was sexual immorality— at least in the view of H (but see also Gen 9:20–27; 19:4–5).

I am casting out. '*ānî mĕšallēaḥ.* Lohfink's (1994: 195–212) claim that the basic priestly narrative (Pg) and H assume that Israel will not engage in a war of conquest is highly questionable. Even if we disregard Num 31; 33:50–56 as late material (contaminated by deuteronomic ideas), the cumulative evidence of the data on the wilderness camp cannot be gainsaid—for example, the two censuses of able-bodied men, excluding the clergy (Num 1, 26; cf. Milgrom 1990a: 336–39); the organization of the camp, either at rest or in march, for war (Num 2, 10:11–28; Milgrom 1990a: 340–41); the trumpet signals of a war camp (Num 10:1–10; Milgrom 1990a: 372–93).

Nonetheless, there is no doubt that according to Lev 18 and 20, Israel will not wage a war of conquest. Both the metaphors of the land spewing out its inhabitants and, explicitly in this verse, that YHWH himself will drive out the Canaanites *mippĕnêkem* 'from before you' imply that Israel will meet no resistance upon entering the land.

defiled themselves (with RSV). *niṭmĕʾû* (*Nipʿal*), can act as a reflexive of the *Qal*, *ṭāmēʾ* 'become defiled' (v. 25a). One may not deduce from the application of the root *ṭmʾ* to non-Israelites that the pollution incurred is noncultic: non-Israelites living on the land are required to observe all the prohibitive commandments (Num 15:27–31), including the cultic ones (see esp. Num 19:13, 20, and Introduction II O). H, however, adds noncultic sins, such as sexual violations, to the ambience of *ṭāmēʾ*.

25. *Thus the land became defiled. wāttiṭmāʾ hāʾāreṣ*. The rabbis, commenting "It (Canaan) is not like the land of Egypt," aver: "Regarding the land of Egypt, regardless of whether (you, its inhabitants) obey God's will or don't obey God's will, the land of Egypt is yours. The land of Israel is different: If you obey God's will, the land of Canaan is yours; if not, you are exiled from it" (*Sipre*, Eqeb 38).

Shadal, clearly unaccepting of the notion that the land can become defiled by human sin, suggests that *hāʾāreṣ* here should be rendered "people" (on the questionable model of Gen 41:57b). He did not notice, however, the distinction that the text makes between land becoming defiled and people becoming defiled: the former, as here, uses the *Qal* (*tiṭmāʾ*; cf. v. 27b) with the land; the latter text uses the reflexive for the people, *Nipʿal* (*niṭmĕʾû*, v. 24b) and *Hitpaʿel* (*tiṭṭammĕʾû*, v. 24a)—they defile themselves.

H has taken the ubiquitous notion that homicide pollutes the land (e.g., Gen 4:10–12; Num 35:33–34; Deut 21:1–9; Milgrom 1972) and applied it to other violations. The change is in keeping with H's terminological characteristic to metaphorize. Thus whereas homicide literally pollutes the area where the blood is spilled, in H, sexual violations metaphorically pollute the entire land.

What are the boundaries of "the land"? Since priestly theology holds that its eastern boundary is the Jordan River (Num 34; cf. Ezek 48), the tribes of Reuben and Gad, settled in Transjordan (Num 32), are living on impure land (Josh 20:7–8; 22:19). Hence the laws incumbent on God's land, such as the firstfruit of trees (19:23–25), the first grain (23:10–22), and the sabbatical and jubilee (25), do not apply to them. But what of YHWH's ethical demands? And what force does the entire complex of prohibitions whose violation leads to exile have for them? Perhaps one has to distinguish between national and individual punishment. The former would not apply to Transjordan, but the latter, the divine penalty of *kārēt* and the jurisdiction of the court, would still be operative (see NOTE on 18:29).

I called it to account for. wā'epqōd 'ālêhā. For this meaning of pāqad 'al, see Isa 10:12; Jer 5:9, 29; 9:24; Hos 4:14; Amos 3:14; Zeph 1:8, 9; 3:7; Zech 10:3. God's intervention is automatic; it is as though he had no choice. In Ezek 18, God's justice mandates the predicted consequence (v. 30a). All God can do is exhort (vv. 30b–32), as he does here. For an expanded treatment, see Schwartz (1987: 103–4).

it . . . for its iniquity. 'āwōnāh 'ālêhā. The antecedent is hā'āreṣ 'the land'. The land, of course, has not sinned, but it has become polluted by the iniquity of its inhabitants.

It can hardly go unnoticed that H's doctrine of land corresponds with P's doctrine of the sanctuary. Both function as the picture of Dorian Gray: as Israel's evil, ostensibly unpunished, continues to mar the face of God's sanctuary, so does the (sexual) evil of the inhabitants of God's land mar the face of the land (vol. 1.258–61). In either case, purgation must take place by either ritual (P) or exile (H).

vomited out. wātāqī'. The root is qy' 'vomit, spit' (cf. Akk. q/ka'u). Problem: the land will not vomit out its inhabitants until Israel gets there (and assists in the process). One expects to read wĕqā'â '(the land) will vomit out'. It is not a *futurum exactum*, which requires 'im or 'ăšer before the perfect (GKC 1060). It must be a perfect (as shown by qā'â, v. 28), as uniformly rendered by the Aramaic translations: wĕrôqînat 'emptied' (*Tg. Onk.*); ûpĕlāṭat 'disgorged' (*Tg. Ps.-J.*); wĕ'etgallêt 'exiled' (*Tg. Neof.*). Thus this linguistic slip betrays the time of the writer (Wellhausen 1963: 152–53).

Alternative approaches have attempted to eliminate the chronological discrepancy. Presumably, one such attempt is by the LXX prosōchthisen 'aggrieved' (also in v. 28). However, no such meaning for qā'â is attested. Another such attempt is to regard qā'â as a metaphor not of exile, but of rejection; that is, the land has rejected the Canaanites, and they are ripe for conquest. This interpretation ostensibly is supported by the participle mĕšallēaḥ '(I) am casting out'. That is, God, as yet, has not cast out the Canaanites. Once again, however, no such meaning "reject" for qā'â is attested. The discrepancy stands.

From the standpoint of history, the metaphor itself is inaccurate. There is no biblical or extrabiblical evidence that Israel expelled any group of Canaanites. That exile is clearly what the priestly tradition had in store for the Canaanites is unmistakably implied by Num 33:55 (H?). Either the writer was unaware of history, or he just did not let the facts interfere with his powerful image.

Perhaps the reason for using this metaphor was to create a polemic with a fundamental axiom of Canaanite religion: the land will vomit out its inhabitants not because they neglected fertility rites, but because of their immoral behavior. The rabbis pick up this theme: "Exile comes upon the world for idolatry (Deut 29:23–26), incest (Lev 18:25), bloodshed (Ps 106:38–46), and (for the neglect of) the sabbatical year (Lev 26:34)" (*m. 'Abot* 5:9; *'Abot. R. Nat*[2]. 41; cf. *b. Pesaḥ* 25a, 81a; *b. Yoma* 9b). "They (Israel) are exiled and others are settled in their place" (*b. Šabb.* 33a). "A parable is drawn: It is likened to a prince who

vomits out food that his digestive system cannot tolerate. So too the land of Israel can not sustain sinners" (*Sipra* Qedoshim 12:14).

26. *You, however, must keep. ûšĕmartem 'attem.* The exhortation of vv. 4, 5 is
here repeated to include the resident alien among those required to obey these
laws (Ibn Ezra). However, the alien was already adumbrated in the word *hā'ādām*
(see NOTE on v. 5). A structural reason is probably more responsible: to create
an inclusio with vv. 1–5. The emphasis of *'attem* 'you' is to differentiate Israel's
required behavior from the actual behavior of "the nations" (v. 24) who preceded them on the land (Dillmann and Ryssel 1897).

commit none of these abominations. wĕlō' ta'ăśû mikkōl hattô'ēbōt hā'ēlleh.
The use of *lō'* rather than *'al* to indicate the negative indicates that this is a command, not an exhortation (contrast v. 24a). The word "abominations" does not
refer to the specific prohibition labeled as such (v. 23), but to all of them (an
injunction repeated in vv. 27, 29; cf. *Sipra* Aḥare 13:18). As pointed out in the
INTRODUCTION to this chapter, the blanket use of *tô'ēbâ* to cover all the prohibitions is one of the indications that the peroration, vv. 24–30, is a subsequent
contribution.

neither the citizen nor the alien who resides among you. The alien, just as the
previous inhabitants, the Canaanites, is also required to observe these prohibitions because he, too, lives on the land (Ibn Ezra). Since the alien was adumbrated in v. 5 (see NOTE) and his inclusion in these laws is integral to the theology of H (see Introduction II O), this clause is clearly not an addition (pace
Cholowinski 1976). For speculations concerning the etymology of *'ezrāḥ* 'alien',
see the NOTE on 19:34.

27. *abominations. hattô'ēbōt.* Schwartz (forthcoming) argues that both H and
D (and Dtr) refer to Molek worship as a *tô'ēbâ* of the Canaanites on account
of which they were driven out of their land (Lev 18:26–27, 29; Deut 12:31;
18:9–12; 2 Kgs 16:3). D and H, however, use the term *tô'ēbâ* differently. Whereas
D categorizes the sacrifice of children (the name Molek does not appear in D,
but cf. 2 Kgs 23:10) among the abominable magical practices of the Canaanites (Deut 18:10–11) involving ancestor worship (see NOTE on v. 21b, and COM-
MENT B), H lists it among the abominable sexual practices of the Canaanites but
specifies it as a desecration of YHWH's name (for the significance, see NOTE on
v. 21b). It is not that H refrains from calling an individual prohibition an abomination; indeed, it designates the very next prohibition, sodomy, as *tô'ēbâ* (v. 22).
Thus there remains little doubt that for H, Molek was not especially a *tô'ēbâ*,
but, as stated, a desecration of the name of YHWH (21b; 20:3b).

people in the land. 'ansê-hā'āres, literally "people of the land." This unique
wording is for the purpose of distinguishing it from the common expression *'am
hā'āres,* which, in the priestly texts, refers to Israel (4:27; 20:2, 4) and, in H,
probably to its functioning executive body (see NOTE on 20:2).

before you. lipnêkem. Is the intent of this preposition spatial or temporal? A
temporal sense would require the verb *hāyû* 'were'. Thus the sense is spatial: Israel is at the moment not in the land but outside it.

and the land became defiled. wattiṭmā' hā'āreṣ. This use of *tāmē'* is metaphoric; otherwise, purificatory rites would have been prescribed (see INTRODUCTION to vv. 24–30).

28. *So let not the land vomit you. wĕlō'-tāqî' hā'āreṣ 'etĕkem.* Contrast this with *wĕlō'-tāqî' 'etêkem hā'āreṣ* (20:22). Here the emphasis is on "you"—that is, you, Israel, may suffer the fate of your predecessors—whereas there the emphasis is on *hā'āreṣ* 'the land' because the focus is on Israel's impending settlement on the land (20:22bβ; N. Shaked).

for defiling it. bĕṭam'ăkem 'ōtāh. Note that H consistently refrains from calling the land holy (a much later designation; Davies 1976: 29, n. 27). The reason, I submit, is that H is a priestly document. If the land were a sanctum (*qōdeš*), then ritual impurity—menstruation, for example—would automatically defile the land, mandating Israel's expulsion.

is vomiting out. qā'â. The cantillation mark indicates that the Masoretes read it as a participle, not a perfect. It would, then, correspond with the participle *mĕšallēaḥ* 'is casting out'. The process of the Canaanites' expulsion is already beginning, even before Israel reaches Canaan. Joosten (1994: 211, n. 65; 1996: 152, n. 65) correctly objects that "the participle usually requires the subject to be explicitly represented." Ibn Ezra (followed by Ḥazzequni) justifies the accentuation, claiming that it marks the past of *q'h* (forcing the assumption that the subject *'ereṣ* is, in this case, masculine). However, the other form of the verb in this verse *wattāqî'* indicates that the root is *qy'* and, hence, *qā'â* should be accented on the first syllable. Thus it should be should be read as a perfect, thereby revealing once again the later time of the author.

the nation. haggôy. The LXX, Pesh., and *Tg. Neof.* read the plural *haggôyim* 'nations', found in v. 24. A similar situation exists in the closing pericope to chap. 20 (vv. 22–28): singular *haggôy* (v. 23) is read by the Versions and Sam. as *haggôyim*, corresponding with the plural *hā'ammîm* 'the peoples' (vv. 24, 26). However, since *haggôy* is followed by two plural words *'āśû* and *bām* (v. 23), there the emendation *haggôyim* is warranted; here it is arguable.

29. *such persons shall be cut off. wĕnikrĕtû hannĕpāšôt hā'ōśōt,* literally "the persons who commit," repeating the verb *'āśâ.* The repetition is for emphasis. Whereas the punishment of exile is total, falling on guilty and innocent alike, the punishment of excision will befall only the sinners. H may have a deeper agenda in stating its theological belief: a polemic against P. In the latter's theology, the advertent and the inadvertent sinner share the ultimate punishment: both are brought down by their pollution of the sanctuary and the community's abandonment by God (vol. 1.258–64). H, however, maintains that there is a distinction: not only is the presumptuous evildoer exiled with his people, but he personally will suffer termination of his earthly line and excision from his clan in the afterlife (vol 1.457–61). This general penalty for the miscreants differs from that in chap. 20, which prescribes graded penalties, depending on the severity of the crime, a strong indication that these two chapters represent different sources (see INTRODUCTION to 20:9–21). It is also possible that the H tradent responsible for the exhortation (vv. 24–30) was stating, on the model of the Molek

(20:4–5; also the sabbath, Exod 31:14), that whoever the court fails to put to death (20:9–16) will be punished by YHWH with *kārēt*.

How much pollution can the land tolerate before it vomits out its residents? How many violations are required before they cause the exile of the nation? The text is silent. Perhaps H is following P's model of the pollution of the sanctuary. Just as it can be presumed that YHWH tolerates a low level of pollution in the sanctuary as long as it is purged by the purification offerings of inadvertent wrongdoers (Lev 4) and advertent miscreants (by the high priest, Lev 16) but will abandon the sanctuary (and the nation) if the pollution level of the sanctuary reaches a point of no return (vol. 1.254–61), so the progressive pollution of the land ultimately leads to its regurgitation of the pollution together with its inhabitants. H, then, has merely borrowed P's theology of the sanctuary and applied it to the land. The penalty of *kārēt* is discussed in detail in vol. 1.457–61 (see also chap. 20, COMMENT A, and NOTE on 20:3).

30. This verse forms an inclusio with the opening exhortation (vv. 1–5; cf. *ûšĕmartem*, *ʿăśôt mēḥuqqôt*, *na ʿăśû* with vv. 4, 5) and is also linked with the prohibition section: *ḥattô ʾăbôt* (cf. v. 22) and *tiṭṭamměʾû* (cf. vv. 19, 20, 23), terms that abound in the entire closing exhortation (vv. 24, 25, 26, 27 [twice], 28, 29).

So you will heed my prohibitions. ûšĕmartem ʾet-mišmartî. The usual rendering of *mišmeret* as "charge" ("an address of instruction or admonition," Funk and Wagnalls) must be totally rejected. This term means "taboo, prohibition" (Saadiah), as can be inferred from its associated verb *lĕbiltî ʿăśôt* 'not to commit', part of a negative command. This conclusion is enhanced by the verb *šāmar*, literally "guard," and the original meaning of the idiom *šāmar mišmeret* 'perform guard duty', which evolves into "keep under guard, safeguard" (Milgrom 1970: 8–14, esp. nn. 41, 43). It is therefore no accident that this idiom, when it does not convey its primary meaning of "perform guard duty" (and before it evolves into the later meaning "serve in a [priestly] unit"), generally refers to prohibitions, especially when its object is "YHWH" (e.g., 8:35; 22:9; Num 9:19, 23; 18:7a, 8 [all priestly texts]; cf. Milgrom 1970: 10–11).

of these statutory abominations. mēḥuqqôt ḥattôʿēbōt. Perhaps the laws and norms of the nations are described as *ḥuqqôt*, not as *mišpāṭîm* 'jurisprudence', because obviously much of the latter is acceptable.

before you. lipnêkem. Soltero (1968) argues that this word proves that v. 30 could not have been written by the author of vv. 25–29 since it proves that Israel is already in its land. However, as demonstrated in the NOTE on v. 27, *lipnêkem* can be understood spatially, not temporally.

and not defile yourself by them. wĕlōʾ tiṭṭamměʾû bahem, repeating *ʾal-tiṭṭamměʾû bĕkol-ʾēlleh* 'Do not defile yourself in any of these' (v. 24a) in chiastic relationship (M. Hildenbrand). Thus the peroration (vv. 24–30) is stylistically enveloped, with emphasis not on the pollution of the land, but on one's person.

I (who speak) am YHWH your God. ʾănî YHWH ʾĕlōhêkem. I have rendered this divine declaration to correspond with its rendering in v. 2 (and in v. 4) in order to indicate that it is an inclusio to the entire chapter and that it is a closing reminder that these prohibitions stem from the God who issued the Decalogue. "R. Ishmael says: The incest laws are severe since they begin and end with 'the Lord' " (*Sipra* Aḥare 13:3).

COMMENTS

A. Did H Permit Intermarriage?

The absence of a ban against intermarriage among the sexual prohibitions of Lev 18 and 20 demands an explanation. After all, the violation of these prohibitions causes impurity—not a cultic concept (see NOTE on 18:24)—both to the land and to those who reside on it (vv. 24–30). Moreover, these sexual violations are expressly attributed to the Canaanites (vv. 3, 24, 27–28), with whom Deuteronomy (7:3–4) and deuteronomistic (Josh 23:12; 1 Kgs 11:1–2) and protodeuteronomic sources (Exod 34:11–17; Langlamet 1969; cf. Caloz 1968; Reichert 1972) explicitly prohibit Israel to intermarry.

Maccoby (1996: 156) has argued that (1) the silence in Leviticus concerning intermarriage, as its absence of any injunction against murder, may be purely accidental; and (2) "The presence of idols among the holy people would be an inevitable result of intermarriage with idolaters." Hence the prohibition against idols (26:1). However, whereas homicide is not an issue in Leviticus—in view of H's obsessive concern for legitimate sexual unions (chaps. 18 and 20; see below)—intermarriage would have been forthrightly condemned and prohibited. As for idolatry, as discussed in the Introduction II D, H holds the same position as the eighth-century prophets, who also voice no polemic against idolatry. Furthermore, in the case of Molek worship, its devotees were in the main worshipers of YHWH and thus were no threat to "the holy people." Finally, 26:1 (and 19:3) is an echo of the Decalogue, and is not a contemporary reflection of religious mores in the time of H.

This glaring omission of intermarriage in H (and in P as well; see below) is especially striking to a social anthropologist: "What is unusual in the biblical laws of purity is they do not set members of the congregation apart from one another. The laws specify prohibited degrees of closeness, but not intermarriage with outsiders or lower classes" (Douglas, forthcoming). Indeed, the need for *Jubilees* (30:10), the rabbis (*b. Meg.* 25a; *Tg. Ps.-J.* on 18:21), and other Second Temple sources (e.g., Philo, *Laws* 3.29) to concoct a forced interpretation of Molek worship as a ban against intermarriage can be attributed to the embarrassment of not finding intermarriage among the prohibited sexual liaisons (see NOTE on 18:2; cf. Vermes 1981; Cohen 1983). How can we account for its absence?

The answer, I submit, can be found only by facing the fact that there is no absolute ban against intermarriage in preexilic times. Even Deuteronomy limits the prohibition against intermarriage to Canaanites (Deut 7:3–4), Moabites and Ammonites (Deut 23:4–7), but not to others (expressly exempting Egyptians and Edomites, Deut 23:8–9). The priestly sources (H and P), on the contrary, express neither opposition to nor prohibition of intermarriage. Endogamy is not a prerequisite for holiness, and, as noted by Kugel (1996: 23), God has separated Israel from the nations so that Israel will not follow their ways (20:23, 24b). Otherwise, contact with them—presumably including intermarriage—is not proscribed. (Note that Num 33:50–56 [probably H] exhorts Israel to expel the Canaanites [cf. Exod 23:27–33] but is conspicuously silent on intermarriage [contrast Exod 34:11–17; Deut 7:3–4].) Of course, evidence of aversion to exogamous marriage on ethnic grounds exists (e.g., Gen 27:46–28:2; Judg 14:3), but it does not achieve legal codification until the postexilic age, as will be discussed below.

D's obssession with the Canaanites may stem from its probable origin in North Israel, where Canaanite enclaves and contacts (e.g., with the Phoenicians) abounded and where the fear of religious syncretism with Canaanite religion is amply attested (e.g., 1 Kgs 18; 2 Kgs 1:2–6; 10:18–29). The H source, however, would not possess that fear because of its unique theological position. Its only concern, as demonstrated throughout its legislation, is the maintenance of the purity of the land. As a consequence, even the resident alien, the *gēr*, who observes all the prohibitive commandments, is permitted to remain on the land and is accorded complete civic equality (with the exception of land inheritance; see chap. 17, COMMENT B) with the Israelite. During the period of the monarchy, with full political control in the hands of the Israel and the Canaanites reduced to a small subservient minority (particularly in Judah, the probable provenance of H), intermarriages—the relatively few that would occur—would have been one-directional: the *gēr* would have become a worshiper of YHWH, a (possibly zealous) follower of his laws (e.g., Uriah, 2 Sam 11:11).

This state of affairs would have radically changed in the postexilic era. The relatively few returning exiles would have found the land occupied by many of the neighboring peoples. Their socioeconomic and political situation would be best described by the deuteronomic curse: "The alien in your midst shall rise above you higher and higher, while you sink lower and lower; he shall be your creditor, but you shall not be his; he shall be the head and you the tail" (Deut 28:43).

Under these circumstances, intermarriage would also have been one-directional—pointing the other way. The new *gēr*—politically independent, socially secure, economically better off—would have become a desirable spouse. Israel, though in its own land, was now threatened with assimilation. Thus among Ezra's first tasks was to stem this assimilationist tide. Without the benefit of an explicit legal precedent, he had to create a halakhic midrash (Ezra 9:2, 12), combining D's declaration that the people Israel are holy (Deut 7:6, etc.) (i.e., a sanctum) and P's dictum that the desecration (*maʿal*) of a sanctum merits divine punishment, but in the case of inadvertence—Israel being innocent of Ezra's "law"—the sin is expiable by the dissolution of the illicit marriages, followed by an *ʾāšām* offering (Lev 4:14–16; cf. Jer 2:3; Mal 2:11). For the details of this exegetical tour de force, probably the first inner biblical midrash, see the discussion in Milgrom (1976a: 70–74 [= vol. 1.359–61]).

"I think your analysis may help to explain why intermarriage was so common in the postexilic community, when the issue was confronted first by Ezra and then Nehemiah. The Jews must have thought that there was no prescriptive or prohibitive law on the subject so far as the written text was concerned. Apparently they weren't intermarrying with specific groups that were interdicted by the Deuteronomic Code" (D. N. Freedman, personal communication).

I began with the observation that in chaps. 18 and 20 and, indeed, everywhere else in the priestly texts, there is not a single ban against intermarriage. Ezra, it turns out, had to invent a halakhic midrash in order to create one. A by-product of this analysis now becomes obvious: chaps. 18 and 20, if not all of P and H, cannot be a product of the postexilic age.

B. Were the Firstborn Sacrificed to YHWH? To Molek? Popular Practice or Divine Demand?

Many scholars have conjectured that originally Israel sacrificed its firstborn males to YHWH (literature cited in de Vaux 1964: 70, n. 69). Its purpose would be akin to that of the firstfruits of the field, namely, to induce greater fertility (cf. Morgenstern 1966: 63–64). However, one can only side with de Vaux's (1964: 71) categorical rejection: "It would indeed be absurd to suppose that there could have been in Israel or among any other people, at any moment of their history, a constant general law, compelling the suppression of the firstborn, who are the hope of the race." And if one would point to the plethora of child burials in the Punic colonies as possible evidence of sacrifice, the paucity of infant jar burials in ancient Israel would provide evidence to the contrary. Besides, as demonstrated by the excavations at Carthage, children found in a single tomb probably came from the same family (Stager and Wolff 1984: 47–49).

Most of those who maintain sacrifice theory turn to purported textual sources, particularly Exod 22:28–29:

mĕlē'ātĕkā wĕdim'ăkā lō' tĕ'aḥēr bĕkôr bānêkā titten-lî kēn-ta'ăśeh lĕśōrĕkā lĕṣō'nĕkā šib'at yāmîm yihyeh 'im-'immô bayyôm haššĕmînî tittĕnô-lî

[28]You shall not delay the first (processed) fruits of your vat and granary. You shall give me the firstborn among your sons. [29]You shall do the same with your cattle and your flocks: Seven days it shall remain with its mother; on the eighth day you shall give it to me.

Since the most recent and comprehensive advocacy of this position has been advanced by Fishbane (1985: 181–87), I shall deal with his arguments seriatim:

1. The phrase "You shall do the same with your cattle and your flocks" (v. 29a) does not, as Fishbane claims, disrupt the syntax linking vv. 28b and 29b. If v. 29b were the continuation of v. 28b, one would have expected the legist to have added v. 29a at the end, yielding: "You shall give me the firstborn among your sons: Seven days it shall remain with its mother; on the eighth day you

shall give it to me. You shall do the same with your cattle and your flocks." On the contrary, the fact that v. 29b follows v. 29a shows that the two phrases are connected; that is, the injunction to give "it" to God after the eighth day refers to only the animal, not to the human firstborn. Moreover, the very examples of the *kēn-tāʿǎśeh* formula adduced by Fishbane (1985: 177–81) — Deut 22:1–3 (cf. Exod 23:4) and Exod 23:10–11 (cf. Lev 25:47) as well as its other attestations, Exod 26:4, 17; Deut 20:15; Exek 45:20 — demonstrate that it applies to only the cases that follow. Thus v. 29 is a harmonious writing, and if there is an addition in Exod 22:28–29, it is all of v. 29.

2. The syntax of v. 29 (MT) is not "grammatically awkward." The lack of a *waw* connecting *lĕšōrĕkā lĕṣōʾnĕkā* indicates that each noun is to be treated separately so that the following singular verbs are correct. (Indeed, even if a *waw* were present, it could mean "or" [e.g., Exod 21:15].)

3. The attempt to interpret Num 18:15a as connoting the sacrifice of the first-born human males is misbegotten. The verb *yaqrîbû* here does not mean "will sacrifice," but "will contribute, donate" (e.g., Num 7:2, 10–12, etc.).

4. Ezek 16:21 and 23:39 do not speak of the firstborn; Ezek 20:25–26 is discussed below.

It is crucial to keep in mind that the verb *nātan* 'give' in sacrificial contexts (occurring twice in Exod 22:28–29) is neutral. In no way does it imply that the "given" object need be sacrificed. The three occurrences of this verb in Lev 18:20, 21, 23 certainly do not mean "sacrifice." Indeed, in the Molek prohibition (v. 21), which clearly refers to a sacrifice, an additional verb *lĕhaʿǎbîr* has to be added to denote a sacrifice (see also Ezek 16:21). The same holds true for *nātan* in many other sacrificial contexts (e.g., Exod 30:12, 13; Num 18:12). And, of course, the Levites who are "given" to the priests (Num 3:9; 8:19) are not sacrificed; neither is Samuel, who is "given" to God (1 Sam 1:11). That *mattānâ* 'gift' can refer to firstborn sacrifice (Ezek 20:31; cf. Levenson 1993: 31) is countered by Num 18:6, 7, where it refers to the dedication of the Levites and priests to the sanctuary (see also Exod 28:38; Deut 16:17; Brin 1994: 215–17). Finally, just as the "first (processed) fruits of your vat and granary" (for the rendering of *mĕlēʾātĕkā* and *dimʿǎkā*, see Milgrom 1976a: 61, n. 216) are "given" — that is, dedicated to the priests but not to the altar — so are the firstborn. How the first-born is "given," whether as human or animal, is not stated. Thus the meaning of *nātan* in Exod 22:28–29 is equivalent to *qaddēš* 'dedicate' in Exod 13:2 (see below).

Levenson's (1993: 3–31) thesis that before the advent of the seventh-century prophets, Jeremiah and Ezekiel, YHWH not only approved of but also demanded the sacrifice of the firstborn is subject to question. He adduces as evidence the following four cases: the binding of Isaac (*ʿǎqēdâ*, Gen 22), the vow of Jephthah (Judg 11:29–40), the sacrifice of Mesha (2 Kgs 3:26–27), and the accusations of the prophets (Ezek 20:25–26; Mic 6:6–8).

To start with, the basic fact must be set forth: but for the case of the *ʿǎqēdâ*, God does not demand the sacrifice of the firstborn. Jephthah's vow is no different from the war *ḥērem* (e.g., Num 21:1–3; cf. chap. 27, COMMENT F); both are conditioned by *do ut des,* a bargain with God, repaying God for granting victory over the enemy. Mesha pays his god in advance. His act is not unique. Classical sources report the frequent sacrifice of children in cities under siege in Phoenicia and its North African colonies (for a survey of the evidence, see Weinfeld 1972b: 133–40). To be sure, these sacrifices are premised on the widespread belief that human sacrifice, especially of one's own child, is the most efficacious gift of all and, as evidenced by the narratives about Jephthah and Mesha, that it works. This fact stands out in the case of Mesha, since the lifting of the siege effected by his sacrifice totally cancels Elisha's victory prophecy to the forces of Israel and their Edomite ally (2 Kgs 3:18). Again, these narratives only reflect popular belief. Indeed, even the great prophets, in their opposition to this practice, never deny that it could be efficacious.

To be sure, Abraham's sacrifice of Isaac is explicitly demanded by God. Levenson (1993: 21), correctly in my view, citing archaeological evidence from Punic tophet urns of animal bones that were found alongside urns of children's bones, concludes that "the lamb or kid *could* take the place of the child, but at no period was the parent *obligated* to make the substitution. This strikes me as essentially the situation in Genesis 22, where Abraham is *allowed* to sacrifice the ram instead of Isaac but never *commanded* to do so."

As a result of this statement, Levenson is forced to conclude that the firstborn "given" to God in Exod 22:28 is commutable to an animal. In effect, Levenson is admitting that the verb *nātan* means "dedicate" (Speiser 1963). To be sure, *in theory*, the father has the option of sacrificing his firstborn. But is that what God wants? The only such example is the story of the *ʿăqēdâ*. Abraham could not have been shocked — in fact, he did not demur — when commanded by God to sacrifice Isaac, since child sacrifice occurred in his world, if not frequently, certainly in extremis. Abraham, however, could not exercise this option. He could not take along a substitute animal (note Isaac's question and Abraham's reply, Gen 22:7–8). Isaac may have intuited that he was the intended victim, but in effect he asked his father: Don't you have a substitute animal? And Abraham, in replying that God will provide the animal, was actually hoping that at the last minute God would change his mind and allow for an animal. By this reading, the suppressed prayer of the two protagonists surfaces into view, and the tension mounts. God *demanded* the sacrifice of Isaac, and Abraham complied. Thus he passed the test of faith. Why, then, does the story not continue (and end) with the divine blessing (vv. 15–19); why the intervening story of the ram (vv. 12–14)? The key is that God, *not Abraham*, provided the animal. It was an indication that, henceforth, the option of animal or child, as practiced by Israel's neighbors, remains theoretical for Israel. God, however, prefers the sacrifice of an animal.

Abraham's test was not that Isaac's death would have been a violation of the divine promise of progeny. According to the epic (JE) tradition, no such promise had been given to Abraham. Gen. 17 is H, and God's intention in Gen 18:17–18 is undisclosed. As for the vague promise of Gen 12:2, it could have been and was fulfilled through Ishmael (note the common expression *gôy gādôl,* Gen 12:2;

21:18). The promise of progeny is bestowed on Abraham as a reward for his unflinching faith (Gen 22:16–18).

"I gave them laws that were not good and rules by which they could not live" (Ezek 20:25–26; see also v. 31). Rather than denying that God ever sanctioned human sacrifice, as does his older contemporary Jeremiah (Jer 7:31; 19:5; 32:35; see NOTE on 18:21b), Ezekiel uniquely takes the tack that God deliberately gave such a law in order to desolate the people. The only way to justify Ezekiel's theodicy is that the people misinterpreted either Exod 22:28b (de Vaux 1964: 72) or Exod 13:1–2 (see below), or that God deliberately misled them in order to punish them (Greenberg 1983a: 368–70; Hals 1989: 141), on the analogy of God hardening Pharaoh's heart or Israel's heart (Isa 6:9–10; 63:17), but not that "YHWH once commanded the sacrifice of the firstborn but now opposes it" (Levenson 1993: 8). If that were the case, the prophet would have said so, as he did whenever a person radically altered his behavior (cf. Ezek 18).

Thus Ezekiel does not contradict Jeremiah's view that the people were mistaken in believing that God demanded human sacrifice; he supports it by the example of the firstborn males, whom the people sacrifice because they erroneously assumed that it was God's will (or because they did not realize that it was God's condign punishment).

"Shall I give my firstborn for my transgression, the fruit of my body for my sins?" (Mic 6:7b). This verse unambiguously states that the practice of sacrificing the firstborn was known and commonly thought to be desired by God. Its function is piacular—in a time of crisis (pace Ackerman 1992: 140), but not for fertility. Ackerman's citation of votive sacrifices of children as indicated in Phoenician and Punic stelae cannot be used as evidence to the contrary. First, it is methodologically unsound to base an argument (in our case for biblical Israel) on the practices of another culture without additional supporting evidence. Then, one might ask: Are not all vows responses to crises, which must be exceptionally great if the sacrifice is one's own child? Finally, Ackerman's only textual support that child sacrifice was a frequent occurrence in Israel is the plural *bannĕḥālîm* (Isa 57:5), a reference to many wadis where child sacrifice took place. Assuming that this difficult verse and its equally difficult context speak of child sacrifice (accepted in chap. 20, COMMENT C), it is still precarious to draw any conclusion from a single verse, much less a single word. In my opinion (equally conjectural) the plural form *bannĕḥālîm* 'in the wadis' suggests that with the official (under Manasseh) Molek site in the Valley of Hinnom permanently defiled by Josiah (2 Kgs 23:10), postexilic Israelites were forced to continue their *private* Molek worship in other wadis (see Introduction II D). This does not imply, however, that child sacrifice occurred frequently.

Ackerman (1992: 161) categorically states that Exod 13:1–2, 13, 15; 22:28; 34:19–20; Num 3:13; 8:17–18; 18:15 refer to child sacrifice, all without substantiation. Exod 13:2; 22:28; Num 18:15 have been refuted above. Exod 13:13, 15; 34:19–20 call for redemption, not sacrifice, and Num 13:13; 8:17–18 deal with the substitution of the firstborn by Levites (Milgrom 1990a: 17–18). In all these cases, redemption is for service, not sacrifice, and even here it is the result of Hannah's vow! It therefore was optional and rare, not mandatory and frequent, and it is categorically rejected by God. In any event, Micah's question reflects popular belief, not divine law.

Fishbane (1985: 181–82, n. 90) also adduces Exod 13:2: "Consecrate to me every firstborn; man and beast, the first issue of every womb among the Israelites is mine." As shown by Brin (1971: 148, n. 22), what man and beast have in common is the sanctification of their firstborn (see chap. 27, COMMENT D), which is explicated by the second statement that they must be transferred to the domain of God. But nothing is said concerning the *method* of sanctification (on which see Exod 13:12–13). Although Exod 13:2 can be interpreted as referring to an earlier practice of dedicating the firstborn to lifelong service in the sanctuary (cf. Rashbam)—an interpretation grounded in the priestly texts and in ancient Near Eastern parallels (see chap. 27, COMMENT E)—it in no way allows for or alludes to the sacrifice of the firstborn. All that can be said is that the verb *pādâ* 'ransom' used in connection with the firstborn (Exod 13:13, 15; 34:20; Num 18:15–17) implies that *in theory* the firstborn should be sacrificed. Israel's God, however, has decreed that they should be ransomed.

Furthermore, it is significant that the priestly laws exclusively use the verb *pādâ* rather than its near synonym *gā'al* for the redemption of the firstborn (Exod 13:13; Num 3:46–51; 18:15–17); *gā'al* signifies that the dedicated object originally belonged to the donor, whereas *pādâ* implies that, from the outset, it was the property of the sanctuary—that is, of YHWH (see NOTES on 27:27, and Milgrom 1990a: 152). Such is the case in Num 18:15. The first half *kol-peṭer reḥem . . . bā'ādām ûbabbĕhēmâ yihyeh-lāk* 'The first issue of the womb . . . human or animal shall be yours' is a general law. It stipulates that *theoretically*, the firstborn belongs to the priest. That is, the meat of the sacrificial firstling is a priestly prebend, and the firstborn is a servant of the sanctuary (on Num 3, see Milgrom 1990a: 17–18, 22–24). The second half of the verse *'ak pādōh tipdeh 'ēt bĕkôr hā'ādām* is a (later?) qualification. *In practice*, the priest shall see to it that the human firstborn is redeemed.

Finally, the suggestion that the Molek cult was dedicated to the sacrifice of the male firstborn must be dismissed out of hand. As recognized by Mosca (1975: 236–37, cited by Heider 1985: 254), daughters as well as sons were sacrificed to Molek (Deut 18:10; 2 Kgs 23:10; Jer 7:31; 32:35), and if 2 Chr 28:3; 33:6 are credible witnesses, in addition to the firstborn, children of the same family were sacrificed (Day 1989: 67). Moreover, Stager's (1980: 4–5) excavations at Carthage show that in earlier centuries, only single-child urns are in evidence, but in the fourth century, one out of three burial urns contained two or three children from the same family! Ackerman's (1992: 138–39) proposal of an evolution from firstborn to multiple-child sacrifice, based on this Carthagenien evidence, is unwarranted. First, there is no evidence that the single-child urns were of only firstborn. Second, no support be mustered for her thesis from biblical or ancient Near Eastern texts.

In sum, there is no evidence that the firstborn, except in crisis situations (e.g., 2 Kgs 3:27), were sacrificed; there is no indication that Israel's God ever demanded or even sanctioned this practice (except in popular belief); and there is no connection between the firstborn and the Molek.

C. Carmichael on Chapters 18 and 20

Calum Carmichael (1997) has recently applied the technique he honed in his many studies on Deuteronomy (for a trenchant critique, see Levinson 1990) to the priestly source, in particular three H chapters: Lev 18–20. Leaving aside his treatment of chap. 19, I shall focus on his radical theory concerning the methodology, order, and purpose of the forbidden sexual unions, chaps. 18 and 20.

Carmichael maintains that the laws of the Pentateuch, uniquely among the law corpora of the ancient Near East—or anywhere else—do not arise out of society's problems, but are pure literary creations, the product of a legist's musings over the narrative traditions of Israel's distant past. He explains the putative lack of order and inner logic in these lists by means of the following literary allusions: father, 18:7a (Ham and Noah, Gen 9:20–21); mother, 18:7b (Lot's daughters and their father, Gen 19:30–38); father's wife, 18:8 (Reuben and Bilhah, Gen 35:22); half sister, 18:9 (Abram and Sarai, Gen 12:13); grandchild, 18:10 (Lot's daughters and Abraham, Gen 19:30–38); half sister from the same father, 18:11 (Abraham and Sarah, Gen 20:12); aunt, 18:12–13 (Amram and Jochebed, Exod 6:20); paternal uncle's wife, 18:14 (Amram and Jochebed?, Exod 6:20); daughter-in-law, 18:15 (Judah and Tamar, Gen 38); sister-in-law, 18:16 (Onan and Tamar, Gen 38:9); wife and her daughter, 18:17a (Judah and Tamar, Gen 38); wife's granddaughter, 18:17b (Shelah and Tamar, Gen 38:11); two sisters, 18:18 (Rachel and Leah, Gen 30); menstruant, 18:19 (Sarah, Gen 18:11–12; Rachel, Gen 31:35); adultery, 18:20 (Sarah and Abimelech, Gen 20:3); Molek, 18:21 (Abraham and Isaac, Gen 22); sodomy, 18:22 (Sodom, Gen 19:5), bestiality, 18:23 (Shechem and Dinah, Gen 34); Molek, 20:1–5 (Judah and Tamar?, Gen 38); mediums, 20:6 (Judah and Tamar?, Gen 38); respect for parents, 20:7–9 (Judah and Tamar, Gen 38; Jacob and his sons, Gen 37:26–34); adultery, 20:10 (Joseph and Potiphar's wife, Gen 39); father's wife, 20:11 (Reuben and Bilhah, Gen 35:22); daughter-in-law, 20:12 (Judah and Tamar, Gen 38); sodomy, 20:13 (Judah and Tamar?, Gen 38); wife and her mother, 20:14 (Tamar with Onan and Shelah, Gen 38); bestiality, 20:15–16 (Dinah and Shechem, Gen 34:2, 31); half sister, 20:17 (Abraham and Sarah, Gen 12, 20); menstruant, 20:18 (Sarah, Gen 18:11); aunt, 20:19 (Amram and Jochebed, Exod 6:20); uncle's wife, 20:20 (Isaac and Sarah, Gen 20:12); sister-in-law, 20:21 (Onan and Tamar, Gen 38); Egyptian mores, 18:3; 20:25 (Joseph and his brothers, Gen 43:32); mediums, 20:27 (Onan and Judah?, Gen 38:9).

An overview of this list will immediately reveal that the narrative association is questionable. Moreover, Carmichael avers that the author of the lists for chaps. 18 and 20 grouped his narratives by incident. If so, he was erratic. The many allusions to the Tamar episode (twelve in all) are scattered in 18:15–17; 20:1–9, 12–14 and 20:21, 27, separated by many other narratives. Those that fall in the life of Abraham, ten in number, are in 18:7b, 9–11, 20–22; 20:17–18, 20; they are interrupted by Reuben and Bilhah, 18:8, and after v. 11 they resurface in vv. 21–22. In chap. 20, they are discontinued by Joseph and Potiphar's wife (v. 10), Reuben and Bilhah (v. 11), and Amram and Jochebed (v. 19). The same irregularity is present in the other groupings. This means that the writer free floats from one allusion to the next wherever his midrashic imagination takes him.

To illustrate the associative links (and leaps) made by Carmichael's imagined author, I shall focus on the Tamar and Abraham passages. There are only two obvious relationships contained in the narratives: Tamar the daughter-in-law of Judah (18:15; 20:12) and Tamar the sister-in-law of Onan (18:16; 20:21). According to Carmichael, it is the intercourse between son and father's wife (18:8; 20:21) that leads to the father and the son's wife (20:11)—via a circuitous route—and it is the "body uncleanness" of Sarah (20:19–20) that accounts for the impurity (*niddâ*) of Onan's intercourse with Tamar (20:21). In chap. 18, these two prohibitions are generated by different narratives: the daughter-in-law (18:15) by Amram's union with Jochebed (18:14), and the sister-in-law (18:16) by Tamar's union with Onan (18:15).

If any of these associative links seem questionable, our bewilderment increases exponentially when the narrative background for the laws themselves proves abstruse. Tamar's relations with two generations of men, Judah and Onan, trigger the opposite situation of a man having relations with two generations of women (18:17a), and prepubescent Shelah—of female status in the mindset of the lawgiver—"prompted him to come up with the third generation" (Carmichael 1997: 37), namely, the prohibition against marrying the granddaughter of his wife (18:17b).

The alleged cult-prostitute pose adopted by Tamar is the presumed background for the Molek and medium prohibitions (20:1–5), as well as the prohibition against sodomy (20:13) (on the nonexistence of cultic prostitution in Israel and the ancient Near East, see NOTE on 19:29). Tamar's cohabitation with a father and son prompts the legist to think of a contrasting situation, a man who marries a wife and her daughter (20:14). The rule against mediums (20:27) derives from Tamar's deceptive means to produce seed for her dead husband, Er.

The same bewilderment accompanies us as we examine the alleged references to Abraham and Sarah: Lot's daughters lying with their father is what prompts the equivalent relationship between a son and a mother (18:7).

The very thought of Abraham the granduncle of Lot's daughters (Gen 19:30–38)—a permissible union—triggers in the legist's mind the impermissible union of a man and his granddaughter (18:10). The sexual offense of Dinah with the son of an ass (Hamor, Gen 34), having prompted the rule against bestiality (20:16), is now associated with Sarah's near sexual offense with Abimelech (Gen 20:2), all because Abraham passed her off as his half sister (Gen 20:12), henceforth a forbidden union (20:17). Sarah's lack of sexual pleasure in her postmenopausal condition (Gen 18:11) leads the legist to the ordinary situation of a woman's sexual pleasure during menstruation, which he hastens to prohibit (20:18).

These examples should suffice to illustrate how the alleged lawgiver worked. Duplications of the prohibitions in chaps. 18 and 20 stem from different aspects of the same narrative or from different narratives: narratives featuring the woman trigger equivalent male situations (18:7, 17a; 20:14); and unusual second-generation relations suggest a third generation (18:10, 17b). The intertextual link between a prohibition and a proper name (20:16), the opposite sexual condition (20:18), two sexual offenses against women (20:16, 17), the many-stepped associations tying two slightly similar prohibitions (18:8; 20:11), the purported uncleanness of a purported sexually obsessed matriarch (20:19–20), and the use of the term *niddâ* 'impurity' in the prohibition immediately following (20:21)— these are some of the associative leaps that typify the mental acrobatics employed by this presumed legist to concert his list of forbidden unions.

Unfortunately, Carmichael makes two basic philological errors that undermine his narrative associations. Rendering *môledet* as "born," he deduces that 18:9 refers to Sarai, who was born abroad (*ḥûṣ*)—outside Canaan—and that 18:11, a case that ostensibly repeats in part v. 9, refers to Gen 20:12, where Abraham states that he and Sarah have the same father. In addition to the complicated exegesis needed to overcome the purported redundancy between v. 9 and v. 11, one is astounded to learn that the *place* of birth is a factor in determining the legitimacy of a marriage. All of Carmichael's difficulties, however, vanish once it is realized that he mistranslated *môledet*, which means "kin group, clan." Thus v. 9 states that the half sister (from the mother's prior marriage) is from either the father's clan or another clan, whereas v. 11 states that the woman is a stepsister (not a half sister); there are no parents in common. However, if the mother is from the father's clan, then the woman is related and, hence, a sister (see further NOTE on v. 11). Thus 18:9 and 11 are two different cases, and they have nothing to do with the relationship between Abraham and Sarah. Carmichael is also in error regarding the term *dōdâ* (18:14). It refers to the wife of the paternal uncle (*dôd*; 20:20); it cannot mean either a father's or a mother's sister (Carmichael 1997: 170–71).

As I have demonstrated, there exists a discernible order in the two lists. Consanguinity and affinity are the principles that govern the primary relationships in 18:6–18, and they are followed by miscellaneous sexual practices in 18:19–23 (see INTRODUCTION to 18:6–23). In chap. 20, another principle is operative: the penalties. They are precisely graded according to their severity (see INTRODUCTION to 20:9–21). Thus one does not have to wonder with Carmichael (1977: 8) why the menstruant is found between the half sister and the aunt (20:17–19). The menstruant had to be placed with the half sister because both violations are punished by *kārēt*, whereas the violation with an aunt is threatened with the ambiguous *ʿăwōnām yiśśāʾû* 'they shall bear their punishment' (see its NOTE).

Above all, instead of searching for the origin of law in the historical literature of Israel, look—as with all laws, of all peoples, at all times—for the contemporary societal problems confronting the legist himself. To be sure, narratives do generate law, but these are the cases facing the legist and his generation, not some literary allusion from the distant, legendary past (see INTRODUCTION to 24:10–23).

19. RITUAL AND MORAL HOLINESS

TRANSLATION

Opening: Call to Holiness

¹YHWH spoke to Moses, saying: ²Speak to the entire Israelite community and say to them: You shall be holy, for I, YHWH your God, am holy.

Religious Duties

³You shall each revere his mother and his father, and keep my sabbaths: I YHWH your God (have spoken).

⁴Do not turn to idols, and molten gods do not make for yourselves: I YHWH your God (have spoken).

⁵When you sacrifice a well-being offering to YHWH, sacrifice it so it may be accepted on your behalf. ⁶It shall be eaten on the day you sacrifice (it), or on the next day; but what is left by the third day must be consumed in fire. ⁷But if it is eaten at all on the third day, it is rotten meat; it will not be acceptable. ⁸Anyone who eats of it shall bear his punishment, because he has desecrated what is sacred to YHWH; that person shall be cut off from his kin.

⁹When you reap the harvest of your land, you shall not destroy the edge of your field in reaping, and the gleanings of your harvest you shall not gather. ¹⁰Your vineyard you shall not pick bare, and the fallen fruit of your vineyard you shall not gather. For the poor and the alien shall you leave them: I YHWH your God (have spoken).

Ethical Duties

¹¹You shall not steal; you shall not dissemble, and you shall not lie to one another. ¹²And you shall not swear falsely by my name, lest you desecrate the name of your God: I YHWH (have spoken).

¹³You shall not exploit your fellow, and you shall not commit robbery. The wages of your hireling shall not remain with you until morning. ¹⁴You shall not insult the deaf, and before the blind you shall not place a stumbling block, but you shall fear your God: I YHWH (have spoken).

¹⁵You shall not do injustice in judgment. You shall not be partial to the poor or favor the rich; in righteousness shall you judge your fellow. ¹⁶You shall not go about as a slanderer among your kin; you shall not stand aloof beside the blood of your fellow: I YHWH (have spoken).

¹⁷You shall not hate your brother (Israelite) in your heart. Reprove your fellow openly so that you will not bear punishment because of him. ¹⁸Rather, you shall not take revenge or nurse a grudge against members of your people. You shall love your fellow as yourself: I YHWH (have spoken).

Miscellaneous Duties

¹⁹You shall heed my statutes.

You shall not let your cattle mate with a different kind; you shall not sow your field with two kinds of seed; and clothing made of two kinds of yarn you shall not put on yourself.

²⁰*If a man has sexual intercourse with a woman who is a slave assigned to another man, but has not been ransomed or given her freedom, there shall be an inquest; they shall not be put to death because she has not been freed.* ²¹*But he shall bring to the entrance of the Tent of Meeting, as his penalty to YHWH, a ram of reparation offering.* ²²*And the priest shall make expiation for him before YHWH with the ram of reparation offering for his wrong that he committed, so that he may be forgiven of his wrong that he committed.**

²³When you enter the land and plant any kind of fruit tree, you shall treat its foreskin with its fruit as foreskin. Three years it shall be forbidden to you; it shall not be eaten. ²⁴In the fourth year, all of its fruit shall be sacred, an offering of rejoicing to YHWH. ²⁵In the fifth year, you may use its fruit that its yield may be increased for you: I YHWH your God (have spoken).

²⁶You shall not eat over the blood. You shall not practice augury or divination. ²⁷You shall not round off the side-growth on your head, and you shall not destroy the edge of your beard. ²⁸Gashes in your flesh you shall not make for the dead, and tattoos you shall not put on yourselves: I YHWH (have spoken).

²⁹You shall not degrade your daughter by making her a prostitute so that the land may not be prostituted and the land be filled with lewdness.

Closing

³⁰You shall keep my sabbaths and my sanctuary you shall revere: I YHWH (have spoken).

³¹Do not turn to ghosts and do not search for wizard-spirits to become impure by them: I YHWH your God (have spoken).

³²In the presence of the elderly you shall rise, and thereby you will show respect to the aged; you shall fear your God: I YHWH (have spoken).

Appendix

³³When an alien resides with you in your land, you shall not oppress him. ³⁴The alien residing with you shall be to you as a citizen among you. You shall love him as yourself, for you were aliens in the land of Egypt: I YHWH your God (have spoken).

³⁵You shall not do injustice in judgment, (namely,) in measures of weight or capacity. ³⁶You shall have an honest scale, honest weights, an honest ephah, and an honest hin.

---

*Vv. 20–22 are an insertion from the *P* source.

Closing Exhortation

I YHWH am your God who freed you from the land of Egypt. [37]You shall heed all my statutes and all my rules, and you shall do them: I YHWH (have spoken).

Comment
Holiness

INTRODUCTION

Chapter 19 differs from all other priestly pericopes (in both P and H). Whereas each of the others expounds a unified theme, this chapter comprises a miscellany of laws (ritual and ethical, apodictic and casuistic, directed to the individual and to the collective; see Schwartz, forthcoming). Its diverse nature can be explained not only on the obvious grounds that it has no common theme (or themes), but by its opening statement (v. 2), namely, that the purpose of all the enumerated laws is to set the people of Israel on the road to holiness. Thus this chapter opens with a command to Israel to be holy and then specifies how holiness is to be achieved. The call to holiness is found only in chaps. 19–22 (19:2; 20:7, 8, 21; 21:16, 23, 22:16, 32) and in two other H passages (11:44–45; Num 15:40) at the beginning or end of units. The peroration *'ănî YHWH* 'I YHWH' is found eighteen times in this chapter and throughout chaps. 18–26. The laws incorporated into chap. 19 were chosen for their aptness to be subsumed under the rubric of holiness or its negation, impurity and desecration. The holiness breakdown of each law is discussed in the COMMENT on holiness. The structure of chap. 19 usually suggested is that it comprises three sections that can be subdivided into fourteen units, each closed by "I YHWH," framed by an introduction and a closing exhortation:

A. Introduction (vv. 1–2a)
B. Religious duties (vv. 2b–10)
    1. Be holy (v. 2b)
    2. Honor parents and the sabbath (v. 3)
    3. No idolatry (v. 4)
    4. On food, sacrificial and ordinary (vv. 5–10)
C. Ethical duties (vv. 11–18)
    5. Honesty (vv. 11–12)
    6. No exploitation (vv. 13–14)
    7. Justice in court (vv. 15–16)
    8. Love your fellow (vv. 17–18)
D. Miscellaneous duties (vv. 19–37)
    9. No mixed breeding (vv. 19–25)
    10. No pagan practices (vv. 26–28)

11. No prostitution; revere the sanctuary (vv. 29–30)
12. No necromancy (v. 31)
13. Respect the aged (v. 32)
14. Love the alien (vv. 33–34)
15. Honest trading (v. 36)
16. Closing exhortation (v. 37)

These sixteen units are equally divided between those that end with *'ănî YHWH* 'I YHWH' (units 5–8, 10, 11, 13, 16) and those that close with the longer formula *'ănî YHWH 'ĕlōhêkem* 'I YHWH your God' (units 1–4, 9, 12, 14, 15). Expressed another way: the religious duties (units 1–4) have the long formula, the ethical duties (units 5–8) have the short formula, and the miscellaneous duties (units 9–16) have three of each. The third section, the miscellaneous duties, are set apart from the two preceding ones in that they are enveloped by an inclusion *'et-ḥuqqōtay tišmōrû* 'You shall heed my statutes' (v. 19aα) and *ûšĕmartem 'et-kol ḥuqqōtay* 'You shall heed all my statutes' (v. 37a; Wenham 1979).

Alternatively, Magonet (1983) proposes to divide the chapter into three different sections (vv. 1–18, 19–29, 30–37), each of which is headed by the verb *šāmar* 'heed'. Moreover, he notes that the first and third sections contain the same phrases:

v. 3b	*'et-šabbĕtōtay tišmōrû*	v. 30a	*'et-šabbĕtōtay tišmōrû*
v. 4a	*'al-tipnû 'el-hā'ĕlîlīm*	v. 31a	*'al-tipnû 'el-hā'ōbōt*
v. 14c	*wĕyārē'tā mē'ĕlōhêka*	v. 32c	*wĕyārē'tā mē'ĕlōhêka*
v. 15a	*lō'-ta'ăśu 'āwel bammišpāṭ*	v. 34b	*wĕ'āhabtā lô kāmôkā*
v. 18c	*wĕ'āhabtā lĕrē'ăkā kāmôkā*	v. 35a	*lō'-ta'ăśû 'āwel bammišpāṭ*
v. 19a	*'et-ḥuqqōtay tišmōrû*	v. 37a	*ûšĕmartem 'et-kol-ḥuqqōtay*

Thus vv. 1–18 and 30–37 represent two parallel panels with two of the elements in chiastic relation, thereby locking the panels (for similar examples, see vol. 1.846–47, 59–60, and Milgrom 1990a: XXVI–XXVIII). The chapter, therefore, takes on an AXA' pattern, the center X being the intermediate vv. 19–29.

The two proposals outlined above share a premise: the formula *'ănî YHWH* (*'ĕlōhêkem*) marks the end of a unit. It is this premise that vitiates the proposals. There are four clearly defined units that do not end with this formula (vv. 5–8, 19, 20–22, 29). But as pointed out by Schwartz (1987: 118), these units have a common denominator: they terminate in the third person and, hence, cannot be followed by a formula whose first-person subject is addressing a second-person object. That is, even if the author/editor wished to end this unit with the formula, he could not do so for stylistic reasons. Thus the units in this chapter are to be decided strictly by their content. Schwartz (1987: 115) divides the chapter into eighteen units flanked by a heading and a closing:

1. The heading (v. 2aβ,b)

2. Unit 1 (v. 3)	11. Unit 10 (vv. 20–22)
3. Unit 2 (v. 4)	12. Unit 11 (vv. 23–25)
4. Unit 3 (vv. 5–8)	13. Unit 12 (vv. 26–28)
5. Unit 4 (vv. 9–10)	14. Unit 13 (v. 29)
6. Unit 5 (vv. 11–12)	15. Unit 14 (v. 30)
7. Unit 6 (vv. 13–14)	16. Unit 15 (v. 31)
8. Unit 7 (vv. 15–16)	17. Unit 16 (v. 32)
9. Unit 8 (vv. 17–18)	18. Unit 17 (v. 33–34)
10. Unit 9 (v. 19)	19. Unit 18 (vv. 35–36)

20. The closing (v. 37)

This division commends itself, first, by its symmetry: both the first half (the heading and units 1–9) and the second half (units 10–18 and the closing) end with the injunction to heed all of God's statutes (*et-ḥuqqōtay tišmōrû*, v. 19aα; *ûšĕmartem 'et-kol- ḥuqqōtay*, v. 37aα). Indeed, the fact that v. 19 contains this injunction is a clear sign that there is a break after this verse (see its NOTE). Moreover, this injunction contains the same words that form an inclusion for chap. 18: Its introduction (vv. 1–5) ends with these words (*wĕ'et-ḥuqqōtay tišmĕrû*, v. 4aβ; *ûšĕmartem 'et-ḥuqqōtay*, v. 5aα), and its closing (vv. 26–30) begins with these words (*ûšĕmartem 'attem 'et- ḥuqqōtay*, v. 26aα). The only change that I have made in Schwartz's (1987: 115) division is in assigning v. 13 to the previous unit (see NOTE on "I YHWH [have spoken]," v. 12).

More important, however, is that this structure allows for all the units to fall under the heading *qĕdōšîm tihyû* 'You shall be holy' (v. 2aβ). That is to say, all the following units must be regarded as Israel's mandatory commandments for achieving holiness. Since, as will be shown, these units comprise ethical as well as ritual commandments—indeed, more of the former (units 1*, 4–8, 13, 16–18) than the latter (units 1*–3, 9–12, 14–15), we are given a glimpse of the revolutionary step taken by H in proclaiming that holiness, hitherto limited by P to the sacred sphere (the sanctuary) and its officiants (the priests), is now within reach of every Israelite provided that he or she heeds the cultic prohibitions and fulfills the ethical requirements specified in this chapter (see COMMENT, and Introduction I H).

Schwartz (1987: 120–22) also detects an editorial seam revealing a stage in the growth of the chapter. Holding the units on the *gēr* (vv. 33–34) and honest trading (vv. 35–36) to be supplements (see NOTES), he finds that the chapter's conjectured original close (vv. 30–32) forms an inclusion with its opening (vv. 3–4):

A *'îš 'immô wĕ'ābîw **tîrā'û***   B' *'et-šabbĕtōtay tišmōrû*

B *wĕ'et-šabbĕtōtay tišmōrû*   (A') *ûmiqdāšî **tîrā'û***

   'ănî YHWH** 'ĕlōhêkem* (v. 3)   ***'ănî YHWH (v. 30)

C *'al-tipnû 'el-hā'ĕlîlîm*   C' *'al-tipnû 'el-hā'ōbōt*

C *wē'lōhê massēkâ lō' ta'ăśû lākem*   (C') *wĕ'el hayyiddĕ'ōnîm 'al-tĕbaqqĕšû lĕṭāmĕ'â bāhem*

   'ănî YHWH** 'ĕlōhêkem* (v. 4)   ***'ănî YHWH (v. 31)

                                   (A') *mippĕnê śêbâ tāqûm*

                                     (A') *wĕhādartā pĕnê zāqēn*

                                        ***wĕyārē'tā** mē'ĕlōhêka*

                                        'ănî YHWH (v. 32)

Vv. 30–32 not only use the same vocabulary as vv. 3–4 (boldface), but also reveal how the one commandment to revere the parents (v. 3aα) is extended to the commandment to respect all elders (v. 32a; cf. Philo, *Decalogue* 165–67, who includes elders in the fifth commandment). Similarly, the single commandment to keep the sabbath (v. 3aβ) is repeated and supplemented to revere the sanctuary (v. 30a). That the love of the alien (vv. 33–34) is an extension of the love of one's fellow (v. 18) and that honest measures concretize the commandment not to "do injustice in judgment" (occurring in both v. 15aα and v. 35a) are explained in the NOTES on these verses. If this analysis proves correct, then chap. 19 exhibits a two-stage development: originally, it consisted of the heading and sixteen units (vv. 2aβ,b–32) plus the closing exhortation (v. 37, which also acts as an inclusion with v. 19); subsequently, it was supplemented by units 17 and 18 (vv. 33–36).

Crüsemann (1996: 326–27) has proposed the following division, based on the work of his pupil, A. Ruwe:

vv. 1–2	Holiness	vv. 36b–37	Exodus and fulfillment (?)
v. 3a	Parents and elders	vv. 31–32	Ancestral spirits (?)
v. 3b	Sabbath	v. 30	Sabbath
v. 4	Foreign (?) deities	vv. 26b–29	Foreign deities (?)
vv. 5–8	Sacrifice	v. 26a	Sacrifice (?)
vv. 9–10	Planting and harvesting	v. 23–25	Planting and harvesting
vv. 11–18	Ethics	v. 20–22	(?)

v. 19   Fulfillment by Israel

The attempt to construct an introverted structure founders on many forced parallels in the bipartite division, some of which I have indicated by question marks. Note as well that vv. 33–34, the *gēr*, and vv. 35–36, business ethics, are unaccounted for and that vv. 19 and 37 should not be separated because they form an inclusio for the second division.

Does this chapter have an organizing principle? The scholarly consensus holds that its original core comprises a reformulation of the Sinaitic Decalogue or an independent one of two decalogues. The latter position is taken by, among others, Mowinckel (1937), Rabast (1948: 11–15), Morgenstern (1955: 1–27, 39–66), Reventlow (1961: 65–78), Kilian (1963: 57–65), Sellin and Fohrer (1968: 69), Auerbach (1966: 266–68), and Elliger (1966), who argues for a dodecalogue. It invariably involves an anatomical dissection and verse rearrangement that undermine its plausibility. Besides, Scripture is unanimous in asserting that Israel was the recipient of a single Decalogue (Schwartz 1987: 182–83). The former position, that this chapter is built on the Sinaitic Decalogue, rests on a firmer foundation. The table below illustrates six attempts to find the Decalogue. These lists, both ancient and modern, are nearly identical. However, an examination of some of these parallels reveals that they are grounded on exegetical quicksand. For example, that v. 16 addresses the crime of murder (no. 6) is questionable (see its NOTE). That the prohibitions against prostitution (v. 29) and mixtures (v. 19) or the case of the betrothed slave-woman (vv. 20–22) all allude to adultery (no. 7) is far-fetched. The same holds true for the purported references in this chapter to nos. 9 and 10. The obvious objection to these parallels is that if chap. 19 had the Decalogue in mind, why was it exemplified with such rare, ambiguous cases? Would anyone who heard or read this chapter have thought of these allusions without looking for them in advance?

Nonetheless, there is a strong basis for maintaining that vv. 3–4, 30–32 reflect nos. 1, 2, 4, and 5, and that vv. 2, 36b had the prologue of the Decalogue (Exod 20:2; Deut 5:6) in mind. Note, first, that nos. 1, 2, 4, and 5 occur in near reverse order (5, 4, 1, 2) in vv. 3–4 (parents, sabbath, idolatry, images of YHWH). The claim that we have here a perfect chiasm and, hence, an intentional reference to the Decalogue (Schwartz 1987: 184, followed by Weinfeld 1985a, mistakenly omit no. 1) is vitiated by the position of no. 1. A stronger argument is the reappearance of nos. 2/1, 4, and 5 in vv. 30–32 (where their order is 4, 5, 2/1), even though their

TABLE 1. Six attempts to find the Decalogue.

X	R. LEVI (*LEV. RAB.* 24:5)	IBN EZRA (1961)	KALISCH (1867–72)	WENHAM (1979)	WEINFELD (1985A: 10–11)	HARTLEY (1992)
1	2b	2b	4a	4	—	—
2	4b	4	4b	4a	4a, 31	4b
3	12	12	12	12	12	12
4	3b	3b	3, 30	3, 30	3b, 30a	3, 30
5	3a	3a	3	3	3a, 32	3
6	16	16b	16	16	16	16
7	29	20–22	29	20–22, 29	19–25, 29	29
8	11	11a	11	11, 13	11a	11a
9	16	11b	11, 16	15–16	11b	11b
10	18	13a	18	17–18	35–36	17–18

grouping does not form a chiasm with either vv. 3–4 or the Decalogue. Rather, as explained above, the possibility that vv. 30–32 may have served as an inclusion for the original core of this chapter makes better sense as an attempt to place greater emphasis on these four Decalogue commandments.

Moreover, the appendix vv. 33–36 ends with a restatement of the prologue to the Decalogue (Exod 20:2; Deut 5:6), forming an inclusion with v. 2b (see its NOTE). Thus the H tradent responsible for the appendix must have been fully aware of the fact that the ending of the chapter, which he had before him (vv. 30–32), formed an inclusion with vv. 3–4 because of its citation of the Decalogue. He, therefore, decided to do the same when he inserted his addition by making a reference to the prologue of the Decalogue (v. 36b), thereby enclosing the beginning of the chapter (v. 2b). Whereas the quotations from the Decalogue are straightforward (hence, unambiguous), the reference to the prologue involves a revolutionary change: the God who freed Israel from Egypt (v. 3b) is defined by the quality of holiness, which can and should be emulated by his people through their fulfillment not only of the Decalogue but of the additional commandments he has enjoined upon them in this chapter (see further NOTE on v. 2aβ, b).

Schwartz (forthcoming) holds that vv. 11–12 in addition to vv. 3–4, 30–32 bear resemblances to commandments of the Decalogue. Since he (1996a; 1997) also maintains that the priestly tradition contained no Sinaitic story of the giving of the Decalogue, he (forthcoming) can account for its allusion in Lev 19 only as follows: "From the raw material that molded this chapter were also included certain elements in the nonpriestly traditions that form part of the Decalogue transmitted at Sinai."

Weinfeld (1985a: 10; 1991: 250–51) derives from the rabbinic statement *parāšâ zû ne'ĕmrā' bĕhaqhēl* 'this chapter was recited (by God) during *haqhēl*' (*Sipra* Qedoshim, par. 1:1) that it was part of the Sinaitic revelation, since the latter is called *yôm haqqāhāl* 'the day of assembly' (Deut 9:10; 10:4; 18:16). In that case, however, one would have expected the rabbis to use the deuteronomic term *yôm haqqāhāl* and not *haqhēl*. The latter, more likely, refers either to the same word in Exod 35:1 (the instructions to keep the sabbath in connection with the construction of the Tabernacle) or to the septennial reading of portions of Deuteronomy (Deut 31:12, according to *m. Soṭ.* 7:7)—in any event at occasions other than the Sinaitic revelation. Thus I disagree with R. Levi (*Lev. Rab.* 24:5) that the Decalogue is embodied in this chapter, but I heartily agree with the majority of the rabbis that this chapter is important *šerôb gûpê tôrâ tĕlûyîn bāh* 'because most of the Torah's essential laws can be derived from it' (*Sipra* Qedoshim, par. 1:1).

Nonetheless, there can be no doubt (contra Schwartz) that H was aware of the Decalogue and alluded to it in vv. 2–4 (and in the inclusio vv. 30–32). Note the following:

1. The only other time that "I YHWH your God" (v. 2) occurs at the head of a group of laws is in the Decalogue (Exod 20:2, Deut 5:6). Whereas in

the Decalogue YHWH identifies himself as the God of the Exodus, here he is identified as God the holy.

2. The very fact that commandments 1, 2, 4, 5, are reversed in vv. 2–4 alludes to Seidel's law, namely, that the author of Lev 19 is referring to an earlier list of these commandments, the Decalogue.

3. The puzzle concerning the omission of commandment 3 can now be solved. The legist only wanted to focus on an aspect of *šāw'* the false oath. He therefore brought it down to its proper context, v. 12.

Thus, the first five commandments are accounted for. It therefore stands to reason that the author of Lev 19 knew the Decalogue and made use of it.

It will be noted that Lev 19 refers to other laws in P—for example, vv. 8–10 and its parallel in 7:16–18; vv. 11–12, 20–22, and 5:20–26, sacrilege against an oath; vv. 3b, 30a, the sabbath, and Gen 2:1–3; Exod 16:23; 20:8; Deut 5:12. Lev 19 also shows strong connotations with laws in H, but in every case Lev 19 is the source from which the others are derived: charity for the poor, vv. 9–10 and 23–27 (see its NOTE); the sabbath and the sanctuary, v. 30 and 26:2 (see its NOTE); the only occurrence of *'ĕlîlîm* in the Torah, v. 4aα and 26:1aα (see its NOTE). It is no accident that the derivative verses, 23:22 and 26:1–2, are attributable, in my opinion, to Hr, the exilic and final H stratum. But it also shows the influence that this cardinal chapter exerted on later tradents.

NOTES

Vv. 1–2. Opening: Call to Holiness

2. *to the entire Israelite community.* '*el- kol- 'ădat bĕnê- yiśrā'ēl.* The LXX, possibly supported by 11QPaleoLev (36–37, 103), omits *kol.* A simple haplography occurred: the scribe's eye jumped from the "l" and the end of '*el* to the "l" at the end of *kol*, with the result that the word *kol* was lost in the process (D. N. Freedman, personal communication). This is the only place in Leviticus where the term *'ēdâ* occurs in a commission speech (contrast 4:13, 15; 8:3–5; 9:5; 10:6). This fact alone should suffice in favoring the MT. Namely, this chapter is of such extreme importance that Moses was commanded to recite it "to the entire Israelite community." Other commission speeches containing this expression are clearly intended to reach every responsible Israelite. Thus instructions for preparing the paschal sacrifice (Exod 12:3), for assembling the building materials for the Tabernacle (Exod 35:1; cf. v. 20), and for taking a census of all able-bodied men (Num 1:2, 18; 26:2) are also addressed "to the entire Israelite community."

This unique heading in Leviticus provides one of the reasons why its author(s) wished to communicate the notion that this chapter is central to the entire book (see Introduction I M). The rabbis also stress this fact: "Holiness [i.e., chap. 19] was not only given to priests but to priests, Levites and Israelites" (*Seder Elijah*

Rab. 145); this chapter was recited to the entire Israelite community "because most of the commandments are dependent upon [*tĕlûyim*; i.e., derivable from] it" (*Sipra* Qedoshim, par. 1:1), because the Decalogue is contained in it (*Lev. Rab.* 24:5; see above).

ʿēdâ is P/H's distinctive term for the entire Israelite nation — men, women, and children. In this usage, it occurs more than 100 times in the early narratives (e.g., Exod 16:1; 17:1; Num 16:22) and laws (e.g., Exod 12:19, 47; Num 1:53). It can also refer to all adult males (e.g., Num 14:1–4; 31:26, 27, 43), especially those bearing arms (e.g., Judg 20:1). Finally, *ʿēdâ* can be used of tribal leaders meeting as an executive body (e.g., Exod 12:3; Josh 22:14–16; Judg 21:10, 13) and acting on behalf of the entire community. Thus the *ʿēdâ* brings to trial and punishes violators of the covenant, be they individuals (e.g., Num 35:12, 24–25), cities, or tribes (e.g., Josh 22:16; Judg 21:10). It also crowns kings (1 Kgs 12:20) and even reprimands its own leaders (Josh 9:18–19).

The *ʿēdâ* was an ad hoc emergency council called together by the tribal chieftains whenever a national transtribal issue arose. Once the monarchy was finally established in Israel, the *ʿēdâ* fell into disuse and disappeared. It was replaced by the synonymous *qāhāl* (Milgrom 1979a). Another synonym for *ʿēdâ* is *môʿēd* (Num 16:2; cf. 1:16), an even more precise term for "council," attested in an eleventh-century account of the Egyptian Wen-Amon (*ANET* 29) in regard to the assembly called together by the king of Byblos (on the Phoenician coast) and in even earlier documents from Ugarit (north of Byblos; *UT* 137:14, 31). The nature and history of the biblical *ʿēdâ* closely corresponds to, and has been greatly illuminated by, the premonarchic and early monarchic political systems of the Sumerian city-states, located near the Persian Gulf, in the third millennium B.C.E. (Jacobsen 1943, 1957; Evans 1958; Milgrom 1979a).

Nonetheless, in this verse *ʿēdâ* unambiguously means the entire people of Israel. Its unique placement here underscores the importance of the prescriptions that follow: they are quintessentially the means by which Israel can become a holy nation.

You shall be holy, for I, YHWH your God, am holy. qĕdōšîm tihyû kî qādôš ʾānî YHWH ʾĕlōhêkem, literally "holy shall you be, for holy am I YHWH your God." Emphasis is clearly placed on the word "holy." This term is discussed in detail in vol. 1.729–32 in the NOTES on 11:44–45 *wĕhitqaddištem wihyîtem qĕdōšîm kî qādôš ʾānî . . . wihyîtem qĕdōšîm kî qādôš ʾānî* 'You shall sanctify yourselves and be holy, for I am holy . . . and you shall be holy, for I am holy'. Because of their emphasis on holiness, their other distinctive vocabulary, and their placement in chap. 11, these two verses were assigned to H (vol. 1.695–96). In that context, the prohibitions against touching and eating impure animal food, holiness is attained by separation and abstention, as emphasized by the rabbinic comment on those verses: "As I am holy you should be holy; as I am separated you should be separate [*pĕrûšîm* > Pharisees]" (*Sipra* Shemini 12:3). This is how the rabbis also interpret Lev 19:2 (*Sipra* Qedoshim, par. 1:1) by stating that "Israel's behavior is different from that of other nations" (*Num. Rab.* 10:1) and by connecting this verse with the preceding chap. 18, namely "from illicit sexual unions" (*Lev. Rab.* 24:6; cf. *y. Yeb.* 2:4). Indeed, the rabbis refine this negative aspect of holiness: "Sanctify yourselves in what is permitted to you" (*b. Yeb.* 20a), which Ramban explicates: "One should lessen sexual relations . . . sanctify himself by minimizing wine (intake) since the text calls the Nazirite 'holy' . . . also he should guard his mouth and tongue from defiling himself by vulgar overeating and from despicable talk." That is, holiness implies abstentions even within the performance of positive acts. Thus the *imitatio dei* implied by this verse is that just as God differs from human beings, so Israel should differ from the nations (20:26), a meaning corroborated by the generalization that encloses this chapter (v. 37): Israel is holy only if it observes YHWH's commandments (Schwartz 1987: 112–13). According to Greenberg (1979: 301, n. 56),

> Abraham son of Maimonides (14 cent., on Exod 19:6) offers this enlightened comment: The essential meaning of this is: Within every community, even among idolaters, there are some pious, ascetical worshipers—such as nowadays, the priesthood among the Hindus and the Christians—while the rest of the community are abandoned to licentiousness. . . . Therefore God said, "You must all be holy"; that is, "Among you it must not be that some are pious and ascetical while others are abandoned to license and transgression."

To be sure, the holiness command here differs from all others in that it heads a chapter and thereby constitutes a generalization (contrast the specific contexts of the other *qādōš* attestations, 11:44–45; 20:7; 21:7–8; cf. Abravanel): "When he (the Lord) says 'be holy' the holiness of all the commandments is meant" (*Sipra* Qedoshim 10:2). However, when we scan the contents of this chapter, although most of the commandments are negative (about thirty), many are positive (about fourteen). Thus holiness implies not only separation from (*qdš min*) but separation to (*qdš lě*), and since YHWH is the standard by which all holiness is measured, the doctrine of *imitatio dei* takes on wider dimensions: "It is comparable to the court of the king. What is the court's duty? To imitate the king!" (*Sipra* Qedoshim, par. 1:1). Moreover, since the ethical commandments are also generators of holiness (e.g., v. 2a, 9–11, 13–14, 16–18, 29a, 32–36), the rabbinic deduction is obvious: "As he (the Lord) is gracious and compassionate (cf. Exod 34:6) so you should be gracious and compassionate" (*Mek.* Shira, par. 3; *b. Šabb.* 133b). Obviously, the commandments prescribed in this chapter do not apply to the deity (e.g., abstain from idolatry, revere parents, how to sacrifice, refrain from cursing the blind or spreading gossip). Similarly, when Matthew states, "Be perfect as your heavenly father is perfect" (5:48), and then defines perfect as "sell your possessions and give (the money) to the poor" (19:21), he obviously does not mean that his definition applies to God. Rather, the observance of the commandments will lead Israel, negatively, to be set apart from the nations (cf. 20:26), as God is set apart from his creatures (the primary meaning of the root *qdš*; see COMMENT) and, positively, to acquire those ethical qualities, such as those indicated in the divine attributes enumerated to Moses (Exod 34:6), cited by the rabbis, above. This dual obligation of both withdrawal and participation inherent in the nature of the deity was fully captured by Buber (1964: 96): "God is the absolute authority over the world because he is separated from it and transcends it but He is not withdrawn from it. Israel, in imitating God by being a holy nation, similarly must not withdraw from the world of the nations but rather radiate a positive influence on them through every aspect of Jewish living."

The positive aspect of *imitatio dei* is spelled out in the book of Deuteronomy:

'ōśeh mišpaṭ yātôm wě'almānâ wě'ōhēb gēr lātet lô leḥem wěśimlâ wā'ăhabtem 'et-haggēr kî-gērîm hěyîtem bě'ereṣ miṣrāyim

[18]He (YHWH) executes justice for the fatherless and the widow, and **loves** *the alien*, giving him food and clothing.
[19]**Love the alien**, therefore, for you were *aliens* in the land of Egypt.

The term "aliens" occurs three times (Deut 10:18–19). Since YHWH related to you with love when you were aliens in Egypt, you should relate to aliens in your midst with love. Note that the *gēr* 'alien' is pulled out of the standard formula *gēr yātôm wě'almānâ* 'alien, fatherless and widow', so it can be governed by the verb *'āhab* 'love'. This emphasizes that since the alien is not an Israelite, he should not be treated with hostility or with indifference, but with love. The rationale is *imitatio dei*. Love, meaning compassionate deeds (see NOTE on 19:18), is specified as the basic essentials for life: food and clothing.

In Lev 19:33–34, *imitatio dei* is stated, rather implied, prohibitively. "Since YHWH redeemed you from oppression when you were aliens in the land of Egypt, so you should not oppress him but 'redeem' him by granting him equivalent civil rights" (see COMMENT).

Thus both aspects of *imitatio dei*, performative and prohibitive, are specified in the two cited passages through the medium of YHWH's love of the alien. This bivalent quality of love is neatly caught by Nasuti (1986:16): "On the one hand, a connection is made with the Egyptian situation and Israel's continuing status as former sojourners / slaves is emphasized. At the same time, a connection is made with the God who liberated them from Egypt and an imitation of that God's actions and attributes is mandated. The Pentateuch laws work to preserve both identities. Put in another way, the laws work to define Israel's present identity in terms of its past status and its future goal."

Here, Schwartz (forthcoming) demurs that *imitatio dei* is a misbegotten concept, since Israel's requirements for achieving holiness are obviously different from the holiness of God, to whom Israel's commandments do not apply. Nonetheless, if one is careful not to take *imitatio dei* literally, but rather to follow the *text* of 19:2 literally, namely, strive for holiness, *qědōšîm tihyû*, and thereby approach God's holiness, *kî qādôš 'ānî*, then the concept can be maintained: *imitatio dei* means live a godly life.

Thus, on the one hand, Israel should strive to imitate God, but, on the other hand, it should be fully aware of the unbridgeable gap between them: "(One may think that) one can be (holy) like me? Therefore, it is written *kî qādôš 'ānî* 'for I am holy' " (*Lev. Rab.* 24:9). This ostensibly enigmatic statement is clarified by the Masoretic pointing of the word "holy": when it refers to God, it is written *plene, qādôš,* but when it refers to Israel, it is defective (the same holds true in 11:44–45; cf. 20:7, 26; 21:7–8; Num 6:5, 8). The Masoretes continually and meticulously distinguish between divine and human (Israelite, priestly, Naziritic) holiness when the two are compared, allowing "full" holiness (*plene*) to be attributed only to God. Thus the Masoretes, too, imply the doctrine of *imitatio dei*: observance of the divine commandments leads to God's attribute of holiness, but not to the same degree—not to God, but to godliness.

Schwartz (forthcoming) rightly points to the expression *kî qādôš 'ănî* (11:44, 45; 19:2; 20:26) as indicating the total otherness of God, his unbridgeable distance from man (cf. Lev 10:3; Josh 24:19; Isa 6:3; Ezek 28:22; Hos 11:9). This numinous, irrational, and ineffable aspect of the deity (cf. the classic treatment of Otto 1958) is probably the root meaning of *qādôš* as applied to God, and the notion of separateness would then be derivative (Jensen 1992: 48, n. 4; Joosten 1996: 123).

As noted by Morgenstern (1955: 10–12), this verse parallels the preamble to the Decalogue, a view supported by the inclusio (v. 36b), which is precisely the opening line of the Decalogue (Exod 20:2; Deut 5:6; see INTRODUCTION). This chapter, therefore, stands in sharp contrast to the previous chapter, which is actually headed by YHWH's self-declaration, as found in the Decalogue (18:2b). The importance of this change cannot be overestimated: for H, the God of the covenant is demanding more than obedience to his commandments (v. 37). He is also stating the rationale or, rather, the goal, the end product of the commandments. Obedience produces godliness, a quality encapsulated in the word *qādôš* 'holy'. Just as the priests, who are innately holy, are qualified to enter into God's presence (*qĕrōbay* 'those near to me', 10:3), so Israel, in following all YHWH's commandments (19:37), will attain holiness (v. 2), thereby also qualifying for perpetual admission into the presence—that is, the providence and protection—of God.

Finally, this verse also embodies H's response to the prophetic indictment against the social and economic injustices prevailing in the land, unwittingly— and at times, brazenly—supported by the priesthood (see Introduction II K, L). Indeed, it is H's counterchallenge to the prophets. First, H adopts Isaiah of Jerusalem's staccato emphasis on holiness as God's quintessential attribute: YHWH is *qĕdôš yiśrā'ēl* 'the Holy One of Israel' (Isa 1:4; 5:19, 24; 10:20; 12:6; 17:7; 29:19; 30:11, 12, 15; 31:1), *hā'ēl haqqādôš* 'the holy God' (5:16), and *qādôš* 'holy' (6:3 [thrice])—for a total of fifteen times. Isaiah also attributes holiness to Israel, but only to *hanniš'ār bĕṣiyyôn wĕhannôtār bîrûšāla(y)im qādôš yē'āmer lô* 'whoever remains in Zion and is left in Jerusalem will be called "holy" ' (Isa 4:3). That is, only after the apocalyptic purge of the wicked (cf. Isa 1:24–25; 3:1–15; 5:8–30; 6:11–13) will those who survive qualify, upon their repentance (*šĕ'ār yāšûb*, Isa 10:21–22), to enter the New Zion (Isa 4:3–4; 33:14–16; Milgrom 1964: 167–72). H, however, rejects this gloomy forecast. The entire Israelite community (*kol-hā'ēdâ*)—including the worst sinners among them—is

capable of attaining the requisite holiness that will enable it to remain and pros-
per in God's presence, namely, in the promised land. (In effect, the land is holy,
though H refrains from using that term; see NOTE on "the land is mine," 25:23,
and Introduction II I.) H, therefore, produces a program constituting both commandments (e.g., chap. 19) and reforms (e.g., chap. 25) by which socioeconomic
injustices will be eliminated, thereby obviating the need for a nationwide purge
of the wicked (details in Introduction II K).

I, YHWH your God. *'ănî YHWH 'ĕlōhêkem.* The full formula is found eight
times in this chapter, once beginning and ending with YHWH's self-declaration
(vv. 2, 36) and six times attached to specific laws (vv. 3, 4, 10, 25, 31, 34). However, as noted above, this first verse (v. 2) is in reality a specific commandment:
that Israel should be holy. Thus there are seven laws (vv. 2, 3, 4, 10, 25, 31, 34)
ending with YHWH's self-declaration (v. 36). We should also note that, similarly, the short formula *'ănî YHWH* 'I YHWH' is also found eight times, seven
times attached to specific laws (vv. 12, 14, 16, 18, 28, 30, 32) and once ending
with a generalization (v. 37). Thus the variation between the two formulas is not
arbitrary. They are equal in number, but contextually they make two parallel
panels: $7 + 7 \parallel 7 + 1$. As noted by Schwartz (1987: 118–19), the distribution is
generally based on grammatical grounds: the long form containing the same
plural *'ĕlōhêkem* is attached to commands in the second plural (vv. 3, 4, 10 [cf.
9aα], 25, 31, 34), but verses in the second singular carry the shorter form (vv.
12, 14, 16, 18, 32). Unfortunately, this neat distinction breaks down in the case
of three verses (28, 30, 37). Thus Schwartz's (1987: 119) justification for their
exceptional nature is unconvincing. The formulas serve only a structural function: to fuse the disparate laws of this chapter into an aesthetic unity.

This is not the formula's only function, however. More significant is that in
this verse—the preamble or general heading of the entire chapter—it formu-
lates a definition of the deity. YHWH is *qādôš.* Henceforth, whenever the formula apears, the holiness of YHWH will be implied (see INTRODUCTION to vv.
10–11, and the end of the COMMENT).

Whereas the long formula serves as a marker for ending a law (discussed in
NOTE on v. 4), here, in this opening verse (and in v. 36), because of its distinctive use of *kî,* it forms part of a motive clause. The many other attestations of
this full formula preceded by *kî* (e.g., Exod 6:7; 16:12; Lev 11:44; 20:7; 24:22;
25:17; 26:1; Ezek 20:20) suffice to explain why the plural *'ĕlōhêkem* occurs in
a singular context. The midrash, however, has a more charming answer:

> R. Joshua ben Levi taught in the name of R. Simeon ben Yohai. By terming
> himself "thy God" [Exod 20:2], the Holy One, blessed be He, provided Israel
> with a loophole whereby extenuation would be asked for them. For at first
> they had risen up to say "All that YHWH has spoken we will faithfully do"
> (Exod 24:7), but then later they said (of the golden calf) "This is thy God, O
> Israel" (Exod 32:4); hence God was about to destroy them, as is said "There-
> fore he said that he would destroy them. . . . Moses, his chosen, stood before
> him in the breach, to turn back his wrath, lest he should destroy them" (Ps

106:23). And Moses said to the Holy One, blessed be He: Master of the universe, was it not *to me alone* that you said on Mt. Sinai "I am the Lord *thy* God?" . . . The Holy One, blessed be He, according to R. Joshua of Siknin citing R. Levi, replied: Moses, you speak well in defense of my children. In a bygone time I used to address the children of Israel using the singular "thee"—"I am the Lord thy God." Henceforth I shall speak to them as "you," using the plural, "I the Lord your God" (Lev 19:2)—in the plural, so as to enjoin every one of you. (*Pesiq. R.* 21:14)

V.3. Unit 1: Revere Parents and Keep the Sabbath (Ethics and Cult)

each (of you). *'îš*. This word before a plural has individualizing force (cf. LXX; Saadiah, Ibn Ezra), as in *'îš 'îš 'el-kol-šĕ'ēr bĕśārô* [sing.] *lō' tiqrĕbû* [pl.] 'No one shall approach anyone of his own flesh' (18:6); *lō' tignōbû* [pl.] *wĕlō'- tĕkahăšû* [pl.] *wĕlō'- tĕšaqqĕrû* [pl.] *'îš ba'ămîtô* [sing.] 'You shall not steal; you shall not lie; you shall not deceive one another' (19:11).

revere. *tîrā'û*. The reference to the Decalogue is obvious, and it helps to explain the reversal of object and verb in this verse:

Exod 20:12 (Deut 5:16)	Lev 19:3
kabbēd 'et- 'ābîkā wĕ'et-'immekā	*'îš 'immô wĕ'ābîw tîrā'û*

This chiastic relation is enhanced by another chiasm: the reversal of the order of the sabbath and parents commandments of the Decalogue (Exod 20:8–12; Deut 5:12–16) in this verse (Paran 1989: 10; cf. Hoffmann 1953; Paton 1897: 53; Schwartz 1987: 126). Thus the conviction, stated in the introduction to this chapter, that its author had the Decalogue in mind is further corroborated. More important, the fact that this one verse combines a quintessentially ethical commandment with a quintessentially ritualistic one is proof, corroborated by the rest of the chapter, that in H's value system both ethics and ritual are of equal rank.

The verbs *yārē'* and *kibbēd* are frequently attested in parallel stichs (e.g., Isa 25:3, 29:13; Pss 22:24; 86:11–12). However, the difference between them should not be ignored. The verb *yārē'* acknowledges the inferiority of the subject; the verb *kibbēd* acknowledges the superiority of the object (see esp. Mal 1:6; Schwartz 1987: 125). Moreover, *kibbēd* generally implies a positive act of homage (Num 22:17–18; Judg 13:17; 2 Sam 10:3; Isa 43:20; Prov 3:9), whereas *yārē'* evokes awe or fear of punishment and, hence, implies refraining from certain actions (Isa 58:13, however, uses *kibbēd* for abstentions). The rabbis exemplify this distinction regarding behavior toward one's father: *yārā'* means to abstain from bad acts, such as interrupting him, contradicting him, or occupying his seat; *kibbēd* means to act on his behalf, such as feeding him, dressing him, and supporting him (*Sipra* Qedoshim, par. 1:10, *y. Pe'a* 1:1; cf. *b. Qid.* 31b). Perhaps *yārē'* was chosen because of the juxtaposition of the sabbath, which is kept (*šāmar*) by abstentions

(Schwartz 1987: 126–27; for the negative connotation of *šāmar*, see NOTE on 18:4). However, since the meaning of *yārē'* here is not "fear," but "revere" (see below), positive acts toward parents are also implied (see further Weinfeld 1991: 310–11). In a comprehensive review of the entire corpus of relevant ancient Near Eastern texts, Greenfield (1982) has demonstrated that Akkadian *palāḫu* (= Heb. *yārē'*) concretizes its basic meaning of "revere" one's parents by specifying to house, feed, dress, bewail, and bury them. Similarly, Akkadian *kubbutu* (= Heb. *kibbēd*) means "honor" one's parents by treating them well. Tigay (1996: 357, n. 100) notes that in Nuzi-Akkadian adoption contracts, "revere" (in text no. 3) is replaced by "provide food and clothing" (in text no. 2; cf. *ANET* 219–20).

The verb *yārē'* means both "fear" and "revere," as does its Akkadian equivalent *palāḫu* (Grüber 1990a: 412–16). These two connotations can generally be distinguished: followed by the preposition *min*, it means "fear" (e.g., vv. 14, 32); followed by the *nota accusativa 'et*, it means "revere" (e.g., vv. 3, 30; Ehrlich [H] 1899–1900; Albertz 1978).

his mother and his father. The order is reversed in the LXX, Pesh., and *Tg. Neof.*, possibly to harmonize it with the Decalogue. Elsewhere, the mother precedes the father only in 21:2 (see its NOTES). What could be its rationale here? Some critics (e.g., Kilian 1963; Elliger 1966; Snaith 1967) claim that it makes no difference. Baentsch (1903) suspects that it is a reflex of an earlier matriarchy. The rabbis posit the following reason: "A man honors his mother more than his father because she sways him with persuasive words. Therefore in the commandment to honor (Exod 20:22) he (God) mentions the father before the mother. . . . A man is more afraid of his father than his mother because he teaches him the Torah. Therefore in the commandment (Lev 19:3), he mentions the mother before the father. . . . Scripture thus declares that both are equal, the one as important as the other" (*Mek.* Bahodesh 8). An analogous interpretation has been proposed by moderns: respect for parents, especially for the mother, had diminished and, therefore, had to be stressed (Porter 1976; Noth 1977). Albertz (1978: 372–73) has explained the first position of the mother in light of the husband's concern that his wife be taken care of if he predeceases her, and Levine (1989) suggests that in familial contexts, deference is shown to the mother (e.g., 21:2, mourning; Gen 35:18, naming of children). However, the most plausible answer is the structural one, mentioned above: the Decalogue is inverted both in the order of father and mother and in the order of the sabbath and parents commandments to indicate that the author has the Decalogue in mind (Paton 1897: 53; Seidel 1978: 2; Weiss 1984: 96; Paran 1989: 10).

Cholewinski (1976: 259–61) cites H's use of the purportedly "religious" *yārē'* instead of *kibbēd* and the placement of the mother first as evidence for the lateness of H relative to D's version of the Decalogue, to which Paran (1989: 10) responds that the *Pi'el* of *kbd* is never found in H (and the *Nip'al* is attested only once in P in connection with God) and that H's changes may be nothing but a stylistic variation of the Decalogue of Exod 20 (not of Deut 5, which itself is a variation of Exod 20).

Respect for parents and other family authorities was a sine qua non in the ancient world. For example, note this sensitive statement in the Sumerian hymn concerning those unacceptable to the goddess Nanshe: "a mother who shouts at her child, a child who talks obstinately to his mother, a younger brother who talks arrogantly to his elder brother, talks back to his father" ("Nanshe Hymn," ll. 168–71 [Heimpel 1981: 93]). For biblical examples, see Gen 45:11; Ruth 4:14–15 (cf. Tob 4:3; 14:13; Ben Sira 3:1–16). One should not overlook, though, a different perspective concerning filial duties to the father recorded in the *Epic of Aqhat* (CTA 17 I: 26–33):

> who erects the stela of his god-of-the-father, in the sanctuary the symbol of his ancestor; who, on earth, makes his smoke emerge, on the dust, tends his place; who crushes the jaws of those who revile him, and drives away those who act against him; who takes him by the hand in his drunkenness and supports him when he is sated with wine; who eats his emmer in the temple of Baal [and] his part in the temple of El; who plasters his roof in the [fou]l season, and washes his garments when they are dirty.

This text presupposes a time when the father will no longer be able to care for himself. He is concerned that his son will keep up the ancestral cult (cf. 2 Sam 18:18; Absalom, having no son, erects the stela himself) at the sanctuary and at the family hearth; will defend his honor; will hold him up whenever drunk (cf. Gen 9:21–27); will celebrate festival meals at the sanctuary (cf. 1 Sam 1:4–5); and will perform mundane but essential tasks, such as doing roof repairs and laundering the father's clothes (translation and discussion in van der Toorn 1996b: 154–65).

H's own omission of the Decalogue's promise of longevity (Exod 20:12b; Deut 5:16b) is not due to H's reluctance to attach a material reward for observing God's commandments (Falk 1990: 139, contradicted by v. 25; see its NOTE), but more likely is an indication that H may have had a leaner version of the Decalogue, prior to its deuteronomic additions.

and keep my sabbaths. wĕ'et- šabbĕtōtay tišmōrû, literally "and my sabbaths you shall keep." The same phrase occurs in Exod 31:13, in a passage (vv. 12–17) that also must be assigned to H (see Introduction I E). This verse exemplifies the structure that is encountered in legal statements: this and that; this and not that; this, namely this. The object occurs before the predicate frequently in this chapter (vv. 2, 3, 4, 5, 9, 10, 14, 15, 19, 28, 30, 31, 32). Its purpose may be aesthetic, to create a chiasm or semantic, to create emphasis (cf. GKC 142f and note).

Why were the fourth and fifth (sabbath and parents) commandments of the Decalogue chosen to head the list? As indicated above, the inversion (the first and second commandments follow in the next verse) implies consciousness of the Decalogue. An ancillary purpose may have been to illustrate from the start that ethics (respect for parents) and ritual (observance of the sabbath) are of equal importance. Indeed, it is their resemblance to their counterparts in the

Decalogue that accounts for their presence here. Just as obedience to the Decalogue, according to the older sources, transforms Israel into a "holy nation" (Exod
19:6, cf. 22:30)—by which is meant that Israel will be different from the nations—so Israel can become holy by observing his commandments. For the
priestly (H, in my opinion) origin of the sabbath commandment, see Weinfeld
(1991: 303–5).

It is no accident that the sabbatarian and parental models in the Decalogue
are also juxtaposed (commandments 4 and 5). The sabbath ends in the duties
toward God; the parental commandment heads the list of the duties toward persons. Philo (*Decalogue* 106–7) elucidates this linkage: "This (parental) commandment he (God) placed on the borderline between the two groups of five,
it is the last of the first set in which the most sacred injunctions are given, and
it adjoins the second set, which continues the duties of man to man. The reason I consider is this, we see that parents by nature stand on the borderline between the mortal and the immortal."

Philo (*Decalogue* 120) further postulates that parents are indeed gods, the difference being that God created the world, while parents can create only single
likenesses. This point, as Weinfield (1991: 311) reminds us "has roots in Greek
philosophy, where the point is made that ancestors are like gods (Plato, *Laws*
11.931a–d) and that honor should be given to the parents such as given to the
gods (Aristotle, *Nicomachean Ethics* 9.2.8). Such ideas are alien to genuine Jewish thought. Jewish sages express the idea that parents *share* with God the creation of the human being (*b. Qidd.* 30b), in other words, they are partners with
God in creating man (cf. Gen 4:1), but they are not like him." The Bible itself,
one might add, would be inimical to this Greek notion because it is redolent of
ancestor worship.

The basic meaning of the verb *šāmar* is "guard" (Milgrom 1970: 8–15; for
complete references, see Elliger 1966: 256, n. 6), and it is frequently found with
the sabbath as its object (19:30; 26:2; Exod 31:14, 16; Deut 5:12; cf. Isa 56:2,
4, 6; Jer 17:21; Ezek 20:19–20; 44:24). In the context of the sabbath, it connotes
the existence of prohibitions that must not be violated. The fact that none are
mentioned here implies that they are assumed. One does not have to look farther than two other H passages (Exod 31:12–17; 35:2–3) and three P passages
(Exod 16:25–30; Num 15:32–36; Decalogue, Exod 20:10) to find the referent:
the general prohibition against work, exemplified by gathering manna and wood
(Exod 16:25–30; Num 15:32–36) and lighting a fire (Exod 35:3).

The plural *šabbĕtōtay* has been explained as including the holidays (*môʿădîm*;
Kalisch 1867–72; Dillmann and Ryssel 1897). However, the sabbath is always
distinguished from the holidays (23:38; Ezek 44:24; 45:17; Neh 10:34; 1 Chr
23:31; 2 Chr 2:3; 8:13; 31:3; see NOTES on 23:3). It refers either to the seventh
day, the seven-day week ending with the sabbath (see NOTES on 23:11, 14), or
to the seventh year (23:15; 25:8; 26:34, 35, 43; Isa 56:4; Ezek 20:12–24; 22:8,
26; 46:3; 2 Chr 36:21), and, as pointed out by Schwartz (1987: 127), the verb
šāmar is never used with the holidays. Rather, *šāmar* is a stylistic earmark of H
(19:3, 30, 37; 20:8, 22; 22:9, 31; 23:38; 25:18; 26:2; Exod 31:13) and the passages

influenced by H (Isa 56:4; Ezek 11:20; 18:19, 21; 20:18, 19, 21; 37:24; 2 Chr 33:8). In these passages, it is always found with a suffix or as a construct. The plural and first-person suffix always refers to God; one never finds the singular *šabbattî* (Schwartz 1987: 127). In other texts, the plural occurs as an absolute, referring to only the seventh day, always in conjunction with months (e.g., Ezek 45:17; 46:3; Neh 10:34; 1 Chr 23:31; 2 Chr 2:3; 8:13; 31:3; cf. Paran 1983: 217).

I, YHWH your God (have spoken). *'ănî YHWH 'ĕlōhêkem.* Many wish to correct the Masoretic cantillation to read "I YHWH am your God" (Ibn Ezra, Wessely 1846, on Exod 20:2; most moderns and translations). However, as I have contended (see NOTE on 18:4), the Masoretes (and the Versions) are correct: not that one should read "I am YHWH your God," which is equally meaningless (except as YHWH's self-declaration; see NOTE on v. 2), but as H's equivalent expression for the prophets' *nĕ'ûm* YHWH 'the declaration of YHWH'.

The purpose of this ending has been variously explained: (1) to emphasize the author as God; (2) to provide a rationale for the commandments (Abravanel); (3) to link this and the rest of the chapter to its first occurrence in v. 2, thereby teaching that only by following the commandments in toto can Israel become holy (Schwartz 1987: 117); and (4) as a warning of God's wrath in the wake of violating these commandments (*Sipra* Qedoshim, par. 1:10), which the halakha tempers by ruling that in order to save a person's life the sabbath may be violated (see the examples in *t. Šabb.* 15:11–17). As indicated by the proposed rendering of this declaration, I hold that reasons 1 and 4 are the most probable: the author of the commandments is God, who will punish their violators.

All the laws in chap. 19 are unenforcable in human courts; hence, the emphatic *'ănî YHWH:* God will enforce them. Note that this formula is absent in vv. 5–8 because in the law the divine punishment *kārēt* is specified.

The sabbath is holy because God sanctified it (Gen 2:3; Exod 20:11; 31:15; 35:2; Neh 9:14). But for H, and H-influenced passages, it is incumbent on Israel to sanctify the sabbath (Exod 20:8; Deut 5:12,; Jer 17:24, 27; Ezek 20:20; 44:24; Neh 13:22) and not to desecrate it (Ezek 20:13, 16, 24; 22:8; 23:38; Neh 13:15–18), which accounts for the inclusion of this unit under the rubric "You shall be holy" (v. 2bα). The contrast of *his* parents, *my* sabbaths, and *your* God emphasizes the covenantal relationship between a person and his parents, on one hand, and between Israel and its God, on the other (Schwartz 1987: 125).

V. 4. Unit 2: Worship of Other Gods and Images of Israel's God

As will be discussed in units 12 and 15 (vv. 26–28, 31), certain forms of idolatry, such as Molek and ancestor worship, negate the holiness of YHWH, the God of life. Moreover, this unit is clearly a reworking of the first and second commandments (see INTRODUCTION, and NOTE on v. 3a).

Do not. *'al.* Bright (1973) prefers the LXX, which apparently reads *lō'*, because MT's *'al* is an immediate but temporary negative particle, whereas *lō'* is used in permanently lasting prohibitions. Overlooked, however, is the probable stylistic reason for choosing *'al*, namely, to create the assonance *'al . . . 'el . . . 'ĕlîlîm.* Also it is possible that *'al* was chosen over *lō'* to indicate that this prohibition is only a warning, since there is the lesser, divine penalty of *kārēt* (as indicated by the sequence of death–*kārēt* in the penalties of 20:9–16, 17–19) for "turning" to idols, (cf. 20:6), but not the death penalty mandated for serving as a necromantic medium (20:27; see below and NOTE on v. 31).

turn to. tipnû ʾel. What constitutes turning? Among the suggested answers are (1) to pay them attention (2 Sam 9:8; Boleh 1991–92); (2) literally, to look at them (*Sipra* Qedoshim, par. 1:10; *b. Šabb.* 149a), even in one's mind (Ibn Ezra, Ramban, citing *pānâ lēb*, Deut 29:17; 30:17); (3) to worship them (*Sipra* Qedoshim, par. 1:10; *b. Qid* 3:6; *y. ʿAbod. Zar.* 3:1), not in thought (*lēb*), but actively; and (4) for help or blessing (Deut 31:16–20; Hos 3:1; Ps 40:5; esp. Isa 45:22). Such, indeed, is its meaning in v. 31, where *tipnû ʾel* is parallel with *těbaqšû* 'seek, inquire' (Schwartz 1987: 128–29).

idols. hāʾělîlîm. In the Torah, this word is found only in H, here and in 26:1; fourteen times in the prophets; and in Pss 96:5; 97:7; with the verb *ʿāśâ* 'made' in Isa 2:20; 31:7; Hab 2:19; in the former two verses out of silver and gold. The definite article here stands in contrast with *lō- taʿăśû lākem* 'Do not make idols for yourselves' (26:1) because, in that verse, the idols have yet to be made; here they are already made; that is, they are definite (cf. Isa 2:18, 20; Schwartz 1987: 129).

This term is a derogatory epithet, one of the *šēmôt hamměgûnîm* 'derogatory names' (*Sipra* Qedoshim, par. 1:11), like *šiqqûṣîm* (Ezek 20:7, 8) and *gillûlîm* (26:30; see its NOTE), a meaning supported by its Semitic cognates: Akkadian *ulalu* 'powerless', Syriac *ʾalîl* 'weak, feeble', and Arabic *ʾalal* 'useless'. Others derive it from *ʾal* 'nothingness, worthlessness' (Job 24:25), as an artificial creation in assonance with *ʾělōhîm* and *ʾēlîm* 'gods' (Dillmann and Ryssel 1897; Snaith 1967), or as a diminutive of *ʾēl* with the meaning of "little god, godling" (Preuss 1974: 285). It also functions as an adjective *rôpěʾê ʾělîl* 'ineffectual physicians' (Job 13:4), *qesem weʾělîl* (K: *wʾlwl*) 'empty divination' (Jer 14:14; Levine 1989).

and molten gods. wěʾlōhê massēkâ. This derives from *nāsak* 'cast, forge' (Dohmen 1985). The unexpected chiastic structure of this verse may be a sign that this unit is closed (Schwartz 1987: 127) or is based on other grounds: these "gods" are not other gods (Rashi), referred to in the first half of this verse, but refer to images of Israel's god, YHWH (Ibn Ezra, Wessely 1846)—that is, to the second commandment of the Decalogue and its explication *lōʾ taʿăśûn ʾittî ʾělōhê kesep wěʾlōhê zāhāb lōʾ taʿăśû lākem* 'With me you shall not make any gods of silver, and gods of gold you shall not make for yourselves' (Exod 20:23; cf. Deut 27:15). This aniconic proscription is precisely what was violated by the golden calf. That is why the similarly worded prohibition *ʾělōhê massēkâ lōʾ taʿăśeh- lāk* 'Molten gods you shall not make for yourself' (Exod 34:17) occurs in the cultic calendar of Exod 34:17–26, but not in the cultic calendar of Exod 23:10–19. The former passage follows after the narrative of the golden-calf apostasy (Exod 32:1–6), but the latter passage occurs before it (Hoffmann 1953; Toeg 1977: 70).

The Babylonian obsession to make cult images of their deities (cf. Hallo 1983) penetrated early into Israel, to judge by the story of Micah's molten cult statue of YHWH (Judg 17–18) and Amos's lampoon of Babylonian astral deities worshiped in North Israel (Amos 5:26; cf. Paul 1991: 194–98).

Hendel (1988) has suggested that it was the antimonarchic tradition in early Israel that gave birth to its aniconism. Specifically, to seat an image of YHWH on the cherubim (though in Israel's theology, he was indeed *yōšēb hakkĕrūbîm*, 1 Sam 4:4), in view of the fact that in the ancient Near East images of gods and kings were indeed seated on cherubic thrones, "would have served to legitimate a kingship that had no place in the universe of early Israel" (Hendel 1988: 381). Mettinger's (1995) exhaustive study of aniconic stelae in the ancient Near Eastern civilizations provides the more satisfying answer that Israel's aniconism is derivative of a standing-stone (*maṣṣēbâ*) cult prevalent in Bronze Age Syria and Palestine. He concludes that although aniconism is not an Israelite innovation, "the express veto on images belongs to Israel's *differentia specifica*" (Mettinger 1995: 196).

In this regard, I would point to the startling absence of *maṣṣābôt* in this verse's blanket aniconism, as well as in the Decalogue (Exod 20:3–6; Deut 5:7–10), Num 33:52 (H), and Deut 27:15 (the Gerizim-Ebal covenant ritual is eighth century; cf. Fishbane 1985: 161–62; Tigay 1996: 486–89). That is, in eighth-century Judah there was no opposition to the *maṣṣēbâ* as long as it was not a sculptured image. It can hardly be overlooked that such eighth-century or older passages as Gen 28:18, 22; 31:51–52; Exod 24:4; Isa 19:19; Hos 3:4; 10:1 take for granted the cultic use of the *maṣṣēbâ* (cf. Driver 1929: 248–49). Only beginning with the deuteronomic (Josianic) reform of the seventh century do we find a blanket prohibition of all representations of the deity, even those bearing no images—for example, Exod 23:24 (cf. Durham 1987: 334); Exod 34:13 (cf. Ginsberg 1982: 64–66); Lev 26:1 (see its NOTE); Deut 7:5; 12:3; 16:22; 2 Kgs 18:4; 23:14. The rabbis were fully aware that they were disqualified only at a later period, "although the pillar was beloved as a means of worship by the patriarchal, it was objectionable in the time of their descendants" (*Sipre* Deut. 146).

A "molten god" was made by pouring molten metal either into a cast or over a wooden frame. The latter apparently describes the metal-plated idols mentioned in Scripture (e.g., Deut 7:25; Isa 30:22; 40:19–20; 44:9–20; Jer 10:3–4). Indeed, the golden calf was, in most likelihood, fashioned the same way because it could be burned (Exod 32:20). The description of the making of Micah's idol (Judg 17:4) is ambiguous. The idol, however, consisted of 200 shekels. Assuming the mean weight of a shekel, 12 grams (Powell 1992: 906), Micah's idol contained roughly 5 pounds of silver. If the idol was made of solid silver, it was not more than a figurine (in the category of Micah's *tĕrāpîm*), hardly worthy of "a house of God" (Judg 17:5). Thus this idol, too, must have been plated with silver.

On the basis of the fact that silver and gold melt, Philo (*Laws* 1.25–26) interprets "molten gods" as referring to wealth. Was he reluctant to condemn his idolatrous neighbors?

One further question remains: Why is the normal term for idol, *pesel*, omitted (cf. 26:1)? Ibn Ezra suggests that this term is covered by the synonymous *'ĕlîlîm*. However, the term *pesel* etymologically means "something sculpted" (Dohmen 1989), which would be fashioned not of metal (*massēkâ*), but of wood or stone. To be sure, the *pesel*, be it of wood or stone, can be metal plated (see above). Perhaps that is why Michah's idol is called by the term *pesel*, on the one hand (Judg 18:20, 30, 31), and by the hendiadys *pesel ûmassēkâ* 'a (silver-) plated carved image', on the other (Judg 17:3–4; 18:14; for the rendering, see above, and Judg 18:17–18, if not a corrupt text, reflects a broken hendiadys).

Thus Ibn Ezra's proposal is probably correct. The term *pesel* is covered by the pejorative *ʾĕlîlîm* and, as argued in the INTRODUCTION, is a reference to the first commandment, the prohibition to worship other gods. The term *ʾĕlōhê massēkâ*, however, echoes the second commandment, referring to images of Israel's god. It can be no accident that the images associated with YHWH are indeed molten—for example, the cherubim (Exod 25:18) and the copper snake (Num 21:6–9; 2 Kgs 18:4b; cf. Milgrom 1990a: 175, 459–60).

Vv. 5–8. Unit 3: The Well-Being Offering

The glaring contrast between the preceding paraphrases of the Decalogue (vv. 2–4) and the ostensibly picayune sacrificial detail discussed in this unit has led most commentators to suggest that these verses are a secondary interpolation by a later redactor (e.g., Dillmann and Ryssel 1897; Wellhausen 1963: 155; Baentsch 1903; Elliger 1966; Cholewinski 1976. Eerdmans [1912] alone defends its integrity). To be sure, it has all the earmarks of an independent law: it is a new topic; begins with *wĕkî*; follows the attested closure formula in this chapter, *ʾănî YHWH ʾĕlōhêkem* (v. 4b); and ends with the frequently attested penalty clause (v. 8b). Thus the question of what this unit is doing here must be addressed. Even the commentators who regard this unit as an intrusion have to face this question. Yet, to my knowledge, none of them does (with the exception of Schwartz 1987: 133–34, who independently comes to some similar conclusions).

Ibn Ezra suggests that this unit is intimately connected with the preceding one dealing with idolatry and that both units repeat the warning of 17:3–7 not to offer the well-being offerings to satyr gods. His explanation, however, cannot possibly be correct, since this unit assumes that the sacrifices are brought to YHWH and is concerned with only their consumption.

Carmichael (1977: 72, 84) surmises that the *šĕlāmîm* pericope here is prompted by Joseph's meal with his brothers, despite the fact that the latter is not a sacrifice. For a critique of Carmichael's methodology, see chap. 18, COMMENT C.

The answer, I submit, lies in the nature of the sacrificial procedure detailed in this unit. It speaks of the *šĕlāmîm* and the need of the offerer to beware *lest he desecrate it*. It must be kept in mind that the *šĕlāmîm* is the only holy object (*qōdeš*) that the lay person is allowed to handle. And he is most likely to be tempted to desecrate it when, after the two-day limit for its consumption has expired, a portion of it remains. (After all, how much of a whole animal can a family consume in two days?) Moreover, he is allowed to bring the sacred meat home and eat it with his family as long as they all are in a pure state (7:19b).

In a sense, the sacred meat has transmitted the holiness of the sanctuary into the home. Thus the family must treat every act of eating a meat meal as a sacred rite. In my opinion, it foreshadows and supplies the precedent for the rabbinic doctrine (but not innovation!) that the home had replaced the nonexistent Temple (*m. Ber.* chaps. 6–7; *b. Ḥul.* 105a). S. Greenberg suggests an associative link between the previously mentioned sabbath (v. 3aβ) and this sacrifice, so that holiness embraces both time and space. This conjunction becomes explicit by the coupling of sabbath and sanctuary (replacing this sacrifice?) in v. 30. In any case, it is holiness that is uppermost in the legists' mind, holiness that is commanded to the entire people of Israel. For this reason, the author/redactor inserts this unit close to the overarching command "You shall be holy" (v. 2a). And his logic is unassailable: after laying out his paraphrase of the most important (for him) part of the Decalogue (commandments 5, 4, 1, 2), he then proceeds to caution his people: you cannot begin to climb the ladder of holiness unless you take precautions that the one sanctum you have a right to possess is never desecrated.

Supporting my view is the fact that although this unit is a near verbatim repetition of 7:16–18 (discussed below), the major difference between the two is that this unit adds a rationale: *kî-'et-qōdeš YHWH ḥillēl* 'because he has desecrated what is sacred to YHWH' (v. 8aβ). Thus it is the fear of cultic desecration, which totally and irrevocably cancels the degree of holiness reached by the Israelite, regardless of how many of the ensuing commandments he has faithfully observed, that is responsible for the insertion of this unit near the head of the list.

The preceding question gives birth to a new one. If, indeed, the consumption of the *šĕlāmîm* offering is the only sacred act performed by the laity, why is not the *tôdâ*, the thanksgiving offering (listed separately by H, 22:29–30)— also eaten by the lay offerer—not included here? That it is not included under the category of *šĕlāmîm* is made certain by the two-day consumption period stipulated here, whereas the *tôdâ* must be eaten in the same day it is offered (7:15; 22:30). In contrast, P reckons the *tôdâ* as a *šĕlāmîm*, as demonstrated by its double construct *zebaḥ tôdat šĕlāmāyw* 'his thanksgiving sacrifice of well-being' (7:13, 15; for the purported challenge it poses to my theory of the chronological priority of P over H, see NOTE on 22:29). The answer is that H deliberately transposed the *tôdâ* pericope to 22:29–30 in order to create an inclusio for chaps. 19–22 (also recognized by Schwartz 1987: 133–34). H's redactoral hand is revealed by the fact that the order of the two sacrifices in P (7:11–15, 16–18), following Seidel's (1978) law that quotations of an earlier statement are cited chiastically: the *tôdâ*, first in P's list (7:11–15), is relegated to last in H (22:29–30).

The wording of the concluding bracket of the inclusion reveals a conscious attempt to duplicate the vocabulary of the opening bracket: both warn that the "YHWH's *qōdeš*" (*qōdeš YHWH*, 19:8; *šēm qodšî*, 22:32) may be desecrated (*qōdeš YHWH ḥillēl*, 19:8, *wĕlō' tĕḥallĕlû 'et-šēm qodšî*, 22:32; C. Hayes). It is no accident that the *tôdâ* was placed at the end of chap. 22. It marks the final time that the term *qādôs / qōdeš* is applied to an Israelite, whether a lay person or a priest.

The redactor is therefore saying that a "little Book of Holiness," the holiness of persons, is confined to chaps. 19–22. The root *qdš*, it will be recalled, does not occur in chaps. 17–18. To be sure, it recurs after chap. 22 regarding time (festivals, chap. 23; jubilee, 25:10, 12), sacred food and space (the Bread of Presence, 24:9), and sanctified animals, land, money, and *ḥerem* (27:10, 14–23, 25, 28). The ramification of this glimpse into the composition of Leviticus is discussed in the Introduction I F.

One final question must be asked: If the innovation of vv. 5–8 lies in concluding v. 8, why the need to repeat the *Vorlage*, 7:16–18, in the preceding vv. 5–7? Moreover, the unit vv. 11–13, as will be demonstrated, is also dependent on its P *Vorlage*, 5:20–26, but in contrast to 19:5–8, it does not repeat the *Vorlage* at all. The answer lies in the formulation of each law. On the one hand, there is no way of understanding v. 8 without restating its entire cultic context. Vv. 11–13, on the other hand, form an independent, novel law founded on new postulates, so that the inclusion of its *Vorlage* (5:20–26) would only blur (and probably distort) the innovations it contains (on the relationship between 5:20–26 and Num 5:5–8, see Licht 1982).

That vv. 5–8 are based on 7:16–18 (P) has been partially demonstrated in vol. 1.14–15. A comprehensive comparison (TABLE 2) of the two passages follows (in literal translation), which shall demonstrate that H is more than the borrower; it has reformulated P into a model of conciseness, clarity, artistry, and innovation.

1. In line 1, P's votive and freewill offerings are subsumed under the well-being offering, thereby freeing the *tôdâ* 'thank offering' from its (awkward) inclusion as a well-being offering (cf. 7:11, 15a) for an inclusio to chaps. 19–22, containing *all of God's holiness demands* on Israelite behavior. That the *tôdâ* can be regarded as a discrete sacrifice is evident from other biblical passages (e.g., Jer 17:26; 2 Chron 29:31; 33:16) and rabbinic literature (e.g., *m. Zebaḥ.* 5:6–7). In distinction from the votive and freewill offerings, it must be eaten on the same day it is sacrificed and it is accompanied by cereal offerings, including one of leavened bread, one of each to be given to the priest as a "gift [*tĕrûmâ*] to YHWH" (7:11–15).

2. In lines 3–4, H simplifies P's repetitive (and confusing) verbiage [bracketed] with just one of the latter's words, *wĕhannôtār*. Thereby, it also removes the offending *wĕhannôtār* in v. 16, which makes sense only by deleting its conjunctive *waw* (see NOTE on 7:16). H, however, adds *lirṣōnĕkem tizbāḥûhû* so that 19:5 corresponds with its inclusio, 22:29.

3. In line 5, H alters P's "on the third day" to "by the third day," thereby insisting that the remainder must be burned *before* the onset of the third day.

4. In line 6, H trims down 7:18aα by removing superfluous *mibbĕśar-zebaḥ šĕlāmāyw* [bracketed] since the antecedent is unambiguously *wĕhannôtār* (v. 17aα; l. 4).

5. H deletes P's line 9, thereby removing the ambiguity concerning the antecedent of lines 8–11 (it must be *wĕhannôtār*, l. 4) and the vexsome syntax of *hammaqrîb*, which might be understood as the subject of line 8, yielding "he who offered it will not be acceptable."

TABLE 2. Comparison of vv. 5–8 (H) and 7:16–18 (P).

19:5–8 (H)	7:16–18 (P)
1. ⁵wĕkî tizbĕhû zebah šĕlāmîm laYHWH	1. ¹⁶wĕ'im-neder 'ô nĕdābâ zebah qorbānô
2. lirṣōnĕkem tizbāhûhû	2. bĕyôm haqrîbô 'et-zibhô yē'ākēl
3. ⁶bĕyôm zibhăkem yē'ākēl ûmimmāhŏrāt	3. [ûmimmāhŏrāt (wĕ)hannôtār mimmennû yē'ākēl]
4. wĕhannôtār	4. ¹⁷wĕhannôtār [mibbĕśar hazzābah]
5. 'ad-yôm haššĕlîšî bā'ēš yiśśārēp	5. bayyôm haššĕlîšî bā'ēš yiśśārēp
6. ⁷wĕ'im hē'ākōl yē'ākēl	6. ¹⁸wĕ'im hē'ākēl yē'ākēl mibbĕśar zebah šĕlāmāyw
7. bayyôm haššĕlîšî	7. bayyôm haššĕlîšî
8. piggûl hû'	8. lō' yērāṣeh
9.	9. [hammaqrîb 'ōtô lō' yēhāšēb lô]
10. lō' yērāṣeh	10. piggûl yihyeh
11. ⁸wĕ'ōkĕlāyw 'ăwōnô yiśśā'	11. wĕhannepeš hā'ōkelet mimmennû 'ăwōnāh tiśśā'
12. kî-'et-qōdeš YHWH hillēl	
13. wĕnikrĕtâ hannepeš hahi(w)' mē'ammêhā	
1. ⁵When you sacrifice a well-being offering to YHWH,	1. ¹⁶If the sacrifice he offers is a votive or freewill offering
2. sacrifice it so it may be accepted on your behalf.	2. on the day of his sacrifice it shall be eaten
3. ⁶On the day you sacrifice it, it shall be eaten, or on the next day;	3. [(and) on the morrow (and) the remainder of it shall be eaten]
4. but as for the remainder,	4. ¹⁷But as for the remainder [of the sacrificial flesh],
5. by the third day it shall be consumed by fire.	5. on the third day it shall be consumed by fire.
6. ⁷If it is eaten at all	6. ¹⁸If any of the flesh of his sacrifice of well-being is eaten at all
7. on the third day,	7. on the third day,
8. it is rotten meat;	8. it will not be acceptable;
9.	9. [it will not be accredited to him who offered it.]
10. it will not be acceptable.	10. It will be rotten meat,
11. ⁸Anyone who eats it shall bear his punishment,	11. and the person who eats of it shall bear his punishment.
12. because he has desecrated the sacred object of YHWH;	
13. that person shall be cut off from his kin.	

6. H acknowledges its dependence on P by creating a chiasm in lines 8 and 10, a stylistic device locking two parallel panels (e.g., Gen 1:6–8, 20–23; Num 20:7–13; 21:6–9, 16–18; cf. Milgrom 1990a: 463–67); it also changes the incurrence of *piggûl* from the imprecise future to the immediate present (*yihyeh* > *hû'*).

7. H changes the subject of line 11 to masculine because it needs *nepeš* for its *kārēt* formula (l. 13).

8. In lines 12–13, H adds, as its wont, a motive clause (e.g., 19:12, 14, 20, 29, 34) and penalty (e.g., 20:2, 3, 5, 6).

9. This pericope says nothing about the need for the sacrifice to be *tāmîm* 'unblemished'; the same holds true for the inclusion, 22:29–30. Neither is the term *tāmîm* present in the antecedent text, 7:11–18. In the latter case, the reason is obvious: this criterion is missing in all of chaps. 6 and 7 because these chapters are dependent on their predecessors, chaps. 1–4, which unfailingly stipulate that each sacrificial animal must be *tāmîm* (e.g., 1:3, 10; 3:1, 6; 4:3, 28, 32; cf. 14:10). However, there is no such excuse for the H versions of the *šĕlāmîm* / *tôdâ*, since their explicit goal is *lirṣōnĕkêm* 'for your behalf' (19:5; 22:29), concerning which the unblemished (*tāmîm*) requirement is indispensable. The reason for its absence is now transparent: the *Vorlage* of both sacrifices (7:11–18) also omits this criterion. Perhaps that is why H has to devote a special section, which includes the *šĕlāmîm* (22:17–25), to emphasize that *tāmîm* is essential for *rāṣôn*.

10. Finally, most of the H law (19:6–8) is in the third person, in contrast to its context (vv. 2–4, 9–19) written in the second person, for which there is but one explanation: it follows its *Vorlage* (7:16–18). Further comments are in the NOTES.

5. *When. wĕkî.* The mark of a new law, it is casuistic in form so that it can stress the notion of acceptability to God (*rāṣôn*) in the apodosis (vv. 5, 7).

you sacrifice. tizbĕḥû. The writer changes the third-person address in 7:16–18 to second person. Whereas the former addresses the priests and the offerer is in the third person, here the injunction addresses the offerer (Wenham 1979). In priestly texts, the verb *zābaḥ* is used only with its cognate accusative *zebaḥ* (17:5, 7; 19:5; 22:29). Elsewhere, it means "slaughter," which in P and H is expressed by *šāḥaṭ* (details in NOTES on 9:4 and 17:5).

a well-being offering. zebaḥ šĕlāmîm. For the discussion, see the NOTE on 17:5; that this compound is not a conflation of two sacrifices, see vol. 1.217–18. Here the *šĕlāmîm* concerns the votive and freewill offerings, whose consumption is permitted for two days (7:16). The discussion of the thanksgiving offering (*tôdâ*), which must be eaten the same day, is postponed until 22:29–30, for the reasons cited above.

to YHWH. laYHWH. The recipient, YHWH, has to be specified, perhaps because Israelites were wont to offer the sacrifices whose meat they wished to eat (i.e., *šĕlāmîm*) to chthonic goat-demons (17:7; see chap. 17, COMMENT A). "R. Simeon b. Azzai says: Come and see, in the entire Torah not a single sacrifice is associated with the names *'ĕlōhîm, ĕlōhêkā, šadday,* or *ṣĕbā'ôt,* but only with the unique name YHWH, in order not to provide an opening for heretics to operate" (*Sipre* Pinhas, 143).

so it may be accepted on your behalf. lirṣōnĕkem (with *Tgs.,* Saadiah, Rashi "appaisement"). How? By offering unblemished animals (22:19–25; Rashbam); by following the commandments (Ḥazzequni). Alternatively, render it "to gain for yourselves" (S. Rattray), an infinitival use of *raṣâ Qal* with a person as a direct object (cf. Ezek 20:40–41; 43:27; Mal 1:8). "Not for my sake do you sacrifice but for yours" (b. Menaḥ 110a). The subject here is the sacrifice, as demonstrated by the phrase lō' yērāṣeh 'it (the sacrifice) will not be acceptable' (v. 7bβ; cf. 1:4; 7:18; 22:23, 25, 27 [all Nip 'al]). For other attestations of rĕṣōnĕkem, see 22:19, 29; 23:11. Without a suffix, it appears as lĕrāṣôn lāhem (Exod 28:38) and lĕrāṣôn . . . lākem (Lev 22:20; cf. 22:18; Isa 56:7; Jer 6:20). Therefore, lirṣōnĕkēm is equivalent to lĕrāṣôn lākem 'acceptable on your behalf'. On the various meanings of rāṣâ, see further Rendtorff (1967a: 253–60).

sacrifice it. tizbāḥūhû. In typical priestly style, the verb is repeated, but in chiastic relation to its first appearance (cf. 23:11; Exod 12:8, 14; 30:1). The added effect of this repetition is to stress that the responsibility for the sacrifice's acceptance to YHWH rests with the offerer, not the priests (contrast 7:16–18).

6. on the day you sacrifice (it). bĕyôm zibḥăkem. The Vorlage in P has bĕyôm haqrîbô 'et-zibḥô (7:16), indicating that H was intent on abbreviating its source (see NOTE on "it will not be acceptable," v. 7).

or on the next day. ûmimmāḥŏrāt. Read umimmāḥŏrātô, the waw lost by haplography with the following word wĕhannôtār (Ehrlich 1908). The mem of the preposition is equivalent to beth (see Note on 7:16).

but what is left. wĕhannôtār. This is the technical term for the sacrificial portion eaten or used by the laity (the paschal offering, Exod 12:10; the anointing oil, Lev 14:18, 29; the thanksgiving offering, Lev 22:30; the consecration offering, Exod 29:34; Lev 8:32 [during their consecratory rites, Aaron and his sons are theoretically laymen]; the well-being offering, Lev 7:17; 19:6; and the manna, Exod 16:19, 20). What all these substances have in common is their cultic status; they are qodāšîm 'lesser sacred things'. A different term nôteret was devised, probably by priestly legists, for the meal offering (2:3, 10; 6:9; 10:12) because it falls under the category of qodšê qodāšîm 'most sacred things' that are eaten only by priests (see NOTE on 2:3).

by the third day. 'ad-yôm haššĕlîšî. The counterpart phrase in P is bayyôm haššĕlîšî 'on the third day' (7:17). The difference in meaning might be this: according to this verse, if the offerer sees that some sacrificial meat will not be eaten by daybreak, he must burn it at once and not wait for daybreak. Perhaps such reasoning led to the rabbinic principle of intention: the sacrificial meat one does not intend to eat must be burned. If, however, one eats it beyond its legal time, it was so intended from the start, thereby invalidating the entire sacrifice (see below).

7. But if. wĕ'im. This particle marks a subunit (see NOTE on 1:3).

it is eaten. hē'ākōl yē'ākēl. That is, if, despite the law, the meat is eaten (Wessely 1846; Hoffmann 1953). The absolute infinitive is used to emphasize an antithesis (GKC § 113 O–P; cf. Exod 21:5; 22:3). The Sam. reads 'ākōl (Qal) yē'ākēl, which is possible, but it parts from its P Vorlage (7:18).

it is rotten meat. piggûl hû'. The meat has been desecrated, as explicitly stated in the next verse (and so I rendered this word as "desecrated meat" in 7:18), but perhaps I should side with the rabbis who claim that "its appearance changes" (b. Pesaḥ 82b) and that it is "disgusting because it has begun to decay" (Greenberg 1983a: 107; cf. Tg. Onq., Saadiah, Rashi, Ibn Ezra). Similarly termed expressions, such as *ḥesed hû'* (20:17), *zimmâ hi(w)'* (18:17), *tebel hû'* (18:23), and *niddâ hi(w)'* (20:21), are all derogatory in meaning (Schwartz 1987: 132). It has been suggested that the equivalent Akkadian term is *anzillu* (Sum. *an-zil*), synonym of *ikkibu* 'abomination, taboo', especially since the semantic equivalent of Sumerian *an-zil kú* in Akkadian is *asakkam akālum* (= Heb. *'ākal qōdeš*, Jer 2:3), literally "eat the sanctum" or "violate the taboo" (Klein and Sefati 1988: 132–33).

Thus *piggûl* is also a pejorative, but it is still a technical term, limited to sacrificial meat eaten after its legal limit. Thus, on the one hand, when Ezekiel asserts that "*piggûl* meat has never entered my mouth" (Ezek 4:14b), he, as a priest, is referring to sacrificial meat, which could have been from purification and reparation as well as from well-being offerings. But, on the other hand, when Isaiah of the exile describes an idolatrous (probably chthonic) rite involving the eating of *měraq* (Q) *piggûlûm*, he clearly leaves the priestly ambit to extend this pejorative to "broth (made) of forbidden animals" (Isa 65:4).

In the context of Lev 19, the rationale for *piggûl* becomes clear. Holiness requires the fulfillment of the divine commandments, which are life-producing (*wāḥay bāhem*, 18:5aγ). The antithesis of holiness-life is impurity-death, and therefore the corpse (Num 19) or anything that symbolizes death, be it the loss of life forces (Lev 15) or the appearance of decay and approaching death (Lev 13–14 and *piggûl*), must be eschewed.

it will not be acceptable. lō' yērāṣeh. It takes a whole sentence for P to make the same assertion; *hammaqrîb 'ōtô lō' yēḥāšēb lô* 'It shall not be accredited to the one who offers it' (7:18). Instead of P's technical (but mechanical, mathematical) term *ḥāšab*, H chooses the more sentient term *rāṣâ* to express divine acceptance (cf. Deut 33:11; Hos 8:13; Mal 1:10).

There is a later usage of *rāṣâ* 'desire', borrowed from Aramaic (cf. Hurvitz 1972: 73–78) and found only in the books of Esther, Daniel, Ezra–Nehemiah, and Chronicles and a few psalms—all postexilic works (Bendavid 1972: 6, 62). As plausibly proposed by Paran (1989: 295–96), signs of the transition can be detected in Malachi's addition of the object *miyyedkem* (Mal 1:10, 13), whose corresponding verb is regularly *biqqēš* 'request' (e.g., 1 Sam 20:16; 2 Sam 4:11; Isa 1:12) or *lāqaḥ* 'take' (e.g., Gen 33:10; Judg 13:23; 1 Sam 25:35). The *Nipʿal* of *rāṣâ* 'be acceptable', strictly a priestly usage (1:4; 7:18; H, 19:7; 22:23, 25, 27 [P]; for H's unique connotation of the *Qal* and *Hipʿil* [26:34, 41, 43], see NOTE on 26:34), is also attested in the eighth-century prophetic books (Hos 8:13; Amos 5:22) and as late as the exile (Ezek 20:41; Isa 60:7), but not beyond.

Rabbi Eliezer asks rhetorically: "Since the meat is (sacrificially) fit, can it be invalidated retroactively?" (*b. Zebaḥ.* 29a). Thus the rabbis declare that the sacrifice was invalid from the beginning because the offerer had intended all along to eat of it on the third day. Perhaps the primary reason why the rabbis introduce the principle of intention is because they oppose the principle of retroactivity. The Karaites, to the contrary, accept it (*Keter Torah* on 7:18), and they are right. Retroactivity is clearly present in other legal statutes—indeed, in the priestly laws themselves. For example, repentance for an advertent sin against

God retroactively converts the advertent sin into an inadvertent one, rendering it eligible for sacrificial expiation (5:20–26; Num 5:6–8; see vol. 1.373–78).

Ironically, the rabbis themselves admit that retroactivity operates in this latter case: "Because he has confessed his brazen and rebellious deeds it is as if they become unintentional ones before him" (*Sipra* Aḥare, par. 2:4, 6; cf. *t. Yoma* 2:1). But they do not allow it elsewhere, that is, they do not say that the act of eating sacrificial flesh beyond its time limit retroactively invalidates the sacrificial procedure (which took place two days earlier). Apparently, they have made a special exception for acts of repentance, which they call *taqqānat haššābîm* 'a remedy for the repentant' (*m. Giṭ.* 5:5), in order to encourage miscreants to repent.

8. *Anyone who eats of it. wĕ'ōkĕlāyw*, literally "and those who eat of it." However, the *MT* represents a distributive plural—that is, every one of its consumers (Ibn Ezra)—and therefore there is no necessity to emend the word to *wĕ'ōkĕlô* (Sam.).

shall bear his punishment. 'awōnô yiśśā'. Alternatively, it can be rendered "shall bear his sin" (see NOTE on 17:16). The accepted rendering is the "consequential meaning of a behavioral term" (vol. 2.339–45). It is preferred here because it is immediately defined as the punishment of *kārēt*. That these two terms are equivalent here, see *Sipra* Ṣaw 13:19.

In all passages containing the phrase *nāśā' 'awōn / ḥēṭ'*, where the subject is man, the crime lies outside the jurisdiction of the human court and is punishable only by God (e.g., 5:1, 17; 20:20; 22:16; 24:15), through either death (e.g., Exod 28:43) or *kārēt* (here).

because he has desecrated what is sacred to YHWH. kî- 'et- qōdeš YHWH ḥillel. This is the rationale, which is absent in the *Vorlage*, 7:16–18. As mentioned in the INTRODUCTION to vv. 5–8, this rationale explains why this unit has been placed near the top of the list of commandments in chap. 19. Because the *šĕlāmîm* is a sanctum—the only one permitted to the lay Israelite—its desecration will nullify whatever holiness has been achieved by observing the other commandments. Thus this unit connects with the general command that heads the chapter 'You shall be holy' (v. 2). Also, as mentioned, this phrase forms an inclusion with *wĕlō' tĕḥallĕlû 'et- šēm qodšî* "You shall not desecrate my holy name" (22:32), encompassing all the injunctions in chaps. 19–22 that detail how all Israelites, priests and laity alike, can attain holiness.

At what point does the *šĕlāmîm* offering become sacred? Ibn Ezra's answer, once the suet is offered up, is not correct. Rather, it is when the priest, together with the offerer, performs the elevation (*tĕnûpâ*) rite with the sacrificial pieces (see NOTES on 7:30 and, vol. 1.461–72). How long does its sanctity last? According to this verse, it lasts as long as it exists. Thus it must be either eaten or eliminated (by burning); otherwise, even in a putrefied state, it technically is still *qōdeš* 'holy'! The result of allowing the meat to remain beyond its legal time is that the entire sacrifice is invalidated. No wonder, then, that H places its emphasis on the offerer, for it lies within his responsibility that he and all those whom he has invited to partake of the sacrifice must eliminate their sacrificial portion by ingestion or fire before the third day. It is, thus, hardly imaginable that the offerer parcels out the sacrificial meat and lets the participants go their merry way. Rather, a feast at or near the sanctuary is presumed, lasting one or two days while the meat remains under the supervision of the offerer (and, perhaps, the priest).

The sacred food must be eliminated lest it putrify or contract impurity; in either case, not only is its offerer punished by *kārēt*, but the entire community stands in jeopardy of destruction by God. (For the fatal consequences of impurity—holiness contact—see vol. 1.254–61, 443–56, 976–85.) This background can illumine the otherwise abstruse law of the Qumran sectaries: "One must not let any dogs enter the holy camp, since they might eat some of the bones of the sanctuary while the flesh is on them (the bones). For Jerusalem is the camp of holiness" (*MMT* B 58–60). Lurking behind this law is the mortal fear that the dogs will bring the still sacred meat in contact with some form of impurity (e.g., a carcass), pollute all Jerusalem (which for the Qumranites is equal in sanctity to the Temple), and place all of Israel under the threat of destruction.

that person shall be cut off from his kin. wĕnikrĕtâ hannepeš hahî' (K: *hhw'*) *mē'ammêhā.* The word *nepeš*, which is feminine in gender, often refers to male persons. For the distribution and meaning of this *kārēt* formula, see vol. 1.457–60. It is a fitting end to a law (e.g., 17:4, 9, 14; 20:18). But in chap. 19, units close with the statement of divine authorship *'ănî YHWH* (*'ĕlōhêkem*; see NOTE on v. 2b). Why is this closing formula missing here? As has been correctly pointed out by Schwartz (1987: 118), it occurs in only second-person prescriptions; as indicated by the second-person suffix on *'ĕlōhêkem*, it has to be directed to "you." It would, therefore, be incongruous grammatically to attach it to a prescription ending in the third person. That is why this formula is absent in vv. 19, 22, and 29.

Vv. 9–10. Unit 4: Horticultural Holiness and Required Gifts to the Poor and Alien

Attempts have been made to find the logical connection between this unit and the preceding ones:

1. As you give God the suet of your well-being offering, give to the needy—at God's behest—of your produce (Ibn Ezra).
2. In contrast to the well-being offering, which is completely eliminated (by ingestion or fire), the field and vineyard should not be stripped, but some produce should be left for the needy (Hoffmann 1953).
3. Since the offerer of the sacrifice cannot possibly consume the entire animal in two days, but must invite others to his feast, so a portion of the field's produce should be left for the needy (Shadal).

Perhaps the placement of this unit here may have more to do with the following verses than with the preceding ones. Vv. 11–18 are characterized by their purely ethical nature. The preceding verses (2–8) deal with religious duties. This unit belongs to both categories: not to harvest the entire crop is a religious duty; leaving the remainder for the poor is an ethical duty. Thus vv. 9–10 form a bridge between the two categories.

The roots *qdš* 'holy' and *ḥll* 'desecrate' do not appear in this unit. Their very absence is significant: an indispensable step toward the achievement of holiness is concern for the indigent. Stated differently: as will be demonstrated in the COMMENT, the formula *ʾănî YHWH ʾĕlōhêkem*, with which this unit ends (v. 12bβ), as do most of the others (vv. 9–10, 13–14, 15–16, 17–18, 32, 33–34, 35–36), is synonymous with otherness or holiness, as explicitly defined in the generalizing principle *qādôš ʾănî YHWH ʾĕlōhêkem* 'I, YHWH your God, am holy' (v. 2). YHWH has symbolically taken the poor and alien into his domain. Hence anyone who disobeys his commandments concerning their care are desecrating, as it were, his holiness. This theme runs through all the ethical commandments (vv. 11–18). The implication is clear: YHWH is the protector of the defenseless, and only those who follow his lead can achieve holiness.

These two verses comprise a symmetrical structure:

Opening	*ûbĕquṣrĕkem ʾet-qĕṣîr ʾarṣĕkem*	
Prohibitions	1. *lōʾ tĕkalleh pĕʾat śādĕkā liqṣōr*	2. *wĕleqeṭ qĕṣîrĕkā lōʾ tĕlaqqēṭ*
	3. *wĕkarmĕkā lōʾ teʿōlēl*	4. *ûpereṭ karmĕkā lōʾ tĕlaqqēṭ*
Prescription	*leʿānî wĕlaggēr taʿăzōb ʾōtām*	
Close	*ʾănî YHWH ʾĕlōhêkem*	

Opening	⁹When you [pl.] reap the harvest of your land,	
Prohibitions	1. you shall not destroy the edge of your field in reaping,	2. and the gleanings of your harvest you shall not gather.
	3. ¹⁰Your vineyard you shall not pick bare,	4. and the fallen fruit of your vineyard you shall not gather.
Prescription	You shall leave them for the poor and the alien:	
Close	I YHWH your [pl.] God (have spoken).	

Prohibitions 1 and 3 deal with reaping; prohibitions 2 and 4, with gleaning— thus forming two parallel panels. The first and last commandments (no. 1 and prescription) are structured differently from those in between: the former begin with the verb; the others, with the object (cf. vv. 19, 26–28; Paran 1989: 129). The entire unit begins and ends with verbs in the plural; those in between are in the singular.

An abbreviated form of this unit is found in 23:22. That vv. 9–10 have been copied and abridged is proved by use of the same singular verbs within a chapter that employs only the plural, and by the fact that it is clearly an appendix to the previous unit (23:15–21). For details, see the NOTE on 23:22.

9. *When you reap the harvest of your land.* The structure of vv. 9–10, charted above, indicates the necessity of this opening clause: it balances v. 10b; other-

wise, it would be superfluous. As noted by Joosten (1994: 68; 1996: 49), when dealing with the harvest of *the land*, the plural is used (*'arṣĕkem*)—that is, all of Israel is addressed—but when referring to the *individual's* field (*śādĕkā*), the singular is used (but see the anomaly of *bĕ'arṣekā*, 25:7). Interestingly, the root *qṣr* occurs four times in 23:22 and three times in 23:10, forming an envelope structure for the entire section on the grain festivals (M. Hildenbrand).

destroy. tĕkalleh. In priestly texts, this verb is found in the *Qal* (Exod 39:32) and the *Pi'el* (16:20; 19:9; 23:22; 26:16, 44; Gen 2:2; 6:16; 17:22; 49:33; Exod 31:18; 40:33; Num 4:15; 7:1; 16:21; 17:10, 25; 25:11). It has both a positive and a negative meaning: "complete an act" or "destroy." An example of the former is *'ad 'im-killû 'ēt kol-haqqāṣîr* 'until all the harvest is completed' (Ruth 2:21; cf. Isa 24:13). The latter connotation is illumined in this chapter by *wĕlō' tašḥît 'ēt pĕ'at zĕqānekā* 'You shall not destroy the edge of your beard' (v. 27). Since the object of *killâ* identifies the direction of the action (GKC § 114m), both renderings are possible. However, whereas the object in the passage from Ruth is "the harvest," the object of "destroy" in v. 27 is the same as in this verse—the edge (*pĕ'â*). The likelihood, therefore, is that the verb *killâ* in the verse should be rendered "destroy" (cf. Schwartz 1987: 135, 277, n. 14). In either case, the verb *killâ* is essential, since no measure is specified for the leftover portion.

Note that the imperative of this initial prohibition comes before the object, whereas in the following three prohibitions, the imperative follows the object. As pointed out by Paran (1989: 144–49), this is a priestly stylistic device to emphasize a novel law (see NOTES on 23:18; 26:1).

edge of your field. pĕ'at śādĕkā. Hebrew *pē'â*, as it cognates Ugaritic *p't* and Akkadian *pātu*, means "side, edge, corner" (e.g., *pĕ'at negeb* 'southside', Exod 27:9). It should not be rendered (as in most translations) "edges," namely, as a distributive. Only one side is intended, as translated in *Tg. Ps.-J. 'ûmānā ḥădā'* 'one furrow', probably at the far end of the field, as more precisely translated in *Tg. Yer. 'ôman 'ôḥăray'* 'last furrow'. The rabbis find practical reasons for this specification:

> R. Simeon said: There are four reasons why the Torah said that *pē'â* should be at the end of the field: so that he will not rob the poor, keep the poor waiting, give the wrong impression, cause deception. How (can he) rob the poor? By waiting until no one is around and then telling his relative "come and take this *pē'â*." Cause the poor to wait? The poor might sit and keep watch on his field all day, thinking "now he will set aside *pē'â*, now he will set aside *pē'â*;" however, if he sets aside the end of his field, the poor man does his work all day and at its end (comes) and takes it. Give the wrong impression? People may pass by his field and say "See this person has harvested his field and has left no edge for the poor despite the Torah's injunction 'Do not destroy the edge of your field'." Cause deception? So that they (the field owners) should not say "we have already given" or they will not leave the (part whose crop is) good but only the bad. (*t. Pe'a* 1:6; cf. *Sipra* Qedoshim 1:10; *b. Šabb.* 23a, b [bar.])

The rabbis ordain that the *pē'â* should minimally be one-sixtieth of the field, but more should be set aside, taking into account the size of the field, the abundance of the yield, and the abundance of the poor (*m. Pe'a* 1:2).

in reaping. liqṣōr. This is an adverbial phrase (Kalisch 1867–72), equivalent to *běquṣrekā* 'in your reaping' (23:22). The latter imitates and repeats the opening verb *běquṣrěkem.* Hence, this verse, containing the more difficult wording, is the original. Some would metathesize this verse to read *lō' těkalleh liqṣōr* (e.g., Buleh 1991–92), but then, as stated above using the example of Ruth 2:21, the rendering would be "do not complete harvesting . . .", whereas the intention of this verse is to forbid the destruction of the (far) edge of the field. Rabast (1949: 19), Reventlow (1961: 69), and Kilian (1963: 40) delete *liqṣōr* for metric reasons. However, it was clearly in the text when the interpolator of 23:22 "simplified" its form to *běquṣrěkā* (Paran 1983: 85, n. 110). Besides, the verbs *qāṣar / liqqēṭ* are found again in parallel stiches (cf. Isa 17:5). Whereas H speaks of only the grain harvest *qāṣîr,* the rabbis extend this rule to other crops (cf. *m. Pe'a* 1:4–5; *Sipre* Deut. 284).

It should never be forgotten that concern for the underprivileged—the poor, the widow, the orphan, and the alien—is consistently reiterated throughout Scripture (Exod 22:20–23; 23:9; Lev 19:33–34; Deut 15:7–11; 24:14,17; 27:19; Jer 7:6; 22:3; Zech 7:10). The prophets repeatedly rail against their neglect and exploitation (Isa 1:17, 23; 3:14–15; 10:2; Jer 5:28; Ezek 16:49; 18:17; 22:7, 29; Amos 8:4; Mal 3:5; cf. Pss 82:3; 94:6). What is sometimes forgotten, however, is that concern for the exploited is equally characteristic of the Torah literature—in all its sources, as cited above.

the gleanings. wěleqeṭ. The verb *lāqaṭ* means "collect, gather piecemeal" (e.g., manna, Exod 16:17–27; Num 11:8; Ps 104:28, *Qal*; gourds, 2 Kgs 4:39, *Pi'el*; people, Isa 27:12, *Pu'al*). The derived nominal form *leqeṭ,* therefore, fits the rabbis' definition: "That which falls (from the reaper) during the harvest" (*m. Pe'a* 4:10). The act of harvesting explains its occurrence: the reaper grabs a bundle of sheaves with one hand and swings his scythe with the other. Such an image is clearly portrayed by the Psalmist: "with which the reaper does not fill his hands or binders of sheaves their arms" (Ps 129:7) and by the prophet: "And it shall be as when reapers gather standing grain and their arms harvest the ears, and as one gleans [*kîmělaqqēṭ*] ears in the Valley of Rephaim" (Isa 17:5). Ancient iconography confirms this picture.

Inevitably, stalks will be dropped during the harvesting. Deut 24:19 forbids the owner to return to the field in order to retrieve them. They belong to the poor: "When are all men permitted to glean from the field? After the last of the gropers [*hannāmôṣôt*; i.e., the old who grope with a stick to find every last stalk] are gone" (*m. Pe'a* 8:1; cf. *b. B. Meṣ.* 21b). The rabbis, however, add to the owners' responsibility to the poor. On the basis of the verse "When you reap the harvest in your field and overlook [*wěšākaḥtā*] a sheaf [*'ōmer*; i.e., a bundle of stalks tied by the reapers], do not turn back to get it" (Deut 24:19a), the rabbis decree (by reading *wěšākaḥtā* as the beginning of the apodosis) that the landowner *must* leave behind at least one sheaf (the duty is called *šikěḥâ*), but if he has left three or more sheaves, they are attributed to his negligence and remain his property (*m. Pe'a* 6:5).

Provision for gleaning was a concern from earliest times: "During your daily harvesting, as in 'days of need,' make the earth supply the sustenance of the young and the gleaners, according to their number [that is, presumably, he must leave the fallen kernels for needy children and the gleaners to pick], (and) let them sleep (in your field) as (in) the (open) marshland. (If you do so) your god will show you everlasting favor" (*Farmers' Almanac*, ll. 80–84; Kramer 1963: 341). Concern for the poor, the widow, and the orphan is widespread throughout ancient Near Eastern codes and edicts. Israel, however, is unique in its solicitude for the *gēr*, the alien.

It surely is of interest to note the impact of this law on the contemporary American scene. An article in the *Los Angeles Times* (Aug. 31, 1983) under the headline "Needy Americans Gleaning Unwanted Agricultural Harvest" reports that "active gleaning programs have now taken hold in 11 states . . . that take its guidance from Lev 19:9–10 . . . in response to what the General Accounting office calls an 'unmet need' for food among Americans who do not qualify for government food systems."

10. *pick bare. tĕʿōlēl.* Three interpretations have been proposed:

1. A denominative from *ʿōlēl* 'nursling, infant' (e.g., Lam 2:11), in the form of a privative *Piʿel* (e.g., *wĕšērešĕkā* 'will uproot you', Ps 52:7; Ibn Ezra); that is, remove the tiniest unripe grapes. Remote.
2. Corresponding to Arabic *ʿalla* 'do a second time' (Baentsch 1903; Noth 1977; Snaith 1967), based on *lōʾ tĕʿōlēl ʾaḥărêkā*, literally "do not pick after you" (Deut 24:21), which, however, may only imply "do not completely pick" (Schwartz 1987: 277, n. 18).
3. From *ʿālel* 'treat severely', hence "strip bare" (*RSV*), in which case its meaning would parallel *tĕkalleh* 'destroy', v. 9 (Elliger 1966) — accepted as my rendering.

That the nominal formation *ʿōlēlōt* refers to the leftover grapes is certified by its usage *kĕʿōlēlōt ʾim-kālâ bāṣîr* 'like gleanings when the vintage is completed' (Isa 24:13); *ʾim bōṣĕrîm bāʾû lāk hălōʾ yašʾîrû ʿōlēlôt* 'If vintagers came to you they would surely leave some gleanings' (Ob 5). Thus *ʿōlēlôt* in the vineyard is the semantic equivalent of *pēʾâ* in the field.

The rabbis define it as a vine branch that has neither "shoulder" (*kātēp*) nor "pendant" (*nātēp*) (*m. Peʾa* 7:4). They define "shoulder" as stalks (*pĕsîgîn*) growing off the top of the main stem and bearing grape clusters, and "pendant" as grapes growing in a branch on the bottom of the stem (*t. Peʾa* 3:11). But they consider the few grapes singly scattered on the stem as *ʿōlēlôt* (cf. Levine 1989; Boleh 1991–92). R. Judah, however, basing himself on Isa 17:6 "only *ʿōlēlôt* shall be left of him . . . two berries or three on the topmost branch," sets an upper limit of three berries, above which the group of grapes is considered a cluster (*y. Peʾa* 7:4). According to the newly published Qumran text 4Q270 (Baumgarten 1995), the limit is ten berries.

the fallen fruit. ûperet. In addition to leftover grapes (above), the poor are entitled to the grapes that fall to the ground during the grape harvest (*m. Pe'a* 7:3). This term is a *hapax*; it is the semantic equivalent of *leqet* (v. 9).

your vineyard. karmĕka. Technically, the term *kerem* also includes the olive orchard (e.g., Judg 15:5). However, the verb for "picking bare" the olive trees is *pē'ēr* (Deut 24:20), not *'ōlēl* (Deut 24:21).

For the poor and the alien. All three commandments in this verse begin with the object, emphasizing the source of the produce and, here, the recipients of the produce.

In the priestly texts, this is the only place (and in its copy, 23:22) where the poor are mentioned. D reserves gifts from the produce for the orphan and widow, namely, of the tithe (Deut 14:29; 26:12, 13), of the harvest (Deut 24:19–21), and during the Festivals of Weeks and Booths (Deut 16:11, 14). The others who are poor are excluded from these compulsory gifts and, instead, are to be granted loans (Deut 15:7–11; 24:12; cf. Exod 22:24 [JE]), the assumption being that the poor can work off their debts, but the orphan and widow cannot. H, however, does not discriminate among these groups. As long as they are poor, they are entitled to glean from the crops. But an endowed widow or an "adopted" orphan would definitely be excluded.

Alternatively (and preferably), H does not mention the widow and the orphan because during its time (mainly, the latter half of the eighth century), the kin group (*mišpāḥâ / bêt 'ābôt*; see Milgrom 1979a: 79–81) and the household (*bêt 'ab*; see Milgrom 1979a:79–81) were tightly controlled (see INTRODUCTION to 18:6–23). The widow and orphan automatically would have been taken care of by the nearest relative(s) of the deceased. The cracks in patriarchal control barely visible in the eighth century (cf. Isa 1:17, 23; 10:2) become a searing fissure a century later, when increasing latifundia and urbanization led to the dissolution of family and clan structure, leaving the widow and orphan an open prey to exploitation (Jer 7:6; 15:8; 22:3, 16; Ezek 22:7, 25).

The question remains: if D takes pains to list the Levites among society's underprivileged (Deut 12:19; 14:29; 16:14; 26:11–13), why doesn't H do likewise? Why is the Levite conspicuously missing from H's humanitarian concerns? The dating of H mainly in the eighth century (for the few exceptions, see NOTES to 23:1–3, 11*, 16*, 39–43; 26:1–2) provides the answer. The Levites are gainfully employed in Judah's regional sanctuaries, residing in their own compound in the Levitic cities (25:32–34; Num 35:1–8). The influx of Levites among the northern refugees has hardly begun, and it is a century before D's (Josiah's) centralization throws Judah's Levites among the ranks of the unemployed.

Carmichael (1997: 74) makes the cogent point that the equivalent instruction in Deut 24:19–22 is impractical because it relies on the landowner's amnesia rather than his duty. However, he is in error in presuming that Joseph's "generosity" in feeding the people of Egypt with the grain he had stored during the years of plenty prompted our legist to formulate an equivalent law for Israel. The alternative and most likely explanation of Joseph's administrative reforms is that their aim was to subjugate Egypt and the Egyptians under Pharaoh's control, a view apparently adopted by H (see NOTE on 25:43).

Here is the first instance of "not this, but this" (cf. vv. 15, 17, 20–21, 33–34, 35–36), which implies, in this case, that one should make it possible for the poor to glean (Schwartz 1987: 135). Therefore, the text begins with prohibitions and climaxes with a new prescription (Kilian 1963). The rabbis point out that the landowner cannot chose his poor in order that they will feel grateful to him (*t. Pe'a* 2:13). Note that the alien (*gēr*) is considered among the poor, a sign that he is landless and has no independent source of income (contrast 25:47; see its NOTE).

them. *'ōtām.* This refers to all four compulsory gifts of vv. 9–10: the edge of the field (*pē'â*), the fallen stalks (*leqeṭ*), the leftover grapes (*'ōlēlôt*), and the fallen grapes (*peret*).

I YHWH your God (*have spoken*). "For YHWH will take up their cause and despoil them who despoil them of life" (Prov 22:23, cited by Rashi).

Vv. 11–13. Ethical Duties

This is an organic section concerning deeds (vv. 11–13), speech (vv. 14–16), and thought (vv. 17–18; cf. Ibn Ezra on Exod 20:2). The unit on deeds (vv. 11–13) can be subdivided into furtive deeds (vv. 11–12) and nonfurtive deeds (v. 13). The chances are, I submit, that H has not innovated these ethical prescriptions, but has selected them from another (perhaps oral) source in order to group them under the rubric of holiness. Just as H hasn't invented the procedure with the *šĕlāmîm* (vv. 5–8), but has borrowed it from P (7:16–18) to subsume it under the rubric of holiness, so H may have borrowed and expanded all the commandments in this chapter (from P?) for this purpose.

These ethical commandments had a profound influence on the rabbis who expounded and expanded them, as detailed in the NOTES. They had no less an impact on early Christianity, as exemplified in the epistle of James. As Johnson (1982: 399) has demonstrated, "James made conscious and sustained use" of vv. 12–18, as follows:

19:12	Jas 5:12	19:16	Jas 4:11
19:13	Jas 5:4	19:18a	Jas 5:9
19:15	Jas 2:1, 9	19:18b	Jas 2:8

If one loves one's fellow as oneself (2:8), one avoids treating people with partiality (2:1, 9), defrauding others or holding back a hireling's wages (5:4), uttering oaths and dissembling (5:12), slandering others (5:9), and speaking evil of them (4:11). But as Hartley 1992: 325) has cautioned, James's ethical pronouncements are actually "filtered through the teachings of Jesus."

The intermingling of ritual and ethics is not unique to Israel. It abounds in Mesopotamia—for example, *Šurpu*, tablet II (Reiner 1958; cf. vol. 1.21–23), "A Bilingual Hymn to Nanurta," ll. 3–7 (Lambert 1960: 119), and the "Nanshe Hymn," ll. 136–71 (Heimpel 1981: 90–93). What, however, is unique to Israel—rather, to H—is the subsumation of ethics as well as rituals under the rubric of holiness. Here H takes a major step forward. Whereas the two other biblical codes that raise the issue of holiness restrict its application to ritual commandments (abstention from sabbath labor and idolatry [essence of the covenant, Exod 20:3–11 (JE); Deut 5:7–15 (D); eating carcasses, Exod 22:30 (JE); Deut 14:21 (D); idolatry and mourning rites; Deut 7:5–6; 14:1–2 (D)]), H lists ethical prescriptions alongside ritualistic ones as determinants of holiness (see COMMENT).

Vv. 11–13. Unit 5: Deeds

The subunit furtive deeds consists of three sentences (11a, 11b, 12) composed according to the rule *kol haqqāṣār qôdēm* 'The shorter (statement) precedes' (Friedman 1971: 122; Avishur 1979: 33, nn. 40–41; cf. Cassuto 1959: 111–12), also attested in Akkadian (Ehelolf 1916: 3) and Ugaritic (*UT* 135–37). This rule also holds in biblical poetry (Gordis 1945; Paran 1983: 149–56).

Many of the categories in vv. 11–13 are found in 5:20–26 (P), and there can be little doubt that the latter passage was clearly in the mind of the writer (H) of the former (details in Milgrom 1976a: 84–101). However, whereas 5:20–26 deal with one theme, the illegal expropriation of property, it will be shown that vv. 11–13 break out of the constricting mold of the punishment for specific acts of expropriation by converting them into basic ethical prohibitions. This distinction is clearly recognized by the rabbis: "because it is written *wĕkiḥeš bāh* 'and he has dissembled about it' (5:22) we learn the punishment. Where (is there) the warning (that it is forbidden)? 'You shall not lie' " (19:11; *Sipra* Qedoshim, par. 2:3).

11. *You shall not steal. lō' tignōbû.* *Tgs. Ps.-J.* and *Neof.* begin this verse and the next with "my people Israel," thereby taking note that the prohibitions are voiced in the plural. The category of theft (*gĕnēbâ*) is missing in 5:20–26, where instead we find *gĕzēlâ* 'robbery'. The reason is that vv. 11–12 deal with furtive acts, whereas 5:20–26 deal with undisguised, open use of force. The category of robbery is listed among the nonfurtive acts of v. 13 (Milgrom 1976a: 89–93). This criterion is the common denominator of all the prohibitions in chap. 19. These violations may elude human jurisdiction. But God will assuredly punish, as implied by the *'ănî YHWH* ending of each section (vv. 3, 4, 10, 12, 14, 16, 18, 25, 28, 30, 31, 32, 34, 36). In Mesopotamia as well, the thief falls under a divine curse (*Šurpu* II.61, 83–85; III.58 [Reiner 1958]).

What is the nature of the theft: is it persons (i.e., kidnaping) (as in Exod 21:16; Deut 24:7; and possibly the Decalogue, Exod 20:15), or is it property (as in Exod 21:37–22:3)? "Scripture refers to theft of property. You say thus, but perhaps it is not so, Scripture referring to the theft of human beings? I will tell you: Go forth and learn from the thirteen (hermeneutic) principles whereby the Torah is interpreted, (one of which is that) a law is interpreted by its general context. Of what does the text speak? Of money matters (vv. 11–13); therefore this too refers to (theft of) money" (*Mek.* Yitro 8; *b. Sanh.* 86a [bar.]). Baḥya infers the same from the fact that the prohibition is written in the singular (Exod 21:16; Deut 24:7).

Why is the *'atnaḥ* placed here? Saadiah suggests that theft is different from the crimes of lying and deceiving because the prohibition of stealing applies to all persons, whereas lying and deceiving apply to only the *ʿāmît* 'neighbor'—a dubious distinction (see below). Schwartz (1987: 139) surmises that the first listed crime, "stealing," is a generalization and the following crimes itemize it, resulting in desecration. As will be shown the context of vv. 11–12 is far broader than theft. The simplest answer, I submit, emerges from a grammatical consideration: the verb *gānab* never takes the preposition *bě*; hence the pausal mark under this word.

you shall not dissemble. welō'-tĕkaḥăšû. A distinction has to be made between *kiḥēš bě* and *kiḥēš lě.* The former means "deny a truth, dissemble"; the latter means "affirm a nontruth, lie" (= *šiqqēr*; see below). An example of *kiḥēš bě* is *kiḥăšû baYHWH wayyō'mĕrû lō'-hû'* 'They denied God and said "Not he" ' (Jer 5:12; cf. Hos 9:2 LXX; Hab 3:17; Job 8:18). An example of *kiḥēš lě* is *kî-kiḥaštî lā'ēl mimmā'al* 'For I would have lied [not "denied," NJPS, NAB] to the God above' (Job 31:28; cf. 1 Kgs 13:18). In property matters, the distinction is clearer: *kiḥēš bě* connotes "I don't owe it to you," whereas *kiḥēš le* (= *šiqqēr* 'lie') connotes "You owe me." Thus *kiḥēš bě* implies a negative statement, a denial. It is found in many contexts: religious (Josh 24:27; Jer 5:12), private (Lev 5:21–22) and public relations (Zech 13:4), and court testimony (Lev 5:21–22).

you shall not lie. wĕlō'-tĕšaqqĕrû. As noted above, both *kiḥēš* and *šiqqēr* connote deception. *kiḥeš bě*, on the one hand, refers to the desire to keep what you unlawfully have; you therefore *deny* that it belongs to someone else. *šiqqēr*, on the other hand, refers to the desire to want something that belongs to someone else; that is, you *affirm* that it belongs to you. The difference, then, is that in the former you deny a *truth*; in the latter, you affirm a *lie*.

The terms *šiqqēr, šeqer* do not occur in Lev 5:20–26 for the same reason that explains the absence of *gānab, gĕnēbâ*, accounted for above. Lev 5 is limited to cases of misappropriation of property, actual fraud. Lev 19, however, adds the terms *gānab* and *šiqqēr* to cover all kinds of deceitful claims, an indication that Lev 19 builds on and is later than Lev 5. For further examples, see below.

The root *šqr* occurs six times in Scripture, and here, too, a distinction is manifest, depending on whether the preposition is *lě* or *bě*. The preposition *lě* occurs in the only case of the verb in the *Qal. 'im-tišqōr lî ûlĕnînî* 'you will not deal falsely with me and my offspring' (Gen 21:23). With the exception of this verse, four other instances are in the *Pi'el* followed by the preposition *bě* and things as the object: God's word (1 Sam 15:29), covenant (Isa 63:8; Ps 44:18), and faithfulness (Ps 89:34). Thus, even from these few examples, it is possible to extrapolate the rule that *šāqar* (*Qal*) takes the dative of a person (*lě*), whereas *šiqqēr* (*Pi'el*) takes the accusative of a thing and requires *bě*. In other words, one lies *to* a person, but lies *about* a thing.

However, this rule is ostensibly shattered in this verse, where the object of *šiqqēr* is *baʿămîtô* 'to another, to his neighbor'. One should have expected *laʿămîtô!* I suggest that the answer lies in the fact that *baʿămîtô* is the object of two verbs *kiḥēš* and *šiqqēr*, and the necessity to comply with the requirement that *kiḥēš* be followed by *bĕ* necessitated the attachment of *šiqqēr* to the same preposition.

to one another. *ʾîš baʿămîtô.* For the meaning of *ʿămît*, see the NOTE on 18:20. The same law as 18:20 is found in 20:10, where the term *rēaʿ* is used. In chap. 19, *ʿămît* is found in vv. 11, 15, 17, where it alternates with *rēaʿ* 'fellow' (vv. 13, 16, 18) and is parallel with *bĕnê ʿammekā* 'your compatriot'. In 25:14, *ʿămît* is used twice alongside of *ʾaḥ* 'brother, kinspeople, fellow Israelite'. Hence the four terms *ʿămît*, *rēaʿ*, *ʾaḥ*, and *ben ʿam* are used synonymously for "compatriot, fellow citizen" (Zobel 1987). Ezekiel replaces *ʿămît* in similar contexts with *ʾaḥ* 'brother, fellow citizen'. Thereafter, in exilic and postexilic biblical literature, *ʿămît* disappears, indicating that it is a preexilic term (Hurvitz 1982: 74–78).

Clearly, all these synonyms refer solely to Israelites. That the ethical persons intended by these ethical demands are not limited to Israel is mandated by vv. 33–34, which apply them to the resident alien (see NOTES). What, however, of the *ben-nēkār* 'the foreigner'? Are we to infer that the Israelite is free to lay aside any of the ethical rules in dealing with him? Here is where abstract logical reasoning leads astray. The forgotten factor is that the H school probably had no contact with foreigners. Sequestered in the Jerusalem Temple or, at best, having visited regional sanctuaries and the surrounding countryside, the only persons *of concern* were Israelites. It was their spiritual status, which priestly teaching tried to elevate, that ultimately determined whether YHWH would remain in his sanctuary, in his land, and among his people. It is hardly accidental that the only mention of the foreigner is as the sender, not the presenter, of sacrifices (22:25). Contrast Isaiah of Jerusalem, a contemporary in my opinion, and his wide-ranging knowledge of the surrounding nations and of the empires beyond. But, then, that is a quintessential distinction between the priest and the prophet, whose commission, in Jeremiah's words, is *nābîʾ laggôyim nĕtattîkā* 'I have appointed you a prophet to the nations' (Jer 1:5).

The lengthening of the final sentence in a series is typical poetic style (e.g., Isa 33:18; 40:24, 28; 42:2; Jer 9:24–25; Paran 1989: 213–21). The fact, however, that the prohibition of the following v. 12 is even longer is one of the indications that it concludes the series.

12. *And you shall not swear falsely by my name.* *wĕlōʾ-tiššābĕʿû bišmî laššāqer.* The rabbis see in vv. 11–12 a series of connected events: "If you have stolen, you are likely to deny, then to lie, and end by taking a false oath" (*Sipra* Qedoshim, par. 2:5; cf. Philo, *Laws* 4.40). Most likely, their perception is based, in part, on the established sequence in the case of the misappropriation of property in 5:20–26: the crime (five varieties), denial (*kiḥēš*), and false oath (vv. 21–22; cf. Milgrom 1976a: 86–89; vol. 1.337–38). If the rabbis are right, then the *waw* would be purposive and would have to be rendered "thereby."

Nonetheless, the rabbis' interpretation must be rejected. First, as noted above, the verb *šiqqēr* has been added, which—even if we limit the unit to property cases—would imply not that the accused denied (*kiḥēš*) possessing property of another, but that he went on the offensive and issued a false counterclaim, namely, that his accuser possessed his property—a contingency that shatters the purported sequence in vv. 11–12. Besides, in all other attestations of false oaths in Scripture, it stands by itself as a grievous sin, e.g., *hăgānōb rāṣōaḥ wěnā'ōp wěhiššābēaʿ laššeqer wěqaṭṭēr labbaʿal* 'Will you steal, murder, commit adultery, swear falsely, and make offerings to Baal' (Jer 7:9; cf. Jer 5:2; Zech 5:4; Mal 3:5).

Indeed, the Qumran sectaries, even when they model themselves on the law of Lev 5:20–26, also make the false oath an independent category: *W'M YŠBʿ W'BR WḤLL 'T HŠM W'M B'LWT HBRYT [N]Š[Bʿ LPNY] / HŠPTYM 'M 'BR 'ŠM [HW'] WHTWDH WHŠYB WL' YŚʿ [ḤT' WL'] / [Y]MWT* 'And if he took an oath and violated (it), he would desecrate the Name. But if he [takes an] oath by the curses of the covenant [before] the judges, if he violates (it) [he] becomes guilty. He shall confess and make restitution and then he will not bear [iniquity and he will not d]ie' (CD 15:3–5).

The importance of H's innovation cannot be overestimated. By unhitching the false oath from the crimes of misappropriation (Lev 5:20–26 [P]), H declares that the latter in themselves are sinful, not just against persons and, hence, adjudicable in the courts, but against YHWH by preventing his holy presence from residing among Israel (see NOTES on 26:11–12). It is only when Israel is striving for a life of holiness, as encapsulated by the commandments of this chapter, can YHWH's otherness (termed *qĕdûšâ* 'holiness', see NOTE on v. 2) be sustained on earth.

Just as commentators have found the prohibition against theft (v. 11a) to echo the eighth commandment of the Decalogue and the prohibition against lying (v. 11b) to paraphrase the Decalogue's ninth commandment (false witness), so they find the false oath in this verse to be imitative of the Decalogue's third commandment *lō' tiśśā' 'et-šēm-YHWH 'ĕlōhêkā laššāw'* (Exod 20:7). The third commandment has been rendered variously as "You shall not make wrongful use of the name of the Lord your God" (*NEB, NRSV*); "You shall not take the name of the Lord, your God, in vain" (*KJV, NAB*). *NJPS*, however, renders "You shall not swear falsely by the name of the Lord your God," thereby equating *šeqer* 'lie' with *šāw'*. But are they equivalent?

Most commentators believe that they are equivalent (see INTRODUCTION; see also Pedersen 1926: 413–14; von Rad 1962: 1.183–84). So too the rabbis (*Sipra* Qedoshim, par. 2:6; cf. Rashi and Ibn Ezra on Exod 20:13 and Deut 5:18), except that, in one view, an oath called *šāw'*, swears on the past, and one called *šeqer*, swears on the future (*b. Šebu.* 20a). In general, the rabbis define *šāw'* as an aspect of falsehood:

1. It differs from an accepted truth (e.g., the stone pillar is made of gold).
2. It projects an impossibility (e.g., seeing a flying camel).
3. It annuls a commandment (e.g., not to build a booth, cf. 23:42).
4. It involves swearing contradictory oaths, inevitably having to violate one of them (*m. Šebu.* 3:8–9).

The accepted meaning of *šāw'* (whose etymology is unknown) is "useless, worthless." Mowinckel (1921: 50–57) proposed that *šāw'* also means "magic, evil" (e.g., Hos 10:4; Job 7:3), and in that sense it refers in the Decalogue to the illicit use of God's name (but see Childs 1974: 11).

In any event, it is clear that in the Decalogue, the use of God's name is forbidden over a wide area, including oaths, prayers, curses, and blessings, if its purpose is worthless, false, magical—in a word, if its use is inimical to the revealed will of God. Here, however, the prohibition deals with lying oaths. I would agree that its range is not limited to property, as in 5:20–26. It constitutes a generalization. Lying oaths are forbidden in any situation: on the witness stand for any crime or in private exchange with one's fellow. Thus it must be concluded that our verse and the third commandment are not equivalent (cf. Schwartz 1987: 139). D. N. Freedman (personal communication) comments that "the case is limited in the Decalogue by the explanatory gloss, namely, that Yahweh will not acquit, a formal legal term, anyone who misuses the name . . . the focus is on jurisprudence." However, YHWH is the subject of *niqqâ* 'acquit' mostly—and logically—in cases that cannot be adjucated in court (e.g., Exod 34:7; Num 4:18; Nah 1:3).

Herein may lie the reason why H had to omit the third commandment from his reprise of the first half of the Decalogue at the head of this chapter. He wanted to focus on only *šeqer*, an aspect of *šāw*', and perforce had to place it here, where he needed it in connection with his supplementation (vv. 11–12) to 5:20–26.

Interestingly, the Qumran sectaries (CD 15:3–5) apparently relate "lie" to W'BR . . . 'M 'BR; that is, the oath itself is not a lie, but it is a lie because it was not fulfilled.

It should not be forgotten that since an oath was always taken in the name of a deity, its violation was considered a mortal sin not only in Israel, but also among Israel's contemporary and anterior neighbors. For Mesopotamia, see the *māmītu* of Šurpu III.19–26; VIII.35–44 (Reiner 1958) and its discussion in Brichto (1963: 71–76) and the text and ritual of the fifth "house" in Laessøe (1955: 52–67). Among the Hittites, perjury is listed with blood, impurity, and mutilation among the four ways of polluting a house and requiring purification (*KUB* VII, 41, cited in Engelhard 1970: 76), evidence that a false oath is considered an offense against the gods requiring expiation or punishment in its wake. For the Greeks, see Jones (1956: 136–39) and the remarks by Heinemann (1932: 92–96). And for Israel, suffice it to cite *hôṣēʾtîhā něʾum YHWH ṣěbāʾôt ûbāʾâ ʾel-bêt haggannāb wěʾel bêt hannišbāʿ bišmî laššāqer* . . . 'I have sent it forth—declares YHWH of Hosts—and (the curse) shall enter the house of the thief, and the house of the one who swears falsely by my name, and it shall lodge inside their houses and shall consume them to the last timber and stone' (Zech 5:4).

lest you desecrate the name of your God. wěḥillaltā ʾet-šēm ʾělōhêkā. This is the rationale for the prohibition against taking a false oath. Notice how different it is from the rationale for the illicit use of God's name in the third commandment of the Decalogue. There it is a threat of punishment that acts as a deterrent. Here, the result, desecration, is the deterrent. God's name is the only sanctum other than the meat of the well-being offering (discussed in vv. 5–8) that can be utilized by the laity. Its desecration nullifies whatever holiness has been achieved through the observance of the other injunctions in this chapter. For this reason, the well-being offering was given such play in this chapter. Now once more, the Israelite is warned that his attempt to climb the ladder of holiness is futile if he commits an act of desecration for which *there is neither remedy nor expiation* (contrast 5:20–26).

P's term for desecration is *māʿal*, which implies trespassing or encroaching on the divine sphere. Its emphasis is on the subject, the encroacher, who either trespasses on God's property or violates an oath (using God's name, also his property). H's equivalent term is *ḥillēl* 'desecrate'. Here the emphasis is on the object, God or, rather, his name (see below); the sinner, by his incursion into the divine sphere, reduces God's realm of holiness, desanctifying or desecrating it (Milgrom 1976a: 16–21). For a detailed discussion of the distinction between P's *maʿal* and H's *ḥillēl šēm YHWH*, see vol. 1.366–67.

The particle *wĕlōʾ* at the beginning of the prohibition against swearing falsely (v. 12a) also applies to the second half of the verse, hence the rendering "lest" (e.g., 22:9; cf. Driver 1892: 133, § 115). However, the desecration of the divine name results from the false oath, not from violating the prohibitions listed in v. 11. Knohl (1995: 176, n. 24) hesitatingly suggests that v. 11 is also included, in conformance with his theory that for H the violation of any of God's commandments constitutes a desecration of his name. Note, however, that the latter concept is explicitly limited by H to specific offenses—for example, Molek worship (18:21; 20:3), idolatrous mourning customs (21:6), and the desecration of sancta, especially sacred food (22:1–16). Knohl's (1995: 184, n. 45) claim that the charge of desecration in 22:31–32 applies to the violation of every commandment cannot be sustained: it refers to only the cultic sins enumerated in the preceding pericope addressed to the Israelites (vv. 17–30; see NOTE on 22:32). Indeed, it can be shown that the eighteen other occurrences of *ḥillēl šēm YHWH* 'desecrate the name of YHWH' in the Bible always occur in a cultic context (Milgrom 1976a: 86, n. 302). As for the term *maʿal* (26:40) describing the violation of the covenant (26:15), which may refer to all of God's commandments, perhaps H has chosen this P term (see above) over its own term *ḥillel* to indicate that this case indeed is a generalization. (For an alternative explanation, see NOTE on 26:40.)

The rabbis stress the severity of this offense: "R. Johanan b. Beroka said: He that desecrates the name of heaven in secret shall be punished in public: In desecrating the Name it is all the same whether it be done inadvertently or wantonly" (*m. ʾAbot* 4:4).

The wording of this clause gives rise to four questions:

1. Why is the verb expressed as *wĕḥillaltā* instead of *wĕlōʾ tĕḥallēl?* The answer is clear: the latter phrasing would transform this clause into a prohibition, whereas it is intended to convey a result, namely, that a false oath automatically causes the desecration of God's name.

2. Why is the verb *wĕḥillaltā* in the singular, in contrast to the plural formation of the other verbs in this unit (vv. 11–12)? The LXX indeed reads it as a

plural. Many commentators (e.g., Dillmann and Ryssel 1897; Elliger 1966) therefore regard this clause as an editorial interpolation. Schwartz (1987: 140) suggests that the plural would imply that desecration will emanate from false oaths taken by many; hence the singular is used to indicate that each one who swears falsely causes desecration. M. Hildenbrand opines that the singular is influenced by the singular of *ḥillēl* in the flanking chapters (18:21; 20:3), in contrast to its uniform plural attestation elsewhere (21:6; 22:2; Ezek 20:39; 36:20–23; Mal 1:12).

3. Why is not the name of God written in the first person, *šĕmî* 'my name', as it appears in the first half of the verse? Perhaps the text wishes to emphasize that not only *my* name but the name of *your* God (*'ĕlōhêka*) is desecrated. That is, the responsibility for desecrating God's name falls on Israel (Schwartz 1987: 140).

4. Why is the name of God desecrated rather than God himself? The answer is that the expression *šēm 'ĕlōhîm* is a euphemism for YHWH. To the Israelite mind, it is inconceivable that God himself can be desecrated—that is, be diminished in his holiness. Moreover, even the verb *ḥillēl* 'desecrate' is somewhat of a euphemism. Cases where the sancta are actually defiled (*ṭm'*) are, in fact, described as causing the desecration (*ḥll*) of God's name. For example, contact with the dead defiles (*ṭm'*) the priest (21:1–5) but leads to the desecration of God's name (21:6). A striking case is Molek worship, which pollutes (*ṭm'*) the sanctuary but desecrates (*ḥll*) God's name. The ostensible exception of the verb *ṭimmē'* in Ezek 43:7–8, stating that YHWH's name is defiled, can be regarded as an aberration (see NOTE on 20:3) or as an expression of horror that corpses (of kings)—the corpse being the severest impurity—are interred adjoining the Temple. Alternatively, deuteronomic theology may have influenced Ezekiel: the Temple is defiled because the name of God resides in it (e.g., Deut 12:11; 14:23; Schwartz, personal communication). In any case, the use of the euphemism *šēm* (the origin of D's name theology) and the reluctance to use *ṭimmē'* 'pollute', which conveys the impression that the very person of YHWH has been impacted by impurity, indicate only too clearly that H is just as opposed to anthropomorphistic notions of God as is P, if not more so (see Introduction I J).

I YHWH (have spoken). The LXX and Pesh. add *'ĕlōhêkem* 'your God'. However, it would appear both stylistically awkward and logically redundant after the singular *'ĕlōhêka*; perhaps for the same reason it is omitted in vv. 14, 32.

A more bothersome question is the occurrence of this clause here rather than at the end of v. 13, which terminates the unit. The likely answer is that v. 13 deals with nonfurtive crimes, which, because they are known, fall under the responsibility of the court. Vv. 11–12, however, deal with furtive crimes, and although they escape the notice of the authorities, they are known to God, who will exact retribution from the offender (Wessely 1846). Assuming this interpretation is correct, it serves as strong evidence that the main function of this phrase is to warn Israel that no violation of God's commandments will go unpunished.

13. *You shall not exploit. lō'- ta'ăšōq*. The general connotation of the verb *'āšaq* is "oppress, extort" (e.g., Jer 21:12; 22:3; cf. Deut 28:29, 33; 1 Sam 12:4;

Hos 4:2; Amos 4:1; see Milgrom 1976a: 101, n. 376). H adopts this connotation. P, as is its wont, has a more specific meaning in mind: witholding payment or property that has come into one's possession *legally* (5:21, 23). In this case, there is no need for the miscreant to take an oath (contrast 5:22, 24), since he freely admits possessing the other's property or money (Bekhor Shor).

your fellow. rēʿăkā. In the priestly texts, the term *rēaʿ* is found only in H (19:13, 16, 18; 20:10). It is indistinguishable from *ʿāmît* (v. 11); both bear the connotation of "fellow, companion," as illustrated by "placing each piece opposite its companion" (piece, *rēʿēhû*) (Gen 15:10).

The term *rēaʿ* can also refer to a non-Israelite (cf. Gen 38:12, 20; Exod 11:2; 1 Chr 27:33), and that broader range is intended here, since the hireling, who exemplifies this ruling (see below), is not restricted to the Israelite (Deut 24:14; but see NOTE on "fellow," v. 18b).

and you shall not commit robbery. wĕlōʾ tigzōl. This term in 5:21, 23 (P) has been explained as taking someone's property by force; hence the property is being withheld from its owner *illegally* (Milgrom 1976a: 9a; cf. Radak, Bekhor Shor, Maimonides, "Theft and Loss" 1:3–4; Wessely 1846). The verbs *ʿāšaq* and *gāzal* are frequently found together (Deut 28:29; Jer 21:12; 22:3; Ezek 18:18; 22:29; Mic 2:2; Ps 62:11; Koh 5:7). The distinction is neatly caught by the rabbis: "What is meant by *ʿōšeq* and *gezel*? R. Hisda said: 'Go and come again, go and come again'—that is *ʿōšeq* [i.e., continually deferring payment]; 'I have (what is yours), but I will not give it to you'—that is *gezel* (*b. B. Meṣ.* 111a).

Why does this prohibition follow "your fellow" instead of preceding it? Saadiah (on v. 11) argues that *ʿōšeq* 'extortion, witholding' applies to only an Israelite (*rēaʿ*), but robbery applies to everyone—an interpretation that is vitiated by the meaning of *reaʿ* and *śākîr* in this verse (see NOTES). The answer may rest purely on stylistic grounds. By ending v. 13a with *lōʾ tigzōl*, a chiasm is created with *lōʾ tignōbû*, which begins v. 11 and also has no object. Moreover, the MT is essential, for it allows the *waw* to be explanatory: don't withold from your fellow, for it is robbery. Thus departing from P's nuanced distinction of legally versus illegally withheld property, H leans toward the broader, more generalized connotation of these terms: oppression and robbery. The realization that all of v. 13a is a single sentence also solves two stylistic problems simultaneously: it explains why the shorter *lō tigzōl* follows the longer *lōʾ-ta ʿăšōq ʾet-rēʿăkā*, and it sets up the entire unit (vv. 13–14) as a series of prohibitions of increasing lengths: vv. 13a, 13b, 14a (Schwartz 1987: 141–42).

The wages of. pĕʿullat. This is the consequential meaning of *pĕʿullâ* 'work' (Jer 31:16; 2 Chr 15:7). For a similar usage, see Isa 40:10; 49:4; 61:8; 62:11; Prov 10:16; Sir 36:21. Masculine *pōʿal* undergoes the same transformation: work (Ps 104:23; Job 24:5) and wages (Jer 22:13; Job 7:2). On the phenomenon of consequential meaning, see vol. 1.339–45.

your hireling. śākîr ʾittĕkā. In priestly texts (mainly H), this term is found in 19:13; 22:10; 25:6, 40, 50, 53; Exod 12:45. That the hireling could be either Israelite or non-Israelite is explicitly stated by a similar law in Deuteronomy: *lōʾ-ta ʿăšōq* śākîr 'ănî wĕ'ebyôn mē'aḥêkā 'ô miggērĕkā 'ăšer bĕ'arṣĕkā biš'ārêkā 'You shall not oppress a needy and destitute hireling, whether a compatriot or alien, in any of the communities in your land' (Deut 24:14). For a discussion of the socioeconomic status of the hireling, see the NOTE on 25:40. There, however, the "slave" is on a long-term hire until the jubilee or until he repays his loan. Here, the subject is the day laborer, who is one of the poorest members of society. He works only intermittently and consequently is in the greatest need of his daily wage for the support of his family (Telushkin 1997: 459).

shall not remain. lō'-tālîn. The verb is Qal, not Hip'îl (Rashi). Rashi is correct, since the Qal is intransitive. All the ostensible exceptions are also Qal (Deut 21:22–23; Jer 4:14; Job 24:7), even wĕlō' yālîn 'et-hā'ām 'and he will not spend the night with the troops' (2 Sam 17:8; where 'et = with). Furthermore, if tālîn were second person, 'ittĕkā 'with you' would be superfluous (Leibowitz 1983: 240).

Some forty MSS, the LXX, Sam., and Tg. Ps.-J. seem to read wĕlō'. However, the absence of the waw may indicate that v. 13b is a continuation and exemplification of v. 13a, namely, an illustration of the way a neighbor can be exploited and robbed by withholding his wages.

The similar law of Deut 24:14–15 states that the daily wage must be paid by sundown (cf. Matt 20:8), whereas this law implies that the payment may be delayed until the following morning. The rabbis harmonize the difference by claiming that both laws offer a concession to the employer: this verse states that the day laborer's wage can be delayed until dawn, whereas Deut 24:14–15 speaks of a night laborer whose wages can be delayed until sundown (m. B. Meṣ. 9:11; Sipra Qedoshim, par. 2:12; Sipra Deut. 299). Ramban, however, holds that both laws are identical, this one merely stating that the day's wages should not be postponed until the morning and implying that they should be paid at sunset— that is, the end of the workday. This, indeed, is the interpretation found in wisdom literature: "Do not say to your fellow, 'Come back again. I'll give it (the wages) to you tomorrow' when you have it with you" (Prov 3:28).

Care for the hireling is reflected in other texts (Jer 22:13; Mal 3:5; Job 7:2). The possibility exists that Jer 22:13 (note bĕrē'ēhû, ûpō'ălô) has been influenced by this verse (Leibowitz 1983: 241).

As mentioned above (v. 12bβ), although this verse marks the end of the unit (vv. 11–13), it does not end with 'ănî YHWH because it describes nonfurtive acts—extortion, robbery, withholding wages—which can be adjudicated in a human court.

V. 14. Unit 6: Exploitation of the Helpless

You shall not insult. lō'-tĕqallēl. The verb qillēl and its nominal form qĕlālâ are antonyms of bērēk 'bless' and bĕrākâ 'blessing', respectively (e.g., Gen 27:12; Deut 11:26; 23:6; 30:1, 19; Josh 8:34; Neh 13:2). It also possesses a wider range of meaning, including "abuse, disrespect," and it is the antonym of kibbēd 'honor, respect', just as Akkadian *qullulu* 'diminish, discredit, ridicule' is the opposite of *kubbutu* 'respect'. Which meaning prevails here?

Brichto (1963: 120–22) opts for the wider meaning, not only in this passage but everywhere in Scripture. Supporting Brichto is the fact that the curse formula invariably begins with another verb *'ārûr* 'cursed', never with *mĕqullāl*. It can be shown, on the one hand, that H itself employs this wider connotation in 20:9, a context of illicit sexual unions, where "disrespect, dishonor" (euphemisms for incest) makes sense but where the notion of cursing is totally out of place. On the other hand, it seems more likely that in the episode of the blasphemer, the meaning of *qillēl* is strictly limited to "curse" (see NOTES on 24:11, 15–16).

Sforno argues that since a physical obstacle is placed before the blind (v. 14aβ), one should expect that the effect of *qillēl* is to generate physical harm, which a curse can achieve (cf. Weinfeld 1976: 186–89), but not verbal abuse. Thus the crime against cursing the deaf is that, not hearing the curse, he can take no countermeasures to ward it off (Hempel 1915: 38–39, cited in Brichto 1963: 120–21). But Brichto is correct in claiming that there is no evidence that the victim had to be within hearing range of a curse for it to be efficacious. This certainly holds true for Balaam attempting to curse Israel from a mountaintop. (It is, however, true that the victim had to be seen for the curse—or blessing— to be effective [Milgrom 1990a: 193–94], but this has no relevance for the deaf.)

The literal meaning of the text is a prohibition against playing cruel practical jokes, saying mean things in front of the deaf, or tripping the blind. Thus the appended "but you shall fear your God" takes on enhanced meaning: although the deaf does not know he was insulted nor the blind who hurt him, God does know and will punish accordingly (Telushkin 1997: 459). D's reading of this law logically follows: "Cursed is he who misdirects a blind person on his way" (Deut 27:18).

The choice, then, is difficult. And it is only H's penchant for generalizations (in sharp contrast to P; see Introduction I C, II B) that tips the scales in favor of a broader definition of *qillēl* 'insult, abuse, ridicule' (see further NOTE on 20:9). Indeed, as will be argued below, it is hardly conceivable that H literally meant that one is only forbidden to place a stumbling block before the blind. Moreover, the Egyptian "Teachings of Amenemope" (twelfth century B.C.E.), chap. 25, reads, "Do not laugh at a blind man and do not mock a cripple" (Brunner 1978: 61), indicating that "stumbling block" probably has a wide-ranging connotation. The rabbis, in fact, extrapolate from this prohibition that no one, not just the deaf, should be subject to verbal abuse (*m. Šebu.* 4:13; *Sipra* Qedoshim, par. 2:13; *b. Sanh.* 66a; cf. Rashi, Rashbam, Ramban). Nonetheless, they have extended this prohibition beyond its plain meaning. That the verse ends with the admonition "but you shall fear your God" implies that the weak and helpless, namely, the deaf and the blind, are under divine protection. This warning is given again in similar circumstances: the elderly (v. 32), cheating in land transactions (25:17), interest on loans (25:36), and exploiting the indentured Israelite (25:35–36; Schwartz 1987: 149). Stewart suggests (1994) that the metaphoric usage of disabilities so prevalent among the rabbis may rest on a firm biblical basis:

Jebusites: "You shall not come (in) here for blind people and lame will repel you . . ." (2 Sam 5:6bα)

David: ". . . the lame and the blind hateful to David. Therefore they say: 'The blind and the lame shall not come into the (God's) House.' " (2 Sam 5:8aβ,b)

It can hardly go unnoticed that David's reply is turned by the narrator into an etiological explanation for the exclusion of defective animals and priests from the Temple (see 21:18–20: 22: 22–24).

Stewart further suggests that a "deep semantic structure" underlies the terms "deaf" and "blind" in our verse, whereby they stand as partonomic metonymies for all non-*mûm* (deaf) and *mûm* disabilities, thus anticipating the selective list of disabilities of both priests (21:18–20) and sacrificial animals (22:22–24). He supports his claim by pointing to the function of the word-pair "deaf and blind" in Sumerian, Akkadian, and Hittite sources—for example, *ú.ḫub.me.en dul.la.ab ibí nu.un.du₃ / [su]-uk-ku-ka-ku katmāku ul anaṭṭal* 'I am deaf, I am [i.e., my eyes are] covered, I cannot see' (CAD 15:362). While the Sumerian and its Akkadian gloss may suggest total disability, the Hittite curse calls for the incapacitation of an enemy army: "[Whoever breaks these oaths betrays the king of Hatti land, and turns his eyes in hostile fashion upon the Hatti land,] Let these oaths seize him! Let them *blind* this man's army and make it *deaf*! Let them not *see* each other, let them not *hear* each other" (KBo VI 34 i 15–22; Ehelolf 1930: 394; ANET 343c). Stewart justifiably asks, "If an army cannot see nor communicate with itself, is its disability somehow less than complete?"

the deaf. ḥērēš. Since the deaf cannot hear a curse, they cannot ward it off by a blessing (Judg 17:2; Ps 109:28). The likelihood, however, is that the term "deaf" stands for all the helpless (*b. ʿAbod. Zar.* 6a, b; Maimonides, *The Book of Commandments,* § 317; Ramban). *Tg. Onq.* renders *dělāʾ šāmaʿ* 'one who cannot hear', thus broadening the prohibition to include those who are unaware of the curse or abuse and cannot take countermeasures to avert or refute it. Since such persons also fall under the category of helpless, they indeed may have been intended to be included by the writer—provided that "curse" be broadened to include verbal abuse.

Deafness is not considered a defect (*mûm*) that disqualifies a priest from officiating at the altar (for a possible explanation, see chap. 21, COMMENT B). Philo (*Laws* 4.197) interprets *kōphon* (LXX) as a "deaf-mute," as indicated by his explicit statement "those who have lost the power of speech" (4.198). The rabbis extend this term to cover all live persons (*Sipra* Qedoshim 2:13).

the blind. ʿiwwēr. "One who is blind about anything. . . . Do not give him advice that is not suitable for him" (*Sipra* Qedoshim, par. 2:14; cf. Rom 14:13), which the rabbis generalize to include all forms of temptation. For example, "Do not give a Nazirite a glass of wine or a severed animal's limb (containing its blood) to a descendant of Noah [i.e., a non-Israelite; cf. Gen 9:4]" (*b. Pesaḥ.* 22b), or "lend a person money without witnesses, thereby tempting him to cheat" (*b. B. Meṣ.* 75b).

This statement begins with the indirect object, thereby indicating the end of the unit (Schwartz 1987: 268, n. 77; see also vv. 4aβ, 28a, 30a). For the word-pair *ʿiwwēr / ḥērēš*, see Isa 29:18; 35:5; 42:18; 43:8.

place a stumbling bloc. tittēn mikšōl. This is a metaphoric expression, in keeping with the meaning of "the blind." Ezekiel's phrase *mikšôl ʿăwōnām*, literally "stumbling block of their iniquity," is also applied metaphorically, referring to idolatry (7:19; 14:3, 4, 7), unrepented transgression (18:30), and illegal shrines (44:12) as the causes for Israel's downfall. Similarly, *mikšôl* is a metaphor for "adversity" in "Those who love your teaching enjoy well-being; they encounter no *mikšôl*" (Ps 119:165). Deuteronomy's version of this prohibition is more specific: *ʾārûr mašgeh ʿiwwēr baddārek* 'Cursed be he who misdirects a blind person on his way' (Deut 27:18). Contrast Job's claim: "I was eyes to the blind" (Job 29:15).

but you shall fear your God. wĕyārēʾtā mēʾĕlōhêkā. The *waw* is adverbial, and what follows is not a new command, but a rationale covering the entire verse. Driver (1881: 150–59) claims that when the perfect with a sequential *waw* follows an imperative, it indicates a new command. This is not so; see *wĕḥāyû* 'that they may live' (Num 4:19; cf. 2 Sam 11:15; Schwartz 1987: 281, n. 42).

This phrase reappears in v. 32 and in 25:17, 36, 43, but nowhere else. They all deal with the exploitation of the helpless: elders, and indebted Israelites forced to sell their land from whom usury and enslavement are exacted. The rabbis also apply this verse to those whose "deafness" and "blindness"—that is, weakness—are exploited (*Sipra* Qedoshim 2:14).

As noted by Stewart (1994), "in the ancient Near East, conspicuously absent are laws protecting disabled people. For sure the Code of Hammurabi rewards the successful physician who heals an eye (§§ 215–17) or a broken bone (§§ 221–23). Hammurabi also grants compensation for failed eye operations (§§ 218, 220). Indeed, if a seignior loses an eye, the physician loses his hand. Likewise, the law of talion allows compensation for accidental (or deliberate) eye loss or broken bones at the hand of a seignior (§§ 196–99). Outside of the codes, Mesopotamian medical texts and incantations show a concern for healing eye-disease (Scheil 1918), muteness (*Šurpu* v:1–6, 15–16), lameness (*Šurpu* vii:24), and various ear troubles (Thompson 1931). In Israel, the law has moved beyond compensation for injury (Exod 21:23–25; Lev 24:19–20; Deut 19:21) or prescriptive medicine to nonmonetary, ethical protections for a class."

The expression *yārē min* 'fear of (punishment)' should not be confused with *yārēʾ ʾet* 'revere' (Abravanel; Wessely 1846; Dillmann and Ryssel 1897; Hoffmann 1953; for a comprehensive discussion of the concept "fear / reverence of God," see Fuhs 1990). Indeed, *min* may imply *lipnĕ* 'in the presence of (God)'; that is, your crime, which you think is committed surreptitiously, is known by God (Gruber 1990a: 419). Those who are exploited cannot defend themselves, but God will come to their aid (Ramban, Bekhor Shor); he will hear them when

they cry out (Deut 24:15)—be they Israelites or resident aliens (Exod 22:20–22).
The defense of the poor is an aspect of the divine holiness that Israel must emulate to attain its holiness (see further NOTE on 25:36).

Vv. 15–16. Unit 7: Injustice and Indifference

The God of justice will not tolerate injustice. This is another aspect of YHWH's
attribute of holiness. V. 15 is constructed chiastically (M. Hildenbrand), as follows:

A   *lō'-taʿăśû ʿāwel bammišpāṭ*   A   *You shall not do injustice in judgment;*

B   *lō'-tiśśā' pĕnê-dāl*   B   *You shall not favor the appear-*
                                            ance of the poor;

B'   *wĕlō' tehdar pĕnê gādôl*   B'   *You shall not show deference to*
                                            the appearance of the rich;

A'   *bĕṣedek tišpōṭ ʿămîtekā*   A'   *in righteousness shall you judge your*
                                            fellows.

This ABB'A' construction encloses the *appearance* of the rich and poor in
the court of *justice.* Judges are warned to *judge* the case on its merit without any
regard of the *appearance* of the litigant, whether rich or poor.

15. **You shall not do. *lō'-taʿăśû.*** This is the only plural verb in this unit (vv.
15–16). The Sam. betrays its harmonistic, hence secondary, tendencies by reading the singular. Ibn Ezra opines that it refers to judges and witnesses, as do the
rabbis (*Sipra* Qedoshim 4:1), thereby confining this verse to the judicial process.
Others (e.g., Noth 1977) claim that this first prohibition is addressed to the entire community and refers to personal relations, as the case cited in v. 35, where
this prohibition is repeated and exemplified by prescribing honest business practices, a viewpoint endorsed here (see NOTE on *ʿămîteka* 'your fellow' v. 17).

injustice. ʿāwel. This is the opposite of *ṭôb* 'good' (Pss 37:1, 3; 53:2); *'emet*
'truth' (Mal 2:6), *yôṣer* 'uprightness' (Pss 92:16; 107:42; Prov 29:27), *tāmîm*
'blameless' (Gen 17:1; Ezek 28:15), *'ĕmûnâ* 'faithfulness' (Deut 32:4), *ṣĕdāqâ*
'righteousness' (Ezek 18:24), and *mišpāṭ* 'justice' (Isa 61:8). The *NJPS* confines
this prohibition to judicial procedure, rendering "You shall not render an un-
fair decision," following the rabbis (see above), who exemplify: "so that one (litigant) will be sitting and the other standing; one (allowed to) speak all he wants,
the other who is told (by the judge): 'make it short' " (*B. Šebu.* 30a).

in judgment. bammišpāṭ. This is the opposite of *ʿāwel* 'injustice'—for example, *ʿad mātay tišpĕṭû-ʿāwel* 'How long will you judge unjustly' (Ps 82:2; cf. Ezek
33:15–16; Ps 7:4–9; 2 Chr 19:6–7). This crime "leads to five things: It pollutes
the land, desecrates the sabbath, removes the divine presence, defeats Israel by
the sword, and exiles it from its land" (*Sipra* Qedoshim 4:1). For the rabbis, this
is the *cause célèbre* for the curses of Lev 26:14–38.

You shall not be partial to the poor. lo'-tiśśā' pĕnê dāl. See also Exod 23:3.
"And this comes from one who has filled practically his whole legislation with

injunctions to show pity and kindness . . . bidding us give wealth to the poor, and it is only on the judgment seat that we are forbidden to show them compassion" (Philo, *Laws* 4.72–76). The absence of the *waw* at the beginning of this statement might imply that it exemplifies the previous prohibition (Leibowitz 1983: 266), thereby supporting the view that the latter is also addressed to the judges (but see NOTE on *ʿămîtekā* 'your fellow', v. 17). The expression *nāśāʾ pānîm*, literally "lift the face," is apt for one whose face has "fallen," namely, the *dāl*, the weaker party (cf. Gen 19:21; 32:21; 1 Sam 25:35), but this idiom is also used for the stronger, respected party (Job 32:21; 34:19; Lam 4:16); contrast *hādar pānîm* (below). Deuteronomy uses the neutral expression *hikkîr pānîm*, literally "recognize the face" (Deut 1:17), which applies to all parties, rich and poor alike (Gruber 1983b).

or favor the rich. wĕlōʾ tehdar pĕnê gādôl. Since *hādār* is a synonym for *kābôd* 'honor' (Isa 35:2; Ps 145:12), the expression *hādar pānîm*, literally "honor the face" (found only here, v. 32, and Lam 5:12) is apt for dealing with respected parties. The effect of both statements is that of a merism: do not show favoritism to anyone.

This admonition is found throughout the law codes of the ancient Near East—for example, "He (the *bēl madgalti* 'commander of the border guards') should not decide it (the case) in favor of a superior" (von Schuler 1957: col. 3: 30:31; cf. HL § 172, Ur-Nammu §§ 162–68).

Because of the contrast with *dāl* 'the poor', *gādôl* here must mean "the rich" (*Sipra* Qedoshim 4:3); so too "he (Barzillai) was a very rich [*gādôl*] man" (2 Sam 19:33) and "a rich [*gĕdôlâ*] woman" (2 Kgs 4:8). It can also mean "important," as in "Moses himself was a man of great importance [*gādôl*]" (Exod 11:3; Boleh 1991–92). On the basis of the use of *ʾebyōnĕkā* 'your poor' (Exod 23:6), many scholars emend Exod 23:3 *wĕdāl* (*loʾ tehdar bĕrîbô*) to *wĕgādōl*, yielding "you shall not honor [note the verb!] the rich in his dispute" (Knobel 1995; Childs 1974; cf. *BHS*). If this emendation is accepted, then H (this verse) has fused JE (Exod 23:3, 6) into a rhythmic couplet. However, as suggested by Paran (1989: 131, n. 127), it is possible that H understood that *taṭṭeh*, literally "bend" (the judgment of your poor) in Exod 23:6 implies favoring the rich, in which case Exod 23:3 need not be emended. As to why H changes JE's *ʾebyōn* to *dāl*, it chose *dāl* and *gādôl* for their alliterative effect. Magonet (1983: 158) opines, however, that this is the reason why H uses *gādôl* instead of *ʿāšîr* 'rich', the usual complement of *dāl* (e.g., Exod 30:15; Prov 10:15; 22:16; 28:11).

in righteousness shall you judge your fellow. bĕṣedeq tišpōṭ ʿămîtekā. For *bĕṣedeq*, Tg. Onq. renders *bĕqûštāʾ* 'in truth'. Note that v. 15aα and b complement each other: *lōʾ ʿāwel = ṣedeq* (see also Deut 25:15–16; 32:4; Ezek 3:20; 18:24, 26; 33:15–16, 18; Zeph 3:5; Ps 7:4–9; Prov 29:27, etc.).

A similar instruction is found in Deut 1:16; 16:18, but the difference should not be overlooked. In Deuteronomy, the address is to the judges; here, it is to *ʿămîtekā* 'your fellow'—that is, to everyone—in all one's personal dealings.

16. *You shall not go about as a slanderer. lōʾ-tēlēk rākîl.* This idiom is found again in Jer 6:28; 9:3; Prov 11:13; 20:19. For *hālak* 'go about', see GKC § 118q.

The adjective *rākîl* stems from the noun *rōkēl* 'merchant, peddler' (Ezek 27:15; Song 3:6; Saadiah, Radak, Ramban, Abravanel), perhaps a variant of *rāgal* 'slander, calumniate' (Ps 15:3; Sir 4:28; 5:4). A slandermonger like a peddler transfers gossip and wares from one to another (Rashi). In Mesopotamia, the slanderer is cursed by the gods. He is described as one "who pointed (his) finger (accusingly) [behind the back of] his (fellow-man) [who calumniated], spoke what is not allowed to speak . . . gossip" (*Šurpu* II 7–9). Aramaic *'ākal qirṣā'* (cf. Dan 3:8; *b. Ber.* 58a; *Tg. Onq.*), as Akkadian *karṣî akālu* (*CAD* 8.222–23), means "defame, calumniate" (Lipinski 1990). This meaning is clearly projected in Prov 11:13: *hôlēk rākîl mĕgalleh-sôd wĕne'ĕman-rûaḥ mĕkasseh dābār* 'A slanderer gives away secrets, but a trustworthy person keeps a confidence' (see also Prov 20:19), and is expressly stated in Jer 6:28: *kullām sārê sôrĕrîm hōlĕkê rākîl* 'They all are arch-liars [cf. Akk. *sarru* 'fraudulent' (*CAD* 15:180–82)], slanderers'.

The rabbis interpret this verse similarly: *zû rĕkîlût lĕšôn hāra'* 'This is peddling slander [lit. "the evil tongue"] (*y. Pe'a* 1:1; cf. *Sipra* Qedoshim 4:5; *b. Ket.* 46a). "Of him who slanders, the Holy One, blessed be He, says: He and I cannot live together in the world. . . . Whoever speaks slander increases his sins even up to (the degree of) the three (cardinal) sins: idolatry, incest (including adultery), and the shedding of blood. . . . Slander about third (persons) kills three persons; him who tells (the slander), him who accepts it, and him about whom it is told" (*b. 'Arak.* 15b; cf. *Tg. Ps.-J.*). The Qumran sectaries narrow the range of this expression to denote the informer: *KY YHYH 'YŠ RKYL B'MW WMŠLYM 'T 'MW LGWY NKR* 'If a man informs against his people, and delivers his people up to a foreign nation' (11QT 64:6–7).

Alternatively, *NJPS* renders "deal basely with" on the grounds that "in such passages as Jer 6:28 and Ezek 22:9 the wickedness of the people is surely more grievous than that of talebearing" (Orlinsky 1969: 217). The LXX also projects a similar rendering: "practice deceit." Nonetheless, tale bearing that constitutes slander and calumny leads to severer consequences, as explicated in the second half of the verse. The *Siprar* (Qedoshim 4:6), which records the view that the entire unit (vv. 15–16) deals with judicial procedure, interprets this statement to imply "As one of the judges is leaving, he should not say (to the convicted person) 'I acquitted (you) but my colleagues convicted (you), but what could I do, they outnumbered me'" (cf. Leibowitz 1983: 273). Philo (*Laws* 4.183), following the LXX, writes in a simlar vein: "The law lays upon anyone who has undertaken to superintend and preside over public affairs a very just prohibition when it forbids him to walk with fraud among the people."

among your kin. bĕ'ammêkā. The Sam., Versions, and sixty-six MSS read *bĕ'ammĕkā* 'among your people'. Ehrlich (1899–1900) (H), however, justifies the MT on the grounds that a merchant plies his wares within his clan or tribe. However, Ezekiel's substitution of *bāk* for this idiom (22:9a) indicates that he, at least, felt that this prohibition indicted his entire people (cf. Hurvitz 1982: 68–69). Hoffmann (1953) renders "against your people," regarding the *beth* as signifying hostility, an interpretation confirmed by 1QS 7:8, which replaces *bᵉmyk* with BR'HW '*against* your fellow', thereby confirming this prohibition to members of the Qumran community. Ezekiel, however, uses *hāyû bāk*, which can only be rendered "were *among* you" (22:9a).

you shall not stand aloof beside the blood of your fellow. lō' ta'ǎmōd 'al-dam rē'ekā. Various interpretations have been proposed for this obscure statement. They differ mainly on the rendering of *ta'ǎmōd 'al*:

1. Do not "stand idle" when your fellow is in danger. Thus "if you are in a position to offer testimony on someone's behalf, you are not permitted to remain silent" (*Sipra* Qedoshim 4:8, *Tg. Ps.-J.*; see NOTE on 5:1). "If one sees someone drowning, mauled by beasts or attacked by robbers one is obligated to save him, but not at the risk of one's life" (*b. Sanh.* 73a). In contrast, "contemporary American law is rights-, rather than obligation-, oriented. For example, if you could easily save a child who is drowning, but instead stand by and watch it drown, you have violated no American law. Under biblical law, however, you have committed a serious crime" (Telushkin 1997: 461).

2. Do not "arise against" your fellow to kill him (*Tg. Onq.*; *Lev. Rab.* 24:5; Ibn Ezra; Maimonides on Deut 7:1; Ramban; Hoffmann 1953; cf. Dan 8:25; 11:14; *Tg. Neof.*; *b. Sanh.* 73a).

3. Do not "profit by" the blood of your fellow (Ehrlich, citing *ḥāyâ 'al ḥereb* [Gen 27:40] as equivalent to *'āmad 'al ḥereb* [Ezek 33:26], thereby connoting that *'āmad 'al* means 'live by' [cf. *m. 'Ab.* 1:2]). That *'āmad* can denote "survive," see Exod 21:21 (*NJPS*; Orlinsky 1969: 217).

These interpretations presume that there is no connection between v. 16a and v. 16b. However the absence of the *waw* before *lō'* betokens that the two halves are linked (Bekhor Shor). And as pointed out by Magonet (1983: 157), since the two prohibitions in v. 15aβγ form a complementary pair, the two in v. 16 should do likewise; namely, the first prohibits slander, which may put someone in danger, and the second prohibits standing by when your fellow is in danger. Thus the unit (vv. 15–16) focuses on a common theme (*Tgs. Onq.*; *Ps.-J.*; Ibn Janaḥ, Kalisch 1867–72; Driver and White 1894–98; Elliger 1966; Snaith 1967; cf. Schwartz 1987: 145). This consideration leads to the conclusion that

4. False slander may result in a person's conviction in court, in keeping with the injunction "Keep far from a false charge; do not bring death on the innocent and the righteous" (Exod 23:7a). Hence v. 16aα forbids the act (slander), and v. 16aβ gives the rationale: slander leads to death. This interpretation closely resembles no 1.

your fellow. rē'ekā. This term must refer here to an Israelite, since it parallels *'ammêkā* in the first part of the verse (note the similar conclusion for *rē'ekā* in v. 18).

M. Hildenbrand notes the word play in the standard idiom *tēlēk rākîl*, where the letters *k* and *l* are reversed, which may have influenced the use of *ta'ǎmōd 'al-dam*, where the letters *m* and *d* are reversed. If correct, it would explain the obscurity of the latter expression. The verbs chosen for this verse are also kerygmatic: your very walking (*hālak*) can lead to ruinous gossip (*rākîl*); your mere standing (*'āmad*) can be at the expense of someone's blood (*dām*).

Vv. 17–18. Unit 8: Reproof and Love

17. The section on ethical duties reaches its climax with this final unit. Ramban perceives a chiastic structure: vv. 17a, 18aβ being general commands, and vv. 17b, 18aα, the details. Also the two commands (vv. 17a, 18aβ) are exact opposites: *lōʾ tiśnāʾ* and *wěʾāhabtā* 'Do not hate . . . but love'. A more precise analysis finds that the two verses of the unit form parallel panels (Schwartz 1987: 145; cf. Saadiah, Bekhor Shor):

	17	18
Prohibition	*lōʾ tiśnāʾ ʾet- ʾăhîkā bilbābekā*	*lōʾ-tiqqōm wělōʾ-tiṭṭōr ʾet-běnê ʿammekā*
Remedy	*hôkēaḥ tôkîaḥ ʾet-ʿămîtekā*	*wěʾāhabtā lěrēʿăkā kāmôkā*
Rationale	*wělōʾ-tiśśāʾ ʿālāyw hēṭʾ*	*ʾănî YHWH*

	17	18
Prohibition	You shall not hate your kinsperson in your heart	You shall not take revenge or bear a grudge against members of your people
Remedy	Reprove your fellow openly	You shall love your fellow as yourself
Rationale	so that you will not bear punishment because of him	I YHWH (have spoken)

This unit focuses on one's thought, the perils of which were sensitively apprehended by the rabbis, who declare that *śinʾat ḥinnām* 'causeless hatred' was responsible for the destruction of the Second Temple (*b. Yoma* 9b).

hate . . . in your heart. tiśnāʾ bilbābekā. As pointed out by Kugel (1997:351–52), wisdom tradition interprets this clause to mean that the outlawed hatred "in the heart" is covered under a veil of lying hypocrisy (cf. Prov 10:18; 26:24–25).

A comparable prohibition illumines the sentence differently: *wěʾîs ʾet-rāʿat rēʿehû ʾal taḥšěbû bilbabkem*, literally "And do not contrive evil each man against his fellow" (Zech 8:17a; cf. Matt 18:15–17), which demonstrates the equivalence of *ḥāšab raʿ* 'contrive evil' and *śānēʾ* 'hate'. Thus hate is not just an emotion, but implies a mental activity, namely, plotting countermeasures. Perhaps that is why "in your heart" has to be added, which also emphasizes its cerebral component.

This warning is aptly illustrated by the case of Absalom, who hated his half brother Amnon for raping Tamar, Absalom's sister and Amnon's half sister. His hatred was so deep that "Absalom didn't utter a word to Amnon good or bad" (2 Sam 13:22). Two years later, Absalom's repressed but mounting anger caused him to have Amnon murdered (vv. 28–29).

Maimonides (*The Book of the Commandments*, Prohibitive, no. 302) adds, "But if he reveals to him his hatred and the other thus knows that he is his enemy, he doesn't transgress this prohibition but 'Do not take revenge or nurse a grudge' (v. 18aα), and he also transgresses the performative commandment 'You shall love your fellow as yourself' (v. 18aβ). However, the heart's hatred is the greater sin."

Qumran paraphrases this prohibition by WŚN' 'YŠ 'T R'HW 'and each man hating his fellow' (CD 8:6), since it follows the statement WNQWM WNYṬWR 'YŠ L'ḤYHW, literally "and taking revenge and bearing a grudge each man against his brother" (CD 8:5–6), which obviously is a paraphrase of the following verse in the MT (v. 18a)—again limiting the application of this injunction to members of the sect (not *běnê 'ammekā* 'members of your people' [MT], but 'YŠ L'ḤYHW 'one man against his brother', or fellow members of the sect).

brother (Israelite). *'āḥîkā*. Note that in the section on ethical duties (vv. 11–18), *rea'* appears three times (vv. 13, 16, 18) and *'ămît* three times (vv. 11, 15, 17), but *'āḥ* only here. It is doubtful if it is limited to members of one's kin group or clan (as argued by Cross [1998: 4]). Its probable intent is to include all Israelites, particularly those belonging to other clans. If *'ahika* were limited to 'your kinsman' this would imply that Israelites from other clans would be the responsibility of *their* kinsmen. Thus v. 17 would also imply that one is free to hate any Israelite who is not ones own kinsman. This is certainly not the intention of 19:17. Nor is it the intention of *'āḥîkā* in 15:25. The broader meaning of *'āḥîkā* is also found in 25:25–55. It is a reminder that the one whom you might hate (and the impoverished one who turns to you, chap. 25) is "your brother." See further the NOTE on 25:25.

Reprove your fellow openly. hôkēaḥ tôkîaḥ 'et-'ămîtekā. This is the answer to the prohibition against harboring hatred.

The verb *ykḥ* (Hip'îl) is generally found in a forensic sense, in judicial procedure, where it has the sense of "set right." It is also found in a nonlegal, pedagogic sense as "reprove," which characterizes its use in this verse (details in Gruber 1990b). But since this strophe (vv. 15–16) deals with dispensing justice, this verse may be focusing on the court behavior of witnesses (complementing the address to judges in v. 15), namely, that slander can lead to false convictions, even death (Crüsemann 1996: 323–24).

From the language of a lawsuit, *hôkîaḥ* develops the extensive meaning of "reprove, reproach"—for example, *wĕtôkîḥû 'ālay ḥerpātî* 'then reprove me with my disgrace' (Job 19:5). More to the point is the advice of wisdom: *'al-tôkaḥ lēṣ pen-yiśnā'ekā hôkaḥ lĕḥākām wĕye'ĕhābekā* 'Do not reprove a scoffer, for he will *hate* you; reprove a wise man, and he will *love* you' (Prov 9:8; cf. 19:25b; 28:23; cf. *b. Yeb.* 65b), and especially *ṭôbâ tôkaḥat mĕgullâ mē'ahăbâ mĕsuttāret* 'Open reproof is better than concealed love' (Prov 27:5). "Whoever heeds discipline [*mûsār*] is on the path to life, but one who ignores a rebuke [*tôkaḥat*] goes astray" (Prov 10:17). The nouns *mûsār* and *tôkaḥat* are synonymous, as shown by their frequent occurrence in tandem throughout Proverbs (3:11; 5:12; 6:23; 10:17; 12:1; 13:18; 15:5, 10, 32), where they mainly "represent verbal censure or oral reproof" (Branson 1990: 129).

That Prov 10:17 may be a reflex of Lev 19:17 is indicated by the verse that follows: "He who conceals hatred [*mĕkasseh śin'â*] has lying lips, while he who utters slander [*môṣî' dibbâ*] is a fool" (Prov 10:18). These two verses present vv. 16 and 17 of our chapter in reverse order, in keeping with Seidel's (1978) law that quotations of earlier statements are cited chiastically. If the association of these two passages is correct, it offers further evidence that *tēlēk rākîl* (19:16) is equivalent to *môṣî' dibbâ* 'utter slander'.

The infinitive absolute *hôkēaḥ* before the verb *tôkîaḥ* is used to lay emphasis on an antithesis (GKC § 113p). The opposite of hating in the heart is reproving in the open (i.e., to his face), a point that is indeed underscored in Prov 27:5. In other words, *tôkaḥat mĕgullâ* 'open reproof' (Prov 27:5) is equivalent to *hôkēaḥ tôkîaḥ*. One detects in this phrase a natural resistance or reluctance to bring one's grievances out in the open, especially, to the offending party directly. To overcome this psychological barrier, the offended party must be urged, a nuance betrayed by the addition of the infinitive absolute (S. Greenberg). Hence, I have rendered (with Hartley 1992) the infinitive absolute as "openly." Note also that open reproof not only dispels hate, but engenders love (Prov 9:8). Thus it throws light on the meaning of "love your fellow" (v. 18). The latter injunction is neither wishful nor impractical. One of the ways to love your fellow, according to this unit (vv. 17–18), is to reprove him openly for his mistakes. And, conversely, the only admissable rebuke is that which is evoked by love, not by animosity, jealousy, or lust for power (M. Aron, personal communication).

Abraham is the role model for exemplifying the virtue of reproof; *wĕhôkīaḥ 'abrāhām 'et- 'ăbîmelek* 'Then Abraham reproached Abimelech (about the well of water which the servants of Abimelech had seized)" (Gen 21:25). The importance of having leaders in every community and every age who will "openly rebuke" is stressed by the rabbis: "R. Tarfon said: 'By the Temple service, if there is anyone in this generation capable of reproving.' R. Eliezer b. Azariah said: 'By the Temple service, if there is anyone in this generation who is capable of receiving reproof.' R. Akiba said: 'By the Temple service, if there is anyone in this generation who knows how to reprove' " (*Sipra* Qedoshim 4:9).

The sectaries of Qumran make reproof a cardinal requirement for its members *LHWKYḤ 'YŠ 'T 'ḤYHW KMṢWH WL' LNṬWR MYWM LYWM* 'to reprove each man his brother according to the commandment [i.e., Lev 19:17] and "not to bear a grudge" (v. 18a) from one day to the next'. However, the one giving reproof (for a capital offense) must also report it to the overseer (*MBQR*), who dutifully records it (CD 9:17–19; cf. 9:2–8, discussed below). Need it be said that this was hardly the intention of the priestly legist, who contemplated that the reprover would share his complaint with no one else.

For a comprehensive review of reflexes of this verse in intertestamental and rabbinic literaure, see Kugel (1987).

so that you will not bear punishment because of him. wĕlō'- tiśśā' 'ālāyw ḥēṭ'. For this idiom, see *Tg. Onq.* (also *Tgs. Ps.-J., Neof.*), 22:9, and Num 18:32. The *waw* is purposive, and *'ālāyw* means "because of him," *bĕ'iṭyô* (*Tg. Onq.*). It should not be overlooked that the expression *nāśā' 'et / lĕ 'āwōn / ḥēṭ'* outside of the priestly texts generally connotes "forgive" (Gen 18:24; 50:17; Exod 23:21; 32:32; Num 14:18, 19; Josh 24:19; 1 Sam 25:28, etc.; cf. BDB *nāśā'*, 2b, 3c). This meaning cannot be found in the priestly texts, where it always denotes "bears sin / punishment" (see NOTE on 17:16), a meaning found elsewhere only in Ezekiel (4:4, 5, 6; 14:10; 18:19; 44:10, 12), whose dependence on P, and especially on H, can be fully demonstrated (see chap. 20, COMMENTS B, C, and D), and once in Second Isaiah (53:12), whose wide-ranging familiarity with priestly idioms has been demonstrated by Paran (1989: 330–39).

Two rationales have been suggested by this rendering: if you do not reprove him, you will bear his punishment. Support is mustered from Ezekiel's admonition *wĕlōʾ dibbartā lĕhazhîr rāšāʿ middarkô hārĕšāʿâ lĕhayyōtô hûʾ rāšāʿ baʿăwōnô yāmût wĕdāmô miyyādĕkā ʾăbaqqēš* ʿ(If) you do not speak to warn the wicked man of his wicked course in order to save his life—he, the wicked man, shall die for his iniquity, but I will require a reckoning for his blood from you' (Ezek 3:18; cf. v. 19; 33:8; Bekhor Shor). However, Ezekiel's words are addressed to "the watchman" (v. 17; 33:7). Even so, Qumran held every member of the sect responsible to fulfill this injunction (CD 9:6–8; see below). Alternatively, the rationale is that you yourself are likely to take action against him, which may prove sinful (Schwartz 1987: 147).

Douglas (1966: 105) reports that among the Lele, "better than harboring a secret grudge, anyone with a just grievance should speak up and demand redress lest the saliva of his ill-will do harm secretly" (cursing consists of uttering words and spitting: unspit saliva withheld in the mouth has the power to do harm).

Two more literal readings of this clause have also been proposed: "And do not carry (his) sin against him" (*Keter Torah*; Mendelssohn 1846); that is, do not carry a grudge against him (cf. v. 18a); and "and you should not put upon him (his sin)"; that is, do not embarrass him in public (*Sipra* Qedoshim 4:8; *Tg. Ps.-J.*; *b. ʿArak.* 16b).

Another rendering is implied by Sir 8:17a: "Reproach is a friend **before getting angry**." That is, by not reproaching your friend, your anger may lead you to harm him and **because of it incur sin.** In this rendering, *ʿālāyw* refers to the implied anger.

At Qumran, reproof was not only a moral duty, but a prerequisite for all offenses:

WKL ʾYŠ MBYʾW HBRYT ʾŠR YBYʾ ʿL RʿHW DBR ʾŠR Lʾ BHWKḤ LPNY ʿDYM . . . ʾM HḤRYŠ LW MYWM LYWM WBḤRWN ʾPW BW DBR BW BDBR MWT ʿNH BW YʿN ʾŠR Lʾ HQYM ʾT MṢWT ʾL ʾŠR ʾMR LW HWKḤ TWKYḤ ʾT RʿYK WLʾ TŚʾ ʿLYW ḤṬʾ

Any man from among those who have entered the covenant who shall bring a charge against his fellow that is not without reproof before witnesses . . . if he kept silent about him from day to day, and accused him of a capital offense (only) when he was angry with him, his (the accused's) punishment is upon him (the accuser), since he did not fulfill the commandment of God who said to him "Reprove your fellow openly so that you will not bear punishment because of him (Lev 19:17)." (CD 9:2–8)

The translation is mainly that of Schiffman (1983: 89; cf. 99–102, nn. 4–32). The sect apparently interprets the infinitive absolute *hōkēaḥ* not as emphasis but to mean "before witnesses" (as does the Vg: *Sed publice argue eum*). It, further, in keeping with Num 30:15, whose wording it borrows, ordains that the rebuke must be delivered the same day—that is, by sunset (1QS 5:24–6:1; Eph 4:26; Heb 3:13; *m. Ned.* 10:8; *Sipre Zuṭa* 30:17; but see Milgrom 1990a: 354). Moreover, Qumran clearly follows the first interpretation, cited above, that if the accuser allows the deadline for reproof to pass, he is to be punished. In other words, it does not leave the punishment for lack or delay of reproof in the hands of God, but incorporates it into its judicial system (for the nature of the punishment, see NOTE on "bear a grudge," v. 18). This passage also implies that for a first offense, the offender is only reproved, but he is tried if he repeats his offense (Schiffman [1983: 92] notes the parallel rule in Matt 18:15–17). The manner of the reproof is also specified by Qumran:

LHWKYḤ 'YŠ 'T R'HW B'[MT] W'NWH W'HBT ḤSD L'YŠ 'L YDBR 'LYHW B'P 'W BTLWNH 'W B'WRP [QŠH 'W BQN'T] RWḤ RŠ' W'L YŚN'HW [B'R]L[T] LBBW KY' BYWM YWKYḤNW WL'YŚ' 'LYW 'WWN

To reprove each his fellow in truth, humility, and lovingkindness to a man: Let him not speak to him in anger or complaint or stub[bornly or in passion] (caused) by an evil disposition. Let him not hate him intrac[tab]ly, for on that very day shall he reprove him so that he will not bear punishment because of him. (1QS 5:25–6:1)

Again, the rendering is mainly Schiffman's (1983: 93), and the restorations are those of Licht (1965: 136). This passage emphasizes, in the language of Mic 6:8, that the reproof must be offered in the spirit of love and kindness (cf. *T. Gad* 6:3–7; Gal 6:1; 2 Thess 3:15). The passage continues with a clarification concerning the requirement of witnesses:

WGM 'L YBY' 'YŠ 'L R'HU DBR LPNY HRBYM 'ŠR LW' BTWKḤT LPNY 'DYM

And also, let no one bring a charge against his fellow before the assembly which is not with reproof before witnesses. (1QS 6:1)

Thus judicial procedure at Qumran required that charges could not be brought before the court, which constituted the full assembly of the sect, unless witnesses (other than those who saw the offense) would testify that they had reproved the offender for a similar offense. In many ways, Qumran's reproof resembles and anticipates rabbinic *hatrā'â* 'warning', which provided that no one might be convicted of an offense without first having been warned. A major difference between the two, as pointed out by Schiffman (1983: 97), is that for the sect reproof *followed* a first offense, whereas for the rabbis reproof was essential for even a first offense.

18. *you shall not take revenge or nurse a grudge. lō'-tiqqōm wĕlō'-tiṭṭōr.* This prohibition may be connected with the previous verse since both (vv. 17–18) form a

unit. Both vengeance and grudge-nursing are products of hate, the former in deed and the latter in thought (cf. Rashi, Rashbam, Ḥazzequni), connecting with v. 17a. Neither vengeance nor grudge-nursing is permitted even if the reproof proves ineffectual, and the harm done has not been effaced (Ginzburg 1966), connecting with v. 17b. The rabbis distinguish between the two concepts:

> "You shall not take vengeance." What is the extent of vengeance? One says to another: Lend me your sickle, and the other refuses. On the morrow, the latter says: Lend me your axe and the former replies, I shall not lend (it) to you since you did not lend me your sickle. Hence it is written "You shall not take vengeance."

> "You shall not nurse a grudge." What is the extent of nursing a grudge? One says to the other: Lend me your sickle and the former replies, Here, take it, I am not like you who didn't lend me your axe. Such behavior is condemned by "You shall not bear a grudge." (*Sipra* Qedoshim 4:10–11; cf. *b. Yoma* 23a)

This finely honed example, I submit, does not convey the intensity of the anger and rage embedded in the term *nāṭar*, which has to match that of *nāqam* 'avenge, take revenge'. In poetry, *nāṭar* is paralleled by *šāmar* 'guard (one's anger)' (Jer 3:5; cf. v. 12b; Ps 103:9). It should not be overlooked that the Akkadian cognates *nadāru* and *šamāru*, respectively, are synonyms, meaning "be angry, rage." Thus when it is said of Jacob *wĕ'ābîw šāmar 'et-haddābār*, it implies that when told by Joseph that he was destined to bow down to him, "he (Jacob) became enraged at the matter" (Gen 37:11; translated *nāṭar* by Tg. Onq.). Similarly, the usual rendering for *nāṭar* 'bear a grudge' is appallingly weak when it follows *nāqam* 'avenge': it implies a reaction of equal intensity. Thus *nōqēm YHWH lĕṣārāyw wĕnôṭēr hû' lĕ'oyĕbāyw* 'the Lord takes vengeance on his enemies; he rages against his foes' (Nah 1:2, with *NJPS*). By the same token, *nāṭar* in our verse, which also follows *nāqam*, implies "seethe in anger," which I have tried to capture by rendering "nurse a grudge."

Westbrook (1988: 97), following Driver (1931b: 362–63), also takes *nāṭar* as the cognate of Akkadian *nadāru* 'be angry, rage', not suppressing the anger (i.e., "nursing a grudge"), but releasing it in the form of "savage slaughter performed by wild beasts, animals and robbers" (*CAD* 11:1.59–60), which leads Westbrook to render *lō'-tiṭṭōr* as "do not slaughter (the sons of your people)." This interpretation is incongruous with the sensitively nuanced ethical prescriptions that dominate chap. 19. Furthermore, it is difficult to conceive that the priestly legist would say that one of the rungs on the ladder of holiness is refraining from embarking on a murderous rampage.

The root *nqm* implies extralegal retribution, which, although forbidden to men, may be exacted by God. Indeed, "the sign of a saintly, noble person [is] that he commits his *nqm* to God (David, 1 Sam 24:12; Jeremiah, Jer 15:15; etc.). For YHWH is properly God of *nqm* (e.g., Nah 1:2; Ps 94:1); to him belongs the ultimate redressing of all wrongs, and by whatever means he wills" (Greenberg

1983b: 13), unless he explicitly assigns the task to humans (Num 31:2, 3; cf. Josh 10:13; 1 Sam 14:24; 18:25). There are only four more attestations of *nāṭar* 'bear a grudge' (rather than "watch, preserve"), and unanimously the subject is God (Jer 3:5, 12; Nah 1:2; Ps 103:9).

Qumran's exegesis of this prohibition is contained within its statement on reproof, cited above:

*W'ŠR 'MR L' TQWM WL' TṬWR 'T BNY 'MK . . . WHBY'W BḤRWN
'PW 'W SPR LZQNYW LHBZWTW NWQM HW' WNWṬR W'YN KTWB
KY 'M NWQM HW' LṢRYW WNWṬR HW' L'WYBYW*

As to that which he (God) said "You shall not take vengeance or nurse a grudge against members of your people" (Lev 19:18a) (any man who . . .) brings it (the charge) when he is angry (with him) or relates it to his (the accused's) elders to make them despise him, is taking vengeance and nursing a grudge. Is it not written that only "he (God) takes vengeance on his adversaries and rages [see above] against his enemies" (Nah 1:2)? (CD 9:2–8)

Qumran clearly associates this prohibition with the previous verse, namely, that if a member of the sect spots an offense and does not offer reproof that same day (see above) but, instead, offers it in anger (cf. 1QS 5:25–6:1, cited above) or accuses him before the offender's elders, he is guilty of violating the prohibition against taking vengeance and nursing a grudge. This injunction is stated explicitly and succinctly in another passage *LHWKYḤ 'YŠ 'T 'ḤYHW KMṢWH WL' LNṬWR MYWM LYWM* 'To admonish each his fellow according to the commandment and not to nurse a grudge from one day to the next' (CD 7:2–3).

That the sect regards this prohibition not just as an admonition punishable only by God (cf. Sir 28:1), but as a rule subject to judicial examination and punishment, is shown by the fact that its violation is accompanied by a penalty:

*W'ŠR YṬWR LR'HW 'ŠR LW' BMŠPṬ WN'NŠ ŠŠH ḤWDŠYM ŠNH 'HT
WKN LNWQM LNPŠW KWL DBR*

And whoever nurses a grudge against his fellow who is not being judged [cf. Schiffman 1983: 108–9, n. 87] shall be fined for six months [one year; cf. Schiffman 1983: n. 89]. And so also for him who takes vengeance for himself (regarding) any matter. (CD 7:8–9)

Thus it seems clear that Qumran interpreted the injunction *lō'-tiṭṭōr* as connected with the requirement of reproof in v. 17. That is, if a person neglects or refuses to offer reproof, he is guilty of nursing a grudge. There is, however, no comparable statement that would explain Qumran's exegesis of *lō'-tiqqōm* 'You shall not take vengeance'. Perhaps it is contained in a section that has not been preserved.

In any event, it is manifest that Qumran enforced Lev 19:18a. Schiffman (1983: 98) is fully justified in concluding that "widespread references [to this verse] in the scrolls show that this was a cornerstone of the sect's legal system."

against members of your people. ʾet-bĕnê ʿammekā. Nah 1:2 uses the preposition *le* instead of the direct accusative. The term ʿammekā (cf. 20:17) should not be rendered "kin, clan" (contra Lipinski 1986). To be sure, H frequently uses *ʿam* 'people' where it intends ʿammim 'kin' (e.g., 17:9, 10), but it strains belief to posit that H forbids vengeance against only one's kin and, by its silence, permits it against one's tribe and nation.

(*Rather*) *You shall love.* wĕʾāhabtā. The juxtaposition of the two halves of this verse prompts R. Hillel to declare, "That which is hateful to you, do not do to your fellow" (*b. Šabb.* 31a), as the central tenet of the Bible (and Judaism). Bekhor Shor asks, however: How does God expect one who has been wronged to the point of wanting to take revenge to love one's fellow? Bekhor Shor finds the answer in the final, overlooked clause of this verse: " 'I YHWH'. Let your love for me overcome your hatred for him . . . and keep you from taking revenge, and as a result peace will come between you."

How can love be commanded? The answer simply is that the verb ʾāhab signifies not only an emotion or attitude, but also deeds. This is especially true in Deuteronomy, which speaks of convenantal love. The gēr is "loved" by providing him with food and shelter (Deut 10:18–19). God is "loved" by observing his commandments (Deut 11:1; cf. 5:10; 7:5–6, 9), and God, in turn, "loves" Israel by subduing its enemies (Deut 7:8; cf. Weinfeld 1972d: 8–13).

"Covenantal love," as Moran (1963) has demonstrated, is found and, perhaps, originates in suzerainty treaties. To select one example out of many, the closest to Lev 19:18b is "You will love Ashurbanipal . . . as yourselves" (*ki-i nap-šat-ku-nu la tar-ʾa-ma-ni*)" (*VTE* col. 4: 266–68 [Wiseman 1958: 49]). Thus ʾāhab also carries the meaning of "reach out, befriend"—a love that can be commanded (see also Levenson 1985: 75–80; Anderson 1991: 9–12). Indeed, as pointed out by Crüsemann (1996: 324), the very context of this strophe (vv. 17–18) implies that love must be translated into deeds.

The medieval exegetes come to the same conclusion by noting that ʾāhab takes the preposition *le* (also in v. 34), which they render as "for, on behalf of, for the sake of" (Ibn Ezra[2], Ramban, Bekhor Shor); that is, do good as you would do for yourself. To be sure, *lamed* frequently is the sign of a direct object, as *hārĕgû lĕʾabnēr* '(they) slew Abner' (2 Sam 3:30; Ibn Ezra; cf. 2 Chr 19:2; GKC § 117B; Joüon 1923: 125k), as prevalent in Aramaic (e.g., Ezra 5:9). Furthermore, the antonym of "love," namely, "hate," also can take the *lamed* (cf. śōnē lô, Deut 4:42; Ḥazzequni). Nonetheless, where the expression ʾāhab lĕ is applied to the alien (vv. 33–34), it means to do him good, treat him kindly (*Qarne ʾOr*, citing R. Leib Shapira). Malamat (1990) makes the interesting point that all four attestations of ʾāhab le imply doing, not feeling (see 19:18, 34; *kî ʾōhēb hāyâ ḥîrām lĕdāwid kol-hayyāmîm* 'For Hiram had always been an ally of David', 1 Kgs 5:15; 2 Chr 19:2, where ʾāhab is paralleled with ʿāzar 'help').

That ʾāhab implies deeds was caught by both Hillel and Jesus: Hillel, negatively, "What is hateful to you do *not do* to others" (*b. Šab.* 31a; *y. Ned.* 9; cf. Sir 28:4), and Jesus, positively, "Do unto others as you *would do* unto yourselves (Matt 7:2; Luke 6:13; Rom 13:8–10). Qumran, as well, insists that love must be translated into deeds: *L'HWB 'YŠ'T 'ḤYHW KMWHW WLHḤZYQ BYD 'NY W'BYWN WGR* 'To love each his brother as himself by supporting the poor, the destitute, and the convert' (CD 6:20–21; by the end of Second Temple times, the term *gēr*, in a legal context, meant "convert," as in the LXX). The change from *rēʿăkā* 'fellow' to *'ḤYHW* 'his brother' limits the scope of this injunction to members of the sect.

Recently Szubin (forthcoming B) has demonstrated that *'āhab* and its cognates *rêmu* (Akk.) and *rĕḥēm* (Aram.)—as well as its antonym in *śānā'*—carry precise legal meanings, namely, of preference and promotion to an exclusive status of primacy. Thus when the Bible portrays Jacob "loving" Rachel and "hating" Leah (Gen 29:30–33), the reference is to the legal status of the two wives rather than Jacob's emotions toward them. Although this legal connotation has no direct application to *'āhab* and *śānā'* in vv. 17–18, it indicates the broad semantic range covered by these verbs: emotion, obligation, change of status. Indeed, the term *śānā* in the Elephantine documents denotes the formal act of divorce (see also Deut 24:3; Judg 15:2; Isa 60:15; Mal 2:14–16; Yaron 1961: 101–2; Fitzmeyer 1971: 162). That is, just as " 'love' towards one's lord or spouse requires some form of contractual obligation, 'hate' involves a formal renunciation of such responsibility (Anderson 1991: 11).

Schwartz (1987: 147) claims that "love" in our verse is not a command, but a consequence. That is, the prefixed *waw* is purposive: by obeying the prohibitions of vv. 17–18a, you will come to love your neighbor. However, it strains credulity to posit that the H legist actually believed that kindly reproof suffices to generate love. Nonetheless, this precisely is the interpretation cited in one rabbinic passage: "If someone is chopping and in doing so cuts one hand, does he avenge himself on the other hand which held the knife by cutting that hand too? Since all Israelites form one single body, anyone who takes vengeance on his fellow punishes himself. Therefore the answer to any injustice one has suffered is not revenge, but love: 'and you shall love your fellow as yourself' " (*y. Ned.* 9:4). Maimonides (*Laws of Homicide* 13:14) excludes the evildoer as an eligible recipient of love on the basis of *yir'at YHWH śĕnō't rā'* 'To fear YHWH is to hate evil' (Prov 8:13; cf. *b. Pesaḥ.* 113b). This verse, however, speaks of evil, not the evildoer.

your fellow. rēʿăkā. Some commentators take this term to embrace everyone, including non-Israelites, a meaning that it clearly possesses in Exod 11:2 (Ḥazzequni; Hoffmann 1953; cf. *Jub* 20:2). There is also no doubt whatsoever that Jesus and the rabbis gave this injunction a universal context (Luke 10:25–37; details in Kaufmann 1953: 2.1945: 573–74, n. 7). However, the fact that love for the resident non-Israelite, the *gēr*, is reserved for v. 34 implies that *rēaʿ* here means "fellow Israelite" (*Sipra* Qedoshim 8:4; Mishnah R. Eliezer 16; cf. Derrett 1971; Kellermann 1990, who point to the object paralleled in this verse *bĕnê ʿammekā* 'members of your *people*'; for other rabbinic interpretations, see Neudecker 1990: 499–503). The term *rēaʿ* can also mean "ally" (1 Sam 30:26), "friend of the king" (1 Kgs 4:5), or "neighbor" (Prov 25:17), but in each of these cases it refers to an Israelite (so, too, "friend," 4 Macc 2:13).

Kugel (1997: 457) holds that Jesus' condemnation of the Pharisees in his Sermon on the Mount "You have heard that it was said, 'You shall love your neighbor and **hate your enemy'** " (Matt 5:43) is an interpretation of Lev 19:18. Although the meaning *reʿa* 'friend' is attested, it is nonexistent in early rabbinic sources.

As noted by Wenham (1979) and Magonet (1983), the four units that compose the section on ethical duties exhibit a buildup of near synonymous terms to designate the Israelite:

vv. 11–12	*baʿămîtô*		
vv. 13–14			*rēʿăkā*
vv. 15–16	*ʿămîtekā*	*bĕʿammêkā*	*rēʿekā*
vv. 17–18	*ʿămîtekā*	*bĕnê ʿammekā*	*lĕrēʿăkā ʾāḥîkā*

as yourself. kāmôkā. A number of renderings of this word have been proposed, each of which changes the meaning of the injunction:

1. Muraoka (1985) suggests that it is adjectival, modifying the noun, and is equivalent to *ʾăšer hûʾ ʾîš kāmôkā* 'who is a person like you' (Deut 5:14; 18:15). He was anticipated by Wessely (1846), who adds "who is like you," since he too was created by God. Ehrlich (1908) nuances it differently: "who is the like of you"—that is, an Israelite, in contrast to the alien (v. 34; see also Derrett 1971).

2. Most commentators (including myself) understand *kāmôkā* as adverbial, modifying the verb: "Love (the good) *for* your fellow as you (love the good for) yourself," shortened to "Love your fellow as yourself." This interpolation is earliest attested in *Jub* 30:24: "And among yourselves, my sons, be loving of your brothers as a man **loves himself**, with each man **seeking for his brother what is good for him**, and acting together on the earth, and loving each other as themselves." Ehrlich (1908) objects: the adverb would then be *kĕnapšĕkā* (1 Sam 18:3; 20:17; cf. *VTE* 4:266–68). In rebuttal, however, *wĕʾāhabtā lô kāmôkā* 'you shall love him (the alien) like yourself' (v. 34) demonstrates that in a similar context, *kāmôkā* modifies the verb, not *lô*, and must be adverbial.

3. Ullendorf proposes the *kāmôkā* is a brachylogy of "for he is yourself," but Mathys (1986: 9, cited in Hartley 1992: 305) points out that *kāmôkā* does not function as a clause.

4. Kugel (1997: 456) cites two examples illustrating that a reflexive sense is intended:

> The way of life is this: First, you should love the Lord your maker, and secondly, your neighbor as yourself. And whatever you do not want **to be done to you**, you should not do to anyone else. (*Didoche* 31:1–2)

> And love your neighbor; for what is hateful to you yourself, do not do to him, I am the Lord. (*Tg-Ps. J.* on Lev 19:18)

Both interpretations are based on older versions, the most celebrated is R. Hillel's reply to the challenge of a potential convert to teach him the entire Torah while standing on one foot: *dĕʿălāk sānēʾ lĕḥăbĕrāk loʾ taʿăbēd* 'What is hateful to you do not do to your fellow' (b. Šabb. 31a; ARN ʿ 15, 61). Note that this version is cited as early as Tob 4:15: "What you yourself hate, do not do to anyone."

A most illuminating exposition of this injunction is recorded in the names of R. Akiba and Ben Azzai: "R. Akiba says: This is (the most) basic . . . law in the Torah. Ben Azzai says: (Rather) 'When God created man, he made him in the likeness of God' (Gen 5:1), so that you should not say: 'Since I despise myself, let my fellow be despised with me; since I am cursed, let my fellow be cursed with me.' This is a more basic law" (Sipra Qedoshim 4:12; cf. y. Ned. 9:4; Gen. Rab. 24:7). Ben Azzai, in my opinion, decisively tops R. Akiba (and Jub 20:2; 36:34; Philo, Laws 2.63; Matt 22:37–40; Mark 12:20–31; Luke 20:27–28). If you do not love yourself, asks Ben Azzai, how can you be expected to love someone else? Having penetrated beyond the outer rational capabilities of the human being to his possibly disturbed psychic condition, he proposes his therapy: first, make such a (and every) person aware of the fact that he is of ultimate worth because he bears the likeness of God, that regardless of his condition he has the divinely endowed potential to achieve joy and fulfillment in life, and only then, after having learned to love himself, will he be capable of loving others.

Israel Baʿal Shem Tov, the eighteenth-century founder of Hasidism, would have taken issue with Ben Azzai. His sanguine view of human nature led him to rephrase the golden rule as follows: "Just as we love ourselves despite the faults we know we have, so should we love our fellows despite the faults we see in them" (cited in Telushkin 1997: 466). This injunction (v. 18b) falls in the middle of chap. 19, containing thirty-seven verses. It is "the culminating point" of H as well as the apex of Leviticus (see Introduction II H), the central book of the Torah (Radday 1981: 89). Within its own pericope (vv. 11–17), it serves as the climax in the series of ethical sins: deceit in business (vv. 11–12), oppression of the weak (vv. 13–14), evil judgment, and hatred leading to planning and executing revenge. The remedy: doing good (love). The result: a giant step toward achieving holiness.

Vv. 19–29. Miscellaneous Duties

According to Magonet (1983) these verses occupy the center of the giant introversion that describes this chapter (see INTRODUCTION). They deal with man's relationship with his possessions: animals, crops, clothing (v. 19), slaves (vv. 20–22), land (vv. 23–25), body (vv. 26–28), and daughter (v. 29).

V. 19. Unit 9: Mixtures

You shall heed my statutes. ʾet- ḥuqqōtay tišmōrû. The noun ḥuqqâ stems from the root ḥqq 'fix / determine by carving out / writing'. As examples, see "carve" (Isa 22:16; 49:16; Ezek 4:1; 23:14), "fix limits" (Isa 5:14; Jer 5:22; Prov 8:27, 29), "fix allotments" (Gen 47:22; Ezek 16:27; Prov 30:8; 31:15; Job 23:14), and "fix a law" by inscribing it (Isa 10:1; 30:8; Pss 2:7; 94:20). In the priestly texts (P and H), the noun *ḥōq* means "allotment, portion," whereas the feminine *ḥuqqâ* means "law, decree" (see NOTE on 10:13). Schwartz (1987: 286, n. 3) holds (with others) that there is no substantive difference between *ḥuqqâ* and *mišpāṭ* (citing 18:3–5; Num 9:14; Ps 81:5). However, *mišpāṭ* in H, which stands mainly for the jurisprudence emanating from the human court, tends to deal with performative injunctions, whereas *ḥuqqâ*, being a divine decree, focuses more on prohibitions (see NOTE on 18:4 and the use of *'āśâ* 'do' with *mišpāṭ* and *šāmar* 'heed, guard' with *ḥuqqâ*).

As Schwartz (1987: 286–87) points out (contra Heinisch 1935; Gerstenberger 1996: 273), v. 19a is the introduction not to the rest of the chapter, but to only the rest of this verse, which deals with the mixture of substances differentiated by nature: animals and plants. Hence the term *ḥuqqôt* represents the laws of creation (Jer 31:35; 33:25; Job 28:26; 38:33; cf. Ramban, Bekhor Shor): "Because of the laws [*ḥuqqîm*] that I have established [*ḥāqaqtî*] in my universe, henceforth they are forbidden to the first man" (*y. Kil.* 1:7).

H's prohibition against mixtures needs to be compared with the equivalent prohibition in D:

Lev 19:19b	Deut 22:9–11
bĕhemtĕkā lō'-tarbîa' kil'ayim	*lō'-tizra' karmĕkā kil'āyim [pen-tiqdaš hamĕlē'â hazzera' 'ăšer tizrā' ûtĕbû'at hakkārem]*
śādĕkā lō'-tizra' kil'ayim	*lō'-taḥărōš bĕšôr-ûbaḥămōr yaḥdāw*
ûbeged kil'ayim ša'aṭnēz lō' ya'ăleh 'ālêkā	*lō' tilbaš ša'aṭnēz ṣemer ûpištîm yaḥdāw*
You shall not let your cattle **mate with a different kind;**	**⁹You shall not sow your vineyard with a second kind of seed, [else the fullness, from the seed you have sown and the yield of the vineyard, may not be used].**
you shall not sow your field with two kinds of seed; and clothing made of two kinds **of yarn you shall not put on yourself.**	¹⁰You shall not plow with an ox and ass together. **¹¹You shall not wear cloth combining wool and linen.**

As already observed by Ramban, D explains and expands H. Fishbane (1985: 58–63) substantiates Ramban's insight by pointing to D's use of *mĕlē'â* 'the (full) crop'. This term describes the firstfruits in two different verses, but in different senses: in Exod 22:28 (E), it refers to the firstfruits of grain (LXX; *Mek.*; *b. Tem.* 4a [Fishbane's n. 43 needs correction: Ibn Ezra on this verse identifies *mĕlē'â* with wine, and *Tem.* IV.1 > *Tem.* 4a]), and in Num 18:27 (P), it refers to the firstfruits of the vat. Therefore, D, according to Fishbane, is forced to say the *mĕlē'â* refers to both the yield of the sown seed and that of the vineyard.

Fishbane's (1985: 58–63) conclusion is correct, but his argument is in need of correction. The term *mělē'â* refers to the firstfruits of the vat, not only in Num 18:27, where the identification is explicit (*min hayyāqeb* 'from the vat'), but also in Exod 22:28 (with Haran 1962b), where the parallel term *dema'* refers to the grain (Milgrom 1976a: 61, n. 216), leaving *mělē'â* to be identified with the vat. That *mělē'â* means "fullness" is supported by *Gen. Rab.* 14:7, which renders it *bišlēmûtô* 'in its totality'. In Deut 22:9, however, *mělē'â* is used in its literal sense "fullness," to include both the produce of the seed and that of the vine (Kutscher 1956–57; contra Haran 1962b) to indicate that the entire crop of this overcultivated field is forfeit to the sanctuary (for an explanation of this forfeiture, see below).

Fishbane (1985: 62, n. 45) makes the plausible suggestion that D is not an expansion of H, but a limitation, namely, that H's law of mixed seed *only* applies when it is sown in a vineyard, thereby, in effect, rendering H's law nearly unenforceable. In view, however, of H's more restrictive rule concerning mixed seed in garments (see below), it is hard to conceive of D's purported leniency regarding the sowing of mixed seed. In any case, whether D is more severe or more lenient than H, it is clear that D is commenting on H.

D changes breeding different animal species (H) to plowing with them. Fishbane (1985: 59, n. 38) conjectures that D intends a double entendre, since "plowing" is a common Near Eastern euphemism for sexual intercourse (citing Judg 14:18, and Kramer 1963: 494–95; see also Carmichael 1982). However, this does not explain why D changed H's law instead of just supplementing it. Clearly, D must have opposed H on this matter. H's law would forbid mating a horse with a donkey. D, therefore, reflects a later time when the use of mules became widespread (see below).

D explicates H's enigmatic term *ša'aṭnēz* as referring to the mixture of wool and linen. Theoretically, D could be *limiting* *ša'aṭnēz* to only wool and linen. But, as explained below, the only attested mixture in fabrics was that of linen and wool; hence D's addition is explicative. D's law, however, also has a polemic in mind. D follows this prohibition with a command concerning the necessity to attach tassels (*gĕdīlîm*) at the corners of one's outer garment (v. 12). The two injunctions (vv. 11–12) must be understood as a unit: the required tassels may not be composed of wool and linen. D is thus opposing H's demand that each of the tassels (customarily made of linen) should contain a violet thread (perforce made of wool; see below and Milgrom 1983b; 1990a: 410–14).

As indicated in the comparison of Lev 19:19b and Deut 22:9–11, the first two prohibitions in H and D stand in chiastic relation, a possible sign that one source is citing the other. The preceding points argue that D is expounding and expanding H.

19. *your cattle.* The pentateuchal sources do not consider the horse as livestock. Only Deut 17:16 and 20:1, dealing with the law of the king and the cavalry of the enemy, respectively, mention horses—indicating that only royalty and the aristocracy possessed horses (S. Rattray). Mules, the offspring of horses and asses, are first attested after King David (2 Sam 13:29; 18:9; 1 Kgs 1:33; 18:5,

etc.). Dillmann and Ryssel (1897) make the unlikely suggestion that, to avert the prohibition, mules may have been imported (cf. 1 Kgs 10:25; Isa 66:20; Ezek 27:14). Besides, as noted by Bertholet (1901) and Hartley (1992), nowhere in Scripture are mules ever disparaged. If the reconstruction of *MMT* B 76 (cited below) is correct, then the Qumran sectaries rendered *běhēmâ* as "pure cattle," thereby excluding impure animals, such as the horse and donkey, from the prohibition against mixtures, contra the rabbinic view (*Sipra* Qedoshim 4:15).

It is of utmost significance that the cherubim flanking the Ark were mixtures (Ezek 1:5–11), as were the divine guardians in Mesopotamia (cf. Freedman and O'Connor 1982: 330–34). This is the initial indication, which will be corroborated in the two following prohibitions, that mixtures belong to the divine realm, on which the human being (except for divinely designated persons, the priests) may not encroach.

mate. tarbîaʿ. Related and, perhaps, derived from the verb *rābaṣ* 'lie down', *rābaʿ* means 'copulate, breed' (Harris 1990: 2.606–607; see NOTE on 18:23).

a different kind. kilʾayim. The cognates *kelʾē / ētu* (Eth.) and *kilallān* (Akk.) mean "both, pair, two," and Ugaritic *klʾat ydh* (*UT* 1231) means "his two hands" (Zipor 1987: 134). The *Tg.* render *ʿêrûbîn, ʿîrěbûbîn* 'mixtures'.

The most favored explanation for the prohibition against mixtures is that it is a violation of the order God brought into the world by separating the species (Gen 1) and, hence, a symbol of disorder, the reversal of creation (*b. Qid.* 39a; *b. Sanh.* 60a; Ibn Ezra, Ramban, Bekhor Shor; Kalisch 1867–72; Dillmann and Ryssel 1897; Douglas 1966: 53; Magonet 1983; Houtman 1984; Schwartz 1987: 151). This theory could explain the mating prohibition, but as pointed out by Boleh (1991–92), it has no relevance for the two following prohibitions because mixed seeds in the ground are not "mated" (i.e., grafted), but are kept apart!

Another popular explanation is that mixtures in nature are symbolic of mixtures of human beings, thus a prohibition against intermarriage and assimilation (Ehrlich 1899–1900 [H]; cf. *Num. Rab.* 10:3; Wenham 1979; Carmichael 1982; Eilberg-Schwartz 1990: 123; cf. also Carmichael 1995; 1997: 87–104; Milgrom 1996a). Interestingly, this precisely is the interpretation adopted by the Qumran sectaries:

WʿL HZWNWT HNʿSH BTWK HʿM WHMH B[NY ZRʿ] QDŠ MŠKTWB
QWDŠ YŚRʾL WʿL BH[MTW HṬHWR]H KTWB ŠLWʾ LRBʿH KLʾYM WʿL
LBWŠ[W KTWB ŠLWʾ] YHYH ŚʿṬNZ WŠLWʾ LZRWʿ ŚDW WK[RMW
KLʾY]M [B]GLL ŠHMH QDWŠYM WBNY ʾHRWN Q[DWŠY QDWŠYM
Wʾ]TM YWDʿYM ŠMQṢT HKHNYM W[HʿM MTʿRBYM WHM]
MTWKKYM UMṬMʾY[M] ʾT ZRʿ[HQWDŠ WʾP] ʾT [ZRʿ]M ʿM HZWNWT

And concerning the mixed marriage [based on 21:7] that is being performed among the people, and they are s[ons of holy [seed], as it is written "Israel is holy" [cf. Jer 2:3]. And concerning [his (i.e., Israel's) pure ani]mal, it is written that one should not mate two species (19:19aβ) and concerning his clothes [it is written that they should not] be of mixed stuff (19:19b); and one must

not sow his field and vine[yard with mixed specie]s (19:19aγ; Deut 22:9a) because they (Israel) are holy, and the sons of Aaron are m[ost holy]. But you
know that some of the priests and t[he laity intermingle and they] unite with
each other and pollute the [holy] seed and their [i.e., the priests'] own [seed]
with forbidden women. (*MMT* B 75–82)

Thus Qumran bases its ban on intermarriage on the prohibition against mixtures. Note, however, that the text, in reality, speaks of *intra*marriage, between
lay and priestly Israelites. Here, too, the assumption is that the priests belong to
the sacred realm, and just as the lay Israelite is forbidden to enter the sacred
realm (according to the Temple Scroll, the innermost, priestly court is off limits to the laity), so the priest is forbidden to marry an Israelite. In this respect,
Qumran is not only severer than the Torah, which imposes such a restriction
only on the high priest (21:14b), but also severer than Ezekiel, who, at least,
permits the priest to marry an Israelite virgin (Ezek 44:22; see NOTE on 21:7aα).

It is hard to believe, however, that a prohibition against intermarriage would
be expressed metaphorically. To the contrary, the question should be reversed:
Why is there no explicit prohibition against intermarriage in H, particularly in
chaps. 18 and 20 dealing with illicit sexual unions, where such a prohibition
could be expected (see chap. 18, COMMENT A)? This point suffices to vitiate
Carmichael's (1995) charming but flawed exposition of this verse (see INTRO-
DUCTION to 24:10–23).

As intimated above, the most plausible explanation, in my estimation, is that
mixtures belong to the sacred sphere, namely, the sanctuary, as do its officiants,
the priests (cf. Jos. *Ant.* 4.208). Thus the lower cover of the Tabernacle and the
curtain closing off the adytum are a mixture of linen and wool (Exod 26:1, 31).
The high priest's ephod, breastplate, and belt contain the same mixture (Exod
28:6, 15; 39:29); for the ordinary priest, this mixture is limited to his belt (Exod
39:29); and the Israelite is conceded this mixture by the insertion of a single
blue thread of wool in his linen tassels (Num 15:39), as recognized by the rabbis *middĕšēš kîtnā' tĕkēlet 'amā'* 'since linen is flax, blue must be wool' (*b. Yeb.*
4b), and as astutely perceived by Bekhor Shor *dĕhawwâ lêh kĕmištammēš kĕšar-
bîṭô šel melek* 'It is as if it (the tassel) served him (the layman) as a royal scepter'.
Knohl (1995: 186) sees an analogy between the violet cords of the layperson's
tassel and the high priest's turban (Exod 28:36–37). However, the high priest's
violet cord is only an accessory to bind the holy gold plate to the turban. Nonetheless, a connection between the two can be deduced. Whenever Israel sees the
blue thread in any of his tassels (Num 15:37–41 [H]), he is reminded of the
blue cord *banding* the plate that bears the inscriptions "holy to YHWH" (Exod
28:36–37 [P]), and thus he is constantly called to seek holiness by fulfilling the
divine commandments (S. Tupper, personal communication). Once again, H
has overruled P: holiness is not the exclusive property of the priesthood; it is attainable by all of Israel. It is not even mentioned among the high priest's garments in Lev 8:9, indicating its auxiliary nature. The pericope Num 15:37–41,
indisputably attributable to the hand of H, echoes H's primary goal to set Israel

on the path of holiness (v. 40b). Thus departing from P's consistently rigid separation between the priesthood (whose garments symbolize the right to enter the sacred sphere) and the laity (barred from entering the sacred sphere, i.e., the inner sanctuary), H prescribes that all (lay) Israelites insert a woolen thread into the linen tassels of their outer garments as a perpetual, visible sign that they must strive for a life of holiness (cf. Milgrom 1983b; 1990a: 410–14).

Of the three colors in the Tabernacle curtains and priestly clothing, the blue is always listed first, thereby signifying its greater importance (cf. Exod 25:4; 26:1, 31, 36; 27:16; 28:5, 6, 8, 15, 33, etc.; note, however, that its primacy breaks down in 2 Chr 2:6, 13). Furthermore, the high priest's robe and the uppermost Ark cover are composed of *tĕkēlet kālîl* 'pure blue' (Exod 28:31; 39:22; Num 4:6), indicating the high priest's unique responsibility to officiate at the inner sancta and, on Yom Kippur, to enter the Holy of Holies. Even more telling evidence of the higher status of the blue over other colors is that a blue cloth covers all the inner sancta during the wilderness journeys. But only the Ark is covered on top with a blue cloth (as a symbol of the divine presence, it is crucial that it always be visible), whereas the inner sancta (the table, incense altar, and candelabrum) are bedecked with fewer cloths, the uppermost being of leather (details in Milgrom [1990a: 25–28] on Num 4:5–14, and 4:10–14). Thus the priestly (H) command to add a blue thread to the fringes that must be worn by all Israelites indicates H's avid desire to inspire all Israelites to aspire to a life of holiness—the theme of this chapter.

Above all, this explanation clarifies the insertion of this prohibition in this chapter. Israel is commanded to be holy, but is warned that it is not allowed the privilege of breeding different animals, sowing mixed seed, or wearing fabrics of mixed seeds—for these are reserved for the sacred sphere and, in the case of clothing, to the priests. The mythology of the ancients was rife with mixtures: hybrid animals (cherubim) guarding temple entrances and flanking royal thrones; gods mating with humans and animals or changing into human form. There are biblical allusions to this background, as in the myth of celestial beings mating with earth women (Gen 6:1–4). Cherubim exist in Israel's cult—more precisely, inside the sanctuary, in woven form, on the inner curtains and veil of the Tabernacle; carved on the inner walls and doors of the Solomonic Temple; and, in sculpted form, inside the adytum of both sanctuaries. Being ensconced inside the sanctuary, all these cherubim were visible to only priests (the cherubim inside the adytum to no one), who were admitted to their presence because they too, wearing garments of mixed seed, symbolically became cherubim (see below), qualified to attend to the service of YHWH. The cherubim themselves, however, were not visible to the laity; they could not become objects of worship.

Mixtures, then, characterize the holiness of the sacred sphere and those authorized to enter or serve in it. The laity, however, dare not cross its boundary. No differently from the cherub guarding the entrance to the sacred garden (Wright forthcoming), so armed Levites guard the entrance into the sacred enclosure, *wĕhazzār haqqārēb yûmāt* 'and the unauthorized encroacher will be put to death' (Num 1:51; 3:10, 38; 18:7; cf. Milgrom 1970: 1–22).

Thus there is no need to explain this prohibition as a metaphor for disorder or intermarriage. It is but a warning to the Israelite that his holiness is not achieved by penetrating into the sacred realm, but by practicing the proper ritual and ethical behavior as specified in this chapter.

you shall not sow your field with two kinds of seed. śādĕkā lō'-tizra' kil'ayim. The LXX substitutes "your vineyard" for "your field," thereby harmonizing with Deut 22:9 and implying that this prohibition is limited to the case of planting a vineyard with diverse seed. It is not referring to cross-pollination, but to mixing different seeds in the same field; they are difficult to harvest (J. Kessel) and, in some instances, injurious to one another. Thus, for example, peach and almond trees affect each other adversely in close proximity (Dalman 1933: 3.238; but cf. Luke 13:6).

and clothing made of two kinds of yarn. ûbeged kil'ayim. Whereas *kil'ayim* ends the two previously stated prohibitions in this verse, it begins it in the third and final prohibition, where it is expanded at length—a typical example of a stylistic device called "closing deviation" (Paran 1989: 211, 213–22). For examples in H, see 21:1–3 (see NOTE on v. 4); 25:6–7; 26:1, 9.

At Kuntillet 'Ajrud in the southern Negev, four mixed fabrics of wool and linen were found. Red wool yarn was interwoven with blue linen yarn to form the end knot of a textile piece (Stager and Wolff 1981: 98, 100, n. 6; cf. Sheffer 1978). Also a "considerable quantity of red and yellow cloth" made of linen and wool was discovered in the "Midianite tented shrine" at Timna (Rothenberg 1972: 151–52). However, fabric made of wool and linen, forbidden to the lay Israelite, was permitted to, indeed enjoined upon, the priest (cf. Jos. *Ant.* 4:208; *m. Kil.* 9:1). As acutely observed by Bekhor Shor, eating blood and suet was forbidden because they were offered on the altar; so, too, *ša'aṭnēz* because it belongs to the same sphere.

This discrepancy between the priesthood and the laity led R. Joshua of Siknin to declare in the name of R. Levi that this is "one of four statutes that the Impulse to evil impugns (which seeks to discredit the word of God by pointing to those verses in Scripture that take exception to, or contradict, the statute). The second of the four statutes absolutely proscribes the mixture of diverse kinds: 'You shall not wear cloth combining wool and linen' (Deut 22:11), and yet, as the Impulse to evil points out, Scripture says elsewhere that a linen cloak with wool tassels is permitted (Num 15:38–39; cf. *b. Yeb.* 4b). Here too, Scripture does not acknowledge the exception to the statute, but simply enjoins obedience to all the decrees: 'You shall keep my decrees' (Lev 19:19)" (*Pesiq. Rab Kah.* 4 [Braude and Kapstein 1975: 78]. The rabbis, however, did not acknowledge the possibility of the diachronic growth of the material even within the same tradition. Thus in this case, the absolute prohibition in H against wearing "clothing made of two kinds of yarn" was modified by a subsequent H tradent (Num 15:38–39), allowing the lay Israelite to suspend on his outer garment tassels made of linen and wool.

The question naturally arises as to why H placed the tassels pericope (Num 15:37–41), which nearly all critics agree stems from his pen, at so far a remove. This question is part of a larger discussion in the Introduction (I E) of H's redactorial activity outside Leviticus. A summary here will suffice. This pericope ends the reconnaissance of Canaan unit (Num 13–15), but is inseparable from the Korahite rebellions unit (Num 16–18). It forms an envelope with the beginning and end of Num 13 by declaring in 15:39 *wĕlōʾ tātûrû*, literally "do not scout" (opposed to *wĕyātūrû* 'so they will scout', Num 13:2), *ʾaḥărê ʿênêkem* 'following your eyes' (opposed to *wannĕhî bĕʿênênû kaḥăgābîm* 'we were in our own eyes like grasshoppers', Num 13:33). In brief, looking at the blue-corded tassels will prevent Israel from disobeying God, as exemplified by the scouts chosen to reconnoiter Canaan.

The tassels pericope also points forward to the Korahite rebellions. Korah's argument against the Aaronides was ostensibly irrefutable *kol-hāʿēdâ kullām qĕdōšîm*, literally "the entire congregation, they are all holy" (Num 16:3). This, indeed, is a basic plank in the theology of D (not H, pace Knohl 1995: 81), which maintains that Israel is biologically, genetically holy because of YHWH's covenant with the patriarchs. This rebellion is ended by the divine incineration of the pretenders to the priesthood (Num 16:35). Korah's theological challenge, however, is not answered in the unit. The H redactor provides it at the unit's beginning. Israel can be holy, but only if it fulfills the divine commandments—the quintessential kerygma of H. Holiness is not endemic; it is not genetically endowed; it must be acquired and sustained by lifelong obedience to YHWH's will by caring each day to treat one's fellow as the bearer of the divine image—the message of Lev 19.

The earliest rabbinic sources, perhaps dating back to biblical days, taught that the tassels are *šaʿaṭnēz*, a mixture of wool and linen (LXX, *Targ. Jon.* to Deut 22:12; cf. Rashi; Ibn Ezra on Deut 22:12; *b. Men.* 39b–40a, 43a; *Lev. R.* 22:10). In fact, white linen cords and dyed woolen cords were found in the Bar Kockba caves, proving that the rabbinic teaching was actually observed. However, the wearing of *šaʿaṭnēz* is forbidden to the Israelite (Lev 19:19; Deut 22:11), patently because it would resemble some of the priestly garments made from a blend of linen and wool (e.g., Exod 28:6; 39:29; colored cloth is wool). In fact, the high priest's linen turban (Exod 28:39) is bound by a *pĕtîl tĕkēlet*, a violet woolen cord (Exod 28:37). Also the Tabernacle's inner curtains were composed of this "forbidden" mixture (Exod 26:1; cf. Milgrom 1990a: 410–14). Thus, as noted by Josephus (*Ant* 4.208), *šaʿaṭnēz* is forbidden because it is a holy mixture reserved exclusively for priests and forbidden to nonpriests (cf. Jos. *Ant* 4.208). That *šaʿaṭnēz* is forbidden because it is holy can be derived from the injunction "You shall not sow your vineyard with a second kind of seed, else the crop—from the seed you have sown—and the yield of the vineyard [literally] will become sanctified [*yiqdaš*]" (Deut 22:9); that is, it will belong not to you, but to the sanctuary. However, early in the rabbinic period it was taught—perhaps stemming from a biblical practice—that every Israelite would wear tassels made of *šaʿaṭnēz* (see also Tosafot on Deut 22:11). Thus the tassels, according to the rabbis, are modeled after a priestly garment that is taboo for the rest of Israel!

The tassels, then, are an exception to the Torah's general injunction against wearing garments of mixed seed. But in actuality, inhering in this paradox is its ultimate purpose. The resemblance to the high priests's turban and other priestly clothing is no accident. It is a conscious attempt to encourage all Israel to aspire to a degree of holiness comparable to that of the priests. Indeed, holiness itself is enjoined upon Israel (Lev 19:2; cf. 11:44; 20:26). True, Israelites not of the seed of Aaron may not serve as priests (cf. 17:5), but they may—indeed, must—strive for a life of holiness by obeying God's commandments. Hence they are to attach to their garments tassels containing one violet cord, a woolen thread among the threads of linen. Indeed, the use of mixed seed in the prescribed garments reveals a gradation in holiness: the outer garments of the high priest are *ša ʿaṭnēz*; the belt of the ordinary priest is *ša ʿaṭnēz* (Exod 39:29; cf. *b.* Yoma 12b); and the fringes of the Israelite are *ša ʿaṭnēz* by virtue of one woolen thread. The fact that the cord is woolen and violet marks it as a symbol of both priesthood and royalty, thereby epitomizing the divine imperative that Israel become "a kingdom of priests and a holy nation" (Exod 19:6). Moreover, when the Ark was carried in the wilderness march to Canaan, it was covered by a blue (*tĕkēlet*) cloth (Num 4:6). Thus it served as Israel's collective woolen blue thread, an insignia, an outward sign, and reminder that Israel was called to holiness (S. Tupper, personal communication). For a complete discussion, see Milgrom (1990a: 410–14).

ša ʿaṭnēz. The etymology of this untranslatable word is a subject of speculation. Albright (cited by Lambdin 1953: 155) suggests that it is of Egyptian origin: **š ʿd-nǧ < š ʿd* 'cut' + *nǧ* 'thread'. The LXX renders *kibdēlos* 'woven falsely'. Görg (1980) justifies the LXX on the basis of an Egyptian etymology: either *šḥt* 'weave' + *n ʿdz* 'false' or *s ʿdz* 'falsify volume / weight' + *N3 ʿ* 'fabric' (Coptic). It is probably a lexical gloss (Elliger 1966; Fishbane 1985: 59) clarifying the meaning of "clothing of two kinds of yarn," and is itself in need of explication: "combining wool and linen" (Deut 22:11). Most likely, the term *ša ʿaṭnēz*, well known in the time of H, fell into desuetude by the time of D and, therefore, had to be explained.

put on yourself. ya ʿăleh ʿālêkā, literally "ascend on you." Deut 22:11 says simply *tilbaš* 'wear' (cf. Ezek 44:17). The emphasis may be *not* "on yourself," but *yes* on the priests. Perhaps it might signify *not* on your garments, but *yes* on your tassels (hanging from your garments). However, the latter deduction is unwarranted, since "on yourself" does not mean "on your garments." Therefore, the probability is that the absolute prohibition here was subsequently modified by an H tradent. The rabbis derive from this phraseology that although mixed garments may not be worn, they may be made and sold (*b.* Yoma 69a).

This prohibition may suffice, all by itself, to explain why the redactors of the priestly material (probably H; see Introduction I H) found it necessary to include all the sundry details on the prescriptions for and consecration and donning of the priestly clothing as well as the prescriptions for and consecration and construction of the Tabernacle (Exod 25–31, 35–40; Lev 8). The people, instructed categorically to avoid mixed seed in their garments, would have been shocked to find the priests flagrantly violating this prohibition in the sanctuary—defying YHWH's instructions in his very presence. It thus was necessary to explain that their garments, in all their detail, stemmed from explicit divine commands, which qualified their wearers to officiate in the Tabernacle that housed a visible, inner curtain composed of the identical mixed seed—thereby indicating that both priests and Tabernacle belonged to the divine sphere.

The absence of *ʾănî YHWH* 'I YHWH (have spoken)' is due to the switch to the third person, as in other units (vv. 8, 22, 29).

Vv. 20–22. Unit 10: The Betrothed Slave-woman

This case is based on the ambiguous status of the slave-woman. Had she been free, she would have been subject to the laws governing a betrothed woman, which in all codes, biblical and nonbiblical alike, prescribe death for her paramour (e.g., Deut 22:23–27; LE 26; CH 130). With this penalty, this case is in full accord, for, on the one hand, the statement "they shall not be put to death because she has not been freed" (v. 20b) implies that if her infidelity took place after her manumission, her paramour (and she) would have been put to death. On the other hand, had she remained a slave and had not been betrothed to another, then the question of the death penalty would not have arisen at all. Instead, since a slave is considered chattel in all the law codes of the ancient Near East, her owner should have been awarded damages (e.g., LE 33; U 7739, 2; cf. Finkelstein 1966; Szlechter 1967). In this case, surprisingly, the Bible does not compensate the owner at all. Herein is revealed the true marginality of the case: on the one hand, because she is betrothed, the master is, in effect, only her partial owner and therefore not entitled to compensation; on the other hand, because she still is a slave, the laws of adultery are not applicable and their penalties cannot be imposed on her paramour.

Before investigating the particulars of this complex case, a question of higher priority must be addressed: Why is it here? Lev 19 does not deal with case (casuistic) law or, for that matter, with any adjudicatable law! Boleh (1991–92) suggests that its purpose is to teach that whoever wishes to be holy (v. 2) must beware of fornicating with a slave-woman. If so, then why are we given these marginal circumstances, which would rarely occur together? Why not state the prohibition without these restrictive elements? The answer, I submit, lies in the sacrifice. It is an *ʾāšām* 'a reparation offering', prescribed for cases of *maʿal* (5:14–26), which has determined its placement here. That P's *maʿal baYHWH* is equivalent to H's *ḥillēl šēm* YHWH 'desecrated the name of YHWH' has been demonstrated (see NOTE on 18:21). This case, therefore, falls into the same category as the other prohibitions in this chapter, whose violation prevents one from achieving the goal of this chapter—the attainment of holiness. Its wording, style, and content are quintessential hallmarks of P. H has, therefore, incorporated this case into chap. 19 for two reasons: it completes H's comprehensive portfolio on P's *ʾāšām*, and, being a case of sacrilege, it belongs in chap. 19.

It is, then, the *ʾāšām* offering that holds the clue to the import of this pericope. But that, too, is subject to question. If the ambiguous status of the slave-woman allows her paramour to be exempted from all monetary penalties, why must he seek divine forgiveness by a sacrifice? Moreover, even assuming that his act constitutes an offense against God (as yet undefined), it has been committed advertently, and by priestly standards, he should be barred from sacrificial expiation (Num 15:30–31; cf. vol. 1.369–70). Finally, the deliberately committed wrongs of 5:20–26; Num 5:6–8 may not be held up as a precedent, since the mitigating factors of repentance and confession are not present (details in vol. 1.365–78). Indeed, the term *biqqōret* 'inquiry' (v. 20bα) implies that the slave-woman's status is investigated and her paramour is tracked down, judged, and found guilty. Yet although the court must turn down the owner's demand for compensation, it has no hesitation in demanding an expiatory sacrifice from the guilty seducer. Surely, there must have been a clear-cut sin against God, and to find it a closer scrutiny of the case is warranted.

20. *If a man.* Elliger's (1966) notion that the slave-woman's paramour was none other than her owner must be rejected, because the text would have read *wĕhî' šiphātô* 'who is *his* slave'. Moreover, the judicial inquiry would have been superfluous, since her owner was surely aware of her exact status.

woman. *'iššâ.* Westbrook (1988: 107) renders "a married woman." If that were the case, then the text would have read *'ēšet 'îš.* Note that the construct *'ēšet* in the adjoining incest laws (18:11, 14, 16, 20; 20:10, 21) stands for a married woman, whereas the absolute *'iššâ* always refers to any woman (18:17, 18, 19, 22; 20:13, 14, 16, 18; cf. 15:18, 19, 25).

a slave. *šiphâ.* This term is derived from *mišpāhâ* 'kin group, clan', as *famula* and *famulus* (female and male slave) are related to *familia* (Cohen 1978–79: XLI). This is the only legal case where *šiphâ* appears instead of *'āmâ*; the probable reason is aesthetic and stylistic, to create an alliteration with *hupšâ, huppāšâ* (Schwartz 1987: 153). Otherwise, *šiphâ* (e.g., Hagar, Gen 16:1, 3; 25:12; Bilhah, Gen 35:25; Zilpah, Gen 35:26) and *'āmâ* (Hagar, Gen 21:10, 13; Bilhah, Gen 30:3; Bilhah and Zilpah, Gen 31:33) are equivalent and enjoy the same legal status (Lev 25:44). The rabbis differ on her status: R. Akiba holds that she, an Israelite, is betrothed to a Hebrew slave. R. Ishmael says that she, a non-Israelite slave, is betrothed to a Hebrew slave. Others (R. Meir in *b. Hor.* 13b) maintain that she is a non-Israelite slave betrothed to a non-Israelite slave (*Sipra Qedoshim* 5:2; *m. Ker.* 2:5; *b. Ker.* 11a). Thus all the possibilities are exhausted. The likelihood, however, is that the unqualified *šiphâ*, betrothed to an unqualified *'îš* and eligible for redemption, is an Israelite slave betrothed to an Israelite freeman (with Ibn Ezra). But if so, it would contradict one of the main tenets of H's legislation, which abolishes slavery for all Israelites (see INTRODUCTION to 25:39–43)! This argument thus augments the non-H terminology and style of this pericope, which leads to the conclusion that it most likely is an insert from another source, namely P (italicized in the translation). The reason for H's utilization of this law is explicated below.

assigned. *nehĕrepet.* The meaning seems clear but the etymology is in dispute:

1. *HALAT* cites MAOG II 3, 44–45, l. 39, for an Akkadian cognate *harup* 'betrothed' (unmentioned in *AHw* and *CAD*).

2. The LXX renders *diapephulagménē* 'reserved, kept' from *diaphulassein*, which also renders *šāmar* and *nāṣar* 'keep, reserve'.
3. Westbrook (1988: 106) claims that *ḥrp* is related to *ʿrb* 'pledge'.
4. Ben-Hayyim (1936) finds a cognate in Ethiopic Geʿez *pḥr* and cites a live idiom in talmudic Palestine: "In Judah a betrothed woman is called *ḥărûpâ*" (*b. Qid.* 6a).
5. Finally, and most likely, Kutsch (1986) suggests the Akkadian cognate *ḥarāpu* 'be early' (cf. Jewish Aram. *ḥărap* [*Aphel*] 'do something early'; *ḥarāpā* 'premature' [e.g., early rains; *CAD* 6.90]; *ḥarîpûtā* 'youth' [cf. Job 29:4], and he concludes that as *ḥōrep* is the early part of the agricultural season, before the fruition of summer, so *neḥĕrept* refers to the premarital status—"espoused, given early to a man"—which points to the Akkadian antonymous pair *ḥarāpu / apālu* 'be early' / 'be late' (cf. *ʾāpîl*, Exod 9:32).

Hence the exact rendering would be "assigned in advance" (Levine 1989)—that is, in advance of redemption or manumission. Levine plausibly suggests that enigmatic *ḥērēp napšô lāmût* (Judg 5:18) should, therefore, be rendered "(Zebulun is a tribe that) *precipitously exposed itself* to death."

Loewenstamm (1980a: 94) recognizes that *ḥărûpâ is not completely equivalent to **ʾărûsâ 'betrothed' but is of lesser legal force. He is probably right. The verb *ʾāras* (e.g., Exod 22:15; Deut 22:23) carries with it the death penalty if the betrothed woman is seduced or violated. Thus the probability is that *ḥārap* is a special usage to designate the betrothal of a slave where the penalties are not as severe.

to another man. lĕʾîš. Westbrook (1988: 107) claims that she is betrothed to her owner and, therefore, repoints the word as *lāʾîš* 'to the man', hence rendering the entire clause "a *married* woman, she being *pledged* to *the* man" (note the three speculative or emended words). This, too, must be rejected. If correct, the text would have read *lô* 'to him' instead of emended *lāʾîš*.

but has not been ransomed. wĕhopdēh lōʾ nipdātâ. Elliger (1966) and BHS would read the absolute infinitive *hippādōh* (Nip ʿal) to correspond with the Nip ʿal verb *nipdātâ* (though the correct infinitive absolute would be *nipdōh*, GKC § 51i). However, the use of the Hop ʿal infinitive absolute is also attested— for example, *hoḥŏrab neḥĕrbû* (2 Kgs 3:23; Driver and White 1894: 30; GKC § 113w; Kilian 1963: 47, n. 46).

The *waw* indicates contrast: although she is betrothed, she is not redeemed. The Hop ʿal / Nip ʿal combination expresses two contrasts: the owner's obligation to enable her to be ransomed (Hip ʿil in Exod 21:8; Hop ʿal here) and the prospective bridegroom's obligation to ransom her (Schwartz 1986: 346–47). That is, the betrothed man *must* ransom her in order to marry her (as does her owner if he wishes to marry her, Exod 21:8), but has not yet done so. An example might be that a marriage document or agreement has been signed, but not yet fulfilled (cf. Neufeld 1944: 68–75).

I use the rendering "ransom" for *pādâ* instead of the customary "redeem" (e.g., Schwartz 1986: 246–47) because, in the priestly texts, the latter translates only *gā'al* and refers to the obligation of the owner or his nearest relative (the *gō'ēl*) to redeem his lost property. Anyone else performing the same act would be a *pôdeh* 'ransomer' (see NOTE on 27:27).

Rabbinic sources designate her as *pĕdûyâ wĕ'ēnâ pĕdûyâ* 'redeemed but not redeemed' and characterize her status as *ḥeṣyâ šipḥâ wĕḥeṣyâ bat ḥôrîn* 'partly slave and partly free' (*b. Giṭ.* 43a–b; *b. Ker.* 119). For a full discussion of the rabbinic terminology and its application to the status of Elephantine Tamet in Kraeling 2, see Szubin (forthcoming A).

or given her freedom. *'ô ḥupšâ lō' nittan-lāh.* Read *ḥupšāh* (*mappiq* in the *he*; Saadiah, Ehrlich 1966), yielding "her freedom" (but cf. GKC § 91e cases without the *mappiq*). Otherwise, it would be a *hapax*, which Boleh (1991–92) claims refers to a technical document of manumission. However, the masculine verb *nittan* favors the former interpretation.

The expected term for manumission is *šillaḥ laḥopšî* (e.g., Exod 21:26–27). Perhaps the term *nātan ḥopeš* is used to indicate that she is released gratis; indeed, the particle *'ô* introducing the phrase indicates an alternative (GKC § 162a); namely, she attains her freedom in some other way than by ransom (Schwartz 1986: 247). The final clause in this verse *kî lō' ḥuppāšâ* confirms the existence of an alternative, either by ransom or by manumission.

an inquest. biqqōret. There are four main interpretations of this unique term: 1. "Indemnity" (Speiser [1960: 33–36], followed by NJPS, Noth [1977], HALAT, Barth [1975: 219], Cohen [1978: 129, n. 54; 1978–79: XXXVI, II. 56], Levine [1989] [cf. Ibn Janaḥ, Ramban, Kimḥi, Shadal], on the basis of Akk. *baqrum*, which Speiser claims was "actually translated *Schadenersatzpflicht* by M. San Nicolò" [1922: 154–75]). However, as pointed out by Loewenstamm (1980a: 95)—and my own investigation has verified—San Nicolò clearly distinguishes between the clause containing the claim (*baqrum*) and the clause asserting the *Schadenersatzpflicht*, or responsibility, for the claim (e.g., CH § 279). Indeed, the alleged meaning of "indemnity" for the Akkadian cognate is not attested at all (cf. *AHw* s.v. *b/paqāru*, 105a). Besides, since two persons are subject to inquiry, the master and the betrothed, the text would have specified who is meant (the Sam. does add *lô*, but from the further change to *yāmût* [instead of the pl. *yāmûtû*], it seems clear that neither master nor betrothed is intended, but her ravisher).

A variation on this interpretation is supplied by Westbrook (1988: 105), who claims that *biqqōret tihyeh* means "there is an *actio in rem*"; that is, the owner has the right to claim his property back. However, part of the objection still stands: one would have expected this phrase to be followed by a specification of the owner (e.g., *la'dōnêhā*, cf. Exod 21:4–5). However, Westbrook's point that the owner is entitled to some compensation is a valid one, but that would probably be determined during the judicial investigation (see no. 3).

On the basis of *ul ibbaqar* 'may not be reclaimed / recovered' (CH § 188), Friedman (1996: VIII) reaches a similar conclusion, but holds that the recovery or release is not by the owner (of his slave), but by the offenders "from a claim on principle of the death penalty allowing them to redeem themselves by making a guilt offering." This interpretation must be rejected because it does not fit any of its verbal attestations (see below); the "recovery / release" sought is not a material and concrete claim, but "a claim in principle of the death penalty," a strange legal usage of the term "release"; and only the paramour is required to bring an *ʾāšām* offering, not the woman!

2. "Punishment" (i.e., lashes—for her, not for him: *m. Ker.* 2:4; *Sipra* Qedoshim 5:4; *Tg. Ps.-J.*; *b. Mak.* 22a; *b. Ker.* 11a; cf. Vg). However, there is no indication in the text as to who is punished and how; this rendering is unsupported by any etymology; the punishment is never the subject of a sentence (Loewenstamm 1980: 97; Schwartz 1987: 154–55); and one would expect a *waw* added to the following *lōʾ* to indicate a contrast: lashes but not death.

3. "Inquest" (LXX; *Tgs. Onq., Neof*; Rashi₂, Ibn Ezra, Rashbam, Dunash 1855; Menahem 1854; Karaites Loewenstamm 1992: 222–29). Note the use of the verb *biqqēr* in *lōʾ-yĕbaqqer hakkōhēn lāśśēʿār haṣṣāhōb* 'The priest shall not search [i.e., examine] for yellow hair' (13:36). The rabbis themselves, although interpreting *biqqōret* as "lashes" (no. 2), acknowledge—within the same context— that *biqqēr* means "inquire, examine": "Whence do we know that the term *biqqōret* implies lashes? . . . R. Ashi says: It denotes she shall be examined [*bĕbiqqûr tihyeh*]" (*b. Ker.* 11a). In fact, the Qumran sectaries follow this very interpretation of the verb *biqqēr* in describing the judicial examiner of a suspected adulteress (paraphrasing Deut 22:13–21):

KY YWṢW ʾYŠ ŠM Rʿʿ ʿL BTWLT YSRʾL ʾM [BYWM] QḤTW ʾWTH YWʾMR WBQRWH [. . .] NʾMNWT WʾM LW KḤŠ ʿLYH WHWMTH WʾM BŠ[QR] ʿNH BH WN ʿNŠ ŠNY MNYM [. . . WLʾ] YŠLḤ KL YMYW KWL . . .

If a man defames a virgin Israelite, if [on the day] he marries he charges (she is not a virgin), *they shall examine her* [*ûbiqqĕrûhā*] as to her fidelity, and if he has not lied about her, she shall be put to death. But if by a [lie] he has humiliated her, he shall be fined two minas [cf. Deut 22:19] [. . . and he cannot] divorce her for the rest of his life, all . . . (4Q159 [*DJD* V 1968:8, pl. II])

A number of objections have been voiced to this interpretation. The first is that there is no need to state that there is a judicial inquiry. The fact that it is a capital case—its outcome can be death—automatically implies that it is thoroughly investigated (Ramban, Wenham 1979). My answer (1976a: 129, n. 460) is that the deuteronomic code demands, precisely in capital cases where inquiry is self-evident: "you shall investigate and inquire and interrogate thoroughly" (Deut 13:15, the apostate community; cf. Deut 19:18, false witnesses; and 17:4, idolatry).

The deuteronomic evidence I have adduced has also been challenged: there, positive findings result in her death; here, it states explicitly "they shall not be put to death"; also there a rumor had to be investigated; here, the facts were known (Schwartz 1987: 289, n. 26). My rebuttal is that the two cases are in this matter completely analogous: the slave-woman and her paramour are not put to death only if the judicial inquiry *verifies* her half-free half-slave status. In Deuteronomy as well: only if the case cited is verified by judicial investigation is the stated penalty carried out. For example: *kî-yāqûm ʿēd-ḥāmās bĕʾîš laʿănôt bô sārâ* 'If a man appears against another to testify maliciously and gives false testimony against him' (Deut 19:16), and if the subsequent inquiry proves that this is indeed true, then the stated consequences follow (vv. 17–19).

A refinement of this position has recently been proposed by Szubin (forthcoming C). The purpose of the inquiry is to investigate her precise status—that is, the amount paid of her ransom or extent of her manumission. The more the ransom has been paid or the more she is free, the more her liaison borders adultery, requiring an expiatory *ʾāšām* (see NOTES on v. 21). If, however, it is determined that she is mainly a slave, no sin against God has been committed and an *ʾāšām* is not required.

According to this interpretation, the dividing line between slavery and freedom is fluid, to be determined by each court; otherwise, it would be stated in the text. It is questionable, however, whether a priestly legist (from the school of either P or H) would have formulated such a nebulous law by which a sin against God would be determined by a secular court, even if priests were represented on it (on the model of Deut 17:8–12). Furthermore, the text provides no options. It states categorically that if the court's investigation determines that she is partially free and partially a slave, regardless of the degree, the death penalty does not apply, but an *ʾāšām* is required.

4. "A distinction, differentiation" (Ibn Ezra; Ehrlich 1966; Schwartz 1987: 156; cf. *Unterscheidung* [Buber 1964]), on the basis of Arabic *baqara* 'split' [*HALAT*, s.v. *bqr*] and *lōʾ yebaqqēr bên ṭôb lāraʿ* 'he shall not distinguish between healthy and emaciated' (27:33). This view is challenged below.

A brief survey of the few attestations of the verb *biqqēr* is in order:

1. In *ûmizbaḥ hannĕḥōšet yihyeh-lî lĕbaqqēr* (2 Kgs 16:15) and *ûlĕbaqqēr bĕhêkālô* (Ps 27:4), *biqqēr* may have the meaning "*investigate* the entrails of a sacrifice" (Mowinckel 1967: 1.146) or, more likely, be a denominative from *bōqer* 'morning', yielding "spend the morning." Thus "I will offer the morning sacrifice on the bronze altar" (2 Kgs 16:15) and "to spend the morning in his Temple" (Ps 27:4).

2. *wĕʾahar nĕdārîm lĕbaqqēr* may be rendered "and *to investigate* (the content of) vows afterward" (Prov 20:25b).

3. *wĕdārâštî ʾet-ṣōʾnî ûbiqqartîm kĕbaqqārat rōʿeh ʿedrô . . . kēn ʾăbaqqēr* 'I shall *search* for my flock and *seek* them *out*. As a shepherd *seeks out* his flock . . . so I will *seek out*' (Ezek 34:11–12). A few verses earlier, *dāraš* 'search' is used in parallel with *biqqēš* 'seek' (v. 6; Greenberg, personal communication). The parallel use of *dāraš* 'search', *biqqēš* 'seek', *biqqēr* (three times) indicates that "seek out" (a synonym of "investigate") is the proper rendering for *biqqēr*.

4. *bĕṭerem taḥqôr ʾal tĕsallēp baqqēr lĕpānîm wĕʾahar tazzîp* 'Do not find fault before you *investigate; examine* first and then, criticize' (Sir 11:7 [Genizah]). The parallel of *biqqēr* and *ḥāqar* 'investigate' requires no comment.

5. The main role of the *MBQR* in QL (e.g., CD, 1QS) is to *examine* new-comers to the sect (e.g., 1QS 6:14).

6. In Rabbinic Hebrew, *biqqēr* clearly means "investigate" (e.g., *m. Tam.* 3:4; *t. Ḥag.* 1:8; *Mek.* Bo 5); so too in Biblical Aramaic (Ezra 4:15, 19; 5:17; 6:1; 7:14) and in Jewish Aramaic (*b. Ket.* 106a; *y. Ber.* IV, 7b; *y. Beṣ* II, 61c).

7. As explicated at the beginning of the discussion of no. 3, *lō᾽ yebbaqēr hakkōhēn* must be rendered "The priest shall not search / examine / investigate (for yellow hair)" (Lev 13:36).

Therefore, to render *lō᾽ yĕbaqqēr* in Lev 27:33 as "he shall not distinguish" not only flies in the face of all other attestations of *biqqēr*, but makes no sense: What does "distinguish" mean? And for what purpose? Hence, the rendering "He must not look out for" (*NJPS*) or "There shall be no inquiry (whether it is . . .)" (*NEB*) or "He must not seek out (the healthy as against . . .)" (my ren-dering; see NOTE on 27:33) is to be preferred. Indeed, even if the alleged Ara-bic etymology *baqara* 'split' is correct, one can readily grant that the develop-ment from concrete "split" to abstract "decide, examine" is logical. The hapax *biqqōret*, therefore, must be rendered "inquest." An official investigation must take place to determine the exact status of the woman and to determine the ex-act compensation due her owner.

they shall not be put to death. lō᾽ yûmĕtû. The Sam. reads *biqqōret tihyeh* [*lô*] *lō᾽ yûmāt(w)*, which applies to only the paramour and harmonizes with the other singular verbs. The implication is that they (the slave-woman and paramour) are punished in some other way (Dillmann and Ryssel 1897), which the rabbis spec-ify as lashes (*m. Ker.* 2:4; see no. 2). Thus the meaning of the entire verse is that whereas all cases of fornication with a married woman constitute a capital crime, in this case if judicial examination proves that the woman is technically still a slave, the death penalty cannot be imposed.

The fact that the law stipulates that she (too) is not put to death indicates that she had sexual intercourse with her paramour or seducer. Had she rather been raped (as claimed by Gerstenberger 1996: 274, among others), she would not have been put to death, even if she were a free person (cf. Deut 22:25–27).

because she has not been freed. kî-lō᾽ ḥuppāšâ. The verb form is a *hapax*; its pattern, however, is not *Puʿal* (Schwartz 1987: 154), since there is no *Piʿel* for this verb, but must be passive *Qal* (IBHS § 22.6b).

21. *as his penalty. ᾽ăšāmô.* For this meaning, see 5:6, 15, 25, and vol. 1.339–45.

to the entrance of the Tent of Meeting. ᾽el-petaḥ ᾽ōhel môʿēd. All sacrificial an-imals must be brought there to be readied for sacrifice (1:3; 3:2, 8, 13; 4:4, 14; 17:4, 9). Surprisingly, this stipulation is missing for the *᾽āšām*, the reparation of-fering. Either it is taken for granted—an unlikely possibility in view of its un-wavering occurrence in all other sacrificial texts—or its absence carries special meaning. The *᾽āšām* differs from all other sacrifices in that the required animal may be commutable into money according to the value fixed by the sanctuary, *bĕʿerkĕkā* (5:15, 18, 25). That is why the text of these latter two verses states that the *᾽āšām* is brought directly *᾽el-hakkōhēn* 'to the priest' and not "to the entrance of the Tent of Meeting," which would imply that he is bringing an animal, as in this case. The rabbis, however, asseverate that monetary substitution is also permissible in this case (*Sipra* Qedoshim 5:6).

It must be assumed from the outset that the purpose of the investigation (*biqqōret*) is to determine whether adultery has been committed. This is underscored by the otherwise superfluous passage "they shall not be put to death because she has not been freed" (v. 20b). The postulate from which the investigation proceeds is that betrothal and marriage are equally subject to the rules of adultery. In both cases, the adulterers must die (for the betrothed, see Deut 22:23–27; LE 26; CH 130; for the married woman, see Deut 22:22; CH 129–32; MAL 12–23; LH 97).

Moreover, throughout the ancient Near East, adultery is conceived as a crime not just against the husband, but also against the gods. Witness these three Genesis narratives (Gen 20:6; 26:10; 39:9b). Not only do all of them specify that adultery is a sin against God, but the specification itself is made to or by a non-Israelite. Thus the narrator assumes that Israel shared with its neighbors the conviction that adultery was an affront to the deity. This is confirmed by yet another bit of evidence from the first narrative (Gen 20:9). That not only the king but his entire kingdom stands to suffer for the crime makes it certain that the wrath of God has been aroused. This is made doubly certain by the description of the adultery as *ḥăṭā'â gĕdōlâ* 'a great sin'. It is now known that this is a technical term for adultery throughout the ancient Near East. In Egypt, four ninth-century marriage contracts label adultery as the "great sin" (Rabinowitz 1959). In Babylonia, as Loewenstamm (1962a) has noted, the adulterer is listed among those who have offended Ninurta by his "weighty sin" (*ra-ḫu-ú aš-ti a-wi-lim a-ra-an-šu kab-[tum-ma]*), ("A Bilingual Hymn to Ninurta," l. 4 [Lambert 1960: 119]), "he who covets his neighbor's wife will [. . .] before his appointed day" (*šá a-na al-ti tap-pi-šú iš-šu- [ú] [īnē-šú] i-na u₄-um la ši-ma-ti ú-šá- [. . .]*), ("The Šamaš Hymn," ll. 88–89 [Lambert 1960: 130–31]), and adultery is specified as one of the sins that Marduk punishes (*a-na al-ti ib-ri-šu a-la-ku pu-uz-zu-ru* 'to visit the wife of one's friend secretly'; *a-na bît tap-pe-e-šú i-te-ru-ub a-na aššat tap-pe-e-šú iṭ-ṭe₄-ḫi* 'he had entered his neighbor's house, had intercourse with his neighbor's wife'; (*Šurpu* IV.6, II. 47–48 [Reiner 1958: 25, 14]). Finally, by plausible inference, the *ḫiṭṭu rabū*, on account of which the king of Ugarit extradites his wife from her native land and has her put to death, can only be adultery (*PRU* IV.129–48; cf. Moran 1959). Thus the identification of the "great sin" as adultery in both Israel and its environment plus the explicit claim in Genesis that Israel's neighbors reckoned adultery as a sin against the deity lead to the conclusion that adultery was considered throughout the ancient Near East as both a civil and a religious crime, a "great sin" against the gods. Further confirmation of Israel's view is provided in H itself, where adultery is included among the sexual offenses for which God banishes Israel from their land and sentences them to *kārēt* (18:20, 25–30).

Herein I believe lies the reason for sacrificial expiation. Sexual relations with someone else's betrothed constitutes adultery, a "great sin" against the Deity. How is his wrath to be assuaged? Priestly thought admits to only two ways: death for intentional sins; sacrifice for inadvertences. However, as noted, although there can be no question of intention in our case, the death penalty is not applicable because the betrothed woman is still a slave. How else shall expiation be made to God? The answer is sacrifice. It comes by default; there is no alternative.

If sacrificial expiation is necessary, why the *'āšām* offering and not another expiatory sacrifice, say the *ḥaṭṭ'āt* or *'ōlâ* (e.g., Lev 1:4; 14:20; 16:24)? An enticing solution suggests itself: the betrothal was solemnized by an oath, and its violation through adultery would therefore constitute *ma'al*, a crime against God that, as shown, under mitigating circumstances is expiable by an *'āšām*.

Ostensibly, this hypothesis is buttressed by the Bible itself. Jacob and Laban enter into an oath concerning the marital status of Laban's daughters (Gen 31:53–55). The technical term for covenant, *běrît*, is used to describe this oath between Jacob and Laban as well as the marital relationship in general (Prov 2:17), whose violation God is called on to witness (Mal 2:14). Indeed, Israel's covenant with God is pictured in terms of a marriage to which God has bound himself by oath (Ezek 16:8). Finally, the only time the word *ma'al* is used outside the sacral sphere of sancta and oath violations is in the case of adultery (Num 5:12, 17). Thus if an oath of fidelity were affixed to the betrothal rite, as the Bible seems to say, then the requirement of an *'āšām* in the case of adultery with a betrothed slave might be justified (favored by Falk 1964: 129–30, 148–49, 156).

Unfortunately, under close scrutiny, the "if" crumbles. First and foremost, although countless marriage contracts and laws from the ancient Near East are known, not a single one to my knowledge stipulates an oath. Indeed, it seems that in Babylonia, betrothal and marriage contracts were not even written, except when additional stipulations had to be made (cf. Greengus 1969). In the Bible, originally at least, marriage (Ruth 4:10–11) and betrothals (Hos 2:21–22) also were oral transactions (contra de Vaux 1961: 33). To the contrary, ancient Near Eastern laws—except for the Bible—allow the injured husband the right to mitigate or even waive the death penalty against the adulterer (e.g., CH 129; MAL 14–16; LH 192–93; *ANET* 171, 181, 196). As for the purported biblical evidence, it leads to no such conclusion. The pact between Jacob and Laban concerns Jacob's marriage to others, Rachel and Leah having long been Jacob's wives. The term *běrît* in the other citations is a literary usage and carries no legal force. The oath in Ezek 16:8 is taken by God, whereas it should have been expected of the bride, Israel, for it is her status, not the husband's, that determines if the action is adultery. The same anomaly is encountered in Mal 2:14, where the husband rather than the bride violates the covenant. The use of *běrît*, then, will not admit any deductions concerning an alleged marital oath. As for the *ma'al* of the suspected adulteress (Num 5:11–31), it is committed against her husband (vv. 12, 17), whereas all other occurrences of this term refer to sins against God. Thus *ma'al* in this passage, as *běrît* in those cited above, is a literary metaphor and has no legal value. Finally, turning to our case, if the violation of the alleged betrothal oath is responsible for the penalty, why is the paramour liable at all—he did not take the oath!

Is there, then, no way of accounting for the *'āšām?* I believe there is. The one fact that survives the demolition of the evidence adduced is that adultery in the ancient Near East had a religious dimension. Since it was considered a "great sin" and a "sin against God," then it can be presumed that the contracting of betrothal and marriage—even without an oath—was a religious as well as a civil act, subject to the jurisdiction of the divine. The betrothal and marriage rites might be conceived as covenants if there were a mutual exchange of *verba solemnia*, even though an oath formula was not used. (On the likelihood of such a verbal exchange, see, for Babylonia, Greengus 1969: 514–520; Lackenbacher 1971, esp. 151, 153; for the Bible, see Ruth 4:10–11 and Hos 2:21–22; cf. 2:4aβ. Perhaps the idiom *hālak 'aḥărê* was part of the declaration made by the bride; see Yaron [1963: 14–15] on *warki . . . alāku;* LE 59; Weinfeld, 1972b: 100, n. 25.) The fact that ancient Near Eastern codes permit the monetary composition of adultery does not render it likely that its religious aspect had any influence on the legislation. However, this does not hold true for Israel. The death sentence for adultery in the Bible may not be commuted. This points to the unique element that distinguishes Israel from its neighbors. All biblical sources agree that the prohibition against adultery was incorporated into the national covenant at Sinai to which every Israelite swore allegiance (Exod 24:1–8; Deut 5:24–26) and all subsequent generations were bound (Deut 29:9–14). The reaffirmation of the Sinaitic covenant on a periodic basis is demanded by Deuteronomy (31:10–13) and is attested as having occurred during the days of Joshua (24:1–28), Josiah (2 Kgs 23:1–3), and Ezra (Neh 8:1–12). Indeed, when both Hosea and Jeremiah score Israel for violating the Sinaitic covenant, they specify the sin of adultery (e.g., Hos 4:2; Jer 7:9). The testimony of Jeremiah is particularly striking, since he expressly pinpoints adultery as the cause of Israel's national doom (Jer 5:7–9; 7:9–15; 29:23a). Thus there is no need to search for an apparently nonexistent marital oath at the time of marriage. All Israelites were considered bound by the Decalogue, and hence the breach of any of its provisions could be regarded as *ma'al.* In other words, rather than an individual oath at the time of betrothal, the Bible predicates a collective oath against adultery when Israel became covenanted with its God (on allusions to the Sinaitic oath in Jer 5:7; 23:10, see Milgrom 1976a: 136, n. 490). Knohl (1995: 184, n. 46) claims that, according to my reading, H would label every intentional sin as a *ma'al* requiring expiation by a reparation ram (I have, however, assigned this pericope to P; see below). This is a misreading of my theory. First, it must be kept in mind that I have proposed an unsubstantiatable hypothesis for a baffling crux. Then, my hypothesis, even if correct, limits the range of the sins to those heard at Sinai, to which Israel bound itself by oath. Thus both H's acceptance of JE's Sinaitic account and Israel's response to God's revelation by oath are only assumptions. In any case, the sins subject to *ma'al* would be those in the Decalogue (and possibly the Book of the Covenant)—but not any other sin! See further the Introduction II F, P.

This, then, is the background for the *'āšām* of Lev 19:20–22. The seducer of the betrothed slave-woman is indeed guilty of adultery, if not in the sight of man, then in the sight of God, and although her slave status renders the death penalty inoperable, the "great sin" against God still must be expiated. As in all cases of desecration where sacrificial expiation is allowed, the offender must bring an *ʾāšām*.

Schwartz (1987: 290, n. 38) objects to my theory on the grounds that the *ʾāšām* should have been enjoined for the violation of all other commandments of the Torah. In rebuttal, first, let me emphasize that the *Sinaitic* covenant is limited to the Decalogue (and, possibly, the Covenant Code). Second, let me reemphasize the nature of our case. It falls into the gray area between a free person and a slave, in which the laws of adultery do not apply. The other commandments and laws have their stipulated penalties. Presumably, if thievery (kidnaping, according to some; Exod 20:15) would also present such a marginal case, the *ʾāšām*, I submit, would be mandated. I cannot, however, conceive of such circumstances. (Involuntary homicide, indeed, presents such a possibility, but its expiation is different; Num 35:20–28; Deut 19:1–9.)

In sum, the resolution of the crux of the *ʾāšām* brought by the paramour or seducer of a slave-woman rests on the assumption that in Israel adultery was considered a violation of the Sinaitic covenant. In the ancient Near East, although adultery was considered a sin against the gods, it had no juridical impact, whereas in Israel its inclusion in the covenant guaranteed legal consequences. The death penalty for clear-cut adultery could never be commuted. However, in the case of Lev 19:20–22, where investigation shows that the betrothed slave-woman had not been emancipated, her paramour or seducer could not be punished. He is not an adulterer because she is not a legal person. Nevertheless, he has offended God by desecrating the Sinaitic oath and must bring his *ʾāšām* expiation. For further details, see Milgrom (1977a).

The burden of proof, therefore, falls on those who hold that this case is exceptional. Indeed, it is. As pointed out by Schwartz (1987: 157), the offender—in this case, the paramour—has committed his offense knowingly, deliberately. This defies the cardinal principle of the expiatory sacrificial system that only inadvertently committed wrongs are eligible for expiation. Only one exception is allowed: before he has been apprehended, he voluntarily confesses his crime (Num 5:6–8, and see Milgrom 1976a: 117–19, and vol. 1.301–3). In this case, however, the stipulation for neither monetary commutation (*bĕʿerkĕkā*) nor confession (*wĕhitwaddâ*) is present. Hence the offender is denied the option of monetary equivalence and must go to the trouble of purchasing an unblemished ram and bringing it "to the entrance of the Tent of Meeting" for his expiation.

reparation offering. ʾāšām. This sacrificial requirement presumes that the offense of the paramour involves a sin against the deity in the form of a desecration. And this is precisely the reason why this law entered chap. 19. As elaborated in the COMMENT on holiness, all of this chapter's laws fall under the rubric of holiness or its violation. Thus, it is the *ʾāšām* penalty that qualifies this law for inclusion in chap. 19.

22. *for his wrong that he committed . . . of his wrong that he committed. ʿal-ḥaṭṭāʾtô ʾăšer ḥāṭāʾ . . . mēḥaṭṭāʾtô ʾăšer ḥāṭāʾ.* The fourfold repetition of the root

ḥṭ' emphasizes that although she is a slave, his act is sinful and requires expiation (Schwartz 1987: 157). The rabbis explain the repetition positively: although he sinned willfully, his sin is considered an inadvertence, qualifying it for sacrificial expiation (*Sipra* Qedoshim 5:7).

so that he may be forgiven. wěnislaḥ lô. H is careful to keep P's formula (e.g., 4:20, 26, 31, 35; 5:10, 13, 16, 18, 26)—using the *Nipʿal* rather than the *Qal* (*wěsālaḥ lô* 'and he [God] will forgive him') to underscore that the sacrifices lack automatic efficacy: forgiveness is only by the grace of God (see NOTE on 4:20).

The unit, vv. 20–22, does not end with the customary *'ǎnî YHWH*, probably for the same reason that this ending is also not found in vv. 8, 13, 19, 29: it is apposite with only a direct address (see NOTE on v. 13). If this unit proves to be an interpolation from another source (see below), it would also constitute another reason for the missing ending.

As conjectured above, this unit belongs in chap. 19 because of the *'āšām* requirement, which presupposes that desecration, hence, a diminution of holiness, has taken place. However, the formulation of this law and its exaction of a penalty (the *'āšām*), despite the fact that no other unit in chap. 19 contains a penalty, have given rise to the suggestion that this unit stems from elsewhere. Dillmann and Ryssel (1897) suggest that by its content, it belongs with 20:10 (the adultery prohibition). Eerdmans (1912) even conjectures that originally it was a marginal note at 20:10, which was later inserted into the right-hand column, chap. 19, at this place. Nonetheless, the fact that in Deuteronomy, the law of mixtures is followed by the pericope on rape (Deut 22:11–12, 13–29) suggests that if this unit is an interpolation, it was deliberately inserted here in order that it, too, would follow the unit on mixtures (v. 19). In any event, its content—its concern with desecration—qualifies it to be placed under the injunction: "You shall be holy" (v. 2).

Knohl (1995: 114–15) claims, on the basis of the deviations from the *'āšām* laws of 5:14–26, that "whereas PT is precise in its formulations of terms, H frames its laws with far greater freedom." He rejects the possibility that this pericope was taken bodily out of P. As I see it, his only seemingly valid argument is the difference in language: where vv. 20–22 describe the sacrifice as *'êl 'āšām* and *'êl hā'āšām*, P resorts to *lě'āšām* (5:15, 18, 25). He is demonstrably wrong. First, *'êl hā'āšām is* the language of P (5:16b)! As for *lě'āšām* (5:15, 18, 25), P had no other choice because it inserted the words *tāmîm min-haṣṣō'n bě'erkěkā* between *'ayyil* and *'āšām*, thereby rendering the construct *'êl 'āšām* impossible. Nor is this construct found anywhere else (including the arguably H passage Num 5:5–8; cf. Knohl 1995: 86–87). Thus there can be no linguistic objection to attributing this pericope to P.

Knohl would also argue that the absence of the term *tāmîm*, especially in a case requiring an *'āšām* sacrifice, is out of step with P's rigid requirements (contrast 5:15, 18, 25). However, one should note that the full formula in these cited verses is *tāmîm min-haṣṣō'n*, and the latter half of the formula is also missing. Above all, this formula is also missing elsewhere—for example, Num 6:12—in a passage that is unmistakably P. Thus it may be concluded that P is not adverse to using shorthand wherever it feels that the omitted words are self-understood. (Note, for example, that P omits the vital requirement of hand-leaning from the inaugural blood sacrifices [chap. 9, discussed in vol. 1: 579].) As for the other factual differences, I have demonstrated that they are not in conflict with P, since they form the data for an entirely new case.

Therefore, since there is no indication of H's terminology or ideology in vv. 20–22, I assign this pericope in its entirety to P (so indicated by the italicized text in the translation). Undoubtedly, H inherited a larger body of P material. The cases of 5:14–26 hang together because all of them allow for *bĕ'erkĕkā*, the substitution of money for the animal. The marginal case of 19:20–22, however, belongs to another part of the unused P corpus because it requires a sacrifice. This is what H chose. It fits perfectly into the main purpose of chap. 19. It is an example of desecration, not of an ordinary oath (cf. 5:20–26), but of the oath taken at Sinai; it adumbrates the Decalogue, as do vv. 3, 4, 11, 29–32 (see their NOTES).

Vv. 23–25. Unit 11: Horticultural Holiness (Continued)

As concern for the poor during harvest time (vv. 9–10) is an essential character-istic of a holy people, so is the dedication of the first yield of the fruit trees to the sanctuary. Other firstfruits (e.g., the grain, must, oil, and firstlings) are not men-tioned because it is presumed that people are aware of them and, in the main, observing them. But waiting for an additional, fourth, year to enjoy the fruit of one's trees may have found few adherents. Hence its mention here and its promise of a reward. R. Akiba neatly captured the issue: "The Torah addressed (man's) temptation [*yēṣer*] so that he should not say: For four years I sorrow over it in vain" (*Sipra* Qedoshim, par. 3:9). This unit is headed by an introversion (v. 23), which points timewise to the remainder (vv. 24–25), as follows (M. Hildenbrand):

```
23   wĕkî-tābō'û 'el-hā'āreṣ
     A    ûnĕṭa'tem kol- 'ēṣ ma'ăkāl
          B    wa'ăraltem 'orlātô 'et-piryô
               C   šālōš šānîm
          B'   yihyeh lākem 'ărēlîm
     A'   lō' yē'ākēl
24   ûbaššānâ hārĕbî'ît . . .
25   ûbaššānâ haḥămîšît . . .
```

The ABCB'A' structure forbids the eating (*'kl*, AA') of the firstfruit of trees, re-ferring to it by the metaphor "foreskin" (BB'), for a period of three years (C). The center C leads into the timing of vv. 24–25, which terminates with the di-vine promise of an increased yield.

23. *When you enter the land.* As noted by Rofé (1988: 10), the opening word *kî* means "when" everywhere it begins a similar protasis (19:23; 25:2; Num 15:2; Deut 7:1; 12:29; 26:1). The LXX adds *'ăšer YHWH 'ĕlōhêkem nôtēn lākem* 'which

YHWH your God gives you'. Elliger (1966) suggests that this addition is authentic because it complements the long form of the divine self-declaration *ʾănî YHWH ʾĕlōhêkem* 'I YHWH your God (have spoken)' (v. 25b). Zakovitch (1978: 440, n. 16) agrees on the authenticity of the addition on the grounds that all other attestations of this formula contain it (cf. 14:34; 23:10; 25:2; Exod 12:25; Num 15:2; Deut 17:14; 26:1; 27:3; 31:7). Schwartz (1987: 291, n. 1) supports the MT because in all other attestations of this formula, in his opinion, the stress is on God's promise of the land, whereas this verse is concerned with only the fruit of trees. His argument must be rejected, since in other H passages (e.g., 14:34; 23:10; 25:2), the divine land promise is equally irrelevant.

The scales would seem to be tipped in favor of the LXX addition. Even if so, one should take into account that the LXX is in the third person, whereas in all other H occurrences, God speaks in the first person (cf. 14:34; 23:10; 25:2; Num 15:2). Thus if the LXX is, indeed, authentic, it offers evidence that this unit (vv. 23–25) is not originally H, but is an interpolation from another source.

fruit tree. *ʿēṣ maʾăkāl.* The term *ʿēṣ* also comprises shrubs (cf. Gen 1:11–12; Dillmann and Ryssel 1897), including the grapevine (called *ʿēṣ-haggepen*, lit. 'grape-vine tree', Ezek 15:2, 6). A rabbinic view holds that this term applies to only the grapevine (*b. Ber.* 35a; *PRE* 29), which cannot be justified.

you shall treat its foreskin with its fruit as foreskin. *waʿăraltem ʿorlātô ʾet-piryô,* literally "you shall treat as foreskin its foreskin with its fruit." This is a cognate accusative construction, in which the verb is a denominative (GKC § 117 p-r). The function of this construction has been variously interpreted:

1. "Make / declare it as foreskin"; however, a *Piʿel* would have been expected.

2. "Regard it as foreskin," emphasized by *yihyeh lākem* 'it shall be . . . to you'—that is, you shall regard it (Ibn Ezra).

3. The entire construction is metaphoric for "forbidden"; that is, the fruit of the first three years is a despicable covering on the tree, like the foreskin (Wessely 1846, followed by NJPS).

4. Do not pluck ("circumcise") the fruit ("Leave it," Pesh.)—the most commonly accepted interpretation among the moderns (Knobel 1857; Dillmann and Ryssel 1897; Baentsch 1903; Ehrlich 1908; Heinisch 1935; Noth 1977; Elliger 1966; Mayer 1989). The objection to this interpretation stems from horticultural science. Allowing immature fruit to remain not just for one but for three years would sap the energies of the juvenile tree, resulting in its stunted growth and reduced productivity (see below).

5. "Pluck (the fruit)"; compare *tigzĕrûn* 'cut' (*Tg. Ps.-J.*; Aramaic for *mwl* 'circumcise'), *tĕpārĕkûn* 'remove' (*Tg. Neof.*), *tĕbattĕlûn* 'destroy' (*Tg. Sam.*), *ûtĕrahăqûn rāḥāqāʾ* . . . *mĕrāḥēq lēʾăbādā* 'must reject . . . must be rejected to be destroyed' (*Tg. Onq.*; the latter clause renders *ʿărēlîm,* lit. 'as uncircumcised;' see below). The LXX renders in a similar vein *perikatharieîte tēn akatharian* 'purge its impurity', followed by Philo (*Laws* 3:50), referring to circumcision, "purified and trimmed like plants." Driver and White (1894–98) were surely correct when they wrote, "The produce is not regarded as sacred tribute any more than the firstling of an ass, of which the neck is to be broken" (cf. Exod

13:13; 34:20). That is, the fruit technically belongs to God, since it is the first yield, but it is unworthy, impure; hence it must be discarded, destroyed (cf. Ramban). Heinisch (1935) objects: in that case, the text would have stated *ûmaltem* 'you shall circumcise (the fruit)'! However, this would imply that the operation would be performed on the fruit. Before his objection can be fully answered, an investigation into the nature of the construction is warranted.

Rashi renders it literally "you shall close its closing (the meaning being that) it shall be (as it were) closed up and barred so that no benefit may be derived from it" (cf. Rashbam, Ramban, Abravanel). Ramban points out that this, too, is the extended meaning of the adjective *ʿārēl* in the metaphors *ʿerel-lēb* (Ezek 44:9), *ʿaral śĕpātāyim* (Exod 6:12), and *ʿărēlâ ʾoznām* (Jer 6:10), namely, that the heart, lips, and ear, respectively, are closed, blocked (cf. *Lev. Rab.* 25:7). Moreover, the antonym *pittaḥ hassĕmādar* 'the blossoms have opened' (Song 7:13) implies that the plant had been "closed"; it had not been "opened" to yield its bloom and fruit (Ramban).

Believing that the text explicitly states that the foreskin (*ʿorlātô*) is its fruit (*piryô*), Eilberg-Schwartz (1990: 251, n. 11) deduces that the tree symbolically stands for the penis. This interpretation clashes with the following plural predicate adjective *ʿărēlîm*, literally "uncircumcised," for two reasons: its antecedent is most likely the immediately preceding noun *piryô* 'its fruit', not the further removed *ʿēṣ* 'tree', and the alleged demand that the tree remain uncircumcised implies that its foreskin and fruit should remain on the tree! Moreover, the particle *ʾet* is not the sign of the accusative, but is the preposition "with."

Thus we must conclude that the foreskin is the fruit while it is enclosed in its bud, and *Keter Torah* has it right when it interprets this cognate accusative construction as "Don't let the fruit ripen (open) but pluck it while it is closed." The closed bud, then, is the foreskin that should be plucked before the fruit (i.e., the penis) emerges. I checked with the Berkeley Horticultural Nursery, and this is precisely what is done. The juvenile tree is *not pruned*—the branches are not thinned or trimmed (contra Eilberg-Schwartz 1990: 151–52)—but its buds are removed (alternatively, the buds are allowed to flower, and only those that are pollinated and bearing fruit are removed [S. Rattray]). That is why, in answer to Heinisch's (1935) objection, the text could not use the verb *nāmal* 'circumcise (the fruit)' since the incipient fruit inside its bud (or flower) must be removed.

The meaning (and literal rendering) of this command is, therefore: since "you shall treat as foreskin its foreskin with its fruit," pluck it before the fruit emerges.

Thus the use of the circumcision metaphor is apt. It is not a "modern abstraction" (Wellhausen 1963: 157), but analogously to the term *nāzîr* 'Nazirite', which is applied to untrimmed vines of the sabbatical and jubilee years (25:5, 11), the circumcised fruit provides another example of how religion penetrated into folk idiom (Dillmann and Ryssel 1897).

forbidden. *ʿărēlîm*, literally "uncircumcised." The plural is now comprehensible, since it refers to both parts of the closed bud: its foreskin and its fruit. The noun *pĕrî* is always a collective (the pl. *pērôt* is never attested). Its singular form is responsible for its verb *yihyeh* 'shall be' also being in the singular, precisely as in v. 24 (where the Sam., however, reads *yihyû*).

The term *'ārēl* is always derogatory (e.g., Judg 14:3; 15:18; 1 Sam 14:6; 17:26, 36; 31:4; 2 Sam 1:20; 1 Chr 10:4; cf. Gen 34:14; Josh 5:9). Hence the rendering "forbidden" is apt.

24. *sacred.* The firstfruits of produce belong to God (Num 18:12–13), as do the tithe, according to H (Lev 27:30), and the firstlings (27:26; Exod 13:2, 12; Num 18:17). However, the fruit of trees during their first three years is unworthy as an offering to God (cf. Ibn Ezra, Bekhor Shor, esp. Ramban), and like the impure firstling, according to the epic tradition (Exod 13:13), it must be destroyed (cf. Driver and White 1894–98; but the priestly tradition allows impure firstlings to be redeemed, 27:27; Num 18:15). Interestingly, the Babylonians regarded the fruit of the first four years as unfit for food (CH § 60).

Concerning the fourth year yield of fruit trees, there exists a wide disagreement in the sources. The rabbis prescribe that it may be eaten in Jerusalem or redeemed to buy food in Jerusalem, just like the tithe of Deut 14:22–27 (*y. Pe'a* 7:6; cf. Jos. *Ant.* 4.227, contra Schwartz 1987: 292, n. 14). As pointed out by Kister (1992: 578), the rabbis based their ruling, in blatant contradiction to Scripture, on the ancient practice of consuming the firstfruits of the annual grape harvest at the sanctuary (cf. Judg 9:27; Isa 62:8–9; cf. *m. Ma'aś. Š.* 5:1–5; *PRE* 29). Indeed, the rabbinic view that this verse refers to only "vineyards of the fourth year" (*b. Ber.* 35a) is also derived from ancient practice: Deut 20:6; 28:30; Jer 31:5 speak solely of the desanctification (*ḥll*, i.e., the release of the crop for common use) of the grape harvest (Kister 1992: 580). Lev 19 extends this custom to all fruit trees to imbue it with religious significance, namely, that all produce belongs to God (Philo, *Virtues* 159; cf. Knohl 1988: 23).

The desanctification of the *annual* wine crop must not be confused with the fourth-year desanctification of the produce of new vines. As indicated, the former is intimated by Judg 21:19–21 and Isa 62:9; the latter, possibly by Deut 20:6; 28:30 and Jer 31:4–5. Since Deut 20:6 refers to a temporary deferral from the army for the sake of desacralizing (*ḥll*) a vineyard, Tigay (1996: 187) wonders, "If Deuteronomy has that law [Lev 19:23–25] in mind, this would amount to a five-year deferral from the army." There are two possible answers that are actually one. If D is conforming to the law of Lev 19:23–25, then one could argue that the farmer was called up to serve in the people's army (Milgrom 1985c: 132–33) just before he was about to harvest his fifth-year crop. D, however, may be following a deviant tradition that the farmer desacralizes his crop the first year by bringing the best of his harvest to the sanctuary as a firstfruits offering. The term *ḥillēl* 'desacralize' certainly implies a sanctuary ritual, and perhaps the attested frivolity attending this event (see below) may be the reason that H shifts the celebration to the fourth year and demands that the *entire* crop be dedicated to YHWH (see NOTE on "an offering of rejoicing"). As cogently argued by Kislev (1997), the annual festival may have been observed throughout Second Temple times: "Rabban Simeon b. Gamaliel said: There were no happier days for Israel than the fifteenth of Ab and the Day of Purgation, for on them the daughters of Jerusalem used to go forth in white raiments . . . to dance in the vine-yards. And what did they say? 'Young man, lift up your eyes and see what you would choose for yourself: Set not your eyes on beauty, but set your eyes on family' " (*m. Ta'an.* 4:8).

It is hardly an accident that Ab 15 falls at the height of the grape harvest, and it was marked by drinking wine, dancing, and choosing (originally seizing, Judg 21:20–21) brides. Moreover, the Qumran sectaries preserve a ritual that the annual wine desanctification is observed at the Temple by everyone "young and old" imbibing the new wine (11QT 21:4–7). The wine, of course, was first offered on the altar—as required of a firstfruit offering—before it was desanctified and available for common use (see also *Jub* 7:1–6, 36).

Thus it may be conjectured (Kislev's reconstruction, which I amend slightly) that behind the law of 19:23–25 lies a popular folk custom to celebrate the first-fruits of the vine. It is first observed with the wine of the fourth-year produce of a new vine, which was brought to a regional sanctuary, where part was offered on the altar and the remainder imbibed by the offerer, his family, and guests. Thereby the vine became desanctified (*ḥll*; Deut 20:6; 28:30; Jer 31:4) for common use. Thereafter, the first wine (*rē'šît*; cf. vol. 1.190–91) of every annual yield was brought to the sanctuary, where it underwent a similar rite: libation on the altar followed by a celebration (*ḥll*) characterized by drinking (inebriation), dancing (orgy), and choosing or seizing women (sexual license).

H's opposition to the bacchanalian excesses of this annual rite is codified in the law of vv. 23–25. The annual firstfruits festival of the vine is abolished (rather, ignored). The one-time fourth-year observance of desanctification of the new vine remains. But its *Sitz im Leben* is obliterated, first, by imposing the rite on all fruit trees and, second, by prescribing that the entire fourth-year yield is transferred to the sanctuary, postponing its common use to the fifth year. The term *hillûlîm* is shifted in emphasis from its orgiastic implications of "unbridled rejoicing" to "rejoicing with praise (of God)."

The annual observance survives in Qumran's Temple Scroll denuded of its orgiastic tendencies. The rabbis preserve a reminiscence of the annual rite by mandating, in contradiction to the plain meaning of the text, that the fourth-year produce be limited (i.e., restored) to the grape harvest and that it belong not to the sanctuary but to the owner. In contrast to Qumran, however, but in keeping with the intention of H, the rabbis ignore the annual firstfruits festival. Indeed, they express the view that the firstfruits of wine were not accepted (*m. Ḥal.* 4:11; *Sipre* Deut. 297).

The sectaries, however, follow the plain meaning of the text: the fourth-year fruit is sacred, and hence it belongs to the priests, presumably to be eaten by them in the inner court (11QTª 38:1–7; 4QDᶜ2ii6; cf. Qimron 1987: 33) after an initial offering on the altar (11QT 60:3–4; 4QMMT B, 62–64; cf. *Jub* 7:35–37). *Jubilees* also seems to bear another tradition in its story of Noah, namely, that wine made by Noah from the fourth-year yield during the seventh month was kept until New Year's Day (the first of Nisan) of the fifth year, offered on the altar, and then drunk by Noah and his sons (*Jub* 7:1–6; contrast

7:36). In this passage, *Jubilees* has preserved a protorabbinic view that the fourth-year produce is consumed by the laity—but only in the fifth year, once it is redeemed by a sacrificial libation. I would suggest that *Jubilees* has interpreted "In the fifth year you may use its fruit [*piryô*]" (v. 25a) to be referring to the produce of the fourth year, thereby remaining true to its methodology of following Scripture rather than popular custom. *Jubilees'* interpretation is echoed in the *Genesis Apocryphon* WŠRYT LMŠTYH BYWM ḤD LŠT' ḤMYŠYT' 'and I (Noah) began drinking it on the first day of the fifth year' (12:15). Thus differing traditions were incorporated in *Jubilees* (contrast the harmonistic attempts by Albeck 1930: 33, and Baumgarten 1987b: 198).

A similar transformation occurred with tithes and firstlings: the older priestly laws ordain that these gifts belong to the sanctuary—that is, the clergy (27:26–27, 30–31; Num 18:15–18, 21–24)—whereas the newer deuteronomic law prescribes that their owners consume them at the sanctuary (Deut 14:22–23; 15:19–20). However, although the latter can be attributed to the consequences of sanctuary centralization, they may, just as in the case of the firstfruits of the vineyard, rest on older, local traditions (cf. Kaufmann 1937: 1.145, 47; Weinfeld 1973: 130; Kister 1992: 580–81).

The declaration that the fourth-year fruits are holy is probably responsible for the incorporation of this unit in Lev 19. Perhaps precisely because the nation-at-large was not bringing its fourth-year fruits to the sanctuary, the priestly legists inserted this provision in Lev 19 as a reminder that the achievement of holiness is thwarted unless it is observed. In this regard, the unit resembles vv. 5–8, which also deals with the time that sacred food may be eaten (Magonet 1983). Finally, it should be noted that I have decided against the Masoretic cantillation, moving the *'atnaḥ* from *piryô* to *qōdeš* (see below).

an offering of rejoicing. hillûlîm. This word is related to Akkadian *alālu* 'to shout *'alala'* (*CAD* 1/1: 331–32); *elēlu* 'jubilation' (*CAD* 4.80). The pejorative use of this root in *hôlēlîm* (‖ *pō'alê 'āwen* 'evildoers', Ps 5:6; ‖ *rĕšā'îm* 'wicked', Ps 73:3) and *hōlēlôt* (‖ *śiklût* 'folly', Koh 1:17) provides grounds for the assumption that originally this term described the unbridled, orgiastic celebration characterizing harvest time (probably reflected in Judg 19:22) before it became sublimated into praises sung to God at the sanctuary (cf. Isa 62:9; Joel 2:26). A vestige of the revelry implied by this term is its use in Rabbinic Aramaic *hillûlā'* 'wedding, wedding feast' (*b. Ber.* 6a, 31a; *b. Giṭ.* 57a). Indeed, a rabbinic tradition has preserved the rule that the fourth-year grapes had to be brought to Jerusalem and not allowed to be exchanged for money at home in order to ensure the element of *hillûlîm* 'revelry, jubilation' (*t. Ma'aś. Š.* 5:14, 16; *m. Ma'aś. Š.* 5:2; cf. Albeck 1952: 403).

The Sam. and *Tg. Sam.* read *ḥillûlîm*, the term used for the desanctification of the vineyard by offering its firstfruit to YHWH, thereby permitting their use for human consumption (Deut 20:6; 28:30; Jer 31:4). The rabbis and Aramaic translators were also aware of this rendering: *lō' mitmannĕ'în daršînān rabbānān bên hê' lĕhet* 'The sages did not refrain from interchanging *hêh* and *ḥet* in exegesis' (*y. Pe'a* 7:6). The halakha is stated specifically by *Tg. Ps.-J.: ûbĕsattā'*

*rĕbî'ātā' yĕhê kol 'inbêh < qûdšê tusbĕhān qădām YHWH> mitpĕraq min
kahănā'* 'On the fourth year all of its produce shall be <holy for praise before
YHWH, to be> redeemed from the priests'. As pointed out by Kister (1992: 577,
n. 21), Geiger (1857: 181–84) was probably correct in regarding *qûdšê tušbĕhān
qĕdām YHWH* as a doublet from *Tg. Onq.* However, the targum may be reflecting the opinion cited in *b. Ber.* 35a, "Whatever requires song (of jubilation,
hillûlîm) requires desanctification [*hillûlîm*]." That redemption from the priest
is not an innovation of *Tg. Ps.-J.* but transmitted by ancient targums is shown
by *Tg. Neof.*, which renders *hillĕlô* (Deut 20:6) in its margin as *pirĕkēh min
kahănā'* 'redeemed it from the priest' (Kister 1992).

Tg. Sam. interprets *hillûlîm* and *hillĕlô* (Deut 20:6) as *mĕšabbĕhîm* and
tišbĕhennâ, respectively, namely, as "praise" (cf. Tal 1981: 2.84, 377). Similarly,
the LXX (on Deut 20:6; Jer 31:5) also renders the verb *hillel* as "praise." Thus
in ancient times, both readings "desanctification, redemption" and "praise" were
preserved.

Nonetheless, it is clear which of the two readings is original in the MT. Read
as *hillûlûm* 'desanctification, redemption', it would have to be followed by
mēYHWH 'from YHWH', not by *laYHWH* 'to YHWH'. However, that this reading was even proposed demonstrates that, as I maintained above, the *'atnah* belonged (against the MT) under *qōdeš*; otherwise, the phrase *qodeš hillûlîm* 'sanctity of desanctification' would be an oxymoron.

Thus the preservation of the term *hillûlîm* adumbrates its origin in the jubi-
latory folk festival that accompanied the annual grape harvest. Further, it renders plausible that subsequently the word *qōdeš* was added by an H tradent in
order to specify that the entire crop, not just its firstfruits, must belong to the
sanctuary and, thereby, to excise the rite of its erstwhile bacchanalian character.

to YHWH. Implying that it is a priestly prebend (Ibn Ezra). I believe that
Goldberg (1977: 39) has it right by calling the priestly transformation of the
fourth-year yield as *bikkûrîm* 'firstfruits', that is, the very first edible yield belongs
to God.

25. *you may use* (with NJPS). *tō'kĕlû*. For this broader meaning of *'ākal* 'eat',
see Gen 3:17; Deut 20:14; Isa 61:6; Hos 10:13; Job 31:39; Koh 5:10; Ottosson
(1974: 239); and Akkadian *akālu* (CAD 1/1: 251–53).

its yield. tĕbû'ātô, literally "what comes in" (cf. *ûtĕbû'at hakkerem* 'the yield
of the vineyard', Deut 22:9; Num 18:30; Ps 107:37); similarly, Akkadian *erbu*
'harvest' derives from *erēbu* 'enter', and Aramaic *'ālaltêh* (Tg. Onq.) stems from
'ălal 'enter'. As pointed out by I. Kislev (1997), the term *tĕbû'â* applies to produce of the field, but to no other fruit except the vine. According to Colton
(1968: 3.496), Philo (*Plant.* 2.137) renders *prosthema humin* (LXX) as "his [i.e.,
God's] yield."

may be increased. lĕhôsîp. Elliger (1966) emends it *lĕha'ăsîp* 'to gather in', in
agreement with the Sam. *lĕhassîp* (Tg. Sam. *limĕkannĕšāh* 'to gather'). This
emendation should be rejected not only because the verb *'āsap* (Hip'îl) is unattested (and meaningless!), but because it would imply that the bounty of pro-

duce (which, presumably, God would gather in) would be limited to the fifth year. That a single year's produce will make up for the dearth of the following three years is, indeed, what is promised for the faithful observance of the consecutive sabbatical and jubilee years (25:20–22; cf. *Sipra* Qedoshim, par. 3:10). But God's blessings for depriving oneself of/from a year's crop extends over many years (Ezek 44:30; Prov 3:9–10) and many endeavors (Deut 15:9–10).

Horticultural facts also correspond with the biblical injunction regarding the taboo concerning the fruit of the juvenile tree. In the land of Israel, fruit trees reach maturity only after several years: an average of five years for date palms, five to seven years for figs and pomegranates, three to six years for grapes, and four to five years for almonds (bibliography in Eilberg-Schwartz 1990: 150–52). Ancient sources confirm this practice. In Babylonia, a date orchard ripens in five years (CH § 60)—not four years (Eilberg-Schwartz 1990: 150–52)—and a rabbinic source testifies that grapevines ripen in five years, figs in six, and olives in seven (*t. Šebi.* 1:3).

The import of this unit was neatly captured by Philo (*Virtues* § 157–59). His exposition of the text is in boldface (although his claim that the young trees need to be pruned [*Virtues* § 156] is in error):

> Thus many farmers during the spring season watch the young trees to **squeeze off at once any fruit they bear** before they **advance in quality and size**, for fear of weakening the parent plants. For, if these precautions are not taken, the result is that when they should bear fully ripened fruit they bring forth either nothing at all or abortions nipped in the bud, exhausted as they are by the laborer of prematurely bearing crops which lay such a weight upon the branches that at last they wear out the trunk and roots as well. But after three years when the roots have sunk deep in and are made firmly attached to the soil, and the trunk supported as it were on immovable foundations has grown and acquired vigour, **it will be able to bear fully in the fourth year . . . . But in this fourth year**, he commands them not to pick the fruit for their own enjoyment but to **dedicate the whole of it as a firstfruit to God**, partly as a thank-offering for the past, partly **in hope of fertility to come and the acquisition of wealth to which this will lead**.

Vv. 26–28. Unit 12: Eschewing Death and the Dead

Neither the word nor the subject of holiness is mentioned in this unit. There is no need. The God of holiness / life negates all forms of impurity/death, of which the corpse is the chief repository (vol. 1.270–78; 986–1000). Abstaining from rites in which the dead are consulted or worshiped is therefore indispensable to achieving holiness. There are seven prohibitions in this unit, the first five introduced by *lō'* and the sixth and seventh, beginning with the object, comprise a lengthened "closing deviation" (Paran 1989: 211–12; for the similar pattern in 9:8–10, see Paran 1989: 206–7). For examples of the closing deviation in this chapter, see vv. 4b, 14aβ, and 19b.

26. *You shall not eat over the blood.* lō᾽ tōʾkĕlû ʿal-haddām. There are three regnant interpretations of the idiom ʾākal ʿal haddām (also found in 1 Sam 14:33–34; Ezek 33:25):

1. The preposition ʿal in this idiom means "with," as attested in another case of ʾākal ʿal (Exod 12:8; cf. 1 Sam 14:33–34 LXX). Thus this injunction prohibits eating blood with anything (Saadiah; Baentsch 1903; Elliger 1966) or, specifically, with meat (Noth 1977). In the latter case, this prohibition would virtually be equivalent to ʾākal ʾet haddām 'eat blood' (17:10–14; Deut 12:16, 23–25; Gen 9:4; Pesh.; Dillmann and Ryssel 1897). The objection to this interpretation is obvious: ʾākal ʿal meaning "eat with" is always used with a direct object naming the other substance being eaten (Exod 12:8; Num 9:11; Hartley 1992). In passing, one should note the LXX *epi tōn oréon* 'on the mountains', reading ʿal-hārîm for ʿal-haddām (hrm < hdm), in consonance with Ezek 18:6, 11, 15; 22:9 — for which, however, there is neither textual nor exegetical warrant. Besides, the LXX is inconsistent: in 1 Sam 14:33–34 it renders ʿal(ʾel) — haddām as "with the blood."

2. ʿal means "over" ("near, at"; with ʾākal, see 2 Sam 9:7). This interpretation is held by the rabbis, giving ʿal a metaphoric sense ᾽ōkēl min habbāśār wĕhaddām bammizrāq 'eating of the flesh while the blood is still in the sprinkling bowl' (b. Sanh. 63a; cf. Sipra Qedoshim 6:1; Tg. Ps.-J.) — that is, before the blood has been offered to God on the altar. This interpretation is in accord with one of the basic tenets of the sacrificial system, that God must receive his portion (via the altar) before man (1 Sam 2:15–17, 29 LXX).

Indeed, this rationale fits the story of Saul's warriors, caught "eating over the blood" (1 Sam 14:32), because Saul, thereupon, improvises an altar (vv. 33–35) so that the slaughter of the animals will be a proper sacrifice (Brichto 1976: 39). The rationale for Saul's action would be provided by Lev 17 (esp. vv. 10–14): the blood of the slain animals must be drained on the altar to atone for human life (Schwartz 1987: 161–62).

However, the intrusion of priestly sacrificial procedures into the story of Saul is suspect. Whereas H forbids common slaughter and demands that initially all meat for the table must be an authorized sacrifice, all other sources (including P) allow for common slaughter (see NOTES on 17:3–4). Moreover, H's sophisticated rationale for the blood prohibition (17:11), labeling common slaughter as murder (vol. 1.704–13), can hardly be what Saul had in mind when he improvised a field altar (see further chap. 17, COMMENT A). The rabbinic answer, cited above, is thus also refuted.

3. By rendering ʿal literally as "over," the sense of the prohibition is clarified by its context: "According to its plain meaning, it is derivable from its context: 'You shall not practice augury or divination' " (Rashbam). As amplified by Ramban:

They would pour the blood (of the cattle) and let it gather into a pit. Demons would gather there, according to their opinion, and eat at their tables to tell them future events . . . and the people (1 Sam 14:33) would inquire of demons or of witchcraft to know their way and what to do. They would eat *over* [my emphasis] the blood in order to perform this craft. Therefore Scripture states "(Saul) said 'You have acted heretically' " (1 Sam 14:33), that is, the Lord wrought for you this day this great salvation, but you inquire of no gods. This is heresy! (see also Ibn Ezra and Radak on 1 Sam 14:32–35; Maimonides, *Guide* 3:46; and NOTES on 17:7)

Thus the expression "eating over blood" may signify a form of divination, namely, chthonic worship involving the consultation of ancestral spirits, as developed with ancient Near Eastern parallels, especially from the Grecian sphere, by Grintz (1966). His exegesis of 1 Sam 14 faces certain difficulties (see chap. 17, COMMENT A), but the case remains strong, as perceptively noted by the rabbis, that this prohibition deals with some form of magic that borders on idolatry.

If this explanation proves correct, it will be of a piece with other prohibitions against ancestor worship, which is one of H's deepest obsessions (see NOTES on 17:7; 18:21; 19:31; 20:1–6, 27; chap. 20, COMMENTS B and C; and Introduction II C).

You shall not practice augury. lōʾ těnaḥăšû. This *Piʿel* verb is found in Gen 30:27; 44:5; Lev 19:26; Deut 18:10; 1 Kgs 20:33; 2 Kgs 17:17; 21:6 (= 2 Chr 33:6). Its etiology is moot, such as related to *lāḥaš* 'whisper' from the common biradical *ḥš* 'sound softly, whisper (a charm)' (Sauermann 1955; Fabry 1985); a denominative from *nāḥāš* 'snake',—that is, observing the movements of a snake (Dietrich and Loretz 1980).

According to Ibn Ezra, this is "augury by means of cards, sticks, (other) acts and movements (whichever come first) or days and hours (that prove propitious)." The Pesh. states dogmatically "with birds." Some examples cited by the rabbis are cries of weasels, twittering of birds, bread falling from the mouth, and a stag crossing one's path (*b. Sanh.* 65b–66a; cf. *Sipra* Qedoshim 6:2).

In Mesopotamia, two kinds of augury were practiced: active, by devising techniques, and passive, by observing natural phenomena. Before 1500 B.C.E., two favorite techniques were lecanomancy (oil patterns on water in a basin; cf. Gen 44:5) and libanomancy (incense patterns); these gave way during the first millennium to sortilege (throwing lots; cf. Josh 18:8, 10) or belomancy (shooting arrows; cf. 2 Kgs 13:14–19) and rhabdomancy (releasing sticks; cf. Hos 4:12). Two favorite (passive) observations were organ formations (extispicy), especially in the liver (hepatoscopy), and astrology (cf. Isa 47:13). One verse in Ezekiel lists three such methods practiced by Nebuchadnezzar: *qilqal baḥiṣṣîm šāʾal battěrāpîm rāʾâ bakkābēd* 'He has shaken (before throwing) arrows, consulted teraphim, and inspected liver' (Ezek 21:26). The Hittites preferred throwing lots, inspecting the liver, or observing the flight of birds; the Egyptians specialized in interpreting oracles and dreams.

Divination (*qesem*), of which augury (the reading of omens) is a branch, must be scrupulously distinguished from *kiššûp* 'sorcery': the latter attempts to alter the future; the former, to predict it (cf. Kaufmann 1938: 1. 350, n. 1; 458, n. 1). The magician who claims to curse or bless is a sorcerer, whereas the one who foretells events but cannot affect them is a diviner. In Israel, sorcery is not only banned (Deut 18:10), but punished with death (Exod 22:17). Mesopotamian laws also hold that sorcery (*kišpu*) is a capital crime, but these refer to black magic—for example, hexing an individual and other such antisocial behavior (e.g., MAL § 47; CH § 2). Sorcery also had a legitimate place in Mesopotamian society, in exorcising demons and countering the effects of black magic (e.g., *Šurpu, Maqlu*). In biblical religion, sorcery in any form was, by definition, deemed ineffectual since all events were under the control of one God. It was also deemed heretical because any attempt to alter the future purported to flout and overrule the will of God. A sorcerer's technique (still not fully understood) is both condemned and ridiculed by Ezekiel: "Woe to those who sew cushions on the joints of every arm, and make rags for the head of every stature to entrap persons . . . sentencing to death persons who should not die, and to life persons who should not live, as you lie to my people who listen to lies!" (Ezek 13:18–19). Yet despite the official ban on sorcery (rather, because such legislation was necessary), we infer that it was widely practiced (see 2 Kgs 9:22; Jer 27:9; Mic 5:11; Mal 3:5; 2 Chr 33:6).

Divination is predicated on the assumption that the course of events is predictable: its advance notices are imprinted in natural phenomena or discernible in man-made devices. The following forms of divination are mentioned in Scripture: casting of lots (sortilege; 1 Sam 14:42–43), interpreting oil or water patterns in a cup (hydromancy or oleomancy; Gen 44:5–15), inspecting the shape of a sacrificial animal's liver (hepatoscopy; Ezek 21:26), and consulting (still unidentifiable) teraphim (Judg 17:5; 18:14; Hos 3:4; Ezek 21:26; Zech 10:2) or the spirits of the dead (necromancy; 1 Sam 28:9; Isa 8:19; 19:3; 29:4). In the Bible, the king of Israel consults the prophets performing divination before engaging the Arameans at Ramoth-gilead (1 Kgs 22:5). Indeed, throughout the ancient Near East, divination was widely practiced before battles in order to ascertain the will of the gods. Thus King Hammurabi of Babylon sends his *bārû*-diviner to "gather omens" before attacking Shabazum (ARM 1.11; cf. *ANET* 482). The Hittites divine by stars and birds, and the ancient Greeks consult diviners before military decisions are taken (e.g., Homer, *Iliad* 1.60–120; Xenophon, *Anabasis* 5.6.29).

Divination could be tolerated in Israel (contra Kaufmann 1960: 87–92) since, theoretically, it was not incompatible with monotheism—the diviner could always claim that he was only trying to disclose the immutable will of God. Divination was practiced and permitted not only in Egypt (Joseph, Gen 44:5) and Aram (Laban, Gen 30:27), but also in Israel (Jonathan, 1 Sam 14:9–10; Eliezer, Gen 24:14). As acknowledged by Rashi, "An omen that is not according to the form pronounced by Eliezer, Abraham's servant, or by Jonathan son of Saul is not a (permitted) divination" (*b. Ḥul.* 95b); that is, to interpret an event as an omen of good or evil is not prohibited. Indeed, according to one source, the prophet originally was called a diviner (1 Sam 9:9). Thus the diviner, in contrast to the sorcerer, was *never subject to sanctions*, either judicially or divinely. The exception was the necromancer, who was executed judicially (Lev 20:27) because he laid claim to the sorcerer's power to raise up the dead even against their will (1 Sam 28:15); his clients, however, were punished by kārēt (Lev 20:6). Molek worship was singled out as a greater capital crime (20:1–5) because it constituted both murder and a desecration of YHWH's name (see NOTES on 18:21, and chap. 20, COMMENT B). However, other diviners, summed up by the terms mĕnaḥēš 'augurer' and mĕʿônen 'diviner' (19:26), were prohibited but not sanctioned, hence tacitly accepted by H. Yet certain religious circles condemned divination as an abominable heresy (Deut 18:10–12; 1 Sam 15:23)—not that they doubted its efficacy. Rather, God had granted Israel the special boon: he communicated with them directly, through either prophets or dreams (Num 12:6; Deut 12:6–8; 13:2–6). The case of Balaam is illustrative of the pentateuchal nonpriestly sources. Although a pagan, Balaam was a worshiper of YHWH (Num 22:13, 18–19; 23:12, 26), and YHWH responded positively to him (22:20) and negatively, when he attempted to play the sorcerer by "compelling" YHWH to curse Israel against his will—something that Balaam knew full well was bound to fail. Balaam reaches the full stature of an Israelite prophet when he abandons his divinatory techniques and seeks a direct revelation (Num 24:1; cf. 23:23; details in Milgrom 1990a: 471–74). It should also be noted that both the priestly and the nonpriestly Tent of Meeting functioned as a vehicle for oracles (e.g., Exod 33:7–11; Num 7:89; 11:16–17; Milgrom 1990a: 386–87). But Moses and his successors, the prophets, were vouchsafed a direct revelation without recourse to divination. Nonetheless, the official cult did sanction one divinatory medium: the Urim and Thummim carried on the (high) priest's ephod (Exod 28:30–35; 1 Sam 2:28; 14:3; 23:6, 9; 28:6, 30:7). Cryer's (1994: 297) claim that the Temple priests practiced hepatoscopy is completely unfounded. He justifiably corrects those who aver that the caudate lobe was used in divination by pointing out that the entire liver (hepatoscopy) as well as the other extra were employed not realizing, however, that he contradicts himself. As I have written, "the rest of the liver . . . would also have been consigned to the altar" and not allowed to be eaten (vol. 1.208 on Lev 3:4).

or divination. wĕlōʾ tĕʿônēnû. There are as many interpretations as interpreters of the etymology: (1) a denominative of ʿānān 'cloud', namely, observing the shapes and movements of clouds (e.g., ʿônĕnîm, Isa 2:6; Jer 27:9; Mic 5:11; Ibn Ezra[1]); (2) a Polel verb from the root ʿwn, hence mĕʿônēn (Deut 18:10; Ibn Ezra[2]); (3) a denominative of ʿayin 'eye', thus the rabbinic term for hypnotist mĕʾaḥāz ʿēnayim, literally "he who seizes eyes" (b. Sanh. 65b); (4) a denominative of ʿônâ 'season', that is, "one who calculates the times and hours, saying: 'Today is propitious for setting forth; tomorrow for making purchases'" (R. Akiba, b. Sanh. 65b); (5) related to Arabic ġannat 'nasal twang', the sounds made by a necromancer (BDB; Snaith 1967; Hartley 1992); (6) related to Arabic ʿunna 'appear', thus one who causes to appear (i.e., raises spirits); and (7) from Ugaritic ʿnn, Canaanite ʿanini (Egyptian ḏd) 'recite (charms)' (Albright 1968: 122, n. 30).

The ʿônēn / mĕʿônēn is always coupled with the mĕnaḥēš (Deut 18:10; 2 Kgs

21:6; 2 Chr 33:6), and each probably involves a different technique of divination for the Deuteronomist, whereas H regards their practice as typical. Blenkinsopp (1995: 12–13) has proposed that the *ʿōněnâ* of Isa 57:3, rendered "sorceress" on the basis of the purported etymology no. 6, engages in some sexual activity in the cult of the dead. This and all the other interpretations are sheer speculation.

The coupling of the verbs *niḥēš* and *ʿōnēn* undercuts Cryer's (1994: 284–86) claim that *niḥēš* is the "all-purpose verb" for "divination by all means of unexpected 'signs.'" To be sure, *niḥēš* is the sole verb used in Gen 30:27; 44:5, 15; Num 24:1; 1 Kgs 20:33, but it is grouped with a host of other divinatory verbs in Deut 18:10; 2 Kg 21:6 (= 2 Chr 33:6), where, however, it occurs in tandem with *ʿōnēn*, as in our verse. Moreover, when the Deuteronomist sums up his list of nine magical practices (Deut 18:10–11), he cites only two of them: *měʿanĕnîm* and *qōsĕmîm* (v. 14). Indeed, when Ezekiel mentions the various divinatory means employed by Nebuchadrezzar (Ezek 21:26), he uses *qāsam* by itself (vv. 27–28, 34). Thus if one wished to choose an "all-purpose verb," it should be *qāsam*.

First, let it be noted that *qāsam* shares the stage with *niḥeš* (Num 23:23; 2 Kgs 17:17; and Num 22:7, balancing Num 24:1). Ezekiel also couples it with *ḥāzâ*, which by all accounts is a general term (Ezek 13:6, 9, 23; 22:28; cf. Jer 14:14) as does Micah (Mic 3:6–7). Here, again, in Micah's summary verse *qāsam* occurs by itself (Mic 3:11). Indeed, the fact that *qāsam* outnumbers *niḥēš* twenty-one to ten suffices to indicate which is the more general term. In truth, however, both terms are mercurial; we cannot be sure whether they are general or specific, since the context is not determinative. But even where they occur in divinatory catalogues, their precise meanings remain nebulous.

27. *You shall not round off. lōʾ taqqîpû.* The verb *nāqap* (*Qal*) means "go round" (the year, Isa 29:1). The *Hipʿil hiqqîp* therefore means transitive "circle, surround" (e.g., Josh 6:3, 11; Ps 48:3, 13) and in this verse "cut around" (LXX; cf. M. Cohen 1993: 300–301). The nominal form *tĕqûpâ*, then, logically, denotes "cycle, circle" (Exod 34:22; 1 Sam 1:20; Ps 19:7). Others derive the verb from Arabic *naqafa* 'smash', citing Isa 10:34; Job 19:26, leaving the *Hipʿil* to be rendered "cut, destroy."

the side-growth on your head. pĕʾat rōʾšĕkem. This tonsure is defined by the rabbis as "equalizing the sides in back of the ear with the forehead" (*Sipra* Qedoshim 6:3; *b. Mak.* 20b)—that is, forming a perfect circle (cf. Jos. *Apion* 1.173). The (Arab) bedouin are described by Jeremiah as *qĕṣûṣê pēʾâ* 'whose (temples') side growth is clipped' (Jer 9:25 [which the Tg. renders *maqpê pātāʾ*]; 25:23; 49:32; cf. Homer, *Iliad* 2:542; Herodotus 3:8; Smith 1927: 325, n. 2). The singular *pēʾâ* is a collective and is equivalent to the plural *pēʾōt* 'temples' or, as explained in *Keter Torah*, "the cheek of each temple." The word *pēʾâ*, in general, means "edge"; it can also mean "corner," but not in this chapter (see NOTE on v. 9). This tonsure is clearly illustrated in a fourteenth-century Egyptian tomb painting of captive Ethiopians (*EBWL* 1987: 139, fig. 3).

The function of this haircut becomes clear when vv. 27–28 are compared with three similar verses (in bold print):

1. *lōʾ taqqîpû pěʾat rōʾšěkem wělōʾ tašbît ʾet pěʾat zěqānekā wěśeret lānepeš lōʾ tittěnû bibśarkem*
   You shall not round off the side-growth on your head, and you shall not destroy the edge of your beard. Gashes in your flesh you shall not make for the dead (vv. 27–28aα).

2. *loʾ-yiqrěḥû(yqrḥhK) qorḥâ běrōʾšām ûpěʾat zěqānām lōʾ yěgallēḥû ûbibśārām lōʾ yiśrětû śārātet*
   They (the priests) shall not make any bald patches on their heads, or shave off the edge of their beards, or make gashes in their flesh (21:5)

3. *lōʾ titgōdědû wělōʾ-tāśîmû qorḥâ bên ʿênêkem lāmēt*
   You shall not gash yourselves or shave the front of your heads for the dead (Deut 14:1b)

4. *wěrōʾšām lōʾ yěgallēḥû*
   They (the priests) shall not shave their heads (Ezek 44:20aα)

The prohibitions given the priesthood (21:5) are nearly the same enjoined upon the laity. The two initial prohibitions (v. 27a; 21:5aα) seem, at first sight, to be contradictory: chap. 19 proscribes the removal of only the side locks, while chap. 21 prohibits making bald patches in any part of the head. The contradiction disappears once the different addressees are recognized: whereas only the side locks are forbidden to the laity, the entire head is forbidden to the priesthood. This conclusion is supported by Deut 14:1bβ: "You shall not shave [lit. "put baldness"] the front of your heads [lit. "between the eyes"]," a tonsorial art practiced, for example, by the ancient Greek tribe, Abantes (Homer, *Iliad* 2.542). Here, again, the prohibition against baldness is enjoined upon the laity, but this time not at the temples, but on the front part of the head (see Deut 6:8 and Ug. *qdqd* ‖ *bn ʿnm*). It would seem that H and D reflect the same tonsorial custom — to shave part of the scalp. Implied is that shaving other parts of the scalp was permitted. Indeed, that Isaiah avers to his fellow Judeans "My Lord God of Hosts summoned on that day to weeping and mourning [lit. "breast beating"], to baldness [*qorḥâ*] and girding with sackcloth" (Isa 22:12) may indicate that baldness not only prevailed as a mourning rite, but even could claim divine approval (see also Isa 3:24; Amos 8:10). The priests, however, as 21:5 avers, and as Ezek 44:20 confirms, are forbidden to shave any part of the head.

The deuteronomic passage just cited is significant because it explicitly states the purpose of this rite: *lāmēt* 'for the dead'. That we are dealing with a pagan mourning rite is confirmed by Isa 15:2bβ (= Jer 48:37a): *běkol-rōʾšāyw qorḥâ kol-zāqān gěrûʿâ* 'On every head [reading *kol-rōʾš* with Jer 48:37] is baldness and every beard is shorn [reading *gědûʿâ* with many MSS]'. The Moabites depicted here are manifestly engaged in mourning, and it is these rites that are expressly forbidden to the Israelites (Ibn Ezra; see also Jer 47:5; Ezek 27:31). The deutero-nomic prohibition is headed by "You are children of YHWH your God" (Deut 14:1a). As noted by von Rad (1966: 101), a contrast is thereby struck between the prohibition against the worship of the dead and the worship of Israel's God. Similarly, as observed by Blenkinsopp (1995: 11–15), a contrast is established between eight prohibited foreign practices (Deut 18:9–14), five of which prob-ably refer to ancestor worship, and prophetic mediation for Israel (v. 15).

Moreover, the hair symbolized the life force of the individual, and locks of hair were laid in tombs or funeral pyres in pre-Islamic Arabia (Smith 1927: 324, n. 1) and ancient Syria (Lucian, *De Dea Syria* 60) as well as brought to the sanc-tuary as dedicatory offerings (details in NOTE on 21:5). In other words, these pro-hibitions ban idolatrous rites. However, they are so entrenched in Israelite life (cf. Ezek 7:18; Mic 1:16) that H and D are forced to limit baldness to part of the head, leaving the total proscription of baldness (of any degree) to the priests (21:5; Ezek 44:20). In any event, it should be clear that the ban on cutting hair at the corners and gashing oneself for the dead properly belongs to the priest-hood (21:5), to judge by its rationale (21:6; cf. Greenberg 1975: 102–3). That H and D follow suit (though in less extreme form) is due to their extension of (priestly) holiness to all Israel. Carmichael (1976: 4) opines suggestively that D's motivation for prohibiting the removal of hair and lacerating the flesh "for the dead" (Deut 14:1) is to separate life from death (see also Carmichael 1979)—a postulate that dominates P (vol. 1.766–68, 1000–1004).

The verb *taqqîpû* 'round off' implies that the side locks may not be removed, even with scissors (Wessely 1846), and many Orthodox Jews will leave their side locks untrimmed throughout their lives. The rabbis, however, basing themselves on the verb *yĕgallēhû* 'shave' in the priestly prohibition (21:5), proscribe only the use of a razor (*Sipra* Qedoshim 6:5; *Mo'ed Qat.* 3:5).

and you shall not destroy the edge of your beard. wĕlō' tašhît 'et pĕ'at zĕqānekā. The LXX, Sam., and Pesh. read the plural *tašhîtû* in consonance with the plural verbs in the rest of the unit, which leads Elliger (1966: 24a), with many mod-erns, to follow suit and change this prohibition into the plural (see the pointed opposition of Kornfeld 1952: 55–68) This prohibition is repeated in 21:5, cited above, expressed as *lō' yĕgallēhû* 'Do not shave off (the edge of the beard)'. The two, however, are not equivalent. Israelites are forbidden to "destroy" their beards, which they would be wont to do in time of emotional stress and anguish, particularly in mourning: "I rent my garment and robe, **I tore hair out of my head and beard,** and sat desolate" (Ezra 9:3). The priests, however, are forbid-den to "shave" their beards, a deliberate act, performed for aesthetic or idola-trous reasons (as pagan priests).

In some ancient societies, including Israel, the beard was the prized symbol of manhood, and its mutilation was considered the greatest disgrace and pun-ishment (2 Sam 10:4–5; Isa 7:20). Among the Greeks, an old Spartan law for-bids the ephori, from the moment of their taking office, to clip their beards; and those who fled before the enemy in battle were forced to appear in public with half-shorn beards (cited by Kalisch 1867–72).

Taking the singular *pĕ'at* as a collective, the rabbis ordain that there are five "edges" on the beard: two on each side (on the upper and lower cheek) and the tip (*m. Mak.* 3:5; *Sipra* Qedoshim 6:5). Their interpretation might find support in a description of a Ugaritic rite of mourning: *yhdy.lhm.wdqn* 'he cut (his) cheeks and beard' (*CTA* 5 VI:19; Lewis 1989: 100), which Gibson (1978: 73) actually renders "he shaved (his) side-whiskers and beard" (a fuller text is cited below). However, Loewenstamm (1980: 459–62) has shown that *hdy* is related to Arabic *had'a*, *hadda* 'lacerate', and *dqn* (Heb. *zaqan*) also denotes "chin" (cf. Lev 13:2a–30; 14:9). Hence the rendering should be "he cut his cheeks and chin" (contra Anderson 1991: 62, n. 6) and is part of the laceration process described in the entire context (ll. 18–22; see below).

28. *Gashes. wĕśeret.* The fact that the object is first in this verse is a sign that the unit is coming to an end (as vv. 4b, 14aβ, 19b; Paran 1983: 148; Schwartz 1987: 293, n. 3). The noun *śeret* and its denominative *śārat* (21:5; Zech 12:3; see below) are related to Akkadian *šarāṭu* 'tear to pieces' and Arabic *šarata* 'slit'. Its meaning in BH is the same, as verified by the comparable expressions in the mourning prohibitions, cited above: *yiśrĕṭû śārāṭet* (21:5b) and *lō' titgōdĕdû* (Deut 14:1bα). That *gdd* I (*Hitpolel*) means "cut, gash" is established by its Semitic cognates, Akkadian *gadādu* 'chop' (*CAD* 5.8) and Old South Arabic *gdd* (*HALAT* 1.169), and, above all, by its biblical contexts—for example, *wayyitgōdĕdû kĕmišpāṭām baḥărābôt ûbarĕmāhîm 'ad-sĕpok-dām 'ălêhem* 'They (the Baal priests)—, —— themselves, according to their practice, with knives and spears until blood streamed over them' (1 Kgs 18:28). There can be no doubt that the missing word is "gash," and we have every reason to concur with R. Yoshi that *śārat* is equivalent to *hitgōdad* and also means "gash" (*b. Mak.* 21a).

That gashing oneself was a Baal-cult rite is also demonstrated in the Ugaritic text *KTU* 1.5; 6.11–12 (cf. Spronk 1986: 245). A much later survival in the same geographic area as Ugarit is reported by Lucian (*De Dea Syria* 50): the Galli priests and their devotees gash their arms (note *yādayim gĕdūdōt* 'gashed arms', Jer 47:5). Lacerating the body, however, is more often recorded as a rite of mourning (Deut 14:16; Jer 16:6; 41:5; 47:5; 48:37). This is also true in the Ugaritic texts, an example of which follows (biblical citations indicate parallels):

10. *ḫlq. zbl. b'l. arṣ.*
11. *apnk. lṭpn. il* (12) *dpid.*
    yrd. lksi. ytb (13) *lhdm*[.]
    [*w*]*l. hdm. ytb* (14) *larṣ*[.]
    yṣq 'mr (15) *un. lriš.*
    'pr. plṭt (16) *l. qdqdh.*
    lpš. yks (17) *mizrtm.*
    ġr. babn (18) *ydy.*
    psltm. by'r
19. *whdy. lhm. wdqn.*
20. *yṭlṭ. qn. dr'h*[.]
    yḥrṭ (21) *kgn. qp lb.*

kʿmq yṯlṯ (22) *bmt.*
yšu. gh [.] *wyṣḥ*
bʾl. mt

"the prince, lord of the earth, has perished."
Thereupon Latipan kindly god
came down from his throne (Isa 47:1; Jon 3:6), sat on the footstool;
and from the footstool, he sat on the ground (Ezek 26:16).
He poured straw of mourning on his head
dust of wallowing on his crown (Ezek 27:30).
For clothing he covered himself with a loincloth (Amos 8:10),
he cut his skin with a stone (Exod 4:25; Josh 5:2–3)
incisions with a razor,
he gashed (his) cheeks and chin,
he raked the bone of his arm (Jer 48:37)
he plowed his chest like a garden
Like a valley he raked his back.
He raised his voice and shouted:
Baal is dead." (*CTA* 5 VI:10–23; *ANET* 139; cf. 19 IV:173, 184)

The close association of these mourning rites with the worship of Baal, as attested in 1 Kgs 18:28, may be responsible for their proscription in H and D.

Laceration as a mourning rite seems to have been universal in the ancient Near East. It is attested as early as the *Epic of Gilgamesh* (VIII, 11, 21 [*ANET* 88a]). Herodotus (4.71) reports that at the bier of his king a Scythian "chops off a piece of his ear, crops his hair close, makes a cut all around his arm, lacerates his forehead and his nose and thrusts an arrow through his left hand." Homer offers evidence of similar rites (*Iliad* 2.700; 11.293; 19.284). For the pre-Islamic Arabs, see Smith (1907: 249). Anthropologists and folklorists have provided evidence of its widespread practice among primitive peoples (Gaster 1969: 590–602).

That laceration (and tonsure, v. 27) were common mourning rites in Israel is attested by Jer 16:6: *ûmētû gĕdōlîm ûqĕṭannîm bāʾāreṣ hazzōʾt lōʾ yiqqābērû wĕlōʾ-yispĕdû lāhem wĕlōʾ yisgōdēd wĕlōʾ yiqqārēaḥ lāhem* 'Great and small alike shall die in this land. They shall not be buried; and no one shall lament them, nor lacerate and tonsure themselves for them'.

Schmidt (1996: 287, 290) suggests a plausible rationale for laceration rites during mourning: "self-mutilation might be more appropriately viewed as an attempt to assuage the envy which the dead possesses for the living by inflicting suffering on oneself or as a desperate attempt to disguise oneself from ghosts on the haunt by making one unrecognizable. . . . Thus, self-mutilation as mourning so blurred the worlds of life and death in the tightly constricted and distinct worlds mapped out in the priestly and dtr legislations that they were singled out for censorship" (see also Feldman 1977: 79–108; for other explanations, see Tigay 1996: 136). The binary opposition of life–death is congruent with the thrust of the entire chapter (and, indeed, most of P and H) whose central theme is the opposition of holiness / life to impurity / death.

In the same vein, Gerstenberger (1996: 276–77) plausibly suggests that these rites were dedicated to underworld deities, whereas "Yahweh was the God only of life and of the living, and not of the deceased (Pss 6:6; 88:6)." Nonetheless, it should not be forgotten that certain acts of mourning were considered legitimate: weeping and lamenting (e.g., Gen 50:1–3), tearing the clothes (Gen 44:13), wearing sackcloth and ashes (2 Sam 3:31; Ps 35:13), and composing lamentations and eulogies (2 Sam 1:17–27).

It should not be overlooked that virtually the identical prohibition is enjoined upon priests (21:5). Tigay (1996: 136) offers the rationale that self-inflicted bald spots and gashes would desecrate priests "because they are comparable to bodily defects." However, 21:16–23 lists only priests who bear *permanent* defects. The signs of laceration and self-inflicted baldness are temporary and rapidly disappear. Temporary defects, such as facial boils, are not even discussed. Presumably, until such visible blemishes heal, they would disqualify a priest from officiating. They would probably fall into the same category as drunkenness (10:9), nakedness (Exod 28:42–43), and unwashedness (Exod 30:19), which incur death by divine agency if the priest would dare officiate while displaying any of these conditions. Also, the mourning rites prohibited to Israelites are self-inflictions. But blemishes caused by birth or disease (21:18–20), the result of natural causes, detract from a priest's holiness, but have no effect on Israelites. Simply, the rationale is straightforward: those who are holy (priests) and those who aspire to holiness (Israel) are desecrated by these practices (see COMMENT).

for the dead. lānepeš. The word nepeš 'person' can also denote "corpse" (e.g., 21:1; Num 5:2; Hag 2:13), but it is an abbreviation for nepeš mēt 'a dead person' (21:11; Num 6:6). The qāmaṣ under the *lamed* instead of a *pataḥ* in a nonpausal word is puzzling. Ibn Ezra suggests that the change was made for easier pronunciation. I submit, however, that the cantillation is responsible: the rĕbî'a (under lānepeš), which acts more like a pausal accent, slowing down its pronunciation (but see GKC § 102h, i).

and tattoos. (ûkĕtōbet) qa'ăqa'. The etymology of this hapax is unknown. Tg. Onq. renders rûšmîn ḥārîtîn 'incised signs', or brands. It was customary to brand a slave with his owner's name (e.g., Babylonia, CH §§ 226–27; Elephantine [with a yod], Cowley 28). In Egypt, captives were branded with the name of a god or Pharaoh; the former captives belonged to the priesthood, and the latter to the state (Breasted 1906: 3.§414; 4.§405). Thus devotees of a god would also be branded with its name. This clearly is the interpretation of both Philo (*Laws* 1.58) and the rabbis (t. Mak. 4:15). Lucian (*De Dea Syria* 59) reports that stigmata of the god were branded on the heads and necks of its adherents. Smith (1907: 249–51) avers (also reported in the ḥadīth, Bokhāri 7.58) that pre-Islamic Arab women would tattoo their hands, arms, and gums.

It should not be overlooked that this prohibition bans the legally accepted practice of marking a perpetual Israelite slave (Exod 21:6 [SE]; Deut 15:17 [D]). This fact alone should indicate that H abolishes the statute of perpetual slavery, and, as demonstrated by 25:39–43 (see NOTE), H abolishes Israelite slavery entirely. Since H maintains perpetual slavery for a resident alien or foreigner (25:44–46), it can be presumed that it also permitted such slaves to be tattooed. This practice is confirmed by the rabbis *harôšēm ʿal ʿabdô šellōʾ yibraḥ pāṭûr* '(The owner) who marks his slave so that he does not run away is exempt (from the prohibition on Lev 19:28)' (*t. Makk.* 4:15, a reference I owe to Greengus). Thus instead of searching (in vain) for a mourning rite to explain the juxtaposition of tattooing to laceration, tattooing should be regarded as an independent prohibition aimed, perhaps among other objectives, at the abolition of slavery in Israel.

A probable reference to this rite is found in Isa 44:5: *wĕzeh yiktōb yādô laYHWH* 'this one will incise on his hand "belongs to YHWH" '. Indeed, the rabbis record the opinion that a person does not violate this prohibition *ʿad šeyyiktōb šēm haššēm šenneʾĕmar ʿûkĕtōbet qaʿăqaʿ lōʾ tittĕnû bākem ʾănî YHWH* 'until he incises (his flesh) with the name of the Name (of YHWH), for it is written "and tattoos you shall not put on yourselves I YHWH" ' (v. 28b; *m. Mak.* 3:6), interpreting "I YHWH" that it is YHWH's name that is forbidden; otherwise, a tattoo is permissible. But as Albeck (1953: 4.467) points out, the Tosepta records a variant and, probably, more correct tradition that the rabbinic prohibition is restricted to tattooing the name of another god (*t. Mak.* 4:15; cf. Philo, *Laws* 1.58).

In contrast, according to the biblical codes (H and D), the Israelite wears phylacteries on his arm and forehead as a sign of his adherence to his God (Exod 13:9, 16; Deut 6:8; 11:18; cf. Rashbam on Exod 13:9 and Ibn Ezra's counteropinion), but he may not disfigure his body made in the divine image (Wenham 1979), connecting the two halves of v. 28, interpreting tatoos as a mourning rite for the dead (but see above).

you shall not put. lōʾ tittĕnû. The Temple Scroll clarifies *LWʾ TKTWBW* 'you shall not write/inscribe' (11QT 48:9). Since the two prohibitions in this verse employ the same verb *tittĕnû*, it would have been possible, and preferable in normal prose, to write them as a single prohibition: *wĕśereṭ lānepeš ûkĕtōbet qaʿăqaʿ loʾ tittĕnû bākem*, proof of H's poetic style in composing a rhythmically balanced, double prohibition (cf. Paran 1989: 130).

V. 29. Unit 13: Prostitution, Cultic or Secular?

Cultic prostitution, meaning intercourse with strangers as a sacred rite to increase fertility, is nonexistent in the ancient Near East. This is the conclusion arrived at by the most recent investigators of the subject (Hooks 1985; Gruber 1983a; 1986; Goodfriend 1992; van der Toorn 1989a; 1992). The following is their evidence:

The Mesopotamian data show that the *qadištu*, the alleged cult prostitute, was most often a wet nurse or a midwife. Even when this term refers to a prostitute who plied her trade in the temple area, she was not part of its personnel. She could marry, could bear children, and did not wear a veil (cf. Tamar, Gen 38:14). Her profits were a source of income for the temple, but not as a part of a fertility ritual. The same obtained in Israel (see below). The only exception is the Neo-Babylonian Ishtar temple of Uruk, which hired out members of its lower female personnel as concubines, but the relations between the hierodule and the man were conducted in the latter's home. The purpose was pleasure for the man and income for the temple, but it was not a fertility rite.

The Bible is alleged to speak of cultic prostitution as a historical fact on the basis of Gen 38:20–23; Deut 23:18–19; 1 Kgs 14:23–24; 15:11–12; 22:47; 2 Kgs 23:7; Hos 4:13–14—all on the assumption that the term *qādēš / qĕdēšâ* stands for a "cult prostitute." The parallelism between *qĕdēšâ* and *zônâ* in Gen 38, Deut 23, and Hos 4 makes it clear that the *qĕdēšîm* did engage in sexual activities. The fact that at one point *qĕdēšîm* had special rooms in the Jerusalem Temple (2 Kgs 23:7), something intolerable to the deuteronomic reformers, indicates that their practice was condoned and encouraged by the clergy, but the motive was economic, not cultic.

Judah's friend Hirah the Adullamite inquires about the whereabouts of the *qĕdēšâ* (Gen 38:21), putting a better face on Judah's rendezvous with the supposed *zônâ*, for then as a devotee of a sanctuary, her wages would have been transmitted to its coffers. There is no doubt that sexual debauchery is frequently associated with sanctuaries, especially at festivals, as testified by Hos 4:13–14 (cf. Exod 32:5–6; Num 25; Ps 106:28–31). Van der Toorn (1992: 510–11) cites the Mesopotamian case of a young woman who is violated "at a festival of the city" (MAL A §55) and the analogous case of the wine festival of Shilo, where the Benjaminites are allowed to seize their wives by force, and the possible vestige of this rite on the fifteenth of Ab (in the middle of the wine harvest), when Israelite girls dressed in white, danced in the vineyards, and invited the boys to make their choice (*b. Ta'an.* 26b). Van der Toorn also offers the attractive proposal that women would have recourse to prostitution as a means of paying their sacrificial vows, which their husbands either were unaware of or denied (cf. Num 30:8–9), a situation that may describe the adulterous woman of Prov 7:14.

In any event, the prostitute's fee *'etnān / 'etnâ* may have provided the Temple with a significant income (Mic 1:7), but it was condemned by the Deuteronomist (Deut 23:19) and derided by the prophets (Isa 23:17–18; Ezek 16:31, 34, 41; Hos 9:1). Priests were forbidden to marry prostitutes, and their promiscuous daughters were burned (Lev 21:7, 14), which presupposes that an Israelite was permitted to marry a former prostitute (cf. Hos 3:1–3).

In sum, there is no evidence of cultic prostitution in the ancient Near East (see also Gruber 1983a; Westenholz 1989). Some prostitutes may have worked in the service of the temple, but not as a cultic functionary engaged in fertility rites. An ancillary conclusion that Molek worship involved sacrificing to Molek the children who were newly born to cult prostitutes (Elliger 1955: 17; Zimmerli 1979: 1.344) must be dismissed out of hand (see also NOTE on "to be sacrificed," 18:21 [end]).

You shall not degrade. *'al-tĕḥallēl.* The use of *ḥillēl* here is figurative, not "desecrate" but "degrade" (Gen 49:4; cf. Isa 23:9, where *lĕḥallēl* is paralleled by *lĕhāqēl* 'disgrace' and is the antonym of *nikbaddê* 'honored'; Boleh 1991–92). In that case, however, why does not the text say straightway *tazneh* 'make (her) a prostitute' (v. 29b; cf. 21:9)? The choice is deliberate, and it accounts for the inclusion of this prohibition in this chapter: she belongs to a people whose goal is holiness, and her father is depriving her of her right and duty to attain this goal (Wessely 1846). Note the similarity between the daughter of an Israelite and the daughter of a priest (21:9): the latter will also degrade (lit. "desecrate") her father (see NOTE on 21:9), and both equally must strive for holiness. Weinfeld (1983b) proposes a secondary meaning of *ḥillel* 'throw to the ground' (e.g., Pss 74:7; 89:40), especially in a case of rape (Ezek 28:7–8, 16; Lam 2:1–2), which would account here for the association of *ḥillēl* and *zānâ*.

MT *'al* is questioned by Bright (1973), which turns this prohibition into an exhortation (contrast vv. 11–19, 26–28, and see NOTES on vv. 4a, 31). He may be correct in preferring LXX *lō'*. Note as well that this verse switches to the singular, which Abravanel explains as being addressed to the fathers as individuals, since each has control over his daughter.

by making her a prostitute. lĕhaznôtāh. As most every other *Hipʿil*, this one is transitive (e.g., Exod 34:16; 2 Chr 21:11, 13), but Hosea uses it intransitively (Hos 4:10, 18; 5:3). The *lamed* here is equivalent to the *beth* of means, as *tĕkalleh . . . liqṣōr* (v. 9) = *bĕquṣreka* (23:22). Another example of this *lamed* is *'ereṣ kî teḥṭā' lî lim'ōl-ma'al* 'If a land were to sin against me by committing sacrilege' (Ezek 14:13a; Boleh 1991–92).

The *Hipʿil* has also been explained as implying permission, "by permitting her to become a prostitute" (Collins 1977). The difference between the two interpretations of the *Hipʿil* is that the former (accepted in the translation) implies a profit motive on the part of the father—one that would accord with the situation described in Hos 4:13–14, where daughter-prostitutes (*zōnôt*), presumably under their fathers' orders, ply their trade at the sanctuary. What father, however, would not look askance at his daughter's promiscuity, knowing that her bridal price as well as her reputation are considerably diminished?

so that the land may not be prostituted. wĕlō'-tizneh hā'āreṣ. Land (*'ereṣ*) is a metonym for "people of the land" (*'anšê hā'āreṣ*) (cf. Gen 41:36, 57; Ezek 14:13; esp. Hos 1:2 *zānōh tizneh hā'āreṣ* 'the (people of) the land will surely stray [lit. "will be prostituted"]'). Alternatively, *'ereṣ* can be rendered "civilization," as a metonym for the cultural milieu (Zipor 1991, citing Gen 6:11–13). However, when *'ereṣ* is the object of an action (e.g., polluting), the land alone is intended, in keeping with H's theology that the promised land is polluted by Israel's sins (see INTRODUCTION to 18:24–30, and Introduction II I). Thus in *watahănîpî 'ereṣ biznûtayik* 'and you polluted the land by your harlotries' (Jer 3:2), only the land is intended (see below).

and the land be filled with lewdness. ûmālĕ'â hā'āreṣ zimmâ. As a result of prostitution, the land will be filled with lewdness (Saadiah). Here, again, "land" is a metaphor for "people" (Wessely 1846, citing *mālĕ'â hā'āreṣ dē'â 'et-YHWH* 'the (peoples of) land will be filled with the knowledge of YHWH', Isa 11:9) or a possible metonymy for "civilization" (Zipor 1991, citing *watiššāḥēt hā'āreṣ lipnê hā'ĕlōhîm wattimmālē' hā'āreṣ ḥāmās*, which, he claims, can be rendered "the civilization became corrupt before God and the civilization was filled with lawlessness," Gen 9:11; cf. v. 13).

For *zimmâ* 'lewdness', see the NOTE on 18:17. In H, it has only a sexual connotation (20:14; Judg 20:6; Jer 13:27; Ezek 22:11; 23:35; Job 31:11). The term *zimmâ* may deliberately have been chosen because its nationwide indulgence leads to exile (18:17; 24–28: D. Stewart, written communication). There is no doubt that *zimmâ* bears the metaphoric meaning "lewdness" in many of its twenty-eight attestations. I suggest, in addition to that in H it carries the legal connotation of "plotting, scheming." This sense certainly fits the sexual crimes of a woman–daughter or mother arrangement (18:17; 20:14). It may also apply here. After all, what does "the land filled with lewdness" really mean? Rather than relying on the admittedly weak explanation that land is a metaphor for people, perhaps this rationale should be understood literally: the land will be filled with similar scheming; fathers everywhere will follow this example and begin to prostitute their daughters.

The absence of *'ănî* YHWH (*'ĕlōhêkem*) to signify the end of the unit is due to the third-person ending (see NOTE on v. 8).

V. 30. Unit 14: Sabbath and Sanctuary

The sabbath took on heightened importance for the prophets of the seventh century who declared that its observance was essential as an antidote to the rampant assimilation under King Manasseh (Zeph 1) and, hence, a determinant of Israel's national destiny (Jer 17:19–27; Greenberg 1971a). It became indispensable to Israel's survival during the Babylonian Exile when all the festivals were suspended because of the loss of the Temple (see NOTES on 23:3). This may be the reason why this verse is repeated verbatim in 26:2, which (as explained in its NOTE) serves the purpose (with 26:1) of summoning up the essence of the Decalogue and of adding the weekly sabbath to the septennate as factors in Israel's national survival.

It can be demonstrated that the sabbath pericope that heads H's festival calendar (23:2aβ–3) is an exilic composition (see NOTE on 23:3). Similarly, the transitional passage 26:1–2, in which the sabbath injunction is ensconced, must also be assigned an exilic provenance. The same chronological verdict must be rendered for the sabbath pericopes that head the prescriptive and descriptive texts of the Tabernacle construction (Exod 31:12–17; 35:1–3). The same dating, however, does not hold for this verse, since it equates the sabbath with the sanctuary. Because the sanctuary exists, the verse is preexilic.

It is instructive to observe Ezekiel's literary technique in turning this verse into a weapon for his indictment against Israel: *ṭimmĕ'û 'et-miqdāšî bayyôm hahû' wĕ'et šabbĕtôtay hillēlû* 'on the same day they defiled **my sanctuary** and desecrated **my sabbaths**' (Ezek 23:38; cf. 20:16, 24). Here, I submit, is a reference to the Molek cult practiced at the foot of the Temple Mount, which also enabled its adherents to worship at the Temple on the very same day (details in NOTE on 20:3).

The sabbath is indispensable to achieving holiness, for by observing it Israel sanctifies it, as expressly commanded in the Decalogue (Exod 20:8; Deut 5:12;

cf. Ezek 20:20), and by violating it, Israel desecrates it (Ezek 20:16, 21, 24; 22:8; see NOTE on v. 3b). Reverence for the sanctuary adds a new aspect to holiness in this chapter, indicating that holiness has both a spatial and a temporal dimension.

This verse begins the close (vv. 30–32) of what may have been the original chap. 19, since it forms an inclusion with its opening (vv. 3–4), as follows: v. 30a = v. 3b (the sabbath); v. 31a ‖ v. 4a (the only two occurrences of *'al-tipnû* in this chapter); and v. 32a ‖ v. 3a (for content), respect for parents and the elderly (Schwartz 1987: 120–23; cf. Hoffmann 1953, and INTRODUCTION). It cannot be overlooked that vv. 3 and 30 present the chiastic structure abcb'ac. The repetition in v. 30 is near complete, but for bb', which share only a verb *tîrā'û*, but their content differs. Since *miqdāšî* (v. 30) replaces *šabbĕtōtay* (v. 3), it might not be far afield to suggest that the observance of YHWH's sabbaths (sacred time) is complemented by fulfilling all the laws concerning the sanctuary (sacred space).

my sanctuary. miqdāšî. Sanctuary here refers to the *temenos*, the sacred precincts (Arab. *ḥaram*), as it does in 12:4; 20:3; 21:12 (cf. Milgrom 1970: 23, n. 78). At the end of the First Temple period, the people frequented the Temple on the sabbath (Ezek 46:3). The priority of the sabbath over the sanctuary in this verse is the basis for the rabbinic rule that the sabbath may not be violated, even for the building of the sanctuary (*Sipra* Qedoshim 7:7). Indeed, the placement of the sabbath commandment (Exod 35:1–3 [H]) at the head of the instructions to erect the Tabernacle also serves the same purpose. The sanctuary here refers to the area of the Temple, an indication of its preexilic provenience. As pointed out by Otto (1995a: 96), it is significant that H uses the verb *yāra'* 'revere' only with its object the sanctuary (19:30; 26:2), parents (19:3), and God (19:14, 32; 25:17, 36, 43). The elevation of the sanctuary alongside the Decalogue's parents (Exod 20:12) indicates the importance of the Jerusalem Temple to the H legist.

To be sure, the Aramaic *Tgs.* (followed by most commentaries) render the term as *bêt miqdāšî* 'my Temple (building)' (also in 26:2 and elsewhere), which Hurvitz (1995: 166–68) has demonstrated occurs only once in Scripture (2 Chr 36:17) and becomes the standard phrase for the entire Temple complex in Second Temple times. However, as I have shown (1970: 23, n. 78), the Chronicler has coined the expression *bayit lammiqdāš*, which can only be rendered "a house of the sacred precinct" (1 Chr 28:10). This indicates that the Chronicler distinguished between the Temple building and the *miqdāš*, the larger sacred area that contained it, in consonance with biblical usage.

On the basis of *Tg. Ps.-J.* and on the analogy to v. 3, Paran (1989: 119) proposes that *miqdāšî* should be rendered "my sanctums," in support of which he adduces 16:33; Num 18:29, and Ezek 45:4. His proposal must be rejected outright: the purported analogy with v. 3 escapes me, and the absolute form of the noun in 16:33 and Num 18:29 should probably be vocalized *miqdēš* (see Ehrlich [1908] on 16:33). Note as well that its form in Num 18:29 is *miqdĕšô*, not *miqdāšô*, which shows that the Masoretes were also intent on distinguishing between "sancta" and "sanctuary." As for Ezek 45:4, its text is in disarray (cf. Zimmerli 1983: 466). Finally, the rendering "my sanctums" would probably have been vocalized as a plural, *miqdāšay*, as in 21:23, or *qŏdāšay*, as in Ezekiel's reworking of this verse (22:8). The contrast between *šabbĕtōtay* and *miqdāšî* is between sacred time and sacred space. The singular *miqdāšî* reflects the perspective of Jerusalem, but not that it is the only legitimate sanctuary. The other sanctuaries dedicated to the worship of YHWH are not invalidated, but their holiness does not rank with that of the Jerusalem Temple.

you shall revere. tîrā'û. In other words, Israel is not to desecrate or pollute the sanctuary. Note that this verb is precisely the same that is used for the rephrasing of the parental commandment of the Decalogue (v. 3aα). H seems to be reminding the reader that reverence is not only a moral obligation in regard to parents, but also a cultic one in regard to the sanctuary, and of equal importance.

What constitutes irreverence? The rabbis were not content with the obvious desecration / pollution proscription; they added the following fine points: entering with the staff in hand, shoes or dust on feet, and money in belt; using the Temple Mount as a shortcut; or spitting on it (*m. Ber.* 9:5; *Sipra* Qedoshim 7:9; *b. Yeb.* 6b). After the Temple's destruction, the rabbis maintained that this injunction still holds: one should walk backward when leaving the Temple Mount, never sleep or defecate in an east–west direction, or duplicate the building or its sancta (*b. Ber.* 5b; *b. Yoma* 53b; *b. Menaḥ* 28b; cf. Maimonides, *The Temple Service,* "the Chosen House," chap. 7).

The sectaries of Qumran affix this injunction to the prohibition against illicit unions: *LHZHR] MKWL TʿRWBT [H]GBR WLHYWT YRʾYM MN HMQDŠ* '[guard against] all illicit unions and (thus) be reverent of the sanctuary' (MMT B 48–49). In their view, the violation of the sexual prohibitions of chap. 18 not only brings in its wake the capital penalties of chap. 20, but coevally defiles the sanctuary.

V. 31. Unit 15: Consulting the Dead

Necromancy was as pervasive in Israel as in the ancient Near East. Because it was associated with ancestor worship, it was deemed a form of idolatry in the biblical codes (H and D) and therefore banned. Obviously, idolatry in any form detracted from the holiness of God and would block Israel's attempt to strive for holiness. The discussion of ancestor worship is reserved for chap. 20, COMMENTS B and C.

Another motivation may underlie the official opposition to consulting ghosts and wizard-spirits. It was presumed that they could read the future. Thus their activity was a form of divination. As I argued (1990a: 471–73), divination as opposed to sorcery was a legitimate practice, since it did not attempt to change the divine decisions (i.e, sorcery), but only to read them in advance of their announcement—in other words, to predict the future. Thus these magicians were in competition with the prophets, who claimed the role of authorized conveyers of YHWH's will, and with the priests, who in their turn restricted divination to the operation of the Urim and Thummim. Thus there may have also been an economic factor that accounts for the repeated official opposition to these competitive diviners (19:31; 20:6, 27; Deut 18:10–12; cf. Olyan 1997b: 85).

ghosts . . . wizard-spirits. hā'ōbōt . . . hayyiddĕ'ōnîm. The precise meaning of both terms is moot. As discussed in chap. 20, COMMENT B, arguably they can stand for the spirit of the dead, the means of consulting them, or the necromancer, the expert consulting them (see also NOTES on 20:6 and 27).

The *yiddĕ'ōnî* never occurs alone, but only in tandem with *'ōb* (20:6, 27; Deut 18:11; 1 Sam 28:3, 9; 2 Kgs 21:6; 23:24; Isa 8:19; 19:3; 2 Chr 33:6); the *'ōb* is attested by itself (1 Sam 28:7, 8 [= 1 Chr 10:13]; Isa 29:4; Job 32:19). Despite MT's cantillation, the two terms are not in tandem since, as indicated in the translation, each term belongs to a different sentence (Ehrlich 1908; cf. Kilian 1963; Noth 1977). Melamed (1964) has demonstrated that in poetry, hendiadyses can be split, and, as demonstrated, H's style has poetic characteristics (see Introduction I D). However, this pair is not a hendiadys, since the terms are not equivalent: *'ōb 'ô yiddĕ'ōnî* "ghost *or* wizard-spirit" (20:27).

Do not turn to. 'al-tipnû. One would have expected the durative *lō'*, indicating a permanent prohibition, and not the time-bound *'al*, indicating immediately—more a warning than a prohibition (Schwartz 1987: 297, n. 21). However, as explained in the NOTE on v. 4aα, this prohibition may indeed be only a warning against divine retribution, since there was no juridical penalty in "turning,"—consulting spirits (and other forms of idols)—only in serving as their mediums. Moreover, this verse is modeled after *'al-tipnû 'el-hā'ĕlîlīm* (v. 4aα), and for stylistic reasons, assonance with *'el* and *hā'ĕlîlīm* may have taken precedence (see NOTE on v. 4aα).

The verb *tipnû* is also puzzling; one would have expected the more precise verb *dāraš* or *šā'al*, both meaning "inquire" (e.g., *dāraš*: Gen 25:22; Exod 18:15; 1 Sam 9:9; 28:6; 2 Kgs 8:10; esp. Deut 18:11 and Isa 19:3; *šā'al*: Num 27:21; Judg 1:1; 18:5; 20:18, 23, 27; esp. 1 Sam 28:6 and 1 Chr 10:13). Again, the reason is stylistic: to create an inclusion with v. 4aα. This verb is found again in a similar context in 20:6, where neither an ideological nor a stylistic reason exists for its usage. This leaves as the only remaining answer that chap. 20, or at least 20:1–8, was composed by the author of chap. 19.

do not search for. wĕ'el . . . 'al-tĕbaqqĕšû. Again, the negative particle *'al* is chosen over *lō'*, since this injunction is less a prohibition than an exhortation, whose consequence is the long-range divine penalty of *kārēt* (20:6), but not the immediate juridical death penalty reserved for those who serve as mediums (20:27)—equivalent to officiating as idolatrous priests.

The expression *biqqēš 'el* is unattested (except in dissimilar 1 Sam 25:26). Most likely, this preposition was chosen to balance the same one in the first half of the verse—a stylistic nicety (Ehrlich 1908). The verb *biqqēš* is frequently used as a synonym of *dāraš*, which does occur with the preposition *'el* (Deut 4:29; cf. Judg 6:29; Ezek 34:6; Pss 24:6; 38:13; 105:4), but there is a shade of difference between them: *biqqēš* 'seek, search' (e.g., Exod 33:7) implies making an effort (to find a medium), while *dāraš* 'inquire, investigate' implies that the effort has proved successful.

to become impure by them. lĕṭām 'â bāhem. For this usage of the *beth* of means, see 5:22, 26. This expression cannot be the object of *'al-tĕbaqqĕšû:* no one seeks impurity! Therefore, it is to be understood adverbially: "Don't turn / seek them whereby you will be defiled."

H's "impurity" is metaphoric; no purificatory rites are prescribed. Neither can the penalty be erased: for polluting the land, expulsion is mandated for the people (18:25) and *kārēt* for the individual (18:29). The same penalty of *kārēt* holds for individuals turning to mediums (20:6). Note, however, that although punishment by God is certain, there is no punishment by man. The use of *tāmē'* has another function: as the fatal antonym to *qādôš* 'holy', it deserves a place in this chapter as one of the injunctions whose violation nullifies the achievement of holiness.

Consulting the dead is a form of idolatry according to the rabbis: "If you contaminate yourself by them, take note of what you are exchanging, what [i.e, the Lord] for what [i.e., the dead]" (*Sipra* Qedoshim 7:11). H's obsessive concern with this practice is indicated by its thrice-repeated mention (19:31; 20:6, 27). For its significance in dating H, see the Introduction II C.

V. 32. Unit 16: Respect for Elders

This verse is the counterpoint to respect for parents (v. 3a) and, thus, continues and expands the grand inclusion (vv. 30–32 and vv. 3–4; see INTRODUCTION). It is divided into two statements like its model (v. 3a); it is also structured chiastically and expressed positively (contrast vv. 4, 9, 14.31). As pointed out by Schwartz (1987: 169), the parallel cola are not synonymous; otherwise, the common word *zāqēn* 'aged' would be first together with the more general verb *wĕhādartā* 'and you will respect' (as A words; cf. Ginsberg 1945: 56; Held 1957: 6–8; Boling 1960: 223–24). Moreover, the use of *pĕnê* in both stiches and the lack of synonymity in their verbs militate against calling this verse poetic (Paran 1989: 110).

In the presence of. mippĕnê. That is, as soon as you see him.

the elderly. śêbâ. Akkadian *šībtu* (pl. *šībâtu*) and Ugaritic *šbt* (*UT* 2407) mean "gray hair, old age" (*AHw* 1228a); *šbt dqn* (*UT* 51 [*CTA* 4] V:66) is probably to be rendered "hoary old age" (Cassuto 1951b: 86; Loewenstamm 1980: 34). *śêbâ* is found in parallel with *ziqnâ* 'old age' (Isa 46:4; Ps 71:18), but these terms are not always synonymous—for example, *zāqantî wĕśabtî* 'I have grown old and gray' (1 Sam 12:2); *wĕhădar zĕqēnîm śêbâ* 'The majesty of old men is their gray hair' (Prov 20:29).

Ibn Ezra points out that the text does not say *'îš śêbâ* 'an old man' but *śêbâ*, or *all* old men (cf. Ramban). One cannot help wondering if old women are excluded (cf. Ruth 4:15).

you shall rise. tāqûm. Rise out of respect. Job testifies, "When I passed through the city gates to take my seat in the square, young men saw me and hid, **elders rose and stood**; nobles held back their words. They clapped their hands to their mouths; the voices of princes were hushed; their tongues stuck to their palates" (Job 29:7–10; cf. also Exod 18:13; 1 Kg 22:19). "What constitutes the rising that the Torah states (in) 'Before the elderly you shall rise'? One should stand before him and ask and reply (standing) within four cubits (of him, for then it is evident that he is rising in his honor)" (t. Meg. 4:24). Noth (1977) conjectures that originally this text meant that "one should make room for an old man if he wants to sit or lie down," forgetting that Scripture treats the elderly as a seated king before whom one stands. The LXX reads *apo prosōpou polioū exanastēsē*, which, according to Colson (1968: 455 n.a), Philo read as "rise up away from the hoary head," leading him to comment: "the young are commanded not only to yield the chief seats to the aged but also to give place to them as they pass" (*Laws* 2.238; 7.454–55).

and thereby you will show respect to the aged. wĕhādartā pĕnê zāqēn (cf. Lam 5:12). This is not an independent injunction (see INTRODUCTION to v. 32), but an illustration of the previous general statement (Schwartz 1987: 297, n. 30). The rabbis also understand it this way, as shown by their other examples: "What constitutes the respect that the Torah meant in 'you shall show respect to the aged'? One does not stand in the place where he usually stands, speak in his stead, nor does one contradict his words. One behaves toward him with fear and reverence; in buying and selling, entering and leaving, they (the elderly) have priority over all others" (t. Meg. 3:24; cf. Lieberman 1962: 1203; cf. also *Sipra* Qedoshim 7:14, and more examples in b. Qid. 32b–33b). This sense of *hādar* 'give priority' is precisely that in v. 15 (Wessely 1846; for greater detail, see Warmuth 1978; Olyan 1996a).

The rabbinic bias that this injunction is limited to men may not be the sense of Scripture. Note that *zāqēn* is a collective for men and women in Josh 6:21; Jer 51:22; Ezek 9:6, and elsewhere.

The rabbis also state that *'ēn zāqēn 'ellā' ḥākām 'zāqēn* (here) means wise' (*Sipra* Qedoshim 7:12; cf. Tg. Ps.-J., and R. Issi in b. Qed. 33a). For this verbal extravagance, they have biblical precedent (e.g., Prov 16:31; Job 12:12; 32:7). They showed respect to all the elderly, however. R. Johanan would even rise before the heathen aged, saying "How many troubles have passed over these" (b. Qed. 33a). Contrast the attitude of the Dead Sea sectaries, who listed 'YŠ Z[QN] KWŠL 'the feeble old man' among those whose physical blemishes or impurities disqualified them from admission to the 'DH, the assembly of the eschatological community (1QSa 2:7–8). Philo (*On the Sacrifices*, 77), however, resorts to attributes of character: "by an elder is meant one who is worthy of honor, and respect, and of preeminence, and examination of whom is committed to Moses, the friend of God, whom you know to be the elders of the people" (Num 11:16).

you shall fear your God. wĕyārē'tā mē'ĕlōhêka. The same warning is found in v. 14. Both the blind and deaf (v. 14) and the aged (v. 32) cannot enforce the dignity they merit, but God will punish those who deny it (Dillmann and Ryssel 1897). "What if one shuts his eyes and makes believe he didn't see him (the elderly)? Therefore it is written: 'you shall fear your God'" (Rashi). The preposition *min* before *'ĕlōhêkā* implies divine retribution (Wessely 1846). Levi's

(1975) argument that this phrase translates as "you shall show reverence for your departed ancestors" is vitiated by v. 14: the ancestral spirits are not known to take special interest in the blind and deaf.

Vv. 33–34. Unit 17: the gēr

This unit has been diagrammed by Schwartz (1987: 18):

wěkî-yāgûr 'ittekā gēr bě'arṣěkem	lō' tônû 'ōtô
kě'ezrāḥ mikkem yihyeh lākem	
haggēr haggār 'ittekem	wě'āhabtā lô kāmôkâ
kî-gērîm hěyîtem bě'ereṣ miṣrāyim	'ănî YHWH 'ĕlōhêkem

The rule of equality before the law for alien and citizen alike (24:22; Exod 12:49; Num 15:16, 29) is bounded by an envelope structure contrasting the alien in Israel's land with alien Israel in Egypt-land. Hence Israel should not oppress the alien, but love him. These two contrasts project the theology of this unit: *land* (Israel and Egypt) and *behavior* toward the alien, negative in not cheating him and positive in loving him (M. Hildenbrand).

Care for the gēr 'resident alien' is mentioned in every code but P (Exod 20:10; 22:20; 23:9 [JE]; Lev 19:10, 33–34; 23:22; Num 35:15 [II]; Deut 1:16; 5:14; 10:18–19; 14:21; 24:14–22; 27:19 [D]). Our verse is echoed in Deut 10:19: wa'ăhabtem 'et-haggēr kî-gērîm hěyîtem bě'ereṣ miṣrāyim 'You shall love the alien, for you were aliens in the land of Egypt'. It is voiced in the plural in contrast to its adjoining verses that are all in the singular. The reason can only be that our verse is also in the plural. Hence, in this instance, D has clearly borrowed from H. That the status of the alien in H (regarding permitted foods) influenced the dietary laws of D, see chap. 17, COMMENT B.

Bultmann's (1992: 177–79) proposal that vv. 33–34 are a conflation of three literary stages (vv. 33, 34aγ, b; 'ittěkā, v. 33aα*; v. 34aγ, b) reflecting two discrete concepts of the gēr must also be rejected (see NOTE on "you shall love him as yourself," v. 34, and chap. 27, COMMENT B).

In discussing the gēr in chap. 17, COMMENT B, I rebutted van Houten's (1991: 151–55) argument that the Israelites who remained in the land during the Exile were considered impure by the returnees, and that made them gērîm (241). Here, I wish to refute her argument that early Israel incorporated into its tribal system large ethnic entities such as the Calebites (following Gottwald 1979: 555–84), the Gibeonites, and the Shechemites (following Blenkinsopp 1966; 1972: 14–27) and such individuals as Doeg the Edomite (1 Sam 21:8), Uriah the Hittite (2 Sam 11:3), and Ittai the Gittite (2 Sam 15:21) (van Houten 1991: 60, n. 1). Yet she herself admits that these groups were considered second-class citizens (61), and, as I pointed out (1982b: 175), the fact that the ethnic appellation was affixed to the above-named individuals indicates that they were aliens (gērîm) and that only after generations—and in some cases, centuries—they were absorbed into Israel only through the process of intermarriage. (Kaufmann [1977: 670–72] makes a strong case that the Calebites, however, were not *gērîm*, but Israelites. That is, they were "charter members" of the confederation called Israel in pre-Mosaic times.)

In a paper presented in Jerusalem, Dandamayev (1990) described the legal status of aliens in sixth-century Mesopotamia. They were deprived of civil rights: they could not be members of the *puḫru* (city assembly), own property, or have access to the Babylonian temples. Indeed, the temples were not interested in proselytes with whom they would have to share privileges; *there was no proselytism.* Instead, the aliens made up their own assemblies (e.g., the Egyptians under Cambyses; Ezekiel and the elders, Ezek 8:1). Thus not only in Israel but elsewhere in the ancient Near East, aliens were kept ethnically apart and only subsequently absorbed through intermarriage. For details on the legal status of the Israelite *gēr*, see chap. 17, COMMENT B.

33. *with you. ʾittĕkā.* The Sam. and the Versions read *ʾittĕkem* (pl.). However, in the legal codes there are frequent occurrences of change in number—for example, *lōʾ tĕʿannûn ʾim- ʿannēh tĕʿannēh* (Exod 22:21–22); *ûbĕquṣrĕkem . . . lōʾ- tĕkalleh* (Lev 23:22); *taʿăbōdû . . . lōʾ-tirdeh* (Lev 25:46; see also 21:7; 25:31, noted by Driver 1911: 232).

you shall not oppress him. lōʾ tônû ʾōtô. The root *ynh* appears in Old Aramaic (Sefire) meaning "oppress, afflict" (cf. Old Assyrian *wanāʾum* 'put pressure on, afflict'). The verb *hônâ* (*Hipʿil*) also denotes "oppress" (Exod 22:20; Deut 23:16; Isa 49:6; Jer 22:3) in regard to the powerless (Ahuvya 1973; Ringgren 1990), often to land (Ezek 45:8; 46:18), and to loans (Ezek 18:7–20; 22:7, 29 ‖ *gāzēl* 'theft'; *ʿōšeq* 'exploitation'). In 25:14, 17 it connotes "cheat" (in a business transaction; see NOTE on 25:14), a meaning that is unique in the Bible. The rabbis confirm the biblical distinction among *laḥaṣ* 'oppression', *ḥāmās* 'violence', and *ʾônāʾâ* 'deception' (cf. Exod 22:20; Jer 22:3): *hammĕʿanneh ʾet haggēr ʾōbēr bišlōšâ laʾwîn, wĕhallôḥăṣô ʿōbēr bišnayim* 'He who *deceives* an alien violates three prohibitions, but he who *oppresses* him violates two' (*b. B. Meṣ.* 59b), keeping in mind that for the rabbis the term *gēr* also means "proselyte." Moreover, they interpret the verb *hônâ* (and noun *ʾônāʾâ*) as (*ʾônāʾat*) *dĕbārîm* 'deception through words', or cheating, which they expand to include such ideas as shaming him because of his former status (*Sipra* Qedoshim 8:2; *b. B. Meṣ.* 58b).

The juxtaposition of this prohibition with the following one, dealing with deception in business (vv. 35–36), makes it likely that the latter is an illustration of the cheating mentioned here.

in your land. But not in the diaspora, where Israel has no authority. In fact, Israel's status in exile is that of a *gēr*, the same status it had in Egypt (v. 34aβ), the patriarchs had in Canaan (Gen 15:13; 23:4), and Moses had in Midian (Exod 2:22; 18:3). It is no accident that those who join the Israelites in Babylon are not termed *gērîm*, but *bĕnê nēkār* 'foreigners' (Isa 56:3, 6; Isa 14:1 is not an exception, since the "foreigners," now settled in Israel's land, are *gērîm*).

34. *as a citizen. kĕʾezrāḥ.* The etymology is unknown. Possibly it is related to *mitʿāreh kĕʾezrāḥ raʿănān* 'well-rooted like a robust native tree' (Ps 37:35 NJPS)—

that is, "one whose lineage has 'roots' in the land" (Levine 1989). Thus the term stands for "native," a connotation supported by the expression kol-hā'ezrāḥ bĕyiśrā'ēl (23:42), where it is uncoupled with the gēr. Israel in exile had no gērîm; in reality, Israel was the gēr and the Babylonian, the 'ezrāḥ (that Israel was then in exile, see NOTE to 23:42). Elsewhere, the term 'ezrāḥ is always in tandem with gēr (16:29; 17:15; 18:26; 19:34; 24:16, 22; Exod 12:48, 49; Num 9:14; 15:13, 29, 30; Jos 8:33; Ezek 47:22). Note that all the cited verses are priestly or priestly influenced texts.

You shall love him as yourself. wĕ'āhabtā lô kāmôkā. The counterpart to v. 18, this is the same command regarding Israelites. Here, however, the command is practical, not platonic (Wellhausen 1963: 155; Elliger 1966): it specifies cheating him (tônû) in business dealings (vv. 35–36). This verse also confirms the practical implication of "love": it must be expressed in one's behavior (see NOTE on v. 18).

That this phrase is dependent and a near quotation of its counterpart in v. 18 is shown by the switch to the singular wĕ'āhabtā within a plural context and by the use of the dative lô, which matches lĕrē'ăkā (v. 18), instead of the Nota accusativa 'et as in wa'ăhabtem 'et-haggēr (Deut 10:19). Thus, contra Bultmann (1992: 179), the singular formation belies its derivation from Deut 10:19, which is voiced in the plural and lacks the dative.

Schwartz (1987: 171–72) points out that there is a reciprocal relation between the alien and the Israelite: it is incumbent on the Israelite to love him (Deut 10:19), not to oppress him (Exod 22:20; 23:9), support him (19:10 = 23:22; Deut 14:28–29; 24:19), include him in festival celebrations (Deut 16:11; 26:11), allow him to rest on the sabbath (Exod 20:10; 23:12), and provide him safety (Num 35:15). It is incumbent on the alien to follow the same sacrificial procedures as the Israelite (Exod 12:48–49; Lev 17:8, 12, 13; Num 9:14; 15:14, 29), observe the same prohibitions (16:29; 18:26), and receive the same punishments (20:2; 24:6, 22).

Schwartz (1987: 298, n. 18) further observes that the ethical category (the Israelite's obligations) is nonpriestly, whereas the cultic category (the alien's obligations) is priestly. This distinction is in need of correction. First, chap. 19 (a priestly text) emphasizes the obligation of the Israelite to treat the alien ethically (vv. 10, 18, 34). Also the alien has to sacrifice like the Israelite only when he has violated a prohibition (Milgrom 1982b) and must bring an expiatory sacrifice (Num 15:29), but he is exempt from all other sacrifices, including the pesaḥ, which requires that he be circumcised (Exod 12:49) and be in a state of ritual purity (Num 9:6–7, 13–14). Note that he need not bring a well-being offering—that is, food for the table—since he is exempt from offering the blood of this sacrifice on the altar (see NOTES on 17:4 and 11). Finally, protection for the alien from the blood redeemer, a noncultic command (Num 35:15), is obviously a priestly text.

Schwartz (1987: 172) also claims that the injunctions directed to the alien (the second category) are interpolations, additions to the existent laws. There is much merit to his claim. Arguably, it may hold for Exod 12:48–49; Lev 16:29; Num 9:14, where these verses are parts of larger appendices (Exod 12:43–49;

Lev 16:29–34; Num 9:9–14); for Lev 18:26 and Num 15:14–16, which themselves may be interpolations; or for Lev 17:8, 10, 12, 15, into which the prescription for the alien may have been inserted (I doubt it). But if the injunction
to abstain from Molek worship (Lev 20:2), incumbent on the Israelite, falls all
the more so on the alien, then the law of blasphemy (Lev 24:16) must also fall
on the alien, if for no other reason than that this law is based on a case involving an alien (v. 10). Thus, at least in these cases, the law regarding the alien is
integral to the text.

for you were aliens in the land of Egypt. This rationale is used elsewhere to
muster support for the alien (Exod 22:20; 23:9; Deut 10:19; 23:8). As plausibly
suggested by Joosten (1994: 83–84; 1996: 59–60), the similarity of wording in
all these attested cases indicates that H was influenced by the weight of the legal tradition (Exod 22:20; 23:9; Deut 10:19).

Vv. 35–36a. Unit 18: Business Ethics

The opportunity (and, hence, the temptation) to cheat in commercial transactions was greatest with the measuring instruments used by the seller. Thus the
focus of this unit is on honest scales, weights, and other measuring instruments.
The declarative statement here for honest measures is repeated in Deut
25:13–16, beginning with a prefatory warning against dishonest measures and,
in typical deuteronomic fashion, ending with a promise of reward for observing
this commandment and condemnation for its violation:

*lō'-yihyeh bĕkîsĕkā 'eben wā'āben gĕdôlâ ûqĕṭannâ lō'-yihyeh lĕkā bĕbêtĕkā 'êpâ
wĕ'êpâ gĕdôlâ ûqĕṭannâ '**eben šĕlēmâ wāṣedeq yihyeh-lāk 'êpâ** šĕlēmâ wāṣedeq
yihyeh lāk lĕma'an ya'ărîkû yāmêkā 'al hā'ădāmâ 'ăšer-YHWH 'ĕlōhêkā nōtēn
lāk kî tô'ăbat YHWH kol-'ōśēh 'elleh kōl 'ōśēh 'āwel*

[13]You shall not have in your pouch alternate weights, larger and smaller. [14]You
shall not have in your house alternate measures, a larger and a smaller. [15]**You
must have** completely **honest weights and** completely **honest measures**, if
you are to endure long on the soil that YHWH your God is giving you. [16]For
everyone who does those things, everyone **who deals dishonestly** [lit. "**who
does injustice**"], is abhorrent to YHWH your God.

There is little doubt that D is a borrowing and expansion of H. The core of
the H passage is contained in Deut 25:15a (boldface). The rest is an expansion,
as indicated by the addition of *šĕlēmâ* 'completely' and the transferal of *'ōśēh
'āwel* 'who deals dishonestly' (lit. "who does injustice") to the end of the passage. D's hypothetical, original formulation is unrelated to D's *'eben šĕlēmâ* 'un-
finished stone' (Deut 27:6; cf. 1 Kgs 6:7; Olyan 1996b: 165, n. 17). Rather, I
side with McKane (1970: 301–2, 438–39) that it stems from universal wisdom
literature (see also Weinfeld 1972d: 267–69).

Dishonest measures are vigorously condemned both in prophecy (Hos 12:8;
Amos 8:5; Mic 6:10–11) and in wisdom (Deut 25:13–16; Prov 11:1; 16:11; 20:10,

23). A pointed indictment by Amos (8:4–5) is directed against those who hypo-critically observe the sabbath while using false weights and measures:

šim ʿû-zōʾt haššōʾăpîm ʾebyôn ûlĕhašbît ʿăniy[wK]ê- ʾāreṣ lēʾmōr mātay ya ʿăbōr haḥōdeš wĕnašbîrâ šeber wĕhaššabāt wĕniptĕḥâ-bār lĕhaqṭîn ʾêpâ ûlĕhagdîl šeqel ulĕʿawwēt mōʾzĕnê mirmâ

Listen to this, you who trample the needy, annihilating the poor of the land, saying, "When will the new moon be over so that we can sell grain; and the sabbath, so that we may open the grain (bins), making the ephah too small, and a shekel too large, and distorting with false scales.

Since wisdom teachings are prevalent throughout the ancient Near East, it occasions no surprise that the same concern for honest business practices is found outside Israel, for example "picking up a small weight instead of a large weight, picking up a small measure instead of a large measure" "Nanshe Hymn," ll. 142–43 [Heimpel 1981: 91]; see also the Code of Ur-Nammu, ll. 143–49; the Edict of Ammisaduqa, §18 [*ANET* 523–28]; Šurpu II. 37 (Reiner 1958: 14), 42–43; *BWL* 132:107–21. For Egypt, see the Protestation of Guiltlessness, A 22–26 [*ANET* 34]; "The Instruction of Amen-em-Opet" 16 [*ANET* 423b]). In Hellenistic times the situation altered radically. Agoranomi were appointed in all Greek states; they regulated the markets and punished those who cheated es-pecially by false weights and measures (cf. Philo, *Laws* 4.193; Colson, Loeb 1968: 8.437).

As aptly noted by Knohl (1991: 33), chap. 19 constitutes the priestly (H) an-swer to Amos, emphasizing the importance of keeping the sabbath (vv. 3b, 30aα) and employing honest business practices (for details, see Introduction II H, J).

This unit is connected with the preceding one (vv. 33–34): it is an illustra-tion of how the *gēr* can be exploited (Ibn Ezra). Hence, as the preceding unit is a supplement, making the *gēr* the beneficiary of Israel's love, initially reserved for fellow Israelites (v. 18), so this unit must be a supplement (Schwartz 1987: 174).

35. *You shall not do injustice in judgment. lōʾ-ta ʿăśû ʿāwel bammišpāṭ.* This is a repetition of v. 15a, another indication that this unit is a supplement. Thus as vv. 33–34 supplement v. 18, so vv. 35–36 supplement v. 15a. The difference be-tween the two units should not be overlooked: in v. 15a, the focus is on court-room justice; here, it is on just business dealings. As succinctly summarized by the rabbis, "every measurer is a judge" (*Sipra* Qedoshim 8:5).

in measures. bammiddâ. The rabbis hold that land measures are meant, whereas Saadiah and the moderns maintain that this word refers to length and width. Schwartz (1987: 74) proposes that it is a general term referring to all mea-sures, followed by the specific reference to weight and capacity, and he points to the use of *middâ* in other contexts where the verb *mādad* 'measure' refers to capacity, both wet and dry (Exod 16:18; Jer 33:22; Hos 2:11; Job 28:25; Ruth 3:15; Schwartz 1987: 300, n. 8). In favor of Schwartz's interpretation is the following verse (v. 36), which exemplifies this rule and mentions only measures of weight and capacity, saying nothing about measures of distance. Just as telling is Deut 25:13–16, which also distinguishes between weights (*'eben*) and measures of capacity (*'êpâ*), but also omits any reference to distance.

or capacity. ûbamměśûrâ. Either wet or dry (Saadiah, Rashi, Ibn Ezra [cf. *Yahel 'or*], Shadal), as shown by *mayim biměśûrâ tišteh šiššît hahîn* 'water you will drink by measure: one-sixth of a hin' (Ezek 4:11; cf. v. 16), the hin being a liquid measure.

36. *honest. ṣedeq.* The genitive expresses the character of the noun in construct and is to be translated as an adjective (GKC § 128p; Joüon 1923: §§ 129–30). The nuance of "honest, true" is confirmed by the parallelism of *śiptê-ṣedeq* 'truthful speech' and *wědōbēr yěśārîm* 'and one who speaks honestly' (Prov 16:13). The staccato effect of the fourfold repetition of *ṣedeq* in this verse hammers away at the quintessential necessity for honest business practices. Deut 25:15 adds the adjective *šělēmâ* for further emphasis. The rabbis turn the adjective into a verb so that it becomes a synonym of *yaššēr* 'straighten, rectify': *ṣaddēq 'et hammō'znayim yāpeh, ṣaddēq 'et hā'ēpôt yāpeh, ṣaddēq 'et hahîn yāpeh* 'Correct the scales exactly, correct the *ephahs* exactly, correct the *hin* exactly' (*Sipra* Qedoshim 8:7), thereby adding greater responsibility on the seller.

scale. mō'znê. The construct of the dual *mō'znayim.* The dual is necessitated by the nature of the scale. It consisted of two cups suspended from a crossbar, originally held by hand and subsequently supported on a stand. In one cup was a stone (later, an iron) weight (*'eben*), and in the other, the goods to be weighed (for an ancient illustration, see *EBWL* 141). The precise terminological equivalent is attested in Akkadian *zibānit (la) kitti* 'true scales'. The same equivalence is exhibited in Mesopotamian measures of weight and capacity: *aban kitti* 'true weights' and *kur kitti* 'true kor'. For the conjectured numerical amount of these terms and others, see vol. 1.890–901 and Powell (1992).

Ezekiel clearly cites this verse but updates it to include a new measure: *mō'znê-ṣedeq wě'êpat-ṣedeq ûbat-ṣedeq yěhî lākem* 'You shall have honest scales, and an honest ephah, and an honest bath' (Ezek 45:10), and he immediately (v. 11) explains that the ephah and the new measure, the bath, are equivalent and equal to one-tenth of a homer, a known measure (cf. 27:16). For other instances of Ezekiel's dependence on the priestly writings, especially of H, see chap. 26, COMMENTS C and D.

Vv. 36b–37. Closing Exhortation

36. (*I am YHWH your God*) *who freed you from the land of Egypt.* The customary unit ending *'ănî YHWH 'ĕlōhêkem* is herewith supplemented. Perhaps its purpose is to connect, as do vv. 35–36a, with the unit on the *gēr* (vv. 33–34), as a reminder that since Israelites were once *gērîm* in Egypt, they should take note of the feelings of the *gēr* (Exod 23:9) and not exploit him (Exod 22:20). Alternatively, and preferably, it may be regarded (with Hoffmann 1955) as the be-

ginning of the closure to chaps. 18 and 19. It is of significance that this statement contrasts with the opening of chap. 18: *'ănî YHWH 'ĕlōhêkem kĕma 'ăśēh
'ereṣ-miṣrayim 'ăšer yĕšabtem-bāh lō' ta 'ăśû* 'I am YHWH your God. As is done
in the land of Egypt where you dwelt you shall not do' (18:2b–3a). In fact, v.
36b can now be seen as the rationale for 18:3a and, indeed, for all of chap. 18:
do not follow Egyptian mores because YHWH has freed you from the land of
Egypt so that you should serve him (cf. 25:42, 51) by observing his laws (chaps.
18–19). This rationale is followed by v. 37, which, as will be shown below, echoes
18:4–5, thus providing a grand enclosure for chaps. 18 and 19, the opening exhortation to chap. 18 (vv. 2b–5) and the concluding exhortation to chap. 19 (vv.
36b–37). Moreover, this observation would explain why the long coda (v. 36b)
does not follow the ending of the chapter (v. 37) where logically, emotionally,
and rhetorically it belongs: the closing exhortation was constrained to follow the
sequence of verses in 18:2b–5. And conversely, it explains why v. 37 ends with
the attested formula—and the short one at that— *'ănî YHWH*. For, as stated, vv.
36b–37 enclose 18:2b–5, which also ends with *'ănî YHWH!*

In sum, this closing formula serves a dual purpose: to close the final unit (vv.
35–36a) and to begin the closing exhortation (vv. 36b–37).

v. 37. **You shall heed all my statutes and all my rules, and you shall do them.**
ûšĕmartem 'etkol- ḥuqqōtay wĕ'et-kol-mišpāṭay wa 'ăśîtem 'ōtām. This statement should be compared with *'et-mišpāṭay ta 'ăśû wĕ'et-ḥuqqōtay tišmĕrû . . .
ûšĕmartem 'et-ḥuqqōtay wĕ'et mišpāṭay . . . ya 'ăśeh 'ōtām* 'My rules alone you
shall observe and my statutes shall you heed . . . you shall heed my statutes and
my rules . . . does them" (18:4–5). The many boldface words of v. 37 speak elo-
quently of this verse's conscious imitation of all the cited words of 18:4–5. What
is new is the twice-repeated particle *kol* 'all'. Thus the close of the inclusion is,
in effect, saying: not only should the prohibitions of chap. 18 be observed, but
all the injunctions of chap. 19 (Hoffmann 1953).

It also should not be overlooked that the beginning of the concluding exhortation of chap. 20 also uses the same phraseology: *ûšĕmartem 'et-kol-ḥuqqōtay
wĕ'et-kol-mišpāṭay wa 'ăśîtem 'ōtām* 'You shall heed all my statutes and all my
rules and do them' (20:22a). Thus a giant inclusion is effected for chaps. 18–20.
Furthermore, since chap. 20 is both a parallel and a complement to chap. 18,
this inclusion locks these three chapters into an AXA' pattern, whose significance is discussed in the Introduction I A. Moreover, it should be noted that
smaller versions of this inclusion are found in 18:26, 30; 19:19a, and 20:8, effectively dividing these three chapters into five large sections, discussed in the
Introduction I A. Finally, it may be surmised that it was the H tradent responsible for the appendix (vv. 33–37) who is also to be credited with the grand design of chaps. 18–20, supplying it with the inclusions 18:2b–5, 26–30; 19:36b–37;
20:22–26 and the section breaks 19:19a and 20:8, discussed in the Introduction
I A, F.

I YHWH (have spoken). 'ănî YHWH. This deliberate imitation of 18:5b is a
further indication that vv. 36b–37 form an inclusion with 18:2b–5, especially
with vv. 4–5 (see above).

COMMENT

Holiness

In the Semitic languages, the concept of "holy" is expressed by the root *qdš*. In Akkadian, the D-stem *quddušu* means both "to purify" and "to consecrate" (persons, buildings, divine images, ritual appurtenances; *CAD*). Through euphonic metathesis, *dš* = *šd* (cf. GAG § 36b), the verb *qašādu* denotes G-stem (mostly as a stative) "become, be pure"; D-stem (*quššudu*) "purify, consecrate"; adjective *qašdu* 'pure, holy' (*AHw* 906); and *quššudu* 'most holy' (*AHw* 930). These derivatives of *qdš* are, almost without exception, found in a religious-cultic context containing a qualified subject of places and persons that have been "purified" and thereby "consecrated"—that is, brought in close relationship to the deity. This would account in the Bible for the ablutions required before a theophany (Exod 19:10, 14, 22; Num 11:18; Josh 3:5; 7:13; 1 Sam 16:5 [all *Pi'el* and *Hitpa'el*]—that is, purification is a prerequisite for holiness. That the stem *qdš* in BH can denote "purify," without a cultic association, see 2 Sam 11:4, which is also *Hitpa'el*, although it can hardly be an accident that ablutions are required in all cases of impurity, such as in the case of Bathsheba's purification following her menses, before access to the sanctuary or sacred food is permitted. Similarly, the "sanctification" required before fasting (Joel 1:14; 2:15) or waging war (Jer 6:4; 51:27–28; Joel 4:9; Mic 3:5) also denotes ablutions so that God may be present in the war camp or with the people (cf. 2 Kgs 10:20; Joel 2:16). On the basis of the aforementioned verses, Schwartz (forthcoming) claims that the *qdš* also means "appoint, designate." However, as indicated, all these verses presume the appearance of God, which requires purification. Furthermore, *ʾispû-'ām qadd'šû qāhāl* (Joel 2:16) clearly implies that *after* the people are gathered, they are "sanctified." As Wolff (1977: 51) rightly comments, " 'Sanctify' (*qdš pi'el*) means here: to make complete preparations (Josh 3:5 [hithpa'el]) for worship activity, which involves desisting from work, food, and sexual intercourse." All the above citations, it should be noted, are from non-priestly sources (see below). In West Semitic inscriptions (e.g., Ugaritic), *qdš* as a verb means "consecrate" but not "purify," as is possible in Akkadian texts. In either case, the consecration of people or objects to the deity implies no moral dimension (on the etymology, see further Kornfeld and Ringgren 1989).

An examination of Semitic polytheism (and, indeed, of any primitive religion) shows that the realm of the gods is never wholly separate from or transcendent to the world of man. Natural objects such as specific trees, rivers, stones, and the like are invested with supernal force. But this earthbound power is independent of the gods and can be an unpredictable danger to them as well as to man. Holy is thus aptly defined, in any context, as "that which is unapproachable except through divinely imposed restrictions" or "that which is withdrawn from common use."

In opposition to this widespread animism, we notice its absence from the Bible. Holiness there is not innate. The source of holiness is assigned to God alone. Holiness is his quintessential nature (see NOTE on 20:3), distinguishing him from all beings (1 Sam 2:2). It acts as the agency of his will. If certain things are termed holy—such as land (Canaan), person (priest), place (sanctuary), or time (festival day)—they are so by virtue of divine dispensation. Moreover, this designation is always subject to recall. Thus the Bible exorcises the demoniac from nature; it makes all supernatural force coextensive with God. True, as in the polytheistic religions, the sancta of the Bible can cause death to the unwary and the impure who approach them without regard for the regulations that govern their usage. Indeed, although biblical *qādôš* attains new dimensions, it never loses the sense of withdrawal and separation (vol. 1.731; see NOTES on 20:25), as will be demonstrated below.

The following analysis is limited to the pentateuchal codes (JE, D, P, and H). Diachronically, these four codes can be considered as two: JE leading to D, and P leading to H (see Introduction II R).

In P, only the sanctuary, its sancta, and those authorized to serve them (the priests) are holy by virtue of being sanctified with the sacred anointment oil (Lev 8:10–11, 15, 30). A temporary status of holiness is also bestowed on the Nazirite as a consequence of his vow of abstinence (Num 6:2–8), especially the prohibition against shaving or trimming his sanctified hair (cf. Num 6:5, 7, 9, 18). Prior to the selection of Aaron and his descendants, the firstborn served as priests, to judge by the tradition, acknowledged by P, that they were "sanctified" by God (Num 3:13; 8:17). To be sure, P maintains that they were replaced by Levites, not by priests. However, the Levites did not inherit the firstborn's holiness. In fact, P goes out of its way to deny the term *qādôš* 'holy' to the Levites and employs, instead, the neutral verb *nātan* 'assign' (Num 8:16; 18:6; cf. Milgrom 1990a: 63–64)—an indication of the enduring obsession of the Aaronide priests to deny priestly status to the Levites. The Kohathite Levites, it should be noted, were warned on pain of death not to touch the covered inner sancta, but to carry them by their poles and frames (Num 4:15; cf. 2 Sam 6:6–7). They were forbidden even to look at them while they were being covered (Num 4:20; cf. 1 Sam 6:19). In other words, in regard to the sacred sphere the Levites were laymen.

The term "holy" (rather, *miqrā' qōdeš* 'a proclamation of holiness') is also bestowed on the fixed festivals (Num 28–29) because they are characterized by the prohibition against work. This term is, therefore, absent from the injunctions concerning the new moon (Num 28:11–15), which is not a day of rest. It is also missing in P's prescriptions for the sabbath (Num 28:9–10), despite the fact that it is the day of rest par excellence. In this case, a different consideration prevails: the sabbath is not proclaimed—it automatically falls every seventh day—and, hence, the term *miqrā'* (from *qāra'* 'proclaim') does not apply (vol. 1.20–21).

In sum, the root *qdš* in all its forms (Pi'el *qiddēš* 'sanctify [by ritual]'; Hip'il *hiqdîš* 'consecrate [by transfer from common to sacred status]'; adj. *qādôš* 'holy'; noun *qōdeš* 'sacred place or object') bears the basic meaning "set apart for God," and applies in P to only *certain* space, persons, and time.

Most recently, Kugler (1997: 15, 22) has challenged the consensus that holds that severe impurity pollutes the holy and instead he propounds the reverse: "Contact between the sanctified and impurity never actually damages the holy in Leviticus 1–16. In fact the opposite seems to be true, where the concern to separate the holy from the impure is evident . . . it is probably for the protection of the impure person from the effect of the holy . . . there is no unequivocal expression of deep concern in Leviticus 1–16 about the invasion of the sanctuary of things impure."

First and foremost, the very P whose theology Kugler (1997) attempts to comprehend postulates that holiness, except for the innermost sanctums, is not contagious to humans (for substantiation, see vol. 1.443–56). I shall cite three examples:

1. Gershonite Levites dismantle, cast away, and reassemble the Tabernacle curtains. The Levites are laymen, and the inner curtains (Num 4:25), according to P, are most sacred (Exod 30:20). Yet the Levites can handle them with impurity! Clearly, their holiness is not contagious to humans.
2. The trespasser upon sanctums must atone for his sacrilege by a fine and sacrifice (Lev 5:14–16), but he is unaffected by his contact with "the most sacred."
3. A person handling sacred meat, even if it is "most sacred," is not infected with holiness (Hag 2:12).

Other examples are cited in vol 1.447–450. The upshot of the matter: all the sanctums outside the inner sanctuary possess no contagious holiness, and the formula *kol-hannogēaʿ yiqdāš* (Exod 29:37; 30:26–29; Lev 6:11, 20), on which Kugler relies, must be rendered "whatever [not "whoever"] touches . . . shall become holy." These sanctums are contagious to objects, not persons. P's great innovation is that it has defused the altar (lying in the outer court, not inside the sanctuary), rendering it noncontagious to persons (Exod 30:28–29) and thus denying it the power to grant asylum to criminals (for the demonstration, see Milgrom 1990: 504–9).

As for Kugler's (1997: 20) contention that in P the sanctuary and its sanctums are "unaffected by the impurity of the general population," what is Lev 16 (an entire chapter!) all about? Why indeed the urgency and emergency to purge (*kippēr*) the sanctuary? There is no need to waste time with an investigation. The text is unambiguous and explicit: *wěkipper ʿal- haqqōdeš miṭṭumʾot běnê yiśrāʾēl* 'Thus he shall purge the adytum of the pollution of the Israelites' (16:16aα). And this verse ends *wěkēn ya ʿăśeh lěʾōhel môʿēd haššōkēm ʾittām bětôk ṭumʾōtām* 'and he shall do likewise for the Tent of Meeting which abides with them in the midst of their pollution' (v. 16b). Can there be any doubt that *ṭumʾâ* 'impurity' has invaded the sanctuary building and penetrated into the Holy of Holies? Thus the sanctums, even the most powerful, prove ineffectual to repel the incursion of impurity. Kugler (1997: 20), therefore, is fundamentally in error in regard to the relationship between holiness and impurity in P and, as will be shown below, equally erroneous in H.

According to Kugler (1997: 20), H maintains that every Israelite is holy; hence if he contacts impurity, he "stands no chance of survival." To be sure, H postulates a metaphoric, nonritualistic impurity, such as sexual violations (Lev 18, 20), that is cultically irremediable (see INTRODUCTION to 18:24–30). However, H does not negate P's cultic impurity, but supports it. H, for example, appends to Lev 16 its own laws, turning P's emergency rite (16:2–3) into an annual one that enjoins abstention from work and fasting upon the entire people (16:29–34a). But it also acknowledges the indispensability of purging the sanctuary of Israel's impurity (v. 33). This means that even the *deliberate* polluter need not die, but can hope that his penitence on that day will effect absolution. Moreover, 15:31 (H) states that polluting the sanctuary incurs death. But if the people are holy, they should be sentenced to death upon contracting impurity! Again, Num 15:22–31 (H) enjoins the purification offering for all inadvertent sins. But if Israel is intrinsically holy, its sacrifice should be of no avail, since it is automatically doomed! The answer, as expounded in the NOTES on 19:2, is that the laity is not inherently holy, but can become holy by following the commandments. For all Israelites (including priests! see NOTE on 21:15), holiness is not static, endemic, but a goal to be attained (by the laity) or sustained (by the priests).

In H, the root *qdš* occurs sixty-six times in chaps. 19–23 (*Nip'al* [once]; *Pi'el* [nine times]; *Hip'îl* [twice]; *Hitpa'el* [once]; adjective *qādôš* [ten times], substantive *qôdeš* [thirty-six times]; *miqdāš* [seven times]). However, as demonstrated by Zimmerli (1980), God's holiness is implied by his self-declaration *'ănî YHWH* (*'ĕlōhêkem*) 'I (am) YHWH (your God)', especially when it is followed by his salvific action *'ăšer hôṣē'tîkā mē'ereṣ miṣrayim* 'who has freed you from the land of Egypt'. The addition of these two formulas enlarges the compass of H to Lev 18–26. (Concerning the remaining chaps. 17 and 27, see Introduction I E, NOTES on chap. 17, and chap. 27, COMMENT B.) Furthermore, the root *qdš* referring to God and the two formulas are attested within P contexts, inside and outside Leviticus, in passages also attributable to H (Lev 11:43–45 [see vol. 1]; Exod 6:2–8, 29; 7:5; 12:12; 29:43–46; 31:12–17; Num 3:13, 44–50; 14:26–35; 15:37–41; 35:34; see Introduction II G).

H introduces three radical changes regarding P's notion of holiness. First, it breaks down the barrier between the priesthood and the laity. The attribute of holy is accessible to all Israel. This implies, as aptly noted by Greenberg (1990: 370), that just as the priests qualify for service by learning and obeying the rules of their order, so the folk-priesthood of Israel must learn and follow the divine law commanded to them. Second, holiness is not just a matter of adhering to a regimen of prohibitive commandments, taboos; it embraces positive, performative commandments that are ethical in nature. Third, all of Israel, priests included, enhance or diminish their holiness in proportion to their observance of all of God's commandments (see NOTE on 20:8). The key to these changes is a new understanding of the holiness of God as expounded in Lev 19.

Chap. 19 opens with the imperative: "You shall be holy, for I, YHWH your God, am holy" (v. 2αβ,b). As pointed out in its NOTE, this chapter is thereby radically different from the preceding one, which is headed by the divine self-declaration "I am YHWH your God" (18:2b). This formula opens the Decalogue (Exod 20:2α; Deut 5:6a). In chap. 19, however, H has altered the formula to emphasize YHWH's holy nature and that Israel should emulate it. The chapter then enumerates some thirty commandments grouped into eighteen units (see INTRODUCTION) by which the goal of holiness can be attained. H accepts the prophetic dictum that righteousness is a quintessential component of holiness (Isa 5:16; with Knohl 1995: 214) and fleshes it out in a series of commandments that are a mixture of both rituals and ethics, the latter taking predominance. Thus holiness is no longer just a matter of "divinely imposed restrictions," but also embraces positive ethical standards that are illustrative of God's nature: as he relates to his creation, so should Israel relate to one another (details in NOTE on v. 2). Thus all the commandments enumerated in chap. 19 fall under the rubric of holiness. A parade example is the *šĕlāmîm* prescription (vv. 5–8). It is a repetition of P (7:16–18), but in its rationale (v. 8) it adds the terms *qōdeš* and its antonym *ḥillēl*. But before entering into a detailed analysis of chap. 19, the concept of holiness in the JE and D codes needs to be discussed.

It initially comes as a surprise that H never designates God's land as holy. Perhaps (as suggested in NOTE on 25:23), if the land were a sanctum, it could be polluted by all forms of impurity—deliberate, accidental or unconscious. Thus H's metaphoric concept of impurity must break the nexus between impurity and its remedy, ritual purification: the pollution of the land is irreversible by ritual means (see INTRODUCTION to 18:24–30). A more fundamental reason, however, is H's rejection of the notion that holiness inheres in nature. In this regard, it differs sharply with P. Whereas P declares that it was Moses who sanctified the Tabernacle and its priests (with the anointment oil, Lev 8 [P]), H states emphatically "I will sanctify [*wĕqiddaštî*] the Tent of Meeting and the altar, and I will consecrate ['*ăqaddēš*] Aaron and his sons to serve me as priests" (Exod 29:44 [H]).

Thus H implies that neither the oil is *inherently* sacred nor its manipulator, Moses, is responsible for the sanctification, but sanctification is generated solely by God's condescending presence (*wĕniqdaš bikbōdî*, Exod 29:43b [H]). In H's view, God does endow Israel with the power to sanctify—not objects, but time. The festivals are *miqrāʾê qôdeš* (lit. "proclamations of holiness"), whose dates on the calendar are fixed by Israel's decrees (except for the sabbath, which is independent of the calendar and which was preordained by God to be holy, Gen 2:3). The concession is significant: with time, in contrast to the land, there is no fear of inherent holiness, a notion that can imply a source of power independent of that of God. H also differs sharply from earlier JE and its subsequent evolution into D (see Introduction I I).

To be sure, Nicholson (1982: 80–83) followed by Blum (1990: 51–53) claim that Israel at Sinai was actually consecrated as priests and a holy people (in fulfillment of Exod 19:6) by the sacrificial blood dashed on them (Exod 24:8a). What consecratory power, however, resides per se in blood? The analogy of the priestly consecration (Lev 8:30) actually undermines their case. The sacrificial blood sprinkled on them and their vestments comes from the altar. That is, the most sacred altar must first transfer its sanctity to the blood (cf. Exod 30:28–29; see vol. 1.443–56, 532–34) before it can sanctify the priestly consecrands. Although the Sinaitic covenant rite is still a mystery, it may be related to the other JE covenant account (Gen 15:17), where God (in Jer 34:18, the people) passes through severed halves of animals as a sign that he has bound himself by the covenant that he struck with Abraham (cf. Weinfeld 1975a: 262–63; 1975b: 77–78). For a similar covenant rite in the ancient Near East, see Sefire I A 39–40 (*ANET* 660; cf. 532–33). This, indeed, is what the Sinaitic text explicitly states: "This is the blood of the covenant" (Exod 24:8). The blood, then, has not made Israel priests, but confirms that Israel is bound by the covenant (Exod 24: 3–4). The problem with this solution is that blood plays no part in the Abrahamic covenant (or in Jer 34:18). The enigma of the blood rite remains unresolved (cf. Hasel 1981). In any case, it does not sanctify the people. Israel, as the text states explicitly, is an aspirant of holiness (Exod 19:6; cf. 22:30), not its possessor.

Rendtorff (1991: 467) astutely remarks that Israel's "sanctification" is associated with the Exodus (Exod 19:4–6), and that a similar association is recorded in Lev 11:44–45. The latter, however, confirms not that Israel *is* holy, but that H, like JE before it, enjoins Israel to *become* holy. Rendtorff also points to the proliferation of the root *qdš* in the Sinaitic account (Exod 19:10, 14, 22), which ostensibly affirms Israel's sanctity. However, as demonstrated in vol. 1.445, 602–3, JE's *Pi'el* and *Hitpa'el* denote "purify / purify oneself," not "sanctify / sanctify oneself," precisely as Israel proceeds to do by laundering its garments.

Gerstenberger (1996: 282) correctly contrasts the ethical holiness prescribed by Lev 19 with its ritual counterpart: "(Ex. 19:10ff., 22; Num. 11:18; Josh. 3:5; 7:13; 2 Chron. 30:15–20) . . . [which] traditionally includes ablutions, abstinence rites, and sacrifices (?), and often extends over a specified period of time." Note, however, that these citations are all from epic sources, whereas in P these cultic preparations are called "purification" (*ṭhr*). Thus, in this matter, H is consistent with its P heritage. Instead, it polemicizes with the popular notion of a time-bound "consecration." Purification (*ṭhr*) eliminates impurity, leading to the state of the common (*ḥōl*), a condition required for contact with the holy sphere. H pursues this forward movement further, demanding that the common be transformed into the holy (see Figure 3 and discussion, below). H's ethical stance on holiness is clearly reflected in the priestly challenge to pilgrims at the entrance to the Temple precincts, as recorded by the Psalmist: "Who shall stand in his holy place? He who has clean hands and a pure heart" (Ps 24:3–4; cf. Isa 33:15; 33:14–15, and vol. 1.731).

The epic tradition (JE) has proposed that Israel could become a holy people, but only if it would accept the covenantal obligations of the Decalogue (Exod 19:5–6), the two distinctive elements of which are the rejection of idolatry and the observance of the sabbath (Exod 20:3–11). Implied, therefore, is that nonobservance disqualifies Israel from attaining a holy status (contra Schwartz, forthcoming), a position that anticipates H. In this matter, D differs sharply from its demonstrated reliance on E (Milgrom 1976h). The epic tradition also adds abstention from *ṭĕrēpâ* 'torn flesh (by prey)' as a holiness requirement (Exod 22:30). This prohibition is contextually tied to the requirement to dedicate the first of the crops and the womb of both humans and beasts to YHWH (vv. 28–29), which by implication are also holy (Knohl, personal communication). These three injunctions—abstention from idolatry, sabbath labor, and torn flesh—are therefore JE's prescription for holiness.

D incorporates them in its holiness prescriptions by its repetition of the Decalogue (Deut 5:7–15), its emphasis on the rejection of idolatry (Deut 7:6; 14:2), and its full dietary code (Deut 14:3–21, esp. v. 21). D may not be original. It may have followed the initiative of eighth-century Isaiah, who referred to the survivors (one-tenth) of God's purge of Israel as *zeraʿ qōdeš* 'a holy seed' (Isa 6:13; G. D. Cohen, cited by Greenberg 1996: 31). Nonetheless, the translation of this idea into law, incumbent on all Israel and not just for a surviving remnant, is the innovation of D. Moreover, D institutes a change of its own: Israel *is* a holy people by virtue of its covenant, and perhaps from the days it was founded by the patriarchs (Deut 7:6–8; 10:15; Schwartz, forthcoming).

In any event, D surely follows the view of its forerunner E that Israel was initiated/"consecrated" into the covenant at Sinai (Exod 24:1–8 [E]). The priests (P/H) harbor no such tradition. Only they were consecrated (Exod 29; Lev 8), not the people. The people have to "earn" their consecration by obeying YHWH's commandments. To be sure, D also acknowledges that Israel's retention of its holy status is dependent on its adherence to YHWH's commandments (Deut 26:17–19; 28:9). This condition recalls H's view of the priesthood: although priests are genetically holy, they diminish, and can even forfeit, their holiness by their violation of the commandments. And conversely, by observing the commandments, they augment their holy status (see NOTES on "I YHWH sanctify them / him," 21:8 LXX, 15; 22:9, 16). Thus for H, holiness is a dynamic concept, toward which all of Israel, priests and laity alike, must continually strive: priests to retain it, lay persons to attain it (see below).

Schwartz (forthcoming) claims (contra Milgrom 1976h: 5; Knohl 1995: 183, n. 43) that since Israel's holiness is transmitted from the forefathers genetically, it is unconditional. In rebuttal, I concede that this view may be implied by the static status of Israel in Deut 7:6; 14:2, 21. However, it is blatantly qualified in the later chapters (by a tradent?) so that if Israel adheres to the commandments, only then *will* God fulfill (*yĕqîmĕkā*) his promise of holiness to the forefathers (26:18–19; 28:9). Hence D moves toward convergence with H on the issue of Israel's holiness.

Nonetheless, this overlap in goal should not mask D's innovation. Whereas H, in agreement with JE (cf. Exod 19:6), regards holiness only as an ideal toward which Israel should aspire, D establishes Israel's holiness as inherent in its biological nature. Thus from the diachronic viewpoint, D has extended H's axioms regarding priestly holiness to all of Israel. Knohl (1995: 183, n. 43) adds a further nuance: in D, holiness is the *reason* for the prohibitions; in H, the prohibitions are the *means* for holiness. Both D and H, however, condition priestly holiness (H) and Israel's holiness (D) on obedience to God's commandments.

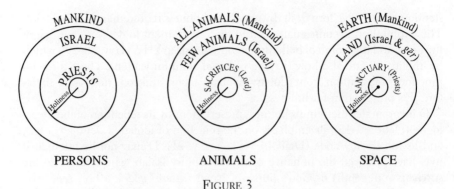

FIGURE 3

As has been demonstrated (vol. 1.698–704), D's diet laws are modeled on Lev 11, and the attachment of the holiness ideal to Israel's diet is also the contribution of H (see NOTES on 11:43–45). H also bans idolatry and emphasizes the sabbath as part of its holiness prescriptions (20:1–8; 19:3, 30; 26:2a). H, however, goes much further: it adds many other regulations, ritual but mainly ethical, as itemized in chap. 19 (see below), and enjoins the wearing of distinctive tassels as a daily mnemonic that Israel can attain holiness by observing YHWH's commandments (Num 15:37–41 [H]; see Milgrom 1990a: 410–14). Moreover, it polemicizes against P's dogmatic insistence that priestly holiness is unchanging and permanent by implying that the violation of YHWH's commandments bars not only Israel from attaining holiness but also priests from retaining it (see NOTES on 21:6, 8, 15; 22:9). H's dynamic concept of holiness is best explained by resorting to Figure 3 (also found in vol. 1.722–25, 32).

In P's world view, the tripartite division of human race corresponds to its three covenants with God: humanity (Gen 9:1–11, including the animals), Israel (via the patriarchs, Gen 17:2; cf. Lev 26:42), and the priesthood (Num 25:11–13; cf. Jer 33:17–22). The comparison of these three congruent sets of concentric circles reveals, first, that priests, sacrifices, and sanctuary (the innermost circles) must be unblemished and unpolluted. They are deliberately set apart from the middle circles, implying that the realms of priests, sacrifices, and sanctuary must never be fused or confused with the realms of Israel, edible animals, and holy land, respectively. Humankind is permitted all animals for its diet, with the proviso that their blood is drained (Gen 9:3–4). Israel (the gēr is H's innovation) must be in a state of ritual purity to enter the sanctuary or partake of sacred food (Lev 7:20–21; 12:4). Priests are bound to a severe regimen of conduct, especially in regard to mourning and marriage, to warrant their office as sanctuary officiants, and the high priest must live by an even higher standard. These rules are found in H (21:1–15), but it must be presumed to be operative in P (see NOTE on 21:7).

H breaks apart this static, immutable picture. It declares that the innermost circles are neither fixed nor frozen. All three innermost realms are capable of a centrifugal movement, enabling them to incorporate their respective middle circles. According to H, although priests are innately holy, all Israel is enjoined to achieve holiness. Not that Israel is to observe the priestly regimen or attain priestly status in the sanctuary. Rather, by scrupulously observing YHWH's commandments, moral and ritual alike, lay Israel can achieve holiness, and priestly Israel can retain it. Indeed, as detailed in the NOTE on 20:8, Israel's holiness is neither inherent nor automatic (as implied by D), but a reciprocal process. God sanctifies Israel in proportion to Israel's self-sanctification.

Signs of this mobility are reflected in the animal sphere: H insists that the blood of permitted nonsacrificial animals (game) must be buried so that the animal's life force can be returned to its creator (see NOTE on 17:14). Sacrificeable animals, however, must be slaughtered (and sacrificed) at the altar. H has abolished profane (i.e., common) slaughter. Henceforth, all slaughter must be sacred. That is, every animal must be brought to the sanctuary. It is transferred from the domain of the profane to the domain of the sanctuary.

H also harbors an old tradition that the entire camp in the wilderness cannot tolerate severe impurity (Num 5:1–4; cf. 31:19). This tradition is echoed in D, which explicitly stipulates that the camp must be holy (Deut 23:10–15). It is H, however, that extends this view, logically and consistently, to the future residence of Israel—the promised land. Hence impurities produced by Israel by violating YHWH's prohibitions pollute not only the sanctuary, but the entire land. Because God dwells in the land as well as in the sanctuary (e.g., 25:23; 26:11; cf. Josh 22:19; Hos 9:3–4), the land cannot abide pollution (e.g., 18:25–30; cf. Num 35:33–34). It is, therefore, no accident that H enjoins upon both the Israelite and the resident alien (*gēr*)—that is, all who live on the land—to keep the land holy by guarding against impurity and following the prescribed purificatory procedures (e.g., Num 15:27–29; 19:10b–13; the *gēr* is an H addition, as explained in Introduction II I) so that YHWH will continue to reside in it and bless the land and its inhabitants with fertility and security (26:3–12).

The dynamic catalyst that turns H's view of YHWH's covenant from a static picture into one of flux is its concept of holiness. For H, the ideal of holiness not only is embodied in a limited group (priests), animals (sacrifices), and space (sanctuary), but affects all who live on God's land: persons and animals, Israel and the *gēr*.

There is one other obligatory dimension for Israel—time. Figure 4 contains only two concentric circles. The holiest day is the sabbath; it is YHWH's (Exod 16:23; 20:10; 35:2; 23:3). It was sanctified at creation (Gen 2:3), and its observance is theoretically available to all persons, but is obligatory for every Israelite household and every living thing in his charge (Exod 20:8–11). The sabbath's holiness is defined by the stoppage of all labor.

The festivals are not YHWH's. They are *miqrā'ê qōdeš,* literally "proclamations of holiness" (see NOTE on "sacred occasions," 23:3) because they, too, require the stoppage of labor (but, with the exception of the Day of Purgation, not to the same degree as the sabbath). Set by the lunar calendar, they do not occur with the regularity of the sabbath. Therefore, it is the responsibility of Israel to fix these days (*môʿēd*) and proclaim them (*miqrā'*). In P's calendar, the sabbath is not a *miqrā' qōdeš;* it falls automatically on every seventh day and need

FIGURE 4

not be proclaimed. New moon is not a "sacred occasion" for a different reason: it is a workday (Num 28:11–15).

H declares the sabbath a *miqrā' qōdeš* (Lev 23:3). Israel was in exile. Being subject to the Babylonian calendar, whose days were ordered by the month—not the week—the exiles might have overlooked the advent of the sabbath; it had to be proclaimed.

In the priestly system, the nations were not required to observe time. Only the prophets, in their eschatological visions, project a period when all peoples will pilgrimage to Jerusalem to worship YHWH on sabbaths and new moons (Isa 66:23) and on the Festival of Booths (Zech 14:16).

Figure 4 contains no arrow and, hence, no movement. In the time dimension, H is not dynamic in relation to P in contrast with the dimensions of person, animals and space (above). H accepts P's concept of the holy sabbath and festivals and the obligation of Israel to sanctify them by the same differentiated work stoppage. H differs with P only by proclaiming the sabbath (and in some minutiae detailed in NOTES on chap. 23).

Schwartz (forthcoming) visualizes the divine presence touching Israelites, and sanctifying them. This image is misleading. Just as YHWH's presence in the sanctuary does not continue to sanctify the priests who serve within or the layperson when he enters, neither does his presence in the land sanctify its inhabitants. Indeed, as the blessings of Lev 26:11–13 indicate, YHWH's walking about (*wĕhithallaktî*, v. 12) the land is for the purposes of fertility (vv. 1–5a, 9–10), and protection (vv. 5b–8). Israelites and priests alike are sanctified by virtue of their own effort, namely, by their adherence to the divine commandments.

As noted above, the commandments, the observance of which generates holiness, are performative as well as prohibitive, ethical as well as ritual. In contrast with P, which touches on the dangerous, even fatal aspect of the sancta (e.g., 10:1–4; Num 4:15, 17–20), H focuses exclusively on the beneficial aspects of divine holiness. It generates blessing and life; it is the antonym and ultimate conqueror of impurity, the symbol of death (vol. 1.733, 766–68, 1000–1004). This dynamic power of holiness can also be represented diagrammatically:

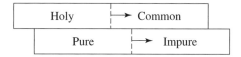

Persons and objects are subject to four possible states: holy, common, pure, and impure. Two of them can exist simultaneously: pure things may be either holy or common; common things may be either pure or impure. (These relationships are represented in adjoining boxes in the diagram.) However, the holy may not come into contact with the impure. (Their respective boxes do not touch.) These latter two categories are mutually antagonistic. Moreover, they are dynamic; they seek to extend their influence and control over the other two categories: the common and the pure. In contrast to the holy and impure, the common and pure are static. They cannot transfer their state; they are not contagious. Indeed, in effect they are secondary categories. They take their identity from their antonyms. Purity is the absence of impurity; commonness is the absence of holiness (cf. Paschen 1970: 64). Hence the boundaries between the holy and the common and between the pure and the impure are permeable, represented by a broken line. There is no fixed boundary. Israel by its behavior can move the boundaries either way. But it is enjoined by H to move in one direction only: to *advance the holy* into the realm of the common and to *diminish the impure*, thereby enlarging the realm of the pure. This accounts for the formulaic expression *bên qōdeš lĕḥōl ûbên-tāmē' lĕṭāhôr* 'between holy and common and between impure and pure' (Ezek 44:23; cf. Lev 10:10). Besides the fact that it exemplifies the priestly affection for chiasm, ABB'A' (cf. 11:47; 20:25), it emphasizes that the first member in each clause (AB') is dynamic and the second, static (BA').

I submit that the same rationale or, more precisely, its complement obtains here. The bodily impurities enumerated in the impurity table (vol. 1.986–91) focus on four phenomena: death (4, 5, 7, 11), blood (2, 3, 8), semen (3, 10), and scale disease (1). Their common denominator is death. Vaginal blood and semen represent the forces of life; their loss, death (vol. 1.766–68). In the case of scale disease, this symbolism is made explicit: Aaron prays for his stricken sister, "Let her not be like a corpse" (Num 12:14). The wasting of the body, the common characteristic of all biblically impure skin diseases, symbolizes the death process as much as the loss of blood and semen. The antonymy of life (*qādōš*) and death (*ṭāmē'*) is graphically underscored by the rationale for not engaging in certain mourning rites for the dead (Deut 14:1–2): *kî 'am qādōš 'attâ* 'for you are a holy people'. (The previous word is *lāmēt* 'for the dead', making the juxtaposition—rather, the opposition—of holy and death striking.)

Thus *ṭum'â* and *qĕdûšâ*, biblical impurity and holiness, are semantic opposites. And as the quintessence and source of *qĕdûšâ* resides with God, it is imperative for Israel to control the occurrence of impurity lest it impinge on the realm of the holy God. The forces pitted against each other in the cosmic struggle are no longer the benevolent and demonic deities who populate the mythologies of Israel's neighbors, but the forces of life and death set loose by man him-self through his obedience to or defiance of God's commandments. Among all the diachronic changes that occur in the development of Israel's impurity laws (vol. 1.986–1000), this clearly is the most significant: the total severance of im-purity from the demonic and its reinterpretation as a symbolic system remind-ing Israel of its imperative to cleave to life and reject death.

Hartley (1992: LX) writes that "another polarity inherent to the holy is that of whole / defective." This undoubtedly holds within the sanctuary, where priests and sacrifices must be unblemished. But outside the sanctuary, this antinomy does not prevail. In fact, Israel's access to the sanctuary or to sacred food is independent of any physical defect (*mûm*). Note that in the detailed program for achieving holi-ness (chap. 19), there is no mention of any physical imperfection. One may, how-ever, say that by not following this program, Israel sustains *moral* imperfection.

Lev 19 provides the prescription to effect this transformation. Under the call to holiness (v. 2), it enumerates sixteen units containing commandments by which holiness can be achieved. The first two units echo the Decalogue. The sabbath (v. 3b) must be sanctified (Exod 20:8–11; Deut 5:12–15), and parents must be honored, revered (v. 3a; Exod 20:12; Deut 5:16); the worship of other gods and images of Israel's God (v. 4) are strictly forbidden (Exod 20:3–6; Deut 5:7–10); and as proposed by the epic tradition—which H has adopted (see In-troduction II G)—obedience to the covenantal Decalogue renders Israel a *gôy qādôš* 'a holy nation' (Exod 19:6).

Unit 3, the well-being offering (vv. 5–8), expressly mentions the terms *qōdeš* 'sacred' and its violation, *ḥillēl* 'desecrate' (v. 8). Unit 4, horticultural holiness (vv. 9–10), lacks these terms, but its inclusion under the call to holiness is sig-nificant. The emulation of God's holiness, *imitatio dei*, must include material-izing God's concern for the indigent. Also, setting aside part of the harvest might be equivalent to firstfruits and tithes; thereby, symbolically, YHWH has assigned some of his due to the poor. Unit 5, ethical deeds (vv. 11–13), includes oath desecration (*ḥillēl*, v. 12), implying the concomitant diminution in holiness. The remainder of this ethical series (vv. 14–18) includes unit 6, exploitation of the helpless (v. 14); unit 7, injustice and indifference (vv. 15–16); and unit 8, re-proof and love (vv. 17–18), all of which emphasize the divine attribute of com-passion, essential to his holy nature. As neatly encapsulated by the rabbis: "As he (the Lord) is gracious and compassionate (cf. Exod 34:6) so you should be gracious and compassionate" (*Mek.* Shira, par. 3; *b. Šabb.* 133b). "As he clothes the naked (Gen 3:21), you should clothe the naked; as he nurses the sick (Gen 18:1), you should nurse the sick; as he comforts the mourners (Gen 25:11), you should comfort the mourners; as he buries the dead (Deut 34:5), so you should bury the dead" (*b. Soṭ.* 14a).

Unit 9, mixtures (v. 19), proscribes the breeding of different animals, sowing mixed seed, or weaving fabrics made from mixed seed because these mixtures are reserved for the sacred sphere: the sanctuary and the priests. Unit 10, the betrothed slave-woman (vv. 20–22), involves a reparation offering prescribed in cases of *desecration* (5:14–16). Unit 11, horticultural holiness (vv. 23–25), focuses on the fruit of the fourth year, which is declared *qōdeš* 'sacred' and belongs to YHWH (v. 24). Unit 12, eschewing the chief form of impurity, death and the dead (vv. 26–28), is essential in adhering to the God of holiness—life. Unit 13, prostitution (v. 29), is a form of desecration (cf. 22:7, 9). Units 14–16, sabbath and sanctuary (also 26:2), consulting the dead (also 20:1–7), and respecting elders (vv. 30–32), parallel the opening verses (vv. 3–4) and, hence, echo the Decalogue, the basic prescription for holiness. Units 17–18, the *gēr* and business ethics (vv. 33–37), as explained in the INTRODUCTION to this chapter, are appendices.

To recapitulate, in Lev 19, H, in effect, writes a new "Decalogue." YHWH's self-declaration becomes a call to holiness, followed by a series of commandments (addressing the most pressing problems in H's time; see below) by which holiness may be achieved.

Schwartz (forthcoming) offers the following reasons for denying that the binding theme of Lev 19 is holiness:

1. Eight units out of eighteen do not have the root *qdš* (vv. 9–10, 13–14, 15–16, 17–18, 20–22, 32, 33–34, 35–36).
2. The term *qdš* or its antonym *ḥll* occurs in the rationale, not in the body of the law.
3. Why must the term *qdš* in some laws be sought elsewhere (e.g., sabbath, Gen 2:2; mixed seed, Deut 22:9, mourning rites, Deut 14:1–2)?
4. The nature of holiness in Lev 19 is not homogeneous; contagious in relation to mixed seeds (v. 19), a notion alien to H; static concerning the sanctuary (v. 30) and the sacrifices (v. 8); and dynamic in regard to YHWH (v. 2).

I shall respond seriatim:

1. Schwartz overlooks the basic fact that the formula *ʾănî YHWH* (*ʾĕlōhêkem*), which terminates these units (with the exception of vv. 20–22, which stem from P; see NOTES), is a declaration of YHWH's otherness or holiness. This identification is made explicit in the chapter's title *kî qādôš ʾănî YHWH ʾĕlōhêkem* (v. 2b; cf. 11:44, 45, 20:26; 21:8). And since this formula is found throughout chaps. 18–26—that is, in every chapter of the H corpus except the first and last (chaps. 17, 27)—it provides irrefutable justification for referring to those chapters as the Holiness *Corpus* or *Supplement*.
2. It is not quite true that the terms *qdš* and *ḥll* are found only in the rationale (see vv. 29, 30). Besides, that they would be in the rationales is precisely the point. H wants to show that these laws fall under the rubric of holiness.
3. It is of no consequence that the term *qdš* is found in other passages, since Lev 19, as demonstrated (see INTRODUCTION) is patently borrowing from these passages. Besides, these units conclude with *ʾănî YHWH*—the holiness equivalent.

4. H does not deny the protean nature of holiness—for example, contagious, as in P (20:3), dynamic (*mĕqaddeš*, chaps. 20–22), and static (*miqrā' qōdeš*, the festivals, chap. 23).

As proposed in the NOTES on 19:2 and Introduction II G, the basic text of Lev 19 (vv. 1–32) and, indeed, the bulk of H reflect the priestly response to the indictment by the prophets of the eighth century (especially by Isaiah of Jerusalem) of Israel's cultic and socioeconomic sins. Isaiah's revelation of the thrice-repeated declaration of YHWH's holy nature (Isa 6:3), to judge by the prophet's reaction (v. 5), indicates to him that the divine imperative for Israel is to be ethical: "YHWH of hosts shall be exalted by his judgment and the holy God shall be shown holy by his righteousness" (Isa 5:16), a statement that is both a prediction of doom upon unrighteous Israel (vv. 24–30; cf. Milgrom 1964: 167–72) and an indictment of the moral failings of Israel's corrupt judicial leaders, who blur the distinction between right and wrong (5:20) and pervert justice for the sake of bribes (5:23). Isaiah's indictment of the leadership includes the prophet *and the priest* (28:7), but it is especially directed against the civil leaders (3:14) and the rich (5:8), who rob the poor and seize their land. That is to say, for Isaiah the Trisagion implies that YHWH, who governs his world by justice, expects Israel to do the same. In Isaiah's gloomy forecast, only those who do not participate in these social evils will survive the forthcoming purge, and these few— provided they truly repent—will be called *qādōš* 'holy' and be admitted into the New Zion (4:3; cf. Milgrom 1964: 167–72).

The text of H testifies that its priestly authors have been stung by their fellow Jerusalemite's rebuke. Their response is twofold: First, they adopt Isaiah's revelation that YHWH's holiness implies that Israel must be ethical, and then they go beyond Isaiah by prescribing specific commandments (Lev 19) by which holiness can be attained and—as will be shown in the NOTES on chap. 25—by prescribing a revolutionary program that will reverse the extant socioeconomic wrongs (Lev 25). Second, H takes issue with Isaiah's pessimism concerning Israel's inability to repent. (Note that after pronouncing Israel's irrevocable doom in chap. 6, Isaiah never again calls on his people to repent; cf. Milgrom 1964: 167–72.) In chap. 19, H brims with hope that all Israel will heed the divine call to holiness, and hence there is no reason to anticipate a purge of the nation (the dour forecast of chap. 26 has not yet dawned; see further Introduction II G).

The rabbis follow up on H's insight and extend it into new dimensions. To be sure, they accept the Torah's basic notion that holiness implies separation and withdrawal, and, hence, they interpret the injunction to be holy to mean that Israel must separate itself from the nations of the world and its abominations (20:26; cf. *Mek.* 63a; *Sipra* Qedoshim 93b; *Lev. Rab.* 23 [end]), but they add, in agreement with H: "Be holy, for as long as you fulfill my commandments you are sanctified, but if you neglect them you become profaned" (*Num. Rab.* 17:6), and "when the Omnipresent enjoins a new precept upon Israel, he adds holiness to them" (*Mek.* de-Kaspa 20); and the rabbis exemplify these statements by specifying that holiness is added to Israel by observing the sabbath

(19:3b, 30a; *Mek.* de-Shabbata 1) and by wearing tassels (Num 15:37–41; *Sipre* Num. 115).

The rabbis also enjoin a superior kind of holiness termed by Schechter (1898: 7–10), ḥăsîdût 'saintliness': "Sanctify yourselves even in what is permitted" (*b. Yeb.* 20a), which Ramban elaborates (on 19:2, Schechter's paraphrase), as follows:

> According to my opinion, by the talmudic term pĕrîšût 'separatedness', is not (just) meant abstaining from illicit sexual unions, but something which gives to those who practice it the name pĕrûšîm 'Pharisees'. The matter (is thus): The Torah has forbidden illicit sexual unions as well as certain kinds of food, but allowed intercourse between man and his wife as well as the eating of meat and the drinking of wine. But even within these limits can the man of (impure) appetites be drenched in lusts, become a drunkard and a glutton, as well as use impure language, since there is no (distinct) prohibition against these things in the Torah. Therefore the scripture, after giving in detail the things forbidden absolutely, concluded with a general law (of holiness) to show that we must also abstain from things superfluous. As for instance, that even permitted sexual intercourse should be submitted to restrictions (of holiness), preserving it against degenerating into mere animal lust; that the drinking of wine should be reduced to a minimum, the Nazir being called holy because he abstains from drink, and that one should guard one's mouth and tongue against being defiled by gluttony and vile language. Man should indeed endeavor to reach a similar degree of holiness to R. Chiya who never uttered an idle word in his life . . . the scripture warns us to be clean, pure, and separated from the crowd of men who taint themselves by luxuries and ugliness.
>
> Finally, note this expansion of the Decalogue's prohibition against adultery: "The eye of the adulterer waits for nightfall" (Job 24:15) teaches us that an unchaste look is also to be considered as adultery; and the verse "so that you do not follow your heart and your eyes in your lustful urge" (Num 15:39) teaches that an unchaste look or even an unchaste thought are also to be regarded as adultery. (*Lev. Rab.* 23:12; cf. Matt 5:27)

Ramban was unaware of the archaeological evidence—the profusion of stone vessels from the second century B.C.E. through the second century C.E., especially in Jerusalem and its environs but also throughout the land—that ordinary people were observing a form of nonsacred purity, in handling not just sacred food (prescribed by Scripture, Lev 7:19–21), but ordinary, daily food (E. Regev, unpublished paper). Stone is impervious to impurity, and thus the abundance of jars, mugs, pitchers, bowls, and measuring cups for containing the food and drink for daily meals indicates the extent to which the people-at-large, and not just the pharisees, went in order to conduct their lives according to a more stringent form of purity.

Furthermore, the sectaries of Qumran prescribe a nonbiblical, one-day ablation for the corpse-contaminated (11QT 50:13–16; cf. Milgrom 1978: 512–18;

vol. 1.968–76), also adumbrated in Tob 2:9; Jud 12:6–10, so that he or she would not be contaminated by food or drink. Archaeology confirms this practice by its unearthing of ritual baths (*miqwā'ôt*) built alongside burial caves and graveyards, which must have served the same purpose.

What drove the common people to adopt such stringent measures? Alon (1977: 231–34) is most likely correct in attributing their motivation to the biblical commandment for all Israel to become holy (Lev 19:2; cf. Exod 19:6; Deut 14:2, 21).

20. PENALTIES FOR MOLEK WORSHIP, NECROMANCY, AND SEXUAL OFFENSES

TRANSLATION

¹And YHWH spoke to Moses: ²Say further to the Israelites:

Penalties for Molek Worship

Any man from among the Israelites, or among the aliens residing in Israel, who dedicates any of his offspring to Molek, must be put to death; the people of the land shall pelt him with stones. ³And I myself will set my face against that man and cut him off from among his people, because he dedicated his offspring, thus defiling my sanctuary and desecrating my holy name. ⁴And if the people of the land indeed shut their eyes to that man when he gives of his offspring to Molek by not putting him to death, ⁵I myself will set my face against that man and his family, and I will cut off from among their kin both him and all who whore after him in whoring after Molek.

Penalty for Necromancy

⁶And if any person turns to ghosts and wizard-spirits to whore after them, I will set my face against that person and I will cut him off from among his kin.

Opening Exhortation

⁷You shall sanctify yourselves and be holy, for I YHWH am your God. ⁸You shall heed my statutes and do them: (Thereby) I YHWH make you holy.

Penalties for Sexual Violations

⁹If any man dishonors his father or his mother, he must be put to death; he has dishonored his father or his mother—his bloodguilt is upon him.

¹⁰If a man commits adultery with a married woman—committing adultery with his (Israelite) neighbor's wife—the adulterer and the adulteress must be put to death. ¹¹If a man lies with his father's wife, it is the nakedness of his father that he has uncovered; the two of them must be put to death—their bloodguilt is upon them. ¹²If a man lies with his daughter-in-law, the two of them must be put to death; they have committed a perversion—their bloodguilt is upon them. ¹³If a man lies with a male as one lies with a woman, the two of them have done an abhorrent thing; they must be put to death—their bloodguilt is upon them. ¹⁴If a man marries a woman and her mother, it is a depravity; by fire they shall burn him and them, that there be no depravity among you. ¹⁵If a man has sexual relations with a beast, he must be put to death, and you shall kill the beast. ¹⁶If a woman approaches any beast to mate with it, you shall kill the woman and the beast; they must be put to death—their bloodguilt is upon them.

¹⁷If a man marries his sister, the daughter of either his father or his mother, so that he sees her nakedness and she sees his nakedness, it is a disgrace; they shall be cut off in the sight of their people. He has uncovered the nakedness of his sister; he shall bear his iniquity. ¹⁸If a man lies with a woman in her infirmity and uncovers her nakedness, he has laid bare her source and she has exposed the source of her blood; the two of them shall be cut off from among their kin. ¹⁹You shall not uncover the nakedness of your mother's sister or your father's sister, for that is laying bare his own flesh; they shall bear their punishment. ²⁰If a man lies with his uncle's wife, it is his uncle's nakedness that he has uncovered. They shall bear their sin: they shall die childless. ²¹If a man marries the wife of his brother, it is repulsive. It is the nakedness of his brother that he has uncovered; they shall remain childless.

Closing Exhortation

²²You shall heed all my statutes and all my regulations and do them, so that the land to which I bring you to settle in will not vomit you out. ²³You shall not follow the statutes of the nations that I am driving out before you. It is because they did all these things that I loathed them ²⁴and said to you: You shall possess their land, and I myself will give it to you to possess, a land flowing with milk and honey. I YHWH am your God who has set you apart from other peoples. ²⁵So you shall distinguish between the pure and the impure quadrupeds and between the impure and the pure birds. You shall not defile your throats with a quadruped or bird or anything with which the ground teems, which I have set apart for you to treat as impure. ²⁶You shall be holy to me, for I YHWH am holy; therefore I have set you apart from other peoples to be mine.

Appendix: Penalty for Mediums

²⁷A man or a woman who is a medium for a ghost or wizard-spirit shall be put to death; they shall be pelted with stones—their bloodguilt is upon them.

Comments

Comparison of chaps. 20 and 18, COMMENT A; ancestor worship in the Bible and its world, COMMENTS B and C; and the current misuse of 18.22 (homosexuality), COMMENTS D, E, and F.

NOTES

Depending on how one views the function of vv. 7–8, the structure of chap. 20 falls into one of two patterns: (1) the two main subjects, Molek worship and illicit sex relations, open with *'îš* *'îš* (vv. 2, 9) and close with an exhortation to holiness (vv. 7–8, 26; Wenham 1979) or (2) the main subject, illicit sex relations (vv. 9–21), is encased by two exhortations (vv. 7–8, 22–26) and flanked by two crimes punished by stoning (2, 27; Dillmann and Ryssel 1897; Hoffmann 1953; Hartley 1992). Molek worship (vv. 2–5) begins the entire chapter in order to create a grand introversion with chap. 18, where it occurs near the end of the prohibitions (18:31; Douglas 1995: 253). This chapter consists of a grand introversion (M. Hildenbrand, following but amending Bullinger 1974: 161):

A   Worship of chthonic gods (Molek and necromancy, vv. 1–6)
  B   Sanctification (v. 7)
    C   Exhortation for obedience (v. 8)
      X   Penalties for violation (vv. 9–21)
    C'   Exhortation for obedience (vv. 22–25)
  B'   Sanctification (v. 26)
A'   Worship of chthonic gods (necromancy, v. 27)

AA' have necromancy in common. As explained in "must be put to death," v. 2, Molek worship is placed at the head of the list because it entails the severest penalties: (immediate) death and *kārēt*. The juxtaposition of Molek with necromancy also demonstrates that they show the common characteristic of being forms of chthonic worship (see COMMENT B). They also exhibit the same vocabulary in their penalties (*môt yûmāt*, vv. 2, 27, and *rāgam bā'eben*, vv. 2, 27).

BB' share the vocabulary of sanctification *wihyîtem qĕdōšîm* and the motive *kî* (*qādōš*) *'ănî* YHWH (vv. 7, 26). In vv. 8 and 22, CC' contain the common admonition *ûšĕmartem 'et-ḥuqqōtay* and the positive command *wa 'ăśitem 'ōtām*. The end of v. 8 *'ănî* YHWH *mĕqaddiškem* is balanced in the remainder of C' by the fourfold use of *hibdîl* (vv. 24, 25 [bis], 26), thereby expressing the quintessential characteristic of holiness in signifying separation, God from humans and Israel from other humans (see COMMENT on chap. 19). On this structure, see the Introduction I A. For the outline of the prohibitions, see further the INTRODUCTION to vv. 9–21.

2. *Say further to the Israelites. wĕ'el-bĕnê yiśrā'ēl tō'mar.* In the NOTE on 17:8, it was pointed out that this is one of seven cases of the divine speech formula where the subject and the object are inverted (Exod 30:31; Lev 9:3; 20:2; 24:15;

Num 11:18; 18:26; 27:8). In all but this case, the inversion indicates a change of addressee. This is only one of five cases where the phrase *'el- bĕnê yiśrā'ēl* begins with a *waw* (Exod 30:31; Lev 9:3; 20:2; 24:15; Num 27:8). Perhaps the H redactor had some other purpose in mind, namely, to alert the reader that this chapter is a continuation of chap. 18, where the same subjects, Molek and forbidden sex relations, are discussed (cf. Kalisch 1867–72).

Vv. 2aβ–5. Penalties for Molek Worship

2. *Any man. 'îš 'îš.* The doubling has individualizing force (GKC § 123c), as in 15:2; 17:3; 18:6.

from among the Israelites. mibbĕnê yiśrā'ēl. The Sam. has *mibbêt* 'from the house of (Israel)', as in 17:3, 8, 10 (cf. Ezek 14:7). However, *mibbĕnê* is attested in the same chapter and more frequently elsewhere (17:12, 13; Num 15:26, 29; 19:10, etc.) and is preferred.

the aliens. haggēr. Those who live on the land are subject to the divine prohibitions (see chap. 17, COMMENT B) and explicitly to sexual prohibitions (18:26; Ibn Ezra). The inclusion of the *gēr* proves that the intermarriage theory for the Molek prohibition propounded by the rabbis cannot be right. Its rationale must be some prohibition to which the *gēr* is subject—that is, some form of idolatry (see COMMENT B).

in Israel. bĕyiśrā'ēl. An old designation for the people of Israel (e.g., Gen 34:7; 49:7; Exod 18:1, 9; Num 23:21). In the priestly texts, it is found forty-two times (BDB; e.g., 22:18; 23:42; Num 1:3, 45; 3:13; 18:14, 21; 25:3, 4; 32:13). That it refers to the people and not to the country, a later designation, is shown by the alternative formulations: *bĕtôkām* 'in their midst' (17:8, 10, 13; Num 15:26, 29; 19:10), *bĕtôkĕkem* 'in your midst' (16:29; 17:12; 18:26; Exod 12:49; Ezek 47:22), *'ittĕkem, 'immāk, 'immākem* 'with you' (19:34; 25:6, 45).

dedicates. yitten. For this rendering, see the NOTE on 18:21.

any of his offspring. mizzar'ô. The attachment of *zera'* with Molek (also in v. 4) undercuts the explanation of its use in 18:21 that it refers to spilled, wasted (i.e., incestuous) seed or that it follows the usage of *zera'* in v. 20. More likely, in my opinion, this term was chosen so as to refer to all the children over which the addressee, the head of the family, has control, including the grandchildren and great-grandchildren who are living in his house (e.g., Gen 46:7). The preposition *min* has a partitive sense (GKC §119 w, n. 2).

to Molek. H's obsession with this specific form of idolatry is evident by the lengthy treatment here (vv. 2–5) (see COMMENT B).

must be put to death. môt yûmāt. Two capital crimes have been committed, idolatry and murder (filicide; Bekhor Shor), and murder must be punished by man (Num 35:31–33; cf. Deut 13:7–11; Ehrlich 1908). Molek worship constitutes murder, since the sacrificed child is burned to death (see NOTES on 18:21, and COMMENT B), as is explicitly stated in Ps 106:38: *wayyišpĕkû dām nāqî dambĕnêhem ûbĕnôtêhem 'ăšer zibbĕḥû la'ăṣabbê kĕnā'an wattehĕnap hā'āreṣ bĕdāmîm* 'They **shed** innocent **blood,** the **blood** of their sons and daughters, whom they sacrificed to the idols of Canaan so **that the land was polluted** with **bloodguilt'**. See Num 35:33 on homicide, where the same vocabulary (boldface) obtains.

Moreover, the crimes of Molek worship and necromancy are not listed according to their previous order (18:21 and 19:31, respectively), but are placed at the head of chap. 20 (vv. 1–6), because the entire chapter is ordered according to the severity of the incurred penalties (Hoffmann 1953). The death penalty is prescribed for the violator of the Molek prohibition, as in the cases that follow (vv. 9–16). In the instance of Molek, however, God supplements death with *kārēt*, the termination of the line (v. 3a), and failing immediate action by the judicial authorities, God will personally intervene *wĕśamtî* / *wĕnātattî 'et-pānay* (vv. 5a, 6b) by imposing *kārēt* on the violator's family and followers (v. 5). The rationale is specified: his crime against God is that he polluted YHWH's sanctuary and desecrated his name (v. 3b). The issue is that YHWH's name is invoked by the Molek worshiper, under the erroneous impression that Molek worship is sanctioned by YHWH (see NOTE on 18:21). The sanctuary (clearly the Jerusalem Temple) has been defiled, possibly because the worshiper would likely ascend from the Valley of Hinnom to worship YHWH in the Temple—both on the same day (Ezek 23:38–39; see NOTE on v. 3). The necromancy prohibition (v. 6) is coupled with Molek (vv. 1–5), even though its *kārēt* punishment technically belongs with the other *kārēt* penalties (vv. 17–18), because Molek and necromancy share the motivation—ancestor worship (see COMMENT B). These two prohibitions are disconnected from the sexual prohibitions by an exhortation to observe God's commandments (vv. 7–8) in order to correspond to the list of sexual prohibitions of chap. 18, which is headed by a similar exhortation (18:1–5; see INTRODUCTION to vv. 7–8).

the people of the land. *'am hā'āreṣ* (i.e., the adult male populace-at-large). This phrase must be distinguished from the ostensibly synonymous expression *'anšê hā'āreṣ* (18:27), which refers to non-Israelites. That the public becomes the miscreant's executioner assumes that there were witnesses (Ibn Ezra). The rabbis, however, presumably on the basis of 24:16 (see NOTES), claim that those who live on the land and who therefore suffer by his crime (18:29; 20:22) must put him to death (*Sipra* Qedoshim, par. 4:4; Rashi, Ramban). If so, then the *gēr*, who also resides on the land, participates in the execution (cf. van Houten 1991: 43). However, according to 4:27 (see its NOTE), the *'am hā'āreṣ* is limited to the Israelites (cf. 4:2). *Tg. Onk.* explicitly renders *'ammā' bêt yiśrā'ēl* 'the people of Israel'. And where Deuteronomy prescribes stoning, it specifies *kol hā'ām* 'the people' (Deut 13:10; 17:7)—the Israelites. Nor can one say that the different terminology is due to the varying viewpoints of the sources involved, namely, that P (and D) restricts the executioners to Israelites, whereas H, on the basis of its claim that the resident aliens are subject to the prohibitions, makes them also responsible for carrying out the punishment for their violation. On the contrary, the case of the blasphemer (24:10–23) limits the lapidary execution to the *'ēdâ* (vv. 14, 16) and explicitly directs the law to and describes its fulfillment by the Israelites (vv. 15, 23). Finally, had the text wished to include the *gēr*, it might have used the expression *'anšê hā'āreṣ* (as in 18:27). Thus the very word *'am* clearly implies a group that belongs to a single people, in this case, Israel. The term, therefore, must be the functional equivalent of the wilderness *'ēdâ* in the settled land (cf. Joosten 1996: 46, but see below). Is there any evidence for its existence?

The term *'am hā'āreṣ* also bears a specific technical meaning, referring to a political group in the kingdom of Judah composed of loyal supporters of the Davidic dynasty (e.g., 2 Kgs 11:14, 18, 19, 20; 21:24; 23:30; cf. 14:21; cf. Talmon 1967; 1971; Tadmor 1968: 20–23), and possibly that is its meaning here (Levine 1989). If so, it would betray the time of the writer (H), who abandoned (accidentally?) his fiction of the wilderness *'ēdâ* and substituted the corresponding body operative in his own day (so theorizes Joosten 1994: 59–64; 1996: 42–47). Why the alteration (or lapse)? It may be surmised that Molek worship was felt by the writer to be so threatening to the worship of YHWH that he pressed upon those responsible for its prosecution, his contemporary political body, the *'am hā'āreṣ*, to take action. If correct, this conjecture would add further evidence for the composition of H during the latter part of the Judaen monarchy when Molek worship was rampant (see Introduction II C).

However, my joy at this further support for the preexilic provenance of (most of) H must be tempered by two objections:

1. Clearly, *'am hā'āreṣ* in 4:27 represents a different entity than *'ēdâ* in the same chapter, v. 13, where it probably refers to the populace, the commoners (see its NOTE). Even though Lev 4 is P and not H, it is hard to believe that *'am hā'āreṣ* bears such disparate meanings in the priestly traditions.

2. Supporting P's notion of *'am hā'āreṣ* is the fact that there is no proof that this term in Kings reflects a fixed, ongoing, *political* body. The evidence points to only some powerful socioeconomic (not necessarily political) force that rose up *sporadically* on behalf of the House of David.

Neverthless, the entirely different and contradictory connotation of *'am hā'āreṣ* in the postexilic books gives certainty that this pericope must be of preexilic provenance (Weinberg 1992: 62–74).

As a possible way out of this impasse, I would like to suggest tentatively that the term *'am hā'āreṣ* is equivalent in both H and P. It refers to any unofficial, unauthorized body of Israelites, in contrast to the *'ēdâ* (in its restricted meaning; Milgrom 1990a: 335–36), which is authorized and official, probably a representative body of all the tribal and clan chiʿftains. In reality, we are dealing— to use a derogatory term—with a lynch mob. Its actual, if not infrequent, occurrence is implied in the ordeal of the suspected adulteress (Num 5:12–31; cf. Milgrom 1990a: 346–54) and attested in such recorded cases as Judg 19:22 (cf. Gen 19:4); 1 Sam 11:12.

The sin of the Molek worshiper is exceptionally grievous because of its severe consequence: pollution of the sanctuary and desecration of the name of YHWH (for the latter, see NOTE on 18:21). The sinner must be killed *immediately*; any delay jeopardizes the welfare of the entire nation. Hence the prolonged judicial process necessary for the summoning of the *'ēdâ* may, in this singular incident, be bypassed. After all, witnesses are not required. If he is not caught in flagrante delicto, the erection of the Topheth and, above all, the charred remains of his child are evidence enough.

For an excellent summary of the various groups dealing with the administration of family law, see Gerstenberger (1996: 302–3, small print).

shall pelt him with stones. yirgĕmūhû bā'āben. Lapidary execution is carried out, according to the several legal codes, on the following criminals: blasphemers (24:16; cf. 1 Kgs 21:9–14), necromancers (20:27), sabbath violators (Num 15:35–36), *ḥērem* violators (Josh 7:25), idolaters (Deut 13:11; 17:5), incorrigible children (Deut 21:21), adulterers (Ezek 16:40; 23:47), a bride who does not disclose she was not a virgin (Deut 22:21), a man and a betrothed woman who engage in consenting sex (Deut 22:24), and an ox that gores a person (Exod 21:28–29). The rabbis describe this execution in detail:

> When he was about ten cubits from the place of stoning they used to say to him "Make your confession," for such is the way of them that have been condemned to death to make confession, for everyone that makes his confession has a share in the world to come. For so we have found it with Achan. Joshua said to him, "My son, pay honor to the Lord, the God of Israel, and make confession to him. Tell me what you have done: do not hold anything back from me." Achan answered Joshua, "It is true I sinned against the Lord, the God of Israel, and this is what I did" (Josh 7:19–20). Whence do we learn that his confession made atonement for him? It is written, "And Joshua said, 'What calamity you have brought upon us! The Lord will bring calamity upon you this day'" (v. 25) — "this day" you will suffer calamity, but in the world to come you will not suffer calamity. If he knows not how to confess they say to him "Say, my death be an atonement for all my sins. . . ."
>
> When he was four cubits from the place of stoning they stripped off his clothes. A man is kept covered in front and a woman both in front and behind. So R. Judah. But the Sages say: A man is stoned naked but a woman is not stoned naked. The place of stoning was twice the height of a man. One of the witnesses would knock him down on his loins so that he would fall on his heart. Then the (second) witness would turn him over on his loins (to see) if he died; but if not, the second (witness) took the stone and dropped it on his heart. If he died, that sufficed; but if not, he was stoned by all of Israel, for it is written, "Let the hands of the witnesses be the first against him to put him to death, and the hands of the rest of the people thereafter" (Deut 17:7). (*M. Sanh.* 6:2–4a; see Albeck 1953)

The rabbinic mode of execution is based on two principles: "Love your neighbor as yourself" (19:18) is applied to even a condemned criminal, whom you love by giving him the most humane death possible (*b. Sanh.* 45a, 52a), and the body should not be destroyed or mutilated, unchanged as when God takes a life (*b. Sanh.* 52a). Stoning is confined to the seventeen cases where the Bible prescribes it or where it can be inferred (Exod 22:17, 18; Lev 18:7; 20:2, 9, 10, 11, 12, 13, 15, 16, 27; 24:14; Deut 13:11; 17:5; 21:21; 22:24). However, instead of having all the people kill the convicted person, the rabbis devised a "stoning place" where he is pushed to his death (*m. Sanh.* 6:4). This place must not be too high, which might cause mutilation, or too low, which might prevent instantaneous death (*b. Sanh.* 45a).

The execution is performed by the witnesses to the crime in conformance with Deut 17:7. However, in two respects rabbinic stoning differs with its biblical antecedent: the criminal is thrown upon stones instead of being stoned, and the general public is excluded from the execution, thus eliminating all traces of *vindicta publica* (Cohen 1971: 142–43).

Nevertheless, it must be conceded that this rabbinic jurisprudence is purely academic. The right of the Sanhedrin to impose capital punishment was annulled by the Romans "forty years before the destruction of the Temple" (*b. Sanh.* 41a; *y. Sanh.* 1:18a).

3. *And I myself.* This emphasis is expressed by beginning the sentence with *wa ʾănî.*

will set. ʾ*ettēn.* The use of this verb instead of its synonym *śām* (cf. v. 5) creates a stylistic measure-for-measure punishment: if anyone dedicates (*yittēn*, v. 2) his offspring to Molek, God declares "I will set [ʾ*ettēn*] my face against that man," thus distinguishing this from other uses of the same expression (17:10; 26:17).

set my face against. ʾ*ettēn ʾet-pānay bā.* The force of this expression is neatly captured by the rabbis: "I will turn [*pôneh*] from all my other affairs and occupy myself (solely) with him" (*Sipra* Qedoshim, par. 4:5). *Tgs. Onk.* and *Neof.* render "face" as *rôgĕzay* 'my anger'. For the difference between this expression followed by the preposition *be* (unfavorable; e.g., Ps 34:17) and the preposition ʾ*el* (favorable; e.g., Num 6:26), see the NOTE on 17:10. The former expression is used with only God as the subject (17:10; 20:3, 6; 26:17; Ezek 14:8; 15:7); the latter's subject can also be man (Dan 9:3; 10:15; 2 Chr 20:3).

and cut him off. wĕhikrattî. The punishment of excision falls into the measure-for-measure category: if the Molek worshiper thought that by sacrificing one of his children, he would be granted many more (Ramban, Abravanel), God will see to it that death will terminate his line. Also, he hoped that the progeny Molek would grant him would guarantee earthly immortality. Instead, he will be denied access to his deceased ancestors. That is, he will be "cut off" from the past as well as the future.

Wellhausen (1963: 156) believes that this verse, imposing *kārēt*, contradicts death by stoning (v. 2), which vv. 4–5 glosses. The cogency of this view is immediately dispelled once it is realized that *kārēt* is not a *substitute* punishment in the event that the people do not stone him (rendering the opening *waw* as "or"; cf. Bekhor Shor[1]). That option is discussed in vv. 4–5. Thus *kārēt* must be an *additional* punishment: he will suffer both execution and excision (Shadal; cf. vol. 1.460). However, if the people fail to stone him, then his family and all those who protected him will also suffer *kārēt* (vv. 4–5). The conjunctive *waw* of *wa'ănî* undermines an alternative explanation that if the miscreant worships Molek in secret (Ibn Ezra, Bekhor Shor[2])—an unsubstantiated assumption— then God will intervene with *kārēt*.

My solution also resolves the crux of Exod 31:14, which prescribes *môt yûmāt* (execution) and *kārēt* (excision) for sabbath violators. Again, the punishments are aggregates, not alternatives. That the *kārēt* punishment perhaps means more than excision of the line, but also implies deprivation of life after death, see vol. 1.457–61.

thus. lĕma'an. For this usage, see Ehrlich 1908; Joüon 1923: § 169g.

defiling my sanctuary. ṭammē' 'et-miqdāšî. This is the first (and in the Torah, the only) explicit statement that idolatry pollutes the sanctuary (see Jer 7:30; 32:34; Ezek 5:11; 23:38). To be sure, P implies that the violation of prohibitive commandments, of which idolatry is surely one, pollutes the sanctuary (see NOTE on 16:16), but P's only explicit statement to this effect is in regard to the ritual impurity of genital fluxes (15:31). Nonetheless, that H regards Molek worship, which takes place outside the sanctuary, capable of polluting the sanctuary indicates that it accepts and continues P's doctrine of "Dorian Gray"; that is, severe impurity committed anywhere registers on the face of the sanctuary (vol. 1.254–61).

On the one hand, it is possible to argue on the basis of Ezek 23:38–39 that the impurity generated by idolatry and Molek worship, in particular, is not areal in character but is transmitted through direct contact. The relevant passage follows:

ṭimmĕ'û 'et-miqdāšî **bayyôm hahû'** *wĕ'et-šabbĕtôtay ḥillēlû ûbĕšaḥăṭām 'et-bĕnêhem lĕgillûlêhem wayyābō'û 'el-miqdāšî* **bayyôm hahû'** *lĕḥallĕlô*

On the same day they defiled my sanctuary and desecrated my sabbaths. **On the very day** that they slaughtered their children to their fetishes, they entered my sanctuary to desecrate it.

Twice, the prophet tells us that on the very day (boldface) they sacrificed their children to their idols, they also worshiped in the Temple. This feat, taken literally, could be accomplished only for Molek worship, which took place at the Topheth in the Valley of Hinnom located immediately below the Temple (see COMMENT B).

Abetting this interpretation is the fact that one sanctuary is singled out, which can be only the Jerusalem Temple. Molek worship was not practiced at or near other sanctuaries. Furthermore, this is the single case in H of sanctuary defilement *by the people.* Otherwise, it is committed only by priests (21:12, 23; cf. v. 9). If, indeed, the *'am hā'āreṣ* were the authoritative executive body operative in the time of the writer (but cf. NOTE on v. 2), one could understand the legal basis for indicting Molek worshipers with the charge: testimony can be brought that they were seen entering the Temple.

On the other hand, the juxtaposition of the defilement of the sanctuary and the desecration of God's name could lead to the conclusion that the sanctuary is polluted by idolatry whenever it is practiced. For if the desecration of God's name can occur anywhere (e.g., by a false oath, 19:12), even in exile (Ezek 36:20–21), so can the desecration of God's sanctuary. However, there is no other indication that H maintains P's doctrine that the sanctuary can be polluted from afar (vol. 1.254–61). Even H's metaphoric notion of impurity requires direct contact. For example, the land can be polluted only by those living on it. Nonetheless, Ezekiel holds to a metaphoric concept of impurity (see INTRODUCTION to 18:24–30), as shown by his shift in contiguous verses between the verbs *ḥillēl* and *ṭimmēʾ*, to describe the deleterious effect of idolatry on the sanctuary. That these two verbs have lost their precise technical meaning for Ezekiel is further illustrated by the fact that God's name can be either defiled (*ṭimmēʾ*) or desecrated (*ḥillēl*) with no apparent change in meaning (Ezek 43:7, 8). H, too, reveals imprecision regarding these two terms (see NOTES on 21:4, 9, 12).

However, this does not mean that the two terms are synonymous, even for Ezekiel (as claimed by Paran 1983: 74, n. 57). Whereas a sacred object (e.g., the sanctuary, sacrificial food) may be either desecrated (through illicit use; see NOTES on 5:14–16) or defiled (e.g., by contact with an impure person, 22:3–7), sacred time (e.g., the sabbath) can be only desecrated (Exod 31:14; Ezek 20:13, 16, 24; 22:8; 23:38). Indeed, Ezekiel's singular use of *ṭimmēʾ* regarding the name of God is confined to 43:7, 8, but elsewhere in his book *ḥillēl* is consistently attested (13:19; 20:9, 14, 22, 39; 22:26; 36:20, 22, 23; 39:7). Since only objects can be defiled, to speak of the defilement of God (or his name) would objectify him, and would constitute an anthropopathism—indeed, a heresy—which the priestly writers assiduously avoided. I therefore suggest that Ezek 43:7–8 is an aberration. It is but another example of (later) Ezekiel accepting and at the same time further despecifying the concepts and terms of (earlier) H.

Finally, it must be emphasized that one may not extrapolate from the prophetic notion of idolatry for H. H neither condemns nor sanctions idolatry except Molek worship (18:21) and necromancy (20:6), which differ from all other forms of idolatry by being forms of ancestor worship and being associated with the name of God (see COMMENTS B and C, and NOTE on "and thereby not desecrate the name of your God," 18:21). Nonetheless, the importance of this verse should not be overlooked. It is the first time that any non-YHWHistic worship is condemned using either the verb *ṭimmēʾ* or the adjective *ṭāmēʾ*. I would suggest that it constitutes a precedent for the seventh-century prophets to extend H's limited usage of *ṭimmēʾ* to idolatry in all its forms and consequences, namely, that idolatry, henceforth, will become a factor in Israel's destiny (see Introduction II D).

and desecrating my holy name, literally "the name of my holiness" (22:32). This indicates that holiness is the quintessential nature of YHWH, which distinguishes him from all other beings (cf. 1 Sam 2:2; COMMENT on chap. 19; and NOTES on 18:21; 19:2, 12). It is ironic yet characteristic of H that it, rather than P, adopts a "name" theology (adumbrating D and clearly showing that H precedes D) and the use of *ḥillēl* 'desecrate' instead of *ṭimmēʾ* 'pollute', proving that

H is just as opposed to anthropomorphism as P, if not more so (see Introduction II Q).

The Molek and necromancy prohibitions are tied together not only by their content (worship of chthonic deities; see COMMENT B), but also by their parallel paneled structure in vv. 4–6.

Case: Molek
wĕ'im ha'lēm ya'līmû 'am hā'āreṣ 'et- 'ênêhem min- hā'îš hahû' bĕtittô mizzar'ô lammōlek lĕbiltî hāmît 'ōtô (v. 4)

   Punishment

  A *wĕśamtî 'ănî 'et-pānay bā'îš hahû' ûbĕmišpaḥtô*
    B **wĕhikrattî** *'ōtô wĕ'ēt kol- hazzōnîm 'aḥărāyw liznôt 'aḥărê hammōlek*
    C **miqqereb 'ammām** (v. 5)

Case: Necromancy
wĕhannepeš 'ăšer tipneh 'el- hā'ōbōt wĕ'el-hayyiddĕ'ōnîm liznôt 'aḥărêhem (v. 6a)

   Punishment

  A' *wĕnātattî 'et-pānay bannepeš hahi(w)'*
    B' **wĕhikrattî** *'ōtô*
    C' **miqqereb 'ammô** (v. 6b)

The paneled structure is contained in the punishment. The identical vocabulary is marked in boldface. Note that the remaining words in A' *wĕnātattî . . . bannepeš hahi(w)'* are paralleled by precise synonyms in A *wĕśamtî . . . bā'îš hahû'*. The lengthened form in ABC is attributable to the inclusion of his family and followers. Otherwise the two cases, Molek and necromancy, are bound by the identical structure.

4. *indeed shut their eyes. ha'lēm ya'līmû . . . 'et-'ênêhem.* If they engage in a cover-up (cf. *Sipra* Qedoshim, par. 10:13; *Tg. Ps.-J.*). For the idiom, see Isa 1:15; Ezek 22:26; Prov 28:27. The infinitive absolute before the verb stresses the willful action of the people (Hartley 1992).

5. *I myself. 'ănî.* The pronoun underscores God's resolve (see NOTE on "And I myself," v. 3), but herein follows the verb *wĕśamtî* in chiastic relation to wa'ănî 'ettēn (v. 3; D. N. Freedman, personal communication).

will set my face against. wĕśamtî . . . 'et-pānay bā. For God as the subject, see Jer 21:10; 44:11; Ezek 15:7b. The equivalence of *śām* and *nātan* in this expression is best illustrated by their occurrence in the same verse (Ezek 15:7). For its meaning, see NOTE on v. 3.

and his family. ûbĕmišpaḥtô. Not the nuclear family (*bêt 'āb*), but the kin group (*bêt 'ābōt*; Milgrom 1979a). "R. Simeon said: If he sinned, what sin did his family commit? But this shows you that there is not a family containing a tax-collector [tax-collectors had the reputation of being thieves and extortionists], in which they are not all tax-collectors; or containing a thief, in which they are not all thieves; because they protect him!" (*Sipra* Qedoshim, par. 10:13; *b. Šebu.* 39a; cf. *Tg. Ps.-J.*). *Tg. Onk.* renders *ûbĕsaʿadôhî* as "his collaborators." However, the expression *heʿĕlîm ʿayin* / *ʿênayim*, literally "shut the eye(s)," implies that the family is guilty even if it ignored the crime and did nothing (e.g., 1 Sam 12:3; Isa 1:15; Prov 28:27). Although collective punishment is a basic doctrine in the priestly texts (cf. Milgrom 1990a: 444–48, and NOTES on 24:14), it probably does not apply here, since by their silence the family members acquiesced in his crime (see below). Deuteronomy's doctrine of individual punishment (Deut 24:16), cited by van der Toorn (1996b: 359) as a refutation of all prior notions of collective punishment, is, however, limited to adjudicatory crime, not sins against God. Note that the "scoundrels" (*bĕnê bĕliyyaʿal*) who induce the inhabitants of a city to worship other gods are not punished, but all the inhabitants are put to the sword, including the innocent among them (Deut 13:13–17)—an unambiguous example of collective punishment.

Indeed, it can be shown that Israel's priests actually (and brazenly) delimit YHWH's freedom to enact collective punishment (Milgrom 1990a: 423–25). Finally, that collective punishment does not even operate in our case is argued in the following NOTE.

Noth (1977) argues, on the assumption of the contagion of capital crimes, that this is a case of collective punishment, akin to the punishment meted out to all of Achan's family and animals that were stoned together with him (Josh 7:24–25). And Bertholet (1901) makes the point that it is precisely this law that generated Ezekiel's doctrine of individual retribution (Ezek 3:16–21). But this case proves nothing of the kind. The chances are that Achan's family was privy to the concealment of the loot in the *family tent* and did not inform the authorities, precisely as in our case. That the entire family is implicated in the crime is proved by the next clause, and therefore they deserve the same punishment (see below).

Abravanel finds a hint of another measure-for-measure punishment in this verse: the father thought that by sacrificing his child to Molek, he was gaining protection for the rest of his family; instead, all of them are destined to die.

and I will cut off . . . both him and all who whore after him. wĕhikrattî ʾōtô wĕʾēt kol-hazzōnîm ʾaḥarāyw. But what of his family? The rabbis, followed by Wessely (1846), suggest that the family is not inflicted with *kārēt*, but with a painful suffering, a lesser punishment (*Sipra* Qedoshim, par. 10:14; *b. Šebu* 39b). On the contrary, the absence of his family in this sentence (v. 5b) can only mean that it is assumed to be included among "all who stray after him"; that is, the family acquiesced to his idolatrous act or actually joined him in the worship of Molek. Thus vv. 4–5 stand in contrast with vv. 2–3. In the latter case, the fact that only the miscreant is stoned proves that the family did not protect him and, hence, was not punished.

As cogently pointed out by Cohen (1972: 121), this case proves conclusively that *kārēt*, as claimed by many scholars, cannot be judicial punishment of excommunication.

whore after . . . whoring after. hazzōnîm 'aḥărāyw liznôt 'aḥărê. See the NOTE on 17:7.

hammōlek. That Molek is always preceded by a definite article is proof that Molek was a god, at least according to the Masoretes. However, as the object of *liznôt 'aḥărê*, the identification of Molek as a god is irrefutable. To argue that the entire expression is a later gloss (Noth 1977; Lipinski 1988: 153, n. 10; Smelik 1995: 140–41) is an act of desperation (see NOTE on 18:21, and COMMENT B).

from among their kin. miqqereb 'ammām. This again implies a measure-for-measure punishment: for seeking to placate his ancestral spirits (*'ammîm*) by worshiping Molek, God will cut him off from them (J. Kessel). The fluidity between the singular *'am* and the plural *'ammîm* in H is noted in 17:10. The connection between Molek worship and necromancy is adumbrated by the juxtaposition of v. 6 and explored in COMMENT B. That the use of *qereb* in the *kārēt* formula betrays the hand of H, see the NOTE on 17:4.

V. 6. Penalty for Necromancy

This verse provides the penalties for the prohibition stated in 19:31; similarly, 20:9–21 provides the penalties for the prohibitions of 18:6–23. Thus all chaps. 18–20 are thematically linked, a fact further underscored by their introverted (ABB'A') structure—sexual regulations (18:6–20, 22–23), Molek worship (18:21), Molek worship (20:2–5), sexual regulations (20:9–21; Douglas 1995: 251)—and by their inclusio: 18:4, 5, 26, 28; 20:22–23. As pointed out by Yaron (1995: 455, n. 27), Molek worship and necromancy occur together among the grave transgressions of Manasseh (2 Kgs 21:6 = 2 Chr 33:6).

And . . . any person. wĕhannepeš. The *waw* is copulative, indicating the connection between the subject of necromancy with the preceding one on Molek worship. Their relatedness is also underscored by the similar vocabulary: *zānâ* (v. 5), *nātan pānîm b* (v. 3), *hikrît miqqereb 'am* (v. 5). See the discussion in COMMENT B.

The subject switches from *'îš* 'man' (vv. 2, 3, 4, 5) to *nepeš* 'person' to include the liability (and susceptibility) of women (see also v. 27).

to ghosts and wizard-spirits. 'el-hā'ōbōt wĕ'el-hayyiddĕ'ōnîm. As indicated in COMMENT B, these terms are capable of three interpretations: (1) the means (i.e., pits) of conjuring up the dead spirits (probable origin of *'ōbôt*), but inapplicable here because of its conjunction with *yiddĕ'ōnîm*; (2) the conjured spirits; and (3) the conjurers (necromancers). The die is cast in favor of no. 2 for two reasons. First, its associated verses 19:31 and 20:27 use the telltale idioms *lĕṭom'â bāhem* 'to be defiled by them' (i.e., the spirits) and *yihyeh bāhem* 'is a medium for' (lit. "has in them"). Second, the idiom *liznôt 'aḥărê* 'to whore after' is followed by the name of a god: Molek (v. 5), goat-demons (17:7), Baalim (Judg 8:33), and foreign *'ĕlōhîm* (Exod 34:15, 16; Deut 31:16; Judg 2:17; 1 Chr 5:25). Note that the dead are also called *'ĕlōhîm* (e.g., 1 Sam 28:13).

turns to . . . face against. tipneh 'el . . . pānîm b. The same root is deliberately used as an exemplification of divine measure-for-measure punishment: a person's turning (facing) *to* forbidden practices is matched by God's turning (facing) *against* such a person. The death penalty specified in v. 27 is not implied here (pace Levine 1989). The cases are not equivalent: *kārēt* is prescribed for turning to a medium; death, for being one.

him . . . his. *ʾōtô . . . (ʿamm)ô.* Although *nepeš* is feminine, it can occasionally be treated as masculine (e.g., 2:1; 17:15–16; Gen 46:22; Ezek 13:20; Ibn Ezra). Thus there is no need to harmonize with the Sam. *ʾōtâ, ʿammâ.*

Vv. 7–8. Sanctification and Opening Exhortation

Scholars differ about whether these two verses connect with the preceding or following pericopes. Elliger (1966) even proposes dividing these two verses: v. 7 with vv. 1–6 and v. 8 with vv. 9–21, the latter on the basis of 19:2, the theme of holiness that introduces the rest of the chapter. I submit that chaps. 18–20 were subjected to an artful H redaction: chap. 20 was chiastically balanced with chap. 18, thereby setting chap. 19 as the center of Leviticus (if not the entire Torah) and necessitating a corresponding symmetry between the flanking chaps. 18 and 20 (see COMMENT A, and Introduction I M). Thus the sexual prohibitions of 20 had to be supplied with opening and closing exhortations (vv. 7–8, 22–26) to match those of chap. 18 (vv. 1–5, 24–30).

7. This verse stands in chiastic relation with 11:44aα (H; see its NOTE). This correspondence is not accidental. It stresses the negative aspect of holiness, not the *imitatio dei* of chap. 19, but the aspect of distinctiveness, separateness. Israel must keep itself apart from the immoral practices of other nations, just as it eschews their dietary practices (chap. 11). This function of the diet laws is made explicit at the end of our chapter (vv. 25–26), where the theme of separation (*hibdîl*) is the explicit bond and common denominator between dietary habits and nationhood.

Thus this verse can best be seen as the opening exhortation regarding the illicit sexual practices that follow (vv. 9–21), corresponding to the opening exhortation of 18:1–5, which explicitly admonishes the Israelites not to follow the (sexual) mores of their Egyptian and Canaanite neighbors. These same peoples are also rife with necromancy (see COMMENT B) and ancestor worship (see COMMENT C). Perhaps, then, vv. 7–8 should also be regarded as a bridge, connecting the two seductive practices that perpetually threaten to assimilate Israel with its neighbors: idolatry and sexual license.

You shall sanctify yourselves and be holy. wĕhitqaddištem wihyîtem qĕdōšîm. This statement could only have been made by H (also 11:44): Israel can achieve holiness only by its own efforts. YHWH has given it the means: the commandments. All other occurrences of this *Hitpaʿel* are nonpriestly, where the meaning is different, namely, "purify oneself" (vol. 1.965–67). The one exception is Ezekiel, who was heavily influenced by H (see chap. 26, COMMENTS B and C). However, he has God speak in the first person *wĕhitgaddiltî wĕhitqaddištî wĕnôdaʿtî* literally "I will make myself great and make myself holy and (thus) become known" (Ezek 38:23). Whereas Israel makes itself holy by obeying

YHWH's commandments, YHWH makes himself holy by his might—in this instance, by his devastation of Gog. That is, the nations will now acknowledge his greatness and holiness (cf. Ezek 36:23–30, 36). Here holiness means YHWH's dissimilarity, total otherness, the realization of which inspires wonder and awe (see NOTE on 19:2, and chap. 19, COMMENT).

for I YHWH am your God. In view of 11:44aγ, one must conclude that this declaration is a paraphrase of *kî qādōš 'ǎnî* 'for I am holy' (Saadiah, Ibn Ezra) or is an introduction to v. 8b (see below).

8. *You shall heed my statutes and do them. ûšěmartem 'et-ḥuqqōtay wa 'ǎśîtem 'ōtām.* This refrain is found in 18:4–5 and 20:22a (and 19:37), indicating that it forms part of an opening exhortation parallel to that of chap. 18 and that it forms an inclusio with the closing exhortation of chap. 20.

(Thereby) I YHWH make you holy. 'ǎnî YHWH měqaddišěkem. The *Pi'el* of *qdš* takes the following persons as the object: Israelites (20:8; 21:8 [but see its NOTE]; 22:32; Exod 31:13; Ezek 20:12; 37:28), priests (21:23; 22:9, 16), and high priest (21:15).

The significance of this usage cannot be underestimated. It is a *Pi'el* causative (GKC § 52g) "make holy"; that is, following God's commandments makes Israel holy. Israel is not innately holy; it is commanded to strive for holiness: *qědōšîm tihyû* 'You shall become holy' (19:2). Holiness for Israel is achieved by following God's commandments, of which the sabbath is the paragon example. The very act of sanctifying the sabbath (Exod 20:8) enables Israel to "know that I YHWH am making you holy" (*Pi'el, měqaddišěkem;* Exod 31:13b, echoed in Ezek 20:12). Of course, what is true for the sabbath applies to all of God's commandments (22:32). That we are confronted by a distinctive H usage is shown by the different connotations of the *Pi'el* in P, "sanctify *through ritual*" (e.g., Exod 28:3; 29:1, 33; 30:29, 30), and where this notion of "make holy, consecrate"—that is, transfer to the Deity—is expressed only by the *Hip'il* (e.g., Exod 28:38; Num 3:13; 8:17).

Here H serves as a polemic against P, which rigidly reserves the notion of *qādôš* solely for the priests, Nazirites, and sanctums (see vol. 1.48, and applicable verses). To be sure, H—also a priestly school—does not deny the genetically transmitted holiness of the priesthood. But even this holiness, limited to the exclusive prerogative of the inherited priesthood to officiate at the altar, can be sustained only by the priests' adherence to a rigorous ritual code (see chap. 21, and Introduction II G). Israel, however, achieves holiness by its obedience to all the revealed commandments, ritual and moral alike.

In fact, all four pentateuchal codes differ on the concept of holiness. P, as indicated, limits holiness to consecrated objects and persons, namely, sanctums and priests. By their one-time consecration by Moses (Lev 8), their holiness is permanent and is automatically bequeathed to their male descendants. (Each high priest, however, must undergo consecration; see vol. 1.555.) D, on the contrary, declares that all Israel is inherently holy (Deut 7:6; 14:2; 26:19). Thus holiness in both P and D is static. In contrast, H's concept is dynamic. Lay persons can attain it, and priests must sustain it, for holiness is diminished or enhanced by either violating or obeying the divine commandments. In my view, the dynamism of holiness is not entirely the innovation of H. It is adumbrated in JE, where holiness is achievable by observing the Decalogue and the firstfruit and firstborn offerings (Exod 22:28–30; see chap. 19, COMMENT). H expands these requirements to all of God's commandments.

By the same token, one should not gloss over H's distinctive innovation, one directed to members of H's own priestly class. No differently from Israel, God also is *mĕqaddēš* of the priests (21:23; 22:9, 16) and even of the high priest (21:15). Indeed, it is not enough for the priests to abstain from ritual impurity themselves (e.g., 22:9). They, like their fellow Israelites, must obey all of God's commandments (see chap. 19, COMMENT) and must beware lest they become "impure" by causing Israelites to sin (e.g., 22:16)—and *thereby diminish their own holiness.*

Holiness is no longer a priestly prerogative. It is available to and attainable by everyone. What could have motivated H to legislate such a far-reaching doctrine? Here only a surmise can be attempted. If, as argued (see Introduction I F), H is mainly the product of the end of the eighth century, holiness may be another plank in H's overall program to rectify the socioeconomic injustice prevailing among the people. The growing number of small farmers who lost their inherited land to rapacious creditors (25:25–43) must have produced widespread destitution and despair. In practical terms, H proposed a land reform, the laws of the jubilee, as laid out in chap. 25. However, it would take effect only in fifty years. What of the immediate need to raise morale and hope? H's answer: its revised doctrine of holiness. It was not like its predecessor P's holiness. It would not qualify one to serve YHWH inside his earthly sanctuary. It was a spiritual, metaphysical holiness. It brought one into the presence of the one proclaimed "I am holy" (11:44, 45 [H]; 19:2; 20:26; 21:8). It made one equal to "the holy ones" (cf. Ps 89:6, 8) who serve YHWH in his divine realm. Neither financial success nor social prestige nor priestly pedigree was a prerequisite for its attainment. Only adherence to the divine commandments was required. By observing them, an Israelite would become holy.

It should also not be forgotten that there was an ethnic exclusivity to the divine gift of holiness. Only a member of the covenant community could qualify. This contrasts with H's position on the *gēr*. H accorded him the full civil rights and religious privileges enjoyed by the native Israelites (see chap. 17, COMMENT B), but it denied him holiness. Strive as he may to worship YHWH with zeal and to observe all his commandments, he still could not become holy.

It should not go unnoticed that the participial expression "YHWH the sanctifier" is the first of seven occurrences in H (20:8; 21:8, 15, 23; 22:9, 16, 32). It is also noteworthy that the outer two are directed to Israel (rather, to all of Israel, including the priests); the second, third, fifth, and sixth occurrences refer to the priesthood (reading 21:8 with the LXX; see its NOTE); and the fourth, the middle occurrence, probably refers to the sanctums (see its NOTE). It is also no accident that the two outer passages are extensive, giving initially the method by which God sanctifies all of Israel, namely, by their following his command-ments (20:7–8), and closing with the rationale for YHWH's indisputable right to impose his holiness demands on Israel, namely, by freeing them from Egypt-ian bondage and, thereby, acquiring his lordship over Israel (22:32–33; see NOTE on 25:43). This motif, YHWH the sanctifier, also shows that 21:1–22:16, the unit on the priests, was not inserted at random into the H corpus but is inte-grally and inextricably bound to its surrounding pericopes (chap. 20 and 22:17–33). Moreover, vv. 7–8 effectively connect this chapter with the preced-ing one, chap. 19, by neatly capitulating the latter's program of holiness: if you (Israel) sanctify yourself by following my commandments, I YHWH will sanc-tify you. Thus a reciprocal relationship has been spun. Israel's sanctification is neither inherent nor automatic (implied by D), but proportionate to Israel's self-sanctification (cf. Hartley 1992: LXI).

YHWH the sanctifier motif reappears outside Leviticus in Exod 31:13 (H) and in Ezek 20:12, citing H's sabbath prescription (above) and Ezek 37:28 (based on and expanding 26:11; see chap. 26, COMMENT B).

H's achievement (at least in its demands) cannot be fully appreciated unless one realizes that H, in effect, has democratized all of Israel. The priests, to be sure, reign supreme in the cult: the sanctuary is their exclusive province; the al-tar is their monopoly. However, to retain their privileges, the accident of birth is only necessary, but not sufficient. As much as Israel is enjoined to attain ho-liness condition, the priests are enjoined to sustain it.

The deeper implication of the *Pi'el* participle *meqaddēš* derives from its dy-namic thrust: observing God's commandments adds to one's holiness and, con-versely, disobeying them subtracts from one's holiness—for priests and laity alike. Both equally must strive to attain or sustain holiness: *qĕdōšîm tihyû* (19:2). The historical or socioeconomic conditions that motivated H to formulate this doc-trine are discussed further in the Introduction II G.

Vv. 9–21. Penalties for Sexual Violations

The order of the prohibitions clearly differs from that in chap. 18 because its organizing principle is also different. Chap. 18 is ordered by family relation-ships: the closest (vv. 7–11), parents (vv. 12–14), their wives (vv. 15–16), wife (vv. 17–18); and by nonrelatives: menstruant (v. 19), married woman (v. 20), Molek worship (v. 21), sodomy (v. 22), bestiality (v. 23). Chap. 20, though, is ordered according to punishments, based on the severity of the crime: death (three kinds of adultery, vv. 10–12; sodomy, v. 13; mother–daughter, v. 14; bes-tiality, vv. 15–16); excision (half sister, v. 17; menstruant, v. 18; aunt, v. 19?); childlessness (wife of paternal uncle, v. 20; sister-in-law, v. 21; Hoffmann 1953). For other distinctions between these two chapters, see COMMENT A.

That the prohibitions of chap. 20 follow a logical order suffices to dismiss

Daube's (1941) theory that they comprise three sets of synchronically developed prohibitions, representing an original code (vv. 10–16) and two appendices (vv. 17–18, 19–21) dating from different (but not necessarily later) periods. Similarly, Douglas's (1994: 293) proposal that chap. 20 rearranges the prohibitions of chap. 18 in an alternating pattern (vv. 9, 10, 13, 15, 18 and vv. 11, 12, 14, 19, 20, 21) is neither precise nor informative. Ezek 18:5–9 is modeled on the positive statements of the death sentences (*môt yûmat*) of vv. 10–16 (Schulz 1969: 163–92). For the dependence of Ezekiel on H, see chap. 26, COMMENTS C and D.

The prohibitions, as mentioned above, are listed according to their punishments. They are as follows:

The Fundamental Cause: Dishonoring Parents (v. 9)

A. Prohibitions carrying the death penalty (vv. 10–21)
   1. Adultery (v. 10)
   2. Incest (vv. 11–12)
     a. Sex with father's wife (v. 11)
     b. Sex with daughter-in-law (v. 12)
   3. Male homosexuality (v. 13)
   4. Marriage to a woman and her mother (v. 14)
   5. Bestiality (vv. 15–16)
     a. By a male (v. 15)
     b. By a female (v. 16)
B. Prohibitions carrying the excision penalty (vv. 17–19)
   1. Marriage to a sister (v. 17)
   2. Sex during menses (v. 18)
   3. Sex with paternal or maternal aunt (v. 19)
C. Prohibitions carrying the childlessness penalty (vv. 20–21)
   1. Sex with uncle's wife (v. 20)
   2. Marriage to a sister-in-law (v. 21)

The structure of these prohibitions (following Hartley 1992: 360) consists of four elements: I case; II penalty; III reason; IV declaratory formula. Their distribution among the prohibitions is shown in the following list:

v. 9	I, II, III, IV	v. 16	I, II (twice), IV
v. 10	I, II	v. 17	I (expanded), IV, II, III, IV
v. 11	I, III, II, IV	v. 18	I, III (thrice), II
v. 12	I, II, III, IV	v. 19	I, III, IV
v. 13	I, III, II, IV	v. 20	I, III, IV, II
v. 14	I, IV, II, III	v. 21	I, IV, III, II
v. 15	I, II (twice)		

M. Hildenbrand also finds that the prohibitions are organized by an introverted structure, as follows (amended):

A   *Family relations*
Adultery (v. 10)
Father's wife (v. 11)
Daughter-in-law, *tebel* (v. 12)
  B   *Nonfamily relations*
Homosexuality, *tôʿēbâ* (v. 13)
    C   *Family relations*
Wife and her mother, *zimmâ* (v. 14)
      X   *Nonfamily relations*
Bestiality: man and beast (v. 15)
Bestiality: woman and beast (v. 16)
    C'   *Family relations*
Sister, *ḥesed* (v. 17)
  B'   *Nonfamily relations*
Menstruant (v. 18)
A'   *Family relations*
Parent's sister (v. 19)
Uncle's wife (v. 20)
Brother's wife, *niddâ* (v. 21)

This structure is symmetrically balanced, AA' (three verses each); BB' and CC' (one verse each), and X (two verses). Its attractiveness rests in AA'. Only the third in the series bears a condemnatory term: sex with a daughter-in-law is called *tebel* (v. 12). Sex with a brother's wife is called *niddâ*, the very term we would have expected for the menstruant (v. 18). Condemnatory vocabulary is also registered in CC' and in B, but not in B', where logically it should be. The answer, Hildenbrand suggests, is structure: *niddâ* has been moved from its rightful place in v. 18 to v. 21 in order to provide the precise symmetry for AA'.

The weaknesses in this construction should not be overlooked: the alternation of family–nonfamily is meaningless, and the placement of bestiality in the center is inexplicable, particularly in view of its lack of a condemnatory term (contrast 18:23).

9. The fact that a law regarding dishonoring parents heads a list of prohibited sexual unions is hardly an accident, but, on the contrary, is crucial in understanding the provenance of the entire list. It reflects a patriarchal society that relates all familial relationships, by the twin principles of consanguinity and affinity, back to one's father and mother. It adverts to the unstated premise that dishonoring parents—that is, the breakdown of obligations to one's father or mother—is able to lead to the breakdown of relationships with the other members of the familial chain, including the sexual taboos. This supposition may also explain why in 18:7 incest with the mother is glossed by a reference to the father, even though both are subsumed under *šĕʾēr bĕśārô* in the preceding verse

(v. 6), as an allusion to the premise that without respect for parents, all other family relationships are liable to collapse.

If. kî. This particle does not indicate the beginning of a casuistic law (a fact certified by the following *ʾăšer*), but marks this opening verse as a generalization for the following list. By the same token, only this opening verse contains the double *ʾîš ʾîš*, again to set off this first law as a general heading (Hoffmann 1953). There is also merit in Ehrlich's (1908) suggestion that, as in narrative (e.g., Gen 21:30; 22:16–17; 26:22), *kî* here introduces the direct speech of God (cf. GKC § 157b).

dishonors. yĕqallēl. The opposite of the Decalogue's *kabbēd* 'honor' (Exod 20:12; cf. Brichto 1963: 132–37, esp. 135), this is correctly rendered by *Tg. Neof.* as *yĕzalzēl ʾîqrēh* 'holds cheap the honor'. So too Philo (*Laws* 2.248): "And even if while making no assault with his hands he uses abusive language . . . or in any other way does anything to dishonor his parents" (cf. LXX; Matt 15:4; Mark 7:10).

This meaning for the root *qll* prevails in the *Qal* (e.g., 1 Sam 2:30), *Nip ʿal* (e.g., 2 Sam 6:22), and *Hip ʿîl* (e.g., Isa 23:9). To be sure, *Pi ʿel* usually denotes "curse." But there are two texts where *qillēl* indisputably means "dishonor, abuse, insult" (for the difference, see NOTE on "cursing," 24:11). The first is the case of Shimei, who heaps abuse on David (2 Sam 16:5–13, *qillēl* occurring six times), and the other is the case of Eli's sons (1 Sam 3:13), who dishonor God (*mĕqalĕlîm lāhem*, a *Tiqqûn Sôpĕrîm* for *ʾĕlōhîm*; cf. LXX; Radaq) by fattening themselves on the sacrifices before the suet (God's portion) is consumed on the altar (1 Sam 2:29 LXX; cf. vv. 15–16; vol. 1.197). This latter text is especially compelling because the antonym *kibbēd* 'honor'—the proper behavior toward God—is attested twice (vv. 29, 30). Similarly, the noun *qĕlālâ*, which usually means "curse," also can denote "contempt, insult" (e.g., 2 Sam 16:12; Deut 21:23).

An earlier, but more concise, prohibition is found in the Covenant Code: *ûmĕqallēl ʾābîw wĕʾimmô môt yûmāt* (Exod 21:17). H has most likely expanded it to form a chiasm by adding to *yĕqallēl* the changed verb pattern *qillēl*. For the legal and sapiential reflexes of this prohibition in Scripture, see Deut 21:18–21; Prov 20:20; compare Matt 15:4; Mark 7:10. Rabbinic legislation, however, restricts the application of this law to cursing one's parents (*m. Sanh.* 7:8; *Sipra* Emor 9:6).

he must be put to death. môt yûmāt. Not at the whim of the parents, but by the decision of the authorized court. The explicit statement of Deut 21:18–21 to that effect is not its innovation, but is already implicit in the earliest legislation (Exod 21:17). The form of death is not specified. The only attested methods of judicial execution are stoning (e.g., v. 2) and burning (v. 14). The latter is specified because it was rare (21:9; cf. Gen 38:24). That stoning is intended by this phrase is confirmed in v. 2, where it is specified because of the exceptional composition of the executioners (see also 24:16; Num 15:35).

That a father *theoretically* had the authority to put a son to death even for noncapital offenses, see Exod 21:15; Deut 21:18–21 (cf. Gen 38:24). Indeed, the very absence here of any statement regarding the executioner can lead to the assumption that the sentence rested exclusively with the family patriarch, who had absolute control over all those who lived together as a *bêt 'āb*, literally "father's house," under his authority (see INTRODUCTION to 18:6–23). However, the prohibition against copulating with one's daughter-in-law (v. 12; 18:15) is clearly directed to the father. Thus there is no alternative but to presume that the elders of the *mišpāḥâ* 'kin group' or, in a later period, of the city (Deut 21:19) would constitute the judiciary (see NOTE on "the people of the land," v. 2).

he has dishonored his father or his mother. *'ābîw wě'immô qillēl.* The chiastic repetition of this sentence emphasizes the horrendous nature of the act (Ibn Ezra).

his bloodguilt is upon him. *dāmāyw bô.* This idiom is attested only in this chapter and in Ezek 18:13. It is synonymous with *dāmô běrō'šô*, literally "his blood is on his head" (Josh 2:19; 1 Kgs 2:37; Ezek 33:4). The latter idiom uses the singular *dām* and implies that the metaphor is probably based on the primitive belief that the blood of the illicitly slain refuses burial, but encircles the head of the slayer, as if to call out: "This is the murderer." The former idiom, however, uses (but not always, cf. 17:4) the plural *dāmîm*, which may indicate an attempt to alter the concrete notion of blood to the abstract concept of bloodguilt (Reventlow 1960). Koch (1962), however, maintains that the concrete meaning is intended. The fear of automatic retribution persists: the blood of the slain (and presumably the slain's spirit) will hound the murderer until he, too, is slain.

In any event, this idiom in legal contexts provides further proof that the miscreant is condemned and executed by the court of elders. For it assures the court-appointed executioner that he will not be held responsible for slaying the convicted person—his blood(guilt) remains with him. It is significant that this idiom is not found in D. Even though family and sexual crimes are adjudicated by elders of the city (e.g., Deut 19:12; 21:20; 22:17–18), they are not given a free hand, but are closely supervised by state-appointed officers (Deut 21:2) and judges (Deut 25:1–3) in every community ("in all your gates," Deut 16:18; Stulman 1992; Blenkinsopp 1995: 4). No longer is there fear of divine or human retribution for taking the life of a person. The responsibility for the execution of a criminal by the clan elders henceforth devolves on the state and its officials. This, I submit, is telling evidence that the family laws in D reflect a later period than those preserved in H. Moreover, if centralization of worship advocated by D goes hand in hand with statewide control of judiciary, as claimed by Blenkinsopp (1995), the absence of the latter in H may also presuppose the absence of centralization. Family law adjudicated by the family head but executed by the elders of his community would then reflect the period prior to or in disregard of cultic centralization (see chap. 17, COMMENT D).

Finally, this idiom also implies that the death penalty will befall the miscreant whether or not the elders put him to death. The death sentences prescribed in vv. 9–16 are therefore parallel to that explicitly stated for Molek worship (vv. 4–5): unless the authorities execute the convicted party, God will. Crüsemann (1996: 317) also includes the intervening case, inquiry of the dead (v. 6), in this category. However, the specified penalty is *kārēt*, and human action is, by implication, forbidden.

A stylistic note. This idiom is found in the capital cases specified in vv. 11, 12, 13, and 16, but it is missing in vv. 10, 14, 15. In the latter, however, the *môt yûmāt* clause is followed by a rationale. This is not true in our verse: *môt yûmāt* is also followed by the rationale *'ābîw wĕ'immô qillēl* concluding with *dāmāyw bô*. A possible reason is that this initial case sets the pattern for those that follow: even where a rationale seems to have replaced the *dāmāyw bô* clause, the latter is understood. All executioners of the court's death penalty should have no fear of human or divine retribution.

10. *committing adultery with his (Israelite) neighbor's wife. 'ăšer yin'ap 'et-'ēšet rē'ēhû*. This ostensibly additional clause has been variously explained:

1. It is original, but the prior clause containing *'ēšet 'îš* had to be added after the term *rēa'* fell out of use (Geiger 1857, cited by Kalisch 1867–72).
2. This clause was added lest *'ēšet 'îš* be interpreted as one's own wife (Ehrlich 1908; but see 18:8).
3. This clause is necessary to include an engaged as well as a married woman.
4. It supplies the motive, stressing the gravity of the crime, following the model of v. 9a (Ibn Ezra). In that case, however, one would have expected this clause to read *'et-'ēšet rē'ēhû nā'ap*.
5. It forms a "word chain," a stylistic device, found in biblical poetry (Berlin 1987, cited by Westbrook 1990: 549, n. 28). However, this text is as far from poetry as imaginable.
6. The purpose of this clause is to limit the jurisdiction of the law to an Israelite (*Sipra* Qedoshim 10:8; *b. Sanh.* 52b [bar.]), as does the equivalent term *'ămîtĕkā* in the corresponding law (18:20). For the meaning of *rēa'* as Israelite, see the NOTE on 19:18. "The initial formulation of the law has been restricted to manageable proportions" (Fishbane 1985: 169, Carmichael's [1997: 155, n. 9] objections notwithstanding).

The final interpretation has been adopted in my translation.

Gerstenberger's (1996: 295) proposal, that whereas 18:20 (as all the prohibitions of chap. 18) refers to relations within the kin group, this verse refers to other Israelites, is refuted by Ezekiel's replacement of *'ămît* (18:20) with *rēa'* (Ezek 18:6, 15). Also, the use of this term in basic ethical prohibitions (19:11) points to the inclusion of all Israelites.

the adulterer and the adulteress must be put to death. môt-yûmat hannō'ēp wĕhannō'epet. The singular verb indicates that originally only the paramour was put to death; the wife was added later (Daube 1941; Noth 1977; Phillips 1981: 6). The LXX and Pesh. skirt this problem by reading the verb as a plural; their reading, however, can be dismissed as a harmonization. Frequently, however, when the verb precedes the subject there is no agreement between them (GKC, 1450; Goodfriend *ABD* 1.84), though Fishbane (1994:25, n. 2) suggests that the death penalty is a "frozen technical term."

The wording of this law (and its rewording in Deut 22:22) makes it clear that the plaintiff is not the husband, who might be willing to accept compensation (cf. Prov 6:32–35), but the community, which must carry out the death sentence (Loewenstamm 1968: 631–32). McKeating (1979: 58–59) raises the possibility that the formulation of this law guarantees that the wife can be put to death only if the same end is meted out to her paramour.

The death penalty for adultery purportedly conflicts with another priestly text (Num 5:12–31 [P]), where the punishment for a woman's adultery is sterility. If a suspected adulteress is proved guilty by the prescribed ordeal, then "the spell-inducing water (she is made to drink) shall enter into her to bring on bitterness, so that her belly shall distend and her thigh shall sag" (v. 27; cf. v. 28). The paradox is clear: the adulteress, proved guilty by the ordeal—that is, by God himself—is not punished with death! True, her punishment is just, "poetically" just. She who opened her womb to illlicit sex is doomed to be permanently sterile. Yet the gnawing question remains: Having been proved guilty of adultery, why is she not summarily put to death? Could it be that our text (H) is rectifying a bizarre (and ostensibly illogical) verdict of P? A close examination of the case, however, reveals that there is no contradiction at all.

The key to the answer lies in the fact that the guilty wife was unapprehended by anyone. That this element is the most significant in her case is shown by the fact that it is cited four times in her indictment, each in a different manner: (1) "unbeknown to her husband," (2) "she keeps secret" (or "it was done clandestinely"), (3) "without being apprehended," and (4) "and there is no witness against her" (all Num 5:13). These clear redundancies, among others, even led one critic to assert that their purpose is "to give weight to what might (and all too correctly!) be seen as a transparent charade . . . to protect the woman as wife in the disadvantaged position determined for her by the mores of ancient Israel's society" (Brichto 1975).

This stylistic inflation, however, may have been deliberately written with a judicial purpose in mind: to emphasize the cardinal principle that the unapprehended criminal is not subject to the jurisdiction of the human court. Since the adulteress has not been apprehended—as the text repeats with staccato emphasis—then the community and, especially, the overwrought husband may not give way to their passions to lynch her. Indeed, even if proved guilty by the ordeal, they may not put her to death. Unapprehended adultery remains punishable only by God, and there is no need for human mediation. The punishment for this sin against man (the husband) and God is inherent in the ordeal. Supportive evidence may also be adduced from the absence of the technical verb for committing adultery, nā'ap, which is found in the Decalogue (Exod 20:14; Deut 5:18) and H (Lev 20:10, four times in this one verse!). Thus although the legist expressed the woman's infidelity in four different ways, it may be no accident that he refrained from using the legal term nā'ap, for he wished to dissociate this woman's fate from the death penalty imposed for adultery. The glaring omission of the term nā'ap is then but another indication that jurisdiction in this case lies outside the human court (details in Milgrom 1990a: 346–54).

11. *father's wife.* His own mother is assumed (*Tg. Ps.-J.*); hence this verse is parallel to 18:7, 8 (Dillmann and Ryssel 1897; Elliger 1966). The implication of the missing mother needs to be underscored. It means that incest with one's mother is such an egregious crime that the death penalty is taken for granted. This supposition can also explain the missing daughter and full sister from this list—and also from chap. 18. Sex with mother, daughter, or sister was abhorred in the ancient Near East (see INTRODUCTION to 18:6–23), the rare exception in Egypt notwithstanding (see NOTE to 18:3). Thus, I submit, S. Rattray's theory (see INTRODUCTION to 18:6–23) is fully substantiated: these three missing persons are the addressee's *closest relatives*; they are subsumed under the phrase *šĕʾēr bĕśārô*, literally "flesh of one's flesh." Hence they need not be itemized either in the prohibitions (the mother's inclusion in 18:7 is explained in its NOTE) or in the penalties. Their proscription and punishment are assumed. It is only the borderline, arguable cases that are interdicted and sentenced.

it is the nakedness of his father that he has uncovered. ʿerwat ʾābîw gillâ. This phrase emphasizes the egregious nature of this crime (Ibn Ezra). Rather, it provides the required motive clause, as in 18:8b.

the two of them . . . upon them. Her culpability presumes her consent.

12. *a perversion. tebel.* On the assumption that the root is *bll* 'mix', Rashi (on 18:23) comments that the seed of the father and son have been mixed (see also *Sipra* Qedoshim 10:10). The term, however, is obscure (see NOTE on 18:23).

Other condemnatory terms in this list are *tôʿēbâ* (v. 13, 18:30β) and *zimmâ* (v. 14 [bis]). They reflect Israel's shame culture, acting as a deterrent, which prevails in Deuteronomy (Daube 1969). The same three terms also occur in 18:17b, 22bβ, and 23bβ. There are major differences between these two lists: chap. 20 adds penalties in case the deterrents fail.

13. *male. zākār*, rather than *rēʿēhû* (i.e., his fellow Israelite). This absolute ban on homosexuality contrasts strikingly with the Hellenistic and Roman world, where homosexuality was sanctioned with those of inferior status, such as slaves, foreigners, and youths.

an abhorrent thing. tôʿēbâ. The same condemnatory term is used for this offense in 18:22.

the two of them. šĕnêhem. Emphasizing the culpability of the passive partner (Ehrlich 1908), presuming, of course, that he gave his consent.

they must be put to death. Those opposed to homosexual rights, in general, and to professing gays and lesbians in the military, in particular, have resorted to the biblical interdiction of their practice on pain of death. In an op-ed piece, James Michener provides this rebuttal:

Two other verses from the same chapter of Leviticus bring into question the relevance of these edicts today. Verse 9 warns: "For every one that curseth his father or his mother shall be surely put to death" [*KJV*]. Would we be willing to require the death sentence for boys who in a fit of rage oppose their parents? How many of us would have been guilty of that act at some point in our upbringing?

Just as perplexing is Verse 10: "And the man that committeth adultery with another man's wife . . . the adulterer and the adulteress shall surely be put to death." Can you imagine the holocaust that would ensue if that law were enforced today? . . .

We do not kill young people who oppose their parents or execute adulterers. (*New York Times*, March 30, 1993)

As Michener notes, the biblical ban on homosexual acts must be considered in the context of all the other forbidden behaviors of Lev 18 and 20. Furthermore, it must be kept in mind that these regulations were binding only in Israel (and its resident aliens, 18:26), but *not in other countries*. Thus prima facie, it is illegitimate to apply these prohibitions on a universal scale. However, it cannot be argued on the basis of the perorations (18:1–4, 24–30; 20:22–26) that their purpose was solely to distinguish Israel from the nations (Parker 1991; Anderson 1993). Note that lesbianism, though prevalent and known, was not banned (contrast Rom 1:26).

Israel's territory was pocketed by numerous Canaanite enclaves, not to speak of more populous nations on its borders. It was therefore understandable that Israel was obsessed with increasing its birth rate without endangering harmonious relations within the extended family, especially among those who lived in the same household (see chap. 18, COMMENT A). The theme of procreation is also stressed by Philo (*Laws* 3.39).

Concerning the illegitimate use of the biblical prohibition against homosexuality in certain modern circles, see COMMENT D.

14. *marries.* yiqqaḥ, from lāqaḥ. For this usage, see Gen 11:29; Exod 21:10; Deut 20:7 (cf. *Sipra* Qedoshim 10:12; Dillmann and Ryssel 1897). Note that the Akkadian semantic cognate aḥāzu 'take' also means "marry." See also NOTES on "marries," vv. 17, 21, and NOTE on 18:17b.

Ramban, however, renders the word as "seize" on the presumption that women, living in the household and under the authority of the addressee, are vulnerable to his passion. But if so, why is not lāqaḥ used in 18:17a; 20:11, 12, which speak of women in similar circumstances? Conversely, why is lāqaḥ used for the sister-in-law (v. 21), who patently resides independently, in her late husband's home? Moreover, it may be asked, chap. 20 is not squeamish in labeling the sex act by the verb šākab (vv. 11, 12, 13, 18, 20), so why is it not employed here? Finally, the fact that both women are put to death implies that they gave their consent (i.e., in marriage). But if he exercised his authority to "seize" them, the possibility exists that they were forced and, hence, not culpable (cf. Deut 22:26).

a depravity. zimmâ. The same term is used for condemning the marriage with mother and daughter (18:17b).

by fire they shall burn. bāʾēš yiśrĕpû. Daube (1947: 79) has argued that the bestiality cases that follow (vv. 15–16) must be an appendix, since their punishment is *môt yûmat*; that is, punishment by fire ostensibly has brought to an end the *môt yûmat* series. However, bestiality is an old taboo, attested at length

not only in the Hittite Code (HL §§ 187–200), but also in older biblical legislation (Exod 22:18), where the penalty is also *môt yûmat*. It therefore is not a
priestly innovation. Moreover, its place in the list is logical: death to three human offenders (v. 14) precedes death to a human and a beast (vv. 15, 16). This
is an indication that the legist classified the laws of chap. 20 not only according
by penalty, but also according by case. This answer also suffices for Hoffmann's
(1953) query about why sodomy (v. 13) and bestiality (vv. 15–16) are not bracketed together; that is, why v. 14 does not come before v. 13.

Execution by burning is attested in early narratives (Gen 38:24; Judg 14:15;
15:6; see NOTE on 21:9). Hartley (1992) suggests that burning may have followed
execution (by stoning), as attested in the case of Achan (Josh 7:15, 25), in order
to deprive the miscreant of a decent burial. However, there is no evidence that
the remains of Achan and his family were not interred. Morever, the rabbis cite
a case of a priest's daughter (cf. 21:9) where burning was carried out (*m. Sanh.*
7:2; probably by Sadducees, *b. Sanh.* 52b) in opposition to the method approved
by the rabbis (*m. Sanh.* 9:1).

and them. wĕ'ethen. The fact that the initial marraige was legal gives rise to
the debate between R. Akiba and R. Ishmael concerning the meaning of this
term and to my suggested solution that the marriage with both was contracted
simultaneously (Kalisch 1867–72; see NOTE on "a woman and her daughter,"
18:17b). Ehrlich (1908) adds a stylistic argument. If the women were married
sequentially, the text would have read *kî yiqqaḥ 'iššâ 'et-bittāh 'ô 'iššâ 'el-'immāh*,
on the model of *wĕ'iššâ 'el- 'ăḥōtāh lo' tiqqaḥ* (18:18). The severity of the punishment, death by fire, predicates that the two women conspired with the man.
Perhaps it was reckoned as a form of harlotry, which may have put this case into
the same category as the priest's daugther who committed harlotry (21:9). More
likely, it merited death by fire because it was *zimmâ*, which should be rendered
not as "depravity" but as "scheme, plot," as attested in many occurrences of the
verb *zāmam* (e.g., Gen 11:6; Deut 19:19; Pss 31:14; 37:12). It therefore is no accident that *zimmâ* occurs once again in the lists of sexual violations, the similar case of a mother–daughter connivance (18:17b; see its NOTE). And if the only
other occurrence of *zimmâ* in H (19:29) also bears this meaning (see its NOTE),
then one can possibly conclude that in H it has only this technical quasi-legal
connotation.

15. *has sexual relations*. This is a euphemistic translation of *yittēn šĕkobtô b*
(for details, see NOTE on 18:23).

he must be put to death. This penalty already is enjoined in Exod 22:18. Contrast HL § 187–200, in which bestiality with a horse and mule was permitted
(§ 200A), perhaps because these animals were taken on long trips (e.g., military
campaigns) during which normal sex was impossible (Moyer 1983: 26, n. 25).

and you shall kill the beast. wĕ'et-habbĕhēmâ tahărōgû. The rabbis offer several rationalizations:

1. The animal now being disposed or trained for bestiality will lead a person
   into sin (*Sipra* Qedoshim 11:5; *m. Sanh.* 7:4).

2. "So that the animal, when passing through the market, will not prompt the remark: 'This is the one' " (m. Sanh. 7:4; cf. Sipra Qedoshim 10:8; Lev. Rab. 27:3).
3. The Torah enjoined the proscription of all the (idolatrous) places and the destruction of its (Asherah) trees (Deut 12:2) because they are reminders of man's shame(ful acts) (Sipra Qedoshim 11:5).

That is, according to the rabbis, the death of the beast serves as a moral lesson to man. It is more likely, however, that the animal dies because it has sinned, as does the goring ox (Exod 21:28–32). Perhaps there also existed the fear that the animal might produce a monster (D. N. Freedman, personal communication).

The change of verb from *hûmat* to *hārag* clearly indicates that instead of death being a judicial process, it is a summary execution. There are only three cases where *hārag* is a positive requirement in the pentateuchal legal corpora (20:15, 16; Deut 13:10). As shown by Levinson (1995: 60, n. 50), Deut 13:10 reflects Neo-Assyrian treaties dealing with threats to the sovereign (to God in Deut 13:10), which employ the semantic equivalent to *hārag*, *duāku* 'kill', and the suspected rebel is summarily put to death without judicial process. Similarly, in Israel, if someone, be he a family member or close friend, promotes apostasy in secret (no witnesses!), he must be killed without delay (Deut 13:7–11; contra Tigay 1996: 132).

16. *approaches. tiqrab.* This verb has a sexual connotation (see NOTE on 18:6). It indicates that she is the initiator. Contrast *ta 'ămōd* (18:23b).

to mate with it. lĕrib 'â 'ōtāh. This is strong evidence that *lĕrib 'āh* (18:23) should be corrected (minus the *mappiq*) to *lĕrib 'â* 'for mating' (Driver and White 1894–98, on 18:23).

you shall kill the woman. wĕhāragtā 'et- hā'iššâ. On the basis of threats to As-surbanipal, the sovereign, in Neo-Assyrian treaties (VTE 12, ll. 130–46; ANET 535–36) and Zakutu, Levinson (1995) has shown that Akkadian *dâku / duâku* is semantically equivalent to *hārag* in Deut 13:10, whose context (vv. 7–12) also deals with a threat to Israel's sovereign, YHWH. All three cases speak of summary execution bypassing judicial process. The same verb *hārag* has been used in the previous verse, which deals with the execution of a beast. Here, however, it is applied to the woman. Implied is that if the woman is caught in flagrante delicto, she is summarily put to death, in contrast to the male (v. 15), who is given a proper trial (Joosten 1994: 70–71; 1996: 51–52).

they must be put to death. môt yûmātû. This death sentence implies a judicial process in contrast to the verb *hārag*. It contradicts the earlier sentence on the woman, and it is nonsensical when applied to the beast. I would suggest that it represents a later attempt to rectify the unfounded discrepancy in the punishments for the crime of bestiality pronounced on the man (v. 15) and the woman (v. 16). The two cases are identical, since both the man and the woman initiate the act and are caught in flagrante. The plural form, if not an outright error, may be a lame attempt to refer back, past the object *bĕhēmâ*, to the subject *wĕʾiššâ*, as well as including a statement that follows that they (pl.) incur bloodguilt. In any case, the result is a jarring grammatical and illogical construction.

their bloodguilt is upon them. This sentence is missing in v. 15; the beast is passive and, hence, blameless (Bekhor Shor; Prado, cited by Shadal). Why, then, is the animal put to death? Shadal (in *Hamishtadel*) cites "I will require it of every beast" (Gen 9:5). But this verse's antecedent is human lifeblood—that is, a case of homicide. Perhaps, then, this sentence refers to the man and woman who commit bestiality (vv. 15–16; Wessely 1846; Elliger 1966). However, since unwarranted killing of an animal does generate bloodguilt (see NOTE on "bloodguilt," 17:4), the text of v. 16 should be accepted at face value: the executioner of the beast (as well as the woman) incurs no bloodguilt. More likely, however, this clause is directed to the execution of the woman. Even though she can be put to death without a trial (see above), her executioner will incur no bloodguilt.

17. *marries.* *yiqqaḥ.* See the NOTES on 18:17 and 20:14. Presumably, the addressee thought that marriage with a half sister was not a violation. Indeed, if she is a stepsister—that is, both her biological parents are of a different clan—marriage with her is permitted (so it must be inferred from 18:11; see its NOTE). Besides, the relationship of Abraham to Sarah (Gen 20:12) and that (desired) between Amnon and Tamar (2 Sam 13:13) as well as its repeated prohibition in the codes (18:9, 11; 20:17; Deut 27:22) indicate that marriage with half sisters indeed was practiced, as it was with half sisters on the father's side in Athens and with full sisters in Egypt (Philo, *Laws* 3.22–23; cf. Colson 1968: 7. 633).

Sexual congress with a full daughter or sister is missing, just as in chap. 18. However, this chapter lists penalties. Surely, incest with a full sister (same father and mother) or daughter (issue of his loins) should incur the death penalty. The only solution that occurs to me is that these two unions were not subject to *human* sanctions. A full sister and an unmarried daughter are under the complete control of the addressee. These unions would be conducted secretively. Even if they became known, who would or could prosecute him? Perhaps this explains their nonspecificity in 18:6, in which they are subsumed but unnamed by the term *šĕʾēr bĕśārô* (see its NOTE). Nonetheless, although the perpetrator cannot be penalized by a human court, he is subject to *kārēt* in the divine court (18:29).

so that he sees her nakedness and she sees his nakedness. This double-euphemism is employed to indicate that the marriage was desired and consummated by both parties (*Sipra* Qedoshim 11:11).

The *Sipra*'s insight is confirmed by Melcher (1996: 94): this sentence is exceptional because *wĕrāʾâ ʾet-ʿerwātāh* 'he sees her nakedness' does not mean he has jurisdiction of her sexual organs (as in 18:10, 14, 16). Instead, it indicates an equality between man and woman. Both are equally guilty in their sexual behavior. Supporting Melcher is the fact that this is the only prohibition in chaps. 18 and 20 that uses the verb *rāʾâ*, a synonym of *gillâ* and hence a euphemism for an illicit sexual act (see NOTE on "shall approach," 18:6).

a disgrace. ḥesed; qĕlānā' 'shame' (*Tg. Onk.*); herpâ 'shame' (Gen 34:14) is rendered ḥisûdā' (*Tg. Onk.*). This homonym of ḥesed 'goodness, kindness' is attested twice more in Scripture: "Defend your right against your fellow, but do not give away the secrets of another, lest he who hears it will reproach you [yĕḥassedĕkā], and your bad repute never end" (Prov 25:9–10); "Sin is a disgrace [ḥesed] to any people" (Prov 14:34).

they shall be cut off in the sight of their people. wĕnikrĕtû lĕ'ênê bĕnê 'ammām. This is a measure-for-measure punishment: they cohabited in secret; therefore, they will be punished in public. Analogously, "You (David) acted in secret, but I will make this happen in view of all of Israel and in broad daylight" (2 Sam 12:12). Implied is that the community will witness that they will die prematurely (correcting vol. 1.458): they will not receive a proper burial, and/or their children will die before them; that is, their line will be cut off. It is probably an ellipsis of wĕnikrĕtû (mē'ammêhem) lĕ'ênê bĕnê 'ammām 'they will be cut off (from their kin) in the sight of their people'. For a discussion of the meaning of kārēt, see the NOTE on 17:4, and vol. 1. 457–61.

The legal implication of kārēt here is that marriage with a half sister cannot be punished by a human court. Would, then, marriage with a full sister be subject to môt yûmat? Not according to Magonet (1996: 151), who claims that the death penalty is invoked in cases that are the equivalent of adultery (vv. 10, 11, 12, 20 [sic]), whereas kārēt is applied to cases of incest where adultery does not occur (vv. 17–18). This distinction, however, is based on the untenable assumptions that all the kārēt victims are single, and that 'arîrîm 'childless' (v. 20) implies the execution of the perpetrator.

he shall bear his inquity. 'awōnô yiśśā'. The singular is puzzling, since both are culpable and punishable by kārēt. The LXX and Pesh. indeed read the plural (as in v. 19bβ). This idiom is a declaratory formula (IV), not a penalty (II) (see INTRODUCTION to vv. 9–21). For its meaning, see the NOTES on 17:16 and v. 20b.

18. *a woman in her infirmity.* 'iššâ dāwâ. This refers to not just a menstruant (niddâ), but a woman with any genital flow. Note that the term dāwâ is used to describe the parturient, niddat dĕwōtāh 'her menstrual infirmity' (12:2). That is, the first part of her infirmity (seven or fourteen days) is equivalent in severity to her menstrual period. Thus this rule is more comprehensive than its counterpart (18:19), which is limited to the menstruant.

Another reason for the avoidance of the technical term niddâ in this law is so it should not be confused with its figurative application in v. 20.

he has laid bare. he'ĕrâ. A synonym of gillâ, usually found in the Pi'el (e.g., Isa 3:17; 22:6; Zeph 2:14; Ps 137:7), this is the word from which the noun 'erwâ 'nakedness' is derived.

her source. mĕqōrāh (i.e., her genitalia; see NOTE on 12:7). The noun māqôr stands for the female pudenda. A male's genitalia require a different terminology: "When a man with a discharge is healed of his discharge" (15:13). Thus it is not surprising that māqôr is also a metaphor for a wife (Prov 5:18).

The basic meaning of māqôr (root qwr) is "fountain, well, source" (Hos 13:15

‖ *maʿyān*; Jer 2:13; 17:13), namely, a source of flowing liquid (e.g., *mĕqôr dimʿâ* 'a fount of tears', Jer 8:23). Ugaritic *mqr* (*KTU* 1.14 V:217) and *qr* (*KTU* 1.19 III:152) have the same meanings.

Daube (1947: 78–80) declares vv. 17–18 an appendix since they more logically belong with vv. 10–13. True, but chap. 20 is ordered not by subject matter, but by penalty, and vv. 17–18 begin a new penalty.

A further question (posed by S. Greenberg): Does the fact that the cause for the woman's guilt is given only in *this* case imply that in all the other cases, originally only the male partner was guilty because he could force himself on the unwilling woman (note the prohibitions in chap. 18, which are directed to the male, not the female)? The answer lies in the sociological dynamics of the ancient Israelite household. Since the family lived in close quarters around a common courtyard (see INTRODUCTION to 18:6–23), the victimized woman could have called out for help (cf. Deut 22:23–26). Also, the male victimizer would have been deterred by certain retribution from her clan. Thus chap. 20 presumes the compliance of the woman, and, hence, she is put to death. D. Stewart (forthcoming dissertation) points out that Ezek 18:6 adopts the same sequence as Lev 20:18–19: "(A righteous man) will not defile his neighbor's wife. Nor will he have sex with a menstruant." Ezek. 22:10 adds that the *rape* of a menstruant is as severe a crime as sex with a father's wife (Lev 18:7). Note than an explanation is given in this verse for him as well as for her because, exceptionally, this is the only case (between two people) in this list that strictly is not incest: the woman may even be unmarried! Thus the death sentence for both sexual partners requires explanation. As for the wording of chap. 18, as pointed out (see NOTE on 18:6), the incest laws are directed to the man because he initiates the sexual act. D. Stewart argues cogently (dissertation, forthcoming) that this verse presumes the woman. Even if she were married (not to speak of single or widowed) her consent is required. "H subverts the notion of 'wife as property' ."

In the NOTE on 15:24, I suggested that the reason P declares the man impure for seven days if he engages in sex with a menstruant, but impure for only one day in all other sexual liaisons (15:18), is that loss of life is symbolically oozing out of both partners. Or, sex during this period cannot lead to conception (Eilberg-Schwartz 1990: 182–85; Biale 1992:28:31). It does not, however, explain why H regards the copulative act as a capital crime (by the divine court) warranting *kārēt*. The answer may lie in the designation of the menstruant as *dāwâ* 'infirm' (20:18; cf. Lam 1:13; 5:17) and her condition as *niddat dĕwōtāh* 'her menstrual infirmity' (12:2). That is, by imposing such a drastic penalty, H is creating a deterrent that will protect the woman from unwanted advances by her husband during her period of weakness (R. Gane). This explanation would therefore coincide with the overall rationale behind the entire list of forbidden sexual unions—to prevent the family head (the addressee) and other dominant males from taking advantage of the woman. Thus sex during her physical infirmity (menstruation) is a symbol of sex during her *figurative* infirmity, if widowed or divorced and a vulnerable prey to the males in her household (see NOTE on 18:7 [Ziskind 1988]).

It might be thought that the reason that P (15:24) prescribes seven days of impurity, whereas H (20:18) prescribes *kārēt*, is that P deals with inadvertences and H deals with advertences (R. Gane). It is more likely, however, following Abravanel (see NOTE on 15:24), that P is concerned with the nature of the generated impurity, not with its penalties. Indeed, certain acts described in chap. 15 are clearly deliberate (e.g., sex! v. 18). Indeed, intention plays no part whatsoever in chap. 15; whether advertent or inadvertent, they generate impurity. Chap. 20, however, focusing solely on sexual intercourse, is limited to advertences.

Vv. 19–21. Ezek 22:10–11 lists father's wife, menstruant, adulterer, daughter-in-law, and half sister (‖20:11, 18, 10, 12, 17, respectively), but vv. 19–21 do not. Some conclude that vv. 19–21 must be later than Ezekiel (Daube 1947: 80; Fishbane 1985: 293). But Ezekiel also omits 20:13, 14, 15, 16. Clearly, he has selected the most egregious heterosexual crimes. Besides, vv. 19–21 are placed at the end of the list because their penalty, in the compiler's schema, is the least severe.

19. *You shall not uncover. lo' tĕgallēh*. Daube (1947: 80–81) regards this law as an appendix because of its switch to apodictic style and to second person. V. 19b, however, reverts to the third person. Contamination from 18:23 may be responsible (Schwartz, personal communication). Perhaps v. 19a was intended to warn against contracting a levirate marriage, under the assumption that such unions were permitted if their purpose was to provide children (Shadal), or to forestall the reasoning that if marriage to a niece was permitted, so was marriage to an aunt (Ibn Ezra), particularly in view of the precedent set by Amram, Moses' father (Exod 6:20).

It is more likely, however, that the change of person is part of an overall attempt to distinguish this prohibition from all the others by its content, style, and vocabulary (M. Hildrenbrand). It is the only prohibition bearing the sole penalty of *'ăwōnām yiśśā'û* 'they shall bear their punishment'. It is the only prohibition in this list that does not begin with *'îš 'ăšer*. Instead, it uses the phrase *wĕ'erwat 'ăhôt*, which reflects the beginning of the same prohibition in 18:12–13. This is one striking indication that the H redactor edited the list of chap. 20 with the text of chap. 18 before him (see COMMENT A). That he had 18:12–13 in mind is further supported by his use of *šĕ'ēr* solely in this prohibition.

your mother's sister or your father's sister. The aunts are listed chiastically in relation to 18:12–13 (reversed in LXX and Sam). Perhaps the mother is mentioned first here to indicate that the penalty (hence, the violation) is equal to that of the father (*Sipra Qedoshim* 11:4).

for that is laying bare his own flesh. kî 'et-šĕ'ērô he'ĕrâ, literally "for he has laid bare his own flesh." The switch of subject from second to third person indicates that the focus has moved from the person to the act. For the metaphoric use of *šĕ'ēr* 'flesh' meaning a close blood relative, see the NOTES on 18:6, 12. This clause stresses that these aunts are not the uncles' wives (affines), but their (consanguineous) sisters.

they shall bear their punishment. The penalty is unspecified. The position of v. 19 between *kārēt* violations (vv. 17–18) and *'ărîrî* violations (vv. 20–21) leaves the impression that the legist was unsure as to which group this law belongs. The idiom *nāśāʾ ʿāwōn* is explicated in the NOTE on 17:16.

20. *uncle's wife.* *dōdātô.* This term can also describe the father's sister (Exod 6:20), but not here. Note that the mother's brother's wife is excluded. Since she is neither a blood relation nor an affine, marriage with her is permitted (see NOTE on 18:14).

They shall bear their sin. The impression given by 19:8 that the expression *nāśāʾ ʿāwōn/ḥēṭʾ* is synonymous with the *kārēt* penalty is refuted here, where it is associated with the *ʿărîrî* penalty. Thus the expression is not a penalty but a declaratory formula stating that punishment is sure to follow. For fuller discussion, see the NOTE on 17:16.

childless. *ʿărîrîm.* This rendering (given by LXX, *Tgs.*) is ostensibly refuted by Jer 22:30, which declares Coniah (= Jehoiachin) as *ʿărîrî* in spite of the fact that his line did continue (1 Chr 3:17–18). Many commentators attempt to resolve this contradiction by arguing that Jehoiachin will not be literally childless but kingless; that is, his progeny would no longer sit on the Davidic throne. On the basis of Driver's (1939: 115) etymological claim that *ʿărîrî* means "stripped" and that in Jer 22:30 it means "stripped of honor/rights," McKane (1986: 550) proposes that here it also denotes "stripped of rights," though he admits that in Gen 15:2, it implies that Abraham is "stripped" of children. Ehrlich (1908) (on 15:2 [H]) comes to the same conclusion, though he derives its meaning from an Arabic cognate signifying "disgrace," and he cites Rachel's comment at the birth of Joseph: "God has taken away my disgrace" (Gen 30:23).

Westbrook (1990: 568, n. 97) suggests that here and in v. 21, the crime is the childless husband's consent and collusion with the addressee to provide a child, and the punishment is therefore "measure for measure": childlessness. In that case, however, the crime would have been adultery, punishable by death (v. 10). Hence this law presumes that the woman is divorced or widowed. Perhaps, indeed, their hope is for children, and it will be frustrated by God.

The Bible speaks univocally about the presence of children (especially males) as the divine reward for obeying his commandments: "Lo, sons are a heritage from YHWH, the fruit of the womb a reward" (Ps 127:3); "Your wife shall be a fruitful vine within your house; your sons, like olive saplings around your table. So shall the man who reveres YHWH be blessed" (Ps 128: 3–4; cf. v.1). Conversely, note the despair to the point of desperation of the barren wife, a motif that runs through the stories of the favorite spouse (Rachel, Gen 30:1; Hannah, 1 Sam 1:5–11; cf. Sarah, Gen 16:2; Rebecca, 25:21) in contrast to the fecundity of the concubines and other wives (Hagar, Gen 16:4; Keturah, 25:1–2; Leah, Bilhah, Zilpah, 29:31–30:21; Peninah, 1 Sam 1:2). The penalty of *ʿărîrî* is one step less severe than *kārēt* (vv. 17–19; see NOTES on v. 17; 17:4; and vol. 1. 457–60); both, however, predicate childlessness.

It is hardly coincidental that, just as reflected in this chapter, the withholding of progeny serves as a divine punishment for sexual violations. For Abimelech's almost consummated adultery, God imposes barrenness on his wife and concubines (Gen 20:17–18). A suspected adulteress is struck with sterility (Num

5:22, 27). In chap. 20 as well, the violation of its sex code is a sin against the Deity, who punishes the guilty parties even when the judicial officials are unauthorized to do so.

How do the punishments *'ărîrî* 'childless' and *nikrāt* 'excised' differ from each other? The difference, I would suggest, is slight but crucial. The one who is *nikrāt* not only suffers the termination of his lineage, but is "excised" from joining his ancestors (rather than being *ne'ĕsāp 'el 'ammāyw* 'gathered to his fathers'). The one who is *'ărîrî* 'childless' joins his ancestors. But what good does it do him? Like the *nikrāt*, he can only echo Absalom's lament: "I have no son *ba'ăbûr hazkîr šĕmî* 'to keep my name in remembrance' (2 Sam 18:18; cf. Isa 56:4–5)—that is, to perform the ancestral rites (see COMMENT C). Alternatively, one can define *kārēt*, with the rabbis, as premature death (before age sixty; *b. Mo'ed Qaṭ.* 28a) plus excision of the line, whereas the *'ărîrî* also suffers excision but might live a full life.

21. *marries. yiqqaḥ.* For this rendering, see the NOTE on v. 14. *Tg. Ps.-J.* adds "during his lifetime," making it a case of adultery, in order to obviate a contradiction with the permitted marriage to a levir (Deut 25:5). Does this verse reject the levirate institution? Elliger (1966) answers in the negative, on the presumption that this law speaks of a case where the woman already had a child and is ineligible for marriage with a levir (Deut 25:5). However, the lack of such specification would argue the reverse: Leviticus's opposition to the levirate, support for which is the penalty that they will be childless. Perhaps this is the reason the penalty is the lesser *'ărîrî* rather than *môt yûmat* (cf. v. 12) or *kārēt* (cf. v. 17), because the levir thought that marriage with a widowed and childless sister-in-law was not only permitted, but even mandatory. A better answer is that this is a classic case of measure for measure. They thought that the levirate marriage would produce a child. Instead their marriage will be childless.

The Samaritans, according to the rabbis (*b. Qid.* 76a), condoned levirate marriage only with a childless widow whose husband died after the betrothal. However, if her husband died after the marriage was consummated, levirate marriage was prohibited.

repulsive. niddâ. The rabbis claim that this term is mentioned only with a (widowed) sister-in-law because of its correspondence with her case: sexual relations are permitted postmenses and with a levir (*Sipra* Qedoshim 12:7; cf. Ibn Ezra).

On the basis of the etymology (see NOTE on 12:2), Saadiah and Ibn Ezra claim that the couple should be banished (citing Isa 65:5; Job 18:18). However, it should be apparent that H uses this term metaphorically: it is a foul, odious, repulsive act. Here H parts with P's specific, cultic *niddâ* 'menstrual impurity' (15:19, 20, 26, 33). This metaphoric use is subsequently found in Ezek 7:19–20; Lam 1:17; 2 Chr 29:5 (Greenberg 1995: 75). It is another instance in H's portfolio of metaphoric meanings given to P's precise terminology. Perhaps this constitutes an additional reason why the term is avoided in the case of the menstruant (v. 18) because of the likely confusion with its metaphoric use.

The sectaries of Qumran express this prohibition, as follows: *LW' YQḤ 'YŠ*

ʾT ʾŠT ʾḤYHW WLWʾ YGLH KNP ʾḤYHW BN ʾBYH ʾW BN ʾMW KY NDH *HYʾ* 'a man shall not marry his brother's wife, nor shall he uncover his brother's skirt, be it his father's son or his mother's son, for this is impurity' (11QT 66:12–13), a combination of Lev 18:16; 20:21 and Deut 23:1, with the additional specification that marriage with a half brother is also forbidden.

they shall remain childless. ʿărîrîm yihyû. The difference in the verbs yāmūtû (v. 20) and yihyû (v. 21) is explained by the rabbis as follows: he will either bury his children or not have any (*Sipra* Qedoshim 11:9; *b. Yeb.* 75a).

The fact that kārēt and ʿărîrî are discrete penalties is an assurance that kārēt, the prior and hence severer penalty, means more than ʿărîrî, the termination of the line. In addition, kārēt most likely refers, as its antonymous expression "gathered to his or her kin" suggests, to being "cut off from the (departed) kin," in other words, the deprivation of afterlife, probably by lack of proper burial (see COMMENT C, and vol. 1.457–61).

Vv. 22–26. Closing Exhortation

The switch to the second-person plural is reminiscent of the exhortations of chap. 18. The resemblances are enhanced by the employment of similar vocabulary. In particular, as will be shown in the NOTES, vv. 22–23 are carefully constructed so that each verse opens and closes with language from the opening and closing exhortations of chap. 18. Thus while the two lists of prohibitions are independent compositions (so I argue in COMMENT A), it would seem that the H redactor appended this exhortation to chap. 20 with those of chap. 18 in mind.

22. This verse is modeled on v. 8a, and both hark back to 18:4–5. V. 22b is a verbatim quote of 18:28aα (except for the metathesis of subject and object). Thus v. 22a closes the unit vv. 9–21 as v. 8 closes its unit vv. 1–7. Or, conversely, vv. 8a and 22a envelop the list (vv. 9–21). Similarly, v. 22b also closes the list vv. 9–21, as 18.28aα (as part of the peroration) closes the list vv. 6–23. The similar wording in v. 22a and 18:4–5 forms an envelope for the pivotal chap. 19 and its chiastic flank of prohibited sexual liaisons and Molek worship: chaps. 18 and 20.

23. This verse follows 18:3bβ, v. 23aβ is the exact citation of 18:24bβ, and v. 23bα imitates 18:27a.

the nations. haggôy. One MS, the Versions, and the Sam. read plural haggôyim; however, 18:28 also reads the singular haggôy, adding support to my supposition that the writer of this exhortation (vv. 29:22–26) had the text (or at least the exhortations) of chap. 18 before him. The singular may be a collective. However, 18:24 contains the precisely equivalent phrase haggôyîm [pl.] ʾăšer-ʾănî mĕšallēaḥ mippĕnêkem. The die is cast in favor of the latter, since it is followed by plurals ʿāśû and bām.

that I loathed them. wāʾāquṣ bām. This is the only new element in vv. 22–23. The primary meaning of the root qwṣ probably is "be disgusted (with food)" (Galatzer-Levy and Gruber 1992: 80, anticipated by *Sipra* Qedoshim 11:16), as exemplified by *wĕnapšēnû qāṣâ balleḥem haqqĕlōqēl*, literally "our throats have come to loathe this miserable food" (Num 21:5b). Wessely (1846) rightly distinguishes between *qāṣ be* 'loathe' (e.g., Gen 27:46) and *qāṣ mippĕnê* 'dread' (Exod 1:12; Num 22:3; Isa 7:16).

24. *and said to you. wā'ōmar lākem.* The promise of the land is attested in many places (e.g., Exod 3:8; 6:8; 13:5; 33:1–2; Lev 14:34; Num 13:27; 14:8; 16:13, 14), but the only priestly texts in this list are Exod 6:8 and Lev 14:34, which also are the only ones that do not contain the expression "a land flowing with milk and honey" (see below). The probability, therefore, exists that the H redactor here, who uses this idiom, was aware of the epic tradition (JE) of the Tetrateuch.

You shall possess. 'attem tîrĕšû. The primary meaning of *yāraš* is "possess" (cf. 25:46). The connotation "inherit" is a subsequent development (Levine 1989).

I myself (will give it). wa'ănî. This is added for emphasis (instead of the expected cohortative *wĕ'ettĕnennâ*). It also balances the other pronominal subjects: *'ănî* 'I (bring you)' (v. 22); 'I (am driving out)' (v. 23), and *'attem* 'You (shall possess)' (v. 24).

a land flowing with milk and honey. This figure is generally taken as a metaphor for fruits as pure as milk and as sweet as honey. Recently, the proposal has been made that this expression is to be understood literally: it contrasts YHWH with Baal, the fertility god of the Canaanites, who ordains that *šmm. šmn. tmṭrn/nḥlm. tlk. nbtm* 'the heavens rain fat/oil and the wadis flow with honey' (*KTU* 1.6 III:12–13). "In this YHWH may have been doing one better than Baal—if Israelites valued dairy products over vegetable fat" (Stern 1992: 555). This is the only place in the priestly texts where this expression occurs; hence many regard it as a Dtr interpolation (but see Propp 1996: 475, n. 66).

honey. dĕbaš. Akkadian *dišpu* and Arabic *dibs* refer to "honey" from either wild bees or dates. In the Bible, the latter is generally meant (cf. Deut 8:8, where *dĕbaš* replaces missing "dates"; Joel 4:18, where milk and *'āsîs* 'fruit juice' stand in parallel; and Gen 43:11, where *dĕbaš* is included among vegetable products).

I YHWH am your God. This is the beginning of a new sentence whose thought runs on into v. 25: just as I have separated you from the nations, so must you distinguish among the animals (Ibn Ezra, Bekhor Shor; Wessely 1846; Ehrlich 1908). YHWH's self-declaration formula functions as an inclusio with v. 7b.

Vv. 24b–26 comprise an ABB'A' construction, combining three major H themes into a theological program: separation from the nations, by observing the dietary laws, propels Israel on the road to holiness.

A   24b*'ănî YHWH 'ĕlōhêkem*
    'ăšer-hibdaltî 'etkem min hā'ammîm

B   25a*wĕhibdaltem bên-habbĕhēmâ haṭṭĕhōrâ laṭṭĕmē'â ûbên-hā'ôp haṭṭāmē' laṭṭāhōr*

B'   25b*wĕlō'- tĕšaqqĕṣû 'et-napšōtêkem babbĕhēmâ ûbā'ôp ûbĕkōl 'ăšer tirmōś hā'ădāmâ 'ăšer-hibdaltî lākem lĕṭammē'*

A'   26*wihyîtem lî qĕdōšîm kî qādôš 'ănî YHWH wā'abdîl 'etkem min-hā'ammîm lihyôt lî*

A ^{24b}I YHWH am your God
    who has set you apart from all peoples
     B ^{25a}So you shall distinguish between the pure and the impure
        quadrupeds and between the impure and the pure birds.
     B′ ^{25b}You shall not defile your throats with a quadruped or bird or any-
        thing with which the ground teems, which I have set apart for you
        to treat as impure.
A′ ^{26}You shall be holy to me, for I YHWH am holy;
    therefore I have set you apart from other peoples to be mine.

Four separations (*hibdîl*) are arranged chiastically. AA′ separates Israel from the nations so it can achieve holiness. BB′ provides the method: separation between pure and impure animals and abstention from the latter's flesh. In effect, H has completed its interpolation into chap. 11, where it adds holiness to swarmers (vv. 43–45; see NOTES). Here the dimension of holiness is extended to the entire dietary system. Thus H (a subsequent tradent) supplements chap. 19. It declares that eschewing impure flesh is indispensable to attaining holiness. A most logical assumption: impure (*ṭāmēʾ*) is the antonym and mortal enemy of holy (*qādōš*). Moreover, the separation of Israel from the nations accomplished by Israel's separation from much of the animal world consumed by the nations helps complete the divine process of creation (see NOTE on v. 26, and Introduction II B).

    set . . . apart. hibdaltî. The first of four occurrences of this verb in the exhortation (vv. 24, 25 [twice], 26). Followed by the preposition *min*, it means "set apart" the nations (vv. 24, 26; 1 Kgs 8:53), Levites (Num 8:14; 16:9), idolaters (Deut 29:20), foreigners (Isa 56:3), and those of mixed descent (Neh 13:3)— from Israel. Followed by *bên . . . bên* (10:10; 11:47; Gen 1:4, 7, 14, 18; Exod 26:33), *bên . . . l* (v. 25a; Gen 1:6; cf. Ezek 22:26; 42:20), or *bên . . . lĕbên* (Isa 59:2), it means "distinguish." It is perhaps no accident that in this pericope the subject of the former is God (vv. 24, 26), and of the latter, Israel (v. 25a): God sets apart one species from another, but Israel distinguishes within the same species.

    There is also a *Nipʿal* (reflexive) usage *nibdal . . . m*, which is of postexilic provenance, referring to the separation of not only Israel from gentiles (Ezra 9:2; 10:8, 11; Neh 9:2), but also (contra Elliger 1966) protoproselyte non-Israelites from gentiles (Ezra 6:21; Neh 10:29).

    The connection between separation and creation is demonstrated by the frequent use in the creation story of the same verb *hibdîl* (Gen 1:4, 7, 14, 18). Separation creates order, and the distinctions between the elements must be maintained lest the world collapse into chaos and confusion. What holds for nature also holds for humanity. The separation of Israel from the nations is a sine qua non for the maintenance of order *within the human world* (see further NOTE on v. 26).

    Moreover, the diet laws associate separation with holiness. The doctrine of holiness is extended from the concept of *imitatio dei* (see NOTES on 19:2 and v.

26a) to the concept of separation. Just as God's holiness is a model and mandate for Israel, so is God's act of separation—first in the creation of the world (note the predominance of *hibdîl*, Gen 1:4, 7, 14, 18) and subsequently in the creation of Israel. In the latter case, however, the injunction is stronger. Whereas holiness is God's *nature* and is apprehensible solely from his self-revelation, separation is the result of his *act*, visible in the creation of the world (nature) and in the creation of Israel (history). Thus both positive holiness (*imitatio dei*) and negative holiness (separation) must be reckoned as cardinal planks in H's theology: they are the divine imperatives for Israel. Israel is enjoined to live a life of imitation and separation, the former by fulfilling God's commandments, and the latter by separating from impure food as a reminder to separate from the destructive folkways of other peoples. Indeed, as I have argued (vol. 1.731), separation is inherent in holiness. The word *qādôs* 'holy' means both "separate from" and "separate to." Israel's attainment of holiness depends as much on Israel's resistance to the moral impurity of others (symbolized by abstention from impure foods) as on its adherence to the attributes of God's being (concretized in his commandments). The identification of holiness with separation is further emphasized in the chapter's structure, whereby sanctification (v. 8b) and separation (vv. 24–26) form balanced elements (CC′) in the chapter's ABCXC′B′A′ structure (see INTRODUCTION).

It should not be overlooked that, according to H, Israel is equally obligated as the priests to distinguish between the pure and the impure (cf. 10:10), another indication of the democratic thrust in H.

25. *So you shall distinguish between the pure . . . quadrupeds.* The verb here is *wĕhibdaltem*, literally "you shall set apart," which matches God's *hibdaltî* 'I have set apart' (vv. 24b, 25b; cf. 26b). And as noted by Zimmerli (1980: 502), both the divine and the human acts of separation are essential for Israel to safeguard its holiness.

The juxtaposition of the dietary prohibition and the holiness and separation requirements (v. 26) does not categorically mean that Israelites may not dine at the same table with others (Gerstenberger 1996: 291), but that they must be wary of the meat being served. A deeper implication, however, can be drawn from the association of both the holiness and dietary demands with the moral life, one well understood in Hellenistic times: "An additional signification (of the diet laws) is that we are set apart from all men. For most of the rest of mankind defile themselves by their promiscuous unions, working great unrighteousness, and whole countries and cities pride themselves on these vices. . . . But we have kept apart from these things" (Letter of Aristeas 151–52; see also *Jub* 22:16).

The sociocultural implications of separation through ritual have been fully drawn by Turner (1979: 75–85), who postulated that many rituals arise to prevent the breakdown of the social order. As encapsulated by Moore and Myerhoft (1977: 17, cited in Gorman 1990: 26–27), "every ceremony is par excellence a dramatic statement against indeterminacy in some field of human affairs. Through order, formality, and repetition it seeks to state that the cosmic and social world, or some particular small part of them are orderly and explicable and for the moment fixed."

Thus it may be assumed that in eighth- and seventh-century Judah there was increased contact with the surrounding nations. It may, in particular, have been the allure of the Assyrian Empire, which had annexed North Israel and subjugated Judah, that gave rise to a wave of assimilation, which the diet laws through their symbolism of separation attempted to stem.

between the impure and the pure birds. One would have expected the reverse order in view of the preceding clause. In both attestations of this chiasm (11:47; 20:25), *ṭāmē'* precedes *ṭāhôr* when the impure species are less numerous, and *ṭāhôr* (or its equivalent, as in this verse) precedes when the pure species are less numerous. The reason is that one always sets aside the lesser quantity from the larger one (Ḥazzequni on 20:25). Thus the permitted creatures are fewer than the forbidden ones, whereas the impure creatures (by touch, not by ingestion!) are fewer than the pure ones. Similarly, in v. 25, pure quadrupeds are fewer than impure ones (Deut 14:4–5), whereas impure birds are fewer than pure ones (see NOTE on Lev 11:13). Ḥazzequni's insight is corroborated by another chiastic structure involving *ṭāmē'* and *ṭāhôr*, that with *qōdeš* and *ḥōl* (10:10; Ezek 22:26; 44:23): the smaller quantities of *qōdeš* and *ṭāmē'* precede the larger quantities of *ḥōl* and *ṭāhôr*, respectively.

The conclusion of v. 25 is illuminating: *'ăšer-hibdaltî lakem lěṭammē'* 'which I have set apart for you to treat as impure'. In this verse and, indeed, in H, to which this verse belongs, the distinction preserved in P that *ṭāmē'* refers to defilement by contact (see also 5:2) and not by eating (for which *šeqeṣ/šiqqēṣ* is used; see NOTE on 11:11, and Milgrom 1992), is no longer upheld: *šeqeṣ/šiqqeṣ* and *ṭāmē'/ṭimmē'* are indistinguishable, both referring to ingestion (cf. 20:25; 22:8), as in 11:44. The same holds true for the terminological distinction between the permitted animals: edible ones are *hanne'ĕkelet* 'that may be eaten', and those whose contact does not defile are *haṭṭāhōr* 'pure'. This distinction is consistently preserved in the P sections: *'ākal* (11:2, 3, 4, 9, 21, 22; see esp. 34 and 39); *ṭāhōr* (11:32, vessels; 36, water; 37, seed). Later, this differentiation is effaced in H (and in D; see vol. 1.698–704), where *ṭāhōr* describes edible animals (20:25).

It cannot but be noticed that the category of fish is missing (contrast 11:9–12, 46aβ). It is another bit of evidence that fish was a food commodity that rarely appeared on the menu of early Israel (see NOTE on 11:12).

quadruped. běhēmâ. This rendering (rather than "beast") is guaranteed by its distinction from "bird" and "anything with which the ground teems" (i.e., land swarmers; see 11:41–43a).

defile your throats. těšaqqěṣû 'et-napšōtêkem. For the justification of this rendering, see the NOTE on 11:43. Both verses stem from the pen of H because P's limitation of the root *šqṣ* to non-*ṭāmē'* animals (11:9–23, 41–42) is applied in H indiscriminately to all forbidden animal food (Milgrom 1992: 108–109).

or anything with which the ground teems. ûběkōl 'ăšer tirmōś hā'ădāmâ. In 11:44bβ (H) this category is called *šereṣ* '(land) swarmers'. It is not the object of *wěhibdaltem* 'you shall separate' (v. 25a) because there are not pure swarmers; all are forbidden.

to treat as impure. lěṭammē'. Sam., LXX, and Pesh. read *lěṭum'â* 'as impurity'. However, the declarative *Piʿel* is well attested for *ṭm'* (see NOTE on 13:3). The significance of maintaining this reading is not trivial: it continues H's theological postulate that it is Israel's responsibility to realize on earth the divine attributes holiness (qdš) and separation (bdl). God has by fiat created pure and impure animals. It is now for Israel to live a holy life by distinguishing every day at mealtime between impure and pure animals and thereby remind itself to make distinctions between practices that enhance holiness and those that desecrate it.

26. Sanctification. *You shall be holy to me, for I YHWH am holy. wihyîtem lî qĕdōšim kî qādôš 'ānî YHWH.* A partial inclusio with *wĕhitqaddištem wihîytem qĕdōšîm kî 'ānî YHWH* (v. 7) and a fuller inclusio with *qĕdōšim tihyu kî qādôš 'ānî YHWH* (19:2), thereby locking chaps. 19–20 into a single unit. The formula here contains the additional word *lî* 'to me' in order to complement and balance *wā'abdîl . . . lihyôt lî* 'I have set (you) apart . . . to be mine', at the end of the verse. That Israel is God's possession and, therefore, *obligated* to follow his commandments turns unambiguously explicit in the divine demand that the enslavement of Israelites be abolished: *kî-lî bĕnê-yiśrā'ēl 'ăbādîm* 'for the Israelites are my slaves' (25:55a).

therefore I have set you apart from other peoples. wā'abdîl 'etkem min-hā'ammîm. This is a repetition of the same phrase in v. 24b, thereby locking in separation (also *hibdîl*) with impure foods (v. 25) as a prerequisite for partaking of God's nature of holiness (v. 26a; see also 11:44 [H]).

The full implication is drawn by the R. Eleazar b. Azariah: "No one should say, I do not want to wear a garment of mixed seed, I do not want to eat pig flesh, I do not want to engage in illicit sex. I indeed want (them), but what I can I do? My father in heaven imposed these (prohibitions) upon me: 'I have set you apart from other peoples to be mine.' Thus one separates himself from sin and accepts the yoke of heaven" (*Sipra* Qedoshim 11:22).

The same juxtaposition of holiness and separation is found in Deut 7:6; 14:2, but there, instead of H's verb *hibdîl* 'separate', which as noted in v. 24 is redolent of creation (Gen 1:1–2:3 [P]), D resorts to its characteristic verb *bāḥar* 'close' (Paschen 1970: 48). The difference is significant. For D, Israel's election is traceable to God's demonstrable love of the patriarchs (Deut 4:37; 7:8). For H (as for P; see Milgrom 1992c), the choice of Israel is a continuation (and climax!) of the process of creation. The implication is clear: just as God created order out of chaos in the *natural* world by his act of separation (*hibdîl*, Gen 1:4, 7, 14, 18), so the separation of Israel from the nations is essential not just for Israel's survival, but for an orderly *human* world.

to be mine. lihyôt lî. This concluding phrase turns v. 26 into a chiasm. By virtue of YHWH's act in separating Israel from the nations, Israel belongs to YHWH and is obligated to follow his demands to lead a holy life.

Appendix: Penalty for Mediums

27. There are two explanations for this appendix. The first is that it was deliberately removed by the author/editor of chap. 20 from its original context dealing with the *'ōb* and *yiddĕ'ōnî* (after v. 6) for structural reasons: to create an in-

clusio for chap. 20 (in the same way that v. 26 functions with v. 7; see above). This verse would have been chosen because of its verbal and contextual linkage with v. 2b (cf. *bā'eben yirgĕmû 'ōtām* and *yirgĕmūhû bā'āben*; Hoffmann 1953). A different structural reason has been proposed by Carmichael (1979: 132): to provide a transition to the next chapter, which also begins with forbidden association with the dead.

The other explanation is that given by Daube (1941), who argues on the basis of his studies of early Roman law codes (e.g., *Lex Aquila*, ca. 287 B.C.E.) that legists did not insert new laws in their logical place but tacked them on the end (see below for a recent attempt to date this insertion).

who is a medium for. kî-yihyeh bahem, literally "who has in them." This certainly corresponds with the LXX rendering *engastrimuthos*, literally "one who speaks from his stomach," or a medium, the Vg *pythonicus*. The rabbis describe how it was done: "The *'ōb* practitioner is a Python who speaks from his armpit and the *yiddĕ'ōnî* is one who speaks from his mouth" (*m. Sanh.* 7:6). The Qumranites clearly follow this ventriloquist interpretation: "Every man in whom [*bô*, not "over whom"; Rabin 1954: 58] the spirits of Belial obtain dominion so that he teaches rebellion shall be judged in the same manner as *hā'ōb wĕhayiddĕ'ōnî*" (CD 12:2–3). Rouillard and Tropper (1987: 239) have argued that this verse is an interpolation dating from Hellenistic times, on the basis of their supposition that belief in mediums did not exist before then. Theirs, however, is an argument from silence.

Alternatively, some argue that *bahem* should be rendered "with them," referring to the instrumental meaning of *'ōb*—for example, Hoffner's (1967) "pit" (see NOTE on v. 6). However, the difficulty with this interpretation is that it forces the term *yiddĕ'ōnî* into a similar interpretative mold as *'ōb*, and there is no philological or evidentiary support for it connoting an instrument.

Adopting the given translation makes sense in view of v. 6: one who turns to a necromancer is punished by *kārēt*, but one who acts as one (i.e., as a medium) is summarily put to death (cf. *Sipra* Qedoshim 9:13). Thus this chapter clearly distinguishes between a "user" and a "pusher."

In sum, it is possible that v. 27 is an appendix, but there is no evidence that it dates from Hellenistic times.

Yaron (1995: 454–55) has proposed that the punishment, death by stoning, was accidentally omitted from v. 6 and, hence, a later tradent inserted it here. However, the two cases are not identical: *kārēt* (v. 6) must be distinguished from *môt yûmat* (v. 27), as demonstrated in the NOTE to "and cut him off" (v. 2).

COMMENTS

A. The Relationship Between Chapters 20 and 18

The critics are evenly divided as to whether chap. 20 is a continuation of chap. 18 or is an independent composition. Those who hold the former view point to obviously related items.

1. Both deal with the same prohibitions: Molek (20:2–5; 18:21) and adultery (20:10; 18:20), for example, and both contain a list of twelve prohibitions.

2. The prohibitions are described by the same condemnatory vocabulary: Molek worship *ḥll Pi'el šēm YHWH* (20:3; 18:21); the illicit sexual unions are *glh Pi'el 'erwâ* (20:11, 17–21; 18:6–20) and constitute *tebel* (20:12; 18:23), *zimmâ* (20:14; 18:17), and *tô'ēbâ* (20:13; 18:22); and YHWH's *ḥuqqôt* and *mišpāṭîm* (20:22; 18:4, 26) are directed against Canaanite mores (20:23; 18:3b, 24), the practice of which causes the land to vomit out (*lěhāqî'*) its inhabitants (20:22; 18:25, 28).

3. The linguistic and stylistic correspondences are apparent in all the prohibitions and exhortations. Even the structure of the two chapters follows a similar pattern: exhortations (20:7–8, 22–26 and 18:2b–5, 24–30) flanking the prohibitions (20:9–21 and 18:6–23). Also the two chapters are connected by the reversed object and subject in 20:2 (see its NOTE).

4. Not only does chap. 20 complete chap. 18 by adding the penalties for sexual violations, but in one case, it may be argued, the legist of chap. 20 clearly must have had chap. 18 before him: he felt the need to explain the euphemism *'erwat 'ēšet-ābîkā lō' těgallēh* 'You shall not uncover the nakedness of your father's wife' (18:8) by *yiškab 'et-'ēšet 'ābîw* 'lies with his father's wife' (20:11; Paton 1894: 120). However, this point is invalidated by the fact that chap. 20 regularly uses *šākab* for sex between humans (vv. 11, 12, 18, 20) and *lāqaḥ* for those prohibitions involving marriage (vv. 14, 17, 21; see below). A better argument is that the construction and vocabulary of v. 19 indicated that H utilized 18:12–13 as the basis for composing v. 19 (see its NOTE). This point, too, is not decisive. All it can mean is that H reworked v. 19 with 18:12–13 in mind; the two lists can still be independent compositions.

An equally strong (and probably stronger) case can be made that both chapters represent independent traditions (Schwartz 1987: 56–60). Two parallels are not infrequently encountered in Scripture (e.g., Gen 1–2; 1 Sam 24 and 26; 2 Sam 22 and Ps 18; cf. the Synoptic Gospels; Gerstenberger 1996: 288).

1. A number of prohibitions contained in chap. 18 are missing from chap. 20: mother (18:7), granddaughter (18:10), two sisters (18:18). Also the mother–daughter prohibitions are differently construed: in 18:17, the wife's daughter and granddaughters and in 20:14, the mother-in-law. Two prohibitions in chap. 20, ghosts and wizard-spirits (v. 6) and dishonoring father or mother (v. 9)—not even sexual crimes—are absent in chap. 18.

2. Some of the same laws are worded differently, such as sex with a menstruant (cf. 20:18 and 18:19; Wellhausen 1963: 155).

3. The form of the prohibitions is different: in chap. 18, it is second-person apodictic; in chap. 20, it is third-person casuistic. However, the change of form may be due to a change of theme, as explained in the INTRODUCTION to vv. 9–21.

4. Although chap. 20, like chap. 18, concerns the father's house, it probably is addressed to the community, which has the responsibility for carrying out the punishment (Hartley 1992: 332).

5. As pointed out by Gerstenberger (1996: 289), Lev 20 refers to earlier chapters (20:6, 27 to 19:26; 20:9 to 19:2; 20:25 to chap. 11, etc.), thus raising the possibility that the author of chap. 20 "used the preceding texts [including chap. 18] to present to the congregation previously treated topics from a new perspective." The redactor also indicates that chap. 20, in its entirety, is related to chap. 18 by reversing the position of subject and object in the heading of chap. 20 (v. 2) and joining the two chapters with a connective *waw*.

6. The penalties are different and cannot be reconciled: in chap. 18, the miscreants are punished with *kārēt*, but in chap. 20, the punishments are graded: *kārēt*, extirpation by God (vv. 17–18, possibly v. 19 [see its NOTE]), is preceded by severer (immediate) execution by judicial authorities (vv. 9–16) and followed by less stringent childlessness (vv. 20–21; see NOTE on v. 21). M. Hildenbrand asks whether chap. 20 may not be assuming that *kārēt* also applies to each violation in the list. This possibility can hardly be envisaged. If *kārēt* were taken for granted by the author of chap. 20, there would be no need to specify it in vv. 17–18. Moreover, as in the case of Molek worship (vv. 2–5), one would have expected a similar formulation in vv. 10–14: if the death penalty is not carried out by human hands, YHWH's *kārēt* is certain to follow. Nonetheless, as in chap. 18, innocent and guilty alike suffer exile (v. 22b; cf. 18:28). It is no accident that the rabbis also added idolatry to the sins of incest and murder as constituting the three most egregious capital crimes: "By a majority vote, it was resolved in the upper chambers of the house of Nithza in Lydda [probably during the Hadrianic persecutions following the failure of the Bar Kochba revolt, 132–35 C.E.] that in every law of the Torah, if a man is commanded: 'Transgress and suffer not death' he may transgress and not suffer death, excepting idolatry, incest, and murder" (*b. Pesaḥ* 25a; *b. Sanh.* 74a; *y. Šebi* 4:2). They would have found their biblical support in 18:21, 28; 20:1–6, and, especially, Ezek 36:18–19, which expressly specifies idolatry as polluting the land and leading to exile.

7. The rationales are also different: chap. 18 dwells negatively on the sins that will lead to exile, while chap. 20 speaks positively of the effect of observing the prohibitions: it will lead to separation from other nations and achieving holiness (v. 26). Schwartz (1987: 56–60) also adds terminological omissions in each of the chapters, such as *môledet bayit 'ô môledet ḥûṣ* (18:9) from 20:17, and *ṭimmē' miqdāš* (20:3) and *zānâ* (20:5) from the parallel prohibition in 18:21. These distinctions, however, are not valid. The author of the *supplemental* chap. 20 was not bound to copy chap. 18 verbatim, but had the literary privilege of adding or deleting words as he pleased. The missing *prohibitions* (no. 1) and the contradiction in penalties (no. 5) are what is decisive in determining that the chapters are independent compositions.

A separate but allied question is why the H redactor of Leviticus did not join these two chapters together. Why, indeed, were they separated by chap. 19? Douglas (1995; 1999), in her structural analysis of Leviticus, makes the trenchant point that chap. 19 is the center of the book and chaps. 18 and 20 mark the turning point. She is correct, though I differ with her terminology. Moreover, I cast the redactor's net even wider: Lev 19 is the center of the Torah (see Introduction I M). In any event, the respective positions occupied by chaps. 18 and 20 serve an aesthetic as well as an ideological purpose—to set off and highlight the centrality of chap. 19.

My conclusion is that the H redactor used the subject of sex and Molek violations to create an introverted structure with chap. 18, because he had (but did not compose) two independent and slightly variant lists, which he flanked chiastically with admonitory but differently worded exhortations and thereby projected Lev 19 as the fulcrum for the entire Torah.

B. The 'ôb, yiddĕʿōnî, Molek, and Necromancy

A spate of recent investigations of the term 'ôb has not yielded a consensus on its meaning. It has variously been interpreted as the spirit of the dead, the medium (necromancer) who communicates with it, or the apparatus employed for that purpose. The last interpretation has been championed by Gadd (1945: 88–89), Vieyra (1961), and, more comprehensively, Hoffner (1967), who have concluded that biblical 'ôb is derived from Sumerian ab, Hittite a-a-bi, Ugaritic 'eb, and Akkadian abu, denoting the ritual pit for sacrificing to chthonic deities. Further support is now available from the recently excavated Emar texts that on the twenty-fifth day of the month Abî, an offering was made "before" the abû, which is also designated "at the gate of the grave" (Fleming 1995: 146).

This interpretation was opposed by Schmidtke (1967), who argued that Hebrew 'ôb was equivalent to Akkadian eṭemmu 'spirit', and could also refer to the necromancer (1 Sam 28:3, 9; 2 Kgs 21:6). He was followed by Lust (1974), who, on philological grounds, argued that 'ôb was related to 'āb 'father', hence the "ancestral spirit." Hoffner's (1967) view was vigorously defended by Ebach and Rüterswörden (1977; 1980), who argued that in 1 Sam 28 the term 'elōhîm is reserved for "spirit" (v. 13), whereas the expression bā'ôb (v. 8b) utilizes the beth instrumenti to designate the means of conjuration. At the same time, Margalit (1976) also came to the support of the etymological equation proposed by Gadd, Vieyra, and Hoffner, but emended it slightly by asserting that ab (Sum.) = apu (Akk.) = a-a-b/pl (Hitt.) = ab (ab-) = 'o(w)b 'pit, mundus', though proposing that the original meaning was replaced metonymously by "necromancer" and "spirit-of-the-dead" (a view also suggested by Vieyra (1961) and Hoffner 1967).

Spronk (1986: 253) concurred that 'ôb refers to a spirit and an object, though the latter is not a pit but an image, just as 'ăšērâ stands for both the goddess and her cult image, and nepeš could refer both to the "life/soul" and (in Aramaic) to a stele representing the dead. Finally, Rouillard and Tropper (1987) independently adopted the same view that 'ôb denotes mainly "spirit" (19:31; 20:6; Deut 18:11; 1 Sam 28:7, 8; Isa 8:19; 19:3; 29:4; 1 Chr 10:13–14) or "image" (1 Sam 28:3, hēsîr; 2 Kgs 21:6, 'āśâ; 2 Kgs 23:24, bi'ēr) and that Lev 20:27 and Job 32:19 stem from Hellenistic times, when the idea of a medium engastrímuthos (LXX) "Buchrednern" prevailed (cf. pîtôm [= puthōn] m. Sanh. 7:7; see NOTE on v. 27).

Rouillard and Tropper's proof texts form the basis for my brief analysis. The beth in the term šā'al be (Hos 4:12; 1 Chr 10:13) is always the beth instrumenti and cannot be rendered "vom Totengeist" *'from* the spirit of the dead' (1987: 237). This conclusion follows inescapably from this term's scriptural attestations: *ʿammî bĕʿĕṣô yišʾal*, literally "My people will inquire *by* its stick" (Hos 4:12); *šāʾal battĕrāpîm* 'inquired *by* its Teraphim' (Ezek 21:26). The instrumental *beth* is clearly evident in *wĕlōʾ ʿānāhû YHWH . . . gam bāʾûrîm* 'YHWH did not answer him . . . *by* the Urim' (1 Sam 28:6). In other words, the stick, the teraphim, and the Urim are instruments for consulting the divinity. Even the expression *šāʾal baYHWH* 'consult YHWH' (e.g., Judg 1:1; 18:5; 20:18, 23, 27; 1 Sam 10:22; 14:37, etc.) implies the use of oracular means (through the legitimate means specified in 1 Sam 28:6).

Moreover, the verbs *hēsîr* 'remove' (1 Sam 28:3), *ʿāśâ* 'made' (2 Kgs 21:6), and *biʿēr* 'burn, remove' (2 Kgs 23:24) imply an object (contra Schmidtke 1967), as does the expression *baʿălat ʾôb*, literally "possessor of an *ʾôb*" (1 Sam 28:7). The question still remains, however, whether *ʾôb* represents an image or an oracular pit. The former option is strictly hypothetical (image of what?). The latter is supported by the evidence from the entire ancient Near East, as just discussed, to which can be added the data from the Greek world (see chap. 17, COMMENT A).

However, where *ʾôb* is the direct object of *šāʾal* (Deut 18:11, though the *beth* may be implied) and in expressions like *pānâ ʾel* 'turn to' (19:31; 20:6), *dāraš ʾel* 'consult' (Isa 8:19; 19:3), *wĕhāyâ kĕʾôb mēʾereṣ qôlēk* 'Your voice will be like that of an *ʾôb* from the underworld' (Isa 29:4), the *ʾôb* probably denotes "spirit" or "necromancer." That *ʾôb* denotes "spirit" has firm evidence to support it. It makes better philological sense that it derives from *ʾāb* 'father, ancestor' (Lust 1974). Its linkage with *yiddĕʿōnî*, literally "knowing (one)," indicates that it, too, is a departed spirit. The expression *pānâ ʾel* 'turn to' (19:31; 20:6) can only refer to a spirit (see NOTE on 20:6). Finally, *baʿălat ʾôb* (1 Sam 28:7) need not mean "possessor of an *ʾôb*," as translated above. There is a firmer basis for rendering it "master of an *ʾôb*" because of its parallelism with the Sumero-Akkadian name for necromancer *lú gidim-ma* and *ša etemmi* 'master/(master) of the spirit in the dead' (MSL 12.168:356; MSL 12.226:14; cf. Tropper 1995). Thus it is probable that *ʾôb* originally meant "spirit," but through metonymic association, it referred to the conjurer as well as the medium.

The term *yiddĕʿōnî* proves more refractory not only because of the paucity of semantic cognates in the ancient Near East, but also because we have no description (as does the *ʾôb* in 1 Sam 28 and elsewhere) of its modus operandi. The only aid we have is its root *ydʿ* 'know', which is also attested in Ugaritic. Thus an incantation text form Ugarit (RIH 78/20, ll. 8–10) reads *aphm kšpm dbbm ygrš ḥrn ḥbrm uglm dʿtm* 'Forthwith (?) sorcerers, enemies! / Horon will expel the binders / And the youth soothsayers' (Avishur 1981: 22–23) and *ktrm ḥbrk wḥss dʿtk* 'Kothar is your spell-caster and Hasis your knower' (i.e., one who knows ghosts or spirits; KTU 1.6 VI 49–50; Smith 1984). Thus *yiddĕʿōnî* would seem to refer to a necromancer. Spronk (1986: 254–55), however, avers that *yiddĕʿōnîm* qualifies dead spirits as "those who are knowing," but offers no evidence except the word play in *kî- ʾattâ ʾābînû kî ʾabrāhām lōʾ yĕdāʿānû* 'Surely, you are our **father**, though Abraham **know** us not' (Isa 63:16), which he claims, following Duhm (1922: 438), is an allusion to *'ôb* and *yiddĕ'ōnî*, namely, that Israel receives its revelation directly from YHWH, the father (i.e., the true *'ôb*-spirit), and not from departed Abraham, who is not a *yiddĕ'ōnî*. The word play may indeed exist; however, *yiddĕ'ōnî* could just as well be the necromancer as the (wizard) spirit. In any event, whatever the meaning of *yiddĕ'ōnî*, in all cases where it is coupled with *'ôb* (e.g., 19:31; 20:6, 27; Deut 18:11; 1 Sam 28:3, 9; 2 Kgs 23:24; Isa 19:3), the two terms would have to refer to the same genre. Thus further discussion must focus solely on the meaning of *'ôb*.

According to Hoffner (1967), the modus operandi of the *'ôb* (i.e., ritual pit) consisted of the following:

1. It was dug at a favorable spot.
2. It was employed at night (1 Sam 28:8).
3. Food offerings were lowered into the pit; honey was conspicuous (see NOTE on 2:11), but the blood of sacrificial animals was most valued (1 Sam 14:32; see chap. 17, COMMENT A).
4. The purpose of these offerings was to lure spirits up out of the grave to obtain information (Isa 8:19); in one Hittite text, a silver ladder was lowered.
5. The spirits appeared anthropomorphically and could therefore be recognized (1 Sam 28:14).
6. The spirits squeaked like birds and cooed like doves (Isa 8:19; 29:4; cf. 59:11; van der Toorn 1988: 209–12).
7. After the consultation, the pit was sealed to prevent the spirits from escaping.

For the purpose of this survey, it need only be added that the offerings to the spirits were not just for consulting them, but also for placating them; the ancients feared the malevolence of disgruntled spirits. Also, the *'ôb* was not the only means of contacting the dead. A favored instrument was the human skull, as attested as early as ancient Babylonia (e.g., *BM* 36703 II, ll. 3[1]–6[1], 10[1]) and as late at the Babylonian Talmud (*b. Sanh.* 65a; cf. Finkel 1983–84).

The juxtaposition of the *'ôb* and *yiddĕ'ōnî* with the Molek prohibition (20:1–6) gives cause to suspect that Molek is a god of the underworld. This suspicion is fully supported by evidence from Israel and its antecedent neighbors. Heider (1985: 124–33) has demonstrated the close association of the *mlkm* with the *rpum*. The latter unquestionably have a chthonic character and, in many cases, are the ancestors of the living (Rin 1993). The *rpum* are invited to share a ritual meal and are implored to bless the royal dynasty (RS 34.126). Departed kings are expected at the feasts held for *rpum* (*KTU* 1.161), and the *rpum* gather with some gods at a seven-day feast in a funerary setting (*CTA* 22.2). King Asa is condemned because he consulted (*dāraš*) "doctors instead of YHWH" (2 Chr 16:12), but perhaps *rōpĕ'îm* should be vocalized *rĕpā'îm* "shades."

Day (1989: 46–55) has expanded Heider's evidence, first, by demonstrating that the god Malik is equated with Nergal, the Mesopotamian god of the underworld, in two texts (48, nn. 72–73), and, then, by citing evidence from

Palmyra that Phoenician Melqart (*mlk* + *qrt* 'king of the city') is identified with Nergal. He also adduces Isa 57:9, "You journeyed [Day 1989: 51] to Molek [MT *melek*] with oil and multiplied your perfumes; you sent your envoys far off and sent down even to Sheol." Finally, to Day's evidence can be added the fact that Akkadian *malku* can stand for a netherworld god or demon (*CAD* 10/1.168–69; cited by Tigay 1986: 11, n. 30) and that Ugaritic Malik appears in the theophonic element of personal names in two snake-bite charms (*KTU* 1.100:41; 1.107:17) and as resident in *ʿttrt* (Ashtoret in the Bashan) also assigned to the underworld deity *rpu* (Heider 1995: 1093, disputed by Day 1995: 49–50). Thus Molek reigns in the underworld.

In Leviticus, the verb *zānâ* 'whore' is used metaphorically in only three instances: the worship of satyrs (17:7), the worship of Molek (20:5), and consulting ghosts and wizard-spirits (20:6). These three acts have in common the practice of necromancy. In the pentateuchal sources, *zānâ* is a metaphor for the worship of other gods (e.g., Exod 34:15–16 [JE/D]; Num 15:39 [also H!]; Deut 31:16 [D]) and is frequently expanded by the prophets (e.g., Jer 3:1–3; 6–9; Ezek 6:9; 16:16–17; Hos 1:2; 2:7; 4:10, 12, 15), but the term is conspicuously absent from the writings of the eighth-century Judahite prophets (for implications, see Introduction II D). Furthermore, as noted in COMMENT A, chap. 20 stands in chiastic relation with its companion list of illicit sexual unions, chap. 18. The latter registers a prohibition of Molek worship (18:21), but not of necromancy. In my view, the H redactor felt that he could tack on necromancy to Molek (20:1–5, 6) because both practices were cut of the same cloth: they dealt with ancestor worship. Thus there remains little doubt that necromancy is a form of idolatry in H (in fact, the only form; see Introduction II C) and that it is limited to chthonic worship (see also NOTE on "after whom they stray," 17:7).

The location of Molek worship in *gê' hinnōm* gave rise to the tradition that hell is called Gehenna (see also Quran 43:72, where Mālik is an agent of hell). Since Mount Zion is equated with paradise (e.g., Ps 46:5), it follows plausibly that the deep valley beneath it would be identified with the underworld (cf. Isa 14:12–15), and it is perhaps no accident that the nearby valley is called Rephaim, or "shades" (e.g., Josh 15:8; 18:16; cf. Montgomery 1908). Finally, Job 18:13–14 may be rendered: "By disease his skin is consumed [reading *yēʾākēl bidĕwê*], the firstborn of death consumes his limbs. He is torn from the tent in which he trusted, and is brought to the king of terrors," in which case death is portrayed as king (*melek*), a possible allusion to Molek.

There is sufficient biblical evidence to support the thesis that in preexilic times, according to popular belief, the dead existed outside of YHWH's realm (cf. Isa 38:18–19; Pss 6:6; 88:11–13; 115:17; cf. Xella 1982; van der Toorn 1991). However, voices arose in the eighth century, stemming from prophets (e.g., Isa 8:19–20) and priests (e.g., Lev 19:31; 20:6), that, in opposition to this dualism, extended YHWH's domain into the underworld and condemned Molek worship as "a desecration of the name of God" (see NOTE on 18:21b). However, monotheism is theoretically entirely consistent with ancestor worship, since the departed spirits, even if semidivine and capricious, are subject to YHWH's overall control. Moreover, if van der Toorn (1996a) is proved correct—and I believe he is—that theophoric names embody family gods, then the continued attestation of these names in the biblical onomasticon implies that the cult of the ancestors endured throughout preexilic (and, even later) times, indeed into rabbinic times (cf. *b. Sanh.* 65). In any event, caution is recommended because a name can persist after its original meaning has long been forgotten (e.g., ʿAnat in modern Israel, Beulah among African-Americans). In any event, as Isa 57:9 testifies (if *melek* > *mōlek*; see COMMENT C), the worship of the underworld god Molek persisted into postexilic times. In other words, the battle against necromancy formed a distinct phase in the monotheistic revolution, a battle—to judge by the biblical record—that was never won.

C. Ancestor Worship in the Biblical World

Both archaeology and written records supply unambiguous evidence for the prevalence of ancestor worship in the ancient Near East. Excavations at Ebla have revealed a Middle Bronze sanctuary and an adjoining graveyard devoted to the *rpʾum*, the deceased ancestors (on which see below). Their worship included the consumption of ritual foods, rites in which the names of the dead were recited, offerings of animal and vegetable sacrifices, and the worship of small cultic images of royal ancestors (Matthiae 1979).

Regarding possible archaeological remains of ancestor worship among the Canaanites, it has been argued by Beck (1990), following Kirkbride (1969), that the schematic statues found alongside the stelae in Hazor are ancestor idols and their function is equal to that of stelae, thus strengthening the arguments in favor of the interpretation of the Stelae Temple at Hazor as related to the cult of the dead (Beck 1990: 94).

It has long been claimed that the clearest archaeological evidence of ancestor worship is the clay pipe of the Ras Shamra (Ugarit) tomb, extending from the surface into the funeral vault below by which libations were brought down to the deceased (Schaeffer 1929: 50; sketch in Schaeffer 1938: fig. 42; Lewis 1989: 98). However, it is now clear that the alleged Ugaritic tomb is an urban dwelling, and the so-called libation pipe is probably the normal installation for the disposal of water in houses (Pitard 1994). Nonetheless, one cannot gainsay the widespread literary references to this device: "On this day stand before Šamaš and Gilgamesh [gods of the underworld]. . . . I will pour cool water down your water pipes; cure me that I may sing your praises" (KAR 227 iii 14–15, 24–25, cited in Bayliss 1973: 118); "May Šamaš never let the pipe for him receive cool water down below in the netherworld" (CAD *arūtu* 1.2:324); "May Šamaš uproot him from the land of the living and leave his ghost to thirst for water in the world below" (CAD *eṭemmu* 4.399a = CH, Epilogue 34–40). In Sumerian temple hymns, Enegi is described as the "big pipe of Ereškigal's underworld"—an allusion to the clay tube into which liquids for the dead were poured (Lambert 1980). The bleak conditions of the Mesopotamian underworld are detailed by Kuwabara (1983: 224–31). One should also not overlook the possibility that the holes found in the floors of the preexilic graves excavated in Samaria may have served as receptacles for drink offerings to the dead (Sukenik 1940). One must keep in mind, however, that the libation of water (*naq mê*; cf. *CAD* 11/1.337) and other liquids as well as the food offerings (*kispu*; cf. *CAD* 8.425–27) for the spirits of the dead should not be misconstrued as feeding them (see further below).

The person in charge of pouring down the water was the *pāqidu* 'caretaker': " 'Have you seen him whose ghost has no *pāqidu?*' 'I have seen (him). He has to eat the dregs of the pot and scraps of food thrown down in the street' " (*Gilgamesh* 12, ll. 153–54); "I inflicted restlessness on their ghosts. I deprived them of funerary offerings and pourers of water" (Streck, *VAB* 7, 56 vi 75; *CAD* 4.399; 21.156d). A Nuzi will (YBC 5142) states that a father bequeaths to his daughter his gods and the care of the dead spirits (cf. Paradise 1987: 204, 211). In Ugarit, that person is "one who sets up the stelae of his divine ancestor in the sanctuary" (*KTU* 1.17 I:26–34; de Moor 1986, corrected in Lewis 1989: 54).

The ancestor cult is also represented by the *kispum* offering: "Hurry, write to the king that they are to offer the *kispum* sacrifices for the shade [*eṭemmu*] of Yaḫdun-Lim" (*ARMT* II, 40). However, as shown by Tsukimoto (1985), the *kispum* rite was almost always limited to the royal line. The Aramean practice of providing food offerings to the dead is reflected in the Panammu inscription: "May the soul of Panammu eat with you and may the soul of Panammu drink with you (Hadad). Let him always invoke the soul of Panammu with Hadad" (*KAI* 214, ll. 17–18; cf. Greenfield 1973). Note that the soul (*nbš*) of Panammu is ascribed the ability to eat and drink and to do so in the company (*'im*, 'with') of his god Hadad.

The only text that describes the liturgy of a funerary rite is from Ugarit (*KTU* 1.161). Ammurapi III (ca. 1200 B.C.E.) initiates a cult of the dead in memory of his father, Niqmaddu III. The dead kings (*mlkm*) and the *rp'm* are summoned with this refrain: *qru (qritm). rpi. arṣ* 'summon (you summon) the Rephaim of the Netherworld'. The main points of this text, as analyzed by Lewis (1989: 95–97), are:

1. It took place at night (*ẓlm*) and had a twofold function: to render services for the deceased and to secure favors from them.
2. The *rp'm* refer to the long-dead ancestors and the *mlkm*, the recently dead rulers.
3. The invocation is an essential service to be rendered to the deceased (see below).
4. The personified furniture (throne, footstool, etc.) mourns for the dead king.
5. Šapsu is responsible for the libations and offerings reaching the deceased.
6. The ritual probably lasts seven days and entails multiple offerings.

Samuel's ghost is termed *'ĕlōhîm* 'divinity' (1 Sam 28:13; cf. Isa 8:19). This, too, has been illuminated by Ugaritic (*CTA* 6 VI:44–47, where *ripm* 'the ghosts', *ilnym* 'the divinities', *ilm* 'the divine ones', and *mtm* 'the dead' are all in parallelism; by *KTU* 1.113, "The Ugaritic King list," verso, where the divine determinative is placed before the name of each deceased king; cf. Ackerman 1992: 150). Gilgamesh is advised to provide for the daily cult to his god and his dead father: "Cool water you should sprinkle for Šamaš, be mindful of the divine Lugalbanda" (Tablet III, Old Babylonian Version V. 42–43). Lugalbanda, Gilgamesh's father, has the divine determinative attached to his name.

Recently, texts from Emar in North Syria stemming from the Late Bronze Age have confirmed the equivalence of Akkadian *ilānu* 'gods' and *mētim* 'deceased' in a number of passages:

DINGIR.MEŠ-*ia* (= *ilānīya* 'my gods'), *ù me-te-ia*

DINGIR.MEŠ-*ia* ᵈm[i]-t[i-ia]

DINGIR.MEŠ-*ia* BA.UG₆-*ia* (= *me-te-ia*)

DINGIR.MEŠ *ù mi-ti ša* PN *a-bi-šu-nu*

DINGIR.MEŠ *ù me-te ša* PN *a-bi-šu-nu*

A typical statement (Akkadianized) is *ilānīya u mētēya lū tunabbi* 'Let her (the daughter) invoke my gods and my dead' (Huehnergard 1985). The expression "my gods and my dead" should be understood as a hendiadys (Lewis 1989: 50; van der Toorn 1995: 38). That is, the dead are called "gods" because of their role as guardians of their descendants.

The obvious purpose of the ancestor cult was to secure favors from the deceased for the present life: "Come (O dead ancestors), eat this, drink this, (and) bless Ammiṣaduqa the son of Ammiditana, the king of Babylon" (cf. Finkelstein 1966). A second equally important purpose was to invoke the name of the dead (*šuma zakāru*): "The invocation in the funerary cult was the only means available to most people to perpetuate their names after death" (Bayliss 1975: 117). Panammu entreats his sons *wyzkr ʾšm pnmw, wyzkr ʾšm hdd* 'to invoke the name of Panammu as well as Hadad' (*KAI* 214.16, 21). For the exact BH cognate *hizkîr šēm*, see 2 Sam 18:18 (see also Exod 23:13; Josh 23:7; Ps 20:8).

Schmidt's (1996a: 10) thesis that "care for or feeding of the dead typically carries with it the implicit notion that the dead are weak; they have no power to affect the living in a beneficial way" has been decisively refuted by citations brought by Lewis (1996). Two examples from Egypt and Mesopotamia follow:

How are you? Is the West taking care of you [according to] your desire? Now since I am your beloved on earth, fight on my behalf, and intercede on behalf of my name. . . . Remove the infirmity of my body! . . . I will then deposit offerings for you. [Wente #340: "A Man to a Deceased Relative" (Early Dynasty 12)]

You are the ghosts of my relatives. . . . I have made for you a funerary offering; I have poured you (a libation of) water . . . before Shamash (and) Gilgamesh stand forth and judged my care. . . . May I, your servant, live; may I get well. . . . Let me give (you) cold water to drink via your water pipe. Keep me alive that I may praise you. [Surlock #85: *KAR* 227iii 6–24; *LKA* 89, 90.1–18; Si. 7–47.1–12]

There was also a negative purpose to this cult, to prevent the malevolent behavior of the dead spirits (cf. Bayliss 1973: 116; Hallo 1993: 184–85). If the ancestors were not regularly and properly fed, they were condemned to a diet of excrement (Xella 1980), which would have aroused their irrepressible wrath. In Mesopotamia, the *kispum* was offered at the new and full moon because it was commonly accepted that on these occasions the departed spirits would ascend to the earth seeking the people's offerings. Thus there was a need for magical prescriptions to expel them: "The exorcists appeased them by seeing to their legitimate needs on the one hand, and on the other hand neutralized them by banishing them to the netherworld" (Hallo 1992: 399). Thus there are texts that advise how to avert evil brought on by accidental contact with a ghost (Finkel 1983–84).

Before 1970, many scholars denied the existence of an Israelite cult of the dead. A typical example is de Vaux (1961: 61), who states after the barest discussion: "We conclude that the dead were honored in a religious spirit, but that no cult was paid to them." Kaufmann (1946: 2.544–54; 1960: 311–16) treats the subject extensively, and he, too, concludes that "the realm of the dead, the rites of death and burial . . . play no part in the religion of YHWH" (544, 311). To be sure, both eminent scholars are correct, but for the wrong reasons. References in Scripture to the cult of the dead do not exist, but only because they were deliberately omitted or excised. Nonetheless, a number of hints emerge from the texts that indicate that ancestor worship was alive and well. The most unmistakable reference is the libations (*nesek*) in Isa 57:6 (Kaufmann overlooks Ps 16:4, cited below), but Kaufmann (1946: 2.556, n. 5) summarily dismisses it because "it refers to the customs of the Jews in exile"! The manifold notices of necromancy are equally rejected simply on the grounds that it was banned. The mantic powers of the dead are admitted, but "they have no power to help the living or to deliver them from trouble" (Kaufmann 1946: 2.549–50; 1960: 313).

Kaufmann (1946: 2.549; 1960: 313) astutely recognizes that D's proscription of giving consecrated food to the dead (Deut 26:14) implies that offerings of common food are permitted, and then he adds "from which it is clear that the law does not regard such gifts in the light of offerings. Such concern for the *well-being of the deceased* in the grave, grounded in the belief that it is possible still to be in touch with and *benefit him*, is not the cult of the dead [my emphasis]." Why? Is it not more plausible that the purpose of these offerings is *do ut des*, not just to "benefit him" but to benefit *from* him? Indeed, what purpose did it serve to offer food (*minḥâ*, Isa 57:6) and drink to the dead? If just for respect and veneration, why not bring flowers, light candles, or *pray* "for the well-being of the deceased"?

Thus there must be a reciprocal purpose to the offerings. There is no escaping the fact that they comprise the same ingredients as the sacrifices, which, whether devotional or expiatory, are for the purpose of benefiting not the deity, but the offerer.

The chances are, however, that the biblical writers, though fully aware of the popular interpretation of the food offerings to the dead, put a different face on it by regarding them as acts of veneration. What choice had they, considering that any attempt to ban them would have been totally ignored by the populace? The hitherto long, uninterrupted tradition in the ancient Near East, that worshiping the dead would guarantee their guardianship of and benefactions to their living descendants, continued unabated. The pure YHWHists, represented by H and D, could do no more than mask this practice with an interpretation compatible with their theology, similar to the one expressed by Kaufmann (1960: 314): "Burying the deceased in a family grave, giving him food, raising a monument for him, and the like, are deeds of devotion toward the dead through which the living maintained a connection with them." An equivalent example of ritual masking (which I owe to Moshe Greenberg) is Maimonides's (*Mishneh Torah*, Idolatry 11:11–12) treatment of incantations:

> Whoever is bitten by a scorpion or snake is permitted to recite a charm over the bite, even on the sabbath, in order to calm his spirit and bolster his courage, even though it is of no help whatever. Since it is life threatening, it was permitted him [cf. *b. Sanh.* 101a] so that his mind does not become deranged. [However, those who] recite a charm over the injury and [add] a verse from the Torah . . . they are among the deniers of the Torah (heretics) for, they turn the words of the Torah, which are only cures for the spirit, into cures for the body. . . . But the healthy person who reads (Torah) verses and Psalms so that he will be protected by the merit of his reading them and be saved from woes and injuries—it is permitted (him)

Although reciting a spell (*ḥōbēr ḥeber*) is forbidden (Deut 18:11; Maimonides, *Mishneh Torah*, Idolatry 11:10), Maimonides had to concede to the widespread use of such charms, not as cures but as psychological supports, and if a Torah verse was co-opted, it served as an apotropaic, a verbal amulet. Thus no differently from Maimonides, the biblical authors had to improvise an acceptable rationale that could mask the real reasons why the people-at-large utilized them.

Similar subterfuge, however, could not be afforded to the necromancer. He infringed on the sole sovereignty of YHWH. He usurped YHWH's exclusive authority to direct Israel's destiny via his appointed agents, the prophets, and it is no accident that the wholesale ban against all mantic practitioners (Deut 18:10–14) is followed by a designation of the prophet as the only legitimate carrier of YHWH's message (Deut 18:15–22; cf. 13:2–6).

Therefore, there exists a world of difference between the guardian-dead and the diviner-dead, the necromancer. The former was a family benefactor who would focus his blessing on his living descendants. The latter, however, might misread God's intention and mislead an entire nation. For example, the king might consult a necromancer, such as an *'ôb* or a *yiddĕʿōnî* (1 Sam 28) rather than a true prophet or the official oracle, the Urim and Thummim (Deut 33:8; 1 Sam 14:41 LXX) and as a result die in battle with his army (1 Kgs 22:10–23) or cause the destruction of the state and the exile of its inhabitants (Jer 28:1–11). The necromancers, like false prophets, thus had to be extirpated (Lev 20:27; Deut 13:2–6; 18:20), if for no other reason that Israel might be preserved.

A deeper, politically motivated cause may lie beneath the ban on necromancy, however. The cult of the dead was a potential and potent threat against the political establishment, the state, which had endorsed the worship of YHWH as the sole legitimate cult in Israel: "The ancestors might inspire resistance to the leadership of the national administration, or even foment revolution. The suppression of necromancy was not an act of demonstrated piety on the part of Saul, but an attempt to secure the state monopoly on divination" (van der Toorn 1996b: 318–19). Ancestor worship was the bastion of family religion, and it would have been a prime, indispensable objective of the monarchy from its inception with Saul to ban the former (1 Sam 28:9) and contain the latter so that the worship of YHWH could become the national religion of Israel.

Were these instructions effective? Not at all. The prohibitions against necromancy proved a dead letter (see below).

During the past quarter century, there have been a spate of publications dealing with traces of ancestor worship in the Bible. Following the lead of Brichto (1973), the major treatises of Spronk (1986), Lewis (1989), and Bloch-Smith (1992a) have appeared, and smaller contributions—to name but a few—of Dahood (1970: 73–74), Halevi (1975), Pope (1977: 210–29), M. S. Smith and Bloch-Smith (1988), Lang (1988), van der Toorn (1988; 1990; 1991; 1996a; 1996b), Levine (1993), and Smith (1993). The obvious passages are Lev 19:31; 20:5, 27 (see COMMENT B); Deut 18:9–14; 26:14; 1 Sam 28; 2 Sam 18:18; Isa 8:19–20; 19:3; 29:4; 57:6–9; 65:4. To be sure, these unanimously speak of the dead, not of the ancestors. However, it is only logical that in the cult of the dead one always turns to the ancestors, not to the dead in general. Aside from emotional and devotional bonds, a practical motivation dominates: ancestors bestow favors on kin who provide *constant* worship. Of these passages, the clearest is Isa 8:19–20a, which also associates ancestor worship with necromancy:

> When they say to you: Consult *hā'ōbôt* and *hayyiddĕʿōnîm* who chirp and mutter; shall not a people consult its ancestral spirits [*'ĕlōhāyw*], on behalf of the living, (consult) the dead [*hammētîm*] for an oracle and a message?

Two more passages merit quotation because their connection with the cult of the dead was only recently investigated:

> Among the dead [*ḥallĕqê*] of the wadi is your [fem. sing.] portion [*ḥēleq*]
> They, they are your lot
> Even to them you poured libations,
> and brought offerings
>   . . .

On a high and lofty mountain
You have placed your bed/grave [miškāb]
There too you have gone up
To offer sacrifice
Behind the door and the door post
You have put your indecent symbol/mortuary stela [zikkārôn]
You tried to discover (oracles) from me (by) bringing up (spirits).
You have mounted and made wide your bed/grave [miškab].
You have made a pact for yourself with them [the dead of v. 6],
You have loved their bed/grave [miškāb],
You have gazed on the indecent symbol/mortuary stela [yād].
You lavished oil on the (dead?) king/Molek [see COMMENT B]
You multiplied your perfumes
You sent your envoys from afar
You sent (them) down to Sheol. (Isa 57:6–9; Lewis 1989: 156, 147–51; cf.
Ackerman 1992: 102–9, 143–55)

As to the deified dead [qĕdôšîm; cf. Ps 89:6–8] who are in the underworld
. . .
I will have no part of their bloody libations;
Their names will not pass my lips
. . .
For you will not abandon me to Sheol
Or let your faithful ones see the Pit. (Ps 16:3a, 4aβb, 10; cf. Spronk 1986:
334–37)

Some of these renderings are admittedly conjectural, but their general context, in my opinion, is ancestor worship. The common denominator between
these two passages is that libations are poured for the dead. These link up with
the libations for the dead in Israel's environment. This does not imply, however,
that in Israel the purpose of offering food and drink to the dead was to nourish
them. Rather, it was an act of veneration, no different from sacrifices to YHWH,
in order to beseech their help (see further below). Also, the mention of "those
who slaughter children in the wadis" (Isa 57:5) may be an indication that private, surreptitious Molek worship continued after its official cult in the Valley
of Hinnom was exterminated (2 Kgs 23:10; see NOTE on 18:21).

Van der Toorn (1990: 211–17) has marshaled strong arguments showing that
teraphim were used in divinatory practices related to ancestor worship (see the
comprehensive analysis of Loretz 1992). First, on the basis of 1 Sam 15:23; Ezek
21:26; and Zech 10:2, teraphim are mentioned in conjunction with qesem 'soothsaying'. Furthermore, a comparison of 2 Kgs 23:24 with Deut 18:11 indicates
that hattĕrāpîm is equivalent to hammētîm 'the dead'. The dead, however, are
also called 'ĕlōhîm 'god(s)' (1 Sam 28:13; Isa 8:19), and in the Ugaritic "Hymn
to Shapash," mtm and 'ilm are in synonymous parallelism (Spronk 1986:
162–63). As demonstrated by Rouillard and Tropper (1987: 355–56), the
teraphim are closely related to the 'ōbôt, which are divinatory in function.

There is no condemnation of teraphim in 1 Sam 19:13, 16, and Hos 3:4. Hence it was quite normal to consult the dead on behalf of the living. Thus it can be reasonably concluded that the teraphim were ancestor figurines used in divination.

Ostensibly, one objection surfaces. Teraphim (pl.) were placed under Rachel's saddle pillow. These must have been relatively small (1 foot, maximum). How can only one of these ("a plural of excellence," cf. Joüon 1923: §136d; GKC §145h), less in size than 20 percent of a person, be mistaken for David? Fully aware of this problem, van der Toorn (1990) hypothesizes that the dim light in the bedroom, the mosquito net (*kĕbîr*) over the bed, and the fear of contagion combined to fool Saul's messengers. This rationale is contrived and unnecessary. Teraphim were not limited in size or shape; the one in David and Michal's bed could have had a large enough head to ward off any suspicion of deceit.

Most recently, van der Toorn (1996a: 1–11) has also mounted a convincing case that in kinship names, *'ăbî* 'father of', *'āḥî* 'brother of', *'ammî* '(paternal) uncle of' are not only theophoric elements, but are references to deified ancestors venerated because they care for their descendants beyond the grave.

Thus far, Bloch-Smith (1992a) has written the most comprehensive and compelling treatise on the Israelite cult of the dead by combining pioneering archaeological research with the biblical evidence. I differ with her, however, on the section entitled "Feeding the Dead" (122–26).

She (1992a: 149) opines that in eighth-century tombs "the lamps provided light, the jars held liquids, the bowls foodstuffs and the juglets scented oils. . . . Following interment, family members or others would offer sacrifices to propitiate the dead and beseech blessings, perhaps on a regular basis." True, food remains have been found in the Iron Age tombs of Gezer, Aitun, Lachish, Akhzib, Tel Bira, and Beth Shemesh, and pits for "receptacles of offering connected with the cult of the dead" have been discovered in Samaria (Crowfoot 1942: 21–22). But have any of these tombs proved to be Israelite? Why have no food remains turned up in Iron Age tombs in and around Jerusalem (cf. Rahmani 1981: 174, 231–34)? Rather, I would agree with Spronk (1986: 241, n. 5) that these "gravegoods [served] as provisions for the afterlife, helping to make the stay in the netherworld bearable." As for the food remains (in the Shephelah and the valley, but not in Jerusalem), they may be vestiges of food deposited there at the time of burial for "the journey." That is, the utensils and other objects placed in the tombs were intended as furnishings for the afterlife domicile, but food placed there was a one-time act at the time of burial for the rite of passage into the netherworld.

Neither would I conclude from the single case of Joshua, who was buried *bigĕbûl naḥălātô* (Josh 24:30; Judg 2:9), that the tomb served as "physical marker of the family claim to the land" or as "territorial boundary markers, as in the case of Rachel, *bigĕbûl binyāmin* ('on the border of Benjamin')" (Bloch-Smith 1992a: 111; cf. 1 Sam 10:2). But *gĕbûl* means not only "border," but also "territory" (e.g., Num 21:12, 22, 23; cf. Milgrom 1990a: 176; Ottosson 1975: 363). Furthermore, I must dispute Bloch-Smith's (1992a: 112) claim that "the Decalogue commandment to honor (*kabēd* [sic]) your father and mother (Exod 20:12;

Deut 5:16) may refer to the filial obligation to *maintain ownership of the family property with the ancestral tomb* so as to provide 'honor' after death as well as in life (Brichto 1973: 20–32; Milgrom 1976c: 338) [my emphasis]." Brichto refers to only memorial rites, not to a putative function of maintaining ownership; I, too, speak solely of memorial rites.

Concerning Deut 26:14, Bloch-Smith (1992a: 123; cf. 1992b: 220) writes: "The dead were 'divine beings' (*'elōhîm*), and so consecrated, tithed food was considered their due." However, the "poor tithe" of Deut 26:14 was mandated for every third year. Giving of the tithe to the dead (or eating it in a state of impurity) is not proscribed for the other two years. Thus it was not the "due" of the dead; it was a matter of voluntary ancestor worship motivated by personal impulse or need. It is important to note that while Deuteronomy opposes the practice of *consulting* the dead (Deut 18:11), it offers no objection to *feeding* the dead, though not as an obligation (lest the dead wreak their malice on their descendants), but as an act of veneration (see below). But at the Temple, to which the ordinary tithe was brought (Deut 14:23), there was no fear that it would be given to the dead or eaten in impurity. For a discussion of the various tithes, see chap. 27, COMMENT G.

There is no clear evidence that the *zebaḥ hayyāmîm/mišpāḥâ* (1 Sam 1:21; 2:19; 20:6, 29) involved sacrifices to the dead. If this were so, why didn't Elkanah observe the sacrifice at the family tomb or at the local family sanctuary (as David was wont to do)? Why didn't Elkanah sacrifice and pray to his dead, as he did to YHWH (1 Sam 1:3, 19, 21)?

There is not a shred of evidence that Asa's spice-filled tomb and *śĕrēpâ gĕdôlâ* 'great burning' (2 Chr 16:14) or that Hezekiah's *kābôd* (2 Chr 32:33) "probably involved post-mortem activities" (Bloch-Smith 1992a: 127). These rites took place at the time of the funeral, and the term *śĕrēpâ* is never used in the Bible for a burnt offering (also contra Levine 1993: 475–76). The sacrifices for the dead reported in Isa 57:7 (see above) are surreptitious and illicit, and *mĕsārĕpô* (Amos 6:10) probably means "his embalmer" (Paul 1991: 215), not "who is to burn incense for him" (*NJPS*).

I would be remiss if I did not express my admiration for Bloch-Smith's brilliant resolution of the crux *ûpĕquddat kol-hā'ādām yippāqēd 'ălêhem* (Num 16:29), usually rendered "if their lot be the common fate of all mankind" (e.g., *NJPS*), which she renders "if these men are cared for by all men" (1992b: 220–21). Thus the denial of postmortem care *paqād* to the Korahite rebels (and to Jezebel, 2 Kgs 9:34–37; cf. Lewis 1989: 120–22) is linked up with the Akkadian *pāqidu*, the one responsible for providing regular offerings to the deceased ancestors (cf. Finkelstein 1966: 115).

But I cannot accept her thesis that the function of this ancestral cult was to "feed the dead" because "nourishment in the afterlife was of paramount importance" (Bloch-Smith 1992b: 218; cf. 1992a: 108, n. 1). These offerings were too infrequent to provide "nourishment." Rather, I side with Brichto (1973) that, in Israel, the sacrifices and invocations associated with ancestral worship served as acts of veneration. No differently from sacrifices to YHWH, the objective of the cult of the dead was to implore their help on behalf of the living (van der Toorn 1996a; 1996b: 206–35), perhaps to propitiate them from doing harm— but not to feed them.

According to Bloch-Smith (1992a: 131–32; 1992b: 223), the historic purpose of the death-cult legislation of the late eighth to the seventh century B.C.E. was to strengthen the two main institutions of the central government, the monarchy and Temple: religiously, by purifying and centralizing worship; economically, by ensuring the livelihood of the priesthood (and prophets?); and politically, by breaking down the clan fidelities that were fostered by the ancestral cults. She has the correct century for the introduction of this legislation (vol. 1.26–35), but her reasons are subject to question. The opposition to necromancy is apparent as early as Saul's day (1 Sam 28:9, 21, even if v. 3 is declared a Dtr gloss); even the pro-Davidic deuteronomistic editor is forced to admit that Saul was a zealot for YHWH (Milgrom 1990a: 430). Then, the food offerings to the dead are paltry compared with the sacrifices offered to YHWH. Note that they constituted only a part (*mimmenû*) of the poor tithe (Deut 26:14). The political motive, to break the bonds of clan loyalties, is possible, but conjectural. The main reason, the only one I submit that fits all the evidence, is religious: chthonic worship, exemplified by royal support of the Molek cult and resort to necromantic mediums, reached a crescendo in the late eighth to the seventh century (see COMMENT B). Moreover, during this period Jerusalem was flooded with refugees from the north bringing with them syncretistic cults and officiants (see Introduction II D). Finally, two minor corrections. D prohibits the people as well as the priests and prophets from consulting the dead through mediums; Deut 18:10–11 is encased in a second-person singular passage: "when you (Israel) enter the land" (v. 9); "YHWH God will raise up for you (Israel) a prophet" (v. 15). And *wĕyārē'tā mē'ĕlōhêka* 'you shall fear your God' (19:32) cannot mean "you shall fear your ancestors" (Bloch-Smith 1992a: 126–27, following Halevi 1975: 101–10), not only because elsewhere (19:14 [the same chapter!]; 25:17, 36, 43) it commands the fear of YHWH, but also because it would present a strange contrast: do not consult the dead (19:30), but fear them by showing respect to the elders. And why, in particular, would dishonoring the aged stir up the wrath of the dead?

In sum, Bloch-Smith (1992a; 1992b) and those scholars who preceded her were absolutely right in pointing out that the cult of the dead was rife in biblical Israel. It was bitterly fought by the monotheistic circles, as evidenced by the prophetic tirades and the priestly and deuteronomic legislation: a good example of the effect of suppressing any positive attitude to the cult of the dead is the Masoretic revocalization of the original *rōpĕ'îm* 'benefactors' (Ug. *rāpi'ūma*; still preserved in LXX *iatroi* in Isa 26:14; Ps 88:11) as *rĕpā'îm* 'impotent ones' (van der Toorn 1996b: 225). The Masoretes may have kept *rōpĕ'îm* in 2 Chr 16:12 because, in contrast to YHWH in this verse, it meant "physicians." However, it is also possible that it actually referred to the dead, and as pointed out by Smith (1990: 130) the verb *dāraš* 'consult' is regularly used for divination. Thus King Asa consulted with dead spirits instead of seeking divine help. (Although YHWH is the ultimate and assured healer, there is no disparagement of human healers in Scripture, Exod 15:26 notwithstanding.) But it was never entirely suppressed, as the following postbiblical evidence demonstrates: "Be generous with bread and wine on the graves of virtuous men, but not for the sinner" (Tob 4:17); "Good things lavished on a closed mouth are like food offerings put on a grave" (Sir 30:18); "They slaughter their sacrifices to the dead [cf. Ps 106:28b], and to the demons they bow down. And they eat in tombs [cf. Isa 57:7]" (*Jub* 22:17). The term *eidōlothuton* (1 Cor 8:1), generally rendered as "food offered to idols," is plausibly interpreted by Kennedy (1987: 228–30) as "meal for the image of the deceased" or a "funerary meal/offering" (cf. Ps 106:28b; *m.* (*'Abod. Zar.* 2:3).

According to Lieberman (1965: 509), "Since there is no doubt that the ancient Jew engaged in these superstitious practices (*Sem* 8:7), the rabbis, who were not able to uproot them, had to reinterpret the meaning of the customs and impart to them a reasonable significance. It was permitted to place the personal belongings of the deceased beside his body, not because he is in need of them, but because the scene arouses the grief of the onlookers" (cf. Alon 1970: 103–5). Furthermore, "the sprinkling of wine and oil on the dead (see *Sem* 12:9) was tolerated by the rabbis, because of their odoriferous properties" (Lieberman 1965: 509, n. 20). The talmudic rabbis state that it was customary to visit the graveside of pious individuals so that "the departed will intercede for mercy on behalf of the living" (*b. Ta'an*, 16a, 23b; cf. *b. Soṭa* 34b; *b. B. Meṣ.* 85b). Rabbinic texts portray the custom of *hištaḥût* 'prostration' at the gravesite in order to engage in petitional prayers, as practiced by biblical figures, tannaim, and amoraim. An example of the former is "Caleb held himself aloof from the plan of the spies and went and prostrated himself on the gravesite of the patriarchs, saying to them: 'My fathers, pray on my behalf that I may be delivered from the hands of the spies' " (*b. Soṭ.* 34b).

Gravesites played a central role in times of drought and famine. Jews would gather to pray for rain at the Cave of Maḥpelah in Hebron and the grave of the legendary Hawmaturye Ḥoni ha- Ma'aged in Far'am (Vilnay 1951: 2.69–74). Jewish mystical tradition justified this practice by theorizing that the soul of the *saddîq* 'righteous person' is an active presence at the gravesite, a listening ear ready to relay messages upward. Therefore, in times of emergency, the community goes to the graveyard to beg the righteous for their intercession (cf. Zohar 3.71b; Gelber, forthcoming).

But the tenth-century C.E. Karaite scholar Sahl ben Mazli'ah complained: "How can I remain silent when some Jews are behaving like idolaters? They sit at the grave, sometimes sleeping there at night and appeal to the dead: 'Oh, Rabbi Yose ha-Gelili! Heal me! Grant me children!' They kindle lights there and offer incense" (cited in Pinsker 1968: 32). The sixteenth-century code of Jewish law (Isserles, *'oraḥ ḥayyim* 459:10; 481:4) discouraged the practice of praying to the dead, limiting it to special occasions: the anniversary of the death, the new moon, and the fast of the ninth of Ab.

Many Hasidic circles, however, would visit the graves of their rabbis frequently, even building rooms called *'ōhǎlîm*, literally "tents," over the graves to pray there whenever they desired the heavenly intervention of their departed rabbis (*EJ* 10:934). It is customary among them even to this day that on the anniversary of their rabbis' death, they partake of food and drink at the graveside. Indeed, the holy rabbi of Stretyn, J. Z. H. Brandwein (d. 1854), ordained that Jews should celebrate with food and drink at the graveside of R. Simeon b. Yoḥai at Meron (in the Galilee) on the anniversary of his death (Sperling 1957: 58)— a rite that thousands of Hasidic pilgrims fulfill annually. However, this custom originated much earlier. According to R. Ḥayyim Vital (1963: 191), the disciple of Isaac Luria (sixteenth century), his master "brought his small son there together with his whole family . . . and they spent a day of feasting and celebration." Indeed, distances are no obstacle. Every year, hundreds of followers of R. Nachman of Bratslav in Israel charter planes and arrange for housing and food in Uman, Ukraine, for their annual visit to their rabbi's grave on the anniversary of his death.

This is the Hasidic tradition of East European (Ashkenazi) Jewry. Jews from the Islamic countries, especially from North Africa, are even more deeply immersed in ancestor worship, in a form known as *hillula*, an annual pilgrimage to the grave of a revered rabbi-saint on the anniversary of his death. The influence of a corresponding custom among the Muslim majority is obvious: "The graves of saints are visited as sacred places for worship. . . . It was believed that through the pilgrimage to the grave, prayers said there, and votive offerings, one could obtain his intercession on behalf of the petitioners" (Goldziher 1971: 281). A similar belief obtained among the participants in the *hillula*: "According to popular thought the belief developed that the *zaddik* (saint) in whose memory the celebration was held would intervene with God on behalf of his followers. Accordingly, persons who suffered from physical or mental illnesses might undertake a pilgrimage to the site of the *hillula* in the hope and belief that their suffering would be lessened" (Deshen 1977: 110–11). In many respects, the Hasidic pilgrimage and the North African *hillula* are no different from pilgrimages to the shrines of Catholic saints in Europe. The Jewish pilgrimages, however, reveal a special feature that distinguish them from their Muslim and Catholic counterparts: the feasting and food offerings.

The etymology of the term *hillula* discloses the reason for this difference. It stems from Aramaic *hillula*' 'wedding' (*b. Ber.* 31a; *b. Sanh.* 105a) and is related to biblical *hillûlîm* 'jubilation' (Judg 9:27). Indeed, a *hillula* is marked by a memorial feast at which the participants drink and eat in a holiday spirit. Moreover, "the women place the food and liquids directly upon the grave: the food is thought to thereby absorb mystic, healing powers, and after it is consumed, offered to others, or taken home. Some of them also pour oil or scented water upon the grave and then smear it over their face and body; this scent is also believed to have special powers" (Weingrod 1990: 27). Is this evidence not a sublimated vestige of the ancient rite of the cult of the dead?

In view of the leech-like hold that the ancestral cult has exhibited down to the present time, even in the most sophisticated monotheistic religion, is it any wonder that the ancient priests of Israel were reluctant to ban the worship of the ancestors outright, knowing that they would only alienate the very people they were charged to bring to the worship of YHWH? Wherever they had control— *within* the sanctuary—they succeeded marvelously. For example, they transformed the *ḥaṭṭā't*, in the pagan world a magical instrument to inoculate the sanctuary against incursions by demons, into an offering to eradicate the pollution of the sanctuary effected by the wrongdoing of an individual or a community (see chap. 4, COMMENTS B and C). They partially desanctified the altar so that it was no longer contagiously holy to persons, and thereby ended the hoary tradition of altar asylum for criminals (Milgrom 1990a: 504–9). They forbade libations on the inner golden altar (Exod 30:9b), though the existence of golden libation vessels (*qĕśôt hannāsek*, Num 4:7) on the golden display table (Exod 25:29; 37:16) indicated the probability that libations of ale (Milgrom 1990a: 45, on Num 6:3; 240, on Num 28:7) were poured in the inner altar. This prohibition most likely was based on the priestly apprehension that offerings on God's table might be regarded literally as "God's food" (*leḥem 'ĕlōhîm*, 21:6, 8, 21; cf. Ps 50:12–13).

Once, however, the ritual left the sanctuary and became public, the priests lost control. A parade example is the failure of the Holiness School to suppress the rituals for rain, which originally dominated the three festivals of the seventh month: the first, tenth, and fifteenth through the twenty-second days. The absence of a natural feature in the description of these festivals (23:23–35), in contrast to the spring festivals (23:9–22), and the description of the seven-day festival in nonpriestly sources (*'āsîp* 'ingathering [of crops]', Exod 23:16; 34:22; cf. *'sp* Gezer Calendar, l. 1) should immediately send a warning signal that some element dealing with nature was excised from the text.

Nonetheless, what was suppressed or excised was ignored, perhaps defiantly, by the people. During the seven-day festival, they would circumambulate the altar each day with branches, lay them on the altar, beat them on the altar, and libate water on the altar—all to the accompaniment of the blowing of the shofar. These rites are not recorded in the Torah, but the rabbis were cognizant of them, and they fully admitted that their goal was to supplicate God for rain. Furthermore, since both the prophet Joel and the Mishna Ta'anit remind us that in times of severe drought, communities would sound an *alarm*, calling for a general *fast* and *assembly* for prayer, it is possible that all three seventh-month festivals—day 1, sound an *alarm*; day 10, *fast*; day 22 (climaxing the seven-day festival), *assembly*—formed a single unified ritual for providing (initially magically, subsequently through prayer) adequate rain in the coming agricultural year.

In passing, it should be noted that many centuries later the rabbis also opposed, at times vehemently, some folkways of the people. Seventeen famous examples compose the six customs followed by the Jews of Jericho that the rabbis opposed in principle, but in practice refrained from protesting against three of them (*m. Pesaḥ.* 4:8; cf. also *b.* '*Erub.* 96a [bar.]; *b. Ket.* 3b).

With this experiential background of Israel's religious leadership, ranging from the early priesthood to the rabbinic sages, I can postulate that it was an astute decision of the Holiness School not to polemicize directly against the ancestral cult. Besides, there were aspects that they surely wanted to preserve, such as veneration of the departed with the hope to join them after death in the family grave (note *yēʾāsēp ʾaḥărōne ʾel ʿammāyw* 'gathered to one's kin' [e.g., Num 20:24], the exact opposite of *nikrat mēʿammāyw* 'cut off from his kin' [Lev 17:9]). They were not about to throw out the proverbial baby with the bath water.

Schmidt's (1996a) published, revised dissertation has just come to my attention. His thesis is that

> the dismal netherworld existence of the dead as portrayed in both biblical and extra-biblical sources . . . suggests the strong likelihood that mortuary rites performed for the benefit of the ghosts located there [in the netherworld] maintained the sufferableness of that existence and no more . . . they do not presuppose the supernatural beneficent power of the Syro-Palestinian or, more specifically, the Israelite dead. . . . That belief was a late foreign introduction motivated in part by the combination of prolonged social crises, the failure of traditional religion, and intrusive contact with other cultures. . . . It came to be ritually expressed in a belatedly adopted Mesopotamian form of divination, namely, necromancy. (280, 275)

The book is an exhaustive examination of the relevant extrabiblical and biblical textual evidence, the latter including Isa 8:19–23; 19:3; 28:7–22; 29:4; Deut 14:1; 18:11; 26:14; 1 Sam 28:3–25; 2 Kgs 21:6; 23:24; Isa 57:6; 65:4; Jer 16:5. It is impossible here to do a comprehensive review of his book, which it manifestly deserves, but some serious objections concerning the biblical material need to be addressed:

1. A methodological question: Schmidt admits that the spirits of the dead can turn actively malevolent to the living. If they have the power to be harmful, why can't they be beneficent?

2. Surprisingly, there is no discussion of Lev 18–21, especially those verses dealing specifically with cultic rites for the dead: 18:21; 19:26–28, 31; 20:1–6; 21:1–4!

3. Schmidt categorically concludes that most of the verses he cites are products of a deuteronomistic edition in the exilic and postexilic age, but none of them were composed earlier than the reign of Manasseh. However, nearly always his dating and ascribed authorship are subject to question. For example, Williamson (1994), building on Clements (1982: 95)—both unmentioned by Schmidt—argues, plausibly in my mind, that the redactorial hand evident throughout Isa 1–39 is that of (Deutero-)Isa 40–55. Most revealingly, however, is that none of Schmidt's cited Isaiahic passages are singled out by Williamson as having undergone redaction.

D. Homosexuality: Its Biblical Misuse in the Current Debate

The case of homosexual relations, as suggested in the NOTES on 18:22 and 20:13, specifically addresses the fear of a stagnant birth rate. This behavior would, moreover, undermine God's promise to Israel, enshrined in all covenantal promises that Israel's population would multiply (e.g., 26:9; Gen 17:6–7 [H]). However, particularly now, when the paramount issue is not birth increase but birth control; when population explosions, especially in underdeveloped countries, is a major cause of the famines and wars that ravage the earth, does this biblical criterion (for ancient Israel!) carry universal validity?

I elaborated on this matter in *Bible Review* (1993c; 1994d) in a more personal vein, which, with a noteworthy addition, should prove germane to the reader reprinted in COMMENT E below.

E. Who Says Homosexuality Is a Sin?

On Yom Kippur, September 25, 1993, my synagogue invited me to explain the afternoon scriptural reading: the list of forbidden sexual liaisons in Leviticus 18. I chose to focus on what is today one of the most frequently quoted passages in the entire Bible: "Do not lie with a male as one lies with a woman; it is an abomination" (v. 22).

What I said may be both good news and bad news to my Christian friends, depending on their position on gay and lesbian rights: This biblical prohibition is addressed only to Israel. Compliance with this law is a condition for residing in the Holy Land, but not elsewhere (see the closing exhortation, vv. 24–30). Thus, it is incorrect to apply this prohibition on a universal scale.

Moreover, as pointed out by my student David Stewart, both occurrences of the prohibition (18:22; 20:13) contain the phrase *mishkeve 'isha,* an idiom used for only *illicit* heterosexual unions. Thus carnal relations are forbidden only with males who are of the equivalent degree of the females prohibited in these lists. For example, the prohibited relations would be nephew–aunt, grandfather–granddaughter, and stepmother–stepson, but also nephew–uncle, grandfather–grandson, and stepfather–stepson. This implies that the homosexual prohibition does not cover all male–male liaisons, but only those within the limited circle of family. But homosexual relations with unrelated males are neither prohibited nor penalized.

But I spoke to my fellow Jews, who are required to observe this prohibition. What is the rationale for this prohibition? In a previous column (1992), I noted that the Bible's impurity rules are part of a symbol system representing the forces of life and death. Israel is required to avoid these impurities and adhere to the laws commanded by God, who promotes the forces of life. Thus in the same chapter we read, "You shall heed my statutes and my rules, by doing them one shall live" (18:5). A man who discharges semen, whether intentionally or otherwise, is declared impure and must purify himself by bathing (a sort of re-baptism) before he is permitted to enter the Temple or touch sacred (sacrificial) food [see NOTES on 15:16–18]. Why? Because semen stands for life, and the loss of semen symbolizes the loss of life.

Note also that in the entire list of forbidden sexual unions, *there is no prohibition against lesbianism.* Can it be that lesbianism did not exist in ancient times or that scripture was unaware of its existence? Lesbians existed and flourished, as attested in an old (pre-Israelite) Babylonian omen text (TCS 4, 194:XXIV 33'; Bottéro and Petschow 1975) and in the work of the lesbian poet Sappho (born c. 612 B.C.E., during the time of the First Temple), who came from the island of Lesbos (hence lesbianism). But there is a fundamental difference between the homosexual acts of men and women. *In lesbianism there is no spilling of seed.* Thus life is not symbolically lost, and therefore lesbianism is not prohibited in the Bible.

My argument ostensibly can be countered by a more comprehensive biblical injunction. The very first commandment, given to Adam and repeated to Noah, is "Be fruitful and multiply and fill the earth" (Gen 1:28 and 9:1, 7). The descendants of Noah—the entire human race—are duty-bound to fulfill this commandment. But the truth is that we have not only filled the earth, we have over-filled it. This does not mean, however, that the commandment should be thought of as no longer in force—especially among Jews, who have lost a third of their numbers in our lifetime. I recall an incident during a premarital interview from the early years of my rabbinate. The starry-eyed bride declared her noble intention to have twelve children to compensate for the tragic loss of six million killed in the Holocaust. "But madam," I gasped, "must you do it all by yourself?"

I have since come to regret my flippant reply. This couple regarded their forthcoming marriage as a sacrament not just between themselves, but with the Jewish people. The problem has worsened for American Jews. Because intermarriage is rife and the Jewish birth rate is low, American Jewry, once at zero population growth, has dipped into the minus column. Were it not for a steady stream of converts, the extinction of American Jewry would be even more imminent. For us the divine command, "Be fruitful and multiply" is truly in force.

To Jewish homosexuals I offer an unoriginal solution. As compensation for your loss of seed, adopt children. Although adoption was practiced in the ancient world (as attested in Babylonian law), there is no biblical procedure or institution of adoption. As a result the institution of adoption is absent from rabbinic jurisprudence. Yet there are isolated cases of a kind of pseudo-adoption in the Bible. For example, Abraham, long childless, complains to God that Eliezer of Damascus, his steward, will inherit him (Gen 15:2). And barren Rachel beseeches her husband Jacob, "Here is my maid Bilhah—go in to her that she may bear on my knees and that through her I too may have children" (Gen 30:3). Adoption is certainly a possibility today. Lesbian couples have an additional advantage. Not only do they not violate biblical law, but through artificial insemination each can become the natural mother of her children.

Thus from the Bible we can infer the following: Presumably, half of the world's homosexual population, lesbians, are not mentioned. Over ninety-nine percent of the gays, namely non-Jews, are not addressed. This leaves the small number of Jewish gays subject to this prohibition. If they are biologically or psychologically incapable of procreation, adoption provides a solution.

I hope the Eternal, in love and compassion, will then reckon their spilled seed as producing fruit.

F. How Not to Read the Bible

I have decided to respond to the letters written by Ms. Joanna Saidel and Dr. Donald Wold because they challenge me on my own turf. Ms. Saidel makes three points: 1. Though Sodomites were non-Israelites, they were destroyed for their homosexuality; 2. Subsequent "Sodomites" were purged by King Asa and his son Jehoshaphat (1 Kgs 15:12; 22:47); 3. Non-Israelite nations residing in the land were expelled because of their sexual immorality, including homosexuality (Lev 18:24–30; see v. 22).

In rebuttal to all these objections, I have cited a simple fact: The ban on homosexuality and the other illicit unions applied solely to the residents of the holy land, as Saidel herself emphasized by italicizing the explicit biblical statement "in all these the nations are defiled, which I have cast out before you" (Lev 18:24). This verse applies to the people of Sodom and to subsequent "Sodomites" who lived within the bounds of the holy land. What is the symbolism of the holy land? It is the sphere of God as much as his Temple in Jerusalem. In this theology, all those who live in God's extended Temple, the holy land, are accountable to a higher moral and ritual standard. Now I want to amplify this conclusion on a deeper level.

In this same chapter, Lev 18, Israel is enjoined "You shall not imitate the practices of the land of Egypt where you dwelt, or of the land of Canaan to which I am taking you" (v. 3). If it were incumbent on all nations to observe these sexual prohibitions, as Saidel claims, one would have to conclude that the Egyptians would be just as culpable for the violation of these laws as the Canaanites. To be sure, the Egyptians are punished for Pharaoh's refusal to release Israel from bondage, and the prophets repeatedly excoriate Egypt for their ongoing crimes against Israel. But not once do they condemn them for their sexual deviations. Ezekiel, for example, is familiar with the pentateuchal literature, especially the last chapters of Leviticus, including chap. 18. He is also fully aware of Egypt's sexual appetites (Ezek 16:26), but in the four lengthy chapters describing their crimes and forthcoming punishment (chaps. 29–32), not once does he mention any of the several violations of Lev 18, let alone homosexuality. The conclusion is obvious: since the Egyptians do not live in the holy land, their sexual aberrations are not sins against God and, hence, not subject to divine sanctions.

I now turn to the question: Why was Sodom destroyed? It is true that they practiced homosexuality (hence the term "sodomy"). Is that the reason? Let us examine the text closely. God intervenes because "they have acted altogether *according to the outcry* that has come to Me" (Gen 18:21). The angels are more explicit: "the *outcry against them* before YHWH has become so great that YHWH has sent us to destroy it" (Gen 19:13). Outcry, then, implies the reaction of those who are persecuted and oppressed by the Sodomites. Their suffering is not identified. But some notion can be extrapolated from the behavior of the Sodomites to the angels (Gen 19:1–9): their inhospitality—rather, their homicidal xenophobia (contrast Abraham's reception of the angel, Gen 18:1–8) and their violence as exhibited by their intent to commit homosexual rape. Additional illumination is provided by Ezekiel: "This was the sin of your sister Sodom: she did not support the poor and the needy" (Ezek 16:49). Thus Sodom's homosexuality has to be seen in the larger context of its heartlessness and brutal acts to the unfortunate in their own society.

Further light on the homosexuality of the Sodomites is reflected from its mirror image, the incident at Gibeah (Judg 19). Residents of the Benjaminite town of Gibeah want to violate a Levite who has been given hospitality by one of its residents. Instead the Levite sends out his concubine who is ravished by the townsmen until she dies. The other Israelite tribes demand the extradition of the guilty townsmen. The Benjamites refuse and under the battle cry "an outrage has been committed in Israel" (Judg 20:6, 10) the tribes attack the Benjamites and decimate them.

In this version, non-Israelite Sodom is replaced by Israelite Gibeah. But the crime is the same: gang rape ending in homicide. To be sure, homosexuality features in both incidents, but its purpose is not sexual fulfillment; it only serves as an instrument of violence. Sodom is evil because it is the epitome of inhumanity and brutality, not because it practices homosexuality. What might we ask would have been the case if Sodomite and Gibeahite homosexuality had been practiced by consenting adults? According to Lev 18, ultimately they would have been expelled from the land, but they would not have provoked the wrath of YHWH (or of the Israelites) to destroy them.

One who interprets Scripture and, above all, one who lives by it is obligated to understand what it says. Theoretically, the Hebrew Bible should be read in Hebrew and, if not, at least in a reliable translation. Unfortunately the King James Version, which Ms. Saidel relies on—with all its glorious cadences—is often inaccurate. The "Sodomites" whom King Asa purges from the land (1 Kgs 15:12) are called *qĕdēšîm*, which means "the consecrated ones," not "Sodomites." In this case, unfortunately, modern translations aren't much better: "temple prostitutes" (NAB); "male prostitutes" (*NJPS, NRSV, NEB*). The chances are this term refers to cultic devotees of some sort, but not temple personnel who engage in prostitution. Indeed, there is no evidence that temple-sponsored prostitution existed anywhere in the ancient Near East, all the more so in Israel! [Goodfriend 1992; van der Toorn 1992]. It may very well be that a *"consecrated* one" would have engaged in prostitution for the benefit of a sanctuary. It was thus only logical that under Israel's strict moral code the income derived from prostitution could not be donated to the Temple (Deut 23:18–19; Eng. 17–18).

Finally, a personal note. I am not for homosexuality, but I am for homosexuals. I grieve for their plight—their pariah status and their discrimination in the workplace and the military. But when the Bible is distorted to make God their enemy, I must speak out to set the record straight. I return to my contention that there is only one deduction to be derived from Lev 18 and 20: The ban on homosexuality is limited to male Jews and inhabitants of the holy land. The basis for the ban, as I have submitted, is the need for procreation, which opposes, in biblical times, the wasting of seed.

In response to Dr. Wold's letter I begin with a personal note. It is good to know that my erstwhile student, though fully (and successfully) engaged in business, has kept up with biblical scholarship, and is about to publish a book on the subject of homosexuality. I shall respond to his arguments briefly:

1. That the Bible says God penalizes Israel for homosexuality does not imply that he approves of it for the rest of the world. But when God punishes Israel for it, he punishes no one else—unless they reside in the holy land. The parade example is Egypt, which is accused of the illicit sexual practices of Lev 18 but is never punished for any one of them (see above). I believe there is only one conclusion to be drawn from the Hebrew Bible: if God never penalizes homosexual non-Jews living outside the holy land, why should we?

2. I cannot fully share Wold's confidence that Ham's act against Noah (Gen 9:20–27) "was almost certainly homosexual rape." Upon awakening from his drunken stupor Noah cursed the younger son for what had been done to him. Ambiguity multiplies explanations. Among the many there is one that reflects the Greek myth of the castration of the god Uranus, not by spousal wrath, but by Kronos, the young son who would displace him. But most commentaries stick to the plain meaning of the text: Ham proceeded to publicize his father's nakedness to his brother instead of covering him, a lapse of filial respect that the brothers did not emulate when they covered him while walking backwards so as not to look.

3. Does Wold wish to infer from the command "be fruitful and multiply" (Gen 1:28; 9:1, 7) that single people and childless couples will suffer punishment?

4. True, the term *ha'adam*, which heads Leviticus 18, is generic for all humanity in the creation story (also noted by reader Riccio). But Lev 18 is part of the Priestly Code where that same *'adam* is used to designate those who offer sacrifices (Lev 1:2) and develop scale disease (Lev 13:2; erroneously rendered "leprosy"). This generic term includes Israelite men and women and, probably, the resident alien. For of certainty, sacrifices to Israel's God are not permitted outside the land (see Josh 22:19; Amos 7:17), and those who suffer scale disease outside the land are not subject to the mandated quarantine and purificatory rites.

5. If Wold were right that "sex with a menstruant is forbidden because she cannot conceive during her period" it would also be forbidden during pregnancy and after menopause. The Hebrew Bible affirms human sexuality: Barzillai the Gileadite declines King David's offer to live out his years at the royal residence: "I am now eighty years old. Can I tell the difference between good and bad (a euphemism for sexual activity)? Can your servant taste what he eats and drinks? Can I listen to the singing of men and women?" (2 Sam 19:36). Barzillai is no longer capable of enjoying wine, women, and song. However, if at age eighty he were still capable of sensual pleasure, is there any doubt that he would have accepted the king's invitation?

21. INSTRUCTIONS FOR THE PRIESTS

TRANSLATION

¹YHWH said to Moses: Say to the priests, the sons of Aaron, and say to them:

Mourning

None shall defile himself (mourning) for any dead person among his kin, ²except for his closest relatives: his mother, his father, his son, his daughter, and his brother; ³also for his marriageable sister, closest to him, who has no husband, for her he may defile himself. ⁴But he shall not defile himself among his kinspeople, thereby desecrating himself.

⁵They shall not make any bald patches on their heads, or shave off the edge of their beards, or make gashes in their flesh. ⁶They shall be holy to their God and not desecrate the name of their God; for they offer the gifts of YHWH, the food of their God, and so must be holy.

Marriage

⁷They shall not marry a promiscuous woman or one who was raped, nor shall they marry a woman divorced from her husband. For each (priest) is holy to his God, ⁸and you must treat him as holy, since he offers the food of your God; he shall be holy to you, for I YHWH who sanctifies you am holy.

Addendum on a Priest's Daughter

⁹When the daughter of a priest desecrates herself by harlotry, it is her father whom she desecrates; she shall be burned by fire.

The High Priest

¹⁰The priest who is preeminent among his fellows, on whose head the anointing oil has been poured and who has been ordained to wear the (priestly) vestments, shall not dishevel his hair or rend his vestments. ¹¹He shall not go in where there is a dead body; even for his father or mother he shall not defile himself. ¹²He shall not leave the sacred area so that he not desecrate the sacred area of his God, for the distinction of the anointing oil of his God is upon him. I (who speak) am YHWH.

¹³He is to marry a young virgin. ¹⁴A widow, a divorcee, a raped woman, or a harlot: these he shall not marry. Only a young virgin of his kin may he take to wife ¹⁵that he not desecrate his offspring among his kin, for I am YHWH who sanctifies him.

Blemished Priests

[16]YHWH spoke to Moses: [17]Speak to Aaron and say: A man of your offspring in any generation who has a blemish shall not be qualified to offer the food of his God. [18]No one at all who has a blemish shall be qualified: a man who is blind, lame, disfigured, or deformed; [19]a man who has a broken leg or broken arm, [20]or who is a hunchback, or a dwarf, or has a discoloration of the eye, a scar, a lichen, or a crushed testicle. [21]Every man among the offspring of Aaron the priest who has a blemish shall not be qualified to offer YHWH's gifts; having a blemish, he shall not be qualified to offer the food of his God. [22]He may eat the food of his God, of the most holy and of the holy. [23]But he shall not enter before the veil or officiate at the altar, for he has a blemish. And he may not desecrate my sanctums. (Thereby) I am YHWH who sanctifies them.

Subscript

[24]Thus Moses spoke to Aaron and his sons and to all the Israelites.

Comments

The structure of chap. 21, COMMENTS A and B; mourning customs, COMMENT C; and blemished priests in the world of the Bible, COMMENT D.

NOTES

Chaps. 21–22 form a single unit: both deal with instructions for the priests. To be more exact, chap. 22 continues the priestly instructions of chap. 21 through half the chapter, but devotes the second half to instructions for the laity (22:17–33).

The redactor of chaps. 21–22 ordered his materials to form a thematic introversion (M. Hildenbrand):

A   Relation of a priest to his family for sacrifice (21:1–15)

   B   Blemishes of priests who sacrifice (21:16–23)

      X   How a priest should avoid desecration of sacrifices (22:1–16)

   B'   Blemishes of animals for sacrifice (22:17–25)

A'   Relation of an animal and its family for sacrifice (22:27–28)

The eligibility of priests and animals for the altar is detailed in AA', but is limited to one aspect—their respective relations to family. The parallels between BB' are obvious (see COMMENT B). X makes a perfect conceptual center, by merging the priest with animals in regard to his sacrificial food. Moreover, this is the only section with indications of penalties for transgressing these laws (*kārēt*, 22:3; *yiśʾû ḥēṭ*ʾ, 22:9; *ʿāwōn ʾašmâ*, 22:16).

Several cogent reasons have been put forward to explain the positioning of these two chapters after chaps. 19–20. I prefer Ibn Ezra's explanation: as Israel is adjured to be holy (19:2; 20:26), so are its priests (Ibn Ezra). I prefer this explanation because it places emphasis on the *Piʾel* present participle *měqaddēš*, attached to the priests (21:8 LXX, 15; 22:9, 16, 32; cf. 20:8 [Israel]), which teaches that just as Israel must strive to *attain* holiness, so the priests must strive to *maintain* holiness. It is also no accident that *měqaddēš* is a structural divider of both chapters (see below).

Bekhor Shor suggests that the previous chapters, explicitly the sexual prohibitions, separate Israel from the nations (18:3; 20:24), whereas chaps. 21–22 separate, within Israel, the priests from the laity. Douglas (1995, 1999), who studied the structural links of the entire book of Leviticus, points out that chaps. 21–22 reverse the order of chaps. 1–7: whereas the latter prescribe the animal sacrifice first (chaps. 1–5) and the priestly instructions second (chaps. 6–7), the former put the priests first (21:1–22:16) and the animals second (22:17–30; see Introduction I L).

Chaps. 21–22 are divided into six sections, each of which ends with the verb *měqaddēš* plus a suffix (21:8, 15, 23; 22:9, 16, 32). The suffixes—that is, the objects of the four inner verbs (21:15, 23; 22:9, 16)—refer to the priests; the suffixes of the two outer verbs (21:8; 22:32) address the Israelites, though in the case of 21:8, the suffix disturbs the sense of the verse (see NOTE).

There is a common denominator to both chapters: blemishes. That is, self-alteration (for mourning, vv. 4–5), marriage with a "defective" woman (vv. 7, 14), outwardly appearing physical defects (vv. 17–20), partaking of sacred food while impure (22:3–7), or permitting it to unauthorized others (22:10–12) constitute blemishes. They desecrate the priest's holiness (vv. 6, 15, 21, 23b; 22:2, 9, 15) and bar him or his offspring (in the case of illicit marriage, v. 15a) from officiating in the sanctuary. Israel is commanded to beware of blemished sacrifices (22:17–25) since, just as in the case of blemished priests, they are not eligible for the altar.

The consummate artistry in the structure of chap. 21 is detailed in COMMENTS A and B, where it is demonstrated that the alleged redundancies that ostensibly predominate in the chapter are in reality instrumental to the complex sophisticated craftsmanship that characterizes the entire chapter so that there cannot be found even one superfluous word in the entire chapter. Wellhausen (1963: 157) faults chaps. 21–22 because they omit the mention of *ʾōhel môʿēd* 'the Tent of Meeting', implying that these chapters stem from a much later age. However, it should first be pointed out that this term is abundantly present in the rest of H (cf. 17:4, 5, 6, 9; 19:21; 24:3). Moreover, it is implied, for example, by the term *pārōket* 'veil' (21:23). And when the entire structure is scanned (see COMMENTS A and B), it becomes clear that the term is not needed.

The content of chap. 21 may be outlined:

A. Purity of the priests (vv. 1–15)
   1. Introduction (v. 1a,bα)
   2. Prohibitions against mourning (vv. 1bβ–6)
      a. For relatives (v. 1bβ)
      b. Exceptions (vv. 2–3)
      c. Prohibitions restated (v. 4)
      d. Prohibited mourning rites (v. 5)
      e. Priestly holiness enjoined (v. 6)
   3. Prohibited marriages (vv. 7a–8)
      a. Enumerated (v. 7a)
      b. Holiness rationale (v. 7b)
      c. Obligation of the laity (v. 8)
   4. Addendum: the priest's daughter (v. 9)
B. Purity of the high priest (vv. 10–15)
   1. Identification of the high priest (v. 10a)
   2. Prohibitions against mourning (vv. 10b–12)
      a. Prohibited mourning rites (v. 10b)
      b. For everyone, including parents (v. 11)
      c. May not leave the sanctuary (to follow the bier) (v. 12aα)
      d. Rationale: desecration of sanctuary (v. 12aβ,b)
   3. Prohibited marriages (vv. 13–15)
      a. Enumerated (vv. 13–14)
      b. Rationale: desecration of his lineage (v. 15a)
C. Blemishes that disqualify priests (vv. 16–22)
   1. Introduction (vv. 16–17a)
   2. The blemishes (vv. 17b–21)
      a. Basic rule (vv. 17b–18a)
      b. Enumerated (vv. 18b–20)
      c. Basic rule (v. 21)
   3. Concession to blemished priest (v. 22)
D. Prohibitions of blemished high priest (v. 23)
   1. To officiate in the sanctuary (v. 23a)
   2. Rationale: desecration of sanctuary (v. 23b)
E. Compliance report: Moses delivers God's commands (v. 24)

Vv. 1a, bα. The Introduction

Say . . . and say. 'ĕmōr . . . wĕ'āmartā. The imperative *'ĕmōr* is equivalent to customary *dabbēr* 'speak', and is attested elsewhere (e.g., Gen 45:17; Ex 6:6; 7:19; 8:1, 12). This introductory formula applies to vv. 1–15.

the priests, the sons of Aaron. hakkōhănîm bĕnê 'ahărōn. According to Ramban, the customary address *'ahărōn ûbānāyw* 'Aaron and his sons' is used when the priestly duties in the sanctuary are prescribed. The laws of mourning and marriage, described here, however, apply to the priesthood even when they are off duty. Wessely (1846), in disagreement with Ramban, claims that since the following verses (vv. 1–9) apply to ordinary priests but not the high priest, Aaron is therefore excluded.

Both exegetes are, in my opinion, partially wrong. Wessely overlooks the fact that the laws of the high priest (vv. 10–15) are subsumed under this introduction. Ramban does not take in account that the same formula, but in reverse order, *běnê 'ahăron hakkōhănîm*, occurs when the priestly cadre, with the exception of the high priest, is addressed as a body in the performance of its cultic duties (e.g., 1:5, 8, 11; 2:2; 3:2; Num 10:8). I would suggest that this unique formulaic occurrence, beginning with the word *hakkōhănîm* 'the priests', is intended to stress that the following laws refer to the *status* of the priests rather than to their *functions*—and here Ramban is correct—a matter that should concern the priests at all times, even when they are outside the sanctuary.

In the priestly tradition, the priesthood is hereditary, limited to the descendants of Aaron. According to the Deuteronomist, the entire tribe of Levi is eligible (Deut 10:8; 18:1–2, 6–7; cf. Judg 17:7, 12–13; 18:4, 19). In this respect, Israel differs radically from its neighbors. In Egypt, for example, the priesthood had a lay character. Priests were in office for a limited time, perhaps three months a year; thereafter, they returned to their normal occupations (Sauneron 1960: 15). In Mesopotamia, the priestly officials were appointed by the king. To be sure, the temple's head priest would probably have recommended the appointment of a member of one of the extant priestly families or, in the case of a priest's death, the deceased's son or relative (Saggs 1984: 210), but the appointment ultimately rested with the king, not the temple. And his selection could well have been from a nonpriestly family (Jeroboam's appointments, 1 Kgs 12:31; 2 Chr 11:13–16). A text from Hellenistic Babylon indicates, however, that the craft of an astrologer was hereditary and that the candidate had to be examined for an adequate knowledge of his craft (McEwan: 1981: 16–20). But even on the assumption that a Hellenistic text totally reflects ancient practice, it must also be realized that astrologers, though members of a temple's staff, did not officiate at the sacrificial rites *inside the Temple*. Why, then, was Israel's priesthood limited to one family (or tribe)?

A practical reason surfaces at once. If a priest was court appointed, then his office could be bought. So it indeed occurred with annoying frequency in Egypt (Sauneron 1960:15), precisely as it occurred during Israel's second commonwealth, when the high priest was chosen by the (foreign) ruler—for a price.

However, there is a more positive reason: the unique function of Israel's priest. First, he was bound by many prohibitions, as detailed in chaps. 21–22. Above all, he had to know the laws of impurity (e.g., the laws of scale disease, chaps. 13–14; cf. Deut 21:5) *and live them* lest their violation pollute the sanctuary (consequences of which are spelled out in chap. 4, COMMENTS B and C). Moreover, the priest had to be a master of Torah, the entire compendium of Israel's revealed law, so that he could teach it to his fellow Israelites (10:10–11; cf. Deut 33:10; Jer 18:18; Ezek 7:26; Mal 2:6–9; 2 Chr 17:8–9).

The conclusion is self-evident. Eligibility for the priesthood required extensive schooling, on the one hand, and disciplined practice, on the other. No wonder that the rabbis preserve the tradition that the sons of priests, at an early age, must practice the laws of impurity (*b. Yeb.* 114a). Israel's neighbors, in contrast, were "the simple executors of a daily religious ceremony which was performed far from the eyes of the profane . . . it called for very limited training to be admitted into the ranks of the 'purified' " (Sauneron 1960:16).

Vv. 1β–6. Prohibitions Against Mourning

Most commentators have understood these verses as a polemic against the cult of the dead (e.g., Baentsch 1903; most recently, Hartley 1992). Eerdmans (1912) objects on the grounds that the priest may defile himself with his father and mother, the very ones he is likely to venerate in a cult of the dead. Thus it is hardly likely that "this law eliminated a funerary role for the Israelite priesthood" (Levine 1989). Instead, Eerdmans proposes that the intent of these verses is to forbid the self-mutilation of the priest (v. 5) except with his named close relatives (vv. 2–3). Welch (1925) rightly objects to Eerdman's proposal that v. 5 would then have been listed first as the general law and the exceptions (vv. 2–3) would have followed. Welch then states his conclusion—a correct one, in my opinion—that only v. 5 can be understood as opposing the cult of the dead, but he is at a loss to explain the underlying purpose of vv. 1bβ–4.

All these scholars are right. A polemic may underlie these verses against the Egyptian cult, which was obsessed with death and the afterlife and which contained in every temple a cadre of special priests involved in the funerary rites (Bergman 1995: 63). Also, underlying these verses is the lethal contact between holiness and impurity, which, if not expunged quickly (lest it fester) and effectively (by the ordained purificatory rites), can lead, in the priestly view, to the destruction of Israel (vol. 1.254–61, 307–18, 766–67, 953–1004). The priests are innately holy—an axiom that H, a priestly document, accepts, even as it tries to qualify it (see NOTES on "who sanctifies you," v. 8, and "who sanctifies him," v. 15). Therefore, theoretically, they should not come into contact with or even be under the same roof as a corpse (see NOTE to 14:35; chap. 15, COMMENT F). If this prohibition applied to everyone, all the more so, therefore, to priests. As pointed out by Levine (1992: 316), this law effectively ruled out any funerary role for the priesthood. That priests had to observe stricter rules than lay persons regarding corpse contamination was known in other cultures as well. For example, an inscription from the island of Kos (§ 5, cited in Weinfeld 1988: 275) warns priests against contact with a corpse or *entering a house containing a corpse.* However, a concession—and that is all it is, a concession—is granted to the ordinary priest, but not to the high priest (v. 11), that he may defile himself with his closest kin. It is assumed that the priestly mourner undergoes the required seven-day purificatory rite (Num 19:14, 16; Ezekiel requires an additional week, terminating with a purification offering, Ezek 44:26–27) before he may resume his priestly functions.

The rabbis were fully aware of the anomaly that these verses of Leviticus presume the purificatory rites prescribed only in Num 19, as expressed by the following midrash:

He (Moses) spoke before him, "Lord of the universe, if these (the priests) are defiled wherewith do they regain their state of purity?" He gave no answer, and at that time, the face of Moses changed [i.e., he was crestfallen, thinking he was unworthy to receive the instruction]. When, however, he (God) reached the chapter of the Red Cow (Num 19), the Holy One, blessed be He, said to Moses, "Moses, when I made to you the statement, 'Say to the priests' (v. 1bα) . . . I gave you no answer. This is the method of their purification" (Num 19:17). He (Moses) spoke before him, "Lord of the universe, is this purification [i.e., how can ashes remove corpse contamination]?" The Holy One, blessed be He, replied, "Moses it is a statute (*ḥuqqâ*, Num 19:2), and I have made a decree, and nobody can fathom my decree" (*Koh. Rab.* 8:5).

Elsewhere, I have analyzed "The Paradox of the Red Cow" (1981: 62–72 [= 1983: 85–95]; vol. 1.270–78) and have proposed that, theoretically and perhaps originally, the purificatory rite for corpse contamination belonged in Leviticus in the unit dealing with severe impurities (chaps. 12–15), where it is also presumed. However, since it has been reworked so that contaminated persons could remain in their homes (contrast the *mĕṣōrāʿ*, 13:46) and that the purificatory rite might resemble (artificially) a purification offering, it was removed (or absented) from Leviticus and placed in Numbers.

Ezekiel's version of the priestly law of mourning differs somewhat in its wording, but not in its substance. Note that its sequence of persons (21:2b–3) is identical: *kî ʾim-lĕʾāb ûlĕʾēm ûlĕbēn ûlĕbat lĕʾāḥ ûlĕʾāḥôt ʾăšer-lōʾ- hāytâ lĕʾîš yiṭṭammāʾû* (Ezek 44:25b). In particular, the setting off of the sister in a discrete, identically worded clause leaves the impression that Ezekiel (or his tradent) had 21:2–3 before him. Although Ezekiel concurs concerning the permitted persons for purposes of attending to their burial, he differs sharply concerning the purificatory rites (Ezek 44:26–27; cf. vol. 1.284, 979, 986). See further the NOTE on 21:7.

1. *shall defile himself.* *yiṭṭammāʾ*, Hitpaʿel. The purificatory period would last for seven days (Num 19:19), as for a lay person. But Ezekiel lays upon the priest an additional week, terminated by a purification sacrifice, before he may resume his priestly duties (Ezek 44:26–27). The contrast between Mesopotamia and Israel is striking: "The Mesopotamian texts hardly refer to the defilement incurred by contact with a human corpse. The ideal of a swift and proper burial of the dead is apparently owing more to a concern for the welfare of the ghosts (*eṭemmū*) of the deceased than to a fear of contamination" (van der Toorn 1985: 37). Conversely, Israel was obsessed with fear of contamination of the dead (the most potent of all impurities; cf. vol. 1. 270–278, 997) for precisely the opposite reason: to wean Israel from the worship of the dead (see Introduction II C).

for any dead person. *lĕnepeš*. The word *nepeš* has a wide semantic range (cf. Wolff 1974: 10–25; Seebass 1986) including "person." It can also mean "dead body" (22:4; Num 5:2; 6:11; 9:6, 7, 10; Hag 2:13), but it is clearly an ellipsis of *nepeš mēt* 'a dead person' (v. 11; Num 6:6; cf. Num 19:11, 13). In Aramaic (*napšāʾ*, DISO 183–84) and in Rabbinic Hebrew (e.g., *y. Šek* 2:5), it signifies "a gravestone, a funerary monument" (Avigad 1954: 66–70; Haberman 1955–56; Negev 1971; Lewis 1989: 162, n. 4).

among his kin. *bĕʿammāyw.* Bekhor Shor renders "for his kin," claiming that the preposition *beth* is equivalent to *lamed.* However, as pointed out by *Keter Torah*, the *beth* should be assigned one of its normal meanings, "among," and it is so rendered here (and in v. 4).

Rashbam takes *bĕʿammāyw* as part of the subject, rendering "anyone among the priestly group should not defile himself for any person." The Sam. and *Tgs. Onk, Ps.-J.* render the singular *bĕʿammô* 'in his nation', which adulterates the force of the prohibition. The confused LXX sows its confusion throughout the chapter, by employing three nouns *ëthnos* (v. 1), *laos* (vv. 4, 15), and *genos* (v. 14). Josephus (*Apion* 1.31), in an apparent reference to this verse, renders *ex homoethnos* 'out of his own race/stock', adding informatively "but he must investigate her pedigree, obtaining the geneology from the archives."

2. *closest.* *haqqārōb ʾēlāyw* (cf. Num 27:11), literally "closest to him." Emphasis is laid on the fact that the direct closeness must be with the mourner, not via another—for example, his paternal uncle via his father (Bekhor Shor).

his . . . relatives. *liš ʾērô*, literally "flesh (relatives)" (see NOTE on 18:6a). Thus the wife is automatically excluded (Rashbam on v. 4). The rabbis, however, maintain that *šĕ ʾērô* means "his wife" (*Sipra* Emor, par. 1:4; *b. Yeb.* 22b; cf. *Tg. Ps.-J.*; also Engelken 1990: 28), but Weiss (1924: 1.46, n. 2) contends that this is a late midrash on *šĕ ʾēr* of Num 27:11 in order to derive the law that a husband may inherit from a wife (which the rabbis subject to a tortuous exegesis; cf. *B. Baba Bat.* 111b). *Seper ha-Mibḥar* offers a logical objection. If *šĕ ʾērô* meant "his wife," it should have been immediately followed by *lĕ ʾimmô* 'his mother'.

The rabbis disagree as to whether a priest can choose not to defile himself for his wife. R. Akiba says he must defile himself; R. Ishmael says he may. Their controversy most likely reflects long-standing opposition to the rabbinic identification of *šĕ ʾēr* with the wife: "The wife of Joseph the priest [a Sadducee?] died on Passover eve and when he refused to defile himself for her [*lîṭāmēʾ lāh*] the sages dragged him (to her) and defiled him against his will" (*Sipra* Emor, par. 1:12).

Hartley (1992) has revived this interpretation by arguing that God's instructions to Ezekiel (a priest) not to mourn for his wife (Ezek 24:15–18) indicates that normally a priest would be permitted to mourn for her. Hartley is correct, but he draws the wrong conclusion. Lev 21:1 does not forbid a priest to mourn; it only forbids him to defile himself, meaning that he cannot come into the presence of the corpse. But he still might be allowed to "lament or weep or let (his) tears flow . . . observe . . . mourning for the dead . . . (remove) turban . . . sandals . . . cover over (his) upper lip and . . . eat the bread of mourners" (Ezek 24:15–17). It is these mourning practices, patently permitted to other priests in mourning, that God denies to Ezekiel. See also the NOTE on v. 4.

his mother, his father. The same order as in 19:3. The Pesh., however, reverses it. Here it serves an aesthetic rather than a heuristic function: to create a chiasm with the high priest's pericope where the same expression surfaces (v. 11; see COMMENT A).

3. *marriageable* (*sister*). *habbĕtûlâ.* By this rendering, I wish to imply that she is young and nubile, as in English "maiden" and German *Jungfrau.* It cannot mean "virgin" (the customary rendering); otherwise, the next clause would be redundant, and the specifications for a bride (v. 7) would simply have read "he shall marry a *bĕtûlâ*" or would have followed the wording of v. 14.

Here, I follow Wenham (1972; supported by Engelken 1990: 27), who argues persuasively, first, that its cognates in Ugaritic (e.g., *btlt 'nt,* describing promiscuous Anat!) and in Akkadian (*batultu,* CAD 2.173–74) consistently mean "an adolescent, nubile girl," and second, that biblical narrative (e.g., Gen 24:16; Est 2:2–3, 17), poetry (e.g., Joel 1:8), and law (e.g., Deut 22:20–21) support the same rendering. For the definitive demonstration that Akkadian *batultu* and Hebrew *bĕtûlâ* refer to adolescence, see Landsberger (1968; but see NOTE on v. 13).

Wenham's (1972) case for the *locus classicus,* Deut 22:20–21, is eminently worth summarizing. The death penalty for the unfaithful bride would make sense only if her offense took place after her betrothal (or marriage); if unbetrothed, she escapes punishment. Her *bĕtûlîm* is therefore a pregnancy test; the elders produce her blood-stained clothing to prove that she was menstruating (and, therefore, was not impregnated) during the betrothal period. Indeed, if the parents had to exhibit her bridal sheets (the customary interpretation), how could they have gotten them?

Tsevat (1975b) adds further that in Semitic languages, the term "virgin" must be expressed by a circumlocution, *ša zikaram la īdûma* (e.g., CH § 130), the exact equivalent of *'ăšer lō'-yādĕ'û miškab zākār* 'who have not had carnal relations with a man' (Num 31:18). A more striking parallel, I submit, is *bĕtûlâ wĕ'îš lō' yĕdā'āh* 'a young woman whom no man had known sexually' (Gen 24:16) because it also proves that a *bĕtûlâ* is not necessarily a "virgin" (cf. Ehrlich 1908 [H]). The case of the high priest, however, merits separate treatment (see NOTE on v. 13).

closest to him. haqqĕrôbâ 'ēlāyw. This refers to a full sister (not a half or step-sister; cf. 18:9, 11; Ibn Ezra). This clause matches the equivalent clause in v. 2. It is therefore a mistake to render "close to him because she has not married" (*NJPS, NPSV*), not only because it misses this nuance, but also because it breaks with the parallel clause of v. 2.

Ehrlich (1908) presumes that this clause implies that the sister is dependent on the addressee (or on his brother; Engelken 1990: 28). However, if that were the case, it would have also qualified the mention of his daughter, who (it must therefore be assumed) may be married. The exemptions here are his *šĕ'ēr* 'flesh', which includes his daughter, not his father's *šĕ'ēr* (i.e., his sister), except under these special circumstances.

who has no husband. 'ăšer 'lō'-hāyĕtā lĕ'îš, as in *wĕhāyĕtā lĕ'îš 'aḥēr* 'she becomes another man's wife' (Deut 24:2; cf. also Ruth 1:12). The rabbis probably render this clause as "who had no husband," namely, that she was no longer a virgin (*Tg. Ps.-J.; Sipra* Emor par. 1:11; cf. Rashi). However, as indicated by Gen 24:16 and Num 31:18, cited above, the verb *yāda'* would have been used to include nonmarital intercourse.

4. *among his kinspeople. baʿal běʿammāyw.* The enigmatic term *baʿal* has been variously interpreted:

1. Since *baʿal* means "master" (e.g., Exod 21:3, 28; 22:7), it refers here to the priest. Aramaic *rabbāʾ* 'master' (*Tgs. Onk., Neof.*) also denotes "priest" (e.g., *rabbāʾ demidyān*, Exod 2:16, *Tg. Onk.*). Thus the priest-master should not defile himself for his kinspeople. Wessely (1846) objects that this interpretation makes this verse a repetition of v. 1b! However, see no. 4.

2. *baʿal* is part of the object. Hence "He shall not defile himself (for) a master among his kinspeople"—that is, for a high priest (Bekhor Shor, Ḥazzequni, Wessely (1846), Shadal; cf. *Tg. Neof.* margin). However, the preposition *lamed* 'for' must be added or assumed, and the verse is misplaced since the laws concerning the high priest are discussed later (vv. 10–15).

3. The rabbis who hold that *šěʾ ērô* (v. 2) means "his wife"—that is, her burial is permitted to him (*Sipra* Emor, par. 1:4; see its NOTE)—are forced to interpret *baʿal běʿammāyw* as "a husband (may not bury) his invalid wife," basing themselves on the following word *lěhēḥallô* 'thereby desecrating him' (interpreting the verb as a *Hipʿil*, not as a *Nipʿal* reflexive; *Sipra* Emor, par. 1:15; *b. Yeb.* 90b; see below). No comment is needed.

4. A number of emendations have been proposed: the LXX reads *exápina* 'suddenly', as in *kěballaʿ* (cf. Num 4:20 LXX), and some moderns conjecture that it is a haplography of *libě ʿullat baʿal* 'for a married woman' (e.g., Baentsch 1903); that is, a priest may not defile himself with the wife of one of his kinspeople. This verse, however, now becomes superfluous in view of the precise limitations enumerated in v. 3.

5. I concur with another emendation, that of Paran (1983: 152–53), which because of its attractiveness I cite separately. He proposes that *baʿal* should be deleted as a partial dittography of *běʿammāyw*. He supports his proposal by pointing out that *baʿal* never appears alone, but always in a construct (e.g., *běʿullat baʿal*, Gen 20:3; *baʿal ʾiššâ*, Exod 21:3) or with a suffix (e.g., *baʿalāh* Deut 24:4). Would not then v. 4 become a clone of v. 1b? Precisely, he argues, in order for vv. 1b, 4 to effect an inclusio for vv. 2–3, which contain seven instances of enumerated exceptions, each of which is prefixed by a *lamed*. He points to 22:10–13, which also illustrates an inclusio structure. I shall also demonstrate that the twelve enumerated priestly blemishes are enveloped in a double inclusio (see NOTE on vv. 17b–21, and COMMENT B). Here, however, the repetition is more than aesthetic. It adds the rationale for the prohibition in the ensuing infinitive.

thereby desecrating himself. lěhēḥallô. This is a *Nipʿal* infinitive (e.g., Ezek 20:9, 14, 22) with reflexive force (Ibn Ezra). H presents its rationale at the end of a commandment (e.g., vv. 7b, 8aβ, 8bβ, 12, 15) or at its repetition. Thus, as demonstrated at 19:8, when H repeats P's law of *šělāmîm* procedure (19:5–7), it adds the rationale, indeed the identical one as in our verse: desecration.

Normally, we would have expected the word *lěhiṭṭāměʾô*, since contact with the dead results in defilement, pollution. The verb *hillēl* 'desecrate' was chosen deliberately to emphasize the effect of the pollution on the person of the priest: he is desanctified and, hence, disqualified to handle or be in the presence of sanctums—in other words, to serve as a priest. Joosten (1994: 175; 1996: 127) suggests that this usage "implies the risk of impurity coming in contact with the holy abode of YHWH." He is on the right track (see below).

It must, however, be admitted that P's precise distinction between *ṭimmē'* 'pollute' and *ḥillēl* 'desecrate' begins to dissolve in H and even more so in Ezekiel. It has already been noticed that the pollution (*ṭm'*) of the land in H is a metaphoric, nonritual concept (18:25, 27; cf. Ezek 23:17) and that idolatry (i.e., Molek worship) pollutes the sanctuary (20:3), again a nonritualistic usage. (Note that Ezekiel uses for the same offense *ḥillel* [e.g., 23:39], and he is technically correct.) The name of God is desecrated (*ḥll*; e.g., 18:21; 20:3); the only exception is a passage in Ezekiel that uses *ṭm'*, not incidentally in a passage dealing with corpse-contamination of the sanctuary (Ezek 43:7–8). YHWH's *mišmeret*, which I render "proscriptions" (22:9), are desecrated (*ḥll*) in a pollution (*ṭm'*) context (22:3–8), again a metaphoric usage, but here once more the reference is to YHWH (*mišmartî* 'my proscriptions'), which can be only (in H) desecrated, not polluted. In the same chapter (22:15), sanctums (*qodāšîm*) are in danger of being desecrated (*ḥll*) by nonpriests, vv. 10, 13b—this time a correct, precise usage.

These examples illustrate the fluidity of P's technical terms in H, a subject that is taken up in the Introduction I C.

5. (*They shall*) *not. lō'*. The LXX, Sam., and Pesh. read *wělō'*, thereby connecting v. 5 with vv. 1–4 and implying that even the *šě'ēr*, the named, closest relatives of the deceased, who may defile themselves in attending the burial rites, still are forbidden to engage in the mourning practices prohibited in this verse (Welch 1925). Ehrlich (1908) suggests that the original *waw* fell out because of haplography.

make . . . bald patches on their heads. yiqrěḥû(h K) *qorḥâ běrō'šām*. The Ketib *yqrḥh* has probably been influenced by the adjoining cognate accusative *qrḥh* (Hartley 1992). The switch from singular to plural may be for the purpose of emphasizing that these rites are forbidden to all priests, including those who may attend funeral rites (vv. 2–3).

The LXX adds *lāmēt* 'for the dead', perhaps due to the influence of Deut 14:1. This verse, which imposes this ban on all Israelites, qualifies it by limiting it to *bên 'ênêkem* 'the front of your heads' (*NJPS*; cf. NAB). As recognized by the rabbis (*Sipre* Deut. 96), this prohibition applies to only rites of mourning; it does not apply at other times. There are clear references in Scripture that this was an idolatrous practice (e.g., among the Moabites, Isa 15:2; the Philistines, Jer 47:5; and in general, Bar 6:30–31; see COMMENT C). But it was widely indulged among the Israelites, evoking apparently no censure from the prophets (e.g., Isa 3:24; 22:12; Jer 16:6; Ezek 7:18; Amos 8:10; Mic 1:16; Job 1:20)!

Shedding tears and hair awards honor to the dead (Homer, *Odyssey* 4.197). On the death of their leader, Persians cut off their hair and that of their animals (Herod. 9.24). Locks of hair were placed on the bier, corpse, or tomb. It was customary for pre-Islamic Arabs to deposit their shorn hair at a tomb of a revered saint (Goldziher 1971: 249). An analogy persists in the custom of present-day

Hasidim who pilgrimage to Meron in the Galilee on Lag ba-Omer in order to cut their children's hair for the first time at the purported tomb of R. Simeon bar Yoḥai.

The purpose of cutting hair for the dead is most likely the same as that of the well-attested donation of hair to the sanctuary. Since hair continues to grow throughout life (and appears to do so for a time after death), it was considered by the ancients to be the seat of a man's vitality and life force, and in ritual it often served as his substitute. A bowl dating from the ninth century B.C.E. found in a Cypriot temple contains an inscription on its outside surface indicating that it contained the hair of the donor. It was placed there, if the reconstructed text is correct, as "a memorial" to Astarte, as a permanent reminder to the goddess of the donor's devotion.

The offering of hair is also attested in later times in Babylonia (*ANET* 339–40), Syria (Lucian, *De Syria Dea* 55, 60), Greece (Meuli 1946), and Arabia (Smith 1927: 331, 483). Lucian's (*De Dea Syria* 60) comment merits quotation: "The young men make an offering of their beards, while the young women let their 'sacred locks' grow from birth, and when they finally come to the temple, they cut them. When they have placed them in containers, some of silver and many of gold, they nail them up to the temple, and they depart after each inscribes his name. When I was still a youth I, too, performed this ceremony and even now my locks and name are in the sanctuary." Absalom, we are told, was wont to cut his hair *miqqēṣ yāmîm layyāmîm* (2 Sam 14:26). If this phrase is rendered "annually at the yearly feast" (cf. 1 Sam 1:21), then the possibility exists that Absalom offered up his shorn hair at the sanctuary.

What I am suggesting is that shaving the head or cutting the beard for mourning the dead is simply an aspect of the cult of the dead. Let us keep in mind that these rites are not the impulsive, anguished acts of grief (contrast Ezra 9:3). Shaving and polling hair is performed carefully, deliberately. And, I submit, there is good chance that this hair—the symbol and essence of life—was offered as a sacrifice to the god(s) of the dead (on the sacrifice of hair, see Milgrom 1990a: 356–57). Israel's priests and, in particular, H, intent on eradicating the pervasive and tenacious cult of the dead (see chap. 20, COMMENT C), would have spared no effort to inculcate that these mourning rites were forbidden by YHWH.

Indirect supporting evidence may be derived from the fact that the ordinary priest is not forbidden to dishevel his hair and rend his clothes, as is the high priest (v. 10b; see NOTES on 10:6). The ordinary priest is therefore permitted to indulge in all other rites of mourning that do not involve cutting his hair (or his flesh; see below). Thus there has to be a specific reason why the removal of hair is proscribed. I submit that lurking in the background is the cult of the dead, a possibility that, I believe, will be enhanced by the prohibition to gash the flesh (see below).

or shave off the edge of their beards. ûpĕ'at zĕqānām lō' yĕgallēḥû. This prohibition is functionally equivalent to that imposed on the laity: *wĕlō' tašḥît 'et pĕ'at zeqānekā* 'You shall not destroy the side-growth of your beard' (19:27b). Ezekiel telescopes the two prohibited mourning rites for the priest into a single statement *wĕrō'šām lō' yĕgallēḥû* 'They shall not shave their heads', but then adds *ûpera' lō' yĕšallēḥû* 'They shall not let their hair go untrimmed'. Ezekiel imposes the severe restriction placed on the high priest (Lev 21:10bα) on all priests and adds on a positive note *kāsôm yiksĕmû 'et-rā'šêhem* 'They shall (always) keep their hair trimmed' (Ezek 44:20). Aaron's sons have been given a similar prohibition (10:6), not because they anticipate Ezekiel but because, exceptionally, they have been anointed with the sacred oil of anointment and are, therefore, equivalent in holiness to the high priest (see NOTES on 10:6).

Cutting or shaving the edge of the beard was practiced in mourning (Jer 41:5) and was a regular practice among some of Israel's neighbors (e.g., Jer 9:25; 25:23).

or make gashes in their flesh. ûbibśārām lō' yiśrĕṭû śārāṭet. The same prohibition holds for the laity (19:28; see its NOTE). It is repeated here because it disqualifies the priest (Ibn Ezra) or because pagan priests engaged in such a practice in the cult (1 Kgs 18:28; Hoffmann 1953). However, as pointed out in the NOTE to 19:28, this practice was commonly followed by worshipers at the altar as a means of offering up their life, symbolized by the blood, to their god(s). In this respect, it was functionally equivalent to pulling or shaving the hair and, as part of the funeral rites, may have served as an integral element in the cult of the dead.

The prohibition against tattooing (19:28aβ) is lacking here. Rather than suggesting that it was not considered a mourning rite (Elliger 1966), it might have been encompassed by the prohibition against gashing the flesh, since it, too, involved blood-letting incisions (Smith 1927: 334).

6. *They shall be holy to their God. qĕdōšîm yihyû lē'lōhêhem.* Note the similar injunction to the laity *wihyîtem lî qĕdōšîm* 'You shall be holy to me' (20:26). Thus both have to aspire to holiness: the priests to retain it, the laity to attain it. Note that both vv. 6 and 26 (and all other references to the holiness quality of Israel, adjectival *qādōš*) use the *lamed* of possession with the object, God, implying that both priests and laity should (imperfect *yihyu*) aim to belong or remain (in the case of priests) in the divine sphere (see also vv. 7, 8, priests; Num 15:40, Israel; and Num 6:8, the Nazirite; Milgrom 1990a: 355–58).

The consistent use of *qādōš* with *lamed* in connection with Israel contrasts sharply in regard to the Deity, who is described as *qādōš* without a *lamed* or any other modifier. For the ostensible exception of the priest at the end of this verse, see below; and for the unique usage of *qādōš* in v. 8, see its NOTE.

their God . . . their God. 'ĕlōhêhem . . . 'ĕlōhêhem. It is obvious that when a suffix is required, *'ĕlōhîm* rather than YHWH will be used. As Tigay (1996: 239) points out, the expression "your God" or so-and-so's God is employed when speaking to or about priests, prophets, and kings, "because their offices were established by God and they were considered especially close to Him." It is also consistently found in H following the verb *yārē'* 'fear' (19:14, 32; 25:17, 36, 43). The reason may be that the term *yir'at 'ĕlōhîm* 'fear of God' has the wider meaning of proper moral or ethical conduct, applicable to Israelite and non-Israelite alike (cf. Gen 20:11; 42:18; Deut 25:18; Job 1:1, 8) and, hence, the general term for God *'ĕlōhîm* is employed. It also occurs once after *qillēl* (24:15, but see its

NOTE) and *qinnē'* (Num 25:13). It is also used when it is preceded by YHWH and the latter is preceded by *'ănî* 'I', or *lipnê* 'before' (e.g., 23:28, 40; Num 10:9, but not in v. 10 because it is followed by *'ănî* YHWH). R. Simeon b. Azzai says, "Come and see. In all sacrificial contexts of the Torah *'ĕlōhîm, 'ĕlōhêkā, šadday, ṣĕbā'ôt* never appear, only the special name YHWH, in order not to leave an opening for heretics to exploit" (*Sipre* Num. 143).

for they offer the gifts of YHWH, the food of their God. kî 'et-'iššê YHWH *lehem 'ĕlōhêhem hēm maqrîbîm.* Note the similar language of Num 28:2: *'et-qorbānî laḥmî lĕ'iššay . . . lĕhaqrîb lî* '(You shall be punctilious) to offer to me . . . my offering, my food, for my gifts'. That this verse also stems from the pen of H, see the Introduction I E. The term *lehem* 'food' is found nine times in chaps. 21–22 (21:6, 8, 17, 21, 22; 22:7, 11, 13, 25) and is characteristic of H, which is not averse to using anthropomorphisms.

The ostensibly redundant apposite phrase "the food of their God" is necessary (also in v. 21) to include the *ḥaṭṭā't*, which is not an *'iššeh*, among the sacrifices offered by the priest (see NOTE on 23:8).

and so must be holy. wĕhāyû qōdeš. 11Q PaleoLev, Sam., and the Versions read the plural *qĕdōšîm*, balancing the opening of the verse. The word *qōdeš* is a noun, but it is also employed adjectivally, with the high priest's gold plate (Exod 28:36; 39:30), and once with the priests (Ezra 8:28). The MT is therefore preferred because it has the more difficult reading (Sun 1990). That holiness is ascribed to the priests without the required object "to God / YHWH" perhaps is responsible for the change in vocalization from adjectival *qādōš*, which would imply that the holiness is inherent rather than acquired, to the nominal *qōdeš*. The rabbis correctly deduce from this clause that a priest can lose his holiness and disqualify himself (*Sipra* Emor 1:6). The root *qdš* appears seven times in vv. 6–8.

Vv. 7–9. Prohibitions Concerning Marriage

Ezekiel differs markedly from H. Whereas H permits a priest to marry a divorcee or a widow, Ezekiel expressly prohibits them, permitting only an Israelite virgin or the widow of a priest (Ezek 44:22). Is it possible that Ezekiel's stricter law echoes an earlier one of P that H suppressed in favor of its own law? Indeed, a more basic question rears its head: Why are other laws concerning the person of the priest, such as the purificatory rites incumbent on the priests, found in H (22:3–9) but missing in P? Again, is it possible that Ezekiel's severer law (Ezek 44:26–27) reflects an older P law supplanted by H? This possibility, though intriguing and entirely plausible, must be rejected. When H differs with P, it does so polemically: it states its law without suppressing the older version—for example, concering the *'āšām* (Num 5:6–8; cf. Lev 5:20–26) and the *ḥaṭṭā't* sacrifices (Num 15:22–26; cf. Lev 4:12–21; vol. 1.264–69; Knohl 1995: 171, n. 18, 176–79). In that way it pays honor to its priestly forbearers, while it differs with them respectfully.

The answer, I suggest, may simply be revealed in the organizational structure for Leviticus. H, I have maintained, integrates the laws of P into its overall redaction of the book of Leviticus. Chaps. 21–22, dealing with priestly matters, have been reworked by H in order to accentuate the doctrine of holiness, and then sandwiched between chaps. 19–20 and chap. 23, which emphasize the holiness incumbent on the laity. It is, therefore, no accident that the key root *qdš* is packed into these chapters sixty-six times. Thus the editorial plan of H, not its purported difference with P, is responsible for the surfacing priesthood laws in H. As for Ezekiel, it could well be that his dissenting laws are not his concoction, but stem from some earlier sanctuary, and they were rejected by the Jerusalem Temple, which emerged from the Josianic reform as the only legitimate sanctuary in the land (tentatively, see Gardiner 1881; Margaliot 1951; Haran 1968b; McConville 1983).

7. *a promiscuous woman.* *'iššâ zōnâ.* According to R. Akiba (*b. Yeb.* 61b) but the sages render other opinions (see also *Sipra* Emor 1:7). The reason for the prohibition is also practical: the priest would never be sure that the offspring would be his (Hartley 1992).

In Second Temple times, the lineage of a woman marrying a priest was carefully investigated (Philo, *Laws* 1.101 [who insist on a virgin, the high priest's requirement of Lev 21:13]; Jos. *Con. Ap.* 1:31–36; *m. Qidd.* 4:4; *t. Qidd.* 5:4; but see Lieberman 1967: 295). The precedent, however, had been set at the beginning of this period when the exiles returned from Babylon (Ezra 2:61–63). The sectaries of Qumran were even stricter: they imposed the priestly prohibition on all Israel *LHZYR MN HZWNOT* 'to refrain from whores' (CD 7:1). But in their view, the *zōnâ* also includes the gentile, as two recently published Qumran documents make clear:

W'L HZWNWT HN'SH BTWK H'M WHMH B[NY 'DT TMYMY] QDŠ MŠKTWB QWDŠ YŚR'L W'L BH[MTW HTHWR]H KTWB ŠLW' LRB 'H KL'YM W'L LBWŠ[W KTWB ŠLW'] YHYH Š'ṬNZ WŠLW' LZRW' ŚDW WK[RMW KL'Y]M WBGLL ŠHMH QDWŠYM WBNY 'HRWN Q[DWŠY QDWŠYM W']TM YWD'YM ŠMQṢT HKHNYM W[H'M MT'RBYM WH'M] MTWKKYM WMṬM'Y[M] 'T ZR' [HQWD]Š [W'P] 'T [ZR']M 'M HZWNWT

And concerning the mixed marriage [cf. Segal 1989: 51, n. 27] that is being performed among the people, and they are s[ons of a congregation perfect in] holiness, as it is written, Israel is holy. And concerning [his (Israel's) pure ani]mal it is written that one should not let it make two species, and concerning his clothes [it is written that they should not] be of mixed stuff; and one must not sow his field and vine[yard with mixed specie]s because they (Israel) are holy and the sons of Aaron are [most holy a]nd you know that some of the priests and [the laity are mixing and] intermarrying and defiling the [holy] seed [as well] as [their own see]d with outside women. (*MMT* B 75–82)

LHGY 'M BṬHRT [HQW]DŠ KY' ṬM'YM [HMH
B 'LWT LBNY HNKR WLKWL HZNWT 'ŠR [
R'[WY] LW LH'KYLM MKWL TRWMT HQ[DŠM

To give (them) access to the [sac]red purities because [they] are impure [. . .
fornicating with gentile men and to all the promiscuity which [. . .
(It is) pro[per] for him to let them eat from all the sa[cred] *těrûmôt* [. . .
4Q513, frag. 2, col. II [Baillet 1982: 287–95, corrected by Baumgarten 1985:
394]

As interpreted by Baumgarten (1985: 393–95), "fornication" is charged against
the priests, who, therefore, are unworthy of eating sacred *těrûmâ* (the first portion of every crop set aside for the priests; cf. Num 18:11–12) and touching "the
sacred purities" (i.e., the sectaries' joint meals). The second line, echoing *ûbā 'al
bat-'ēl nēkār* 'and espoused [lit. "had sexual intercourse with"] daughters of alien
gods' (Mal 2:11), apparently refers to mixed marriages with women from priestly
households. From this, we can plausibly deduce that the impure priests were
also guilty of marrying gentiles. This change is intimated by the term *ZNWT*,
one of the three nets of Belial, attributed to the warning by the patriarch Levi
(CD 4:16–17; although it is applied to polygamy and niece marriages, 4:21,
5:8–11), and is confirmed (boldface) in the Greek text of the Testament of Levi
(9:9–10): "Be on guard against the spirit of **promiscuity,** for it is constantly active and through your descendants it is about to pollute the sanctuary. Therefore take for yourself a wife while you are still young, a wife who is free of blemish or pollution, **who is not from the race of alien nations."**

Thus the Qumranites are far stricter than the Torah and even Ezekiel (44:22).
They ban the priests from marrying lay Israelites (the high priest's prohibition, Lev 21:14b; cf. Philo, *Laws* 101), and they prohibit both from marrying
gentiles.

It is illuminating that other cultures also ordain severe marital requirements
for their priestly class. In Hindu law, for example, the first wife of a Brahman
must be a virgin of a pious and healthy family of his own caste (cf. the rule for
the high priest, Lev 21:13–14), must have no reddish hair or any deformed limb,
and must have a pleasing and auspicious name, "whose gait is graceful like that
of a flamingo or young elephant" (Manu 3:6–12).

or one who was raped. wahălālâ. This problematic term has received many interpretations:

1. The rabbis (and halakha) declare that this woman is the product of a forbidden marriage (enumerated in chaps. 18, 20). Philo (*Laws* 1.101) avers that
a priest should marry "a pure virgin whose parents and grandparents and ancestors are equally pure, highly distinguished for the excellence of their conduct
and lineage." Although Colson (1968: 1.158) is correct in asserting that this requirement has no scriptural authority, it accords, according to Belkin (1940:
236), with the tannaitic ruling that the priest must be certain of her ancestry
four generations back (*m. Qid.* 4:3).

2. Many modern translations, on the basis of its asyndetic link with *zōnâ* in

v. 14, render it as a hendiadys—for example, "a woman degraded by harlotry" (*NJPS*); "a woman who has been defiled" (*NRSV*). Weinfeld (1983b) offers a philological argument in favor of the hendiadys hypothesis. He finds that the verb *ḥillēl* is associated with trampling or throwing to the ground. For example, *higgîaʿ lāʾāreṣ ḥillēl mamlākâ wĕśārêhā* 'he brought (them) to the ground; he has dishonored the kingdom and its leaders' (Lam 2:1–2); *ḥillaltā lāʾāreṣ nizrô* 'you have dragged his dignity in the dust' (Ps 89:40b *NJPS*; see also Isa 23:8; Ezek 28:7–8, 15). Furthermore, he argues that *ḥll* and *znh* appear together, as in "Do not profane your daughter by making her a harlot (19:29; 21:7, 14). Thus he concludes that *ḥalălâ*, connoting "disgrace, defame," can be an attribute of *zōnâ*. Nonetheless, I must reject the hendiadys hypothesis. The term *zōnâ* is precise enough and requires no descriptive attribute. After all, is there a category such as a *zōnâ* who is not degraded or disgraced? Moreover, that the order of these two words is reversed in v. 14 can be explained only by the ascending order of the prohibitions (see NOTE on v. 14).

3. Snaith (1967) renders "used (by a man)," based on the use of the root *ḥll* to permit the use of firstfruits after the priestly portion has been removed (e.g., Deut 20:6; 28:30; Jer 31:5). Besides being a nonpriestly usage, this interpretation is invalidated by the fact that an ordinary priest is permitted to marry a "used" widow. For the same reason, "a girl who has lost her virginity" (*NEB*; Wenham 1979) is also invalidated.

4. Levin (1984) derives this term from conjectured *mĕḥōlĕlôt* 'dancers' (1 Sam 18:6), or women devoted to sacred prostitution.

5. Zipor (1987) argues that *ḥalălâ* means "cultic prostitute," normally expressed by *qĕdēsâ* (e.g., Deut 23:18), a term that, for obvious reasons, would not be used in a priestly text. However, the notion that sacred prostitution existed in Israel or even in the ancient Near East has been vigorously and convincingly refuted by Gruber (1983a; 1986), Hooks (1985), Goodfriend (1989; 1992) and van der Toorn (1989a; 1992) (see NOTE on 19:29).

6. "One who was raped," the translation accepted here. First it should be noticed that the prohibited women are listed in descending order of their defect. Thus *ḥalălâ* must be less offensive than a *zōnâ* and more offensive than a *gĕrûšâ* 'divorcee'. This means that if she was willing, she is a *zōnâ*, but if forced, she is a *ḥalălâ* (Ehrlich 1908; Elliger 1966; Kornfeld 1972). Then, on the basis of the root *ḥll* I 'desecrate, profane', Ezekiel exclaims *wĕʾattā ḥālāl rāšāʿ nĕśîʾ yiśrāʾēl* 'You, O desecrated one, wicked one, prince of Israel' (Ezek 21:30). Adding to that notion is *ḥll* II 'pierce'. Thus the *ḥālāl/ḥalălâ* is "the desecrated pierced one," or "raped."

In the ancient Near East, rape was considered a stigma. In the laws of Ur-Nammu and Sumer, deflowering is described in the context of rape (*ANET* 524, 526). In Israel, however, there is no stigma attached to a raped (or seduced) single girl (Deut 22:28–29)—if she is the daughter of a layman. But a stigma may very well exist if she is the daughter of a priest. (She may even be suspect of complicity.) Consider the case of a husband who finds that his bride is not a virgin; for her deception, she is put to death. However, a priest's daughter who is neither married nor betrothed, but just promiscuous, is burned by fire (v. 9). Finally, in view of the high degree of purity demanded of priest's bride in Second Temple times (see above), it is altogether plausible that in the biblical period, rape disqualified a woman from marrying a priest.

marry . . . marry. yiqqāḥû . . . yiqqāḥû. As pointed out by Paran (1979: 130), the two prohibitions could have been combined as objects of one of the two identical verbs, as indeed happens in v. 14. The only possible reason for the doubling is aesthetic, to convey a rhythmic effect (see NOTE on 19:28).

a woman divorced from her husband. wĕ'iššâ gĕrûšâ mē'îšāh. Why is she, but not a widow, forbidden? Clearly, divorce must be a stigma, though a lesser one (last on the list). The exemption of the widow would, therefore, indicate that the prohibition focuses on reputation, not on virginity. The purity of the priestly line is thus not only a matter of biology (i.e., in-breeding), as demanded by Ezek 44:22. The divorcee may be suspected of other deficiencies: she may be pregnant, barren (B. Leigh), or unfaithful (Abravanel). None of these changes would have been levied against a widow.

The school of Shammai allows only marital infidelity as grounds for divorce, based on *'erwat dābār* (Deut 24:1), which it interprets as sexual misconduct. The school of Hillel, however, broadens the interpretation of this phrase (*b. Giṭ.* 90a). R. Yishmael b. Yossi, in apparent agreement with Shammai, uses *'erwat dābār* as a reason for Israel's exile (*'Abot R. Nat.*[1] 38).

For each (priest) is holy to his God. kî-qādōš hû' lē'lōhāyw. The switch in number is not surprising; it is characteristic of H (e.g., 22:8–9).

Whereas Israelites are enjoined to strive for holiness (19:2; 20:26), priests are inherently holy, though they, too, must strive to maintain it (see NOTES on "must be holy," v. 6, and "sanctifies him," v. 15).

8. *and you must treat him as holy. wĕqiddaštô.* Israel is apostrophized in a second-person address (Moses relays God's message to the priests, not to Israel, v. 1). Nowhere in the priestly texts are priests referred to in the third person when the address, in the second person, is to the Israelites (Wellhausen 1963: 156–57). Noth (1977) declares this verse secondary. It clearly does not fit the structure of the chapter (see COMMENT A). If so, why was it inserted? Perhaps for a stylistic or aesthetic reason: it brings the number of *qdš* forms in vv. 6–8 up to seven. More likely, it adds a new element: the laity's responsibility to the priest.

Kugler (1997: 27) argues that "the authors of Leviticus 17–26 were not particularly pro-priestly." This one word *wĕqiddaštô* belies his conclusion. Besides, H does not deny any of the perquisites granted him by P. To the contrary, H takes pains to allow the blemished priest the priestly portions of all the sacrifices (21:22), indicating the extent to which the H school is concerned about the welfare of its fellow priests.

The rabbis cite two opinions:

1. Since the text does not use the *Hitpa'el* reflexive *wĕyitqaddēš* 'he shall keep holy', but the *Pi'el* active *wĕqiddaštô*, Israel is responsible for the priest's maintaining his holy status, even if he is unwilling (*Sipra* Emor 1:13). Thus, connecting this verse with the previous one, Israel must prevent him from entering

into a forbidden marriage. Or, put in a more positive way, each Israelite (sing.) must see to it that his daughter qualifies for marriage with a priest.

2. "One should not see him while he is naked, at the barber, or in the bath house. . . . However, he is permitted to invite others to bathe with him" (*t. Sanh.* 4:1). "The school of R. Ishmael taught: (Give him precedence) to open proceedings, to say grace first, and to choose his portion first" (*b. Giṭ.* 59b; cf. 1QS 6:3–4, 8). In other words, show him the respect due his status.

In P, *qiddēš* (*Pi ʿel*) denotes "sanctify (by ritual)" (e.g., priests, Exod 28:3; 29:1, 33; sanctums, Exod 29:44; 30:29). The unique connotation "treat as holy" occurring here is a sure sign of H, which typically bestows metaphoric meanings to P terms (see Introduction I C; NOTE on "sanctifies you"; and NOTE on 20:8).

Gerstenberger (1996: 315) correctly observes that this verse (rather, this word) proves that Israel is the real addressee of this chapter. It is cut of the same cloth as v. 24—both interpolations by an H tradent. It affirms that priestly behavior, as prescribed in the chapter, falls under Israelite supervision.

sanctifies you. *mĕqaddiškem.* This word presents two problems that are really one: the suffix. It is plural and refers to Israel, and neither the word's form nor its referent can be countenanced by the content of the verse. Ibn Ezra suggests that the plural is used because it refers to the sanctification of the priests as well as the laity; Ramban (followed by Knohl 1995: 191) adds that Israel is sanctified through the priests. These explanations are patently forced.

The LXX, Sam., and 11QPaleoLev read *mĕqaddšām* 'sanctifies them', referring to the priests (cf. v. 15; 22:9, 16; followed by Driver and White 1894–98; Dillmann and Ryssel 1897). The third-person plural might be explained as a minor inclusio for vv. 5–8, which also begin with the priests in the third-person plural. How, then, can the "error" *mĕqaddiškem* be accounted for? Was it, perhaps, inserted to balance the same word in 22:32 in order to create an inclusio for chaps. 21–22?

The sense of the *Pi ʿel* is explored in the NOTE on 20:8, where Israel is addressed. If the emendation is accepted, the significance is amplified: the priests, no differently from the laity, must work at holiness. Even though the priests are born holy, they can easily defile their status if they ignore or violate the marital specifications listed in v. 7, just as they can do so by violating the mourning practices listed in vv. 1–6 (see NOTE on "and so must be holy," v. 6).

The ancient Near East may have known something parallel to the fluctuating holiness of Israel's priests. According to the Sumerian *Nanshe Hymn* (Heimpel 1981; Gane 1998: 2), the goddess Nansha would review "the men on the attendance list" each year and terminate the service of unfaithful workers. "She would be calling for eyewitnesses among them to a runaway of hers, the witnesses to (one) of hers who had absconded from the temple, and shaking the head she would be discontinuing his position and box (of records)" (ll. 106–9). Similarly, the goddess Inanna would maintain a review of her servants on New Year's Day, "the day for rites for reviewing loyal servants and performing correctly the rites of the last day of the worker" (Jacobsen 1987: 122).

Akkadian literature records refer not only to yearly review and reappointment of temple officials, but also to their promotion and demotion on New Year's Day (Heimpel 1981: 68; van der Toorn 1989b: 5).

The differences with H should not be overlooked. Chief among them is the total absence of evaluations for the people. Israel alone had covenantal obligations to its Deity, whose fulfillment was meticulously noted, according to H, by its status of holiness.

9. *desecrates herself by harlotry.* tēḥēl liznôt. This Nipʿal reflexive does not mean "begins" (Pesh.), which would be vocalized tāḥēl, Hipʿil (Ibn Ezra). Ordinarily, it would have read tēḥal (e.g., Isa 48:11); the ṣērê is due to the ḥet.

The rabbis cannot accept that the death penalty—an excruciating one, by fire—is imposed on a single, unattached woman; they differ only on whether she was betrothed or married (*Sipra* Emor 1:15; *b. Sanh.* 50b, 51b).

I must reckon with the possibility that by "harlotry," premarital sex is intended. It has been shown that although some societies may be permissive in sexual matters in regard to commoners, they are restrictive in regard to royalty. For example, the Samoans prescribe the death penalty to royal girls who engage in premarital sex (Cohen 1969: 673). Thus, as far as H is concerned, JE and D's laxity (Exod 22:15–16; Deut 22:28–29), which it apparently accepts (note H's silence in chaps. 18 and 20), does not apply to daughters of its royalty, the priests. (D does prescribe the death penalty for premarital sex only when knowledge of it is withheld from the groom, Deut 22:20–21; cf. Shadal; for the possibility that Deut 22:20–21 is a later interpolation, see Rofé 1988: 144–51).

it is her father whom she desecrates. ʾet-ʾābîhā hîʾ mĕḥallelet. In this verse, the twice attested ḥll apparently takes on a metaphoric connotation, typical of H (e.g., cf. maʿal 26:40 with 5:15; Weinfeld 1983b: 197).

The rabbis declare likewise: "If he (the father) was regarded as holy, he is now regarded as profane [ḥōl]; if he was treated with respect, he is now treated with contempt; and men say, 'Cursed be he who begot her, cursed be he who brought her up, cursed be he from whose loins she sprung' " (*b. Sanh.* 52a). Note also Saadiah's translation "whom she shames." Nevertheless, I render both instances by the verb's technical meaning: "desecrate." The fact that she "sprang from the loins" of a priest means that she partakes of his holiness, which she diminishes, as would a priest (v. 7), by her promiscuity. Indeed, as a member of a priest's family, she literally absorbs holiness by partaking of her father's portion of holy (but not most holy) sacrifices (10:14; Num 18:11, 19; cf. Lev 22:10–13). Thus "her purity was more criticized than that of Israelite women" (Countryman 1988: 38). To be sure, ḥll, indeed, is metaphoric regarding the priest, since in no way does it disqualify the father from officiating in the sanctuary. However, as the rabbis well recognize, her action casts a stigma on her father. In all likelihood, he has no desire to be seen in the company of his fellow priests; it is *as though* he were disqualified.

Recently published 4QLevᶜ reads ʾet bêt [ʾābîhā] (as does *Tg. Ps.-J.*) as "her father's house" (Tov 1995: 264), which points to a total metaphoric usage of ḥillēl 'desecrate' in this context.

Gerstenberger (1996: 314) rightly asks why Leviticus speaks only of errant daughters and not of disreputable priests (1 Sam 2:12–13, 22–36; 1 Sam 8:1–3), and why women are excluded from the priesthood. He wrongly answers that this "attests the priestly prejudice against women." Such prejudice is undoubtedly present in Scripture, but it has nothing to do with Gerstenberger's questions. First, the cited example of Eli's sons proves that dishonorable sons not only dishonor their father, but can cause the disqualification of his line. Second, the woman's ineligibility for the priesthood is based on purely practical grounds: the impurity of her menses disqualifies her from serving for one week out of every four (and as much as three months during parturition). Extreme caution should be exercised in attributing prejudice, especially where it can be shown that none exists.

she shall be burned by fire. The unfaithful *married* or *betrothed* daughter of a layman (20:10; Deut 22:23–24) was put to death by stoning, whereas even a promiscuous *single* daughter of a layman was probably stigmatized socially, but was unpunished by the court. However, the older practice for punishing adultery was death by fire (Gen 38:24; Judg 15:6). The Samson incident (Judg 15) shows that the instigator of the adultery, in this case the father, is also burned. Note that in contrast to the lay bride, who is stoned at her father's house (Deut 22:21), indicating his culpability in fomenting the deceit that she was a virgin, the burning of the priest's daughter does not take place at the father's home; he is not held responsible for her harlotry.

> The manner in which burning is executed is as follows: He who was thus condemned was lowered into dung up to his armpits. Then a hard cloth was placed within a soft one, wound around his neck, and the two loose ends pulled in opposite ends forcing him to open his mouth. A wick was then lit, and thrown into his mouth, so that it descended into his body and burned his bowel. R. Judah said: Should he, however, have died at their hands (being strangled by the bandage instead of by the wick), he would not have been executed by fire as prescribed. Hence, it was done thus: His mouth was forced open with pincers against his wish, the wick lit and thrown into his mouth, so that it descended into his body and burned his bowels.
>
> R. Eleazar b. Zadok said: It once happened that a priest's daughter committed adultery, whereupon bundles of faggots were placed round about her and she was burned. The sages replied, that was because the court at that time was not learned in the law. (*m. Sanh.* 7:2)

In contrast to the Sadducees, who believed in literal burning (see also *Jub* 41:25), the Pharisees held that "the soul [*nĕšāmâ*] is burned, but the body is intact" (*b. Sanh.* 52a). However, R. Eleazar witnessed (probably before the destruction of the Second Temple) a priest's daughter being burned alive. That Achan and his family were burned after they had been killed by stoning (Josh 7:15, 25) is an exceptional case—probably to deprive them of normal burial rites.

Vv. 10–15. The High Priest

These verses clearly constitute a unified structure containing six prohibitions in which the negative particle *lō'* and a verb end each prohibition, except in the sixth, where they begin the prohibition as a "closing deviation" (Paran 1983: 149). Also the entire pericope is enclosed by the term *šemen hammišḥâ* 'anointing oil' (see further COMMENT A).

10. *The priest who is preeminent among his fellows. wĕhakkōhēn haggādôl mē'eḥāyw.* According to Hoffmann (1953), this is the full title of the high priest, whereas *hakkōhēn haggādôl* is its abbreviation. However, the Masoretic cantillations indicate that it is not a title, but a description (Elliger 1966). Moreover, that it must be further defined (v. 10aβγ) proves that it is not a title. The expression may be explained by the possibility that H refers to a practice or an event where the son who was anointed as high-priest designate *hammāšîaḥ taḥtāyw* (6:15; cf. 16:32) did not succeed, due to a change in the priestly line. Alternatively, the expression may be explained as the transitional stage between P's preexilic *hakkōhēn hammāšîaḥ* 'anointed priest' (4:3; vol. 1.231) and subsequent *hakkōhēn haggādôl* 'high priest' (Num 35:25, 28 [H?]; Josh 20:6; 2 Kgs 12:11; 22:4, 8; 23:4; Hag 1:1, 12, 14; 2:2, 4; Zech 3:1, 8; 6:11; Neh 3:1, 20; 13:28; 2 Chr 34:9). However, the latter title is attested by its exact cognates in antecedent cultures: *rb khnm* (Ugarit), *šangû rabû* (Assyria), and *pāšišu rabû* (Elam). Thus it is preferable to take this expression as a description.

To this very day, many scholars hold that the title *hakkōhēn haggādôl* is a postexilic creation (e.g., Dommershausen 1995: 71) and that its four attestations in 2 Kgs are "later modifications" (de Vaux 1961: 378). As evidence, de Vaux cites the parallels in Chronicles, where 2 Chr 24:11 (= 2 Kgs 12:11) has *kōhēn hārō'š* 'the chief priest'; 2 Chr 34:14,18 (= 2 Kgs 22:4, 8) has *hakkōhēn*, and "the Greek version of 2 Kg 23:4 also presumes the reading *hakkōhēn*." His evidence is invalidated for three reasons:

1. The adjectives *hārō'š* and *haggādôl* are virtual synonyms and interchangeable. Thus if Seraiah was called *kōhēn hārō'š* (2 Kgs 25:18 = Jer 52:24), he just as well could have been called *hakkōhēn haggādôl*. Indeed, this is precisely the case in 2 Kgs 12:11 and 2 Chr 24:11 (cf. Cogan and Tadmor 1988: 138).

2. 2 Kgs 22:4, 8 and 2 Chr 34:14, 18 have to be compared *in context*. As 2 Kgs 22:4 introduces Hilkiah, his full title is essential. In v. 8, he is mentioned alongside Shafan the Scribe; as the latter is given a title, so is the former. In contrast, 2 Chr 34:14, 18 refer to Hilkiah as *hakkōhēn* because he already has been introduced (v. 4); thereafter, he remains *hakkōhēn* or is untitled throughout the chapter (vv. 14, 15 [bis], 18, 20, 22).

3. De Vaux's (1961) evidence of the Greek for 2 Kgs 23:4 is taken from the Syrohexapla, ostensibly based on the oldest Greek text. However, he failed to observe that Origen put asterisks around the entire phrase *hakkōhēn haggādôl* (correctly noted by BHS), not just around *haggādôl* (cf. Šanda 1912). According to this reading, Hilkiah had no title at all. Considering that he is followed by mention of *kōhănê hammišneh* 'priests of the second order', Hilkiah's superior status had to be stated. This Greek text must therefore be rejected.

In sum, at the end of the First Temple period, two synonymous titles for the high priest are in currency: *kōkĕn hārō'š* and *hakkōhēn haggādôl*. Our verse Lev 21:10 is disqualified as evidence since it is a description, not a title. One may suggest, however, that its use of *haggādôl* may be an allusion to the title. In any event, the reference to the anointment of the high priest with the sacred oil squarely puts this verse into a preexilic setting, since the anointment oil was not used in the Second Temple. (The same deduction can be made for P's title *hakkōhēn hammāšîaḥ* 'the anointed priest', 4:3; cf. vol. 1.231.)

on whose head the anointing oil has been poured. *'ăšer-yûṣaq 'al-rō'šô šemen hammišḥâ.* A clear reference to *wayyiṣōq miššemen hammišḥâ 'al rō'š 'ahărōn* (8:12 [P]), this is another indication of the lateness of H in relation to P. Pouring oil on the head of a high priest or priestess as part of the consecration rites is neither unique nor original with Israel. A similar rite was performed at the installation of Baal's high priestess at Late Bronze Emar (fourteenth to thirteenth century B.C.E.; Fleming 1990: 56, 59). The purpose of mentioning this specific rite is to distinguish the high priest, who exclusively, as at Emar, is anointed on the head, from ordinary priests, who are anointed only on their clothing (8:30). Thus there is no basis for positing the two rites as stages in a development from anointing only the high priest to including all the priests (de Vaux 1961: 105; Noth 1967). Rather, both rites can more plausibly be understood as parallel customs (Fleming 1995: 143).

and who has been ordained to wear the (priestly) vestments. *ûmillē' 'et-yādô lilbōš 'et-habbĕgādîm.* Note the similar phraseology *wa'ăšer yĕmallē' 'et-yādô* (*lĕkahēn taḥat 'ābîw*, 16:32 [H]) in contrast with the description of the high priest's officiating garments (Exod 28; 29:5–6; Lev 8:7–9 [P]) and the specification of the length of the consecration rites, *kî šib'at yāmîm yĕmallē' 'et yedĕkem* (8:33b [P]), which again leads to the conclusion that H is dependent on P. The idiom *millē' yād* 'ordain' is explained in the NOTE on 8:33b.

The definite article on *habbĕgādîm* 'the vestments' means his prescribed officiating vestments. Other garments, even for such special occasions as the unique Yom Kippur rites, must be specified *wĕlābaš 'et-bigdê habbād bigdê haqqōdeš* 'He shall put on the linen vestments, the sacral vestments' (16:32 [H]).

shall not dishevel his hair. *'et-rō'šô lō' yiprā'.* Ramban connects v. 10b with v. 11 so that it refers to only the time of mourning (cf. *bĕša'at 'ănîqê* 'in the time of distress', *Tg. Ps.-J.*). Wessely (1846), however, argues that since v. 10b precedes v. 11, it is not limited to death but applies always. Ezek 44:20, where it stands as an independent prohibition, clearly has no time limit. Maimonides ("Entry into the Sanctuary" 1:10) refers to v. 12 as justification for this permanent ban—he may never leave the sacred precincts (but see below).

For the rendering "dishevel" as against "bare" (LXX), see the discussion in the NOTE on 10:6. Ezek 44:20 *ûpera' lō' yĕšallēḥû* 'and they shall not let their hair hang loose' (NAB) confirms this rendering, though it applies to every priest, a clear indication that Ezekiel's rule is later (cf. Fishbane 1985: 295, n. 11).

This act of mourning would entail the removal of the turban (8:9) and remaining bareheaded (cf. 10:6; 13:45) during the mourning period. Also, as pointed out by Gerstenberger (1996: 311), the prohibitions of vv. 5 and 10b must be understood cumulatively.

or rend his vestments. ûbĕgādāyw lō' yiprōm. For the possible distinction between the ostensible synonyms *qaraʿ* and *pāram*, see the NOTE on 10:6.

The high priest donned ordinary clothes when he left the sanctuary (Maimonides, *Temple Service,* "Temple Vessels" 1:5, 5, 7; cf. *m. Hor.* 3:5 and *b. Hor.* 12b). Thus when Mark 14:63 declares that the high priest rent his clothes because of Jesus' blasphemy, these were not his sacred vestments since the blasphemy was uttered in the high priest's home (v. 53). Gerstenberger (1996: 312) expresses surprise that Ezra, a priest, rent his clothes (Ezra 9:3, 5). However, he was not in mourning but in dismay, and, above all, these were his ordinary clothes, not priestly vestments. To be sure, Josephus (*Wars* 321–22) relates that priests (not the high priest) threatened to tear their sacred garments. However, the people's horrified reaction indicates that normally it was not and could not be done.

11. *He shall not go in where there is a dead body. wĕʿal kol-napšōt mēt lō' yābō'.* The preposition *ʿal* does not mean "on account of" (Levine 1989); "go near" (Pesh.) is a better rendering. It was probably chosen because the corpse is prostrate (Dillmann and Ryssel 1897), and a living person stands "over" it. Thus Pharoah *ʿōmēd ʿal-hayĕʾōr* 'stands by the Nile' (Gen 41:1), i.e., stands above its water level (see also Isa 6:2; Zech 4:14; Ps 1:3). An apposite analogy would be *bāʾ ʿal haḥălālîm* 'came upon the slain' (Gen 34:27), since, obviously, the slain are prostrate on the ground.

The plural construct *napšōt* interchanges with singular *nepeš* (e.g., Gen 46:15; 2 Sam 19:6), so there is no need to change over to the singular *nepeš* (LXX, perhaps under the influence of Num 6:6; see below). As pointed out in the NOTES to 19:28b and 21:1b, *nepeš* by itself can be elliptical for the full expression *nepeš mēt* 'corpse'. The word *mēt* is not an adjective (Ibn Ezra), but a noun (cf. Gen 23:3). And *yābō'* 'enter' implies that the corpse is inside an enclosure (Num 19:14b).

The principle of areal impurity or, to be more exact, overhang, is operative here. The severe impurity of the corpse (and the *meṣōrāʿ*; see NOTE on 14:46) fills the house in which it lies (vol. 1.986–1000).

The same prohibition is enjoined upon the Nazirite: *wĕʿal-nepeš mēt lō' yābō'* (Num 6:6b; note the sing. *mēt*). It is not a coincidence. In his or her taboos, the Nazirite approximates the greater sanctity of the high priest:

1. He or she may not become contaminated by the dead in the immediate family (Num 6:7; Lev 21:11; contrast the ordinary priest, vv. 1–4). Note the precise verbal similarity of their respective prohibitions: *ʿal-nepeš mēt lō' yābō' lĕʾābîw ûlĕʾimmô . . . lō' yiṭṭammāʾ lāhem bĕmōtām kî nēzer ʾĕlōhāyw ʿal-rōʾšô* 'he shall not go in where there is a dead body. Even for his father or mother . . . he shall not defile himself for them, for the distinction of his God is upon his head' (Num 6:6b–7); *wĕʿal kol-napšōt mēt lō' yābō' lĕʾābîw ûlĕʾimmô lō' yiṭṭamāʾ . . . kî nēzer šemen mišḥat ʾĕlōhāyw ʿālāyw* 'He shall not go in where there is a dead body; even for his father or mother he shall not defile himself

. . . for the distinction of the anointing oil of his God is upon him' (Lev 21:11, 12b). The only substantive difference is the addition of the qualification *šemen mišḥat* for the high priest, since he and not the Nazirite is anointed with the sacred oil (v. 12).

2. For the Nazirite, as for the high priest, the head was the focus of his or her sanctity (Num 6:11b; Exod 29:7; note the similar motive clauses, Num 6:7b; Lev 21:12b; and contrast the consecration rite of the ordinary priest, Lev 8:30).

3. The Nazirite abstained from intoxicants during the term of the vow (Num 6:4), actually a more stringent requirement than that of the high priest, whose abstinence, like that of his fellow priests, was limited to only the time he was inside the sacred precincts (Lev 10:9).

even for his father or mother he shall not defile himself. lĕ'ābîw ûlĕ'immô lō' yiṭṭammā'. Following the general rule in v. 11a, the specific case of v. 11b is enunciated for purposes of emphasis—"even for" (cf. Paran 1989: 128). The gradation in the corpse-contamination taboo is now complete: Israelites may contact the dead without restriction; priests, with only close relatives; and the high priest, with no one. What happens if the Nazirite or high priest *accidentally* contacts a corpse? The former contingency is foreseen by the priestly texts: the Nazirite vow is terminated and after the purification period, the Nazirite begins his or her term anew (Num 6:9–12). Nothing equivalent is said about the high priest. Presumably, his journeys outside the sanctuary were few and carefully supervised. Yet, presumably, accidents could and did happen (e.g., the death of Nadab and Abihu *within* the sacred precincts, 10:2). His place would immediately be taken by the son *hammāšiaḥ taḥtāyw* (6:15; 16:32), who had been anointed beforehand, precisely for that purpose. Thus Philo (*Laws* 1.113) exaggerates when he claims that "no one else is allowed to perform the functions of a high priest."

It was customary for sons to bury their father (e.g., Gen 25:9; 35:29; 50:12–13). Who, then, bore the responsibility of burying the father of the high priest? Obviously, it would fall on the priest's brother. If he had no brother, then on his paternal uncle. No other blood (priestly) relative would be eligible (vv. 1–4). What if the high priest had neither a brother nor a paternal uncle? Judging by the case of Nadab and Abihu (10:4), the burial would be conducted by a non-priestly member of his tribe, namely, a Levite.

12. *He shall not leave the sacred area. ûmin hammiqdāš lō' yēṣē'*. That *miqdāš* does not mean the sanctuary building but the *temenos*, the sacred area, see Milgrom (1970: 23–24, n. 78, correcting Knohl 1995: 63, n. 10). In his note, Knohl disputes my thesis, claiming that *miqdāš* should be given the customary rendering "sanctuary house." This verse proves the fallaciousness of his rendering. If it were true, then the high priest would be free to roam in the sanctuary courtyard, thoroughly polluting its sacrificial altar and the other sanctums stored within its quarters. The same criticism holds for the other attestations of *miqdāš* in H. The people are warned to revere the sanctuary (19:30; 26:2) because by entering it (but not the building, which is off limits to them!) they may pollute it (20:3). In punishing Israel, God will "make your sanctuaries desolate" (26:31),

not just the inner sanctums but, again, the altar and the other stored sanctums, located in the sacred area, as well the priests who work there preparing the public sacrifices and assisting the people with their private sacrifices.

Knohl misunderstands my remark on Exod 25:8. I admitted only the *possibility* that *miqdaš* in that verse might mean the sanctuary building, but he overlooked the continuation of my sentence: "but from the following verse *miqdaš* is defined as *hammiškān wĕ'et . . . kol-kēlāyw* 'the Tabernacle and all its furnishings', i.e., all the objects of the sacred area of which the Tabernacle is but one."

Does this prohibition imply that the high priest may never leave the sacred area? Kalisch (1867–72) replies in the affirmative: the high priest resides permanently in the sacred precincts, as Eli did in the Shilonite sanctuary (1 Sam 1:9; 3:2). Although Samuel slept inside the sanctuary itself (1 Sam 3:3), Eli must have slept nearby for Samuel to think that it was Eli who called him during the night. This "proof" is patently weak. Undoubtedly, Eli resided nearby, but with his family. The likelihood, then, is that the high priest's quarters adjoined the sanctuary, but were not within the *temenos*, the sacred area. Joshua, like Samuel, resided inside the sanctuary, "a youth would not stir out of the tent" (Exod 33:11b). It is no accident that both Joshua and Samuel are explicitly referred to as *na'ar* 'youth' (1 Sam 3:1), that is, they were unmarried.

However, the sanctuary envisioned by P (which I have surmised was the one at Shilo; vol. 1.29–32) implies that the high priest could leave the sacred premises. During the week-long consecration service, Aaron and his sons are enjoined: "You shall not go outside the entrance of the Tent of Meeting for seven days" (8:33a). And, more relevantly, on the day following the consecration rites, at the death of Nadab and Abihu, Aaron and his remaining sons are warned: "You must not go outside the entrance of the Tent of Meeting, lest you die, for YHWH's anointing oil is upon you" (10:7). Both these verses imply that ordinarily, the high priest may leave the sanctuary premises. Our verse, then, must be connected to the previous one (contra Gerstenberger 1996: 315–16). It is part of the high priest's mourning prohibitions: he may not leave the sanctuary to *follow the bier.*

There is no doubt that at the end of Second Temple times, the high priest's private quarters were located outside the premises of the sanctuary (e.g., Mark 14:53–54; see NOTE on "or rend his vestments," v. 10). This fact is confirmed by the rabbis (cf. *m. Yoma* 1:1). Moreover, the rabbis discuss the high priest's behavior when he suffers the loss of a family member: "If a death happens in his family, he must not walk immediately behind the bier (even though he does not contact the corpse), but when they (the mourners) disappear, he may show himself; when they appear (in one street), he must be hidden (be one street behind the cortege). He may go with them as far as the entrance of the gate of the city. So holds R. Meir. R. Judah said: He must not leave the sanctuary, because it is written 'He shall not leave the sanctuary' " (*m. Sanh.* 2:1). The *Sipra* adds "for any reason" (Emor, par. 2:5), but the *Tosefta* counters "while he officiates" (*t. Sanh.* 4:1). The amoratic sages ask: "Surely R. Judah's argument is correct? R. Meir will tell you: In that case (if the verse is taken literally) he must not (leave the Temple) *even for his house* [my emphasis]! Hence, this is the meaning of *ûmin hammiqdāš lō᾽ yēṣē᾽*: He must not depart *miqqĕdûšātô*, from his sacred status" (*b. Sanh.* 19a). Thus the controversy between R. Meir and R. Judah rests on only whether the high priest can leave the sanctuary to follow the bier. But all of rabbinic tradition concurs that, otherwise, the high priest may leave the sacred precinct and, moreover, that he resides outside.

The text naturally assumes that if a death occurred at his home while he was officiating at the sanctuary, then he would not be allowed to return to his premises, but would be quartered on the sanctuary grounds (with Elliger 1966) for the week of mourning while his home would undergo ritual purification (cf. Num 19:18–19).

Belkin (1940: 83) cogently suggests that Jesus applied the high priest's absolute prohibition of mourning to his disciples: "To another (disciple) he said, 'Follow me.' But he said, 'Lord, first let me go and bury my father.' But he said to him, 'Let the dead bury their own dead, but for you, go and proclaim the kingdom of God' " (Luke 9:59–60).

Whereas Jesus, in keeping with Scripture and in the tradition of Philo (*Laws* 1.114), claims that the high priest must remain totally free from obligations and desires to mourn, the rabbis, as indicated above, relented by allowing the high priest to mourn for his close kin, provided that it did not interfere with his official duties.

Knohl (1995: 52, 68), following Dillmann and Ryssel (1897), argues that 10:6–7, prohibiting Aaron and his sons from engaging in mourning rites and leaving the sanctuary, is a "standing order" to all priests on duty. He correctly adds (69, n. 26) that, in this case, Aaron's (remaining) sons have equal status with their father because they, too, were anointed with the sacred oil (vol. 1.610–11). This in itself, however, implies that subsequent generations of priests (but not the high priest) were exempted from this prohibition, which neatly corresponds with the fact that high priests, but not ordinary priests, continued to be anointed (vol. 1.610–11). Moreover, if this indeed were a standing order, we should expect to find the formula of permanence *ḥuqqat ῾ōlām lĕdōrōtêkem*, precisely as in the immediately following prohibition against imbibing spirits while on duty (vv. 8–9). Finally and foremost, the mourning prohibition in our chapter applies solely to the high priest, implying that it does not apply to other priests, which accords earlier (vv. 1–4) with the blanket permission granted to ordinary priests to mourn for their closest blood relatives—without any regard as to whether they were on duty.

Thus 10:6–7 cannot be a standing order; it applies solely to Aaron and his sons, but not to their descendants. One need not side with Wellhausen (1963: 140, 147) and Kuenen (1886: 85, n. 21) that this would imply that the consecration service had not been completed, and is contrary to 9:1. The death of Nadab and Abihu indeed occurred the following day, at the inaugural service. Aaron and the other sons were then warned neither to engage in mourning within the sanctuary nor to exit the sanctuary to follow the bier. But this prohibition does not apply to subsequent generations of priests, except to the high priest, as explicitly stated in our verse.

It must be more than a coincidence that the text reads *ûmin-hammiqdāš lōʾ yēṣēʾ*, whereas Aaron and his sons are warned, during their consecration, *mippetaḥ ʾōhel môʿēd lōʾ tēṣĕʾû* (8:33aα [P]). The first priestly consecration took place in the Tent of Meeting, whereas H's focus is on subsequent generations (note the occurrence of *miqdāš* in 19:30; 20:3; 26:2). That the Tent of Meeting is recorded in 17:4, 5, 6, 9; 24:3 is because their contexts are explicitly set against the wilderness background; 19:21, the only other attestation, is part of a pericope (vv. 20–22) that is an interpolation from P (see its NOTE).

desecrate. yĕḥallēl. Note, again, the imprecision of H, which uses *ḥillel* 'desecrate' in the case of corpse-contamination instead of the precise verb *ṭimmēʾ* 'defile, pollute' (see also NOTES on vv. 4, 9, and 22:9). The high priest would defile the sanctuary on his return from the funeral. Direct contact is required by H for the transmission of impurity (see NOTE on 20:3).

for the distinction of the anointing oil of his God is upon him. kî nēzer šemen mišḥat ʾĕlōhāyw ʿālāyw. This awkward clause containing three words in construct can be explained as an expansion of *kî šemen mišḥat YHWH ʿălēkem* (10:7aβ [P]), an indication that H is later than P. The term *nēzer* has been added (from 10:9). It could not be used in 10:7 because that verse included Aaron's sons, who were not anointed on their heads, or in Num 6:7, the case of the Nazirite, for a similar reason; here, however, the text is limited to the high priest (Ehrlich 1908). The change from *YHWH* to *ʾĕlōhāyw* is explicable by the suffix on the latter (so, too, in Num 6:7, and see NOTE on "their God," v. 6). This verse proves that each high priest was required to undergo the consecration rites (Exod 29; Lev 8), during which his head would be anointed with the sacred oil, whereas Aaron's sons were anointed (on their bodies and vestments, but not on their heads, Exod 29:21; Lev 8:30) but not the priests thereafter (vol. 1.554–55). The high priest held office for life (Num 20:22–29; cf. Jos. *Ant.* 20:229).

The root of *nēzer* means "set apart, dedicate (for a sacred purpose)." Thus the dedication of the Nazirite's hair (Num 6:4, 5, 7, 8, 11, 12), his or her most distinctive outward sign, is responsible for the name *nāzîr*. Referring to the high priest's distinctive headgear, it carries the secondary connotation "diadem, crown" (see NOTE on 8:9). Here, however, it bears a more abstract notion (typical of H!), since it refers to the effect of the anointing; hence the rendering "distinction" (with NJPS).

I (who speak) am YHWH. ʾănî YHWH. Thus the section that deals with the high priest's laws of mourning comes to an end. For the rendering, see the NOTES on 18:1, 4, 5.

13. *a young virgin. ʾiššâ bibĕtûlêhâ,* literally "a woman in her adolescence," akin to English "maiden" and Chinese/Korean *chonyo* (B. Leigh). When the text wishes to state that the girl is a virgin, it adds the phrase *lōʾ-yādĕʿâ ʾîš* 'who has not known a man' (Judg 11:39; 21:12; cf. Gen 24:16). Here, however, that she is a virgin is assumed; for the sake of clarity, it is added in the translation. The plural form is abstract, signifying a state—for example, the synonym *nĕʿûrêhâ* 'her youth' (22:13). Note the parallelism of *nĕʿûrêhen/bĕtûlêhen* (Ezek 23:3) and *šĕdê nĕʿûrayik* (Ezek 23:21) / *daddê bĕtûlêhen* (23:3) in describing a harlot, and the

frequent pairing of *bāḥûr* and *bĕtûlâ* (Deut 32:25; Isa 23:4; 62:5; Jer 51:22, etc.), whose connotation can only be "young man" and "young woman." The LXX adds *'ek toû génous autoû* (= *mē'ammāyw* 'from his kin'). But this addition is decidedly wrong; it would render v. 14b superfluous. Is it possible that the high priest was unmarried at the time of his election? Yes, since he is appointed the high-priest designate in the lifetime of his father (6:15; 16:32), when he himself is young. The rabbis derive from the singular *'iššâ* that he had only one wife (*b. Yeb.* 59a). For the meaning of *bĕtûlâ/bĕtûlîm*, see the NOTE on v. 3.

Gerstenberger's (1996: 313) surmise that priests could marry only virgins because prior sex with another man would "infect her with an alien power, one possibly incompatible with the holiness of YHWH's temple," is refuted by the fact that all priests (except the high priest) could marry widows (see NOTE on v. 7). The high priest's restriction may be explained as a concern for the purity of his line; note that his bridal choice is limited to the daughter of a priest (v. 14b). This, too, is Ezekiel's concern: he extends the *bĕtûlâ* rule to all priests, but allows marriage to a priest's widow (Ezek 44:22; see below).

14. The undesirables are given in ascending order, reversing the descending order prevailing for the ordinary priest (v. 7). The reason for the change is to begin with the innovation, the widow (Wessely 1846), and to parallel the inverted order of the mourning rites for the priest and high priest (see COMMENT A). Moreover, v. 14b is a circular inclusio, in chiastic relation to v. 13. The rationale, v. 15, stands outside this structure (Paran 1989: 161).

A widow. *'almānâ*. According to Ezekiel, a priest is permitted to marry the widow of only a priest (Ezek 44:22b), whereas H, by its silence, permits his marriage to any Israelite widow (see NOTE on v. 7). Ezekiel's stricter rule could be anticipated in view of his severe prohibitions regarding mourning (Ezek 44:26–27). Widowhood was considered a reproach from God (Isa 54:4), and widows themselves possessed low self-esteem (Ruth 1:13, 20).

a raped woman, or a harlot. *waḥălālâ zōnâ*. The reversal of these two terms from their position in v. 7 indicates that they are two separate entities, the harlot being more undesirable in view of the ascending order of undesirable women. The LXX and Sam. read *wĕzōnâ*, correctly in my opinion.

Only a young virgin of his kin. *kî 'im-bĕtûlâ mē'ammāyw*. The wording in Ezekiel is *kî 'im-bĕtûlōt mizzera' bêt yiśrā'el* 'only young virgins of the stock of the House of Israel' (Ezek 44:22bα). The change from kin to nation shows that Ezekiel is later than Leviticus (contra Levine 1989). However, in another respect Ezekiel's rule turns out stricter than that of Leviticus. By insisting on virgin status for the priest's bride, he thereby excludes widows (except those of priests). Philo (*Laws* 1.107) adds, in agreement with the rabbis (*m. Yeb.* 4:4), that a betrothed woman is also forbidden to the high priest "even though her body is that of a maid intact." The rabbis' basis is legal. Since a betrothed woman requires a writ of divorce before she can remarry (*Sipre Deut.* 270), she would automatically be forbidden to an ordinary priest.

That *mē'ammāyw* means "of his own kin" is recognized by Philo (*Laws* 1.110), "a priestess descended from priests" (cf. Jos. *Con. Ap.* 1:31; *Keter Torah*). Ehrlich

(1899–1900 [H]) provides a logical reason: Since intermarriage is forbidden, from whom else should a high priest choose his bride? It is obvious that his choice is limited to his people! However, Ehrlich's reasoning has to be amended: marriage to non-Israelites was not forbidden (only stigmatized; see chap. 18, COMMENT A). The converse argument, that this prohibition implies that intermarriage by Israelites is permitted (Joosten 1994: 121; 1996: 85), is equally unjustified. All that can be inferred is that Israelites may marry outside their kin group. The situation changed radically in the Babylonian Exile (and afterward) when intermarriage became rife. Hence out of fear that priests might marry widows of non-Israelites, Ezekiel imposed a requirement of virginity on priestly brides, insisting that they stem from *"the stock* of the House of Israel" (Ezek 44:22bα).

In Second Temple times, endogamous marriages are frequently attested, not just for high priests. R. Tarphon's mother's brother was a priest (*y. Yoma* 1.38d; *y. Hor.* 3.47d). Both of John the Baptist's parents were of priestly families (Luke 1:5). The rabbis themselves frowned on the "intermarriage" of a priest and an Israelite: "The marriage of a daughter of a priest to an Israelite is bound to result in a bad marriage" (*b. Pesaḥ* 49a). As discussed in the NOTE on "a promiscuous woman," v. 7, the sectaries of Qumran regarded marriage into nonpriestly families as *kil'ayîm* '(forbidden) mixed seed' (*MMT* B 76–78), a view that is echoed in the rabbinic literature: "As their vineyards are being sown with mixed seed [*kil'ayîm*], so their (the priests') daughters are being sown with mixed seed" (*y. Sot.* 1:8; cf. Urbach 1988: 309).

15. *desecrate.* This verse is the inverse of v. 9. In v. 9, the daughter "desecrates" her father; in v. 15, the father desecrates his daughter and his other offspring (see COMMENT A). However, whereas the desecration in v. 9 is metaphoric, here it is literal, and the consequences are severe: the daughter is disqualified from partaking of sacred food (*m. Ter.* 8:1; *Sipre Zuṭa* on Num 18:11), and the son, in addition, is disqualified from officiating in the sanctuary (*Sipra* Nedaba par. 4:6).

among his kin. bĕ'ammāyw. That is, all his relatives are stigmatized.

who sanctifies him. mĕqaddĕšô. Here the participle is explicitly applied to the high priest, implying that although the priests are innately holy, they can diminish or even lose their holiness by their actions. This view, stressed by and unique to H, is specified in 20:8 for Israel, 21:8 LXX for priests, and here for the high priest.

Joosten (1994: 134, 178–79, 183; 1996: 97, 129, 132) claims that God consecrates the priests, especially the high priest, by means of their presence in the sanctuary, under the assumption that a holy object is contagious. Such a belief persists in folk tradition regarding the Ark (1 Sam 6:19; 2 Sam 6:6–7) and in the priestly tradition regarding the sanctums while they *are being moved* (Num 4:15, 20; Milgrom 1990a). Thus the numinous, dangerous power of holiness indeed is contagious. But the priests themselves categorically deny that the sanctums are able to transmit their holiness to persons. The oft-repeated priestly formula in regard to the sanctums *kol-hannōgēa' yiqdaš* 'all who touch (them) become holy' (e.g., Exod 30:29; Lev 6:11) does not induce persons (Milgrom 1981d: 278–310). The five cases where God sanctifies the priests are found solely in negative contexts: forbidden marriage (21:8, 15), blemished priests (21:23), defiling sacred foods (22:9), and profaning them by giving them to ineligible Israelites (22:16). Not a single case speaks of priests absorbing holiness by their service in the sanctuary. Rather, by observing the divinely ordained prohibitions, they avoid *diminishing* their holiness. How, then, does God continue to sanctify them? The remaining two "God the sanctifier" passages (20:8; 22:32) provide the clue. Their address to Israel surely includes the priests, the latter pericope expressly so (22:18). Thus it must be concluded that God continues to sanctify the priesthood, first, if it refrains from diminishing its holiness by acts of desecration and, second—together with all Israel—if it follows God's commandments. Indeed, the divine summons to Israel *qĕdōšîm tihyu* 'Be holy' (19:2) followed by the summation and summit of God's commandments (19:3–4, 9–18, 34) is also addressed to the priests.

Vv. 16–23. Blemished Priests

The requirement that priests bear no physical blemish is not limited to Israel, but is attested universally. Examples from Israel's neighbors are cited and discussed in COMMENT D. These examples also include moral requirements. I cite one to underscore the paradox: according to Plato (*Laws* 6.759), a prospective priest "must be screened to see to it that he is sound of body and of legitimate birth, reared in a family whose moral standards could hardly be higher." Regarding Israelite priests, Josephus (*Ant.* 3.279) remarks: "Nor is it only during sacred ministrations that their purity is essential: they must see to it also that their private life be beyond reproach." The obvious question remains: Why is the biblical list of priestly blemishes restricted to the physical body, whereas blemishes of character and piety are omitted? Indeed, one scholar concludes flatly that H "attaches more importance to the freedom of priests from physical effects (21:16 ff) than to moral character" (Elliot-Binns 1955: 26). A possible answer is that moral and spiritual requirements are subsumed under the root *qdš*: since Israel is required to be a moral and devout people in order to attain holiness (detailed in chap. 19), ipso facto, the same holds true for Israel's priests. Indeed, since H itself places great emphasis on disregard for the sabbath (19:3, 30; 26:2), ethical abuse (19:11–16), sexual malpractice (18:7–30; 20:9–24), and violation of YHWH's commandments, in general (18:3–5; 26:3), "Leviticus 21f. do not represent a complete collection of priestly instructions, but at best an extraordinarily fragmented one" (Gerstenberger 1996: 312). The lacuna, however, is so gaping that to assume it is taken for granted will not do. This problem and its possible solutions are discussed in COMMENTS B and D.

As will be argued in COMMENT B, the list of blemishes for priests (21:17–23) was compiled to match that for sacrificial animals (22:22–24). Since animals have only physical imperfections, but no moral ones, the compiler of the priestly defects was constrained to limit himself to physical imperfections. To be sure, the prohibited animals also could have included stolen ones, a defect that Malachi makes sure to include (Mal 1:13; cf. *m. Giṭ.* 5:5), but, in reality, this defect is that of the offerer and not of the animal, and it therefore does not belong in this list.

Interestingly, the sectaries of Qumran, also taking for granted that the moral requirements for members of the sect fall equally on their priests, "update" the biblical list of disqualifications with new provisions. The fragment 4Q266 has been reconstructed and translated by Baumgarten (1992: 506–7):

<pre>
     .N WKL '[ŠR NQL B   ṬRWR DBR]
     [L'] PṢL DBRYW LHŠMY' [QWLW L' YQR' BSPR]
     [HTWRH] LMH YŠYG BDBR MWT [   ]
          ḤW HKHNYM B'BWDH ['YŠ]
5   MBNY 'HRWN 'ŠR YŠBH LGW'YM [   ]
     LHLLH BṬM'TM 'L YGŠ L'BDT [HQDŠ   ]
     MBYT LPRWKT W'L YWKL 'T QDŠ H[QDŠYM   ]
     'YŠ MBNY 'HRWN 'ŠR YNDD L'B[D 'T   ]
     'MW BYŚWD 'M WGM LBGW{D} .M.['YŠ MBNY]
10   'HRWN 'ŠR HP<Y>L ŠMW MN H'M T W[   ]
     BŠRYRWT LBW L'KWL MN HQWDŠ [   ]
     MYŚR'L 'T 'ṢT BNY 'HRWN .M [   ]
     'T H'WKL W<ḤBY> WḤB BDM [   ]
     BYḤŚ<Y>M WZH SRK MWŠB [   ]
     HQWDŠ [BMHNY]HM [W] 'RYHM BK[
          ŠB
</pre>

1 And anyone w[ho speaks too softly(?) or with a staccato voice]
2 [not] dividing his words so that his voice may be heard, [shall not read from the book of
3 the Torah], lest he cause error in a capital matter . . .
4 his brothers, the priest in the service . . . [Any man]
5 of the Sons of Aaron who was in captivity among the gentiles . . .
6 to profane it with their uncleanliness. He may not approach (officiate at—J.M.) the [holy] service . . .
7 within the curtain and may not eat the most holy [offerings] . . .
8 Any man of the Sons of Aaron who migrates to serve . . .
9 with him in the council of the people and also to betray . . . [Any man of the Sons]
10 of Aaron who caused his name to lapse from the truth . . . [walking
11 in the stubbornness of his heart to eat of the sacred . . .
12 from Israel the counsel of the Sons of Aaron . . .
13 the one who eats shall incur guilt for the blood . . .
14 in genealogy. And this is the order for the session of . . .
15 of holiness in their cam[ps] and their towns in a[ll

What is of relevance here are the three innovative rules that add to the biblical priestly disqualifications:

1. The Torah reading, apparently a priestly function at Qumran (on only a few occasions, according to Jos. *Ant.* 4:209), had to be declaimed loudly and distinctly.

2. Priests in foreign captivity were not permitted to officiate in the Temple or partake of the offerings. Baumgarten (1992) cogently suggests that the prohibition *kol-nĕbēlâ ûṭĕrēpâ . . . lōʾ yōʾkĕlû hakkōhănîm* 'Priests are forbidden to eat . . . anything that died or was torn by beasts' (Ezek 44:31) included meat of forbidden animals (Lev 11), which a captive priest was most likely to do (note the exception cited in Jos. *Life* 14). In a similar vein, 4Q513 states categorically that daughters of priests who had sexual intercourse with aliens were also denied access to the *tĕrûmâ*, the priestly portion of produce (see NOTE on v. 7).

3. Priests who voluntarily migrated to foreign countries as well as apostates were excluded from "the council of the people" and the priestly portions. (On other provisions of this text, see Baumgarten 1992: 509–13).

17. *Speak to Aaron.* Aaron and future high priests are responsible for using these criteria to weed out those priests ineligible to officiate in the sanctuary.

man. ʾîš. But not a minor or a woman. According to the rabbis, a priest must be twenty years of age (*Sipra* Emor, par. 3:1; cf. *b. Ḥul.* 24b), though adolescent novitiates (*pirḥê kĕhûnâ*) served on the watches (*m. Tam.* 1:1) and kept the high priest awake on Yom Kippur eve (*m. Yoma* 1:7). In theory, a priest was permitted to officiate once he entered adolescence (*b. Ḥul.* 24b [bar.]). Indeed, Aristobulus was only seventeen years old when he was appointed high priest by Herod (Jos. *Ant.* 15:51). To be sure, Samuel "served YHWH" (1 Sam 2:11, 18; 3:1) while still a child. However, there is no evidence that he actually officiated at the altar. Rather, since he slept near the Ark—probably in the inner sanctum—he probably was assigned to guard it.

Women were excluded from the priesthood probably out of fear of menstrual pollution, a reason that is expressly cited for the Ethiopians: "At the sacrifices in honor of Helios and Selene, the purest deities, the attendance of women was prohibited, in order to protect the sacred act even from involuntary pollution" (Heliod. 10:4, cited by Kalisch 1867–72: 573, n. 9).

a blemish. mûm. In the priestly texts, it can be both human (21:17, 18, 21 [twice], 23; 24:19, 20) and animal (22:20, 21, 25; Num 19:2). The Greek terms *kolobós* 'blemished' and *téleisos* 'unblemished' (= Heb. *tāmîm*) were assiduously avoided by the LXX, probably because of their pagan association. Instead, it used the similar-sounding Greek word *nōmos* 'fault', and for *tāmîm* it coined the word *ámomos* (Licht and Leibowitz 1962).

The base meaning of *mûm* is "physical deformity" (cf. Deut 17:1; 2 Sam 14:25; Song 4:7; Dan 1:4). It is also attested for moral deficiencies (Prov 9:7; Job 11:15), but these two citations stem from wisdom literature, where the term acquires an extended meaning. Thus the limitation of *mûm*, by definition, to physical defects signifies that moral defects, which may also have disqualified a priest (see COMMENTS B and D), were not the concern of this list.

In the Second Temple, blemished priests were employed in the Wood Chamber (located in the northeastern corner of the woman's court, the farthest from the Temple building) to remove worm-eaten wood from the altar stockpile (*m. Mid.* 2:5). Before being admitted to their office, priests were closely inspected by the Sanhedrin (*m. Mid.* 5:4; cf. Jos. *Ant.* 14:366; *Con. Ap.* 1:31), not by the high priest, which v. 17a would imply (see above). "A priest in whom was found a disqualification [e.g., that his mother had been a divorcee] used to put on black undergarments and wrap himself in black, exit, and depart" (*m. Mid.* 5:4). A blemished priest, however, could sound the trumpets (in certain instances; *Sipre* Num. 75; cf. *t. Soṭa* 7:16; *y. Yoma* 1:1) and pronounce the priestly benediction from the porch (*t. Soṭa* 7:8).

"One in whom no disqualification was found used to put on white undergarments and wrap himself in white and go in and minister along with his brother priests. They used to make a feast because no blemish had been found in the seed of Aaron the priest, and they used to say thus: Blessed is the Omnipresent [*hammāqôm*, lit. "the place"], Blessed is He, because no blemish has been found in the seed of Aaron. Blessed is He who chose Aaron and his sons to stand to minister before the Lord in the Holy of Holies" (*m. Mid.* 5:4).

shall not be qualified. loʾ yiqrab. It can be shown that the verbs *qārab/nāgaš ʾel* mean "encroach" wherever penalties are invoked (Milgrom 1970: 33–37). In particular, there are four cases where a disqualified priest encroaches on pain of death: if he failed to wash himself (Exod 30:20; 40:32), was drunk (Lev 10:9), was improperly dressed (Exod 28:43), or was blemished (Lev 21:17, 18, 21 [twice], 23; though the death penalty is not cited; cf. the rabbinic controversy, *Sipra* Emor 3:11). For details, see Milgrom (1970: 38–43) and Gane and Milgrom (1990). The rabbis impose another restriction on the blemished priest: "(In the area) between the vestibule (of the Temple) and the altar, blemished priests and those with disheveled hair are not permitted to enter" (*m. Kel.* 1:9), on which Maimonides (*Book of Commandments*, prohibition 69) comments: "Whoever (among the priests) deliberately enters (the area) inside the altar, even if it was not for the purpose of officiating, is punished with lashes." However, the commentators Bartinoro, Rabad, Samson of Sens (on this mishna), and Ramban (on 10:9) claim that this prohibition is only rabbinic in origin, but according to Scripture, the blemished priest may enter. This view is confirmed by Josephus (*Wars* 5.228), who affirms that blemished priests are admitted to this area, but not to the altar or inside the sanctuary.

However, when *qārab/nāgaš ʾel* is used positively, it takes on the opposite meaning "qualify, have access" (e.g., Exod 12:48; 28:1; Ezek 43:19; 44:16; for other examples, see Milgrom 1970: 33–35). This meaning is confirmed by its antonyms, Aramaic *rěḥēq* and Akkadian *reqû*, which are used in legal texts to denote "relinquish rights and claims" (Muffs 1969: 48–50, 118–19). This meaning of *qārab* 'qualify, be eligible' is substantiated in the QL. For example, *WK'ŠR YṢʾ HGWRL ʿL ʿṢT HRBYM YQRB ʾW YRḤQ* . . . 'and according to the decision of the council of the congregation, he shall either *qualify* or be *rejected*' (1QS 6:16; cf. 6:18–19; 9:15–16). The same holds true in Rabbinic Hebrew:

maʿăśêkā yĕqārĕbûkā ûmaʿăśêka yĕraḥăqûk 'your deeds will bring you *acceptance* and your deeds will *reject* you' (*m. ʿEd.* 5:7); *lĕraḥēq ûlĕqārēb* 'to reject or accept' (*m. ʿEd.* 8:7; cf. Lieberman 1951: 200–201, nn. 8, 26; Ben Yehuda 7:6550).

This rendering should lay to rest once and for all the usual rendering of *qārab* as "approach" in most cultic contexts. Still Zimmerli (1980: 504) avers that blemished priests endanger the divine spheres "beim Herantreten zum Heiligen" (in approaching the holy). That this claim is patently false is demonstrated by the concession granted the blemished priest to eat most sacred food (v. 22), which *must be consumed within the sacred court* (cf. 6:9, 19; 7:6)!

A similar error attends Klawans's (1995: 292–93) attempt to deduce that since non-Israelites were profane (*ḥll*), they must have been excluded from the sanctuary, as were blemished (*ḥll*) priests. Again, blemished priests were barred from officiating, but not from entering the sanctuary. Moreover, H expressly permits the *gēr* to offer sacrifices (Num 15:14), and for violating prohibitive commandments, he *must* offer sacrifices (Num 15:30–31; see NOTE on 22:25), which means he had access into the sanctuary court. Also his statement that "the status of non-Israelites as profane is implied when Israel is called sacred" (n. 34) is challengeable; for H, Israel is not inherently holy, but it can achieve holiness by observing YHWH's commandments. Finally, H's holiness is metaphoric, not cultic, implying that Israel still may not partake of sacred food: it remains ritually profane (see chap. 19, COMMENT). Consider, however, that a zealous worshiper of YHWH, such as the *gēr* Uriah the Hittite (2 Sam 11:11), climbs the ladder of holiness prescribed in chap. 19. Will he, too, become holy? The question remains open.

the food of his God. leḥem ʾĕlōhāyw. See the NOTE on v. 6. That *leḥem* must frequently be rendered "food," see Gen 3:19; 31:54; Exod 2:20; Num 14:9; Dan 5:1.

Vv. 18–20. The Twelve Blemishes

These are general categories (Abravanel), according to the rabbis who expand them to 142 blemishes. A major criterion is appearance (*b. Bek.* 43a,b); for example, the blemished priest is permitted to offer the priestly blessing as long as his defect is not visible—on his face, hands, or (being barefoot) feet (*t. Soṭa* 7:8). Maimonides (*Temple Service.* Temple Entry 8:17) claims that the twelve blemishes are ranked in decreasing severity of appearance: missing limbs (blind, lame), truncated limb (*ḥārum*), elongated limb (*śārûaʿ*), and broken limb (*šeber*), followed by aesthetic criteria: hunchback (*gibbēn*), spotted eye (*daq, tĕballūl*), scarred skin (*yallepet, gārāb*), and swollen testes (*mĕrôaḥ ʾāšek*). A few of his renderings will be contested below, but his major flaw is that the testes are not visible (see NOTE on v. 20b).

18. *kî.* Untranslated, not because it is lacking in the LXX but because its function is asseverative (e.g., Isa 7:9; GKC 159ee).

shall be qualified. lōʾ yiqrab. For the sake of symmetrical structure, one is tempted to add *lĕhaqrîb ʾet-ʾiššê* YHWH to balance v. 17b (see COMMENT B). However, the truncated *lōʾ yiqrab* is grammatically acceptable, since the verb *qārab* does not require an object (e.g., *hazzār haqqārēb yûmat,* Num 1:51; 3:10).

blind. *'iwwēr.* The absence of deaf and dumb from this list means that obvious defects are not listed; thus the blind must be the one-eyed (Elliger 1966). Alternatively, with the rabbis, these are general categories from which the rest can be derived. Strikingly, the Qumran sectaries also name only the blind among the blemished persons prohibited from entering the Temple-city (11QT 45:12–14), where clearly they also included the defects of Lev 21. This is explicitly stated in another Qumran document: "Anyone halt or blind or lame, or a man in whose body is a permanent defect" (1QM 7:4; cf. 1Qsa 2:3–9, and Yadin 1983: 1.289–91). The Qumranites, it should be noted, also included deafness as a defect (*MMT* B 52–54), a restriction that the rabbis opposed *(t. Ter.* 1:1; cf. Lieberman 1962: 5.1267). Another possibility, the one I favor, is that this list is arbitrary, to match the twelve animal defects with equivalent ones for the priests (see COMMENT B). This explanation is also compatible with that of the rabbis: they may be general categories.

lame. *pissēaḥ,* from *pāsaḥ, pissēaḥ* (P'el) 'strike against' (1 Kgs 18:21, 26; Isa 31:5); *nipsaḥ* (Nip'al) 'strike oneself' (2 Sam 4:4); see also Akkadian *pessû,* *pessātu* 'bodily injury (to man and beast)'. The precise injury is moot: one of his legs is paralyzed (Saadiah); lame in either one or both legs (*Sipra* Emor, par. 3:6). Ehrlich (1987: 152), however, claims that it means lame in one leg, since it is translated in the *Tgs.* by *ḥăgîr.* Supporting his interpretation is that Mephibosheth is described as *ûpissēaḥ šĕtê raglāyw* 'lame in both legs' (2 Sam 9:13; also as *nĕkēh raglayim,* 2 Sam 4:4); namely, *pissēaḥ* without qualification denotes lame in one leg. Furthermore, the Qumranites distinguish between *ḥiggēr* and *pissēaḥ* (1QM 7:4; 4QDᵇ; Milik 1959: 114) as do the rabbis (*m. Pe'ah* 8:9; although *pissēaḥ* is omitted in MS Cambridge). Otto (1988) is unconvincing in his claim that it refers to an injured extremity, hands or legs.

The rule deriving from David's conquest of Jebusite Jerusalem *'iwwēr ûpissēaḥ lō' yābô' 'el-habbayit* (2 Sam 5:8b) is best rendered "blind or lame (priests) may not enter into the house (of YHWH LXX)." The only way this prohibition can refer to all Israelites is to assume that *habbayit* refers to the Temple complex (Olyan 1996b: 168, n. 30). In either case, whether priests or Israelites, this rule would clash with the priestly texts, which not only allow blemished priests to enter the Tent of Meeting (prototype of the Temple building), but offer no objection to blemished Israelites from entering the sanctuary court (see NOTE on v. 23a). Presuming that this rule refers to priests, it would imply that the actual practice of the Jerusalem Temple was stricter than that demanded by P, which I have proposed stems from the legislation of a prior regional sanctuary (vol. 1.29–35). Although H focuses on the Jerusalem Temple, it also posits the existence of other legitimate sanctuaries (see chap. 17, COMMENT D) and tacitly agrees with P, not with 2 Sam 5:8b. That only two blemishes are singled out need not be taken as an additional contradiction; the blind and the lame are general designations for blemishes, not an exhaustive list. Note that they head the blemish lists for both priests and sacrificial animals (vv. 18–20; 22:22–24, where *šābûr 'ô-ḥārûṣ = pissēaḥ;* see NOTE on 22:22).

disfigured. *ḥārūm.* This translation is an educated guess. This *hapax* has been variously interpreted: (1) "short limbed" (Ibn Ezra) or "amputated limb" (Ibn Janaḥ; cf. Abravanel) because it should be the opposite of adjoining *śārûaʿ*; (2) from *ḥrm* 'destroy' (27:29; Num 21:2): since "the nose is the glory of the face," it refers to a destroyed nose (cf. *b. Yeb.* 102a; Ramban); or "his nose is either flattened, blocked, petite, or elongated, Aba Yosi says: one who is able to paint both eyes with one stroke" (*Sipra* Emor, par 3:8; *m. Bek.* 7:3; *b. Bek.* 49b [bar.]; cf. *Tg. Neof*). The LXX renders "stumped-nose," and *Tg. Ps.-J.* renders "mutilated nose"; (3) considering Dillmann and Ryssel's (1897) rightful observation that the nose is too limited a feature, perhaps the entire face (cf. Akk. *arāmu* 'to stretch' [e.g., the skin, *CAD* 1.2:228]); (4) on the basis of Arabic *ḥarama* 'split nostrils, ear, or lip' (Ibn Janaḥ), perhaps a "split nose" (cf. *heḥĕrîm*, Isa 11:15), though Dillmann and Ryssel's objection still stands.

deformed. śārûaʿ. Again, there are a variety of interpretations: (1) one limb longer than the other (cf. *mēhiśtārēaʿ*, Isa 28:20; Rashi, Ibn Ezra); (2) an extra limb (Abravanel): the Athenian priest had to be *aphelés* 'one who has neither too much nor too little in his body' (Kalisch 1867–72); (3) a dislocated hip (= longer leg?) (*Sipra* Emor 3:9); (4) mutilated ears (LXX, Pesh.); (5) from Arabic *šaraʿa, ašraʿ* 'long-nosed' (Snaith 1967). I have chosen the most comprehensive (hence, safest) conjecture: "deformed."

19. *broken leg or broken arm. šeber regel ʾô šeber yād.* Presumably unhealed. Indeed, Ezekiel specifies that God will break Pharaoh's arms, and they will not heal (Ezek 30:21–25). The question is what of a break in another part of the body, such as the collar bone? Surely *šeber* by itself implies it (24:20; see its NOTE). The answer is that the blemishes are limited to only those that are visible or noticeable (see COMMENT B, and vol. 1.722–23).

20. *a hunchback. gibbēn.* This translation agrees with that in the LXX. The rabbis offer two interpretations: "One who has no eyebrows or has only one eyebrow, this is the *gibbēn* of the Torah. R. Dosa says: one whose eyebrows lie flat (overshadowing the eyes). R. Ḥanina b. Antigonus says: One who has a double back or a double spine" (*m. Bek.* 7:2; Sipra *Emor*, par. 3:12; *b. Bek.* 43b).

The first interpretation is derived from root *gbb*, as in *gabbōt ʿênayîm* 'eyebrows' (14:9; rendered by *Tg. Onk.* as *gĕbînê ʿênôhî*); the second, from root *gbn*, as in *hārîm gabnunnîm* 'jagged mountains' (Ps 68:17; cf. *b. Meg.* 29a; Saadiah, Ibn Ezra, Radaq).

a dwarf. daq. The interpretations vary. Assuming that the previous word *gibben* refers to the eyes, as does the following *tĕballul bĕʿênô*, the rabbis render "a spotted pupil" (*b. Giṭ.* 56a; *b. Bek.* 38b); Rashi translates *tiole*, Old French for "web" (i.e., a membrane in the eye); and *Tg. Ps.-J.* renders "thin (i.e., no) eyebrows." Many moderns prefer "thin (body)," as the cow of Pharaoh's dream (Gen 41:3–4), the authorized incense (Lev 16:12), and the manna (Exod 16:14). *Tgs. Onk., Neof.* and the Pesh. render "pygmy," and the Akkadian cognate *daqqu* means "small" (*CAD* 3.107), on which the accepted translation is based.

a discoloration of the eye. tĕballul bĕʿênô. The noun pattern is similar to *tĕʿaššûr* (Isa 41:19). On the assumption that the root is *bll* 'mingle, mix' (2:5), *Tg. Onk.* renders *ḥîlîz* (from Rabbinic Heb. *ḥillāzôn* 'worm'); that is, a line of white has entered the pupil (cf. *Sipra* Emor, par. 3:13; *b. Bek.* 38 a,b [bar.]). But see Akkadian *balālu* 'to be spotted'. Ibn Ezra suggests that it is related to *tebel* (20:12), which he derives from *blh* 'be worn out, decay'; hence his rendering: "impaired." On its surmised relation to the animal blemish *yabbelet*, see the NOTE on 22:22.

a scar. gārāb. "A moist *šěḥîn* (boil)" (Rashi on Deut 28:27), assuming that *gārāb* and *šěḥîn* (Deut 28:27) are related, but not synonymous. The rabbis reverse the meaning of these two words, declaring that *gārāb* is a potsherd, or a dry boil (*Sipra* Emor, par. 3:15).

Akkadian *garābu* means "scab, scale-disease" (*CAD* 5.46). That is, it refers to a general category and not a specific kind of skin ailment. This, I submit, is the reason why *gārāb* is not included among the types of *ṣāraʿat* in Lev 13. Nevertheless, *gārāb* should not be equated with *ṣāraʿat*; otherwise, Lev 21, a *priestly* text, would have used the latter term. I would surmise that *gārāb* is more inclusive than *ṣāraʿat*, for it would include types of scale disease, such as as the *yallepet*, that are not impure.

lichen. yallepet (cf. *lichēn*, LXX, i.e., tetter, eczema, and *impetigo*, Vg). Akkadian *liptu* A 2, 3 (*CAD* 9.201–2) means "disease" and "(dissolved) spot." Some rabbis hold that it (and not *gārāb*) is dry, like a potsherd (*b. Bek.* 419 [bar.]). Resh Lakish suggests that its name implies that it clings to the body; presumably, he traces its root to *lpp* (see *Tg. Onk.* on *wayyěhabbēr* 'and he attached', Exod 36:10, 16).

I would surmise that here we are dealing with a specific kind of *gārāb* that, differently from any kind of *ṣāraʿat*, is not impure.

a crushed testicle. měrôaḥ ʾăšek. The hapax *ʾešek* means "testicle" in cognate languages: Akkadian *išku* (*CAD* 7.250) and Ugaritic *ušk* (*UT* 132.1.2). Deuteronomy employs the synonym *pěṣûaʿ-dakkâ* (23:2). The rabbis differ on the meaning of the hapax *mārôaḥ*. R. Ishmael (deriving it from the root *mrḥ*; Ibn Janaḥ) maintains that it means *nimrěḥû* 'crushed' (*m. Bek.* 7:5; *Sipra* Emor, par. 3:15; *Tg. Onk.*), whereas R. Akiba (deriving it from *rwḥ*; Menaḥem, Rashi on *b. Bek.* 44a) holds that it means "has wind," is swollen, enlarged (*m. Bek.* 7:5; *Sipra* Emor, par. 3:15). In either case, it implies that at least one testicle is impaired (LXX, Pesh; *m. Bek.* 7:5). Another rabbinic opinion explains that the impairment is the lack of sperm cells (*b. Bek.* 52; *y. Soṭa* 26b). If the root is *mrḥ*, the word is probably a past participle that should read *měrûaḥ* (Dillmann and Ryssel 1897; Ehrlich 1908). If the root is *rwḥ*, it should be vocalized as the noun *merwaḥ*.

This defect proves that the common denominator of the list is not an aesthetic or a visual criterion (Elliger 1966). Rather, it can be shown that this defect was arbitrarily chosen to match its equivalent number in the animal list (22:24; see COMMENT B). Alternatively, one can argue that it reflects the priests' aversion to their castrated counterparts in the pagan world (Kalisch [1867–72] cites the Galli and Megabyzi).

21. *the offspring of Aaron. mizzeraʿ ʾahărōn.* The change of person from second (*mizzarʿăkā*, v. 17) is typical for H (e.g., 22:3–4).

shall not be qualified. lōʾ yiggaš, correctly rendered by *Tg. P.-J. yitkaššēr*. The verbs *nāgaš* and *qārab* are synonyms. For *qārab*, see the NOTE on v. 17b, and for *nāgaš*, see Milgrom (1970: 34–35). The switch to *nagaš* is mandated by the need of an auxiliary for *lĕhaqrîb* (twice in this verse).

YHWH's gifts . . . the food of his God. ʾiššê YHWH . . . leḥem ʾĕlōhāyw. This is another piece of evidence that the latter explains the former: the term *ʾiššeh* means "food gift" (see NOTE on 1:9). However, a more important reason for adding the ostensibly redundant clause (v. 21bβ) is to include the *ḥaṭṭāʾt* offering, which is not an *ʾiššeh* (see NOTE on 1:9), among the sacrifices offered up by the priest (see also NOTE on 23:8). For further proof that *ʾiššeh* cannot mean "fire offering," its usual rendering, see the NOTE on 7:30. The chiasm effected by v. 21a and b is essential to the structure (see COMMENT B).

22. *of the most holy. miqqŏdšê haqqŏdāšîm.* The distinction between most holy and holy offerings is not the innovation of P or H; 1 Sam 21:6 shows that the Bread of Presence, which falls in the category of "most holy" (24:9), was in local sanctuaries of premonarchic Israel and ordinarily was not removed from the sanctuary (1 Sam 21:6; Eerdmans 1912: 105).

It is also no coincidence that the provincial priests of the destroyed cult places, who were not permitted to officiate at the Jerusalem Temple, were permitted to partake of sacrificial leavened bread (2 Kgs 23:9). In effect, they were treated as blemished priests. Note, however, that they could not partake of sacrificial meat—a restriction that Deut 18:1 categorically rejects (see also v. 8).

the holy. haqqŏdāšîm. The Qumran text 4Q266, discussed in the INTRODUCTION to vv. 16–23, apparently differs with—rather, reinterprets—this verse:

W'YŠ] MBNY 'HRWN 'ŠR YŠBH LGWYM[   ]
LHLLH BṬM'TM 'L YGŠ L'BWDT [HQWDŠ   ] MBYT
LPRWKT W'L YWKL 'T QWDŠ H[QDŠYM

Any man] of the Sons of Aaron who was in captivity among the gentiles . . . to desecrate it with their impurity. He may not qualify for [the holy] service . . . inside the veil and may not eat the [most] holy offerings. (4Q266, 11.4–7)

Assuming that the reconstruction is correct, this text provides a new disqualifying defect for priests: being taken captive by gentiles. But, ostensibly, it also compromises this verse by placing a ban on eating most holy food (i.e., the meat of the purification and reparation offering; see 6:22; 7:6). I say "ostensibly" because the missing end of l. 7 might contain the needed information. The possibility, however, must be entertained that this statement was followed by *W'T HQDSM*, in keeping with the MT of our verse: *miqqodšê haqqŏdāšîm ûminhaqqŏdāšîm.* This reconstruction would result in a blatant contradiction of the MT. However, it refers to a priest who had been in captivity, and the sect probably follows the view expressed in Scripture that foreign territory is *ṭāmēʾ* 'impure' (Josh 22:19; Amos 7:17; cf. *b. Šabb.* 14b [bar.]). Thus a priest taken into captivity not only has a bodily defect, but is impure, and he would be forbidden any contact with the sacred.

Also puzzling is the ban on serving inside the veil (i.e., in the adytum). It implies that ordinarily a priest may do so. This would openly defy the prohibition on priests entering the adytum, not to speak of officiating in it—a prerogative reserved solely for the high priest on Yom Kippur (16:2, 32–33)! But again, the lacuna at the end of l. 6 may have contained the needed correction. It is hard to conceive that the "fundamentalist" sectaries of the Dead Sea would blatantly contradict Scripture. The alternative is to conjecture that the invention of a new, nonbiblical disqualification—captivity among the gentiles—allowed them the right to depart from Scripture. If so, then it is possible that they ranked captivity as a greater disqualification than a blemish. But this explanation would apply to only the ban on partaking of most holy offerings.

23. *But he shall not enter before the veil. 'ak 'el-happārōket lō' yābō'.* Not "behind the veil" (Haran 1978: 206, n. 1), which would have been expressed as *mibbêt lappārōket.* Nor are the two expressions equivalent, as claimed by Knohl (1995: 116). Hence this prohibition applies to only the high priest (Ibn Ezra, Abravanel; see Milgrom 1970: 40: n. 154)—that is, to his ritual acts inside the shrine: daily at the menorah and incense altar (Exod 30:7–8), weekly at the table (Lev 24:5–9), and, in cases of impurity generated by him and the people, at the incense altar and *before the veil* (Lev 4:3–21). The prohibition, however, would cover all the other rites of the high priest inside the shrine because all the inner sanctums stand close to the veil: the incense altar *lipnê happārōket* (Exod 30:6), the menorah *miḥûṣ lappārōket* (Exod 27:21; Lev 24:3), and the table *miḥûṣ lappārōket* (Exod 26:35). Note that *lipnê*, meaning "directly in front, center," is used solely for the incense altar, which stood between the menorah and the table in the center of the shrine. (Note, however, that the purification blood is aspersed *'et-pĕnê hakkāpōret* 'against [i.e., toward] the veil', Lev 4:6, 17.)

If this prohibition had all the priests in mind, it would have been worded *'ak 'el-'ōhel hammô'ēd lō' yābō'* 'But he shall not enter the Tent of Meeting' (cf. Exod 28:43; 30:20; 40:32; Lev 10:9). There is a fundamental distinction between these two "enterings": *'el-happārōket* 'to the veil' is the language of officiating; *'el-'ōhel hammô'ēd* 'to the Tent' is the language of entering (cf. Milgrom 1970: 40–41). The implication of this distinction is that although the blemished high priest (and, of course, all priests) is forbidden to officiate inside the shrine, he and his fellow priests would not be prohibited from entering the shrine for the purposes of covering the sanctums for the journey, in particular (Num 4:1–14), and of cleaning, repairing, or assisting in the shrine, in general. This concession follows logically from the priestly system of scaled taboos: if blemished priests are allowed contact with most holy food, they should not be denied contact (but only to minister) with any other most holy object, namely, the sanctums inside the shrine (and the sacrificial altar). In this respect, blemishes would constitute a lesser disqualification than other defects, where it is explicitly stated: a priest may not *enter the Tent* if he is improperly washed (Exod 30:20; 40:32), intoxicated (Lev 10:9), or improperly dressed (Exod 28:43; see NOTE on Lev 10:9). The rabbis, however, are more severe in this matter. They prohibit the blemished priest from entering the shrine even for noncultic purposes, such as doing repairs, though, paradoxically they permit the lay Israelite to enter (*Sipra* Emor 3:11; *b. 'Erub.* 105a [bar.]).

or officiate at the altar. wĕ'el-hammizbēaḥ lō' yiggaš. For this rendering of the verb *nāgaš* in the context of the altar, see Milgrom (1970: 41–42). But to whom does this prohibition apply, to all blemished priests or to only the blemished high priest? If the former, then two objections rise to mind: first, it would create a redundancy with v. 21, and second, the sudden switch from the high priest to the priest would be inexplicable. Thus the reference must be to the high priest and is a continuation of his prohibitions: if he is blemished, he may officiate neither inside the shrine nor at the altar. The Bekhor Shor, who, correctly, associates all of v. 23 with the high priest, avers that the altar mentioned here is the inner, incense altar and that the entire verse is directed to the high priest's purgation of the shrine of Yom Kippur (Milgrom 1970: 41, n. 158). However, this interpretation must be rejected, since the high priest's service at the inner altar (not limited to Yom Kippur; see 4:3–20) is subsumed in the prohibition against officiating inside the shrine (v. 21aα). The only answer, in keeping with other instances of the same prohibition (Exod 28:43; 30:20), is that it refers to the sacrificial altar located in the courtyard. The entire verse then reads: a blemished high priest may not officiate in the sanctuary, either inside the shrine or outside, at the sacrificial altar.

One further reason supports the interpretation of all of v. 23 as referring to the high priest: the structure of chap. 21. As noted, vv. 1–15 contain regulations dealing with priestly restrictions on mourning and marriage: vv. 1–9 concern the priest; vv. 10–15, the high priest. The third and final subject of this chapter is priestly blemishes (vv. 16–23). Should we not expect that this subject, too, should also contain provisions for the priest and high priest—and in that order? Since vv. 16–22 clearly apply to the ordinary priest, v. 23 must refer to the otherwise missing high priest. True, the high priest is not expressly mentioned, as in v. 10. But consider that the blemishes pericope has its own introduction (vv. 16–17a). Whereas the introduction to the laws of mourning and marriage is addressed *'el-hakkōhănîm* 'to (all) the priests', the introduction to the blemishes is addressed to *'îš mizzar'ăkā* 'any man *of your seed*' (v. 17bα), an expression that includes, and perhaps emphasizes, the direct descendant of Aaron in his high priestly office. Perhaps it is no accident that the following impurity disqualifications, though voiced in the singular (22:3–8), are introduced by the plural *mikkol-zar'ăkem* '*all* your seed', an indication that the entire priestly cadre is being addressed. In any case, the interpretation of v. 23 as referring to the high priest solves both contextual and structural problems in this chapter.

desecrate (my sanctums) yĕḥallēl ('et-miqdāšay). This verb is used precisely and correctly: a blemish desecrates, desanctifies; it does not *mĕṭammē'* 'pollute'. The verb *ḥillel* is H's term for P's *ma'al*, which also refers to sanctum desecration (Milgrom 1976a: 16–21, 86–89). What happens when a sanctum is desecrated? The law of 5:14–16 declares that a person who desecrates a sanctum must pay its assessed value plus a 20 percent fine. This implies that the desecrated sanctum is discarded. But the altar and the inner sanctums of the sanctuary are obviously not replaced. If desecrated, how, then, can they be reused? The text provides no answers, so we have to resort to logic. If polluted sanctums, a worse condition, must be purged with the blood of the purification offering (Lev 4, 16), should we not expect that desecrated sanctums must be reconsecrated? Perhaps other consecrating rites will provide a clue. On Yom Kippur, the sacrificial altar must be both purified and consecrated (wĕṭiḥărô wĕqiddĕšô, 16:19). That is, it first must be neutralized—have its status changed from impure (ṭammē') to common (ḥōl); its impurity is removed (wĕṭiḥărô) by daubing it with blood of the purification offering. Then, its status must be changed from common (ḥōl) to holy (wĕqiddĕšô) by sprinkling it with the blood (for details, see NOTE on 16:19). The initial consecration of the sanctuary also calls for a double rite, but with sacred oil, not sacred blood; that is, the sanctums are both anointed and sprinkled (8:10–11). This provides a more apt analogy, since the sanctums require consecration, not purification from impurity. Perhaps, then, desecrated sacred furniture of the sanctuary had to be reconsecrated with the sacred oil of anointment. However, without further evidence, this conclusion remains a surmise.

my sanctums. miqdāšay. Three renderings of this word have been proposed: (1) the LXX presupposes another text miqdaš 'ĕlōhāyw 'the sanctuary of his God'; (2) "sacred precincts," a spatial designation, a clearly attested usage (e.g., 12:4; 16:33; 20:3; 21:12 [twice]; 26:2 [= 19:30], Num 19:20), also in the plural (Jer 51:51; Ps 68:36); and (3) the previously mentioned veil (sanctums of the shrine) and (outer) altar (Bekhor Shor).

The first interpretation must be rejected out of hand as an unsupported emendation; it may have arisen out of fear that the MT might imply multiple sanctuaries. This, I shall propose, is the precise meaning of the plural miqdĕšêkem (26:31), where the reference, however, is to pre-Hezekian multiple sanctuaries (see the NOTE), not to the one authorized sanctuary referred to in this verse.

The second interpretation, "sacred precincts," is plausible because, as noted, it is amply attested in many priestly texts. Elsewhere, I find it difficult to distinguish between the second and third interpretations. For example, the plural of miqdāš found in Jer 51:51; Ezek 21:7; 28:18; Pss 68:36; 73:17 can be rendered as either "sacred precincts" or "sanctums" (Milgrom 1970: 23, n. 78). Here, however, I prefer the third interpretation, "my sanctums," because it fits the context of the verse and because of the meaning of the verb that follows:

sanctifies them. mĕqaddĕšām. The antecedent of the suffix is problematic. The usual interpretation is that it refers to the priests (as in vv. 15 and 8 LXX). This would mean, however, that the priests are referred to in the plural in the context of a single priest. The problem is not unsurmountable. The switch of person is again attested with the same verb mĕqaddiškem/ mĕqaddĕšām (LXX) in a singular context (vv. 7–8). However, I prefer the interpretation that the antecedent is the veil and altar, the sanctums specified in the beginning of the verse (Dillmann and Ryssel 1897). God initially sanctified them (Exod 29:43–44) by means of his kābôd (Lev 9:6, 23) and continues to sanctify them (hence, the participle) by his presence.

V. 24. Subscript

24. *Thus Moses spoke to Aaron and his sons and to all the Israelites.* wayĕdabbēr mōšeh 'el-'ahărōn wĕ'el-bānāyw wĕ'el-kol-bĕnê yiśrā'ēl. This compliance report

contains a major problem. Moses, indeed, had been commanded to speak to Aaron (v. 17) and to his sons (v. 1), but nowhere in chap. 21 is there any statement that Moses was supposed to speak to the Israelites. Wessely (1846) proposes that this verse fills in the addressees missing in the prior headings: *wayyĕdabbēr*, *'ahărōn*, and *bĕnê yiśrā'ēl* in v. 1 and *bĕnê 'ahărōn* in v. 17; however, no such purpose is attested in any other compliance formula. Dillmann and Ryssel (1897) suggest that it is intended to be a compliance subscript for chaps. 20–21 or 17–21, both addressed to the Israelites; however, they admit that it should have followed chap. 22, which is addressed to all three—Aaron, his sons (vv. 1, 17), and the Israelites (v. 17)—and which lacks a compliance subscript.

Thus the statement "to all the Israelites" is an interpolation. The rabbis claim that it alerts the Israelites to the need of warning the priests to be on guard that no disqualified priest invalidate their offerings (*Sipra* Emor 3:12). Ehrlich (H) adds that it is a warning to the Israelites lest their own encroachment invalidate their sacrifices. But this verse *in its entirety* may be the work of the redactor. D. Stewart has noted that YHWH speaks to Moses seven times in 17:1–21:24 (17:1, 8aα; 18:1; 19:1; 20:1; 21:1, 16), the first time to all three constituencies (Aaron, his sons, Israel, 17:1). It would have been the redactor who added 21:24 as a summary compliance statement containing the same three. As further signs of symmetry, one should note that the center, 19:1, contains the expanded addressee *kol-'ădat bĕnê yiśrā'ēl* and that the first and last three fall in the same chapters (17 and 21).

My own (tentative) reasoning is that it is a statement by the H redactor that priestly disqualifications, in all other cultures the private responsibility of their priestly elites, are—as all of God's commands—the concern of all Israel (see NOTES on 23:44; 26:46; 27:34; see the extensive NOTE in 17:2). That this represents the quintessential viewpoint of H is strikingly demonstrated by H's appendix to chap. 16, vv. 29–34a (vol. 1.1054–59). The body of chap. 16 (vv. 1–28 [P]) is addressed to the high priest, Aaron, via Moses (v. 2). But in the appendix (vv. 29–34a [H]), the address shifts to the plural, to Israel—without any introduction or proleptic preparation (Gorman 1990: 66; vol. 1.1054–55). In this appendix, Israel is given collateral commandments (self-denial and cessation from labor, *lākem* [bis], vv. 29, 31). In addition, a seemingly irrelevant summary of the high priest's rites is cited (vv. 32–33), followed by a notice that his performance (*zō't*) is a binding statute *for Israel* (again *lākem*, v. 34a). This can only mean that the high priest's precise performance in purging the sanctuary and transferring its impurities as well as Israel's sins to a scapegoat is *ultimately the responsibility of the entire community*. Thus the impeccable appearance and behavior of the ordinary priest, as detailed in chap. 21, is a fortiore Israel's responsibility. The two H pericopes are related: all priests, including the high priest, are answerable to the people.

Moreover, as pointed out by Gerstenberger (1996: 307–8), the behavior of priests was not a matter of indifference to the public. Reprehensible priestly deeds, such as those exhibited by Eli's sons, involving illicit ritual procedures and sexual practices (1 Sam 2:12–17, 22 LXX), became the subject of gossip. The prophets frequently berated the priests on similar grounds (e.g., Hos 4:4–11;

Mal 1:6–13). The question, however, remains: Why was this verse not placed at the end of chap. 22? Perhaps it was not essential there, since 22:17–23 is explicitly addressed to all of Israel. Furthermore, the first part of chap. 22 (vv. 1–16) deals with cases of impure priests or ineligible members of their household eating sacred food—acts that are furtive and, hence, removed from the purview of the Israelites. The priestly disqualifications of chap. 21, by contrast, be they contact with the dead or illicit marriages or bodily defects, are all subject to observation and can, therefore, be assigned to the Israelites as their supervisory responsibility.

COMMENTS

A. Parallelism and Inversion in Lev 21:1b–15 (Christine E. Hayes)

Lev 21:1b–15 can be divided into two pericopes. The first (vv. 1b–9) contains a series of laws and exhortations for the ordinary priests, while the second (vv. 10–15) contains a related series of laws and exhortations for the high priest. These two pericopes exhibit striking structural features attesting to the writer's conscious attempt to interlock the laws for priest and high priest so as to create a coherent unit. Beyond its patent aesthetic and mnemonic purpose, this interlocking structure also serves an exegetical purpose, as will be indicated below.

There are two independent formal principles at work in the construction of Lev 21:1b–15: parallelism and inversion. The parallelism is apparent primarily at the macro level. Each of the two pericopes contains four major units arranged in parallel order (vv. 1b–9: A, B, C, D ‖ vv. 10–15: A', B', C', D'). The inversion is apparent at the micro level. Within each parallel unit, overlapping or identical material generally appears in inverse order.

Parallel Structure

Both pericopes can be subdivided into four units in parallel sequence:

Unit		First pericope (vv. 1b–9)	Second pericope (vv. 10–15)
A//A'	Prohibitions concerning corpse defilement and mourning rites	A = vv. 1b–5	A' = vv. 10–11
B//B'	Exhortations concerning holiness	B = v. 6	B' = v. 12
C//C'	Marriage prohibitions	C = v. 7	C' = vv. 13–14
D//D'	Statement concerning intergenerational desecration	D = v. 9	D' = v. 15

The parallelism in unit B‖B' (v. 6 ‖ v. 12) is quite extreme, extending to the micro level. Vv. 6 and 12 contain four clauses each, and these clauses are functionally parallel:

1. The first clause in each case charges the priest or high priest to remain in a condition or place of holiness.
2. The second clause contains a prohibition against defiling a certain sanctum (God's name or the sanctuary).
3. The third clause contains the rationale for the preceding clauses, a rationale connected with the party's special function or status.
4. The fourth clause is a final exclamation.

Unit B (v. 6)

a. *qĕdōšîm yihyû lē'lōhêhem*
b. *wĕlō' yĕhallĕlû šēm 'ĕlōhêhem*
c. *kî 'et-'iššê YHWH leḥem 'ĕlōhêhem hēm maqrîbīm*
d. *wĕhāyû qōdeš*

Unit B' (v. 12)

a'. *ûmin-hammiqdāš lō' yēṣē'*
b'. *wĕlō' yĕhallēl 'ēt miqdaš 'ĕlōhāw*
c'. *kî nēzer šemen mišḥat 'ĕlōhāyw 'ālāyw*
d'. *'ănî YHWH*

Inverted Structure

Wherever identical material appears in the parallel units, there is a marked tendency toward inversion as a second-order interlocking device (with the distinct exception of unit B‖B', which features parallelism at the micro level; see above). Because the laws for an ordinary priest and a high priest are different, the parallel units in the two pericopes do not contain entirely identical material—but where an overlap occurs, inversion is featured.

First pericope (vv. 1b–9)		Second pericope (vv. 10–15)	
Unit A		**Unit A'**	
vv. 1b–4	Corpse defilement	v. 10	Mourning rites
v. 5	Mourning rites	v. 11	Corpse defilement
(v. 2)	"mother, father . . . ")	(v. 11)	" . . . father or mother")
Unit B		**Unit B'**	
v. 6a	Be holy	v. 12a	Remain in holy precinct
v. 6b	Do not defile God's name	v. 12b	Do not defile the sanctuary
v. 6c	Because . . .	v. 12c	Because . . .
v. 6d	Be holy!	v. 12d	I am YHWH!
Unit C		**Unit C'**	
v. 7	Promiscuous	vv. 13–14	Divorced
	Raped		Raped
	Divorced		Promiscuous
Unit D		**Unit D'**	
v. 9	Daughter (desecrates)	v. 15	Father (desecrates)
	Father		Daughter

In unit A, vv. 1b–5 contain the prohibitions of corpse-contamination followed by the prohibition of certain mourning rites, while vv. 10–11 in unit A' contain similar prohibitions in reverse order; that is, the prohibition of certain mourning rites precedes the prohibition of corpse-contamination. In addition, the terms "mother" and "father" are inverted.

In unit B, there are no inversions. On the contrary, there is extreme parallelism (see above) and for good reason. Unlike the other units, unit B∥B′ contains one sentence with four clauses tightly arranged in a sequence of logical progression that cannot be inverted and remain coherent.

In unit C, there is a minimal overlap of material, since the second pericope contains additional exhortations relevant to only the high priest. Nevertheless, the material that does overlap does exhibit inversion. Specifically, the list of prohibited women (promiscuous, raped, divorced) appears in the second pericope in reverse order (to begin with the innovation, the widow [Wessely 1846]; see NOTE on v. 14—J.M.).

In unit D, the inversion is not merely formal, but ideational. In units A and C, we find purely mechanical inversions of disparate items that do not affect the general idea being conveyed: in A, first corpse defilement and then mourning rites are prohibited; in A′, mourning rites are prohibited before corpse defilement; in C, three categories of prohibited women are listed; and in C′, the list is inverted. In none of these cases does the inverted order affect meaning. However, in unit D∥D′, subject and object are inverted, and this change does indeed affect meaning. To be specific, the inverted word order results in the creation of an inverted idea: whereas v. 9 refers to a daughter who desecrates (i.e., disgraces) her father, v. 15 refers to a father who desecrates (i.e., disqualifies) his offspring. Thus the *idea* of "child desecrating parent" is inverted in the second pericope and is transformed into the *idea* of "parent desecrating child." (Note that the same verb *ḥillēl* is employed by the two verses.)

Exegetical Implications

The structural interlocking of these two pericopes has exegetical implications. Otherwise, obscure issues are illuminated by comparing the verse in question with its twin in the corresponding pericope. I submit that

1. V. 10 prohibits the two actions in question *qua mourning rites,* just as its twin in v. 5 clearly does (hence I have referred to both as "mourning rites" in the analysis presented above).
2. V. 15 is speaking of the high priest's desecration of his offspring *by means of prohibited sexual activity,* just as its twin verse (v. 9) clearly refers to the intergenerational effect of *prohibited sexual activity.*
3. V. 8 is an interpolation (as might have been inferred from the sudden change in voice) since it has no twin in the corresponding passage.

B. The Priestly Blemishes (21:17b–21): Structure and Meaning

A   a   *ʾîš mizzarʿăkā lĕdōrōtam*

       x   *ʾăšer yihyeh bô* **mûm**

          b   *lōʾ yiqrab lĕhaqrîb leḥem ʾĕlōhāyw* (v. 17b)

a₁   *kî kol-'îš*

   x   *'ăšer bô-**mûm***

       b₁   *lō' yiqrāb* (v. 18a) [*lĕhaqrîb 'et-'iššê* YHWH]

       X   Twelve **blemishes** (vv. 18b–20)

A' a₁' *kol- 'îš*

     x   *'ăšer- bô **mûm***

   a' *mizzera' 'ahărōn hakkōhēn*

       b₁' *lō' yiggaš lĕhaqrîb 'et-'iššê* YHWH (v. 21a)

       x   ***mûm** bô*

       b'   *'ēt leḥem 'ĕlōhāyw lō' yiggaš lĕhaqrîb* (v. 21b)

A   a   A man of your offspring in any generation

     x   who has **a blemish**

       b   shall not be qualified to offer the food of his God (v. 17b)

   a₁ No one at all

     x   who has **a blemish**

       b₁   shall be qualified (v. 18a) [to offer YHWH's gifts]

       X   Twelve **blemishes** (vv. 18b–20)

A' a₁' Every man

     x   who has **a blemish**

   a' among the offspring of Aaron the priest

       b₁' shall not be qualified to offer YHWH's gifts (v. 21a);

     x   having **a blemish**

       b'   he shall not be qualified to offer the food of his God (v. 21b)

The many fine points in this sophisticated structure are almost too numerous to mention. The most glaring and, hence, most important point is that it consistently keeps the key word "blemish" (x) in the middle (boldface): in each of the two panels (axb; a₁xb₁); in each of the two chiasms (a₁'xa'; b₁'xb'); and in the overall structure (AXA') not by the word "blemish" but by enumerating twelve of them.

The twelve blemishes (X) are enveloped by twelve clauses (axb; a₁xb₁; a₁'xa'; b₁'xb'), which themselves are of equal number (4a + 4b + 4x). Thus the number twelve is the structural key to the pericope. This implies that twelve blemishes are enumerated not because there are no more. Rather, the enumerated twelve are generic categories from which specific blemishes of each genre can be derived. Thus the rabbis are justified in adding many others to this list (*b. Bek* 43a,b; Abravanel; cf. NOTES on 22:22–24).

The two panels of A and the two chiasms of A' are totally interlocked by similar or synonymous wording arranged chiastically. Thus a + a₁ = a₁' + a', and again b + b₁ = b₁' + b' (note that in each equation, the positions are inverted:

a₁' precedes a', and b₁' precedes b'). The final chiasm b₁' x b' (vv. 21aβ,b) is
itself an introverted structure:

c   *lō' yiggaš lĕhaqrîb*
d   *'et- 'iššê YHWH*
   x   *mûm bô*
d'   *'ēt leḥem 'ĕlōhāyw*
c' *lō' yiggaš lĕhaqrîb*

Note that in this final chiasm, there are subtle changes: the verb *nāgaš* is substituted for *qārab*, and the x clause reads *mûm bô* instead of *'ăšer bô mûm*.

I have added the clause *lĕhaqrîb 'et- 'iššê YHWH* to v. 18a (b₁ in the diagram)
in order to yield two occurrences of *yiqrab lĕhaqrîb* in A and to balance the two
occurrences of *yiggaš lĕhaqrîb* in A'. However, the absence of this clause in the
MT may be due to the artistry of the author, who wished to break up the mo-
notony of repetition. Besides, the verb *qārab* can stand alone without an object,
as in the formula *hazzār haqqārēb yûmat* 'The stranger who encroaches shall be
put to death' (Num 1:51; 18:7).

The remarkable thing about this structure is that it accounts for every word.
Its many redundancies, which are the despair of the critics (inducing them to
drastic deletions), are witnesses to the work of a master craftsman. Such skill is
evident in other H passages, but not, in my opinion, to the same superlative degree (see Introduction I A).

There are two major questions regarding the blemishes themselves:

1. Why are they limited to the body with nary a word, not even a hint, concerning disqualifying moral and religious defects, which surely are more
   important considerations?
2. Granted the limitation to physical defects, why were more such obvious
   defects as deafness and muteness omitted?

The answers to both questions rest on a fundamental premise: the list of disqualifying blemishes in priests is matched by the same number (twelve) of equivalent blemishes of sacrificial animals (22:22–24). Hence since moral standards
are not applied to animals, none are required of priests (in this list). In effect,
not only have structural considerations determined the composition of the pericope on animal blemishes, but the blemishes themselves have been arbitrarily
chosen to match the structure of an equivalent list of disqualifying blemishes in
sacrificial animals. However, I have reserved COMMENT D for another and, for
me, a more acceptable answer.

The patent arbitrariness of this list is further illustrated by the second question: the omission of other obviously impairing and ostensibly disqualifying defects such as deafness and muteness. The rabbis, I submit, (unintentionally) provide the correct answer. Occasionally, they will use such expressions as *mar'ît
hā'ayin* 'appearance' (*m. Bek.* 7:3; cf. 7:5). To be sure, among the 142 blem-

ishes listed by the rabbis appear the deaf and the mute (for priests and, explicitly, not for animals; *m. Bek.* 7:6). However, the rabbis are not bound by H's structural criteria, and even though appearance seems to be the standard for a disqualifying defect, they were not going to exempt an obviously impaired priest such as a deaf-mute.

There exists one blemish among the twelve that patently cannot be observed: a crushed testicle. This ostensible flaw is, in actuality, proof of the artificiality of the list. Indeed, it does not fit the criterion of appearance. But it had to be chosen in order to correspond to the list of blemished animals, where injured (and exposed) genitals appear in four different forms (22:24).

It should not come as a surprise that the selection of the twelve blemishes of animals and persons eligible for the altar is based on appearance. A similar criterion also determines the skin diseases declared *ṣāra'at* (vol. 1.1000–1003). The priestly system of impurities / blemishes is thereby affirmed as an arbitrary set of rules reflecting some higher values—in the case of impurity, that Israel should choose life (God's laws) over the forces of death (the violation of God's laws), and in the case of blemishes, that YHWH's sphere of holiness demands moral and ritual perfection.

A comparison of the two lists, blemish for blemish, is discussed in the NOTES on 22:22–24. Here it shall suffice to deal with the larger, more fundamental question: the purpose of composing two lists of the same number of approximately the same blemishes, one for priests and the other for animals. The key to this answer is that these animal blemishes apply to only sacrificial animals, those that will be offered up by the priests on the altar. That priests were subject to the same requirements as their sacrificial animals was also demanded in other cultures: "A priest whose body has a blemish is to be avoided like something of ill omen. . . . This is an object of censure even in sacrificial victims: how much more so in priests!" (Seneca, *Controversiae* 4:2). Seneca thus alludes to the belief current throughout the ancient Near East that physical deficiencies are signs of bad omens. So it is explicitly stated in Babylonian birth omens: birth defects, both animal and human, portend catastrophe (von Soden 1952, cited by Gerstenberger 1996: 319). That this was not the case in Israel is shown by the fact that blemished priests, though prohibited from officiating at the altar, could enter the sanctuary and eat most holy portions (see NOTES on vv. 22 and 23; cf. *m. Kel.* 1:8).

The lesson is clear: those who qualify to function in the sacred sphere, whether human or animal, must admit to a more rigid standard than those who live outside. Thus Israelites who are not holy but must aspire to holiness are limited to relatively few animals for their table (Deut 14:4–5 enumerates ten quadrupeds, and Lev 11 and Deut 14 make allowance for some fish and birds), whereas the altar, "the table before YHWH" (Ezek 41:22), permits only three quadrupeds and two birds (cf. Lev 1). Non-Israelites are given unlimited access to the animal kingdom, but they are restricted by one law: the prohibition against ingesting blood (Gen 9:4).

These criteria form the basis of P's dietary laws, discussed in vol. 1.718–36.

H's transformation of P's system is also discussed there and elaborated in greater detail in the Introduction II B, G.

C. Mourning Customs in the Biblical World

The most detailed account of mourning in the ancient Near East is found in the description of El's reaction to the news of the death of Baal:

[w]l. hdm. yṯb (14) larṣ[.]	he sat on the ground (cf. Isa 58:5; Jer 6:26; Ezek 27:30)
yṣq. ʿmr (15) un. lriš.	he poured earth (?) of mourning on his head (cf. Job 2:12)
ʿpr. plṯt (16) l. qdqdh	the dust in which he wallowed on his skull (cf. Ezek 27:30)
lpš. yks (17) mizrtm.	for clothing he covered himself with a loin-cloth (cf. Amos 8:10)
ġr. babn (18) ydy.	he scratched (his) skin with a stone knife (cf. Josh 5:2–3)
psltm. byʿr	he made incisions (?) with a razor
(19) yhdy. lḥm.wdqn	he gashed (his) cheeks and chin (cf. 1 Kgs 18:28; Hos 7:14)
(20) yṯlt. qn. drʿh[.]	he raked (?) his collar-bone (cf. Job 31:22)
yḥrṯ (21) kgn.ap lb.	he plowed (his) chest like a garden
kʿmq. yṯlt (22) bm	the raked (?) his back like a valley (cf. Jer 16:6)
yšu. gh[.] wyṣḥ	he lifted his voice and shouted: (cf. Jer 46:12)
bʿl. mt. . . .	"Baal is dead . . . " (KTU 1.5 VI:13–22; cf. 1.5 VI:31–1.6 I:5)

Appended to the translation are some of the biblical parallels—selected from actual practices, not laws—that indicate the similarity of mourning rites in Israel and Ugarit (see also *Epic of Aqhat* 171–74). But lest one think that the similarity is limited to the Canaanite or Northwest Semitic ambiance, I shall confine my remaining examples to the Greco-Roman civilization, and concentrate on mourning regulations for priests:

> They (the Galli) observe a period of seven days [cf. Num 19:14], then they enter the sanctuary. If they enter before this time, they commit a sacrilege. In such matters, they abide by the following customs: If anyone of them sees a corpse, he does not enter the sanctuary that day. On the following day, after purifying himself, he enters. When the corpse is that of a relative, they observe thirty days, shave their heads [contrast Lev 21:4a] and then enter the temple. (Lucian, *De Dea Syria* 52)

> (At the death of a Scrutineer), the priests and priestesses will bring up the rear; they are of course banned from other funerals, but provided the oracle

at Delphi also approves, they shall attend this one, as it will not defile them. (Plato, *Laws* 12:947)

Among the Greeks, pollution extended to a house in which death had occurred, to relics of the dead (cf. Num 19:14–16), and even to kin; in ancient Rome, even though the relatives were separated from the deceased by many miles they became contaminated (cf. Parker 1983: chap. 2). In Rome, no priest or augur was permitted "to engage in ceremonies of the dead" (Tacitus, *Annales*, 1:62). A priest delivered a funeral oration behind a curtain, but he was not forbidden to view the corpse (Dio Cass. 56:31); however, the Flamen Dialis (the high priest) "never approached a place where there was a tomb with ashes [cf. Num 19:15], and never touched a corpse, though he was permitted to attend to funeral rites" (Gell. 10, 15). Moreover, cyprus boughs were placed before a house containing a corpse "lest a Flamen Dialis enter unwittingly and defile himself" (Serv. ad Aen. 6:176). Finally, to cite one culture outside the Mediterranean littoral, a Hindu Brahman is considered defiled for "having voluntarily followed a corpse" (Manu 5.103).

How startling is the contrast with ancient Egypt, where the grave and the dead were sacred (*SDB* 9:430–52; cf. Gevaryahu 1960: 50) and where an inscription could read "Whoever enters this tomb after he has purified himself is as though he has purified himself for the temple of the great god" (Bonnet 1952).

Thus there are grounds for the theory that the prohibition imposed on Israel's priesthood against contact with the dead is a continuation of H's polemic against Egyptian practices. Just as chaps. 18 and 20 explicitly declare the incestuous unions practiced in Egypt taboo for all Israelites (see NOTE on 18:3), so the severe impurity generated by contact with the dead, in general (Num 19), and the prohibition against contact with dead enjoined upon priests (absolute for the high priest, modified for ordinary priests, 21:1–4, 10–12), in particular, may be construed as being partially directed against Egypt, where the cult of the dead was espoused and ministered by the Egyptian priesthood. However, the fact that Egypt is a solitary exception in the ancient Near East and that other societies share many of Israel's taboos in contacting the dead and mourning for them makes it likely that another rationale lies behind this legislation. Moreover, as pointed out by Eerdmans (1912), the fact that priests are conceded the right to defile themselves for their deceased parents—the very ones venerated in a cult of the dead—makes it even more unlikely that these prohibitions on mourning have anything to do with the cult of the dead. As argued elsewhere in this commentary, behind all the priestly rules of impurity lies the pedagogic goal of teaching the people of Israel that its divinely revealed laws promote life and reject death (see INTRODUCTION to vv. 1b–5, and vol. 1.307–19, 766–68, 1000–1004).

D. Blemished Priests: A Comparative Survey

One should not be surprised to find that the ancients took pains to compose detailed lists of the blemishes that disqualified their priests and all others (e.g., the Mesopotamian *bâru*, or diviner) who claimed to have access to the gods. After all, they also required physical perfection for royal attendants (Dan 1:4) and leaders (e.g., Absalom, 2 Sam 14:25). In fact, is modern society much different? Recall how President Franklin Roosevelt's paralyzed legs were carefully (and successfully) hidden from the American public during his long political career.

The sectaries of Qumran modeled their list on Lev 21. But they were also punctilious about spelling out some of the latter's obvious lacunae. For example:

WKWL 'YŠ MNWG' [B'ḤT MKW]L ṬWM'T H'DM 'L YB' BQHL 'LH
WKWL 'YŠ MNWG'B['LH LBLTY] HḤZYQ M'MD BTWK H'DH WKWL
MNWG' BBŚRW NK'[H RGLYM] 'W YDYM [PS]Ḥ 'W ['W]R 'W ḤRŠ
'W 'LM 'W MWM MNWG' [BBŚRW] LR'WT 'YNYM 'W 'YŠ Z[QN]
KWŠL LBL[T]Y HTḤZQ BTWK H'DH 'L YB[W'W] 'LH LHTYṢB [BTWK]
'DT ['NW]ŠY HŠM KY' ML'KY QDŠ [B'D]TM

And no man smitten with human impurity shall enter the assembly of these (men), no man smitten with any of them shall be confirmed in his office in the midst of the congregation. No man smitten in his flesh, or paralyzed in his feet or hands, or lame, or blind, or deaf, or dumb, or smitten in his flesh with a visible blemish; no old and tottery man unable to control himself in the midst of the congregation; none of these shall come to hold office among the congregation of the men of renown, for the Angels of Holiness are [with] their [congregation]. (1QSa 2:4–9 [Vermes 1987: 102])

The eschatological community portrayed in these regulations (priestly in leadership, but not in membership) must pass muster as though it consisted of only priests in order to qualify for being in the presence of the holy angels. These requirements are supplemented by another, as yet unpublished, Qumran fragment:

WKWL HYWTW 'WYL [WM]ŠWG' 'L YBW WKWL PTY WŠWGH WKH
'YNYM LBLTY R'WT [W]HGR 'W PSḤ 'W ḤRŠ 'W N'R Z'ṬWṬ '[L
YBW<'>] 'YŠ [M]'LH 'L TWK H'DH KY ML'K[Y] HQWD[Š BTWKKM]

Fools, madmen, simpletons and imbeciles, the blind [lit. "those who, being weak of eye, cannot see"], the maimed, the lame, the deaf, and minors, none of these may enter the midst of the community, for the holy angels (are in the midst of it). (4QD[6] 17I:6–9; Milik 1959: 114)

On the special requirements for the priests of Qumran, see 4Q266 (discussed in INTRODUCTION to vv. 16–23); on the omission of the lame, mute, and moral defects from the biblical list, see the INTRODUCTION to vv. 16–23, and COMMENT B; and for other Qumranic disqualification lists, see 1QM 7:4–5; CD 15:15–17; and 11QT 45:12–13.

The Mesopotamian documents are rich with bodily disqualifications, particularly as they pertain to the *bāru*, the diviner. They are summarized by van der Toorn (1985: 29), with my comments and sources in parentheses: "who is not of pure descent (preferable to "descendant of a free [*ellu*] man," CAD 2.123a), or is not perfect as to his appearance and his limbs (BBR 24:30; CAD 4:106), who is cross-eyed (*zaqtu*, CAD 21.64a), has chipped teeth (BBR 24:31), a mutilated finger (*nakpu*), who suffers from any disease of the testes (?) or of the skin." Another Mesopotamian text specifies that only if the diviner "is without blemish in body and limb may he approach (*iteḫḫi*) the presence of Šamaš and Adad where live inspection and oracle (take place)" (Lambert 1967: 132, ll. 22–29).

The candidate for the priesthood (*nišakku* or *pašīšu*) in Enlil's temple has to be inspected "from the edge of his head to the tips of his toes" and not have a face disfigured by mutilated eyes, irregular features, or brands (Borger 1973: 164: I, 11–12; 165: I, 33, 41–42). What is of special significance in this text is its concern for proof that he has no police record, but not for personal morality, namely, that he is not "a bloodstained person, who has been apprehended in theft or robbery? (*kiššatu*); a condemned person who has been thrashed or lashed" (Borger 1973: 165: I, 29–32).

I have not found an equivalent list for the Hittite world. Surely, one must have existed, since the Hittite laws declare unambiguously that bestiality with a horse or mule is permitted, but that person may not approach the king, *nor may he ever become a priest* (HL § 200A; cf. Hoffner 1973: 85, n. 2; Moyer 1969: 61). Moreover, an unfavorable omen is on one occasion attributed to "two mutilated men (who) came into the temple" (*ANET* 497, corrected by R. Stefanini).

To judge from Egyptian papyri of the Roman period, which undoubtedly preserve ancient practice, there were priestly specialists in the temples whose function was to inspect sacrifices. They were called *sphragista* 'seal bearers' because they would stamp the animal without blemishes (cf. Licht and Leibowitz 1962). The Greeks also required physical perfection in both animals and priests (Plato, *Laws* 6.759–60).

Finally, turning to the ancient Hindu culture outside the ambience of the Near East, Brahmans born with a bodily defect or receiving one before the sixteenth year are excluded from the holy caste and from the rite of consecration. Also excluded are liars; calumniators; those who are passionate or quarrelsome, malicious or spiteful, haughty or averse to prayer; those who are blind or deaf; those whose teeth are large; and those who have any symptom that threatens to undermine life or health (Manu 2.176; 5.138, 143; Zend-Avesta 21.92, 93; Vendid 2.80 ff, cited in Kalisch 1867–72: 472, 571, n. 14).

The absence of any moral requirements in amply attested Mesopotamian texts (akin to those in the Hindu culture) is striking, particularly since one text, cited above, requires only that the aspirant for the priesthood not be a criminal. Still, in view of the same silence in Lev 21, we should not be too hasty in concluding that moral qualities were not required of Babylonian priests. Indeed, the clue may be hidden by the fact that both lists, Mesopotamian and biblical, were written by priests who may have taken moral requirements for granted. After all, the prophet, an outside observer, and a critical one at that, could lambaste the priest for his moral dereliction (e.g., Hos 4:6–8) and heap paeans of praise for his moral perfection (Mal 2:4–7). Still, one cannot but harbor the suspicion that because the biblical priesthood was hereditary, it too—no differently from its Mesopotamian counterpart—would disqualify a priest on moral grounds only if he were apprehended and convicted of some egregious criminal act.

22. INSTRUCTIONS FOR THE PRIESTS AND LAY PERSONS

TRANSLATION

[1]YHWH spoke to Moses, saying: [2]Instruct Aaron and his sons to be scrupulous concerning the sacred donations that the Israelites consecrate to me so they do not desecrate my holy name, I am YHWH. [3]Say (further) to them: Throughout your generations, if any man of your offspring, while he is impure, encroaches upon the sacred donations that the Israelites may consecrate to YHWH, that person shall be cut off from my presence: I YHWH (have spoken).

Concerning Sacred Food

[4]Any man of Aaron's offspring who has scale disease or a chronic discharge [or is contaminated by a corpse], may not eat of the sacred donations until he is pure. [One who touches anything contaminated by a corpse, or] If a man has an emission of semen, [5]or if a man touches any swarming thing by which he is made impure or any human being by whom he is made impure whatever (be) his impurity, [6]the person who touches any of these shall be impure until evening, and he shall not eat of the sacred donations unless he has washed his body in water [7]and the sun has set. Then, he shall be pure; and afterward he may eat of the sacred donations, for they are his food. [8]He shall not eat of any animal that died or was torn by beasts to become impure by it. I YHWH (have spoken). [9]They shall heed my prohibition lest they bear sin by it and die thereby when they desecrate it; I am YHWH who sanctifies them.

[10]No lay person shall eat sacred food; neither may a priest's resident hireling eat sacred food. [11]But if a priest purchases a person with money, he may eat of it; and those born into his household may eat of his food. [12]If a priest's daughter marries a layman, she may not eat of the sacred gifts; [13]but if a priest's daughter is widowed or divorced and without children, and returns to her father's house as in her youth, she may eat of her father's food. But no lay person may eat of it.

[14]If any (lay) person inadvertently eats of a sacred donation, he shall add one-fifth of its value to it and pay to the priests the (combined) sacred donation. [15]They (the priests) shall not desecrate the sacred donations of the Israelites that they set aside for YHWH [16]by causing them (the Israelites) to bear the penalty of reparation when they (the Israelites) eat their (own) sacred donations; for it is I YHWH who sanctifies them (the priests).

Concerning Blemished Sacrificial Animals

[17]YHWH spoke to Moses, saying: [18]Speak to Aaron, to his sons, and to all the Israelites, and say to them:

Whenever any person from the house of Israel or from the aliens in Israel presents an offering for any of their vows or any of their freewill gifts, which may be presented to YHWH as a burnt offering, [19]to be acceptable on your behalf (it must be) a male without blemish, from cattle, sheep, or goats. [20]You shall not present any that has a blemish, because it will not be acceptable on your behalf.

[21]And whenever any person presents, from the herd or the flock, a well-being offering to YHWH for an expressed vow or as a freewill offering, (it must be) perfect in order to be acceptable; it shall not have any blemish. [22]Anything blind, (has a) broken (limb), is maimed, (has) a seeping sore, a scar, or a lichen—such you shall not present to YHWH; you shall not put any of them on the altar as a food gift to YHWH. [23]You may, however, sacrifice as a freewill offering a herd or flock animal with an extended or contracted (limb), but it will not be accepted for a votive offering. [24]You shall not offer to YHWH (an animal) with bruised, crushed, torn, or cut-off (testicles). You shall not do (this) in your land. [25]And from the hand of a foreigner, you shall not offer the food of your God from any of these. Because of deformities and blemishes in them, they will not be accepted in your behalf.

Additional Criteria for Sacrificial Animals

[26]YHWH spoke to Moses, saying: [27]Whenever an ox or a sheep or a goat is born, it shall remain seven days with its mother, and from the eighth day on it will be acceptable as a food-gift offering to YHWH. [28]However, no animal from the herd or from the flock shall be slaughtered on the same day as its young.

[29]When you sacrifice a thanksgiving offering to YHWH, sacrifice [it] so that it will be acceptable on your behalf. [30]It shall be eaten on the same day; You shall not leave any of it until morning. I YHWH (have spoken).

Exhortation

[31]You shall heed my commandments and do them. I YHWH (have spoken). [32]You shall not desecrate my holy name that I may be sanctified in the midst of the Israelites. I am YHWH who sanctifies you, [33]your deliverer from the land of Egypt to be your God; I am YHWH.

Comment
The Structure of Chapter 22.

NOTES

Chap. 22 clearly is a continuation of chap. 21, which ends with priestly blemishes and continues here with priestly impurity. The previous chapter closes with a concession to blemished priests that they may partake of sacred food (21:22), but in this chapter that privilege is denied to impure priests (Bekhor Shor).

The chapter is divided into three sections, each of which is headed by a discrete divine address: to the priests via Moses (vv. 1–2aα), to the priests and Israelites via Moses (vv. 17–18a), and to no special audience (v. 26). The catchphrase *ʾănî YHWH* acts as a structural marker (M. Hildenbrand): v. 2 (ending the introductory formula); v. 3 (ending the general principle of the following laws); v. 8 (ending the first law section); v. 9 (ending the first subsection, dealing with the priests); v. 16 (ending the second subsection, dealing with the priests and ending the first major section of the chapter); v. 30 (ending the last section on the laws); v. 31 (ending the third section of the chapter, vv. 17–31); v. 32 (ending the envelope for the chapter; vv. 2, 32); v. 33 (end of chapter). The chapter's content can be outlined:

I. Topic: priests should be scrupulous when impure not to officiate or eat sacred food, and not to allow the nonpriest to eat it (vv. 1–16)
   A. Introductory formula (vv. 1–2aα)
      1. Basic command: scrupulousness regarding sacred donations (v. 2aβ,b)
   B. General law: encroachment on sacred donations in a state of impurity punishable by *kārēt* (v. 3)
   C. Specific law: eating sacred food (vv. 4–16)
      1. In regard to impure priests (vv. 4–9)
         a. Who are the sources of impurity (v. 4)
         b. Who touch an impure source (vv. 5–6a)
         c. The required purification (vv. 6b–7)
         d. Prohibition against eating from a carcass (v. 8)
         e. Peroration (v. 9)
      2. In regard to nonpriests (vv. 10–16)
         a. General law: lay persons forbidden to eat sacred food (v. 10a)
            (1) So too a priest's resident hireling (v. 10b)
            (2) But a priest's slave is permitted (v. 11)
            (3) So too the widowed or divorced childless priest's daughter (vv. 12–13a)
         b. General law (v. 10a) repeated (v. 13b)
      3. Reparation required for inadvertently eating forbidden sacred food (vv. 14–16)
         a. A 20 percent penalty (v. 14)
         b. A warning to the priests (vv. 15–16)
            (1) To prevent the Israelites from incurring this reparation (vv. 15–16a)
            (2) Rationale: holy priests are enjoined to sustain their holiness (v. 16b)
II. Topic: blemished sacrificial animals (vv. 17–25)
   A. Introductory formula (vv. 17–18a)
   B. Burnt offerings (vv. 18b–20)

    C. Well-being offerings (vv. 21–24)
       1. Must be unblemished (v. 21)
       2. Disqualifying blemishes (vv. 22–24)
    D. Prohibition against offering such animals gotten from foreigners (v. 25)
  III. Topic: additional criteria for sacrificial animals (vv. 26–33)
    A. Introductory formula (v. 26)
    B. Humanitarian safeguards concerning mother and young (vv. 27–28)
       1. First week together (v. 27)
       2. Not to be slaughtered on same day (v. 28)
    C. The thanksgiving offering (vv. 29–30)
    D. Exhortation (vv. 31–33)

Vv. 2–3. Introduction

2. *Aaron and his sons.* See the NOTE on 21:1.

be scrupulous. wĕyinnāzĕrû. Nipʿal reflexive of *nzr*, which followed by *min* means "separate oneself from"; compare *wĕyiprĕšûn* (*Tg. Onk.*; cf. *Sipra* Emor, par. 4:1). Thus *wayyinnāzēr mēʾaḥăray* 'broke away [lit. "separated himself"] from me' (Ezek 14:7). If, however, this verb is followed by the preposition *lamed*, then it means "separated for, to" or "attach." Thus *wayyinnāzĕrû labbōšet* 'they (Israel) attached themselves *to* shamefulness' (i.e., Baal, Hos 9:10; cf. Num 25:3). Similarly in the *Hipʿil*: the Nazirite vows *lĕhazzîr laYHWH* 'to separate himself *for* YHWH' (Num 6:2); *miyyayin wĕšēkār yazzîr*, if "he will separate himself *from* wine and ale" (v. 3). See also *wĕhizzartem . . . miṭṭumʾātām* 'You shall separate (the Israelites) from their impurity' (Lev 15:31), in a context similar to this one.

Other renderings are extensions of the basic meaning: *yizdahărûn* 'beware' (*Tgs. Ps.-J., Neof.*); *prosechō* 'give heed to' (LXX); 'abstain' (Pesh.). Hence the rendering "be scrupulous concerning" is adopted in the translation. As the following verse specifies, the context of this command is the apprehension lest the priests contact sancta in a state of impurity (cf. Tosefot on *b. Zeb.* 15b, s.v. *ʾellāʾ*).

sacred donations (*that the Israelites*). *qodšê* (*bĕnê yiśrāʾēl . . . ʾăšer hēm*), literally "the sacred donations of the Israelites . . . that they." For the syntactical peculiarity that compels this rendering, see below.

What precisely are these "sacred donations"? Dillmann and Ryssel (1897) hold that they refer to sacred food eaten *outside* the sanctuary, as indicated by the context of vv. 11–13. These, then, would fall under the category of rabbinic *qŏdāšîm qallîm*, literally "minor sacred offerings," such as the well-being offering and the priestly prebends from the crops (rabbinic *tĕrûmâ*). Since most sacred offerings (rabbinic *qŏdšê qŏdāšîm*), such as the meat of the purification and reparation offerings, are eaten inside the court, the purity of the priestly consumer is taken for granted. However, the use of the verb *yiqrab* 'encroach' in v. 3 implies otherwise. If the defiled priest is inside the sanctuary, he is liable to encroach on the divine sphere. Eerdmans (1912) also wishes to delimit this term to the (minor) sacred offerings on the grounds that most sacred offerings, such as the purification and reparation offerings, are omitted from the discussion of the animal blemishes (vv. 17–25). However, the burnt offering is clearly a most sacred offering, and it is explicitly featured (vv. 18–19). That the expression *qodšê bĕnê yiśrā'ēl* can refer to all the offerings to the sanctuary is proved by its occurrence in Num 18:8, where it heads up the list of both the sacred and the most sacred offerings (vv. 9–19). See, however, its use in v. 15.

Thus one must conclude that the term "sacred donations" in v. 2 is all inclusive, denoting both the sacred and the most sacred offerings (as in 21:22; with *Sipra* Emor, par. 4:5; *Keter Torah*; Wellhausen 1963; Elliger 1966; Porter 1976). This conclusion will be even more evident by the expression "he may not eat of the sacred donations" (v. 4), which surely refers to *all* sacred food (*Seper Hamibḥar*; cf. Exod 28:38 [twice]; Num 5:9, 10; 18:8; see NOTES on 5:15, 16).

that the Israelites consecrate to me. 'ăšer hēm maqdîšîm lî. This clause is moved up from the end of the verse (2bα) for the sake of clarity: "Metathesize the verse to interpret it" (Rashi). Ibn Ezra, however, justifies the order of the MT, claiming that its sense is that of an independent clause (as if it begins with a *waw*, i.e., *wa 'ăšer*), implying that both *qodšê bĕnê yiśrā'ēl* 'the sacrifices of the Israelites' and "those that they consecrate to me" (i.e., their sacred gifts) must not be desecrated by the priests.

Ibn Ezra's proposal might be countered by the fact that the verb *hiqdîš*, found forty-four times in a cultic context, never takes a sacrifice as its object. However, two passages containing this verb clearly imply that sacrifices are included: the following verse (22:3) and Exod 28:38. Thus Ibn Ezra's explanation is plausible, but even if the *waw* at its beginning is added (or intended), the syntax remains difficult. This clause should still precede *wĕlō' yĕḥallĕlû . . .* 'so that they do not desecrate . . .' (v. 2aγ). This conclusion is supported by the repetitive inclusio, v. 15, which envelops the unit vv. 1–16 (see its NOTE, and COMMENT A).

The rabbis, who also hold that this clause is independent, claim that it refers to the priests' own offerings, in contrast to those of the Israelites. Galil (1987: 155) suggests that the syntactic awkwardness of this clause indicates that it is a later appendage. However, it is essential to the very structure that he himself proposes (see COMMENT).

Kugler (1997: 10) claims that this clause shows that H, in contrast to P, grants Israel the power to consecrate its sacrifices. This cannot be correct. First, since this clause is part of the protasis rather than the apodosis, it is not the language of a polemic. To the contrary, it takes for granted that Israelites were *always* empowered to consecrate their offerings. Furthermore, since the subject of this verse is encroachment on the sacred, it is not limited to altar sacrifices, but covers all dedications to the sanctuary, such as property (27:14–25) and *ḥērem* items (27:28–29), which are consecrated by the owner's declaration (note the same use of the *Hip'îl, m/yaqdîš,* 27:14–19). That this is not H's innovation is shown by the *ḥērem* imposed on Jericho, whereby all its possessions are declared holy (Josh 6:18–19). See further, chap. 27, COMMENT D.

consecrate. maqdîšîm. For the meaning of the *Hip'îl* of *qdš* 'consecrate', referring to the transfer of the common to the realm of the holy, see the NOTE on 27:14.

so they do not desecrate my holy name. wĕlōʾ yĕḥallĕlû ʾet-šēm qodšî. Even though the context of the following verses (vv. 3–8) is that of defilement, the verb employed here is not the expected ṭimmēʾ because its object is God's name. As explained in vol. 1.254–60, impurity is conceived as a physical entity, a miasma that attaches itself to the defiled object, in particular, the sanctuary. In order to avoid the gross anthropomorphism that God can actually be defiled, two euphemisms are employed: the first—the more obvious—is that it is not God but his name that is damaged; the second is that his name is not physically polluted but desecrated; that is, its holiness is diminished or desecrated. Twice, however, the verb ṭimmēʾ is used (Ezek 43:7, 8), but the context is the sanctuary, which the Israelites are indeed polluting by their burial practices. For other aspects of this expression, see the NOTE on 18:21. In this case, another reason for using the verb ḥillēl is to create an inclusio with v. 16 and, especially, with v. 32.

I am YHWH. ʾănî YHWH. Structurally, this multivalent expression acts as the inclusio of this chapter (vv. 2, 33). Here its function is to identify the author of the "holy name." Alternatively, it could be rendered "I YHWH (have spoken)," as in v. 3 (see NOTES on 18:4, 5).

3. *Say (further) to them.* ʾĕmōr ʾălēhem. As indicated by the cantillation mark (rĕbîaʿ), what follows is the direct speech to the priests (cf. Num 6:23; 14:28). Thus the impression is thereby created that the previous v. 2 constitutes the general notion of scrupulousness regarding the sacred donations falling under the control of the priests. Moses and Aaron are free to word this generalization as they please. But beginning with this verse, the *ipsissima verba* of YHWH's commands (i.e., his laws) must be recited. The switch to second person is another indication that the following verses constitute a direct address to the priests.

The same function was displayed by waʾălēhem tōʾmar in 17:8aα, which distinguished between the private aside to Moses (17:5–7) and the law(s) promulgated to Israel (17:8–10, 15–16). So, too, the private remarks of God to Moses and Aaron revealing the end of his patience with Israel's rebelliousness (Num 14:26–27) are followed by ʾĕmōr ʾălēhem and the punitive decree that they should deliver to Israel (vv. 28–35).

Throughout your generations. lĕdōrōtêkem. This adverbial phrase is placed first to emphasize that the divine decree that follows is permanent (Bola).

while he is impure. wĕṭumʾātô ʿālāyw. This clause is advanced toward the beginning of the verse in the translation, since it modifies yiqrab 'encroaches'. That is, his impurity is that which qualifies his handling of sancta as encroachment. The question needs be asked: Why a clause instead of the simple adjective ṭāmēʾ? In other words, why doesn't the text read kol-ʾîš ṭāmēʾ 'any impure man'? The answer resides in a finely nuanced distinction in the priestly vocabulary. The adjective ṭāmēʾ means "*remains* impure," either permanently or until the prescribed purificatory rites are followed (*Sipre* Num. 126; NOTE on 11:4), but it would exclude time-limited impurities, such as those included in vv. 5–7. Therefore, the priestly lexicon employs the circumlocution ṭumʾātô ʿālāyw (7:20) or ṭumʾātô bô (Num 19:13).

This phrase is found only once again (7:20 [P]), where, most likely, it bore the connotation "while it [i.e., the flesh] is impure." The meaning of the phrase took on its present connotation by the addition of 7:19b—mostly the work of an H tradent (details in Knohl and Naeh 1994).

encroaches. yiqrab. Rashi (followed by *NJPS* and some moderns, e.g., Hartley 1992) renders "eats," probably because of the content of the following pericope (vv. 4–16). However, the term *qārab 'el* in a cultic prohibition means "encroach" (details in NOTE on 21:17, and Gane and Milgrom 1990). It implies the illegitimate use of a sacred object (vol. 1.351–56). The effect is *maʿal,* P's term for desecration (see NOTE on 19:8). I would only add a personal note that it was my difficulty in understanding this verse that led me to abandon temporarily my study of Leviticus and turn to Numbers, where this verb in the *Qal* proliferates. The result was my first book, *Studies in Levitical Terminology* (1970), culminating in the publication of my commentary on Numbers (1990a), even before I could devote my full energies to Leviticus.

(shall be cut off) from my presence. wĕnikrĕtā . . . millĕpānay. The priest is defined as one who *ʿōmēd lipnê YHWH* 'stands before YHWH' (Deut 10:8; 18:7; Judg 20:28)—that is, in the sanctuary. In the priestly texts, the expression *millipnê YHWH* always refers to the sanctuary (9:24; 10:2; 16:12; Num 17:11, 24; 20:9; cf. 1 Sam 21:7). It also has the extended meaning of the (prophetic) service of YHWH (Jon 1:3; contrast 1 Kgs 17:1; 18:15; 2 Kgs 3:14; 5:16; Jer 15:19). When it is told of Cain that "he went away *millipnê YHWH*" (Gen 4:16), the reference may be to the Garden of Eden, where the divine presence resided.

The full expression *nikrat millipnê YHWH* is used by the Deuteronomist to refer to the Davidic throne (1 Kgs 8:25; cf. 2:4; 9:5). Jeremiah (who was a priest) distinguishes very precisely between the king and the priest in this regard: "There shall never be an end [*lōʾ-yikkārēt*] to men of David's line who sit upon the throne of the House of Israel. Nor shall there ever be an end to the line of levitical priests *before me* [*wĕlakkōhănîm halwiyyim lōʾ-yikkārēt ʾîš millĕpānāy*], of those who present burnt offerings and turn the meal offering to smoke and perform sacrifices" (Jer 33:17–18). Thus the king will not be cut off from the throne, and the priest will not be cut off from the divine presence in the sanctuary.

The priest is also differentiated from the lay person in regard to encroachment on sancta. The latter is put to death (*yûmat,* Hip'il; e.g., Num 18:7), whereas the priest suffers *kārēt,* implying the end of his line (vol. 1.457–61; see NOTE on Lev 20:3), or death by divine agency (*yāmût, Qal;* 22:9; Num 18:3). That this punishment of *kārēt* falls on all the violations enumerated in vv. 4–8, see the NOTE on "bear sin by it," v. 9. However, the lay person is subject to the same *kārēt* penalty as the impure priest for contacting the sacred (7:20). The difference between them lies only in regard to eating from a carcass or torn beast: the lay person undergoes ablutions (17:15); the priest is subject to death (22:8–9).

I YHWH (have spoken). The formula *ʾănî YHWH* marks the end of YHWH's direct, second-person address to the priests. The rules that follow are given in the third person, as is the case in normative casuistic law.

Vv. 4–16. Concerning Sacred Food

This topic is the logical sequence to that of priestly blemishes (21:16–23). Whereas the latter disqualify a priest from ministering in the sanctuary, they do not bar him from partaking of sacred food (21:22). But the impure priest is barred from eating (indeed, contact with) sacred food under pain of *kārēt* or death (see NOTE on v. 9).

Vv. 4–9. Priests eating sacred food

4. *Any man.* ʾîš ʾîš. This is a distinctive H expression (cf. 17:3, 8, 10, 13; 18:6; 20:2, 9; 22:4, 18). To be sure, P also uses this expression (15:2). However, it should be noted that when P begins a casuistic law with ʾîš ʾîš or ʾîš (ʾiššâ), the relative conjunction *kî always* follows (e.g., 12:2; 15:2, 16, 19, 25). H, on the contrary, generally uses the relative conjunction ʾăšer (e.g., 17:3, 8, 10, 13; 20:2, 9, 10–21; 21:17, 18, 19, 21; 22:5, 18; contrast 24:15). This verse, however, is an apodictic prohibition, and no relative conjunction is required.

has scale disease. ṣārûaʿ. The passive participle, as in 13:44, 45; 14:3; Num 5:2, but in 14:2 and elsewhere, *mĕṣōrāʿ* the *Puʿal* participle is used, meaning "struck with scale disease" (e.g., Exod 4:6; Num 12:10; 2 Kgs 5:27; 2 Chr 26:20) or as a noun, a certified scale-disease carrier (e.g., 2 Sam 3:29; 2 Kgs 5:1; 7:3, 8; 15:5 [= 2 Chr 26:21]; 2 Chr 26:23). P is characterized by greater precision than H, since P uses *sārûaʿ* in its true participial sense "struck with scale disease," but not yet certified as one (13:44, 45; 14:3), whereas H indiscriminately uses it to designate the certified carrier (22:4; Num 5:2 [H]; see NOTE on 13:44).

Saadiah correctly notes that the impurities in vv. 4–5 are listed in descending order of severity (on which see below). It has been shown that ancient Israel and its Near Eastern contemporaries were aware of many diseases and had diagnosed them (Zias 1991), which gives further support to the theory that Israel's impurity laws, in general, and the skin diseases, in particular, are part of a symbolic system (vol. 1.766–68, 1000–1004).

chronic discharge. zāb. The order of impurity carriers is determined by decreasing severity. Paran (1989: 266–67) contrasts this with the curse zāb ûmĕṣōrāʿ (2 Sam 3:29), which, for a stylistic reason (the shorter word first) lists the zāb initially.

[*or is contaminated by a corpse*]. [o ṭāmēʾ lannepeš or ṭĕmēʾ nepeš (Hag 2:13)]. I have added this clause on the basis of kol-ṣārûaʿ wĕkol-zāb wĕkōl ṭāmēʾ lānāpeš (Num 5:2). This impurity carrier is required here, since, like the ṣārûaʿ and zāb, a seven-day purificatory period is mandated, keeping in mind that a priest is permitted to become defiled by the corpse of a near blood relative (21:1–4). Indeed, logic dictates its restoration: if a corpse-contaminated lay person is forbidden to contact sacred food (7:21), all the more so a corpse-contaminated priest!

The possibility may be entertained that this clause mistakenly was transferred after the word *yiṭhar* (i.e., to the end of the [original] verse), and the words *wĕhannōgēaʿ bĕkol*- were prefixed to it in order to parallel *yiggaʿ bĕkol-šereṣ*

(v. 5a). Thus the clause became included among the one-day impurities (see NOTE on "One who touches anything contaminated by a corpse," v. 4bα).

may not eat of the sacred donations. baqqŏdāšîm lōʾ yōʾkal. The idiom *ʾākal bĕ* (Exod 12:43) is equivalent to *ʾākal min* 'eat of' (Saadiah; cf. v. 6bα). The sacred donations, as comestibles, are of three kinds: *qodšê qŏdāšîm* 'most sacred' (enumerated in Num 18:9–10), *qŏdāšîm* '(less) sacred' (enumerated in Num 18:11–18; see NOTE on 21:22) and, using rabbinic terminology, *tĕrûmôt*, which the rabbis limit to the required agricultural donations (but in the priestly writings refers to all sanctuary offerings; cf. Num 18:11, 19, 26; see NOTE on Lev 22:12).

Except for the tenth of the tithe assigned to the priests (Num 18:26), no measure is assigned for the mandated agricultural donations (cf. Num 18:12–13). The rabbis, however, prescribe the following: "(If a man is) generous [*ʿayin yāpâ*], (he separates) one-fortieth (of his produce). The House of Shammai say, 'one-thirtieth.' And (if he is) average [*habbênônît*], (he separates) one-fiftieth (of his produce). And (if he is) miserly [*harāʿâ*], (he separates) one-sixtieth (of his produce)" (*m. Ter.* 4:3; cf. *t. Ter.* 5:3a).

The contaminated priest obviously has to subsist on nonsacral food during the period of his impurity. He need not, however, be faced with hunger or starvation (Gerstenberger 1996: 324). If necessary, he has access to the sanctuary's store of monetary fines (v. 16; 27:13, 27, 31) with which to purchase his basic dietary needs. It must be kept in mind that none of the "severe" impurities are long-lasting (contra Gerstenberger 1996; see NOTES on chaps. 13–15).

until he is pure. ʿad ʾăšer yiṭhār. No time limit is cited, as in the case of the one-day impurities (v. 6), since the duration of the impurity is indeterminate. The purificatory period, however, is the same: seven days. The Qumran sectaries prescribe eight days for scale disease (see NOTE on 14:11). The same apparently holds true for the *zābâ*, as can be conjectured from the unpublished fragment D^b9II:3–4: WHYʾH ʾL TWKL QWDŠ WʾL T[BWʾ] ʾL HMQDŠ ʿD BW HŠMŠ BYWM HŠMYNY 'she (the *zābâ* [cf. 15:25, 28]) shall not eat sacred food nor shall she e[nter] the sanctuary until sunset on the eighth day.'

[*One who touches anything contaminated by a corpse, or*]. *wĕhannōgēaʿ bĕkol-ṭĕmēʾ-nepeš ʾô.* I have chosen to delete this clause on the following grounds:

1. This case is covered by v. 5b.
2. The list of the one-day impurity bearers should logically begin with the person as the source of the impurity—that is, the emitter of semen (v. 4bβ)—as is the case with the major impurity bearers (v. 4a). Thus the subjects would progress logically: *ʾîš ʾîš* (v. 4a), *ʾô ʾîš ʾăšer-tēṣēʾ* (v. 4b), *ʾô ʾîš ʾăšer yiggaʿ* (v. 5a); that is, those who are the source of their impurity are followed by those who are contaminated by a source.
3. The order of the secondarily contaminated, touching a *šereṣ* 'swarming thing' followed by touching *bĕʾādām* 'an (impure) man' (v. 5), is precisely the order found in 5:2–3.

Gerstenberger (1996: 325) is mistaken in claiming that this clause clashes with Num 19:11–12 (P), which prescribes a seven-day purification. The latter verses deal with the corpse-contaminated person. This clause, however, focuses on a third-degree transmission of impurity: anything contacting a corpse-contaminated person or object is impure for one day (Num 19:22). In the matter of impurities, H does not differ with P.

If a man has an emission of semen. The law of 15:16, 18 (P) is presumed, another indication that H is later than P.

5. *touches any swarming thing by which he is made impure. yigga' bĕkol-šereṣ 'ăšer yiṭmā'-lô.* The qualification "by which he is made impure" is a clear indication that the reference is to the eight enumerated swarming animals of 11:29–31. Only these eight swarmers defile by touching them (11:31). All other swarmers fall under the category of *šeqeṣ*: they are forbidden as food, but they do not defile (see NOTE on 11:11; for greater detail and analysis, see Milgrom 1992a; 1992b). This is but another instance of H presupposing P. Recently published 4QLev^c reads *ṭāmē'* after *šereṣ* (as do LXX and Sam.) "an impure swarming thing" (Tov 1995: 265), a total redundancy in view of the following clause "by which he is made impure." Apparently, Qumran wished to make explicit that there was also a pure, edible category of swarming animals (e.g., locusts, 11:21–22).

The question disturbingly remains: Why are the carcasses of quadrupeds omitted, since they also defile (5:2; 7:21)? And since the lay person defiled by quadrupeds is forbidden to touch sacrificial flesh, all the more so the defiled priest! In my opinion, there is only one plausible answer. It places emphasis on the fact that P (rather, P$_1$; vol. 1.61–63) forbids the lay person to make contact with only the carcasses of *impure* quadrupeds (see NOTES on 5:2; 7:21) but, by implication, permits contact with the carcasses of pure quadrupeds (see also NOTE on v. 8). The text of H, then, takes for granted that the priest will avoid at all costs any contact with an impure carcass; note the account of a priest and a Levite bypassing a (supposed) corpse (Luke 10:30–32). However, contact with the forbidden *šereṣ* is nigh unavoidable, since the priest may encounter the dead *šereṣ* in the sanctuary itself (cf. *m. 'Erub.* 10:15). Hence the priests are instructed on the required purificatory procedures for touching a dead *šereṣ*.

By the same token, sanctuary animals—which by definition are pure—surely might have died in the sanctuary. Why, then, is there no prohibition against touching the carcasses of pure animals? To be sure, this subject is taken up in v. 8. But the prohibition there is against eating such carcasses, not touching them. Indeed, if touching them were prohibited, it surely would have been mentioned instead (as in vv. 5–6), since it is the more inclusive category, embracing eating. Therefore, one must conclude that although the priest is forbidden to eat of such a carcass, he is permitted to touch it. This must be the case, since the sacrificial animal becomes a carcass (*nĕbēlâ*) the moment it is slaughtered. And yet there is no indication that touching it renders the priest impure. Otherwise, he would not be able to continue officiating! This would not be a problem for P, which declares that only carcasses of *impure* animals defile (5:2; 7:21;

cf. vol. 1.297). If, however, I am correct in attributing 11:39–40 to H (see NOTE on "He shall not eat," v. 8), then the problem of a priest handling a sacrificial carcass could be resolved only by presuming that the holiness of the animal or of the priest himself overrides and cancels the impurity of the carcass. This conclusion accords with the one other H passage dealing with carcasses of pure animals, 17:15–16, which states that the Israelite (and resident alien) who eats of carrion (of pure animals, 17:13–14) must undergo purification. That is, the lay person is not forbidden to eat of carrion, but he is required to undergo ritual purification. The priest, however, is subject to a more stringent rule: he is forbidden to eat it. (Presumably, both lay person and priest are permitted to touch it.) This point is discussed further in the NOTE on v. 8.

or any human being by whom he is made impure whatever (be) his impurity. ʾô bĕʾādām ʾăšer yiṭmāʾ-lô lĕkōl ṭumʾātô. Here, too (as in the case of šereṣ), the additional clause lĕkōl ṭumʾātô 'whatever his impurity' (for the expression, see NOTE on 5:3) implies that only certain humans defile. Who are they? Clearly, they must be those identified and discussed in chaps. 12–15: the parturient (chap. 12), mĕṣōrāʿ (chaps. 13–14) zāb (15:1–15), the menstruant (15:19–23), the man who has sexual intercourse with a menstruant (15:24), and the zābâ (15:25–30). Saadiah would also include unspecified things, such as the couch, seat, and saddle of the zāb (cf. 15:5, 6, 9), but as Bekhor Shor and Abravanel correctly observe, the source of the impurity has to be human. The *Sipra* (Emor 4:4) and *Tg. Ps.-J.* add the corpse and the corpse-contaminated person. But anyone touching these would undergo a seven-day purification, which is precluded by the purificatory procedures that follow (vv. 6–7; see also NOTE on "One who touches anything contaminated by a corpse," v. 4bα).

Once again, a precise knowledge of P's impurity system must be attributed to H. One other bit of evidence points to H's knowledge of not just the laws of P, but also their text: the order of these secondary impurity carriers is the priest who touches an animal carcass (the šereṣ; v. 5a) and the priest who touches a human source (v. 5b). Should not, however, the human logically precede the animal? This is precisely the order found in 5:2–3 (P). Finally, the use of ʾādām, whereas throughout the chapter ʾîš is employed (ten times; cf. vv. 3, 4 [thrice], 5, 12, 14, 18 [twice], 21), can be explained only as a citation from 5:3 (cf. 7:21 [P]).

6. *the person. nepeš.* A repetition of the subject of v. 4b is necessitated by the four long intervening clauses (Hoffmann 1953). The subject of the pericope begins with ʾîš (vv. 4–5) and ends with nepeš, which leads Noth (1977) and Porter (1976) to deduce that vv. 6–7a,bα applied originally to lay persons. However, it must be kept in mind that H not only is the redactor of P, but also is not averse to utilizing either its texts (see NOTES on 17:3–4 and 19:20–22) or its idioms (see NOTES on 23:4–36). Thus the writer begins properly in v. 3 with ʾîš (priests are only males), and in the same verse switches to nepeš because he uses one of P's idioms wĕnikrĕtā hannepeš, a practice he regularly follows (Gen 17:14; Exod 12:15, 19; Lev 19:8; 22:3; 23:29; Num 9:13; 15:30; 19:13 [all H, according to Knohl 1995]; see Introduction I E). Similarly, although the writer continues with ʾîš in vv. 4–5, he again switches to nepeš ʾăšer tiggaʿ (v. 6), probably be-

cause he has in mind P's similar phraseology in 5:2 and 7:21. One should not presume, as does Knohl, that H is consistently nonchalant about using P's precise terminology (see Introduction I C).

touches any of these. tigga ʿbô. This refers to any of the persons who defile, except the emitter of semen (v. 4bβ), who contaminates things but not persons (see NOTE on 15:17). I have rendered *bô* as "one of these" (with Saadiah). Equally acceptable would be "them" (LXX). But the renderings "such" (*NJPS*), "such as these" (*NAB*), and "such a thing" (*NEB*) are inaccurate because only these enumerated impurity bearers (vv. 4b–5) and no others transmit a one-day impurity.

unless he has washed his body in water. kî ʾim-rāḥaṣ bĕśārô bammāyim. The vocalization (pausal, lengthened *qāmaṣ*), versification (it ends the verse), and all translations (to my knowledge) place a period at the end of this clause. This, I believe, is what gave rise to the rabbinic concept of *ṭĕbûl yôm*, referring to the status of the person between the time he has bathed and sunset, during which he is allowed to eat the least sacred of the sacred foods, namely the second tithe (see NOTE on "all the tithes from the land," 27:30). Thus the rabbis ordain: "The *ṭĕbûl yôm* may eat of the (second) tithe (and the priest who is *ṭĕbûl yôm* may eat his [tenth of] tithe, Num 18:26); after sunset he (the priest) may eat of *tĕrûmâ* [see NOTE on "he may not eat of the sacred donations, v. 4], and after he has brought his atoning sacrifice (on the following day), he may eat of the sacred food [i.e., the flesh sacrifices]" (*m. Neg.* 14:3; *b. Yeb.* 74b).

Why is laundering, the usual component of bathing, omitted here? The answer is that precisely in the cases of one-day impurities (vv. 4b–6), no laundering is required for those who *touch* the impurity bearers (but not for those who eat or carry them). For the *šereṣ*, see 11:31; the impure quadruped, 11:24–27; the pure quadruped, 11:39; and the menstruant, 15:19. However, after touching the *zāb* (15:7), his bed or seat (15:5, 6), or the objects underneath the menstruant (15:21)—items not listed in vv. 4b–5—laundering is required.

7. *and the sun has set. ûbāʾ haššemeš.* The *waw*, I submit, is copulative, not sequential. The plain meaning of the text is that there is no *ṭĕbûl yôm* (contra the rabbis); that is, the concession to allow the priests any sacred food during the interval between bathing and sunset is nonexistent. The first part of the verse (v. 6a) distinctly states that impurity lasts until evening. The verse then adds the quintessential information that evening alone does not suffice, but it must be preceded by bathing (v. 6b). However, bathing by itself also does not suffice; the bather must wait until sunset before he may partake of any sacred food (see also the ostensible exception discussed in the NOTE on "after that [i.e., bathing] he may reenter the camp," 16:26).

The question also arises: Why is this clause even needed, since it already has been stated that "the person who touches any of these shall be impure until evening" (v. 6a)? It is needed for explanatory and rhetorical purposes: both to define evening as sunset and to emphasize that eating in the evening is a special concession granted the priests, as stated in the rest of the verse.

for they are his food. kî laḥmô hûʾ. This is clearly the language of concession; implied is that ordinarily the priest would have to wait longer before being allowed to eat sacred food. But how long and for what reason? Ralbag and Sforno, following the rabbinic distinction, namely, sunset for těrûmâ (agricultural donations) and the following morning for sacrificial flesh (m. Neg. 14:3), claim that logic would dictate that all sacred food (produce and meat alike) should have to wait for morning, the end of the calendar day (see NOTE on 23:5), but since a priest may be totally dependent on sacred food for his sustenance, he is allowed to eat some of it—the agricultural portion (těrûmâ)—after sunset the previous evening.

Following this rabbinic reasoning but from another angle, it also can be argued that originally the purificatory process of the priest was severer than that of a layman: instead of having to wait until the sunset of the day of his ablution, he would have to wait until the following morning. Indeed, such a more stringent rule prevails in Ezekiel's system, which mandates that a corpse-contaminated priest not only must undergo the Torah's seven-day purification with the ashes of the red cow (Num 19:19), but must wait an additional week and on the following day bring a purification offering (Ezek 44:25–27). Thus it is possible to conjecture that for a minor, one-day impurity Ezekiel probably would have waived the purification offering, but he might have required that the purified priest wait until the following day before being allowed to eat sacred food. That Qumran's system was even more rigorous, examine its purificatory requirements for the měṣōrāʿ (see NOTE on 14:11) and the zābâ (see NOTE on "until he is pure," v. 4).

8. animal that died or was torn by beasts. něbēlâ ûṭěrēpâ. For the meaning of these terms, see the NOTES on 17:15. The juxtaposition of this verse and the preceding verses is explained by Wessely (1846) to mean that priests are conceded all sacred food (following a one-day impurity) by the evening of their day of ablution, but not if their food stems from an animal that died (něbēlâ) or was torn by beasts (ṭěrēpâ). H's rule for the priests is more stringent than its rule for lay persons, who are allowed to eat něbēlâ or ṭěrēpâ, provided they undergo purification (17:15–16).

It must be assumed that the dead animal (něbēlâ), of which a priest might eat, would most likely be a sacrificial animal awaiting slaughter inside the sanctuary. But how can one conceive of a ṭěrēpâ occurring with a sanctuary animal? Perhaps the expression originates in oral and, later, literary usage: něbēlâ ûṭěrēpâ frequently occur in tandem as an idiom (cf. 7:24; 17:15; Ezek 4:14; 44:31). Moreover, the consequence of the Hezekian and Josian reforms would have been rampant unemployment among the priests of the abolished local sanctuaries, who no longer had access to sacred meat (note the concession of the minḥâ in the form of unleavened bread, 2 Kgs 23:9) and who, therefore, would have been tempted by (or unaware of) eating něbēlâ or ṭěrēpâ. Note that Ezekiel, while in exile, proclaims (exceptionally?) "I have not eaten něbēlâ or ṭěrēpâ from my youth until now" (Ezek 4:14).

Ezekiel's prohibition is more precise: kol-něbēlâ ûṭěrēpâ min-hāʿôp ûmin-habběhēmâ lōʾ yōʾkělû hakkōhănîm (44:31). He clearly refers to the sacrificial animals, both the quadrupeds and the birds. He could not be referring to game, which would be worded ḥayyâ ʾô-ʿôp (cf. 17:13) and is ineligible for the altar.

He shall not eat . . . to become impure by it. lo' yō'kal lĕṭāmĕ'â-bāh. What about touching? Surely, since the priest should avoid impurity of any kind, why doesn't the text say *lo' yigga'* (cf. vv. 4–6), which would have included eating a fortiori? Only one answer, I submit, is possible: the priest is, in fact, permitted to touch the carcass of an animal that has died (*nĕbēlâ*) or was torn by a beast (*ṭĕrēpâ*)! The point already was made (see NOTE on v. 5) that animals awaiting slaughter may have died of natural causes. It is possible also to conceive of a *ṭĕrēpâ* occurrence on sanctuary grounds (by an incited bull?). In either case, the carcass would have to be removed immediately. The priests called on for the removal would, of course, become impure (as do the laity, 11:39–40) and would be barred from their service for the rest of the day while they underwent purification.

The difference, then, between the laity and the priesthood is that the laity is warned not to touch a carcass, but no sanctions are involved. Touching a carcass, according to P_1 (see NOTE on v. 5), is not even prohibited. Thus the warning is only a "fence" to prevent the violation of the prohibition against eating of a carcass (analogous to Gen 2:17, 3:3; see NOTE on 11:8). Touching an impure carcass (*ṭāmē'*, but not *šeqeṣ*) renders one impure, according to P_2 (11:24–28), but touching a pure carcass renders one impure according to only the isolated view, which I called P_3 (11:39–40; see vol. 1.691–98 and the discussion below).

The prohibitions for the priesthood are the concerns of H. The lay person who eats of an animal's carcass need but undergo purification (17:15–16), but the priest who does so is subject to death by divine agency (v. 9). Regarding the touching of a carcass, however, the law for both is the same: there are no penalties if the required purification is observed.

In vol. 1.681–82, 93–94, I argued, on the basis of this verse, that since the priest is forbidden only to eat of a carcass, he may touch a carcass with impunity. Hence, 11:39, which states that touching the carcass of a pure animal is defiling, can stem neither from P nor from H, and must be the interpolation of a later P tradent (whom I called P_3). I herewith change my mind, for two reasons:

1. The conclusion, deduced above, that a priest may touch a carcass does not ipso facto mean that he does not become impure.
2. The rule of 11:39 that one who touches a carcass becomes impure does not mean it is forbidden to touch a carcass.

Thus 11:39–40 are perfectly in accord with H (but not with P; see NOTES on 5:2; 11:40). Both agree that the one who touches a carcass, be he lay person or priest, is rendered impure. If he bathes, his impurity lasts until sunset (implied by 11:39b, 22:6a; see their NOTES). The existence of P_3 has proved chimerical, for which I am most grateful. I no longer have to agonize over whether this alleged third priestly stratum was interpolated into the text of Lev 11 before or after H's redaction (vol. 1.696). Lev 11:39–40 must also be part of the H stratum, and the view that the school of H is subsequent to (and the redactor of) all of P remains unchallenged.

In sum, H's impurity rules for the priesthood are equivalent to those for the laity regarding contact with sacred donations in a state of impurity (v. 3), regarding purificatory procedures for major (v. 4a) and minor impurities (vv. 4b–7), and regarding contact with carcasses of (pure) animals (v. 8, by implication). However, in regard to the *eating* of the last, there is a major difference: lay people need only purify themselves (17:15–16), but priests are subject to death by divine agency (vv. 8–9).

It is of interest to observe the exegetical distress that this verse has caused traditional Jewish exegetes who wonder why the verse is needed in view of the same prohibition incumbent on the laity (Exod 22:30). The talmudic rabbis either are openly nonplussed or come up with a fanciful halakhic distinction (*b. Menaḥ.* 45a). Ibn Ezra, while refuting another fanciful reason, proposes that this verse teaches that priests who violate this prohibition are disqualified from officiating. *Yahel 'Or* adds, in supporting Ibn Ezra, that a similar reason explains why the same mourning customs forbidden to the laity (19:27–28) are also forbidden to priests (21:5), namely, to bar violators from officiating. (But the rites are not equivalent; see NOTE on "You shall not destroy the edge of your beard," 19:27.) Eliezer of Beaugency (twelfth century) speculates (on Ezek 44:31) that priests had to be warned separately so, in addition to their sacrificial prebends, they would carefully inspect the gifts of meat from the laity. Radak (also on Ezek 44:31) simply suggests that priests must be given a separate warning because they minister in holy space. He presumably implies that the priest's pollution has severer consequences.

Radak's reasoning makes sense. However, as argued above, once we compare the two H sources dealing with this subject (17:15 and 22:8 [Ezek 44:31]) and omit from consideration Exod 22:30 (not a priestly text), the difference between the prohibitions for laity and priesthood is readily apparent.

I YHWH (have spoken). *'ănî YHWH.* This forms an inclusio with the same formula at the end of v. 3, thereby enclosing the laws of vv. 4–8a.

9. This hortatory verse is appended to the laws of vv. 4–8 as a warning to the priests that because of their status any impurity prohibition they violate is deserving of capital punishment at the hands of God. The wording of this verse parallels that of v. 16, thereby indicating that both verses end their respective pericopes.

They shall heed my prohibition. *wĕšāmĕrû 'et-mišmartî.* For this idiom, see the NOTE on 18:30. The antecedent of "my prohibition" is neither the sanctuary (Ibn Ezra) nor all sacred donations excluding carcasses (v. 8; *Sipra* Emor 4:14). Once it is understood that the term *"mišmeret* of YHWH" refers to a prohibition (Milgrom 1970:10–12), then the immediately preceding v. 8 is the referent (see NOTE on "lest they bear sin by it").

lest they bear sin by it. *wĕlō'-yiś'û 'ālāyw ḥēṭ'.* For this idiom, see the NOTE on 19:17, and for this technical meaning of the verb *nāśā'*, see the NOTE on 17:16. This meaning of the verb recurs in v. 16, thereby indicating the parallel construction of the two pericopes that compose the larger unit on sacred food (vv. 4–9, 10–16; see COMMENT).

What is the antecedent of *ʿālāyw*, literally "by/because of it" (also of *bô* and *yĕhallĕlûhû*)—all with masculine suffixes? It cannot be *mišmartî*, which is feminine! Opinions range widely: (1) *leḥem* (v. 7b; Hoffmann 1953; Noth 1977; Elliger 1966); (2) *haqqŏdāšîm* (v. 7b, taken as a singular; Wessely 1846; Shadal; Dillmann and Ryssel 1897; Bertholet 1901); (3) *mišmeret* (v. 9, treated as masculine; Kalisch 1867–72); (4) *šēm qodšî* (v. 2; D. N. Freedman, personal communication); and (5) most probably, since the penalty for encroaching on (eating or touching) sancta while being impure is *kārēt* (vv. 3–7), the penalty for eating carcasses, *presumably in a state of purity* (v. 8), is death by the hand of God (v. 9). Therefore, the suffixes of the terms *mišmartî* and following *ʿālāyw*, *bô*, and *yĕhallĕlûhû*, correctly in the singular, refer to the *single prohibition* against eating forbidden carcasses (v. 8).

and die. ûmētû. In the priestly lexicon, the *Qal* of *mwt* always refers to death by divine agency (Milgrom 1970: 5–8). It is distinguished from *kārēt* (v. 3), a severer penalty that calls for the extinction of the miscreant's line and, possibly, his exclusion from the company of his forbears (vol. 1.457–61).

Abravanel, who correctly observes that these two punishments are not synonymous, claims (incorrectly) that in this chapter, *kārēt* is enjoined for the impure priest who encroaches on sacred donations (v. 3) and death (*mwt*), if he eats of sacred food (vv. 4–7). Abravanel is corrected in *Keter Torah*, which cites 7:20, where *kārēt* is prescribed for an impure Israelite who eats of sacred food. The distinction, as outlined in the previous NOTE, is that *kārēt* is prescribed for any advertent violation of sacred donations by an impure priest, whether by encroaching (v. 3), eating (v. 4a), or touching (vv. 4b–7), whereas death is imposed on even a pure priest if he (advertently) eats of carrion (vv. 8–9). Thus *kārēt*, a severer penalty, is prescribed for a severer crime, encroachment. The text presumes that if these violations occur inadvertently, the penalty consists of the appropriate remedial sacrifice, a purification offering (4:1–5:13). Again, H's knowledge of P's sacrificial system is taken for granted.

It should not go unnoticed that the penalty for the priest is much severer than that for a lay person for a similar violation. Indeed, the lay person who eats carrion is impure for one day (11:39–40), and if he fails to purify himself, he is subject to a purification offering (see NOTES on 5:2; 17:16). In reality he suffers no penalty at all; his sin is remediable. But the priest's sin is unexpiable: he will suffer death.

The magnified risk of priests who work inside the sacred sphere is best illustrated by the tragedy of Nadab and Abihu (10:1–3; see their NOTES). Gerstenberger (1996: 306) supplies an apt modern parallel: "The x-ray physician is far more at risk than is the patient. Thus those who work directly at the hearth of danger must implement heightened precautions."

thereby. bô. The *beth* of means. The rendering "(die) in it" (NRSV), referring to the sanctuary, cannot be right, since the consumption of lesser sacred donations (e.g., produce, the prebends of the well-being offering) is shared by the priest with his family outside the sanctuary.

when they desecrate it. kî yĕhallĕlûhû. Should not the proper verb be *ṭimmēʾ*, since most of the preceding verses posit that the violation is committed by an impure priest? If, however, the exegesis is accepted that v. 9 refers to only the violations of v. 8 and not to the impurities mentioned in vv. 4–7, the use of the verbs may possibly be justified. The offending priest who eats carrion is initially pure. He is not like the priest described in the previously mentioned violations (vv. 3–7), who, in a sense, has committed a double violation: he has become impure and, in that state, has contacted or partaken of sacred food. Thus the priest who eats carrion has committed the lesser crime, and his penalty is also the lesser: death instead of *kārēt* (i.e., the end of his line; see above).

Nonetheless, the use of the verb *ḥillēl* is imprecise because eating carrion renders the priest impure (v. 8aβ)! The only possible answer, then, is that H has fused (or confused) the terms *ḥillēl* and *ṭimmē'* which it also did in 21:12, proving again that H frequently breaks down P's precise terminological distinctions. Why has it done so in this case? Perhaps its reason is simply aesthetic: to create an inclusio with vv. 2 and 15, which warn the priests lest they *yĕḥallēlû* 'commit desecration'.

I am YHWH who sanctifies them. 'ănî YHWH mĕqaddĕšām. As recognized by the rabbis, this sentence terminates the previous pericope (*b. Sanh.* 83b). That is, the death penalty promulgated by this verse does not apply to any of the subsequent violations (enumerated in vv. 10–16).

Who or what is the antecedent of "them"? Wessely (1846) claims that it is the previously mentioned *qŏdāšîm* 'sacred donations'; since they are holy, their contact with impurity is lethal. This identification is unlikely. God does not sanctify the sacrifices; Israel does, as expressly stated in this chapter: "the sacred donations that the Israelites consecrate to me" (v. 2; see also v. 3).

Furthermore, the change of object from singular to plural indicates, on purely grammatical grounds, that the referent is the plural subject of all the verbs in this verse, namely, the priests. Logic also dictates that the priests are the antecedent: since the priests are holy, their contact with impurity can be fatal. Once again, the consistent use of the participle *mĕqaddēš* indicates H's basic theology: though priests are innately holy, they can enhance or diminish (and even suspend) their holiness by keeping or violating YHWH's prohibitions (*mišmeret*). Hence the priest's sanctification is an ongoing (participial) process (see NOTE on 21:15).

Vv. 10–16. Nonpriests Eating Sacred Food

Since the previous section deals mainly with a priest eating sacred food (vv. 4–7), the next section concerns itself with other persons who may (or may not) eat sacred food (Abravanel).

This section is similar in structure to the previous one (vv. 2–9). Note the following parallels:

1. Vv. 2 and 9 form an inclusio; both are warnings to the priest ("be scrupulous"/"heed") lest they profane (*yĕḥallĕlû*) God's name or prohibitions. Similarly, vv. 10a and 13b constitute an inclusio (vv. 14–16 extend the thought of v. 13b).

2. V. 15 forms an inclusio with v. 2, and v. 16 with v. 9, thereby locking the two sections (vv. 2–9, 10–16) into a single pericope.

3. The final verses of each section (vv. 9, 15–16) are voiced in the plural (as is v. 2) and terminate with the identical phrase, *'ănî YHWH mĕqaddĕšām* (details in COMMENT).

10. *lay person.* This is the usual translation of *zār.* But according to the content of vv. 10–13, the definition of *zār* is more restricted to one who is neither a servant nor a family member of a priest—that is, an outsider (Dillmann and Ryssel 1897; Ehrlich 1908). This same usage is found in Deut 25:5.

shall eat. yō'kal. The subject of vv. 10–13 is the eating of sacred food, indicated by the sevenfold occurrence of the verb *'ākal* (Paran 1983: 105). Akkadian *akālu* (CAD A1, 252) and rabbinic *'akāl* (e.g., *m.* 'Abot 5:19) can mean "enjoy" (see also Job 21:25), or benefit from. The lay person may not benefit from sacred food assigned to priests.

sacred food. qōdeš. Clearly this must refer to the priestly prebends that may be shared by the priest's family (i.e., the lesser sacred offerings). They would consist of produce (first-ripe fruits [*bikkûrîm*] and first-processed fruits [*rē'šît*]), the breast and right thigh of the well-being offering, the firstling, the *ḥērem,* and the tithe of the produce and of the flock and the herd (Num 18:11–19, 26; Lev 27:30; 33). The most sacred offerings—cereal, purification, and reparation (chaps. 2, 4, 5; cf. Num 18:9)—would be excluded. It must be kept in mind that P differs with H in regard to the tithe: P assigns the crop tithe to the Levites (Num 18:21–24) and a tithe of the tithe to the priests (Num 18: 26–32), and it knows nothing of an animal tithe (see chap. 27, COMMENT G).

a priest's resident hireling. tôšāb kōhēn wĕśākîr. This compound has bedeviled commentators over the ages. The rabbis identify the *tôšāb* with a lifelong slave and the *śākîr* with a manumitted (six-year) slave (*Mek. RŠbY* on Exod 12:45; *Sipra* Emor 4:17; *b. Qidd.* 4a [bar.]). Abravanel claims that the *tôšāb* is a slave and the *śākîr* is a one- to three-year hireling. *Tg. Neof.* identifies the *tôšāb* with the *gēr* (*tôšāb*) '(resident) alien' and the *śākîr* with a hired laborer. Philo (*Laws* 1.120) takes the LXX rendering of *tôšāb* '*paroikos*' to mean "a dweller near a priest" (i.e., neighbor) and *śākîr* to mean a "hired servant." Moderns do no better. The common denominator of all the explanations, ancient and modern, is that the terms *tôšāb* and *śākîr* refer to two discrete socioeconomic entities. I select at random from the modern translations: "bound or hired laborer" (*NJPS, NRSV*), "tenant or hired servant" (*NAB*), "a stranger lodging (with a priest) or a hired man" (*NEB*).

To my knowledge, Melamed (1944–45: 175–76, 79) is the only scholar who has recognized that this compound encapsules a hendiadys. He came to this conclusion on the basis of his carefully honed arguments that the analogous compound *gēr wĕtôšāb* 'resident alien' is also a hendiadys (25:23, 35, 45, 47; Gen 23:4; Ps 39:13; the evidence is cited in NOTE on 25:23). That the compound *tôšāb wĕśākîr* is a hendiadys is discussed in the NOTE on 25:40 and is fully demonstrated in Milgrom (1999). Here let the main points suffice:

1. The word *tôšāb* never appears by itself (*mittōšābê* [1 Kgs 17:1] is probably a dittography; cf. LXX).
2. Although *tôšāb wěśākîr* are two words, they take a singular verb (e.g., Exod 12:45).
3. They can occur without a connecting *waw* (e.g., Lev 25:40).
4. Both words always contain the same prefix (e.g., *kěśākîr kětôšāb*, 25:40; *wěliśkîrěkā ûlětôšāběkā*, 25:6).
5. The order of the two words is interchangeable (cf. Exod 12:45 and Lev 25:40).

As for the broken hendiadys encountered here, it is necessitated by its being a double construct, two *regens* and one *rectum*, as is *kěḥuqqat happesaḥ ûkěmišpāṭô* (Num 9:14).

Since the hireling is a nonpriest, he is included in the term *zār*. Why is he mentioned? Since he resides on the priest's property, like the slave, one might deduce that he, too, may benefit from the priest's sacred food. How, then, can the hireling and his family subsist? It must be presumed that his wages suffice to buy an adequate supply of nonconsecrated food for their alimentary needs. For the economic and social status of the resident hireling, see the NOTE on 25:40.

11. *But (if a priest).* *wě(kōhēn).* The *waw* is adversative.

purchases a person with money. *yiqneh nepeš qinyan kaspô*, literally "purchases a person, the purchase of his money." The slave was bought (*kaspô* 'his money'), not acquired by indenture, which for an Israelite may not result in slavery (see NOTES on 25:39–43). The rabbis aver that the double use of the root *qnh* is deliberate—to emphasize that the slave is not an Israelite (*b. Yeb.* 70a). Philo (*Laws* 1.126–27) offers two practical reasons why a chattel slave is entitled to the priest's sacred provisions: he "has no other resources but his master," and "if they do not take them openly, they will pilfer them on the sly."

and those born into his household. *wîlîd bêtô*, literally "and one born . . ." The Sam., LXX, Pesh., and *Tgs. Onq.* and *Ps.-J.* read the plural *wîlîdê* 'and those born . . .', an emendation necessitated by the following plural clause *hēm yō'kělû*, literally "they may eat." The MT may have arisen because of the two preceding *yods* (Hartley 1992). This phrase is followed by *hēm* 'they' (omitted in the translation). Its force is: only they among the nonpriests (note the analogous use of *hî'*[K *hw'*] in the next verse).

Does the slave have to be circumcised, as in the law of the paschal sacrifice (Exod 12:44)? One would certainly think so, since the slave is permitted to eat sacred food, including the sacrificial meat of the well-being offering and the firstling. Of course, H may be assuming that God's command to Abraham to circumcise his slaves (Gen 17:13; cf. vv. 23, 27) could be taken for granted. But its inclusion in the law of the paschal sacrifice and its exclusion in this law regarding the priest's sacred food is most puzzling.

Hallo (1995: 88, citing Kraus 1939) suggests that the functional and semantic equivalent of *yělîd bayit* in Akkadian *w/īlid bītum* 'house-born slave' remains permanently a slave unless the master voluntarily chooses to release him, in contrast to the free citizen who becomes a slave through indebtedness or otherwise and can gain his freedom "by purchasing his freedom, by judicial review of his status, or by royal edict." The similarities and significant differences between the free citizen of Mesopotamia and of Israel (because the Israelite "slave" can accumulate sufficient funds to pay off his debt) are discussed in the INTRODUCTION to 25:39–43.

In any event, this phrase proves that the institution of slavery was fully accepted by H in regard to non-Israelites (25:45–46), whereas it was totally prohibited in regard to Israelites (see INTRODUCTION to 25:39–43).

12. The principle here is the same as in 21:3. The daughter of a priest who marries out loses her priestly privileges.

she. hî'(K *hw'*). The pronoun is added for emphasis: as opposed to other family members, she may no longer eat sacred food. The use of the pronoun is analogous to that of *hēm* in v. 11, but in an opposite sense: *they*, the born and bought slave, may eat sacred food, whereas *she*, the priest's daughter, may not.

of the sacred gifts. bitrûmat haqqŏdāšîm. The same idiom is found in Num 18:19, but in the plural *tĕrûmōt haqqŏdāšîm.* Bula would compare this construction with *bêt 'ăbōtām* (e.g., Num 7:2; the *rectum* is pluralized, not the *regens*). The analogy, however, is incorrect. The compound *bêt 'ābōt* is treated as a single word. This idiom is also found in 4Q513 (frag. 2, col. II, l. 3), as restored by Baumgarten (1985b: 398, n. 15): *R'[WY] LW LH'KYLM MKWL TRWMT HQ[DŠYM]*, which, if correct, is clearly derived from this verse.

The use of this unusual compound instead of the expected *qŏdāšîm* may be explained on stylistic and aesthetic grounds—to limit the occurrences of *'ākal qōdeš* to seven (see NOTE on v. 14).

13. *but if a priest's daughter. ûbat-kōhēn.* The *waw* is adversative. Since this verse is a continuation of v. 12, there is no need to repeat the information that she had been married to a layman.

without children. wĕzera' 'ên lāh. Whether male or female (*Seper Hamibḥar*). Elliger (1966) presumes that if she had children, they would be expected to care for her, but he does not take into account the possibility that her children may be minors. Rather, if she were widowed, she and her children would be cared for by her late husband's clan (Philo, *Laws* 1.130). If divorced, she would face hardship, being rejected by both families, his and hers. If his family also rejects her children, they would suffer her fate. However, an Israelite married to a priest would experience the opposite fate. If widowed, she and her children would continue to be supported by her late husband's family; that is, they would continue to eat sacred food. And if she were divorced, at least her children would retain that privilege.

and returns to her father's house. wĕšābâ 'el-bêt 'ābîhā. The accent mark on the final syllable of *wĕšābâ* indicates that *waw* is copulative, that the verb is a participle (*Seper Hamibḥar*), and that, hence, the clause is part of the protasis. That is, if she returns to her father's house, then she will be supported. Rashi (followed by Levine 1989) renders the verb as a sequential *waw* 'she may return', making it the beginning of the apodosis, which is also grammatically possible.

This rule reflects customary law: Tamar returned to her family (Gen 38:11), and Ruth and Orpah were requested by Naomi to return to their respective families (Ruth 1:8–16; Dillmann and Ryssel 1897).

as in her youth. kin 'ûrêhā. Apocopated form of *kĕbin 'ûrêhā* (Kalisch 1867–72), it is exemplified by *kabbōr* 'as with lye' (Isa 1:25), elided from *kĕbabbōr* (Shadal).

eat of her father's food. millehem 'ābîhā tō'kēl. The rabbis aver: her fare is limited to *tĕrûmâ* (i.e., produce; *Sipra* Emor 6:1), but if she has a son from a priest she may continue to eat sacrificial flesh (i.e., the breast and right thigh of the well-being offering) as before (*b. Yeb.* 86a). The unexpected use of *lehem* instead of *qōdeš* was necessitated by the legist's desire to limit the occurrences of the idiom *'ākal qōdeš* to seven (see NOTE on v. 14).

But no lay person may eat of it. wĕkol-zār lō'-yō'kal bô. This is a repetition of v. 10a, except that the *waw* here is adversative and the object *qōdeš* is replaced by *bô*, which adds the nuance "of." But why the repetition? Stylistically, it forms an inclusio with v. 10a, thereby enclosing the list of those who may or may not benefit from sacred food. But it also connects semantically with the following passage (vv. 14–16; Wessely 1846), which continues the same thought, answering the question about a lay person who eats sacred food. Schwartz (personal communication) suggests that the repetition stresses that if she had children, they would be lay persons. The most likely explanation (with Wessely 1846) is the obvious one: serious penalties befall such a person, as detailed in vv. 14–16 (see also NOTES on 5:14–16). Dire consequences are spelled out for a similar case in Zoroastrianism:

> If indeed a wicked man partakes (of this sacrifice), or a prostitute, or a listless man who does not chant the Gāthās, who destroys life and withstands this Zarathrustian religion of Ahura [i.e., a *zār*], the bright glorious Tištrya denies him help. Simultaneously famine will come over the Aryan lands, simultaneously hostile armies will fall upon the Aryan land, simultaneously the Aryan lands will be struck with a hundred blows through fifty, with ten thousand blows through a thousand, with a hundred thousand blows through ten thousand blows. (*Yašt* 8:59–61 [Panaino, with some changes])

14. (*If*) *any (lay) person. wĕ'îš.* "An Israelite (lay person)" (*Tg. Ps.-J.*). The fuller expression *'îš zār* is reduced because the subject *zār* is mentioned in the previous sentence (v. 13b), which introduces this case (see also Milgrom 1976a: 63, n. 221).

inadvertently. bišgāgâ. For an exposition of this term, see the NOTE on 4:2.

eats of a sacred donation. yō'kal qōdeš. This expression is the *Leitwort*, the quintessential theme of the entire pericope (vv. 1–16), appearing a total of seven times (vv. 4, 6, 7, 10 [twice], 14, 16).

Although *'ākal* literally means "eat," it may also serve as H's equivalent of P's *mā'al min haqqōdeš* 'trespasses on sancta' (5:15)—that is, commits sacrilege. This is surely what Jeremiah had in mind: *qōdeš yiśrā'ēl laYHWH rē'šît tĕbû'ātōh kol- 'ōkĕlāyw ye'šāmû* 'Israel was holy to YHWH the first / best of his harvest; all who ate of it will be punished' (Jer 2:3; on the root *'šm*, see vol. 1.339–45). Here, *'ākal* means "destroy" (as in 26:16; see its NOTE; cf. Fishbane 1985: 302, n. 27, opposing Milgrom 1976a: 70). However, Fishbane has overlooked the significance of the expression "the first / best of his harvest." To be sure, *'ākal* means "destroy." But this is its metaphoric, extended meaning. Jeremiah's play on our verse makes it certain that he is employing *'ākal* also in its basic meaning of "eat." The *rē'šît* 'first / best' is holy and belongs to the Deity (cf. Num 18:12), and its consumption or destruction by the *zār* 'alien' (i.e., Israel's enemies) constitutes desecration for which they will be punished (*ye'šāmû*). Jeremiah's use of this verb provides further evidence that he had our passage in mind (*'ašmâ*, v. 16). Thus *'ākal* in Jer 2:3 is a double entendre: "eat / destroy" (Kugel 1996: 22). However, the attempted equation of *'ākal qōdeš* with Akkadian *asakka akālu* is doubtful (Milgrom 1976a: 25–27).

he shall . . . pay. wěnātan. For evidence that *nātan* also has the meaning "pay," see the NOTE on 27:23. According to the rabbis, if a lay person deliberately eats sacred food, he pays no fine since he is subject to death by divine agency (*m. Ḥal.* 1:9; *m. Bik.* 2:1; cf. *m. Ter.* 3:7; *Sipre* Deut. 63).

the (combined) sacred donation. 'et-haqqōdeš. Saadiah renders this phrase "for the sacred donation." Ibn Ezra gives two interpretations. The first suggests the rendering "with the sacred donation." His second explanation states correctly that the one-fifth fine is also sacred. Thus the sacred donation paid to the priest consists of both the principle and the penalty. That this reading is correct is verified by the wording of the penalty for accidental sacrilege with sancta, on which this case is based: *wěnātan 'ōtô lakkōhēn* 'When he gives it to the priest' (5:16), where "it" (sing.) refers to both the principle and the one-fifth fine. Thus the translation of *NJPS* "he shall pay the priest for the sacred donation, adding one-fifth of its value" cannot be correct.

15. *They (the priests) shall not desecrate. wělō' yěhallělû.* This *Piʿel* verb has the force of a *Hipʿil* "they shall not permit the desecration" (GKC § 52g). Ehrlich (1908) suggests that some of the priests might be tempted to mislead the Israelites in order to increase their *'ăšām* prebends (cf. Hos 4:8).

the sacred donations of the Israelites. qodšê běnê yiśrā'ēl. Although this phrase in the parallel verse (v. 2) is arguably inclusive of all individual offerings, most sacred and sacred alike, here the context (vv. 10–16) clearly determines that this term is limited to sacred food eaten by the priest's family outside the sanctuary precincts (i.e., the sacred offerings).

This conclusion also provides evidence for believing that no *'ăšām* offering is involved in the penalty and, hence, there is no contradiction between this case (vv. 14–16) and the ostensibly similar case of 5:14–16 (see NOTE on "the penalty of reparation," v. 16).

which (they). 'ēt 'ăšer. This relative construction is explicated by its equivalent in parallel v. 2, *'ăšer hēm* 'which they' (see further COMMENT A). Saadiah holds that it begins a new object (as though it read *wě'ēt 'ăšer*), which must be rejected (see below).

they set aside. yārîmû. The corresponding verb in the parallel verse is *maqdīšîm* 'consecrate' (v. 2), which proves (contra Saadiah) that *'ēt 'ăšer yārîmû* is not a new object, but an apposite, explanatory clause. Note that the structure of v. 15 follows that of v. 2, demonstrating that the *sense* of v. 2 requires reordering the sequence as aα, aβ, bα, bβ.

16. *by causing them (the Israelites) to bear the penalty. wĕhiśśî'û 'ōtām 'āwōn.* This clause is interpreted in three ways:

1. Israelites transmit punishment to priests by causing them to sin (Abravanel [second explanation]). This interpretation is patently wrong, since the subject (from vv. 14–15) continues to be the priests.

2. The object is the Israelites (the interpretation accepted here). The *Hip'îl* implies that the subject (the priests) is causing someone *else* to bear the penalty (Ibn Ezra, Bekhor Shor, Ramban, Abravanel [first explanation], *Keter Torah*). This usage is precisely echoed in QL: ŠLW' Y[HYW] MSY'[Y]M 'T H'M 'WWN 'so that (the priests) should not *let the people* bear punishment' (*MMT* B 12–13; see also 26–27).

3. The Temple Scroll contains a different interpretation of vv. 15–16. It is part of a longer passage that merits quotation at length (with slight changes):

W'ŚYTH MQWM LM'RB HHYKL SBYB PRWR 'MWDYM LḤṬ'T WL'ŠM MWBDLYM ZH MZH LḤṬ'T HKHNYM WLŚ'YRYM WLḤṬ'WT H'M WL'ŠMWTMH WLW' YHYW M'RBYM KWLW 'LH B'LH KY MWBDLYM YHYW MQWMWTMH ZH MZH LM'N LW' YŠWGW HK-WHNYM BKWL ḤṬ'T H'M WBKWL 'LW 'ŠMWT LŚ'T ḤṬ' 'ŠMH

You shall fashion a place west of the sanctuary roundabout, a colonnaded stoa for (animals reserved for) purification and reparation offerings so that the purification offerings of the priests, the he-goats, the purification offerings of the people and their reparation offerings will be kept apart from each other and one kind will not mix with the other. Indeed, their locations shall be separate from each other in order that the priests shall not err with any of the purification offerings of the people or with any of these reparation offerings for which they will bear grievous sin (11QT 35:10–15).

Among the unusual installations prescribed by the Temple Scroll for the inner court of the temple compound is the *PRWR*, or stoa, the colonnaded structure to the west of the sanctuary, whose purpose, as expressed in the quotation, is to keep apart the purification offerings of the priests and the he-goats from the purification offerings of the people and their reparation offerings. The four enumerated sacrifices need be clarified:

1. *Purification offerings of the priests.* These must refer to the purification offerings brought on behalf of the priests. Their cause may be the inadvertent wrongdoing of an individual priest, requiring a female of the flock or two birds (4:27–35; 5:11–13), the inadvertent wrongdoing of the high priest, requiring a bull (4:3–12), or the ritual for a specific occasion such as the purification bull

sacrificed on behalf of the priests at the annual priestly consecration (8:14–17; cf. 11QT 15:18–16:3) and the purification calf offered on behalf of the priests at the initiation of the Tabernacle cult (9:8–11). Some of these sacrifices are burned outside the camp (cf. 4:12; 8:17; 9:11)—though normally they would constitute a priestly perquisite (6:19, 22; cf. 10:18)—either because it is improper for the priests to benefit from sacrifices brought for their own wrongdoing or because the blood of the purification animal is used to purge the sanctuary (6:23; 10:18).

2. *He-goats.* These clearly refer to the purification offerings required in the fixed cult of the calendar year for the inauguration of the public cult, new moons and festivals (Lev 9:3; Num 28:15, 22, 30; 29:5, 11, 16, 19, 22, 25, 28, 31, 34, 38; cf. 11QT 14:18; 17:13–15; 18:4–6; 25:5–6, etc.). They can also include the purification offering of the *nāśîʾ*, the tribal chieftain (Lev 4:22–26) and of the individual (Num 15:24–26). The he-goats are eaten by the priests, since they are brought on behalf of the Israelites (Lev 10:16–18; Jos. *Ant.* 3:249; cf. *m. Men.* 11:7; *b. Men.* 100a).

3. *Purification offerings of the people.* These refer to the purification offerings of the individual Israelite brought for inadvertent wrongdoing (Lev 4:27–35; 5:1–13) or for severe ritual impurity (birth, 12:6–8; leprosy, 14:10, 19, 30; gonorrhea, 15:14–15, 29–30, etc.). These animals are either females of the flock or birds and are eaten by the priests (6:19–22). If provision also has to be made for the inadvertent wrongdoing of the entire community, then a bull is set aside and then is burned outside the camp (4:13–21).

4. *Their reparation offerings.* The *ʾāšām* is an individual sacrifice brought for inadvertent sacrilege committed against either YHWH's sancta or his name. The sacrificial animal is always a ram or a male lamb and is eaten by the priests (7:6).

Now it is possible to understand how the priests could make a mistake with purification offerings. Both they and the people would use the same animals—females of the flock, birds, or bulls—for their personal offerings. Moreover, as noted, the he-goat either could be offered for the community in the regular cult or could be brought by the chieftain and individual for their individual inadvertence, thereby providing another opportunity for sacrificing the wrong animal. The consequences of admixture would be severe. A sacrifice offered for the wrong party would automatically be invalidated (cf. *m. Zebaḥ.* 1:1–3). Furthermore, defilement might occur because it would be offered improperly, for it would be possible for a purification offering to be eaten by the priest when it should have been incinerated and vice versa.

The author of the scroll would have been quite aware of the dire consequences of such an error, since such a notorious case is cited in the Torah: Aaron and his remaining sons burn the people's purification offering instead of eating it, bringing down on them the wrath of Moses (10:16–20; vol. 1.261–64). Moreover, according to the Temple Scroll, the priests are admonished in an explicit statement in the Torah not to allow the admixture of purification animals. Indeed, the final statement in the quoted passage (35:13–15) can be understood only as the scroll's exegesis of Lev 22:15–16. The two passages follow side by side:

Lev 22:15–16	11QT 35:13–15
wĕlō' yĕḥallĕlû 'et-qodšê bĕnê yiśrā'ēl . . . wĕhiśśî'û 'ōtām 'āwōn 'ašmâ bĕ'oklām 'et-qodšêhem	LM 'N LW' YŚWGW HKWHNYM BKWL ḤṬ'T H 'M WBKWL 'LW 'ŠMWT LŚ'T ḤṬ' 'ŠMH
They (the priests) shall not desecrate the sacred donations of the Israelites . . . by causing them (the Israelites) to bear the penalty of reparation when they (the Israelites) eat their (own) sacred donations.	in order that the priests shall not err with any of the purification offerings of the people or with any of these reparation offerings for which they will bear grievous sin

Elsewhere I have demonstrated (1976a: 63–64) that this biblical text should be rendered "They (the priests) shall not permit the sacred donations of the Israelites . . . to become profane by causing them (the Israelites) to incur the penalty of reparation when they (the Israelites) eat their (own) sacred donations." However, the author of the scroll understood this passage differently. He took the particle as a reflexive, referring back to the priests. Indeed, this is precisely how many of the Versions understood it (e.g., "so shall they bring upon themselves the iniquity of trespass," LXX; similarly Tgs. Onk., Ps.-J., and Neof.). It is also found in early rabbinic exegesis: "this is one of the three occurrences of 'et that R. Ishmael interpreted as reflexive. By the same token wĕhiśśî'û 'ōtām 'āwōn 'ašmâ (Lev 22:16): Others do not bring it (the punishment) on them; rather, they bring it on themselves" (Sipre Naso 32). It is interesting that the two other occurrences of 'et that R. Ishmael identifies as reflexives, Num 6:13 and Deut 34:6, are equally incorrect: yābî' 'ōtô (Num 6:13) has to be rendered as a passive, and wayyiqbōr 'ōtô (Deut 34:6), which R. Ishmael reads as "He (Moses) buried himself," should be rendered "He (God) buried him."

In keeping with the interpretation of 'ōtām as a reflexive, the author of the scroll would have rendered the Leviticus passage as follows: "The priests shall not desecrate the sancta of the Israelites . . . by bringing on themselves a grievous sin when they (the priests) eat their (own) sancta." As indicated, the priests may not eat any of the expiatory sacrifices that they bring on their own behalf. The only way in which such an error could happen would be through the intermingling of the purification offerings of the priests and the people, resulting in the priest mistakenly eating a priest's animal, thinking that it belongs to the people. Thus Lev 22:15–16 warns, according to its interpretation by the Temple Scroll, that Aaron's mistake can happen at any time unless steps are taken to keep apart the purification offerings of the priests and the people.

According to Yadin's (1983) rendering, the scroll also prescribes that the reparation offerings of the people be segregated from the priests' purification animals. However, there is no point in such a ruling. Even if these animals intermingled, there is no chance of error because the reparation animals can be only rams or male lambs, from which the purification offerings may never be taken (cf. *m. Zebaḥ.* 8:2). For the solution to this problem, I propose a different rendering. The antecedent of WL'ŠMWTMH 'their reparation offerings' (35:12) is not just the people, but also the priests. Thus the reparation animals of the priests and the people must be segregated from each other. Indeed, this interpretation would correspond to the stated program of the stoa LHT'T WL'ŠM: for the separation of the purification *and* the reparation animals. It would also correspond with the end of the passage BKWL ḤṬ'T H'M WBKWL 'LW 'ŠMWT, which I would render "with every purification offering of the people and with all these reparation offerings," thus framing the entire passage in an inclusion. It is gratifying that Yadin (1983: 2.151) accepted my interpretation.

For the idiom *nāśā' 'āwōn*, see the NOTES on 5:1, 17, and Zimmerli (1954: 8–12). The prefixed *waw* of *wĕhiśśî'û*, I take as a relative conjunction meaning "when."

the penalty of reparation. '*āwōn* '*ašmâ*. This can be rendered, alternatively, as "the penalty of punishment" (see NOTE on 4:3); the idea is that when priests sin, they cause the people to suffer (cf. Segal 1989). This expression is a hapax and, as generally rendered, is a tautology, since both words connote punishment for sin. It will hardly do to render it "iniquity and guilt" (*RSV*) or a "severe guilt" ("eine Verstärkung des einzelnen Begriffes," Elliger 1966: 294, n. 35). "Guilt requiring a penalty payment" (*NJPS*) and "guilt and its penalty" (*NEB*) are probes in the right direction, but the idiom remains abstruse: the penalty/payment is still unspecified.

However, it may be that *'ašmâ* alludes to the sacrificial penalty of the *'āšām*. This possibility is suggested by another verse: "their reparation offering [*w'šymm* > *w'šmm*; cf. BH³, and 1 Esdras 9:10] was a ram of the flock for their [*'ašmātām*] sacrilege" (Ezra 10:19). In the postexilic literature, *'ašmâ* connotes a sin against God (e.g., Ezra 9:6, 7, 13, 15; 10:10; 2 Chr 24:18) and converges on *ma'al*. Hence the translation "sacrilege." This late usage is absent in P, where *'ašmâ* is infinitive Qal (e.g., Lev 4:3; 5:24, 26) or possibly a nominal form like *'āšām*, conveying the consequential meaning of "penalty" (4:3) or "reparation" (22:16). Here, then, is another cultic term in P that is preexilic. Since *'ašmâ* in Ezra is associated with an *'āšām* offering, the same may hold true for Lev 22:16. *Sefer Hamibḥar*, *Keter Torah*, Abravanel, Ehrlich (only tentatively), and *NRSV* maintain that the context deals with the *'āšām* sacrifice. So, apparently, did the Qumran sect, according to their Temple Scroll.

Nonetheless, this meaning is far from certain. The doubt stems not only from morphological considerations, but from the context. What is the nature of the sancta that are defiled? The term *qōdeš* is nonexplicit, but its context (vv. 10–16) speaks of only sacred food that is brought into the priest's home and is consumed by his household. Thus most sacred food (*qodšê qŏdāšîm*) is automatically excluded, since it may be eaten by only male priests within the sacred precinct. Food of lesser sanctity, *qōdeš*, according to P can include only the following: crop donations, the right thigh and breast of all animals slaughtered for their meat (i.e., offered as *šĕlāmîm*), the firstling, the *ḥērem*, the crop and animal tithe, and the tithe of the Levites. These are expressly stipulated as prebends for the priest's household (Num 18:11–19, 25–29; Lev 27:30–33).

Thus the possibility exists that since sancta of a lower order are involved, the penalty for their expropriation is reduced. The penalty of one-fifth is still maintained for changing the status from sacred to profane, but no *'āšām* offering is required. It is not considered a *ma'al* against God. This is the interpretation of the Tannaim (e.g., *Sipra* Emor 6:3–7). Eating is a lesser sin than encroachment (*qārēb*; Dillmann and Ryssel 1897). Whereas the latter is punishable by *kārēt* (v. 3), the former is subject to the lesser penalty of death by divine agency (*mwt*, v. 9) for eating carrion (v. 8). Thus no reparation offering would be required, and vv. 14–16 would not be in contradiction to 5:14–16. Reinforcing this conclusion is the fact that the sancta no longer belong to God, but to the priest, underscored by the explicit reference to the sancta in the priest's home (vv. 10–13). Thus since God has not been slighted, sacrificial expiation would not be required. *'ašmâ* would then simply mean "reparation"—another example of the consequential *'āšām* (vol. 1.339–45)—referring back to the required restitution (v. 14b). Thus one may not cite *Ludul* II 19 (*BWL* 289) and *Šurpu* II 77 (Reiner 1958) as analogies, since they (probably) speak of accidently eating the food of one's god.

No conclusion can be drawn concerning the requirement of an *'āšām* offering in Lev 22:14–16. All that is certain is that desanctification has taken place and that the standard penalty of principal plus one-fifth is imposed.

who sanctifies them (the priests). *mĕqaddĕšām*. Hoffmann (1953) opts for the *qŏdāšîm* 'the sacred donations' as the antecedent of the pronoun on the basis of his exegesis of v. 9. However, it was demonstrated that the pronominal suffix of this verb in v. 9 refers to the priests. Moreover, the parallelism of vv. 9 and 16 mandate that the referent here, in v. 16, is also the priests. Note that both verses are codas: in v. 9, the priests die if *they* desecrate; in v. 16, the priests inflict "the penalty of reparation" on the Israelites by causing *them* to desecrate. Finally, the participle *mĕqaddēš* is appropriate for only persons (priests and lay persons), but not sacrifices, which are consecrated by their offerers.

Vv. 17–25. Blemished Sacrificial Animals

After forbidding blemished priests to officiate at sacrifices (21:16–23) and impure priests (and nonpriests) to eat sacred food (22:1–16), the text turns to the topic of blemished animals. The list of animal blemishes (vv. 22–24) matches the list of priestly blemishes (21:18–20; see chap. 21, COMMENT B).

This pericope contains no mention of the purification (*ḥaṭṭā't*) and reparation (*'āšām*) offering, which leads some exegetes to conclude that H did not know of them (e.g., Wellhausen 1963: 157; Snaith 1967). This conclusion is unwarranted. This pericope explicitly limits itself to votive (*neder*), free-will (*nĕdābâ*), and thanksgiving (*tôdâ*) offerings (see below), which exclude purely expiatory offerings. Moreover, that an offerer would bring a blemished animal for *his expiation* is simply inconceivable. Finally, the historical books record that the offerer would most likely buy his expiatory animals from the sanctuary (2 Kgs 12:17; vol. 1.177), and H may reflect this practice. (Is this the reason why these expiatory sacrifices are missing in Deuteronomy [e.g., 12:6]?). The finely crafted structure of this pericope is discussed in the COMMENT.

Vv. 17–21. Blemishes Prohibited

18. *Speak . . . and to all the Israelites. dabbēr . . . wĕ'el kol-bĕnê yiśrā'ēl.* There are three recipients of Moses' speech: Aaron, his sons, and the new component— Israel. The significance is clear: both the priesthood and the laity are held responsible for detecting sacrificial blemishes by the offerer, when the animal is chosen, and by the priest, when the animal enters the sanctuary grounds. This threefold address is also found in 17:2–3, which stresses that both lay offerers and priestly officiants are responsible for carrying out H's fundamental tenet: all meat for the table must initially be sacrificed on the one legitimate altar so that its blood will ransom the offerer's life from the charge of murder (17:11; see NOTES).

from the house of Israel. mibbêt yiśrā'ēl. The LXX and a number of *Tg.* MSS read *mibbĕnê.* The MT, however, should be favored because of the many attestations of *mibbêt* in H (e.g., 17:3, 8, 10).

an offering. qorbānô, literally "his offering." The individual's sacrifice cannot be presented by proxy.

the aliens. haggēr. The Sam., Versions, and fourteen MSS add *haggār* 'who dwell' (cf. *Sipra* Emor, par. 7:1). The non-Israelite resident who worshiped Israel's God (1 Sam 21:8; 2 Sam 11:11) was subject to the same sacrificial laws (cf. Num 15:14–16).

their vows. nidrêhem. Here begins a switch to the plural, which continues through v. 20. The switch from plural to singular is attested in the vow pericope of Num 15 (vv. 2–3, sing.; vv. 4–10): "the lawmaker is instructing all individual members of the community to fulfill all their individual commitments, even though these have been made apart from one another and at different times throughout the year" (Berlinerblau 1996: 55). H's knowledge of the rules for the votive and freewill offerings is presumed (7:16–21 [P]).

their freewill gifts. nidbôtām. The distinction between votive and freewill offerings is set forth in chap. 27, COMMENT C. It is supplemented here by the nuanced (and significant) rabbinic distinction:

> When are they accounted votive offerings? When he says, "I pledge myself to a burnt offering." And when are they accounted freewill offerings? When he says, "this shall be a burnt offering." Wherein do votive offerings differ from freewill offerings? (In nothing) save that with votive offerings he is answerable for them (and must replace them) if they die or are stolen, but freewill offerings he is not answerable for them if they die or are stolen. (*m. Qinnim* 1:1)

This distinction is logical. A freewill offering refers to an animal at hand: "*this* shall be a burnt offering." Therefore, once the offerer sets it aside, it belongs to the priests, and its loss is their loss. The votive offering refers to a conditional (hence future) payment—it depends on the fulfillment of the vow—and thus he is responsible if the animal is stolen.

which may be presented. '*ăšer yaqrîbû*, literally, "they will present." This is a virtual passive (GKC §§ 144–45; Hartley 1992).

as a burnt offering. This is an addition to the laws of P. Just as 7:11–18 (P) supplement chap. 3, describing three purposes of the well-being offering (*šĕlāmîm*), so here H specifies two purposes for the burnt offering (*'ōlâ*). But P has already stated a/the function of the burnt offering—for expiation (1:4). H now cites two other functions, votive and freewill—for expressing happiness. Is H supplementing or supplanting P? I think the latter. The expiatory function of the *private* burnt offering has effectively (not theoretically [P]) been replaced by the purification and reparation offerings. Public burnt offerings, however, retain an expiatory function (details in vol 1.172–77).

Strikingly, the burnt offering is not assigned a thanksgiving function. And, indeed, in all the attestations of the *tôdâ* in the Bible, none involves a burnt offering. In fact, the term *tôdâ* is usually compounded with the term *zebaḥ* (7:12, 13, 15; 22:29; Pss 107:22; 116:17; 2 Chr 33:16), implying that it always was a form of *šĕlāmîm* (see chap. 3, COMMENT). To be sure, the requirement that the *tôdâ* be accompanied by a bread offering, part of which was leavened (7:13) and, hence, ineligible for the altar, makes it impossible for a burnt offering to take place. However, a rationale for not offering the entire animal (*'ōlâ*) as a sign of thanksgiving escapes me.

19. *to be acceptable on your behalf. lirṣōnĕkem.* This clause is part of the object. In all its attestations, *rāṣôn* is part of the apodosis (e.g., 19:5; 22:21, 29; see NOTE on 21:23). It is placed at the head of the verse and is changed to the second person for emphasis. It is another example of the possessive suffix actually representing a genetive predicate: *lirṣōnĕkem = lĕrāṣôn (yihyeh) lākem*, as demonstrated by Kogut (1994: 35–36, 46–47; 84–86; e.g., Ps 115:5–7; suggested by Schwartz, personal communication). Note *Tg. Onq. lĕra'ăwā' yĕhê lĕkôn* on v. 19 and *lĕra'ăwā' lêh* for *lirṣōnô* (1:3). Its meaning is clarified by the parallel apposition, in a similar context, of *lō' yērāṣeh* and *lō' yēḥāšēb* 'it will not be accredited' (7:18). An even more illuminating parallel is found in Mal 1:8, "if you present a lame or sick animal—doesn't it matter? Just offer it to your governor: Will he accept you (*hăyirṣĕkā*)? Will he show you favor [*hăyiśśā' pānêkā*]?" From this citation, two things can be derived. First, to be acceptable (*rāṣôn*) to God (or the governor), the sacrifice (or the gift) must be unblemished. Second, the terms *rāṣâ* and *nāśā' pānîm* are semantically equivalent, so that the function of the burnt offering is to elicit the favor of the deity.

This pericope contains seven occurrences of the root *rṣh* (vv. 19, 20, 21, 23, 25, 27, 29), indicating its importance. It is no accident that this term appears with the burnt offering (22:19–20; Jer 6:20; cf. Isa 60:7) and the well-being offering (19:5; 22:21, 29), but never with the purification or reparation offering. These latter two sacrifices serve strictly expiatory purposes (vol. 1.176–77, 254–61). Their offerers approach God under the burden of sin; they seek his pardon, not his pleasure. For a discussion of the etymology of *rāṣâ*, *rāṣôn*, see the NOTE on 1:3.

(*it must be*). These words (with *NJPS*) must be added, since the verse has no verb. The words that follow are an explicative clause in apposition; but without a verb, expressed or implied, the verse makes no sense. Perhaps, the implied (or missing) verb is *taqrîbû* 'you shall present' to contrast with *lo' taqrîbû* 'You shall not present' (v. 20). Then, vv. 19–20 will be exact semantic opposites.

a male. The indispensable requirement of the burnt offering (1:3, 10), but it is waived (together with the unblemished requirement) if the animal is a bird (vol. 1.167).

without blemish. tāmîm. This adjective is derived from the verb *tāmam* 'be complete' (cf. 23:15; Deut 31:30). The adjective precedes the noun, as in *yĕraqraq ḥārûṣ* 'bright green gold' (Ps 68:14; *Keter Torah*; see GKC § 132b). The same requirement prevailed in Mesopotamia (Thureau-Dangin 1921:10, ll. 2–3; Falkenstein and von Soden 1953: 275), Hattia (Gurney 1952: 150–51), and Egypt (Blackman 1951: 479–80) and is echoed in the prophetic charge that people were offering up defective animals (Mal 1:8–14). According to Philo (*Laws* 1.66), the officiating priest scrupulously checked the sacrificial animal for blemishes, even examining concealed parts not a biblical requirement; see the discussion below). D, which avoids any mention of sacrificial rites, is nonetheless concerned about sacrificial blemishes (17:1).

Douglas (1966: 51–52; 1972: 76–77) correctly emphasizes that *tāmîm* 'wholeness, completeness' is the hallmark of holiness. On the basis of that insight, Olyan (1996b) has aptly concluded that stones of the altar (Exod 20:21–22 [24–25] [JE]; Deut 27:5–6 [D]; Josh 8:31 [Dtr]; and, by extension, stones of the Temple building, 1 Kgs 6:7) must also be whole, or unaltered (in priestly usage *'ên bāhen mûm*; cf. Num 19:2). Thus not only priests and sacrificial animals, but also inanimate materials within YHWH's domain must be distinct and separated from the outside domain of the common (*ḥōl*) by bearing (symbolically) the quality of completeness that characterizes YHWH. Olyan (1996b: 167, n. 27) also points out that instead of *tāmîm*, nonpriestly texts resort to a different but synonymous term, *šālēm* (Deut 27:6; cf. Josh 8:31) or, expressed negatively, *lō' gāzît* 'not hewn' (Exod 20:25). But see the INTRODUCTION to 19:35–36a.

What for me is equally significant is the corollary conclusion deriving from Olyan's (1996b) study, namely, that the nonpriestly, epic sources (JE, D, Dtr) are equally adamant about setting a boundary—indeed, the same boundary—between the sacred and the common.

Why does H and not P name the blemishes? P surely had criteria (even if they were not the same); the qualification *tāmîm* is attached to each of the sacrificial quadrupeds (1:3, 10; 3:1, 6; 4:3, 23, 28, 32; 5:15, 18, 25). The probable answer is that P takes them for granted, and it finds no need to list them because the examination of the animal is done by the sanctuary priest. H, however, will have nothing to do with priestly exclusivity. It regards the inspection of the animal to be the shared responsibility of the lay offerer and the officiating priest, as indicated by the inclusion of the Israelites in this address (v. 18a).

Thus H supplements and refines a major theme of P. In P, the purity of the sanctuary (chap. 16) is marred by impurity (*ṭum'â*) in animals (chap. 11) and humans (chaps. 4–5, 12–15). In H, this distinction moves to the realm of defects (*mûm*) and focuses on the sanctuary's officiants (21:16–23) and its offerings (22:17–30).

The term *tāmîm* is not used as a criterion for priests, even though they, too, must be without blemish, for the simple reason that *tāmîm* applied to persons implies moral perfection (e.g., Gen 6:9; 17:1 [P]). In fact, in D (and other sources), it denotes nothing but moral perfection (Deut 18:13). This may be the reason why in D's two pericopes that speak of the unblemished requirement of sacrifices, the word *tāmîm* is conspicuously missing (Deut 15:21; 17:1, Paran 1983: 195).

from. ba. "in the domain of" (GKC § 199i).

cattle, sheep, or goats. But no birds, despite 1:14–17. Hartley (1992: 361) intuits the correct reason: "since these two kinds of whole (i.e., burnt) offerings are voluntary." Contrast the burnt offering in chap. 1 that is exclusively for expiation (1:4). Expiation being mandatory, the priestly legists had to make some concession to the poor, allowing for birds (1:14–17) and cereal (chap. 2) to substitute for the more expensive quadrupeds. Voluntary offerings, however, being votive and freewill sacrifices, fall under the *šĕlāmîm* rubric. This indirect deduction from the enumerated animals eligible for (burnt and) well-being offerings gives added support to my thesis, which I based on other grounds, that birds were ineligible as well-being offerings (vol. 1.222).

Note that *kĕśābîm* (sing., *keśeb*) "sheep" stands for the genus, whereas *kĕbāśîm* (sing., *kebeś*) refers to the male sheep.

20. *You shall not present. lō' taqrîbû.* The LXX adds "to YHWH," presumably to balance *yaqrîbû laYHWH* 'may be presented to YHWH' (v. 18). But, if as I have suggested, the word *taqrîbû* is to be inserted (or implied) in v. 19, then it becomes the perfect counterpoint, and no additions are necessary.

21. *And whenever any person. wĕ'îš kî.* Because the vow pericope (Num 30) distinguishes between *'îš kî* (v. 3) and *'iššâ kî* (v. 4), Berlinerblau (1996: 135–36, 144) claims that the former expression is not gender-neutral and sanctions only a male votary. This deduction is fallacious. Numbers has to distinguish between male and female votaries in order to expatiate on the way a woman's vow can be annulled by her father or husband. That women initiate and fulfill vows is attested in 1 Sam 1:11; 24–28; Prov 7:14; 31:2. And even if our pericope assumes, in consonance with priestly tradition, that a woman's vow is subject to the approval of her male authority, the fact remains that if a woman makes a vow, she must fulfill it. Hence our pericope applies to her. Indeed, the Nazirite vow (P), expressly permitted to a woman (Num 6:2), is fulfilled not only by specific ablutions, but also by a battery of sacrifices (vv. 10–21) falling exclusively on the vower. Besides, since a woman may offer a sacrifice (see NOTE on "any person among you," 1:2), why not a votive sacrifice?

for an expressed (vow). lĕpallē'-(neder), literally "to express, articulate (a vow)," so *lĕpārāsā' nidrā'* (Tgs. Onq., Neof.) and *lĕhaprîš bĕdibbûrô* (Rashi). There are three other suggestions:

1. A denominative from *pele'* 'miracle', since to make a vow is, in effect, to request a miracle (e.g., Gen 28:20; Num 21:2; Jon 1:16; Ramban). This interpretation has some bearing in the *Hip'îl hiplā'* (Num 6:2; see NOTE on 27:2), but not on the *Pi'el* (22:21; Num 15:3, 18).

2. The LXX renders it "pay, discharge," probably on the basis of the verb *šillēm* 'pay' in similar, but non-P, contexts (e.g., Pss 66:13; 116:18; Prov 7:15). But this rendering would not satisfy the *Hip'îl* usage (27:2; Num 6:2). Ehrlich (1899–1900 Heb.) would overcome this objection by rendering the *Hip'îl* 'to make'. This suggestion is most attractive, since it fits the four given contexts: Lev 27:2; Num 6:2 (*Hip'îl*) are set in a vow-making context, and Lev 22:21; Num 15:3, 8, describing the animals and their sacrificial accompaniments, fit a fulfillment context. However, there is neither an etymological basis nor a philological precedent for such a radical distinction between the *Pi'el* and *Hip'îl* of *pl'*. What, finally, dissuades one from this solution is that *neder* occurs in v. 23, where the subject is clearly the fulfillment of a vow, and yet the expected word *ûlĕpallē'* is missing.

3. It is a by-form of *plh*, meaning "set aside" (Albertz 1976: 414, 416; *HAL*³, 3.876; Levine 1989). But see Conrad's (1987: 572) strictures (cf. Berlinerblau 1996: 177–78).

For the possible distinction between *pille'* (*Pi'el*) and *hiplî'* (*Hip'îl*), see the NOTE on 27:2.

as a freewill offering. *lindābâ*, literally "for a freewill offering." The Sam., Tg. Ps.-J., and one MS omit the *lamed*, thereby adding the freewill offering as an object of the verb *lĕpallē'*, the sense now being "to make (or fulfill) a vow or freewill (declaration)." However, the occurrence of *lĕpallē'-neder 'ô bindābâ* (Num 15:3; note the prefixed *beth*) indicates that the freewill offering is independent of the verb *lĕpallē'*, and the MT here is correct.

it must be perfect. tāmîm yihyeh. The rabbis add that it must be the best (*min hammubḥār*) in his possession (*m. Menaḥ.* 8:1). This clearly is the reason for YHWH's preference for Abel's offering: he gave *mibbĕkōrôt ṣō'nô ûmēḥelbēhen* 'the choicest of the firstlings of his flock' (Gen 4:4). But "perfect" does not mean "unworked." If the latter were a requirement, it would have to be specified (Num 19:2; cf. Deut 21:3).

The possibility exists, with Berlinerblau (1996: 96, n. 3, 101–2), that Mal 1:14 does permit a blemished animal to be a votive offering (contrary to 22:18–20) if there are no unblemished animals in the owner's possession.

Vv. 22–24. The Blemishes

In addition to physical defects, there was universal concern that the sacrificial animal had not been stolen. In the instructions for the priestly staff at the temple of Philae, Egypt, "watchmen and hour-priests must guard against aliens and those who strive against the ordinances of the priests . . . and must inspect everything [i.e., the sacrifices] which are brought in for impurity and for stolen property" (ll. 8–10 [Junker 1959]). And in Israel, the prophet fulminates against those who bring to the temple blemished or stolen animals (Mal 1:13–14a), and subsequently, the rabbis reckon with the category of a stolen animal in their discussion of the prohibited sacrifices (*m. Giṭ.* 5:5).

As noted in chap. 21, COMMENT B, the common denominator among the twelve blemishes listed here is that they are noticeable to any observer. This also holds true for the twelve priestly blemishes (21:18–20), with the exception of "a crushed testicle," which indicates that the list of animal blemishes (22:23–25) is original and the priestly blemishes were chosen subsequently to match the animal blemishes in number and kind (see NOTE on "a crushed testicle," 21:20).

This conclusion compels me to rethink my NOTES on 11:5–6 (vol. 1.648–49), where I implied that the priestly legists erred in labeling the camel, rock badger, and hare as ruminants. It is entirely possible that they knew the truth, but it sufficed that these three creatures *gave the appearance* of ruminants by the sideward movement of their jaws. In other words, appearance was as much a criterion for the prohibited edible animals as for the prohibited sacrificeable animals.

The blemishes form a structural introversion (M. Hildenbrand):

A   a   *ʿawweret ʾô šābûr ʾô-ḥārûṣ ʾô-yabbelet ʾô gārāb ʾô yallepet*
     b   *lōʾ-taqrîbû ʾēlleh laYHWH*
          c   *wĕʾiššeh lōʾ-tittĕnû mēhem ʿal-hammizbēaḥ laYHWH* (v. 22)
          X   aʾ   *wĕšôr wāśeh śārûaʿ wĕqālûṭ*
                x   *nĕdābâ taʿăśeh ʾōtô*
                     cʾ   *ûlĕnēder lōʾ yērāṣeh* (v. 23)
A'   aʾʾ   *ûmāʿûk wĕkātût wĕnātûq wĕkārût*
     bʾ   *lōʾ taqrîbû laYHWH*
          cʾʾ   *ûbĕʾarṣĕkem lōʾ taʿăśû* (v. 24)

The structure consists of three panels of three parallel lines each, consisting of a first line (a, aʾ, aʾʾ), which deals with animal blemishes, and two following clauses, which specify the action involved (vv. 22, 24; bxbʾ, ccʾcʾʾ). The outer two panels (AAʾ) deal with only blemishes, while the inner panel (v. 23) deals with animals as well as their blemishes, forming an AXAʾ introversion.

The second clause of the panels emphasizes this introversion. The two outer clauses (bbʾʾ) use the exact form of the verb *qārab*: *taqrîbû* preceded by *lōʾ* and followed by *laYHWH*, while the middle clause (X) uses *taʿăśeh* with the verb in the second position (as opposed to the verb's first position in the outer clauses, bbʾ). The middle clause of the middle panel does not contain the negative particle, *lōʾ*. In fact, it is the only positive statement in the section, the only place that allows any kind of offering for a blemished animal. For this reason, it is a fitting center to the entire structure.

The twelve animal blemishes are arranged chiastically in relation to the twelve priestly blemishes of chap. 21. The animal blemishes fall into groupings of six, two, four, whereas the priestly blemishes are listed in groupings of four, two, six (Hartley 1992). The blemishes match in kind as well as in number. There are five clearly identical items: blind, overgrown limb, broken bones (comprising two items in the priestly list), sores, and scab. The remaining items are difficult to match because they are mainly unidentifiable. But the following are possible semantic equivalents: *qālûṭ* 'stunted limb' ‖ *ḥārûm* 'stunted limb' (?) or *pissēaḥ* 'lame'; *ḥārûṣ* 'sty' (?) ‖ *tĕballul bĕʿênô* 'a growth in his eye'; *māʿûk, kātût, nātûq, kārût* 'bruised, crushed, torn, cut (testes)' ‖ *mĕrôaḥ ʾāšek* 'crushed testes'. The variation in terminology may be ascribed to different biological and environmental factors governing each species. Obviously, the exposed testes of the animal would be subject to greater injury than would the covered testes of a man, and a hunchback would be considered a defect only in the upright human, but not in the animal. Nonetheless, mutatis mutandis, the same blemishes that invalidate officiating priests also invalidate animal sacrifices.

According to the rabbis, the reverse is true in the moral sphere: "R. Abba b. Judan said 'Whatever the Holy One, blessed be He, declared unfit in the case of an animal, he declared fit in the case of man. In animals he declared unfit "blind, has a broken limb, is maimed . . . " (Lev 22:22), whereas in man he declared fit "a broken and contrite heart" ' (Ps 51:19). R. Alexandri said: If an ordinary person makes use of broken vessels, it is a disgrace for him, but the vessels used by the Holy One blessed be He, are precisely broken ones, as it is said, 'the Lord is nigh unto them that are of a broken heart' (Ps 34:19)" (*Lev. Rab.* 7:2).

The artificiality of these lists is manifested by their equal number, their chiastic grouping, and the transparent attempts within each list to reach the number twelve (equivalent to the twelve tribes? see NOTE on 24:6a), as by listing broken bones twice in the priestly list and specifying four kinds of injuries to the testes in the animal list. As mentioned above (and developed in chap. 21, COMMENT B), the common denominator of both lists is that all the blemishes are noticeable to any observer. The one exception is "a crushed testicle," which was added to the priestly list to match the animal list in kind. That appearance is the fundamental criterion of these blemishes is demonstrated by the absence of the deaf and the mute from the priestly list, an omission that the rabbis—free of structural constraints—unhesitatingly correct (*m. Bek.* 7:6).

22. *blind*. *ʿawweret*, literally "blindness," a feminine form of the abstract *ʿiwwārôn* (Rashi). Saadiah avers that the animal is ineligible even if it is blind in one eye.

(*has a*) *broken* (*limb*). *šābûr*, literally "broken," a passive participle (rather than the noun *šeber*), probably influenced by the following term: *ḥārûṣ*. These two terms are subdivisions of the term *pissēaḥ* 'lame', which is also second in the list of priestly blemishes (21:18).

is maimed. *ḥārûṣ*, literally "cut, chopped off" (cf. 1 Kgs 20:40), a meaning attested in Akkadian *ḥarāṣu* (*CAD* 6.92–94). Rashi, however, claims that it refers to a defect of the eye or eyelid.

(*has*) *a seeping sore*. *yabbelet*, from *ybl* 'flow' (Dillmann and Ryssel 1897). HAL[3] (2.367) renders "warts" on the basis of Akkadian *ublu* and the LXX. Ibn Ezra suggests that it is related to *tĕballul bĕʿênô* (21:20), presumably from the root *bll* 'mix'.

a scar. *gārāb*. See the NOTE on 21:20. According to Dr. Nancy East of the School of Veterinary Medicine, University of California at Davis (personal communication), it probably is eczema, a dry itchy condition. Both *gārāb* and *yāllepet* (see below) are rare in humans, but very common among domestic animals; afflicted sheep often mutilate themselves in order to scratch.

lichen. yallepet. Perhaps a wet (oozing) condition (see above).

a food gift. 'iššeh. That these animals are possible well-being offerings (v. 21) means that *'iššeh* cannot mean "fire offering," the usual rendering, because the priestly prebends and the rest of the meat, given back to the offerer, are nonetheless referred to as *'iššeh* (see NOTES on 7:30, 35). For the rendering "food gift," see the NOTE on 1:9.

23. *extended. śārûa'.* This has been rendered as "a slipped thigh" (*Sipra* Emor 7:6), hence short legged; *yattîr* 'overdeveloped limb' (*Tgs. Onq., Neof.*); "short-stepped," because one leg is short (Saadiah). They have lameness in common (note that the term *pisseaḥ* [21:18] is lacking here). Since the root *śr'* means "extend" (e.g., Isa 28:20), I propose that the defect is a longer limb. Bekhor Shor holds that the extension resides in the hoof; that is, it is split a number of times. The LXX (cf. Vg, Pesh.) suggests a mutilated ear.

contracted. qālûṭ. Tgs. Onq. and Neof. render *ḥāsîr* 'underdeveloped limb', accepted here. Saadiah renders "long-stepped"; that is, it drags its feet. The LXX (cf. Vg, Pesh.) suggests an amputated, short tail.

sacrifice. ta'áśeh. The Sam. reads the plural *ta'áśû* to conform with the verbs in vv. 18b–33. If correct, then MT was influenced by following *yērāṣeh*.

sacrifice as a freewill offering . . . but it will not be accepted as a votive offering. The reason for this distinction is not self-evident. The following explanations have been offered:

1. The rabbis solve the problem by declaring that the freewill offering accepted from these two blemished animals is not offered up on the altar. Instead, the animals are used for *bedeq habbayit*, literally "Temple repair"—that is, as draft animals. Ramban finds biblical support, claiming that unqualified *neder* is for the altar (e.g., Pss 56:13; 66:13; 116:17–19) and unqualified *nĕdābâ* is for sanctuary improvements (e.g., Exod 35:22, 24; 2 Kgs 12:5; Ezra 1:4). However, his position is decisively refuted by Wessely (1846), who points to Lev 27, which unambiguously states that nonsacrificial animals (27:11–12) can be the result of a vow (vv. 1–8). And, conversely, freewill offerings are recorded as being sacrificed (Ps 54:8; 2 Chr 29:31; 35:8; Ezra 2:68).

2. According to Bekhor Shor, the *śārûa'* and *qālûṭ* are not deformed, but just have a larger or smaller limb; hence they are eligible for the freewill offering, but not for the more exacting requirements of the votive offering. However, a different length in a limb is surely a deformity.

3. Noth (1977) echoes this position, adding that the fulfillment of a vow is mandatory; hence obligatory offerings are more important. However, the fulfillment of a freewill declaration is just as binding.

4. Abravanel, I submit, offers the most plausible reason: the freewill offering, being the result of a spontaneous declaration, falls on the animal at hand, whether of good or poor quality (but not if it is defective). Under these conditions, a concession is allowed for an extended or a shortened limb, the least of

the blemishes. (After all, this limb is not inherently defective, but only so in comparison with others.) But the fulfillment of a vow is set in the future, and the offerer has ample time to find an animal of the finest quality for a votive offering. Hence the votive offering is subject to more rigorous standards than the freewill offering.

24. According to D, impaired testes invalidate persons from belonging to Israel (*qĕhal* YHWH, Deut 23:2), whereas H imposes this ban only on priests (21:20bβ) officiating at the altar (21:17b, 21). Each source legislates in accordance with its theological postulates: D ordains that all Israel is innately holy; H (and P) limits innate holiness to priests. This comparison with D suffices in itself to draw the conclusion (derived from elsewhere; see chap. 19, COMMENT) that H's concept of holiness, which it imposes as a goal on Israel, goes beyond P's limitation of holiness to the altar and the sacrifices and enters into another, moral, dimension.

Note that the four genital blemishes are listed according to their increased severity.

bruised. *ûmā'ûk; mĕrîs* 'crushed' (*Tg. Onq.*). The LXX uses the same word *thladías* 'injured, broken' for both *mā'ûk* (here) and *pĕṣûa' dakkâ*, literally "injured (by) crushing" (Deut 23:2).

crushed. *wĕkātût; rĕsîs* (*Tg. Onq.*; cf. Amos 6:11). For attestations of this root, see Deut 9:21; 2 Kgs 18:4; Isa 2:4.

torn. *wĕnātûq; šĕlîp* 'detached' (*Tg. Onq.*; cf. Num 22:23). For this root, see Josh 4:18; Judg 16:9; Jer 10:20; Koh 4:12. Presumably, this penultimate word reflects a penultimate condition: torn off, detached—but not entirely.

cut off. *kārût; gĕzîr* (*Tg. Onq.*). D employs this past participle not for the testicles, but for the urinary tract, *kĕrût šopkâ* (Deut 23:2)—that is, the penis.

You shall not do (this) in your land. *ûbĕ'arṣĕkem lō' ta'ăśû.* What is the implied referent? It clearly refers to the previously named testicle-impaired animals. But does it refer to animals for sacrifice or to all animals?

Kalisch (1867–72) holds that the gelding prohibition is limited to animals headed for the altar. He argues that since the verb *'āśâ* means "sacrifice" in the previous verse (v. 23), it has the same meaning here (see also 16:9; 17:9; 23:12, 19). Wessely (1846) also observes that these blemishes are listed separately and placed last in the blemish list because they are not only sacrificial losses for God (the altar), but also economic losses for the offerer since gelding improves the animals' quality (see below). Moreover, the progression of the three prohibitions in vv. 24–25 makes sense because gelded sacrifices are their common denominator. Animals in the sanctuary's vicinity (v. 24a), animals anywhere in the land (v. 24b), and imported animals (v. 25) are barred from the altar if they are gelded.

This interpretation, however, ostensibly suffers a severe objection: v. 25 bans all gelded sacrifices—not just in the sanctuary's vicinity. Thus there is no need to extend the gelding prohibition to the land and to imports (vv. 24b–25). For this reason, the rabbis argue that "in your land" (v. 24b) refers not to animals for sacrifice, but to all animals. In other words, H prohibits all gelding (*Tgs.*; *b. Ḥag.* 14b; cf. Jos. *Ant.* 4: 290–91; Vg). Textual support may be deduced from the verbs in v. 24: since *lō' taqrîbû* 'you shall not offer' (v. 24a) refers to sacrificial animals, *lō' ta'ăśû* 'you shall not do' (v. 24b) refers to nonsacrificial animals (Elliger 1966).

There are four problems, however, with this new interpretation:

1. *Structure.* The progression gelded sacrificial animals (v. 24a), gelded nonsacrificial animals (v. 24b), gelded sacrificial imports (v. 25) is broken.
2. *Logic.* Gelded animals for nonsacrificial use could be imported.
3. *Rationale.* Presumably, H prohibits gelded animals in all the land because it extends the holiness of the sanctuary (P) to the entire land. If so, one would rightly ask: Why doesn't H also ban castrated humans in the land? That is, why doesn't H extend the ban on castrated priests (21:20bγ) to Israelites (and resident aliens)?
4. *Economics.* As observed by Wessely (1846), gelding is essential husbandry. His observation is correct, for it can be shown that gelding is necessary for better quality meat, for manageable beasts of burden, and for the production of wool (Wapnish and Hesse 1991: 34–35).

In sum, there must have been large-scale gelding in the land.

We have reached an impasse. If "in your land" (v. 24b) refers to sacrifices (Wessely 1846; Kalisch 1867–72), it is redundant of v. 24a. If it refers to all animals in the land (rabbis; Jos.; Vg), it runs into greater obstacles: structure, logic, rationale, and economics. I tentatively offer this solution. The weight of the arguments tips the scales in favor of limiting all three prohibitions in vv. 24–25 to the gelding of animals for the altar. The one problem to resolve is the purported redundancy of vv. 24a and b. I propose, with due reserve, that "in your land" means *any other sanctuary* in your land. I have argued that H is written from the point of view of an important—probably Jerusalem, the most important—*regional* sanctuary (see chap. 17, COMMENT D). If I am correct, a rigorous logic is preserved in H: gelded animals and castrated priests are barred from the altar, but not from the land. Moreover, a sanctuary could own gelded beasts of burden, castrated priests could benefit from the sacrifices (20:22), and castrated Israelites could offer their sacrifices. Perhaps this implied stance of H influenced the reversal of D's edict barring castrated Israelites from entering "the congregation of YHWH" (Deut 23:2), as prophesied by Isaiah of the exile (Isa 56:3–5).

25. *any of these.* mikkol-'ēlleh. As a continuation of v. 24, the antecedent of the pronoun is the castrated animals. This verse answers the question: What if the animal with defective genitals comes not from the land of Israel, but from foreigners outside the land (Ehrlich 1899–1900 [H])? Thus vv. 24–25 compose a single taboo of increasing range: sanctified animals (v. 24a), all the animals in the land (v. 24b), imported animals (v. 25). The rabbis claim, on the basis of v. 25b, that the referent is not limited to injured testicles (v. 25), but embraces all animal defects (vv. 23–24; cf. *Tgs. Onq.* and *Ps.-J.*). Both views are plausible, but the limitation of v. 24b to animals with impaired testicles (see its NOTE) tips the scales in favor of the former.

And from the hand of a foreigner. ûmiyyad ben-nēkār. In the priestly texts, this term for foreigner is found in Gen 17:12, 27; Exod 12:43. *NJPS* and *NRSV* (following Rashi, Ibn Ezra, Dillmann and Ryssel 1897), add the verb "accept" before this expression, implying that these animals are presented by foreigners as *their* sacrifices. However, the end of this verse *lō' yērāṣû lākem* 'they will not be acceptable on *your* behalf' implies otherwise: these animals were obtained by Israelites from a third party: a foreign source (Dillman and Ryssel 1897; Shadal; Ginzberg 1932; Hartley 1992). That *miyyad* is used in purchase transactions, see 25:14aβ (Ehrlich 1899–1900 [H]). Eerdmans (1912) objects to this interpretation because of its redundancy: if defective animals are forbidden as sacrifices (v. 24a), it is superfluous to add that they should not be bought from foreigners. (Note the similar objection raised by Dillmann and Ryssel [1897] on my interpretation of v. 24b). He ignores, however, that the prohibitions in vv. 24–25 are graded, climaxed here by the notice that gelded animals should not come from abroad.

May the foreigner (*nokrî*) offer sacrifices at the sanctuary? It should be recalled that the *gēr* may sacrifice (17:8–9; Num 15:14) and, for the violation of prohibitive commandments, *has* to sacrifice (Num 15:30–31; see chap. 17, COMMENT B). The *gēr*, however, has a different religious status than the *nokrî*. Precisely because the *gēr* is obligated to observe the prohibitive commandments, he can be trusted as much as the Israelite to enter the sacred compound in a pure state with an unblemished sacrifice. Not so the *nokrî*. He, therefore, can only *send* his sacrifices (which would be carefully inspected), as implied by this verse (see below). Prescribing such a ban, one can imagine the shock waves generated by Isaiah of the exile when he proclaimed *kî bêtî bêt-tĕpillâ yiqqārē' lĕkol-hā'ammîm* 'for my house will be called a house of prayer for all peoples' (Isa 56:7; cf. 1 Kgs 8:41). His tolerant stance did not go unopposed in Israelite circles, even within the priesthood. The prophet-priest Ezekiel explicitly barred the foreigner from entering the Temple precincts (Ezek 44:9). Moreover, his view ultimately prevailed. In Second Temple times, a barrier was constructed around the Temple Mount to exclude entry to gentiles (*m. Kel.* 1:8; Jos. *Ant.* 11.301; 4 Macc 4:11).

However, this verse should not be misconstrued as a warning to the priest against accepting blemished sacrifices *miyyad*, literally "from the hand of" a foreigner who is in the sanctuary to offer his sacrifice. Joosten (1994: 107; 1996: 75), who adopts this interpretation, is forced to ascribe v. 25a as addressed to the priests and v. 25b, to the Israelites. Not only is such an abrupt change of address unverifiable in priestly law, but it is also illogical. The foreigner who sacrifices does so on his own behalf, not for the benefit of the Israelites. Rather, the entire verse is directed to both priests and Israelites, as specified in the heading (v. 18a). Neither group will gain acceptance from God, not the Israelite offerer or the officiating priest. Besides, in H, *miyyad* does not denote "from the hand of," but its legal meaning "from the possession of" (25:14).

That defective sacrificed animals may not be acquired from non-Israelites implies that perfect animals may be acquired. This, indeed, is the halakha of the rabbis (e.g., *m. Šek.* 7:6; *t. Šek.* 3:12; *m. Zebaḥ.* 4:5; *m. Menaḥ.* 5:3; 6:1) and the testimony of historical sources (Ezra 6:8–10; 7:21–22; 2 Macc 3:3; Jos. *Wars* 2:412–17; cf. Knohl 1979), though some of the rabbis limited purchases from non-Jews to certain sacrifices (e.g., *Sipra* Emor 7:2), and others banned these purchases outright (e.g., R. Eliezer in *b.* ʿ*Abod. Zar.* 23a [bar.]; *y.* ʿ*Abod. Zar.* 2:1; cf. Gilat 1980), as did the sectaries of Qumran (*MMT* B 8–9).

deformities . . . in them. mošḥātām bāhem; *hibbûlhôn bĕhôn* 'there are injuries in them' (*Tgs.*), a *muqtal* form (cf. Isa 52:14; Mal 1:14). 11QPaleoLev reads *MŠḤ]TYM HM*, which can be read either as a *Hopʿal* participle "they (the animals) are damaged ones" or as a plural nominal form of *mašḥît, mašḥēt*, or *mišḥat* 'they are corrupt ones' (Freedman and Mathews 1985: 41). Ibn Ezra reminds us that this identical word *mošḥātām* in Exod 40:15 comes from a different root *mšḥ* 'anoint', whereas in our verse, the root is *šḥt* 'be corrupt' (*Nipʿal*).

and blemishes in them, they will not be accepted. mûm bām lōʾ yērāṣû. These words are directly parallel with *bô mûm . . . lōʾ lĕrāṣôn* (v. 20) and stand in chiastic relation with *lĕrāṣôn kol-mûm* (v. 21), thus lending to the entire section (vv. 19–25) an introverted structure. This explains the intrusion of *mûm bām*, which in view of synonymous *mošḥātām bāhem* would be superfluous.

Vv. 26–30. Additional Criteria for Sacrificial Animals

Since these verses clearly continue the topic of vv. 17–25, they must be considered a subunit, an extension of the preceding verses. Their link with vv. 17–25 is further evidenced by the occurrence of the key root *rṣh* seven times in vv. 17–33: 19, 20, 21, 23, 25, 27, 29. Why, then, the need for a new heading (v. 26)? A plausible answer has been suggested by D. Stewart (personal communication): "When topics are freely available to memory, then economy dictates the reduction of their referents. When topics are new to memory and maximally difficult to process, more information must be given."

26. *YHWH spoke to Moses, saying.* Because this verse contains no addressee, it must be assumed that the following passage is meant to be a continuation of the preceding one (vv. 17–25), hence addressed to all Israel, priests and Israelites alike (v. 18).

27. *an ox or a sheep or a goat.* Tg. Neof. (cf. Tg. Ps.-J.) resorts to a midrashic comment:

There was a time in which you remembered for us our offerings which we used to offer and atonement was made for our sins; but now we have nothing to offer of our flocks of sheep, still we can make atonement for our sins; the ox has been chosen before me, to recall before me the merit of the man of the East who in his old age was blessed in all (Gen 24:1); he ran to his cattle-yard and brought a calf fat and good, and gave it to the boy-servant who hurried to prepare it. And he baked unleavened bread and gave to eat to the angels. And immediately it was announced to Sarah that Sarah would give birth to Isaac. And after that the lamb was chosen to recall the merit of the unique man, who was tied on one of the mountains like a lamb as a burnt offering upon the altar: But (God) delivered him in his good mercies (Gen 22) and when his sons pray they will say in their hours of tribulation: "Answer us this hour and listen to the voice of our prayer and remember in our favor the *Aqedah* of Isaac our father." And afterwards the kid-goat was chosen to recall the merit of the perfect man (Gen 25:27b) who clothed his hands with goat-skins and prepared dishes and gave them to eat to his father and he desired to receive the order of blessings (Gen 27). These are the three sacrifices of the three fathers of the world, Abraham, Isaac and Jacob; therefore it is written and specified in the book of the Torah of the Lord: "an ox or a sheep or a goat" (Lev 22:27).

Although prayer and the doctrine of the merit of the fathers replaced the suspended sacrificial rites of atonement, it was, according to the midrash, the "sacrifice" of the three species mentioned in the verses by the fathers that is the source of their atoning power.

seven days. Similarly, a firstling must be permitted to stay with its mother for seven days before it may be transferred to the sanctuary (Exod 22:29). There are many suggestions for its rationale:

1. It is modeled on circumcision (Ibn Ezra).
2. It is considered born after seven days of creation (Sarna 1991: 141).
3. After seven days, one can tell if it is an aborted fetus (*Tg. Ps.-J.*; *b. Šab.* 135a) or if it has a defect invalidating it as a sacrifice (*b. Zebaḥ.* 112b; *b. Ḥul.* 81a).
4. Seven days are the newborn's purificatory period from the mother's impurity (Bekhor Shor). However, the offspring is not impure (see NOTE on 12:3).
5. The provision is humanitarian.

The last is the most frequently proposed rationale, beginning with Philo (*Virt.* 143) and echoed by Clement of Alexandria, Ibn Ezra, Rashbam, and the moderns. The theory is that the newborn should be allowed to suckle for seven days, to spend one sabbath with its mother (Zohar), or to teach Israel not to be cruel to each other (Bekhor Shor). But on the eighth day, it may be brought to the altar, even though it is still suckling! Similar flaws attend the other laws explained by a humanitarian reason (vol. 1.738–39; see NOTE on v. 28). A completely satisfying rationale has yet to be supplied.

with its mother. taḥat 'immô, literally "under its mother." The sense of *taḥat* may be that of *taḥat yad* 'under the authority of' (Gen 41:35) or that of the suckling offspring can mostly be found, literally, "under its mother." *Tg. Onq.* renders *bātar 'immēh* 'after its mother', since the offspring is attached to and follows its mother. Philo (*Virt.* 137) also forbids the sacrifice of pregnant animals until they have delivered, for which there seems to be no similar rabbinic ruling.

on. wāhāl'â. This word has both a spatial connotation (Gen 19:9; Num 17:2; 32:19) and a temporal one (Lev 22:27; Num 15:23; Radaq).

acceptable as a food-gift offering to YHWH. yērāṣeh lĕqorban 'iššeh laYHWH.
Compare *[y]rqy. bh. šy. lhdd. wl'l. wlrkb'l. wlšmš.* "Lui (le sacrifice) sera agreé / sat-
isfaisant comme présent fait à Hadad et El, à Rakib-El et Shamash" ["(the sacrifice) will be acceptable / satisfying to him as a present made to Hadal, to Rakib-El
and Shamash"] (Greenfield 1973: 50), where *rqy* = *rṣh*, and followed by a *lamed*,
it designates the *Nip'al*, and *šy* (*ty* and *itt* in Ug.) = *'iššeh*. Thus the expression
qorban 'iššeh, a hapax in the Bible, is accounted for in Northwest Semitic.

28. *However, no animal from the herd or from the flock. wĕšôr 'ô śeh 'ōtô wĕ'et-
bĕnô*, literally "And the ox or flock animal, it and its young." This prohibition
applies to even the father of the animal (hence the masc. *šôr* and *'ōtô*; cf. R.
Hananiah in *b. Ḥul.* 75b [bar.]; Ramban on 3:12; Maimonides *Temple Service*,
"slaughter" 12:11). So, too, 11QT 52:5–7 (Schiffman 1989a: 489).

Others claim that the prohibition applies to only the mother (*wĕtôrtā' 'ô śêtā',*
Tg. Onq.; cf. *Tg. Neof.*, LXX; the rabbis in *b. Ḥul.* 78b; Saadiah, Rashi, Abravanel). Why, then, did not the text remove the ambiguity by stating *ûpārâ wĕ'et-
bĕnāh* 'a cow and its (fem.) offspring'? The answer falls into the realm of aesthetics: H wanted to continue the style of v. 27 (Bula).

Gerstenberger (1996: 331) claims that this prohibition is limited to a mother
and its male offspring, and he compares it with the injunction not to boil a kid
in its mother's milk (Exod 23:19b; 34:26b; Deut 14:21b; but see vol. 1. 737–42).
It should be obvious that both sexes are included in *šôr* and *bĕnô*, which should
be rendered "ox" and "its young."

The sectaries of Qumran go further: *[W'L H 'BRT] 'NḤNW ḤWŠBYM [Š'YN
LZBWḤ ']T H'M W'T HWLD BYWM 'ḤD* '[And concerning pregnant ani-
mals] We have decided [that one should not slaughter] the mother and the fetus in one and the same day' (*MMT* B 36 versus *m. Ḥul.* 4:5; cf. 11QT 52:5–7;
Schiffman 1989b: 249). Incidentally, the use of *śeh* for "flock animal" belies the
usual limitation of this word to the young.

shall be slaughtered. tišḥāṭû. This is an impersonal imperfect. Sacrificial
slaughter is intended, not only of animals whose meat the offerers will eat (vv.
29–30), but even of their expiatory sacrifices, the slaughter of which is a lay prerogative (see NOTE on 1:5).

Here, too, the humanitarian rationale fails: one may not slaughter the dam
and its young on the same day, but it is surely permitted on successive days.
Similarly, the analogous prohibition against taking the mother bird and her fledg-
lings or eggs together (Deut 22:6) permits them to be taken separately. Nonetheless, the rabbis not only maintain the humanitarian interpretation as an ethical
desideratum, but convert it into a halakhic procedure: "At four periods in the
year (before major festivals in which much meat is eaten) he who sold a beast
to another must inform him 'I sold today its dam to be slaughtered' or 'I sold
today its yearling to be slaughtered' " (*m. Ḥul.* 5:3; *Sipra Emor* 8:10), though
most likely the rabbis were concerned with only the literal fulfillment of the biblical injunction.

Moreover, the tannaitic rabbis sharply rebuke anyone offering a humanitarian rationale in his prayers: "If a man says [i.e., prays] 'To a bird's nest do your

mercies extend', they (the congregation) silence him" (*m. Ber.* 5:3; cf. *b. Meg.* 25a). Three explanations have been suggested for this cryptic statement:

1. The prayer implies that God's mercies have not reached him.
2. He converts the Torah's decrees into mercies (*p. Ber.* 5:3; *p. Meg.* 4:10; Maimonides, *Prayer* 9:7).
3. He limits God's mercies to a bird nest (Albeck 1957: 1.23).

Nonetheless, *Tg. Ps.-J.* does not hesitate to champion a humanitarian rationale: "My people, my children: As our father is merciful in heaven so you should be merciful on earth" (see also *Pesik. R. Kah.* 9). Maimonides (*Prayer* 9:7) echoes the rabbinic view in his law compendium and gives an additional reason: "If (the rationale) were mercy, he (God) should not have permitted animal slaughter at all!" However, in his *Guides to the Perplexed* (3.48), he writes that "animals feel very great pain, there being no difference regarding this pain between man and other animals. For the love and tenderness of a mother for her child is not consequent upon reason, but upon the activity of the imaginative faculty, which is found in most animals just as it is found in man." Although the scholarly consensus is that Maimonides contradicts himself (Seidler 1998), Rubenstein (1959: 86) points out that the rabbis' opposition is limited to prayer, but they would have raised no objection to anyone offering a humanitarian rationale in exegesis or preaching.

29. *you sacrifice. tizbĕḥû.* As Elliger (1966: 301, n. 31) correctly remarks, whereas *zābaḥ* means "slaughter" in other sources, in priestly texts it refers to performing the entire sacrificial procedure. His distinction, nonetheless, requires greater refinement: the verb *zābaḥ* is used only with its cognate accusative *zebaḥ*; that is, it means "sacrifice the well-being offering," of which the *tôdâ* 'the thanksgiving offering' is one example (hence the term *zebaḥ tôdâ*; cf. 7:12, 13, 15; Pss 107:22; 116:17; see NOTE on 9:4).

a thanksgiving offering. zebaḥ tôdâ. Why is the discussion of this offering mentioned here rather than together with the *šĕlāmîm* 'the well-being offering' (v. 21), under which it is subsumed in P (7:11, 13)? The answer lies in structural aesthetics: to form, together with vv. 30–33, an inclusio with chaps. 19–22 (cf. 19:5–6), the very chapters that focus on spatial and personal holiness (noted by Schwartz 1987: 133–34). Note that v. 31 ‖ 18:4–5; 19:37, and that v. 32 ‖ 19:2. The rules for the (two-day) *šĕlāmîm*, given in 19:5–6, are now balanced by the corresponding rules for the remaining *šĕlāmîm*, the *tôdâ* (vv. 29–30; note the similar wording). The near congruence of the wording in these two sections would explain why the animal species mentioned in vv. 19, 21, 27, 28 are not mentioned here: it is due to the clear attempt to follow the wording of 19:5–6. Moreover, since the purpose of vv. 29–30 is to specify the time limit for eating sacrificial meat, it *presumes the knowledge* of 19:5–6.

This explanation also answers the ostensibly troubling question: Could it be that H does not consider the *tôdâ* as a subunit of the *šĕlāmîm?* Abetting this suspicion is that the *tôdâ* bears an independent designation *zebaḥ tôdâ*; one never hears of a *zebaḥ nĕdābā* or a *zebaḥ neder.* Moreover, the distinction is firmly

planted in Scripture (e.g., Jer 17:26; 2 Chr 29:31–33; 33:16) and among the rabbis (*m. Zebaḥ* 5:6–7; cf. 1 Macc 4:54–56). Furthermore, the *tôdâ* stems from a
different motivation (cf. Ps 107) and is subject to a different procedure (7:11–15)
than the other *šĕlāmîm* (7:15–18; 19:5–8). Could it be, then, that H regards the
tôdâ as an independent sacrifice? If so, then P, which subsumes the *tôdâ* under
the rubric *šĕlāmîm*, by creating the ponderous construct *zebaḥ tôdat šĕlāmāyw*
(7:13–15), must be a later development (Levine 1974: 43; Berlinerblau 1996:
152)? At least I thought so (vol. 1.219), leaving me with the unarticulated but
depressing doubt as to whether H is really the successor to P. I am now relieved
of these qualms. The severing of the *tôdâ* from the *šĕlāmîm* pericope (vv. 29–30
versus v. 21) is due not to H's denial of the subsumation of the former under
the latter, but to the structural need to balance the two-day *šĕlāmîm* in 19:5–6
with the one-day *tôdâ* in 22:29–30.

To this stylistic argument Hartley (1992) adds one based on logic: to distinguish the *tôdâ* from the *neder* and *nĕdābâ*, sacrifices that may be offered as an
ʿōlâ, a burnt offering (v. 18). To be sure, there is no *ʿōlat tôdâ*, only a *zebaḥ
tôdâ*. Thus the *tôdâ* could not be included in the pericope of vv. 17–21, but had
to be moved to a separate location. As for the choice of the present locus, the
structural grounds provide the answer. Finally, Knohl (1987: 108; 1995: 119)
points out that the pericope (vv. 17–30 [H]) must be aware of 7:11–18 (P) because it reverses the order of the sacrifices: *tôdâ* after and not before *neder* and
nĕdābâ, following the rabbinic dictum *hāhûʾ dĕsālîq mînêh hāhûʾ mĕpārēš
bĕrêʾšāʾ* 'whatever follows precedes in the explanation' (*b. Ned.* 2b; *b. Naz.* 2a),
which Seidl (1955–56: 150) and Weiss (1962) convert into a principle of biblical exegesis. Other explanations, such as this pericope adds the term *lirĕṣōnĕkem*
(v. 29) to 7:15 (Ibn Ezra) or to distinguish it from the concessions made for the
freewill offering (Noth 1977), are unsatisfactory.

For the function of the *tôdâ* offering and its distinction from the other *šĕlāmîm*,
see vol. 1.218–25.

sacrifice [it]. tizbāḥû. The Sam., LXX, Pesh., and five MSS read *tizbāḥuhû*
'sacrifice it', as in 19:5. The MT here may be a case of accidental haplography
(D. N. Freedman, personal communication).

30. *It shall be eaten on the same day.* This statement explains the previous
clause (v. 29b); that is, your only obligation as an offerer of a thanksgiving offering is to consume or eliminate it the same day, so that "it will be acceptable
on your behalf" (Saadiah). The reason for the severer restriction on the *tôdâ*
(one day instead of two days) is nowhere stated. Perhaps because it is brought
in response to God's salvific acts, it differs from the *neder* and *nĕdābâ*, which
are spontaneous offerings expressing a person's mood or whim. In this respect,
the *tôdâ* is more akin to the *pesaḥ* (Exod 12:10) or the ram of the Nazirite (Num
6:19, according to *m. Zebaḥ.* 5:6) and of the priestly consecrand (Lev 8:32),
which is also offered with loaves of bread and eaten in one day. What they share,
on both the individual and the national level, is the motivation: deliverance.
Hence they are really mandatory, not voluntary, sacrifices, and they are eaten
in one day, as are the mandatory expiatory sacrifices eaten by the priests the
same day (nowhere stated but derived from 10:19b; see vol. 1.402).

The limitation of the one-day requirement to the consumption of the meat (ostensibly here and in 7:15) may have led some opponents of Qumran (but not the proto-Pharisees) to hold that the incineration of the cereal offering (i.e., the unleavened bread loaves), which accompanies the thanksgiving offering (7:12), may be delayed for several days. This is the implication of the language of 4Q MMT B 9–10: [*W'P 'L MNḤT ZBḤ] HŠL[MYM] ŠMNYḤYM 'WTH MYWM LYWM 'N[ḤNW ḤWŠBYM] ŠHMN[ḤH N']KLT 'L HḤLBYM WHBŚR BYWM Z[W]B[ḤM]* 'And also concerning the cereal of the thanksgiving offering which they (the opponents) used to leave from one day to the next we decide that the cereal is to be consumed (on the altar) on the day they sacrifice it'. Interestingly, although the subject is clearly the thanksgiving offering (a one-day sacrifice), the sacrifice is called *šĕlāmîm*, unless the initial lacuna should be read [*W'P 'L MNḤT TWDT ZBḤ] HŠL[MYM]*, in keeping with 7:11.

You shall not leave any of it until morning. Obviously, nothing of the suet should remain either. The suet, however, is not in the hands of the offerer. It is on the altar, and its incineration is the responsibility of the officiating priest, who is not addressed in this verse (or in its probable *Vorlage*, 7:15).

I YHWH (have spoken). 'ănî YHWH. This formula signals the end of the last legal section in this chapter (vv. 26–30).

Vv. 31–33. Exhortation

This corresponds to the concluding exhortations of 18:24–30; 19:37; 20:22–26. One might argue that it refers to vv. 17–30, since it is addressed to Israel (cf. v. 33), implying that its only concern is unblemished sacrificial animals (vv. 17–25; note a similar concern in Mal 1:12–14) and the slaughter and consumption of sacrificial animals (vv. 26–30). However, the priestly tribe (*lēwî*) was also redeemed from Egypt, and vv. 17–30 also address the priests (v. 18). Moreover, v. 32 is a patent attempt to form an inclusio with v. 2 (see COMMENT A). Hence one must conclude that the exhortation (vv. 31–33) applies to the entire chapter. It is also possible that vv. 31–33 continue the inclusio with chap. 19 by referring "to God's commandments as a whole, the compliance with which is holiness, but the failure to comply with which is a desecration of his name" (Schwartz, personal communication). Moreover, since this concluding exhortation stresses the holiness of YHWH, it forms a fitting inclusio for the opening verse of chap. 19, which sets forth the theme of holiness that, as demonstrated, is repeated with staccato emphasis throughout the intervening chapters. Note that whereas, until this point, the details have been given about how Israel can fulfill *qĕdōšîm tihyû* 'You shall be holy' (19:2aβ), this final statement stresses the significance of YHWH's holiness: *kî qādōš 'ănî YHWH 'ĕlōhêkem* 'for I, YHWH your God, am holy' (19:2b).

31. *You shall heed . . . and do. ûšĕmartem . . . wa'ăśîtem.* As explained in the NOTES on 18:4–5, 19:37, and 26:3, the verb *šāmar* means "guard, heed" and, therefore, functions as an auxiliary to a verb of action, in this case *'āśâ* 'do.' The rabbis state the matter succinctly: *zû mišnâ . . . zû ma'ăśeh* 'this is the instruction . . . and this is the action' (*Sipra* Emor 9:3).

my commandments. miṣwōtay. A rare term in H (26:3; 27:34), it is also scarcely attested in P (4:2, 13, 22, 27; 5:17; Elliger 1966: 297).

I YHWH (have spoken). 'ănî YHWH. Hartley (1992) prefers to delete it, with Sam. and LXX^BA, because of its frequency in vv. 31–33. However, it serves effectively as the opening of an inclusio in the exhortation (vv. 31–33) and should be retained.

32. *You shall not desecrate. wĕlō' tĕḥallĕlû.* Abravanel claims that this injunction is addressed to the priests. This can hardly be the case, since God's redemptive act in the Exodus (v. 33) embraced all of Israel. Are all of YHWH's commandments within the purview of the injunction, as proposed by Hoffmann (1953)? Again, the answer is negative: the other eighteen occurrences in H of *ḥillēl šēm YHWH* 'desecrate the name of YHWH' always refer to a specific context (Milgrom 1976a: 86, n. 302). Here, too, the immediate context is intended, namely regarding the Israelite's indispensable responsibility in the sacrificial service: to present an unblemished animal (vv.17–25), its minimal age (v. 27), its slaughter (v. 28), and its consumption (vv. 29–30), and the priests' indispensable responsibility to supervise all these acts.

that I may be sanctified in the midst of the Israelites. wĕniqdaštî bĕtôk bĕnê yiśrā'ēl. YHWH is sanctified when Israel performs his commandments (v. 31), not that he thereby increases his own sanctity (Knohl's [1995: 183] daring suggestion; see also Kugler 1997: 16). Rather, it does so relatively. Israel increasingly regards him with sanctity and is more scrupulous in preventing the desecration of his name (see NOTE on 21:8a). The result is that YHWH's sanctity is more visible, giving the appearance of his increased sanctity.

Wessely (1846) maintains that Israel shall sanctify YHWH's name for the edification of the nations. This unusual role attributed to Israel is more in line with prophetic vision (e.g., Ezek 36:23) than with priestly theology. The plain meaning of the text is that each individual Israelite has the responsibility of sanctifying God's name *within Israel.* Nonetheless, it is understandable how the rabbis used this verse as a basis for martyrdom, namely, that there are certain basic commandments that never should be violated, even when one's life is at stake (*b. Sanh.* 74a, b; *Sipra* Emor 9:4).

I am YHWH. 'ănî YHWH. The absence of the particle *kî* is significant. It assures that this verse, the last of seven occurrences of "YHWH the Sanctifier," forms an inclusio with the first (20:8), which also refers to Israel and is also without the particle *kî*. As already mentioned in the NOTE on 20:8, the first and seventh occurrences are directed to Israel; the second, third, fifth, and sixth, to the priest; and the fourth, probably to the sanctums, forming thereby the following introverted structure:

A   Israel (20:8)

  B, C   priests (21:8 LXX, 15)

  X   sanctums (21:23)

  B', C'   priests (22:9, 16)

A'   Israel (22:32)

That AA′ (20:8; 22:32) are the only ones without the particle *kî* enhances the possibility that this introversion (and the LXX of 21:8) is correct.

who sanctifies you. mĕqaddiškem. The Sam. reads *mĕqaddĕšām* 'who sanctifies them' (i.e., the priests), as it and the LXX read in 21:8. There, however, the context justifies the emendation; here it does not. Since the entire pericope (vv. 17–33) is addressed to the Israelites and the priests (v. 18) in the second person (cf. *lākem* 'to you', vv. 20b, 25b, where the antecedent is unambiguous), the object of God's sanctification is all Israel. Of the six occurrences of God's sanctification in chaps. 21–22 (21:8, 15, 23; 22:9, 16, 32), this final occurrence falls in the only context that also addresses Israel. See the NOTE on 20:8, where the full implication of the participle is expounded.

Let it suffice here to understand the ideological thrust of this verse: if all Israel refrains from desecrating God's name by faulty sacrificial procedures, it will hasten its progress toward the divine goal, the attainment of holiness (see NOTE on 19:2). The only other instance in H that speaks of God's grace in bestowing sanctity on Israel is in connection with its observance of the sabbath (Exod 31:13). The influence of this doctrine on Ezekiel is profound (cf. Ezek 20:12; 37:28).

33. *your deliverer. hammôṣî' 'etkem.* Most translations (e.g., NJPS, NRSV, Hartley [1992] among the most recent) render "who brought you," understanding the word as a perfect participle (e.g., Gen 27:33; 35:3; 43:18; Exod 11:5; Judg 3:25; cf. GKC §116d). However, the decision concerning the nature of the participle can only be inferred from the context. Regarding *hôṣî'* 'freed, delivered', when H intends a perfect, it uses *'ăšer hôṣē'tî* (e.g., 19:36; 25:38, 42, 55; 26:13). Thus, with *hammôṣî'*, a participial noun is intended: "deliverer." Support for this rendering stems from the participle in the previous verse, *mĕqaddiškem.* To render it "who made you holy" is to contravene one of the basic axioms of the priestly establishment: only the sanctuary and its priests are "made" holy. Israel, however, although not innately holy, can strive for holiness (19:2). That is, God provides, through his commandments, the means by which Israel can attain holiness. H, then, is consistent in its use of participles.

This is not to deny that other sources will use *hammôṣî'* as a perfect participle (cf. Deut 8:14, 15; 13:6, 11; Judg 2:12). This participle is attested for H on one other occasion (Exod 6:7), but since it is the eve of the Exodus, the participle is strictly present (or future). The perfect participle is again evident to describe God's redemption of Israel from Egypt in the synonymous use of *hammaʿăleh* (Deut 20:1; Josh 24:17; 2 Kgs 17:7; Jer 2:6; Ps 81:11). This participle is attested once in H (Lev 11:45). Rendsburg (1993) is probably correct in explaining it as a deliberate attempt to form an inclusio in this chapter with *maʿăleh* (vv. 3–6). This does not refute my assertion that 11:43–45 stem from H (as suggested by Rendsburg 1993: 420, n. 9). H, it must be borne in mind, is the redactor, and the inclusio is an example of his editorial artistry. That is, precisely because the P text of chap. 11 used a cluster of *maʿăleh* (four times) at the beginning of the chapter (vv. 3–6), H switched from *hammôṣî* to the synonymous *hammaʿăleh* in *its* addition to the chapter. A relevant deduction follows from this artistic maneuver. The reason for the participle has nothing to do with tense, but stems from stylistic and structural considerations.

This verse gives the appearance of being an addition in view of the fact that the participle *meqaddēš* ends each of six sections that compose chaps. 21–22 (21:8, 15, 23; 22:9, 16, 32). So it appears as an addition in other (probable H) contexts: Exod 29:46; Lev 19:36; 25:38, 55; 26:45; Num 15:41; 33:3. But it is integral to its context in other H texts: 19:34; 23:43; 25:42; Num 33:38. The Exodus is absent in contexts where it would be expected (the Paschal Offering and Festival of Unleavened Bread, 23:5–8; the Second Paschal Offering, Num 9:9–14; the sabbath, Exod 31:12–17 [contrast Deut 5:15]. In the entire cultic calendar of Lev 23, it is found only in an addendum to the Feast of Booths, 23:43). However, I would not label this verse an addition. It marks the end of the holiness chapters (chaps. 19–22), and it is no accident that 22:31, 33 is a chiastic repetition of 19:36b–37, thereby locking these holiness chapters into a unified expression of YHWH's injunction to Israel, priests and laity alike, to adhere to holiness.

COMMENT

The Structure of Chapter 22

This chapter consists of two major topics: the priestly prohibitions regarding sacred food (vv. 1–16) and the prohibitions incumbent on all Israel (priests and laity) regarding sacrificial animals (vv. 17–30), followed by a concluding exhortation (vv. 31–33).

Vv. 1–16 (minus the enumerated impurities, vv. 3–8) constitute a complex introversion of the key clauses (Galil 1987):

```
A    wĕyinnāzĕrû miqqodšê bĕnê-yiśrā'ēl
     wĕlō' yĕhallĕlû (v. 2)
     B    wĕlō'-yiś'û 'ālāyw ḥeṭ' . . .
          kî yĕhallĕluhû
          'ănî YHWH mĕqaddĕšam (v. 9)
          C    wĕkol-zār lō' yō'kal qōdeš
               tôšab kōhēn wĕśākîr lō' yō'kal qōdeš (v. 10)
               D    ûbat kōhēn kî tihyeh . . . (v. 12)
               D'   ûbat kōhēn kî tihyeh . . . (v. 13a)
          C'   wĕkol-zār lō' yō'kal bô (v. 13b)
     B'   wĕlō' yĕhallĕlû
          'et-qodšê bĕnê yiśrā'ēl (v. 15)
A'   wĕhiśśî'û 'ōtām 'ăwôn 'ašmâ
     . . . 'ănî YHWH mĕqaddĕšam (v. 16)
```

The matching sections, the priestly responsibility for the purity of their own bodies (vv. 1–9) and for others ineligible to partake of sacred food (vv. 10–16), are interlocked by matching clauses. Thus the priests are responsible for their daughters (the center, vv. 12–13a) and the laity (vv. 10, 13b) as well as for their own persons that they do not cause the sin (vv. 9, 16) of desecration (vv. 2, 9, 15) to Israel's sacred donations (vv. 2, 15), since YHWH sanctifies them (the priests, vv. 9, 16).

A tighter introversion is represented by vv. 10–13:

A   **wĕkol-zār lō' yō'kal qōdeš** tôšab kōhēn wĕśākîr
    lō'-yō'kal qōdeš (v. 10)
   B   wĕkōhēn kî-yiqneh nepeš qinyan kaspô hû'
      yō'kal bô wîlîd **bêtô** hēm **yō'kĕlû bĕlaḥmô** (v. 11)
      C   **ûbat-kōhēn kî tihyeh** lĕ'îš **zār** hi(w)'
         bitĕrûmat **haqqŏdāšîm lō' tō'kēl** (v. 12)
      C' **ûbat kōhēn kî tihyeh** 'almānâ ûgĕrûšâ
         wĕzera' 'ên lāh
   B' wĕšābâ 'el-**bêt 'ābîhā** kin'ûrêhā **milleḥem**
      'ābîhā tō'kēl
A' **wĕkol-zār lō'-yō'kal bô** (v. 13)

These verses are visibly chiastic in their entirety. Parallel words and expressions are printed in boldface. Furthermore, the key verb 'ākal 'eat' appears seven times in these verses (fourteen times [2 × 7] in the chapter). The subject zār 'stranger' is found in the extremes (AA') and in the center (C). The object qōdeš 'sacred food', its pronominal suffix bô 'it', and its synonym lehem '(sacred) food' together total seven times (A [bis], B [bis], C, B', A'). Finally, the reference to the father's house, bêtô, bêt 'ābîhā, appears in a matching pair (BB').

H's literary artistry reaches a new summit in its structuring of the next pericope, animal blemishes (vv. 17–25, minus the list of blemishes):

v. 18b. 'îš . . . 'ăšer yaqrîb qorbānô
    a. lĕkol-nidrêhem ûlkol-nidbôtām
    x. 'ăšer-yaqrîbû laYHWH
    b. lĕ'ōlâ

v. 19c. lirṣōnĕkem
    y. tāmîm
    d. babbāqār bakkĕśābîm
      ûbā'izzîm
v. 20. lō' taqrîbû [laYHWH]
    kî-lō' lĕrāṣôn yihyeh lākem

v. 21. wĕ'îš kî-yaqrîb
    b'. zebaḥ-šĕlāmîm
    x. laYHWH
    a'. lĕpallē'-neder 'ô
      lindābâ
    d'. babbāqār 'ô baṣṣō'n
    y. tamîm yihyeh
    c'. lĕrāṣôn

vv. 22, 24. lō'-taqrîbû . . . laYHWH
vv. 23, 25. lō' yērāṣû/yērāṣeh lākem

This unit consists of two matching panels, each of which utilizes the same formula for the introduction (vv. 18bα; 21aα) and the conclusion (vv. 20, 22–25). The intervening verses (vv. 18bβ–21) again compose two matching panels, the sacrificial category (vv. 18bβ; 21aα) and the animals (vv. 19; 21aβ, b), which are in chiastic order (axb b'xa' and cyd d'yc'). The pivot centers around which they revolve form the main message of the entire pericope: *tāmîm laYHWH*—YHWH will accept only unblemished animals. Otherwise, as stated in the twin conclusions, the sacrifices will not be accepted. For emphasis, the warning "Do not present . . . it will not be acceptable," stated once in the first panel (v. 20), is stated twice in the second and concluding panel (vv. 22–23, 24–25).

The additional criteria for sacrifice (vv. 26–30), patently directed solely to the lay offerers, do not reflect any internal structure. This is not due to carelessness or neglect on the part of H. Their purview extends far beyond the borders of the chapter—to the similarly structured two-day *šĕlāmîm* (19:5–6; see NOTE on "a thanksgiving offering," v. 29).

Finally, v. 32, the center of the concluding exhortation (vv. 31–33), skillfully echoes the wording of this chapter's opening statement, thereby creating a chiastic inclusio (abcd ‖ b'a'd'c'), which puts H's stamp on the entire chapter as a unity (M. Hildenbrand). Note how its structure mimics, in miniature, that of vv. 18b–19, 21.

v. 2aβb	v. 32
a. *wĕyinnāzĕrû miqqodšê bĕnê-yiśrā'ēl*	b'. *wĕlō' tĕhallĕlû 'et-šēm qodšî*
b. *wĕlō' yĕhallĕlû 'et-šēm qodšî*	a'. *wĕniqdaštî bĕtôk bĕnê yiśrā'ēl*
c. *'ăšer hēm maqdīšîm lî*	d'. *'ănî YHWH*
d. *'ănî YHWH*	c'. *mĕqaddiškem*

It should not be overlooked that this double chiastic relationship binds both priests (v. 2) and Israelites (v. 32) in their common obligation to prevent the desecration of the sacred.